In Session Tonic

IN SESSION

TONIGHT

THE COMPLETE
RADIO 1
RECORDINGS

KEN GARNER

BBC BOOKS

To Magda, Mum and Dad

PICTURE CREDITS

BBC Books would like to thank the following for providing photographs and for permission to reproduce copyright material. While every effort has been made to trace and acknowledge all copyright holders, we would like to apologise should there have been any errors of omissions.

© BBC 25, 29, 97, 103 (Don Smith), 142, 177, 178, 179, 187, 191 (courtesy Radio 1); Bob Conduct 33, 77; H. Goodwin/Radio Times 3; Hear Say Music, Mark Hodkinson 126; Hulton Deutsch Collection 59; Courtesy Andy Kershaw 146-148; London Features International 69, 72/73, 162/163, 171; Courtesy John Peel (photo Pete Saunders) 46/47; Pictorial Press 41, 83, 111, 154, 159; Barry Plummer 11, 14/15, 53, 60, 63, 87, 107, 109, 114, 120 (lower), 133, 139, 157, 160/161, 188-189; Redferns 21 (Val Wilmer), 43, 49, 89, 91 (Val Wilmer), 101 (Erica Echenberg), 104, 112, 121 (Fin Costello), 145, (Dave Peabody), 151 (Tim Hall); Repfoto, Robert Ellis 12/13 (Barry Wentzell), 51, 57, 65, 66 (Barry Wentzell with thanks to Ron Geesin), 79, 93, 95, 119; Retna Pictures 117, 118, 120 (top), 122/123, 131, 165; Savage and Best (photo Andy Catlin) 16; Serious Speakout, courtesy Ivor Cutler 175; Strange Fruit Records 71, 172, 181; Strange Things Archive 55;

With Special thanks to Barry Plummer.

Published by BBC Books,
a division of BBC Enterprises Limited,
Woodlands, 80 Wood Lane, London W12 0TT
First published 1993
© Ken Garner 1993
Foreword © John Peel, 1993
ISBN 0 563 36452 1
Designed by Bill Mason
Set in Perpetua by Goodfellow & Egan Ltd, Cambridge
Printed and bound in Great Britain by Clays Ltd, St Ives plc
Cover printed by Clays Ltd, St Ives plc

CONTENTS

FOREWORD

That the Radio 1 session has been of incalculable benefit to British music over the station's 26-year history, a major part of the BBC's continuing commitment to public service broadcasting and all that sort of stuff, can hardly be disputed.

The publication of this book is, of course, by no means the end of the session story, but it may mark a temporary end to phone calls from its author, usually at key moments in *One Foot In The Grave* or during the football, to check on a title from the second Hard Meat session or to confirm rumours that Bernie Andrews (Whom God Preserve) and I sang backing vocals on the Daddy Long Legs session.

The evidence that this is a work of almost lunatic scholarship is all about you, so much so that there have been numerous occasions on which Ken Garner has been able to put me right on details of what has been, in effect, my life. For example, for years I delighted my fellow

drinkers at the Live And Let Live in Combs and, since the latter's untimely closure, at the Brewers in Rattlesden, with yarns based around the fact that the very first session we broadcast starred Lulu. Ken pointed out that for years I have been lying.

What the boy Garner has not described to you, are the processes by which these sessions are commissioned. There are those, probably a majority of you, who believe that there is in place some system, that meetings are held, that prolonged discussions take place, that charts are pored over. But what tended to happen, at least during the Walters years, was that the great man would phone with a lengthy detailing of the lives and times of his cats and his more off-the-wall relatives, ending with a 'Pinky says we've no one booked for the 4th'. On this cue, John and I would list those bands who had not recorded a session for a spell, eliminating those whose work no longer pleased us or, more rarely, whose new-found celebrity status would mean that their agents, management and record companies would come together in unholy union to frustrate our attempts at a rebooking. We'd also add to the list the names of artistes we had heard and liked on demo tape or record or seen and liked in performance.

Some of these latter experiences – it is fashionable to call them epiphanies but I try to steer clear of that sort of thing – remain with me. There was the morning, for example, on which Walters, plainly excited, insisted that we book without delay a band he had seen the night before. He had seen the Smiths. Altered Images I heard on tape as I detoured across a housing estate in Braintree, Edsel Auctioneer as I drove up the hill out of Buxton towards Manchester.

Considering the perversely random nature of our commissioning of sessions, it is astonishing how few have turned out to be unsatisfactory. There was a band in the 1970s with whom I had worked at a polytechnic in the Midlands somewhere – and a couple of occasions on which the clamour of acclaim from normally reliable sources swayed our better judgement, but apart from those ... nothing.

Obviously it is my wish that before, during and after the campaign for Charter renewal, Radio 1FM will continue to broadcast sessions, that programmes other than those which already do so will feature 'live' music and most importantly, I will still be around to introduce sessions myself. I already have a pretty, little speech ready for the Fall's 25th.

I hope too that Ken Garner will have been able in due time to update this present volume and will be back on the phone to clear up the spelling of the name of the bass player on that all-important second Squit session.

In fact, I think I can hear the phone now. If it's not Ken, it will be Andy Kershaw to tell me about the ten or more potential sessions he recorded in Malawi. Or of course it might be Walters again ...

John Peel

PREFACE

John Peel and I first met on St Valentine's Day 1986. Nothing in my life was ever the same again. But our relationship had already been going on for many years, before that fateful Friday night together in the old Shish Mahal restaurant in Gibson Street, Glasgow.

I started listening to his radio programme some time in 1975. I've been listening fairly consistently ever since, save for a brief sabbatical between 1979 and 1981, when I was a student in London. I like to flatter myself that I am a fairly typical long-standing listener. Long before the idea for this book was born, I had bought the 'Peel sessions' EP releases by the Wedding Present, June Tabor and Ivor Cutler; the Stars of Heaven's Rough Trade mini-LP *Sacred Heart Hotel*, including their first Peel session; the 'Ukrainian recordings' by the Wedding Present; and the Strange Fruit albums by Soft Machine and Microdisney. I have also managed to limit my collection of off-air tapes of programmes and sessions to sixty or so cassettes in a single drawer.

By the time of our curry rendezvous in 1986, I was a research student, editor of the *Glasgow University Guardian* students' newspaper, and contributor of a radio column. My report of our meeting, together with other pieces, led to an invitation to submit a trial article to the *Listener* by the then editor, Russell Twisk. From this developed my freelance work as a writer on music broadcasting, which, in turn, led to my writing this book.

I knew it would be a big job but even I did not realise how big. The Sessionography, in particular, expanded exponentially. However, I can assure readers of the following: every quote in here is genuine; every session date and production credit in the main text or Sessionography has been checked; all track titles and band members' names have been entered as on the session sheet or contract; and any inconsistencies that have arisen in all these matters have been resolved to the best of my ability in the time available.

I shall stop typing soon and put on my headphones for tonight's programme. Apart from directing the reader's attention to my debts to the many people who helped in the preparation of this book, who are listed at the end of the Sessionography, it only remains for me to pay tribute to my wife Magda's patience and advice. I shall finish this book as I have written most of it – with Magda watching television behind me, and Peel, or Kershaw, or Harris, in my ears, I shall type one last crucial point.

K.G., October 1992, Glasgow.

INTRODUCTION

•

THE BASEMENT TAPES

There are two kinds of book about pop music, and our story will fit into neither of them. The easy way into the subject is to describe the career of one group, from early gigs to chart-topping albums. The alternative is to attempt to unlock the meaning of it all by putting a number of bands' experiences into some kind of cultural context. But there is another, often ignored, key to understanding the history of British pop music. It is the key to Room B08, in the basement of Egton House, at BBC Radio 1 in London.

The key is bent. It will only go into the lock if you slide it in from an odd angle. But then it's quite difficult, in the maze of BBC buildings around Broadcasting House, to find Egton B08 in the first place. First you have to squeeze through the permanent mêlée of record pluggers, publicists and security staff filling the Radio 1 foyer; and, ignoring the lift and staircase which lead up to the studios and production offices, head for what appears to be a door to a cupboard under the stairs. Descending the narrow steps beyond, you come to the lift machinery and locker room. Turn left, and B08 is the last door on your right before the boiler room.

Once inside, pulling a cord floods the room in buzzing strip lighting, and confronting you, end-on, is a line of gun-metal uprights of a sliding shelf system. Turning the steering wheels on the ends slides each 8-foot-high unit sideways, opening up a narrow aisle, down which can be glimpsed hundreds of small, flat white boxes lining the shelves.

They are all labelled. At the end of one aisle, on the top shelf, is a box spine that reads 'Hendrix 67 Top Gear'. Near to it are others marked 'Pink Floyd 67', 'Cream 67 + 68' and 'David Bowie 69 + 72'. Further along, there's 'Fleetwood Mac 68', and 'Genesis First Broadcast 20/2/70'.

The boxes on the opposite shelves have rather different names. Here, there's a 'Kathryn Tickell #1 of 4 *Glenaln Hornpipe*'; above it, 'The Real Sounds of Africa #3 of 4 *Mujinga*'; and below, 'The Ukulele Orchestra of Great Britain #1 of 4 *Silver Machine*'. A sticker on the edge of the shelf says 'Andy Kershaw Show'. Most of the next aisle is full of boxes belonging to the 'Evening Show'.

But more than a quarter of the entire room, which also holds tapes of Radio 1 interviews, concerts and notable complete programmes, is taken up with aisles marked 'Peel Sessions'. Scanning these shelves, it's impossible to register all the group names: My Bloody Valentine, Napalm Death, New Order, Pigbag, Pink Floyd, the Slits, Steeleye Span, Terry & Gerry, Richard and Linda Thompson, Twa Toots, the Vibrators, the Wedding Present, Robert Wyatt,

XTC … Each name appears on at least four boxes, and frequently on many more. Bending down and cocking your head to one side to try and read all the names, it's not long before your eyes begin to swim.

The BBC Radio 1 tape archive in B08 contains about 7000 session tapes. Each tape contains one single song recorded in a BBC studio especially for broadcast on a Radio 1 programme. Open up one of the little boxes, and inside you will find an individual $5^1/4$-inch spool, with a small reel of quarter-inch magnetic tape on it. Load it on to a reel-to-reel tape recorder, press play, and, after the short yellow leader tape, one song from the past will blast out of the speakers. When it's over, there will be a short red bit, and that's it.

Each band has traditionally got down, on average, four complete

Family, 16 March 1971,
Studio T1, BBC
Transcription Service,
Kensington House.

numbers on a single recording date, to make up one 'session'. A self-adhesive label on each tape spool merely gives the artist and that particular song title, repeating the rudimentary information scribbled on the outside of the box. What about the recording date? Who played on it? What else did they record on that day, and why? Shouldn't there be more clues to begin to explain how all these tapes came to exist? There are, but they are to be found elsewhere in the BBC, not here in Egton B08.

Singing Christmas carols for John Peel's *Top Gear* in Maida Vale Studio 4, 8 December 1970. Back row (left to right): Marc Bolan, Peel, Robert Wyatt, Mike Ratledge, Rod Stewart, Kenny Jones, unknown Faces' roadie; (front row) unknown friend of ..., Sonja Kristina, Ian McLagan, Ronnie Lane, Ron Wood, Ivor Cutler.

Upstairs, on the third floor of Egton, where the producers and presenters of night-time and weekend shows have had their offices since Radio 1 moved in here in 1970, squeezed on to a single shelf in Room 318 are a dozen tattered lever-arch files labelled 'Peel Sessions'.

Taking down the first of these, sub-titled 'Pre-1976', a shower of dried-up ring reinforcement stickers falls out. On top of the hundreds of sheets inside, so frayed and worn that you hardly dare to touch them, is an almost crumbling page, which reads 'TOP GEAR; TRANSMISSION: 4.7.72; RECORDING: 19th June, 1972; ARTIST: Albion Country Band; PRODUCER: John Walters'. Deciphering the confused scribblings of several hands below suggests that the band recorded two long medleys of traditional English folk dance tunes, and one other song. Gingerly turning the manuscript over, on the back is scrawled the six-strong line-up, headed by 'Tiger H. – bass/vcls', otherwise known as Ashley Hutchings.

Leafing through the frail sheets turns up other classic sessions. Here, on Thursday 1 May 1975, in Studio Maida Vale 4, is John Cale recording songs from what was to be perhaps his finest solo LP, '*Fear*', including the title track, for John Peel's show of the following Thursday.

'A goody', producer Tony Wilson has inscribed, next to his name. The line-up has been entered incongruously, as many of this period are, in the space left at the bottom of the sheet for 'Track 5'.

Further on are details of a session by an 'artiste' apparently called 'Carols', first broadcast on John Peel's *Top Gear* on Boxing Day 1970. An all-star line-up, under the guidance of producer John Walters and pianist David Bedford, sang 'God rest ye merry gentlemen', 'Away in a manger', 'Good King Wenceslas' 'Silent night', and 'O come, all ye faith-

ful'. They are listed with their BBC fees at the top of the sheet. Rod Stewart, who sang 'Away in a manger' solo, and the Faces, got £50 to share; Robert Wyatt and Mike Ratledge of the Soft Machine received £44; Marc Bolan, £20; David Bedford, £16; Sonja Kristina, of Curved Air, and Ivor Cutler, £15 each; but, as a famous DJ's left-sloping hand adds, 'Pig & Peel – nowt'.

Each of the other eleven files contains session sheets for hundreds of other BBC recording dates for Peel. But there have been many other Radio 1 pro-grammes that featured sessions. Mike Hawkes, producer of the mid-evening show for most of the eighties and Peel's producer since 1991, has six lever-arch files like Peel's, stuffed with session sheets. Two years ago a leaking ceiling deposited water on the files, which were stored on top of his office shelves. Delicately cracking apart the now dried-out but swollen files reveals events like the Cure, recorded 26 February 1981 ('Any odd clicking in background of tracks is part of rhythm box sound and intentional,' producer Dale Griffin has appended to the sheet); and Altered Images, for David Jensen, recorded 14 March 1982; who kicked off with 'I could be happy', on which 'Clare [Grogan] would like it to be fully appreciated by the public at large that she played the celeste', as well as singing. 'Tich: lots of drums; John, Tony, Jim: several very pleasant guitars,' reads the rest of the line-up.

Every producer's office on the third floor of Egton has a small corner that is forever a pile of session sheet files. If the decay brought on by time, leaking ceilings and the retirement or departure of former producers has taken its toll on these documents, from 1987 something in another corner of every Radio 1 office is safeguarding the facts about contemporary sessions.

Logging on to Romeo, the computerized 'Radio 1 Music and Editorial Organizer', and selecting 'Sessions', flips up a standard form on which, if you type in a band name, will appear the details of all the band's post-87 BBC recording dates, and some older sessions as well, if it's a well-known group. A few keystrokes will tell you the tracks the band recorded, on which dates, who played on them, and for whom.

Tap in the name of the band Mark Goodier had in session just two weeks ago, and the details will appear. Romeo's records may omit the amusing scribbles on old session sheets, but at least you can work out the line-up. Neither the old files nor the computer screen, however, convey what a session is actually like, then or now. Romeo quickly tells you that in recent months there has been a different band recording for Radio 1 each day of the week. Even as you rummage about in the tapes down in B08, thumb through the 'Peel Sessions' files or call up information on Romeo, someone, somewhere, is recording a BBC Radio 1

session – probably at Maida Vale.

―――――

'Do you know which studio they're in?', asks the commissionaire. He leafs through several sheets of computer printout on his clipboard. 'No John Peel or Spiritualized here, mate; ah, wait, is this it, 7 January, Radio 1, Studio 5?' He gives directions. Studio 5 is almost at the other end of the long building. The only way to get there is to walk all the way round the other studios, through a subterranean maze of corridors.

From reception at street level, the main staircase takes you down 10 feet to

the ground floor. Peering through the porthole window in the doors at the bottom of the stairs reveals the huge Studio 1, in which conductor Andrew Davis is rehearsing the BBC Symphony Orchestra for a Radio 3 recording of Stravinsky's *Requiem Canticles* the following day. Thirty yards along the corridor up the left of Studio 1, another porthole discovers the BBC Singers in the almost as large Studio 2, working up their parts for the same work.

After two confusing changes of direction, a sign appears saying 'Studios 4 & 5 →'. Suddenly, up ahead round a cor-

ner, a soundproof door must have been opened. There's a discordant blast of electric guitar, a thud of drums. A short slope up, and through the next door is Mike Robinson, producer and studio manager, his engineer James Birtwistle, and most of the group Spiritualized, listening in the control room while bass player Willie B. Carruthers tries to get the right level of fuzz distortion on his instrument, for the band's debut session on the *John Peel Show*.

A former roller-skating rink in a genteel residential area of west London is as unlikely a location for a recording

A door through which hundreds of bands have passed: the main entrance, BBC Maida Vale Studios, Delaware Road, London.

15

Spiritualized, as in January 1992, the line-up featured on their debut Peel session.

studio as any. By the time the BBC bought this large tin-roofed building in Delaware Road, the Maida Vale Roller Skating Palace and Club had long since closed down. Seating 2620, the rink opened in 1909, but lost its licence for 'music and dancing – no intoxicants' in 1912. In the 1920s the Ministry of Health used the premises for National Insurance offices. When the BBC opened Studio 1 in 1934, at 110 by 72 feet it was 'the largest broadcasting studio yet constructed in

this country' (*BBC Annual Report 1935*). Studios 2–5 were added the following year. Studios 1, 2 and 3 are still the same shape as they were then.

The attractions of the building were obvious. It was the only available existing structure that could 'relieve the growing pressure on the studios in Broadcasting House [opened in 1932], and provide a studio large enough for the whole of the BBC Symphony Orchestra' (*BBC Annual Report 1934*). Also, Maida Vale Studios are only a short tube journey on the Bakerloo line from Oxford Circus and Broadcasting House, followed by a half-mile walk from Warwick Avenue Underground, which, even on a freezing January afternoon in 1992, isn't unpleasant.

'I've just met Sir Michael Hordern in the lavatory,' says trumpeter Roddy Lorimer, entering the control room. Beyond Studios 4 and 5, at the very end of the building, in the newly converted drama studio, Number 7, Kenneth Branagh and Glyn Dearman are directing *Hamlet* for Radio 3, the first radio co-production of the BBC and Branagh's Renaissance Theatre Company. Today, Sir Michael is playing the Player King to Branagh's Prince Hamlet (Act II, scene ii).

Here in Studio 5, however, Roddy Lorimer, as one of the three-man 'Kick Horns', is playing trumpet on Spiritualized's debut session. He, Simon Clarke (sax/flute) and Tim Sanders (sax) have been hired as special guests by the group. They've backed the band before, on their second single 'Feels so sad' (the early release which led Peel to 'draw a bow at a venture' and ask the band to do a session). Although the Horns have worked together for nine years and played with everyone from the Who to the Rolling Stones, it's their first Peel session too. Nor are they the only non-classical blowers on the premises. On the other side of the building in the green-carpeted Studio 3, Polish jazz trumpeter Janusz Carmello and his quartet are swinging lightly through 'Surrey with the fringe on top' for Radio 2's *Jazz Parade*.

It's 3.30 p.m. and Spiritualized have just laid down the backing track (drums, bass, two guitars and keyboards) for their first number, 'Angel sigh'. Willie is now doing fuzz bass 'drop-ins', at crucial moments replacing his normal sound with a grinding special effect. The rest of the band, Jonny Mattock (drums), Kate Radley (keyboards), Mark Refoy (guitar), and leader Jason Pierce (guitar and vocals) crack open some cans and relax on the huge leather sofa at the back of the control room. Lorimer and Sanders tell jokes while Clarke writes out their horn parts. They won't be needed for at least another hour.

The band have been here since lunchtime. Groups have about 90 minutes to set up their equipment, with the BBC engineer miking up their amplifiers and drums at the same time; recording should start at about 2.30 p.m. and be completed by about 6 p.m. After an hour or so break for dinner in the canteen, they have until almost 1 a.m. to mix the session, which is expected to have produced about 15–20 minutes of original material.

Compared to the time taken these days to record pop music for commercial release (several months for an album is not uncommon), it's no time at all. As soon as Willie has completed his drop-ins, the rest of the band troop back into the studio and, in a couple of takes, blast down the basic tracks for their other two numbers: the long 'Feels so sad', with a specially extended second part to feature a complex, slowly building horn arrangement; and 'Smiles', also to get some wild sax playing later. After the last shuddering guitar chord and squeal of feedback has faded away at the end of 'Smiles', producer Mike Robinson opens up the talk-back. 'That felt a bit frantic, but presumably that's in the nature of the beast.' 'Yeah,' says Jason, blithely.

Jason has already decided to link 'Angel sigh' and 'Feels so sad', written in the same key, into a single 13-minute medley, by means of a swirling sustained drone on the BBC house Hammond organ, to be dropped in by himself ('So we're talking about an eight-bar run-on, are we, roughly?' queries Robinson). It's partly, he claims, a cheeky revenge on

Peel, for having edited on air a very long piece on a record by his previous group, the Spacemen Three. But it also further helps make this Peel session version an original, unique recording, part of the BBC brief.

But when Robinson lets the tape run on after 'Angel sigh', to keep as much of Willie's fuzz bass sustain on from the backing track's final chord as possible, to support the Hammond, suddenly a number by another band blasts in on other tracks. 'Sorry, something left over from last week's session,' shouts Robinson, 'I'll wipe that rubbish off.' Everyone laughs; especially when the band's roadie, from behind Q magazine, chips in, 'That's what they'll be saying about you lot next week.'

By 5 p.m. the Kick Horns are blowing their stuff in the vocal booth, a windowed antechamber at the front of the main studio (the producer at the desk, and band in the studio, can see each other through it). Switching between flute and baritone sax, Clarke is grafting a melody on to the band's guitars, when Robinson points out he's running short of tracks: 'Can you switch from one to the other in one take?'

'You mean one in each hand?'

'Yes, can you do a Jethro Tull?'

'Can *you* stand on one leg?'

'OK, we'll do an overdub. I'll find space for it somewhere. We'll keep the baritone. I like the Piltdown Man sound.'

One hour later, Jason has taken over, replacing the guide vocals he recorded on the backing tracks with more considered renditions. There's a brief level problem with the mike ('We know it's OK, though—not like when the Pixies insisted I find the cheapest and tinniest-sounding mike in the cupboard,' recalls James Birtwistle). As the packed-up Kick Horns are leaving, Mike Robinson suggests to Jason, 'Could you sing about a foot away from the mike?'

'That sounds an interesting subject,' quips Tim Sanders, closing the control-room door behind him.

Recording is all done by 7 p.m. The band have already removed their equipment during the sax and vocal overdubs. Everyone breaks for a meal. By 8 p.m., full of curry, exhausted by a busy day's travelling and playing, the band flake out on the sofa. Robinson, meanwhile, leaps into action again, starting with the drum mix. Jumping about, roll-up between his fingers, he twiddles knobs, punches buttons, plugs in cables, pulls them out again, and fiddles with faders, until the deafening, raw racket coming out of the huge monitors resolves itself into a recognisable drum kit: thud, thud, thud; tish, tish, tish. On the sofa, Jonny Mattock turns and hollers at his neighbour, 'What is he, deaf or something?'

Fairly quickly, however, Robinson and Birtwistle have a basic mix, making full use of the Studio's SSL G Series desk with computer-controlled mixing. Jason asks if he can have backwards reverb on his vocals, a creepy effect whereby the voice seems to be echoing even before words are spoken. He can, but it involves Robinson and Birtwistle carefully turning the 2-inch master tape over on one of the studio's two Studer A80 24-track recorders; playing the tape backwards, recording the reverb over the now unwanted guide-vocal track; then turning the large tape spool over the right way again. It means that the 'Angel sigh/Feels so sad' medley ends up using all 24 tracks on the tape.

There's one final hitch. The drums have to disappear completely in a quiet bit, but the bass drum is still audible. 'I forgot to stop', apologises Mattock. An indecisive debate drags on for some minutes. The only option is to fade the bass drum. 'I think it's OK, but it's not ideal,' ruminates Jason. 'It is meant to be a *session* remember, it's not for a record,' points out Robinson. The band agree. 'Yeah, leave it, it'll do.'

London Underground tubes stop running soon after midnight. At five minutes to twelve, it's time to leave. The Symphony Orchestra, the BBC Singers, Janusz Carmello, Kenneth Branagh and Sir Michael Hordern have long since left the building. The canteen closed hours ago. The coffee machine has run out of cups. There are no cans left in the band's carry-out. Everyone is close to sleep, except Mike Robinson and James Birtwistle.

Robinson is rattling off the mix for 'Smiles' at speed. Birtwistle has filled in the band and track details on the session sheet. He has also dubbed the master mix of 'Angel sigh/Feels so sad' on to a quarter-inch tape spool, put it in a new small white box and labelled it. The final image of the control room is Mike Robinson peering into the computer screen that controls the desk, preparing to push the button, to copy the master version of the last song.

In the past twenty-five years Radio 1 has recorded some 8000 sessions for its evening and specialist music programmes. In 1991, for example, there were 312 of them. At Maida Vale, a Peel session is recorded every Sunday and Tuesday. Andy Kershaw's are done on Thursdays. Studios 4 and 5, and occasionally 3, are block-booked on other days of the week for sessions for Nicky Campbell, Mark Goodier and Tommy Vance. A few are also done at the Golders Green Hippodrome in north London, and at BBC Manchester. Back in the late seventies, Maida Vale engineers did three sessions a week for Peel alone. In 1970 Peel's original weekend show, *Top Gear*, and the nightly *Sounds of the Seventies* pro-

grammes which began that April, between them featured 254 new sessions alone.

But that's not all. Until the late seventies, many daytime programmes had sessions too. There is a simple explanation of why there were so many in the first ten years of Radio 1: needletime.

Until it was eventually abandoned in 1988, needletime was the number of hours of music on record that the BBC and other broadcasters were allowed to play per day. It was allocated by a rights-negotiating company called Phonographic Performance Ltd (PPL), representing the record companies, who had an agreement with the Musicians' Union (MU) over how many hours broadcasters could have. (PPL still sets the rate broadcasters have to pay per hour of recorded music broadcast, but the MU is not involved, there is no longer any limit on the total amount, and stations simply pay per play.)

So limited was the amount granted in 1967 that the new Radios 1 and 2 went on air with only seven hours' total needletime a day. Radio 1 had just three hours of this for its own peak-time programmes: at breakfast, midday and early evening. For the rest of the day it shared programmes with Radio 2, which consisted mostly, if not entirely, of BBC-originated music sessions.

Of these shared programmes, Jimmy Young's two-hour show from 10 a.m. on Friday 13 October 1967, for example, featured only nineteen discs, and songs selected from fifteen BBC sessions, performed by Bob Miller and his Millermen, Alan Elsdon's Jazzband, the Montanas, the Northern Dance Orchestra and Wally Whyton, among others. At 1 p.m. there was *The Joe Loss Show*, with the famous orchestra and featured vocalist Ross McManus performing live from the Playhouse Theatre, Northumberland Avenue, with guests the Nashville Teens.

Pete Brady's show at 2 p.m. drew on no less than 24 sessions, recorded by the likes of the Button-down Brass, and Maureen Evans with the Harry Stoneham Trio.

Even in the new service's own programmes, the limited needletime meant that sessions were still needed. Only Tony Blackburn at breakfast had 100 per cent needletime. David Symonds' show, at 5.33 p.m. on that Friday, had six new sessions, from the Marmalade, Eric Burdon and the Animals, the Swinging Blue Jeans, Cliff Bennett and the Rebel Rousers, Jimmy James and the Vagabonds and the Flowerpot Men. There were also repeat broadcasts of tracks from seven other sessions.

This book is not a history of all BBC popular music recordings. Such a project would take a lifetime to research, and thousands of the sessions celebrated would be of little historical interest. There are books that need to be written about the BBC's historic recordings of jazz, folk, blues, and country & western music, but this is not one of them. Even such works would omit thousands of light entertainment music sessions, recorded to fill airtime tomorrow and be forgotten the day after.

This is the story of the handful of BBC producers, engineers and presenters who chose to use the combination of limited needletime and the BBC's extensive recording operations to push pop music forward; who created evening and weekend programmes based on session recordings of the newest groups; who booked in bands who didn't in many cases even have a record out yet; who, by sheer perseverance, changed from within a BBC system not then sympathetic to feedback, guitar distortion and 10-minute blues workouts.

It's the story of the classic sessions they helped create, and the groups they helped to change pop music for ever. Not

every evening session has been a classic, but there's been a high strike rate. When Hendrix, Bowie, Fleetwood Mac and Genesis recorded their first BBC sessions, very few people had heard of them. They had just released or were about to release their first records. They had played a few underground concerts. But they were booked in; with the result that millions of radio listeners, for whom these groups were then only acts they had read about in the music papers, had their first opportunity to hear what they actually sounded like.

Almost by accident, this quest for broadcasting exclusives created a unique sound archive. It was never meant to exist, and the sessions certainly weren't recorded with a view to building a historic tape library. They were and still are made for radio listeners. Each session is and was designed as an event, something unique to one night's programme.

From a listener's point of view, this means that the classic sessions are not necessarily those debut recordings by bands who go on to achieve superstar status. A first broadcast is just one kind of unique session. There are classic sessions where musicians hire unexpected guests; which involve startling, one-off arrangements; feature either disturbingly short or seductively long numbers; consist entirely of surprising cover versions; or which are simply funny.

Whatever it is, when you tune in of a night and catch a new session, somewhere, deep in the back of your mind, you know you are hearing something extraordinary; something you would not otherwise have heard were it not for the BBC, Radio 1, and DJs like John Peel.

——————

'Right, in tonight's programme we've got sessions from Leatherface and Spiritualized and three hours, by and large, of tomorrow's hits today, starting

——————

Ray Davies of The Kinks. One of the pop bands featured many times on the old Light Programme and in the first months of Radio 1.

with *this*': a grungy guitar noise comes out of the radio, later revealed to be a song called 'Baby say Unh!' by the Gories, on Estrus Records of Bellingham, Washington.

The next record is 'the first African record I ever played on the radio, back in 1971', 'Tickey Dopies' by Sipho Bhengu. 'Jill Furmanovsky, the photographer, gave me that, and whenever I see her pictures in the papers they remind me of that record.' After this, we get a hostile techno record, 'Thrash,' by Cybersonik; followed by the racing, catchy opener from Leatherface in session, 'Peasant in paradise'; a London rap record from Point Blank; 'and the programme's got off to such a roaring start that I forgot to tell you what things are included in it. Well, there are three tracks from the forthcoming LP from P.J.Harvey, three from the Meathooks, and three from Pavement.'

It's 11.20 p.m. on John Peel's show of Saturday, 14 March 1992. After numbers from the Fall, King Tubby and Crane, Brian Deacon tells us in the 11.30 p.m. news that a helicopter has crashed into the North Sea next to Shell's Cormorant Alpha platform, 'in a snowstorm with winds up to 52 knots, and waves up to 10 metres'. The death toll in the Turkish earthquake has risen to 500. Seven new opinion polls suggest Labour and the Conservatives are neck and neck, on this first weekend of the 1992 general election campaign. Kevin Keegan has confirmed he will stay as manager of Newcastle United until the end of the season.

Liverpool lost to Crystal Palace 1–0 at Selhurst Park that afternoon, prompting loyal supporter Peel to grumble two records later, 'These days every team seems to be Liverpool's bogey team.' Soon after the P.J. Harvey exclusive, Peel says, 'This is Spiritualized, and "Angel sigh" and "Feels so bad" '(*sic*).

On the desk in front of him he will push the 'Start' button for 'Tape 1', and wham up the fader. Next door in the control room, one of the tape machines lined up along the back wall, with a quarter-inch reel on it cued up at the end of the yellow leader tape, at that moment will have whirred into action. The first radio transmission of Spiritualized's session, the '1st TX', is under way.

Thirteen minutes later, as the final blast of the horns reverberates away into the ether, he says, 'Well, I wasn't sure what to expect from this, but that was rather ripping, I think.' An hour later, after the wild saxophone solos and howling wah-wah guitar of 'Smiles' have ended, he asks 'Is this a freak-out that I see before me?'

Looking out the window while picking up the telephone, I may not see a freak-out, but the revellers emerging rowdily from Volcano nightclub into the mid-March snow-clad streets of Glasgow, mean that the radio in my house has to stay loud; at which volume the Spiritualized session definitely sounds 'ripping'.

On the other end of the phone line in London, Simon Clarke is 'very pleased with the session'. He was impressed by 'the whole day' at Maida Vale and 'how quickly the engineers got a really good sound', because he's found engineers in other broadcasters' studios not so sympathetic.

Jason, at home in Rugby, said, 'We were lucky. Mike Robinson really got behind what we wanted to do. We don't get a lot of studio time, and here was someone else paying for a whole day, so we took as much advantage of it as we possibly could, and decided to do something different.'

The group's debut album, *Lazerguided Melodies*, released by Dedicated Records two weeks after the programme, contains very different versions of two of the three session tracks. 'Feels so sad' is not on it. The band weren't touring to support it until the end of April, so saw the broadcast of their session as the best kind of promotion of the group's potential. 'I believe our album will sound as good in ten or twenty years' time, and I wanted the same thing for the session.'

Later that night, on the radio, Peel agrees. 'Two storming sessions tonight, from Leatherface and Spiritualized. Next weekend, on Friday it's sessions from the Family Cat and th'Faithhealers, on Saturday, Papa Sprain and Silverfish. Coming up next on 1FM, Lynn Parsons. Thanks very much for listening, goodnight.'

A few days later, Pinky, Peel's programme assistant, typed Spiritualized's session details into the Romeo system. She printed out one copy, and put it in the current session sheet file. The tapes, in their boxes, went away into a steel cupboard in Peel's office.

They will stay there for several months, or even years, for possible repeat broadcast. Eventually, when the cupboard can take no more boxes, a batch of old tapes will be taken downstairs to the basement. Phil Lawton, Radio 1's archivist, will put the white boxes labelled 'Spiritualized' on the appropriate shelf. There the tapes will remain, locked away in B08.

To tell the story of Radio 1's session broadcasts from the beginning, however, depends on a different kind of tape, in a different kind of archive. The session tapes in B08 are not the complete story, because the collection is not complete. Many tapes were wiped for re-use in the 1970s. Then, blank tape was judged in some quarters of the BBC to be a more valuable commodity than any pop music recorded on it. Nor can session sheet files be relied on absolutely, for many of the older sheets have been lost.

Nevertheless there is one piece of BBC paperwork that remains sacrosanct. It is the programme-as-broadcast sheet, or 'PasB'. For talk programmes, it transcribes the script. For music shows, it lists every item that was played, in order; giving artist, title, duration, composer and publisher; with label and catalogue number, for commercial records; and pre-recording date for BBC-originated material.

At BBC Written Archives in Caversham every PasB is kept, right back to the Corporation's first day of radio broadcasting in 1922. Those since the 1950s undergo transformation on to microfilm in order to save space.

Twenty-five years of BBC Radio 1 takes up a single short metal shelf. One small reel inside a cardboard box holds the PasBs for every programme on the network for a two-month period. You load up tape 'No.1' on a microfilm reader, switch on the screen and magnifier, and, turning the control knob firmly clockwise, fast forward into the past.

2

BERNIE'S TUNE

The first Peel sessions were nearly the last. But it wasn't the chosen groups, or even the sessions themselves, that were under threat. The list of acts featured on the first edition of *Top Gear* on Radio 1, broadcast from 2–5 p.m. on the second day of the new network, Sunday, 1 October 1967, introduced by joint 'comperes' Pete Drummond and John Peel, were: Tomorrow featuring Keith West; the Move; Traffic; the Pink Floyd; Tim Rose; and Big Maybelle and the Senate. On the following week's *Top Gear*, on 8 October, it was the turn of Procol Harum; Lou Rawls, Maxine Brown and the Johnny Watson Concept; Denny Laine and the Electric String Band; the Crazy World of Arthur Brown; and the Idle Race. But the comperes that day were Pete Drummond and Mike Ahern. Of Peel there is no trace on the PasB. It wasn't so much the bands being featured that Radio 1 wasn't sure about, as Peel.

The fact that Peel got any work at all was largely thanks to a man who was himself regarded by many of his superiors as a thorn in the BBC's flesh: Bernie Andrews, a producer in the radio Popular Music department, at its headquarters in the Aeolian Hall, Bond Street. Bernie had been listening to the pirate stations, and also sounding out his music business and underground band contacts throughout the summer of 1967, about who they thought would be a good presenter for his new show. 'I knew it was him I wanted to do the programme,' he recalls.

He couldn't just hire Peel outright, however. Just as the forty-six DJs hired to launch Radio 1 were only on eight-week contracts, all knowing that many would be weeded out thereafter, so Bernie was originally instructed to try out a different compere for *Top Gear* in each of the first six weeks. Instead, Bernie suggested to Robin Scott, the controller of the new Radios 1 and 2, a double-headed show,

John, Paul, George ... and Bernie. The Beatles record for *Saturday Club* at The Playhouse Theatre, Northumberland Avenue, 17 December 1963.

using one professional anchorman with a different guest 'DJ' each week. Scott agreed.

Peel had written requesting work to Mark White, deputy head of BBC Radio's Gramophone department, from the pirate Radio London office on 27 July, two weeks before it was to close down on the eve of the Marine Offences Act becoming law, on 15 August. He enclosed a tape of his late-night *Perfumed Garden* show, which he'd developed since returning to Britain from America in early spring 1967 and landing a job on the station.

'Basically, the programme is a forum for the "better" sounds in popular music, with the emphasis on the music rather than myself,' Peel wrote; 'by "better music" I mean the West Coast groups and British groups that are trying to do something new and imaginative. Obviously I hope that there is some possibility of my continuing with what I

believe to be an important programme,' he concluded. White replied on 1 August, saying he had forwarded the tape to Mary Cotgrove, who ran BBC Radio's audition unit. It then went to John Simmonds in the Light Entertainment department, and subsequently disappeared.

Nothing came of this formal approach except, perhaps, 'more than a little reluctance to give me work,' reflects Peel; 'they were probably passing the tape around for their own amusement'. Bernie remembers that his first suggestion of Peel was greeted by his superiors with remarks like, 'No, not *him*.' As late as 8 August a provisional station line-up still had a blank space next to *Top Gear*, in which an administrator had scribbled 'Mike Ahern? Mike Raven?'

But Bernie was determined, and had a secret ally: the new controller himself, Robin Scott. 'Whilst I had from very early on wanted John Peel to do quite a lot of things, I think there was a feeling in house,' Scott acknowledges, 'that maybe John was almost too much his own man to let loose.' Two weeks before launch Peel was booked for a *Top Gear* rehearsal on 13 September; and on the 26th Bernie confirmed his presentation line-up to his department: Drummond as anchorman, with Peel as guest DJ, followed by Mike Ahern, Tommy Vance and Rick Dane. About weeks five and six, Bernie said nothing. He knew that his joint-compere format could establish Peel, surreptitiously, as the programme's regular voice after the first four weeks. 'I was very glad when it shook down, that afternoon programme, and became his show,' Scott recalls, 'but it was a shaky start.'

Listening to that first show, you can see Scott's point. Yet, once again, it's not the sessions that are shaky. The thirty-six session tracks are generally excellent. Every other day from 21 September, the show's two session-recording teams, Bernie Andrews with engineer Dave Tate, and co-producer Bev Phillips with engineer Pete Ritzema (Bernie would also do extra ones with Pete), had been working hard in studios like the Playhouse Theatre, 201 Piccadilly (formerly 'The Stage Door', a Lyons tea-house), and Maida Vale 4, recording bands.

Traffic, who Bernie remembers being ear-splittingly loud – 'I think Stevie Winwood brought in three Leslie cabinets' ('Well, at least two,' says Pete Ritzema) – got down a swirling version of 'Hole in my shoe'. Tomorrow 'featuring Keith West', with Steve Howe on guitar and Twink on drums, recorded their summer hit 'My white bicycle', with Bernie ringing the bicycle bell live on the transmission, opening up a mike in the control room: 'We completely forgot to put it on at the session.'

On Monday, 25 September, the Pink Floyd had completed a first session

at the second attempt, including versions of 'Scarecrow' and 'Set the controls', and possibly the band's only live attempt at their next single, 'Apples and oranges' (not broadcast until the session repeat on 5 November). A previous Pink Floyd session at the Playhouse on the afternoon of 28 July, which Bernie had attempted to produce for *Saturday Club*, had to be abandoned when Syd Barrett, not in the best of health, walked out. 'I have memories of Syd getting upset that either we couldn't play loud or long enough or something, then the whole thing becoming rather disastrous,' says Floyd's drummer Nick Mason. When Patrick Newman, Light Entertainment bookings manager, noted for his dry sense of humour, learned of the cancellation, he wrote to the band's management asking 'whether you'd be good enough to find out which gentleman "freaked out" (this strange expression was heard about the studio), together with any explanatory comments which come to mind.'

Bernie also used his 60 minutes' needletime to the full. The first record was 'Love bug leave my heart alone' by Martha and the Vandellas. Amidst new releases from Donovan, the Idle Race, Procol Harum and Blossom Toes there were several records Peel had brought back from California, including Country Joe and the Fish, the Mothers of Invention, the Velvet Underground and Nico, and Captain Beefheart and his Magic Band.

What makes the programme awkward is the nervousness of Drummond and Peel. Although they had worked together at Radio London and had the same manager (Clive Selwood of Elektra Records), they were nevertheless in competition, and it shows. Each tries to outwit the other with amusing remarks, and silly 'BBC' voices are adopted frequently.

Peel remembers it being 'a rather

fraught way of making programmes'. Sitting at a table in a talks studio in Broadcasting House, with records and tapes played in from the control room, the formality compared to 'self-op' on the pirate ships was unnerving. 'I think we had to give a written cue for the end of our links as well,' he says.

This formality, however, was the price Bernie had to pay to get Peel on air. He had the sessions. He had the mix of records. He knew Peel was the missing link. The subsequent reputation of both Peel and those first sessions have proved Bernie right, but at the expense of public recognition of his own contribution. 'It was always Bernie's show,' says his co-producer, Bev Phillips.

The way Bernie organised and ran BBC recording dates in the sixties established precedents without which the sessions celebrated in this book might never have taken place. Ask any BBC engineer about sessions in the early days, and back will come the reply, 'Ah, now, the person you really *must* talk to is...' He was so insistent on how things should be done that he retained the name *Top Gear* from a previous programme of his. He even re-recorded its old signature tune, first heard in 1964, performed by Sounds Incorporated, and composed by 'J. Woodhouse, A. Boyce', otherwise known as Bernie himself, 'I hummed it', and his chief producer, Jimmy Grant, 'he played it'. And that name takes us back to the beginnings of rock'n' roll sessions at the BBC.

When Bernie Andrews joined the BBC in October 1957 at the age of 24, rock'n' roll may have been in full swing in the USA but it was barely beginning to encroach on the BBC. The Gramophone department operated a policy of giving airplay priority to British recordings of popular tunes; although in many ways admirable, this meant that original records from Elvis Presley and Little Richard were passed over in favour of covers by British dance bands. The originals would turn up only when specifically requested on programmes like *Family Favourites*.

There was one small sign of the way ahead. A 30-minute pre-recorded programme, *Saturday Skiffle Club*, had been launched on the Light Programme at the beginning of June that year, taking over the daily 10 a.m. theatre organ spot. The producer was Jimmy Grant of the Light Entertainment department, a skilled jazz musician; and the presenter Brian Matthew, a new BBC staff announcer who had left his job as an actor at the Old Vic the year before. 'The folk and jazz elements of skiffle at first made up the entire repertoire of the acts,' Grant remembers, 'but then some of the groups began introducing pop tunes such as Everly Brothers numbers, but I cannot recall whether amplifiers were ever brought into the studio.' That was yet to come.

On his way to his BBC engineering induction course on his first day that October, Bernie bumped into another new recruit outside the Langham Hotel: Johnny Beerling, a former studio technician at RAF Aden, and today controller of Radio 1. They started out working the same shift in the old control room in the Broadcasting House sub-basement. After a few months they went separate ways, Johnny becoming a studio manager, and Bernie moving into tape recording, a parting that would ten years on see Johnny producing the new Radio 1's top-rated *Tony Blackburn Show* and Bernie in charge of the most rebellious item in the schedule, *Top Gear*; but they have always remained friends.

The department that Bernie moved into in summer 1958 was a relatively new one, 'XP-Ops', or transportable tape machines, for playing in pre-recorded items (inserts) from the control cubicle during programme transmissions, and for location recording at BBC theatres. At first, American Ampex recorders were used; but after a few months the department standardized on EMI TR90s, single-track mono quarter-inch, 15ips tape recorders, then new, and still the staple music-recording machine in BBC outside studios in the first years of Radio 1. The only other tape machines the BBC used in the late 1950s were also mono, BTR-2s. These huge green units, designed in the 1940s and known affectionately as 'battleships' or 'ovens', certainly weren't portable, and were mainly used to tape complete programmes for later broadcast. But in 1958, recording by tape at the BBC was only just becoming the norm. Jimmy Grant remembers producing many programmes in the mid-1950s 'with inserts played in on 78 r.p.m. acetate discs'.

In summer 1958, the high listening figures for *Saturday Skiffle Club* prompted Jimmy Grant's boss, Jim Davidson, head of Light Entertainment, to ask Grant to put together a two-hour live programme with quite a small budget aimed at a younger audience, with half an hour's needletime. This was one of the many firsts for the show that would eventually run until January 1969, *Saturday Club*.

For the Gramophone department, which controlled needletime and kept nearly all of it for its own programmes (a few minutes went to Home Service programmes like *Desert Island Discs* and *Down Your Way*), to give some of it to a rival music programme-making department was unprecedented. Before, music shows from Davidson's department were all live or pre-recorded sessions.

'There must have been some reluctance to lose control of needletime to another department,' reflects Grant. 'I was instructed to take my list of records every week to Jack Dabbs, a producer in the Gramophone department, for approval. It was clear from the start that he wasn't concerned which records I had chosen, and we left it that I would consult him if I had any problems. Things might have been different if a less amenable gramophone producer had been chosen for me to see.'

This meant that for the first time a producer was free to play the latest genuine rock'n' roll records from America, if only nine or ten each week. The rest of the show would be made up of four pre-recorded sessions, put down at the Playhouse, 201 Piccadilly, the Paris, or Maida Vale; and one live band. On the first edition, on 4 October 1958, the guests were Terry Dene and the Dene Aces; Humphrey Lyttelton and his Band in the 'Jazz Cellar' (who also recorded the signature tune, 'Saturday Jump', written by Grant under another alias, Eddie James, and later re-recorded by Ted Heath); Gary Miller; Johnny Duncan and his Blue Grass Boys; and Russell Quaye's City Ramblers. Record requests were featured in 'Cats' Call'.

If none of this seems the sound of rock'n' roll rebellion, it was nevertheless new for the BBC Light Programme of the late 1950s. Trad, bluegrass, folk and the beginnings of R & B were all regarded as fringe cults, and to put them all together into one Saturday morning show was positively radical.

As a BBC technical production, it was a total innovation. It was the first radio programme to combine live music, records and pre-recorded sessions, all of which would be presented live from Studio 3A in Broadcasting House. Grant, Matthew, their studio manager (live sound) Ron Belchier and first XP operator Pete Dauncey could look down from the control cubicle into the main studio on the floor below, where the live band, normally a trad jazz group, would be playing. In 1959, when Pete Dauncey left for an engineering course, Bernie took over as regular XP-op, Johnny Beerling came in as grams studio manager, cuing up the records, and this team ran the show for the next two years.

But the show would never have been possible without yet another liberating development: the Musicians' Union agreement in 1956 to allow live music sessions to be pre-recorded. Before that, since the opening of Broadcasting House in 1932, every music show was live. The only music recording that went on was of complete programmes on to transcription disc, for a single re-broadcast on the Empire Service, or, later, General Overseas Service, forerunners of today's World Service.

During the war the union had allowed 'substitutional' recording, the recording of a complete show at or after a final rehearsal, in case the Blitz prevented the show going out live from a London studio. The union didn't want to risk the lives of its members, even for the sake of a principle. Many old BBC theatres were destroyed in the bombing. Indeed, it was to cover the loss of St George's Hall to enemy action in September 1940 that the Corporation acquired the tiny Paris Cinema in Lower Regent Street, 'for largely service audiences'; this was still in use for Radio 1's classic *In Concert* recordings in the 1970s (today it's used for BBC radio comedy shows).

Once hostilities were over, the union clamped down. 'MUSICIANS ACT AGAINST RECORDED BROADCASTS,' announced the front page of the *News Chronicle* on 1 March 1946. The union,

Making radio shows in 1959, in Studio S1, sub-basement, Broadcasting House: (left to right) tape operator Bernie Andrews with two TR90s; studio manager Johnny Beerling, today Controller of Radio 1 FM, at the mixing desk; *Roundabout* producer Jack Singleton (standing); and presenter and guitarist Ken Sykora.

under general secretary F. Dambman, argued that instead of recordings, all shows should be live, creating jobs for demobbed musicians returning to civvy street from the forces. Under the new Labour government the union had strong political sympathy, and won. The BBC agreed to abolish all pre-recording of complete programmes of music.

This merely created confusion over bands playing a number or two in a variety show, which was then recorded for repeat broadcast. The union, under new general secretary Hardie Ratcliffe, tried to get tough on this in 1954, and sought to ban *all* 'pre-recording' at the BBC.

It was unsuccessful, and in this lay the seeds of its undoing. For during the crisis negotiations the BBC's head of programme contracts, W. L. Streeton, having been asked to investigate the implications of tape recording, pointed out to his superiors in a confidential memo that it was now possible 'to make up a pre-recorded programme by a series of sessions at each of which we both rehearse and pre-record. This would involve the MU recognizing a new type of session, somewhat akin to a transcription, film or gramophone recording session.' The BBC negotiators raised it with the MU immediately. Nothing happened, but two years later the point was eventually conceded. The 'pre-recording' session was created, just in time for *Saturday Club*.

Not that this new type of session was anything like as informal as Radio 1 sessions today. Every session was to be three hours' rehearsal followed by half an hour's continuous recording, producing some ten or twelve numbers. For *Saturday Club*, this meant two options. Either Jimmy Grant could hire an established band leader or musical director, with up to a dozen session musicians, who would back two star singers, performing five songs each, with the orchestra adding

a couple of instrumentals at the end of the session; or, more problematically, he could hire two self-contained groups, who would both have to set up, rehearse and then record five numbers each, all within three and a half hours.

All this was to be achieved in mono, in one take, with no overdubs, no 'EQ' (tone controls) on the eight-channel BBC Type-A mixing desk, no playback for the acts to hear how they sounded, and no remixing before broadcast. Vocal overdubs were introduced later on, by 'bouncing' the recorded backing track on to a second tape machine and adding the vocals at the same time; but as this was strictly outside the MU agreement it frequently had to be conducted secretly, once any regular MU session men on the date had left for the pub, thinking the session over.

'To be frank, during the early stages of the programme, the SM [studio manager] and I would be pleased if we got five numbers of broadcastable quality from a group in the limited time,' says Jimmy Grant. 'It's worth noting that prior to *Skiffle Club* practically all broadcasters in popular music were trained musicians, with twenty years' or more experience, able to co-operate in the studio with the SM to produce good results in the time available. With *Skiffle Club*, SMs had to learn to cope with inexperienced broadcasters, although, in time, I suppose, talent won through.'

The question of new talent raises the spectre of the BBC Audition Unit. In those days, every artist to be broadcast first had to pass an audition. A band who applied would be booked, along with three other hopefuls, for a three-hour session. Each band would have just 45 minutes to set up, rehearse and record up to three numbers. The unmarked tapes would then be vetted by the Talent Selection Group, a weekly meeting of

Light Entertainment producers, who would aim to pass or fail up to twenty acts in a morning's listening. 'It was generally a very fair system,' says Bernie.

For records, there was an equivalent monitoring body, the Dance Music Policy Committee, later just the Popular Music Policy Committee, which sat in judgment each week on sheet music, albums and singles. It was eventually wound up at the end of 1964, when the absurdity of songs like Cole Porter's 'Love for sale' still being marked 'NTBB' (Not To Be Broadcast) on grounds of 'taste' became too much embarrassing publicity for the BBC to bear.

In the early 1960s *Saturday Club* was easily the top radio show in Britain. Admittedly, it had little competition. In 1960 *Easy Beat* was launched, with a live session included on each Saturday evening's live show from the Playhouse (later it moved to Sunday morning), and the daily lunchtime shows on the Light began to feature guest pop groups; but *Saturday Club* was the biggest weekly showcase.

It also had two very positive things going for it, as regular listener (and later *New Musical Express* staffer) Bob Woffinden recalled on the show's 30th anniversary in the *Listener*: Jimmy Grant's 'painstaking production work ... he always tried to achieve a fast-paced show'; and 'the authority and unruffled professionalism of Brian Matthew, surely one of the outstanding voices in post-war radio'. But if the show was big already, unpredictable events were about to transform it into a legend.

On 7 March 1962 a northern group with a strong local following were booked into the Playhouse Theatre, Manchester, by BBC Light Programme producer Peter Pilbeam for their debut session, to be broadcast on *Teenager's Turn* the following

day. He wrote on their audition report: 'a tendency to play music'. 'Now that was, in those days, high praise, because a hell of a lot of noise came out of most of the three guitars and drums groups,' says Pilbeam. In a tradition continued today by Peel, that group were then just another unsigned band. The Beatles didn't sign to EMI until July.

The week after the Beatles' debut, Bernie Andrews, having acquired a name as the fastest tape editor around, began a three-month 'attachment' as a producer in Light Entertainment, at the suggestion of Jim Davidson himself. It was a breakthrough, for never before had a tape op, or anyone from Engineering, moved straight into production.

Tape operations then came under 'Engineering', and the established BBC promotion route was first to move out of the 'recording channel', the separate room which held the tape machines, into the control cubicle, and become a 'studio manager' or 'SM', who mixed and balanced the sound; and thence a producer. Xp-Ops, however, had brought portable machines into the control cubicle, and talented engineers, like Pete Dauncey and Bernie, with them. Getting into the cubicle was effectively half-way to promotion.

Most producers and SMs at that time, like the acts they were used to recording, were ex-RAF, educated, experienced musicians, with a strong bias towards jazz. Bernie's background, by contrast, was simply that of the ordinary pop fan. In a BBC environment characterised by professionalism, Bernie's common touch was to prove invaluable.

By the time the Beatles did their first session for *Saturday Club*, on 28 January 1963, many things had changed. They had two hits under their belt; Bernie had just become a full-time producer at the Aeolian Hall; and the MU, late in 1962, had agreed to allow 'discontinuous' pre-recording, whereby each number could be rehearsed, then recorded immediately, rather than taping all tracks in a single take at the end of the session. During the negotiations the union told the BBC this was 'the sacrifice of a cherished principle'. 'They undoubtedly spoke from the heart,' noted G. M. Turnell, head of programme contracts. Yet it was clearly what union session men wanted. For a start, verbal directions from the Musical Director didn't have to be remembered for up to two hours, until the red light was finally on.

One more crucial change was under way. Late in April 1963 the BBC floated Popular Music off from Light Entertainment as a separate department, headed by Ken Baynes, with Donald MacLean as his assistant. In May, three chief producers were appointed to over-see the new department's various kinds of programmes. Not surprisingly, considering *Saturday Club*'s pre-eminence, Jimmy Grant was put in charge of pop music. He remained as co-producer of his show, but only had time to produce every other Saturday's transmission. So he delegated the alternate week's transmission, choice of records, session bookings and all session production, save one a week, to his new co-producer: Bernie Andrews. 'Bernie definitely became the supremo for a period,' recalls Brian Matthew, 'and the show changed noticeably.'

His co-producer saw it. 'Bernie excelled in consistently booking top-line British and American groups for the programme and matching studio facilities to their limited availability,' says Grant. 'This was against a background of a new economy regime of block bookings at fixed times, with which he struggled.'

But Bernie did a lot more than this. He had often watched in dismay, on various programmes, as a nervous young group doing their first BBC session (a far more make-or-break career moment than today) would be bustled along – 'That's fine, next number please' – not allowed to hear their takes played back, and generally shown little sympathy. 'They had to do as they were told,' says Bernie, in a mock-authoritative tone, 'and if they didn't, that was the last session they did. You didn't come along and tell *BBC producers* what to do!' The professional, cool atmosphere that worked so well for accomplished jazzers was stultifying for self-taught beat groups. Bernie began to make some changes.

For a start, he invited bands into the cubicle to hear their takes. This was simply not done. At first, horrified SMs of the old school would protest: 'What do you want to ask their opinion for? They're only pop musicians, what do they know about how it should sound?' But helped by his new regular SM, Vernon Lawrence, and later on, Bev Phillips, Bernie established this courtesy.

Bev Phillips was already acquiring a name as the SM for getting a good drum sound. 'Originally for *Saturday Club* there'd just be one mike above the kit, and one on the bass drum as well. Then I'd be at a gig and see a mike on a specific part of the kit and think "hmmm…".'

Bev also developed the tradition of SMs bringing in a personal suitcase of tricks to modify the spartan controls of the BBC desks, a tradition begun by the legendary SM Freddy Harris, who first stuck a fag packet down the back of a standard BBC ribbon mike to help get a good piano sound.

'In the early sixties there was usually only one "Response Selection Amplifier" or RSA (a basic pre-amp) per studio mixing desk, so once you had enhanced the vocal mike, you were technically stuffed,' recalls Bev. 'I used to solder resistors and capacitors between

The very first *Top Gear* session. The Beatles in Studio S2, sub-basement, Broadcasting House, 14 July 1964.

telephone jack plugs housed in my father's tobacco tins in order to create high-pass filters. There was once hell to pay when my boss came round with some engineering top-brass and saw these tobacco tins dangling from the jackfield on the wall.'

Taking more trouble to get a good electric guitar and drum sound, they found they couldn't squeeze two bands into a single session. In a move which was initially criticized by BBC management for encouraging inefficiency, self-contained bands on Bernie's show now got a session each. When the Beatles had done their first *Saturday Club* dates earlier in 1963, they'd had to share the sessions, the first with Alan Elsdon's Jazz Band (22 January), and the third with Kenny Ball and his Band (25 May). (The second was live from 3A on Saturday, 16 March.)

But by the time they came in to record for the show's special fifth birthday edition, on 5 October, they had a session to themselves. That show, produced by Bernie, also featured the Everly Brothers, Joe Brown and Kenny Ball; as well as Frank Ifield, Kathy Kirby, and Tommy Roe singing with the Art Greenslade Orchestra, complete with strings – 'the most expensive pop session ever booked,' recalls Bernie – and won 20.2 per cent of the adult listening population, 'and that's not counting any under-14s.' This classic broadcast is now, thanks to Bernie's foresight in making a complete tape, one of the jewels in the BBC Sound Archive.

'Before the Beatles there weren't many real electric self-contained groups, except perhaps Cliff and the Shadows, and Shane Fenton and the Fentones,' points out Bernie. So the need to allocate more time for electric group recording was an inevitable development, as Jimmy Grant recognises: 'Pop taste changed over the run of *Saturday Club* from middle-of-

the-road, finally polarizing towards beat groups, and, for instance, the small backing group of session musicians later proved unsuitable.'

The session-men system could still come in handy. After the Rolling Stones, minus Charlie Watts and Bill Wyman who were fearful of losing their day jobs, had just failed an audition early in 1963, Bernie got them in that autumn by booking individuals from the group to back Bo Diddley.

Once they were there, he gave them the first of what was to evolve into another mould-breaking innovation. Instead of the standard audition, he did a full session with them, and submitted that to the audition panel, but only *after* it had been broadcast. 'It had to be someone already becoming "big" for the innovation to be accepted,' recalls Mary Cotgrove of Auditions; with her support and Jimmy Grant's, this 'trial broadcast' idea was rapidly adopted as more appropriate for rock acts who were already recording stars. Bill Wyman recalled on the Radio 1 documentary *The Stones at the Beeb* that one member of the panel thought Mick Jagger's vocals 'too black'; but they squeezed a pass. The session went out on *Saturday Club* on 26 October 1963.

Through winter and spring 1964, new bands like the Animals, Manfred Mann and the Kinks joined the Beatles and the Stones as regulars. In his quest for informality, Bernie was now doing such revolutionary things as, for a recording with Trini Lopez of 'If I had a hammer', inviting along an entire participating audience of BBC clerical staff, 'for many of whom it was clearly their first contact with real-life showbiz,' remembers Bev Phillips. Then he borrowed a builder's board for him and Brian Matthew to stamp along authentically behind the Dave Clark Five's 'Bits and pieces' (the audition panel rejected the tape); and in

February 1964, in response to press criticism of the thinness of BBC versions of current hits, Bernie announced he was adding an extra trumpet, sax, two guitars and a second drummer to the show's regular backing band Arthur Greenslade and the G Men. He'd already added vocal backing groups on star sessions for the first time the previous year.

The music press started referring to Bernie as 'ace BBC producer'. In January 1964 the BBC announced that regular adult audience figures for the show had recently trebled to 9 million. The total was much higher. The next month Decca released its *Saturday Club* tribute LP, made up of sessions recorded specially by Jimmy Grant, featuring regular guests. And the show of 14 March won *Saturday Club*'s highest ever audience, 25.1 per cent of the adult listening population.

By now the tide of beat groups was unstoppable. The BBC bowed to the inevitable, and Bernie was asked, at short notice, to produce a new show 'to reflect the group scene, a more progressive version of *Saturday Club*'. 'In other words, it didn't mix skiffle, trad-jazz ... it was pretty hard rock from the word go,' recalls Brian Matthew, who was to present it. Bernie was given a slot, 10 – 11.55 p.m. on Thursdays, a budget of £225 per programme, and – 'quite generous' – 45 minutes' needletime. The first show was to be on 16 July 1964 – but what to call it, and who to book?

'I organised a competition through *Disc*,' says Bernie. Two winners, Margaret Swanson of Edinburgh, and Susan Warne of Welwyn Garden City, suggested *Top Gear*. Their prize, although only Susan could come, was to attend the recording session of the show's first guests, the Beatles, who also recorded some irreverent trailers. The session, on 14 July, came days after the release of both the film and LP *A Hard Day's Night*.

Bernie got the Beatles because by now he'd formed a close friendship with the group.

'I had got to know them very well socially, because I used to share a flat in Shepherd's Street, in Shepherd's Market, in Mayfair – sounds posh, but it was eleven quid a week for four bedrooms, kitchen and bathroom and I wish I still had it! – with a very close friend of George's, Terry Doran, who was a business associate of Brian Epstein. So both Brian and the boys used to come round to see Terry. I wouldn't kid myself they only used to come round to see me. George used to come round for egg and chips. He loved egg and chips. He couldn't go to a café because he'd get mobbed. He didn't want to know about cooking it himself, so he used to come round to Bern's for egg and chips. Paul only came round once, actually. Terry had this mynah bird in a cage just inside the door. When Paul came in, the bird said "Hello Ringo!" I was very embarrassed, because it was the first time Paul had come round.'

Cheeky birds notwithstanding, the first session for *Top Gear* was a classic. The group did five numbers from the new LP, and Paul tore through 'Long tall Sally'. They also clowned about with Brian Matthew, launching 'Bernie's new vessel'. 'When was the accident, then?' says John.

Early in March 1965 it was also Bernie who brought the Stones back from the wilderness with a *Top Gear* session, after they were 'banned' by the BBC in December 1964 for failing to turn up to three recording sessions. The *Melody Maker* of 12 December had proclaimed: 'BBC STORM: 6 MONTH SATURDAY CLUB BAN?' 'We are not going to book them,' a *Saturday Club* office spokesman told the paper. Light Entertainment booking manager Pat Newman wrote in a memo that he would 'dearly love to impose sanctions

The Jimi Hendrix Experience

RECORDED: 6 OCTOBER 1967
STUDIO: PLAYHOUSE THEATRE
PRODUCER: BEV PHILLIPS
ENGINEER: PETE RITZEMA
FIRST BROADCAST: 15 OCTOBER 1967 *TOP GEAR*

TRACKS: 'Little Miss Lover', 'Driving south', 'Burning of the midnight lamp', 'Hound dog', 'Experiencing the blues'.

LINE-UP: Jimi Hendrix, guitar & vocals; Noel Redding, bass & vocals; Mitch Mitchell, drums.

'While at the BBC studios, we were introduced to Stevie Wonder [there to be interviewed by Brian Matthew]. When Mitch nipped off to the loo, some enterprising person suggested an "informal jam" between Jimi and myself, with Stevie on drums. We jammed two segments, then Stevie sang an old R&B song. Of course, they forgot to turn the tape machines off. The jam was aired a couple of times [not on *Top Gear*] and then bootlegged.' (*Are You Experienced?* by Noel Redding and Carol Appleby, © 1990. Published by Fourth Estate Ltd.)

'Stevie wanted to play the drums, to calm down before his interview. Jimi Hendrix and Noel Redding played along with a bit of 'I was made to love her', for about a minute and a half, and then about another seven minutes of mucking about. I don't remember Stevie singing, though. It's not that wonderful, but it is one of those legendary things: Stevie Wonder *did* jam with Jimi Hendrix on that session *and* it's there on tape. I don't think it was ever broadcast.

'Hendrix I remember as being rather shy, giggly and camp. He was very self-conscious about doing his vocals. He insisted on having screens put up round his mike when he was overdubbing his vocals, because, otherwise, he said, Noel and Mitch would make him laugh. But he also did these blues jams on his sessions [e.g. 'Getting my heart back together again' on his second *Top Gear* session, 15 December 1967] where he'd get everyone along from the Hendrix office to join in, which was rather fun.'

PETE RITZEMA

The Jimi Hendrix Experience, 1967: Jimi Hendrix, Mitch Mitchell, Noel Redding

of some sort.' Teddy Warrick, then a producer in the Gramophone department, recalls getting memos from Popular Music telling them not play Stones records; this is backed up by Bill Wyman, who recalls the band's hit single, 'Little red rooster', being omitted from *Pick of the Pops*' Christmas and New Year shows.

For all these reasons *Top Gear* was an enormous success. But it only ran for a year. After six months it was cut to an hour and switched to 4 p.m. on Saturday. It was axed at the end of June 1965. There was a small demonstration outside Broadcasting House and, learning of the impending axe, Bob Dawbarn wrote a feature in the *Melody Maker* on 29 May, 'Is the BBC anti-pop?': 'The BBC, with remarkable generosity, has just parcelled up its Saturday afternoon pop listeners and handed them over to the pirate stations,' he wrote. The pirates, including Caroline and London, had been broadcasting for almost a year.

Bernie, today, can only put the axeing down to his superiors not liking the show. Perhaps *Top Gear* took undeserved blame for the Corporation's struggle to come to terms with the swinging sixties. Bernie got a new show, *Folk Room*. The only live shows left playing any rock were *Saturday Club* and *Easy Beat*.

Yet perhaps the most interesting BBC show of this period (1965 – 67) and which was to run on into the early seventies, couldn't easily be heard in Britain: a short 20-minute programme on the World Service, *Rhythm and Blues*, presented by the late Alexis Korner, and produced by Jeff Griffin, who had taken over from Bernie as XP-op on *Saturday Club* and later followed him into production. Based on one session a week, Jeff recorded bands like the Yardbirds, John Mayall's Bluesbreakers, the Spencer Davis group, Zoot Money and, later, a

classic session in Aeolian 2, on which Alexis jammed, 'brilliantly', according to Noel Redding, on slide guitar with the Jimi Hendrix Experience. 'Bit loud out there, boy, ain't it?' queried Jeff's SM, the 'MIGHTY' Joe Young, the BBC's famous live-jazz engineer, so dubbed by the late jazz critic and broadcaster Peter Clayton.

Bill Bebb, who became *Saturday Club*'s last producer in 1966, remembers the best sessions of that time as being precisely the same kind of rhythm and blues acts that Jeff and Alexis were recording. 'One after another we were doing first broadcasts: the Cream, the Who, Amen Corner.'

There was an extraordinary Tom Jones date at the Paris. He was booked for the afternoon, and Eric Burdon for the evening, but Burdon got muddled, and came along after lunch. 'What's more, he'd told all his mates to come down,' says Bill. 'Gordon Mills [Tom Jones' manager] was flapping because the Squires' organist hadn't turned up, when in stroll Eric's mates: Georgie Fame, Alan Price, Chris Farlowe and Zoot Money. "I think your organ problems are over," I said.' Fame played organ, Price piano, and Farlowe and Money did backing vocals. Gordon Mills told Bill Bebb he would allow this to happen, but, in the interest of building up Tom's career, didn't want the real line-up announced on air. 'Tom loved it,' says Bill.

But in 1966 it was easily the pirates that were leading pop radio, with all-record programming. On 20 December 1966, in the wake of the first reading of its Marine Offences Bill, the Labour government published its White Paper on the future of broadcasting, recommending that the BBC should run a popular music service. And yet what both government and BBC had in mind was hardly a copy of the pirates. In the *BBC Handbook* for 1967, published late in 1966, Frank Gillard, director of Sound Broadcasting, wrote: 'startling changes in BBC Radio in 1967 are highly improbable'.

Some insiders, like Donald MacLean, assistant head of Popular Music, believed listeners wanted to hear popular tunes, and the BBC should commission its own research into a song, not record sales-based, chart, working from which the department's regular orchestras would record cover versions. Others, like Mark White, MacLean's opposite number at the Gramophone department, and Robin Scott, who arrived in March 1967, argued for as much needletime as possible, believing the station should, ideally, be all-record.

But even with another seven hours' needletime granted by the MU and PPL, an all-disc format was impossible. Inevitably, the launch format was a compromise between Scott, White and MacLean, enforced by needletime restrictions. There was one significant breakthrough, however, in the summer of 1967, without which, Scott is convinced, the station would never have got on air: a new deal on sessions negotiated by MacLean and Michael Standing (Controller, Programme Organization Radio), with an MU team led by John Morton.

Essentially, it expanded an experimental deal which had been running for two Light Programme shows since late 1964, making it available for most daytime shows. The 'item recording' agreement allowed producers to use tracks from one session on different days of the week: one at 4 p.m. Monday, the next at 5.30 p.m. Tuesday, and so on, instead of having to put the session out as a lump. This remains the basis of how Mark Goodier and Nicky Campbell use their sessions. 'It meant we could use those items like we might use gramophone records,' says Robin Scott, 'but it also allowed groups not only to play both sides of their current hit, but six other numbers as well.' Nevertheless, 'departmental policy was that sessions were simply a necessity,' says Mark White.

Bernie, however, had a more positive attitude, with a new idea to help make Radio 1 sessions worthwhile. 'To me, it seemed silly to spend $3^1/_2$ hours in a studio, recording material just for one programme, because you used a third of that setting up and getting a balance. So I had this idea for the "double-session". I'd book the studio for seven hours: that gave us twice as much time for recording; the band got twice the fee; and I'd record enough material for two programmes — I'd hold two of the tracks back for a later broadcast.

'I made an undertaking to the groups that if they did a session for me, I would take a lot of trouble over it, as much as I could, and get it how *they* wanted. I'd make sure I'd get the right sort of studio, which was the Playhouse, and the right engineer, who was sympathetic to that kind of music the heavy groups were playing, and that was Pete Ritzema.'

'Bernie was a great innovator,' says Pete Ritzema. 'The double-session was a really radical departure. The people who did those sessions were prepared to hang around for hours and hours, really producing the thing *with* the musicians.'

Bernie knew groups were frustrated with the BBC's mono studios and time restrictions. The double-session implicitly took them and their music seriously. The deal was exclusive to Bernie and the show he created. The *Sounds of the Seventies* shows that came along in 1970 had to make do with the old $3^1/_2$ hour system. When those shows were axed at the end of 1974, leaving only Peel and Walters standing, the double-session they inherited from Bernie became the main kind of Radio 1 session. Every 'session' today is still, technically, two, or even three sessions: 2.30 – 6 p.m. 7.30 – 11 p.m., and, sometimes, extra mixing time to 1 a.m. Bernie's legacy, however, is not only the recording schemes he spun; it lies in the classic recordings they helped him create.

He felt he made one of his very best on the day after that first Radio 1 *Top Gear*, on 2 October 1967. It was the first for a new Birmingham band, the Idle Race, led by Jeff Lynne. For the recording at the Playhouse, extra instruments hired by the BBC included '2 pedal timps, glockenspiel, Wow Pedal' (*sic*). The band had just released their first single and had applied for an audition, but before one could be booked, Bernie called them in for this 'trial broadcast'.

'We'd been going for about eighteen months,' says Jeff Lynne. 'We lived and played mostly in Birmingham, so going down to London to record for the BBC was a major event. We hadn't had much experience of recording, so it was a relief to find it quite easy-going. I thought it was great, you got to record and got paid for doing it. I think the fee just about covered the petrol from Birmingham.

'Bernie got us a good sound. At the time, I was wanting to be a producer myself, so I was learning a lot. I even got some blue corduroy trousers like Bernie's, and wore them for my first attempt as a record producer, the second Idle Race album. From then on, corduroy trousers were always called Producer's Trousers.'

The Idle Race were one of several bands who availed themselves of the BBC's unique phasing technique: the engineer's thumb. 'The BTR machines were the best because of the gap between the heads,' Bev Phillips explains. 'This allowed the engineer's thumb to distort the passage of the tape between the heads,

creating azimuth misalignment.'

That was just the Monday of the first Radio 1 week on air. Tuesday saw the Crazy World of Arthur Brown, with Ron Wood guesting on guitar, pre-recording at Aeolian 2, and Lou Rawls and Maxine Brown at 201 Piccadilly. Wednesday was Denny Laine's Electric String Band at Maida Vale 4, with Bernie and Dave Tate; and Friday the Jimi Hendrix Experience at the Playhouse.

But it wasn't the group's first BBC session. They had done two for *Saturday Club*, in February and March that year. Chas Chandler, Jimi's manager, knew Bill Bebb from his days in the Animals, and had assured him, as Bill recalls, that 'this guy'll blow you away.'

He did more than that. The first session, on 13 February, was in S2, a studio in the Broadcasting House sub-basement, three floors below street level, which had originally been the small Vaudeville studio theatre. 'The SM [Peter Harwood] said "getting a lot of feedback", so I opened up the talkback, and started saying "er, Jimi, we're getting rather a lot … ", when Chas, sitting with me in the control room, leans over and says, "shut-up man, that's his *sound*!",' remembers Bill. 'So quickly I said, "No, everything's fine Jimi, you just carry on." But by now the SM's having kittens. "Just shut it right down," I said; but when he switched off the monitors we could still hear Jimi through the soundproof glass, and we could *see* the glass moving.'

Half-way through the session, a woman appeared behind Bill to complain that the live string quartet broadcast she was doing for Radio 3 from the Concert Hall, two floors above, kept being interrupted by wafts of electric guitar. But, as Bill points out, for this first, and possibly unique Radio 1 & 3 simulcast, 'Jimi didn't even ask for a repeat fee.'

The Bonzo Dog Doo-Dah Band

RECORDED: 8 NOVEMBER 1967
STUDIO: MAIDA VALE 4
PRODUCER: BERNIE ANDREWS
ENGINEER: PETE RITZEMA
FIRST BROADCAST: 12 NOVEMBER 1967 *TOP GEAR*

TRACKS: 'The equestrian statue', 'The Craig Torso show', 'Mickey's son and daughter', 'Death cab for Cutie'.

LINE-UP: Viv Stanshall, vocals, trumpet, tuba & ukelele; Neil Innes, piano, guitar & vocals; Roger Ruskin Spear, saxophone, cornet & xylophone; Rodney Slater, saxophone, clarinet, trombone & tuba; Legs Larry Smith, drums; Vernon Dudley Bohay-Nowell, bass & banjo; Sam Spoons, percussion.

'We'd always do short playlets, made up specially for the sessions. They would be worked out in the BBC studio for the first time. I remember I lived round the corner from Bernie in Muswell Hill, and I used to phone him up the day before a session asking can we have such-and-such effect? Those sessions quickly took the format of three songs and one piece of recitative. I used to invent things just to break all these ridiculous BBC rules: like on the one we did later with Walters, he told us that more than five-or-six seconds' silence was not allowed, so I put about ten seconds into "Sofa head", after saying "Silence is appropriate, and it shall remain appropriate." On that first one with Bernie, 'The Craig Torso show' was a play parodying the new Radio 1 DJs, which we never recorded elsewhere.'

VIV STANSHALL

'They were some of the most creative sessions I ever did, because the numbers were *created* in the studio, with tape editing, effects and so on. As the first ones also ran until 1 a.m., then unheard-of, and the commissionaires at Maida Vale and Piccadilly complained, they also started my undeserved reputation of running all these weird sessions through the night.'

BERNIE ANDREWS

The Bonzo Dog Doo-Dah Band, 1967

The session of 6 October went out on the third Radio 1 *Top Gear*, along with debuts by the Incredible String Band and Skip Bifferty, a session by the Bee Gees, and a 'first' of a different kind from the Who: the first BBC music session recorded outside the Corporation, in a commercial music studio. Bernie remembers he had to fight for permission. The Who were keen to do it, as proved by their agreeing to record five one-off jingles for the show on the date, including 'My favourite station' to the tune of 'My generation'; but had insisted on using stereo facilities at De Lane Lea, rather than BBC mono studios. Bernie went there to produce it on the 10th. Soon afterwards, the Who offered to re-do some of their *Top Gear* jingles for regular use on Radio 1, but were prevented by the fact that there was, apparently, 'no MU/BBC agreed basis for a contract'.

All this was going on without Peel. But after the fourth show (featuring the Nice's first session, members of whom had backed Tim Rose's recording two days before), Bernie put him back on air with Drummond for two more Sundays. The 29 October *Top Gear* featured new sessions from the Cream, the Kinks and Jeff Beck, and the debut of Roy Harper, backed by Clem Cattini on drums and Brian Brocklehurst on bass. 'The recording experience was fraught with worrying whether what I was doing would be understood by either the session musicians or the producer and engineer,' says Harper; the session ended up 'a compromise, but quite a happy one. What I managed to get together with the bass player on 'Zengem' was excellent. The most important thing I gained, I think, was how quickly something adequate could be knocked together when necessary.'

Peel was beginning to have quite an influence on the bookings. There had been the Incredible String Band and then,

for 5 November, the debut session by Tyrannosaurus Rex. Two of the six numbers Marc Bolan and Steve Peregrine-Took played on the 30 October recording at 201 Piccadilly, 'Highways' and 'Pictures of purple people' (the latter not broadcast until the repeat on 4 February 1968), did not appear later on the group's first album.

Although Peel was already a fan and friend of Bolan, the audition panel were not so sure about the tape when it was presented to them the day after the trial broadcast. 'Crap, and pretentious crap at that,' said one producer. They scored two 'No' votes; but, demonstrating the fairness of the system, six said 'Yes', and the group passed, as 'a contemporary folk/blues duo' with the proviso that 'the panel thought them suitable only for specialist programmes such as *Top Gear*'.

Perhaps it's no coincidence that two days after the panel met it was suggested to Bernie informally by one of his superiors that perhaps he shouldn't use Peel again. Bernie acted immediately. He telephoned Clive Selwood [Peel's manager] and booked Peel for a further seven weeks. From 12 November, for the next three months, *Top Gear* was to be co-hosted by Peel with Tommy Vance. There was hell to pay for Bernie when the Popular Music department found out. But by then it was too late.

Initial audience research on the network's first month, which appeared internally from the second week of November, showed that the 'sizeable minority' who liked *Top Gear* felt Peel had 'a good voice' and was 'more sincere' than other DJs. The duty office summarized its calls up to 21 November, saying that 'many of the suggestions for Radio 1 were from supporters of DJs such as John Peel and Tony Prince'.

Peel and Vance's first show featured no

less than three first broadcast sessions: the Gun, Peter Green's Fleetwood Mac and the Bonzo Dog Doo-Dah Band, recorded successively on 6, 7 and 8 November. And the next week it was Brian Auger's Trinity, Honeybus, and a session by Lulu, which has become an innocent subject of controversy.

For years Peel has believed that this was on his first show, and held it up as an example of what he recalls as the programme's original brief, 'to look over the horizons of pop', which never, in truth, existed in writing. Like all BBC radio producers then, Bernie was never given a formal brief: 'they knew what I was about,' he says. In fact, Bernie booked Lulu partly at the suggestion of Donald MacLean, to reassure him that *Top Gear* was open-minded, and partly because she was going through an R&B phase. 'It was actually a bloody good, ballsy session,' Bernie recalls. 'I think if Peel heard it now he'd be quite surprised.'

Two more debut sessions followed on the 26th: Family and Elmer Gantry's Velvet Opera. So the scoops went on: Ten Years After and Fairport Convention on 10 December (along with a storming soul session from Gladys Knight and the Pips, backed by the Johnny Watson Concept, including then session guitarists Jim Sullivan and Jimmy Page – 'they were knocked out by the guitar playing,' recalls Pete Ritzema); and the Soft Machine on the 17th, all of these being trial broadcasts.

That Softs debut was of the three-piece that had just released their first LP, including Kevin Ayers on guitar and bass, and they did 'Clarence in Wonderland', later a staple of Ayers' solo BBC sessions. As Robert Wyatt was to sing on their second session, eighteen months later, 'though each little song was less than three minutes long, Mike [Ratledge] squeezed a solo in somehow'.

And then on Christmas Eve it was David Bowie's turn. Two years earlier, on 2 November 1965, his group, David Bowie and the Lower Third, had auditioned but been rejected by the Talent Selection Group, with comments on his report such as: 'a singer devoid of personality' and 'amateur sounding vocalist who sings wrong notes'.

Now he was back with his debut album on Deram, in his Anthony Newley phase. Bernie liked it a lot. 'I phoned up Ken Pitt [then Bowie's manager], and the three of us met for lunch to discuss it. David wasn't too keen to do things from the LP, because to him it was already old stuff; but he did some of them, plus new songs ('In the heat of the morning', for example). It was very good for a first session: he did almost everything first take.' Bernie booked a fifteen-piece version of the Art Greenslade Orchestra, complete with four-piece violin section to back Bowie, on that 18 December recording at 201 Piccadilly. This time, the tape passed the audition panel.

That same show featured Hendrix's last BBC date, again produced by Bev Phillips at the Playhouse with Pete Ritzema engineering, including, to get things going, a special Radio 1 jingle at the start of the session. Improbably, Jimi complains 'Radio 1 – You stole my gal!'

January 1968 brought two noteworthy soul sessions: one by P. P. Arnold, with a backing band including uncredited vocalists Madeline Bell and Dusty Springfield; and one from the first British multiracial band, the Foundations (both on the 14th). Then Fleetwood Mac did a session with guest singer Eddie Boyd, producing nine numbers in all (21st). Fellow Blue Horizon act Chicken Shack did their first the next week, including a cover of Freddy King's 'San-Ho-Zay' (28th).

The same month also saw one of

Bernie's most cunning ruses. Captain Beefheart and his Magic Band were in the UK on tour, and Peel was keen to get them in. Unfortunately, as Americans, they fell foul of the then Ministry of Labour rules on work permits.

In support of the MU, the Ministry stipulated that only musicians from countries whose radio stations offered reciprocal bookings for British acts could play at the BBC. As American radio didn't do live sessions, no American bands could be recorded in the UK. Solo artists could be booked, if backed by British musicians. But Beefheart had an all-American band. Bernie persuaded the Ministry that, as the name suggested, this was a touring band of magicians. They got permission, as a 'Variety' act.

The session itself, on 24 January at Maida Vale, featured 'Sure 'nuff'n'yes I do'. Dave Tate, the engineer, remembers having to suspend a mike over Beefheart, who insisted on singing lying on his back. Later, on the band's second and final BBC radio date, in May, at the Piccadilly, Bernie recalls Beefheart being entranced by the sound made by the control cubicle light switch. 'Oh, isn't that great,' he said, switching the fluorescents on and off for three or four minutes.

But that first Beefheart broadcast, on 4 February, was notable for another reason. It was the first *Top Gear* Peel presented on his own. The show was cut to two hours, ending at 4 p.m. Needletime was cut to 45 minutes. Each week's show now needed only two, not three or four new sessions. Bev Phillips left at the beginning of March to become a producer on the teatime David Symonds show. Soon after, Bernie moved Peel to self-op studios in Broadcasting House, meaning he could play the records himself.

But this, and some other good news, had been coming to Peel for a while. As early as 5 December 1967 a meeting of

the Popular Music department had confirmed that Peel would be the sole *Top Gear* presenter 'from Week 6'. Even earlier, an idea from another producer, in a different department, meant that by March 1968 Peel – who had barely got past the first cut of DJs in November – now had not one, but two programmes. That producer was John Muir.

Muir had joined the BBC from the RAF as a technical operator in 1961, and followed the usual route into Studio management, then, just before Radio 1 was

Peel comes to the end of another *Night Ride*, 1 a.m., Thursday 4 July 1968. On that Wednesday night's show, listeners had just heard 'Death Letter' by Son House, followed by a poem 'Ode to 166' read live by Geoff Hill, then the title track of the Spontaneous Music Ensemble's 'Karyobin' LP. As this picture was taken, Peel was closing the show with the final piece in Ron Geesin's debut session, 'Devised now'.

launched, won a production attachment in the Recorded Programmes Department, or Service (RPS).

Today it's known as Archive Features. The idea is to make programmes from non-needletime archive material, such as recordings by the BBC and other broadcasters; in other words, programmes costing little in copyright payments.

Muir discovered there was a wealth of under-used, non-needletime world music recordings. He was toying with the idea of putting them together with poetry and acoustic sessions when, about a month into Radio 1, he met Clive Selwood. 'Peel thinks they're going to sack him,' he told Muir. 'Any programmes going?' Muir immediately suggested making a pilot. Peel did it, the tape was submitted; nothing happened.

Muir became worried: his attachment, on which he was producing middle-of-the-road editions of RPS's after-midnight show *Night Ride*, ran out at the end of March. Late in 1967 he asked his boss, Harold Rogers, about the delay. The tape must then have got through to

Robin Scott, the controller. On 1 January 1968 he told the Popular Music department: 'RPS has produced a *Perfumed Garden* type show, which I am considering for a late-night slot'. Peel and Muir got the first hour, midnight to 1 a.m. of the Wednesday *Night Ride* strip, from 6 March.

The show would become a cult to rival *Top Gear*. Each edition had a guest poet live, and one session act, normally a solo, acoustic artist or duo. John Muir, with SM Roger Derry, pre-recorded most of these on Monday afternoons or evenings in S1, the tiny sub-basement studio in Broadcasting House celebrated as the site of the world's first experimental television broadcast, on 22 August 1932. It also sits right on top of the Bakerloo tube line, and sessions occasionally had to be stopped as trains rumbled below.

'This is the first of a new series of programmes on which you may hear just about anything,' Peel said, introducing the Incredible String Band, and Adrian Mitchell. In those first few weeks, people like the new Mersey poets, Roger McGough, Brian Patten, and the 'Liverpool Scene', Andy Roberts and Adrian Henri, were featured.

When his attachment ended after the first four shows, Muir handed Peel over to Denis O'Keefe, a fellow SM on attachment to RPS. Some weeks *Night Ride* threw up startling double bills: Champion Jack Dupree and Christopher Logue; the Occasional Word Ensemble and Roy Harper; Ron Geesin and Mike Cooper – debuts for the last two.

Through spring and summer 1968 the show also featured first sessions from Shirley and Dolly Collins, Stefan Grossman, Michael Chapman, John Martyn, Bridget St John, Dave Kelly, and Ian A. Anderson, today editor of *Folk Roots* magazine: 'I took along harmonica player Steve Rye. He wasn't credited as there apparently wasn't the budget to pay him, but he was heard on the tapes,' he says. Many of these acoustic country-blues acts, like Anderson, had started on the south-west club scene the year before.

'Mike Cooper and I had suggested Gef Lucana of Saydisc in Bristol start a blues label called Matchbox, and when its first compilation LP *Blues Like Showers of Rain* came out in July 1968, everything went silly,' says Anderson. 'John Peel, then as now, the first to spot something good happening at the roots, played it every week on *Night Ride* and had most of the artists guesting.'

But what made the show a *cause célèbre* at the time was something quite different. Pete Carr took over production in October 1968, and decided to make the show more satirical. His first edition featured Richard Neville of *Oz*. On 6 November, John Wells, then author of 'Mrs Wilson's Diary' in *Private Eye*, came in and said to Peel, among other things, that people who had spoken to Harold Wilson had said that he wasn't interested in the Nigerian war because it would lose him too many votes.

Across London in No. 10 Downing Street the Prime Minister, apparently, was listening. He was evidently not pleased. Shortly after the broadcast, the Labour chief whip, John Silkin, complained to Sir Hugh Greene, director-general of the BBC. On the following Monday morning, the 11th, the headline on the front page of *The Times* read: 'BBC AT FAULT OVER SLUR ON WILSON'. 'The complaint is understandable. We were at fault,' the BBC apologized, via the newspaper. On the following Wednesday Peel read out a written BBC apology, but was allowed to dissociate himself from it. A few weeks later, Pete Carr got the attachment to television he'd been seeking. John Muir was put back in charge.

Not that things calmed down. On his first show back on, Muir found Lennon and Yoko Ono holding up to the mike a cassette recording of the heartbeat of Yoko's baby, which had later miscarried. A Baptist minister, the Rev. John McNicol, complained to the BBC that the interview was in bad taste. *The Times* of 17 December, under the headline 'LATE NIGHT SHOW "SUGGESTIVE"', said the BBC was to investigate the complaint. Nothing, however, came of it. Muir and

Peel carried on.

In January 1969 Muir recorded Tim Hart and Maddy Prior, the duo that would end up in Steeleye Span, and the next week he captured Pete Brown and the Battered Ornaments in session. But, in the wake of the Wilson affair, the show, never liked by some senior executives, was now definitely out of favour. Shortly after Muir left to take up a contract producer's job in Popular Music in March and Pete Ritzema, by now himself

One of the few bands to do two sessions for John Peel's *Night Ride:* The Incredible String Band in 1969.

on attachment as a producer, took over, the Wednesday Peel *Night Ride* was moved, in April, to a mid-evening slot, 8.15 – 9.15 p.m. 'They moved it to kill it,' says Pete Ritzema, and he should know.

Nevertheless it was allowed to continue, under sentence of death, before finally being axed in September. Ritzema and Peel made use of the stay of execution. Interviewing Tony van Den Burgh on 28 May about a forthcoming Radio 4 programme on VD and the problem of people acknowledging the disease, Peel, to help the argument, admitted he'd had it. There were complaints, but Peel survived.

Other interviewees that summer included a young Richard Branson, and Ralph Steadman. Ivor Cutler did what was to be the first of more than a score of Radio 1 sessions; and the Paris was booked on 12 May 1969 for what would prove to be Pink Floyd's fifth and final BBC studio pre-recording date (they later did two concerts), on which they performed 'Daybreak', 'Cymbeline', 'Green is the colour' and 'The narrow way', broadcast on 14 May. Still confusing Floyd completists years later, these takes were promptly repeated by Peel on the *Top Gear* of 1 June.

Pete Roche, a poet and regular guest, livened up the penultimate show no end. 'At first, I thought he was perhaps changing into something, as you do,' says Peel. 'All of a sudden there was this naked figure in the studio saying "Hi John, look at me",' recalls Pete Ritzema. After a moment's shocked pause, fellow guest Viv Stanshall exclaimed, 'I say, what a *good* idea!'

The last night, 24 September 1969, featured the debut of Kevin Coyne's first band, Coyne Clague. He, like many others given their first break in *Night Ride*, would return to record for Peel again.

'A very good blues singer' was the Audition panel's verdict on Kevin Coyne's debut appearance, with Coyne Clague, on the last Peel Wednesday night show in '69. Coyne went on to do several sessions in the 70s.

The management of Radio 1 may have killed the show; but the idea of giving Peel a late-night slot, originating from John Muir and backed by Robin Scott, was far from dead.

Back in March 1968 there was no sign of a threat hanging over either of Peel's new, solo-DJ programmes. Audience figures published later would show *Top Gear* regularly winning 1.6 million listeners in the first quarter of 1968. Peel and Bernie were really getting into their stride. That summer would prove to be their finest hour. Once on his own, Peel's manner relaxed and the programmes sounded much more confident. After Bev's departure, Bernie produced all the sessions, normally with Pete Ritzema at the Playhouse on Mondays, and with Dave Tate, and, from July, Allen Harris, at 201 Piccadilly on Tuesdays. Bernie and Pete would, alternatively, sometimes use Maida Vale 4 on Wednesdays.

Harris had been one of the two regular XP-ops on the *Top Gear* sessions since the beginning, sharing running the tape machines at the Playhouse and Piccadilly with Bob Conduct who, today, is in charge of all Radio 1 and 2's sound engineers.

'The Playhouse was good for loud groups,' Bob Conduct explains. 'The irregular shape of the unconverted theatre, with all its velvet-upholstered seating, even when empty, absorbed a lot of the volume.'

As you entered the back of the stalls from the foyer, the control room, for producer and SM, was on the right, and the recording channel, with the tape recorders, on the left. The layout was similar at the Piccadilly, except that the two cubicles were at the front of a small balcony, reached by a spiral staircase up from the stalls.

Things had developed since Bev

Joe Cocker and the Grease Band

RECORDED: 20 MAY 1968
STUDIO: STUDIO 1, 201 PICCADILLY
PRODUCER: BERNIE ANDREWS
ENGINEER: PETE RITZEMA
FIRST BROADCAST: 9 JUNE 1968 *TOP GEAR*

TRACKS: 'Something's coming on', 'Marjorine', 'Mr Bus driver', 'I shall be released', 'With a little help from my friends'.

LINE-UP: Joe Cocker, vocals; Chris Stainton, bass guitar; Tommy Eyre, keyboards; Mickey Gee, guitar; Tommy Reilly, drums.

The first ever recording of the group's new stage favourite, 'With a little help from my friends'. Producer Bernie Andrews saved it, and first put it out on the repeat on 14 July. It was only recorded commercially later that summer, released in September, and later became a UK and US number 1, and was famously captured on film at Woodstock, but that was more than a year later.

52

Joe Cocker

2

Phillips had brought in his customized tobacco tins, but recording was still mono. The Playhouse mixing desk now had four RSAs (Response Selection Amplifiers), or BBC EQ circuits. It was also the Type-B desk, which allowed you to mix at high level, every mike having its own valve amplifier. Piccadilly had a rebuilt Type-A, with 'quadrant pots' instead of rotary faders. These were rather bizarre, Flash Gordon-style levers which moved through 90 degrees.

Not that bands necessarily disliked the antiquated atmosphere of the theatres. Pete Ritzema remembers Tim Buckley, after his memorable first session for *Top Gear* on 4 April 1968, at the Piccadilly, wanting ·to make an album there. Then he asked, 'This place *is* stereo, right?' At this point the plan collapsed.

Nevertheless there could be technical problems which no one could blame on the BBC's ageing recording equipment. Gilbert O'Sullivan, then just known as Gilbert, had made his first record on CBS, 'Disappear', and on the strength of it Bernie booked him for a debut recording at the Piccadilly on 14 May, backed by the sixteen-piece Keith Mansfield Orchestra.

'He was worried about coming in, because he'd only ever performed with his own piano, which was half a tone out,' says Bernie. 'So I OK-ed an extra £8 porterage to bring his piano in from his flat in Bayswater. Then when the musicians went to tune up with the piano, they went mad. They all had to de-tune down to it. He did about three or four songs, and it turned out OK. Afterwards, he played another three numbers on his own at the piano, and really got into it. I think that session was much better than anything he did subsequently.'

On the same show as Joe Cocker's debut

repeat in July, listeners also heard Leonard Cohen's only BBC radio session. 'We expected him to come in and sit in the corner in denims and be rather sombre,' recalls Peel, ' instead of which he appeared in a rather nice suit and really took charge of everything: "I want the singers over there where I can maintain eye contact; and if we could have those screens here please...", just a very organized guy.'

Also there at the Piccadilly that day was Ashley Hutchings of Fairport Convention, a big Cohen fan, who had asked Bernie if he could come and listen. 'It was a strange reworking of the old BBC session system, because Bernie had booked this pick-up band of contemporary notables, including Dave Cousins on banjo. I just sat there enthralled at the back of the stalls. Cohen walked out for a break and I had a word with him. He was a really nice guy.' One month later the Fairports would do their only ever recording of their stage favourite, Cohen's 'Suzanne', in the same studio.

In the space of four weeks that summer, Deep Purple, Free and Jethro Tull all made their first radio appearances, on *Top Gear*. 'I recall finding Bernie a jolly soul, who, if nothing else, put everyone at ease,' says Ian Anderson of Tull. 'We did a third of the act we were doing then at the Marquee and the blues clubs, and Mick Abrahams' interpretation of 'Cat squirrel'.

'I do remember the position the programme held within the otherwise chaperoned world of radio. It was all there was. The importance of *Top Gear* was that it created a volatile atmosphere, which reflected what was going on. At the time there was growing competition, albeit friendly rivalry, between the Marquee bands. And that was a cruel indication that out there was a manipula-

Fairport Convention

RECORDED: 26 AUGUST 1968
STUDIO: STUDIO 1, 201 PICCADILLY
PRODUCER: BERNIE ANDREWS
ENGINEER: PETE RITZEMA
FIRST BROADCAST: 1 SEPTEMBER 1968 *TOP GEAR*

Ian Matthews,
Simon Nicol,
Ashley Hutchings,
Martin Lamble,
Sandy Denny,
Richard Thompson

55

TRACKS: 'If you feel good you know it can't be wrong', 'Fotheringay', 'Gone gone gone', 'Eastern rain' ('Suzanne', first broadcast 29 September 1968)

LINE-UP: Sandy Denny, vocals; Ashley Hutchings, bass & vocals; Martin Lamble, drums; Ian Matthews, vocals; Simon Nicol, guitar; Richard Thompson, guitar & vocals.

'The care and attention that was paid to tracks was wonderful, particularly on "If you feel good"; I remember recording a kazoo and speeding it up on tape, just to get the right ragtime effect. And we took ages to record one tiny insert that was a musical joke. This involved breaking a cup, which wasn't as easy as it sounds, because it had to be just the right kind of smash, and then inserting it into the song after the line "put down your coffee mug". The whole operation took up about an hour and several BBC cups. We never recorded a lot of those tracks we did for radio sessions. We'd put down things we liked to do on stage, and we were doing a lot of cover versions then. "Suzanne" was a stage favourite, and audiences would cheer the moment we announced it; but that BBC session was the only recording we made of it. The arrangement was all based on rhythm. Martin was going round the kit with beaters, and the two guitars, drums and bass were all doing different patterns. It was a masterpiece of rhythmic interplay, and Bernie did a great job on the production.'

ASHLEY HUTCHINGS

Tim Hardin

RECORDED: 15 JULY 1968
STUDIO: STUDIO 1, 201 PICCADILLY
PRODUCER: BERNIE ANDREWS
ENGINEER: PETE RITZEMA
FIRST BROADCAST: 28 JULY 1968 *TOP GEAR*

TRACKS: 'Reason to believe'*, 'Don't make promises', 'Danville Dan', 'Hang on to a dream'.
LINE-UP: Tim Hardin, piano, guitar & vocals; with the Spike Heatley Quintet. *solo.

'The backing group had already packed up and gone, we were all getting ready to go home, and he suddenly decided he wanted to record "Reason to believe". The equipment was switched on again, and he recorded it just playing piano. He was having severe drug problems then, and it was an amazingly emotional performance: it was a very emotional moment, one of those *real* moments.'

JOHN PEEL

'There were tears on that session. Tim Hardin was in a pretty bad way on heroin. He'd done two or three songs with this semi-jazz type backing band, and he was having a hell of a job to carry on. Some of the numbers with the band I couldn't use because he had to keep stopping to go round the back for another fix. We gave up, I thought I had just enough for a session, but then he asked to do "Reason to believe" at the end. It became so pathetic almost, listening to him try and sing this song, when he was in such a state himself, it actually brought tears to my eyes. In the middle, Peel came up the spiral staircase into the control room. He'd been sitting listening alone in the front row of the stalls, but said he couldn't stay down there any longer, he was finding it too upsetting.'

BERNIE ANDREWS

Tim Hardin was found dead of a heart attack in his Los Angeles apartment on 29 December 1980.

Tim Hardin

tive world. That rather chummy friendliness, that Peel and Bernie's show captured, was inevitably beginning to get frayed, as bands became successful, harsh realities were coming home to roost, and record sales began to be significant.'

Ian Anderson suggests that in the scene's success lay the beginning of its end. Hindsight is an easy thing, but he's right. Many, like Peel, were sensing it even then. In the *Melody Maker* late in July, Peel lamented the inverted snobbery into which the 'Underground' was slipping: 'The extraordinary thing is, if anybody gets anything done, he becomes unpopular.' His and Bernie's programme would soon suffer a similar fate within the BBC. *Top Gear* was about to achieve its greatest success. Yet six months later it would be dealt a body blow.

When the *Melody Maker* published the results of its 1968 Readers' Poll, in late September, John Peel won Top Disc Jockey, and *Top Gear* won Top Radio Programme. Radio 1 management was stunned. They had assumed that Tony Blackburn, who came second, would win. Bernie himself was 'gobsmacked'. The *MM* itself was sure: 'The idea that *Top Gear* is a minority appeal programme has been exploded.' 'JOHN PEEL – A VICTORY FOR THE MUSIC' read the headline; 'probably more letters to *MM* mention Peel than any other artist or deejay'. Peel claimed his contribution was simply 'to let people hear what other people are doing'. Bernie paid tribute to the programme's session sound engineers. 'A lot of our success is due to their efforts and the way they take a personal interest in getting things right.'

They carried on doing so. That autumn Ritzema and Harris were joined as Bernie's SMs by Bob Conduct, who moved up from XP-op; two of the earliest sessions he did were Van der Graaf

Generator's first, and Caravan's first, recorded on the last day of the year. For Bernie, it was a career highlight to rank with the Idle Race. 'It was one of those where I didn't care what anyone else thought: I know they're bloody good, and *I'm* going to book them!' Caravan founder member Richard Sinclair's memories are mainly to do with the Maida Vale canteen. 'David [Sinclair] and I were both on macrobiotic diets, but the canteen didn't have gamasio salt or brown rice. Man, what a downer. Not a lentil in sight.'

The very next show, 12 January 1969, featured the radio debut of Yes; and the week after that it was the turn of Jon Hiseman's Colosseum. 'Having already played with the New Jazz Orchestra, Georgie Fame, and John Mayall's Bluesbreakers, to say nothing of Graham Bond, I knew those BBC recordings were a normal and essential part of getting a band born,' says Jon Hiseman.

'The radio shows were important in that we could record a number, and then find people would clap in recognition on the first concerts following transmission,' he remembers. 'John and Bernie were particularly generous to us, and we took the shows very seriously; though the recording of material at the BBC at that time was definitely a technique that had to be developed, because, technically, the BBC lagged far behind commercial recording studios. But, because of the speed of work, the very quick balance-and-play system, a good live band could get very good results.'

Just how good was to be proved again early in March. Almost exactly a year before, *Top Gear* had featured the Yardbirds' last BBC session. Now, on 3 March 1969, Bernie did Led Zeppelin's first, at the Playhouse. He was renewing a relationship with Jimmy Page, who had also turned up on many of Bernie's BBC dates, as one of the top session guitarists

The first of many. Peel is named 'Top DJ — British' in the September 1968 Melody Maker Readers' Poll. He has won the Poll in every year but two since then.

Danny Kirwan,
Jeremy Spencer,
Mick Fleetwood,
Peter Green,
John McVie

CLASSIC · SESSION

Fleetwood Mac

RECORDED: 27 AUGUST 1968
STUDIO: STUDIO 1, 201 PICCADILLY
PRODUCER: BERNIE ANDREWS
ENGINEER: ALLEN HARRIS
FIRST BROADCAST: 1 SEPTEMBER, 13 OCTOBER, &
24 NOVEMBER 1968 *TOP GEAR.*

TRACKS: 'A mind of my own', 'I have to laugh', 'You're the one', 'Preachin' the blues' (all first broadcast 1 September 68); 'You need love', 'A talk with you', 'Bo Diddley', 'Wine whisky women' (all first broadcast 13 October 68); 'Crutch and Kane', 'If you be my baby', 'Crazy for my baby' (all first broadcast 24 November 68).

LINE-UP: Peter Green, guitar & vocals; Jeremy Spencer, guitar & vocals; Danny Kirwan, guitar & vocals; John McVie, bass guitar; Mick Fleetwood, drums; and guest, Christine Perfect, keyboards & vocals.

A classic session for three reasons: the band's first recording with new member Danny Kirwan; a special guest appearance by Christine Perfect, then with Chicken Shack but also John McVie's wife-to-be; and a staggeringly productive work-out, eleven numbers, totalling 33 minutes 50 seconds of music, in what Bernie put down as the first 'Triple Session' for Radio 1: 'Once we set the tapes rolling, they just played and played.' 'Most of the numbers were recorded straight down in one go, live, with no overdubs,' says Allen Harris.

Recorded the day after the Fairport Convention 'Classic Session' in the same studio, and first broadcast on the same show: just a typical week on *Top Gear.*

in London. The group had already conquered America, but their first album was not released in Britain until later that month and, save for *Top Gear*, UK audiences were then indifferent. 'They were very loud, but it was very good,' says Bernie.

In the same month Bernie finally updated his signature tune. Sounds Incorporated had re-recorded 'Top Gear' in 1967, with an organ replacing the original reed section. Then, late in 1968, it was re-done by jazz guitarist Joe Moretti. But at last Bernie got what he was looking for from the Nice. On their session of 5 March, Keith Emerson slowed it down and radically rearranged it. Allen Harris used buckets of swirling echo on the recording. The new sig was first used on 16 March, and remained Peel's *Sounds of the Seventies* hallmark until October 1975. It was to be almost Bernie's final contribution, and yet, ironically, one of the longest-lasting.

About this time, the Popular Music department, in its staffing plans for the third quarter of the year, allocated to Bernie a weekly *Music While You Work* session for Radio 2. The department thought that Bernie was not pulling his weight by working solely on his own programme. Other producers would do their own projects and yet also have general duties, day-to-day session work for other programmes, meetings and so on. Bernie refused to do it.

He argued that this extra work would mean he would only be able to spend forty hours a week on *Top Gear*, which would mean an unacceptable drop in the programme's award-winning quality. The department relented slightly, and put Bernie on 'standby', the producer to be called on in emergencies. Bernie said this too was impractical. At the end of March he was told, at short notice, to stand in for a colleague on a Radio 2 session. Bernie insisted his work producing *Top Gear* meant he was unavailable. The department took him off *Top Gear*.

'TOP GEAR PRODUCER IN BBC SHAKE-UP' read the headline on page 3 of the next week's *Melody Maker*. According to the paper, Bernie was believed to be unhappy about the decision, but unable to comment. It understood that the reason for his removal was 'the BBC not wanting him to devote so much of his time to the one programme'. Peel told the paper that Bernie worked six days a week, often into the small hours, on the show. 'It seems a rotten thing to take Bernie off *Top Gear*,' he said. 'After all, it was his programme. He deserves credit for making it such a success.'

He was given other work. In June he produced the Joe Loss Orchestra for Sam Costa, the Ian Wright Quartet, the cinema organ recorded in Leicester Square, the Johnny Douglas Orchestra, and Ken Moule and his Music, and other sessions for *Sounds Like Tony Brandon*. The following spring he launched the Monday evening *Sounds of the Seventies*, with David Symonds. Late in 1972 executive producer Teddy Warrick reunited him with Peel for a Thursday edition of *Sounds of the Seventies*, where he temporarily rediscovered his old flair, producing the first sessions by Queen, Camel, Hatfield and the North, and Richard and Linda Thompson. During 1974 he produced Alan Black's Saturday night show *Rock On*. In his last years at Radio 1 he became most well known as producer of Annie Nightingale's request show.

But it's fair to say that Bernie was never the same man again after he was taken off the programme he had created. His relationship with BBC management became increasingly acrimonious throughout the seventies. He has now taken early retirement.

'I suppose I would have played things slightly differently, looking back,' he says, 'made an effort to put on a suit, go to some meetings, been a bit more flexible'.

Mention his name today and you get different reactions. Former BBC managers will roll their eyes to heaven, grimace ironically, and say, not unkindly, things like 'a creative genius, of course, but impossible to manage, in fact, a pain in the arse to manage'. Pop musicians, almost without exception, will exclaim, with laughter and delight, 'Bernie Andrews! How is the old fellow?' When Andy Peebles interviewed John Lennon for Radio 1 on 6 December 1980, the first thing Lennon . said was, 'How's Bernie?' 'All of the producers we worked with at the BBC were helpful, but Bernie was particularly kind,' remembers Simon Nicol of Fairport Convention.

His track record speaks for itself. In the first eighteen months of Radio 1 he and Peel's one weekly programme featured more than seventy-five first broadcasts of new pop and rock groups. That list includes almost everyone from that generation of the British rock scene. He invented the double-session and the trial broadcast. It was he who first invited bands to 'come and have a listen'.

Many other BBC SMs and producers not mentioned in this chapter worked with the Beatles, the Stones, and other pop giants of the fifties and sixties. But most of them fall into two distinct camps. There are those for whom it was a day's work like any other; and there are those younger SMs and producers whose great days lay ahead, in the seventies and eighties. It is no disrespect to them to say that, as far as pop and rock sessions go, Bernie Andrews is the key figure in BBC history. Jimmy Grant started the ball rolling, and Bernie ran with it. No one else was there at the beginning and yet still delighting in booking the wildest groups in the late sixties.

Perhaps the only thing he lacked was the ability to sing the BBC's song as well as his own rebel yell. That skill – to be able to play the tune the BBC wanted to hear and at the same time preserve a corner of the Corporation for the musically uncompromising – was to be found in ample measure in his successor as John Peel's producer, John Walters.

CLASSIC · SESSION

Love Sculpture

RECORDED: 16 SEPTEMBER 1968
STUDIO: STUDIO I, 201 PICCADILLY
PRODUCER: BERNIE ANDREWS
ENGINEER: ALLEN HARRIS
FIRST BROADCAST: 6 OCTOBER 1968 *TOP GEAR*

TRACKS: 'The rebel', 'Wang dang doodle', 'Promised land', 'Sabre dance' ('Don't answer the door', first broadcast 3 November 1968).

LINE-UP: Dave Edmunds, guitar & vocals; John Williams, bass guitar; Bob 'Congo' Jones, drums.

'We recorded "Sabre Dance", all six minutes of it, and I couldn't believe it: it was one of those "first take" numbers, we did do another take, but we couldn't improve on the first. I programmed it intentionally early in the programme: I wouldn't normally, but rather close with it, especially if it was a long number. Now by this time, Peel was doing the transmissions by himself, and I would be at home. For the last item in the show, I put in a six-minute record, which could be cut, because I knew what was going to happen: as soon as "Sabre dance" went out, the phone rang, and I knew it was Peel, and what he was going to ask. "Take out the last song, and you can play 'Sabre Dance' again," I said. And that was the first and only time a pre-recorded session item was played twice in the same programme. The reason it hadn't been done before was because it incurred an immediate full repeat fee. But "Sabre Dance" justified it. Parlophone picked up on it, re-recorded it, rush-released it, and had a hit [entered Top 40 on 27 November 1968, reached Number 5, 14 weeks on chart]. But Dave Edmunds always said that first BBC version was the best recording.'

BERNIE ANDREWS

'We did a live session for John Peel's *Top Gear* [their first, in April 1968], and suddenly we were signed up by EMI, Gordon Mills was managing us, and we had a number 2 hit single.'

DAVE EDMUNDS, IN *SOUNDS*, 1977

3

THE PROGRESSIVE STRIP

Adrian Henri of The Liverpool Scene – the unusual interval act for the first Radio 1 In Concert, Led Zeppelin at The Playhouse, broadcast on *Top Gear* Summer 1969.

He could be heard blowing his own trumpet at the BBC as early as 1966. That was even before he joined the Corporation. As trumpeter in the Alan Price Set, John Walters recorded a session himself for *Saturday Club* that year. Before that he'd been an art teacher in Newcastle. But in early 1967 he was looking for more steady income, and remembered the BBC session. 'The producer seemed to be someone who sat there with a stop-watch timing tracks. I thought I could do that.' He wrote to the Popular Music department, and was called in to see Donald MacLean, with whom he recalls having a relaxed chat. Later that summer, the department invited him to apply for one of the new producers' jobs necessitated by the creation of Radio 1. They wanted him, and they got him.

He spent the first six months, along with Ted Beston and Paul Williams, as a junior 'session' producer on *Scene and Heard*; and later on David Symonds' teatime show. Then, in June 1968, he was given *Savile's Travels*, a Sunday show which preceded *Top Gear*.

When Symonds was taken off daytime, in January 1969, Walters was given his new show, *Symonds on Sunday*. 'I'd felt as a listener, before I'd joined Radio 1, that the live bands were often there just because the BBC couldn't play the records,' he recalls; 'but, particularly when I started *Symonds on Sunday*, I thought, let's do something positive with the live music.' He knew there were acts, like Geno Washington, that were huge in the clubs yet not being broadcast.

As part of this plan, he also booked the first sessions by ex-Jethro Tull guitarist Mick Abrahams' new band Blodwyn Pig, and Mason Wood Capaldi and Frog – scoops which first brought him to the attention of a miffed Peel and, more significantly, his Popular Music departmental chiefs.

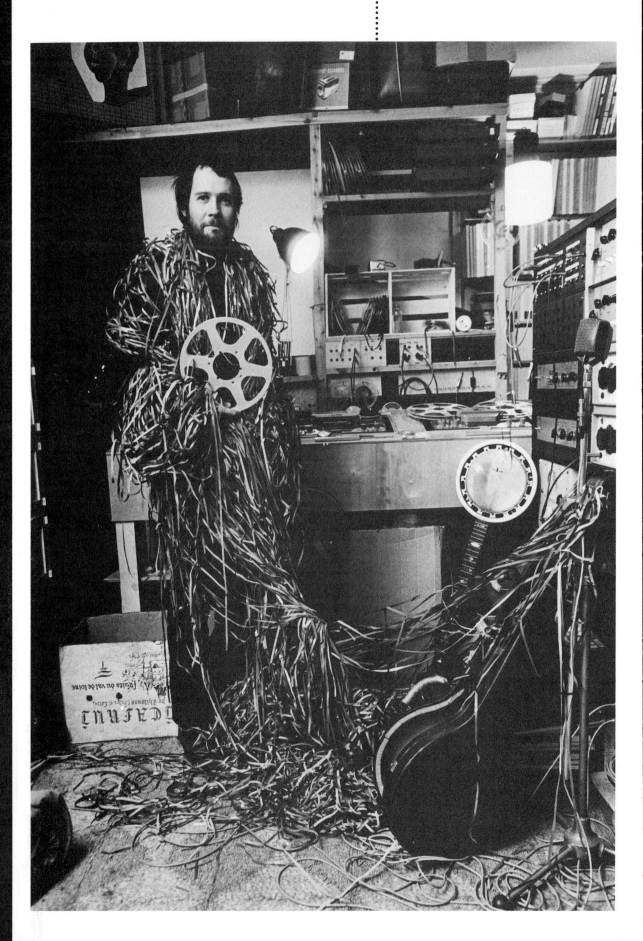

contract, and not MU members. Walters found four unsigned acts – Bridget St John, Sweet Marriage, Welfare State and Ron Geesin – and recorded them (except Welfare State, who provided their own tape of the song 'Silence is requested in the ultimate abyss') through late July and early August in the huge Maida Vale 1. Then the only BBC stereo studio, this was normally reserved for orchestral sessions and still had no overdubbing facilities.

Geesin, a surreal performance artist and musician and later co-composer of Pink Floyd's *Atom Heart Mother*, had first attracted attention with his 1967 LP on Transatlantic, *A Raise of Eyebrows*. He was one of the first musicians of the sixties to experiment with tapes and create music using the techniques of modern recording.

'Ron had a thing on that session where, to get something delayed, or echoed, we had to run the tape across all the heads of four tape recorders, and the tape ran like a washing line all round the control room,' says Walters. The *Top Gear* LP, engineered by Tony Wilson and edited by Mike Franks, also came complete with Peel's rendition on jew's harp of the old signature tune, and a sleeve featuring the bare feet of 'the Pig' ('she snorts when she laughs'), Peel's regular girlfriend of the past year, and later wife, Sheila Gilhooly.

In late September 1969 Peel and *Top Gear* again won the Best DJ and Best Radio Programme categories in the *Melody Maker* poll. Walters was maintaining the strength of the show. Yet, just one week later, Peel's Wednesday ex-*Night Ride* show was axed, and *Top Gear* was shifted again, this time to Saturday afternoons. The following month a poll of 500 *Disc and Music Echo* readers also put Peel top, and 75 per cent of them thought Radio 1 'should promote unknown talent more actively'.

Not for the first, or last, time Peel and Walters were almost alone in championing the unknown. They featured many first sessions early in 1970, including Medicine Head, who were destined to become one of the most BBC-recorded groups and mainstay of Peel and Clive Selwood's Dandelion record label, launched the previous September. 'I remember John Walters did stop talking once during the whole session, something that many *Top Gear*-ists do not believe to this day', says John Fiddler of Medicine Head. On 14 March there was Syd Barrett's first solo session – 'I remember Dave Gilmore asking Syd what he wanted to do throughout,' says Walters – and the Faces' first for Peel on the 28th.

But a week later they were not alone. On Saturday, 4 April a plane-load of British journalists were flown to New York, just to see the new British band Brinsley Schwarz play their first public gig, at the Filmore East. It was an over-the-top hype that rapidly became infamous, defining Seventies excess. It seems fitting that on the following Monday, ushering in a comparable period of excess in rock broadcasting, Radio 1 launched *Sounds of the Seventies*.

———

Bringing in management consultants to improve financial control and contribute to a Policy Study Group on 'the future of national radio' sounds more like the BBC today, but that's what the Corporation did in the late sixties. Consultants McKinsey arrived in November 1968. By spring 1969 they had made their suggestions, and the thinking of the Policy Study Group largely informed the decisions the Board of Management made on future programming, detailed in *Broadcasting in the Seventies*.

This manifesto was published late in 1969, to howls of protest from the arts establishment: its main proposal was to abolish the old 'Third Programme' as a

The first legal Peel Session release, the BBC Records *Top Gear* LP, 1969. Peel in boots, Pig on tip-toe.

separate department. The idea was to make each network more distinct – Radio 4 for talk, Radio 3 for classical music – and 'to achieve a cleaner separation' between Radios 1 and 2, which were still sharing much programming.

An early draft of *Broadcasting in the Seventies* in BBC Written Archives specifically mentions 'a daily specialist "strip" featuring mainly progressive music' on Radio 1. It didn't make the published version, but was trailed in the *BBC Handbook* for 1970. The progressive 'strip' was announced early in March.

Sounds of the Seventies would be a daily, one-hour show, at 6 p.m. from Monday to Friday. Apart from Wednesday's edition – to be a repeat of John Peel's *Sunday Show*, the original

name for Jeff Griffin's *In Concert* series, which had begun in January – each show would take the form of a DJ presenting a mix of records, with two studio sessions taking up half the hour in total. 'We are more than doubling the amount of airtime given to progressive pop,' controller Douglas Muggeridge (who had taken over from Robin Scott in 1969) retorted, in response to tart criticisms expressed by George Melly and Pete Townshend in the *Radio Times* on 19 March.

The original line-up was David Symonds with producer Bernie Andrews on Mondays (although the first three shows were presented by Andy Ferris, Symonds being on holiday); Mike Harding, produced by Malcolm Brown (Tuesdays); Stuart Henry, also produced

Free perform 'Alright Now' on *Top of the Pops*, Summer 1970. But the song might never have been a single without a conversation in a Radio 1 recording studio three months before.

by Malcolm Brown (Thursdays); and Alan Black, produced by John Muir (Fridays).

Symonds' career at Radio 1 was nearing an end, as he dabbled in band management and other interests. His short-lived *Seventies* edition featured sessions by Rare Bird and Gentle Giant, and, in the first show, Bowie's first with the Hype, and the Nice's last — 'my first session balancing for Bernie,' recalls a young engineer of the time, Nick Gomm.

Mike Harding was simply Malcolm Brown's recording engineer. 'I'd been allocated some DJ for the Tuesday I didn't like,' recalls Malcolm. 'I complained to Mark White, who gave me 24 hours to find a replacement.' Harding, a soft-spoken Scot who followed Peel's natural style, was promptly given an audi-

tion. They sent in the unmarked tape, and when Harding was offered work, had to own up. After some argument, he got a trial period, which ended up lasting eighteen months.

Tuesday night became the heavy rock night, with Harding acquiring the distinction of being the only BBC DJ to engineer his own sessions. 'After the show, I'd often dash up to Maida Vale in a taxi, to record the next week's band, in a 7.30 p.m. evening session.' He recorded the first BBC dates by Uriah Heep and Heads Hands and Feet.

Mick Box of Uriah Heep remembers that part of their act caused problems: 'We had a girlfriend with us, with seashells all over her dress, and, being the days of the hippies, she was dancing all

over the studio while we were playing; the engineer told her to sit down as the microphones were picking up the seashells rattling. Quite how come, at our volume, we had no idea. Nevertheless, she sat down.'

Harding, in addition, recorded two sessions with Yes, both in 1970, the second consisting entirely of a 16-minute rendition of 'America'. 'I remember blowing up a piece of gear. They wanted a bass solo effect, and Maida Vale had this little Brenell tape recorder, with a tape loop on it for a single repeat. You certainly weren't supposed to put bass guitars through it. Anyway, we got a good effect, and Chris Squire [Yes's bassist] liked it, but at the end of the session it just fizzled out. There was smoke coming

out of the back.'

As Malcolm Brown's SM, Harding also engineered the sessions for Stuart Henry's edition on Thursday nights. Malcolm Brown, an SM himself on the old Joe Loss lunchtime show at the Playhouse ('mixing guests like the Who in off four mikes') before being promoted for the launch of Radio 1, had previously been producing Henry's *Noise at Nine* on Sunday evenings. Before that, Henry had a Sunday morning show, produced by Aidan Day live from the Paris, which is now chiefly famous for having featured Elton John's first session. 'Stuart did a slightly more melodic, lighter rock show,' says Malcolm.

Yet the first edition featured a classic session by Free, recorded on 2 April at Aeolian 2, which has passed into BBC legend because of a conversation which allegedly took place in the Aeolian's gents toilet. On the session, the band were previewing new numbers from their forthcoming third album *Fire and Water*, to be released that June. The line-up at the urinals is unclear, as Malcolm Brown, Mike Harding and second engineer Mike Franks all have slightly differing versions of events.

Essentially, someone from the band said, 'We're thinking about maybe making that first number a single, but Island Records aren't certain. What do you think?' The BBC team, as a man, said, 'Definitely.' Mike Franks thinks Malcolm Brown might later even have phoned Muff Winwood of Island from the control room, insisting the song be released as a single. The song was 'All Right Now', and the rest, as they say, is pop history.

Fridays, with Alan Black, a former pirate DJ and illustrator, leaned towards jazz-rock, led by John Muir's own taste: he was producing Radio 3's *Jazz in Britain* at the same time. Over the next eighteen months bands recorded included Egg, If,

Quintessence, a famous one-off date featuring Jack Bruce with Chris Spedding and John Marshall, and former solo blues guitarist Mike Cooper, with the Mike Gibbs Orchestra, at the beginning of his move into jazz.

'This orchestra was made up of some of the best British musicians of the time, and there they were playing *my* music, and I was singing with them,' Cooper says. 'I remember Frank Ricotti was brought to the session by his dad – he was probably too young to drive at the time. I also had a friend over from Chile who played the guitar. I decided to invite him to play as well. Mike Gibbs said "fine", but Chris Spedding, who was the guitarist on the session, refused to show my friend the chord charts: probably "Union rules, mate!".'

All this was during a time of considerable political change at Radio 1. In September 1970 the Popular Music and Gramophone departments were abolished, replaced by Radio 1 and Radio 2 departments. Producers from each production department had to choose their preferred network. Jimmy Grant and Bill Bebb opted for Radio 2. Most of the other names above chose Radio 1, and everyone from Popular Music moved out of Aeolian Hall and into Egton House ('They said it was purely temporary, and I'm still in the same office today,' says Jeff Griffin). Mark White became the first head of Radio 1 department. But within a little over a year, he, Donald MacLean and Grant would have retired or left (White went to Radio 2 as head), and Radio 1 found itself with a new hierarchy.

From September 1970 the station had three executive producers, responsible to the head: Doreen Davies, in charge of the middle-of-the-road programmes; Derek Chinnery, looking after mainstream pop; and Teddy Warrick who, in his own words 'was expected to deal with

the sharper end'. (Chinnery became head on White's departure in April 1972, and Johnny Beerling took his old job.)

Having been chief programme organizer in the Gramophone department, Teddy Warrick found himself dealing with sessions, and with independently minded producers like Bernie Andrews, Jeff Griffin and John Walters, for the first time. *Sounds of the Seventies* and *Top Gear* became his main responsibilities, and he was to prove a consistent champion of the new.

Also under Teddy's remit came Jeff Griffin's *Sunday Show*, the one-hour concert first presented by Peel, which evolved into *In Concert* and deserves an entire book of its own, as it lies outside our definition of studio sessions.

Late in August 1970 Peel went on holiday, and although previous concerts could be repeated on the Sundays, Jeff Griffin didn't want to 'repeat a repeat' on Wednesday nights for a month. Instead, he offered four DJ-ed shows to a journalist, Bob Harris, whom he had met earlier in 1970. 'Who do you fancy having in session?' Jeff asked him. Bob chose three new acts, and Elton John: Aubrey Small, Argent, and Wishbone Ash.

Wishbone Ash's 'trial broadcast', recorded on 6 August at the Paris by Jeff Griffin, which went out on Bob's first show, on Wednesday, 19 August, was an instant classic. They blasted down two long versions of 'Errors of my ways' and 'Phoenix', as well as 'Blind eye' (not broadcast), some time before recording and releasing different versions on their first album. The next week it was Elton John's last normal studio session, at the Playhouse; and Argent went out on 9 September.

'At the end of the four weeks, I was feeling so excited about the idea of working for Radio 1, but that was it, there was nothing else in the pipeline at all,' recalls

Bob today, 'and then David Symonds resigned, and suddenly the Monday programme became available, and the BBC offered it to me.'

He kicked off on 12 October with a session from Uriah Heep recorded by John Muir, his producer for the next fifteen months. Muir carried off a neat trick for this new show. Although Radio 1 still had no stereo recording studios, he managed to record the groups in stereo, with the help of a subsidiary department of the World Service based in a side street off Shepherd's Bush Green: the Transcription Service.

The name suggests libraries of monks transcribing by hand the utterances of distinguished contributors to BBC radio discussion programmes. The truth is slightly more complicated. The Transcription Service was set up as part of the World Service, funded by the Foreign Office and not the licence fee, to export BBC programmes to foreign broadcasters: 'cultural diplomacy' was the idea. Many state broadcasters do this but, uniquely, Transcription *charges* for BBC programmes. The annual subscription is not huge, but it's still a measure of BBC quality that stations pay up, and put out the programmes. So the service pays for quite a bit of its operating costs itself; it is possibly the world's oldest broadcasting syndication outfit. As well as distributing ready-made UK BBC shows, Transcription also makes its own programmes, solely for export, and this is where pop music comes in.

When the Beatles and the British sound exploded on to the American pop scene early in 1964, the Transcription Service realised there was money to be made. Using BBC session tapes made for *Saturday Club* and, from July, Bernie's original *Top Gear*, a special weekly 45-minute show, strictly for export only,

was released to America and the world's eager radio stations. It was put together at Kensington House, Shepherd's Bush, Transcription's base. The host was Brian Matthew, who would attend the sessions and record interviews with the stars exclusively for Transcription. The show was pressed up on 12-inch LPs and sent off to subscribing stations by airmail.

The show is still going. It's released today on CD, and has not used BBC sessions as its raw material for many years. But *Top of the Pops*, not to be confused with its television namesake, is still hosted by Brian Matthew, and until he left in spring 1992, was still made by its original producer, Pete Dauncey, the fifth man of the early *Saturday Club* team. Jimmy Grant, Brian Matthew, Bernie Andrews and Johnny Beerling have all played a part in changing the sound of BBC pop radio. As the original tape-op on the show, Pete Dauncey's role has been to export his colleagues' achievements to the world. But his influence has helped change a few things at home too.

Like stereo, or multi-track music recording, for one. Until the early seventies, *Top of the Pops* got most of its raw material by sending along its own engineers, such as Pete Dixon, Dave 'Spot' Mulkeen and Bob Harrison, armed with a portable EMI TR90 tape recorder, to sessions for John Peel's *Top Gear*, *Saturday Club*, Jeff and Alexis' World Service blues show, and others; producing a weekly show on disc meant there simply wasn't time to borrow and copy master tapes.

They would plug in their machine alongside Radio 1's in the recording channel at the Playhouse, Piccadilly, or wherever, and take a direct copy of the session, live. They left the tapes running between numbers, picking up banter between the control room and studio, odd jams and out-takes, so Transcription's copies of classic sessions are frequently the most detailed record of what happened. Back at Kensington House, they would use the tracks to make up the next week's show.

As the Radio 1 studios were mono, *Top of the Pops* had to be released in mono too, much to the frustration of American subscribing stations. Transcription had built its own small stereo studio, T1, in the mid-sixties, recording direct to two-track, but it was used mainly for classical and light music. In early 1970 a new, bigger portable desk was acquired, effectively providing, with a bit of cunning 'lash-up' with cable, 8-track recording.

Pete Dauncey hit on the idea of adding a full stereo session on the flip-side of each edition of *Top of the Pops*, without Brian Matthew's links: 'For Your DJ' read the label. While the main part of the programme would still be in mono on the A-side, stations could dip into the complete session by the featured guest, in stereo, on the B-side. If Dauncey had enough tapes, he could even do a selection of stereo tracks from more than one date. The only problem was getting enough stereo sessions to choose from each week.

John Muir had heard about the new facilities at Kensington House. 'I desperately wanted to do stereo sessions,' he says. In August 1970 he and Pete Dauncey came to an arrangement. Muir would book one or both of the new sessions he needed each week (one for Alan Black and one for Bob Harris) to be recorded at Transcription's stereo studio, T1. Pete Dauncey would produce the Monday evening session with his own engineers, including Bob Harrison and Adrian Revill; and John Muir the Tuesday, or, occasionally, Wednesday evening, mainly with Nick Gomm or John White as SM. Each producer would get instant access to both sessions; Muir to broadcast on Radio 1, and Dauncey to

put out on that week's *Top of the Pops*. By January 1971, the scheme was in full operation.

Dauncey had previously tried other ways of getting sessions in stereo, unsuccessfully. The most infamous experiment was on Curved Air's first session, recorded at Maida Vale 4 for *Top Gear* on 28 April 1970. In the control room, producer John Walters and SM Bob Conduct were recording the group in mono. But Bob was splitting the signals from the mikes, and running them down cable along 50 yards of Maida Vale corridor, to another room, where Pete Dauncey and Bob Harrison were simultaneously recording the same session, but in stereo on a mobile desk.

'Everything went fine until we realized that one of the tracks we'd recorded was just a backing track, and the band wanted to overdub,' recalls Bob Harrison. The mono version could be 'bounced', as normal, to another tape machine, but Dauncey and Harrison would have to do the same, at exactly the same time. 'How the hell would we get the stereo tape in sync?' wondered Pete Dauncey.

Eventually, communicating on headphones, the two engineering teams, with fingers poised on the recorders' capstans (drive wheels) ran both tapes, in sync, against a verbal count, while the band overdubbed. This prompted the telling of the legendary BBC joke, of how the Corporation produced its first 'digital' session.

'In the middle of all this, the new managing director of radio, Ian Trethowan, walks in,' says Bob Conduct. '"My first time at Maida Vale", he says, "but isn't this a silly way to do it?"'

Some, like Walters, thought stereo recording at that time irrelevant. 'For the average listener, it made no difference,' he claims, and he has a point: Radio 1 was

The last days of mono. The Maida Vale 4 control room was still only equipped with BBC-designed mixing desks and mono tape machines in late 1972.

still, after all, only broadcasting in mono, on medium wave. This had always been the argument of administrators. As recently as February 1969 a memo from the Popular Music department had argued that multi-track equipment would unnecessarily increase producer effort, and 'provision of even one multi-track machine would create a demand for more: 2-track would lead to the "need" for 4 tracks, and then 8'. The number of sessions for which double-tracking was 'legitimate' was 'small'.

Muir may now have been able to record his sessions in stereo, but stereo broadcast of them was impossible. Even when *Sounds of the Seventies* won the 10 p.m. to midnight FM slot in October 1971, the strip only got FM mono. Yet

Dauncey and Muir's arrangement still had a part to play.

Muir recalls staging a demonstration for Ian Trethowan early in 1972, showing how stereo transmission could benefit his Transcription sessions. FM stereo broadcasts had just started, but on Radio 3 only, with the odd test transmission on Radio 2. Soon afterwards it was decided that Radios 1 and 2 would at last have to have their own multi-track studios. Two studios would be equipped with Neve 16 – 4 desks, and 8-track Studer A80 1 inch tape recorders. Aeolian 2 was to be one of them. But it was the other chosen location that was effectively to become the home of *Sounds of the Seventies* sessions. A former drama studio complete with false doors and gravel-traps, it was famed as

Genesis

RECORDED: 10 MAY 1971. STUDIO: T1,
TRANSCRIPTION SERVICE, KENSINGTON HOUSE
PRODUCER: PETE DAUNCEY
ENGINEER: ADRIAN REVILL
FIRST BROADCAST: 31 MAY 1971 *BOB HARRIS*

TRACKS: 'Musical box', 'Stagnation'.

LINE-UP: Peter Gabriel, vocals & flute; Mike Rutherford, bass guitar & guitar; Tony Banks, keyboards; Phil Collins, drums; Steve Hackett, guitar.

The band did four radio sessions in BBC studios between 1970 and 1972. Alec Reid produced the first, for *Night Ride*, on 20 February 1970, with the first broadcast on April Fool's Day; this included 'The shepherd,' 'Pacidy' and 'Let us now make love', songs never released on vinyl. After Jonathan Mayhew (drums) and Anthony Phillips (guitar) were replaced by Phil Collins and Steve Hackett, the group did three more, the last two for John Peel, all of them recorded at Transcription Service. This particular session took place a month before they recorded the *Nursery Cryme* LP.

'I remember the sessions being very hurried and musically we would have preferred to have spent more time getting it right. We weren't that happy with the end result, but we look back with affection. I was surprised John Peel recorded some sessions with us as he never did like Genesis.'

TONY BANKS

'It's possible that the May 1971 date was a pre-album session. As 'Musical box' was written in Farnham Maltings during my first rehearsal (it was a writing period, and 'Stagnation' was from the *Trespass* album), it could have been the first studio session by the band with me on drums. Probably the most historical fact of these sessions was the fact that John Peel *almost* liked us then!'

PHIL COLLINS

'The first one, with Alec Reid, sticks in my mind the most. We were just writing and writing then, with very little to work towards, and suddenly that first session appeared, and we had a goal to work towards. I remember being very impressed with the way everyone was worried about the levels not peaking too loud, whereas normally you didn't worry, as long as it sounded good. So I think those sessions are a good vehicle for new acts to get something going. It's one thing I've noticed from travelling round the world to play, that the BBC, not being commercial, and so not having to be *too* concerned about listeners, can do these things. It does stand out in that respect, and it's still true.'

MIKE RUTHERFORD

Phil Collins, Steve Hackett, Peter Gabriel, Mike Rutherford, Tony Banks

the home of *Mrs Dale's Diary* and was located on the ground floor of the Langham Hotel right opposite Broadcasting House: Langham 1.

Only after Langham 1 opened, making multi-track recording available for all Radio 1 producers, did *Sounds of the Seventies* start going out in stereo, on Monday, 6 November 1972. That, however, was more than two years after the T1 stereo tapes first ran for Alan Black and Bob Harris.

It was T1 which hosted two of the most famous debut recordings in 1970 – 72, before Langham 1 opened: the first by the reconstituted Genesis line-up, including Phil Collins and Steve Hackett, on 10 May 1971; and Roxy Music's first, on 4 January 1972.

If there were not so many new bands appearing in the early seventies, those that did were taken up very enthusiastically indeed. A handful of groups were recording new BBC sessions every few weeks. These universal favourites included Stone the Crows, Steeleye Span, Medicine Head, Thin Lizzy and Lindisfarne.

'We became regulars in the canteen and almost had our own coathooks,' says Ray Laidlaw, drummer with Lindisfarne, and later Jack the Lad. Such was the clamour for Lindisfarne that having debuted on *Night Ride* on 6 January 1971, they recorded another two sessions before the end of the month; the second, for *Top Gear*, going out only two days before the third, on *Bob Harris*. 'Lady Eleanor', which was on the first, was to be re-recorded many times.

'One unforeseen source of irritation caused by our popularity with the BBC was having to record the same songs over and over again,' says Laidlaw. 'Every producer wanted the "biggies" and we always pushed for more obscure songs. I remember someone suggesting that we recorded an official BBC version of all of the hits and then just circulated copies around every producer.'

Whoever suggested this might well have been thinking of a kind of BBC date that wasn't openly discussed: the 'network' or 'single' session. In order to get round needletime, right up until the early eighties bands with a new hit single would be booked to come in to re-record it for the BBC, in just $3^1/_2$ hours. This identikit version could then be played several times by the Corporation, thus avoiding using up needletime and paying PPL dues to the record companies.

It sounds an impossible thing to ask of a band today. Many didn't like it then. On the other hand, BBC engineers remember occasions when bands preferred the energy of the quickly-made BBC version. In one or two cases record companies even bought the tapes, deleted the original single, and re-released the BBC tape as the official version.

Thousands of 'networks' took place. Most are lost and forgotten. As time went on and the difficulties of matching the work of weeks in a commercial studio increased, SMs and producers, to please both the bands and BBC bureaucrats, evolved unofficial shortcuts. At first, to meet the perceived requirement for five numbers, five copies of the master of the one song recorded would be made, and labelled 'Take #1', 'Take #2', and so on. Later, a band would sometimes bring in their own unlabelled master backing track, and just add on new vocals and overdubs. Eventually, on occasion – whisper it not – when the BBC producer or SM had gone to the loo, the record company tape would be 'switched', by the band's A&R man, with the contents of the white BBC boxes.

This practice was perhaps just the most extreme manifestation of the music industry's schizophrenia over broadcasting. On the one hand, through PPL, record companies wanted money for their product being broadcast; yet their representatives would do whatever was necessary to bend the rules to get airplay for their artists. Happily, since needletime was abolished in 1988, 'networks' have obviously ceased to be necessary.

Not to be confused with 'networks', well-known pop acts also recorded four-song feature sessions for some daytime shows throughout the 1970s. This accounts for how the BBC came to make Gene Vincent's last recording, on 1 October 1971. 'By that time, Gene's reputation as a hypochondriac preceded him,' recalls Dave Tate, who produced the session for the Johnnie Walker show. 'He was genuinely in a terrible way: limping around the studio, swigging back different bottles of medicine all the time, but he was backed up by a British session band, and they really held him together. But I thought he was as good as ever on his standard songs.' Before the session was broadcast in November, Vincent was dead, at the age of 36. In response to a campaign by his British fan club, this session of his hits was released on BBC Records.

Although Lindisfarne never made their own 'BBC Greatest Hits' tape, the fact that *Sounds of the Seventies* was frequently recording bands who later went on to have hits meant its producers' tape shelves were constantly being raided. Elton John's contract file, for example, shows daytime producers re-contracting, again and again, the early night-time versions of Elton's hits as 'network' sessions for prime time broadcast.

Evening show producers would rarely be interested in re-contracting daytime pop sessions for their shows, but *Sounds of the Seventies* producers would sometimes re-contract from each other, or from the specialist shows. In early 1971 Malcolm Brown twice repeated on Stuart Henry a classic date by blues original Champion Jack Dupree, which he had produced for his other slot, Mike Raven's influential R 'n' B show (which merits its own history). Also popular with other shows was 'Lady Eleanor', produced for Peel by Walters.

'We had a very enjoyable relationship with John Walters, who we knew slightly, as a fellow Tynesider, from his days with the Alan Price Set,' says Laidlaw. 'His constant piss-taking was a great source of amusement and one of the main attractions at Maida Vale. When asked what he would like us to record, the usual answer would be, "Oh just whack down any old shit, it all sounds the same to me anyway." On many occasions we would spend most of our allotted time falling about laughing and then have to record the songs in a bit of a rush.'

Walters and Peel, in the absence of large numbers of new bands, had taken *Top Gear* sessions down a more experimental path. Groups like Chris MacGregor's Brotherhood of Breath, and earlier, in 1970, Ian Carr's Nucleus, had come in.

'Getting on *Top Gear* was a big break, because it got us out of the jazz broadcasting ghetto, and into a wider field of exposure,' says Ian Carr. 'The other thing that surprised and delighted us was that we had more artistic freedom on these non-jazz programmes. Nobody seemed to worry about how long each piece was or whether it was the "right sort" of piece for the programme.'

Peel and Walters also developed the idea of bringing unusual combinations of musicians together on sessions, begun by Peel and Bernie in February 1968 when American singer-songwriter Tim Rose

David Bowie

RECORDED: 21 SEPTEMBER 1971
STUDIO: T1, TRANSCRIPTION SERVICE, KENSINGTON
HOUSE. PRODUCER: JOHN MUIR
ENGINEERS: JOHN WHITE AND BILL AITKEN
FIRST BROADCAST: 4 OCTOBER 1971 *BOB HARRIS*

TRACKS: 'Supermen', 'Oh you pretty things/Eight-line poem', 'Kooks' ('Fill your heart', first broadcast 1 November 1971; 'Port of Amsterdam', 'Andy Warhol', not broadcast).
LINE-UP: David Bowie, guitar & vocals; Mick Ronson, guitar & vocals.

'Bowie had been going through a bad patch. I only know that the morning after the session went out, the record company sent me a huge bunch of flowers.'

JOHN MUIR

'My own feeling then was that Mick Ronson's contribution to Bowie's sound and style was something he was never given enough credit for; and I like to think that duo session was a rare moment of Bowie, in effect, acknowledging that Ronson was not just a sideman, but an integral part of his sound.'

BOB HARRIS

'It was a strange session: two voices, two acoustic guitars or, on some numbers, two electric guitars. The electric guitars sounded very strange as neither Bowie or Ronson had brought in amplifiers; consequently the guitars were direct injected. The fact that they DI'd led me to think they weren't taking the session too seriously. However, it's worth a listen.'

BILL AITKEN

David Bowie, Mick Ronson

recorded one with the Aynsley Dunbar Experience. Christine Perfect (then of Chicken Shack) had made her famous, first guest recording with Fleetwood Mac on 27 August 1968; there was the Christmas Carols concert in 1970; and, in summer 1971, the 'free improvization' session was planned.

Walters wanted to get various musicians to improvize over a backing tape, originally to be a Doris Day record. But what he really needed was someone with no experience of playing an instrument. Chimpanzee! he thought. He was going to get just one, but he could only find two, Bugsy and Rosie, who worked as a double act. He recorded them bashing the piano. The plan then was for Robert Wyatt to play drums, Mike Ratledge keyboards, and Peel and Pig jew's harp. Lennon and Yoko also agreed to take part. But then Lennon went to America and didn't come back. The session never happened. Peel still has a postcard: 'Hang on to the chimps! – John'. 'A couple of years later I read in the paper that the chimps had escaped into a school playground, police marksmen had been called, and they, like Lennon, were shot as well,' says Walters.

Also that year, in another attempt to find new, different sounds for the sessions, Peel and Walters had organized a competition: best demo tape wins a session. The winners were the Cambridge band Henry Cow, and a duo, Paul Savage and John Hewitt. At around the same time, spring 1971, confirming his frustration in an interview with Michael Watts in the *Melody Maker*, Peel laid into Deep Purple, Black Sabbath, Ten Years After and ELP: 'those bands have lost the spark somewhere down the line and are basically going through a routine ... we're going through a very sterile period ... the one distinguishing feature of Progressive music with a capital "P" is that under no circumstances should it progress an inch,

because if it does people don't want to know.' Five months later the *Radio Times* announced: 'Double the radio time for "Progressive Pop".'

Harding was dropped. Henry had recently been replaced by Pete Drummond. Bob Harris kept Mondays. Tuesday became the John Peel's Sunday Concert repeat and a short-lived magazine show, *Ear to the Ground*, with Alan Black. *Top Gear* was pulled into the strip, taking the Wednesday night at first, and, from the beginning of 1972, Tuesdays. Fridays was the record 'Review' show, with Alan Black and Bob Harris.

Instead of four teatime shows every week recording one new session each, the move of *Sounds of the Seventies* to 10 p.m. on FM, from Monday 4 October 1971, meant three shows, each of which needed two sessions a week. From January 1972 that rose to *four* session-based, two-hour shows: Peel got a second show, on Fridays, with producer John Muir (which featured the first two Roxy Music BBC dates), and the Review slot moved to Wednesdays. Jeff Griffin took over producing Bob Harris. All this demanded eight new rock sessions a week. 'Double the radio time' had meant almost doubling the sessions.

The studios, however, still 'looked like the inside of a Lancaster bomber' to a new young Scottish tape op and former Glaswegian rock musician, Bill Aitken. Maida Vale 4 and Aeolian 2, the main rock session studios, 'looked very shabby,' he recalls (sessions were still mono, with a backing track being followed by a 'bounced' vocal overdub, then a second bounce for solos).

The bands agreed. Dave Brock of Hawkwind, a group ahead of its time in the use of electronics, remembers finding the Maida Vale control room, on his first

Top Gear session in August 1970, 'with its grey-painted equipment, like being in a submarine: "Full Ahead Captain!".' The band also did a later session in the Playhouse, which Brock recalls as 'rather overbearing'. Although 201 Piccadilly had been abandoned the year before, the Playhouse was evidently still in use: Rab Noakes remembers his first session for Peel there in May 1972: 'I'd made a few live appearances there before on Radio 1's *Country Meets Folk*, engineered by Chris Lycett. The Peel one was produced by Walters himself, I think, and as a solo performance it probably only took about an hour. But those sessions were often done on the Hank Williams principle, of just calling in to the studio to put down a few tracks between shows.'

Since Tony Wilson had become an attachment producer at Radio 1, along with Dave Tate and Pete Ritzema, in summer 1970, Walters had worked mainly with Bob Conduct as SM and Ian Sharpe as tape op; as Rab Noakes testifies, Walters was still recording most Peel sessions himself, although Pete Ritzema also did some.

But in 1972 Wilson became a full-time producer, and virtually took over session production for Walters. Walters and Ritzema still did a few, but on surviving Peel session sheets from these years 'JOHN WALTERS' has increasingly been scored out, and 'One of Wislon's' [*sic*] scribbled in. In the mid-seventies, Wilson producing, with, by then, SM Bill Aitken, became the standard Peel session production unit. From summer 1973 Wilson was also producing Alan Freeman's famous Saturday afternoon show, on which he would repeat many of his recent Peel productions, always trailed by Fluff as 'Tony Wilson Re-Creations'.

Back in early 1972 Bill Aitken was still a tape op, the third man of the team

recording two stereo sessions a week at Transcription, with producer John Muir and SMs Nick Gomm or John White. This team produced the first two of the *five* sessions Bowie recorded between late September 1971 and late May 1972. They helped him get over the 1971 low of his career, and bounce back with *Hunky Dory* then *Ziggy Stardust*. Every one of these sessions is a classic. At the same time, the T1 team produced the first two Roxy Music sessions.

Aitken had an unusual role to play in *Sounds of the Seventies* legend. For Peel's new Friday night show, 'Muir was daft enough to ask me to write some jingles,' says Bill Aitken. 'Radio 1 took over the FM slot at this time from Radio 2, and if you didn't know where you were on the dial at home, you could be tuning to the wrong station.

'To capitalize on this, the jingle began with Peter Howell [of the Radiophonic Workshop] saying in a very BBC voice "Ladies and Gentlemen – Friday Night is *Boogie* Night!" (polite applause) then I would crash in sounding like a Glasgow drunk doing a pale imitation of Little Richard to the tune of "Keep a knockin'," except the words were "Get your boogie on a Friday night, Auntie Beeb's gonna treat you right, Johnny Peel's really out of sight, Boogie on a Friday and you'll be all right!".'

He had found a vocation. He followed up with the 'John Peel's got nice legs' jingle, and, years later, a series of IDs for Tommy Vance's *Friday Rock Show*, featuring Phil Lynott singing over backing tracks performed by Aitken himself. But the 'Boogie night' jingle remains the most memorable. It was also appropriate: the show featured the first session by the 12-bar-boogie incarnation of Status Quo, on 3 March 1972.

Elsewhere, it was Pete Drummond

on Thursdays who mainly kept the rockier tradition going, no doubt helped by the fact that Malcolm Brown and Mike Harding were still recording the sessions. They'd taped Thin Lizzy's first in July 1971, after Malcolm had a tip-off about 'this band playing in a pub on the Tottenham Court Road', went to see them, and offered them a session on the spot – 'I think we had them in within ten days'; and followed up with studio debuts by Man (13 January 1972) and Nazareth (8 June 1972).

On Mondays Bob Harris and Jeff Griffin were unashamedly producing 'the most laid-back of the nights', according to Bob, featuring many singer-songwriters; but Jeff, with his usual *In Concert* team of SM Chris Lycett and tape op John Etchells ('L.E.G. Productions' as they styled themselves on session sheets), also recorded two sessions with the original ELO in 1972, and the only BBC studio recording by Todd Rundgren.

For Peel and Walters, it was a quiet time. Apart from soloists like Rab Noakes and Martin Carthy, and revivalist folk acts like the High Level Ranters and the Fureys, the only three new name bands to come in in the first nine months of 1972, apart from Roxy Music (who did their third session, with Pete Ritzema, for Walters, on 18 July), were all made up of members of former bands: Matching Mole, Plainsong, and the Albion Country Band. The long-awaited multi-track studio, Langham 1, opened in October that year: Aeolian 2 and the Playhouse had all but done their last rock sessions; and Maida Vale 4 and 5 closed for major refurbishment soon afterwards. Now they were all set up, but where was the new music to come from?

One of the first sessions in Langham 1 was the debut of a very shy, nervous singer-songwriter: Joan Armatrading. The week

after that recording on Tuesday, 31 October, the stereo transmitters were finally switched on.

When a newly promoted Bill Aitken studio-managed his first sessions in Langham 1 on 17 January 1973 – 'Medicine Head in the afternoon, and Frankie Miller backed by Brinsley Schwarz in the evening, both for Bob Harris' – he became 'the first SM to cut his teeth on multi-track'. Most of the production teams had spent September getting stereo experience by doing their sessions at Kensington House.

However, BBC management had made it known that extra remix time was not available. The thinking was still that too much mixing was unproductive, unnecessary work: hence the decision to install 8-track, which 16-track in commercial studios had already rendered obsolete. 'Nevertheless, it was a giant step forward for the Beeb,' says Aitken. Fairly soon after 'the Langham' opened, all *Sounds of the Seventies* sessions were allowed to expand to Peel's 'double-sessions'.

Langham 1 was only ever meant to be a stopgap until Maida Vale could be refurbished, but it was to remain in constant use, fifteen hours a day, until summer 1981. It wasn't initially promising. Sited in a wing of the building that follows the line of Portland Place opposite Broadcasting House, it had an unusual, curved shape; and the traffic meant that bands faced terrible parking problems. Turning left from reception, roadies humping in the gear would push open the door into the tiny control room, which then smashed back on the Studer tape machines, thoughtfully sited behind the door.

'However, Langham 1 is the studio I remember with most affection,' says Aitken, and he is not alone. Sharing the ground floor of the Langham with the

CLASSIC · SESSION

Roxy Music

RECORDED: 4 JANUARY 1972
STUDIO: T1, TRANSCRIPTION SERVICE,
KENSINGTON HOUSE. PRODUCER: JOHN MUIR
ENGINEERS: JOHN WHITE AND BILL AITKEN
FIRST BROADCAST: 21 JANUARY 1972 *JOHN PEEL*

The early Roxy Music line-up that recorded their third and fourth Peel Sessions:
Paul Thompson
Bryan Ferry
Brian Eno
Phil Manzanera
Rik Kenton
Andy Mackay

TRACKS: 'Remake remodel', 'B.O.B. medley', 'Would you believe', 'If there is something', ('Sea breezes', first broadcast 18 February 1972).

LINE-UP: Bryan Ferry, vocals & keyboards; Andy Mackay, saxophones; Brian Eno, synthesizer & treatments; David O'List, guitar; Graham Simpson, bass guitar; Paul Thompson, drums.

Roxy Music's first session, with David O'List on guitar. In May, then with Phil Manzanera, they recorded a second session at Kensington House with Muir, just before their first album was released.

'When the band came into the control room to listen back to the mix, I asked "Where's Dave?" "In the studio," they said, and there he was, lying flat on his back.'

JOHN MUIR

'Despite the strange "lashed-up" control room, the band seemed happy with this session. I remember Eno asking us about phasing effects machines. He was really into gadgets, and the only way then to get a really good flangeing or phasing effect was to play back two recordings of the sound you wanted to phase off separate tape recorders, and knock one slightly out of phase with the other, by rubbing your fingers against the flange of the tape reel. At the BBC, we never had the time to attempt such convoluted techniques. Consequently, we had acquired a little box which attempted to simulate such phasing effects automatically. It didn't work very well, but it was all that was around, and I remember giving Eno the details.'

BILL AITKEN

BBC club, the studio's atmosphere was informal. It was easy to pop out for a pint. 'Strangely, the lack of useful space seemed to work towards an effect of "closeness" rather than being cramped,' Aitken recalls.

At the start of October 1972 Radio 1 had at last completely separated its daytime programmes from Radio 2. *Sounds of the Seventies* was tweaked a bit too: Peel was moved to Thursdays, and reunited with Bernie Andrews as producer; and John Muir launched *The Sequence* on Fridays.

That's exactly what it was. Each week, Muir would pre-record two new sessions, then select tracks from half a dozen other repeats. 'I used to have to lay all the tracks along a stretch of 8-track, and lay Pete Drummond's short voice links on a spare track,' explains Bill Aitken, who worked on the show with Nick Gomm, John White and Margaret Garrard. Muir then booked Langham 1 and experimental musicians, like Bob Downes, Ian Carr, John Stevens, Barbara Thompson, Stan Tracey, Ron Geesin and Eno (once), to come in and improvize connecting sections between the sweeps of four or five tracks in a row, changing the mood, key and rhythm, creating a 'sequence'.

'This was very difficult, and didn't always come off, not least because the tuning could be slightly different from one track to the next, and it was always difficult to figure out exactly when the incoming track might come crashing in,' says Aitken, 'but when it did come off, the links could be quite spectacular.' Aitken also worked on the show's sig, 'I'm in the Moog for love', with fellow SM and Radiophonic Workshop composer, Paddy Kingsland.

Muir's only real scoop for the show was the sole British session by Focus, in March 1973. But his persuading Vincent Price to do the links for three shows in summer 1973 was another great success: 'I was able to go to town with spooky music and effects.' In the *Melody Maker* Readers' Poll of September 1973 *The Sequence* won an honourable eighth place in the Best Radio Show category. At the end of that month it was axed, and replaced with *Rock Speak*, a review show. 'I think, next to Peel's *Night Ride*, it was the most creative thing I did in radio,' says Muir. He left Radio 1 a few months later, when his contract was not renewed.

There may have been new session-based programme ideas like *The Sequence*. There may have been a new multi-track studio. But fewer and fewer new bands were emerging to be recorded. Even Bernie Andrews only turned up a dozen debuts in his fourteen months producing Peel on Thursdays, though these did include Camel, Richard and Linda Thompson, and Queen.

Bob Harris' Monday show could gain a few scoops, since Bob was also now hosting BBC2's *The Old Grey Whistle Test*: while visiting Jesse Colin Young in San Francisco for *Whistle Test*, Bob persuaded him to record a special session for the radio show in his studio shack. He and Jeff, or Pete Ritzema, who produced the show for several months early in 1973 and 1974, featured notable solo BBC recordings by Sandy Denny, and the only one, then, from Bruce Cockburn. Bands they debuted in 1973 – 74 included Greenslade, Frankie Miller, the Average White Band, Wally, Sassafras, Horslips and Dr Feelgood. In addition, after Nazareth's date on 1 August 1973, which included 'Turn on your receiver', Bob and Jeff got the band to re-record the number as Bob's signature tune, from the end of that month. 'We always regarded it as a bit of a feather in our cap,' says Naz

CLASSIC·SESSION

Queen

RECORDED: 5 FEBRUARY 1973
STUDIO: LANGHAM I
PRODUCER: BERNIE ANDREWS
ENGINEER: JOHN ETCHELLS
FIRST BROADCAST: 15 FEBRUARY 1973 *JOHN PEEL*

John Deacon,
Brian May,
Freddie Mercury,
Roger Taylor

TRACKS: 'My fairy king', 'Keep yourself alive', 'Doing alright', 'Liar'.

LINE-UP: Freddie Mercury, vocals & piano; Brian May, guitar & vocals; John Deacon, bass guitar and vocals; Roger Taylor, drums & vocals.

The first of Queen's six BBC Radio I studio sessions. Having done two for Bernie Andrews and Peel's Thursday show in 1973 (which now form the "Queen at the Beeb" CD on Band of Joy Records), and three for Bob Harris in 73–74, the band came back, just for fun, and did a totally unexpected Peel Session in October 1977, at the height of punk.

drummer, Darrell Sweet.

Lee Brilleaux of Dr Feelgood remembers their first two sessions for Bob, in late 1973 and 1974, 'as particularly important to the early career of the band, the early "pub rock" era, and at a time when we were unsigned to a record label. On that first Bob Harris session [24 October 1973], Wilko Johnson put the finishing touches to the lyrics to "I don't mind" literally minutes before the session, and we rehearsed "She does it right", only written twelve hours before, in the van on the way to the studio.'

Peel and Walters, by late 1973, were also picking up on the pub rock beginnings, with the first date by Ducks DeLuxe. But the most noticeable trend on Tuesday nights was the incoming continental experimental groups: Can, who did many sessions; Faust and Tangerine Dream, who supplied special 'private tape' recordings from Germany.

Robert Wyatt remained the most significant home-grown experimenter: of the two sessions he did then for Peel, in late 1972 and 1974, he says, 'Those mark my metamorphosis from adolescent bipedal caterpillar to adult paraplegic flutterby.

'On the '72 one I sang a Danny Kaye version of the sentimental 'Little child', the kind of thing I wouldn't have risked in a more constricted atmosphere, certainly not on record, and a Gilbert and Sullivanish joke about Arts Council grant culture.

'In September 1974 I went into the studio not only legless but, recklessly, without any other musicians or instruments, and just used the equipment to hand [Hammond organ, piano, marimba], to do truly solo versions of a few of my recent songs.' These included the long 'Sea song', and his then new, hit single 'I'm a believer'.

Peel and Walters, unwittingly, also conducted their own broadcasting experiment. Fripp and Eno released their guitar-and-effects LP *No Pussyfooting* in November 1973, and, because of the technology of the recording, Walters agreed to buy in a 'private tape' of the album. But when he put it on in the office, it sounded strangely different. He checked with the record company, but no, it was the right tape. It must be a different take, he thought: 'even better, that's what private tapes were *supposed* to be'.

The two long tracks were broadcast on 18 December 1973. 'Eno was, apparently, driving down the motorway and heard it. He pulled in, phoned up the BBC, and said, "I must speak to John Peel, I think he's playing my album backwards." "That's what they all say," said the switchboard, and refused to put him through,' says Walters. 'We found out later and checked, and he was right! I had no experience of record companies, where tapes are kept on the take-up spool and stored "tail-out", and the record company didn't know the BBC keeps tapes "front-out". Fortunately, only Eno noticed.'

A more intentionally amusing event was Elton John's pub piano session, recorded for John Peel's Christmas Day show in 1973. 'I think the original idea was to do what was very popular then — everyone did their singalong-a-Christmas medley, which, of course, was so inappropriate to Elton,' says Walters: 'and at that time, don't forget, he was just peaking in world-wide popularity, and being seen very much as a serious artist.' Elton agreed to the joke.

Walters got some light ales in to Langham 1, dragged along Peel and various other Radio 1 producers and managers, to get the atmosphere going around the specially-hired upright pub

CLASSIC · SESSION

Joan Armatrading

RECORDED: 31 OCTOBER 1972
STUDIO: LANGHAM 1 PRODUCER: JOHN WALTERS
ENGINEER: BOB CONDUCT
FIRST BROADCAST: 28 NOVEMBER 1972
JOHN PEEL

Joan Armatrading

TRACKS: 'Head of the table', 'Spend a little time', 'Child star', 'Whatever's for us'.
LINE-UP: Joan Armatrading, acoustic guitar, piano & vocals.

The first of eight sessions Joan Armatrading was to record for John Peel up to summer 1976. Bob
Conduct afterwards went round telling all his SM colleagues he'd just done this first session
with an amazing singer-songwriter. Peel had gone along to listen, and sat on the floor. John
Walters remembers that Joan communicated only by whispering to friend Pam Nestor, who
would then talk to him. Gus Dudgeon, who had just produced Joan's debut album, came along
and twiddled knobs.

'I remember being terribly quiet and shy then. John Peel was a big influence on a lot of people's
careers. When he got stuck on someone's stuff I think it made a big difference. There was
certainly a good feeling from having been on his programme. One of my happiest moments
was when, years later, I did "The Secret Policeman's Third Ball", in 1987, I think, afterwards
Peel gave me a great review. That pleased me immensely, because you know sometimes if he
likes you, then you have success, and you stop doing the show, you can think he doesn't like
your stuff any more. So I was really happy to read that, because I've always considered him
to be a big part of my career; I know some people wouldn't think so, but I do.'

JOAN ARMATRADING

Bob Marley and the Wailers

RECORDED: 1 MAY 1973
STUDIO: LANGHAM 1
PRODUCER: JOHN WALTERS
ENGINEER: BOB CONDUCT
FIRST BROADCAST: 15 MAY 1973 *JOHN PEEL*

TRACKS: 'Slave driver', 'Concrete jungle', 'Rasta man'.

LINE-UP: Bob Marley, acoustic guitar & vocals; Peter Macintosh, guitar & vocals; Aston Barrett, bass guitar; Charlie Barrett, drums; Earl Lindo, keyboards; Bunny Livingstone, congos, bongos & vocals.

'When we got them in, people at the time said, "You're not booking that lot, are you?" When Marley arrived at the studio, you realized he was a star; very quiet, and somehow dignified. Of course, all of them were there then, Bunny Wailer, Peter Tosh. I seem to remember it took a lot of time to get started, there was a lot of sitting around, as you'd expect, and, at that time, of course, possessing marijuana was an imprisonable offence; they did everything very discreetly, but you could *smell* it, even through the double doors, in the control room. They were also grinding hash up and putting it in honey. What was I supposed to do? BBC training would probably have told me to call the police. Anyway, that was on their first visit to Britain, years before they were noticed. Only Island and us were on to them then.'

JOHN WALTERS

Bob Marley

piano, and Elton kicked-off with a plinky-plinky medley of Christmas tunes. Then Walters suggested Elton do some other stuff in a pub style. 'Tell you what, I'll do a Bob Dylan medley,' he replied. The resulting, truly jingle-jangle version of "Mr Tambourine Man" was 'the finest interpretation of Dylan's work I've ever heard,' says Walters, 'and that includes Dylan.'

But that wasn't all. He went on to do a selection of pub favourites ('Down at the old Bull and Bush', etc), and then proceeded to do a 'kamikaze act' on his own standards 'Daniel' and 'Your Song'. 'He was so successful he could afford to have a tongue-in-cheek attitude to his own work,' says Walters; 'if anybody was going to have a good time destroying his own work, he might as well get the pleasure himself.' In amidst the sound of clinking beer bottles and the rollicking singalong chorus on 'Your Song', Walters can clearly be heard announcing 'Last orders!'

While pub rock was the only live music beginning, other things were drawing to a close. Family did their last session in May 1973, yet its leaders re-emerged the next year as Chapman-Whitney Streetwalkers. This says it all. Only twenty-four entirely new bands debuted on *Peel* in this period: Be Bop DeLuxe were the only real stars, and the rest consisted of ex-members of defunct groups. There were one-off scoops, solo sessions by Randy Newman and Duane Eddy. And late in 1974, *Peel* experienced a minor soul explosion, with big band dates by Kokomo, Viola Wills and Gonzalez, and Ann Peebles.

Then, quite unexpectedly, three months after the refurbished Maida Vale reopened, with the latest generation of 24 – 4 Neve desks and 8-track Studer A80s, the axe fell on *Sounds of the Seventies*.

'BBC to cut services by tenth in new year', announced the front page of *The Times* on 11 December 1974. Facing a £20 million deficit in March and with uncertainty over the licence fee, in order to save £1 million, BBC television programmes would stop at 11.30 p.m. and Radios 1 and 2 would merge again in the afternoons and after 10 p.m. 'There will be no staff redundancies,' said the BBC, 'but Stuart Henry, Bob Harris, Alan Black and David Simmons, the Radio 1 disc jockeys, will not have their contracts renewed in the new year.'

'Radio 1 Scandal – Rock Off!' screamed the front page of the next week's *Melody Maker*. 'All this in pursuit of savings of less than £500,000 a year, out of a total budget of £140 million,' commented the paper. 'It means the end of Radio 1 stereo programmes,' said Bob Harris. 'Last week I had the best contract from the BBC I'd ever had, and then suddenly, four days later, the whole of the *Sounds of the Seventies* programmes go overboard. It's a really retrogressive step. The only real survivor will be *Top Gear*.'

So once again Peel and Walters were alone. A new early evening strip was hurriedly created, from 5.15 to 7 p.m., and Peel was given Mondays and Thursdays. The other nights, presented by Alan Freeman, Annie Nightingale and Rosko, did not feature sessions. Where there had been eight new 'double-sessions' a week, there were now just Peel's two. In the nine months this regime ran, there were only a dozen new bands in session on Radio 1.

But from Monday, 29 September 1975 it was 'bedtime with Peel', announced the *Radio Times*. Peel was back on FM, from 11 p.m. to midnight, from Monday to Friday. The name *Top Gear*, only retained as a subtitle of his show since 1971, was finally dropped, as was

the sig by the Nice, replaced by 'Pickin' the blues' by Grinderswitch. Of the seven debut sessions before Christmas the most unusual was, perhaps, by SM Bill Aitken.

Aitken played all the instruments himself, recording the numbers in his spare time at a 16-track commercial studio. Peel, Walters and Tony Wilson liked the tape so much that Aitken was given 'a papal dispensation', and his tape including the famous 'Chimney pots', was broadcast on 8 December.

Every night of the week before Christmas that year, an episode was broadcast from Viv Stanshall's *Christmas at Rawlinson's End*. Aitken remembers that the session overran, and everyone wondered if there was enough on tape. Then Stanshall returned a week later. 'He started to perform monologues over the backing tracks, and the effect was hilarious: Tony Wilson, Mike Engles and I were literally falling about in the control room laughing our heads off. I even created some special sound effects for one song: "We are three vivisectionists" (F/X – Splash/Rip/Spurt).'

It was a great broadcasting event. That Christmas, many tuned in every night at 11 p.m. But doing just that – turning on the radio at night to listen to Peel – was soon to become a daily ritual.

4

●

THANKS
TO THE
TWO JOHNS

New Short-Haired Man.
Peel, Walters' office,
circa '79.

How many people were there at the start of punk? Pete Frame's *Rock Family Trees* names only nine. And how many more really bought the idea: got their hair cut, went to every gig, followed the *NME* line? A few hundred more names, perhaps, and not one of them was mine. Most of us heard the news, but at a remove; for most of us live our lives at a remove.

To listen to the radio is to start a private affair. The figures show that most listening is done at home. Unlike the washing up, it is not something we share: most listening we do completely alone. To hear what's new we tune in, because we're alone. To find out about punk we all tuned in to John Peel. The only place anyone could hear it was on Peel. He too, like us, is alone when he's on the air. He finds that guests in the studio put him off his stride. Regular listeners can tell when someone's there. As he so often complains, 'The building's empty tonight';

but he likes it, protest though he may. He says 'It's easier to talk to a microphone than people'. But who are listeners, if not people?

He was alone in other ways by 1975. The cuts had left him a sole campaigning voice. He continued the only way he knew how: by making the records and sessions his personal choice. To which new bands and sounds should he give a voice? And Walters stuck to the line he'd held all along: 'Which bands to record? It's a question of right and wrong.'

So when punk began, listeners were in for a shock. The two Johns' rules meant their choice was clear: if punk was *now*, they would have to drop the old rock. It didn't just happen, it took over two years. But what would one day be a legend was near. We not-so-old rock fans were won round. Our private friend brought us a shocking new sound.

And that's the secret of radio's

TONIGHT

power and style. We lived a revolution from the safety of home. But we only felt safe and immune for a while. By 1978 punk was almost grown: those nine original punks were not alone. Most of us experienced it first through Peel. It was a media event first, and only later, real.

What follows is not the definitive story of that time. It is simply the ordinary listener's story, one person's night-time listening diary. The session sheets have aided my memory, and PasBs also help tell the story. I leave cultural theory to cultural theorists. For this is how punk happened to most of us.

――――

The date is Wednesday 19 May 1976. Most of Peel's show that night was interesting enough. There were tracks from LPs by Supercharge, the Steve Miller Band, Nils Lofgren, Streetwalkers and the Mighty Diamonds. But the last track, all 01' 30" of it, was 'Judy is a punk'; which, as the PasB confirms, is 'Side 1. Band 3. LP: *Ramones*'.

'Every week I used to go down to Virgin Records at Marble Arch, and the manager, I'm sure without the approval of Head Office, used to allow me to take records out "on approval": the ones I didn't want I'd return, and those I did I would have to pay for,' says Peel. 'One week I took out about ten LPs, one of which was the one by the Ramones, and I immediately liked several things about it: first, the simplicity of the name, it having an implication of that romantic Spanish-New York thing; and also because it was a monochrome sleeve. When I put the record on, initially, because of the aggression and brevity of the numbers, I was slightly taken aback, but sufficiently excited, that I started playing it that very night.'

And the following night he went mad, playing the last three tracks on side 2 of the album in a row: 'Let's dance', 'I

don't wanna walk around with you', and 'Today your love tomorrow the world'. On the Friday he restrained himself to playing just 'Havana affair' (S.2 B.2). Through late May and early June, he'd kick off one or two shows a week with tracks from the album like 'I wanna be your boyfriend' and 'Blitzkreig bop'. By the week after the band's British debut at the Roundhouse on 4 July, 'Blitzkreig bop' was being spun three nights in a row. It seemed his mind was made up. Things were changing.

On the Wednesday of the next week, several tracks were played from the Jonathan Richman and the Modern Lovers LP. The next day, the 21st, it was the 101ers' 'Keys to your heart', on a new small British label, Chiswick Records. On the same show there was Dave Edmunds' 'Here comes the week-end'. And throughout late July, Peel spun tracks from Eddie and the Hot Rods' *Live at the Marquee* EP.

But each of these only took up three minutes of an hour-long nightly show. More representative, perhaps, was the broadcast of Eric Clapton's new LP, *No Reason to Cry*, in its entirety, on 6 August. Then, for the next two weeks, each night was devoted to a band's history: the Who, Roxy Music, Fairport Convention, the Soft Machine and the Faces.

Everyone now knows that the Sex Pistols played their first gig in 1975. Retrospectively, their gig reviews, which started appearing in the music papers from February, assume a huge significance. But at the time they simply seemed to offer a glimpse of a bizarre new cult. Early 1976 is more accurately summed up by the new bands Peel had in session: Shanghai, Lone Star, National Health, Racing Cars, Widowmaker, AC-DC, and a couple of sessions from a new jazz-rock ensemble, including a drummer from a well-known progressive group, then just gigging occasionally, Brand X.

'There were no other places that would play Brand X then; it was only people like Peel, who, whilst as " Phil Collins" he probably wouldn't be very interested in what I did, seemed to take a bit of an interest in Brand X,' says Phil Collins today; 'because it was such an odd mixture of music, and it was a growing music, living and breathing – you couldn't record it and say, "That's the definitive version of that song", because it just kept changing or getting better, it would never be the same thing twice, so live sessions made more sense for us.'

Old favourites were still coming in as well. The first session of the year was by Bridget St John; others featured included Moon, Blue, the Jess Roden Band, Elkie Brooks, String Driven Thing, and Caravan. 'I think I was probably relatively happy with the first part of 1976, until we got into the second part,' says Peel. Perhaps the only two bands to continue recording through the early punk era unscathed were Be Bop Deluxe and Thin Lizzy.

'The punk thing never really bothered us,' says Scott Gorham of Lizzy. 'In fact, we embraced it, we were closer to the punk attitude than the pomp rock: other bands would go off-stage, have the towel draped over their shoulders, into the limo, and away. We'd stay and have parties backstage – we were a street-type band. We used to go to those sessions, get a sound, and then basically put it down live, and any overdubs were icing on the cake.'

There were also new bands who, if still drawn from a generation older than the punks about to emerge, had a more back-to-basics approach. In May the Count Bishops, who had the first release on Chiswick at the end of 1975, did a debut session, closely followed by the Roogalator. The next month, Graham Parker and the Rumour did their first.

'I do seem to remember saying in the mid-seventies, prior to punk,' recalls Peel, 'that I would like to see a return to the discipline that was imposed by the $2^1/_4$-minute long single – Jerry Lee Lewis was the example I used at the time – that when you went into a studio you'd got two minutes and fifteen seconds in which you'd got to say everything you'd got to say, *possibly in your life*; and that seemed to me to concentrate the mind wonderfully, and produce quite extraordinarily passionate records.'

Ironically, the first British record which sought to meet this prescription was by one of the older generation: Nick Lowe's 'So it goes', the first release on Stiff, *BUY 1*. Peel played it every night of the week beginning Monday, 23 August 1976.

Meanwhile, the new generation were just appearing above ground. On the Sunday of the Bank Holiday at the end of that week, the Clash played their first proper gig, supporting the Sex Pistols at the Screen on the Green. Then on Tuesday the 31st, the two bands played the 100 Club. In the audience was John Walters.

'When I walked in, I thought, "Well, it's over for these people now, because I've found it. If they were on at the 100 Club and *I* knew about it, it was no longer underground",' says Walters, echoing a comment in Caroline Coon's *Melody Maker* review the next week: 'the private party is over, they're public property now'. 'There were one or two people from record companies there, there was clearly a buzz, and obviously any purity they'd ever had was about to go,' according to Walters.

'Looking back now, the whole punk movement must have been in that room. Nothing was fixed stylistically, people just looked a little odd; but there was a very conscious kicking over of traces. I just remember it being banging and shouting, I'd never seen pogo-ing before, and all this spitting: I thought this was *wonderful*. Then, just as Rotten finished "Anarchy in the UK", Dave Dee, A&R for Warners, shouted to me at the bar "They've got no charisma!"

'But, to my eternal shame, I made one of the only two mistakes I've ever made,' admits Walters. 'I thought, if I book them, I'm going to have to send them to Maida Vale. The engineers will put their fingers in their ears and say this is rubbish; but at least we'll have it on record, what they sounded like. But I looked at them, and all the spitting and banging, and thought, *I* wouldn't like to be in the studio with this lot. It's going to be trouble, and I'd like to have it done, but I wouldn't want to inflict this event on anybody. I'll postpone it, I thought; and by then, of course, it was too late. The old camaraderie of the producers, all mates together, got the better of me for once.'

But there were other new sounds they did book. Aswad's first session was broadcast on Thursday, 2 September; and Deaf School made their debut the following Tuesday. The curious tension of the time was perfectly captured when Peel kicked off on the 29th with the Saints' 'I'm stranded', then devoted the rest of the show to Stevie Wonder's *Songs in the Key of Life* LP.

Things really accelerated at the end of October. In the previous four weeks the Damned signed to Stiff, the Sex Pistols to EMI, and the Vibrators to RAK. On Tuesday, 12 October the Vibrators recorded their first Peel session, before bringing out their first record 'We vibrate', over a month later. Eddie and the Hot Rods' 'Teenage depression' was first played on the 22nd. But the following week changed everything.

On Tuesday the 26th Peel played the Damned's 'New Rose'. It was the first real punk record. If hearing 'Heartbreak Hotel' or 'Tutti Frutti' was the crucial moment for a previous generation, 'New Rose' was, for many of us, the record after which nothing was ever the same again. On the Thursday, the Vibrators' session went out, and Peel closed the week's shows with 'Pressure' from the repeat of Aswad's date, followed by 'Teenage depression'. And in that week's *Melody Maker*, as well as reviews of the Damned and the Rods' singles, details were announced of the first national tour by the Sex Pistols, with the Clash and the Damned.

On Friday, 19 November, a full week before it was released, along with Richard Hell's 'Blank Generation' (and a session by Martin Carthy), Peel played 'Anarchy in the UK'. By then the Damned had been booked to come in for a session, to be recorded on Tuesday, 30 November, just before the tour was due to start on 3 December. But the Pistols appeared on Thames TV's *Today* with Bill Grundy on the 1st and everything went mad.

In the midst of the press hysteria over that weekend, Peel drove to Derby on Saturday the 4th, in an attempt to catch the second night of the tour, only to be met by a sign saying 'Sorry – Not Playing'; and on the Monday John Walters received a phone call from Radio 1 controller, Derek Chinnery.

'He had come out of a meeting and he was calling me from the Council Chamber in Broadcasting House, or the governors' dining room, I think. Somebody had brought up this punk stuff after the Bill Grundy business on the front pages, wanting to check with Chinnery that Radio 1 wasn't getting behind this filth. "I'm just checking that you're not going to be using any, are you?" he said.

The Damned

RECORDED: 30 NOVEMBER 1976
STUDIO: MAIDA VALE 4
PRODUCER: JEFF GRIFFIN
ENGINEER: MIKE ROBINSON
FIRST BROADCAST: 10 DECEMBER 1976 *JOHN PEEL*

Captain Sensible,
Dave Vanian,
Rat Scabies,
Brian James

TRACKS: 'Stab your back', 'Neat neat neat', 'New rose', 'So messed up', 'I fall'.
LINE-UP: Dave Vanian, vocals; Brian James, guitar; Captain Sensible, bass guitar; Rat Scabies, drums.

'I think I was apprehensive about it, because I hadn't seen them before or met them; but, in fact, when we got to the studio, I'm not sure who was more apprehensive, them, about being in a BBC studio, or me about working with them. The amusing thing was quite a few other people had heard that the Damned were in, and every now and again we got people creeping in through the door, looking in through the window to see if they were being sick all over the place or spitting at us. Which they weren't at all, of course; they were four of the nicest blokes I ever got to work with.'

JEFF GRIFFIN

'I just remember it being a very fast session. Five numbers down, and Jeff away back to Radio 1 with the tapes. We finished very early.'

MIKE ROBINSON

10

"Well, we already have, Derek," I said. "What!" he exclaimed. I said we'd played several records, and the audience liked them. "Yes, but you won't be getting them into BBC *studios*, will you?" Well, actually, I said, Jeff Griffin did the Damned for us last week.'

In that week's *Melody Maker*, towards the end of a large feature on the aftermath of the Grundy incident and after reporting that 'Radio 1 is refusing to play "Anarchy in the UK" during the day', the paper pointed out that 'the record has been played by John Peel, who will be devoting his Radio 1 show this Friday to punk rock, with the Damned making their BBC debut.'

Speaking perhaps as much to his concerned superiors as to *Melody Maker* readers, Walters told the paper, 'It's not meant to be a history of punk, but a presentation of the music, after all the remarks about the sociology of the players. It's not like the BBC is jumping on the punk bandwagon, but just some examples of what the actual artists sound like.'

At a time when commercial stations up and down the land were proclaiming bans on punk, that show on Friday, 10 December was a triumph for Peel and Walters, and Radio 1. The Damned's five numbers were interspersed with tracks by Iggy and the Stooges, Richard Hell, Television's 'Little Johnny Jewel', 'I'm stranded', and 'Anarchy in the UK'.

But it was too late to change listeners' votes in the first ever Peel's Festive Fifty, broadcast two weeks later over the Christmas and New Year holidays. 'Stairway to Heaven' was listeners' all-time Number 1. The rest of the poll was dominated by Bob Dylan (four tracks), Hendrix (three), the Beatles (three), Led Zeppelin (another two), and Pink Floyd. The only new insurgent was Jonathan

Richman's 'Roadrunner' at Number 33. Nothing would change overnight, and that included the bands being booked for sessions.

Most of the acts recorded in the first few months of 1977 were tried and tested favourites: the Boys of the Lough, Be Bop Deluxe, John Martyn, Roy Harper, June Tabor, and Supercharge. Big new releases featured included Bowie's *Low*, Pink Floyd's *Animals*, and Steve Gibbons' *Rollin' On*. Looking at the PasBs, there's a sense of a lull after the dramatic events before Christmas. 'Don't forget that in the nature of the session booking process we would be working several weeks, or even a couple of months ahead,' Peel points out.

Maida Vale 4 was used for all Peel sessions at this time. It was 8-track, with Neve 24 – 4 desks adapted, by BBC rules, so the faders went 'up' towards the engineer. This idiosyncrasy was introduced because the studios were also used for live broadcasts, and psychological research by Engineering suggested that the instinctive gesture to shut something off in the event of an accident, or rude word, was to jerk the hand forwards, not back.

Tony Wilson was effectively in charge of Peel session production. He would invariably do the Monday Peel recording session, initially with Bill Aitken, but, increasingly through the punk period, with Dave Dade, as Aitken went on attachments. The two remain a recording team today, on Tony's rock sessions. Mike Robinson was the SM allocated to the Tuesday Peel recording, most often with Jeff Griffin producing. They, too, remain a team, later handling ·Live Aid and the Mandela concerts.

At the beginning of April 1977 Peel's show expanded to two hours a night, starting at 10 p.m. Nick Gomm was the SM allocated to the *third* Peel ses-

John Walters

Eddie and the Hot
Rods completed their
first Peel session in
under two hours.
Possibly only The
Damned were faster.

sion recording now required most weeks, on Wednesdays, and the producer was Malcolm Brown, who had returned to Radio 1 the year before after two years' directing at BBC Television: 'They weren't expecting me back, and had nothing for me to do'. Walters found him something. Through summer 1977 he and Nick Gomm, along with Jeff Griffin and Mike Robinson, were to record some of the key debut punk sessions.

But before that Peel and Pig went to their first punk gig: Generation X at the Roxy, late in January. 'We got spat at as we walked in, and I thought, my goodness, they love me, they accept me,' says Peel. The Pig pogo-ed frantically and both were greatly impressed. Billy Idol and Tony James' band would later record their first session, early in April.

The third British punk record, after 'New Rose' and 'Anarchy', was the Buzzcocks' *Spiral Scratch* EP, which Peel played from 3 February. He was also spinning Talking Heads' 'Love goes to building on fire'; tracks from Television's *Marquee Moon* LP; the Damned's debut LP; Elvis Costello's 'Less than zero'; and the Stranglers' 'Get a grip on yourself/London lady': 'I saw them supporting Patti Smith at the Hammersmith Odeon, and people were getting up and

walking out, always a good sign,' says Peel. The band recorded their first Peel session on 1 March, broadcast on the 7th.

Eddie and the Hot Rods finally came in for their first session in February. 'We started after 2.30 p.m., and I was back handing the tapes to Walters in his office at 4.30 p.m.!' says producer Jeff Griffin. 'They did four fast numbers live, no overdubs, and that was the way to do those bands, because that was the way they played their set, and that way you captured the feel of it. Walters couldn't believe it when I handed him the tapes.'

Once the show had doubled in length the punk bookings increased.

Spring and summer 1977 would bring the final sessions from many old retainers: Medicine Head's last of twenty-one; Caravan (their tenth for Peel alone); and Thin Lizzy (eighteen in all). 'We carried on booking a punk band and a straight band each week for quite some time,' says Walters.

In the last week of April in Maida Vale 4, for example, the Adverts recorded their first on the Monday; the Jam their first the day after; and Medicine Head their last, on the Wednesday. On Monday 9 May John McLaughlin and Shakti were in, but the next day the Damned were back to do their second. On the night of the McLaughlin broadcast, 13 May, Peel also played a record which the BBC later refused to play because of its 'gross bad taste', the Sex Pistols' 'God Save the Queen'.

Back in late April, Peel had received 'a large purple handbill for a beat group who revel in the appellation XTC', as he later reported in his *Sounds* column. He confessed himself intrigued by its promise of 'Twilight! Insects! Iron! Lust! Rays!', and the description of the band's music as 'irritating, itching rhythms, probably more ant music than human stuff'. He went to see them at Ronnie Scott's Upstairs on the 19th, and reported he was 'thoroughly ensnared'. The band did their first session late in June. By the time they came back for a second, late in September, Virgin had signed them up.

On Monday, 25 July Elvis Costello and the Attractions recorded their first session, and the next day it was the turn of the Boomtown Rats. They were booked despite some casual remarks by Bob Geldof to an Irish newspaper earlier in the year which had rather upset Peel, as he reported in his *Sounds* column. 'We have been offered a spot by John Peel,' the Rats told the Irish paper, 'but we won't do it unless it's part of a set of London gigs with planned promotion and publicity.' Commenting on Peel's offer of money to help the band make a record, Geldof said they didn't want to be part of 'Peel's perfumed paradise'. In his autobiography *Is That It?* Geldof acknowledges, regarding Peel, that he 'had made some pointless remarks in the press about ageing hippies, but I doubt if this affected his judgement'.

By early September the debuts were coming thick and fast: Alberto Y Lost Trios Paranoias, the Buzzcocks and the Only Ones in three consecutive shows. Years later, John Perry of the Only Ones told Dave Cavanagh in *Sounds*: 'When somebody who'd never heard the Only Ones wanted to know what we sounded like I'd always play them the Peel Sessions in preference to the studio albums. They're rougher but there's more feel, because the songs were more or less recorded live. You could do more or less whatever you wanted; nobody was at all put out when I wanted to record the sound of my Strat being thrown around the room for the end of "Oh no," they just went out and set up the appropriate mikes. The great thing about recording under those conditions and at that speed is that it shows whether the songs stand up for themselves.'

Walters, meanwhile, had developed a regular diary of weekly punk gigs, to go out and 'lack-of-talent spot': the Croydon Greyhound on Sundays, the Roxy, and the Vortex on Mondays, among others. 'I did most of the going out because it rapidly became obvious that Peel was recognized and would be surrounded, as Uncle John Peel, and they'd all give him tapes – we were their main platform, and they all knew it; and also he was working late anyway, and hadn't got the time.'

But the Vortex went on until 2 a.m., and when a gig featuring the Slits was billed for 15 August, Walters said he'd take Peel down after the show. As early as March, Peel had written in *Sounds* that his 'heart was heavy' because he had yet to see the all-female Slits, already attacked in the *News of the World* simply for their name. 'They were the very essence of punk: banging and shouting, unhindered by any discernible musical ability. We thought the BBC should record them for posterity,' says Walters.

How did the audition panel respond to this absence of 'musical ability' in the punk acts? The panel was still meeting once a week, but since 1967 new acts had been passed with the proviso 'suitable for *Top Gear* only'. Maggie Brown, who had taken over the unit from Mary Cotgrove, recalls the number of tapes submitted direct from rock acts dwindling by the late 1970s, with the advent of cassette demo tapes, which bands increasingly sent direct to Peel.

Audition sessions were still held, and the Talent Selection Group still met, but by the time she left for Programme Contracts department at the end of 1978, Maggie Brown recalls, the unit had all but ceased to do any work for Radio 1. Responsibility devolved on to individual producers. The unit staggered on auditioning ventriloquists and variety acts for Radio 2 shows, until it was eventually abandoned in 1981.

A few weeks before the Slits, Walters had seen Siouxsie 'strutting her stuff, with this blatant Brechtian bellowing', on a multiple bill at the Vortex. Then on 9 October he went to a Siouxsie/Slits double bill at the Croydon Greyhound. Turning up early, and listening to the Banshees' sound-check, he remembers thinking, 'These are memorable tunes, underneath it all. They were actually working as a band; you could see there were certain musical patterns, and

XTC

RECORDED: 20 JUNE 1977
STUDIO: MAIDA VALE 4
PRODUCER: MALCOLM BROWN
ENGINEER: DAVE DADE
FIRST BROADCAST: 24 JUNE 1977 *JOHN PEEL*

Colin Moulding,
Terry Chambers,
Barry Andrews,
Andy Partridge

TRACKS: 'She's so square', 'Crosswires', 'Radios in motion', 'Science friction'.
LINE-UP: Andy Partridge, guitar & vocals; Colin Moulding, bass guitar & vocals; Barry Andrews, keyboards; Terry Chambers, drums.

'I don't think any of us really knew what sessions were about: would we have to play live into the show, we wondered? We were the usual very green and nervous things when we arrived at Maida Vale. I was convinced the backwards faders were a ploy to keep our hands off the desk; and I was astonished by this grey peg-board soundproofing everywhere, the BBC must have had a monopoly on the stuff. On "Radios in motion", I held up a cassette playing radio interference at the start, which we didn't get to use later on the LP version. I can recall sticking my head in through our van window to hear the number going out, just before we did a gig at the Rock Garden on the Friday: a very exciting moment, and I think we were late on stage as a result. Later, confronted by an apathetic audience at the Greyhound, we actually went on and mimed to the Peel tape of "Radios in motion." No one noticed.'

ANDY PARTRIDGE

The Slits

RECORDED: 19 SEPTEMBER 1977
STUDIO: MAIDA VALE 4 PRODUCER: TONY WILSON
ENGINEERS: NICK GOMM AND BILL AITKEN
FIRST BROADCAST: 27 SEPTEMBER 1977
JOHN PEEL

TRACKS: 'Love and romance', 'Vindictive', 'New town', 'Shoplifting'.
LINE-UP: Ari Up, vocals; Tessa Pollite, bass guitar; Viv Albertine, rhythm guitar; Palmolive, drums.

'That was the first time we'd ever been in a studio. Lots of people thought the result better than the album. It was absolutely raw, more raw than any boys' band. I almost can't believe we had that much energy. You don't expect girls of that age to have that much energy: Ari was 14, I think, and the rest of us were all under 20. "Vindictive's" not on any LP, and "New town" was very different when re-recorded. It was also the only recording we made with Palmolive, as an all-girl band. It was years before we made an album.'

VIV ALBERTINE

'It was everyone hitting anything as loudly as possible; vaguely in time, there was a sort of rhythm there, and then this maniac shrieking on top. On stage, at that time, it probably sounded quite good, when it was loud, but, when it came out over little speakers, fairly quietly, it just sounded painful. The tuning of the guitars was all over the place. We couldn't stand listening to these guitars, they were so badly out of tune. So myself and the other engineer, both guitarists to a certain degree, had to go out and tune them ourselves. Every now and then we'd have to go back in and re-tune them, because they didn't have a clue how to. I wonder if we did the right thing.'

NICK GOMM

'The two sessions that they did are both in the Top Ten best sessions of all time. The first one they did is the best one to come out on Strange Fruit. It sums up the spirit of the era.'

JOHN PEEL

The Slits, 1977

they had plans. I booked them.'

———

At the Greyhound that night Walters had met Jordan, former assistant in Malcolm Maclaren's shop Sex, and on 1 December he went to a gig at the Royal College of Art by the band Jordan was managing, Adam and the Ants. 'Adam was all right, although a bit art-school for my taste; and then suddenly Jordan came on stage herself for one number: painted face, hair standing up about a foot in the air, and began to shriek; I thought, get that girl into the studio, and let her shriek to the nation!'

He went backstage after the first half of the set, to fix up a session date with Jordan, and the two spent the entire second half locked in the band room, after Adam inadvertently slammed the door, as he went on stage: 'This prompted much "oh, so that's how you get on the Peel Show" ribaldry when they came off'. The session was conditional on the band doing Jordan's song 'Lou', involving the shrieking, and the recording was set for Monday, 23 January 1978.

'I felt absolutely out of my depth the moment I walked in there, because I'd never done the song in a controlled atmosphere,' Jordan told Walters years later. 'It was a song from the heart, to put it kindly, and you had to work yourself up before each performance of it, to give it its all. To sing a song like that, which is meant to be sung out of control, in a controlled atmosphere, was very difficult for me: I'd never sung it more than once on the trot, obviously. To have to do it two or three times, as I remember, was very hard on the voice, and the emotions.' The band also did 'Deutscher girls'. The official story of Adam and the Ants describes the session, broadcast on 30 January 1978, as a 'landmark' in the group's career.

Now that Adam, Jordan, Siouxsie,

Rich Kids, Subway Sect, the Slits, Chelsea, the Adverts, Generation X and the Damned had been in, all the bands that had emerged out of the original London punk movement had now been featured in session on John Peel – except the Sex Pistols and the Clash. By January 1978 the Pistols were on the verge of collapse, while the Clash were firmly established. They would get a chance later that year.

But what really mattered was that in the wake of the Grundy incident, when according to Jordan 'everyone was scared witless of punk', Peel, Walters and Radio 1, alone, had given it airtime. Most of the above bands were unsigned when they did their first Peel session. No one knew then that they would go on to become stars; and that wasn't the point anyway. They were simply what was happening at the time, and Peel recorded it. By the end of 1977 each night's programme was predominantly punk releases and sessions, mixed in with reggae records.

And by then, Peel and Walters were not quite alone at Radio 1 in giving a break to the new wave of bands. From Autumn 1977, bands like Generation X, XTC (twice), and the Tom Robinson Band (their first), advanced forward in the schedules to do sessions for Dave Lee Travis' tea-time show, led on by DLT's producers Tim Blackmore and Dave Atkey. Later, from spring 1978, after Kid Jensen took over the show, with producer Dave Tate commissioning, and co-producer Pete Ritzema recording many of the bands, this punk bridgehead broke out, with dozens of sessions by acts like Elvis Costello, the Buzzcocks, and the Rezillos; and debuts by the Pretenders, the Police, and in 1979, Simple Minds.

But what happened to the Banshees in 1978 showed the particular importance of Peel sessions. Despite graffiti all over

Elvis Costello recorded
his first Peel session
with the Attractions on
Monday 25 July 1977;
the next day it was the
Boomtown Rat's first.

Siouxsie and the Banshees

RECORDED: 29 NOVEMBER 1977
STUDIO: MAIDA VALE 4
PRODUCER: MALCOLM BROWN
ENGINEER: MIKE ROBINSON
FIRST BROADCAST: 5 DECEMBER 1977 *JOHN PEEL*

Siouxsie and the
Banshees, 1977

TRACKS: 'Love in a void', 'Mirage', 'Metal', 'Suburban relapse'.
LINE-UP: Siouxsie, vocals; Steve Severin, bass guitar; John McKay, guitar; Kenny Morris, drums.

'It was a bit like seeing your picture for the first time, because it was the first time we'd actually "separated" anyone and listened to and laughed at each other. It was terrifying, actually doing the session. You ended up finding how difficult it was to come across good in a recording situation: we came from going "bleaugh!" on stage. You look back and know that the knock-on effect was a help to your career, but at the time it was just a thrill.'

SIOUXSIE

'It was the first real chance we had of getting across to a lot of people and to show that we were actually serious about what we did. At the time, all we were concerned with was being in a decent studio for the first time and hearing the songs. So we didn't really think about how it would help our career.'

STEVE SEVERIN

London saying 'SIGN THE BANSHEES', the record industry wouldn't touch them: 'They hoped it would all go away,' says Walters. On their second session, broadcast on 23 February 1978, the group did 'Hong Kong garden'. Still the record companies weren't interested. Walters and Banshees' manager Nils Stevenson negotiated a deal for BBC Records to bring out a single of the session recording. 'We thought that'd be enough to get them on the fringes of the chart, and that would pull the finger out of the dyke, as it were, and the offers would come flooding,' says Walters.

As soon as the labels heard about this, they jumped. Polydor signed Siouxsie up, and the BBC Records plan was dropped. 'Hong Kong garden' was re-recorded, and promptly shot into the chart late in August that year, peaking at Number 7. Without Peel sessions, it is doubtful that this would have happened so fast.

'Within that year, all these new bands were doing sessions, and they'd never been heard by many people before, they'd just been up and down the country playing to thirty people,' says Steve Severin; 'and then suddenly it was all over the airwaves, and you couldn't really ignore it.'

It would have been difficult indeed to ignore those Peel sessions. By the time 'Hong Kong garden' charted, in the twenty months since the Vibrators' first recording there had been ninety debut sessions on the programme. It matched Bernie and Peel's achievement on *Top Gear* ten years before. But it was by no means over yet.

The very day after Adam and the Ants' debut in January 1978, Wire's first went out; and Patrik Fitzgerald, Magazine, X-Ray Spex, the Mekons and the Flys had followed them before the end of March. The first record played in the show on which the Flys appeared, on 23 March, was 'Suspect device' by Belfast's Stiff Little Fingers. They promptly went into the most easily available small studio, which happened to be the 8-track Studio 1 at the Northern Ireland commercial radio station, Downtown Radio, and recorded a four-song 'private tape' session for Peel, which was broadcast on 13 April. Downtown's engineer Stephen Nelson recorded the tracks; and both he and Downtown Studio 1 would famously figure again on Peel before the year was out.

But April also brought the infamous, aborted session by the Clash. They were booked in on the 24th, with Tony Wilson producing and Bill Aitken engineering. 'Tony was introducing me to two of the band leaders when my eye caught Nicky Headon, who I knew as a good drummer from other bands,' says Aitken, 'and who had a very friendly little mongrel dog, who he used to love so much he would bring it along to sessions, where it would lie patiently at his feet, waiting for him to stop thumping the hell out of his kit.

'"Hi Nicky, how's your dog?" I said. The two leaders immediately started derisively mimicking "How's your dog, ha! ha! ha!" then corrected me: "That's Topper." I felt sorry for Nicky, who looked extremely embarrassed by the whole thing, but couldn't afford not to conform to the collective Clash image.' The band put down some tracks, but became increasingly 'negative', says Aitken, until, towards the end, they told Tony Wilson they wanted to cancel. The explanation given was that 'it wasn't happening'. Aitken, however, is convinced the real reason was his innocent enquiry after Topper's dog.

Altogether more productive and happier were the recordings Viv Stanshall made, mainly with Malcolm Brown pro-

113

ducing, for five *Rawlinson's End* broadcasts on Peel, between 1977 and 1979. One of the most complex, involving two full recording sessions, went out in April 1978. 'I remember on one of those Malcolm was trying to get for me the noise of a haddock being slapped across the back of Henry's head,' says Stanshall. 'He first of all hunted round the broom cupboards at the studios for the right kind of mop, then insisted on exactly the right amount of wetness, before it was slapped on a special piece of lino. He was really quite a wizz with the sound effects, was Malcolm.'

By now, Malcolm Brown was doing the Tuesday and the Wednesday Peel sessions. But when he went on to produce a daytime show that summer he had less time for Maida Vale work. One of his last regular Tuesdays produced the Skids' first session, on 16 May. At the same time, Radio 1 learned that Engineering was not going to release an SM for promotion to producing that year. Controller Derek Chinnery asked if staff knew any good freelance producers.

Walters did. Coincidentally, a few days earlier he had bumped into an old friend and musician from Newcastle. He'd first turned up on Peel sessions as keyboard player in Mick Abrahams' band, and later in his own right as a solo multi-instrumentalist, who had recorded for Peel as recently as June 1977: Bob Sargeant. He was hawking round his production of a demo tape of Rat Scabies' new band, the Whitecats.

Bob Sargeant became the first of the freelance Peel session producers, signifying the beginning of a major change in how sessions were done. His first two, made as trials, were the Boys of the Lough on Wednesday, 24 May, 'live — finished by 6.30 p.m.', and the Rezillos on the 31st 'slightly more problematic'. He started doing the Wednesday Peel

recording session regularly from 5 July.

But the day before the Rezillos, a rather longer-lasting new band had been in the studio for Peel for the first time. 'You don't know me but I know you,' Walters had written to its leader on 15 May, having seen them at the Greyhound, Croydon, the other Sunday. The band seem to have the kind of defiant non-musical approach which ought to be encouraged. 'We might be able to work out something to your advantage,' he wrote. 'P.S. I went to see Siouxsie really but Danny Baker had recommended that I try to catch your performance.' That support band was the Fall.

They were to go on to become the most recorded Peel session band of the punk and post-punk era, and remain Peel's favourite group. Bob Sargeant, another new boy at Maida Vale that week, did their second session that November, and ended up producing their first album, *Live at the Witch Trials*.

Sargeant's beginning regular session production coincided with the last gasps of the old guard. The only pre-punk acts to come in again were Rab Noakes, Roy Harper, Racing Cars and, last of all, Dr Feelgood, broadcast on 18 September along with Stiff Little Fingers' first Maida Vale date, which was almost Malcolm Brown's last Peel production, recorded on Tuesday, 12 September. Even as they were finishing the session that night, across London at Egton House another Northern Irish band was about to make history.

Just who got a copy of 'Teenage kicks' to Peel is unclear. Feargal Sharkey says he had previously contacted Peel about a demo tape the Undertones had sent, so when Terri Hooley's Good Vibrations label of Belfast pressed up 2000 copies of the *True Confessions* EP, he posted one to Peel. Terri Hooley says he spent a Friday unsuccessfully trying to

The Fall's Mark E. Smith: booked for their first session in May 1978, after Danny Baker recommended Walters see them at the Croydon Greyhound. The band did their 20th Radio 1 session in March 1993.

sell the record to major labels in London, and late at night left a copy for Peel at Radio 1.

What happened next has become a pop legend. On Tuesday, 12 September Peel played all four tracks from the EP. 'Isn't that the most wonderful record you've ever heard?' he commented. He was so excited he played 'Teenage kicks' again on the Thursday and Friday. And again two days the following week. Listening to the show in his car as he drove through London was Sire Records' boss Seymour Stein, who, having signed the Ramones and the Rezillos, was looking for more acts. The next day he contacted Good Vibrations and the band in Derry. Within three weeks the band had signed to Sire, and 'Teenage kicks' was rush re-released on Sire on 13 October. Peel used the excuse to play it again that night. 'I still maintain it's the best record ever made,' says Peel today. 'It cost us £100 to record,' says Terri Hooley. And for just another £70 Peel had, in the meantime, already scooped Sire on a further recording by the group.

Before the band had signed, when they still could not afford to come to London to do a session, Peel paid for them to go into Downtown Studio 1, and with Stephen Nelson engineering, do a three-hour 'private tape' session for the show. 'We just drove down to Belfast in an hour and a half and did it,' says Feargal Sharkey.

'The first number they played, I thought, ah, that's a hit record. Then they did another, and I thought, ah, now *that's* a hit record; and every song was like that,' recalls Stephen Nelson. The tracks recorded were 'Get over you', 'Top 20', 'She can only say no', and 'Male model', and the tape was first broadcast on Monday, 16 October. Long thought lost, the tape turned up in summer 1992, when Peel stumbled across it in his attic.

Walters was still picking bands at gigs. On Sunday, 26 November he went to see 'Generation X + support' at the Greyhound, Croydon. 'Generation X had made it by then, and they'd been on tour supported by this band from Crawley,' says Walters. 'I was horrified to learn they were being paid a fiver for the whole band, but the manager was then having to pay Generation X's lighting and sound men a tenner, so it was *costing* them money to play.' Walters booked them. The band was the Cure.

Shortly afterwards, Peel ran his second Festive Fifty, over Christmas 1978, and everything had changed. 'Anarchy in the UK' was listeners' all-time Number 1, and punk records filled the top 10 and dominated the rest of the chart. 'Stairway to Heaven' was the highest pre-punk record, at 14. There were five Sex Pistols songs, four from the Clash, and no less than seven by Siouxsie and the Banshees, reflecting how they had been championed by the show since that first session in December 1977. Five times as many listeners voted as in the first poll two years before.

'The audience of two years ago was an audience growing old with me,' Peel told *Melody Maker*; 'My listeners were in their mid-to-late twenties, either students or ex-students. My existing audience did not come with me as I thought they would, and I developed a whole new audience. Today my audience is a disenfranchized minority.'

On top of all that, the Undertones, perhaps the last pure pop band to explode out of punk, did their first Maida Vale session in January.

Peel's new listeners' Festive Fifty votes may have swung behind the first generation of punk bands, but the music, and Peel, were already, in 1979, definitely in

The Cure

RECORDED: 4 DECEMBER 1978
STUDIO: MAIDA VALE 4
PRODUCER: TONY WILSON
ENGINEER: DAVE DADE
FIRST BROADCAST: 11 DECEMBER 1978 *JOHN PEEL*

4

Laurence Tolhurst
Michael Dempsey
Robert Smith

117

TRACKS: 'Killing an Arab', '10.15 Saturday night', 'Fire in Cairo', 'Boys don't cry'.
LINE-UP: Robert Smith, guitar & lead vocals; Michael Dempsey, bass & backing vocals; Laurence Tolhurst, drums & backing vocals.

'After overcoming the initial disappointment in discovering the great man would not actually be there himself, the experience lived up to expectations. The four songs we recorded captured the spirit far more than the album versions. I found that the producers had exactly the right approach: if it looked like you knew what you were doing, they let you get on with it. It was this lack of meddling that made the results more like the original demos that had secured our recording contract in the first place, just better quality. All songs in the first and second session should be seen as the definitive sound of the early Cure.'

MICHAEL DEMPSEY

CLASSIC · SESSION

The Undertones

RECORDED: 22 JANUARY 1979
STUDIO: MAIDA VALE 4
PRODUCER: BOB SARGEANT
ENGINEER: DAVE DADE
FIRST BROADCAST: 5 FEBRUARY 1979 *JOHN PEEL*

Billy Doherty,
Damian O'Neill,
Feargal Sharkey,
Mickey Bradley,
John O'Neill

TRACKS: 'Listening in', 'Family entertainment', 'Billy's third', 'Here comes the summer'.
LINE-UP: Feargal Sharkey, lead vocals; John O'Neill, rhythm guitar; Damian O'Neill, lead guitar & backing vocals; Billy Doherty, drums; Mickey Bradley, bass guitar & backing vocals.

'We were just a bunch of late teenagers having a good time. I never thought I would still be working in music when I was 24, let alone 34. By January 1979 we were over supporting the Rezillos so we could do a session at Maida Vale. But the biggest thing that struck me at the time was that John Peel had paid for us to do that first tape the previous autumn out of his own pocket. I don't know of any other DJ that I've met who would care to that extent, show that much drive and commitment to the music.'

FEARGAL SHARKEY

The Beat

RECORDED: 24 OCTOBER 1979
STUDIO: MAIDA VALE 4
PRODUCER: BOB SARGEANT
ENGINEER: NICK GOMM
FIRST BROADCAST: 5 NOVEMBER 1979 *JOHN PEEL*

The Beat's
Ranking Roger
does the Ranking
full stop

TRACKS: 'Tears of a clown', 'Mirror in the bathroom', 'Ranking full stop', 'Click click', 'Big shot'.
LINE-UP: Everett Morton, drums; Dave Wakeling, guitar & lead vocals; Ranking Roger, percussion, vocal & styles; David 'Shuffle' Steele, bass; Andy Cox, guitar & optional vocals.

'They were very nervous, it being their first session. I tried to put them at ease. When they started to play it was immediately very fresh and exciting. I particularly thought Dave Wakeling had a great voice. We were trying to get it live and immediate, and as a result the session went very quick, and we had five numbers done by 7.30 p.m. Then the manager rolled in. He said the band had had a chat in the canteen, they were recording a single for 2-Tone in a few days, and would I like to produce it? I think they were simply pleased at having a very well-engineered session.'

BOB SARGEANT

Bob Sargeant went on to produce the Beat's first and second albums.

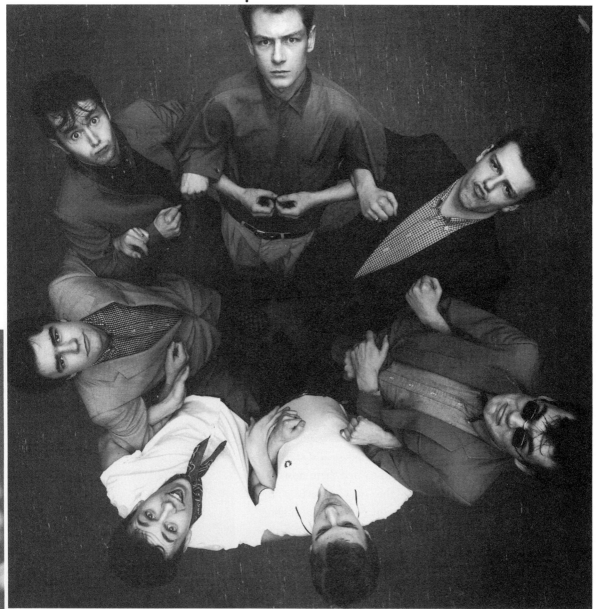

The 2-Tone explosion:
The Specials, Madness
and The Selecter all
recorded first Peel
sessions in 1979.

the post-punk era. Early that year such diverse bands as Tubeway Army, the Gang of Four, Joy Division, Big in Japan, the Raincoats and Linton Kwesi Johnson recorded first sessions.

Trevor Dann and John Sparrow, two new junior staff producers at Radio 1, were packed off to Maida Vale once a week to produce Peel sessions from early 1979 for the next year and a half. Trevor Dann remembers it as a thin time. 'Some of the groups were hideously unlistenable. I remember a series of utterly wretched groups, all of which I thought then were forgettable, and indeed who are now forgotten. The exceptions were Echo and the Bunnymen, who I thought were great; Psychedelic Furs, who overcame initial nervousness to do a good session; and Simple Minds.'

It was also the year when Walters feels he made his other 'mistake' on session booking: the first was not having the Sex Pistols; the second was going ahead with a session by the Police. 'I'd seen the Police in a pub and turned them down as far too retro – they were clearly going back to playing proper tunes, and singing proper songs – and although they had a following, I thought "*No*".

'Then Peel was knocked out with them at a Dutch festival ('They played particularly well,' says Peel), and we got them in. They did a good session, but if you follow the philosophy of the programme, they shouldn't have been on: they summed up conformity, whereas punk was all about nonconformity.'

But there were non-conformist musical movements appearing in the aftermath of punk: the ska revival, first embodied by the Specials, and later Madness, the Selecter and the Beat; the mod revival, through the Monitors, the Chords and Secret Affair; and, as *Sounds* called it in March, 'The new Merseybeat': Echo and the Bunnymen,

the Teardrop Explodes, Pink Military and Orchestral Manoeuvres in the Dark, all of whom debuted on Peel in 1979.

Of these, perhaps the 2-Tone bands, led by the Specials, produced the most exciting sessions, purely because their music thrived on live performance. On the night their debut session went out in May, the Specials, in Leeds for a gig, rushed into a second-hand shop to buy a radio to listen in; Peel repeated the session three times before September. Early

Orange Juice — Edwyn Collins resisted BBC producer John Sparrow's advice to sing 'Falling and Laughing' through a megaphone.

in August, Madness recorded a version of 'The Prince' that, with Bob Sargeant's production and Mike Robinson's mixing, surpassed the record. Pauline Black of the Selecter remembers that 'half the band arrived late, and the other half *very* late' for their debut in October: 'It was a terrible rush, but we rowed our way through it, like everything else, ending up doing the fourth number "Danger" totally live.' Then at the end of the month came the Beat.

By the first week of the new decade such was the multiplicity of styles emerging that the show had established a different kind of equilibrium: new bands and independent records weren't just playing '1 – 2 – 3 – 4!' frantic punk, but enough of a variety for Peel's show to become a mix again. In the first week of January 1980, UB40, Bauhaus and Simple Minds all had their first Peel sessions broadcast.

But although an average of five new

bands were still being recorded each month in 1980, far fewer of them went on to become famous household or even cult names. Perhaps the one truly transcendental band to appear was the Birthday Party. 'I saw them at the Moonlight Club in West Hampstead,' says Peel, 'and they were stupendous, a revelation. It was also one of those gigs where you know, instantly, that this band are going to be worshipped by a certain sector of the listening public.' Their first broadcast was on 25 September.

'We'd been working at home in Australia for a couple of years, made a couple of records, then came to start from scratch in London in 1980,' remembers Mick Harvey of the Birthday Party. 'We picked up a deal with 4AD, and released two singles, but only did about eight gigs in all that year, around London. So the session was very good exposure for the band. It certainly contributed to us gaining popularity! I must admit, though, I always remember being amused at how all the engineers and producers would break off for their lunch and tea-breaks no matter what.'

From late that year and into early 1981 there was also a wave of Scottish bands, starting with Altered Images closely followed by Orange Juice, Fire Engines, Josef K. and the Associates. Edwyn Collins remembers Orange Juice recording 'Falling and laughing' 'at breakneck speed compared with the Postcard single and Polydor album versions. 'I don't know why that was, I think it was because we were very enthused to be doing our first Peel session. The producer John Sparrow suggested I sing "Poor old soul" through a megaphone. He thought it sounded like a twenties song, a Bonzo Dog Doo-Dah Band kind of song. I don't know where that guy's head was at! "Poor old soul" and "You old eccentric" are the two outstanding tracks from the

session.' Both are now out on CD.

That first date for Orange Juice was one of the very last recorded in the old 8-track Maida Vale 4. It closed down at the beginning of November 1980 for conversion to 24-track. For over a year, a team of Bob Conduct, Bob Harrison and Bill Aitken had been investigating what equipment should be chosen. They eventually plumped for a new desk design from SSL, a company in Oxford. In the end the BBC ordered quite a number of desks from SSL, which made the company's name. In fact, so pleased were they with the sale that they offered Bill Aitken a job, which he took in 1981.

But in the meantime, while Maida Vale 4 and 5 were being converted, sessions were temporarily relocated at Langham 1 for eight months. Bands would turn up and be astounded by what the engineers got out of the ageing 8-track equipment. Ageing it was: the monitors were in a particularly bad way, having been hammered for fifteen hours a day for ten years. Session sheets of this time are covered in engineers' doodles of exploding speakers, and credits like 'Another Blast from the Pit'. This, however, was where New Order, with Tony Wilson producing and Dave Dade balancing, recorded their famous first Peel session in January 1981.

By then, for various reasons, the number of Peel sessions being recorded had slipped back to two a week. And when Walters launched his own series, *Walters' Weekly*, early that year, Chris Lycett, who had begun his career at Radio 1 playing in 'grams' (records) for *Top Gear* in 1967, took over producing John Peel's programme for two years.

'I did the Wednesday evening show, pre-recorded, to keep my hand in,' says Walters, 'but looking back it does seem to be a very slack period. It seemed to be a million and one live bands called

"Dance" something. Punk had already become a bit of a historic thing. It was a trough after a peak.'

———

That might have meant that many of the bands who did sessions in those years would be forgotten. There might well have been a succession of 'utterly wretched' bands for Trevor Dann to record. The impact of the punk explosion may indeed have passed and the frequency of shock waves in the aftermath declined. But, thanks in part to the Peel sessions, something in pop music-making had changed for ever.

The years of the punk sessions did not just repeat Peel and Bernie's success of ten years before, in tapping an underground well of new music. Hand in hand with the establishment of independent record labels, those sessions permanently changed bands' perspective on worthwhile musical or career ambitions. From now on, a Peel session became as much an achievement in itself as a means to advancement. Those punk sessions had so great an impact that to record one as a new band was to gain a permanent place in an alternative tradition. Bands knew their names would be added to an unwritten musical roll of honour.

Being in a band became just part of a way of life. Playing in a band was to take part in a new kind of folk music. Recording your demo tape in your bedroom was its own reward, but getting to do the same on a Peel session was more than enough public acclaim. Anything that followed was an unexpected bonus.

From punk on, Peel sessions were not only rare and exclusive early recordings of later superstars. Peel and Walters were not 'picking winners'. They were giving space and time, fairly cheaply, to whoever seemed to have something to say at a particular moment. You could pick the story of any band's first session and it would be worth telling. Here, just two will have to do.

For example, how Que Bono got their booking in summer 1981 is now one of the few things people remember about them at all. 'Our singer, Jane, had the idea to send our demo tape to Kenny Dalglish, Peel's hero at Liverpool FC, asking him to forward it to Peel, endorsing our request for a session,' says guitarist Alan Maskell. Dalglish did so. 'We got a phone call from Peel, saying for sheer cheek, could we do a session?'

The recording itself, at Langham 1 on Tuesday, 9 June, was beset by difficulties. 'We couldn't put certain things through certain channels, because they didn't work,' says Maskell. 'Even though this studio is only due to be used for a few more weeks, the monitors have deteriorated beyond all hope,' despairing producer Dale Griffin scribbled on the session sheet. Nevertheless, the session, broadcast on the 16th, was 'a highlight of the band's career,' says Maskell: 'our later self-financed single was incorrectly pressed; six months later we had a blazing row; I left; and the band split up soon after.'

And then there's the story of the band, like Que Bono, from Lancashire, who had their first session broadcast the very next night, and who had been in Langham 1 the day before them: the Chameleons. The story told by Mark Burgess of their first, classic session, says more about the value of Peel sessions than the rest of this book. So I leave the telling to him.

The Chameleons

RECORDED: 8 JUNE 1981
STUDIO: LANGHAM 1
PRODUCER: TONY WILSON
ENGINEER: DAVE DADE
FIRST BROADCAST: 17 JUNE 1981 *JOHN PEEL*

The later, stable line-up
of the Chameleons that
recorded most of their
Radio 1 sessions:
Dave Fielding,
Reg Smithies,
John Lever,
Mark Burgess

TRACKS: 'The fan the bellows', 'Here today', 'Looking inwardly', 'Things I wish I'd said'.
LINE-UP: Mark Burgess, bass & vocal; Dave Fielding, guitar; Reg Smithies, guitar; Brian Schofield,
drums.

'We began by simply wanting to record a session for John Peel. It wasn't that we saw this as a stepping stone to success or anything; no, all of the bands that we had grown up admiring had all recorded sessions for John Peel, and that was our main incentive. I personally never dreamt that we would get a response to the first tape we sent in. I don't think any of us did. We didn't have a regular drummer, and recorded the songs on Reg's old blaster without drums and sent it off.

'A few weeks later back came a letter: *Enjoyed the tape, sounds like something worthwhile is going on, if you do a studio tape be sure to send me a copy. Regards, John Peel.*

'We sold everything we didn't need to make the recording: mike stands, PA amps, everything except our guitars and back line. Having recorded the demos, Dave and I boarded a train to London and spent the afternoon sitting on the steps of the BBC waiting for John Peel to walk past. Finally John did go by and we accosted him. Once he had established that he wasn't being attacked he became very sympathetic. He told us to give him an hour with the tape. When he came back we had a hard time convincing him that it was actually us on the tape. He seemed convinced we were playing some sort of practical joke on him, that we would suddenly declare the tape to be the work of some already established band and belittle his considerable reputation as an "underground" music guru.

'A few days later on the following Monday, at 9 a.m., the phone rang at my parents' house and I dashed downstairs to answer it. It was John Peel! He told me he liked the tape and wanted to book us for a session, then handed me over to Chris Lycett. He told me we could wait until Maida Vale was finished and do the session in 24-track, or do it immediately in the old Langham 8-track. I consulted with the others and we decided not to wait. A date was set the next day.

'We still didn't have a permanent drummer, but a local heavy-metal drummer we knew who'd played with us before, Brian Schofield, said he'd help us out. We didn't know anyone in London so it meant a ride down, record the session, then back to Manchester. That meant leaving Middleton at 6 a.m. We made it to Langham 1 by 10 a.m.

'I remember Tony Wilson as a very nice guy, but very quiet. Whenever he spoke to his engineer, Dave Dade, it was always in hushed tones. We were all very nervous and overawed by it all but Tony and Dave were very good with us. It was the first time we had worked with a producer or engineer, so for us the results sounded rather stunning. "Looking inwardly" then had no title or lyrics, we just had the raw idea, but we didn't want the technicians to know: Dave or Reg kept them busy with guitar parts, while I lay under the grand piano with a pad and paper scribbling away. I was enjoying myself so much though, that at one point, during the take, I just threw them away: "*I don't need these lyrics, what am I doing here?*"

'I remember the night the session was broadcast vividly. We all met up at Alastair's [roadie's] flat shortly before 10 p.m. We were doubly excited because the evening before John had wound up his show by telling the story of how Dave and I turned up on the BBC steps with the demo, and then urged everyone to tune in to hear a "remarkable" session. We had been stunned. On the evening of the broadcast he heaped even more praise on the group. None of us could believe it.'

MARK BURGESS

Within days the Chameleons were signed to Virgin Publishing and CBS Records. They released one single, and were then dropped over an argument about who should produce their LP. The band eventually recorded three albums for small independent labels in the mid-1980s, and several more Radio 1 sessions, then broke up. Most people regard their Radio 1 sessions as their finest recordings.

5

FILLING
THE
IN-FILL

B ut it wasn't just punk bands who took the music business into their own hands in the late seventies. Other kinds of groups, taking their lead from the punks, started making their own records; releasing them on their own labels; and, as a direct result, getting attention, in the form of press write-ups and BBC radio sessions, without the help of the established record companies. On 22 November 1978 the singer in a Sheffield heavy metal band sent the band's self-produced debut EP to Geoff Barton of *Sounds*. The week before, Radio 1 had launched a new weekly radio show that would soon become a vital and unique national outlet for the new wave of bands, led by that Sheffield group, Def Leppard: the *Friday Rock Show*, with Tommy Vance, produced by Tony Wilson.

As well as still recording one Peel session a week, Tony had continued producing Alan Freeman's Saturday after-

noon show through the seventies. When Fluff left in summer 1978, Tony recalls there being a slight hiatus before a presenter and slot were found for a planned new 'rock show'. A pilot was done with Tommy Vance, which Tony was pleased with, but still no time was pencilled in. When they were finally given what had been Peel's Friday night spot, from 17 November, it was not ideal. But the show quickly acquired a solid audience, 'slightly higher than any other weekday in that slot,' says Tony proudly; before acknowledging that the 'metal' fans only had one night to tune in *en masse*, rather than Peel's listeners who were then spread over four nights.

For almost the first full year of the show there were no new sessions. But the early PasBs name famous guests on their first page, so these clearly weren't just all-record programmes. Tony and Tommy would mix in with each week's new releases a classic session from the

Peel and *Sounds of the Seventies* archives: Hendrix, Fleetwood Mac, Yes, Deep Purple and Genesis sessions were much featured, later followed by Tony's own Peel productions from the early seventies, of the likes of Rory Gallagher and the Climax Blues Band. It was at this time that Tony started sorting out the surviving Radio 1 session tapes, cataloguing, restoring and collecting together all the notable ones he could find, some years before the station created the proper archive in B08. Many old Peel session sheets consequently acquired the scribbled addendum, 'Tony has tapes'.

Those first 'from the archive' features were timely. 'I liked the way they repeated the old sessions, I think they created variety, and educated listeners and musicians at an important time,' says guitarist Paul Samson, whose eponymous group was at the forefront of the new metal bands in 1979. Samson put together a package tour of clubs that spring, with Iron Maiden and Angelwitch as support; and it was Geoff Barton's *Sounds* review of the London date, at the Camden Music Machine in May, that gave the movement its name: in a centre-page spread flashed as 'the page for idiots who play cardboard guitars' the subheading introduced 'The New Wave of British Heavy Metal' – which rapidly shrank, in use, to the inelegant acronym 'NwoBhm'.

'As with so many musical "movements", that cumbersome phrase was a mistake, sprung from a drunken lunchtime with *Sounds* editor Alan Lewis,' says Geoff Barton today. But NwoBhm stuck, and the *Friday Rock Show* was there ready to champion it. Summer and autumn 1979 were a hectic time for Tony Wilson: 'I'd started taping the Reading Festival each year, and that August and September we broadcast the Scorpions, Steve Hackett and Whitesnake

recorded there live.' Two days before Whitesnake, the last of the Reading tapes, went out, Tony and engineer Dave Dade recorded the first *Friday Rock Show* session, on 3 October, with Def Leppard. It went out on the 26th, although it wasn't the band's first: Jeff Griffin had recorded them for Andy Peebles' new mid-evening show that summer.

But Leppard were the exception to the rule. In the next few months all the NwoBhm bands debuted on the *Friday Rock Show*: Samson and Iron Maiden before the end of the year; and Girl (from Ireland), Saxon, Angelwitch, the Tygers of Pan Tang, Trespass, More, Toad the Wet Sprocket, Girlschool, Diamond Head and Sweet Savage in 1980. Most of them were unsigned when they came into Maida Vale.

'Our first session helped us a lot,' says Kim McAuliffe of Girlschool. They had been supporting Motorhead on a tour in 1979, and ended up being signed by their manager and record label. But that 'nationwide radio' broadcast, on Friday, 1 August 1980, really made the general public sit up, she recalls.

In 1981 Tony Wilson picked up on Spider, a Liverpool band who had moved to London and were gigging everywhere around town. 'We didn't think of ourselves as part of the NwoBhm thing, we were really I suppose the second wave,' says Spider's leader, bassist Brian Burrows. There was a shaky moment for Brian early on at their first *Friday Rock Show* session recording, on 10 June, when his younger brother Robby, the band's drummer, said 'We don't work with anyone who wears a tie' to Tony Wilson, who was sporting a snazzy leather tie that day. 'I thought, oh no, here's this legendary rock session producer, and here's my kid brother laying down the law to him,' remembers Brian; 'what's he gonna do? Throw us out? We'll never record at the BBC again!' But Tony, ever diplomatic, removed the offensive garment.

In the end the session went so well that when the band was later offered a record deal they asked Tony to produce their first album in his spare time. 'He was really the only person we knew and trusted,' says Brian. Tony did the record. The band came back to do a second radio session in 1986, and thus became the only rock band so far to do two sessions for the *Friday Rock Show* with the same line-up.

In fact, only 11 bands in all have recorded more than once at Maida Vale for Tommy Vance. 'We've sort of made it a general rule not to re-book bands, just to keep bringing in new people and keep the sessions fresh,' says Tony. 'The rule's more or less held up over the years: those few bands who have come in again, it's been four or five years later, and with a very different line-up.'

By 1982 the NwoBhm had died down: 'Once the first bands had all been signed up, the movement kind of lost its momentum,' says Geoff Barton. But there were still enough new bands and rock styles coming along for Tony Wilson to justify continuing to record new sessions – quite apart from all the concerts and festivals he taped for broadcast. In early 1982 Tony went to Lombard Studios in Dublin to record the Mama's Boys, and the week after that first broadcast, featured the debut session by Marillion.

Later that year, Terraplane came in to Maida Vale (members of whom have gone on to greater things, as Thunder), and the next year Tony and Dave Dade went to Germany to record two new metal bands there, Eloy and Accept. At the same time, the show began recording *new* sessions by rock legends still working, such as Gillan and Gary Moore.

The success of some of these sessions perhaps helped prompt the launch of a new Thursday night show with Tommy Vance, also produced by Tony Wilson, *Into the Music*, at the beginning of October 1984. As well as sessions from new, melodic, less straight-ahead metal groups, *Into the Music* also featured new recordings from veterans like Roxy's Phil Manzanera and Andy MacKay (The Explorers), and the Climax Blues Band's guitarist Peter Haycock. Martin Colley, a Maida Vale producer-engineer, who had followed Dale Griffin and Harry Parker into sharing rock session production with Tony and Dave Dade, remembers some of these as excellent sessions, which have been rather forgotten in both rock and Radio 1 history. Bands featured in the short, one-year life of *Into the Music* included Virginia Wolf and Beltane Fire. 'There were some excellent bands who didn't quite make it,' says Martin Colley.

The *Friday Rock Show* continues to feature about twenty new bands in session each year. As well as keeping broadly to his one-session-only-per-band rule, Tony Wilson explains that the number of sessions is also kept to this level because he spends a full day's session recording, and likes to go back and mix the raw tapes the following week, using his four Maida Vale bookings each month regularly this way: record – mix, record – mix.

'It's not something I'm prepared to compromise over,' says Tony. 'Rock sessions are liable to be lengthier and more complex than punk sessions.' As a senior producer at Radio 1, and certainly the longest-serving continuous session producer at the station (he was still producing Peel sessions in 1983), his views carry some weight. It's also worth pointing out that, as a result of other organizational changes at Radio 1 detailed in the final chapter, Tony is now unique in being the *only* producer who still goes to Maida

CLASSIC · SESSION

Samson

RECORDED: 17 OCTOBER 1979
STUDIO: MAIDA VALE 4 PRODUCER: TONY WILSON
ENGINEER: DAVE DADE
FIRST BROADCAST: 2 NOVEMBER 1979
FRIDAY ROCK SHOW

Paul Samson

TRACKS: 'Big brother', 'Six foot under', 'Hammerhead', 'Take it like a man'.
LINE-UP: Paul Samson, guitar; Bruce Dickinson, vocals; Chris Aylmer, Bass; Thunderstick, drums.

'We were very inexperienced then, and the studios seemed very "BBC" and official, like, you weren't allowed to put your feet on the desk. But I do remember that "Big brother" had a rock guitar solo in the verses, and Tony Wilson asked me if I could "track" the guitar part, meaning record it again note for note, and you put one take in the left-hand speaker and the other on the right. I said OK and did the whole thing in one take, without a mistake; or, if I did make one, it was a harmony anyway! And that clearly astonished Tony. I think from then on we had his respect, and the session went fine.'

PAUL SAMSON

Marillion

RECORDED: 29 JANUARY 1982
STUDIO: MAIDA VALE 6 PRODUCER: TONY WILSON
ENGINEER: DAVE DADE
FIRST BROADCAST: 26 FEBRUARY 1982
FRIDAY ROCK SHOW

TRACKS: 'Forgotten sons', 'Three boats down from the candy', 'The web'.
LINE-UP: Fish, lead vocals; Diz Minnitt, bass; Steve Rothery, guitar; Mark Kelly, keyboards; Mick Pointer, drums.

'We were playing small clubs everywhere in summer 1981, and then did our first date at the Marquee in October. About the same time we tried Tony Wilson out with a couple of tapes, and then he came down to a gig, and the session was on. You had to be fully rehearsed to do those sessions, there wasn't time to mess about, and I think that's very good for encouraging professionalism in bands. I remember getting lost with all the FX we could get on the vocals. The broadcast itself was one of the key career moments for the band: basically, we were able to turn professional in March, and headlined a tour of Scotland on the strength of the session shortly afterwards. We weren't signed to EMI until September that year, and until then, having done the Radio 1 session was a major feather in our cap, in promoting the fact that there was a definite buzz about the band.'

FISH

Fish of Marillion

Vale himself to record sessions for his programme.

The general move away from programme producers doing their own sessions, which today leaves Tony a curious survivor, was, of course, begun when he himself took on doing the Peels for Walters in 1972. But it was another set of changes at Radio 1, in the late seventies, which really accelerated this trend, and opened up a whole new session-recording area in the 1980s. It was the development that led to Jeff Griffin scooping the *Friday Rock Show* to record Def Leppard's first session. It was when Radio 1 connected up the teatime show with Peel at 10 p.m., and finally filled 'the in-fill'.

———

'Radio 1 on 247 is now joining Radio 2': for years the station had shut down at 7.30 p.m., only to come back at 10 p.m. with Peel. How to fill what was called 'the in-fill' period had occupied planners for some time, when, in autumn 1978, to coincide with the frequency shift to 275 and 285 metres, the budget became available to begin evening programmes.

From Monday 13 November, Andy Peebles, a new DJ from Manchester, under producer Jeff Griffin, started a show at 8 p.m.; Kid Jensen was given a one-hour documentary slot, *Stayin' Alive*, from 7 to 8 p.m.; and Mike Read launched a Saturday-night live show from Manchester. Both Peebles and Read were to feature sessions by new bands. Unfortunately, things didn't settle down quite as planned.

Three weeks into the filled-in 'in-fill', Radio 1 had to empty it again. A dispute with an engineering union over pay for controlling the extra hours' transmission prevented the evening broadcasts. Having barely had time to book its first sessions, the new evening show was suspended. It was re-launched, once the dispute was over, in February 1979.

But there were more changes to come. After five months, during which Jeff recorded the Leppard debut, Andy Peebles was moved into a daytime show, and Mike Read, produced by Chris Lycett, took over the weekday evenings. Read kicked off on 16 July 'with sessions from John Miles, Cowboys International and Straight 8'. Lycett, who had spent two years as an attachment producer doing an odd mixture of looking after the lunchtime show and recording a few Peel sessions, brought the same kind of pop & punk mix to Read's show, with some famous sessions by the Revillos and Madness. One night a week came live from a college in the North. Produced by Tony Hale, Radio 1's man in Manchester, this included many live bands.

This too, however, was a comparatively short-lived arrangement. Late in 1980 Lycett formed a triumvirate with Peel and Walters to handle Peel's shows and *Walters' Weekly* for the next couple of years; the evening show, from 1 September, was handed to producer Mike Hawkes. He was the man who would bring continuity to the slot, remaining in charge for most of the eighties. Presenters came and went (starting off with Read himself, nipping off to the *Breakfast Show* only three months later), but Mike stuck it out. Fronted successively thereafter by Richard Skinner, David Jensen, Muriel Gray (one week), Richard Skinner (again, six weeks), Janice Long, Simon Mayo and Liz Kershaw, the *Evening Show* became one of the delights of Radio 1 listening between 1980 and 1988.

'Because of all the changes, the slot was barely established when I took over,' says Mike. 'Peel had a clear identity and a reputation built up over years. The *Evening Show* then *didn't* — it had already had a variety of presenters, who didn't quite have the authority of Peel.' Mike, a veteran of the old Gramophone department, who had produced Noel Edmonds' *Breakfast Show*, Gambaccini's US chart show, and *Rosko's Round Table*, consequently took upon himself the 'eyes and ears' role of the slot: listening to records, going to gigs and booking sessions.

Having started in Gramophone department in the 1960s, he had no background in live music engineering. So the sessions had to be produced by someone else. Walters had started the 'independent session producer' ball rolling with Bob Sargeant in 1978, followed by Dale Griffin, formerly known as Buffin, Mott the Hoople's drummer, who started at Maida Vale in spring 1980.

The veteran session producers by now had little time for Maida Vale work, and fewer engineers were being released for promotion to production at Radio 1. But at the same time new programmes like the *Evening Show* were demanding more new sessions. So the independent producers became essential.

From the start of the decade, names like Barry Andrews, Dale Griffin, John Porter and John Williams pop up again and again in the blank space alongside the word 'Producer' on *Evening Show* session sheets (and Peel's as well). Yet, there is no trace of Mike Hawkes' name on them, even though it was he who commissioned them.

He also gave his sessions greater prominence on air. Lycett had been recording a session a week for Read, stripping it across the four daily editions, putting out one track a night, plus one from each of a couple of repeat sessions, via the item recording agreement. Mike, in contrast, from April 1981, started featuring a complete session every night. Each week's shows would feature two new sessions and two repeats.

Mike's enthusiasm for dance music and reggae quickly became apparent, as bands like the Belle Stars, Aswad, and Clint Eastwood and General Saint joined the likes of the Alarm, the Higsons, the Farmers Boys and the Passions as frequent guests in session on the show in the early eighties. There were also one-offs which were to prove famous with the advantage of hindsight: a debut appearance by the original Depeche Mode, including Vince Clark, recorded in the old eight-track Langham 1 on 11 June 1981 (three days after the Chameleons' first there); Culture Club, and the Eurythmics, both in as early as July 1982, before either had their first hits; and three sessions by U2, the first in September 1980.

Another favourite at that time was Simple Minds, who recorded several times for David Jensen, and used the sessions to try out new numbers on British listeners. In February 1982 they recorded 'Promised you a miracle' for Radio 1, followed by 'Glittering prize' that August, and 'Waterfront' the following September. 'We'd literally just returned from our first tour of Australia and went straight to the studio to record that session,' remembers Jim Kerr. 'This was the first time anyone in the UK had heard "Waterfront".'

Freelance session producer John Porter also remembers a classic session, in June 1983, by Elvis Costello and the Attractions, one of Mike's favourites. 'Elvis was not exactly in the best of health, but it was wonderful in the end,' says Porter. He did a cover of Percy Mayfield's 'Danger zone', as well as 'Pills and soap', 'Shipbuilding', and a medley of 'Big sister's clothes' and the Beat's 'Stand down Margaret'. The recording date was Thursday, 9 June, general election day. Elvis's plea on his final number was too late. By the time it was broadcast on the 21st, Mrs Thatcher and the Conservatives were back in power with a historic majority.

Mike Hawkes can also claim, with some confidence, to have discovered Howard Jones. He saw him playing in a pub in their mutual home town of High Wycombe: 'I thought lumme, this is rather good.' Howard was booked for a session, which was first broadcast on 21 March 1983. On the session sheet producer Dale Griffin scribbled a note to David Jensen: 'David – it's worth mentioning on air that the highly talented Mr H. Jones has yet to sign a record deal – wake up out there!' Howard's manager, David Stopps, remembers the session vividly. 'I can clearly remember Dale turning to me during the first number, "New song", and saying "*That's* a hit record".' Which, of course, it was; but not until that September.

Another future hit heard first on David Jensen's programme that year was an early version of Frankie Goes to Hollywood's 'Relax', recorded at Maida Vale in February (the band had already debuted what would later prove their second hit, 'Two tribes', on their first Peel session, broadcast the previous December). The Jensen recording was broadcast, although Mike Hawkes made a cautious note to himself, in case of complaints. He wrote 'lyrics?' on the box containing 'Relax – Shoot it in the right direction', as the track was then called. 'I thought, are they singing what I *think* they're singing? We broadcast it though, and that was ages before the rumpus over the single (it didn't enter the charts until the end of November).'

Late in spring 1983, and before the 'Relax' controversy, another new band was to receive extraordinary attention through Radio 1 evening sessions, also involving questioning over lyrics. But it was Walters, not Hawkes, who first picked up on the phenomenon that was the Smiths.

It was one of the first things he did when he resumed producing Peel full time. After Chris Lycett moved to the *Breakfast Show* at the New Year, Trevor Dann had stood in as Peel's producer for the first two months of 1983, and then in March Peel did some shows from BBC Radio Merseyside. Walters was back in charge of all four Peel shows, Monday – Thursday, by late April. And on 6 May he went to see the Smiths at ULU, the University of London students' union venue.

'They were a late replacement as a support act. I'd heard there was a buzz about them in Manchester, and Scott Piering [then handling the Smiths' promotion] told me about the gig at the last minute. He said "I think you should see this band." There was a scattering of people there. I was standing next to Scott, and felt there was a kind of charisma there on stage, so I thought we'd better have a session.' He offered the band one there and then. That's the way Walters tells it, but Peel remembers him returning to the office in a *highly* enthused state.

By the time they went into Maida Vale 5 on 18 May, the Smiths had released their first one-off single on Rough Trade, 'Hand in glove'. Their Radio 1 producer that day, Roger Pusey, was then doing quite a few Peel sessions, and according to him 'they do stand out as being one of the better ones, certainly one of the ones we got the most out of at the session'.

Engineer Nick Gomm admits he was initially slightly put off by Morrissey's singing, but then, to be honest, many of us were, at first. That didn't prevent Nick doing an atmospheric live mix. The first number recorded, 'What difference does it make', would later be the band's third single; but that version was to feature several overdubbed layers of guitars, and some members of the band were reportedly more fond of this original, more straightforward, Peel session recording. Years later, drummer Mike Joyce told writer Johnny Rogan: 'the Peel version is the way I wanted it to be'. It was the first time the band had even attempted to record both this number and 'Reel around the fountain' (they had made a demo of 'Miserable lie', and 'Handsome devil', the fourth song recorded on the 18th, was the B side of the single).

The session went out on the last day of May. In the middle of a tour late in June they finally signed to Rough Trade permanently, and a few days later recorded a second Radio 1 session, this time for David Jensen, commissioned by Mike Hawkes, on Sunday 26th. Three numbers were completed, with Dale Griffin producing.

But it was the second session for David Jensen that was to prove a turning point. Mike Hawkes booked this one soon after repeating the first on 20 July, and the recording was set for 25 August. By then Peel had already repeated the first session twice, the second time the very night before this third Maida Vale date for the band.

One notable thing about the recording on the 25th was that it was the first time the band met and worked with independent producer John Porter; although he had, coincidentally, already been asked, earlier that month, by Rough Trade boss Geoff Travis to remix tracks for the band's first album, following the unsuccessful Troy Tate-produced sessions in June and July.

'I had listened to the tapes a few days before the BBC session,' reflects John Porter; 'then, having met the band and got on well with them at Maida Vale, particularly Johnny, I think that, knowing we liked each other, and that it would be all right, I suggested to Geoff we simply re-record the album tracks; and I think

we did that very soon, perhaps only a couple of weeks after that Jensen session.' Geoff Travis thinks he only agreed the re-recording of the album after Johnny Marr had spoken highly of Porter to him, following the BBC date.

Porter would later produce the Smiths' last two BBC sessions, both for Peel, one in 1984 and the other in December 1986. 'We were working together quite a lot, and tried to make the BBC sessions as easy, and as painless, as possible. We'd try and get it good, but not get too hung up about it. I think all the numbers were done very quickly, in just a first or second take. We'd get the band sound set up, and Morrissey would come in, perhaps only for a couple of hours, and we'd just do the numbers in a very straightforward way. We never really laboured that much over them.'

The working relationship that the band first developed with Porter in BBC Maida Vale studios in August 1983 was later to prove highly creative; it produced their first album and several singles, including 'How soon is now?' On the 25th, with Mike Robinson engineering, they recorded 'I don't owe you anything', 'Accept yourself', 'Reel around the fountain' and 'Pretty girls make graves'.

But again with baffling coincidence, on the morning of the 25th the *Sun* published a story headlined 'Child Sex Song puts Beeb in a Spin'. The article claimed that some of Morrissey's lyrics were about paedophilia, although it mistakenly referred to the words of 'Reel around the fountain' as belonging to 'Handsome devil'. Just where the paper got the idea that the BBC had already expressed reservations about either of these songs is unclear, since both of them had been broadcast, either from the single or the sessions, some time before. What the article did was to precipitate the offence

The Smiths

RECORDED: 14 SEPTEMBER 1983
STUDIO: MAIDA VALE 4 PRODUCER: ROGER PUSEY
ENGINEER: TED DE BONO
FIRST BROADCAST: 21 SEPTEMBER 1983
JOHN PEEL

TRACKS: 'This night has opened my eyes', 'Still ill', 'This charming man', 'Back to the old house'.
LINE-UP: Morrissey, vocals; Johnny Marr, guitar & harmonica; Andy Rourke, bass; Mike Joyce, drums.

This was the first ever recording of 'This charming man', and the other songs were also new. Geoff Travis of Rough Trade popped in to Maida Vale, heard 'This charming man', and immediately recommended it be the next single: 'It was certainly the first time I'd heard the song, and I remember saying that's a fantastic track, it'd make a great single, and the band said "that sounds OK by us"; a sort of happy, casual but serious decision, as things were then with the group. It was a really golden time for the group, around that session, they were just getting into the first flowering of their most creative period.'

By the time the re-recorded commercial version was released in early November, Peel had broadcast this session three times. 'You couldn't buy pre-release publicity like that,' says Scott Piering, then handling the Smiths' promotion. The single went straight into the charts.

How the band felt about the session can be deduced from the fact that all four tracks, including the unique, acoustic version of 'Back to the old house', appeared on the compilation album *Hatful of Hollow* the following year. The album reached Number 7 on its release in November 1984, and spent almost an entire year in the Top 100. This session version of 'This night has opened my eyes' is the only recording of the song that has been commercially released.

Andy Rourke, Johnny Marr, Mike Joyce, Morrissey

it claimed to report, a not uncommon occurrence in tabloid journalism.

'The way I remember it,' says John Walters, 'Derek Chinnery [Radio 1 controller] got the wind up, and finding out they were doing a session, asked Mike Hawkes if either of these songs was included,' says Walters. Mike is not certain of the order of events in the week following the recording. 'Chinnery might have asked me, "What's all this about?", or I might have approached him. One way or another, he got to hear the lyrics of "Reel around the fountain". I was arguing we should broadcast it, but as even I felt it *was* ambiguous, it was decided that as we weren't certain, we would not broadcast it on the first time out.' This was an upset for the band, who were seriously contemplating making it their next single.

But things ultimately turned out to the band's advantage. Walters was outraged when he heard about the dropping of 'Reel' from the broadcast. 'I got the tape out, and, on my reading of it, it was clearly about heterosexual love. And that's not the point anyway: why should Radio 1 be concerned about what the *Sun* says about anything?' He phoned Scott Piering and immediately offered the band a second Peel session. 'The message came back from the band "Morrissey won't forget this",' says Walters. And less than two weeks later, on 14 September, they delivered a classic session.

Roger Pusey did check with the band about the lyrics of 'This night', but correctly points out that this is what every Radio 1 session producer has to do: 'The only way round it is to make a joke of it: "Look, I'm sorry, this is the BBC, we have to tell you you can't use the F-word", and so on. It's only sensible to know exactly what it is that is being sung and broadcast, to enable Radio 1 to disregard scare stories in the tabloids about allegedly corrupting pop songs.'

After their first session, Morrissey and Marr had made some disparaging remarks to the music press in July about BBC recordings (admittedly before they got to work with John Porter and Mike Robinson), and these were reprinted years later in *Q* magazine. 'It was very, very cold,' said Morrissey; 'You can feel the weight of the BBC bearing down on you the whole time you're there,' said Marr.

But what cannot be denied is the quality of the work they eventually produced under these constraints. Inevitably – because the BBC is an institution, and Maida Vale studios are imposing, and sessions have to be done against the clock – they can be a traumatic experience. Yet, perhaps more than any other band, what the Smiths put into those sessions in 1983 and, crucially, what they got out of them, demonstrates how what might seem an oppressive way of working to today's bands can actually produce results that, in some ways, say more than months and months of work in the studio. On reflection, Johnny Marr today says that the sessions did give the band 'the opportunity to record our new songs very quickly.'

Thanks to Walters, Peel and Mike Hawkes' enthusiasm, and, in a curious back-handed way, the *Sun*'s hysteria, the Smiths had a new session broadcast or repeated every couple of weeks for seven months: twelve transmissions in all. Tuning in, you felt, as so often when hearing Peel sessions, a witness to pop history in the making: you knew everybody would be talking about *that session* the next day. You can still hear the group's unique character echoing in those session tapes today. In 1987 journalist Nick Kent said on *The South Bank Show*: 'In ten years' time the Smiths will be viewed in the same way that the Beatles are now viewed.' He was exaggerating. But not much.

Just one discrepancy in the two bands' careers is that the Smiths didn't record their first BBC session in the old Manchester Playhouse. In fact, the Smiths didn't do any in their home town, which is surprising, and not just because they were so characteristic of where they came from. It's also strange because BBC Manchester is traditionally where Broadcasting House sends troublemakers. They have their revenge, however, by making troublesome, interesting programmes. That includes programmes for Radio 1.

Like the city's periods of dominating British pop, Manchester-based productions for Radio 1 have come and gone over the years. In the late sixties, every Thursday lunchtime on Radio 1 was *Pop North*, live from the Playhouse in Hulme, with the Northern Dance Orchestra live on stage, and guests like Terry Webster, Mike Curtis and the Mal Craig Three, all produced by John Wilcox. BBC TV's *Top of the Pops* was also sometimes broadcast from Hulme. Then, in the early seventies, the Playhouse hosted dozens of sessions for the Radio 1 Club. When Tony Hale arrived in 1973, this influence had dwindled: there were frequent outside broadcasts across the North, but no regular show from Manchester.

'The place was mainly being used by the Northern Dance Orchestra for Radio 2,' says Tony. 'They'd be doing six sessions a week at the Playhouse; but two days a week, Mondays and Wednesdays, we'd move in when they finished, at 2.30 p.m., and do a session for one of the afternoon shows.'

But in the mid-seventies things started getting more adventurous. Tim Blackmore, then producing DLT's tea-time show, started getting Manchester to do two of the sessions he needed each week. This unwritten arrangement for Manchester to supply raw musical material to the teatime and early evening shows was to continue for over a decade.

The early Manchester punk scene provided some notable locally-recorded sessions in the late 1970s, for Kid Jensen's tea-time show, including one by the Buzzcocks. 'Martin Hannet used to come and help out at the Playhouse occasionally,' recalls Tony Hale.

Dire Straits 'couldn't get arrested' says Tony, before he brought them up to do their first and only Radio 1 studio session at the Playhouse in April 1978 (they later did one *In Concert* at the Paris).

The big break, however, was the launch of Mike Read's Saturday night show early in 1979. This would involve pre-recording two or three sessions a week, and then transmitting the show live. This was followed by Al Matthews' soul show, live from the Playhouse, featuring large soul bands (like Light of the World, and Central Line) on stage, and a dancing audience: demanding work for the regular Mancunian SMs, David Fleming Williams, Dick Wilson and Tony Worthington (joined in the eighties by Paul Smith and Steve Robertshaw).

Later that year some money became available to buy studio time at Strawberry Sound, 10 c.c.'s studio in Stockport, and a number of name bands were able to do sessions in more modern surroundings. This too, established a precedent in the Manchester recording operation: of doing sessions in commercial studios, if the budget permitted. Soon after John Leonard took over from Tony Hale in 1982, a new Saturday night show was planned, featuring exclusively northern bands in session, with a new local presenter: Janice Long.

'I'd had a show on BBC Radio Merseyside, and I got the message that Derek Chinnery and Johnny Beerling at

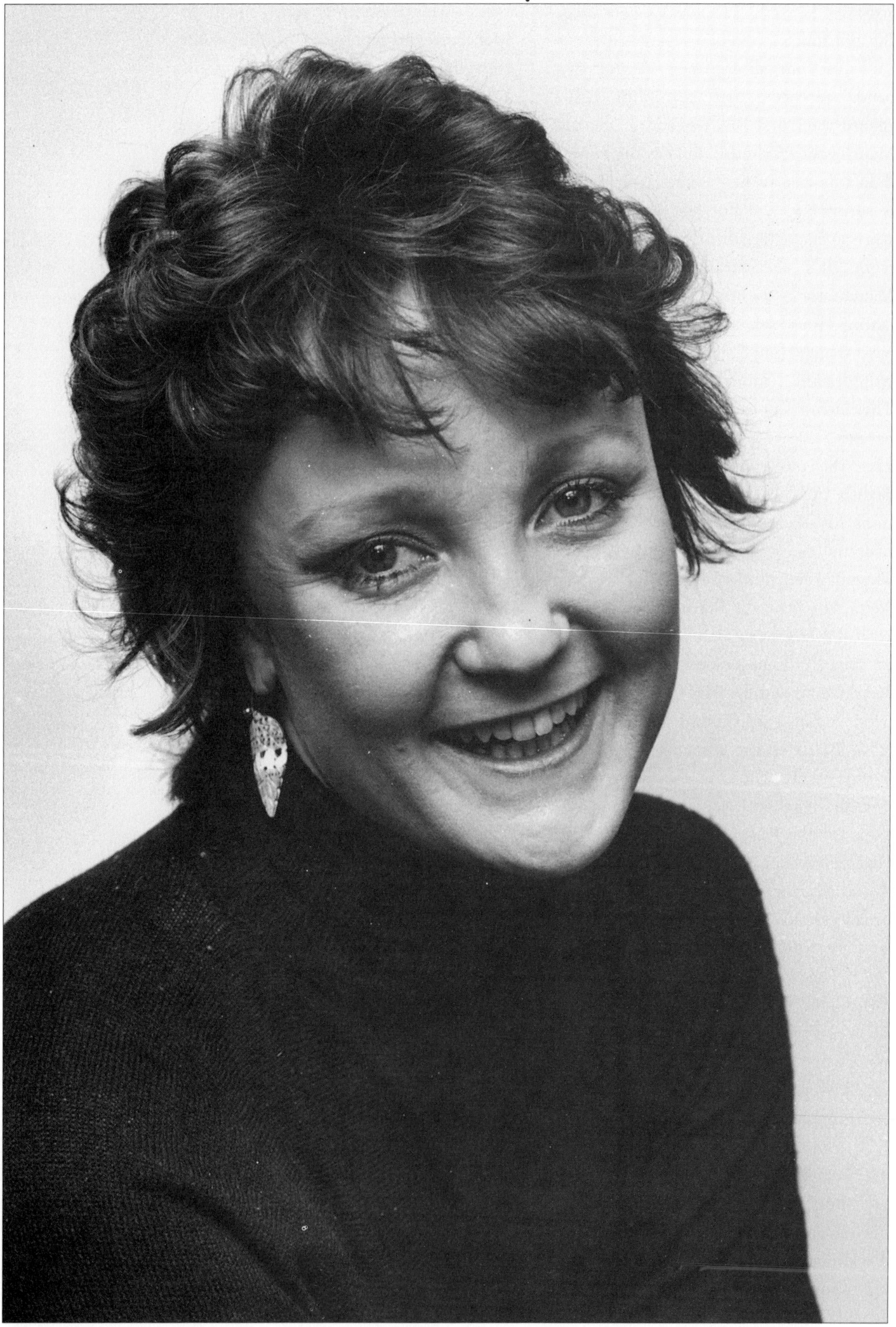

that time were keen to get programmes done in Manchester,' says Janice Long. She was snapped up for the network, and with John Leonard, and Dave Shannon or David Treadway co-producing, her $2^{1}/_{2}$ hour show first went out on 4 December 1982.

Two bands were featured each week, the first of note, the one that Janice recalls really starting things moving, being A Flock of Seagulls. They also recorded some jingles for Janice. This launched a hectic, exciting period for her. 'I'd do the show on a Saturday night, then rush back to Liverpool to go to a gig, or sometimes more than one, to pick up on all the bands.'

Throughout that spring and summer those in session included Aztec Camera, Felt, It's Immaterial, the Pale Fountains, Kissing the Pink, the Room, Carmel and Cook da Books. In June there was a con-cert tape of OMD, and a live outside broadcast from the Leadmill in Sheffield on 3 September, featuring the Lotus Eaters. By then Leonard and Dave Shannon, and freelance session producers Nick Barraclough, Clive Gregson (for-merly of Any Trouble), and Ian Wilson and Des Tong (both late of Manchester band Sad Café), had started doing some of the sessions at Moonraker Studios in Manchester.

And Janice had been noticed. In October that year production of her show was transferred to London, with Phil Ward-Large as producer, although Leonard and the Playhouse in Manchester continued to supply some of the record-ings.

The Manchester recording connec-tion lapsed when, almost a year later, in August 1984, Janice was allocated the weekday evening show slot (after David Jensen's sudden departure to Capital Radio in June, the show had been tem-porarily hosted by various presenters).

Mike Hawkes had always had a few sessions done in Manchester, most of them in 1981 – 82, including dates at the Playhouse by Fashion, the Electric Guitars, Syncopation and the Chameleons. Mark Burgess of the Chameleons recalls finding the old Hulme theatre 'rather like that television theatre in *A Hard Day's Night*' (indeed it had scarcely changed since the Beatles' debut session there in 1962, save for the intro-duction of eight-track equipment in the 1970s); instinctively he guessed it was the kind of place BBC staff were sent for punishment.

Compared to Maida Vale, with its SSL 24-track desks since summer 1981, in 1984 the Playhouse was past its prime. In 1985 the BBC faced facts and started abandoning the theatre for good. John Leonard transferred virtually all Radio 1 sessions to the commercial 24-track studio Yellow 2, in Stockport, in summer that year. Re-mixing could be done at Broadcasting House Manchester, if neces-sary.

By then, Leonard had won a slot for a new hour-long weekly show from Manchester, to feature sessions recorded at the new location. The presenter was a local Lanchashire lad, too. He had been Billy Bragg's roadie, then became one of the presenters of BBC 2's *Whistle Test* in 1984. He did a pilot for Radio 1, with Trevor Dann at BBC Radio Cambridge, after Stuart Grundy phoned him at the *Whistle Test* office. Radio 1 listened to the pilot, and sent Andy Kershaw to Manchester.

He must be the only Radio 1 DJ ever to have been so busy he missed his own first show. 'I was roadie-ing for the Bruce Springsteen gig at Roundhay Park in Leeds that day, so I didn't even hear it,' says Andy. His programme had been pre-recorded at Broadcasting House Man-

Janice Long: her Saturday night show in 1983 was one of BBC Manchester's well-liked contributions to Radio 1 output.

chester, as it was to be for the next three months. That first show, at 6.30 p.m. on Saturday, 6 July 1985, kicked off with 'Join my gang' by the Long Ryders, and featured the Screaming Blue Messiahs in session.

The next week was the Live Aid concert, but Andy was back on the 20th with the Ramones. Through the summer he featured other new sessions by Brendan Croker, Richard Thompson, and Robyn Hitchcock and the Egyptians, most recorded at Yellow 2, and all indicative of Andy's personal taste for rootsy music. In fact, this list of early session guests, quite by chance, could almost be said to reflect the perceived brief of the show.

'As far as Radio 1 is concerned it's still a "rock" show,' says Andy. It certainly looked like that when Andy was switched to the Thursday night 10 p.m. – midnight slot from 3 October that year, replacing the axed *Into the Music*, and relocated to Radio 1 in London: the trailer in *Radio Times* read 'A new programme of rock music'.

'My sister took a call at the flat some time in September (I was still living in London and commuting back to Manchester to do the show): "YOU ARE BEING TRANSFERRED TO WALTERS".' Walters later said of Andy Kershaw's arrival into his and Peel's private domain of Egton 318 that it was as if someone had entered the room and let a bluebottle out of a jar. Or, more fancifully, as if Peel and himself, like an ageing couple facing each other across the table, no longer making love but knowing what they meant, suddenly had an unexpected child. At that time Walters had not tidied his office for fifteen years. He knew instantly where everything was, 'but there definitely wasn't room for three people in there. I had to sit on a box of records, or, more often, the upturned bin,' remembers Andy.

Up to Christmas 1985 the session guests remained predominantly electric Anglo-American guitar groups, still recorded at Yellow 2 by John Leonard and his colleagues. The summer sessions were repeated, as well as new sessions from the Doctor's Children, Surfin' Dave, Champion Doug Veitch, Thrashing Doves, the High Five, Green on Red, the Godfathers, and the first Radio 1 session by the Wedding Present, first broadcast on 28 November. 'My main memory,' reflects David Gedge of the Wedding Present, 'appears to consist of arguing with the producer about the loudness of the singing: "You'll never get anywhere with vocals that low!" said Clive Gregson.'

It also took a while to build up enough repeats to fill his two-hour show each week, 'so Walters said, "Until you're ready, just pull out some old ones you fancy off the shelf there".' This was how Andy came to repeat Arthur Crudup, the Buzzcocks and Bob Marley and the Wailers in those first weeks; and to this mix of new guitar bands and old blues and reggae was added another element, detectable even in Andy's first London show, when he played 'Hatisitose' from the Bhundu Boys of Zimbabwe; 'Charming Trinidad' by the Roaring Lion; and 'Jesus is the answer' by the Staple Singers.

'I clearly remember thinking, even when I was driving up to Manchester to do the shows in that summer, there was no point duplicating the records Peel was playing,' says Andy, 'so I emphasized those areas you were then just getting the odd flash of on Peel.'

One area he made his own early on was what was known as 'the Paisley Underground', new twangy guitar bands from the West Coast of the US, like the Long Ryders and Green on Red, who came to Britain in 1985. Folk artists com-

ing back into attention, such as Dick Gaughan and Martin Carthy also did sessions.

'The programme really found its feet after about six months' broadcasting from London,' says Andy. The African, Caribbean and Bulgarian records became more noticeable throughout 1986, but sessions for these bands took a little longer to get organized. For American bands, the BBC was still then restricted by the Department of Employment (DoE) which, through an understanding with the Musicians' Union, granted permits for live or media work only if a balance of reciprocal bookings was possible.

But even musicians from other countries about which the MU were less sensitive would still have to wait for their permit applications to be processed by the DoE, then cleared by the union. This took time, even if most encountered no objection. Effectively, the whole procedure made trying to bring a non-EC band in for a session more trouble than it was worth. 'But Andy rode coach and horses through all that,' remembers Peel, with a wicked twinkle in his eye.

'We just kept on booking the international acts until people stopped arguing,' says Andy. Some of the first beneficiaries were the Bhundu Boys of Zimbabwe, recorded for Peel; and Somo Somo, recorded in Manchester for Andy Kershaw, both in July 1986. Later, with most of Andy's sessions now done at Maida Vale, were to come Taxi Pata Pata; the West African kora players Dembo Konte and Kausu Kouyate; Jonah Moyo; the Real Sounds of Africa; Balkana; Kanda Bongo Man with Dally Kimoko on lead guitar ('*What* a band!' producer Dale Griffin exclaimed on the session sheet); Nusrat Fateh Ali Khan; S.E. Rogie; Baaba Maal; Remmy Ongala and Orchestra Super Matimila; Mahlathini and the Mahotella Queens; Salif Keita; and the

Four Brothers. In fact, just about every significant African artist to visit Britain since 1986 made their first broadcast on Andy's show.

'The Bhundu Boys were really the ambassadors for African music in Britain,' says Andy. Few who heard their early sessions, and Peel and Andy's eulogies on air, will forget how their promise that we would not be disappointed if we went to see them was fulfilled.

The author will never forget seeing the Bhundu Boys on a snowy January

Andy Kershaw
celebrates winning the
Sony Radio Award for
Specialist Music
Programme with his
friend Biggie Tembo,
then guitarist and
singer with Zimbabwe's
Bhundu Boys.

night in 1987 at Fury Murray's in Glasgow; and how two strangers bumped into in the queue, also drawn there by the DJs' recommendations, went on to become close friends: the kind of thing that only happens at exhilarating African gigs.

'What was most satisfying about developing those sessions by bands from around the world was the feeling of being a fan in a position of power,' says Andy; 'the two best examples of that being what happened to Ali Farka Touré and Ted

Hawkins. I'd heard a record of Ali's, which had arrived from Paris. I remember standing next to a woman called Ann Hunt at a gig at the Town and Country Club, who said she was going to Mali. I asked her to look for him. Within six months he was here and did a session.'

The response from listeners was huge. 'And if I'd not asked Ann, and later gone to Mali myself, Ali would still be sitting in Timbuktu and hardly anyone would have had the chance to see and hear him play. It's great that, through

Zairean guitarist Diblo Dibala recording for Andy Kershaw and John Peel at BBC Maida Vale on 19 July 1992, an event he later celebrated in the track 'Matchatcha Wetu' on his 1993 album *OK Madame*.

BBC sessions, I could make these ideas a reality.'

An earlier example of someone whose music caught listeners' imagination was Ted Hawkins. Peel had played a track or two from his album, which had been shelved by Rounder Records in LA for twenty years. 'Then I was in Nashville for *Whistle Test* in April '86,' says Andy. 'I was at the airport, supposed to be going to Atlanta, and when I reached the desk I heard myself saying, "To LA, please", it was that spontaneous: I was going to look for this man. And I found him, and recorded him playing two songs. We

broadcast them, and such was the response, I went back and did some more.' Ted Hawkins later toured Britain several times, and recorded more formal sessions at Maida Vale.

Later in 1986 Pete Lawrence of Cooking Vinyl brought into the Walters office a cassette 'of this woman he'd recorded at the Kerville Folk Festival in Texas,' recalls Andy. 'We listened to a bit of it, it was a sort of a female Woody Guthrie, and you could hear trucks rumbling by, train whistles in the distance, crickets chirping. Pete wanted to get her over here to re-record the numbers.

Great idea, I said.

'Anyway, the tape burbled on, crickets chirping away; and I suddenly thought, look, if *we're* sitting here enjoying this so much with all this noise on the tape, why not just put it out as it is? It's just the right environment for these songs anyway.' And, later, that's precisely what Cooking Vinyl did, releasing Michelle Shocked's *Texas Camp Fire Tapes*; yet only after they were convinced by the overwhelming response they got, when part of it was heard first as a Radio 1 session. Andy had believed in this idea to the extent of contracting in four of the numbers, which were first broadcast on 25 September 1986.

From the stories of Ali Farka Touré, Ted Hawkins and Michelle Shocked grew the legend about how Andy has radically extended the definition of a BBC session. Armed with just a Sony Pro Walkman, Andy would record musicians everywhere on his increasing overseas trips, then put these out as 'sessions'. 'You have to accept the reality of life say, in a remote Mali village. No one has chequebooks or bank accounts. You can't issue them with a BBC contract. I just pay them cash on the spot.'

The BBC now has cause to be grateful for this wanton disregard for procedure. In 1991 Andy went to Equatorial Guinea, precisely because he had never come across any music from there on record. 'The recordings I did there of musicians have now been put on to CD by BBC Sound Archives. I see all of this as being part of the public service obligation of the BBC. We can introduce people to music they might not otherwise ever hear.'

For all these reasons Andy Kershaw's programme has become essential listening. He has twice won the Sony Radio Award for Best Specialist Music Programme. More recent classic sessions

have come from Orchestra Virunga from Kenya, the Mighty Sparrow, and Diblo Dibala, the amazing Zairean guitarist, who in summer 1992 became the first session guest to debut on both Andy's and Peel's shows on the same night, having recorded eight numbers on the one session at Maida Vale.

But then many of the Africans bands are used to playing all night in hotels, so to have eight hours to record just four or five numbers 'is a holiday', as producer Dale Griffin once told John Walters. Producers and engineers like Dale, Nick Gomm and Miti Adhikari have come to enjoy doing the Kershaw sessions in particular; perhaps none more so than that by B.B. King.

But Andy, like Peel, is still more interested in the music he hasn't yet heard. 'The people I'm interested in haven't actually made any records or tapes; so when they come over to Britain for a folk festival or something, from Africa or the Caribbean, when they record a session for my programme, it's often the first time they've been in a recording studio and made a proper recording.'

One unknown recorded by Peel, if not from so far afield, in February 1985, was Kershaw himself. He appeared as 'guest whistler' on a session by Dawn Chorus and the Blue Tits, otherwise known as his elder sister Liz and her mates. 'We were *terrible*,' says Liz Kershaw, proudly.

She also already had a part-time radio career, of the same vintage as that of her brother: both had appeared on Radio Aire in Leeds during 1982. Coincidentally, she was to follow Andy to Radio 1, first of all hosting *Backchat* with Ro Newton (which, ironically, took the Sunday afternoon slot previously occupied by *Sunday Live*, presented by Andy); and then becoming the last presenter of

B.B. King

RECORDED: 9 MARCH 1989
STUDIO: MAIDA VALE 4
PRODUCER: DALE GRIFFIN
ENGINEER: NICK GOMM
FIRST BROADCAST: 30 MARCH 1989 *ANDY KERSHAW*

TRACKS: 'When it all comes down', 'Go on', 'Paying the cost to be the boss', 'The thrill is gone', 'Ain't nobody's business'.

LINE-UP: B.B. King, guitar & vocals; Caleb Emphrey Jnr, drums; Michael Doster, bass; Leon Warren, guitar; James Toney, piano & Hammond organ; Walter King, saxophone, and musical director; Edgar Synigal Jnr, saxophone; James Bolden, trumpet.

'I'd been listening to his records since I was 13. I didn't think he was coming over that year, but then I saw an ad, and so I asked Walters if we could try and get him. "We can't get B.B. King!" he exploded, but I said, "Oh go on, just make a call." And I couldn't believe it when B.B. agreed to do it: I mean, the fact that this guy could come and record a session for a programme presented by me! But then the best things he's recorded since the mid-60s have been all to do with that kind of session, when there's no time to get precious. The tapes had a fantastic feel, and I heard that B.B. really enjoyed it. That's exactly how he *should* make a record!'

ANDY KERSHAW

'I remember it being particularly great. The whole of Maida Vale was abuzz, everyone knew B.B. King was in the building.'

NICK GOMM

'He came round with all these "B.B. King" badges, and he was giving them to everyone, the commissionaires, the canteen staff. He loved it: he kept saying, "Hey, I should come and record my albums here!".'

MITI ADHIKARI

B.B. King

the eighties *Evening Show*, in April 1988. That, however, was almost four years after Janice Long took it on.

———

'Janice was a fan, and would get very enthusiastic about bands,' says Mike Hawkes. Of all his *Evening Show* presenters, she was the one who came to have the most active influence on the choice of records, and bands booked for sessions. 'We were always going to gigs, and listening to demo tapes; we always worked as a team,' says Janice.

Some of her first guests in session in Autumn 1984 included Ellery Bop, Swans Way, the Blow Monkeys, the Fall, Floy Joy, Red Guitars, Felt, the Room, Cabaret Voltaire, Paul Haig, the June Brides, Brilliant and, at the beginning of 1985, the Loft. Pete Astor's band, and its successor, the Weather Prophets, became favourites of the show and recorded several sessions for Janice.

Bands like the Room, and It's Immaterial, who had appeared two years before on her Saturday show from Manchester and who were still soldiering on, joined groups in session like Furniture, Skeletal Family, Marc Almond's Willing Sinners and the Mighty Lemon Drops in almost defining the sound of Janice's show in the mid-eighties. About this time, as Mike Hawkes points out, the show also acquired the unique distinction of having featured all three incarnations of Ian Astbury and Billy Duffy's band in session: Southern Death Cult, Death Cult and, finally in 1984, the Cult.

But the soul, dance and reggae enthusiasms of her producer were still evident. Janice's time as presenter saw legendary BBC studio recordings by Toots and the Maytals, Tippa Irie, the Trojans, and another of Mike's discoveries, but one that this time inexplicably never really achieved stardom, Hot House. A multiracial, soulful band fronted by talented singer Heather Small, they recorded three sessions for Janice, the first two in spring 1985, some time before they made a record.

'I got a tape, and thought this voice was so distinctive, we've got to have them in,' remembers Mike. On that first session, first broadcast on 7 May 1985, they did 'Don't come to stay', which was championed by Mike and Janice, even more so when it later became a single. But to no avail: despite their enthusiasm, and critical acclaim, Hot House never quite made it. Heather Small and guitarist/songwriter Mark Pringle are now achieving success in M People.

A band who didn't have to change their name or style to break through, and who had been supported by Mike and Janice, was the Proclaimers.

———

Later in 1987 Liverpool's the La's recorded a great debut session for Janice, about the time their first single, 'Way out', appeared on Go! Discs, and some three years before the band finally broke through with their single 'There she goes' and subsequent album, which contained three of the songs featured on the session so long before, including 'Way out'.

Soon after this Mike Hawkes vacated the evening show producer's chair: an era was coming to an end. In October 1987 Phil Ross took over. In an ironic twist of fate, he had been presenter of the music show at BBC Radio Merseyside which Janice had inherited in 1981, when he left to work in BBC Radio Training. More recently, at Radio 1, he had been producing the Saturday afternoon *Sequence* (a job he was to resume in spring 1990); before that he had been in charge of *Sunday Live* and its predecessor *Saturday Live*, from January 1986.

Saturday Live, a teatime show launched in April 1983 and produced originally by Mark Radcliffe and then Phil

Ward-Large, is worth a mention as a programme which featured some famous 'live' sessions 'from the basement'.

This 'basement' was in fact the old Studio S2 in the sub-basement of Broadcasting House. Despite not being a technically ideal venue, it was popular because it was close at hand. Presenters like Richard Skinner and, later, Andy Kershaw, could introduce a record in Radio 1's on-air studios in Egton House, run downstairs through the underground tunnel to BH, down another two flights to the sub-basement and along the corridor to S2, in time to introduce the band at the end of the record.

'It was a really big room and the snare drum echoed terribly,' remembers Mark Radcliffe; 'and there was this antiquated limiter on the desk which would just pack up and go distorted when you put things through it; but I really liked the effect it gave. When I did Peel sessions at Maida Vale, Ted de Bono, who also engineered most of those Saturday Lives in S2, would spend ages trying to recreate this crunching distortion for me on the SSLs.'

These live performances for Saturday Live in the mid-eighties featured bands like the Waterboys, the Fall, the Style Council, Lloyd Cole and the Commotions, James, the Chameleons and New Order: 'they were due on live at 4.30 p.m., and at 3 p.m. only Peter Hook was there with the crew,' remembers Radcliffe. 'The rest of the band were still speeding up the motorway from Bristol in manager Rob Gretton's Audi.' They just made it in time for the show.

Those eventful afternoons were virtually the last rock sessions to be done in S2. In a rather sad fate for the once-grand Vaudeville Theatre, later the wartime control room, and then the site of Jimi Hendrix's first BBC session, the shell of S2 has now been occupied by small, general-purpose talks studios inside Portakabin-like constructions. Stepping outside them, you can see the original ceiling and faded wall fittings of the old studio. Despite the busy activity today inside the Portakabins, there's a sense of something missing. It remains a space, like the mid-evening gap in the Radio 1 schedule used to be, needing something to fill it.

At the end of 1987 Janice took maternity leave to have a baby. She ended up not coming back, as she planned, but that's another story (in short, Radio 1 offered Janice a weekly, hour-long Pick of the Week programme, instead of her four nights a week show, which she declined). In the meantime Radio 1 'new boy' Simon Mayo had stepped in, from January 1988, and he proved so successful that after just four months he was allocated to the Breakfast Show. Liz Kershaw took over in April, but the old Evening Show, unknown to its listeners, was drawing to the end of its life. Some of its last sessions were by the Cardiacs, the Primitives and Voice of the Beehive.

In October 1988 Radio 1 'FM' was launched to most of the country, and everything in the schedules changed, including the shows featuring sessions. The Evening Show disappeared. There was a documentary at 7.30 p.m. every night. Nicky Campbell began a 10.30 p.m. show, featuring one session a week. The station now stayed on air until 2 a.m., initially in the company of Richard Skinner, but from the following summer with Bob Harris; who, with Jeff Griffin producing, also featured a session a week. Between 8.30 and 10.30 p.m. there was simply no room for the old Evening Show. The man who had sat at the other side of the empty 'in-fill period' for years, then watched new DJs bridge it and bring new listeners over to him, was to become the 'in-fill' himself. After $11^1/_2$ years of starting at 10 p.m., John Peel was moved.

The Proclaimers

RECORDED: 4 JANUARY 1987
STUDIO: MAIDA VALE 4
PRODUCER: JOHN ETCHELLS
ENGINEER: MIKE SHILLING
FIRST BROADCAST: 7 JANUARY 1987 *JANICE LONG*

TRACKS: 'Letter from America', 'Beautiful truth', 'Throw the "R" away', 'Joyful Kilmarnock blues'.
LINE-UP: Craig Reid, vocals & percussion; Charlie Reid, vocals & guitar.

'I think the fact that we got this session had its roots in an appearance by Paul Heaton of the Housemartins on Janice's singles review show *Singled Out*, some time in late summer 1986. Paul was asked about Scottish bands, and replied he wanted to find out more about a group called the Proclaimers whose demo tape he had heard. A pal of ours heard the show, got into contact with the Housemartins, they contacted us, and we ended up supporting them on a tour of the UK and Eire in autumn '86. By the end of the year we were getting a fair bit of record company interest. The session we were offered was on a Sunday, so we took the bus down from Edinburgh on Saturday morning. We stayed on a friend's floor on Saturday night. We'd never been in a large studio before, and the size of the Maida Vale complex combined with its history was a bit intimidating.'

CRAIG REID

'I remember being worried about using the guitar I owned at the time. It was pretty bad and the neck was twisted, but we'd been unemployed so long I'd never been able to buy another one. Listening to the tape again, I think it sounds OK; we were a bit restrained but I'd put that down to nerves.'

CHARLIE REID

'Everyone we encountered was friendly enough, although it was the first time we'd encountered the BBC, which provoked a certain degree of amusement on both sides I'm sure ['Throw the "R" away' is a Scottish critique of those, like some at the BBC, who insist on 'standard' English]. Neither of us felt, or still feel, very much at home in recording studios, and as long as we know the feeling of a song is coming across, we're usually happy. Listening to the session again for the first time in five years, I think it pretty much reflects the stage we were at: maybe a bit too much echo, but I seem to remember we liked it at the time. This session, and appearing on *The Tube* later in January, definitely helped us secure the contract we eventually got from Chrysalis.'

CRAIG REID

'Janice Long was a great help to us in those early days, and is one of the most genuine characters in broadcasting. The evening the session was broadcast was certainly a landmark in our development. That feeling of knowing that your songs are being broadcast to the nation never leaves you.'

CHARLIE REID

The Proclaimers signed to Chrysalis a few weeks later; recorded their debut album *This is the Story* in ten days; spent the rest of the year touring; and had a Number 3 hit with 'Letter from America' at the end of the year, a song first aired on this Radio 1 session eleven months earlier.

Craig and Charlie Reid

6 PUTTING THE FUN BACK INTO BEING PRETENTIOUS

He'd always been there. Putting out at least two new sessions a week, with an average of 120 recorded each year, Peel was responsible for more sessions in the eighties than all the programmes explored in the preceding chapter put together. The pile of neat photocopies of Peel session sheets for 1981 – 91 on the desk in front of me stands more than six inches high. There are some 1200 in all. How to begin to tell the story of Peel sessions in the 1980s?

Perhaps the Smiths' sessions have been the most famous since 1981; but the extraordinary events surrounding them are well known and have already been documented. What is not generally known is that another famous band, who did not have hit singles until 1990 (and a Number 1 album early in 1991), actually appeared listed as session guests on the front of a Peel show PasB *before* the Smiths.

'The first session we recorded for Radio 1's John Peel show was first broadcast back in May 1983, believe it or not,' Peter Hooton of the Farm told Walters, years later. It went out on the 17th, two days before the Smiths recorded their first at Maida Vale. 'It was a great opportunity for us, and also managed to help the profile of the band, because in Liverpool at that time, if you did get a Peel session, it was regarded as an achievement; and once you'd got on to that level, you got a bit more attention from the press. You certainly walked round Liverpool as if you were next in line to the throne.'

Interestingly, on that first session could be heard the embryonic idea of what would prove a top 10 hit for the band more than seven years later. '"All together now" was first really demoed on that session,' said Peter Hooton. 'The lyrics and the melody were taken from the song "No man's land"; it's obviously changed quite radically from the original, but the ideas were there.' Similarly, the

Billy Bragg performed
'A13 – trunk road to
the sea' on his first
Peel session in
August 1983.

band's second Peel session, recorded with Mark Radcliffe in February 1984, opened with 'Hearts and minds', not a hit single until 1991.

All in all, 1983 was quite a year for Peel sessions, after a rather uneventful 1982, save for the Cocteau Twins, Trixie's Big Red Motorbike, the Farmers' Boys and Sophisticated Boom Boom (New Order's second session, in May that year, was a private tape, recorded outside the BBC). Early in 1983, before Walters' return in April, there were a few more 'poppy', or unexpected sessions under Trevor Dann's production, including debuts by the Three Mustaphas Three, and Sophie and Peter Johnston ('what lovely people and refreshing light music,' producer Dale Griffin and engineer Martin Colley wrote on the sheet).

But by the summer, on top of the Farm and the Smiths, we had memorable debuts by Billy Bragg and Microdisney, both in August. Bragg performed his now celebrated Anglicized version of 'Route 66', a hymn to Essex: 'A13 – trunk road to the sea'. October brought the first session by James, including 'Hymn from a village'.

Generalizations are dangerous, but all these acts were characterised by a witty melancholic disaffection with the emerging cultural orthodoxy of 1980s Britain. Songs like the Smiths' 'Still ill', Bragg's 'A new England', Microdisney's 'Sleepless' and James' 'Hymn from a village', all first heard on Peel sessions that summer, while not specifically political, conveyed a sense of what was it then to be alive and neither stupid nor a yuppie. The humour of the time was added to by Twa Toots' 'Don't play "A rainy night in Georgia"' and Sudden Sway's 'Let's evolve!', also first heard on Peel sessions in autumn 1983.

Microdisney went on to be *the* Peel session band of 1984. They recorded three in all, including the song with the best chorus of the year, attacking English nostalgia and complacency, 'Loftholdings-wood' ('Aren't you glad you were born in England?'), and three other great songs recorded in April, all now on the band's 'Peel Sessions' album. There were notable dates by Working Week, and the Chameleons (both May); Yeah Yeah Noh's first (August); the Mighty Wah! (September); Bronski Beat (including Jimmy Somerville's solo of 'Puits d'amour', in October); and from Australia's Go-Betweens (October) and the Triffids' thrilling debut (November); but the dominant sound of sessions that year was non-electric: 1984 was the year of cow-punk.

The first of these coarse, rough-sounding acoustic bands to complete a session and have it broadcast was the Boothill Foot Tappers; closely followed by Pogue Mahone, both in April. 'Half of Pogue Mahone turned up completely pissed,' remembers producer Mark Radcliffe, 'and the bass player, Cait O'Riordan, was completely out of it: I think the accordion player re-did her parts after she'd gone. I can remember her sitting with her boots over the back of Ted De Bono's chair, which Ted wasn't too keen on when he was trying to do the mix. I found them quite amiable, despite all that.' One of their four numbers recorded, 'The boys from the County Hell', had so much swearing on it even Peel couldn't broadcast it.

Next came the Skiff Skats (May), and the Men They Couldn't Hang, in July. This first session by the Men featured their rendition of Eric Bogle's anti-war folk standard, 'The green fields of France', which quickly became a highly requested repeat, was later released as a single, and reached Number 3 in Peel listeners' Festive Fifty that Christmas. That

same month also introduced Terry and Gerry, whom the audition panel, had it still been operating, might well have described as 'a humorous contemporary skiffle duo'; their demo tape was picked up by Peel simply for the chance reason that another 'Terry and Gerry' were the Pig's flatmates when Peel first met her.

By the end of the year the formally renamed 'Pogues' had come back for a second date. All the above bands continued to record for Peel in 1985, but other sounds were also emerging, most notably the Jesus and Mary Chain (October 1984), Big Flame (February 1985), the Cookie Crew (May), That Petrol Emotion (June), the Housemartins (July), Freiwillige Selbstkontrolle, or FSK

(August), and the Primevals (September).

'We'd recently won the rap championship for the best rap group of 1985 at the Wag Club, and were doing a series of shows at the big rap festival Rap Attack at the Shaw Theatre, where we think John Peel and John Walters first saw us,' say the Cookie Crew. 'We'd probably only done about four shows, and the session was our first time in any studio that had so much equipment. We didn't have a clue. What was an engineer?

'We took in instrumentals and other people's rap records, had a well-written and rehearsed rap, and sang over the instrumentals.' Debbie, 'Reme-Dee', listened to and recorded every session they did, even though she only had 'a crap

Half of the Pogues (then known as 'Pogue Mahone') turned up at Maida Vale 'completely pissed' recalls producer Mark Radcliffe.

cassette recorder: I will always remember John Peel saying he hoped that one day we'd be making records of our own.' The Cookie Crew first recorded as guests on the Beatmasters' hit 'Rok da House' in 1987, and signed to London Records in 1988.

All that Michael Rooney of the Primevals can remember of his classic first Peel session is being excited at meeting Dale Griffin. A Mott the Hoople fan, he had seen and met them years before at the Maryland in Scott Street, Glasgow: 'I was even sick in their dressing room.' But he didn't get a chance to ask Dale if he remembered him: 'Dale was either on the phone to his garage to get his car repaired, or our French manager was on the line, throughout the day, threatening to kill me over a sum of money.'

Apart from the debut of Half Man Half Biscuit that November, late in 1985 and early in 1986 the most interesting first sessions came from the bands, including the Primevals, later unfortunately labelled 'the shambling bands' by the music press, after a passing comment by Peel. These include the Passmore Sisters (August 1985); Age of Chance (October); Bogshed (November); A Witness (January 1986); and Stump, the Mackenzies and Twang (February).

Perhaps the most memorable of these debuts was that by Stump, with its hilarious portrayal of obese female American tourists, 'Buffalo'; 'most enjoyable newcomers for some time, wethinks,' Dale wrote across the top of the session sheet. Hard on their heels came We've Got a Fuzzbox and We're Gonna Use It (March); the Happy Mondays and Head of David (April); Pop Will Eat Itself (June) and, also that summer, the first by the Bhundu Boys (July); Anhrefn (August); Slab! (September) and the Primitives (October).

None of these, however, acquired

FSK's distinction of getting an unreleased session track into Peel's listeners' Festive Fifty that Christmas. The German band's ironic cover of Dave Dudley's 'I wish I could "Sprechen sie Deutsch"' was voted to Number 33. Commenting on the poll in his *Observer* column at the beginning of January 1987, Peel described the rendition as 'a highlight amongst tracks which, despite their individual merits, make up a rather characterless chart'. If character was lacking in 1986, a movement spearheaded by a band that had just recorded its first session would certainly make up for this in 1987. On 9 December 1986 the Stupids first arrived at Maida Vale. The hardcore holocaust had begun.

———

'We turned up at Maida Vale on our skateboards, and Tommy, the drummer,

The original Bhundu Boys launch their first major label album *True Jit* at an HMV shop in 1987. The group's British success owed much to Peel's championing of the band, recording their first session in July 1986.

had a bad crash outside the doors,' remembers Ed Wenn, alias Ed Shred. Then the Stupids' fourth non-recording member, but singer and bassist-to-be, he came along to the session for the ride. 'We thought of ourselves as young punk rebels, and were all ready to get annoyed with the engineers. We wanted loud guitars and felt sure proper BBC engineers wouldn't understand. We even took the band engineer along to back us up in case.'

Such was the Stupids' radicalism, they didn't have any equipment. The guitar and bass were simply slung over the skateboarders' shoulders. A drum kit was arranged to be delivered to Maida Vale by the guitarist. Unfortunately, the only one he could hire that day was a synth drum kit, not exactly appropriate

for the thunderous sound of hardcore. They took along a small hand-held guitar amp, although a Marshall 100-watt stack was also hired and delivered. 'And the bass was Direct Injected into the desk,' says Ed.

'Dale and Mike Robinson knew what they were doing and got some good sounds out of the kit; but the session, looking back, was OK, not brilliant,' says Ed. Peel's listeners disagreed. Their response, as Peel later wrote in the *Observer* after the first broadcast of the session on 12 January 1987, 'was generally expressed in terms more appropriate to the casualty ward than to music criticism. "It rips," suggested one writer. "The Stupids shred," enthused another. "They truly maim," volunteered a third.'

Peel had started playing the Stupids'

first LP the previous autumn, after Ed had sent him a copy. More importantly, shortly after the session broadcast, Ed, now singing for the band, invited Peel and Walters along to the Stupids' first gig at the Igloo Club, at the King's Head pub in Fulham High Street, on 16 February 1987. Peel's review in the following Sunday's *Observer* alerted everyone to British hardcore, which had been born of British bands watching how American punk had split into myriad forms of 'thrash, speedcore, speedmetal', and which involved 'playing hard, fast, and with commendable brevity and lack of attention to detail'.

On that memorable night the Stupids were supported by Ed's own band Bad Dress Sense, and his and Tommy's collaboration with vocalist Bobby Justice, in the band Frankfurter. As Walters recalls, it was like the heady days of punk: 'The band would get off stage and half the audience seemed to get on'. Most of the 'forty or so revellers ... seemed to be known to members of the band,' Peel wrote. Walters offered Bad Dress Sense a session on the spot. They recorded it a week later, on Tuesday, 24 February, two days after Peel's seminal review, and the same night as Peel repeated the Stupids' debut for the second time. And when Frankfurter did their first session on 16 April, all Tommy and Ed's bands of that night at the Igloo had been in.

'On that Frankfurter one I remember Fred Kay was the second engineer, and she suddenly exclaimed, "I've got it! I *know* what this music is all about!" and

Dale and Mike Engles just watched as she took over the mix', recalls Ed. 'It was a wonderful moment.'

Ed finally played on a Peel session as a full Stupid on the band's second, in May. Then there was a brief lull in the storm, before the Electro Hippies' staggering debut in July. Nine tracks were recorded, none of them over 1' 40", and the last, 'Mega Armageddon death', clocking in at exactly one second only. 'Starts and stops rather abruptly,' Dale added helpfully on the sheet. By now, Walters was regularly going to the handful of London pub gigs that supported hardcore, once again spotting bands. Heresy recorded their first at the end of that month. Then in September came Napalm Death.

Napalm Death's drummer and leader Mick Harris rapidly became a vital figure in the burgeoning hardcore scene after that debut. Following a third session by the Stupids (October), 'the first with the proper recording line-up,' says Ed Shred, and Gore's astounding debut early in November, featuring a 17-minute instrumental medley of four numbers, Mick was back at Maida Vale that same month, but now guesting on drums for Ipswich band Extreme Noise Terror, on their first Peel session. 'It was a different style, a lot slower, with more of a punk than metallic influence, very enjoyable,' he remembers. 'There were eight numbers on that first ENT one too.'

Mick would later play on Unseen Terror's Peel session (March 1988), and several successive ENT and Napalm

6

The Stupids turned up at Maida Vale on 9 December 1986 with skateboards but no equipment.

163

Napalm Death

RECORDED: 13 SEPTEMBER 1987 STUDIO: MAIDA
VALE 5 PRODUCER: DALE GRIFFIN
ENGINEERS: MIKE ENGLES AND ELIZABETH LEWIS
FIRST BROADCAST: 22 SEPTEMBER 1987
JOHN PEEL

TRACKS: 'The kill/Prison without walls/Dead' (0'55"), 'Deceiver/Lucid fairytale/In extremis' (1'45"), 'Blind to the truth/Negative approach/Common enemy' (1'05"), 'Obstinate divide/Life/You suffer' (1'55"). Total time: 5'40".

LINE-UP: Mick Harris, drums & vocals; Shane Embury, bass; Bill Steer, guitar; Lee Dorian, vocals.

'Napalm Death had been around since 1981, although in a totally different style. I joined in 1986, and the sound became faster, more aggressive, with metallic riffs: that's why I joined, to play relatively fast hardcore, with metallic riffs. The band got a new singer, bassist and guitarist early in '87, and the sound became harder, faster, and the guitar sound even denser. Our first LP was done then, came out that July, and Peel took a liking to the shorter tracks: he played "You suffer", which was 0.75 of a second long, three times before we were invited to do the session.

'What happened at the session? Oh God, what can I say? We had to hire equipment — we had no amps, drums, or cymbals — because we hadn't started touring then, and had recorded on equipment available in studios. Anyway, we turned up. "How long are your songs?" Dale asked. "Pretty short, we'll do twelve numbers" we said. Well, that's OK by us, they said, but I could see they weren't sure.

'We literally blasted our way through it. I *really* enjoyed it. I was so happy with the sound that day. It was just a blinding, vicious sound, coming straight back at you. What Dale and the engineers didn't know was that the twelve songs came to only 5' 40" in all, the shortest ever Peel session.

'That first Napalm Death session did really have a huge impact. It was *nearly* perfect. It was like doing a great live recording, but more relaxed, a good experience. I think Peel enjoyed it too: he repeated it three times.'

MICK HARRIS

Lee Dorian, Mick Harris (back), Bill Steer, Shane Embury

Death dates. After he left Napalm Death, his new band Scorn recorded a session in September 1992. But as Ed Shred points out, even as early as summer 1987 the relatively close-knit hardcore scene was fragmenting.

'Hardcore was proud of itself. At first it was very different, and nobody in Britain understood us,' says Ed. 'When we got on Peel, everyone was chuffed. Then everyone thought they could get one. What was a small cliquey thing changed after Peel started playing our records, and everyone started sending him their records. Before that the bands had been making records without a public in the UK. The original scene had changed, and by 1988 I felt we were just going through the motions really. So many bands had said, "Oh wow, *we* can do this" I became a bit sceptical: lots of people had moved to the US.'

Nevertheless, there were still people listening for whom there were still new hardcore bands to discover in 1988. Bolt Thrower (January), Intense Degree (February), Dr and the Crippens (May), Doom (June), and Ripcord (July) all made their debut on *Peel* that year. Later years would bring the likes of Prong, Carcass and Deviated Instinct.

'We never really classed ourselves as a hardcore band,' says Karl Willetts, singer with Bolt Thrower, underlining Ed's point about the fragmenting scene. He joined the band just after their first Peel session, when, on the strength of it, they were offered a record deal by Vinyl Solution. 'It was an exciting period, very different from how it is now. The scene was more integrated: Doom, Napalm Death, Extreme Noise Terror, us, we were all in the same boat.'

Bolt Thrower's first session got them a deal, and their second, in November 1988, got them a better deal, with Earache, and, intriguingly, a deal with Games Workshop, the chain of role-playing games stores. 'We had a track called "Realm of chaos", about this fantasy world of gaming,' says Karl. The company and band ended up sharing artwork for the band's second album, in an unusual bi-media marketing exercise.

The effect of all these radio sessions was to leave most listeners simply stunned. The speed, violence and brevity of the numbers made the shocking punk records of ten years before sound tame by comparison. And while hardcore, in whatever manifestation, did not cross over into mainstream success quite as punk and new wave did, the bands discovered that a self-financing, separate market had grown up around them, particularly in the US.

Certainly no one else on British radio was touching this dangerous stuff – except, of course, Peel's colleague Steve Wright. When the Electro Hippies' session came out on record he started playing it, perhaps as a joke, in his Radio 1 afternoon show. It was a strange kind of testament to Peel sessions' exclusive, vice-like grip on this most vicious animal, born of the decaying remains of punk.

———

Most of those classic hardcore sessions were done by Dale Griffin. But then you can't talk about Peel sessions in the 1980s without mentioning him. He was, of course, doing plenty of other programmes' sessions as well. At one time in the mid-eighties, Dale would often do two *Peels*, a *Friday Rock Show*, an evening show recording or two, and an Andy Kershaw session, six or seven in all, every week. His name is on many, and many of them are classics.

The stories about him are legion, some complimentary, some not. The Maida Vale SMs talk warmly of his professionalism and dedication. 'He would nearly always turn up early, and start setting-up the mikes and rigging the studio, which is not really the producer's job at all,' says Mike Robinson. Several pop and rock bands interviewed for this book looked back with astonishment at how Dale's opinions of the merits of some of their numbers, which they petulantly disregarded at the time, proved exactly right. His ear for a hit is not in question.

But there would be arguments, and what arguments! To sum it all up, it could be said that Dale saw his responsibility to the BBC as an important one: to deliver at least four well-recorded, exciting numbers to make a session, in just one day; and if that meant appearing a hard taskmaster or worse in order to get some of the more relaxed bands through it, then so be it.

'I changed my mind about Dale,' says Ed Shred, 'when I turned up for my third or fourth session. We hadn't even got to the studio when we bumped into Dale in the corridor. "Oh shit, not you lot again," he said. Not a happy day, really. But then he changed and became really friendly, after we'd done a few more. I think once you've gone through some sessions and got his respect he's fine. I'd be really happy now for him to produce any album for me.'

Other musicians would probably disagree, finding a more relaxed, unpressured atmosphere more conducive to recording. But given the unusual time constraints on BBC sessions, who can say that the demanding approach might not, with some kinds of acts, be just as valid? It certainly helped Dale produce some of the most memorable Peel sessions ever, like the Wedding Present's Ukrainian recordings.

But events like those Ukrainian recordings were unusual in featuring so many acoustic instruments. Increasing numbers of sessions in the late eighties were based on drum machines, sequencers and sampling, with acts effectively remixing from their pre-programmed digital tracks.

With the growth of house music, debuts like those by the Funky Ginger (August 1988), A Guy Called Gerald (November), and Where's the Beach (August 1989) became, along with the continuing hardcore bands, some of the most exciting Peel sessions. They were also heard by a significantly larger number of listeners, as they occurred after Peel's move forward to 8.30 p.m., 'which got rather good figures, I seem to recall,' says Walters.

A Guy called Gerald's session was made doubly difficult by the fact that, as Dale pointed out in a note to Walters, it was booked in at the Hippodrome, which had no 'direct injection capability ... it may be a good idea to keep the heavily machine-oriented stuff to MV4'.

Walters later asked Dale if the house, computer-based sessions were by definition more difficult. 'It's only more difficult if they actually haven't got their act together. Unlike a live band, you can't suggest the drummer maybe changes this or changes that. It's really that they need to have done all their programming ahead of time, because it's not something that we can really advise on, because it's all locked up in a machine. It's really down to how together the particular artist is.'

Dale was speaking from bitter experience. The session sheet files reveal that a number of machine-based bands (not including any named above), did indeed, as Dale's scribbled apologies for a session of only one or two short numbers explain, turn up at Maida Vale and only then start programming the drum machine. On a BBC session there simply isn't time for this kind of messing about.

But there is a professional preference among some BBC producers and engineers for live bands. Contrary to

The Wedding Present's 'Ukrainian Sessions'

THE WEDDING PRESENT'S 'UKRAINIAN SESSIONS'
RECORDED: 6 OCTOBER 1987 & 15 MARCH 1988
STUDIO: MAIDA VALE 4 PRODUCER: DALE GRIFFIN
ENGINEERS: MIKE ROBINSON AND FRED KAY
FIRST BROADCAST: 14 OCTOBER 1987 & 5 APRIL 1988 *JOHN PEEL*

TRACKS: 'Tiutiunnyk', 'Yichav Kozak za Dunai', 'Hude Dnipro Hude', 'Katrusya/Svitit Misyats' (6 October 87); 'Minooli Dnee', 'Vasya Vasyl 'ok', 'Zadumav Didochok', 'Verkhovyno' (15 March 88).

LINE-UP: Peter Solowka, mandolin, accordion, tambourine & backing vocals; Len Liggins, vocals & violins, balalaika, sopilka (Ukrainian flute); Keith Gregory, bass; David Gedge, guitar & backing vocals; Shaun Charman, drums (first session only); Ron Rom, backing vocals & handclaps (first session only); Simon Smith, drums (second session only); Roman Remeynes, mandolin & backing vocals (second session only).

'I always thought John Peel sessions were major rock'n'roll events, but as I walk down the diarrhoea-brown corridors of Maida Vale ... I realize my preconceptions are about to be smashed. Dave Gedge greets me: "All right Ron, we're just recording some cover versions of Ukrainian folk songs. We're doing some clapping bits at the moment. Why don't you come and give a hand?" Insanity rules and I agree. Next moment I'm in the studio clapping along and shouting "Hey! Hey! Hey!" at the right moments. A strict woman with a tone of voice that could run a comprehensive school (Fred Kay) barks from the other side of the studio

168

"Stop giggling!" I blush furiously. "If you're going to clap, clap in time," howls another voice (Dale Griffin). "Yes sir" reply the Wedding Present, before breaking into hysterics of laughter.'

RON ROM, IN *SOUNDS*, 24 OCTOBER 1987

'On a previous Peel session we'd recorded "Hopak," a tune I used to play on the guitar that I knew from my childhood, which we'd often play in the band in spare moments to warm up. After we'd done another session we were offered yet another, and felt we wanted to do something different. I suggested doing something radical, an entire session of Ukrainian folk songs, and managed to persuade the others. David asked John if it would be OK.

'We practised four or five songs but the ethnic flavour wasn't coming through, so I drafted in a fiddle player friend of mine, Len Liggins, who had studied Slavonic languages at university, and had always been crazy about everything East European; so he could do all the singing as well.

'After we'd done the first one we realized we'd done something rather good, although we weren't sure Peel would broadcast it. But when we heard it going out, we thought immediately, "we could do it better". Peel was startled and pleased and so we asked if we could do another. But I also got a phone call from this Ukrainian guy, that I knew of vaguely, a musician, saying, "What are you doing destroying this music?" He was quite severe, and said we could improve it. So we invited him to join us on the second one. He was a mandolin player and singer who called himself Roman Remeynes, because his real Ukrainian name is unpronounceable!

'So the second one, in March 1988, was much better: the intense bits more intense, the laid-back bits more quiet. In front were me, Len and Roman doing the fiddly bits, backed by the solid backing of the band. After it had been broadcast, many Ukrainian people said to us they had never heard the final song, "Verkhovyno", played with such intensity. Dale and Mike worked really hard on the second session, and particularly on the mix of "Verkhovyno". Dale normally gets done by midnight, but they were still there mixing it at 2.45 a.m. They put a lot of effort into it and it showed, it was really good.'

PETER SOLOWKA

These *Ukrainski Vistupi V Johna Peela* were released by RCA in April 1989 and reached Number 22 in the album chart, selling over 40 000 copies in the first few months on release. The expanded Wedding Present recorded one more Ukrainian session for Peel. Peter is no longer in the group. He, Len and Roman became the Ukrainians permanently, and released a debut album of their own songs in 1991.

Keith Gregory, Roman Remeynes, David Gedge, Peter Solowka, The Legendary Len Liggins, Simon Smith

what you might expect, to be confronted with a deafening, grungy, distorted hardcore band is just the kind of challenge the SMs relish: it's something they can really get their teeth into, and work hard and fast to capture properly on tape (all of the longer-serving SMs, for example, remember the punk sessions with delight). By contrast, for a trained broadcast sound engineer, a session which involves simply remixing digital tracks is less demanding of their particular skills.

'The only thing with machines is they play the same thing each time,' Dale told Walters. 'You never get a feel from a machine. I don't think even with the best will in the world you can build too much feeling into what's coming out of a machine output.'

As the use of computers in music and on BBC Radio 1 sessions increases, this sounds like a recipe for potential conflict. But then a certain amount of creative conflict need not necessarily be unproductive. A perfect case in point is what turned out to be one of the most extraordinary Peel sessions in their 25-year history, and the most requested session for a repeat broadcast for months: the first session by the Orb.

'For days after that session the phone would keep ringing in the office,' recalls Walters. 'I'd pick it up, and someone would say something like, "Ah, er, hello, er, John Peel played a very long record the other night and I was wondering if you could tell me where to get it; it's by a group called the Auburn session".' They couldn't get it then, but fortunately the Orb-in-Session mix of 'Loving you' is now out on Strange Fruit Records.

But the guitar bands were still coming in regularly, and increasingly American bands would do sessions for Peel: the Pixies, Mud Honey, and Nirvana (October 1989) all recorded at

Maida Vale before they crossed over to become stadium tour acts in the US. He also had the first Russian rock band to record at the BBC, Zvuki Mu, in May 1989, when they visited the UK for a residency on the Renfrew Ferry at Glasgow's MayFest. The best British bands still debut on Peel too, Teenage Fan Club (September 1990) being just one example from the past couple of years.

And old favourites remain loyal. The Wedding Present have completed at least eleven Radio 1 sessions, nine of them for Peel, the most recent in spring 1992, in the midst of their 'Hit Parade' of monthly seven-inch single releases. That recording included 'Softly softly', a song which David Gedge says the band has shelved until now, because attempts to record it in a commercial studio somehow failed to catch the atmosphere of Miti Adhikari's Maida Vale production.

'If I were asked for my favourite session, I would have to say the eighth one we did for Peel [October 1990], where we previewed some of the songs which later formed the core of our best LP *Seamonsters*,' says David Gedge. 'I think the combination of the massive orchestral recording room [Maida Vale 3] and sympathetic technical staff combined magnificently to capture the sound of the band in transition from jangly indie-pop to a darker, more brooding noise.'

But even Gedge's band can't match two other acts for sheer number of appearances in session: the Fall (fifteen for Peel and counting); and the almost annual appearance, since 1969, of Ivor Cutler.

By the time Teenage Fan Club did their first and the Wedding Present their best, Peel had moved again. From Saturday, 29 September 1990 he was back on late nights, and back on weekends. He'd last

been on air at the weekend in 1971. This meant he came on immediately after Fluff or Andy Kershaw; and more recently, having been jiggled forward to Friday nights, after his former *Top Gear* co-presenter Tommy Vance, and the *Friday Rock Show*.

In some ways things have come full circle for their sessions, and in others, changed completely. In the midst of the hardcore holocaust, as one set of the bands migrated to speed-metal, Peel and Tommy both found themselves playing one or two records by the same band. 'Every so often Tommy and I do seem to meet round the back as it were,' says Peel.

As in 1967, the shows with the most dangerous sessions are clustered round the weekend schedules. That doesn't mean Radio 1 is running away from the idea of sessions; far from it. Just as David Symonds' original teatime show featured good non-needletime recordings, produced by Walters, Malcolm Brown, Jeff Griffin and Bev Phillips, so does the show which now occupies the slot. It's even got the word 'session' in its billing: *Mark Goodier's Evening Session*. And the 'Session' is regularly trailed throughout the day.

Yet something is subtly different. Peel is just as important to Radio 1 today as he was on that first awkward Sunday. The station knows its sessions are just as valuable now as they were to Bernie in 1967. The same kinds of thing may be happening at Radio 1 now as twenty-five years ago. But they are being done for entirely different reasons.

Nirvana first recorded for John Peel in October 1989.

The Orb

RECORDED: 3 DECEMBER 1989
STUDIO: MAIDA VALE 3
PRODUCER: DALE GRIFFIN
ENGINEERED AND MIXED BY: JIMMY CAUTY
FIRST BROADCAST: 19 DECEMBER 1989 *JOHN PEEL*

TRACKS: 'A huge ever growing pulsating brain that rules from the centre of the ultraworld (loving you)' (20 minutes 10 seconds).

LINE-UP: Jimmy Cauty, producer & mixing; Alex Paterson, DJ, samples.

'We turned up early and finding nobody about, started setting up the turntables and desk in the control room. Suddenly the producer appeared and bawled us out: "Get this equipment out of here!" He told us to set it up in the studio and come back at 2 p.m. We said we were going to generate a load of samples then mix it off the multi-track, which he didn't seem to get. We were so put off, we went round to a friend's house for an hour. But we were determined to defeat this producer, so we went back, and pulled all the sofas and lamp stands into the middle of Studio 3 and set up a little living-room set in this huge studio, like something out of *Alice in Wonderland*, and got the main lights switched off, to get a good atmosphere. I just started throwing all these samples at Jimmy: waves, birdsong, jets, old sci-fi play excerpts, those 'Aaaahs' off Grace Jones' 'Slave to the rhythm', and Minnie Riperton's 'Loving you', of course (we'd already started this thing of crediting all our samples, and virtually mixing the drums *out* of house music). And Jimmy did this great live mix really quick. I think we were out of the building by 7 p.m.! I think it was the best mix we ever did of that. The head of Geffen Records was over here, and listening to it on Peel while driving had to pull over, he was so knocked out. He tried to sign us for America, but we already had a deal. The whole thing couldn't have been planned: it was just a very vivid day, because we were finding it so entertaining to defeat this producer bloke.'

ALEX PATERSON

'It was almost as if they'd never had an electronic group in. Quite a lot of energy was spent at the beginning just explaining what we were going to do. Everybody was very tense. We knew, in these circumstances, we had to be really good. The other argument was when I said I was going to have to mix it myself, but I persuaded them in the end. There were just two sequences in it, the arpegiatting figure, and a 16s pulse, which I programmed on the spot, and looped everything on to 24 tracks, but there was no structure to it — you do it all in the mix, that's really important, cutting things on and off, trying to build it into an entity. It did get more relaxed later, more people came down, Alex had this living room set-up, a friend of his was videoing everything, and we started laying the sequence of samples and FX down. I just did a non-stop mix through all 20 minutes I'd laid down. It was good having the SSLs, because I could do a pass and it would memorize it on the computer. Even so I think I only did two or three passes. But because it was so long the desk crashed just before the end: the computer's memory ran out just as we'd done the final pass, so it couldn't memorize the last minute and we had to fade it. It was all so difficult that day, but I was always trying to make the thing flow, and I do remember being into it at the time.'

JIMMY CAUTY

Ivor Cutler

RECORDED: ALMOST ANNUALLY SINCE 1969
(21 BY RADIO 1'S 25TH ANNIVERSARY)
STUDIOS: MOSTLY MAIDA VALE 4
PRODUCERS: NUMEROUS
ENGINEERS: NUMEROUS
FIRST BROADCAST: *JOHN PEEL*

TRACKS: See Sessionography
LINE-UP: Ivor Cutler, vocals, piano, harmonium.

'I don't remember how my first Peel session came about. He was playing anarchic tapes then [1969], by the likes of Ron Geesin, and Lol Coxhill. I know he bought a copy of my LP *Ludo* [on Parlophone] in Woolworth's, Stowmarket for 10 shillings, not long after. He stopped playing the others eventually, but kept on playing me. When I asked him why, a couple of times, he just smiled quietly and said nothing. Maybe the Director-General forced him to.

'Jasia Reichardt of the ICA invited me at about that time to write an introduction to a show of sitting rooms they were doing. I wrote a piece called *Life in a Scotch Sitting-Room* for the catalogue.

'After the show, I asked the late Mal Dean, of the free-form "Amazing Band", to illustrate it. He said he would only do one picture, and I'd have to write more if I wanted more pictures. So I did that [two episodes were first broadcast as part of a Peel session on 27 February 1971]; but his work wasn't *simpatico*, so I gave him some money for his trouble, but went on writing episodes, about two per annum, and performing them on stage and radio, until I had twenty. Then greatly daring, I asked Martin Honeysett to illustrate them, and he was perfect, and off I went to Methuen. I've done six books with him now.

'Thanks to Peel, I gained a whole new audience, to the amazement of my older fans, who find themselves among 16-to-35s in theatres, and wonder where they come from. I've also had fan-mail and a lot of work because of the sessions, both gigs and radio. Piers Plowright of Radio 3 heard me on Peel, got in touch and I wrote thirteen plays for him. Neil Cargill got me to do six thirty-minute shows, also for Radio 3. And Andy Kershaw started playing me on his show as well.

'Lastly, I'm a member of the Noise Abatement Society and the Voluntary Euthanasia Society, if you get my meaning.'

IVOR CUTLER

Ivor Cutler

IN SESSION TONIGHT

David, you've been to Maida Vale before, do you remember it?' asks Mark Goodier. 'Do I remember Maida Vale?' wonders David Bowie. 'No, I just remember the money, Mark.' 'Fifteen quid, I think it was,' quotes Goodier from Bowie's last BBC session contract, dated May 1972. Bowie is surprised. 'Was it that much?'

It's some time after 7 p.m. on Tuesday, 13 August 1991 on the balcony inside Maida Vale 5. Tin Machine are about to play five numbers live into *Mark Goodier's Evening Session*. Show producer Jeff Smith has been here since 2 p.m., bringing a desk to set up on the balcony, so Goodier can be on location to chat to the band between numbers; or, as now, before they start. The band arrived at 2.30 p.m. By 6 p.m. they had done a full sound-check with Mike Robinson at the controls; but then, as Jeff Smith recalls, having found the whole thing 'easier than they thought it was going to be', they went straight into the live broadcast without taking a break.

'This is rather different from the way we normally record sessions,' says Goodier. 'All the bands that do our show's sessions come here for a day and they record four tracks and they mix them. Doing the thing completely live, Hunt, is rather different.'

'Yes, it is, I think it's the way to do it,' says Hunt Sales, the band's drummer. 'If there's any mistakes then we kick ourselves later, but the audience I guess can feel part of it, like a live show, that's what radio started out like.'

In the days before *Saturday Club* and the pre-recording agreement, every session was like this. But after thirty years of ever-increasing effort being put into the pre-recording of sessions, the abolition of needletime restrictions has meant that what was once a necessity is now a special occasion to be celebrated.

Mark Goodier has also had a live

session, direct from Maida Vale 5, from PIL ('John Lydon was very nervous,' says Jeff Smith); and Nicky Campbell's show, on 13 March 1991, was presented entirely from the same location, with REM playing several acoustic, live numbers from their new album *Out of Time*.

These one-off events say two very important things about Radio 1 FM in the 1990s, and they are inextricably linked. First, given the changes in the music industry and star system since the 1960s, which have seen recorded product and the rights accruing to it assume total primacy over any notions of regular live performance, only a national station like BBC Radio 1 FM carries the clout to persuade big bands that special live sessions are worthwhile.

Secondly, following on from the above, only a national institution on the scale of the BBC has the resources to do events like these properly. A system of studios, equipment and engineers that can cope with occasions like Live Aid can handle a live session with David Bowie from Maida Vale without breaking stride.

But obviously, as Goodier said to Bowie, it's not the normal way with his sessions. He's had one session a week, playing one track a night, since he started on the teatime show in April 1989, under producer Mick Wilkojc, then Kenton Allen. The *Evening Session* began in October 1990. By then, producer Jeff Smith was in charge.

'I'd put some programme proposals to Stuart Grundy before,' says Jeff, 'and we'd met when I was working at the World Service.' He'd gone off to the commercial radio station TFM in the North-east for a while, where he produced Al Rhodes' respected new music show, before being asked to join Radio 1 on Kenton Allen's departure.

'Mark and I weren't given a definite remit for the show, but we knew it would

John Lydon and PIL with Mark Goodier at their live broadcast for his *Evening Session*, 25 February 1992.

Peter Buck of REM playing on the band's special acoustic Maida Vale set for Nicky Campbell, 13 March 1991.

be fairly new music, with a target audience of 12 – 25.' Radio 1 was conscious that after the old evening show had gone, and with Peel on earlier, there hadn't been a slot for mid-range bands. 'We've had EMF, Ned's Atomic Dustbin, Blur, Cud, the Charlatans, and many others,' says Jeff; 'we often trail the *Session* throughout the day.' They are usually recorded on Saturdays in Maida Vale 4 or 5, with, most often, Martin Colley producing and engineering. Miti Adhikari also does some.

'Sessions are expensive, however, so I've kept to Kenton's plan of one track a night,' says Jeff. 'Most of the response we get is from A&R people from the record companies. The bookings tend to be A&R led, but we try to keep a bit edgy.' In other words, although most of the bands in session are already signed, this has only just happened; or the band are on an independent label; or about to break big; or certainly deserve to, and soon.

'They are primarily guitar bands,

although we have had Banderas, and, more recently the Tyrrel Corporation.' Martin Colley says there have been some problems with electronic bands who are not on top of their equipment, underlining Dale's point that there isn't time to program on site. But an entertaining, impromptu reworking of the session idea, entirely appropriate to computer-based bands, was when Altern-8 came into the on-air studio in summer 1992. They put together a dance track in the course of the show, with listeners nominating drum patterns and keyboard figures, and providing vocal samples over the phone.

Yet it's the guitar bands the fans still seem to go for. When *Vox* magazine gave away a cover-mounted cassette of 'Live and unreleased' band session tracks from the show, the print run was increased and then entirely sold out. That led to a special, 17-track, lavishly packaged CD,

The Best of the Mark Goodier Radio 1 Sessions, released by NightTracks records in 1992. But this was by no means the first official release of Radio 1 session material. The long-dreamed-of goal of getting the classic Peel sessions out on record had been realised six years before, largely thanks to a man we last encountered managing Peel in 1967: Clive Selwood.

At that time Selwood was Elektra Records' man in Britain. He brought the Doors and Tim Buckley to the UK, and signed the Incredible String Band. In spring 1967 Peel's enthusiasm for the last of these, while he was still on the pirate Radio London, led to their meeting. 'Presumably when he realized what a hopeless dickhead I was, I think he probably felt I needed protection,' says Peel. 'I don't think the Selwoods have ever had

EMF launch their debut album on Mark Goodier's *Evening Session*. The band had already done a session for the show.

it in their minds that they were going to make a great deal of money out of being my earthly representatives, and, in fact, they haven't done.' Clive and his wife Shurley still have this role. 'It's never been formalized: I've never signed a contract or anything,' says Peel.

After having directorships of various record companies, Clive spent a year in hospital and then a year at home recuperating in the early 1980s. The state of his health meant he couldn't return to work in the music industry, or work in an office. However, he could run a label for putting out Peel sessions from home. It took a year's planning and negotiations, but Strange Fruit Records was launched in September 1986.

There had been previous attempts to get the sessions out. Peel had a meeting with Richard Branson in the late 1970s, but nothing came of it. Meanwhile, several bands bought the rights to their tapes from BBC Enterprises and released them. Fans and collectors have for years hunted down black-market copies of Transcription Service's *Top of the Pops* discs, containing many old Radio 1 session takes, sold off by radio stations around the world and now selling at huge prices. Unscrupulous operators have also produced bootleg copies of Transcription discs. More openly, bootlegs of fashionable bands' debut Peel sessions could be found on sale around London within days of their first broadcast.

The name of the label that would attempt to bring some sanity to this madness and redirect part of the proceeds to the bands themselves came from the song made famous by Billie Holliday. Clive approached Peel and Walters, who gave the OK, as long the label wasn't 'cherry-picking', and reflected the contents of the whole Peel sessions series. 'I offered both of them a financial stake, but they said no. Neither of them has any involvement,'

says Clive.

Far more problematic was the legal deal for actually getting the records out. Of the dealer price of any Peel session release (the price the shops pay, before adding on their own mark-up and VAT), 20 per cent goes to the distributor, and then a little over 30 per cent in royalties: that includes a percentage and fee to BBC Enterprises; Mechanical Copyright (MCPS); and then the artist's royalty, which forms the largest part of this 30 per cent. 'About 25 per cent of what you pay in the shop comes to us,' says Clive, 'on which we have to do everything.'

Every musician on any session released also has to be a fully paid up member of the Musicians' Union. 'Of course, many of them aren't when they do the session, so we have to pay to join them up, which is another cost to us.'

But the biggest headache is getting permission from the artist or their record company, most often the latter. The commercial release rights to the BBC tapes in principle reside with the artist. However, if at the time the BBC session was recorded the artist had an exclusive recording contract with a record company, then that company has the right to block the release. Most of Strange Fruit's time and effort is spent persuading record companies to waive this blocking right.

'Back in 1985 Peel compiled a list of 300 of his first-choice sessions for release, and we're still trying to get clearance on many of those,' says Clive. 'Luckily, one of the first bands we asked, New Order, said yes, they'd do anything for John, and that really made the series.'

New Order's second Peel session, of June 1982, was the first release on the label (SFPS001), along with other 12-inch vinyl EPs containing sessions by the Damned, the Screaming Blue Messiahs, Stiff Little Fingers, Sudden Sway and the Wild Swans. On that day of release in

THE PEEL SESSIONS

BUZZCOCKS

New Order / Peel Sessions

THE PEEL SESSIONS

THE UNDERTONES

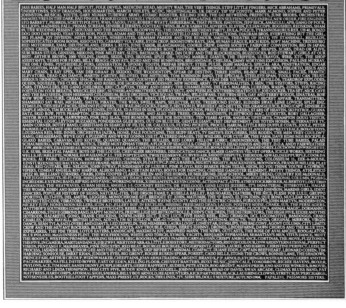

The Peel Sessions were launched on Strange Fruit Records in 1986; first as single session 12-inch EPs only, then as complete CD albums of two or more sessions.

September 1986, 'we shipped 9 tons of vinyl; we'd banked on an average sale of 2000 copies of each release, but shipped 20 000 on day one alone. The New Order one later sold 50 000.'

From then on, four or so sessions were released every month. 'The response far exceeded what we had expected', and led to Clive launching three other related labels: Band of Joy, for any BBC Radio 1 sessions, particularly from the early days and before Radio 1 – releases have included CDs of surviving 1960s sessions by the Yardbirds, Pretty Things and Chicken Shack; then there's Raw Fruit, which released *Friday Rock Show* sessions ('although that's now stopped'); and NightTracks, for evening show sessions featured over the years by David Jensen, Janice Long and Mark Goodier.

But it's Strange Fruit, exclusively for Peel sessions, that has caught record collectors' imagination. Two years ago a marketing drive by the label's American licensee, Dutch East Indies Records, resulted in feature articles on Peel, and the famous sessions appearing in the *Washington Post, Chicago Tribune* and *Los Angeles Times* in the same week. About the same time Clive moved into albums, and complete collections of two or three sessions were put out on CD by bands like the Undertones, the Only Ones, the Buzzcocks and Joy Division.

'The biggest seller though has been the *Queen at the Beeb* album on Band of Joy, which sold 100 000,' says Clive. 'The band were very happy with it; although it's worth pointing out that figure is still only 10 per cent of what a normal Queen album would sell. It's very much a collector's thing.'

There are also the ones that have got away. Pink Floyd, Genesis, the Rolling Stones and Eric Clapton have all repeatedly blocked the release of their sessions.

This despite the fact that bootlegs of radio releases like Transcription Service's current *Classic Tracks* series – a short show on CD featuring, for example, three Genesis BBC session songs – are among the top-selling bootlegs in North America.

Of the major record companies, Polygram and EMI are the most amenable to granting releases for their artists. Virgin said no to everything for years, but has recently relented slightly. But Sony Music (formerly CBS) has never granted permission for anything, save one track by Real People on the *Best of Mark Goodier* CD.

Even if the record company agrees, a handful of artists can effectively prevent the release by demanding ludicrous advances on sales, 'which are never going to be *that* incredible'. Plans for a compilation album of Peel's favourite numbers from the Fall's fifteen sessions for him have lumbered on for the past six years, awaiting final clearance from all parties.

All things considered, that Strange Fruit has released more than 150 Peel sessions in the past six years is quite an achievement. But the deepening recession in 1992 raised a question mark over the survival of the label in its present form, as this book was being completed. One possibility is that Strange Fruit may scale down to become a monthly low-budget release by subscription club, somewhat like the 'single clubs' launched by some independent record companies.

Strange Fruit has been unusual in handling these releases properly, with the interests of BBC Radio 1, the bands and their fans paramount. Royalties are paid. The bands are consulted on the artwork and sleeve notes. Each album is made a worthwhile, collectable record, and contains two or three complete sessions. Not all of these things can always be expected of other record companies.

Very often, having been alerted by Clive's request for clearance to the existence of an early session, a major label will block Strange Fruit's release, then license just one track from the BBC (which they are quite within their rights to do), and add it as a 'bonus track' to a pre-planned compilation. This seems hardly fair on the band, their fans, and the *principle* of Peel sessions: that they are a unique, complete event on one day.

Record companies also generally fail to give precise recording and broadcast information about the session tracks on their releases, merely giving what they are obliged to do, an acknowledgement to BBC Enterprises. Strange Fruit, by contrast, wherever possible credits the original programme, session producer and, last but not least, the session engineer.

It's a common scene. A new band turn up for their first Peel session. They discover their producer-engineer is Mike Robinson – or Mike Engles, or Ted de Bono, or Nick Gomm. In hushed reverence they ask, 'Wasn't it you who did the Damned/the Specials/the Eurythmics/the Smiths' first session?' To which the most common reply is something like 'Er, I think so, but to be honest, I've done so many, they all just become a blur.'

Nick Gomm, 'the Professor of Sound' as Dale Griffin came respectfully to style him on eighties session sheets, has the longest track record. He's been 'doing knobs', balancing and mixing rock sessions, continuously since spring 1970. Along the way he's worked with the Nice, Genesis (their first), Roxy Music, David Bowie, the Beat (their first) and many more.

Just behind him in seniority comes Mike 'Megawatts' Robinson, who started 'knobs' in the early 1970s. Robbo did most of the Damned's early sessions, and has mixed just about everyone you'd care to name since. Then there are Dave Dade, Mike Engles, Ted de Bono, Martin Colley and Miti Adhikari, who all started between 1976 and 1980. There have been many others before and since, but these are the veterans.

It's not surprising that it's hard for them to remember particular sessions. They've been doing a full week's work, a different band or event every day, for all these years. And that is the attraction of the job. 'If you work in a commercial studio, you might be working with just one band on an album for three months, nine months or even a year,' says Mike Robinson, 'whereas we get constant change: big stars one day, new bands the next, which definitely appeals to some of us.'

There are countless recent examples. A few days after mixing the live sound at Michael Jackson's Bucharest concert at the end of September 1992, not only for the BBC but also for the dozens of television and radio stations around the world that were taking the Radio 1 FM 'feed', Mike Robinson was back at Maida Vale producing debut Peel sessions by both the Moles and Huggy Bear. Nick Gomm came back from a tour of Italy with the BBC Concert Orchestra, playing popular operas, to produce and mix Papa Wemba for Andy Kershaw.

On National Music Day, Bob Conduct was showing a party of EC broadcasting dignitaries around Broadcasting House. 'They heard the mix coming back live from the Carreras concert in Bath. They were very complimentary and asked, "How much experience does it take to produce an engineer that skilled in classical music broadcasting?" I had to reply I couldn't say, because the sound was being done by our heavy metal freak, Dave Dade. They were speechless.'

Then there's the job security. 'I would suspect that out of all engineers in this country, 95 per cent do worse than we do financially, and have to work in appalling conditions,' says Miti Adhikari. 'Every SM is occasionally tempted by work outside, but the more you look into it, the more it's a nightmare. I walked into a studio in LA once where Joni Mitchell was supposed to be recording a new album. Her engineer was there, but she hadn't actually been there herself for three months!'

The flip-side of the immediacy and variety of BBC engineers' work is the frustration of knowing their work may be heard only once. 'I think we'd all like that, to know some of our work would last,' says Nick Gomm, thoughtfully. Martin Colley finds it frustrating that the young staff of record companies' A&R departments look down their noses at BBC sessions: 'I think it's simply a historic prejudice they've inherited from their superiors.' It's almost as if the record companies don't believe a recording can be good unless it's done with a famous producer, takes months, and costs hundreds of thousands of pounds.

Yet when you talk to some of the famous producers who have themselves done BBC Radio 1 sessions, you get quite a different story. Bob Sargeant, John Porter and John Williams all speak with delight of their days doing Peel sessions, and believe there is a lesson in them that record companies should not ignore.

'Those sessions give you invaluable experience in dealing with artists,' remembers Bob Sargeant: 'the mood you're in has a great relevance to how it's going to go. I still believe that you're there to help get a certain energy out of a record; and if you get on with it, you'll capture that energy. The tendency to use too much technology and time sours what you're trying to get out.' Using these

rules, honed on punk Peel sessions, Sargeant in 1988 produced Breathe's *Hands to Heaven*, which included three American top 10 singles.

John Porter, who now produces hit guitar and blues albums in Los Angeles for the likes of Buddy Guy and Otis Rush, remembers the sessions fondly: 'I even sort of wish now and again I could go in and do a few like that; not knowing who the band are before you turn up, and having to establish a mood and get a performance there and then. After working for months on one album, it has its attractions.'

'John Porter was a real gent,' says Edwyn Collins of a Janice Long session he did with him in 1984, 'who created the perfect atmosphere for recording. I know from my own production experiences that recording is 80 per cent psychology and 20 per cent technique.'

John Williams, now director of A&R at Chrysalis, agrees. 'The sessions made me realize that it's the performance which is all-important. I realised you didn't have to spend a month or three months in the studio. Towards the end of my sessions career, I worked with the Housemartins, and ended up producing every record they made. I took the same approach there. And we did the first Proclaimers album in ten days like that. I don't produce now, but I like to think I sign bands on the grounds of live performance.'

'What happens today on a lot of sessions,' points out Miti Adhikari, 'is because the bands come in and do it live, and the adrenalin's flowing, and they know they're in a situation where they have to produce the goods, they actually do come out with better performances. Listening to the tracks on a 3-minute basis they sound a lot better than the records; the sound may not be quite as refined, but the performance, the feel, is better. And

I think that's what the bands pick up on. They know what's happening.'

Indeed they do. It would be impossible here to reproduce all the eloquent testimonials to BBC session engineers that I have received from bands. The metal bands are in awe of Tony Wilson and Dave Dade. Grunge bands, or, in fact anyone with a thunderous drum sound, speak highly of Mike Robinson. Billy Bragg asked Ted de Bono to make an album with him. Microdisney wanted Martin Colley to do their records. 'If I had a pound for every time a band has said "how did you do that, it's better than our record", I'd never have to work again,' says Miti Adhikari.

The secret is in the training and speed of work. Disciplined for live, immediate work, a BBC sound engineer might not get quite as good a bass drum sound as if you spent a week on just that in a studio; but he or she will get you 95 per cent of the way there. They have developed their own tricks. Now for the first time some of their historic technical secrets can be revealed.

***

'Most BBC-designed stuff was a bit of a disaster,' says Bill Aitken. Nevertheless, over the years, Maida Vale, and Langham 1 before it, acquired a small arsenal of odd, effective gadgets to meet the urgent demands of sessions.

Three of the most famous were the 'Cyclops', the 'Wilsonic Wireless', and 'The Rotivator'.

The Cyclops, a cyclical panning unit controlled by a single huge knob on the sloping front panel (hence the name) was built for Quad experiments (a handful of sessions were recorded in quadrophonic in the mid-70s) and ended up being used by Tony Wilson on stereo Peel sessions for automatically wobbling instruments' placing in the stereo mix.

Before that, Tony had been the first SM and producer to consider how relevant his stereo mixes were to medium-wave listeners, to the extent of ripping out the contents of an old transistor radio and wiring it up to the mixing desk. Bob Conduct reassembled the tranny's case around the tiny monitor, stuck it on top of the desk, and gave it a sign: the 'Wilsonic Wireless' sat proudly through many classic rock recordings.

'The Rotivator', as explained by Bill Aitken, was a clever echo machine: 'Someone cut an LP shape out of recording tape material, mounted it into a gramophone-like turntable, then fitted record and playback heads, but the playback head was on a swivel, and could be placed anywhere in a 360 degree arc on the disc.' This gave extraordinary variety and sensitivity of echo times. It featured on many sessions in the late 1970s. Mark Burgess of the Chameleons remembers Mike Robinson wheeling it out as late as 1983 for one of their sessions.

But the nickname under which all these gizmos became generically known was first coined after the transforming appearance in Langham 1 of the first Eventide Clockworks Harmonizer. This enabled the pitch of the delayed echo to be changed, creating a harmonic effect. Bob Conduct named the trolley housing it and some of the other gadgets the 'Fairydust Trolley', after a famous comment by Reg Presley of the Troggs on a bad backing track ('What do you expect me to do? Sprinkle some fairydust on the bastard?'). Bill Aitken recalls that when the architect's drawings were laid out for the refurbishment of Maida Vale for the new SSLs in 1980, a small corner was neatly marked 'Fairydust Trolley'.

Developments in digital rack delays in the 1980s have enforced retirement on these BBC inventions. The latest change was the complete conversion of the old Maida Vale 4 and 5 into a composite single-studio complex, with two control rooms, in 1989. The acoustic design was by Harris Grant Associates, with some of the technical work done by Real World, Peter Gabriel's Bath studio. One control room can be used for mixing a concert tape, for example, while the other records a live band.

About the same time, in a pragmatic economy drive, most Radio 1 sessions began switching from having a station or freelance producer and two engineers, to just two engineers, with one of them acting as producer as well. Radio 1 had less staff producers available; the freelancers were costing money; and the engineers were used to the work, so it seemed to make sense. Most of the experienced SMs can produce a session at short notice, although only a few have a regular slot producing. Generally, Mike Robinson does the Tuesday *Peel*, Nick Gomm the Thursday *Kershaw*, Martin Colley the *Goodier* on Saturdays, and Mike Engles the Sunday *Peel*. Miti Adhikari takes on the *Peels* when the two Mikes are away, or off doing concerts. Ted de Bono has produced a lot of weekday late-night sessions, and Dave Dade sometimes does the rock dates on his own, without Tony Wilson.

All of these take place in Maida Vale 4 or 5, except the Sunday *Peel*, which happens in 3 simply because Mike Engles prefers the sound of the large room, with its famous corrugated walls. These were designed when the studio was originally built in the 1930s to give a natural kind of dead sound, instead of soundproofing. Quite a few bands have come to like its character.

Maida Vale 1 is still the largest recording studio in Britain apart from Abbey Road. But, as part of cutbacks, one other music studio will close, although it definitely won't be the modern 4 or 5. But even to come down to three purpose-built music studios makes one wonder at the transformation of BBC Radio recording in the past twenty years. What has happened to all those old studios where rock bands made their first broadcast appearances?

At least the most famous of them has survived as a venue. The Playhouse in Northumberland Avenue, abandoned by the BBC in the 1970s and empty for many years, has now reopened as a theatre.

201 Piccadilly's frontage is taken by a branch of Boots, although what has happened to the actual auditorium is unclear. Simpson's department store next door has moved into much of the space occupied by the BBC studios, particularly where the rear of the building opens on to Jermyn Street. But it's hard to believe the big Studio 1 is now just a store.

The frontage of the old Aeolian Hall at 136 New Bond Street is now Renoir House, a suite of offices, many occupied by Barclay's Bank Corporate department. The hall itself is used by Sotheby's the auctioneers. Where Hendrix, Hawkwind and Free recorded is now the rear part of a large Sotheby's sale room used mainly for auctioning books and collectors' items.

Langham 1 is now the Chukka Bar in the Langham Hilton Hotel, opened after the BBC abandoned the building in the 1980s. Surrounded by imported Raj memorabilia, guests sip their cocktails, blissfully unaware that a few years ago Bob Marley and the Wailers filled the place with the sweet smoke of marijuana.

Studio T1 at Transcription Service, Kensington House, is still there, but has mainly been used for remixing concert tapes since the late 1970s. While S2 in Broadcasting House may be occupied by new, small studios, S1 is still there along the corridor. Until recently it was used as a Radio 2 transmission area: Ken Bruce's

show came from there regularly. In one crucial change, however, the control room and studio area itself have swapped places. What is now the control room is where Peel's *Night Ride* guests recorded their first broadcasts.

The Hippodrome in Golders Green, and the Paris Cinema, Lower Regent Street, are still BBC theatres; the former for Radio 2, although some sessions still take place there. The Paris is a Light Entertainment theatre, for quiz and comedy programmes, although it is used less than it was.

Last of all, the Manchester Playhouse in Hulme was finally closed in summer 1986, after an emotional final show *Farewell to the Playhouse*, recorded on 16 June. Producer Mike Craig assembled a galaxy of showbiz stars whose careers

had begun at the theatre's old variety shows on the wireless: Bob Monkhouse, Ernie Wise, the Beverley Sisters, Les Dawson and the broadcaster Ray Moore. But even Craig couldn't reassemble the Beatles for the show. Today the building is the Nia Cultural Centre, which hosts multicultural gigs, discos and theatrical events.

Many of the key session producers and engineers have retired from the BBC. Bernie Andrews has been gone for ten years. Bev Phillips left Radio 2 for the Mechanical Copyright Protection Society two years ago, and Bill Bebb left Radio 2 about the same time. In the past eighteen months, even John Walters and Malcolm Brown have gone.

But others remain. Pete Ritzema is still producing shows for Radio 1, and

Tony Wilson and Jeff Griffin, as two of the senior producers, keep the importance of sessions high on the agenda. In the 1970s Chris Lycett, now Head of Music, was one of the most respected live music engineers at the BBC. Nor should it be forgotten that controller Johnny Beerling once worked on *Saturday Club*.

'I suppose what's changed in the seven years I've been controller is that sessions have been placed as a positive ingredient in shows that want to reflect music and performances that aren't available on record,' says Johnny Beerling.

'For example, look at the *Stereo Sequence* on a Saturday afternoon (started in 1987), where often they've made a virtue of the session being live, in that case, admittedly simple acoustic sets. At the other extreme, at the beginning of my time as controller, we had Janice Long on the *Evening Show*, trying to present I suppose what would be considered as alternative music and independent bands, a lot of them fairly unknown.

'I think what's happened,' he sums up, 'is that the music that's recorded in session has become more pertinent to the musical style of the particular programme.'

Beerling also thinks it's quite important that session production has devolved on to the engineer, and the 'session producer' has gradually been phased out. Paying the supplementary fee to the engineers makes sense, he says, because recording has become highly technical, and the engineers enjoy and merit the additional responsibility.

'The key thing, though, and it sounds worthy and public service but it's

BBC outside studios past and present: The Paris in Lower Regent Street is still a BBC theatre, mainly for Light Entertainment programmes. The Playhouse, Northumberland Avenue, meanwhile, is now a commercial theatre, but evidently still retains a rock connection.

189

true, is that part of our function is to be a patron of new music. Radio 3 is always talking about commissioning new works by up-and-coming composers; and I do passionately believe that it's part of our function to encourage people to get out there and make music.

'British record companies will also tell you that much of the success of British music around the world is due to that initial nurturing of talent that happens here in the UK, uniquely through Radio 1. It doesn't happen in America. There aren't live radio sessions for new bands there.'

Radio 1 FM is almost continuously in the media news columns these days. In the build-up to the BBC's Charter renewal it has become a political football. In the government's Green Paper on *The future of the BBC: A consultation document*, published in November 1992, a hint is made that the government is perhaps waiting to be convinced of the continuing justification for Radio 1 FM. The first point it makes under the heading 'The scope of the BBC's services' speculates that 'if the range of programmes were to be limited, then the number of BBC services might be reduced. For example, if the BBC is not expected to broadcast popular music, then it might have three national radio channels, rather than five.'

But the BBC's response suggests it recognizes the uniqueness of Radio 1's sessions and concerts, and will argue hard for them. In the Corporation's vision of its future, *Extending Choice*, published just two days after the Green Paper, it says that its overall music and arts programming should aim for 'pop and popular music programming of range, diversity and innovation; specialist music programming; and an emphasis on live performance, new work and ideas.' That seems to cover the Peel sessions.

Some think public service broadcasting for the young means only infor-mation helplines, but Johnny Beerling knows it also includes music that people might otherwise not hear. 'We'll go on doing sessions. I would never see a situation where Radio 1 would become an all-needletime station. I think it would be all the poorer for it.' Ironically, now the station doesn't have to do sessions, it knows the fact that it does is one thing that, today, makes BBC Radio 1 FM unique.

I asked Johnny Beerling how the concept of 'Producer choice' might affect studio bookings for sessions at Maida Vale. 'Maida Vale is only sustainable as a multiple studio complex, and you couldn't have one programme producer, for example, unilaterally pulling out of Maida Vale and going to a commercial studio, even if they could get a better deal, because it would have to be a network decision.' So he sees no reason why Maida Vale 4 and 5, for example, could not quote a competitive internal price that would mean Radio 1 could continue to do all its sessions there.

What is undeniable is the name and reputation the BBC has created for itself around the world from its session and concert recording activities. In the 1950s, when Ted Heath and his Big Band were broadcasting, Heath insisted that the BBC's Freddie Harris do his sound. Dudley Moore, as a jazz pianist, insisted on Joe Young being his engineer.

When Elton John played Barcelona in summer 1992, and Radio 1 were to tape the show, his management rang up Jeff Griffin: 'Just checking it's going to be you and Mike Robinson.' Once they knew it was indeed Jeff and Robbo, they calmly offered to pay for them to bring the Radio 1 mobile, in return for feeding the live sound to all the other stations who wanted the concert. The same thing happened with the Michael Jackson concert in Bucharest.

This kind of esteem and trust in a broadcasting organization's expertise is unique in world pop radio. It would indeed be staggering if the BBC ever forgot what a jewel it has, in its engineers, studios, and the sessions and concerts they record.

Tonight – Saturday, 10 October 1992 – as I finish typing the first draft of this book, John Peel is talking to me and all his other listeners from Berlin. It's unusual, part of an information campaign by the station on work opportunities in Europe. That's one more thing that makes Radio 1 different, by the way.

In session are Munich's Freiwillige Selbstkontrolle (FSK). They have just played an ironic, original waltz on electric guitars, celebrating their home town's new airport, named after the late Franz-Josef Strauss. There's no need for me to tune around. No other pop station will be playing satirical Bavarian waltzes.

By the time you read this at least 250 more new sessions will have been recorded and broadcast on Radio 1 FM, whether on Mark Goodier, Nicky Campbell, the *Friday Rock Show*, Andy Kershaw or John Peel. If you've missed them, never mind. Seven days a week, there is always another band, another band you might otherwise never hear, in session tonight.

Peel broadcasting live from Budapest, the week after his shows from Berlin, October 1992: (left to right) producer Mike Hawkes, Peel, programme assistant Hannah Jones, Radio 1 FM controller Johnny Beerling.

8

THE SESSIONOGRAPHY

A-Z by artist, giving First Broadcast Date; Programme; Tracks; Line-up; Recording date; Studio; Producer and Engineer details of almost 6,000 of the most important BBC Radio 1 sessions featured up to its 25th birthday, 30 September 1992.

In order of number of sessions featured, it includes:

- All 'Peel Sessions'.
  Including those on *Top Gear* (1967–71), John Peel's *Night Ride* (1968–69), his *Sounds of the Seventies* shows, and on all programmes under his own name since.
- All *Sounds of the Seventies* sessions (1970–74)
  As featured on programmes presented by David Symonds, Mike Harding, Stuart Henry, Alan Black, Bob Harris, Pete Drummond, and on *The Sequence* and *Rock On* (other *Sounds of the*

Seventies shows, such as the Record Review and Rockspeak, did not feature sessions).

- All *Evening Show* sessions (1979–88) for which the session sheets survive.
  As featured on programmes presented by Andy Peebles, Mike Read, Richard Skinner, David Jensen, Janice Long, Simon Mayo and Liz Kershaw.
- 400 key early sessions by famous bands for other Radio 1, BBC World Service, Radio 2 and 'Light Programme' shows. These are included to make the session listings for the likes of Jimi Hendrix, Cream, and Fairport Convention complete. Most of them come from the first four years of Radio 1, and can give a vivid picture of the life of a BBC-gigging pop band (see Spooky Tooth, for example). But to be complete on some bands in the early days has also demanded the inclusion of:
  – approximately 20 Light Programme sessions from before the launch of

Radio 1 (in these cases, the programme name has been preceded with the word LIGHT);
– approximately 70 sessions for Alexis Korner's *Rhythm & Blues/Blues is where you hear it* show on BBC World Service (entered as WS R&B);
– a handful of Radio 2 *Night Ride* and *Country Meets Folk* sessions from the early Seventies (programme names preceded by R2).

- All *Andy Kershaw* sessions 1985–92.
- All *Friday Rock Show* sessions 1979–92. and also those on *Into the Music* 1984–85.
- All *Mark Goodier's Evening Session* sessions 1990–92.
- Plus a selection of other programmes' sessions, totalling about 200 in all, covering:
  – tea-time show sessions in the late Seventies by important new wave acts, including debuts by The Police, The Pretenders, and so on;
  – all sessions I could trace for the first ten months of Janice Long's Saturday night show from Manchester (Dec 1982 – Sept 83), and a handful of those from the second year;
  – a couple of dozen sessions from *Saturday Live* in the mid-Eighties by key bands;
  – a sample of Nicky Campbell, Richard Skinner and Bob Harris sessions since 1988, to show the range of music featured, including, for example, Steve Williamson, Capercaillie, the Jeff Healey Band, XTC and REM.

For the purposes of this Sessionography, a session is defined as a pre-recorded single day's work in a BBC studio. Concert tapes, and live in-the-on-air-studio acoustic sets are omitted, save for exceptional circumstances; as are all 'private tape' sessions, which are only included when it is clear beyond doubt, for example, that the numbers were recorded on a specific day, specifically for a Radio 1 programme.

I cannot stress strongly enough that this is not an index of all Radio 1 sessions. That would total many thousand more 'network' session recreations of singles, and hundreds of pop daytime performances in the early years. It would take years to research – and would also prove an impractical document to publish commercially.

This Sessionography is, instead, designed as a *programme* based index: which programmes featured the most important sessions? Once those sessions and bands were noted, the document has been expanded, wherever possible, to include any other sessions these bands did for other shows, *but should not be considered definitive beyond sessions for the key programmes named above.*

So, for example, if an act in the early years did not do one for *Top Gear* or *Sounds of the Seventies*, they will not, as a rule, appear here, even though they may have been in BBC studios dozens of times for other shows (a good example from the sixties would be Cliff Bennett and the Rebel Rousers). Similarly, a band may have done two or three sessions in the eighties for Nicky Campbell or the tea-time shows, but if they did not do any for one of the key programmes listed above, they will not be in here. Space, I'm afraid, is at a premium, even for a book this size.

Because most session sheets from before 1978 do not survive, the Sessionography has therefore been compiled in two halves, merged only at the last minute before going to press:

(i) 1967–1979. This has been based almost entirely on the programme scripts kept on microfilm at Written Archives ('PasBs'), with line-ups and studios provided by then cross-checking with artists' contract files (a carbon is kept of every session contract issued). For a tiny handful of artists, their contract file copies do not appear to have survived. Similarly, a very small number of PasBs evidently never arrived at the archives, because they are not to be found on the microfilm. On the rare occasions when contextual evidence suggests either of these sad fates applies to details of a session below, I have drawn attention to the fact (it has been possible, in several cases when the PasB is missing, to find out what happened, by this date appearing as a '1st TX date' for a session repeat on a later show). Producer and Engineer credits have been obtained almost exclusively by interview, and circulating a draft of this half of the list, inviting claims.

For key bands of these years, their contract files obviously threw up all their sessions, all of which I added in, until they either became simply too numerous to mention (Status Quo), or drifted off into less interesting, day-time single-recreating 'network' sessions (The Idle Race). On these occasions, the symbol [M] has been used below, to denote that there were more sessions contracted, but I judge them to be of dubious interest.

This period is consequently, to all intents and purposes, as 100% complete as could reasonably be expected, for any artist that is included.

(ii) 1980–1992. Based on surviving session sheets, cross-checked, for those since 1988, with Radio 1's Romeo computer system. Also invaluable for recent years have been Tony Wilson's preserved wall calendars of *Friday Rock Show* recording dates, 1979–today, providing a complete chronology to check against; Jeff Smith's programme files for *Mark Goodier's Evening Session*, which similarly enabled a full session list to be compiled; and the wall chart planners from Walters' old office, on which his session recordings and broadcasts were scribbled in for each week's shows. Lovingly preserved by Pinky, they gave a vital, 100 per cent accurate check for every Peel session from 1986; and all of Andy Kershaw's from his beginning in 1985.

Some readers will already have spotted that there is an unchecked gap here. The most problematic years, strangely enough, have been the early eighties, where I have had to rely solely on surviving session sheets (time and resources did not permit a full PasB check – I judged it more important to make 1967–1979 copper-bottomed). This means that:

(a) The *Evening Show* sessions included below are based solely on Mike Hawkes' surviving session sheet files. It is possible that one or two have gone astray. In the 18 months before Mike started producing the show (early 1979 to September 1980 – Andy Peebles and Mike Read), I have only included those sessions I have been able to trace from the sheets Mike inherited; and one or two others I chanced on by accident. For that period, the Sessionography is not complete. However, having found more than 900 session sheets for 1980–88, it is unlikely more than a handful are missing for those years, if any.

(b) It is also just possible that one or two Peel Sessions from those years, 1980–84 have slipped through the net: unlikely, but possible. 1980–1982 is particularly unclear, partly because I was not listening then myself. However, I know, by checking against the PasBs, that by 1977–78 Walters was keeping every bit of paper, and his session sheet files for those years are complete; and I have found more than 130 session sheets for each of the years 1980–82; all of which suggests, once again, that if any are missing (there is an equal chance that none at all are missing), it is unlikely to be more than a dozen in all: not too bad, if I say so myself, out of a total of almost 3000 Peel Sessions.

There is one final question every reader will be asking: do the tapes survive? A good rule of thumb is sessions after 1980 exist, those before don't. Don't forget, this Sessionography is an index of what happened, not what survives. It was once BBC policy to wipe tape for re-use. Technically, it was for many years part of the agreement with the MU that the tapes would be destroyed after six months anyway. A previous incarnation of BBC management used on occasion to enforce this policy with military efficiency.

However, long-standing producers, particularly Bernie Andrews, Jeff Griffin, John Walters, and Malcolm Brown, carefully preserved what they judged to be their most important tapes, wherever possible (sadly, however, Malcolm Brown's *Sounds of the Seventies* tapes were taken and wiped when he was away at BBC TV in the mid-seventies; and similarly, very few John Muir-produced session tapes survive, save some of those recorded at Transcription Service – see below). This accounts for the survival of a fair few classic *Top Gear* and *Sounds of the Seventies* sessions. Later, Walters also safeguarded all the key early punk tapes.

A handful of bands who had a good relationship with those key producers in the early years would occasionally take home a copy of the master tape.

The other way early sessions have survived is thanks to Transcription Service, and the tape copies they took for their *Top of the Pops* programmes. Also, the most famous sessions recorded at their own stereo studio T1 in the early seventies, like those by Genesis and Roxy Music, were preserved.

Today, everything is stored on R-DAT masters, as well as the quarter-inch stereo mixes. Finally, not wanting to be too creepy about it, I think it only fair to put on record the fact that priority being given to preserving the tapes, the setting up of the basement archive, and taking on an archivist at Radio 1 FM in Phil Lawton, were all measures launched in the early years of Johnny Beerling's controllership of the station.

HOW TO READ
THE SESSIONOGRAPHY

FAIRPORT CONVENTION
10/12/67 TOP GEAR *Let's get together, One sure thing, Lay down your weary tune, Chelsea morning.* Judy Dyble (v) Hutchings (b), Martin Lamble (d), Simon Nicol (g), Richard Thompson (gv). 24/11/67 PH BA PR

3/3/68 TOP GEAR *If (stomp), If I had a ribbon bow, Time will show the wiser, Violets of dawn.* Ian Matthews (v) joins. 6/2/68 AO2 BA DT
BA submitted this second session as trial broadcast. 'Unanimous, enthusiastic pass' from panel; 'compared to Harpers Bizarre'.

SYMONDS *If (stomp), It takes a lot to laugh it takes a train to cry, It's alright ma it's only witchcraft,*

Chelsea morning. 11/3/68 PS JW *
Contracts file suggests Matthews first appeared on this date, but Ashley Hutchings thinks it unlikely 'If (stomp)', a Matthews/Thompson song, would have been recorded on previous date without him.
2/6/68 TOP GEAR *Close the door lightly when you got, Where I stand†, Nottamun town, You never wanted me (& Some sweet day†, 30/6/68).* Sandy Denny (v) r.

 28/5/68 PCI BA DT
24/6/68 SYMONDS *Marcie, Night in the city, Jack O'Diamonds, Morning glory.* 18/6/68 MV4 * *
1/9/68 TOP GEAR *If you feel good you know it can't be wrong†, Fotheringay, Gone gone gone†, Eastern rain (& Suzanne†, 29/9/68).* 8 PCI BA PR
8/12/68 HENRY *Meet on the ledge, I... a bird on a wire†, Reno Nevada, Mr. Lacey.* 2/12/... D *
15/12/68 NIGHT RIDE *Things you gave me, Meet on the ledge, Autopsy, Morning glory, Bird on a wire, Mr.Lacey.* 25/11/68 MV4 PC *
22/12/68 TOP GEAR *Meet on the ledge, She moves through the fair, Light my fire, I'll keep it with mine, Billy the orphan boy's lonely Christmas.* 9/12/68 PCI BA PR
6/1/69 SYMONDS *Reno Nevada†, Book song, I still miss someone†, Tried so hard†, Sandy.* 27... V4 c.RB *

Band next appeared live from the Paris on R1 Club 6/1/69, playing 'Bird on a wire', 'Jack O'Diamonds', 'I still miss someone', 'You're gonna need my help'.
9/2/69 SYMONDS ON SUNDAY *Fotheringay, Who knows where the time goes, Shattering live experience†, You're gonna need my help.* 4/2/69 PCI JW TW
6/4/69 TOP GEAR *Cajun woman, Percy's song†, Si tu dois partir va t'en°, Autopsy.* & guest Ric Grech (vi); Matthews out. 18/3/69 PH BA AH&BC

† on 'Heyday' album, Hannibal HNCD 1329. ° On 'I and only' BOJCD025.
27/9/69 TOP GEAR *Sir Patrick Spens, Jigs & reels medley, Tam Lin, The Lady is a tramp, Reynardine.* Dave Swarbrick (vi) r. Grech; & Dave Mattacks (d) r. Lamble [died 12/5/69, after M1 accident]. 23/9/69 MV4 JW TW
27/4/70 SYMONDS *Open the door Richard, The flatback caper, Sir Patrick Spens (& The bonny black hare,*
25/5/70). Dave Pegg (b,fd,mand) r. Hutchings, Denny, from 1/70. 21/4/70 PH BA NG
2/5/70 TOP GEAR *The deserter, Walk awhile, The flatback caper, Poor Will and the jolly hangman (& Doctor of physic, 1/8/70).* 20/4/70 PH JW TW
26/7/70 FOLK ON 1 *Sir Patrick Spens, Medley: jigs and reels, The deserter, Hangman's reel, Bonny bunch of roses (& Dirty linen, Flowers of the forest, Now be thankful, Tam Lin 2/8/70).* 7&9/7/70 AO2 FL *

1 BAND OR ARTIST

In alphabetical order, by surname or first proper word of act's name; except where a band or musician's career merits (eg. Richard Thompson's solo sessions come after those by Richard and Linda Thompson; Brian Auger's Oblivion Express comes after Brian Auger's Trinity).

2 FIRST BROADCAST DATE

The date on which this session was first broadcast. Repeat broadcast dates are not given. Each new date sticking out to the left of the rest of the column represents a new session recording and broadcast.

3 PROGRAMME

The programme on which this session was first broadcast that day (see *Programmes*).

4 TITLES

The songs or tracks broadcast on that day on that programme. Titles linked to form a medley as a single item are separated by oblique slashes. For sessions from 1967–1974, they are normally given in the order they were broadcast (this also applies to tea-time and evening show sessions in the late seventies); for sessions thereafter, in the order they appear on the session sheet (ie. the order in which they were recorded). On rare occasions it has been possible to point out that the track's title when broadcast was later changed by the band, and this more-familiar, final name of the piece has been given in square brackets.

5 LINE-UP

The line-up of the band that recorded these titles.

Instrumentation is as abbreviated, in brackets (see *Instruments*). The full line-up is printed on an act's first session, with only any changes in personnel being given on subsequent sessions, 'r.' meaning 'replaces'. Therefore, if no line-up is shown, it means it is the same as on the band's previous date. All musicians listed after a semi-colon (groups) or an ampersand (solo artists), appear on that session only. Musicians are credited and their names spelt as on the contract carbons or session sheets. Wherever possible, the hundreds of name-spelling inconsistencies that arose on both these kinds of documents have been resolved. The line-ups on contracts, on occasion, also lagged behind band changes by a session or two – BBC contracts were dependent on bands' management keeping them up-to-date – and these errors, where spotted, have also been corrected.

6 RECORDING DATE

The day on which these musicians recorded these titles.

7 STUDIO

The studio in which they recorded on the above date (see *Studios*).

8 PRODUCER

The Radio 1 staff producer, a freelance, or producer-engineer, who produced the session (see *Keys*). Until the mid-1980s, this person's role was primarily setting the atmosphere, advising on content and arrangements if thought necessary, and making sure enough material was recorded in time. Most of the technical sound work belonged to the...

196

9 ➤ ENGINEER

The BBC studio manager or 'SM' who mixed and balanced the sound (see *Producers and Engineers*). If two names are given, linked by an ampersand, it means the first engineer did the balance; and the second was the tape operator (pre-1981), or the one who set up the studio while the first SM controlled the sound (post-81).

...FURTHER DETAILS?

Were all the tracks recorded broadcast on that date? Certain shows used the 'item recording' agreement, playing one song from a session on each daily show through one week. For these shows' sessions, the date given is normally the Monday of that week. On some, it has been possible to give the exact subsequent days of transmission, and these are given in brackets after each title (For list of shows this applies to, see *Programmes*).

10 ➤ Other programmes sometimes

saved some tracks, to put out on the repeat broadcast. These titles are given in brackets, followed by the later date on which they were transmitted. If these were then first broadcast on a different programme, the programme is given in capitals. On rare occasions, it is known that extra tracks were recorded, but never broadcast; these are also given in brackets.

11 ➤ IS THERE ANYTHING ELSE THAT SHOULD BE KNOWN?

Footnotes have been included as deemed appropriate, in chronological order between the sessions. These include: comments of the Audition panel; brief details of other BBC dates for the band (eg concerts); amusing notes from the session sheets; various recollections or anecdotes that didn't fit into the book or arrived too late; and details of sessions that have been commercially released at some

point. Throughout these notes, abbreviations in keeping with those outlined below have been employed, such as 'TX' for 'transmitted, or first broadcast', 'PS' for the Paris Cinema, and 'rec'd.' for 'recorded on'.

OTHER SYMBOLS

12 ➤ † and *†*

tracks that have been commercially released. If a complete session has been released, the dagger appears in roman text immediately after the programme title. If only some tracks from the session have been released, the dagger is printed in italics after those individual track titles. If tracks from one session have appeared on more than one release, the additional symbols ° and ´ are used, where necessary. Details of the release are given in a footnote after the last session from which tracks were drawn, with catalogue numbers where possible.

This does not claim to be a definitive element of the Sessionography, and has partly been compiled with the help of Sue Falconer of BBC Enterprises' Business Affairs department (to whom any band wishing to licence their session tracks for release should write in the first instance); and partly from scouring the author, his friends', and Peel's record collection. It should be pointed out that documentation for releases licenced before the mid-1980s has proved hard to come by.

13 ➤ [M] (not shown on sample)

More BBC Radio bookings followed, but have not been included, for various reasons: either they were for Radio 2; they were simply too numerous for daytime pop shows, and deemed of limited interest; or they were contracted as 'Private Tape' sessions, and consequently were not proper BBC sessions.

14 ➤ c.RB 'Session commissioned by

show's chief producer/editor' ie. this person booked the band, but it is unlikely they produced the recording themselves. This is common for daytime sessions 1967–80.

15 ➤ MR⁻ (not shown on sample)

'Produced and engineered by' the person's initials preceding the symbol. This has happened since the late seventies, but has been common since 1988, and is now normal. If a second engineer is named after this symbol, it means they either assisted setting-up and running the studio; or, if the name given is one of the regular long-standing SMs, they probably also contributed to the mix, but the producer-engineer took responsibility for the final sound.

16 ➤ *'Unknown': applies to Line-

ups, Studios and Producers (all rarely), and Engineers (often).

On unknown line-ups, readers might be surprised to see this applied to some name bands; surely the line-up could be checked from an album, even if it was missed off the sheet? Unfortunately, there is no guarantee the session line-up would have been the same; and there has simply not been time to check the contract files for all artists in recent years. I have therefore followed the old journalistic maxim 'if in doubt, leave it out'.

Finally, uncertainty must also remain over bands who entered their names on the session sheet as pseudonyms. This has resulted in occasional credits in the Sessionography of the kind 'Timmy Bottom Gargler (b) r. Gut Bucket' – when, for all we know, they could be one and the same real person. I think it only fitting that I should advise readers to react to such credits in the spirit which was originally intended: incredulity.

8

197

PROGRAMMES

This is an alphabetical index and guide to any and all those Radio 1, Radio 2, Light Programme and World Service programmes which have any of their sessions featured in the Sessionography. Only some of these programmes have all their sessions included. See introduction to Sessionography for those programmes which are listed 'complete'.

ALL OUR YESTERDAYS
- ALL OUR YESTERDAYS; Sundays, 3–4pm, 1970, presented by Johnny Moran, produced by Bernie Andrews. Revival rock 'n' roll sessions.

ANTHONY
- DAVE ANTHONY, Saturdays, 2–4pm, 1972. Two sessions included only, both from show of 13/5/72, Barclay James Harvest and Atomic Rooster. Produced by Dave Tate.

BLACK
- ALAN BLACK, SOUNDS OF THE SEVENTIES, Fridays 6–7pm, 10/4/70–1/10/71, produced by John Muir; 17/9 & 24/9/71, presented by Steve Bradshaw; 14/8/70, produced by Jeff Griffin; 21 & 28/8/70, produced by Ray Harvey.

BLACKBURN
- TONY BLACKBURN, Mon–Fri, 2–4.30pm, late 70s, produced by Paul Williams. One or two 'Network' sessions included. Item recording.

BRANDON
- SOUNDS LIKE TONY BRANDON, Mon–Fri, 4.15–6.30pm, 27/1/69–April 69; 5.15–7.30pm, April–Sept 69. Editor, Ron Belchier. Session producers Don George, Paul Williams, and Bernie Andrews (not credited in *Radio Times*). Inherited tea-time slot from David SYMONDS (see below). A handful of surprising sessions. Item recording.

BURNETT
- PAUL BURNETT, Mon–Fri, 12.45–2.31pm, late 70s-early 80s, produced Chris Lycett. One or two 'Network' sessions included. Item recording.

CAMPBELL
- NICKY CAMPBELL, Mon–Thurs, 10.30 pm–00.30 am, 3/10/88–1/4/89; 10 pm–midnight, 3/4/89 onwards. Produced by Paul Williams until September 1992. A selection of sessions included. Item recording.

CASH
- DAVE CASH, Mon–Fri, 2–4.15pm, Jan–Sept 1969; then took over BRANDON tea-time slot (above). Editor, Derek Mills; producers Malcolm Brown and Bill Bebb. Belchier's team took over with move to tea-time in September. By March 1970, edited by Ron Belchier or Pam Cox, producers Peter Harwood and Don George. A few unusual daytime sessions
- CASH AT FOUR, Sundays, 4–5pm, late 1970, produced by John Bussell. One session only included, Cat Stevens on 25/10/70. Item recording.

COUNTRY MEETS FOLK
- COUNTRY MEETS FOLK, Saturdays, 5.30–6.30pm, 30/9/67–end 69, produced by Ian Grant, presented by Wally Whyton. Produced by Bill Bebb from 7/6/69. In 1970 moved onto Radio 2 only, 4–5pm Sunday, presented by Johnny Silvo, produced by Bill Bebb.

DLT
- DAVE LEE TRAVIS, DLT, Sundays, 10am–midday, 28/9/69–26/9/71, produced by Paul Williams (DLT inherited the SYMONDS ON SUNDAY slot – see below).
- IT'S DLT OK!, Mon–Fri, 4.30–6pm, 29/9/75–1/4/77, produced by Tim Blackmore; 4.31–7pm, 4/4/77–14/4/78, produced by Dave Atkey from 4/7/77. Item recording.

DRUMMOND
- PETE DRUMMOND, SOUNDS OF THE SEVENTIES, Thursdays, 6–7pm, 2/9/71–30/9/71, produced by Malcolm Brown; Thursdays, 10pm–midnight, 7/10/71–28/9/72, produced by Malcolm Brown; except 13 & 20/7/72, produced by Tony Wilson, and 3/8/72, presented by Alan Black. See also SEQUENCE, ROCK ON.

EASY BEAT

- EASY BEAT, Sundays 10–11.30am, presented by David Symonds, produced by Ron Belchier. Light Programme show, originally presented by Brian Matthew, and on Saturday evenings, which didn't survive onto Radio 1.

EDMONDS

- NOEL EDMONDS' Saturday lunchtime show in 1970, 1–3pm, produced by John Bussell; one or two sessions only included.

FERRIS

- ANDY FERRIS, SOUNDS OF THE SEVENTIES, Mondays 6–7pm, 6/4/70–20/4/70, produced by Bernie Andrews.

FIRST GEAR

- FIRST GEAR, Saturdays 3–5 pm, 8/8/70–29/8/70, produced by John Walters, presented by Johnny Moran. Four weeks of old rock'n'roll records and sessions in the 'Top Gear' slot while Peel was on holiday. These included sessions by Bert Weedon, Marty Wilde, Shakin' Stevens and the Sunsets, and Billy J. Kramer (not listed) and more importantly Fleetwood Mac's famous session of Buddy Holly covers (included).

FOLK ON 1

- FOLK ON ONE, Sundays 7–7.30pm, from 1/10/69, evolved out of MY KIND OF FOLK (see below), produced by Frances Line. Although this title was not entered in *Radio Times* until the show's second year, when it moved to 2.31–3pm Saturdays on 3/10/70 (coming on before TOP GEAR), I have used it throughout. First few months were series of several weeks presented by one artist or act (eg. Peter Sarstedt, Pentangle, Bridget St John, The Liverpool Scene) with guests. Frances Line started to feature just one band each week from 5/4/70, 'with the debut of folk-rock supergroup Fotheringay'. Show ended 27/3/71 (See SOUNDS ON SUNDAY below).

FREEMAN

- ALAN FREEMAN, Saturdays 3–5pm, 30/6/73–26/8/78, produced by Tony Wilson. Mostly repeats of Tony's Peel Session 'Re-Creations', but a few sessions of its own, including the quad experiments.

FRI. ROCK

- THE FRIDAY ROCK SHOW, Fridays, 10pm–midnight, 17/11/78–1/10/88; 10.30pm–12.30am 7/10/88–1/4/89; 10pm–midnight 7/4/89–13/3/92; and

9–11pm from 20/3/92 onwards. Presented by Tommy Vance, produced by Tony Wilson.

GOODIER

- MARK GOODIER'S EVENING SESSION, Mon–Thur, 7.30–9pm, from 1/10/90, produced by Jeff Smith. Show started at 7pm from Monday 9/3/92. Item recording.

GRAY

- MURIEL GRAY, THE EVENING SHOW, Mon–Thur, 7.30–10pm, 1st week July 1984 only, produced by Mike Hawkes.

HAMILTON

- DAVID HAMILTON, Mon–Fri, 2–5pm 1973 & 74, produced by Paul Williams. A small number of 'Network' sessions included. Item recording.

HARDING

- MIKE HARDING, SOUNDS OF THE SEVENTIES, Tuesdays 6–7pm, 7/4/70 – 28/9/71, 6–7pm, produced by Malcolm Brown; 6/4 & 13/4/71 presented by Pete Drummond.

HARRIS

- BOB HARRIS, SOUNDS OF THE SEVENTIES, Wednesdays 6–7pm, 19/8/70–9/9/70, produced by Jeff Griffin; Mondays 6–7pm, 12/10/70–27/9/71 produced by John Muir; Mondays 10pm–midnight (same day and time henceforth), 4/10/71–27/12/71, produced John Muir; 3/1/72–18/12/72, produced by Jeff Griffin; 1/1/73–25/6/73, produced by Pete Ritzema; 2/7/73–21/1/74, produced by Jeff Griffin; 28/1/74–20/5/74, produced by Pete Ritzema; 27/5/74–23/12/74, produced by Jeff Griffin; except 5 & 12/6/72, introduced by Andy Finney, and 19 & 26/8/74, presented by Alan Black.
- BOB HARRIS, Mon–Thur, Midnight–2am, from 2/4/90; Mon–Thur, Midnight–4am, from Jan 91. Produced by Jeff Griffin from 2/4/90; and by Phil Swern from Jan 91. Item recording.

HENRY

- STUART HENRY, Sundays, 10am–midday, 16/6/68–19/1/69, produced by Aidan Day, live from the Paris. Chiefly famous for featuring Elton John's first broadcast, Joe Cocker's audition, and various cock-ups.
- STUART HENRY'S NOISE AT NINE, Sundays, 9–10pm, 27/4/69–21/9/69, produced by Malcolm Brown. Show moved to Sundays 4–5pm from 28/9/69, produced by Malcolm Brown. Then came...

- STUART HENRY, SOUNDS OF THE SEVENTIES, Thursdays 6–7pm, 9/4/70–26/8/71, produced by Malcolm Brown; 13/8/70, 24/6/71, presented by Pete Drummond; 28/1/71 produced by Teddy Warrick.

INTO THE MUSIC

- INTO THE MUSIC, Thursdays, 10pm–midnight, 4/10/84–27/9/85, presented by Tommy Vance, produced by Tony Wilson.

IT'S ROCK'N' ROLL

- IT'S ROCK'N' ROLL, Saturdays, late 70s, 5.30–6.31pm, presented by Stu Colman, produced by Dave Price. One session only included here, Fumble, 24/2/79.

R1 JAZZ WORKSHOP

- JAZZ WORKSHOP, Wednesdays, 9.15–10pm; show of 6/8/69, produced by Roger Eames; one session only included, Jon Hiseman's Colosseum.

JENSEN

- 'KID' JENSEN, Mon–Fri, 4.31–7.30pm, 17/4/78–21/6/80, produced by Dave Tate; with Dave Price, Malcolm Brown, or Pete Ritzema. Item recording.
- DAVID JENSEN, THE EVENING SHOW, Mon–Thur, 7.30–10pm, 5/10/81–30/6/84, produced by Mike Hawkes.

KERSHAW

- ANDY KERSHAW, Saturdays 6.30–7.30pm, from Manchester, 6/7/85–28/9/85, produced by John Leonard.
- ANDY KERSHAW, Thursdays 10pm–midnight, 3/10/85–29/9/88; Thursdays 8.30–10.30pm, 6/10/88–30/3/89; Sundays 9–11pm, 2/4/89–8/3/92; Saturdays 9–11pm, 14/3/92 onwards. Produced by John Walters 3/10/85–June '91, and by Mike Hawkes thereafter.

L KERSHAW

- LIZ KERSHAW, THE EVENING SHOW, Mon–Thur, 7.30–10pm, 18/4/88–1/10/88, produced by Phil Ross.

LONG

- JANICE LONG, Saturdays, 7.30–10pm, from Manchester, 4/12/82–24/9/83, produced by John Leonard and David Treadway; and 1/10/83–22/9/84, from London, produced Phil Ward-Large.
- JANICE LONG, THE EVENING SHOW, Mon–Thur, 7.30–10pm, 3/9/84–31/12/87, produced by Mike Hawkes until September 87, thence by Phil Ross.

JOE LOSS

- THE JOE LOSS SHOW, Fridays, 1–2pm, (inherited by Radio 1 from the Light Programme), 6/10/67–18/10/68, live from The Playhouse. Produced by Ian Grant; produced by Paul Williams from 5/4/68.

LULU'S BACK IN TOWN

- LULU'S BACK IN TOWN, 2–3pm, New Year's Day special, 1/1/71, produced by Don George. Stone the Crows in session.

MAYO

- SIMON MAYO, THE EVENING SHOW, Mon–Thur, 7.30–10pm, 1/1/88–15/4/88, produced by Phil Ross.

MONDAY, MONDAY

- MONDAY, MONDAY, 1–2pm, 2/10/67–14/10/68, presented by Dave Cash, produced by Don George, live from the Playhouse. One or two sessions included only.

MY KIND OF FOLK

- MY KIND OF FOLK, Wednesdays, 7.45–8.15pm, 6/3/68–24/9/69; presented by Alex Campbell, Cyril Tawney, Noel Murphy; produced by Frances Line (today Controller of Radio 2). All-star final show featured The Johnstons, Ralph McTell, Pentangle, Peter Sarstedt, The Spinners and The Strawbs. See FOLK ON 1, SOUNDS ON SUNDAY.

NIGHT RIDE

- JOHN PEEL'S NIGHT RIDE, R1 & 2, Wednesday nights, midnight–1am, 6/3/68–23/4/69. All sessions produced by John Muir, Denis O'Keefe, Pete Carr or Pete Ritzema. Any Night Ride sessions included outside the above dates are not John Peel's Night Ride (see PEEL, TOP GEAR below).
- NIGHT RIDE, R1 & 2, daily, midnight–2am, from 30/9/67. Producers for the period which produced most of the sessions included here (ie. mainly 1970–72) were Derek Mayell, Alec Reid, Denis O'Keefe, Larry Parker, Derek Drescher, and, later, Pam Cox and Geoffrey Mullin.

PEEBLES

- ANDY PEEBLES, THE EVENING SHOW, Mon–Thur, 8pm–10pm, 13/11/78–end of November; & 29/1/79–13/7/79, produced by Jeff Griffin. Item recording.

PEEL

- see TOP GEAR (below) and NIGHT RIDE

(above) for early 'Peel Sessions' 1967–71.

- JOHN PEEL, Wednesdays 8.15–9.15pm, 30/4/69–24/9/69, produced by Pete Ritzema (the last six months of his old Night Ride show, moved forward).

- JOHN PEEL 'WITH *TOP GEAR*', SOUNDS OF THE SEVENTIES, Wednesdays 10pm–midnight, 6/10/71–29/12/71; Tuesdays, 10pm–midnight, 4/1/72–24/12/74; Thursdays, 10pm–midnight 24/1/74–16/12/74. All sessions commissioned by Walters. Sessions produced by: October 1971–June 72, Walters or Ritzema; June 72–September 73, Tony Wilson, Walters, Ritzema; October 73–end 74, Tony Wilson. I have included this brief chronological summary of producers of the Walters-commissioned early 70s 'Peels' because there were many sessions which none of the three could definitely be sure they had done themselves, so these have had to be left as unknown. In addition, in 1972–74, Walters went and did a few at Transcription Service, some of which Pete Dauncey produced. In general terms, after he was joined by Ritzema and Wilson, Walters mainly produced the solo or acoustic acts, save for notable big occasions like Bob Marley's debut, or ones with bands he knew well, like Lindisfarne.

- JOHN PEEL, SOUNDS OF THE SEVENTIES, Fridays, 10pm–midnight, 7/1/72–29/9/72, produced by John Muir; ie 'Friday Night is Boogie Night'. These sessions can easily be distinguished from Walters' Peel commissions, because they were all recorded at Studio T1, Transcription Service, and produced by John Muir or Pete Dauncey.

- JOHN PEEL, SOUNDS OF THE SEVENTIES, Thursdays, 10pm–midnight, 5/10/72–17/1/74, produced by Bernie Andrews; distinguishable from Walters' commissions because all sessions were produced by Bernie Andrews, save one or two by Chris Lycett.

- JOHN PEEL 'WITH *TOP GEAR*', Mondays & Thursdays, 5.15–7pm, 6/1/75–25/9/75. All sessions commissioned by Walters, all produced by Tony Wilson.

- JOHN PEEL. All programmes in simply his own name from the end of September 1975 onwards. From 29/9/75, Mon–Fri, 11pm–midnight; from 4/4/77, Mon–Fri,

10pm–midnight; from 13/11/78, Mon–Thurs, 10pm–midnight; from 1/10/84, Mon–Wed, 10pm–midnight; from 3/10/88, Mon–Wed, 8.30–10.30pm; from 3/4/89, Mon–Thurs 8.30–10pm; from 29/9/90, Sat & Sun 11pm–2am; from 13/3/92, Fri & Sat 11pm–2am. Session producers as identified from session sheets. Up to June 1991, all sessions commissioned by John Walters, except: 1981–2, sessions commissioned by Chris Lycett; and January–March 1983, sessions commissioned by Trevor Dann. From July 1991 onwards all sessions commissioned by producer Mike Hawkes.

PETE'S PEOPLE

- PETE'S PEOPLE, Saturdays 10 pm–midnight (and Sundays from end Sept 1968) 30/9/67–end 69 (at least), presented by Pete Murray, produced by John Hooper. One or two sessions from earliest days only.

POP NORTH

- POP NORTH, Thursdays, 1–2pm, from 3/11/66 (Light Programme) until 17/10/68 (Radio 1). Live from The Playhouse, Hulme, with Bernard Herrmann and the Northern Dance Orchestra, presented by Ray Moore, produced by John Wilcox. Heir to 'The Beat Show' and 'Here we go', produced by Peter Pilbeam, which featured The Beatles' first broadcast.

POWELL

- PETER POWELL, Mon–Fri, 3.32–6.31pm, from 23/6/80, produced Dave Tate, and later, Dave Atkey (or Phil Stannard, on attachment). Several tea-time sessions included here. Item recording.

R1 CLUB

- RADIO 1 CLUB, Mon–Fri, Midday–2pm, 21/10/68–1/10/71. Numerous venues, numerous presenters, numerous producers, but Johnny Beerling was in charge, and out of it came the Radio 1 Roadshow. Each day was live from a different BBC or Theatre location around the UK, with often extra live or pre-recorded sessions piped-in from the home base, the Paris. Not to be confused with 'Radio One O'Clock', the previous Monday Lunchtime show live from the Playhouse, which evolved out of MONDAY MONDAY – see above. Item recording.

RAVEN'S R&B

- MIKE RAVEN'S RHYTHM AND BLUES SHOW, Sundays, 7–7.30pm, 1/10/67–end Mar.

68; 7–8pm, Mar–Oct 68; 7–8.30pm Oct 68–20/4/69; 10–11pm 27/4/69–20/9/69; 7.30–8.45pm 27/9/69–29/3/70; and 7.30–9pm from 5/4/70, which is when sessions start appearing, kicking-off with Chicken Shack. Although Raven's show was produced by Keith 'Boots' Stewart, these sessions, until the end of 1970, were actually those recorded by Jeff Griffin for Alexis Korner's World Service Rhythm and Blues show, and borrowed for domestic broadcast. The exigencies of World Service production meant that the broadcast on Raven was always at least ten days before the session went out on its own programme. This applies to all RAVEN sessions for 1970 (see WS R&B below). From the end of 1970, however, RAVEN had his own sessions, recorded by his new producer, Malcolm Brown. Show moved to Saturdays 5–6.30pm, 3/10/70; programme ended at the end of 1971.

READ

- MIKE READ, THE EVENING SHOW, Mon–Thur, 8pm–10pm, 16/7/79–30/6/80, produced by Chris Lycett. (In July/August 1980, the show was presented by a succession of BBC local radio DJs, and no session sheets survive for these weeks); 7.30–10pm, 1/9/80–26/12/80, produced by Mike Hawkes. Item recording.

ROCK ON

- ROCK ON, SOUNDS OF THE SEVENTIES, Saturdays, 10pm–midnight, 27/10/73–21/12/74; presented by Pete Drummond 27/10/73–30/3/74, presented by Alan Black 5/4/74–21/12/74; produced by Pete Ritzema 27/10/73–19/1/74, produced by Bernie Andrews 26/1/74–21/12/74.

ROMAN

- MARK ROMAN, Saturday, 2–4pm, 27/4/68, no producer credited, one session only.

SAT. CLUB

- SATURDAY CLUB, Saturdays, 10am–midday, 4/10/58 (Light Programme) to 18/1/69 (Radio 1). Sessions included here date from 12/11/66, with Cream's first broadcast, and the earliest one in the whole Sessionography. Presented by Brian Matthew up to launch of Radio 1, and by Keith Skues thereafter. Producer 1966–1969, Bill Bebb, except Keith

Bateson 1/6/68–28/9/68.

SAT. LIVE/SUN. LIVE

- SATURDAY LIVE, Saturdays, 5–6.30pm, April 83–10/1/87; presented by Richard Skinner, Andy Batten-Foster, Andy Kershaw; produced by Mark Radcliffe, Phil Ward-Large, Phil Ross; then Sundays, 2.30–3.30pm, 18/1/87–27/9/87, presented by Andy Kershaw, produced by Phil Ross. Live sessions from S2.

SAT. SEQ.

- THE SATURDAY SEQUENCE, (originally called 'The Stereo Sequence'), Saturdays 3–6.30pm 17/1/87 onwards, presented by Johnnie Walker, Roger Scott, and then Walker again; produced by Kevin Howlett, Jeff Griffin, and now Phil Ross. Occasional acoustic, live or pre-recorded sessions in the studios at Egton House, and one or two from Transcription Service's studio, Kensington House.

SEQUENCE

- THE SEQUENCE, SOUNDS OF THE SEVENTIES, presented by Pete Drummond, Fridays, 10pm–midnight, 5/10/72–28/9/73, produced by John Muir; 20/7/73–3/8/73 presented by Vincent Price.

SKINNER

- RICHARD SKINNER, THE EVENING SHOW, Mon–Thur, 7.30–10pm, 29/12/80–2/10/81, produced by Mike Hawkes (had already done weeks beginning 10 & 17/11/80 for Read); and again, 8/7/84–1/9/84, produced by Mike Hawkes. Item recording until April 81.
- RICHARD SKINNER, Mon–Thur, 12.30am–2am, from 3/10/88; Midnight–2am, from 3/4/89–30/3/90. Produced by Kevin Howlett 3/10/88–30/6/89, and by Jeff Griffin 1/7/89 onwards. Item recording & some live after-midnight sessions from MV3.

SOUNDS ON SUNDAY

- SOUNDS ON SUNDAY, 7–7.30pm, 1/10/72–30/11/75, produced initially by Frances Line, and sub-titled 'Contemporary Folk' (evolved out of FOLK ON 1 – see above). Featured almost concert length sessions. By October 74, folk bias had disappeared, produced by Dave Atkey, presented by Peel, among others. Some shows from Manchester, some shows based on records. In final months, rocky sessions, presented by Peel, produced by Malcolm Brown.

SPEAKEASY

- SPEAKEASY, Saturdays, 5–5.45pm (later, – 6pm), 27/9/69–end of 71; Sundays 3–4pm Jan 72–23/9/73. Presented by Jimmy Savile, produced by Roy Trevithian, with Jeff Griffin, then Ted Beston (from 71). 'Issues' show with live music guests.

STAGE ONE

- STAGE ONE, Sundays, 4–5pm, from 27/4/69, presented by Chris Denning or Ray Moore, produced by Don George. Took over slot when TOP GEAR was moved to Sunday evenings. Two sessions only included: Famous Jug Band and Sam Apple Pie. Ran for only six months.

STUDIO B15

- STUDIO B15, Sundays, 3–5pm, 31/8/80–26/9/82, presented by Adrian Love, David Jensen; produced by Chris Riley and Mary Pett, Chris Longley and Howard Benson. Moved back to 2.30–4pm in 82. Live sessions from Langham 1.

SYMONDS, SYMONDS ON SUNDAY

- DAVID SYMONDS, Mon–Fri, 5.33–7.30pm, 2/10/67–end Feb 68; 4.30–6.25pm, Feb–Jul 68; 4.15–5.45pm, Jul 68–24/1/69. Editor Ron Belchier. Session producers: from 2/10/67 Keith Bateson, Malcolm Brown; from Apr 68 John Walters, Bev Phillips; 29/7/68–24/1/69 Bev Phillips, Jeff Griffin. Item recording.

- DAVID SYMONDS, SYMONDS ON SUNDAY, 10am–midday, 26/1/69–21/9/69. Produced by John Walters 26/1/69–20/4/69, Paul Williams 27/4/69–21/9/69.

- DAVID SYMONDS, SOUNDS OF THE SEVENTIES, Mondays 6–7pm, 27/4/70–5/10/70, produced by Bernie Andrews; except 7/9–28/9/70 produced by Alan Wisher, 5/10/70 produced by John Muir.

TOP GEAR

- TOP GEAR, Sundays, 2–5pm, from 1/10/67; Sundays, 2–4pm, from 4/2/68; Sundays, 3–5pm, from 2/6/68; Sundays, 7–9pm, from 27/4/69; Saturdays, 3–5pm, from 27/9/69–25/9/71 (from 6/10/71, Top Gear was pulled into the 10pm FM Sounds of the Seventies slot. The title was retained as a sub–heading in *Radio Times* until September 1975, but all sessions after 25/9/71 have been simply labelled PEEL – see above). Almost all of these Top Gear sessions count as 'Peel Sessions', but not

all, because: 1/10/67 presented by Pete Drummond & John Peel; 8/10/67 Drummond & Mike Ahern; 15/10/67 Drummond & Tommy Vance; 22/10/67 Drummond & Rick Dane; 29/10/67, 5/11/67 Drummond & Peel; 12/11/67–28/1/68 Peel & Tommy Vance; but from 4/2/68 onwards, Peel sole presenter. Sessions produced by: 1/10/67–3/3/68 Bernie Andrews or Bev Phillips; 3/3/68–20/4/69 Andrews only; 27/4/69–July '70 John Walters; July 70–October 71 Walters or Pete Rizema.

VIV STANSHALL'S RADIO FLASHES

- VIV STANSHALL'S RADIO FLASHES, Saturdays, 3-5 pm, 7/8/71–28/8/71, produced by John Walters, presented by Stanshall with mates including Keith Moon, while Peel was on holiday. Featured debut sessions by Greyhound, Gaspar Lawal.

WALKER

- JOHNNIE WALKER, Saturdays, 2–3.55pm, 26/4/69–21/9/69, produced by John Bussell. One or two sessions included.

- JOHNNIE WALKER, Mon–Fri, 1–3pm, from 4/10/71, produced by Johnny Beerling. A few notable 'Network' sessions featured here. Show replaced R1 CLUB (see above). Item recording. See also SAT. SEQ (above).

WOGAN

- TERRY WOGAN'S afternoon show, 2–4.15pm, in 1969; one or two sessions only included. Editor Derek Mills; session producers Malcolm Brown, Denis O'Keefe. Item recording.

WS R&B

- BBC WORLD SERVICE 'RHYTHM & BLUES' (later renamed 'Blues is where you hear it'), presented by Alexis Korner, produced by Jeff Griffin. Fifteen minute show based on one session, started in 1965, that ran well into early 1970s. Broadcast times varied immensely. Most sessions included here are drawn from 1968–71. For all of 1970, the sessions Jeff and Joe Young recorded for this show were borrowed and first broadcast domestically on RAVEN'S R&B (see above).

YOUNG

- JIMMY YOUNG, R1 & R2, 10am–midday, 2/10/67–onwards, produced by Doreen Davies. One or two sessions only, all from early months. Item recording.

INSTRUMENTS

g	guitar
ag	acoustic guitar
lg	lead guitar
rg	rhythm guitar
b	bass guitar
d	drums
dm	drum machine
k	keyboards
lv	lead vocals
bkv	backing vocals
gv	guitar, vocals
lgv	lead guitar, vocals
glv	guitar, lead vocals
rgv	rhythm guitar, vocals
bv	bass guitar, vocals
dv	drums, vocals
kv	keyboards, vocals
sxv	saxophone, vocals
percv	percussion, vocals
syv	synthesiser, vocals
v	vocals

A 'v' immediately after any instrument, whether separated by a comma or not, means vocals in addition.

Simple multi-instrumental abbreviations are printed closed-up, more complex credits are punctuated by commas, eg 'gkv' = guitar, keyboards, & vocals; 'k,fl,gv' = keyboards, flute, guitar & vocals.

Other instruments

In line-up credits, an instrument or vocal attribution, followed by a dash and number, indicates musician only played on identified track: eg., "Peter Zorn (al-1)" = plays alto sax on first track listed for that session only.

ab	acoustic bass guitar
acc	accordion
afd	african drums
al	alto saxophone
bal	balalaika
barh	baritone horn
bars	baritone sax
bcl	bass clarinet
bfl	bass flute
bgo	bongos
bh	bodhran
bj	banjo
blp	balaphon
bnd	bandoneon
bns	bones
bpp	bagpipes
brs	brass
bsn	bassoon
bsx	bass saxophone
btb	bass trombone
bu	bugle
bz	bouzouki
cel	celeste
cga	conga
ci	citern
cl	clarinet
clav	clavinet
clo	cello
cmp	computers
cnc	concertina
cnt	cornet
co	cor anglais
cru	crumhorn

db	double bass	picc	piccolo	
dig	didgeridoo	pn	pans	
dj	'dj'	pp	pipes	
dob	dobro	prd	band producer	
dro	drones	prg	programming	
dsc	discs	ps	pedal steel guitar	
dul	dulcimer	rec	recorder	
el	electronics	rd	reeds	
elp	electric piano	rp	rapping	
eu	euphonium	sc	scratching	
fd	fiddle	seq	sequencer	
fl	flute	sfx	special effects	
flg	flageolet	sit	sitar	
flh	flugelhorn	slg	slide guitar	
frh	french horn	smp	samples, sampling	
gg	gong	sp	spoons	
gha	ghatiam	ss	soprano saxophone	
glo	glockenspiel	str	strings	
gsy	guitar synthesiser	sty	stylophone	
hbb	human beatbox	su	surbahor	
hca	harmonica	sx	saxophone	
hmn	harmonium	sxl	saxello	
hn	horn(s)	sy	synthesiser	
hp	harp	tab	tabla	
hrp	harpsichord	tamb	tambourine	
jh	jew's harp	tb	trombone	
kor	kora	ti	timbales	
lsg	lap steel guitar	timb	timbal	
lt	lute	tmbu	tamboura	
ly	lyricon	tp	trumpet	
ma	machines	tps	tapes	
mbi	mbira	tr	triangle	
md	musical director	ts	tenor saxophone	
mel	melodica	tst	toasting	
ml	melodeon	tt	turntables	
mll	mellotron	tu	tuba	
mnd	mandolin	tym	tympani	
mnda	mandola	uk	ukelele	
mrm	marimba	vi	violin	
mx	mixing	vib	vibraphone	
ng	ngoni	vla	viola	
npp	Northumbrian pipes	wb	wobble board	
o	organ	wh	whistle	
ob	oboe	wsh	washboard	
p	piano	ww	woodwinds	
perc	percussion	xyl	xylophone	

8

STUDIOS

This list includes all studio locations which appear more than once in the Sessionography.

All BBC Studios are in London unless specified otherwise.

Non-BBC Studios are in italics.

A01	Aeolian Hall, Studio 1
A02	Aeolian Hall, Studio 2
B6	Studio B6, Broadcasting House
B15	Studio B15, Broadcasting House
BEL	BBC Belfast studios
BHM	Broadcasting House, Manchester
BRM	BBC Birmingham
CH	Concert Hall, lower ground floor, Broadcasting House
CM	The Camden Theatre, London
DWN	*Studio 1, Downtown Radio, Northern Ireland*
ED	*Eden Sound, London*
EDN	BBC Edinburgh Studios
EG2	Egton Studio 2, Egton House, Radio 1
FR	*Field recording: country as stated*
HP	The Hippodrome, Golders Green, London
KK	*Andy Kershaw's Kitchen, Crouch End, London*
LH1	Langham 1
MCR	Broadcasting House, Manchester
MR	*Moonraker Studios, Manchester*
MV1	Maida Vale 1
MV3	Maida Vale 3
MV4	Maida Vale 4
MV5	Maida Vale 5
MV6	Maida Vale 6
NW	BBC Newcastle studios
OD	*Odyssey Studios, London*
OS	'Own Studio': (exact location unknown)
PC1	201 Piccadilly, Studio 1
PH	Playhouse Theatre, Northumberland Avenue.
PHM	Playhouse Theatre, Hulme, Manchester
PRIV	*'Private Tape': (studio unknown)*

PS	Paris Cinema, Lower Regent Street
RGS	*Ron Geesin Studio*
RTE	*RTE Dublin, Eire*
S1	Studio S1, Sub-basement, Broadcasting House
S2	Studio S2, Sub-basement, Broadcasting House
S2G	Studio 2, BBC Glasgow
SS	*Strawberry Sound, Stockport, Manchester*
T1	Studio T1, Transcription Service, Kensington House, Shepherd's Bush
T2	Studio T2, Transcription Service (as above)
VS	*Vineyard Studio, London*
WX	*Wessex Studios, London*
Y2	*Yellow 2, Stockport, Manchester*

Note: for some inexplicable reason, the studio locations have been left off all Peel Session sheets for 1987 and the first half of 1988, so these have been entered as unknown. However, for those who are interested, a check with Sound Ops Group 2 has revealed that, in general, these were either Tuesdays, MV4, DG and MR; or Sundays MV5 (or occasionally MV3), DG and ME.

PRODUCERS & ENGINEERS

italics = non-BBC staff

* = Manchester sessions

† = Transcription Service

AA	Adam Askew
AC	Alison Chorley
AD	Aidan Day
ADW	Angie Dowd
AH	Allen Harris
AJ	*Andre Jacquemin*
AK	*Andy Kershaw*
AM	Andy Meeson
AP	Anthony Pugh
AR	Andrew Rogers
ARD	Alec Reid
ARV	Adrian Revill†
AS	Alan Scott
ATA	Anthony Askew
BA	Bernie Andrews
BAI	Bill Aitken
BB	Bill Bebb
BC	Bob Conduct
BH	Bob Harrison†
BJ	Barry Jordan
BN	Baz Newman
BP	Bev Phillips
BS	*Bob Sargeant*
BT	Brian Tuck
BTN	Bob Tanner
BYA	*Barry Andrews*
CB	Clive Burrows
CBM	Colin Beaumont
CCM	Charles Clarke Maxwell
CG	*Clive Gregson**
CL	Chris Lycett
CLN	Chris Lane
CML	Chris Maclean
DD	Dave Dade
DDR	Derek Drescher
DFW	David Fleming Williams*
DG	*Dale Griffin*

DGE	Don George
DH	Douglas Hart
DK	Denis O'Keefe
DM	Dave Mulkeen†
DMC	Dave McCarthy
DMI	Derek Mills
DMY	Derek Mayell
DP	Dave Price
DS	Dave Shannon*
DST	*Des Tong**
DT	Dave Tate
DTH	Dave Thomas
EL	Elizabeth Lewis
FB	Fran Barnett
FK	Fred Kay
FL	Frances Line
GB	Graham Bunce
GF	*Gerry Fitzgerald (RTE)*
GH	Geoffrey Hewitt
GJ	Graham Judd
GP	Graham Puddifoot
GPR	Gary Parker
GT	George Thomas
HP	Harry Parker
IG	Ian Grant
IS	Ian Sharp
IW	*Ian Wilson**
IWI	*Ian Wilson (RTE)*
JB	James Birtwistle
JBE	Johnny Beerling
JBN	John Boon
JBU	John Bussell
JC	John Clark
JE	John Etchells
JG	Jeff Griffin
JH	Jackie Hamilton
JHO	John Hooper
JI	Jim Isaacs
JK	John Knight
JL	John Leonard*
JLB	Julian Best

JLC	Julia Carney
JLN	John Lunn
JLO	Jonathan Leong
JLY	Jane Lyons
JM	John Muir
JMK	Julian Markham
JP	*John Porter*
JRS	James Ross
JS	John Sparrow
JSM	Jerry Smith
JT	John Taylor
JUB	Julian Best
JW	John Walters
JWH	John White
JWI	*John Owen Williams*
JWX	John Wilcox*
JY	Joe Young
KB	Keith Bateson
KBD	Kevin Bird
KH	Kevin Howlett
KJ	Keith Johnson
KR	Kevin Rumble
KS	Keith Stewart
KW	Keith Walker
LM	Louise Musgrave
LP	Larry Parker
LS	Lisa Softley
LWM	Lawrie Monk
MA	Miti Adhikari
MB	Malcolm Brown
MC	Martin Colley
MCO	Mike Costello
ME	Mike Engles
MF	Mike Franks
MFA	Mark Farrar
MG	Margaret Garrard
MH	Mike Harding
MHW	Mike Hawkes
MHY	Martyn Hayles
MP	Mike Page
MPK	Martyn Parker
MR	Mike Robinson
MRD	Mark Radcliffe (* from 87)
MS	Mike Shilling
MW	Mick Wilkojc
MWT	Mike Walter
NB	Nick Barraclough*

NBU	Neil Burn
NF	Nick Fountain
NG	Nick Gomm
NGR	Nick Griffiths
NK	Nick King
NR	Nick Russell-Pavier
PA	Paul Allen
PC	Pete Carr
PCX	Pam Cox
PD	Pete Dauncey†
PF	Paul Fahey
PH	Peter Harwood
PK	Paddy Kingsland
PL	Paul Long
PLA	*Pete Lawrence*
PRB	Paul Roberts
PR	Pete Ritzema
PRS	Phil Ross
PS	Phil Stannard
PSI	Paul Smith [London]
PSM	Paul Smith*
PW	*Peter Watts [BBC SM – 1985; freelance producer 1988–91]*
PWH	Pat Whelan
PWI	Paul Williams
PWL	Phil Ward-Large
RB	Ron Belchier
RC	Richard Crichlow
RD	Roger Derry
RE	Roger Eames
REL	Richard Ellsworth
RF	Rachel Fisher
RG	*Robin Garside**
RH	Royston Herbert
RJ	Ralph Jordan
RK	Ro Khan
RM	Robin Marks
RN	Robert 'Rab' Noakes*
RP	Roger Pusey
RPF	Rupert Flindt
RYK	Ray Kin*
SA	Simon Askew
SB	Steve Bittlestone
SBR	Steve Bridges
SC	Simon Clifford
SCO	Sue Cockburn
SF	Sarah Fletcher

SFX	Stephen Faux
SM	Sue Maillot
SN	*Stephen Nelson*
SP	*Stuart Pickering**
SR	Steve Robertshaw*
TB	Tim Blackmore
TBK	Trevor Barker
TBS	Ted Beston
TD	Tim Durham
TdB	Ted de Bono
TH	Tony Hale*
TVD	Trevor Dann
TW	Tony Wilson
TWN	Tony Worthington*

THE LAST WORD

I can't pretend that this Sessionography will ever be complete: for a start, there will have been at least another 250 sessions between Radio 1's 25th anniversary and the publication date of this book. But there may have been others from before that date that have gone missing from the files. And someone's name, somebody's Gaelic or African song title, is bound to be spelled wrong, despite my best efforts. Corrections and additions can be sent to me c/o the publishers. In the event of a second edition, or some other form of updated appendix being possible in the future, all contributions will be gratefully acknowledged

8

A CERTAIN RATIO
17/10/79 PEEL *Do the du (casse)†, All night party, Flight, The choir.* Simon Topping (v), Martin Moscrop (g), Peter Terrell (g), Jeremy Kerr (b), Donald Johnson (d). 1/10/79 MV4 TW BAI
† On 'Manchester - so much to answer for' SFRCD202.
2/7/81 PEEL *Knife slits water, Day one, Skipscada.* & Martha Lucy. 29/6/81 LHI TW DD
1/12/82 PEEL *Who's to say?, Piu lento, Touch.* Andy Connell (k,perc) joins. 20/11/82 MV4 DG MPK
2/4/83 LONG *I need someone tonight, Si fermir or grido, Don't worry about a thing, Shack up.* * 28/3/83 PHM cJL PSM
7/8/89 CAMPBELL *River's edge, The big E, Backs to the wall, Your blue eyes.* Johnson, Kerr, Moscrop; & Anthony Quigley (ss,k), Flo McSweeney (bkv). 28/6/89 ED HP MPK

ABACUSH
3/1/84 JENSEN *Batta-dem, One day, Pot a cook, Sodom & Gomorah.* Juda, Jena & Peneay (v), Skid Dim (b), Christos (g), Zanz (sx), Zion (d), Mikey (g), Zeb (o,p). 8/12/83 MV4 JP HP

ABANA BA NASERY
28/7/91 KERSHAW *Mapenzi kama karata, Tumeubeba msalaba, Abasiani babulano, Abebunangwe lelo lekhe.* Shem Tube (gv), Justo Omofila (gv), Enos Okola (v, 'bottle scrape'). 4/7/91 MV5 DG JB&EL
9/5/92 KERSHAW *Atisa wangu, Esimiti Khusilenje, Esiesi Siolle, Abakambi, Sumila Omusiele (& Tumeubeba musaldba, Abakhasi bano, Abebi betsingombe, Sowena:* on PEEL later same night). Live from on-air studios.

ABANDON CITY
11/1/85 FRI. ROCK *This won't Hurt, Heavy traffic, When your time comes, Shernlan under my chair.* Adam Smallman, Mark Davis, Shaun Winslow, Philip Ball, Simon Wake. Rec. date unknown MV4 TW DD

MICK ABRAHAMS' BAND
21/11/70 RAVEN'S R&B *Greyhound bus, The way you look, Blues for Ekim Nevar.* Mick Abrahams (gv) & probably: Bob Sargeant (kv), Walt Monahan (b), Ritchie Dharma (d). Files missing. 28/10/70 * JG JY
11/12/70 BLACK *Greyhound bus, Big queen, How can you love me so, Seasons.* 25/11/70 * JM JWH
10/4/71 TOP GEAR *Not to re-arrange, Seasons, Winds of change.* 30/3/71 * JW BC
21/5/71 BLACK *Why do you do me this way, Burning rain blues, Seasons (& Not to re-arrange, 18/6/71).* 19/4/71 * JM *
31/8/71 HARDING *Let me love you baby, You'll never get it from me, Am I blue.* 23/8/71 * MB MH&MF
4/2/72 PEEL *The good old days, Let me love you baby, Absent friends (& Whole wide world, 17/3/72).* 12/1/72 * JW BC
14/9/72 DRUMMOND *Let's get down to business, Boogie train, Cat squirrel, Can't take it anymore.* 4/9/72 * MB MH&MF
10/11/72 SEQUENCE *Let's get down to business, See my way, Cat squirrell.* 19/9/72 TI PD JWH&BAI

THE ABS
8/7/87 PEEL *Grease your Ralph, Hand me down, Fear is the key, Same mistake twice.* Bas (gv), Bryn (gv), Buzz (b), The Rev (d). 28/6/87 * DG ME&MC
9/2/88 PEEL *Rock your tits off!, Concrete hits bone, Ideetapoo!, Cunkers in my cleft. 'Fatty Ashtray' (b).* 31/1/88 * DG JB&ME

AC TEMPLE
29/7/87 PEEL *Blowtorch, Mincemeat, Fraud, America.* Jane Bromley (v), Noel Kilbride (g,v-1,4), Neil Woodward (g), Andy Hartley (b), Jayne Waterfall (d). 19/7/87 * DG MS&MA

AC/DC
21/6/76 PEEL *Live wire, High voltage, Can I sit next to you?, Little lover.* Angus Young (lg), Malcolm Young (rg), Mark Evans (b), Philip Rudd (d), Bon Scott (lv). 3/6/76 MV4 TW *

ACCEPT
19/8/83 FRI. ROCK *Fast as a shark, Princess of the dawn, Son of a bitch, Flash rocking man.* Wolf Hoffman (g), Herman Frank (g), Steffan Kaufmann (d), Peter Baltes (b), Udo Dirkschneider (v). 3/7/83 Dierks Studios, Cologne TW Lou Austin &DD

ACCORDIONS GO CRAZY
6/7/88 L. KERSHAW *Dance the zydeco, Rock'n roll music, Get rich quick, Private number.* Mike Adcock (p,acc,v), Clive Bell (acc,wsh,wh,v), Dean Speedwell (dv), Nicola Hadley (acc,v), Sylvia Hallett (vi,tb,v), Stuart Jones (bv). 3/7/88 MV4 TdB JB

ACE
12/11/74 PEEL *24 hours, I ain't gonna stand for this no more, Rock & roll runaway, I know how it feels.* Paul Carrack (kv), Alan 'Bam' King (g), Phil Harris (g), Tex Comer (b), Fran Byrne (d). 22/10/74 MV4 TW BAI
2/12/74 HARRIS *Why, How long, Know how it feels, Satellite.* 20/11/74 MV4 JG *
31/3/75 PEEL *Sail on my brother, Get ready, Ain't that peculiar, Ain't gonna stand for this no more.* 25/3/75 MV4 TW BAI

DAVID ACKLES
27/10/68 TOP GEAR *Down river, Laissez faire, When love is gone (& Road to Cairo, Be my friend, 24/1/68).* David Ackles & (o), (hmn), (d), 2 (ag) unknown. 1/10/68 PCI BA AH&BC

ACT FUSELI
30/6/84 LONG *Autumn stallions, Behind de clouds, Solange, The deeds.* Dawn Lanton (gv), Steve West (ob), Tony Gammage (clo), Francis Danby (perc). 11/6/84 PHM DS *

ACTION PACT
22/2/82 PEEL *People, Losers, Suicide bag, Mindless aggression, Cowslick blues.* Joe Fungus (d), Dr Phibes (b), Wild Planet (g), George (v). 6/2/82 MV4 DG MR&MC
16/8/82 PEEL *Times must change, Drowning out the big jets, Fools' factions, These are a few..., Protest is alive, Fouled on the footpath.* 7/8/82 MV4 DG MR
4/5/83 JENSEN *Question of choice, The cruellest thief, Gothic party-time, New kings girl.* Sheet says 'Grimly Fiendish' (d), 'Herman' (b,bkv). 24/4/83 MV4 DG ME

ACTION SWINGERS
8/5/92 PEEL *You want my action, Kicked in the head, Hot rock action, Lexicon devil.* Bob Bert (d), Colin Todd (b), Bruce Bennett (g), Ned Hayden (gv). 22/3/92 MV3 DG SA&EL

ACTORS AND FAMOUS PEOPLE
20/3/84 JENSEN *Waterloo, Shape of things, On and on, Promised land.* Nigel Brittain (d), Chris Rowland (b), Martyn Shouler (g), Dave Greenfield (g,bkv), Nigel Allen (k), Mike Brizel (sx), Anne Wilbourn (v). 11/3/84 MV5 DG ME

ADAM AND THE ANTS
30/1/78 PEEL *Deutscher girls, Puerto-Rican, It doesn't matter†, Lou†.* Kurt Van Den Bogarde (Andy Warren) (b), Johnny Bivouac (g), Dave Barbe (d), Adam Ant (glv), Jordan (lv-4 only). 23/1/78 MV4 TW DD
17/7/78 PEEL† *You're so physical, Cleopatra, Friends, I'm a xerox.* Matthew Ashman (rg,p) r. Bivouac; Adam (sty); Jordan out. 10/7/78 MV4 TW DD
2/4/79 PEEL† *Table talk, Liggotage, Animals and men, Never trust a man with egg on his face.* Adam (g-4 only). 26/3/79 MV4 TW BAI&MPK
†† on Strange Fruit SFRCD115.

ADAMSKI
20/2/90 PEEL *Something is happening, Genetic NRG, Rap you in the sound.* Adamski (k,prg). 2/2/90 MV3 DG MA

ADICTS
5/12/79 PEEL *Get addicted, Distortion, Numbers, Sensitive.* Monkey (lv), Mel Ellis (gv), Pete Davison (gv), Kid Dee (dv), Tim Hocking (bv). 20/11/79 MV4 JS MR

ADORABLE
1/6/92 GOODIER *Homeboy, Seasick martyr, Glorious, Summerside.* Robert Dillam (g), Piotr Fijalkowski (gv), Stephen Williams (b), Kevin Gritton (d). 9/5/92 MV4 MC~ JMK

THE ADULT NET
27/10/86 LONG *Waking up in the sun, Spin this web, Sea of rain, Been around.* Brix Smith (gv), O. Kipling (g,k), Ian Broudie (b,d). 1/10/86 MV4 BYA TD

THE ADVENTURES
18/7/85 INTO THE MUSIC *Love in chains, Feel the raindrops, Always, Two rivers.* Paul Crowder (d), Tony Ayre (b), Pat Gribben (gv), Jonathan Whitehead (k), Terry Sharpe (v), Eileen Gribben (v), Spud Murphy (v). 22/6/85 MV4 DG MC
10/10/88 CAMPBELL *Broken land, Trip to bountiful, Drowning in the sea of love, One step from heaven.* & Bob White (pp). 28/9/88 MV4 HP MPK
19/3/90 CAMPBELL *Your greatest shade of blue, Washington deceased, Heaven knows which way, Love's lost town.* Gribben, Gribben, Sharpe, Ayre, Whitehead, & Downs Thompson (vi), Martin Hughes (d) 28/2/90 MV4 PW MPK

THE ADVERTS
29/4/77 PEEL† *Quickstep, Looking through Gary Gilmore's eyes°, One chord wonders, New boys, Bored teenagers.* Laurie Driver (d), Gaye Advert (b,bkv), Howard Pickup (g,bkv), TV Smith (lv). 25/4/77 MV4 TW BAI
† on Strange Fruit SFPS034; ° also on 'Winters of Discontent' SFRCD204.
30/8/77 PEEL *We who wait, New church, Safety in numbers, The great British mistake.* 22/8/77 MV4 MB MR
11/9/78 PEEL *Fate of criminals, Television's over, Love songs, Back from the dead, I surrender.* Rod Latter (d) r. Driver. 21/8/78 MV4 TW DD
12/11/79 PEEL *The adverts, I looked at the sun, Cast of thousands, I will walk you home.* Tim Cross (kv), Paul Martinez (g), Nick Martinez (d) r. Pickup, Latter. 16/10/79 MV4 JS MR

AFFINITY
10/4/70 BLACK *Little lonely man, Three sisters, Mr. Joy, Day in the life.* Lynton Naiff, Grant Serpall, Mike Jopp, Mike Foster, Linda Hoile. 6/3/70 AO2 JM *
23/9/70 R2 NIGHT RIDE *Jumping Jack Flash, I am and so are you, I am a walrus, United States of mind, Three sisters, Night flight.* 2/9/70 MV4 DMY *
4/12/70 BLACK *United States of mind, Coconut grove, Yes man, All along the watchtower (& Night flight, 1/1/70).* 18/11/70 AO2 JM *

AFT
8/11/76 PEEL *Race horses, The great panjandrum wheel part II.* Paul Macdonnell (g), Bob Cross (g), David Ball (d), Trevor Darks (b). 21/10/76 MV4 TW BAI

AGAIN AGAIN
20/12/78 PEEL *Beached, Scarred for life, Here we go, Self employed.* Rob Hutchings (v), Jeff Pountain (rg), Mark Mabon (lg), Roger Payne (b), Mark Broad (d). 12/12/78 MV4 TW MR

AGE OF CHANCE
29/10/85 PEEL *Mob! Hut!, The going going gone man, The morning after the sixties, I don't know and I don't care.* Jan Penny (g), Geoff Taylor (b), Neil Howbs (g), Stevie Elvidge (v). 6/10/85 MV5 DG GB

23/6/86 PEEL *Be fast be clean be cheap, How the west was won, From now on this will be your god, Kiss.* 10/6/86 MV4 MR&FK

4/2/87 LONG *Shut up and listen, Hold on, Who's afraid of the big bad noise, The bible of the motor city beat.* 25/1/87 MV4 JE TdB

13/10/87 LONG *The story of crush collision, We got trouble, Ready or not here we come, D.J. Powercut gets even!* & DJ Powercut (tt). 16/9/87 MV4 HP MPK&MA

AGONY COLUMN
20/6/79 PEEL *Home movies, Dietitian, Love is a blanket expression, Losing my lust.* Malcolm Raeburn (v), Ian Heywood (gv), Bri Tag (b), Jon Rust (d). 12/6/79 MV4 TVD MR

AIRHEAD
20/1/92 GOODIER *Counting sheep, Funny how, They don't know, I might fall.* Michael Wallis (gv), Steve Marshall (k), Ben Kesteven (b), Sam Kesteven (d). 4/1/92 MV4 MC~ FK

AIRRACE
15/11/84 INTO THE MUSIC *I don't care, Do you want my love again, Promised to call, Brief encounter.* Keith Murrell (v), Laurie Mansworth (g), Jim Reid (b), Toby Sadler (k), Jason Bonham (d). 3/11/84 MV4 DG MC

AIRSTREAM
21/10/91 GOODIER *Dream of you, Follow through, Stay with me, Airstream.* Cymon Eckel (v), Jon Male (lg), Rob Wells (rg), Mick Bond (b), Richard Van Spall (k), Martin Duffy (k). 14/9/91 MV5 MC~ CML

BILL AITKEN
8/12/75 PEEL *Chimney pots, Sequel, Ghosts of yesterday, Open up your eyes.* Bill Aitken (all instruments: ag, g, b, sy, o, d, perc, v). 6/75 PRIV BAI BAI

LAUREL AITKEN
12/5/80 PEEL *Big fat man, Rudi got married, Jesse James, Rock me baby/Caledonia.* Laurel Aitken (o,v), Paul Fox (g,bkv), Gary Barnacle (sx,o), Segs (b), Dave Duffy (d,bkv), Malcolm Owen (bkv). 28/4/80 MV4 TW DD

AKABU
28/10/86 LONG *Live up, Motherless children, Work, Life in the ghetto.* Valerie Skeete (v,lg), Vyris Edghill (v), Barbara Grossett (rgv), Caroline Wiliams (k), Collette Coke (k), Diane White (b), Salomi Coke (d). 7/9/86 MV4 BYA *

AHMAD AL-KHLAIL & HAMID MOHAMMED
19/2/69 NIGHT RIDE *Music from Hacha, Nasma, Halla yum abit, Dancing of the north.* * 12/2/69 SI JM *

THE ALARM
23/2/83 JENSEN *68 guns, Unsafe building, Up for murder, We are the light.* Mike Peters (lv,b-1,2), Dave Sharp (gv), Eddie MacDonald (gv,b-3), Nigel Twist (d). 13/2/83 MV4 DG ME

21/5/83 LONG *Legal matter, Third light, What kind of hell, 68 guns.* 16/5/83 PHM cJL TWN
    Contracts suggest sessions recorded for Peter Powell 6/5/83; and Mike Smith, 19/8/83.

15/11/83 JENSEN *Howling wind, Unbreak the promise, One step closer to home (excerpts), Walk forever by my side.* & Alan Shacklock (p). 6/11/83 MV4 DG ME

31/12/83 SAT. LIVE *Declaration, 'Unknown', Deceiver, Blaze of glory, The stand, Where were you hiding when the storm broke.* Live from S2 MRD TdB

25/9/89 GOODIER *Sold me down the river, Devolution working man's blues, Prison without prison bars.* & Mark Taylor (k,bkv). 17/9/89 OD PW TdB

7/5/91 CAMPBELL *Rockin' in the free world, The wind blows away my words, Moments in time, Spirit of '76, God save somebody.* 17/4/91 MV5 PW JB

ALASKA
27/1/84 FRI. ROCK *Coupe de ville, Heart of the storm, Headlines, Sorcerer.* John Marter (d), Brian Badhams (b), Richard Bailey (k), Robbie Hawthorne (v), Bernie Marsden (g). 13/1/84 MV4 TW DD

ALBERTO Y LOST TRIOS PARANOIAS
16/9/77 PEEL *Kill, Gobbing on life, Snuffing in a Babylon, Sid's song, Death of rock and roll.* Bruce Mitchell (d), Tony Bowers (gvb), Bob Harding (gvb), Simon White (g), Chris Lee (bv, other things), Les Pryor (mouth), Jimmy Hibbert (gv, sex appeal). 14/9/77 MV4 MB NG

ALBION COUNTRY BAND
4/7/72 PEEL *New St.George/St. Anne's reel, Rambling sailor, Morris dance tune medley: Morris on, Jockey to the fair, Room for the cuckoo, Princess royal, Morris off.* Tiger H. (bv), Simon Nicol (gv), Dave Mattacks (d), Steve Ashley (wh,hca,rec), Sue Draheim (fd), Royston Wood (v). 19/6/72 PH JW BC

1/3/73 PEEL *I was a young man, The gallant poacher, Medley: Mouresque, London pride, Maid of the hill, So selfish runs the hare, Sheriff's ride.* Hutchings, Nicol, John Kirkpatrick (mnd,cnc,v), Sue Harris (ob,v), Martin Carthy (g,bj,v), Roger Swallow (perc). 19/2/73 LHI BA BC

21/5/73 HARRIS *The new St. George, Harvest home/The gas almost works, I'll go and 'list for a soldier (& Hanged I shall be, not broadcast).* 9/5/73 LHI PR BAI

6/9/76 PEEL *An Estampie, Hopping down in Kent, The horses' brawl, Old Sir Simon the king.* Now 'Albion Dance Band': Hutchings, Mattacks, Nicol, Shirley Collins (v), Eddie Upton (v), John Rodd (cnc), John Sothcott (fd), Phil Pickett (ww), Michael Gregory (d). 22/7/76 MV4 TW BAI

8/6/77 PEEL *Holm's fancy/Cuckolds all awry (instrumental), Poor old horse, Postman's knock, Bourreé (instrumental).* Hutchings, Nicol, Pickett, Gregory, Mattacks, John Tams (lv,ml), Graeme Taylor (g,bkv,elp), Ric Sanders (fd). 31/5/77 MV4 JG MR

20/4/78 PEEL *Time to ring some changes, Rainbow over the hill, Down the road, Albion sunrise/Uncle Bernard's/Bacup tune/Jenny Lind.* Billed just as 'The Albion Band': & Peter Bullock (sy). 11/4/78 MV4 MB *

ALIEN
14/5/89 KERSHAW *Sing in she party, You too rude, Pump it up, Paramin girls.* Alien (v), Lenny Hadaway (g,bkv), Fred Nicholas (b,bkv), Colin Graham (tp), Simon Gunton (tb), Julien Martin (sy). 27/4/89 WX DG NG

ALIEN SEX FIEND
15/5/84 PEEL *Attack, Dead and buried, Hee haw, Ignore the machine.* Nick Fiend (v), Mrs Fiend (sy), Johnny Haha (d), Rodney (g). 2/5/84 MV5 RP NG

3/9/84 PEEL *In God we trust, E.S.T-trip to the moon, Boneshaker baby.* Sheet says 'Yaxi' (g). 25/8/84 * DG MC

ALISHA
6/1/72 DRUMMOND *The harvest, Adam in exile, The dream, The friends (& High street, 24/2/72).* Alisha (ag,v). 22/12/71 MV4 MB *
    'A well-to-do busking lady with an unusual voice and a well-mastered yodelling capacity' Malcolm Brown's report to Audition panel.

ALKATRAZZ
6/8/82 FRI. ROCK *Long time no love, Miles away, Blinded, Communication.* Bob Jenner (g), Craig Stevens (v), Nick Parsons (d), Philip Tame (b), Kirk Pinkney (k). Rec. date unknown * TW DD

ALL ABOUT EVE
26/8/87 LONG *Every angel, Wild hearted woman, In the meadow, Martha's harbour.* Andy Cousin (b), Tim Bricheno (g), Julianne Regan (v), Mark Price (d). 5/8/87 MV4 HP MPK&MP

TERRY ALLEN AND THE PANHANDLE MYSTERY BAND
15/5/86 KERSHAW *Amarillo highway, New Delhi freight train, Give me a ride to heaven, Blue Asian reds.* Terry Allen (pv), Pete Dennis (bv), Bryn Burrows (dv), B. J. Cole (ps), Barry Martin (gv). 29/4/86 Y2 JL&NB SR

ALLEZ ALLEZ
8/9/81 PEEL *Turn up the meter, Papa was, Stripped portrait.* Sarah Osborne (v), Robbie Bindels (d), Roland Bindi (perc), Nico Fransolet (g), Paul Delnoy (b), Christian Debusscher (g). 29/8/81 MV4 DG MC

THE ALLIANCE
4/4/86 FRI. ROCK *We are strangers, Keep in touch, No broken hearts, Trying to forget.* * 7/3/86 MV4 TW *

THE ALMIGHTY
22/9/89 FRI. ROCK *Power, Wild & wonderful, Destroyed, Thunderbird.* Ricky Warwick (gv), Stump Monroe (d), Floyd London (b), Tantrum (lg). 25/8/89 MV5 TW MC

MARC ALMOND
24/2/83 PEEL *Empty eyes, The bulls, Once was, Your aura.* Marc Almond (v) & the Mambas: Ann Hogan (k), Lee Jenkinson (b,bkv), Matt Johnson (g,bkv), & the Venomettes: Ann Stevenson & Virginia Hews (vi), Martin McCarrick (clo,v), Bill McGee (db). 1/2/83 MV4 DD

2/7/84 GREY *Ugly head, Joey Demento, Hell was a city, Black mountain blues.* & The Willing Sinners: McGee, Hogan, McCarrick, Richard Riley (gv), Gary Barnacle (sx), Enrico Tomasso (flh,tp), Steve Humphries (d). 10/6/84 MV5 DG ME

28/1/85 LONG *Always, Traumas traumas traumas, Broken-hearted beautiful, Love and little white lies.* Mark Lockhart (sx) r. Barnacle; Tomasso out. 16/1/85 MV5 DG MPK

2/9/85 LONG *I who never, My candle burns, Medley: Unchain my heart/Black heart.* Tomasso returns; Lockhart out. 18/8/85 HP BYA SC

ALONE AGAIN OR
16/6/84 LONG *Sunshine jazz, Drum the beat, Only, Love takes time.* * 4/6/84 PHM c.PWL *

ALTAN
17/3/88 KERSHAW *Three highlands, Paddy's trip to Scotland-Pinky's-Battlefield, Mo Chleamhnas, Tuirse mo chroi.* Mairead ni Mhaonaigh (vi,v), Paul O'Shaughnessy (vi), Mark Kelly (g), Frank Kennedy (fl), Ciaran Curran (bz). 11/2/88 MV4 DG MWT&JBN

ALTERED IMAGES
14/10/80 PEEL *Beckoning strings, Legionnaire (instrumental), Insects, Dead pop stars.* Clare Grogan (v), Caesar (g), Tony McDaid (g), Johnny McElhone (b), Michael 'Tich' Anderson (d). 7/10/80 MV4 JS MR

10/3/81 PEEL *A day's wait, Idols, Midnight, Jeepster.* 2/3/81 LHI DG DD

23/4/81 SKINNER *Disco pop stars, Sentimental, Who cares, Leave me alone.* & Jim (g). 10/4/81 LHI DG TdB

22/9/81 PEEL *Yellow and it might, Pinky blue, Little brown head, Song sung blue.* Caesar out; & The Allneds (bkv-4). 4/9/81 MV4 DG HP

22/3/82 JENSEN *I could be happy, Forgotten, Love and kisses, See you later.* 14/3/82 MV4 DG ME

ALTERN 8
24/11/91 PEEL *Frequency (sample 8 mix), Give it to baby, Say it ya'll, Activ 8 (LA song mix).* Chris Peat, Mark Archer. 27/10/91 MV3 DG ME&BJ

ALTERNATIVE TV
12/12/77 PEEL *Action Time Vision, Still life, Love lies limp, Life after life.* Mark Perry (gv), Dennis Burns (b), Chris Bennett (d), Kim Turner (g). 5/12/77 MV4 TW DD

27/7/78 PEEL *Nasty little lonely, Going round in circles, Release the natives, The good missionary.* Mick Linehan (g), r. Bennett, Turner. 17/7/78 MV4 TW DD

AMAYENGE

12/7/88 PEEL† *Chibuyubuyu, Munise munise, Free Nelson Mandela, Filiukotuleya.* Peter Banda (d), Darius Mwelwa (gv), John Mwanza (g), Adrick Silokomela (k), Davy Mwape (bv), Kris Chali (lv), Charles Kangwa, Michael Chewe, Francis Zimba, Chanda Kama (afd), Mwangala Mubiana, Alice Mumba (bkv). 5/7/88 MV4 MR~
† on Strange Fruit SFPS067.

6/9/88 PEEL *Madzela madzela, Mbikulo, Children of Africa.* & Alica Mwenge, Irady Lungu, Ajessy Bwalya (v). 11/8/88 MV4 DG MA

AMAZING BAND

17/10/70 TOP GEAR *Find, Amazing march.* Mal Dean (tp), Rob Spall (vi,acc), Top Topham (g), George Jenson (b), Ken Hyder (perc), Mick Brannan (al), Miriam Spall (v). 29/9/70 MV4 JW BC

'A band concerned with experiments in free improvisation; can hardly be failed as there is no real yardstick to measure them by' Walters to Audition unit. Failed: 'Pretentious...boring...a musical confidence trick...rubbish of the first order'.

THE AMAZING BLONDEL

9/1/71 FOLK ON 1 *Willow wood, Springseason, Pavan, Old Moot Hall, Bethelowtn Mission, St. Crispin's day, Love sonnet, Lady Marion's galliard.* John D. Gladwin (lt,db,lv), Edward Baird (lt,g), Terry Wincott (ww,lt,hmn, pp, cru). 29/12/70 * FL *

11/3/71 HENRY *Spring season, Old Moot hall, Pavan, Lady Marion's galliard.* 3/3/71 * MB *

24/5/71 HARRIS *Willow wood, Shepherd song, Almaine.* 4/5/71 TI JM JWH

2/9/71 DRUMMOND *Fantasie lindum.* 25/8/71 * MB *

AMAZULU

7/7/82 PEEL *Fussin' 'n' fightin', Cairo, Neya neya, Amazulu, You'll never walk alone.* Rose Minor (lv), Sharon Bailey (perc), Lesley Beach (sx), Margo Sagov (g), Clare Kenny (b), Debbie Evans (d). 5/6/82 MV4 DG PS

17/1/83 PEEL *Cairo, Tonto, Brixton, Smiley stylee.* Annie Radok (v) r. Minor, Nardo (dv) r. Evans. 8/1/83 MV4 DG MC

23/3/83 JENSEN *Fussin' & fightin', Amazulu, Upright forward looking fashion, The good lord said.* 20/2/83 MV4 DG ME

16/7/83 LONG *Brixton, Cairo, Smilee stylee, Only love.* 4/7/83 PHM c.JL PSM

19/9/83 JENSEN *Point blank, Only love, Moonlight romance, Don't do it.* 8/9/83 MV4 JP MR

THE AMEN CORNER

22/10/67 TOP GEAR *Let the good times roll, Beauty is skin deep, In the pocket, The world of broken hearts, Open the door to your heart, A man's temptation.* Andy Fairweather-Low, Neil Jones, Blue Weaver, Dennis Bryon, Alan Jones, Clive Taylor, Mike Smith, & 2 trumpets. 18/10/67 * * PR

7/1/68 TOP GEAR *I don't want to discuss it, Bend me shape me, The duck, Satisnok the job's worth, Shake a tailfeather.* & 2 trumpets.
1/1/68 * * PR [M: several for Pop North, Summer 68].

AMERICA

28/12/70 HARRIS *James Holiday, Rainy day, Riverside.* Daniel Milton Peek, Lee Mertin Bunnell, Gerald Linford Beckley (all gv). 11/12/70 MV5 JM JWH

19/7/71 HARRIS *Riverside, Sandman, I need you, Three roses, Never found the time.* 24/6/71 TI JM *

14/10/71 DRUMMOND *Desert song, California, Sandman, I need you.* 4/10/71 MV5 MB *

24/10/71 SPEAKEASY *Riverside, I need you, A horse with no name, California.* 22/10/71 Recorded at King's College, Hendon. TB *

AMON DUUL II

29/5/73 PEEL *Marnana, Green bubble raincoat man, Dem guten schonen wahren, The trap.* Renate Kanupp (v), Chris Karrer (p,g), John Weinzierl (g), Danny Fischelscher (d), Peter Leopold (d), Falk Rogner (k). 8/5/73 A02 JW BC

TORI AMOS

16/12/91 CAMPBELL *China, Silent all these years, Leather, Winter.* Tori Amos (pv). 30/10/91 MV4 PW MPK

ANACONDA

17/5/85 FRI. ROCK *Running time, The loser, Heaven is full, Centurion.* Derek Hall (lg,bkv), Kenny McKay (rg), Ian Crockert (b,lv), David McRoberts (d). 12/4/85 MV4 TW DD

AND ALSO THE TREES

26/4/84 PEEL *There was a man of double deed, Wallpaper dying, Impulse of man, The secret sea.* Simon Jones (v), Joe Jones (g), Steve Burrows (b), Nick Havas (d). 7/4/84 MV5 DG MC

IAN A. ANDERSON

21/8/68 NIGHT RIDE *It's hard times, Little boy blue, Rowdy blues, That's all right, Crazy fool woman.* Ian A. Anderson (gv), Steve Rye (hca). 14/8/68 SI DK *

11/10/69 WS R&B *Edges, Paint it black, My babe she ain't nothing but a doggone crazy fool mumble, Mousehunt, Book of changes.* Anderson & John Turner (b), Al Jones (g), Dave Jeffs (fl,hca) (4-Anderson solo). 17/9/69 MV4 JG JY

24/5/70 RAVEN's R&B *Ginger man, Silent night No.2, Edges, The man in the high castle, Please re-adjust your time.* & Ian Hunt only. 8/5/70 * JG JY

3/4/72 HARRIS *Edges, One more chance, Silent night no.2, (& Pretty Peggy O, 8/5/72).* Solo. 14/3/72 MV5 JG BC

13/5/74 HARRIS *A sign of the times, Marie Celeste on down, Baby let me follow you.* Ian A. Anderson's Hot Vultures: self & Margaret Anderson (b). 20/3/74 LH1 PR *

MILLER ANDERSON

21/9/71 HARDING *High tide high water, Alice mercy, Ship to nowhere, To whom it may concern.* Miller Anderson (gv), & 4 unknown (o,p) (b) (d) (fl). 13/9/71 MV5 MB MH&MF

7/1/72 PEEL *Corina corina, Blackbird, Ship to nowhere.* Solo. 13/12/71 TI JM&PD JWH&BAI

13/4/72 DRUMMOND *Mr Horizontal, Monopoly, On a ship to nowhere, Fool's gold.* 12/4/72 MV4 MB MH&MF

21/7/72 PEEL *It takes a lot to laugh it takes a train to cry, Fool's gold, Garden of life, Shadows across my wall.* 20/6/72 TI JM JWH

HARVEY ANDREWS

15/8/72 PEEL *Gift of a brand new day, Unaccompanied, Hey Sunday, I used to revolve at 78 rpm but now it's down to 33.3rpm, Don't know the time.* Harvey Andrews (gv). 17/7/72 PH JW BC&MF

29/12/72 SEQUENCE *Requiem, Gift of a brand new day, Writer of songs, Sweet little fat girl, Unaccompanied.* 28/11/72 TI JM NG

HARVEY ANDREWS AND GRAHAM COOPER

25/5/73 SEQUENCE *Anna my love, Whisky Jack, Down so long it feels like up, For my father.* Harvey Andrews (gv), Graham Cooper (gv). 3/5/73 LH1 JM BAI&MG

14/6/73 PEEL *Whisky Jack, The mallard, Down so long it feels like up, Headlines.* 21/5/73 * * *

ANDROMEDA

17/11/68 TOP GEAR *The reason, Looking for you, Day of the change, Return to sanity.* John Cann (gv), Mick Hawkesworth (bv), Jack Collings (d). 29/10/68 PC1 BA AH

ANDWELLA'S DREAM

1/5/70 BLACK *Just how long, I gotta woman, Hold on to your mind (& Shadow of the night, 26/6/70).* Dave Lewis (p,o,fl,g), Nigel Smith (b,hp), Gordon Barton (d), David McDougall. 20/3/70 A02 JM *

ANGELIC UPSTARTS

30/10/78 PEEL *We are the people, Student power, Upstart,* Youth leader. Mensi (lv), Mond (g), Steve (b), Sticks (d). 24/10/78 MV4 JE MR

1/10/80 PEEL *Guns for the Afghan rebels, Last night another soldier, Kids on the street, Sticks' diary.* Glyn Warren (b) r. Steve. 17/9/80 MV4 DG NG

29/6/81 PEEL *Two million voices, You're nicked, I understand (Pt.3), New values.* Decca Wade (d) r. Sticks, & Simon Lloyd (sx). 23/6/81 LH1 DG MR

ANGELS 1-5

8/7/81 PEEL *Cut and dried, Accident in studio 4, Living for the future, Workface.* Cressida Bowyer (v), Jimmy Cauty (gv), John Cook (bv), Martin Cottis (d). 1/7/81 LH1 CL NG
'That was the last session I went along to,' says Peel; 'I think because the woman singer had been in another band we'd liked before. Now what were they called? ...er...er....' This was also, coincidentally, the last Peel session recorded in Langham 1.

ANGELWITCH

14/3/80 FRI. ROCK *Sweet danger, Angel of death, Extermination day, Angelwitch.* Kevin Heybourne (g,lv), Kevin Riddles (b,bkv,k), Dave Hogg (d,bkv). 20/2/80 * TW *

ANHREFN

4/8/86 PEEL *Action man, Dawns y duwiau, Defaid, Nefoedd un.* Sion Sebon (gv), Rhys Mwyn (b), Dewi Gwyn (g), Hefin Huws (d,bkv). 22/7/86 * DG MR&MS

11/9/89 PEEL *Rude boys, Crafwr, Bach by Ben, Gwesty Cymru.* 8/8/89 MV3 DG MA

ANIMAL MAGIC

2/2/82 PEEL *No sex in heaven, Get it right, Human being, Standard man.* Gill Baker (tp), Rob Boswell (d), Mark Hollis (sx), Mark Tayler (b), James Hill (perc), Howard Purse (gv). 20/1/82 MV4 KH *

14/4/82 JENSEN *Love makes the world go square, Standard man, Life, Guilt.* 1/4/82 MV5 JS MR

ANIMAL MAGNET

26/10/81 JENSEN *Saturday night special, Amor, Survival of the fittest, Game over player one.* Richard Magnet (v), Paul Animal (k), Adrian Chilvers (b), Bosco D'Oliveira (perc), Matthew Whambam (d); & Kevin Byrd (g-2 only). 18/10/81 MV4 DG ME&MC

ANIMAL NIGHTLIFE

2/11/83 JENSEN *Mint condition, Sharkfin soup, The lesson, Love street.* Paul Waller (d), Steve Shawley (b), Flid (g), Mac (perc), Declan John Barclay (tp), John Critchinson (p), Billy Chapman (sx), Dee C. Lee (bkv), Andy Polaris (lv). 13/10/83 MV4 JP TdB

ANNA

10/8/92 GOODIER *MMC/Icon, Still remain, Magic feather, Coming down.* Pete Uglow (gv), Daren Lynch (g), Philip Lynch (b), Cormac Stokes (dv). 18/7/92 MV4 MC~ AA

ANOTHER PRETTY FACE

25/2/81 PEEL *This time it's real, Lightning that strikes twice, Out of control, I'll give you fire.* John Cattwell (g,vi,bkv), Adrian Johnston (d), Alan Muir (b), Mike Scott (v,p,g,vi), Paul Connelly (handclaps). 18/2/81 LH1 CL NG

ANY TROUBLE

6/3/80 PEEL *Girls are always right, Turn up the heat, Second choice, Yesterday's love.* Mal Harley (d), Phil Barnes (b), Clive Gregson (glv), Chris Parks (lg). 27/2/80 MV4 JE NG

APB

11/1/82 PEEL *My love, Higher the climb, Crooner's lullabye, From you and back to you.* Iain Slater (bv), Glenn Roberts (gv), George Cheyne (dv). 23/12/81 MV4 JWI *

2/6/82 JENSEN *Danceability, Crazy grey†, Stop before I go, Out of town.* Nick Jones (perc) joins. 23/5/82 MV4 DG ME
† On Albion 12-inch ION160.

5/1/83 PEEL *Got it in one, Play it, Wondering, Back inside your heart.* 13/12/82 MV4 TW DD

9/5/83 JENSEN *Love and learn, One day, Partners in love.* 1/5/83 MV4 DG ME

24/8/83 Powell *Hypnotic love affair, Don't close the door, Take me to a good place.* [NB. This broadcast date could be unreliable] 9/8/83 MV4 * *

12/4/84 Jensen *What kind of girl, You can't have her, Something to believe in, So many broken hearts.* Mike Craighead (perc) r. Jones. 29/3/84 MV5 JP MPK

THE APOLLINAIRES

25/8/82 Peel *First degree, The feeling's gone, Envy the love, Dance with your heart.* Francis Brown (g), Tom Brown (g), Simon Kirk (perc), Kraig Thurnbar(d), James Hunt (b), Paul Tickle (v); & Chris (tp), Pete (sx), Lawrence (sx), Paul (tb), Stephen (fl). 12/7/82 MV4 TW MC

APRIL 16TH

3/6/88 Fri. Rock *She's mean, Sleepwalking, Let it roll, Rattlesnake shakedown.* Dave Russell, Chris Harris, John Fisher, Lawrence Mills, Eric Puffett. 20/5/88 * HP DD

ARC

13/3/71 Top Gear *Guru, Hello Monday, Great Lager Street.* Mickey Gallagher (elp,o,v), John Turnbull (lgv), Rob Tait (d), Tom Duffy (bv). 1/3/71 PH JW BC

'They must surely top the bill at the News of the World Awards Concert as my brother-in-law plays the keyboards and co-writes much of the material' Walters to Audition panel. Unanimous pass.

ARENA

23/5/85 Into The Music *Some new day, All points in between, Iced under, Know the feeling.* Sion Jones (b,lv), Karl Roberts (g,bkv), Mick King (d,bkv). 27/4/85 MV4 DG MC

ARGENT

9/9/70 Harris *Where are we going wrong?, Rejoice, Aquarius.* Rod Argent (kv), Russ Ballard (gv), Robert Henrit (d), Jim Rodford (b). 27/8/70 PS JG *

Group's trial broadcast on 'John Peel's Concert' 5/7/70 passed by audition panel.

25/1/71 Harris *Sweet Mary, Rejoice, Stepping stone (& Chained, 1/3/71).* 12/1/71 MV5 JM JWH

8/6/71 Harding *Uranus, Sweet Mary, Time of the seasons.* 31/5/71 MV5 MB *

27/9/71 Harris *Heaven, Hold your head up, Keep on rolling, Schoolgirl.* 14/9/71 TI JM JWH

Files suggest band recorded Network Session version of 'Hold your head up' 30/11/71 for WALKER, TX week of 27/12/71.

6/3/72 Harris *Hold your head up, Keep on rolling, Tragedy.* 23/2/72 AO2 JG *

25/4/72 Peel *Tragedy, Rejoice, Keep on rolling, Liar.* 4/4/72 MV4 PR *

12/3/73 Harris *It's only money (pt.2), God gave rock'n roll to you (& It's only money pt.1, 9/4/73).* 7/3/73 LH1 PRorTW BAI&MG

ARIEL

12/11/74 Peel *Rock & roll seas, Yeah tonight, What the world needs now is a new pair of socks, Worm-turning blues, I'll be bone.* John Lee (d), Harvey James· (g), Phil Putt (b), Michael Rudd (gv). 29/10/74 MV4 TW BC

ARK

23/8/91 Fri. Rock *Train, Cover me with rain, Message to the world, Celebrate, Scientific jingle.* Steve (gsy), Pete (g), Gel (b), Paul (d), Ant (v,fl). 12/7/91 MV5 MC~

JOAN ARMATRADING

28/11/72 Peel *Head of the table, Spend a little time, Child star, Whatever's for us.* Joan Armatrading (ag,pv). 31/10/72 LH1 JW BC

5/4/73 Peel *Lonely lady, Alice, City girl, Lazy day.* & possibly Larry Steel (b), Henry Spinetti (d) & unknown (lg). 19/3/73 LH1 BA *

19/7/73 Peel *Spend a little time, Give it a try, Steppin' out, Catchin' up.* Solo. 25/6/73 LH1 BA *

15/1/74 Peel *Some sort of love song, Lonely lady, Freedom.* & Snowy White (g), Mike Tomich (b), Brian Glasscock (d). 14/1/74 TI JW *

25/6/74 Peel *Old but gold, Back to the night, Dry land,*

World's gonna love me tonight. & Peter Zorn (al,fl-1). 20/5/74 LH1 JW *

17/2/75 Peel *Steppin' out, Back to the night, No love for free.* & Jean Roussel (k), Gerry Conway (d), Tony Reeves (b). 4/2/75 MV4 TW BAI

17/7/75 Peel *Back to the night, Tall in the saddle, Body to dust, City girl.* & 'The Movies': Jon Cole (g), Julian Diggle (perc), Gregg Knowles (g), Durban Laverde (b), Dag Small (k), Jamie Laine (d). 10/7/75 MV4 TW BAI

25/8/76 Peel *Kissing and hugging, Down to zero, Help yourself, People.* & Pat Donaldson (b), Jerry Donahue (g), Dave Mattacks (d). 29/7/76 LH1 TW BAI

ARMISTICE

20/6/86 Fri. Rock *Land of the giants, Roses, Lean on me.* Marcus Hutson-Saxby (d), Dean Cowell (b), Julian Jutson-Saxby (lg), Rolf Riley (rg), Alan Pateman (k), Monty Eugene Lindsay (v). 30/5/86 MV4 TW *

THE ARMOURY SHOW

25/8/83 Jensen *Ring those bells, The glory of love, Castles in Spain.* Richard Jobson (v), John McGeoch (gv), Russell Webb (bv,sy), John Doyle (d). 21/8/83 MV4 DG ME

24/12/83 Long *Brave, Jungle of cities, Avalanche.* 15/12/83 PHM c.PWL PSM

19/8/84 Skinner *Sleep city sleep, Kyrie, 19 hours, Waiting for the floods.* 19/8/84 MV5 DG ME

BILLY BOY ARNOLD

14/10/77 Peel *I'm ready, Baby please don't go, Goin' away baby, Oo-wee, I wish you would.* Gordon Smith (g), Bob Hall (p), Bob Davies (b), Ted Tetlow (d). 5/10/77 MV4 TW NG

P. P. ARNOLD

14/1/68 Top Gear *Satisfaction, Tin soldier, If you're think you're grooving, You make me feel like a natural woman, Road to nowhere.* P.P. Arnold (v), & (g), (b), (d), (o,p), (fl,al), (al,ts), (ts,bars) (unknown), & Madeline Bell, Dusty Springfield (bkv). 2/1/68 PC1 BA DT
First solo session had been TX 18/1/68, Pop North [M].

ARSON GARDEN

24/2/91 Peel *Cold, Impossible space, Kathy's in deep, It will soon be over.* Joby Barnett (d), Michael Mann (g), April Combs (v), Chip Starr (b), James Combs (g). 4/12/90 MV5 MR~

ART OF NOISE

18/4/85 Long *From science to silence, Beat box, Moments in love.* J.J. (k), Anne Dudley (k), Gary Langan (k). 31/3/85 HP BYA PW

ARTERY

28/7/81 Peel *The clown, Into the garden, Potential silence, Afterwards.* Mark Goldthorpe (v), Mick Fiddler (g,sx,bkv), Garry Wilson (d,bkv), Neil McKenzie (b), Simon Hinkler (o). 20/7/81 MV4 TW DD

15/2/82 Peel *The ghost of a small tour boat captain, Louise, The slide, The sailor situation.* 30/1/82 MV4 DG MR

AS ABOVE...SO BELOW

23/10/81 Fri. Rock *Out of touch, City in the sea, Flying dreams, Dan the bomb.* Robin Hodge (glv), Phil Hodge (kv), Charlie Noble (b), Dave Ashcroft (d). 2/10/81 * KH TW&AP

ASHMAN REYNOLDS

3/7/72 Walker *Taking off, I wish I knew, Take me home.* Rod Edwards (p), Bob Weston (lg), Keith Boyce (d), Harry Reynolds (g), Aleki Ashman (v). 21/6/72 MV5 PR *

14/7/72 Peel *Came right in, Taking off, I'm tired I'm cold and I'm hungry, Work out the score.* 12/6/72 MV3 JM *

ASLAN

17/9/86 Long *Book of life, Dangerous games, Been so long, Lately.* Christie Dignan (lv), Tony McGuiness (b), Joe Jewell (g), Billy McGuiness (perc), Alan Downey (d). 31/8/86 MV4 BYA SC

ASSAGAI

28/5/71 Black *Cocoa, Beka, Telephone girl, Monday one.*

Raymond Barker (tp), Dudu Pukwana (al), Charles Cheide (b), Terry Quaye (cga), Fred Frederick (ts), Fred Coker (gv), Tony Hicks (d). 22/4/71 AO2 JM *

ASSASSIN

18/3/88 Fri. Rock *So now you know, Ready for the fight, Your kind of loving, Down to love.* Dave Byrne (v), Jon Dillon (g), Mick May (lg), Charlie Hannah (b), Paddy Mooney (d). 4/3/88 MV4 PW MC

THE ASSOCIATES

4/5/81 Peel† *Me myself and the tragic story, Nude spoons, A matter of gender°, It's better this way, Ulcrajiceptimol.* Billy McKenzie (v), Alan Rankine (g,k), Mike Dempsey (b), John Murphy (d). 28/4/81 LH1 DG MR
† on Strange Fruit SFPCD075; ° also on 'Winters of Discontent' SFRCD204.

19/4/82 Peel *Waiting for the love boat, Australia, Love hangover, A severe case of career insecurity.* Steve Golding (d) r. Murphy; & Martha Ladly (v-3). 6/3/82 MV4 DG MR

23/11/83 Jensen *Helicopter, Snap, Don't give me that I told you so look, Breakfast.* McKenzie, Howard Hughes (k), Steve Reid (g); & 'The Whippets' (d). 29/9/83 MV4 JP DG

30/7/84 Skinner *A matter of gender, Message/Speech, Affectionate punch, Kites.* Mckenzie, Hughes, Golding, Martin Lowe (g), Roberto Soave (b), Ian McIntosh (g). 15/7/84 MV5 DG GP

7/10/85 Long *Give, Obsession magnificent, Take me to the girl, Heart of glass.* Lowe out; & 'Mority Von Oswald' (d). 8/9/85 HP BYA PW

ASWAD

2/9/76 Peel *Pressure, Ethiopian rhapsody, Back to Africa, Natural progression.* Brinsley Forde (gv), Donald Griffiths 'Dee' (lgv), Angus Gaye 'Drummie Zeb' (dv), George Oban 'Ras' (b), Courtney Hemmings (kv), Bunny McKenzie (hca,v), Candy McKenzie (v). 10/8/76 MV4 TW BAI&NG

18/12/78 Peel *Behold, Love has its ways, It's not our wish.* Tony Gadd (kv), Donnal Benjamin (gv) r. Hemmings, Griffiths. 10/10/78 MV4 MB TdB

14/6/82 Jensen *Pass the cup, Girl has got to know, African children, Love fire.* Tony Gadd (b) r. Ras; & Bigger Morrison (k), Martin Tatta (lg), Jimmy Haines (lg), Levi (perc), Peter Soweto (tp), Mike 'Bammie' Rose (al). 3/6/82 MV4 JWI AP

24/11/83 Jensen *African children, Recipe, Roots rocking, Cool runnins inna west eleven area.* Forde, Drummie, Gadd; & Michael Rose (sx), Martin Augustine (lg), Clifton Morrison (kv), Eddie Thornton (tp), Henry Tenhui (tb). 17/11/83 MV4 JP TdB&HP

10/10/84 Long *Rebel souls, Gave me your love, Chasing the breeze, Candles.* & Clifton Morrison (k), Martin Augustine (g), Michael Rose (sx), Henry Tenhui (tb), Cecil 'Jimmy' Hayes (g), Eddie Thornton (tp), Roger Guthrie (sx). 13/9/84 MV5 MHY MPK

10/9/85 Long *Janice Strong, Pull up, Nuclear crisis, Wrapped up.* & Clifton Morrison (k), Martin Augustine (g). 28/8/85 MV5 BYA MC

24/1/88 Miss P *Your recipe, Bubbling, Roots rockin', Breezin'.* & Stanley Andrews (lg), Michael Martin (k), with Trevor Walters (lv-1), Janet Kay (lv-2), Adrian De'Allie (lv-3), Ciyo (v-4). 2/1/88 MV5 PW ME

8/9/88 L. Kershaw *Coolkuh, Can't get over you, Rebel soul.* & Stanley Andrews (lg), Michael Martin (k), Carlton Ogilvie (k), Alan Williams (sx), Eddie Thornton (tp), Winston Rollins (tb). 14/8/88 MV4 TdB FK

PETE ATKIN

24/8/70 Symonds *Girl on the train, Touch has a memory, Master of the revels, Rider to the world's end, Laughing boy.* Pete Atkin (gv), Nick Harrison (md) & 8 musicians (unknown). 4/8/70 PH BA NG

Atkin applied for and passed an audition 6/2/70 AO2, produced by John Walters. 'Very clever stuff in the lyrics', remembers Walters. That lyricist, who came along to several of these sessions, was Clive James. Today, Atkin is a senior BBC management figure in Bristol, and Clive James...

3/3/72 PEEL *Driving through mythical America, Apparition in Las Vegas, Wristwatch for a drummer, All the dead were strangers (& The girl on the train, A guitar is a thief in the night, 21/4/72).* * 15/2/72 TI JM *

14/3/72 PEEL *Thief in the night, 30 year man, Uncle seabird, A king at nightfall.* * 6/3/72 PH JW BC

22/8/72 PEEL *The wristwatch for a drummer, Between us there is nothing, All the dead were strangers, Screen freak.* * 31/7/72 PH JW BC&BAI

5/1/73 SEQUENCE *The girl on the train, Sheer quivering genius, A guitar is a thief in the night, The man who walked toward the music, The double agent.* Atkin solo. 28/11/72 TI JM NG

3/4/73 PEEL *Perfect moments, The hypertension kid, The beautiful changes, The last hill that shows you all the valley.* * 13/3/73 LH1 JW BC

9/8/73 PEEL *Ready for the road, Be careful when they offer you the moon, Between us there is nothing, Senior citizen.* * 30/7/73 LH1 BA *

1/1/74 PEEL *The man who walked towards the music, National steel, Pay day evening, An array of passionate lovers.* * 20/11/73 LH1 JW BC

28/5/74 PEEL *Perfect moments, Payday evening, Wall of death, The road of silk.* Pete Atkin (p,elpv), Les Davidson (g), Maurice Adamson (b), Andy Monroe (d). 14/5/74 LH1 TW *

26/11/74 PEEL *Session man blues, I see the joker, Black funk rex, Rain wheels, Nothing left to say.* * 12/11/74 * * *

9/10/75 PEEL *Uncle sea bird, Errant knight, Lonesome Levis lane, Stranger in town.* & Dick Levens, Neil Campbell, Roger Odell. 18/9/75 MV4 * *

ATLANTIS

29/3/73 PEEL *Let's get on the road again, Maybe it's useless, My dreams are the vision of my former life, Rock'n roll preacher.* Ingar Rumpf (v), Jean-Jacques Kravatz (o,p), Karl Heinz Schott (b), Udo Lindenberg (d), Klaus-Georg Meier (g). 19/3/73 LH1 BA *

7/9/73 SEQUENCE *It's getting better, A simple song, A daydream, Drifting wind, Days of giving.* 25/7/73 A02 JM *

ATOMIC ROOSTER

3/1/70 WS R&B *Friday the 13th/Vug, Sly, Decline and fall.* Vincent Crane (o), Carl Palmer (d), Nick Graham (gv,fl). 3 or10/12/69 MV4 JG JY

2/6/70 HARDING *Seven lonely streets, Friday the 13th/Vug.* 26/5/70 MV5 MB MH&MF

30/3/71 HARDING *Tomorrow night, Before tomorrow, Death walks behind you.* Paul Hammond, John Cann r. Palmer, Graham. 22/3/71 MV5 MB MH&MF

26/6/72 WALKER *Stand by me* [possibly Network Session] Crane & Chris Farlowe (v), Ric Parnell (d), Steve Bolton (g). 12/6/72 A02 RP *

10/8/72 DRUMMOND *People you can't trust, All in Satan's name, Stand by me, Vug.* 28/7/72 MV5 MB MH&MF

6/11/81 FRI. ROCK *Death walks behind you, Play it again, In the shadows, Devil's answer.* Crane, Du Cann, Hammond & Spig (b). 16/10/81 * TW DD

ATTIC

10/12/80 PEEL *The axxe, Art 5946 foreign, The ability to speak, Whenever is it.* Robert Bartlett (lv), Pete Coote (gk,bkv), Mark Bushell (d), Steve Austin (b,bkv), Simon Green (gk). 3/12/80 LH1 BS NG

ATTILA THE STOCKBROKER

30/6/82 PEEL *Cocktails/Nigel want to go to C&A's, They must be Russians/Russians in the DHSS/Russians in McDonalds, Death in Bromley/A bang and a Wimpy/The night I slept with Seething Wells, 5th column/Russians at Henley regatta.* Attila (v). 9/6/82 MV4 RP *

29/3/83 PEEL *England are back/Holiday in Albania, Burn it*

down/Eros products, A very silly East European propaganda station/Where you goin' with that flounder in your hand?, Sawdust and empire.* & Steve Drewett (gb), Simon O'Brien (d), Ruth O'Brien (fl), Chris Payne (k,vi,rec,v), Tim Vonce (rec,v), Lin O'Brien (acc), Johnny Smegma (v).* 14/3/83 MV4 JP MC

9/7/85 LONG *Jim, Pop stars, Russians in McDonalds, Russians on the centre court.* Solo. 2/7/85 * JS *

THE AU PAIRS

9/10/79 PEEL *Pretty boys, Come again, Ideal woman, Monogamy.* Lesley Woods (gv), Paul Foad (gv), Jane Munro (b), Pete Hammond (d). 26/10/79 MV4 BS NG

12/6/80 PEEL *Dear John, The love song, It's obvious, Repetition.* 28/5/80 MV4 DG NG

12/1/81 SKINNER *The set up, We're so cool, Unfinished business, Diet.* 8/1/81 LH1 DG MR

28/1/81 PEEL *We're so cool, Armagh, The set up, Headache for Michelle.* 21/1/81 LH1 CL NG

1/9/81 SKINNER *Shakedown, Intact, Pretty boys, Slider.* & Josh Fifer (tp-3). 27/8/81 MV4 DG MR

31/3/82 PEEL *America, Steppin' out of line, Sex without stress.* 15/3/82 MV4 TW DD

24/2/83 JENSEN *Beast of a machine, Lion love, No more secret lives, She runs with honey.* Woods, Hammond, Nicholas O'Connor (kv), Caroline Howes (kv), Jane Morris (perc,v), Graeme Hamilton (tp), Andy Birchall (cl). 31/1/83 MV4 DG MC

AUBREY SMALL

2/9/70 HARRIS *Sleeping people, Maybe tomorrow, Lost my heart to a woman, It's me.* Rod Taylor (elp), Pete Pinckney (gv), Allan Christmas (g,bkv), Dave Young (fl,bkv), Graham Hunt (d). 20/8/70 PS JG *

7/12/70 HARRIS *Broken whisky, What's this all to do with the airport, Country road.* 27/11/70 TI JM JWH

28/6/71 HARRIS *Break up and roll away, I've been a fool too long, Any particular way, She came through.* 15/6/71 TI JM JWH

1/12/71 PEEL *If I were you, Seeing believing, You'll always be a dreamer, You'll agree with me, Questions.* 22/11/71 * * BC

24/4/72 HARRIS *The loser, Someone, Into my life, Another world.* 11/4/72 * JG *

11/9/72 HARRIS *Someone to play to, Once in a while (& Lost my heart to a woman, 23/10/72).* 1/8/72 * JG *

AUDIENCE

7/4/72 PEEL *Trombone gulch, Barracuda Dan, Buy me an island (& Thunder and lightning, 19/5/72).* Howard Werth (gv), Trevor Williams (bv), Anthony Connor (perc,v), Nick Judd (k), Patrick Charles. 13/3/72 TI PD *

MICK AUDSLEY

13/7/73 SEQUENCE *Dawn falls heavily, The commissioner has come, Bridges motorways and dams, The Isle of Dogs.* Mick Audsley (agv). 21/6/73 LH1 JM *

BRIAN AUGER'S TRINITY

6/11/67 WS R&B *Isola Natale, A kind of love-in, Shadows of you, Goodbye jungle telegraph.* Brian Auger, Julie Driscoll & the Trinity. 17/10/67 A02 JG JY

Auger passed audition, A02, 18/10/63, line-up: Brian Auger (p), Rick Laird (db), Phil Kinorra (d). 1st session, Jazz Club, Light Programme, rec'd: the Paris 5/12/63, 1st TX 7/12/63, Prod. Bryant Marriott.

19/11/67 TOP GEAR *A kind of love-in, Save me, shadows of you, Isola Natale, Goodbye jungle telegraph.* 10/11/67 PH *

22/1/68 SYMONDS *Save me, I just got some (23/1), I don't know where you are (25/1).* Auger, Driscoll (v-1,3 only), Dave Ambrose (b), Clive Thacker (d). 15/1/68 PS c.RB *

14/4/68 TOP GEAR *Why (am I treated so bad?), A day in the life, This wheel's on fire, Inside of him, Calze rosse.* Driscoll (v-1,3,4) & unknown (g). 8/4/68 PCI BA PR

20/5/68 SYMONDS *If you live, This wheel's on fire (21/5), A*

kind of love-in (22/5), Shadows of you (23/5). &* Driscoll (v). 10/5/68 PCI c.RB *

28/6/68 JOE LOSS *This wheel's on fire.* 7/6/68 PH PW *

30/9/68 SYMONDS *Old Jim Crow, After loving you (1/10), Take me to the water/I'm going back home (2/10), Road to Cairo (3/10).* Auger and Driscoll only. 23/9/68 PH c.RB *

27/10/68 TOP GEAR *Old Jim Crow, I'm not talkin', Road to Cairo, Lonesome hobo.* 7/10/68 PCI BA *

16/11/68 SAT. CLUB *Tiger, Ellis Island, What you gonna do.* Driscoll out. 12/11/68 PH BB PR

13/1/69 WS R&B *After loving you, What you gonna do, Shadows of you, Ellis Island.* & Driscoll (v-1,3 only). 13/12/68 A02 JG JY

2/3/69 SYMONDS ON SUNDAY *Indian rope man, Ellis Island, Bumpin' on sunset, Take me to the water.* Driscoll (v-1,4 only). 19/2/69 PCI JW *

Files suggest session for WS R&B recorded 3/9/69, untraceable.

BRIAN AUGER'S OBLIVION EXPRESS

8/1/71 BLACK *The light, On the road, Dragon song, Total eclipse (& The sword, 5/2/71).* Brian Auger (o,p,elp), Jim Mullen (lg), Robbie McIntosh (d), Barry Dean (b). 16/12/70 A02 JM JWH

22/6/71 HARDING *Man's wedding, Better land, I wanna take you higher.* 14/6/71 MV5 MB MH&MF

24/9/71 BLACK *Just me just you, Day tripper, Truth.* 6/9/71 TI PD ARV.

18/11/71 DRUMMOND *Somebody help us, Freedom jazz dance, Just me just you.* & Alex Ligertwood (v). 10/11/71 MV4 MB MH&MF

27/4/72 DRUMMOND *Freedom jazz dance, Everyday, Somebody help us.* Godfrey MacLean (d) r. McIntosh. 19/4/72 MV4 MB MH&MF

9/6/72 PEEL *Somebody help us, Blind man, Just me just you.* 16/5/72 TI JM JWH

20/4/73 SEQUENCE *Inner city blues, Freedom jazz dance, Happiness is just around the bend, Somebody help us.* Ligertwood out; Jack Mills (lg) r. Mullen; & Lennox Langton (cga). 27/3/73 TI JM *

AUTO DA FÉ

30/4/83 LONG *Girl boy difference, Blood into life, Sensitive eyes.* * 29/3/83 PHM DS PSM

AUTUMN 1904

5/3/84 PEEL *I heard Catherine sing, The city, Give it time, Innocence.* Keith Falconer (d), Billy Bowie (b), Allan Dumbreck (k), Ross Thom (g), Billy Leslie (v), Lisa Cameron & Indira Sharma (bkv). 25/2/84 MV5 DG MC

THE AVERAGE WHITE BAND

12/2/73 HARRIS *Put it where you want it, This world has music.* Alan Gorrie (bgv), Hamish Stuart (lgv,b), Roger Ball (k,al,bars), Onnie McIntyre (g,bkv), Malcolm 'Molly' Duncan (ts), Robbie McIntosh (d,perc). 31/1/73 LH1 PR BAI

29/7/74 HARRIS *I just can't give you up, Got the love, Just wanna love you tonight (& Keepin' it to myself, 30/9/74).* 26/6/74 LH1 JG BAI&DD

AVO-8

9/6/88 KERSHAW *Fame, Big car, Dangerman, Silver lining.* Jan Hastie & Claire Gourlay (v), George Glen (b), Steve Hastie (g), Kenny Gourlay (d). 12/5/88 MV4 DG NG&MA

THE AVONS

9/10/86 KERSHAW *Trapped, Seeing things, I don't want to talk about Lorraine, In my time.* Barry MacGilty (gv), Mark Kingston (bv), Hywel Jordan (gv), Ed Street (d). 24/9/86 * DST SR

ASTER AWEKE

21/5/89 KERSHAW *Sebubu, Segno, Wolela, Yeshebela.* Aster Aweke (v), Roland Perrin (k), Mike Mondesir (b), Richard Bailey (d), Frank Williams (ts), Ray Carless (ts,bars), Kevin Robinson (tp,flh). 2/4/89 WX PW TdB&MA

KEVIN AYERS

28/2/70 TOP GEAR *Stop this train, Clarence in wonderland, Why are we sleeping, The oyster and the flying fish (&*

Hat Song, no record of TX). Kevin Ayers (g,b,lv) '& Soft Machine, Lyn Dobson': Robert Wyatt (d, p-2, bkv), David Bedford (p), Lol Coxhill (ss), Nick Evans (tb), Elton Dean (al), Lyn Dobson (fl). Hopper (b) & Ratledge (o) also contracted to appear. 10/2/70 MV4 JW TW

3/7/70 BLACK *Gemini chile, Lady Rachel, Colores (& Short departure, 14/8/70)*. & The Whole World: David Bedford (p), Mike Oldfield (b), Lol Coxhill (sx), Nick Fincher (bv). 20/5/70 PH JM *

This line-up first appeared on Peel Sunday Concert, rec'd 7/5/70 PS, TX 17/5/70.

11/7/70 TOP GEAR *Derby day, The interview, We did it again, Lunatic's lament*. 9/6/70 MV4 JW TW

Guested on *Bridget St. John's Radio 1 Folk Show* on 20/9/70. He played 'The oyster and the flying fish', and 'If you've got money'.

6/11/70 BLACK *Currant cake, Derby day, There is loving (& Clarence in wonderland, 27/11/70)*. 21/10/70 AO2 JM JWH

14/4/72 PEEL *Take me to Tahiti, Whatevershebringswesing, Stranger in blue suede shoes, The interview*. & 3 singers (10 in all): including Robert Wyatt, Johnny van Derek. 21/3/72 TI JM JWH&BAI

Contracts suggest Ayers next recorded a session for DRUMMOND 15/5/72 TI, TX 25/5/72. Unfortunately, the PasB is missing, and the session was not repeated.

12/6/72 HARRIS *Oyster and the flying fish, Butterfly dance, Whatevershebringswesing, Queen thing*. and Archibald: Archie Legget (bv). 17/5/72 AO2 JG *

16/4/73 PEEL *Oh what a dream, Shouting in a bucket blues, The interview*. & 3 singers (7 in all). 11/4/73 MV4 PR BC?

30/7/74 PEEL *Another whimsical song, Lady Rachel, Stop this train, Didn't feel lonely till I thought of you*. & the Soporifics: Rabbit (k), Ollie Halsall (g), Archie Legget (b), Freddie Smith (d). 9/7/74 LHI PR BAI

16/11/74 ROCK ON *After the show, Stranger in blue suede shows, Sweet deceiver*. & the Soporifics. 11/11/74 * BA *

22/7/76 PEEL *Star, Mr Cool, Love's gonna turn you round, Ballad of Mr Snake*. & Andy Summers (g), Zoot Money (k,bkv), Charlie McCracken (b), Rob Townsend (d). 13/7/76 MV4 JG MR

AZTEC CAMERA
5/3/83 LONG *Walk out to winter, Queens tattoos, Boy wonders, Just like gold*. * 28/2/83 PHM DS TWN

DEREK B
10/5/88 L. KERSHAW *Bad young brother, All city, Bullet from a gun, We got the juice*. Easy Q (rp), Derek B (dj,rp,dsc), Paul Townrow (prg,k), Robin Boult (gb). 30/3/88 MV4 HP MPK&TdB

B MOVIE
7/4/81 PEEL† *Polar opposites, Welcome to the shrink, Escalator, All fall down*. Graham Boffey (d), Paul Statham (lg), Steve Hovington (bv), Rick Holliday (k). 31/3/81 LHI DG MR

14/4/81 SKINNER† *The devil in me, Nowhere girl, Love me, Disturbed*. 2/4/81 LHI JS *

† on 'Radio Days', Document DCD3.

6/4/82 JENSEN *The great divide, Amnesia, The promised land, Mediterranean*. Hovington (lv); & Mike Peden (b). 28/3/82 MV5 DG ME

8/2/84 JENSEN *No shadow of a doubt, Furnishing the empty dream, Arctic summer, Blind allegiance*. Hovington, Statham, Martin Winter (b), Alan Cash (d,perc). 26/1/84 MV4 JP HP

BABE RUTH
14/12/72 PEEL *Wells Fargo, Bit o'blues, King Kong*. Line-up unknown, files missing. 11/12/72 LHI BA *

22/1/73 HARRIS *The joker, King Kong, Black dog*. 3/1/73 LHI PR *

2/8/73 PEEL *Lady, For a few dollars, Cool jerk*. 9/7/73 LHI BA *

18/2/74 HARRIS *Amar caballero, Isn't that so, Gimmee some leg, Baby pride*. 6/2/74 * JG *

BABES IN TOYLAND
29/9/90 PEEL† *Catatonic, Ripe, Primus, Spit to see the shine*. Lori Barbero (dv), Michelle Leon (b), Kat Bjelland (gv). 9/9/90 MV3 DG ME&RPF

30/6/91 PEEL† *Pearl, Dogg, Laugh my head off, Mad pilot*. 11/6/91 * TdB FK&AC

'At last! A Radio One session with a male:female ratio of 1:5!' scribbled on sheet, presumably by Fred Kay or Alison Chorley. † on Strange Fruit SFMCD211.

22/12/91 PEEL *Handsome and Gretel, Blood, Mother, Dirty*. 18/8/91 MV3 DG MC&PRB

25/7/92 PEEL *Jungle train, Right now, Sometimes, Magic flute*. Maureen Herman (b) r. Leon. 11/7/92 MV4 JB~ DMC

BABY KNIVES
19/7/84 SKINNER *Baby knives, Big drive, Heaven is in your body, Cowboy slide*. Mike Peden, Calum MC~air, Billy Wilcox, John Robertson, Neil Martin. 28/6/84 MV5 MHY MPK

THE BABY SNAKES
13/7/87 LONG *Walk on water, The prophet, You're gonna miss me, Johnny*. Frank Rynne (lv), Colin Byrne (g), Daragh McCarthy (b), Ciaran O'Brien (d). 14/6/87 MV4 PW TdB

BABY TUCKOO
20/4/84 FRI. ROCK *Hot wheels, Awol, Holdin' on, Baby let the good times roll*. Rob Armitage (v), Neil Saxton (g), Paul Smith (b), Andy Barrott (kg), Tony Sugden (d). 6/4/84 MV4 TW DD

BACK DOOR
21/11/72 PEEL *Skilpered widlash, Askin' the way, 32-20, One day you're down the next day you're down*. Colin Hodgkinson (b), Ron Aspery (al), Tony Hicks (d). 30/10/72 TI JW&PD *

8/1/73 HARRIS *Vienna breakdown, Country blues No 1, Adolphus Beal, You gotta good friend (& Captain Crackup, 19/2/73)*. 3/1/73 LHI PH BAI

21/6/73 PEEL *Dancin' in the van, Livin' track, Lieutenant Loose, Back door, Roberta*. 18/6/73 LHI BA *

3/7/73 PEEL *Adolphus Beal, Walkin' blues, It's nice when it's up, Cat cote rag, His old boots*. 26/6/73 LHI JW *

25/10/73 PEEL *His old boots, Blue country blues, Walkin' blues, Adolphus Beal*. 1/10/73 LHI BA *

17/12/73 HARRIS *Human bed, Walkin' blues, Louisiana blues, Fanny Wiggins*. 5/12/73 LHI JG *

12/9/74 PEEL *Slivadiv, The spoiler, The dashing white sargeant, TB, Blakey Jones*. & Dave MaCrae (k). 5/9/74 LHI TW *

Group also recorded several sessions for R2's Jazz Club, and several R1 In Concerts, between 72-75.

BAD COMPANY
13/12/87 FRI. ROCK *Can't get enough, When we made love, This love, Fame and fortune*. Mick Ralphs (g), Simon Kirke (d), Boz Burrell (b), Brian Howe (v). 30/1/87 MV4 TW DD

BAD DRESS SENSE
10/3/87 PEEL *Need to love, Life's demand, Always away, Cynical smile, Never so funny*. Jason Twitch (d), Ed Shred (gv), Nick Schozzer (v), Paul Pizza (b). 24/2/87 * DG MR&TD

BAD MANNERS
6/4/81 SKINNER *Suicide, The Hawaiin adventures of Ivor the engine, Doris, King Skar-Fa*. Buster Bloodvessel (Douglas Trendle) (v), Alan Sayag (hca,v), Louis Cook (g,bkv), Paul Hyman (tp), Andrew Marson (al), Chris Kane (ts), Brian Tuitt (b), Dave Farren (b), Martin Stewart (k). 27/3/81 LHI DG ME

BADFINGER
27/7/74 ROCK ON *Blind owl, No matter what, Perfection, Suitcase*. Pete Ham (lgv), Tom Evans (rgv), Joey Molland (b), Mike Gibbons (d). 22/7/74 LHI BA BC

Passed trial b'cast for Sounds Like Tony Brandon, rec'd 20/1/69 [M:daytime].

BADGER
1/12/72 SEQUENCE *Wheel of fortune, On the way home, Wind of change*. Tony Kaye (o), Simon Foster (b), Tony Parrish (lg), Roy Dyke (d). 24/10/72 TI PD ARV

BADLANDS
13/7/84 FRI. ROCK *Badlands (53rd state), What do you do with your life, Love is*. Paul George (d), Tutt Skillin (v), Murray Ward (b), Dave Flett (g), Mel The Axe (g). 22/6/84 MV4 TW MC

THE BAKER-GURVITZ ARMY
23/1/75 PEEL *Help me, Inside of me, Memory lane*. Ginger Baker (d), Paul Gurvitz (gv), Adrian Gurvitz (bv) & 2 (unknown). 15/1/75 MV4 * *

THE BAKERLOO LINE
20/10/68 TOP GEAR *Rock me, Don't know which way to go, Smokestack lightnin', Eleanor Rigby*. Terry Poole (bv), Clem Clempson (lgv), John Hinch (d). 24/9/68 PCI BA BC

16/2/69 TOP GEAR *Big bear Ffolly, This worried feeling, The last blues, Driving backwards*. 10/2/69 * * *

BALAAM AND THE ANGEL
3/7/85 LONG *Day and night, Warm again, Dark lands, Sister moon*. James Morris (gk), Mark Morris (bv), Des Morris (d), Mich Ebeling (bkv). 23/6/85 HP BYA JB

15/11/91 FRI. ROCK *Just no good, Next to me, What love is, She's not you*. Billed now just as 'Balaam': James, Des & Mark Morris, Ian McKean. 18/10/91 MV4 TW MC

THE BALCONY
24/11/81 PEEL *The lizard hunt, Surprise after surprise, She keeps her secret*. David Palmer (lv), Caroline Henning (bkv), Paul Cavanagh (g), Pete Baker (k), Pete McAsey (b), Bert Gardener (d). 18/11/81 MV4 JWI TdB&MWT

JOHN BALDRY
30/6/72 PEEL *Going down slow, A rake and a rambling boy, How long blues, As long as I can feel the spirit, Mother ain't dead (& Cocaine, 4/8/72)*. 29/5/72 TI JM JWH

Long John Baldry had been doing live Radio 1 sessions since 1968. This was his last session for which a contract exists in BBC archives.

BALKANA
27/8/87 KERSHAW *Mete Moma Dvorove, Mari Irino Irinko, Strandjansko horo, Svatbarski melodii, Stani mi maicho otkachi*. Janka Rupkina, Eva Georgieva, Stoyanka Boneva & Rumen Rodopsky (v), Ognyan Hristov (tapau drum), Rumen Sirakov (mnd), Georgy Mussorchiev (bpp), Kostadin Varimezov (bpp), Stoyau Velchikov (fl,cl), Mihail Stoyanov (fd). (1-Trio Bulgarka only, vocals). 20/8/87 * DG NG&FK

THE BAMBI SLAM
16/3/87 FRI. ROCK *La la la (it's out of hand), Shame of a sad sick psycho, The awful flute song*. Roy (gv), Natalie (b,bkv), Nick Maynard (d,bkv), Linda Miller (clo-1&2). 1/3/87 * DG MR&MFA

15/12/87 LONG *I and I, Falling out, Down, Hot summer nights inter city kitchen hoe-down kinda thang*. Dinah (clo) r. Miller. 21/10/87 * PW MPK

THE BAMBOO FRINGE
20/8/85 LONG *Wave bye bye, The restless heart, Careless talk costs lives, Change your mind*. Gerry Garland (v,sx), Gary McGuiness (gv), Howie Minns (perc,d). 7/8/85 MV4 BYA *

BAMBOO ZOO
3/9/81 PEEL *Fools colours, Look! listen! consume!, Binding wire, Ghost party*. Mick Duffy (gv), Joe Duffy (b), Gordon Holden (d), Paul Shorrock (perc), Russ Entwhistle (g). 28/8/81 MV4 DG ME

THE BAND OF SUSANS
11/10/88 PEEL *I found that essence rare, Child of the moon, Throne of blood, Hope against hope*. Karen Haglof (gv), Page Hamilton (gv), Robert Poss (gv), Ronald Spitzer (d,bkv), Susan Stenger (bv). 4/10/88 MV4 MR~

13/7/89 PEEL *Because of you, Hard light, Which dream*

came true, *Too late*. Mark Lonergan (g,bkv) r. Hamilton. 2/7/89 MV3 DG MR

BANDERAS
25/2/91 GOODIER *First hand, Don't let that man* †, *This is your life, May this be your last sorrow*. Caroline Buckley (lv), Simon Bishop (d), Danny Sanders (k), Colin Smith (g,sx,kv), Sally Herbert (k), David Pollitt (b), Gary Butcher (g), Simon Elms (tp, & WX11). 9/2/91 MV5 MA~ NF

† On 'Best of Mark Goodier' Nighttracks Mark1.

BANDOGGS
13/1/78 PEEL *The taylor in the tea chest/Astley's ride/Up and away, Laird logie, The dragoon and the lady/Grand Duke of York, The swimming song*. Peter Coe (bz,ml,dul,lv-1), Christine Coe (dul,hca,v-2), Tony Rose (cnc,hca,v-3), Nick Jones (fd,g). 14/12/77 * MB NG

THE BANDUNG FILE
20/1/88 PEEL *Handkerchief boy, Tin-legged tap dancer, Addicted to Robert Palmer, Garbage town*. Paul Bacon (v,sx), Steve Attwell (g,bkv), Pete Hendy (b,bkv), Screw Sawney (prg). 12/1/88 * DG MR&PS

BANG BANG MACHINE
15/2/92 PEEL *Justine, Monkey, A charmed life, Say it again Joe*. Lamp (d), Stan Wood (b), Steve Eagles (g), Elizabeth (v). 28/1/92 MV4 MR~

THE BANKROBBERS
13/12/82 JENSEN *The band played on, Where did the days go?, Over the edge, The ballad of Davy Clements*. Seamus O'Neill (d), Joby Fox (bv), John McDonald (g), Liam Carville (kv), Alistair Wallace (tp), Mervyn Crawford (sx). 5/12/82 MV4 DG ME

12/12/83 JENSEN *Going to the moon, Problem page, Why is it?* Fox, McDonald, Carville, Crawford, Julian Watson (d), Spike (tp), Ashley Slater (tb). 4/12/83 MV5 DG ME

BARBEL
12/2/90 PEEL *Shadow of a doubt, (Safe in a) Bubble, World facts, Inferno*. Roger Sinek (d), David Morgan (b), Greg Milton (gv), Alison Williams (o,elp). 2/1/90 MV3 DG MR

30/11/91 PEEL *Kicker, Lay by, Income tax, If I was a rich man*. & Simon Breed (g). 6/10/91 MV3 DG ME&PF

BARCLAY JAMES HARVEST
5/5/68 TOP GEAR *Mr Sunshine, Early morning, So tomorrow, I can't go on without you (& Eden unobtainable, 2/6/68)*. John Lees (gv), Mel Pritchard (d), Les Holroyd (bv), Stuart Wolstenholme (kv). 23/4/68 PCI BA DT
'Unanimous if unenthusiastic pass' from Audition panel.

4/8/68 TOP GEAR *Small time town, Night, Need you so bad, Pools of blue*. 30/7/68 PCI BA AH&BC

5/7/71 HARRIS *Ursula, Galadriel, She said*. 29/6/71 T1 PD ARV

14/1/72 PEEL *Blue John's blues, The poet, After the day*. 20/12/71 * JM *

8/2/72 PEEL *After the day, The poet, Medicine man*. 1/2/72 MV4 PR BC

3/4/72 HARRIS *Child of man, Galadriel, Medicine man (& I'm over you, 8/5/72)*. 15/3/72 AO2 JG *

13/5/72 ANTHONY *I'm over you* [probably Network Session]. 8/5/72 AO2 DT *

9/10/72 HARRIS *Thank you, 100,000 smiles out, Delphi town morn, Medicine man*. Rec. date unknown PRIV * *

24/9/73 HARRIS *Child of the universe, The joker, Untitled No 6, Allergy*. 5/9/73 LH1 JG *

8/8/74 PEEL *Crazy city, Mining disaster, For no-one, Paper wings*. 1/8/74 LH1 TW *

2/9/74 HARRIS *Negative earth, Crazy city, For no-one*. [M: all private tapes] 31/7/74 LH1 JG *

PETER BARDENS
6/10/70 HARDING *The answer, Homage to the god of light, I can't remember*. Peter Bardens (o,v), Andy Gee (g), Steve Hayton (g), Reg Isadore (d), Bruce Thomas (b), Ian Macdonald (sx,fl), Alan Marshall (perc). 29/9/70 MV5 MB MH&MF

THE BARDOTS
6/6/92 PEEL *Caterina, Obscenity thing, Gloriole, Don't let me down*. Neil (d), Steve (b), Chris (g,bkv), Andy (g), Simon (lv). 5/5/92 MV4 MR~

BARK MARKET
14/10/90 PEEL *Happy, Pencil, The patsy*. Rock Savage (d), John Nowlin (b), David Sardy (gv). 30/9/90 MV3 DG MA&PL

THE BARRACUDAS
12/11/81 SKINNER *On the strip, I can't pretend, Somewhere outside, Living in violent times*. Robin Wills (gv), Jeremy Gluck (lv), David Buckley (bv), Nick Turner (dv). 12/12/80 LH1 DG MC

SYD BARRETT
14/3/70 TOP GEAR† *Baby lemonade, Effervescing elephant, Gigolo aunt, Terrapin (& Two of a kind, 30/5/70)*. Syd Barrett (gv), Dave Gilmour (o,b,g), Jerry Shirley (d), [& Alan Styles (g), according to some biogs - not on contract]. 24/2/70 MV4 JW TW

† on Strange Fruit SFPCD043.

1/3/71 HARRIS *Baby lemonade, Domino, Love song*. * 16/2/71 T1 JM&PD JWH

THE BASEMENT FIVE
28/4/80 PEEL *Last white Christmas, No ball games, Immigration, Silicon chip*. J.R. (g), Leo (b), T. (d), D.M. (v). 21/4/80 MV4 TW DD

BASKING SHARKS
3/5/83 PEEL *View from the hill, New industry, Theatre war, Diamond age*. Adrian Todd, Jed McPhail & Martyn Eames (all: sy,dm,v). 25/4/83 MV4 TW MC

BASS DANCE
21/4/88 L. KERSHAW *High class girl, Starbright, Freakout, Africans*. Basil Gabbidon (lv,g), Alex Williams (bkv,perc), David Parry (g), Steve Miller (k), William Minto (b), Colin Gabbidon (d). 23/3/88 MV4 PW MPK

BASTARD KESTREL
15/2/88 PEEL *Pigout, B.S. 3704, Risk, Drinking suicidal*. Chris M. (d), Keith C. (v,b), Dik (gv), Paul C. (g). 7/2/88 * DG *

9/11/88 PEEL *Slob, Dog rabbits, Harry Hausen, Indian train*. Jimmy Perse (d) r. Chris M. 1/11/88 MV4 MR~

BASTRO
29/1/90 PEEL *I come from a long line of shipbuilders, Extrovert, (I've) Ben Brown, Nothing special*. John McEntire (d,bkv), Clark Johnson (b,bkv), David Grubbs (gv). 14/1/90 MV3 DG ME

23/7/90 PEEL *Demons begone, Krakow Illinois, Floating home, Recidivist 2*. 1/7/90 MV3 DG ME&PA

THE BATTERED ORNAMENTS
8/1/69 NIGHT RIDE *Then I must go, Security blues, The week looked good on paper, Water carrier, Station song*. Pete Brown (v), Nisar Ahmed Khan (ts, fl), Peter Bailey (cga), Robert Tate (d), Butch Potter (b), Chris Spedding (lg). 1/1/69 PCI JM *
'Tuneless lead vocalist... a lead voice which could never be called singing... all the tricks serve only to emphasise their mediocrity. ... lyrically meaningless and pretentious... material laughable...awful' Audition panel: Failed.

14/9/69 TOP GEAR *Sandcastle, Slag room, Half past Ladbroke, Going underground*. & Brian Miller (o,v), Brown out. 2/9/69 MV4 JW *
Granted second trial broadcast after Brown's departure. Passed: 'avant-garde hairy group for Top Gear-type shows only'.

BATTLEAXE
13/5/83 FRI. ROCK *Ready to deliver, Running out of time, Mean machine, Shout it out*. Ian McCormack (d), Brian Smith (b), Steve Hardy (g), Dave King (v). 29/4/83 * TW DD

BAUHAUS
3/1/80 PEEL *A god in an alcove, The spy in the cab, Telegram Sam, Double dare°*. Peter Murphy (v), Daniel

Ash (g), David Jay (b), Kevin Haskins (d,perc). 4/12/79 * JS MR
° on 4AD LP 'In the flat field' CAD13.

12/4/82 PEEL *The party of the first part†, Three shadows (pt.2), Departure´*. 13/3/82 MV4 DG MC
´ later released on B side of Beggar's Banquet 12-inch BEG 91T 'She's in Parties'.

22/7/82 JENSEN *Third uncle†, Silent hedges, Swing the heartache, Ziggy Stardust†*. 1/7/82 MV4 JS MR
† released as a single on Beggar's Banquet BEG83T, with 'Ziggy Stardust' as the A side, and reached 15 in Oct/Nov '82. 'Ziggy' now on Band of Joy 'I and Only' BOJCD025.

23/3/83 JENSEN *She's in parties, Terror couple kills colonel, In the nightime*. 17/2/83 JW1 MPK

BB BLUNDER
17/9/71 BLACK *Sticky living, Go and have yourself a good time, Strange love*. Reg King (v), Chris Hunt (d), Brian Belshaw (b), Brian Gooding (g), Nick Judd (elp). 26/8/71 AO2 JM JWH&BAI

27/12/71 HARRIS *Say goodbye, The seed*. Judd out. 6/12/71 T1 PD BH

BE-BOP DELUXE
27/11/73 PEEL *Axe victim, Blusey ruby, Tomorrow the world*. Bill Nelson (gv), Robert Bryan (b), Ian Parkin (g), Nick Dew (d). 6/11/73 LH1 TW BC

23/5/74 PEEL *Third floor heaven, Adventures in a Yorkshire landscape, Mill street junction, Fifteenth of July (invisibles)*. 9/5/74 LH1 TW BAI

17/3/75 PEEL *Maid in Heaven, Stage whispers, Sister seagull, Lights*. Nelson; & Andrew Clark (k), Charlie Tumahai (bv), Simon Fox (d). 11/3/75 MV4 TW BAI

23/2/76 PEEL *Blazing apostles, Crying to the sky, Peace of mind*. 10/2/76 TW MR

25/1/77 PEEL *Mill street junction, Adventures in a Yorkshire landscape, Still shining*. 11/1/77 MV4 TW DD

6/2/78 PEEL *Super enigmatix, Panic in the world, Possession, Love in flames*. 30/1/78 MV4 TW DD

BE-BOP PRESERVATION SOCIETY
11/11/71 DRUMMOND *Ahleucha, Donna-Lee, God child, One bass hit*. * 3/11/71 * MB MH&MF

THE BEAT
5/11/79 PEEL *Tears of a clown, Mirror in the bathroom, Ranking full stop, Click click, Big shot*. Everett Morton (d), Dave Wakeling (g,lv), Ranking Roger (perc,v,styles), David "Shuffle" Steele (b), Andy Cox (g, "optional" vocals). 24/10/79 MV4 BS NG

11/2/80 READ *Rough rider, Hands off, Twist and crawl, Mirror in the bathroom*. Saxa (sx) joins. 17/1/80 MV4 CL *

22/9/80 PEEL *Too nice to talk to, Walk away, Monkey murders (9 Mexicans), New psychedelic rockers*. Blockhead (k-2,3,4 only). 3/9/80 MV4 BS ME

9/2/81 SKINNER *I am your flag, They're all out to get you, Drowning, Dream home in New Zealand*. 30/1/81 LH1 DG PW

29/3/82 PEEL *Spar wid me, Till the end of the party, She's going she's gone, Save it for later, Sole salvation, Patou and Roger a go talk*. & Lionel Martin Jr. (sx), Blockhead out. Rec. Date Unknown PRIV * *

22/4/82 JENSEN *Sounds like sorry, Ackee-1-2-3, It makes me rock, Sugar and stress*. Blockhead returns. 11/4/82 MV5 DG ME

BEATNIGS
7/12/88 PEEL *Suffering, The statement on built-in obsolescence, The mash, Fight fire with water*. Michael (b,v), Andre (k,smp,tps,bkv), Henri Flood (cga,ti,perc), Rond Tse (v,tp,perc), Kelvin (d,bkv,smp,perc). 4/12/88 HP DG ME

JEFF BECK GROUP
18/3/67 LIGHT SAT. CLUB *Let me have you baby, Stone crazy, I ain't superstitious, Hi Ho silver lining, I know I'm losing you*. Jeff Beck (gv), Ron Wood (b), Ray Cook

(d), Rod Stewart (v) [not on contract until 2nd date].
7/3/67 PH BB *

8/7/67 LIGHT SAT. CLUB *Rock my plimsoul, This morning,*
Tallyman. Aynsley Dunbar (d) r. Cook. 4/7/67 PH BB *

16/10/67 SYMONDS *Rock my plimsoul, Let me love you*
(19/10), Walking by the railings (20/10). 9/10/67 PS c.RB *

5/11/67 TOP GEAR *Ain't superstitious, Beck's Bolero, Loving*
you is sweeter than ever, You'll never get to heaven if
you break my heart, You shook me (Tales of Mickey
Waller). Micky Waller (d) r. Dunbar. 1/11/67 MV4 BP PR

29/9/68 TOP GEAR *You shook me, Shapes of things, Sweet*
little angel, Mother's old rice pudding (& Rock my
plimsoul, 3/11/68). 17/9/68 PCI BA *

14/1/72 PEEL *Going down, Got the feeling (& Ice cream*
cokes, 11/2/72). Clive Chaman (b), Cozy Powell (d),
Max Middleton (k), Bob Tench (v), r. Waller, Stewart.
14/12/71 TI JM NG&MF

BECKETT
12/11/73 HARRIS *Rain clouds, Green grass green, Little girl,*
True life story. * 7/11/73 * JG *

10/1/74 PEEL *Rolling thunder, Life's shadow, Tiffany.* *
7/1/74 * BA *

19/8/74 HARRIS *Etchings on velvet, Castle walls, Angela.* *
17/7/74 * JG *

BEDLAM
31/8/73 SEQUENCE *I believe in you, Hot lips, Seven long*
years, The beast. * 17/7/73 * JM *

THE BEE GEES
22/4/67 LIGHT SAT. CLUB *In my own time, New York*
mining disaster 1941, One minute woman, Cucumber
castle (& Mr James, not broadcast*).* Barry Gibb, Robin
Gibb, Maurice Gibb, Colin Peterson (d). 17/4/67 PH BB *
'Rave notices from the Audition panel' noted Jimmy
Grant.

15/10/67 TOP GEAR *In my own time, I close my eyes, New*
York mining disaster 1941, Massachusetts, Mrs
Gillespie's refrigerator, To love somebody, Cucumber
castle (& World, 12/11/67). & Vince Melouney (g) &
'small group'. 9/10/67 PCI BA DT

18/2/68 TOP GEAR *Birdie told me, With the sun in my*
eyes, The Earnest of being George, And the sun will
shine. & Tony Gilbert for the services of 19 musicians,
Bill Shepherd (md) (Bill Shepherd Orchestra) [M].
13/2/68 PH BA *

BEE VAMP
9/11/81 PEEL *Lucky grills, London bridge (is falling down),*
Valium girls, Nigel follows Barry to Bengal, Our eyes
met across the disco floor. Paul Ablett (sx), Jim Paris
(db,b), Martin King (g), Rory Lynch (d).
24/10/81 MV4 DG PS

CAPTAIN BEEFHEART AND
HIS MAGIC BAND
4/2/68 TOP GEAR *Sure 'nuff'n' yes I do, Yellow brick road,*
Abba zabba, Electricity. Captain Beefheart (v), John
French (d), Alex St. Clair (g), Jerry Handley (b), Jeff
Cotton (g). 24/1/68 MV4 BA DT&BC

12/5/68 TOP GEAR *Safe as milk, Beatle bones 'n' smoke'n'*
stones, Kandy korn, You gotta trust us.
6/5/68 PCI BA PR&AH

Both these sessions did take place, they were not,
as legend has it, tapes that Beefheart brought over
from the States with him. However, on the 9/6/68
repeat TX of the 2nd session, 'Beatle bones...' is not
TX, and the show closed with 'You gotta trust us', now
7'25", when on 1st TX it was only 4'00". Neither
Bernie nor Peel recall having played tracks from an
acetate of long takes of these numbers recorded in LA
in late '67 which Beefheart did bring for Peel, which
well-known event perhaps caused all the stories in the
first place. It is more likely that Bernie put out an
edited version of 'You gotta trust us' on the 1st TX,
ending the show with 'Kandy Korn' (8'00") — two
lengthy Beefheart songs were too much for one show.

His diary shows 'Beatle bones...' scored out in 9/6
running order, and a full-length 'You gotta trust us'
stuck in, again ending the show. Peel started spinning
tracks from the 'Strictly Personal' LP on 20/10/68. I can
find no evidence that acetate tracks were TX at all in
'68. Thanks to John Platt for comments.

BEES MAKE HONEY
23/1/73 PEEL *Get on board, The woman from Booterstown,*
Bloodshot eyes, Hanging on hoping strong.
Files missing. 9/1/73 * * BC

18/6/73 HARRIS *Dead flowers, Highway song, Caledonia (&*
Music every night, 23/7/73). * 6/6/73 LH1 PR BAI

26/11/73 HARRIS *Hangin' on, Boogie queen, Dancing in the*
moonlight, Sing me back home. * 21/11/73 * JG *

4/12/73 PEEL *Knee trembler, On Virginia, The sweet taste*
of moonshine, Rocking days. * 13/11/73 * * BC

BEGGAR'S OPERA
1/4/71 HENRY *Festival, Sarabande, Think, Memory.* Martin
Griffiths (v), Richard Gardiner (lg), Gordon Sellar (b),
Alan Park (o), Raymond Wilson (d), Virginia Scott (mll).
24/3/71 MV5 MB MH&MF

7/10/71 DRUMMOND *Time machine, The fox (& Poet and*
peasant, 4/11/71). 29/9/71 * MB MH&MF

BELGIQUE
8/1/83 LONG *Force of habit, School for scandal, Visual*
attack, Come out and cry. * 5/1/83 PHM c.JL TWN

THE BELLE STARS
2/3/81 SKINNER *Stop now, Take another look, Big blonde,*
Iko iko. Jennie McKeown (v), Sarah-Jane Owen (lg),
Stella Barker (rg), Penny Leyton (k), Lesley Shone (bg),
Judy Parsons (d), Miranda Joyce (sx). 27/2/81 LH1 DG *

2/7/81 READ *Miss World, Take another look, Funky chicken,*
Wrap it up. 12/6/81 LH1 DG ME

28/4/82 JENSEN *The reason, Sweet memory, Turn back the*
clock, Burning. Clare Hirst (ts,k) r. Leyton. 8/4/82 MV5 JS *

BELLTOWER
13/1/92 GOODIER *Eyes on the times, Lost in hollow,*
Outshine the sun, Solstice. Britta Phillips (gv), Jody
Porter (gv), Mark Browing (b), Nino Dmitryszyn (d).
14/12/91 MV4 MC~DMC

BELLY
17/8/92 Goodier *Feed the tree, White belly, Gepetto,*
Angel. Tanya Donelly (gv), Fred Abong (b), Chris
Gorman (d), Thomas Gorman (g). 25/7/92 MV5 MA~JLO

THE BELOVED
15/1/85 PEEL *The flame, A hundred words, Idyll, A*
beautiful waste of time. Jon Marsh (kv), Steve
Waddington (g), Tim Havard (b), Guy Gausden (d).
8/1/85 MV5 MRD PW

23/10/85 PEEL *Josephine, Up a tree, So seldom solemn, In*
trouble and shame. 13/10/85 MV5 DG ME

BELTANE FIRE
20/6/85 INTO THE MUSIC *Fortune favours the brave, The*
poacher, Run, Arthur's cave. Stef Edwards (d), Mitch
Caws (db), Carlo Edwards (lg), Clint Bradley (lv,rg).
25/5/85 MV4 DG MC

TONY 'DUSTER' BENNETT
10/4/68 NIGHT RIDE *Worried mind, I've been a fool,*
Everybody got a friend but me, Blues with a feeling. *
20/3/68 * DK *

3/11/68 TOP GEAR *Worried mind, I'm gonna wind up*
ending up, Country jam, Jumping at shadows (& I want
you to love me, Sleeping in the ground, 15/12/68). *
14/10/68 * * *

16/4/69 NIGHT RIDE *Further up the road, What a dream,*
Hot roddin', Rock of ages cleft for me, Morning star
blues, Life is what you make it. * 16/4/69 S2 PR *

6/9/69 WS R&B *Since I've been with you, Bright lights big*
city, Lone wolf blues, Fresh country jam. * 6/8/69 * JG JY

24/1/70 TOP GEAR *Hill street rag, I chose to sing the blues,*
I worship the ground you walk on, I was fooled. &
Tony Mills, Stella Bennett. 9/12/69 PH JW *

23/8/70 RAVEN'S R&B *I love my baby, Scooby Doo, Raining*

in my heart, Church, I'm fully saved today. & Stella
Bennett (4,5) & Tony Mills (3,4,5). * * JG JY

31/3/72 PEEL *I love my baby, Walking pork shops, Country*
breakdown (& I feel so good, Watcha gonna do,
5/5/72). * 28/2/72 * JM *

11/8/72 PEEL *Pride of place, Blue river rising, Let your*
light shine on me (& Back in the same old bag,
22/9/72). * 24/7/72 * JM *

21/9/73 SEQUENCE *Wasted time, Wish that I was wrong,*
Cold chills. * 15/8/73 * JM *

1/11/73 PEEL *Gone Gershwin, Summertime, Them that got,*
Coming home. * 24/9/73 * BA *

BENNY PROFANE
6/6/88 PEEL *Everything, Quick draw McGraw meets Dead*
Eye Dick Rob a bank, Beam me up. Becky Stringer (b),
Robin Surtees (g), Joseph McKechnie (g), Peter Baker
(o), Dave Jackson (v), Dave Brown (d,tamb).
22/5/88 MV4 DG MA

14/2/89 PEEL *Skateboard to oblivion, Pink snow, Fear, Man*
on the sauce. Roger Sinek (d) r. Brown. 29/1/89 * DG *

15/1/90 PEEL *Time Bomb, Hey waste of space, Jerked to*
Jesus, When it all kicks in. Liam Rice (d) r. Sinek.
7/1/90 MV3 DG ME

ANDREW BERRY
1/10/86 PEEL *All alone, God bless (your sister), Take what*
you please. Andrew Berry (gv), Vini Reilly (g,b), Simon
J. Wolstencroft (d). 21/9/86 * DG ME&FK

THE BHUNDU BOYS
14/7/86 PEEL *Manhenga, Writing on the wall†, Chemedza*
vana†, Let's work together, Kuroja chete. Kenny
Chitsvatsva (d), Davie Mankaba (b,bkv), Rise Kagona
(gv), Biggie Tembo (gv), Shakie Kangwena (k,bkv).
6/7/86 HP DG ME&SC
† Released as single 'The Bhundu Boys in London'
JIT-5, in Zimbabwe.

7/1/87 PEEL *My foolish heart, Ndoita sei?, Jig-a-jig, Rugare.*
& the Potato Five Brass section (2,3 only).
21/12/86 * DG ME&FK

12/3/87 KERSHAW *Simbimbino, Hpenyu hwangu, Pedzamuto,*
Shabini. 3/3/87 * HP ME

THE BIBLE
1/12/86 LONG *She's my bible, Glorybound, Slow drag down,*
Winter coat. Boo Hewerdine (lv,g), Tony Shepherd
(k,perc), Dave Larcombe (d), Neill MacColl (g,b-3,4),
Constance Redgrave (b-1,2), Dave Ellingham (sx-4).
5/11/86 MV4 BYA MS

BIG BLACK
6/5/87 PEEL *The Newman generator, L Dopa, Dead Billy,*
Ugly American. Steve Albini (gv), Santiago Durango (g),
David Riley (b). Rec. Date Unknown, Recorded in Chicago * * *

BIG CHIEF
14/12/91 PEEL *Destination poon, Six pack, Bong wrench,*
Into the void. Mike Danner (d), Matt O'Brien (b), Phil
Durr (g), Mark Dancey (g), Barry Henssler (v).
20/10/91 MV3 DG ME

BIG CHILL
13/3/92 FRI. ROCK *Halfway to heaven, Say anything, Ivelo*
wheels, Big chill. John Granger (g), Roy McLoud (b),
Stuart Wright (d), Andy Bassett (gk). 21/2/92 MV4 MC~

BIG COUNTRY
23/8/82 JENSEN *Heart and soul, Close action, Harvest home,*
Angle park. Stuart Adamson (gv), Bruce Watson (g),
Tony Butler (b), Mark Brzezicki (d). 12/8/82 MV4 JWI MR

22/3/83 PEEL *Close action, Inwards, 1000 stars, Porroh*
man. 9/3/83 MV4 JP NG&MS

THE BIG DISH
12/12/85 LONG *Swimmer, Another people's palace, Swing*
chicken, Beyond the pale. Steven Lindsay (gv), Mark
Ryce (lg), John Harper (k), John Burns (b), Raymond
Docherty (d). 27/11/85 MV5 BYA MPK

11/2/91 GOODIER *Give me some time, Warning sign, Twenty*
five years, State of the union. Lindsay, Brian McFie

(g,bkv), Skip Reid (d), Tracy Gilbert (b), Colin Bennick (k). 26/1/91 MV5 MC~

BIG FAYIA
7/12/89 PEEL *Gba nya ma/Nga mone biwe, Kamo ahmadu/Nginamudele, How are you/Lawoseh/Look waiu wowo/Co co rose, Tiawama a kpandei/U deh make make panme, Muana limia/Yawolo yiama/Sandi manya/Heilei nay hun.* The Big Fayia West African mask dance troup of Sierra Leone, featuring: Mustafa Joe (lv-1,2,5), Sidikie J.C. Kortogbou (lv-3), Tamba Musa (shengbi drum-3), Sahr Karimu (kongoma,lv-4), Daniel Lavalie (mendi shengbai, or big drum-5). Recorded 2/11/89, The British Council, Freetown, Sierra Leone. * *

BIG FLAME
16/7/84 PEEL *Debra, Man of few syllables, Sargasso, Breath of a nation.* Alan Brown (bv), Dil Green (d), Gregory Keeffe (g). 10/7/84 MV5 MRD MWT

25/2/85 PEEL *All the Irish must go to heaven, New way, Chanel Samba, These boots are made for walking.* 17/2/85 MV5 DG ME

27/11/85 PEEL *Earsore, Let's re-write the American constitution, Cat with cholic, Every conversation.* 17/11/85 MV5 DG HP

12/5/86 PEEL *Sink (get out of the ghetto blues part I), Xpqwrtz, Three on baffled island, Testament to the slow death of youth culture.* 4/5/86 MV5 DG DD&EL

BIG IN JAPAN
6/3/79 PEEL *Suicide high lie, Goodbye, Don't bomb China now.* Jayne Casey (lv), Ian Broudie (g,bkv,o), Holly (b, bkv), Budgie (d,bkv). 12/2/79 MV4 TW DD

BIG PIG
19/10/87 LONG *Hellbent heaven, Breakaway, Big hotel, Money god.* Nick Disray (v), Sherine Abeyratne (v), Timmy Rosewarne (kv), Oleh Witer (dv), Neil Baker (dv), Adrian Scallione (d), Tony Antoniades (hca,v). Recorded 8/87 in Metropole studios, Melbourne, Australia. * *

BIG SELF
1/2/82 PEEL *When the wind blows, Don't turn around, You're not afraid, Supervisor.* Michael Morris (d), Patrick Sheeran (bv), Bernard Tohill (gv), Jim Nicholl (g). 16/1/82 LHI DG MR

16/2/82 JENSEN *Don't turn around, 4-4 International rescue, War on want, Kamikaze.* 17/1/82 LHI DG ME

BIG SOUND AUTHORITY
8/4/85 LONG *Soul man, Bad town, Hell shaped room, Be true to yourself.* Tony Burke (gv), Martin Wilson (b), Steve Martinez (d), Julie Hadwen (v), Michael Garnochan (k), Kevin White (tp), Greg Brown (sx), Frank Seago (tb). 24/2/85 MV4 BYA *

BINA
3/11/91 KERSHAW *Anjabee, Ah de masti, Agar hai rasm, Mujhe is tarha.* Bina Mistry (v), Jan Steele (g,sx,fl), Marid Castronari (b), Dinesh Pandit (tab), Prakesh Mistry (perc), Kiran Thakrar (sy). 26/9/91 MV5 DG NG&JLC

TONY BIRD
10/12/73 HARRIS *Rift valley, A man and his friends, Athlone incident, Belated summers.* Tony Bird (agv). 7/11/73 LHI JG *

22/7/74 HARRIS *Cars, The cape of flowers (& Bird in a cage, 23/9/74).* [M: In Concerts]. 17/7/74 LHI JG *

BIRDHOUSE
9/3/87 PEEL *Hurricane in my head, Rev it up, Sick boy, Bad love.* Johnny Rev (v), Kathy Freeman (g), Mark Nicol (g), Billy Scarr (b), Max Cantara (d). 22/2/87 * DG ME&PS

BIRDLAND
28/6/89 PEEL *Paradise, White, See no evil, Sugar blood.* Robert (v), Simon (b,bkv), Lee (g,bkv), Kale (d). 6/6/89 ED DG MR

5/2/90 PEEL *All over me, Wanted, Shoot you down, Rock 'n' roll nigger.* Lee (lv-3). 2/1/90 MV5 DG TD

28/1/91 GOODIER *She belongs to me, Letter you know,*

Wake up dreaming†, Exit. Neil Hughes (d) r. Kale. 5/1/91 MV5 MC~

† On 'Best of Mark Goodier' Nighttracks Mark1.

THE BIRTHDAY PARTY
25/9/80 PEEL *Cry, Yard, Figure of fun, King ink.* Nick Cave (v,p,sx), Rowland Howard (g), Mick Harvey (g,o,d), Phil Calvert (d), Tracy Pew (b). 10/9/80 MV4 DG NG&MC

28/4/81 PEEL† *Release the bats, Roland around in that stuff, (Sometimes) Pleasure-heads must burn, Loose.* 21/4/81 LHI DG MR

† on Strange Fruit SFPCD020.

10/12/81 PEEL† *Big Jesus trash can, She's hit, Bully bones, Six inch gold blade.* 2/12/81 MV4 JWI PW

† on Strange Fruit SFPS058.

22/11/82 PEEL *Pleasure avalanche, Deep in the woods, Sonny's burning, Marry me (lie! lie!).* Calvert out. 15/11/82 * DG DD

BITCHES SIN
16/10/81 FRI. ROCK *Hold on to love, Down the road, Fallen star, Strangers on the shore.* Tony Tomkinson (v), Ian Toomey (g), Pete Toomey (g), Dave Newsham (b), Tony Leece (d). 26/8/81 * TW DD

BIVOUAC
25/4/92 PEEL *Drank, Two sticks, Lead, Spine.* Anthony Hodkinson (d), Granville Marsden (b), Paul Yeadon (gv). 8/3/92 MV3 DG ME&AR

BIZARRE INC
10/11/91 PEEL *Controversy, Song for John, 4024, Plutonic.* Meercham (k,mix), Meredith (k,mix), Turner (dm,mix). 1/9/91 OS * *

BLACK
12/1/83 PEEL *Under wraps, As long as it takes, Blue, Stephen for the moment.* Colin Vearncombe (gbv), David Dickie (bk,dm,bkv), David Wibberly (g), Justine Shakespeare & Pauline Dickie (v). 6/12/83 MV4 TW MC

4/7/83 PEEL *It's easy, Fast car soundtrack, Widemouth frog, Why do I do the things I do when they only get me done?* Vearncombe, Dickie, Rachel Furness (vi). 25/6/83 MV4 DG TdB

9/5/84 JENSEN *Skin up, Reunion, Here I am together, Blue.* Vearncombe, Dickie, Gary Dwyer (d), Jimmy Sangster (b). 12/4/84 MV5 JP MPK

12/11/86 LONG *Sometimes for the asking, Everything's coming up roses, I'm not afraid, The sweetest smile.* Vearncombe, Dickie, James Hughes (d), Roy Corkhill (b), Martin Green (sx), Christopher Mark Hutchinson (g). 26/10/86 MV4 BYA TdB

8/2/90 SKINNER *Now you're gone, Brother o'mine, Tracks of my tears.* Vearncombe, Green, Peter Adams (k), Sara Jones (bkv,perc), Tina Warrilow (bkv,perc), Gordon Longworth (g), Steve Price (b), Gavin Harrison (d). 29/1/89 MV4 HP TdB&JL

BLACK AXE
6/3/81 FRI. ROCK *Edge of the world, Shock treatment, Too close for comfort, Night from the blue.* Simon Sparks (lg), Bill Keir (gk), Mike Thorburn (d), Stewart Richardson (b), Chris English (v). 4/2/81 * TW DD

BLACK CAT BONES
6/1/69 WS R&B *Neighbour neighbour, Got a mind to give up living, Baby be good to me.* Paul Tiller (hca,v), Bob Weston (lg), Derek Brooks (g), Stuart Brooks (b), Terry Sims (d). 13/12/68 AO2 JG JY

9/2/69 TOP GEAR *Baby be good to me, I want to know, Train blues, Don't know which way to go.* 13/1/69 MV4 BA *

7/7/69 WS R&B *Save my love, Chasing dreams, Chauffeur.* 10/5/69 AO2 JG JY

10/1/70 WS R&B *Leavin' blues, Feelin' good, Good looking woman.* 10/12/69 MV4 JG JY

21/6/70 RAVEN'S R&B *Drown my life in fear, Four women, Work my body.* 27/5/70 MV4 JG JY

PAULINE BLACK
26/5/82 JENSEN *We the people, Fire, Tell me what the*

others do, Nameless. Pauline Black (v) & The Members: Nicky Tesco (v), Adrian Lillywhite (d,bkv), Nigel Bennett (lg,bkv), J.C. (rg,bkv), Chris Payne (b), Simon Lloyd (al & tp-1,2), Rudi Thompson (ts-1,2), Roots Qunta (k-3,4). 2/5/82 MV4 DG ME&PS

15/11/82 JENSEN *I think I'm losing my faith, Something's burning, Nameless, No woman no cry.* & Joe Cang (b), Matthew Cang (g), Mike McAvoy (k), Dick Cuthell (tp-4 only), Rico Rodriguez (tb-4 only) & Mae McKenna, Lorenza Johnson & Jackie Challenor (bkv). 7/11/82 MV4 DG ME

28/11/83 JENSEN *Dark they were and golden-eyed, The beast, It's a pity, Redemption song.* & Neil Conti (d), Winston Blissett (b), J. J. Belle (k), Ben Barson (k), Phil Reis (perc); & choir: Claire Neilson, Jennifer Simms, Julie Fletcher, Mario Frendo, Errol Brown, Michael Deslandes (bkv). 13/11/83 MV4 DG ME

15/5/84 JENSEN *Street heart, Reasons for living, Pirates on the airwaves, Someone to you.* & Neville Staples (v), Lynval Golding (gv), Phil Graham (d), Wayne Lothian (b), Jeremy Edwards (kg), Brian Clarke (sx,bkv), Eli Thompson (sax,bkv), Roddy Radiation (g). 15/4/84 MV5 DG ME

BLACK ROOTS
27/5/81 PEEL *Confusion, What them a do?, Chanting for freedom, The father.* Charles Bryan (lv), Errol Brown (v), Barry Thompson (perc,v), Cordell Francis (lg), Michael Taylor (k), Arol Thompson (rg), Derek King (b), Trevor Seivwright (d). 19/5/81 LHI DG MR

17/2/82 JENSEN *Starvation, Opportunity, Move on, Oh Jah.* 7/2/82 MV4 DG ME

14/11/83 PEEL *Far over, Strugglin', Africa, Black heart man.* J. Ngozi (rg), Carlton Smith (k) r. A. Thompson, Taylor; & K. Ngozi (cga,v). 7/11/83 MV4 * *

1/2/84 JENSEN *Confusion, Signs and wonders, War, Juvenile delinquent.* As 19/5/81, except C. Smith (k). 22/1/84 MV4 DG ME

BLACK ROSE
17/1/86 FRI. ROCK *Easy lovin' you, Need a lot of lovin', Go for the throat, Get off your high horse.* * 13/12/85 MV4 * *

BLACK SABBATH
29/11/69 TOP GEAR *Behind the wall of sleep, NIB, Black Sabbath (& Devil's island, 21/3/70).* Tony Iommi (g), Ozzy Osbourne (v), Geezer Butler (b), Bill Ward (d). 11/11/69 * JW *

BLACK SLATE
21/9/82 JENSEN *Forward on Pyaka, De yah pon creation, Rasta reggae, Reggae music.* Jack Price (v), Anthony Brightley (k), Chris Hanson (g), Colin McNeish (b), Desmond Mahoney (d). 19/8/82 MV4 JS MR

BLACK UMFOLOSI CHOIR
29/7/90 KERSHAW *Wakhuluma emoyeni, You are mine love, Dlala lo tshaka, Tjakuwangula, Ukhozi lwangithatha, Ntombizodwa.* Thomeki Dube, Dumisani Dube, Milton Ncube, Taurai Tichareva, Benia Phuti, Lucky Moyo, Morgen Moyo, Sotsha Moyo (all v). 12/6/90 MV3 MR~

BLACK VELVET BAND
13/6/88 L. KERSHAW *Domino, Old man stone, When justice came, We plough the fields.* Kieron Kennedy (ag), David Horner (d), Shay Fitzgerald (b), Liam Murphy (g,o,p), Maria Doyle (v). 5/4/88 RTE IWI GF

BLADE
1/12/90 PEEL *The coming is near, It don't mean a thing, Lyrical maniac, Forward.* Blade (v), Renegade (dj). 15/11/90 MV5 DG NG&JLY

BLANCMANGE
23/2/82 PEEL *I would, Living on the ceiling, Waves, Running thin.* Neil Arthur (g,v,el), Stephen Luscombe (k,el). 13/2/82 MV4 DG AP

22/6/82 JENSEN *God's kitchen, Feel me, Kind, Cruel.* & David Rhodes (g). 5/6/82 MV4 DG ME

30/3/83 JENSEN *Time became the tide, Murder, Blind vision, Vishnu.* & the Sapphires: Ruby James, Sylvia Mason James & Vicky St James (bkv). 17/3/83 MV4 JS MR&MS

28/11/85 Long *Believe, Don't you love it all, Lose your love, Paradise is...* . 29/9/85 HP BYA PW

BLANK STUDENTS
23/4/81 Peel *Supercreeper, Don't understand, Passionate rap.* Miles Salisbury (gv), Dog (d), Dom (sx), Harts (b), Horace (unknown). 13/4/81 LH1 TW AP

BLAST FURNACE AND THE HEATWAVES
3/7/78 Jensen *Can't stop the boy, Keep on dancing, South of the river, Write me a letter.* Blast Furnace (lv,lg), Skid Marx (hca), Blitz Krieg (rg,slg), D. Based (b,bkv), Tim Pani (d). 19/6/78 MV5 PR *
Repeated by Peel 11/7/78.

THE BLASTERS
3/9/85 Long *So long baby goodbye, Trouble bound, Red rose, Hoodoo man.* Dave Alvin (lg), Phil Alvin (gv), William Bateman (d), John Bazz (b), Gene Taylor (k), Lee Allen (sx). 21/8/85 MV5 BYA MPK

THE BLAZING APOSTLES
1/5/86 Long *The secrets, Threshold, Worlds apart, Speak out.* Kenny Hutchison (gv), Allan Liddell (g), John Anderson (b), Scott Watson (d). 2/3/86 Recorded in Scotland * *

BLEACH
2/12/90 Peel *Fall, Wipe it away, Seeing, Dipping, Jingle.* Steve Scott (d), Nick Singleton (b,g), Salli Carson (gv). 20/11/90 MV5 MR~
21/7/91 Peel *Decadance, Friends, Surround, Headless.* 4/6/91 MV3 MR~

BLEEDING HEARTS
26/6/92 Fri. Rock *Rock and roll, British boy on sunset, Like a bullet, Holidays in the sun.* Gary Borland (v), Billy Duncanson (d), Duncan Cameron (md), Richard Simpson (g), Bill Cochran (b). 5/6/92 MV5 TW MC

BLESSING
29/10/90 Goodier *Highway five, Let's make love, Birdhouse, Hurricane room.* William Topley (v), Kevin Knowles (b), Mike Westergaard (k), Luke Brighty (g), Jeff Dunn (d), Becky Price, Val Etienne & Shirley Lewis (bkv). 8/9/90 MV5 MC~

BLIND FURY
31/5/85 Fri. Rock *Contact rock 'n' roll, Hard times, Feel just the same, Back inside.* Steve Ramsey (g), Russ Tippins (g), Sean Taylor (d), Graham English (bv), Lou Taylor (v). 26/4/85 MV4 TW DD

BLIND MICE
15/8/88 L. Kershaw *Nothing, His own eyes, Just like we do, It's over.* Craig Quentin (d), Gary Bennett (b), Dave Alexander (g), Guy Hunt (g), Mark Willson (lv). 31/7/88 MV4 TdB TdB&FK

BLISS
28/4/87 Long *All across the world, It's gonna b good 4 u, Light and shade, I walk alone.* Chris Baker (d), Paul Ralphes (b), Paul Sirett (g), Rachel Morrison (v), Patricia Kuecklemann (k,al). 22/4/87 MV4 HP MPK&SC

BLODWYN PIG
2/3/69 Symonds on Sunday *The change song, Ain't you coming home, It's only love.* Mick Abrahams (lg), Andrew Pyle (b), Jack Lancaster (ss, ts, bfl, vi), Ron Berg (d). 24/2/69 A02 JW *
13/4/69 Top Gear *Ain't you coming home, The modern alchemist, It's only love, Mr Green's blues.* 24/3/69 PA AH&BC
12/5/69 WS R&B *It's only love, Dear Jill, Ain't you coming home, Leave it with me.* 16/4/69 MV4 JG JY
13/7/69 Top Gear *Summer day, See my way, It's only love.* 7/7/69 PH JW *
25/10/69 WS R&B *See my way, Summer day, Modern alchemist.* 1/10/69 MV4 JG JY
5/4/70 WS R&B *Worry, Meany morny, Black night.* 4/3/70 MV4 JG JY
14/4/70 Harding *See my way, Worry, Meany morny.* 30/3/70 MV4 MB MH&MF

10/7/70 Black *Rock me baby, Live, Worry, San Fransisco sketches.* 29/5/70 A01 JM *
3/10/70 Top Gear *See my way, Lonely nights, Lovely lady, Lady of liberty.* Pete Banks (gv), Barry Reynolds, r. Abrahams. 14/9/70 PH JW *
9/10/70 Black *Moon's gone, Lovely lady (& Lady of liberty, 20/11/70).* 23/9/70 A02 JM JWH
9/7/74 Peel *Baby girl, Dunstable truck driver, See my way, The leaving song.* Re-formed after 3 years apart: Abrahams, Lancaster, Pyle & Clive Bunker (d). 17/6/74 LH1 TW *

BLOOD AND ROSES
26/4/83 Peel *Theme from 'Assault on Precinct 13', Possession, Spit upon your grave, Curse on you.* Lisa Kirby (v), Bob Short (g,cel), Jez James (b,p,o), Richard Morgan (d). 20/4/83 MV4 RP NG&NR

BLOOD MONEY
1/5/87 Fri. Rock *The third wish, Battle scarred, Caligula, Shape shifter.* Bret Avok (d), Danny Foxx (v), Gramie Dee (g), Dale Lee (b). 10/4/87 MV4 TW MC

THE BLOODFIRE POSSE
3/7/86 Long *Brixton, Be!, Suddenly, Get flat.* Donovan Belnavis (b), Paul Blake (v), Alden Stewart (k), Danny Brownie (g), Carl Ayton (d). 25/6/86 MV4 BYA MPK

BLOSSOM TOES
29/10/67 Top Gear *Listen to the silence, The remarkable saga of the frozen dog, What on earth, Watchmaker.* Jim Cregan (g), Brian Godding (g), Brian Belshaw (b), Kevin Westlake (d) & unknown (tb). 23/10/67 PC1 BA DT
31/3/68 Top Gear *I'll be your baby tonight, Looking up I'm looking back, Love is, The remarkable saga of the frozen dog.* 25/3/68 PC1 BA PR
27/10/68 Top Gear *Wait a minute, Ever since a memory, Peace loving man.* 22/10/68 PC1 BA AH&BC
9/12/68 R1 Club *Postcard, Looking up I'm looking back, Wait a minute, Peace loving man.* 7/11/68 PS DG *
7/9/69 Top Gear *Love bomb, Kiss of confusion, Peace loving man, Indian summer.* 18/8/69 PH JW TW

THE BLOW MONKEYS
13/9/84 Long *Atomic lullaby, He's shedding skin, Waiting for Mr. Moonlight, Professor Supercool.* Tony Kilbey (d), Mick Anker (b), Robert Howard (gv), Neville Henley (sx). 2/9/84 MV5 DG ME

BLOW UP
23/9/87 Long *Scarlett dreams, Miss Mayhem, The heights, Pool valley.* Nick Roughley (gv), Alan Stirner (g), Aziz Hashmi (b), Chris Window (d), Diu Nimmo (tamb). 6/9/87 MV4 PW TdB&JB

BLUE
28/6/73 Peel *Look around, Someone, Little Jody, Wish I could fly.* Hughie Nicholson (gv), Jimmy McCullough (gv), Ian MacMillan (b), Angus 'Timi' Donald (d). 18/6/73 LH1 BA *
9/7/73 Harris *Moonite, Let me know, She wrote me a letter, Little Jody.* 20/6/73 LH1 PR BAI
18/10/73 Peel *Max Bygraves, Sad Sunday, Sittin' on a fence, Too many miles.* 23/8/73 LH1 JM *
30/4/74 Peel *Big bold love, Lonesome, You give me love, Sweet memories.* Robert Smith r. McCullough. 9/4/74 LH1 * *
17/6/74 Harris *Max Bygraves, Atlantic ocean, Lonesome, Mr Moon.* 29/5/74 LH1 JG *
21/8/75 Peel *Dark eyed darling, Round and round, I know how it feels.* Smith out. 14/8/75 MV4 TW *
29/1/76 Peel *I'll be satisfied, Careless kinda guy, Love has gone.* David Nicholson (b,v,p), Dean Ford (v,hca), & Jeff Allen (d,cga,ti) r. Donald. 22/1/76 MV5 TW *
18/11/76 Peel *The shepherd, Another nighttime flight, Charlie black arrow, Tired of loving you (silver dollars).* 9/11/76 MV4 JG MR
15/8/77 Peel *Bring back the love, I'm alone, Tired of loving you, Women.* Hughie Nicholson (g,p,hca,v), David

Nicholson (b,p,v), Ian McMillan (g,b,v,hca), Charlie Smith (dv). 8/8/77 MV4 TW DD

BLUE AEROPLANES
3/3/87 Long† *Cowardice and caprice, Coats, What do you mean?, Shame.* John Langley (d), Gerard Langley (v), Richard Bell (g), David Chapman (g), Nicholas Jacobs (g), Ruth Cochrane (b), John Stapleton (dsc). 15/2/87 MV4 JE TdB
† On Nighttracks SFNT009.
14/3/88 Mayo *Veils of colour, Stripped, 88 out, Breaking in my heart.* Wojtek Dmochowski (g) r. Richard Bell. 14/2/88 MV4 HP TdB
5/3/90 Campbell *Jacket hangs, And stones, Careful boy, Smelley and jazz and leider and love.* G. & J. Langley, Alex Lee (g,bkv-1), Angelo Bruschini (g), Rodney Allen (g,lv-3,bkv-1), Andy McCreeth (b). 15/2/90 MV5 PW MPK

BLUE CATS
19/1/81 Skinner *Gotta be loose, Slap that bass, Southbound blues, Wild night.* Carlo Edwards (lg), Mitchell Caws (db), Stefano Edwards (d), Clinton Bradley (lv), Clive Osborne (sx). 15/1/81 LH1 DG ME

BLUE MURDER
3/1/85 Into The Music *Blue murder, Don't say yes, Promises.* Kirby (gv), Durban Laverde (b), Ted McKenna (d,bkv). 8/12/84 MV4 DG MC

BLUE ORCHIDS
17/12/80 Peel *The house that faded out†, Work, Low profile.* Martin Bramah (g,lv), Richard Goldstraw (g,bkv), Steve Toyne (b), Ian Rogers (d, bkv), Una Baines (k). 8/12/80 LH1 TW NG
† On 'Manchester - so much to answer for' SFRCD202.
5/5/82 Peel *A year with no head, No looking back, Bad education, Sun connection.* Bramah, Baines, Mark Hellyer (b), Toby (d), Philip Rainford (bkv). 17/4/82 MV5 DG MR

BLUE POLAND
7/4/82 Peel *Find out, Household God, Time and motion, Puppet nation.* Neil Morgan (lv), Mel Deeprose (bkv), Nigel Robinson (gv), Chris Larsen (b), Steve Thomas (d,perc). 29/3/82 MV5 JWI DD

BLUE RONDO A LA TURK
7/12/81 Jensen *They really don't, Klactoveesedsteine, The method.* Mark Reilly (g), Chris Sullivan (v), Chris Tolera (v), Geraldo D'Arbilly (d), Kito Poncioni (b), Mike Bynde (cga,perc); & Chris Hunter (sx). 26/11/81 MV4 RB *
11/8/82 Jensen *Change, On the run, It happened one night, Carioca.* & Tony Gordon (ts), Arthur Colins (al,ts), Peter Segona (tp), Danny White (k). 29/7/82 MV4 JS&JWI MC

BLUE ZOO
3/8/82 Jensen *These days, One against one, Different view, Fun.* Tim Parry (g), Andy O. (v), Mike Ansell (b), Micky Sparrow (d); & Matthew Flowers (k), Pete Lancaster (tp). 22/7/82 MV4 JWI MR

DAVID BLUE
3/8/72 Drummond *The house of changing faces, The blues all night long, Another one like me, Come on John (& Looking for a friend, 14/9/72).* David Blue (pgv). 19/7/72 MV4 TW *

RUBY BLUE
30/5/88 L. Kershaw *The child song, Too many suitcases, Away from here, Easy.* Anthony Coote (b), Roger Fife (g), Robert Peters (d, perc), Rebecca Pigeon (v), Erika Spotswood (bkv). 22/5/88 MV4 TdB TdB&FK

THE BLUEBELLS
8/12/81 Jensen *Oh dear, You're gonna miss me, Happy birthday, Goodbye and good luck.* David McCluskey (d), Lawrence Donegan (b), Robert Hodgens (rgv), Russell Irvine (lg), Kenneth McCluskey (hca,v); & Mike Shilling (cel,o-3 only). 29/11/81 MV4 DG ME&MS
9/6/82 Jensen *Some sweet day, Wishful thinking, Sugar bridge, Everybody's somebody's fool.* 27/5/82 MV4 JS *

3/5/83 JENSEN *Young at heart, Red guitars, Learn to love, Small town martyr to love.* & Alan French (k), Pete Thomas (sx). 21/4/83 MV4 JP MR

PSM engineered another Bluebells session in Manchester on 6/2/85, but this has proved untraceable so far.

COLIN BLUNSTONE
20/9/71 HARRIS *Misty roses, Smokey day, Say you don't mind, Though you are far away.* & 7 musicians, including Patrick Halling string quartet (clo, vla, 2 vi, hp, db,ag). 31/8/71 T1 JM JWH

Later, on 30/11/71, recorded session for WALKER backed by Argent, TX last week of the year.

14/11/72 PEEL *Andorra, I don't believe in miracles, How wrong can one man ever be ? (& Say you don't mind, 26/12/72).* Colin Blunstone (v), Derek Griffiths (lg), Pete Wingfield (elp), Terry Poole (b), Jim Toomey (d). 23/10/72 T1 JW BC&NG

19/2/73 HARRIS *She's not there, A sign from me to you, How wrong can one man be?, She loves the way they love her.* 3/2/73 LH1 PR *

27/3/73 PEEL *Pay me later, I want some more, Looking for someone to love.* 6/3/73 LH1 JW BC

6/11/73 PEEL *Wonderful, Weak for you, Shadow of a doubt, Setting yourself up to be shot down.* 22/10/73 T1 JM BAI

24/6/74 HARRIS *Keep the curtains closed today, Beginning, Weak for you, Beware.* & Duncan Brown. 24/4/74 LH1 PR *

BLUR
24/9/90 GOODIER *Hi cool, She's so high, Bad day, Day upon day.* Graham Coxon (g), Damon Albarn (kv), David Rowntree (d), Alexander James (b). 10/8/90 MV5 MA~

5/5/92 GOODIER *Headist, Hanging over, 7 days, Colin Zeal.* 11/4/92 MV4 MC~*

BLURT
9/10/80 PEEL *Cherry blossom polish, Paranoid blues, Ubu, Some come.* Peter Creese (g,tb), Ted Milton (v,sx), Jake Milton (dv). 24/9/80 MV4 BS MR

THE BMX BANDITS
23/6/86 LONG *The day before tommorow, Groovy goodluck friend, Girl in the pink tee-shirt, Strawberry Sunday.* Duglas (v), Sean (gp), Jim (g), Billy (v,tamb), Norman (perc). 8/6/86 MV4 AJ *

9/4/87 LONG *Flipper, Rosemary Ledingham, Figure four, Take five.* Duglas, Billy, Joe (b,k,sx), Gordon (g), Arthur (g), Francis (d). 29/3/87 MV4 HP TdB&MA

BOB
18/1/88 PEEL *Esmerelda Brooklyn, Kirsty, Trousercide, Brian Wilson's bed.* Simon Armstrong (gv), Richard Blackborow (gv,k), Jem Morris (b), Gary Connors (d). 7/1/88 * DG ME&PL

29/3/88 MAYO *Times like these, Smelly summer, Just like you, It was Kevin.* Dean Legget (d) r. Connors. 2/3/88 MV4 HP MPK

15/2/89 PEEL *Who you are, Scarecrow, It was Kevin, So far so good.* 5/2/89 MV3 DG ME

25/9/89 PEEL *Extension 'Bob' please (instrumental), Throw away the key, Bloodline, Wild west 9.* Blackborow (o-1 only); & Harry Parker (p-3 only). 3/9/89 MV3 DG ME

THE BODIES
3/4/80 PEEL *Zone X , Something new, New positions, Subtraction.* Mark Adams (v, sy), The Tanz (b, lg), Leon Thompson (rg), Tony Cobley (d). 26/3/80 MV4 JE NG

THE BODINES
18/11/85 LONG *Scar tissue, Therese, William Shatner, The back door.* Michael Ryan (v,g), Paul Brotherton (g), Tim Burwood (b), John Roland (d). 30/10/85 MV5 BYA MPK

9/7/86 LONG *What you want, Slip slide, Naming names, Long time dead.* 18/6/86 MV4 BYA SC&MPK

24/3/87 PEEL *Skanking queens, Untitled, Tall stories, Clear.* 15/3/87 * DG ME&PS

THE BODYSNATCHERS
14/4/80 PEEL *What's this, Happy timetune, The boiler, The ghosts of the vox continental.* Rhoda Dakar (lv), Miranda Joyce (sx), Stella Barker (g), Sarah-Jane Owen (g), Pennie Leyton (k), Nicky Summers (b), Judy Parsons (d). 8/4/80 MV4 **

28/4/80 READ *What's this, Ruder than you, Rock steady, Too experienced.* 28/3/80 MV4 JE *

File suggests that the band had recorded same 4 numbers two days before, 26/3/80 PHM, TX JENSEN 28/4/80, same night the READ session started going out! A plugger's dream!

8/9/80 PEEL *Hiawatha, Mixed feelings, Private eye, The loser.* 27/8/80 MV4 BS NG

ERIC BOGOSIAN
17/8/83 PEEL *The coming depression, Marios, Fat fighter, Inside inside, Starving children, Cancer dessert, No answers.* Eric Bogosian. 10/8/83 MV4 BYA *

BOGSHED
4/11/85 PEEL *Packed lunch to school, Oily stack, Hell bent on death, Can't be beat.* Tristan King (d), Mike Bryson (b), Mark McQuaid (g), Phil Hartley (v); & Tom Sott (sx-2 only). 27/10/85 MV5 DG TdB

5/3/86 PEEL *The fastest legs†, Adventure of dog†, Summer in my lunchtime, Morning Sir†/Little car.* & Mac Andrassy (sx). 25/2/86 MV4 DG JB

28/7/86 PEEL *Tried and tested public speaker†, Champion love shoes†, Little grafter†, Gather in the mushrooms.* 15/7/86 * DG MR&MA

† on 'Tried and tested public speaker' LP, Shelf3.

4/5/87 PEEL *The gourmet is a baby, Raise the girl, I said no to lemon mash, Loaf.* 14/4/87 * DG MR&JB

26/10/87 PEEL *Six to one and likely, Into me, From the stumble, Duck flight/US bands/Wally Wallah (medley).* 18/10/87 * DG ME&PS

BOLT THROWER
13/1/88 PEEL† *Forgotten existence, Attack in the aftermath, Psychological warfare, In battle there is no law.* Al West (v), Jo Bench (b), Andy Whale (d), Gav Ward (g), Baz Thomson (g). 3/1/88 MV4 DG MWT

16/11/88 PEEL† *Drowned in torment, Eternal war, Realm of chaos, Domination.* Karl Willets (v) r. West. 6/11/88 HP DG ME

4/9/90 PEEL† *Destructive infinity, Warmaster, After life, Lost souls' domain.* 22/7/90 MV3 DG ME&FK

† on Strange Fruit SFRCD116.

BOMB DISNEYLAND
13/9/89 PEEL *Suicide 999, Twisted, Nail Mary, Faster bastard.* Simon (d,bkv), Prud (bv), Mark (gv). 13/8/89 MV3 DG ME

BON JOVI
18/1/85 FRI. ROCK *Breakout, Roulette, Shot through the heart, Get ready/Runaway.* David Rashbaum (kv), Alan John Such (bv), Jon Bon Jovi (lv,g), Ritchie Sambora (lgv), Tico Torres (d). 11/10/84 MV4 TW&DG MR&DD

THE GRAHAM BOND INITIATION
31/1/70 TOP GEAR *Walking in the park, Wade in the water, Love is the law.* Graham Bond (o,al,v), Diane Stewart (cga), Keith Bailey (d), Nigel Taylor (b), Dave Usher (fl,ts,g). 20/1/70 MV4 JW TW

Graham Bond's trio, quartet and the Organisation all did BBC sessions prior to R1. The Organisation's trial broadcast was for WS R&B, Rec'd 19/11/64 at PH, prod. JG, TX 12/12/64.

BOND AND BROWN
23/3/72 DRUMMOND *Macumbe, Milk is turning sour in my shoes, Beakes suite.* Graham Bond (o), Pete Brown (v), Diane Stewart (cga), Eddie Spevock (d), Lyle Harper (b). 15/3/72 MV4 MB MH&MF

BONE
2/5/90 PEEL *Amnesia soup, Bad line to Lebanon, 8 legged enemy, Cannibal sunset.* Danny (b,bkv), Dave (g), Bob (v). 15/4/90 MV3 DG MC

BONE ORCHARD
28/7/83 PEEL *Mankre, The mission, Shall I carry the budgie woman?, Fat's terminal.* Mark Horse (g), Troy Tyro (g), Paul Henrickson (b), Mike Finch (d), Chrissy McGee (v). 18/6/83 MV4 DG MR

BONGOS AND THE GROOVIES
10/7/73 PEEL *Ella, First day of October, Lagos, The station, Eche une.* 8-piece African group. Rec. Date Unknown OS * *

BONGWATER
13/4/91 *The power of pussy, You don't love me yet, White rental car blues, Kisses sweeter than wine.* David Licht (d), Kramer (bv), Dogbowl (g), Randolph Hudson III (g), Ann Magnuson (v). 19/3/91 MV5 MR~

THE BONZO DOG DOO DAH BAND
12/11/67 TOP GEAR *The equestrian statue, The Craig Torso show, Mickey's son and daughter, Death cab for Cutie.* Viv Stanshall (tp,eu,tu,v), Neil Innes (p,g), Roger Ruskin Spear (cnt,ts,xyl), Rodney Slater (al,ts,bars,bsx,cl,bcl, tb,tu), Vernon Dudley Bohay-Nowell (bj,b), Legs Larry Smith (d,tu), Sam Spoons (d,perc). 8/11/67 MV4 BA PR

17/12/67 TOP GEAR *The equestrian statue, Mickey's son and daughter, Rockalyser baby, The monster mash, Jazz delicious hot disgusting cold.* 5/12/67 PH BA PR&BC

5/5/68 TOP GEAR *Do the trouser press baby, Canyons of your mind, I've found the answer, I'm the urban spaceman.* David Clague (b) r. Bohay-Nowell, Spoons. 29/4/68 TX BA PR

21/7/68 TOP GEAR *Young girl, Beautiful Zelda, Captain cool, My pink half of the drainpipe, 11 moustachioed daughters (& Can blue men sing the whites, 18/8/68).* 8/7/68 PCI BA PR&BC

20/10/68 TOP GEAR *Shirt, I'm the urban spaceman baby, The bride stripped bare 'by the Bachelors', Excerpt from 'Brain opera' (& Ready made [E's mad dreg], 1/12/68).* Clague out. 8/10/68 PCI BA AH&BC

2/11/68 SAT. CLUB *Somebody stole my gal, Trouser press, Hello Mabel, Canyons of your mind, I'm the urban spaceman.* Dennis Cowan joins. 29/10/68 PH BB *

13/11/68 R1 CLUB *Humanoid boogie, Rockaliser baby, I'm the urban spaceman, Trouser press, Canyons of your mind.* This one recorded before Cowan joined. 22/10/68 PS * *

21/12/68 SAT. CLUB *My pink half of the drainpipe, Santa Cherie baby, Rhinocratic oaths, I'm the urban spaceman, Eleven moustachioed daughters.* 17/12/68 PH BB *

Next appeared live on R1 Club 19/2/69 PS.

9/3/69 SYMONDS ON SUNDAY *Look out there's a monster coming, Humanoid boogie, Mr. Apollo, Canyons of your mind.* 3/3/69 AO2 JW *

13/4/69 TOP GEAR *Look at me I'm wonderful, Mr. Apollo, Quiet talks and summer walks, Excerpt from 'Brain opera' pt.3.* 31/3/69 PH BA AH&BC

Between recording and TX, appeared live again on R1 Club, 11/4/69 PS.

3/8/69 TOP GEAR† *We're going to bring it on home, Monster mash, Sofa head°, Tent.* 29/7/69 MV4 JW TW

† on Strange Fruit SFPS051; ° also on 'Before the Fall' SFRCD203.

17/8/69 SYMONDS ON SUNDAY *You dun mi brane in, Shirt, Quiet talks and summer walks, Tent.* 11/8/69 AO2 c.PWI

*3rd live appearance on R1 Club 27/11/69 PS.

21/12/69 DLT *Keynsham, I want to be with you, Tent.* Aynsley Dunbar (d) r. Smith. 15/12/69 AO2 c.PWI *

Contracts file suggests a possible final session recording three days later, on 18/12/69 in AO2 for BRANDON, but there is no record of it having been broadcast.

THE BOO RADLEYS
30/7/90 PEEL *Aldous, How I feel, Bluebird.* Steve (d), Tim (b), Martin (g,v), Sice (v). 12/7/90 MV5 DG NG&BJ

7/4/91 PEEL *Alone again or, Something soon she said,*

Foster's van, Eleanor everything. Rob Cieka (d) r. Steve. 12/3/91 MV5 MR~

26/10/91 PEEL Smile fades fast, Towards the light, Lazy day, Boo faith. 5/9/91 MV5 DG NG&PA

THE BOOMERANG GANG
23/5/85 LONG I want you to stay, Shout, Dr Jones, Get up. David Shaw (lv), Simon Tedd (k), Milton (g), Mike Ansell (b), Michael Arthur Sparrow (d). 12/5/85 HP BYA PW

THE BOOMTOWN RATS
3/8/77 PEEL Joey, Neon heart, Looking after number one, Mary of the 4th form. Simon Crowe (d,bkv), Bob Geldof (lv), Johnny Fingers (k,bkv), Garry Roberts (g,bkv), Gerry Cott (g), Pete Briquette (b). 26/7/77 MV4 JG MR

26/5/78 PEEL Like clockwork, Me and Howard Hughes, Living in an island, (Watch out for) the normal people. & Neil Burn (bkv-4 only). 15/5/78 MV4 TW NBU

THE BOOTHILL FOOT TAPPERS
2/4/84 PEEL New river train, Long white robe, Bowl of porridge, I ain't broke. Danny (d), Kevin (agv), Slim (acc), Chris (bj,v), Marnie (wsh,v), Wendy and Merrill (v). 24/3/84 MV5 DG MC

16/4/85 PEEL How's Jack? (part 1), Learning how to dance, Sunday evening, Coloured aristocracy. & Lloyd Winter (db), 'Merrileggs' Heatley (v). 10/3/85 MV5 DG ME

BOOTS FOR DANCING
4/12/80 PEEL Timeless tonight, The pleasure chant, (Somewhere in the) South Pacific, Hesitate. David Carson (lv), Michael Barclay (g), Jo Callis (g), Douglas Barry (b), James Stewart (d), Robert Last (bkv), Hillary Morrison (bkv). 17/11/80 LH1 TW DD

15/7/81 PEEL Shadows of stone, Stand, Wild jazz summers. Carson, Barclay, Mike Bailey (d), Simon Bloomfield (b), Dickie Fusco (perc), Pete Harris (o). 13/7/81 MV4 TW DD

BOSS
30/11/87 LONG Fresh beat, Boss boys, Positive, House party. Dennis Morris (v), Michael Smith (kdv) & the Boss Boys (wh). 15/11/87 MV4 HP TdB

BOSS HOG
30/3/91 PEEL Big fish†, Sugar bunny/Spanish fly†, Red bath. Charlie (d), Jens (d), Jon (gv), Kurt (g), Cristina (v), Remko (perc,'ashtray'). 3/3/91 MV3 DG SA&DMC
† released as a single, NR18795.

THE BOTANY 500
30/10/86 LONG If I ruled the world, You and I, Teaching Jesus. Gordon Kerr (gv), Simon Fildes (b), David Garbraith (g), Sammy McGee (d), Michael Nolan (k). 5/10/86 MV4 BYA TdB

THE BOTHY BAND
26/3/76 PEEL Music of the glen/The humours of Scariff/Poll an Madadh Uisce, Old hag you have killed me/Danny Delaneys/Morrisons, When I was a fair maid, Am bothan a bh'aig Fionnghuala, The maid of Coolmore. Uncertain, save Triona (v-3,5 only). 9/3/76 MV4 JG MR

24/11/76 PEEL The hare in the heather, Bonny Kate/Jenny's chickens, Garrett Barry's/Coppers and brass, Billy Banker/The shores of Loughrea/The laurel tree, Michael Gormans/The Frieze britches/All the way to Galway/Fairhead Mary, Sixteen come next Sunday. Matt Molloy (fl-1 solo), Kevin Burke (fd-2 solo), Paddy Keenan (Uileann pp-3 solo), Fion (v-6 only). 19/10/76 MV4 JG MR

21/3/78 PEEL Lord Franklin, O'Neill's march, The strayaway child, Maids of Mitchelstown. Paddy Keenan (wh, Uileann pp), Micheal O'Domhnaill (g, v-1 only), Trina Ni Dhomhnaill (cl,v-1 only), Matt Molloy (fl), Kevin Burke (vi), Donal Lunny (bz&bh-2 only). 14/3/78 MV4 MB MR

BOURBONESE QUALK
11/3/87 PEEL Sweat it out, Dream decade, Northern soul, Cupid's itch, Call to arms. Simon Crab, Steven Tamza, Mike Kean, Lucia Binto. 31/3/87 OS * *

BOURGIE BOURGIE
25/1/84 PEEL Careless, I gave you love, Here comes that feeling, Breaking point. Ken McDonald (d), Keith Band (b), Ian Burgoyne (g), Michael Slaven (lg), Paul Quinn (v). 18/1/84 MV4 DG NG&PS

BOW WOW WOW
27/10/80 PEEL Radio G-string, Baby on Mars, Uomosex-Al-Apache, Fools rush in. Matthew Ashman (g,bkv), Leigh Gorman (b,bkv), Dave Barbe (d), Annabella Lu-Win (v). 20/10/80 MV4 TW DD&BC

1/2/82 JENSEN Go wild in the country, Golly golly go buddy, Prince of darkness, TV savage. 21/1/82 JS MR

DAVID BOWIE
24/12/67 TOP GEAR Love you till Tuesday, Little bombadier, In the heat of the morning, Silly boy blue, When I live my dream. David Bowie (v), & The Arthur Greenslade Orchestra. 18/12/67 PC1 BA DT

26/5/68 TOP GEAR London bye ta ta, In the heat of the morning, Karma man, When I'm five (& Silly boy blue, 30/6/68). & Tony Visconti (md), Orchestra management Ltd for 14 musicians. 13/5/68 PC1 BA PR&AH

26/10/69 DLT Unwashed and somewhat slightly dazed (& Let me sleep beside you, Janine, not broadcast). & Junior's Eyes: Mick Wayne (g), John 'Honk' Lodge (b), Tim Renwick (g), Graham Kelly, John Cambridge. 20/10/69 AO2 PR DP

6/4/70 FERRIS The supermen, Waiting for the man, The width of a circle (& Wild-eyed boy from free cloud, 11/5/70). & The Hype: Mick Ronson (g), Tony Visconti (b), John Cambridge (d). 25/3/70 PH BA PK
    Bowie had rec'd his 1st Peel Sunday Show Concert 5/1/70 PS, TX 8/2/70.

4/10/71 HARRIS The supermen, Oh-you-pretty things/8-line poem, Kooks (& Fill your heart, 1/11/71; Port of Amsterdam, Andy Warhol, not broadcast). & Mick Ronson (gv) only. 21/9/71 T1 JM JWH&BAI
    Had rec'd 2nd Peel Sunday Concert 3/6/71 PS, TX 20/6/71.

28/1/72 PEEL Hang on to yourself, Ziggie Stardust, Queen bitch, Waiting for the man (& Lady Stardust, 31/3/72). & Ronson, Trevor Bolder (b), Woody Woodmansey (d). 11/1/72 T1 JM NG

7/2/72 HARRIS Queen bitch, Ziggy Stardust, Hang on to yourself, Five years (& Waiting for the man, not broadcast). 18/1/72 MV5 JG *

23/5/72 PEEL Hang on to yourself, The rise and fall of Ziggy Stardust, White light white heat, Suffragette city, Moon-age daydream. & Nick Graham (p). 16/5/72 MV4 PR *

19/6/72 HARRIS Andy Warhol, Lady stardust, White light white heat, Rock and roll suicide. 23/5/72 MV4 JG *
    Files also suggest a Network session for Johnnie Walker, TX 5-9/6/72, rec'd AO2 22/5/72.

THE BOWLES BROTHERS
30/8/76 PEEL Nuts for Charlie, Why the fuss, Disparate Dan, Sweeter than sugar. Brian Bowles (gv), Julian Smedley (g,v,vi), Richard Lee (b), Sue Jones-Davies (v). 5/8/76 MV4 TW * Previous live broadcasts on R2.

14/1/77 PEEL F1 to, Roger the dodger, Samba, Downtown girl. 10/1/77 MV4 TW DD

ALAN BOWN
7/1/67 LIGHT SAT. CLUB Headline news, Love me, The boomerang, Gonna fix you good. 'The Alan Bown Set': line-up unknown. 2/1/67 PH BB *

9/1/67 WS R&B I can't get no satisfaction, Headline news, It's growing, Gonna fix you good, Love me, Do the boomerang. 9/12/66 MV4 JG JY
    The band's first recording for a BBC broadcast, but they had originally failed an audition in June 1965.

8/4/67 LIGHT SAT. CLUB Come on up, Gonna fix you good, Good thing, 98.6, Buddy ain't it a shame.
    * 3/4/67 PH BB *

11/11/67 SAT. CLUB The violin shop, Penny for your

thoughts, Toyland, Tehnicolour dream. Just as 'The Alan Bown': Jess Roden, Jeff Bannister, John Anthony, Alan Bown, Vic Sweeney, Stan Haldane, Tony Catchpole. 24/10/67 PH BB *

3/12/67 TOP GEAR Story book, Technicolour dream, Love is a beautiful thing (& Pandora's golden heebie-jeebies, 31/12/67). 29/11/67 MV4 BA *&BC

7/4/68 TOP GEAR Mutiny, Story book, All along the watchtower, Penny for your thoughts. 20/3/68 MV4 BA *&BC

7/4/70 HARDING Crash landing, My friend, Pyramid. Billed simply from now on as 'Alan Bown': Robert Palmer (v), r. Roden. 27/3/70 MV4 MB MH&MF

22/9/70 HARDING Curfew, Pyramid, Wanton man (& Make us all believe, 27/10/70). 15/9/70 MV5 MB MH&MF

3/8/71 HARDING Stretching out, Find a melody, Hobby horse's head. Gordon Neville (v) r. Palmer. 12/7/71 MV5 MB MH&MF

BOX OF TOYS
28/4/83 PEEL When daylight is over (sunset), Time takes me back, Precious is the pearl, I'm thinking of you now. Andy Redhead (d), Roy Campbell (b), Phil Martin (al,ss,ob,fl), Brian Atherton (kv). 13/4/83 MV4 HP NG

THE BOX
3/2/83 PEEL Out, Strike, The hub, Water grows teeth. Paul Widger (g), Charlie Collins (sx,fl), Roger Quail (d), Peter Hope (d), Andy Newton (d). 24/1/83 * DG MC

7/3/83 JENSEN Old style drop down, Skin sweat and rain, No sly moon, Deeper blue. 27/2/83 MV4 DG ME

BOXER
10/11/75 TOP GEAR Shooting star, California calling, All the time in the world, More than meets the eye. Mike Patto (p,elp,v), Ollie Halsall (g,clav), Keith Ellis (b), Tony Newman (d). 7/10/75 MV4 TW *

GARY BOYLE
31/8/77 PEEL The dancer, Cowshed shuffle, Almond burfi. Gary Boyle (g), Zoë Kronberger (k), Geoff Downes (k), Steve Shone (b), Sergio Castillo (d). 22/8/77 MV4 TW DD

THE BOYS
8/7/77 PEEL Sick on you, First time, Cop cars, Box number, Livin' in the city, Rock relic. Kid Reid (lv,b), Mat Dangerfield (lgv), Honest John Plain (rgv), Casino Steel (pv), Jack Black (d). 3/8/77 MV4 TW NG

15/5/78 PEEL TCP, Brickfield nights, Classified Suzie, Boys. 2/5/78 MV4 MB MR

BOYS IN DARKNESS
18/1/82 JENSEN Semantics, 47 home, Other people think my thoughts, Sad story. Dave Gilhooly (v), Richard Wade (g), Dave Milne (k), Mike McCann (b), Colin Laverty (d). 7/1/81 MV4 JS *

BOYS OF THE LOUGH
7/11/72 PEEL The boys of the lough/Slantigard, Farewell to whiskey, Keenya rua/Morning dew, The lass from Glasgow town. Robin Morton (bh,v), Cathal McConnell (v,wh,fl), Dick Gaughan (gv), Aly Bain (fd). 16/10/72 * JW *
    ...And recorded for Folk on 2 the following day, 17/10/72 PH, prod. FL.

13/3/73 PEEL Shetland wedding marches, Flowers of the forest, Erin I won't say her name/The whinney hills of Leitrin/Joe Ryan's jig, Wee croppy tailor/Boy in the gap/McMahon's reel. 29/1/73 T1 JW *

2/10/73 PEEL A ewe came to our door bleating/Christmas day in the morning, Lovely Nancy, Shetland reels, Mason's reel. Dave Richardson (bj,mnd,ci,cnc), r. Gaughan. 24/9/73 T1 JW NG&ARV

24/9/74 PEEL Jigs: Kincora jig/Behind the haystack, The maid with the bonnie brown hair, The golden slipper/The Stevenstown jig/Johnny McIljohn's reel/Sonny's mazurka, Hounds and the hare. 9/9/74 LH1 JW *

18/11/75 PEEL Medley: The laird of Drumblair/Millbrae, Farewell to Ireland, The darling baby, Dovecote/The

Atholl highlanders, Lochaber no more. & Finlay McNeil.
30/10/75 MV4 TW *

17/1/77 PEEL *Torn petticoat/The piper's broken finger/The
humours of Bally Connell, The lament for Limerick, The
red haired man's wife, The old favourite jig/Bobby
Gardner's jig, Lady Anne Montgomery/The highland man
that kissed his granny/O'Connor Donn's reel.* 9/12/76 MV4
TW *

1/6/78 PEEL *Donal Og, The new rigged ship/Naked and
bare/The Graemsay jig, McConnell's gravel walk/ The
gravel walk, The larks march.* 24/5/78 MV4 BS NG

BOYS OWN
31/3/83 JENSEN *Banksville, Dead end, Crazy about you,
Heart of stone.* Jay Manjay (gv), Paul Davies (gk), Mark
Irving (d,perc). 24/3/83 MV4 JS MR

PAUL BRADY
28/11/78 PEEL *The hunter's purse/The sailor on the rock,
The death of Queen Jane, Jigs, Mulqueeny's
(hornpipe)/Fergal O'Gara (16th chieftain)/Drag her
round the road, Crazy dreams.* Paul Brady (g,v,mnd),
Matt Molloy (fl), Kevin Burke (fd), Micheal O'Domhnaill
(gv). 20/11/78 MV4 TW DD

28/8/86 KERSHAW *Deep in your heart, To be the one,
Back to the centre, The island.* Solo. 26/7/86 Y2 CG TWN

2/4/91 CAMPBELL *Can't stop wanting you, Blue world,
Nobody knows.* & Anto Drennan (g), Trevor Wright (k),
Mick Bolton (k), Tony Molloy (b), Robbie Brennan (d).
20/3/91 MV5 PW MPK

BILLY BRAGG
3/8/83 PEEL† *A new England, Strange things happen, This
guitar says sorry, Love gets dangerous, Fear is a man's
best friend, A13 - trunk road to the sea.* Billy Bragg
(gv). 27/7/83 MV4 * *

4/1/84 JENSEN *Island of no return, Like soldiers do, The
Saturday boy, The man in the iron mask.* & David
Woodhead (flh-4 only). 22/12/83 MV4 DG TdB&MA

21/1/84 SAT. LIVE *New England, Love gets dangerous, To
have and to have not.* Live from S2 MRD TdB

27/2/84 PEEL *Lovers' town†, St Swithin's Day, Myth of
trust, To have and to have not.* & Wiggy (g-1 only).
21/2/84 MV5 MRD TdB

20/9/84 PEEL *It says here, A lover sins†, Between the
wars†, Which side are you on†.* 18/9/84 MV5 MRD TdB

13/10/84 SAT. LIVE *A13 - Trunk road to the sea.* Live from
S2 MRD TdB

2/9/85 PEEL *Days like these†, Jeanne†, The marriage†,
There is power in a union.* 20/8/85 MV5 TdB TdB

18/12/85 LONG *People get ready, A lover sings, Tracks of
my tears, Scholarship is the enemy of romance, Days
like these, I don't need this pressure Ron, A13.* &
Bobby Handley, Bobby Valentino, Wiggy (7 only). Live
from S2 * *

15/9/86 PEEL *Greetings to the new brunette†, Ideology,
The warmest room, Chile your waters run red through
Soweto†.* 2/9/86 * DG MR

19/9/88 PEEL† *The short answer, Valentine's day is over,
Rotting on remand, She's got a new spell.*
30/8/88 MV4 MR~

† on Strange Fruit SFRCD117.

22/11/88 CAMPBELL *She's got a new spell, The short answer,
Ideology.* Live in on-air studio CON K C.PWI *

15/6/91 PEEL *The few, Accident waiting to happen, Tank
park salute, Life with the lions.* & Cara Tivey (pv),
Wiggy (g,b), Grant Cunliffe (g). 12/5/91 MV3 DG *

BRAND X
8/3/76 PEEL *The ancient mysteries, Kubil blitz (& Born
ugly, not broadcast).* John Goodsall (g), Robin Lumley
(k), Percy Jones (b), Phil Collins (d). 26/2/76 MV4 TW BAI

2/8/76 PEEL *Why should I lend you mine when you've
broken yours off already, Malaga virgin.* & Preston
Hayman (perc). 15/7/76 MV4 TW BAI&DD

BRAZIL
17/8/90 FRI. ROCK *Why can't this be love, Sleepless night

(just another), Garden of Eden, Having a good time.
Nigel Harrison (v,perc), Barrie Gledden (g), Robin
Beanland (k), Andrew Greaves (b), David Moore (d).
20/7/90 MV5 MC~

BREED
7/9/91 PEEL† *Splinter, Perfect hangover, Pendulum, Hard
cash.* Steven Hewitt (d), Andrew Park (b), Simon Breed
(gv). 28/7/91 MV3 DG ME&FK

† On Strange Fruit SFMCD213.

THE BREEDERS
7/2/90 PEEL *Hellbound, When I was a painter, Iris,
Fortunately gone.* Kim Deal (agv), Tanya Donelly (gv),
Josephine Wiggs (b), Shannon Doughton (d).
22/1/90 Boston, USA * *

BILLY BREMNER
25/11/81 JENSEN *Cry cry cry, Trouble boys, Musclebound,
Didn't wanna get married.* Billy Bremner (gv), Gavin
Povey (p), James Ellar (b), Bobby Irwin (d).
12/11/81 MV4 JS *

BRENDA AND THE BEACH BALLS
26/8/86 LONG *Yummy ya, Moonbeams, Do you hear me,
Catch a falling star.* Brenda Kenny (v,perc) Steve Jeffries
(k), Bob Jones (g), Freddie Viadukt (b). 10/8/86 MV4 AJ PS

BREWER AND SHIPLEY
14/6/71 HARRIS *Tarkio road, People love each other, Witch
tai to (& Indian summer, 12/9/71).* Mike Brewer, Tom
Shipley. 1/6/71 T1 JM *

THE BRIDEWELL TAXIS
28/10/90 PEEL *Spirit, Whole damn nation, Face in the
crowd, Aegis.* Glenn Scullion (d), Simon Scott (b), Sean
McElhone (g), Gary Wilson (k), Chris Walton (tb), Mick
Roberts (v). 18/9/90 MV5 DG ME&JLO

MARC BRIERLEY
11/9/68 NIGHT RIDE *Matchbox men, Sunlight sleepers song,
Welcome to the citadel, Thoughts and sounds, Hold on
hold on the garden scene looks good on the floor.* *
11/9/68 * DK *

BRIGANDAGE
18/5/83 PEEL *Let it rot, Heresy, Hope, Fragile.* Michelle (v),
Mick Fox (g), Scott Addisson (b), Ben Addisson (d).
14/5/83 MV4 DG ME

ANNE BRIGGS
3/9/69 PEEL *The snow melts the soonest, No one was on
board, Sullivan's John, Go your own way.* Anne Briggs
(agv). 18/8/69 * * *

7/1/72 PEEL *Tangled man, Fire and wire, Hills of
Greenmore.* 19/12/71 PH JM JWH

BETTE BRIGHT AND THE ILLUMINATIONS
15/7/81 SKINNER *Rumour, Some girls have all the luck,
Soulful dress, Shoorah shoorah.* Bette Bright (v), Clive
Langer (g), Paul Pilnick (g), Bob B. Irwin (d), James
Eller (b), Henry Priestman (k), Ian Broudie (g).
26/6/81 LH1 DG ME

LEN BRIGHT COMBO
22/5/86 KERSHAW *Julie, Selina through the windshield,
Swimming against the tide of reason, Young upwardly
mobile... and stupid.* Eric Goulden (gv,o), Russ Williams
(bv,o), Bruce Brand (d). 7/5/86 Y2 DS *

BRILLIANT
8/11/82 PEEL *Colours/Break it down, Bells, Holst.* Marcus
Myers (gv), Youth (b,db), Tin Tin (b), Andy Anderson
(d); & Peter Ogi (k). 11/10/82 MV4 TW MC

26/11/84 LONG *Silent rage, Purple haze, Hesitation, Soul
murder.* Stephanie Holweck, Jake Le Mesurier, Brendon
Beal, June Lawrence, James Cauty, John Chester, Youth.
4/11/84 HP BYA *

THE BRILLIANT CORNERS
21/8/84 PEEL *Tangled up in blue, Sixteen years, My baby's
in black, Trash.* Bob Morris (d), Chris Galvin (b), Davey
Woodward (g,hca,lv), Winston Forbes (bkv).
11/8/84 MV5 DG MC

6/2/85 LONG *Honey whispers none, Across the border, Nine

out of ten unbelievers, Hidden snakes.* & Dan (k).
13/1/85 HP BYA *

5/6/86 KERSHAW *What can I do, Sweet Brendan, I never
said that, Happy capital.* Dan Pachini (tp) joins.
21/5/86 Y2 CG SR

15/12/86 PEEL *Arlington villas, Would it be sad?,
Anticipation, Trust me.* 23/11/86 * DG ME&FK

1/6/87 PEEL *Oh!, Please please please, I'll never be the
one to break your heart, Teenage.* 17/5/87 * DG ME&SC

DEREK BRIMSTONE
12/3/69 NIGHT RIDE *Back in Tobago, Little tin men, Mrs
Fisher and poem, Sing to me, Streets of London, Long
old summertime, Fairytale, Jon Curle's lullabye.* *
4/3/69 * JM *

BRINSLEY SCHWARZ
17/5/70 DLT *Mayfly, Shining brightly, Rock'n roll woman.*
Brinsley Schwarz (gv), Nick Lowe (bv), Bill Rankin (d),
Bob Andrews (ov). 6/5/70 MV5 PR DP

5/12/70 TOP GEAR *Seymour I love you, Funk angel, The
slow one, Rock and roll station.* Ian Gomm (g), Dave
Jackson join. 16/11/70 PH JW BC

9/8/71 HARRIS *Country girl, Range war, Merry-go-round,
What would you do.* Jackson out. 19/7/71 T1 PD *

13/1/72 DRUMMOND *She's got to be real, Unknown number,
Country girl, Nervous on the road.* 5/1/72 MV4 MB *

28/2/72 HARRIS *Unknown number, Wonder woman, Brown
sugar, She's got to be real.* 22/2/72 MV4 JG *

11/9/72 HARRIS *Havin' a party, Nervous on the road, Been
so long, You got us hummin'.* 30/8/72 AO2 JG *

12/12/72 PEEL *Hooked on love, Thirty pounder (do the
cod), Night flight, Hello mamma.* 27/11/72 T1 JW BC

2/4/73 HARRIS *I've cried my last tear, I worry, You never
can tell (& Play that fast thing, 14/5/73).*
28/3/73 LH1 PR BAI

8/10/73 HARRIS *Speedoo (1st TX ROCK ON, 6/10), Small
town big city, Down in Mexico, Murder on my mind.*
26/9/73 LH1 JG *

25/7/74 PEEL *What's so funny about peace love and
understanding (1st TX ROCK ON, 20/7), The ugly
things, You ain't living till you're loving, I'll take good
care of you.* 11/7/74 LH1 TW BAI

19/8/74 HARRIS *I got the real thing, Peace love and
understanding (& Small town big city, In in man,
28/10/74).* 24/7/74 LH1 JG *

20/2/75 PEEL *(You've got to be) Cruel to be kind, We can
mess around with anything but love, Gimme back my
love, Everybody.* 6/2/75 MV4 TW BC

THE BRITISH LIONS
22/5/78 PEEL *One more chance to run, Break this fool,
Wild in the streets.* Buffin (d,bkv), Overend Watts
(b,bkv), John Fiddler (lvg), Ray Major (lg,bkv), Morgan
Fisher (k,bkv). 10/5/78 MV4 TW NG

DAVE BROCK AND FRIENDS
29/1/69 NIGHT RIDE *Diamond ring, When I came home this
morning, Hesitation shuffle, Illusions, Ripley's blues, Roll
on Pete.* Dave Brock (g,v,hca), Mike King, Mike Greig,
Pete Judd. 21/1/69 S1 JM *

Brock telephoned and asked for an audition on
22/10/68. Recorded on MV3 28/11, passed.

BRONCO
7/7/70 HARDING *Time, Bumpers west, Well anyhow.* Jess
Roden (v), Robert Blunt (g), Kevyn Gammond (g), John
Pasternak (g), Peter Robinson (b). 30/6/70 MV5 MB MH&MF

29/12/70 HARDING *Civil of you stranger, House of the rising
sun, Woodstock.* 22/12/70 MV5 MB MH&MF

10/8/71 HARDING *Woman, Old grey shadow, Warminster
3rd part.* 2/8/71 MV5 MB MH&MF

4/9/71 TOP GEAR *Old grey shadow, Time slips away, New
day avenue.* 26/7/71 PH JW BC

24/1/72 HARRIS *Woman, Discernible, New day avenue,
Amber moon.* 19/1/72 AO2 JG *

6/9/73 PEEL *Strange awakening, Turkey in the straw, Steal

that gold. Paul Lockey (lv,g), Dan Fone (kg,hca), r. Roden, Blunt. 13/8/73 LH1 BA BC?

BRONSKI BEAT
16/5/84 JENSEN *Ain't necessarily so, Crazy Maraquitta, Why?, Memories.* Larry Steinbachek (k,dm), Steve Bronski (k,dm), Jimmy Sommerville (v). 6/5/84 MV5 DG ME

2/6/84 SAT. LIVE *Hard train, Small town boy, I feel love.* Live from S2 MRD TdB

15/10/84 PEEL *Close to the edge, Puits d'amour, The potato field, Ultra clone.* 25/9/84 MV5 MRD TdB

10/2/86 LONG *Come on, Hit that perfect beat, In my dreams, Back on me.* John Foster (v) r. Sommerville. 17/11/85 HP BYA NG

BRONX CHEER
2/8/70 R2 COUNTRY MEETS FOLK *KC Moan, Darling be home soon, Surprising find.* Brian Cookman (g,hca,v), John Reed (mnd,g,bj,v), Tony Knight (g,bj,v). 1/8/70 PH BB *

4/5/72 DRUMMOND *Barrelhouse player, The ballad of Reg Purvis, Springdale blues, Back door (& Lazy daze, 29/6/72).* & Charles Johnston. 24/4/72 MV4 MB MH&MF

1/9/72 PEEL *Springdale blues, KC Moan, Surprising find, Adult games, Flash in the park.* 15/8/72 TI JM *

30/4/73 SEQUENCE *No dice, Southern moon, Oh so easy, Walkin', Changes.* Peter Radley (d) r. Knight. 20/3/73 TI JM JWH&GB

ELKIE BROOKS
8/4/76 PEEL *Jigsaw baby, Lilac wine, Try a little love, Where do we go from here.* Elkie Brooks (v), Isaac Guillory (g), Pete Gage (g), Peter Van Hook (d), Steve York (b), Kirk Duncan (k), George Chandler (bkv), Jimmy Chambers (bkv), Lee Van Der Bilt (bkv). 16/3/76 MV4 TW MR [M: previous & subsequent, R1&2]

BROTHERHOOD OF BREATH
24/7/71 TOP GEAR *Union special, Call, Kongi theme, Think of something (& There is a spirit, not broadcast).* Chris MacGregor (p), Louis Moholo (d), Harry Miller (db), Alan Skidmore (ts), Gary Windo (ts), Dudu Pukwana (al), Mike Osborne (al), Nick Evans (tb), Malcolm Griffiths (tb), Mongezi Feza (tp), Mark Charig (tp), Harry Beckett (tp). 13/7/71 MV4 JW BC
Heirs to The Blue Notes, whose radio audition 10/65 was rejected by the Audition panel: 'lacking in precision' 'a cacophony' 'full of inaccuracies'. MacGregor's band did get sessions two years later.
20/6/72 PEEL *Do it, The serpent's kindly eye.* Keith Bailey (d), Evan Parker (ts) r. Moholo, Beckett. 13/6/72 MV4 PR * [M: Jazz shows].

THE EDGAR BROUGHTON BAND
16/3/69 TOP GEAR *Evil, For what you are about to receive, Love in the rain, Why can't somebody love me? (& Crying, 4/5/69).* Edgar Broughton (gv), Stephen Broughton (d), Arthur Grant (b). 27/1/69 PH BA *
'For the extreme sharp end only' Audition panel borderline pass.
10/8/69 TOP GEAR *They carried a star, Aphrodite, Psychopath blues, For the captain (& Medals, 25/10/69).* 4/8/69 PH JW *

11/8/69 WS R&B *Love in the rain, American boy soldier, Put me out to die.* 9/7/69 MV4 JG JY

17/1/70 TOP GEAR *Old Gopher, The moth, There's no vibrations but wait, Officer Dan (& Mama's reward, 4/4/70).* 5/1/70 PH JW BC

26/9/70 TOP GEAR *Freedom, What is a woman for, For Dr Spock, The house of turnabout.* 1/9/70 MV4 JW *

2/10/70 BLACK *Drop out Apache, For Dr Spock, Place of my own (& Evening over rooftops, 6/11/70).* Vic Unitt joins. 17/9/70 TI PD BH

3/7/71 TOP GEAR *Hotel room, Look at the mayor, Mama's reward.* 15/6/71 MV4 JW BC

20/8/71 BLACK *Call me a liar, The poppy song, The house of turnabout, Hotel room.* 9/8/71 TI PD *

17/3/72 PEEL *What a pity/I got mad, Side by side/Sister Angela, Chilly morning mama.* 14/2/72 TI JM *

7/7/72 PEEL *Homes fit for heroes, Gone blue, The rake, Side by side/Sister Angela.* 6/6/72 TI JM JWH

20/7/72 DRUMMOND *Hotel room, I got mad (soledad), Gone blue, Double agent.* 17/7/72 MV5 MB MH&MF

7/8/73 PEEL *Hurricane man/rock'n roller, Green light, Slow down.* 17/7/73 LH1 * *

THE CRAZY WORLD OF ARTHUR BROWN
8/10/67 TOP GEAR *Witch doctor, Nightmare, Devil's trip, I put a spell on you, Time.* Arthur Brown (v), Vincent Crane (o), Drachen Theaker (d); & guest Ron Wood (g). 3/10/67 AO2 BA *

28/4/68 TOP GEAR *Child of my kingdom, Come and buy, Fire†, I put a spell on you.* & (b) unknown. 8/4/68 PCI BA PR
Two further recording dates: 15/7/68 PS, TX 19/7/68 JOE LOSS show; & 30/7/68 PH, TX 3/8/68 SAT. CLUB. Line-up on final session Brown, Carl Palmer (d), Bill Davidson, Sean Nichols. † On 'Before the Fall' SFRCD203.

ARTHUR BROWN'S KINGDOM COME
3/4/71 TOP GEAR *No time, Night of the pigs, Gipsy (& Sunrise, not broadcast).* Arthur Brown (v), Goodge Harris (o), Andrew McCulloch (d), Des Fisher (b), Andrew Dalby (lg), Paul Brown (VCS3 sy). 22/3/71 PH PR *

15/6/71 HARDING *Eternal messenger, Galactic zoo.* Martin Steer (d) r. McCulloch. 7/6/71 MV5 MB MH&MF

3/9/71 BLACK *No time, Space plucks/Creation, Simple man, Metal monster trouble.* 12/8/71 MV4 JW *

14/1/72 PEEL *Night of the pigs, Bathroom.* Phil Shutt (b) r. Fisher; P. Brown out. 28/12/71 TI JM *
Also appeared on BBC African Service 24/2/72.

16/3/72 DRUMMOND *Whirlpool, Love is a spirit, The teacher/The experiment.* Billed just as 'Kingdom Come' from now on. 8/3/72 MV4 MB MH&MF

8/9/72 PEEL *Director general, Time captains.* Steer out; Brown (dm). 29/8/72 TI JM *

19/9/72 PEEL *Van Gogh's not ear, Triangles, Slow rock.* 5/9/72 MV4 * BC

ARTHUR BROWN BAND
24/4/75 PEEL *We've got to get out of this place, Dance, The Lord will find a way, Crazy.* Arthur Brown (v), Chris Nichols (k), Andy Dalby (g), Barry Clark (g), Steve York (b), Charlie Charles (d), Eddy Edwards (perc), George Khan (ss,ts), Stevie & Mutt Lang (bkv), & 10 Gospelaires (bkv-3). 17/4/75 MV4 PR *
Line-up recorded In Concert 23/4/75 PS, TX 17/5/75.

PETE BROWN AND PIBLOKTO
2/5/70 TOP GEAR *The politician, Here comes the old man dressed in flowers, Someone like you.* Pete Brown (v,perc), David Thompson (o,p,sx,perc), Jim Mullen (lg,perc), Robert Tait (d, perc), Steve Glover (b, perc). 21/4/70 MV4 JW *

27/8/71 BLACK *Airplane head woman, Dawn of night wasp, Got a letter from a computer.* 16/8/71 TI JM JWHorBH&BAI

BOB BROZMAN
29/10/89 KERSHAW *Zonky, Stones in my passway, Sister Kate shimmy, Death calypso.* Bob Brozman. 5/10/89 * DG NG&PA

JACK BRUCE
6/8/71 BLACK *The clearout, Theme for an imaginary western, You burned the tables on me, Folk song, A letter of thanks.* Jack Bruce (bv), Chris Spedding (g), John Marshall (d). 20/7/71 TI JM JWH&ARV

TIM BUCKLEY
7/4/68 TOP GEAR† *I'm coming here to stay, Morning glory, Sing a song for you, The troubadour (& Once I was, Hallucinations, 19/5/68).* Tim Buckley (agv), Edward 'Lee' Underwood (gv), Carter C.C. Collins (bgo) [& Tony Carr (d), says PasB, although people don't think he was there]. 1/4/68 PCI BA PR
† on Strange Fruit SFPCD082.
13/10/68 TOP GEAR *Love from room 170, Buzzin' fly, Untitled.* 1/10/68 PCI BA PR&BC

BUDGIE
25/2/72 PEEL *Hot as a docker's armpit, The author, Whisky river, Nude disintegrating parachutist woman.* Burke Shelley (bv), Tony Bourge (g), Ray Phillips (d). 1/2/72 TI JM *

3/11/72 PEEL *Hot as a docker's armpit, Stumble, Young is a world.* & Kidd Brown. 11/9/72 TI JM NG

1/7/76 PEEL *Sky high percentage, In the grip of a tyre fitter's... Myf Isaacs (g) r. Brown. 15/6/76 MV4 TW *

18/12/81 FRI. ROCK *I turned to stone, You're a superstar, She used me up.* Burke Shelley (bv), Steve Williams (d), John Thomas (gv). 27/11/81 MV4 TW DD

BUFFALO TOM
16/7/90 PEEL *Sunflower suit, Birdbrain, Bus, Fortune teller.* Bill Janovitz (gv), Chris Colbourn (bv), Tom Maginnis (d). 5/7/90 MV5 DG NG&RPF

24/2/92 GOODIER *Velvet roof, Staples, Darl, Tall lights fade.* 1/2/92 MV4 MC~ NK

BUILDING 44
11/4/83 PEEL *Azrael, Give me it back, Mr Opium.* Pete Reynolds (v), Kenneth Nelson (sy,v), Tony Jones (bv), Dave Riley (d,perc). 2/4/83 MV4 DG MC

TRIO BULGARKA
12/5/88 KERSHAW *Kazum Elenke, Dva Konya, Tru Byulbyula, Raditse le, Stratt Angelaki.* Janka Rupkina, Eva Georgieva, Stoyanka Boneva (all v). 28/4/88 * DG NG&FK

BULLET
23/12/71 DRUMMOND *Millionaire, Hobo (& No witch at all, 27/1/72).* John Gustafson (b), John Cann (lg), Al Shaw (v), Paul Hammond (d). 24/11/71 MV4 MB MH&MF

BUMBLE AND THE BEEZ
22/10/81 JENSEN *Brown eyes, Smile, Reasons for living, Plastic world.* Michael Riley (v,perc), Simon Walker (vi,k), Nick Page (lg), Dan Lee (rg), Winston Blissett (b). 11/10/81 MV4 DG ME&PS

ERIC BURDON AND THE ANIMALS
2/10/67 WS R&B *Gratefully dead, Hotel hell, Red house, San Fransisco nights.* This line-up unknown: possibly as 21/12 below. 4/9/67 * JG JY [M: previous, Light programme.]

31/12/67 TOP GEAR *All night long, Monterey, Orange and red beans, Anything, Chim chim cheree.* Eric Burdon, John Weider, Barry Jenkins, Danny McCullough, Victor Briggs. 21/12/67 * * *

26/5/68 TOP GEAR *White houses, Monterey, Landscape, When things go wrong (& It hurts me too, 23/6/68).* * 21/5/68 PCI BA DT

THE BUREAU
19/5/81 SKINNER *The first one, Find a way, Looking for excitement, Helpless.* Archie Brown (v), Pete Williams (b), Andy (Stoker) Growgott (d), Jeff Blythe (ts), Steve Spooner (al), Robert Jones (g), Mick Talbot (o), Paul Taylor (tb). 7/5/81 LH1 JS *

BURLESQUE
17/5/91 FRI. ROCK *Friends, Say it's alright, The man in me, Branded.* Steve Proctor (kd), Gee Labanca (gv), Chris Labanca (b). 19/4/91 MV5 TW DD

EDDIE 'GUITAR' BURNS
10/2/72 DRUMMOND *Kansas city, Bottle up and go, The thing to do/ Treat me like I treat you, Wigwam woman.* Eddie Guitar Burns (g), Roger Hill (lg), Dave Pegg (b), Bob Walker (d). 2/2/72 MV4 MB MH&MF

1/12/72 SEQUENCE *Ain't that lovin' you baby, I'm ready, Bottle up and go, Treat me like I treat you.* 26/10/72 LH1 JM *

JAKE BURNS
11/1/84 JENSEN *The company of strangers, Innocent man, Waltz on, Race you to the grave.* Jake Burns (g,lv) and the Big Wheel: Steve Grantley (d,perc), Sean Martin (b,bkv), Nick Muir (k,bkv). 18/12/83 MV4 JP *

5/6/86 LONG *Belfast 14, She grew up, Trapped inside, Breathless.* & Martin, Grantley, Phil Harrison (k), John Ablen (sx), Debbie Doss & Shirley Roden (bkv). 25/5/86 MV4 BYA MR

CLIVE BURR'S ESCAPE

24/2/84 FRI. ROCK *Enough is enough, Romancer, Top of the mountain, Take no prisoners.* Clive Burr (d), Bernie Shaw (v), Tino Troy (g), Chris Troy (b), Alan Nelson (k). 10/2/84 MV4 TW DD

BUTTERFLY CHILD

1/3/92 PEEL *Violin, Led through the Mardi Gras, Ship wreck song, Neptune's fork.* Joseph Cassidy (g,v,b), Gary McKendry (g), Rudy Tambala (prg). [See also PAPA SPRAIN.] 12/1/92 MV3 DG ME&PRB

THE BUTTHOLE SURFERS

12/8/87 PEEL *Florida, Cherub, Graveyard, Shotgun.* * Rec. date unknown, recorded in Texas * * *

27/9/88 PEEL *Blind man, EDG, Neee neee.* Gibby Haynes (v), King Coffee (d), Theresa Taylor (d), Jeff Pinkus (b), Paul Leary (g). 20/9/88 MV4 TdB TdB

BUTTSTEAK

15/5/92 PEEL *Keith meat thief, The kidd, Garnishy wages, I saw him burn his head, Wine dealership, Western opera, It's.* George M. Bowen (gv), Julie McDermott (kv), Jim Glass (g), Scott Hedrick (b), Sergio Ponce (d). 31/3/92 MV4 MR~ PL

BUY OFF THE BAR

13/10/86 PEEL *Peanut butter boy, Commie come back, Too shy to die/That man, Papa's music.* Loet Schilder (d), Marcel van Hoof (b), Paul Hekkert (gv), Ingmar van Wynsberge (g), Theo van Heynsbergen (g), Michael Lemmens (sx,v), Francois Moonen (tamb). 28/9/86 * DG ME

13/7/87 PEEL *Keyboard control, There's no fridge on the Bristol Bridge, In the back, No progression.* Jaj Bouwens (tp), Dirk Shouten (v,tamb) r. Heynsbergen, Moonen. 5/7/87 * DG TD&NG

18/7/88 PEEL *No money for the lavatory, Euroburger, Illegal shed, Go away.* Heynsbergen (tp) returns, Femke Hoyng (tamb,perc) r. Shouten. 3/7/88 * DG FK&MWT

4/9/89 PEEL *Hi America, Pleasure machine, Big sleep.* Dirk Shouten (g,bkv) returns, Theo Van Kempen (tp) r. Heynsbergen. 30/7/89 MV5 DG PL

MC BUZZ B

14/3/90 PEEL *Mr Smooth, Good mourning.* Native Rhythm (prd), Sean Braithwaite (v). 15/2/90 MV3 DG TD

THE BUZZCOCKS

19/9/77 PEEL† *Fast cars, Pulse beat, What do I get?* John Maher (d), Garth Davies (Smith) (b), Pete Shelley (lg), Steve Diggle (rg). 7/9/77 MV4 MB NG

17/4/78 PEEL† *Noise annoys, Walking distance, Late for the train.* Steve Garvey (b) r. Davies. 10/4/78 MV4 TW DD

29/5/78 JENSEN *I don't mind, Love you more, Noise annoys.* 8/5/78 MV5 PR *

23/10/78 PEEL† *Promises, Lipstick, Everybody's happy nowadays, 16 again.* 18/10/78 MV4 BS NG

4/12/78 JENSEN *16 again, What do I get?, Promises.* 16/11/78 PHM DFW TWN

28/5/79 PEEL† *I don't know what to do with my life, Mad mad Judy, Hollow inside, ESP.* Diggle (lv-2). 21/5/79 MV4 TW DD

Band's last BBC contract was live from Manchester Poly on Mike Read 22/5/80. † on Strange Fruit SFRCD104.

BYZANTIUM

7/5/74 PEEL *I'll just take my time, Half way there, Small world.* Jamie Rubinstein (g), Mick Barakan (g), Robin Lamble (b), Steve Corduner (d). 16/4/74 LH1 TW *

3/6/74 HARRIS *Oh darling, October Andy.* 22/5/74 LH1 JG *

CABARET VOLTAIRE

25/6/81 PEEL *Black mask, Greensborough, Walls of Jericho, Jazz the glass.* * Rec.date unknown PRIV * *

18/10/84 LONG *Sensoria, Digital rasta, Kino, Ruthless.* Richard Kirk (gk), Stephen Malinder (bv), Mark Tattersall (d,perc). 10/10/84 MV5 JS MPK

22/10/84 PEEL *Sleep walking, Big funk, The operative.* 14/10/84 MV5 DG ME

6/8/86 LONG *You like to torment me, Hey hey, We've got heart, Sex money freaks.* Mallinder, Kirk only. 27/7/86 HP BYA NG

CACTUS WORLD NEWS

30/10/85 LONG *Church of the cold, Jigsaw street, The porridge, State of emergency.* Eoin Mcevoy (agv), Fergal Andrews (b), Wayne Sheehy (d), Frank Kearns (lg). 16/10/85 MV5 BYA MPK

CADO BELLE

6/11/76 PEEL *Stone's throw from nowhere, Rough diamonds, Got to love.* Maggie Reilly (v), Alan Darby (g), Stuart Mackillop (k), Colin Tully (sx,fl), Gavin Hodgson (b), Davy Roy (d). 26/10/76 MV4 JG MR

R CAJUN AND THE ZYDECO BROTHERS

30/5/92 KERSHAW *Jolie blond, Bon ton roulet, Midland one step, Bosco stomp.* Freddy (d), Clive (g), Chris (acc,lv), Jan (tr,wsh), Sticky (b), Mitch (fd), Beeds (lv,hca). 13/5/92 MV4 DG NG&JB

CAJUN MOON

2/12/75 PEEL *Back again, Calling on, Fiddler John, Losers can be winners.* Allan Taylor (gv), Brian Golbey (fd,v), John Gillaspie (o,clav,v,bombarde). 6/11/75 MV4 TW *

8/1/76 PEEL *Underneath the cajun moon, Mistress music, Sawtooth line, Crowded city.* * 17/6/76 MV4 BAI BAI

JOHN CALE

8/5/75 PEEL *Taking it all away, Darling I need you, Fear, You know more than I know.* Pat Donaldson (b,bkv), Chris Thomas (hrp), Chris Spedding (g,kbv), Timi Donald (d,bkv), John Cale (p,g,v). 1/5/75 MV4 TW *

CAMEL

15/3/73 PEEL *Never let go, Arubaluba, Curiosity, Six ate.* Peter Bardens (v), Andy Latimer (gv), Andy Ward (d), Doug Ferguson (b). 19/2/73 LH1 BA *

3/9/73 HARRIS *The white rider, Earthrise, Lady Fantasy.* 22/8/73 LH1 JG *

JIMMY CAMPBELL AND ROCK'N HORSE

14/9/70 SYMONDS *That's right that's me, So lonely without you, Don't leave me now (& Green-eyed American actress, 16/11/70).* Line-up unknown. 25/8/70 PH BA *
Debuted live 3/5/69 on Country meets Folk, PH [M].

CAMPER VAN BEETHOVEN

30/3/87 LONG *One of these days, Eye of Fatima (part 1), Photograph, Never go back.* Victor Krummenacher (b), Greg Lisher (g), David Lowery (gv), Chris Pedersen (d), Jonathan Segel (vi,k,bkv). 15/3/87 MV4 HP TdB&TD

30/4/87 KERSHAW *Six more miles, Good guys and bad guys, Waka, Sad lover's waltz.* 19/4/87 * DG MWT&FK

CAN

13/3/73 PEEL *Untitled (as 'Up the Bakerloo with Anne Nightingale' on repeat).* Irmin Schmidt (elp,o), Jaki Liebezeit (perc), Damo Suzuki (v), Holger Czukay (b), Michael Caroli (g). 20/2/73 LH1 JW BC
1st UK TX was 3/3/73, on R1 In Concert.

12/2/74 PEEL *Tony wanna go.* Damo out. 29/1/74 LH1 TW (or JW) *

15/10/74 PEEL *Return to BB city, Tape Kebab.* 8/10/74 MV4 TW *

19/5/75 PEEL *Geheim†, Mighty girl.* 14/5/75 MV4 TW *
† On Strange Fruit 'Before the Fall' SFRCD203.

CANDYLAND

18/2/91 GOODIER *Rainbow, Precious, Something to somebody, Kingdom.* Felix Tod (v), David Wesley Ayers (g), Kennediid (b), M.C. Kenzie (d), Colin Payne (k). 2/2/91 MV5 MC~

CANNES

2/5/86 FRI. ROCK *Her eyes, Still the one, Edge of a dream, Tigers of Japan.* Andy Burns (b), Colin Peel (v), Gordon Roberts (d), Dave Senczak (g). 19/4/86 MV4 TW *

CANTON TRIG

20/8/73 HARRIS *Sunday is so beautiful, People in the night, Time to kill, Miss Karen Mutch.* Dave Evans, Dave Fuller (gv), Andy Fuller (perc,v), Rolf Spensley (g,b,elp). 1/8/73 LH1 JG *

Previous broadcasts on 'Folk on 2', from 12/71.

8/4/74 HARRIS *Practical man, Just gotta be you, You've got the gift (& Evening song, 15/7/74).* & Jeannie Roper (v), Sally Anne (v). 27/3/74 LH1 PR *

30/9/74 HARRIS *Living in the night, People like us, First conversation, When you've got to do.* James Warren r. Evans, Roper, Anne. 18/9/74 LH1 JG *

CAPARIUS

8/5/70 BLACK *Independence walk, Ooh baby.* * 18/3/70 * * *

CAPERCAILLIE

25/11/91 CAMPBELL *Fear a bhata, Waiting for the wheel to turn, Coisich a ruin, You will rise again.* Karen Matheson (v), Donald Shaw (k), Marc Duff (wh,bh), John Saich (b), Charlie McKerron (fd), Manus Lunny (g,bz), Ronnie Goodman (d). 23/10/91 MV4 PW MPK

CAPITAL LETTERS

24/1/79 PEEL *Smokin' my ganja, Rasta say, Fire.* Rodrick Harvey (d), Junior Brown (b), George Scarlet (g), Springey (gv), Danny McKen (gv), Earl Lynch (kv), Wenty Stewart (cga), Dell Spence (perc,v), Paulette Hayden (perc,v). 16/1/79 * BS MR

THE CAPITOLS

6/4/87 PEEL *I want to be alone, Who can tell?, Every time, Born yesterday, Failing again.* Phil (d), Jimbo (b), Tank (g), Sue (g,lv), Maria (vi,bkv). 24/3/87 * DG MR&MS

TONY CAPSTICK

18/7/72 PEEL *Sir Thomas of Winesbury, I drew my ship into a harbour, Captain Grant, Foggy dew, Bonny bunch of roses.* Tony Capstick (agv). 26/6/72 PH JW BC
1st appeared on Radio 4 North's 'Local Accent', 19/1/68.

26/12/72 PEEL *Charley, Punch and Judy man, The seeds of love, The only friend I own.* 19/12/72 LH1 JW *

11/6/74 PEEL *Lazlo Faher, Punch and Judy man, McCafferty, Old Mollie Metcalf.* 13/5/74 T1 * *
Also appeared on several Manchester-based folk shows for various BBC networks throughout early 70s.

6/1/75 PEEL *I drew my ship into a harbour, Van Dieman's land, Weak before Easter, Rambling sailor, Hello Hans.* 16/12/74 MV4 * *

CAPTAIN SENSIBLE

29/11/82 JENSEN *Martha the mouth, There ain't no thrilling Maggie (tonight), Happy talk†, The power of love.* Captain Sensible (bgkv '& motorbike'), Dave Ruffy (d), Dolly Mixture (bkv). 28/10/82 MV4 JWI MR
† On 'I and only' BOJCD025.

CARAVAN

5/1/69 TOP GEAR *Green bottles for Marjorie, A place of my own, Feeling reeling and squealing, Ride.* Pye Hastings (gv), Richard Sinclair (bv), David Sinclair (kv), Richard Coughlan (d). 31/12/68 MV4 BA BC
Next appeared live on R1 Club 5/2/69 PS.

3/2/69 BRANDON *A place of my own, Ride (4/2), Green bottles for Marjorie (6/2).* 27/1/69 MV4 c.RB *
2nd appearance live on R1 Club 14/3/69 from the Top Rank Suite, Plymouth.

14/9/69 TOP GEAR *The clipping of the eighth, Why, Excerpt from the daily routine of Maurice Haylett.* 26/8/69 MV4 JW *

14/11/70 TOP GEAR *Golf girl, For Richard, Hello hello.* 2/11/70 PH JW BC
Also recorded special session for Transcription's 'Top of the Pops' show, 9/9/70. TI.

9/4/71 BLACK *Love to love you, In the land of grey and pink, Golf girl, Love song without flute.* 11/3/71 AO2 JM JWH

17/4/71 TOP GEAR *Nine feet underground.* 29/3/71 PH JW BC

2/5/72 PEEL *Waterloo Lily, Love in your eye, The world is yours.* 11/4/72 MV4 * *

30/8/73 PEEL *Head loss, Memory lain Hugh, L'Auberge du Sanglier/A hunting we shall go/Pengola/Backwards.* John Perry (b), Geoff Richardson (vla) r. R. Sinclair (show presented by Alexis Korner). 20/8/73 LH1 BA *

1/10/73 HARRIS *Waffle (Be alright/Chance of a lifetime),*
Cthluthlu, Love in your eye. 12/9/73 LHI JG *

14/2/74 PEEL *Love in your eye, Virgin on the ridiculous,*
Mirror for the day, For Richard.
7/2/74 LHI TW *

3/7/75 PEEL *The show of our lives, Stuck in a hole,*
Dabsong Conshirto. Mike Wedgewood (b,cga) r. Perry.
26/6/75 MV6 TW *

17/5/76 PEEL *All the way, A very smelly grubby little*
oik/Bobbing wide/Come on back/Grubby little oik
(reprise). Jan Schelhaas (k) r. D. Sinclair.
6/5/76 MV4 TW BAI

10/5/77 PEEL *Behind you, The last unicorn, Better by far,*
Nightmare. Dek Messecar (b) r. Wedgwood, Schelhaas
out. 2/5/77 MV4 TW DD

CARCASS
2/1/89 PEEL† *Crepitating bowel erosion, Slash dementia,*
Cadaveric incubator of endo parasites, Reek of
putrefaction. K. Grumegargler (dv), J. Offalmangler (bv),
W. G. Thorax Embalmer (gv). 13/12/88 MV4 DG MR
† On Strange Fruit SFPS073.

16/12/90 PEEL *Empathological necroticism, Foeticide,*
Fermenting innards, Exhume to consume. Bill Steer
(g,lv), Jeff Walker (b,lv), Michael Amoit (g,bkv), Ken
Owen (d,bkv). 2/12/90 MV3 DG ME&DMC

THE CARDIACS
30/12/87 LONG† *R.E.S., Buds and spawn, In a city lining,*
Cameras/Is this the life. Tim Smith (glv), Sarah Smith
(sx,bv), Jim Smith (b,bkv), William D. Drake (k,bkv),
Tim Quay (perc,k), Dominic Luckman (d). 29/11/87 MV4.
† On Nighttracks SFNT013

CARMEL
9/8/83 JENSEN *I thought I was going mad, Hot dog, Willow*
weep for me, The drum is everything. Carmel McCourt
(v), Jim Paris (b,perc), Gerry Darby (d), Alex Webb (o),
Isaac Osapanin (perc), Helen Watson & Ingrid
Mansfield-Allman (bkv). 28/7/83 MV4 DG MR

10/9/83 LONG *Willow, Hot dog, Rue St. Dennis, I can't*
stand the rain. * 5/9/83 MR c,JL *

7/2/84 JENSEN *I thought I was going mad, The prayer,*
Sugar is sweet, Nothing. Carmel, Paris, Darby; &
Watson, Shirley Ladly (bkv-1 only), Isaacs Dankawa &
John Folalin (perc-2 only). 29/1/84 MV4 DG ME

30/4/90 CAMPBELL *Take it for granted, You've lost that*
loving feeling, If birds can fly, God put your hand on
me. & Toyin Adekale (bkv), Ricky Payne (bkv), Fayyaz
Virji (k), Poly Coussee (fl). 4/4/90 MV5 PW MPK

CARNASTOAN
4/1/82 PEEL *Progressive news, Natural man, Give a damn,*
Pirate. Conrad Kelly (d), Eugrall Brown (rg,lv), Neville
King (k,bkv), Anthony Bennett (b,bkv), Nigel Bowen
(bkv). 1/12/81 MV4 TW DD&MC

19/10/82 PEEL *Satan, Trouble on my mind, I don't want to*
lose you, Sufferer. Kelly, King, Bennett, Leo Green
(perc), Neville Brown (lv,rg). 29/9/82 MV4 RP NG

THE CAROL CONCERT
26/12/70 TOP GEAR *God rest ye merry gentlemen, Away in*
a manger, Good King Wenceslas, Silent night, O come
all ye faithful. David Bedford (p), & Marc Bolan, June
Child, Ivor Cutler, Sonja Kristina (& friend unknown),
Rod Stewart, Robert Wyatt, Mike Ratledge, Ron Wood,
Ronnie Lane, Peel & Pig, Kenny Jones, Ian McLagan (all
v). (2-Stewart only; 3-Lane & Wyatt solos; 4-Kristina
only). [Kevin Ayers contracted to appear, but didn't].
8/12/70 MV4 JW BC&IS

CARPENTER JOE
22/5/86 LONG *Path of most resistance, Not for nothing, No*
ordinary Joe, Dangling man. Robert Scott (gv), Russell
Maddox (b), Davy McGarry (g), Max Armstrong (d).
3/4/86 BEL JH JLN

THE CARPETTES
24/7/78 PEEL *Reach the bottom, I don't mean it, Away*

from it all, Indo-China. Neil Thompson (gv), George
Maddison (bv), Kevin Heard (d). 12/7/78 MV4 BS NG

21/12/78 PEEL *Cruel honesty, What can I do, It don't*
make sense, Double platinum, Routine. Tim Wilder (d)
r. Heard. 13/12/78 MV4 BS MR

CARLENE CARTER AND THE CC RIDERS
6/10/81 SKINNER *Billy, Love is a four letter-verb, Tougher*
stuff, I need a hit, Born to move. Carlene Carter (v),
Paul Carrack (p,o,v), Bob B. Irwin (d), James Eller (b),
Martin Belmont (g). 20/9/81 MV4 DG ME

CARTER USM
11/3/91 GOODIER *Sheriff Fatman, Prince in a pauper's*
grave, Sealed with a Glasgow kiss, A sheltered life. Jim
Morrison (g,lv), Les Carter (gv). 2/3/91 MV5 MA RPF

MARTIN CARTHY
30/5/72 PEEL *The false lover won back, King Henry, Died*
for love, Trindon Grange, John Blunt. Martin Carthy
(agv). 22/5/72 PH JW BC
   First broadcast accompanying Shirley Collins on Light
   Programme's Roundabout, 2/61 [M: Folk shows, dozens
   of them].

8/3/73 PEEL *John Barleycorn, Seven yellow gypsies, John*
Blunt (& Trindon Grange explosion, Brigg fair,
26/4/73). 19/2/73 * BA *

14/8/73 PEEL *Thorneymoor woods, Three jolly sneaksmen,*
The famous flower of serving men, The false lover won
back. 6/8/73 PH JW *

7/3/74 PEEL *Lucy Wan, Prince Heathen, Skewball, Geordie.*
28/2/74 LHI JW BC

3/10/74 PEEL *Bonny boy Billy boy, All of a row, The bed*
making, Green wedding. 16/9/74 * * *

28/4/75 PEEL *Sweet Joan, The trees they do grow high,*
The unfortunate sailor, The famous flower of serving
men. 22/4/75 MV4 * *

21/9/76 PEEL *The unfortunate tailor, King Knapperty,*
Willie's lady, Searching for lambs. 7/9/76 MV4 TW MR

16/12/77 PEEL *Willie's lady, Bonnets so blue, William*
Taylor the poacher, Three jolly sneaksmen, Brown
Adam. 7/12/77 MV4 MB NG

25/4/83 PEEL *The devil and the feathery wife, Tatty*
trousers, Lady Dysie, Long John, I sowed some seeds.
18/4/83 MV4 TW *

17/9/87 KERSHAW *When I was young, Rufford park*
poachers, Hommage à roche proulx, Company policy.
9/7/87 * DG TdB&MA

29/9/88 KERSHAW *La cardeuse, Aux anciens parapets, The*
dominion of the sword, The famous flower of serving
men. 15/9/88 MV4 DG TdB

9/9/90 KERSHAW *Sovay, A question of sport, Oh dear oh,*
Carthy's march/The lemon tree. & Dave Swarbrick (fd).
30/8/90 MV3 DG TdB

CASE
11/10/83 JENSEN *I ain't gonna dance, You'll be my fool,*
Let that one go, You know what's good for you.
Derwent (d,bkv), Marc Adams (b), Robert Brook (g),
Mick Donnelly (sx), Matthew Newman (v).
25/9/83 MV4 DG ME

PETER CASE
13/8/89 KERSHAW *Lay down little doggies lay down,*
Travellin' light, Walking bum, Power lust money, Poor
old Tom, Old part of town. Peter Case (gv,hca), Tymon
Dogg (vi-1 to 4 only). 31/7/89 EG2 MHW CBM

CAST OF THOUSANDS
8/5/86 LONG *Blue Connemara, Girl, Nothing is forever,*
Never forget. Greg Terry Short (d), Mark Megennety
(b), Jim Walker (g), David Harvey (v), Lorraine
Coleman (bkv). 27/4/86 BYA SC

CATAPULT
5/10/87 PEEL *Sink me, Hope, Subtle and tip, Undemocratic.*
Stephen Butler (gv), Martin Stebbing (b), Graham Clarke
(g), Richard Knight (d). 27/9/87 * DG ME

THE CATERAN
18/9/86 LONG *Story of shame, Difficult days, Everything to*

you, Last big lies. Tei Davidson (b), Cameron Fraser
(g), Murdo McCloud (g), Andy Milne (d), Sandy
McPherson (v). 10/9/86 MV4 BYA *

THE CATHERINE WHEEL
5/5/91 PEEL *She's my friend, Shallow, Black metallic,*
Painful thing. Neil Sims (d), David Hawes (b), Brian
Futter (g), Rob Dickinson (gv). 9/4/91 MV5 MR~

NICK CAVE AND THE BAD SEEDS
9/4/84 PEEL *Saint Huck, I put a spell on you, From her to*
eternity. Nick Cave (v), Hugo Race (g), Mick Harvey
(d), Barry Adamson (b), Blixa Bargeld (g).
28/3/84 MV5 RP NG

CAVERN
12/3/83 LONG *From me to you, Twist and shout.*
* 28/1/83 PHM c,JL *

CENTRY
26/5/91 KERSHAW *This is a message, The garden, African*
mask. Gil Cang, Nick Raphael. 2/5/91 MV5 PW NG&PA

THE CHAIRS
22/2/88 MAYO *Boys from Slumberland, Shakespeare's*
motorbike, Size 10 girlfriend, Neck of the woods. Dave
Read (k,bkv), Paul Sullivan (g,lv, hca), Trevor
Richardson (b), Kevin Lagen (d). 17/2/88 MV4 HP MPK

CHAKK
17/10/84 PEEL *Cut the dust, Sedative ends, #3 sound,*
Mother tongues. Dee Boyle (d), Mark Brydon (b),
Simeon Lister (sx), Alan Cross (k,tps), Jake Harries (v).
7/10/84 MV5 DG SC

8/8/85 LONG *Big hot blues, Stare me out, Imagination,*
Brain. John Stuart (v) joins. 17/7/85 MV5 BYA *

30/4/86 LONG *Cut the dust, Falling, Swell up, Love trip.*
13/4/86 MV4 BYA SC

THE CHAMELEONS
17/6/81 PEEL† *The fan the bellows, Here today, Looking*
inwardly, Things I wish I'd said. Mark Burgess (bv),
Dave Fielding (g), Reg Smithies (g), Brian Schofield (d).
8/6/81 LHI TW DD

30/6/82 JENSEN° *On the beach, Nathan's face, Up the down*
escalator, View from a hill. Martin Jackson (d) r.
Schofield. 9/6/82 PHM * TWN

14/6/83 PEEL† *Don't Fall, Nostalgia, Second skin, Perfumed*
garden. John Lever (d) r. Jackson, & Alistair Lewthwaite
(k) joins. 8/6/83 MV4 BYA *

11/8/83 JENSEN° *Thursday's child, Pleasure and pain,*
Monkeyland, Singing rule Brittania while the walls close
in. 14/7/83 MV4 JP MR

16/5/84 PEEL† *Dust to dust (Return of the roughnecks),*
One Flesh, Intrigues in Tangiers, P.S. goodbye.
Lewthwaite out. 5/5/84 MV5 DG MR
   † on Strange Fruit SFRCD114.

3/4/85 LONG *Home is where the heart is°, Intrigue in*
Tangiers, View from a hill°, Second skin. Andy Clegg
(k) joins. 13/3/85 MV5 JS MPK
   ° on Nighttracks CDNT001. Sleeve notes are
   incorrect: the Manchester session is included complete;
   'View' from it (complete with someone in the
   Playhouse audibly slamming a door) was broadcast;
   'Escalator', 'Nathan', 'Beach' only recorded in '82.

23/3/85 SAT. LIVE *Pleasure and pain, One flesh, Singing*
Rule Brittania.* Live from S2 MRD TdB
   * on B-side of 'Singing Rule Brittania (while the
   walls close in)' Statik TAK 35.

SHEILA CHANDRA
19/9/92 KERSHAW *Mecca, Kafi noir, Lament of*
Mcrimmon/Song of the banshee, Dhyana and donalogue,
Speaking in tongues I. Sheila Chandra (v).
30/7/92 MV4 MA~ CML

MICHAEL CHAPMAN
12/6/68 NIGHT RIDE *No one left to care, If I bring you*
roses, Sunday morning, One time thing, On my way
again. Michael Chapman (gv). 23/5/68 * JM DK
   When told this trial tape had to be submitted to
   the Audition unit, Chapman wrote in saying he'd

already been on WS R&B on 2/2/68. However, this possible first broadcast has proved untraceable on PasBs. He did guest on a Mike Cooper WS R&B session recorded 14/5/69, and TX 23/6/69 (and again in 1970 – see MIKE COOPER, below).

18/6/69 PEEL *Rabbit hills, No song to sing, Naked ladies in electric ragtime, Not so much a garden more like a maze.* 10/6/69 * PR *

31/8/69 TOP GEAR *Naked ladies in electric ragtime, You say, Postcards of Scarborough, Rabbit hills.* Chapman, Barry Morgan, Jack Asselman, Bruce Barthol (b). 11/8/69 PH JW *

25/4/70 TOP GEAR *Among the trees, Lady on the rocks, Not so much a garden more like a maze (& Landships, Soulful lady, 28/11/70).* & Rick Kemp (b), Ritchie Dharma (d). 7/4/70 MV4 JW *

2/11/70 HARRIS *The last lady song, Rude Louis rides again, On my way again.* & Phil Greenberg (g), Johnny Van Derek (vi). 23/10/70 MV5 JM JWH

16/1/71 FOLK ON 1 *Last lady song, Scholarly man, Lady on the rocks/Song for September, In the valley, She came in like the 6.15.* & Rick Kemp (b), Mick Ronson (g), Alex Atterson (p), Johnny van Derek (vi), Laurie Allan (d). 6/1/71 AO2 FL *

22/12/71 PEEL *Polar bear fandango, Night drive, In the valley, Time enough to spare.* * 13/12/71 * JW *

7/4/72 PEEL *Soulful baby, The hero returns, Shuffleboat river farewell, New York ladies.* * 20/3/72 * JM *

26/1/73 SEQUENCE *Back on the farm, Sea of wine, Wellington the skellington, The hero returns.* * 19/12/72 * JM *

30/10/73 PEEL *The hero returns, Firewater dreams, The dawning of the day, Time enough to spare.* Solo. 16/10/73 LH1 TW BC

23/7/74 PEEL *Time enough to spare, Rock and roll jigley, Banjo song, Firewater dreams.* & 3 unknown. 1/7/74 * * *

20/1/75 PEEL *Waiting for a train, Deal gone down, Party pieces, Among the trees.* * 14/1/75 MV4 TW MR

7/5/76 PEEL *Shuffleboat river farewell, Devastation hotel, Secret of the locks, How can a poor man stand such times and live.* & Brian Chatton (p,elp), Rick Kemp (b), Keef Hartley (d) "recorded on his birthday". 8/4/76 MV4 MB *

12/4/77 PEEL *Among the trees, Dogs got more sense, Secret of the locks, In the valley.* & Rod Clements (b), Keef Hartley (d, dynamic tambourine "from Woolworths"- JG). 15/3/77 MV4 JG MR

17/1/78 PEEL *Falling apart, Dogs got more sense, I'm sober now, Kodak ghosts.* & Andy Ward (d), Rod Clements (b), Brian Chatton (k), B.J. Cole (ps). 10/1/78 MV4 MB MR

CHAPMAN-WHITNEY STREETWALKERS
4/7/74 PEEL *Tokyo rose/Hangman, Systematic stealth, Get out of my life woman, Roxyanna.* * 27/6/74 LH1 TW *

15/7/74 HARRIS *Roxyanna, Burlesque, Call ya, I just wanna make love to you.* Roger Chapman (v), Charlie Whitney (g), Tim Hinkley (k), Mel Collins (sx), Ian Wallace (d), Bob Tench (g), Philip Chen (b). 12/6/74 LH1 JG *

28/8/75 PEEL *Burn it down, Toenail draggin', Crawfish.* John Plotell (b), Mick McBain (d) r. Chen, Wallace, Hinkley, Collins. 21/8/75 MV4 TW MR

18/6/76 PEEL *Daddy rolling stone, Run for cover, Me me horse and me rum.* Billed from now on just as 'Streetwalkers'. 8/6/76 MV4 TW *

11/4/77 PEEL *Chilli con carne, Mama was mad, Crazy charade.* Micky Feat (b,bkv), Dave Dowle (d), Bryan Johnston (k,bkv) r. Plotell, McBain. 14/3/77 MV4 TW DD

CHAPTERHOUSE
7/10/90 PEEL *Falling down, Something more, Inside of me, Treasure.* Ashley Bates (d), Russell Barrett (b), Simon Rowe (g), Stephen Patman (gv), Andrew Sherriff (gv). 23/9/90 MV3 DG MA

22/7/91 GOODIER *Breather†, Feel the same, Autosleeper, Falling down.* 13/7/91 MV5 MC~
 † On 'Best of Mark Goodier' Nighttracks Mark1.

CHARIOT
29/6/84 FRI. ROCK *Love or leave me, Heartless, Vigilante, When the moon shines.* Pete Franklin (gv), Scott Biaggi (lg), Jeff Braithwaite (d), John Smith (b). 25/5/84 MV4 DG MC

THE CHARLATANS
9/4/90 PEEL *Then, Always in mind, You can talk to me, Polar bear†.* Tim Burgess (v), Rob Collins (o), Jon Day (b), Jonathan Brookes (d), John Day (g). 20/3/90 MV4 DG TdB
 † On Strange Fruit 'New Season' SFRCD205.

4/6/90 GOODIER *Some friendly, Indian rope, The only one I know, White shirt.* Martin Blunt (b), Jon Baker (g) r. J. & J. Day. 19/5/90 MV3 MC~ PA

10/2/91 PEEL *Can't be bothered, Between 10th & 11th, Opportunity.* 22/1/91 MV5 MWT~

14/10/91 GOODIER *Weirdo, End of everything, Me in time, (No one) Not even the rain†.* Mark Collins (g) r. Baker. 5/10/91 MV5 MC~
 † On 'Best of Mark Goodier' Nighttracks Mark1.

CRAIG CHARLES
17/3/83 PEEL *Party night, Family way, Thought it was, Music scene, Oh to be in England, In the city.* Craig Charles (v) & Dave Treble (g), Pete Gray (bk), Stuart Gray (d), Alan Peters (tp-1 only). 2/3/83 MV4 RP MWT

14/2/84 PEEL *What can you do, Hands together eyes closed, Consulting his notebook he said..., Adolf Hitler.* & Brian Harcombe (d), Tony Doyle (b), Paul Morgan (g), Alan Peters (tp), Mike Nelson (sx), Jason R. Cunliffe (bkv) (4,5: Charles only). 7/2/84 MV5 MRD TdB

24/12/85 LONG *The nightmare, A seasonal complaint, Opening of the presents, The party.* Charles only. 10/12/85 B6 JS *

CHARLIE
10/5/76 PEEL *Fantasy girls, Prisoners, Summer romances.* * 13/4/76 * JG MR

THE CHARLOTTES
18/10/89 PEEL *Where you're hiding, See me feel, Could there ever be, Venus.* Petra Roddis (v), Dave Fletcher (b), Graham Garfiulo (g), Simon Scott (d). 21/9/89 MV5 DG MA

CHASAR
10/12/82 FRI. ROCK *Underground, Destiny, Visions of time, Devil's revenge.* Jim Marshall (d), Peter Marshall (b), Alec Pollock (g). 19/11/82 * TW DD

CHASE
28/2/85 INTO THE MUSIC *Lost in love, Lies, Rebel with a cause, Stand your sins.* Gary Hunt (d,bkv), John Cunningham (b.bkv), Mark Lathan (g,bkv), Mark Hall (k,bkv), Phil Harvey (v). 2/2/85 MV4 DG DD

THE TOMMY CHASE QUARTET
11/9/86 LONG *Killer Joe, Double secret, Baptist beat, East of the village.* Tommy Chase (d), Kevin Flannegann (sx), Mark Edwards (p), Martin Clute (b). 9/8/86 S2 DG NG

CHEAP 'N' NASTY
30/11/90 FRI. ROCK *Midnight emperor, Retribution, Mind across the ocean, Internal action.* Nasty Suicide (gv), Les Riggs (d), Timo Caltio (g), Alvin Gibbs (b), Mel Wesson (k). 9/11/90 MV5 DD~

THE CHEATERS
TX date uncertain JENSEN *Stop pushing, You, Kick, Drugs.* Mick Brophy (g,hca,v), Stewart Burnet (d,bkv), Neil Cossar (lg,bkv), Malcolm Smart (b,bkv). 10/12/81 MV4 JWI *

THE CHEFS
11/5/81 PEEL *One fine day, I'll go too, Love is such a splendid thing, Northbound train, Springtime reggae.* James McCallum (g), Russ Greenwood (d), Helen McCookerybook (bv), Carl Evans (gv). 5/5/81 LH1 DG MR

10/8/81 SKINNER *Sweetie, You get everywhere, Femme fatale, Let's make up.* 2/8/81 MV4 DG PW

CHELSEA
27/6/77 PEEL *No admission, High rise living, Right to work, Pretty vacant, Blind date.* Gene October (v), James Stevenson (g), Henry Daze (b), Carey Fortune (d). 21/6/77 MV4 JG MR

3/7/78 PEEL *No flowers, Urban kids, Come on, I'm on fire.* Dave Martin (rgv), Geoff Myles (bv), Steve Jones (d) r. Daze, Fortune. 26/6/78 MV4 JG DD

7/9/79 READ *Fools and soldiers, Don't get me wrong (18/9), Look at the outside (19/9), Trouble is the day (20/9).* 24/8/79 * * *

THE CHERRY BOYS
6/4/82 PEEL *Why don't you write?, Don't leave me that way, Come the day, Kardomah café.* Howie de Minzo (d), Keith Gunson (b), John Cherry (g), Jimmy Hughes (k). 20/3/82 MV4 DG MR

2/9/82 PEEL *Only fools die, In the dark, Nightmare, I'll keep on movin'.* 16/8/82 MV4 TW AP

16/12/82 JENSEN *Man to man, Plead sanity, Airs and graces, I remember.* 2/12/82 MV4 JS MR

23/4/83 LONG *Kardomah café, Shoot the big shot, Tell me.* 18/4/83 PHM cJL TWN

CHERRY FOREVER
17/8/91 PEEL *Spook, Down and around, Back to back, Higher than heaven.* Gaz Parker (d), Peter Vaughan (b), Mark Revell (g), David Parker (gv). 30/6/91 MV3 DG TD&AM

CHERRYBLADES
8/6/91 PEEL *On you, Make it mean, Stodge.* Tony Renyard (d), Darrin Woodford (b), Richard Larke (g), Tim Scott (gv). 7/5/91 MV5 MR~

THE CHESTERFIELDS
6/1/87 LONG† *Two girls and a treehouse, What's your perversion?, Oh! Mr Wilson, Love mountain.* Dominic Manns (d), Simon Barber (b), David Goldsworthy (g), Brendan Holden (g), Scott Tracey (perc). 17/12/86 MV4 DG MPK
 † On Nighttracks SFNT003.

3/3/88 MAYO *Twin town, Lunchtime for the wild youth, International walkabout, Let it go.* Mark (gv) r. Holden. 10/2/88 MV4 PW *

THE CHEVALIER BROTHERS
30/3/83 PEEL *Barnyard boogie, Coco beans, Twelfth St. rag, Fat like that.* Ray Irwin (sx,lv), Maurice Chevalier (g,bkv), Roger Downham (vib,bkv), Anders Janes (b,bkv), Ricky Lee Brown (d,bkv). 23/3/83 * RP MC

14/12/83 PEEL *On the tip of my tongue, C jam blues/Now's the time/Three-handed woman, Bartender.* Irwin, Downham, Janes, Patrice Serapiglia (g,bkv), Geoff Brittain (d). 7/12/83 MV4 RP TdB

11/1/88 MAYO *A flash in the pan, Just a gigolo/I ain't got nobody, On the sunny side of the street, Is you is or is you ain't me baby.* Roger Beaujolais (vib,perc), Ray Gelato (ts,lv), Mark Adelman (p), John Piper (d), Clark Kent (db). 16/12/87 MV4 HP MPK

CHEVIOT RANTERS
25/7/72 PEEL *Jigs: Rakes of Kildare/Smash the windows/The tenpenny bit, March: Danish double quadrille, Hornpipes: Ridesdale hornpipe/King of the fairies/Lads of Wickham, Reels: My love she's but a lassie yet/Caddam woods/The rose tree, Waltzes: Mallorea/Whittingham Green lane/The banks of the Tyne.* Bryce Anderson (acc), Jack Thompson (fd), Phil Sutherland (b), Geo. Mitchell (p), Jock Wilson (d). 12/7/72 NW JW *

11/7/74 PEEL *Rants: Corn jigs/Aiken drum/Island dance, Jigs: Traditional air/The frost is all over/Pet o' the pipers, Hornpipes, Waltzes: The lads who were reared among heather/Bonny cragside/The gentle maiden.* 3/7/74 NW JW *

226

JOHN CHIBADURA AND THE TEMBO BROTHERS

22/10/89 KERSHAW *Linda, Five thousand dollars, Chi meso meso, Rufu haru sarure.* John Chibadura (lv,g), Douglas Chibadura & Innocent Makoni (bkv), Mike Gunde (d), Bata Sintrio (g), Charles Ruwizhi (b). 12/10/89 HP DG MPK

6/12/89 PEEL *Shira, Diya wangu, Mukadzi wangu, Amai.* 19/11/89 MV5 DG ME

8/7/90 KERSHAW *Mudzimu yangu, Kugarika tange nhamo, Rudo.* Samson Mukanga (d) r. Gunde; & Jeffery Chavunduka (perc,bkv). 14/6/90 MV5 DG NG

8/9/91 KERSHAW *Kunatsa hama, Zuva refuxa kwangu, Lovemore, Hosana.* & Richard Matimba (sy); Chavunduka out. 8/8/91 MV5 DG NG&PRB

CHICKASAW MUDD PUPPIES

31/3/91 KERSHAW *Raven/Superior, Shannon love Bisquit, Do you remember, Jambalaya.* Brant Slay (wsh,hca,perc,v), Ben Reynolds (gv). 7/3/91 MV5 DG NG&CML

CHICKEN SHACK

28/1/68 TOP GEAR *Lonesome whistle blues, It's okay with me baby, The letter, When the train comes home, San-ho-zay (& My baby she loves me,* not broadcast). Stan Webb (gv), David Bidwell (d), Andy Silvester (b), Christine Perfect (kv). 9/1/68 AO2 BA *

‘Unanimous pass’ from Audition panel; ‘girl singer/pianist received special praise’.

28/4/68 TOP GEAR *See my baby, Waiting on you, Love me or leave me, You done lost your good thing now.* & Rik Gunnell (ts). 17/4/68 MV4 BA PR

29/4/68 SYMONDS *Waiting on you, Every day (30/4), When the train comes back (1/5), You ain't no good (2/5).* Gunnell out. 22/4/68 PH c.RB *

3/6/68 YOUNG *Blues on my mind (4/6), Lonesome whistle blues (5/6), It's okay with me baby (7/6).* Stan (lv-1,2), Christine (lv-3). 9/5/68 PC1 * *

8/9/68 TOP GEAR *Everyday I have the blues, Night life, Side tracked, Mean old world (& It takes a woman to make a man cry, 10/11/68).* 4/9/68 MV4 BA *

Appeared live on The Joe Loss Show, from PH, on Friday 6/9.

29/10/68 WS R&B *Take care of yourself, Have you ever loved a woman, I want to see my baby, Worried about my woman.* 11/10/68 AO2 JG JY

30/12/68 SYMONDS *One room lonesome country shack, Tell me (31/12), Hey baby (1/1/69), Loving loving loving (2/1).* 23/12/68 PH RB *

2/2/69 SYMONDS ON SUNDAY *The right way is my way, Pony and trap, If you believe in what you do, Night is when it matters†.* 27/1/69 AO2 JW TW

29/3/69 WS R&B *Unlucky boy, Lonely without you, The night is when it matters, One room lonesome country shack.* 5/3/69 MV4 JG JY

20/4/69 SYMONDS ON SUNDAY *Look Ma I'm crying, Hey baby†, I'd rather go blind†°.* 14/4/69 AO2 JW TW

° on ‘I and only’ BOJCD025.

22/6/69 TOP GEAR† *Midnight hour, Look ma I'm crying, Things you put me through.* Paul Raymond r. Perfect. 17/6/69 MV4 JW TW

31/8/69 SYMONDS ON SUNDAY *Midnight hour, Tears in the wind.* 25/8/69 AO2 c.PWI *

13/9/69 WS R&B *Things you put me through, Singe, Tears in the wind, Horse and cart.* 20/8/69 MV4 JG JY

Files next suggest the band appeared twice on R1 CLUB, recording on 9/10/69 & 2/1/70. Both of these broadcasts have proved untraceable.

5/4/70 RAVEN'S R&B *Telling your fortune, Diary of your life, Tired eyes, Dribblin'.* 18/3/70 MV4 JG JY

16/6/70 HARDING *Diary of your life, You knew you did what you did, Tired eyes, Telling your fortune.* 9/6/70 MV5 MB MH&MF

15/12/70 HARDING *You knew you did what you did, My way, Telling your fortune.* 8/12/70 MV5 MB MH&MF

8/4/71 HENRY *Poor boy, Crying won't help you now, Imagination lady.* John Glascock (b), Paul Hancox (d) r. Bidwell, Sylvester. 31/3/71 MV4 MB MH&MF

† On Band of Joy BOJCD002. At this stage it is not certain from which of their later sessions some of the tracks recorded more than once are drawn.

THE CHIEFS OF RELIEF

19/11/85 LONG *This is where it all began, Breakaway, The kiss of life, Walkabout.* Matthew Ashman (gv), Lance Burman (b), Duncan Grieg (k), Paul Cook (d). 3/11/85 HP BYA MC

THE CHIEFTAINS

5/9/70 TOP GEAR *Fox hunt, The Munster cloak, Lord Inchiquin, Kerry polkas, Strike the gay harp, An Maighdean mara.* Paddy Moloney (pp), Sean Keane (fd), Sean Potts (wh), Michael Tubridy (fl), Martin Fay (fd), Peader Mercier (bh). 3/8/70 PH JW *

Group's first R1 broadcast was on ‘Country meets folk’ PH 2/8/70.

3/10/72 PEEL *Lord Mayo, Sonny's mazurka/Tommy Hunt's jig, John Kelly's/Merrily kiss the quaker/Dennis Murphy's, Trip to Sligo, Planxty Johnson (& An goach aenas,* not broadcast). * 9/9/72 MV4 JW BC

20/3/73 PEEL *Drowsy Maggie, Planxty Johnson, The Munster cloak, Morning dew (& Lord Mayo,* not broadcast). 10/3/73 T1 JW BC

12/3/74 PEEL *Humours of Bally Connell/Bean an fhir rua/Cherish the ladies, Fanny power, Battle of Aughram, Three Kerry slides.* * 2/3/74 AO2 JW BC

16/10/75 PEEL *Samhra samhra, The humours of Bally Connell/Bean an fhir rua/Cherish the ladies, The humours of Carolan, Slides, 3 polkas.* Derek Bell (Irish hp) joins. 9/10/75 MV4 TW *

15/6/89 SKINNER *O'Mahoney's frolics, Full of joy, Women of Ireland/Chattering magpie, Here's a health, Planxty Browne medley, The iron man.* Paddy Moloney (pp), Sean Keane (fd), Martin Fay (fd), Derek Bell (Irish hp), Kevin Conneff (bh), Matt Molloy (fl). Live from MV3 KH *

29/7/91 CAMPBELL *Love theme from Barry Lyndon/Good morning, The road to sweet Athy, Galicia, Setting sail.* 3/7/91 MV5 PW MA

CHILLI WILLI AND THE RED HOT PEPPERS

19/4/73 PEEL *Friday song, Goodbye Nashville hello London town, Desert island woman, Truck driving girl.* Martin Stone (gv), Philip Lithman (gpv,vi), Paul Riley (bv), Paul Bailey (bj,gv), Pete Thomas (d). 9/4/73 LH1 BA *

28/2/74 PEEL *The natural evolution of the human life form as we know it from stage one to ultimate union with his creator, All in a dream, Choo choo ch'boogie, Fiddle diddle.* 21/2/74 LH1 * *

30/3/74 ROCK ON *We get along, Jungle song, I wanna love him so bad.* 25/3/74 LH1 BA *

8/8/74 PEEL *Fiddle diddle, Just like the devil, Nine to five songwriting man, Streets of Baltimore.* 25/7/74 LH1 TW *

21/9/74 ROCK ON *Wasn't born in Tennessee, Older guys, Midnight bus, Desert island woman.* 16/9/74 LH1 BA *

THE CHILLS

25/11/85 PEEL *Rolling man, Brave words, Wet blanket, Night of chill blue.* Martin Phillipps (gv), Terry Moore (b,bkv), Alan Haig (d), Peter Allison (k,bkv). 12/11/85 MV5 PWL MR

15/4/87 PEEL *Dan Destiny and the silver dawn, Living in a jungle, Rain, Moonlight on flesh.* Phillipps, Justin Harwood (bv), Andrew Todd (k), Caroline Easther (d,bkv). 5/4/87 * DG MR&MA

4/1/89 PEEL *Part past part fiction, Christmas chimes, Effloresce and deliquesce, Dead web.* Jimmy Stephenson (d) r. Easther. 18/12/88 HP DG ME

CHIMERA

23/1/92 GOODIER *Ellis bleeds, Slowburn, Innocence, Heals me (feels so strange).* Eileen Henry (v), Steven Emerson (b), Ted Laverty (g), Willie Wincent (d). 8/2/92 MV5 MC~ SB

CHIN CHIN

14/6/88 L. KERSHAW *Cheat boy cheat, Inescapable, Nowhere to run, Surf beat.* Karen Diblitz (gv), Esther Dick (b,bkv), Beatrice Graf (d). 25/5/88 MV4 PW MPK

CHINA CRISIS

1/4/82 PEEL *Seven sports for all, This occupation, Be suspiscious, Some people I know to lead fantastic lives.* Dave Reilly (d,perc), Gary Daly (v,b,k), Eddie Lundon (g,k). 22/3/82 MV4 JWI *

25/5/82 JENSEN *Hana Hana, You never see it, Animals and jungles, Reflections.* 16/5/82 MV4 DG *

27/1/83 PEEL *A golden handshake for every daughter, Wishful thinking, Watching the rainclouds, Greenacre day.* Daly, Lundon, Gary Johnson (b), Kevin Wilkinson (d), Steve Levy (ob). 15/1/83 MV4 DG MC

5/2/83 LONG *Scream down at me, Red sails, No more blue horizons, No ordinary lover.* * 1/2/83 PHM c.JL TWN

25/10/83 JENSEN *Papua, No ordinary lover, When the piper calls, The soul's awakening.* & Derek Lovelady (sy.p). 20/10/83 MV4 DG MR

18/3/85 LONG *King in a catholic style, Gift of freedom, Strength of character, Wall of God.* Lundon, Daly, Johnson, Wilkinson, Brian McNeil (k). 10/3/85 HP BYA PW

CHINA WHITE

2/2/90 FRI. ROCK *Live for night, Cry freedom, Sweet money, This time.* Hella (lv), Stephanie (bkv), Dave Steel (g), Sean Kelly (g), Mark Lambourn (b), Adrian More (d). 5/1/90 MV5 PW DD

CHINATOWN

25/6/82 FRI. ROCK *City woman, Back on the streets, Caught on the wrong side, I wanna see you tonight.* Steve Prangnell (v), Danny Gwilym (g), Pat Shayler (g), John Barr (b), Steve Hopgood (d). 11/6/82 * TW DD

CHINESE GANGSTER ELEMENT

10/9/84 PEEL *Red, In my body, Red light, This is hell.* Fiona McBean (kv), Mick Haymer (g), Andrew Greaves (g,bkv), Kevin Greaves (d). 1/9/84 * DG NG

TED CHIPPINGTON

17/8/87 LONG *Gay cavalieros, C.B. Savage, Pull up, Driving down the road.* Ted Chippington (v), Micky Harris (b), Cara Tivey (k), Dave Lowe (g), Mark Tibenham (dm). 2/8/87 MV4 HP TdB&MFA

P K CHISALA AND MASUSU

24/6/90 KERSHAW *Eva, Kilanguluka, Sunga Ilyashi.* P. K. Chisala (lv,g), Donald Mwelna (g), John Mulemena (g,lv), Abuild Madichi (b), Evans Blualya (d), Henry Lwanga (bkv). 31/5/90 MV3 DG NG

STELLA CHIWESHE

14/3/88 PEEL *Kachembere, Kana ndikafa, Chapfudzapasi, Vana vako vopera.* Stella Chiweshe (v,mbi,mrm) ‘& the Earthquake’: Virginia Mkewsha, Leonard Gwena, David Tapfuma, Tonderai Zinyawa, Joshua Araketa. 6/3/88 MV4 DG *

20/7/91 PEEL *Chimbochababa, Serewende, Guuarangu, Shungu.* & Earthquake: Gordon Mapika (d), Eric Makakora (b), Ephraim Saturday (g), Chinembira Chidodo (mbi), Leonard Ngwenya & Gilson Mangoma (mrm). 6/6/91 MV5 DG NG&CML

15/8/92 KERSHAW *Mahororo, Ewe mudiwa (broken heart song), Hondende, Sarurawaka, Mbira kwoyedza (mbira at dawn).* & Henry Matimba & Gilson Mangoma (mrm), Joshua Mufunde (g), Ephraim Saturday (b), Albert Ruqizhi (d), Muruva Chikwateri (perc). 4/6/92 MV4 DG NG&PA

THE CHORDS

9/7/79 PEEL *Now it's gone, It's no use, Something's missing, Maybe tomorrow* Chris Pope (lg), Billy Hassett (rg,lv), Martin Mason (bv), Brett Ascott (d). 3/7/79 * MR ME

24/3/80 PEEL *Tumbling down, Happy families, Far away.* 11/3/80 MV4 JE MR

CHORDS

15/8/92 PEEL *Gasping, My dearest friend, Plastic sister, The mirror.* Simone Holsbeek (gv), Marcel Morsink (g,bkv), Marc Fabels (d), Arnoudt Pieters (d). 28/7/92 MV4 MA~ PL

CHRISTIANS IN SEARCH OF FILTH
31/8/82 PEEL *Fast food, Super rich, Work, Gorilla.* Alex Usborne (g), Dan Rubinstein (g), Simon Lewis (d), Akinola (perc), Dave Benady (b), Reed Pimlot (sx), Rick Walker (cl). 11/8/82 MV4 JWI TdB

THE CHRISTIANS
22/7/86 LONG *Forgotten town, Save a soul, One in a million, Why waltz.* Roger, Russell & Garry Christian (v), Bob Roberts (g), Henry Priestman (o,perc), Paul Barlow (d), Tony Jones (b), Dave Dickie (kg). 6/7/86 MV5 BYA *
19/3/87 LONG *When the fingers point, Hooverville, Born again.* Mike Bulger (g) r. Roberts, Dickie out. 11/3/87 MV4 DG JB

KEITH CHRISTMAS
16/12/74 HARRIS *Could do better, Brighter day, Country farm, Song of a drifter.* Keith Christmas (gv), Pearce Kelly (d), Dave Wilkinson (p), Adrian Shaw (b), Andrew Dolby (g). 4/12/74 MV4 JG *

CHROME MOLLY
8/2/85 FRI. ROCK *Lose again, Lonely, Don't fight dirty, Too far gone.* Steve Hawkins (v), Nick Wastell (b), Mark Godfrey (d), John Antcliffe (g). 11/1/85 MV4 TW DD

CHUMBAWAMBA
21/8/92 PEEL *Agadoo, The birdie song, Knock three times, Y viva Espana.* Harry Hamer (d), Julian Walker (b), Boff (g), Danbert (k), Dunston Bruce (perc), Maviy Dillan (tp), Lew Watts (v). 2/8/92 MV4 TdB~ SA

CHICK CHURCHILL
21/1/74 HARRIS *Ode to an angel, Dream of our maker man, Broken engagements, Come and join me.* Chick Churchill, Cozy Powell, Bernie Marsden, Leo Lyons, Gary Pickford Hopkins, & I (unknown). 12/12/73 LH1 JG *

THE CIGARETTES
24/1/80 PEEL *Can't sleep at night, Frivolous disguises, It's the only way to live (die), Valium world.* Rob Smith (g,v,p), Steve Taylor (b,bkv), Adam Palmer (d). 15/1/80 * JS MR

THE CIMARRONS
16/12/75 PEEL *Tradition, Dim the lights, You can't beat us.* * 4/12/75 MV4 * *
13/12/78 PEEL *Rock against racialism, Civilisation, Reggae rockin'.* Locksley Gichie (gv), Franklyn Dunn (bv), Carl Levy (kv), Maurice Ellis (d), Winston Reid (lv). 6/12/78 MV4 BS NG

CINDERELLA MC
5/6/88 MISS P *Future plan, Aids is the kill, Joker lover, Storyteller.* Cinderella (v), Leroy Matthew (k), Dave Fluxy (d), Tony 'Scully' Cooper (k). 26/5/88 MV5 PW JB

CIRCUS
24/4/68 NIGHT RIDE *Who would love her?, Gone are the songs of yesterday, The patience of a fool, Do you dream.* Mel Collins (ts,fl), Alan Bunn (d), Ian Jelfs (lg), Phillip Goodhand-Tait (v), Kirk Riddle (b). 23/4/68 AO2 DK DT
'Outdated, square, rubbish, badly played, out of tune... NO' Unanimous fail from Audition panel.

CITY LIMITS CREW AND THE MUTANT ROCKERS
23/1/85 PEEL *Fresher than ever, Sucker, Money, Keep it on.* Little Stevie Bee & Pretty Boy Gee (rp), Erica Harrold (bkv), Damon Butcher & Ricky Rennalls (k), Paul K. Edgley (g,b-2), Budd Beadle (sx). 15/1/85 MV5 MRD MR

CLAIRE
22/7/87 PEEL *Who haunted Mrs Robbins?, Wife lover killer, Passions for Pamela, Filled with fear.* Ian Wilson (gv), Pete Devine (g), Ian Williams (b), Andy Williams (d), Ian Wilky (perc). 14/7/87 * DG MR&MS

CHRIS CLARK AND THE JOHNNY WATSON CONCEPT
17/12/67 TOP GEAR *Love's gone bad, From head to toe, Do right baby, I want to go back there again, Gotta get you into my life.* * 1/12/67 * * *

CLARK HUTCHINSON
5/2/71 BLACK *They've started complaining, A boat in the morning mist, Spanish OD, Best suit.* Andy Clark (o,v), Mick Hutchinson (lg), Steve Amazing (b), Del Coverley (d). 14/1/71 AO2 JM JWH

JOHN COOPER CLARKE
6/11/78 PEEL *I married a monster from outer space, Readers' wives, Health fanatic, Spilt beans.* John Cooper Clarke (v). 31/10/78 MV4 TW MR
15/3/82 PEEL *Midnight shift, The day my pad went mad, Night people, The new assassin.* & Steve Hopkins (k), Steve Williams (b), Richard Darbyshire (g), Martin Hannet (g), Trevor Spencer (d). 24/2/82 MV4 KH NG
25/6/83 LONG *Health fanatic, The day my pad went mad, I wanna be yours.* * 6/5/83 PHM c.JL *

CLIMAX CHICAGO BLUES BAND
26/5/69 WS R&B *Insurance blues, Times are getting tough, It was a dream, Flight.* Colin Cooper (v,hca,sx,fl,g), Arthur Wood (o,p), Peter Haycock (v,g,hca), Derek Holt (b,o,p), George Newsome (d). 30/4/69 MV4 JG JY
13/12/69 WS R&B *City ways, Hey baby, Louise, One more time.* 12/11/69 MV4 JG JY
26/7/70 RAVEN'S R&B *Looking for my baby, One room country shack, Long loving man, Train.* 8/7/70 MV4 JG JY
3/12/70 HENRY *Spoonful, Papa hat, Morning noon and night, Flight.* Anton Farmer (o,v) r. Wood. 26/11/70 AO2 MB MH&MF
9/1/71 RAVEN'S R&B *So many roads, Everyday, Insurance blues, Long loving man.* 28/12/70 MV5 MB *
20/4/71 HARDING *Going to New York, Come into my kitchen, Train (& Shoot her if she runs, 11/5/71).* 12/4/71 MV5 MB MH&MF
9/10/71 RAVEN'S R&B *Hey mama, Chevrolet, Keep me running.* 29/9/71 MV4 KS *
25/3/74 HARRIS *Reaching out, Amerita, Before you reach the grave.* John Cuffley (d) r. Farmer, Newsome. 20/3/74 LH1 PR *
7/10/74 HARRIS *Milwaukee truck song blues, Amerita/Sense of direction, Losin' the humbles, Right now.* 18/9/74 LH1 JG *
17/10/74 HARRIS *Shopping bag people, Amerita/Sense of direction, Reaching out, Before you reach the grave.* 26/9/74 MV4 TW BAI
2/10/75 PEEL *Devil knows, I am constant, Running out of time, Using the power.* & Richard Jones (k). As 'Climax Blues Band' from now on. 9/9/75 MV4 * MR
8/10/76 PEEL *Couldn't get it right, Chasin' change, Together and free, Mighty fire.* 16/9/76 MV4 TW BAI

CLOCK DVA
7/6/83 PEEL *Sister, Beautiful losers, Dark encounters.* Adi Newton (tp,v), Paul Browse (sx,k), Nick Sanderson (d), John Carruthers (g), Dean Dennis (b). 25/5/83 MV4 BYA TdB

THE CLOSE LOBSTERS
15/7/86 LONG† *Nothing really matters, Heaven rains, Pathetic trivia, Never seen before.* Stewart McFadyen (d), Bob Burnett (b), Graeme Wilmington (g), Tom Donnelly (g), Andy Burnett (v). 29/6/86 MV4 BYA MC
† On Nighttracks SFNT008.
4/1/88 PEEL *Loopholes, From this day on, What is there to smile about?, Mirror breaks.* 15/12/87 * DG MR&MC

CLOUDS
13/4/70 FERRIS *Imagine me, I know better than you, Carpenter.* Billy Ritchie (o), Ian Ellis (b), Harry Hughes (d). 18/3/70 PH BA *

CLOUDS
23/11/91 PEEL *Dude electric cell, Poll tax blues, King of the rocket men.* Balloon (d), Helicopter Hot-Rock (b),

Bruce Starbuck (g), Vim Void (v,g), Doctor Cosmos (sy). 29/9/91 MV3 DG ME&JMK

THE CLOUDS
9/2/87 LONG *Village green, Jenny Nowhere, Round in circles, Thinking.* John Charnley (gv), Bill Charnley (k,bkv), Norman Blake (g), Andy Brady (b), Gino Ionta (d). 1/2/87 MV4 JE TdB

CLOVEN HOOF
10/6/83 FRI. ROCK *Laying down the law, Crack the whip, Return of the passover, Road of eagles.* Steve Rounds (g), Lee Payne (b), Kevin Pountney (d), Dave Potter (v). 27/5/83 * TW DD
21/10/89 FRI. ROCK *Mistress of the forest, Astral rider, Mad mad world, Fox on the run.* Lee Payne (b), Andrew Wood (g), Lee Jones (g), Russ North (v), J.B. (d). 8/9/89 * TW DD

THE COAL PORTERS
3/6/90 KERSHAW *Hey hey Johnny, Roll Columbia roll, What am I doing (in this thing called love), The man who invented the blues.* Billy Frank (d), Ian Thomson (b), Chris Buessem (g), Sid Griffin (g,lv), Toby Petrie (sy). 17/5/90 MV5 DG DD

COBRA
19/1/92 PEEL *Tek him, Be patient, Fulfillment, Yush.* Don Campbell (d), Kenton Brown (b), Tony Phillips (g), Carlton Ogilvie (sy), Tony Thomas (electric perc), Cobra (v). 29/12/91 MV3 DG ME&JRS

COCHISE
14/3/70 TOP GEAR *Velvet mountain, Woodland lifetimes, Past loves.* B.J. Cole (ps), Richard Wills (b), Mick Grabham (lg), Willie Wilson (d), Stuart Brown (v). 3/3/70 MV4 JW *
7/9/70 SYMONDS *Why I sing the blues, Watch this space, China, Down Country girls (home again).* John Gilbert (v), r. Brown. 11/8/70 PH BA PK&NG
7/11/70 TOP GEAR *Love's made a fool of you, Why I sing the blues, Words of a dying man, Moment and the end.* 26/10/70 PH JW BC
19/1/71 HARDING *Country comfort, Love's made a fool of you, Painted lady.* 18/1/71 MV5 MB MH&MF
1/5/71 TOP GEAR *Hummingbird, Why I sing the blues, The dream, Midnight moonshine.* 20/4/71 MV4 * *
24/6/71 HENRY *Dance dance dance, Diamonds, Rick's song (many times), Ray's song (up and down).* 16/6/71 MV4 MB MH&MF

BRUCE COCKBURN
1/1/73 HARRIS *Feet fall on the road, Fall, Sun wheel dance, Dialogue with the devil.* Bruce Cockburn (pgv). 6/12/72 LH1 PR BAI?
Rec'd In Concert following day at The Paris, TX 30/12/72.
26/8/89 SAT SEQ *Shipwrecked at the stable door, Tibetan side of town, If I had a rocket launcher.* 25/8/89 'CON L' onair studios, Egton House KH KBD

JOE COCKER AND THE GREASE BAND
9/6/68 TOP GEAR *Something's coming on, Marjorine, Mr. bus driver, I shall be released (& With a little help from my friends, 14/7/68).* Joe Cocker (v), Chris Stainton (b), Mike Gee (g), Tommy Eyre (o), Tom Riley (d). 20/5/68 PCI BA PR
Recorded onair audition for Aidan Day at R1, 16/5/68, passed by panel 21/5.
16/6/68 HENRY *Mr. bus driver, Just like a woman, Marjorine, Let's go get stoned.* 9/6/68 PS AD *
17/6/68 SYMONDS *Bye bye blackbird, Something's coming on (18/6), Let's go get stoned (19/6), Marjorine (20/6), Come back baby (21/6).* 11/6/68 MV4 C RB *
6/10/68 HENRY *Something's coming on, Can't be so bad.* 30/9/68 AO2 AD *
13/10/68 TOP GEAR *Can't be so bad, With a little help from my friends, Let's go get stoned, Run shaker life.* & 3 singers. 7/10/68 PCI BA *

14/10/68 Symonds *Sandpaper cadillac, Change in Louise (15/10), With a little help from my friends (16/10), Marjorine (17/10)*. Henry McCullough (g), Ken Slade (d), r. Gee, Riley. 4/10/68 PCI RB * [M]

11/10/69 Top Gear *Laudy Miss Clawdy, Darlin' be home soon, Hello little friend, Delta lady*. Alan Spenner (b), Bruce Rowlands (d) r. Slade, Eyre. 29/9/69 PS JW TW

COCKNEY REBEL

11/6/74 Peel *Bed in the corner/Sling it, Mr.Soft, Sweet dreams/Psychomodo*. Steve Harley (gv), Paul Jeffreys (b), Stuart Elliott (d), Milton Ream James (p), Jean-Paul Crocker (vi). 28/5/74 LHI TW *

Group's first R1 broadcast was 'In Concert' recorded 22/1/74, TX 26/1.

THE COCKNEY REJECTS

15/8/79 Peel *East End, Are you ready to ruck, Flares'n slippers, They're gonna put me away*. Stinky Turner (v), Mick Geggus (g), Vince Reardon (b), Andy Scott (d). 8/8/79 MV4 TVD MR

25/2/80 Peel *Cockney rip off, 15 nights, I wanna be a star, Block buster*. Nigel Woolf (dv) r. Scott; & the road crew (v, shouting). 13/2/80 MV4 JE NG

COCO, STEEL AND LOVEBOMB

17/11/87 Long *I want a Salvador Dali crash wall, I don't believe in miracles, Hi honey, Cash on 45*. Ali Butt (v), MC Mike (dsc), Andrew Dobell (tp,kg), Mark Waterman (gb), Christopher (dsc,v) & drummer 'on tape'. 8/10/87 HP HP&ME

THE COCTEAU TWINS

15/7/82 Peel *Wax and wane, Garlands, Alas dies laughing, Feathers oar/Blades*. Robin (g), Liz (lv), Will (b). 21/6/82 MV4 JWI DD&ME

31/1/83 Peel *Hearsay please, Dear heart, Blind dumb deaf, Hazel. & Cindy Talk (Gordon Sharp) (v)*. 22/1/83 * DG HP

4/10/83 Peel *The tinderbox (of a heart), Strange fruit, Hitherto, From the flagstones*. Fraser, Guthrie only. Rec. date unknown OS * *

10/10/83 Jensen *Sugar hiccup, In our angelhood, Musette and drums, My hue and cry*. 2/10/83 MV4 DG ME

5/9/84 Peel *Pepper tree, Whisht, Peep bo, Otterley. & Simon Raymonde (b)*. 29/8/84 * BYA NG

LEONARD COHEN

14/7/68 Top Gear *That's no way to say goodbye, You know who I am, Bird on a wire, So long Marianne (& Dress rehearsal rag, 11/8/68)*. Leonard Cohen (agv) & Tony Gilbert for 5 musicians (including Dave Cousins, banjo) & 3 singers. 9/7/68 PCI BA DT

LLOYD COLE AND THE COMMOTIONS

26/5/84 Sat. Live *Glory, Patience, Perfect skin*. Lloyd Cole (v), Neil Clark (g), Stephen Irvine (d), Blair Cowan (k), Lawrence Donegan (b). Live from S2 TdB MFA

16/7/84 Skinner *Rattlesnakes, Speedboat, Forest fire, Andy's babies. & Joslyn Pook (vi-1,2), Audrey Riley (clo-1,2)*. 5/7/84 MV5 MHY *

12/8/85 Long *Speedboat, Perfect blue, Brand new friend, James*. Live from BBC Edinburgh * *

LLOYD COLE

26/3/90 Campbell *A gift, Don't look back, Sweetheart, Perfect skin*. Lloyd Cole (gv), Robert Quine (lg), Matthew Sweet (g,bkv), Blair Cowan (k), David Ball (b), Dan McCarroll (d). 7/3/90 MV4 PW MPK

COLENSO PARADE

22/7/85 Long *Hallelujah chorus, Too late for anything, Bad blood between us, Anything*. Robert Wakeman (d), Neil Lawson (b), Terry Bickers (g), Linda Clendinning (k), Oscar (v). 10/7/85 MV5 BYA MPK

EDWYN COLLINS

25/8/86 Long *Judas in blue jeans, Wheels of love, Don't shilly shally, You're better than you know*. Edwyn Collins (gv), Malcolm Ross (lg), Dennis Bovell (b), Chris Taylor (d), Alex Gray (k). 13/8/86 MV4 BYA *

SHIRLEY COLLINS

5/3/69 Night Ride *Nelly the milkmaid, Fire and wine, Ramble away, Dreamsong, Lowlands, The finite time, Oliver Woodworm, The spirit of Christmas*. Shirley Collins with the Tinderbox (2,4,6,7,8-Tinderbox only). 28/1/69 S1 JM *

SHIRLEY AND DOLLY COLLINS

8/5/68 NIGHT RIDE *Whitsun dance, Lovely John, Good dog, A blacksmith courted me, Over the hills and far away*. Shirley (v) and Dolly Collins (k). 7/5/68 S1 DK *

[Premiered Anthems in Eden song cycle on 'My kind of Folk' 8/8/68 (M: Folkshows)]

15/3/73 Peel *Nelly the milkmaid, The blacksmith, Morris dance medley, The banks of the bawn*. * 12/2/1973 * BA *

COLON

31/7/90 Peel *Top quality sturdy bargains, Disco bar, Corno, Sex cadet*. Nicky Smith (bv), Phil Reynolds (gv), Selwin Callister (g), Colin Christian (dm). 3/7/90 MV3 MR~

THE COLORBLIND JAMES EXPERIENCE

24/10/88 Peel† *Polka girl, Hey Bernadette, Havoc theme, Wedding at Cana*. Jim McAveney (d), Ken Frank (b), Phillip Marshall (lg), Dave McIntire (sx,cl), John Ebert (tb), Colorblind James (rg,vib,v). 18/10/88 MV4 MR~
† On Strange Fruit SFPCD076.

27/10/88 Kershaw *Considering a move to Memphis, In the diamond mine, Circus girl, If you love each other*. 20/10/88 MV4 DG TdB

27/11/89 Peel *Some night, Rollin' 'n' tumblin', It didn't work out, I'm never gonna hurt the girl I love. same, except 'Joe Colombo' (tb)*. 7/11/89 MV5 DG MR

JON HISEMAN'S COLOSSEUM

19/1/69 Top Gear *The road she walked before, Those about to die, Backwater blues, A whiter spade than Mayall (& Debut, 2/3/69)*. Jon Hiseman (d), Dick Heckstall-Smith (sx), Dave Greenslade (o,vib), Tony Reeves (b), James Litherland (gv). 17/12/68 PCI BA AH

20/1/69 WS R&B *Debut, Backwater blues, A whiter shade of Powell*. 20/12/68 AO2 JG JY

16/3/69 Symonds On Sunday *Walking in the park, Beware the Ides of March, Plenty hard luck*. 24/2/69 AO2 JW TW

24/5/69 Walker *Walking in the park, Disprination, Butty's blues, I can't live without you*. 19/5/69 CM c.JBU *

6/7/69 Top Gear *Elegy, Grass is greener, Hiseman's condensed history of mankind, February's valentine (& Butty's blues, 31/8/69). & Barbara Thompson (sx,fl)*. 30/6/69 PH JW TW

20/7/69 Symonds On Sunday *Elegy, The road she walked before, Walking in the park*. 15/7/69 PCI PWI *

6/8/69 R1 Jazz Workshop *Those about to die, Mandarin, Butty's blues, Grass is greener, Elegy, Debut*. 17/7/69 PH c.RE *

22/11/69 Top Gear *Lost Angeles, Grass is always greener, Arthur's moustache. & Thompson, & Dave 'Clem' Clempson (gv) r. Litherland*. 18/11/69 MV4 JW TW

Last appearance under original name on John Peel's Sunday Show Concert, Rec'd 5/3/70 PS, prod. JG, TX 8/3/70.

COLOSSEUM

7/4/70 Harding *Bring out your dead, Time lament, Daughter of time*. Thompson out. 31/3/70 MV5 MB MH&MF

21/7/70 Harding *Butty's blues, Shades of blue, Rope ladder to the moon, Tanglewood '63, Rebirth*. Louis Cennamo (b) r. Reeves. 28/6/70 PH MB MH&MF

19/2/71 Black *Take me back to doomsday, Skeleton, Pirate's dream, Tanglewood '63*. Mark Clarke (bv), Chris Farlowe (v) r. Cennamo. 20/1/71 TI JM JWH

This line-up had debuted on a second John Peel Sunday Concert, Rec'd 29/10/70 PS, TX 8/11/70, prod. JG.

10/9/71 Black *Jumping off the sun, Sleepwalker, Pirate's dream (& Upon a tomorrow, 11/10/71)*. 2/9/71 T1 JM JWH&ARV

COLOSSEUM II

23/8/77 Peel *Put it this way, Intergalactic strut, Lament,*

The inquisition. Jon Hiseman (d), Gary Moore (g), Don Airey (k), John Mole (b). 15/8/77 MV4 TW DD

1st Colosseum II line-up, with Neil Murray (b), & Mike Starrs, debuted on In Concert 26/6/76.

COLOUR BOX

11/11/82 Jensen *Punch, Kill it, Water up the tap, Bleach*. Martin Young (g,sy), Ian Robbins (dm,g,sy), Stephen Biggs (g,sy), Debbion Currie (v). 31/10/82 MV4 DG ME

5/6/84 Jensen *Low rider, The wanderer, The look of love, You keep me hanging on*. Lorita Grahame (v-3,4), Ray Conroy (v-2), r. Currie. 29/4/84 MV5 DG ME

THE COLOURFIELD

4/2/85 Long *Faint hearts, Castles in the air, Cruel circus, Virgins and philistines*. Pete De Freitas (d), Pete Barrett (k), Terry Hall (v), Toby Lyons (g), Katrina Phillips (bkv), Karl Shale (b), Jim Morrison (g), Tim Whitaker (perc). 23/1/85 MV5 JS MPK

COLOURS OUT OF TIME

26/5/81 Peel *Listen to me now, The waiting, Asylum, 5 4 3 2 1*. Steve Reynolds (v), Dave Roberts (g,bkv), Andy Pennance (g), Philip Bourne (b), John Durrant (d), Clive Williams (o). 18/5/81 LHI TW DD

COME

18/4/92 Peel *Bell, Off to one side, William, Dead Molly*. Arthur Johnson (d), Sean O'Brien (b), Chris Brokaw (g,bkv), Thalia Zedek (gv). 2/4/92 MV4 DG NG&JI

COME IN TOKYO

4/2/82 Peel *Tokyo, Nature call, Walk away, Save me from falling*. Alan Curry (d), Frank Mahon (b), John Gillin (lg), Phil Wylie (rg,lv), John Jenkins (k). 23/1/82 * DG MR

28/9/82 Peel *What lurks behind old satan's door?, Number one, Say you'll never go away again (& Change of style, possibly not broadcast)*. 15/9/82 PHM JL *

2/12/82 Jensen *The day the world fell round your head, Read the news, You can tell everybody, Temper - count to ten*. 21/11/82 MV4 DG ME

10/5/84 Peel *Say you'll never go away again, Turn walk away, Been such a long time waiting for love, It was nothing*. Craig Blade (k) r. Jenkins; Gillin out. 28/4/84 MV5 DG MR

COME TO THE EDGE

6/1/72 Drummond *Xinga, Dorien terilament*. Robin Thompson (sx,k), Morris Pert (perc), Andrew Powell (bk, perc). 5/1/72 MV4 MB MH&MF

THE COMMUNARDS

23/10/85 Long *So cold the night, Don't slip away, America, Forbidden love/La Dolorosa*. Jimmy Sommerville (v), Richard Coles (k). 13/10/85 HP BYA PW

COMPANY 2

20/9/89 Peel *I'm breathing thru this, Bear no malice, Tell it as it is*. Ben Chapman (dj), David Harrow (k), Lee (Stepz) Bennett (v). 20/8/89 MV5 DG ME

THE COMPASS FLOW

14/4/87 Long *Take me away, Standing in the rain, You can take it, Serious mistakes*. Brian Cain (g), Scott Blain (d), Craig Keaney (b), Kenneth Brown (k), Paul MacNeil (v). 4/3/87 MV4 DG ME&TD

COMSAT ANGELS

25/10/79 Peel† *Total war girl, Independence day, Baby, Ju-ju money*. Steve Fellows (lvg), Andy Peake (k,bkv), Kevin Bacon (b), Mick Glaisher (d). 10/10/79 MV4 TVD NG

8/5/80 Peel† *Real story, Monkey pilot, Waiting for a miracle, Home is the range*. 29/4/80 MV4 BS MR

9/2/81 Peel† *Dark parade, Eye of the lens, Be brave, At sea*. 3/2/81 LHI DG MR

13/4/81 Skinner† *Gone, Be brave, Eye dance, Total war (intensified)*. 3/4/81 LHI DG TdB

7/10/81 Peel† *Now I know, Ju ju money, Our secret, Goat of the west*. 28/9/81 MV4 KH HP

23/8/83 Jensen† *A world away, Nature trails, Island heart, Mr Memory*. Paul Robertson (g) joins. 14/8/83 MV4 DG ME

19/11/83 Long *Island heart, Independence day, Nature trails, What else*. 3/11/83 PHM c.PWL PSM

19/8/85 Long† *Forever young, Close your eyes, High tide, Citadel.* Robertson out. 11/8/85 HP BYA DD

    † on 'Time considered' RPM 106, plus tracks from two other RI tea-time sessions not listed here.

CONSOLIDATED

24/11/91 Peel *America No.1, This is fascism, No censorship, Meat kills.* Adam Sherburne (gv), Mark Pistel (k), Philip Steir (d). 8/10/91 MV4 JB~ PL

CONTINUUM

13/8/70 Henry *Bouree-Bach, Appolosis, Release/Approach of judgement (& Invention in A minor, 17/9/70).* Yoel Schwartz (g,fl,rec,hmn), John Warren (g), Dick Wildman (d), Mike Hart (db). 6/8/70 AO2 MB MH&MF

COOK DA BOOKS

14/2/83 Peel *Low profile, Do one, I wouldn't wanna knock it, Falling.* John Leggett (d), Gwen Moran (bv), Peter 'Digs' Deary (gv), Tony Prescott (k). 7/2/83 * JP *

17/9/83 Long *Becoming a stranger, You've got to learn how to fight it, Over cocktails, I'm not the kind.* 12/9/83 PHM DS PSM

28/2/84 Peel *Keep on believing, Golden age, I wouldn't touch you, Hurt me deep inside.* 18/2/84 MV5 DG MC

THE COOKIE CREW

8/5/85 Peel *B the place to be, The cut master swift rap, It's gotta be fresh.* Suzie Q (v), Reme-Dee (v). 28/4/85 MV5 DG ME

23/9/85 Peel *Party people, On the beat, All you people, Radio one tribute, Sipho. '& Sipho Hah!': Sipho Jozana (hbb), Debbie Pryce (rp), Susan Banfield (rp). 10/9/85 * JWI MS

27/4/87 Long *Easy to rock, Top of the head, Busy beat, World class.* & Peggy Lee (human beat box-3,4 only) & The Beatmasters (backing track). 18/4/87 MV5 HP TdB

MIKE COOPER

7/8/68 Night Ride *Leadhearted blues, Tadpole blues, Divinity blues, The way I feel, Maggie Campbell.* Solo (agv). 7/8/68 S2 DK *

30/4/69 Peel *Turtle blues, Death letter blues, Poor little Annie, Electric chair, Oh really.* 29/4/69 PH PR BC

23/6/69 WS R&B *Crow Jane, Death Letter blues, See the fish, Naked ladies and electric ragtime, Unfinished ending.* with Mike Chapman (5; 3,4-Chapman solo). 14/5/69 MV4 JG JY

15/11/69 Top Gear *Spider and the fly, I think she knows me now, Moon going down, Tell me papa.* Mike Cooper (gv), Jo-Ann Kelly (p), Bob Ball (p) (3-Cooper out). 20/10/69 PH JW BC

12/4/70 Raven's R&B *I think she knows me now, Keep looking back, Soulful lady, Blast load.* with Mike Chapman (3,4-Chapman solo). 18/3/70 MV4 JG JY

24/6/70 R2 Night Ride *I think she knows me now, Too late now, Watching you fall, Journey to the East, Turtle blues, Theme in C, Your lovely ways.* 9/6/70 PS DMY *

1/1/71 Black *Don't talk too much, Good times, Watching you fall, Tanglewood 63.* & The Michael Gibbs Band. 9/12/70 AO2 (or TI) JM JWH

2/1/71 Top Gear *Wish she was with me, Black Monday, Take a look around, I've got mine (& Too late now, 20/3/71).* 7/12/70 PH JW BC

26/6/71 Raven's R&B *Turtle blues, Fulton Alan, Black Monday, Blues for Andalusia, Gotta get away.* 16/6/71 MV4 MB *

2/12/71 Drummond *Paper and smoke, Too late now, Song for Abigail, Night journey.* & (sx), (p), (b), (d) unknown. 22/11/71 MV5 MB MH&MF

21/3/72 Peel *3.48, I think she knows me now, Time to time, Few short lines.* Solo. 6/3/72 PH JW BC

21/4/72 Peel *Morning glory, The singing tree, Night journey, Three forty.* Mike Cooper's Machine Gun Company: & Bill Boazman (g), Geoff Hawkins (ts), Les Calvert (b), Tim Richardson (d). 28/3/72 JM *

12/1/73 Sequence *Get a hymn, Wish she was with me, I've got mine, Keep on rolling.* Ian Foster (d) r. Hawkins, Richardson. 12/12/72 TI JM *

14/9/73 Sequence *Saturday night, Sister Anne, Your lovely ways, Slowly but surely.* Solo. 2/8/73 LHI JM *

27/6/74 Peel *Suicide deluxe, Black night crash, Beads on a string.* Mike Cooper & the Trout Steel Band: Mike Cooper (rgv), Terry Clarke (g,bkv), Mike Osbourne (al), Colin Boyd (b), Harry Miller (db), Louis Maholo (d). 20/6/74 LHI PR *

26/6/75 Peel *Wild rover, Blind Willie, Beads on a string, Rock and roll highway.* & Les Calvert (b), Roger Keene (perc,fl). 19/6/75 MV4 * * [See 'Uptown Hawaiins', below].

COP SHOOT COP

24/3/91 Peel *If tomorrow ever comes, Drop the bombs, Slipped clutch, Coldest day of the year.* Tod (b,v-1,2,4), Natz (b,v-3), Cripple Jim (smp), Phil Pyled (d,perc). 26/2/91 MV5 MR~

16/5/92 Peel *Surprise surprise, Nowhere, Rm 429.* & KJ (bkv-3 only). 28/3/92 MV3 DG ME&SCO

JULIAN COPE

10/2/83 Peel *Head hang low, Lunatic and fire-pistol, Hey high-class butcher, The greatness and perfection of...* Julian Cope (gv,sit,k,perc), E.O. Cas (dm), Kate St. John (ww). 5/2/83 MV4 DG TdB

16/1/84 Jensen *Reynard the fox, 24A Velocity Crescent, O king of chaos, Laughing boy.* Cope, St. John, Steve Lovell (g), Donald Skinner (g), John Dillon (d). 5/1/84 MV4 JP *

11/6/84 Peel *Me singing, Sunspots, Search party, Hobby.* Cope, Skinner only. 29/5/84 MV5 MRD ME

31/12/84 Long *Disaster, Christmas morning, Pulsar, Crazy farm animal.* & Joss Cope (kv). 12/12/84 MV5 JS MPK

8/9/86 Long *Shot down, World shut your mouth, Eyes volcano, Planet ride: Transporting.* Cope, Skinner, James Eller (b,bkv), Chris Whitten (d,bkv), Richard Frost (k). 6/8/86 MV4 BYA NG

4/5/91 Peel *Hanging out and hung up on the line, You think it's love, The mystery trend, Soul medley: Free your mind/Everything/Hung up.* & Peggy Suicide: Skinner, Tim Bran (bk), Rooster Cosby (d). 11/4/91 MV5 DG NG&PL

THE COPPER FAMILY

13/4/72 Drummond *Spencer the rover, Sportsmen arouse, The echoing horn, Come write me down, When Spring comes in (& Clodding banks, Babes in the wood, 8/6/72).* * 5/4/72 * MB MH&MF

PHILIP CORDELL

15/1/69 Night Ride *Quality street, When summer's here again, That's a mighty road, Winning in the end, Anna syde.* Philip Cordell (agv). 8/1/69 SI JM *

THE CORPORATION

3/11/82 Peel *Threats and promises, Hard times, Hip talk, Open season.* Paul Winters (gv), Keith Robson (bv), John Alexander (d), Rob MacLagan (sx), Brian Bull (tp,g), Grahame Cusak (perc,cga). 18/10/82 * TW DD

THE CORTINAS

26/7/77 Peel *Defiant pose, Television families, Having it, Further education.* * 16/7/77 MV4 TW DD

ELVIS COSTELLO AND THE ATTRACTIONS

1/8/77 Peel *Less then zero, Mystery dance, Red shoes, Blame it on Cain.* Elvis Costello (lvg), Peter Thomas (d), Bruce Thomas (b), Steve Naive (p,o). 25/7/77 MV4 TW DD

20/3/78 Peel *(I don't wanna go to) Chelsea, The beat, Pump it up, You belong to me.* 13/3/78 MV4 TW DD

17/4/78 Jensen *Lip service, You belong to me, Pump it up, The beat.* 7/4/78 MV5 PR ME

30/10/78 Peel *Really mystified, Radio radio, (I just) don't know what to do with myself, Stranger in the house.* 23/10/78 MV4 TW DD

3/3/80 Peel *High fidelity, Possession, Beaten to the punch, B movie.* 25/2/80 MV4 TW DD

13/10/81 Jensen *Why don't you love me like you used to do?, Tonight the bottle let me down, Colour of the blues, Sweet dreams.* 8/10/81 MV4 JS *

21/6/83 Jensen *Pills and soap, Danger zone, Shipbuilding, Big sister's clothes/Stand down Margaret.* 9/6/83 MV4 JP MR

ELVIS COSTELLO

15/3/89 Skinner *Deep dark truthful mirror, Pads paws and claws, God's comic, Tramp the dirt down.* Costello solo (agv). 14/3/89 EG2 KH PS

THE COUNT BISHOPS

17/5/76 Peel *Takin' it easy, Confessin' the blues, Wang dang doodle, Dust my blues.* Zenon de Fleur (rgv), Johnny Guitar (lgv), Steve Lewins (b), Paul Balbi (d). 4/5/76 * JG MR

27/7/77 Peel *Til the end of the day, Don't start me talking, Hands on the wheel, I want candy.* & Dave (v). 20/7/77 MV4 * NG

COUNTRY GAZETTE

5/3/73 Harris *Durham road, Pretty boy Floyd, Fallen eagle, Hot burrito breakdown, Sounds of goodbye.* Byron Berline (fd,mnd,v), Roger Bush (db,v), Alan Munde (bj), Kenny Wertz (g,lv). 28/2/73 LHI PR BAI

20/3/73 Peel *Virginia darlin', Keep on pushing, I might take you back again, Rawhide.* 5/3/73 TI JW *

22/10/73 Harris *Down the road, Fallen eagle, The black mountain rag, Swing low sweet chariot (& Good woman's love, 3/1/74 PEEL).* Roland White (g,bj,v) r. Wertz. 3/10/73 LHI JW *

3/11/73 Rock On *Never ending song of love, Huckleberry hornpipe, I don't believe you've met my baby, Keep on pushing/Tried so hard/Swing low sweet chariot.* 4/10/73 LHI PR BAI

31/7/75 Peel *Sunday sunrise, Working on a building, The last thing on my mind, Hide your love away, Improve your mind, Dear old dixie.* David Ferguson (fd,v) r. Berline. 22/7/75 TW MR

WAYNE COUNTY AND THE ELECTRIC CHAIRS

18/6/79 Peel *Waiting for the marines, Berlin, C4, Midnight pal.* Wayne County (lv), Henry Padovani (kgb), Elliot Micheals (g), Val Haller (bk), J. J. Johnson (d,tp), David Cunningham (p-2 only). 11/7/79 MV4 TW DD

JIM COUZA AND MACLAINE COLSTON

6/10/88 Kershaw *Cranes over Hiroshima, Liberty/Soldier's joy, Jamie Allen/Blackberry blossom, My old man/1st prelude 'The well-tempered clavier', Poor wayfaring stranger, If you don't love your neighbour then you don't love god.* Jim Couza (dul,lv), Maclaine Colston (dul,g,bkv). 8/9/88 MV4 DG NG&SC

COWS

27/6/90 Peel *Big Mickey, You are so beautiful†, How dry I am†.* Tony Oliveri (d), Kevin Rutmanis (bv), Thor Eisentrager (g), Shannon Selberg (v,bu). 3/6/90 MV3 DG ME&FK

    † On Strange Fruit SFMCD212.

LOL COXHILL

13/6/72 Peel *Felicidad, Whitefield music II, Mood, Whispering.* Lol Coxhill (sx), David Bedford (p), Ted Speight (gp-1) John Walters (mel-4 only). 22/5/72 JM JW BC

10/8/72 Drummond *Jack in the box, Crotchet 96, Tover bal, Mood.* Lol Coxhill (sx) & 2 (unknown). 25/7/72 * * *

19/6/73 Peel *Bath '72, Monk, Fire and rain, Theme for Mrs. Grieg.* 7/5/73 * JW BC

THE LOL COXHILL-DAVID BEDFORD DUO

16/8/71 Harris *Alone on the raft, When the king went riding by, I hab de bloom, Pretty little girl.* Lol Coxhill (sx), David Bedford (p). 27/7/71 TI JM JWH

10/11/71 Peel *Pretty Little girl, Hungerforf, It's easier than it looks, Don Alfonso (& Pretty little girl pt.2, 4/1/72).* 25/10/71 * JW *

COYNE CLAGUE

24/9/69 Peel *The stride, I wonder where, Sixteen women, Get right church.* Kevin Coyne (v), David Clague (b),

Martin Sax (lg), Nick Cudworth (p), Tat Meager (d).
28/8/69 PH PR *

Passed by panel: 'A very good blues singer,' backed by band 'who did not impress the panel so much'. Band changed name to Siren 1/70 (see below).

KEVIN COYNE
27/7/72 DRUMMOND *Araby, Mother where are you now?, Evil island home, Head boy.* Kevin Coyne (gv).
10/7/72 MV5 TW *

30/1/73 PEEL *Mummy!, Smile, Pretty park, Breathe in deep.* 2/1/73 LHI JW BC

18/9/73 PEEL *Karate king, Everybody's saying, The fat girl, Chicken wing.* & Gordon Smith (g). 20/8/73 TI * BC

6/10/73 ROCK ON *Marlene†, I want my crown, Cheat†, Lonesome valley.* & 4 (unknown). 27/9/73 LHI PR BAI

12/11/73 HARRIS *Home on the hill, Chicken wing, Eastbourne ladies.* & 5 (unknown). 24/10/73 LHI JG *

31/1/74 PEEL *Poor swine†, Need somebody†, Araby, Do not shout at me father†.* & Smith, Tony Cousins (b), Chilli Charles (d). 24/1/74 LHI PR BAI

25/6/74 PEEL *Mrs. Hooley go home, It's not so bad, The stride, Blame it on the night.* Terry Slade, Rick Dodds r. Charles. 4/6/74 LHI TW *

26/8/74 HARRIS *Bewitched, Mummy, Another man goes down, Right in hand (& Marjorie Razorblade suite, 4/11/74).* & Tim Penn. 24/7/74 LHI JG *

10/12/74 PEEL *The miner's song†, Evil island home†, Looking for the river, Dance of the bourgeoisie.* Pete Nu (p) r. Penn. 26/11/74 MV4 TW BC&MR

18/3/77 PEEL *You know who, Araby, Rainbow curve.*
7/3/77 MV4 * *

1/3/78 PEEL *That's rock and roll†, Lunatic, River of blood†, I only want to see you smile.* 'all these songs written for and sometimes during the session' KC to Peel. 22/2/78 MV4 * NG

19/9/79 PEEL *A leopard never changes its spots†, Nothing's changed, Memory lane pt.12, Ey up me duck†.* & Bob Ward (g). 5/9/79 MV4 TVD MR

8/7/82 PEEL *Tell the truth, Liberation, You won't like it, I talk to myself, You'll never walk alone.* & Pete Kirtley (ag), Steve Bull (sy). 7/6/82 MV4 TW DD

1/9/88 KERSHAW *The chairman's ball, Witch, Rambling operator, Good boy.* & Robert Coyne (g).
18/8/88 MV4 DG TdB

5/3/90 PEEL *Tear me up, City crazy, We're going to heaven, I couldn't love you†.* & 'Paradie Band': Martin Muller (d), Friedrich Pohrer (b), Hans Pukke (g), Henry Beck (sy). 11/2/90 MV3 DG MA
† On Strange Fruit SFRCD112.

25/3/90 KERSHAW *Daddy, Juliet and Mark, Sunshine home, Back home boogie.* with Paradie Band again.
1/3/90 MV5 DG NG

19/5/91 KERSHAW *Victoria smiles, Dynamite days, Evil island home, Karate king.* & Pukke (g) only.
7/2/91 MV5 DG NG&PL

THE CRABS
3/5/78 PEEL *Victim, Under pressure, Lullabys lie, Don't want your love.* Tony Diggines (lv,rg), Rick Newson (lg), Ricci Titcombe (d), Ashley Morse (b). 26/4/78 MV4 MB NG

THE CRABS ('82)
3/5/82 PEEL *Please ask me out, Love's not that great really, Stalemate, Rape rap, You'll never walk alone.* Sarah Smith, Jeanette Purcell, Karen King, Phil Emby, David Cuff. 21/4/82 MV4 RP *

THE CRAMPS
10/2/86 PEEL *What's inside a girl?, Cornfed dames, Give me a woman.* Lux Interior, Mick Knox, Ivy Rorschach. 11/6/86 Recorded at Ocean Way Recording Studios, Hollywood, CA. * *

12/3/86 LONG *The hot pearl snatch, Hot pool of woman need, How far can too far go?, Oloa from Hell.* *
12/3/86 MV4 BYA *

THE CRANBERRIES
16/2/92 PEEL *Waltzing back, Linger, Want, I will always.*

Dolores O'Riordan (v,ag), Fergal Lawlor (d), Mike Hogan (b), Noel Hogan (g). 16/1/92 MV4 DG NG&KR

CRANE
21/8/90 PEEL *Consumption, The than sets in, Fear of noise, Asleep.* Shawn Richardson (d), Nick Carter (b), Steven Malley (g), Roy Fox (v). 8/7/90 MV3 DG ME&DTH

THE CRANES
19/7/89 PEEL *Focus breathe, E G shining, Starblood, Till tomorrow.* Jim Shaw (d,b,g), Alison Jane Shaw (v), Mark Francombe (g), Simon Tufnal (b). 9/7/89 MV5 DG ME

11/4/90 PEEL *Give, Da da 331, Inescapable.* Matt Cope (g) r. Tufnal. 13/3/90 MV3 DG MR

CRASS
10/4/79 PEEL *G's song, Mother Earth, Bomb, Shaved women, Tired.* Steve Ignorant (lv), Eve Libertine (lv), Phil Free (gv), N A Palmer (g, literal readings), Pete Wright (bv), George Tarbuck (p), Penny Rimbaud (d), Virginia Creeper (tram noises), Alan (Wind and Wit).
28/3/79 MV4 JS NG
'Recorded & mixed by Nick Gomm at 105 decibels'.

THE CRAVATS
9/8/79 PEEL *Welcome, Who's in here with me, Pressure sellers, Precinct, Live for now.* Rob Dallaway (gv), Richard Yehudi (sx, other bits), The Shend (bv), Dave Bennett (dv). 31/7/79 MV4 BS MR

6/10/80 PEEL *Still, In your eyes, You're driving me, Triplex zone.* 23/9/80 MV4 JS MR

18/8/81 PEEL *Rub me out, Terminus, Firemen, Ice cubists.* Shend (b,v-1,3), Rob (g,v-2,4), F-Reg (sx,cl), Dave (d).
10/8/81 MV4 TW DD

15/11/82 PEEL *The station, Working down underground, There is no International Rescue, Daddy's shoes.* Shend (bv), Arthur (lv,g), Baird Smart (sx,cl), '31' (d).
6/11/82 * DG MR

CRAZYHEAD
21/5/87 LONG† *Baby turpentine, Down, Dragon city, Out on a limb.* Ian Anderson (v), Kevin Bayliss (g), Richard Bell (g), Alexander Peach (b), Robert Morris (d).
19/4/87 MV4 PW *
† On Nighttracks SNTCD018.

CREAM
12/11/66 LIGHT SAT. CLUB *Sweet wine, Steppin' out, Wrapping paper, Rolling and tumbling, I'm so glad, Sleepy-time time.* Eric Clapton (gv), Jack Bruce (bv), Ginger Baker (d). 8/11/66 PH BB *

21/11/66 WS BANDBEAT *Spoonful, Sleepy-time time, Rolling and tumbling.* 21/10/66 MV4 JG JY
The group's 1st BBC recording. Also appeared live on Light Programme's 'Monday Monday' 21/11, PH, prod BA

30/12/66 HOME GUITAR CLUB *Crossroads, Sitting on top of the world, Stepping out.* 28/11/66 AO2 BA *
This weekly Home Service show on Thursdays at 2pm was introduced by Ken Sykora, and produced by Bernie Andrews.

9/1/67 WS R&B *Cat squirrel, Train time, Hey Lordy mamma, I'm so glad.* 9/12/66 MV4 JG JY

14/1/67 LIGHT SAT. CLUB *Four until late, I feel free, Train time, NSU, Toad.* 10/1/67 PH BB *
Group next appeared live on 'Monday Monday' again, 16/1/67 PH, prod. KB; then live 25/1 PH 'Parade of the Pops' (Light) prod. Ian Scott; and 'Monday Monday' 27/3/67 PH prod. KB.

3/6/67 LIGHT SAT. CLUB *Strange brew, Tales of brave Ulysses, We're going wrong.* 30/5/67 PH BB *
Next appearance live on Joe Loss Show, 14/7/67 PH, prod. Ian Grant.

29/10/67 TOP GEAR *Take it back, Outside women blues, Tales of brave Ulysses, Sunshine of your love, Born under a bad sign.* 24/10/67 AO2 BA DT
Repeated on SYMONDS Show 30/10 to 3/11; & on WS R&B 18/12/67, after planned session on 28/11 cancelled due to Ginger Baker being ill; & on R1 'Happening Sunday' 3/12/67.

14/1/68 TOP GEAR *Swalbr, The politician, Steppin' out, We're going wrong, Blue condition.* 9/1/68 AO2 BP PC

THE CREATURES
13/10/81 JENSEN *Mad eyed screamer, So unreal, But not them, Wild thing, Thumb.* Siouxsie (v), Budgie (perc).
2/10/81 Polygram studios * *

CRESSIDA
15/6/70 SYMONDS *Depression Winter is coming again, Lima.* Angus Cullen (v), John Culley (g), Peter Jennings (o,p), Kevin McCarthy (b), Iain Clark (d). 2/6/70 BA BA *

CRISIS
8/11/78 PEEL *UK '78, Alienation, White youth, Brickwood hospital.* Phrazer (lv), Doug Pearce (rg,v), Tony Wakeford (bv), Lester Jones (lgv), The Cleaner (d), Dexter (bkv), Virg (bkv). 1/11/78 * MR *

CRISIS ('86)
5/12/86 FRI. ROCK *Battlefield, Spirits, Casablanca, Suicide.* Chris Stock (b), Russ Meehan (gv), Mike Rawsthorne (g), Geoff Lilleyman (d). Rec. Date Unknown MV4 TW *

CRISPY AMBULANCE
19/1/81 PEEL *Come on, Egypt, Drug user drug pusher, October 31st.* Robert Davenport (g), Gary Madeley (g), Keith Darbyshire (b), Alan Hempsall (v).
12/1/81 LHI TW DD

BRENDAN CROKER
27/7/85 KERSHAW *Let that liar pass on by, Good rockin', Hard times.* Brendan Croker & the Five O'Clock Shadows (unknown). 20/6/85 Y2 * SR

13/3/86 KERSHAW *Brownskin gal, That's the way all my money goes, Chains, Don't trade me in.* *
6/3/86 Y2 JL SR

26/2/87 KERSHAW *I walk the line, Lonely one in town, 5 o'clock shuffle, Rail road blues, 5 o'clock swing.* & the Five O'Clock Shadows: Mark Cresswell (g), Marcus Cliffe (b), Davey Curry (d). 4/2/87 * SP SR

18/8/88 KERSHAW *Please baby, Blues stay away from me, Weapon of prayer, That's where I belong.* & Mark Knopfler (gv), Steve Phillips (gv) 'The Notting Hillbillies'.
25/7/88 MV4 TdB MA

8/10/89 KERSHAW *No expectations, Just an old waltz, This kind of life, My government.* & the Five O'Clock Shadows: Cresswell, Cliffe, Mick Weaver (acc,p), Preston Hayman (d), John Porter (g). 14/9/89 OD DG MA

11/11/91 HARRIS *Nothing but time, There'll come a day, Selfmade saviour, What it takes, The great indoors, I guess that says it all, Tomorrow is another day, My government.* Solo. 28/9/91 MV5 TdB~ *

CROSS AND ROSS
30/7/71 BLACK *Blind Willie Johnstone, Petrol fumes and gas leaks, Can you believe it?, Clams.* 22/6/71 TI JM JWH
SM John White's diary has the duo booked-in under their former band name 'Sunburst'.

CROSS SECTION
7/4/82 PEEL *Wounds are too deep, The dole, Too many hills, Where is the love.* Graham Amir (lv,rg), Jr. Spence (d), Lloyd Massett (b), Roddie Gillard (lg), Julie Reid (k,sx), Neil Innes (perc,bkv), Steve Welsby (perc,bkv). 31/3/82 MV5 RP NG

SANDRA CROSS
10/4/88 MISS P *Styler boy, Live in love, Take a look around, Runaround.* Sandra Cross (v) 'with the Ariwa Posse': Bernard Cumberbatch (b), Winston Bennett (lg), Black Steel (b,rg, bkv,prg), The Mad Professor (d), Victor Cross (k,bkv). 11/2/88 MV5 HP DD

CROWBAR
12/12/72 PEEL *Oh what a feeling, Listen sister, Kilroy, Nothing lasts forever.* Nicholas McGowan (tp), Henry Soltys (ts), Pierre Rouchon (tb), Sonnie Ernardi (dv), Kelly Jay (kv), Roland Greenway (bv), John Peter Gibbard (lcv), Rheal Lanthier (lgv), Joey Chirowski (kv).
4/12/72 TI JW *

ARTHUR 'BIG BOY' CRUDUP
14/2/70 TOP GEAR *Sunny road, That's alright, Rock me*

mama, *All I've got is gone, Nobody wants you when you're old and grey.* Arthur 'Big Boy' Crudup (gv).
9/2/70 PH JW TW

CRUELLA DA VILLE
14/5/77 FREEMAN *London lies waiting, Kings and Queens, Schoolday's past loves, We got air.* Bill Flynn (gv), Phil Mitchell (b), Dave Tate (d). 4/5/77 MV4 TW NG

CRY BEFORE DAWN
9/9/85 LONG *Stateside Europe, White strand, Crimes of conscience, The wild geese.* Brendon Wade (pp,wh,v), Pat Hayes (d), Tony Hall (g), Vince Doyle (b).
4/9/85 MV5 BYA MPK

CRY WOLF
4/3/88 FRI. ROCK *Be my lover, Girls like you, Goodbye forever, Light up my life.* Jon Clayton (d), Paul Robinson (b), Nikk Singleton (g), Chris Gyngell (g), Mark Grimmet (v). 20/2/88 MV4 HP DD

CRYER
23/1/81 FRI. ROCK *Spaces, The visionary, Footsteps through time, Cyclone.* Gary Chapman (g,bkv), Stuart Clarke (g), Fez Ferriday (b), Pete Wain (k), Graham Careless (lv), Roger Whitehouse (d). 7/1/81 * TW TdB

CRYS
28/1/83 FRI. ROCK *Pendoncwyr, It's about time, Merched gwillt a gwin, Rockin' along.* Alun Morgan (lg), Scott Forde (b), Nick Samuel (d), Liam Forde (gv).
7/1/83 * TW DD

CUBAN HEELS
23/3/81 SKINNER *Sweet charity, Liberty hall, The old school song, A matter of time.* John Milarky (v), Nick Clark (bv), Laurie Cuffe (gv), Ali Mackenzie (d).
12/3/81 LH1 JS MR
24/3/81 PEEL *Hard times, Walk on water, Work our way to heaven, Old school song.* 18/3/81 LH1 CL NG
15/10/81 PEEL *Call of the wild, The innocents, Matthew & son, Primitives.* 10/10/81 MV4 DG AP

CUD
30/6/87 PEEL† *Mind the gap, You're the boss, Don't bank on it, You sexy thing.* Carl Puttnam (v), Mike Dunphy (g), William Potter (b), Stephen Goodwin (d). 16/6/87 * DG ME&TdB
† On Strange Fruit SFPS045.
24/5/88 PEEL *Treat me bad, Punishment/reward relationship, Living in the past, Everybody works so hard.* 15/5/88 * DG MA&JBN
13/3/89 PEEL *Only a prawn in Whitby, B.B. couldn't C, (I'm the) Urban spaceman, The Epicurean's answer.* 19/2/89 MV3 DG JB&MA
30/9/91 GOODIER *Profession, Oh no won't do†, Purple love balloon, Sometimes rightly sometimes wrongly.*
21/9/91 MV5 MC~ JMK
† On 'Best of Mark Goodier' Nighttracks Mark1.

THE CULT
25/7/84 SKINNER *Ghost dance, Bad medicine waltz, Resurrection Joe, Go west.* Ian Astbury (v), Billy Duffy (g), Jamie Stewart (bp), Nigel Preston (d).
12/7/84 MV5 MHY *
26/6/85 LONG *Spiritwalker, Big neon glitter, Revolution, All souls avenue.* 16/6/85 MV4 BYA PW
4/3/86 LONG *Love removal machine, Conquistador, King contrary man, Electric ocean.* Les Warner (d) r. Preston. 23/2/86 MV4 BYA *

CULTURE
11/1/83 PEEL† *Too long in slavery, Two sevens clash, Lion rock, Armageddon.* Joseph Hill (v), Frederick Thompson (lg), Ronald Campbell (rg), Fez Walker (b), Lewis Daley (d), Harry Powell (perc), Vincent Morgan (k), Evoald (tb), Itico (tp). 11/12/82 MV4 DG MR
† On Strange Fruit SFPS024.
2/1/89 PEEL *Two sevens clash, Fussin' and fightin', Capture rasta.* Norman Douglas, Ian Watson, Joslyn George McKenzie, Francisco Thompson, Albert Walker, Roy

Silvester Dayer, Joseph Hill, Frederick Anthony Thomas.
22/11/88 MV4 MR~
1/8/92 KERSHAW *Fussing and fighting, See them a come, I am not ashamed, Capture rasta.* Joseph Hill (v), Tony Phillips (b), Bigga (sy,bkv), Trevor Fagan (d), Anthony Thomas (perc). 28/5/92 MV4 DG JB&NG

CULTURE CLUB
20/7/82 JENSEN *I'm the boy, Take control, I'm not crazy, White boys can't control it.* Boy George (v), John Moss (d,perc), Michael Craig (b), Roy Hay (g), Phil Pickett (k), Nick Payne (sx), Terry Bailey (tp).
11/7/82 MV4 DG ME

THE CULTURE VULTURES
19/2/87 LONG *Miss Heart Break, Ruby, Chuck in the fire, Each day a battle.* Dave Wiseman (v), Mick Scatley (d), Sean Butler (g), John Catlett (b), Ann Summers (acc).
8/2/87 MV4 JE TdB

THE CURE
11/12/78 PEEL† *Killing an arab, 10.15 Saturday night, Fire in Cairo, Boys don't cry.* Robert Smith (gv), Michael Dempsey (bv), Lol Tolhurst (d,bkv). 4/12/78 MV4 TW DD
† On Strange Fruit SFPCD050.
16/5/79 PEEL *Desperate journalist in ongoing meaningful review situation, Grinding halt, Subway song, Plastic passion, Accuracy.* 9/5/79 MV4 JS TdB
29/8/79 JENSEN *Boys don't cry, Do the Hansa, Three imaginary boys.* 13/8/79 MV5 BS *&MFA
10/3/80 PEEL *A forest, 17 seconds, Play for today, M.* Matthieu Hartley (k), Simon Gallup (b) r. Dempsey.
3/3/80 MV4 TW DD
15/1/81 PEEL *Holy hour, Forever, Primary, All cats are grey.* Smith, Gallup, Tolhurst. 7/1/81 LH1 CL NG
2/3/81 SKINNER *Funeral party, A drowning man, Faith.*
26/2/81 LH1 DG MR
4/1/82 PEEL *Figurehead, A hundred years, Siamese twins (& A hanging garden,* not completed or broadcast).
21/12/81 MV4 KH DD
1/11/82 JENSEN *Let's go to bed, Just one kiss, One hundred years, Ariel.* Smith, Tolhurst (k,dm), Steve Golding (d).
24/10/82 MV4 DG ME&TD
21/9/83 JENSEN *Speak my language, Mr Pink Eyes, Lovecats.* Smith, Tolhurst, Clifford (Andy) Anderson (d), Phil Thornalley (b). 26/8/83 PRIV * *
22/12/84 JENSEN *Banana fish bones, Piggy in the mirror, Give me it, The empty world.* Paul Thompson (g,k,sx), Norman Fisher Jones (b) r. Thornalley. 2/12/84 MV4 JP TdB
7/8/85 PEEL *The exploding boy, Six different ways, Screw, Sinking.* Smith, Thompson, Tolhurst, Gallup (b) returns, Boris Williams (d). 30/7/85 MV5 JWI TdB

CURLY
20/11/73 PEEL *Keeping my motor cool, Rock me roll me, High flying bird.* Steve Farr (ts,fl,v), Stewart Blandameer (al,gv), Dave Dowle (d), Kevin Cantlon (b), Bill Roberts (gv). 29/10/73 T1 JW *

CURVE
31/3/91 PEEL *Ten little girls, No escape from heaven, The colour hurts, The coast is clear.* Monti (d), Dean Garcia (b,seq), Debbie Smith (g), Alex Mitchell (g), Alan Noulder (g-4 only), Toni Halliday (v).
10/3/91 MV3 DG ME&NJ
29/2/92 PEEL *Split into fractions, Die like a dog, Horror head, Arms out.* Noulder out. 11/2/92 MV4 MR~

CURVED AIR
9/5/70 TOP GEAR *Screw, Vivaldi, Hide and seek.* Sonja Kristina (v), Darryl Way (vi,v), Francis Monkman (gk), Robert Martin (b), Florian Pilkington-Miska (d).
28/4/70 MV4 JW BC
Kristina had previously appeared as a member of the cast from 'Hair' on Symonds on Sunday TX 26/1/69.
17/11/70 HARDING *It happened today, Vivaldi, Propositions.* Ian Eyre (b), r. Martin. 10/11/70 MV5 MB MH&MF

18/1/71 HARRIS *Thinking on the floor, Situations, Stretch, Young mother in style.* 5/1/71 MV5 JM JWH
20/2/71 FOLK ON 1 *Thinking on the floor, Situations, Blind man, Melinda, Stretch, It happened today, Young mother in style.* 27/1/71 AO2 FL *

IVOR CUTLER
7/5/69 PEEL *Trouble trouble, Bounce bounce bounce, In my room there sits a box.* Ivor Cutler (v,p,hmn).
5/5/69 S2 PR MH
27/2/71 TOP GEAR *Trouble trouble/I'm going in a field, A second before is not now, Ivor you are beautiful, My father once had, Life in a Scotch sitting-room Vol II episode 2, Sit down/Man with the trembly nose, Life in a Scotch sitting-room Vol II episode 7, (& A lemon on the grass, A seal is a sheep, Two balls/Two fried eggs for sixpence, 8/5/71).* 15/2/71 PH JW BC
24/11/71 PEEL *I believe in bugs/That's what it's all about, Life in a Scotch sitting-room Vol II episodes 1 & 9, The green rain/Mud, If all the cornflakes/I like sitting/When I entered heaven/Poem by my son Jeremy.* 8/11/71 PH JW BC
25/9/73 PEEL *Piano tuner song AD2000, A wag at the flicks, Gooseberries and bilberries, I worn my elbows, Poems from 'Many flies have feathers', Pearly gleam (& Life in a Scotch sitting-room Vol II episode 4, 11/12/73).* 3/9/73 T1 JW BC
28/11/74 PEEL *Railway sleepers/Three sisters, I'm walkin' to a farm/Baby sits, Alone/Lean/The run/What?, Big Jim, Yellow fly/I think very deeply, Song of the sky, Life in a Scotch sitting-room Vol II episode 6.*
14/11/74 MV4 TW BAI
14/10/75 PEEL *Pearly winged fly, Go and sit upon the grass, Sleepy old snake, Little black buzzer, Life in a Scotch sitting room Vol. II ep.11, Fremsley, True humility, Nigerians in a tunnel, I spent ten years, Excitement, A hen runs, A bowled over child, A wooden tree.* 25/9/75 MV4 JW *
31/8/76 PEEL *Bicarbonate of chicken, Barabadabada, In the chestnut tree, Rubber toy, Life in a Scotch sitting room Vol. II ep.5, Lemon flower, Everybody got, The surly buddy (story), I ate a lady's bun, Stubborn vassals, Fish, Living donkey, When I stand on an open cart, Irk (9-14 poems).* 17/8/76 MV4 * MR?
17/8/77 PEEL† *A great grey grasshopper, A suck of my thumb, The shchi, Get away from the wall, The natural height of cloud/If we dug a hole, I had a little boat/I'm going in a field, Life in a Scotch sitting Room Vol. II episode 12/Life in a Scotch sitting-room Vol II episode 13, Jungle tips.* 10/8/77 MV4 TW MR
† On Strange Fruit SFPS068.
12/4/78 PEEL *Three piece suite, Lead bell, The head of a nail/The blonde mouse, A mouse asked a rat/A small mouse beckons, I even know what size/The old lady danced, Life in a Scotch sitting room Vol. II episodes 3 & 8 &14, My face is red, There's got to be something there, The green rain. (3-6 poems).* 3/4/78 MV4 TW DD
27/2/79 PEEL *The obliging fairy, The man with the trembly nose, I love you but I don't know what I mean, Bubu bird, Pass the ball Jim, Examine the contents/A saucer/A lady found an insect/Lunatic/Melon, Gruts for tea, Egg-meat. (6,7,8 poems).* 20/2/79 MV4 TVD MR
22/4/81 PEEL *Pellets, O.K. I'll count to eight, Tomato brain, Step it out lively boys, Counting song, Ready/A land of penguins/Her darling, Oh quartz/How do you do/Dirty sky, Life in a Scotch sitting room - episodes 15 & 16.* 15/4/81 LH1 CL *
3/3/83 PEEL *Pussy on the mat/Blue bear/Women of the world, Halfway through/The wren/Creamy pumpkins, Life in a Scotch Sitting room Vol II. Ep.17 & 18 (& Brenda/Mostly tins/People run to the edge, Bad eye/A doughnut in my hand/Old black dog, 23/3/83).*
23/2/83 MV4 RP NG
22/2/84 PEEL *All the time, The revelation, Her equipment,*

Three men, Just a nuance, Life in a Scotch sitting room Vol II ep.19, Vegetarians, Lemonade, I jumped over a wall, Jelly mountain, My next album, I built a house. 15/2/84 MV5 RP NG

15/7/85 Peel *Back home, I'm fixed, Knockin' at my door, It's snowin', I'm walkin' to a farm, Life in a Scotch sitting room Vol. II Ep.10, Other poems.* 30/6/85 MV5 DG ME

21/5/86 Peel *Bend down yetta, Crunch crunch, A ball in a barrel, One of the best, Questionnaire, Glasgow dreamer #3 & #4, Eggmeat, Jewish jokes, God's blessing, Laughter and disbelief, Bucket and steam, Maturity, Vermin, A new home, Large and puffy, A country door, Are you a Tory?, The curse, Scratch on my back.* 11/5/86 MV5 DG ME

4/6/87 Kershaw *A romantic man, Carry on dancing, The river bends, The book, Dolly, Poems: Intro and local natural sounds, Free wood, Loneliness, Seven, A warm bucket, Glasgow dreamer #14 & #15, A big head.* 21/5/87 * DG TdB&PS

15/6/87 Peel *The shapely balloon, The clever night doctor, The aggressive onion-vendor, Me and my kid brother, The perambulating Scottish collander, A wag at the flicks.* 9/6/87 * DG *

23/6/88 Kershaw *And so do I, Jump in the Clyde, The dishes are dry, A strategy suit with a jelly pocket, Glasgow dreamer #5 & #1, Thunder and lightning, Evergreen moon, Amplification is the curse of civilisation, Picking your nose, Barrel torsos, Emasculated, leather, Their favourite.* 26/5/88 * DG NG&MFA

5/11/89 Kershaw *Glasgow dreamer #2 & #18, Mishap #2 & #3/Tsukiyuki hana, Tree dentist/Stiff as a meringue/A clear lite, Where are my underwriters/Her strange brain/Austin Metro.* 27/7/89 * DG *

6/7/91 Peel *Glasgow dreamer #6 & #8, Beside the fish/Footsteps/Green light, Biltong/A long hard gland/Hee haw, Two coy hinnies/Insect/Seaweed.* 9/5/91 MV5 DG NG&JLC

15/12/91 Peel *Thick coat, Neighbours, Eyes shut tight, What a mistake, Glasgow dreamer #7 & #10.* 31/10/91 MV4 DG TdB&RK

OLD MA CUXSOM
4/9/86 Kershaw *Don't cry darlin', Whip that fool, Timmy car park, Lady Pilkington.* Troy Steel (b), Marcu Gossage (g), Hugh Umbidaligo (v), Colin Smith (k), Mike (d). 20/8/86 * DST PSM

CYMANDE
12/7/73 Peel *Bra, Rickshaw, The message, Zion I.* Patrick Patterson (g), Steve Scipio (b), Sam Kelly (d), Pablo Gonzalez (cga), Joey Dee (v), Derek Gibs (al,ss), Michael Rose (al,fl,bgo), Desmond Atwell (ts). 9/7/73 LH1 BA *

2/7/74 Peel *Crawshay, For baby-ooh, Brothers on the slide, Breezeman.* 11/6/74 LH1 TW BC

ASHER D AND DADDY FREDDY
8/3/88 Peel *Ragamuffin song, Run come follow me, Ragamuffin hip-hop medley.* Asher D & Daddy Freddy (v,rp,tst); & Simon Harris (rg,prg,k). 2/2/88 * DG DD&SC

D NOTES
15/1/83 Long *Lunatic, Broken people, Design for living, Leo.* * 14/1/83 PHM c.JL PSM

D ROSE
22/4/88 Fri. Rock *D Rose, Can you feel it, Step into my living room, To be content.* Rony Rocker (v), Jake Marvin (b), Andy James (g), John O'Leary (d). 8/4/88 * PW DD

D&V
8/10/86 Peel *So you believe in West Minstawoffel, Conscious pilot, Epsilon city limits.* Jet Antcliff (v), Andy Leach (d), Ray Shulman (prg,p), Smuf (b). Rec. date unknown. OS Produced by Ray Shulman & Smuff. *

MICHAEL D'ABO
14/10/74 Harris *My lord, I go where my spirit leads me, Sitting on a wood floor, Papa didn't tell me.* Michael D'Abo (gv). 14/8/74 * JG *

TERENCE TRENT D'ARBY
22/4/87 Long *Seven more days, Wishing well, Never turn my back, Dance little sister.* Clive Mngaza (d), Cass Lewis (b), Thomas 'Blast' Murray (g), Christian Marsac (g,sx), Andy Whitmore (k), Frank Collins (bkv), Ebo Ross (bkv), Terence Trent D'Arby (lv). 15/4/87. MV4 PW MPK

'P.S. Session done as "live", due to band having to rush off to do Anti-Apartheid gig at Royal Albert Hall' PW.

10/8/87 Peel *Soul power, Under my thumb, Heartbreak hotel/Mannish boy.* Terence Trent D'Arby (v), Dave (d), Cass (b), Pete (g), Christine (g,sx), Preston (perc), Ebo & Frank (bkv). 2/8/87 * DG NG&MS

DADDY LONG LEGS
7/2/70 Top Gear *Where have all your clothes gone?, Bad blood mama, Getting high again.* Steve Hayton (v), Kurt Palomski (b), Clif Carrison (d). 26/1/70 PH JW TW
Rec'd Peel's Sunday Concert (& James Armstrong) 14/5/70 PS, TX 24/5/70. Did 2nd Concert 22/4/71 PS (Peter Arnesden, Gary Holderman r. Hayton, Armstrong), TX 2/5/71.

MARTIN STEPHENSON AND THE DAINTEES
20/2/84 Jensen *Slaughterman, Look down look down, Neon skies, Cecil.* Martin Yule (d), Anthony Dunn (b), Martin Stephenson (gv), John Steel (gk), Brian Davidson (vi,vla). 5/2/84 MV5 DG ME

26/6/86 Kershaw *Roll on summertime, Crocodile cryer, Louis, Rain.* Stephenson, A. Dunn, Gary Dunn (g), Paul Smith (d). 4/8/86 Y2 SP SR

19/5/88 Kershaw *Goodbye John, Far-away meadows, Migrants, Matthew.* Smith out. 21/4/88 * DG MA&FK

DAISY CHAINSAW
27/1/92 Goodier *Pink flower, All the kids agree, Hope your dreams come true, I feel insane.* Katy Jane Garside (v), Crispin Gray (g), Vince Johnson (d), Richard Adams (b). 15/1/92 MV4 MA~

DALAI LAMA
19/12/72 Peel *Trying too hard to score, Nimzo witch, Spirit of the living dead.* Kenny George (v,perc), Morris Lares (agv), Temba Matebese (gpo), Andre Abrahamse (b), Bobby Stegnac (cga,perc), Koss Georgiou (lg), Wally Gilek (d), Stuart Spiers (sx,fl). 28/11/72 LH1 * *

DAMACLES
6/12/85 Fri. Rock *Out of luck, White hot, Jealous eyes, Gimme more.* Don Threlfall (d), Paul Henley (g), Danny Clarke (b), Bob Miller (v). 1/11/85 MV4 TW DD

THE DAMNED
10/12/76 Peel† *Stab your back, Neat neat neat, New rose, So messed up, I fall.* Dave Vanian (v), Brian James (g,bkv), Captain Sensible (b,bkv), Rat Scabies (d). 30/11/76 MV4 JG MR
† On Strange Fruit SFPS040.

16/5/77 Peel† *Sick of being sick, Stretcher case, Fan club, Feel the pain.* 10/5/77 MV4 JG MR
Recorded In Concert 19/5/77 PS, TX 21/5/77, prod. JG. † On Strange Fruit SFRCD002.

8/1/79 Peel *Melody Lee, Love song, I'm a burglar, Looking at you.* Captain Sensible (switches to: gv,o); Al Ward (bv) r. James. 20/12/78 MV4 BS NG

29/10/79 Peel *Just can't be happy, Smash it up, Liar, I'm so bored.* Al Ward (lg-3). 22/10/79 MV4 TW DD

11/12/79 Read *Plan 9 channel 7, I just can't be happy today & Noise noise noise (12/12), Drinking about my baby (13/12).* 16/11/79 MV4 JS NG

20/10/80 Peel *Curtain call pt I, Hit or miss, Therapy.* Paul Gray (b) r. Ward. 6/10/80 MV4 TW DD

20/10/80 Read *Dr Jeckyll and Mr Hyde, Blackout, Lively arts, History of the world.* 9/10/80 MV4 CL *

4/8/84 Sat. Live *Stranger in the town, Limit club, Smash it up.* Vanian, Sensible, Scabies only. Live from S2 MRD TdB

6/8/84 Peel *Thanks for the night, Nasty, We love you, Is it a dream?* Bryn Merrick (b), Roman Jug (gk) r. Gray. 7/7/84 MV5 DG MR

6/8/84 Peel *Thanks for the night, Nasty, We love you, Is it a dream?* Dave Vanian (v), Captain Sensible (g), Rat Scabies (d), Bryn Merrick (b), Roman Jug (gk). 7/7/84 MV5 DG MR

20/5/85 Long *Shadow of love, Is it a dream, Street of dreams.* Sensible out. 14/4/85 HP BYA PW

DAN
11/7/88 Peel *Blind Ignorance/Woman of your dreams, Army of fools, Madman and the fool/El amour, A dream come true.* James Clarke (d), Ian Armstrong (b), Ian Wallis (v), Julie Dalkin (v), Sarah Goddard (v). 28/6/88 MV4 MA~ MFA

DANCE FAULT
8/9/82 Peel *Tell me it's fine, No surprise, Toys, Stop.* Jan Smiley (lv), Susan Jones (v), Debbie Knapp (v), Jade Campbell (bv), Penny Pooley (g), Graham Cusak (d). 23/8/82 MV4 DG GP

DANDELION ADVENTURE
18/6/90 Peel *Exit frenzy revisited, Bing Crosby's cathedral, Don't look now, All the world's a lounge.* Geoff (d), Jason (d), Ajay (b), Stan (g), Mark (v). 13/5/90 MV3 DG MFA

DANDO SHAFT
23/8/70 Folk On 1 *Cold wind, The harp lady I bombed, Drops of brandy, Young man, Kallyope driver, Muntaz, Waves upon the ether.* Line-up unknown. 28/7/70 * FL *

31/12/70 Henry *Waves upon the ether, Whispering Ned, Pass it on, Railway, Riverboat.* 17/12/70 T1 PD BH

3/7/71 Top Gear *Coming home to me, Shadows cross the moon, Never mind the rain, Black prince of paradise (& Whispering red, 18/9/71).* 21/6/71 PH JW BC

13/9/71 Harris *September wine, Amarita rising, I heard somewhere, Bushes and briars (& Black prince of Abyssinia, 1/11/71).* 17/8/71 T1 JM JWH

18/1/72 Peel *Road song, I heard somewhere, Melancholie fervour, Don't forget the animal.* 11/1/72 PH JW *

6/11/72 Harris *Now's the time for changing, Gigolo king, Sounds of time.* 11/10/72 * JG *

DANGEROUS
3/1/92 Fri. Rock *Crazy kind of love, No more surrender, As I lay awake.* Robin Goodridge, Stevie Boreham, Paul Watson, Doug Palfreeman, Matt Fowler. 6/12/91 * TW DD

DANGEROUS GIRLS
22/12/80 Read *Summertime blues, Instinct, Dangerous girls, Domestic blisters.* Rob Peters (dv), Rob Rampton (bv), Beetmoll (g,bgo), Mike Occupation (gv). 4/12/80 LH1 CL *

DANSE SOCIETY
30/11/81 Peel *Sanity career, We're so happy, Woman's own, Love as positive narcotic.* Paul Gilmartin (d), Steve Rawlings (v), Lyndon Scarfe (k), Tim Wright (b), Paul Nash (g). 21/11/81 MV4 DG MR

13/9/82 Peel *Clock, Ambition, Godsend, The seduction.* 28/8/82 * DG MC

12/4/83 Jensen *Wake up, The sway, So lonely in your crowd, We know the place.* 3/4/83 MV4 DG ME

29/10/83 Long *Lizard mad, Red light, Where are you now, The night.* 20/10/83 PHM c.PWL *

DANTA
17/4/71 Top Gear *Queen of Sheba, Ebeneza Nwa Nnem, The dead.* Vernon Cummings (cga), Richard Mainwaring (d), Hugh Ashton (b), Helen Denniston (tamb,v), Kenny George (v,perc), Derek Mandel (lg), Ige Adebari (rg), Denny Morris (cga). 6/4/71 MV4 JW BC

18/1/72 Peel *Mau mau, Stormsong, Freeway.* Val McDonald (d) r. Mainwaring. 10/1/72 PH JW BC

21/4/72 Peel *Feeling the heat, Anambra, Flying out.* 4/4/72 T1 JM *

21/9/73 SEQUENCE *Daddy gone, Crossfire, Day, Bushman song.* Cummings, McDonald, Alvin Williams (lv), Mark Ramos (lg), Chas Chiedo (b), Gerry Glene (k).
9/8/73 LH1 JM *

DARK CITY
27/2/85 LONG *For you, Solid gone, Untouchable, Rules of the game.* Richard Lewis (b), Amos Pizzey (gv), Nick Plytas (k), Dave Charles (d), Clem Clemson (g).
22/2/85 MV4 JWI PW
16/9/85 LONG *Live, Calling, Insecure, Squeeze.* Kas (b), Amos Pizzey (v), John Cambridge (g), Theodore Thunder (d), Dave Rose (k), Susie O'List & Jill O'Donovan (bkv).
25/8/85 HP BYA PW

DARKNESS AND JIVE
26/10/82 PEEL *Death in Venice, Guys and dolls, Candle, Rage in a Cage.* Paul Johnstone (gv), Steve Rainey (d), Tony Kennedy (b), Gary McKenzie (sy), Louise McGuckin & Jackie Dear (bkv-2). 6/10/82 MV4 RP NG
8/6/83 PEEL *Shake down, Speak clearly, Jigsaw, Victims.* Johnstone, Rainey, Kennedy, Tony Strong (sy), Jackie Dolly (bkv). 1/6/83 MV4 BYA *

THE DARLING BUDS
8/4/87 PEEL *I couldn't remember, It's up to you, Mary's got to go, The other night.* Andrea (v), Harley (g), Simon (b), Bloss (d). 29/3/87 * DG ME&MWT
2/9/87 PEEL *Shame on you, Think of me, My valentine, Spin.* Chris (b) r. Simon. 23/8/87 * DG MA
7/7/88 L. KERSHAW *You've got to choose, When it feels good, Hit the ground, Just say so.* 29/6/88 MV4 PW MPK
20/2/89 PEEL *The things we do for love, Different daze, She's not crying, It's all up to you (flip flop).*
7/2/89 * DG MR
    Later session for CAMPBELL, not listed.

DAS PSYCHO RANGERS
8/12/86 LONG *Homage, Power station, Intellectual gangsters, Medea tearorists.* Troy Tempest (g), Jules Von Vleet (bk), Bee Decard (v), Steve Honest (bk), Kathy-Anne Joseph (bkv). 3/12/86 MV4 BYA MPK

DATBLYGU
13/5/87 PEEL† *Bagniau Gareth, Carpiog, Cerddoriaeth dant, Nesaf.* David Edwards (gv,o,'toys'), Patricia Morgan (g,p,o,mel,b), Wyn Davies ('more toys', 'rhythmic accompaniments', cel). 26/4/87. * DG ME&TD
17/2/88 PEEL† *Fanzine ynfytyn, Cristion yn y kibbutz, Gwlad arfy nghefn, Dros y pas g eto.* 9/2/88 MV4 DG MC
9/2/91 PEEL† *Slebog bywpeg, Nid chwiwgi pwdin gwaed, Rhag ofnichi anuhofio, Popeth.* 20/1/91 MV3 DG ME&FK
    † on 'BBC Peel Sessions' Ankst 027.
12/6/92 PEEL *Hymne Europa 1992, Dim deddf dim eiddo, Rausch gift suchtiae, Hablador.* Edwards, Morgan, John Griffiths (perc), Al Edwards (d,perc), Eurus Rowlands (d,perc), Rheinallt Ap Gwynedd (b), Peredur Ap Gwynedd (p,g). 3/5/92 MV3 ME~

THE DAVIDSONS
9/2/88 MAYO *Dance like an astronaut, Beautiful, My feet don't touch, Dress me up.* Captain Bliss (v), Efrem Zitblaster Jnr (g,bkv), Duffy (smp), Philby Edwards (b). 20/1/88 MV4 PW NG&MA

THE DAVINCIS
2/2/87 PEEL *Something missing, Ava Gardner, When you're in, New ways to wear coats.* Paul McCormick (gv), Martin Ward (g), Chris Stevens (d), Iain Bickle (d). 18/1/87 * DG ME&FK
10/10/88 PEEL *This is what we look like, Eating gifted children, On and on, Second home.* Steve Ashton (d) r. Bickle. 27/9/88 MV4 MR~

SPENCER DAVIS AND PETER JAMESON
28/9/70 SYMONDS *One hundred years ago, Crystal river, Thinking of her.* Spencer Davis, Peter Jameson.
8/9/70 PH BA PK&NG
    Spencer Davis Group had done countless Light Programme and R1 sessions since 1964.

SPENCER DAVIS BAND
23/3/73 SEQUENCE *Dust my blues, Catch me on the rebop, I'm a man, Keep on running, The edge.* Spencer Davis, Peter York, Eddie Hardin, Ray Fenwick, Charlie McCracklin. 20/2/73 T1 JM NG [M: daytime]

DAWN CHORUS AND THE BLUE TITS
4/3/85 PEEL *Teenage kicks, Photographs, Lovely lips, That silver-haired daddy of mine.* Dawn Chorus (aka Liz Kershaw) (v), Al Thompson (g), David Davies (b); & Damien O'Neill (g), Andy Kershaw (whistling-3).
24/2/85 MV5 DG ME

DAWN PATROL
6/4/90 FRI. ROCK *Slight of heart, Shades of grey, Private dancer, Explicit through implication.* Michelle McCormick (v), George Gillies (d), Steed (g), John Mooney (k), Don McDonald (b). 23/3/90 MV5 TW DD

DAWSON
29/5/90 PEEL *Molicoke cocktail, White colonial, Sort of man, Ad nauseam, From the loins of Mr & Mrs Neurosis, Fifty years.* Jeremy Reid (v,g,b), Alistair Begbie (v,b,g), Richard Dempsey (b), Rhodri Marsden (bsn,perc), Marcus Nichol (tp,perc). 1/5/90 MV5 MA~
18/1/92 PEEL *Face of W Biriyani, Booger hall, A statement of intent, From Bearsden to Baghdad (via the Erskine Bridge).* Reid, Begbie, Dempsey, Robbie McEndrick (d), Craig Bryce (perc), Ceebe Begbie (v-2).
1/12/91 MV3 DG M&RPF

DANIELLE DAX
14/1/86 LONG† *Fizzing human bomb, Pariah, Ostrich, Numb companions.* Danielle Dax (v,sy), David Knight (sy), Ian Sturgess (b,perc), Steve Reeves (g), Martyn Watts (d).
1/12/85 HP BYA PW
    † On Nighttracks SFNT006.
9/5/88 L. KERSHAW *Up in arms, White knuckle ride, Flashback, Whistling for his love.* Dax, Tim York (d), James Piper (g), Steve Cannell (b), Dave Knight (g).
27/4/88 MV4 HP MPK

DC BASEHEAD
8/9/92 GOODIER *2000 BC, Not over you, Do you wanna make love (or what?), Kiss my black ass.* Michael Ivey (gv), Keith Lofton (g), Bill Conway (b), Bryan Hendrix (d), Clarence Greenwood (tt). 15/8/92 MV4 MC~ DMC

DC KICKS
31/5/91 FRI. ROCK *Chained addiction, Too far gone to be wasted, Regrettably yours, What's new.* Carl (v), Mark Steven Johnson (lg), Dick Zap (rg), Richard Page (b), Slack (d). 3/5/91 MV5 TW MC

DCL LOCOMOTIVE
28/4/86 PEEL *Night and day, (Walk under) The big sky, Red, Coast to coast.* Robin Raymond (gv,k), The Shend (b), Disneytime (d). 20/4/86 MV5 DG ME&FK

DE DANNANN
3/2/78 PEEL *Trip to Durrow/The maid behind the bar, The lamentation on the price of the pig, Love will you marry me, The hackler from Grouse Hall, Tom Billy's jig/Sean Ryan's jig/The sandmount reel/The cloghar reel.* Frankie Gavin (fd,wh), Johnny Moynihan (mnd, bz,v), Charlie Piggot (bj,mnd,wh), Alec Finn (bz,mnd,clo), Ringo McDonagh (d), Tim Lyons (v,acc).
25/1/78 MV4 MB NG [M: before this, on R2]

DEACON BLUE
15/6/87 LONG *Raintown, Just like boys, That brilliant feeling, Real gone kid, Suffering.* Graeme Kelling (g), James Prime (k), Ricky Ross (v), Ewen Vernal (b), Douglas Vipond (d), Lorraine McIntosh (v).
3/6/87 MV4 HP MPK&FK

D.O.A.
19/4/84 PEEL *Burn it down, Race riot, A season in hell, General strike.* Joe Keighley (lg,lv), Dave Gregg (g,bkv), Brian Goble (b,bkv,lv-3), Gregg James (d,bkv).
3/4/84 MV5 MRD MR

DEAD CAN DANCE
28/11/83 PEEL *Instrumental, Labour of love, Ocean, Threshold.* Brendan Perry (gv,perc), Lisa Gerrard (v), James Pinker (perc), Scott Roger (b), Peter Ulrich (d).
19/11/83 MV4 DG MC
13/6/84 PEEL *Flowers of the sea, Penumbra, Panacea, Carnival of light.* 2/6/84 MV5 DG MC

DEAD CAR DRIVE
12/7/88 L. KERSHAW *Criminal mind, When you fall, Do do doo, Only jewel.* Ben Dimassa (d), Nina Spencer (lv), Chips Chapman (g), Nick Medlin (b), Dani Medlin (v,perc), Dave Berry (hca). 22/6/88 MV4 HP MA

DEAD FAMOUS PEOPLE
5/7/89 PEEL *Postcard from paradise, How to be kind, Go home stay home.* Donna Savage (v), Wendy Kisstrup (g), Biddy Leyland (o), Jenny Renals (b), Gill Moon (d).
11/6/89 MV3 DG ME

DEAD ON ARRIVAL
15/4/81 PEEL *Murder school, Rest in peace, Helpless, Party games.* Steve Lynn (v), Carol Bayne (v), Paul Denheyer (g), Mark Webb (b), Steve Majors (d). 8/4/81 LH1 CL NG

DEAD OR ALIVE
17/2/81 PEEL *Nowhere to nowhere, Running wild, Flowers, Number 11.* Joe Musker (d), Sue Bagton-James (b), Mandingo Healy (k), Adrian Mitchley (g), Pete Burns (v). 4/2/81 LH1 CL NG
18/3/82 PEEL *Misty circles (parts 1 & 2), Number twelve, Untitled.* Burns, Musker, Mike Percy (b), Wayne Hussey (g), Marty (k). 1/3/82 MV4 TW DD
1/6/83 JENSEN *Far too hard, Give it to me, What I want.* Burns, Hussey, Percy, Steve Coy (perc), Tim Lever (k,sx). 26/5/83 MV4 JP *

DEAF SCHOOL
7/9/76 PEEL *What a way to end it all, Where's the weekend?, Knock knock knocking, Final act.* Enrico Cadillac Junior (aka Steve Allen) (v), Eric Shark (v), Bette Bright (v), Clive 'Cliff Hanger' Langer (k), Steve 'Average' Lindsay (b, p-4), Tim Whittaker (d), Ian Ritchie (sx). 19/8/76 * TW *
15/4/77 PEEL *Boy's world, Hypertension, What a jerk, Capaldi's cafe.* Langer (g) & Max Ripple (k). 29/3/77 MV4 MB MR
8/2/78 PEEL *Working girls, All queued up, English boys, Ronny Zamora.* 11/1/78 MV4 MB NG

DEATH BY MILKFLOAT
17/8/87 PEEL *Breakbone, Mr. Obvious wig, Blood on the car, The front of your face.* Phil Dolby (gv), Jonny Dawe (b,bkv), Steve Kelly (d). 9/8/87 * DG ME&MP
4/7/88 PEEL *Post jazz rumble bumble, Vagrancy, Boxed away, Too much feel, Wrong.* 21/6/88 * MR~

DEATH CULT
27/10/83 JENSEN *Too young, Butterflies, With love, Flower in the desert.* Billy Duffy (g), Jamie Stewart (b), Nigel Preston (d), Ian Lindsey (v). 16/10/83 MV4 DG TdB

DEATH VALLEY BOYS
14/1/90 KERSHAW *Colorblind's 99 year blues, Please don't make me wait, Persian rug, Back to life.* Colorblind James (gv), Joe Columbo (tb), Dave McIntire (cl), Phil Marshall (dob,bj,bkv), Ken Frank (b), Jim McAvaney (perc). 30/11/89 MV5 DG NG

DEDRINGER
1/5/81 FRI. ROCK *Innocent, Long time, So still, Maxine.* Alan Scott (g), Neil Hudson (g), Lee Flaxington (b), Kenny Jones (d), Johnny Hoyle (v). 15/4/81 * TW TdB

DEEP PURPLE
30/6/68 TOP GEAR *Hush, One more rainy day, Help.* Rod Evans (v), Nick Simper (b), Jon Lord (k), Ian Paice (d), Ritchie Blackmore (g). 18/6/68 PC1 BA DT
    'Enthusiastic, unanimous pass' from panel: 'polished, commercial group'.
1/7/68 SYMONDS *Hush, Kentucky woman (2/7), One more rainy day (3/7), It's all over now (4/7).* 25/6/68 MV5 * *
9/2/69 TOP GEAR *Hey Bob-a-roo-bob, Emmaretta, Wring that neck, Hey Joe (& It's all over now, 23/3/69).*
14/1/69 MV4 BA AH

Group also live on R1 Club 6/2/69 from Top Rank Suite Birmingham.

17/2/69 Brandon *Emmaretta, The bird has flown (18/2), Hush (19/2), Hey Bob-a-roo-bob (20/2).* 11/2/69 MV4 * *

1/7/69 Brandon *Lalena, The painter (3/7), I'm so glad (4/7).* 24/6/69 MV5 * *

6/7/69 Chris Grant's Tasty Pop Sundae *The painter, I'm so glad, Hush.* 30/6/69 AO2 c.PWI *

17/8/69 Symonds on Sunday *Ricochet, Bird has flown.* 11/8/69 AO2 c.PWI *

7/9/69 Henry *Kneel and pray, Child in time.* 29/8/69 PC1 MB *

13/10/69 Cash *And the address, The painter (14/10), Child in time (15/10), Kneel and pray (16/10), The bird has flown (17/10).* Ian Gillan (v), Roger Glover (b) r. Evans, Simper. 28/9/69 (PasB says 25/9) MV5 * *

9/11/69 Henry *Speed king, Jon's (or Jam) stew, Livin' wreck.* 31/10/69 MV4 MB *
Recorded 1st Peel Sunday Concert 19/2/70 PS, TX 22/2/70.

28/4/70 Harding *Bloodsucker, Livin' wreck, Hard loving man.* 21/4/70 MV5 MB MH&MF
Group later did R2 South Bank Pops concert from Royal Albert Hall 17/9/70; special session at T1 for Transcription 23/9/70; & 2nd In Concert, rec'd 9/3/72 PS, TX 18/3/72.

SAM DEES' BEAUTY & THE BEAT

14/12/91 Peel *One in a million, Homecoming, Child of the streets.* Sam Dees (lv), Crissy Lee (d), Ruth Bitelli (b), Ayala Ciran (g), Hilary Cameron (k), Sarah Kelly (sx,fl). 7/11/91 MV4 DG NG&PA

DEF LEPPARD

18/6/79 Peebles *Wasted, Answer to the master (19/6), Glad I'm alive (20/6), Sorrow is a woman (21/6).* Pete Willis (g), Steve Clark (g), Rick Savage (b), Rick Allan (d), Joe Elliott (v). 7/6/79 * JG *
Next, In Concert TX 15/9/79, rec'd 22/8/79 PS.

26/10/79 Fri. Rock *Satellite, Rock brigade, Wasted, Good morning freedom.* 3/10/79 MV6 TW *

DEFINITION OF SOUND

26/1/91 Peel *Now is tomorrow, Wear your love like heaven, Moira Jane's cafe, Rise like the sun.* Crispin Taylor (d), Paul Holland (b), Ronnie Simpson (g), Adrian York (k), Kevin Clark & Donald Weekes (rp), Elaine Vassell (v), Angela Henry-Fontaine (bkv). 30/12/90 MV3 DG TD&JSM

10/11/91 Kershaw *Wear your love like heaven, Moira Jane's cafe, Dream girl, Rise like the sun.* Clark, Weekes, Vassell, York, Holland, Tony Remy (g), Frank Tontoh (d). 19/9/91 MV5 DG MA&JRS

THE DEIGHTON FAMILY

2/4/87 Kershaw *Travelling light, Tennessee wig walk, Forked deer/Salt river, Keep the candle burning, Going down the road.* Dave (g,fd,ml,hca), Josie (g), Maya (wh,fl,perc), Arthur (mnd,g), Kathleen (fd), & Rosalie Deighton (fd,perc,mnd). 25/2/87 * * *

17/11/88 Kershaw *Many good men, In my time of dyin', Mama was right, Bonaparte's retreat, Cotton patch rag, When you're smiling.* Rec. date unknown * c.JL SR

15/12/91 Kershaw *I love you because, I can see clearly now, The road to Newcastle, Under the boardwalk, I forgot to remember to forget.* & Angelina Deighton (perc). Rec. date unknown BHM JL SR

DEL AMITRI

24/4/84 Peel *Heard through a wall, Crows in the wheat field, Breaking bread, Deceive yourself (in ignorant heaven).* Justin Currie (bv), Paul Tyagi (d,perc), Bryan Tolland (g), Iain Harvie (g). 31/3/84 MV5 DG MC

27/3/85 Peel *Hammering heart, Ceasefire, This king is poor, Keepers.* 19/3/85 MV5 * *

9/7/90 Campbell *Nothing ever happens, This side of the morning, Spit in the rain, No holding on.* Currie,

Harvie, David Cummings (g,bkv), Andy Alston (p,acc), Brian McDermot (d). 20/6/90 MV5 MPK~

DELIVERY

8/11/69 WS R&B *Harry lucky, Last night, Miserable man, Free at last.* Billed as 'Steve Miller's Delivery': Steve Miller (pv), Phil Miller (g), Lol Coxhill (sx), Pip Pyle (d), Jack Monck (b). 15/10/69 * JG JY

19/4/70 Raven's R&B *My own fault, We were satisfied, Is it really the same?* 1/4/70 MV4 JG JY
Then rec'd Peel's Sunday Concert 3/12/70 PS, Roy Babbington (b) r. Monck, Carol Grimes (v) r. Coxhill; TX 13/12/70.

23/1/71 Top Gear *We were satisfied, Fools meeting, Home made rain.* As 3/12/70. 4/1/71 PH JW BC

5/3/71 Black *Blind to your light, The wrong time, Yes/no sandpaper (& Vuelta Abajo, 2/4/71).* Laurie Allen r. Pyle. 4/2/71 AO2orT1 JM JWH

THE DELMONAS

18/2/85 Long *You did him wrong, Hidden charts, Fever, Twist and shout, Please don't tell my baby.* Louise Baker (v), Sarah Crouch (v), Hilary Wilkins (v), Billy Childish (g), Mick Hampshire (g), Russ Wilkins (b), Bruce Brand (d). 30/1/85 MV5 JS MA

25/4/88 L. Kershaw *The uncle Willy, Nineteen seventy (I feel alright), Kiss me honey honey kiss me, The world keeps going round, You can't sit down, I'll use evil.* Crouch, H. & R. Wilkins, Childish, Hampshire, J Gawn (d), K De Coninck. 3/4/88 MV4 AJ TdB

DELMONTES

3/3/81 Skinner *Lemon verbena tea, B.G.J.M, Use it, Let's forgive.* Julie Hepburn (v), Gillian Millar (k,bkv), Mike Berry (g), Gordon Simpson (b), Berniece Simpson (d). 20/2/81 LH1 DG *

THE DELTA 5

11/2/80 Peel *Delta-5, Colour, Make up, Anticipation, You.* Bethan Peters (bv), Ros Allen (bv), Alan Riggs (g), Kelvin Knight (d), Julz Sale (v). 4/2/80 MV4 TW DD

11/9/80 Peel *Triangle, Journey, Try, Leaving.* 2/9/80 MV4 JS MR

27/7/81 Skinner *Train song, Final scene, Innocent, Sing the praises.* 16/7/81 MV4 JS *

DELTONES

2/6/86 Peel *Stay where you are, Make me smile, Party pooper, Lemon squeezy.* Sandra Brown (d), Julie Liggett (b), Angie Risner (b-1,2), Serena Parsons (g), Sara McGuiness (k), Amanda Fenn, Jacqui Callus & Anna Maria Bianchi (v), Nicky Ford & Gilly Johns (al), Anna Keegan (ts), Penny Leyton (tp). 25/5/86 MV5 DG ME&FK

DEMON

7/8/81 Fri. Rock *Night of the demon, Father of time, One hell of a night, Decisions.* Clive Cook (lg), Malcolm Spooner (g), Paul Riley (b), John Wright (d), Dave Hill (v). 24/7/81 * TW *

25/1/91 Fri. Rock *The lion's share, Don't break the circle, (No more) Hell on earth, Commercial dynamite.* Hill, Steve Watts (k), John Waterhouse (lg), Steve Brookes (g), Scott Crawford (d), Nick Bushell (b). 11/1/91 MV5 MC~

SANDY DENNY

6/9/71 Harris *North star grassman and the ravens, Crazy lady blues, Late November blues, The optimist, Lowlands of Holland.* 24/8/71 T1 JM JWH&NG
Originally applied and passed solo audition at AO1 14/10/66, after mother Ena phoned auditions unit on 18/2/66 and 'rambled on about how good her little girl was'. 1st session recorded 7/11/66 in S2 for WS Folk Music programme, TX 4/1/67, prod. BA. Did 2 more for Light's 'Cellar full of Folk' 3,4/67; & live on Country Meets Folk 30/12/67 PH; & 'My kind of folk' 3/7/68; but by then, she was in Fairport Convention (see below).

11/4/72 Peel *That'll be the day, Love's made a fool of you, Learning the game, Crazy arms, Jambalaya.* & bunch (5) (unknown). 28/3/72 MV4 JW *

Had just rec'd In Concert 16/3/72 PS, TX 25/3/72.

20/11/72 Harris *It suits me well, The music weaver, Bushes and briars, It'll take a long time.* Solo. 25/10/72 LH1 JG *

3/12/72 Sounds on Sunday *The lady, Bushes and briars, It suits me well, Black waterside, The music weaver, The sea captain, John the Gunn.* 9/11/72 AO1 FL *

25/9/73 Peel *Solo, Like an old-fashioned waltz, Who knows where the time goes?* Solo. 11/9/73 LH1 TW *

17/12/73 Harris *Until the real thing comes along, Dark of the night, Whispering grass, Solo.* & Hughie Burns (g), Pat Donaldson (b), Willie Murray (d). 14/11/73 LH1 JG *

THE DENTISTS

2/4/87 Long *Just like Oliver Reed, Both sides now, A strange way to go about things, (We thought we'd got to) Heaven.* Michael Murphy (gv), Robert Collins (g), Alun Jones (d), Mark Matthews (b). 22/3/87 MV4 HP MR

DEPARTMENT S

3/12/80 Peel *Clap now, Ode to Cologne (The stench of war), Age concern, Is Vic there?* Vaughan Toulouse (lv), Michael Herbage (g), Tony Lordan (b), Eddie Roxie (sy), Stuart Mizon (d). 19/11/80 LH1 BS NG

16/2/81 Skinner *Clap now, Monte Carlo or bust, Just pretend, Somewhere between heaven and Tesco's.* Marc Taylor (k) r. Roxie. 5/2/81 LH1 DG MR

29/10/81 Jensen *The fightin' Irish, Of all the lost followers, Age concern, Going left right.* Jimmy Hughes (b) r. Lordan. 22/10/81 MV4 PW *

DEPECHE MODE

17/6/81 Skinner *Boys†, Tora! Tora! Tora!, Photographic, Big Muff.* Dave Gahan (v), Vince Clarke (kv), Martin Gore (kv), Andrew Fletcher (k). 11/6/81 LH1 DG *
† On 'I and only' BOJCD025.

DEPTH CHARGE

23/2/91 Peel *Depth charge US silver fox, War is not good, Under the electrical storm, Laughing at strangers wearing funny shorts.* Saul Kane (prg,smp), Alan Scott (g), Donovan Hart (v-1 only). 27/1/91 MV3 DG ME&FK

THE DESPERATE BICYCLES

10/7/78 Peel *Smokescreen, Skill, Sarcasm, Teacher's prayer.* Dave Papworth (d), Roger Stevens (b), Nicky Stevens (lg), Danny Wigley (lv). 4/7/78 MV4 MB MR

DEVIATED INSTINCT

15/5/90 Peel *Molten tears, Dredger, (Behind) The scaffold, Open wound†.* John Adam Stevenson (d), Steven Harvey (b), Robert Middleton (gv). 17/4/90 MV5 TdB PA
† On 'Hardcore Holocaust II' SFRCD113.

DR DEVIOUS

26/9/92 Peel *Return to cyber space.* Dr Devious (kv), The Diddyman (kv), Cobalt. 6/9/92 MV3 ME~ CML

HOWARD DEVOTO

8/8/83 Peel *Cold imagination, Topless, Some will pay.* Howard Devoto (gv), Dave Formula (k), Alan St. Clair (g), Neil Pyzer (sx,sy), Pat Ahearn (d), Martin Heath (b), Laura Teresa (bkv). 1/8/83/ MV4 TW MC

DEXY'S MIDNIGHT RUNNERS

13/3/80 Peel *(Tell me when my) Light turns green, Breaking down the walls of heartache, The horse, Geno.* Kevin Rowland (lv), A. Archer (gv), J.B. (ts), Steve Spooner (al), Pete Williams (bv), Stoker (d), Andy Leake (o,v), Big Jim Paterson (tb). 26/2/80 MV4 BS MR

20/7/81 Skinner *Let's make this precious, Spiritual passion, Your own, Until I believe my soul.* Rowland, Paterson, Mick Billingham (o,v), Billy Adams (g,bkv), Steve Wynne (b,bkv), Seb Shelton (d), Paul Speare (ts), Brian Maurice (al). 9/7/81 MV4 JS MR

21/7/82 Jensen *Let's make this precious, Jackie Wilson said..., All in all, Old.* Rowland, Shelton, Adams, Billingham, Giorgio Kilkenny (b), Helen O'Hara & Steve Brennan (fd), Nick Gatfield (ts,al), Mark Walters (tb). 4/7/82 MV4 DG ME

DI'ANNO

5/10/84 Fri. Rock *Spiritual guidance, Antigua, Razor edge, Flaming heart.* Paul Di'Anno (v), Paul J. Ward (g), Lee

Slater (g), Kevin Browne (b), Frank Noon (d), Mark Venables (k). 21/9/84 MV4 TW MS&DG

KASSE MADY DIABATE
26/11/89 KERSHAW *Koulandian, Kemba dendi, Barana, Tasri makan.* Kasse Mady Diabete (ng,v), Lassena Kouyate (blp), Mamadou Doumbia (g), Papa Kouyate (perc), Damba Assa Sachko (v), Chantal 'Shann' Evuort (v). 9/10/89 HP DG NG

SONA DIABATE
28/10/90 KERSHAW *M'bote, Kankele ti, M'bore.* Sona Diabate (v), Sayon Diabate (rgv), Sexou Diabate (g), Ibrahima Soumano (bal). 9/8/90 MV5 DG NG

TOUMANI DIABATE
16/2/89 KERSHAW *The group's theme, Gnewalale ode to Toumani, Mousso maramba, Dounya, Koulandjan song for the hunter, Sackodougou.* Toumani Diabate (kor), Moriba Koita (ng), Fadiala Tounkara (g), Fanta Sacko (v). 2/12/88 * * *
19/11/89 KERSHAW *Alaa lake, Djaraby, Dany donfoly, L'arme d'un orphelin.* Toumani Diabate (kor-1,2; ng-3,4). 2/11/89 * DG MWT

THE DIAGRAM BROTHERS
27/3/80 PEEL *Animals, Bricks, Bikers, There is no shower.* Fraser (lv,g), Laurence (g), Jason (b), & Simon Diagram (d). 17/3/80 MV4 TW DD
3/2/81 PEEL *Postal bargains, Those men in white coats, I didn't get where I am today by being a right git, My bad chest feels much better now.* Andy Diagram (b,bkv) r. Jason. 27/1/81 LHI DG MR
22/7/82 PEEL *Hey Dad!, Tracey, You've got to pick a pocket or two, The expert, You'll never walk alone.* 26/6/82 MV4 DG PS

DIAMOND HEAD
28/11/80 FRI. ROCK *Borrowed time, Lightning to the nations, Don't you ever leave me, Sweet and innocent.* Brian Tatler (g), Colin Kimberly (b), Duncan Scott (d), Shawn Harris (v). 29/10/80 * TW PW

DIATRIBE
1/1/86 PEEL *Peace in our time, Student rap, No reason, Burn.* Jonathan Kirby (d), Tim Kirby (bv), Andy Fenn (g). 8/12/85 MV5 DG ME

DIBLO DIBALA
8/8/92 KERSHAW *Matchatcha wetu, Bolingo, Mondo ry, Merci papa (& Laissez passer, Tcheke, Medisance, Extra ball, on PEEL: later same night).* Diblo Dibala (gv), J.P. Kinkazi (rg), Alain Dieng (b), Ringo Avom (d), Serge Bimangou (perc), Emi Laskin (v), Mondo David (v), Gwen Lemmonier, Electra Weston, Laure Anne & Antoinette Yelessa (bkv, dancing). 19/7/92 MV3&4 MA~ SA

JOHNNY DIESEL & THE INJECTORS
5/5/89 FRI. ROCK *Looking for love, Parisienne hotel, Burn, Rat pack.* Johnny Tatt (b), Johnny Diesel (vg), Bernie Bremond (sx), Yak Sheritt (d). 14/4/89 WX TW MWT

DIESEL PARK WEST
28/9/87 LONG *Like princes do, The girl with the name, Jackie's still sad, A house divided.* John Butler (v,ag), Rick Wilson (g,bkv), Mick Salisbury (g), Jeff Beaven (b,bkv), Moth Smith (d,bkv). 26/8/87 MV4 PW *
31/8/88 L. KERSHAW *The bell of hope, Fine Lily fine, I want no mystery, Opportunity crazy.* Rich Barton (g) r. Salisbury. 2/8/88 MV4 HP MR

THE DINNER LADIES
10/12/87 KERSHAW *Muscle in the bud, Waltz, The sea's eating Britain, These knees have seen the world.* Lorraine Bowen (p,rec,bkv), Julia Palmer (clo,bkv), Ben Davies (g,bkv), Mick Jackson (lv). 19/11/87 * DG *
30/8/88 L. KERSHAW *I need a tree to breathe, Waterman, Blackpool for the day, The submariner dreaming.* 17/7/88 MV4 TdB~

DINOSAUR JUNIOR
14/11/88 PEEL *Raisans, Does it float, Leper, Bulbs of passion.* Patrick Murphy (d), Lou Barlow (b), J. Mascis (g). 8/11/88 MV4 MR~

23/3/89 KERSHAW *Quest, Keep the glove, In a jar, Heaven up here.* 1/3/89 OS * *
22/5/89 PEEL *Budge, No bones, Chunks.* 25/4/89 WX DG DD

DION
30/9/89 SAT. SEQ. *Written on the subway wall, I've got to get to you, The wanderer, King of the New York streets, Dripdrop, I wonder why, And the night stood still, Ruby baby, Runaround Sue.* Dion (v), Terry Harr (sx,k,bkv), Paul Harris (k,bkv), Johnny Sambataro (g,bkv), Gabriel Vales (b,bkv), Larry Hirt (d). Live from MV3 PW TdB.
One of Roger Scott's last broadcasts.

DIRE STRAITS
17/5/78 JENSEN *Water of love, Walkin' in the Wild West End, Sultans of swing, Lions.* Mark Knopfler (g,lv), David Knopfler (gv), John Illsley (bv), Pick Withers (d). 13/4/78 PHM TH TWN.
'Mark Knopfler wanted the lights down lower and lower to get the atmosphere,' recalls Tony Worthington; 'so we went down to "reds" on the battens (remember it was still a theatre, with all the lighting controls), then we dimmed the reds, and finally I think we were down to just the emergency lighting only, with Tony Hale biting his nails over the insurance claim if Mark had fallen off the stage'
Later recorded 'In Concert' 19/7/78 PS, TX 22/7/78. All subsequent sessions 'private tapes'.

DIRTY DOGS
14/7/89 FRI. ROCK *Live by the gun, Dirty lies, City of dreams, Dogs of war.* Tony Lawrence (v), Bill Liesegang (g), Harris Joannon (b), Barry Fitzgerald (d). 28/4/89 WX&MV3 PW DD&TD
Changed name to 'Killer Dogs' by repeat on 8/9/89.

DIRTY STRANGERS
27/7/84 FRI. ROCK *You'll have to do better, Diamonds, Hands up, Survival dance.* Alan Clayton (v), Al Symons (g), Mark Harrison (d), Scott Mulvey (k), Ray King (b), John Plain (g), Chris Winter (hca). 6/7/84 MV4 TW DD&MS

DIRTY WEEKEND
24/11/89 FRI. ROCK *Kick it in, Dreaming, Save my soul, Word with you.* Ian Briggs (lv), Adam Crook (lg), Andrew Hough (g,bkv), Howard Potts (b,bkv), Phil Slaven (d). 20/10/89 MV5 HP DD&MC

DIRTY WHITE BOY
29/6/90 FRI. ROCK *Bad reputation, Hammer on the heart, Let's spend mama's money, Badlands.* David Glen Eisley (v), Earl Slick (g), F Kirk Alley (b), Michael Lord (k), Keni Richards (d). 15/6/90 MV5 TW DD&MA

DISLOCATION DANCE
11/8/81 PEEL *Friendship, Remind me of those little things, Shoot out at Dead Man's Creek, It don't mean a thing.* Andy Diagram (tp,bkv), Ian Runacres (g,lv,k), Paul Emmerson (b,bkv), Dick Harrison (d,bkv). 5/8/81 MV4 CL NG
20/1/82 JENSEN *Stand me up, You can tell, Rosemary, Spare concern.* 6/1/82 PHM * *
14/7/82 PEEL *Baby blue, Tyrannies of fun, You'll never never know, Working the midnight shift, The next year I returned to St. Michel but Marie had gone and with her my childhood.* & Kathy Way (v,sx). 12/6/82 MV4 DG TdB

DISPOSABLE HEROES OF HIPHOPRISY
9/5/92 PEEL *Positive, Traffic jam, Language of violence, Exercise.* Michael Franti (v), Rono Tse (perc,v,'taste'), Simone White (d). 24/3/92 MV4 MA~ RK
12/9/92 KERSHAW *Positive, Colour blind, Water pistol man, Financial leprosy.* 19/5/92 MV4 MR~

THE DISTRIBUTORS
21/6/79 PEEL *TV me, We have fun, Melt down, Wireless.* Mick Switzerland (g,k,v,tps), Keith James (gv), Enzo Raphael (bv), Dave Holmes (d). 13/6/79 MV4 BS NG
17/12/81 PEEL *House party, Look at this, Keep looking*

ahead, Motionless. Holmes, James, Robert Worby (g,k), Steve Beresford (b). 14/12/81 MV4 JWI *

DR AND THE CRIPPENS
17/5/88 PEEL *Pink machine gun†/Ballad of farmer Vincent/The garden centre murders†, Peely backwards/Skin tight†/Ode to a slug, Pneumatic geek/Death squad/Jimmy goes to Egypt, Don't look in the freezer°/Mindsurf°/Experiment conclusion°.* Jesus Van Gough (d,bkv), Wayne Crippenski (b,bkv), Tom Crippen (g,bkv), Max Von Reinhart (v), Emily Danger (v-4 only). 8/5/88 * DG MA&JB
† On 'Hardcore Holocaust' SFRCD101; ° On 'Hardcore Holocaust II' SFRCD113.
14/8/89 PEEL *Henrietta's baby, The death of Pinocchio/Kid with the removable face, I'm sop done/Song for Guy, Braindead/Melt.* Danger out. 16/7/89 * DG JB

DOCTOR CALCULUS
28/1/85 PEEL *Programme 7, Killed by poetry, Honey I'm home.* * Rec. Date Unknown * * *

THE DOCTOR'S CHILDREN
3/10/85 KERSHAW *Tomorrow I'll die, Song for gnasher, Rose cottage, Love it miss it.* Rowland Howarth (d), Paul Issott (b), Paul Smith (gv). 26/9/85 Y2 DST SR
21/8/86 KERSHAW *I am the sun†, Harvest moon†, Born to wander, Baby teardrop.* Smith, Howarth, Matthew Woodman (k), Dave Ramsay (b). 9/7/86 SS SP TWN
† On Buffalo BUFF1 12-inch.
21/5/87 KERSHAW *Cowboy song, Sugar Jo, Girl with green eyes, Love's sweet pain.* 7/5/87 * * *
10/6/87 LONG *Soldier Suzy, Kissing sweet, Don't let the snow, Heartache.* Chris Smith (d) r. Howarth. 12/4/87 MV4 HP SC

DOCTORS OF MADNESS
7/12/76 PEEL *Out, Brothers/Suicide city.* Kid Strange (gv), Urban Blitz (vi,g), Stoner (bv), Peter Dilema (dv). 25/11/76 * TW *

JEGGSY DODD
19/8/85 PEEL *Welcome to hillview heights, No place to run, A scouse werewolf in London, Why the clown?, The beer bellied bully boys bash the boys in blue, Who killed New Brighton?, The day my flat turned wierd.* Jeggsy Dodd (v). 6/8/85 MV5 JWI MR

THE DODGEMS
24/9/79 PEEL *Muscle beach, Gotta give it up, Lord Lucan, Science fiction (Baby you're so).* Gary Turner (lvb), Doug Potter (gv), Paul Birchall (k), Charlie Zuber (d). 17/9/79 MV4 BS DD

THE DODGERS
26/5/76 PEEL *Don't let me be wrong, I just wanna love you, Get to you, Help me out.* John Wilson (gv), Tom Evans (bv), Bob Jackson (pv), Dave Powell (d). 11/5/76 * JG MR

DODGY
6/1/92 GOODIER *Lovebirds, As my time goes by, Easy way, Age of not believing.* Nigel Clark (bv), Matthew Priest (d), Andrew Miller (g), Stevie C (k), Chrissie H (smp,perc). 26/10/91 MV4 MC~ SM

DOG FACED HERMANS
18/5/87 PEEL *Shat on by angels [or 'Shore up the enemy'], Malcolm Rifkind's privy, Balloon girl, El doggo speaks.* Marion Coutts (v,tp), Colin McLean (b), Andy Moor (g), Wilf Plum (d). 3/5/87 * DG ME&MA

DOGGO
12/6/72 HARRIS *Nothing more, By surprise, Lovely ways, Next phase.* * 30/5/72 * JG *

DOGS D'AMOUR
12/2/88 FRI. ROCK *Kid from Kensington, I don't you to go, How come it never rains, Everything I want.* Jo (g,bkv), Bam Bam (d,bkv), Steve James (b,bkv,hca), Tyla (g,lv). 22/1/88 * HP DD

THOMAS DOLBY
24/12/81 JENSEN *Urges, Commercial break-up, Radio silence, Therapy/Growth.* Thomas Dolby (sy,lv), Mark Heyward-

Chaplin (b), Kevin Armstrong (gv), Justin Hildreth (d).
25/10/81 MV4 DG PS

BO DOLLIS AND THE WILD MAGNOLIAS
18/8/91 KERSHAW *Meet the boy on the battlefront, Handa wanda, Shoefly, Shallow water.* Theodore 'Bo' Dollis & Joseph 'Monk' Boudreax (v,tamb), Norwood Johnson (bass drum,v), Wilson Victory (gv), Earl Nunez (b), Tiffany Brown & Roy Varnado (bkv).
18/7/91 MV5 DG NG&JB

DOLLY MIXTURE
14/8/79 PEEL *Dolly mixture theme song/Dream come true, He's so frisky, New look baby, Ernie Ball, The locomotion.* Rachel Bor (lv,g), Debsey Wykes (bv), Hester Smith (dv). 7/8/79 MV4 BS MR
20/9/82 JENSEN *Side street walker, Understanding, Dead rainbow, Spend your wishes.* 9/9/82 MV4 JS *
7/11/83 JENSEN *Winter seems fine, Grass is greener, Dust to dust, Whistling in the dark.* 27/10/83 MV4 JP *

LISA DOMINIQUE
15/9/89 FRI. ROCK *Rock & roll lady, All fall down, Somebody special, Time bomb.* Lisa Dominique (v), Marino (g), Ian Spicer (b), Ian Hale (g), Steve Holland.
11/8/89 MV5 TW *

DONOVAN
21/1/68 TOP GEAR *There is a mountain, As I recall it, Lalena, The timber and the crab, Young girl blues.* Donovan (gv) & The John Cameron group (5).
16/1/68 MV4 BA DT&BC
16/6/68 TOP GEAR *Mad John's escape, It's been a long time, The entertaining of a shy little girl, Lalena, Hast thou seen the unicorn? (& Skip-along Sam, 21/7/68).* & John Cameron, David Katz, 14 musicians.
11/6/68 PCI BA DT

DOOM
28/6/88 PEEL† *Symptom of the universe/Multinationals, Exploitation, Circles, No religion, Relief, Sold out/War crimes.* Anthony Dickens (d), Peter Nash (b), Brian Talbot (g), John Pickering (v), Paul Halmshaw (v).
19/6/88 MV5 DG MR
14/3/89 PEEL† *Means to an end/A dream to come true, Natural abuse/Days go by, Life lock/Bury the debt, Life in freedom/Money drug/Fear of the future.* Karl Willetts (v) r. Halmshaw. 7/3/89 MV4 DG MWT
† On Strange Fruit SFPMA203.

JOHN DOONAN
13/8/74 PEEL *3 Irish jigs: Comb you hair and curl it/I have a wife of my own/Any old jig will do, Lament to Oliver Goldsmith, The piper through the meadow strayed, Fiddler round the fairy tree, Jigs: Banish misfortune/Gillian's apples/Morrison's jig, Reels: Jacky Coleman's reel/Brennan's reel.* John Doonan (fd).
22/7/74 TI JW *

DORMANNU
12/6/84 PEEL *Slam, The Dread, Pole.* Simeon Warburton (gv), Wig (b), Cristine Crev (k), Marcus Stott (d), Tinley (g), Dizzy Heights (tst). 30/5/84 MV5 BYA NG

BOB DOWNES' OPEN MUSIC
1/5/70 BLACK *Migration, Don't let tomorrow get you down, Sea shore, Walking on (& Gonna take a journey, 12 /6/70).* Bob Downes & (tpx3), (ts), (bars), (fl), (b), (d), (vib) (unknown). 18/3/70 AO2 JM *
Had done two trio sessions for R1's Jazz Workshop 69,70.
28/8/70 BLACK *There's no time like the present, The word, Go find time (& Hell's angels, 23/10/70).*
22/7/70 AO2 JM JWH [M: Jazz shows]

THE DOWNLINERS SECT
13/10/77 PEEL *Talking about you, Killing me, Richmond rhythm and blues, Show biz.* Paul Holm (d), Keith Grant (lvb), Terry Gibson (lg), Don Craine (rg,bkv), Paul Tiller (hca,bkv). 27/9/77 MV4 MB MR

THE DRAGSTERS
8/1/87 LONG *Shoot me dead, Fine sense of humour, Dead*

skunk, Echo mountain. Billy Harron (g), Ian Boffey (g), Martin Roberts (d), James Jamieson (b), Ian Hoey (lv).
21/12/86 MV4 JE TdB

NICK DRAKE
6/8/69 PEEL *Time of no reply, Cello song, River man, Three hours.* Nick Drake (ag,v). 5/8/69 MV5 PR MH

ROBIN AND BARRY DRANSFIELD
5/6/71 TOP GEAR *Still he sings, Lord of all I behold, Who liveth so merry, The wild rover.* Robin Dransfield (gv), Barry Dransfield (fd,v). 18/5/71 MV4 JW BC
Rec'd trial broadcast for R1/2's 'Folk on Friday' 14/3/70, prod. FL, passed [M: Folk shows].
31/10/72 PEEL *A week before Easter, Hyde Park mansions, The werewolf, Girl of dances.* Barry only (fd,v).
3/10/72 LHI JW BC
21/2/74 PEEL *When it's night-time in Italy it's Wednesday over here, It's dark in here, I once had a dog, The Cutty wren, Lazy afternoon.* Robin only. 14/2/74 LHI JW *
16/4/74 PEEL *Ballad of Dickie Lubber, Old Joe, Up to now (& Daddy please take me to the line, 4/6/74).* Barry only. 1/4/74 TI JW *
17/9/74 PEEL *It's dark in here, Medley: Roaring Mary/The bunch of keys/Silver spire, Up to now, The three muscadets.* Duo. 2/9/74 TI JW *
15/5/75 PEEL *Hey hey, The handsome meadow boy, The fool's song, Fair maids of February.* 8/5/75 MV4 JW *
18/12/75 PEEL *Christmas is coming, What will we tell them, You can't change me now, Violin.* Billed as 'The Dransfields': Robin, Barry & Brian Harrison (b).
27/11/75 MV4 TW *
5/10/76 PEEL *You can't change me now, The ballad of Dickie Lubber, The alchemist and the peddler, The blacksmith pt I.* Billed as 'Dransfield': Robin, Barry, Harrison (b), & Bob Critchley (d). 14/9/76 MV4 JG MR
10/2/78 PEEL *Catch the morning dew, Too much to do, Doctor Spine, Be your own man.* Robin & Barry only.
31/1/78 MV4 MB MR

DREAMTIME
26/10/87 LONG *Insecure, A cold and lonely place, She already knows, I'm happy now.* Rachel Lewis (v), Tony Fellowes (b), Robert Fellowes (g), Alan Day (d).
13/9/87 MV4 HP TdB&SC

DRIVE
25/9/90 PEEL *Grease gun, Road, Drive out, Fire flaps.* Jeff Egerton (d), Dan Pye (b), Iain Roche (gv).
14/8/90 MV5 MR~

THE DRONES
13/12/77 PEEL *Be my baby, The change, Clique, Movement.* M.J. Drone (lvg), Pete Lambert (d), Whisper (b,lv-2), Guss Gangrene (lg). 6/12/77 MV4 MB MR

DROWNING CRAZE
13/1/82 PEEL *In the heat, Keep fit, Out of order, He was.* Simon Godfrey (d), Simon Raymonde (b), Paul Cummins (g), Frank Nardiello (v). 2/1/82 MV4 DG HP

DRUID
18/11/74 HARRIS *The dawn of the evening, Remembering.* Ced Sharpley (d), Neil Brewer (bv), Dane Stevens (lgv), Andy McCrorie (k). 13/11/74 MV4 JG *

**PETE DRUMMOND AND
THE FREQUENTLY-HIGH WAVEBAND**
28/9/72 DRUMMOND *The laughing policeman, Rocking at the BBC, Nonsense, Goodbye.* * ?/9/72 LHI MB MH&MF

DRUNK TANK
11/9/92 PEEL *Stranger danger, Crooked mile, Pin up girl, Accidents.* David Barker (g), Julian Mills (bv), Steve Cerio (d). 18/8/92 MV4 JB~ PL

DUB SEX
4/2/87 PEEL *Then and now, Play street, Kristallnacht, Man on the inside.* Mark Hoyle (gv), Dave Rumney (g), Cathy Brooks (b), Roger Cadman (d). 20/1/87 * DG MR
24/8/87 PEEL *Push!, Voice of reason, Kicking the corpse around, Splintered.* 16/8/87 * DG ME&MC
5/7/88 PEEL *Caved-in, Snapper!, I am not afraid, The big*

freeze. Chris Bridgett (g) r. Rumney.
5/6/88 * DG NG&ME&PS .
8/3/89 PEEL *Swerve†, North by north east, Kumina, Time of life.* & Tim Costigan (g). 26/2/89 * DG MR
† On 'Manchester - so much to answer for' SFRCD202.

DUCKS DELUXE
26/6/73 PEEL *Coast to coast, Pensecola nightmare, Bring back that Packard car, Fireball.* Martin Belmont (lgv), Sean Tyla (gv), Nick Garvey (bv), Tim Roper (d).
12/6/73 LHI CB BC
6/8/73 HARRIS *Sweet music, Nervous breakdown, Come what may, Carol.* 25/7/73 LHI JG *
11/2/74 HARRIS *My my music, West Texas truckin', American mother (& Don't matter tonite, 1/7/74).* & Andy McMasters (kv). 30/1/74 LHI PR *
4/6/74 PEEL *Dancing beat, Fireball, It's all over now, The cannons of the boogie night.* 23/4/74 LHI PR *
27/3/75 PEEL *Paris nine, Jumping in the fire, Something's going on, Amsterdam dog.* Mick Groome (bv) r. Garvey, McMasters ("Brinsley Schwarz joining band next week"-TW). 20/3/75 MV4 TW DD

M. C. DUKE
28/9/87 PEEL *The raw, Funky for you, Free.* M.C.Duke (rp), Simon Harris (d,prg,k,smp). 20/9/87 * DG DG&MFA

JOHN DUMMER BLUES BAND
11/8/68 TOP GEAR *40 days and 40 nights, Travelling man, Standing round cryin', After hours.* John Dummer (d), Dave Kelly (slg,v), T. S. McPhee (gv), John O'Leary (hca), Iain Thomson (b). 2/7/68 PCI BA *
Passed by panel despite 'some criticism' of vocalist.
22/10/68 WS R&B *When you've got a good friend, Sittin' and thinkin', After hours, Little red rooster.*
20/9/68 AO2 JG JY
28/1/69 RI CLUB *I need love, Bulldog blues, When you've got a good friend, Long distance call, I love you honey.* 13/1/69 PS KB *
21/4/69 WS R&B *Riding at daylight, Skin game, Travelling blues, Memphis music.* Adrian Pietryea r. McPhee, O'Leary. 2/4/69 MV4 JG JY
18/5/69 TOP GEAR *Big feeling blues, Skin game, Jungle blues (& A few short lines, Hard times, 6/7/69).*
13/5/69 MV4 JW *
31/1/70 WS R&B *Lady luck, Bullfrog blues, No chance now, Boogie woogie lullaby.* Nick Pickett r. Kelly.
7/1/70 MV4 JG JY
17/5/70 RAVEN'S R&B *Fine looking woman, Going in the out, In the wee wee hours, Nine by nine.* Rec. date unknown * JG JY
12/6/71 RAVEN'S R&B *No chance now, Reconsider baby, Down home girl, I can't be satisfied, Nine by nine.*
2/6/71 MV4 MB *
20/10/71 R2 NIGHT RIDE *No time to lose, Little red rooster, Tonight I'll be staying here with you, Turn my head away, Stranger.* 8/7/71 MV5 DK *
23/10/71 RAVEN'S R&B *Time will tell, Me and your boogie, Fortune and time, Lost love, Ramblin' boy.*
13/10/71 MV4 KS *

JOHN DUMMER OOBLEE DOOBLEE BAND
5/5/72 PEEL *I love you honey, Shake your money maker, Riding at midnight, Walking blues.* Kelly returns, r. Pickett. 1/2/72 PH JM JWH&NG
17/8/72 DRUMMOND *The monkey speaks his mind, Lovin' man, Statesborough blues.* 9/8/72 MV4 MB MH&MF
15/9/72 PEEL *The monkey speaks his mind, Young blood, Be careful, I ain't sorry.* Pat Grover r. Pietryea.
4/9/72 TI JM *
22/3/73 PEEL *Going home, Steel guitar rag, Lovin' man, Undying love.* Pete Emery (lg), Colin Earl (p), Pete Richardson (d) r. Grover. 26/2/73 LHI BA *
13/9/73 PEEL *Keep it in my mind, Bad dream, Good rocking man.* Show presented by Alexis Korner, produced by Clive Burrows. 10/9/73 LHI CB *

DUMPY'S RUSTY NUTS
23/11/84 Fri. Rock *Rip it up, Hot lover, Box hill or bust, Cross keys, Tush.* Graham Dunnell (gv), Kerry Langford (b), Mark Brabbs (d) Nik Turner (fl-4 only).
13/10/84 Great Yarmouth TW DD&DG

THE AYNSLEY DUNBAR RETALIATION
27/11/67 WS R&B *Killing flaw, Love her with a feeling, Cobwebs, Down home Chicago.* Aynsley Dunbar (d), Victor Brox (o,v), John Moorshead (g), Keith Tillman (b). 31/10/67 AO2 JG JY
8/10/68 WS R&B *Call my woman, Tuesday's blues, Watch'n chain, Mean old world.* 23/8/68 AO2 JG JY
1/12/68 Top Gear *I tried, When the devil drives, Call my woman, Mean old world.* Alex Dmochowski (b) r. Tillman. 15/10/68 PCI BA AH&BC
17/3/69 WS R&B *Blood on your wheels, Downhearted, Invitation to a lady.* 19/2/69 MV4 JG JY
30/8/69 WS R&B *Leavin' right away, Ride let it ride, When your fear rides on, Down down down.* [Show changed name to 'Blues is where you hear it' this week]. 6/8/69 MV4 JG JY

LESLEY DUNCAN
28/2/69 Night Ride *Exactly who you are, Look what you've done, Lullabye, Sing children sing, Love song, Sunshine.* Lesley Duncan (ag,v) with Sweet Thursday: John Mark (g), Harvey Burns (d), Nicky Hopkins (p). 19/2/69 S2 JM *
11/10/71 Harris *Rainbow games, Emma, Sing children sing, Mr. Rubin.* * 28/9/71 T1 JM JWH&BAI
21/8/72 Harris *Thunder, Times, Love will never lose you, Queen to your king.* 2/8/72 AO2 JG *
11/11/74 Harris *My soul, The serf, Everything changes, Fortieth floor.* 10/10/74 MV4 JG *

CHAMPION JACK DUPREE
19/6/68 Night Ride *I haven't done no-one no harm, Red beans and rice, Whisky look what you've done to me, Tippin' in, Down-don't worry me.* Champion Jack Dupree (gv). 5/6/68 S1 DK *
5/7/70 Raven's R&B *Chicken shack, Goin' down slow, Nothing I do is right, Schooldays, Ugly woman, Dupree special.* 10/6/70 * JG JY Rec date unkown * * *
23/1/71 Raven's R&B *Shirley May No. 3, State St., Hoolionday, Somebody.* Rec. date unknown.

DURAN DURAN
9/3/81 Skinner *Sound of thunder, Anyone out there, Friends of mine, Careless memories.* Simon Le Bon (v), John Taylor (b), Andy Taylor (lg), Roger Taylor (d), Nick Rhodes (k). 16/1/81 BRM GH *
11/8/81 Powell *Waiting for the night boat, Girls on film, Anyone out there, Like an angel.* 19/6/81 BRM GH *
These two by Duran Duran highlight the forgotten pop sessions done for Radio 1 tea-time shows up to the mid-eighties, by Geoffrey Hewitt, at Radio's Network Production Centre, BBC Birmingham. 'We'd do one every ten days or so for Bruno Brookes or Peter Powell', he recalls. Bands recorded, not in this sessionography, included Erasure, Simply Red and Culture Club. Years before, there had been dozens done in the Old Walker Hall. But no more.

THE DURUTTI COLUMN
7/1/88 Kershaw *English landscape tradition, What is it to me woman, Kangleur Gray, 28 Oldham Street.* Vini Reilly (gp,fx), Bruce Mitchell (d), John Metcalfe (vla), Rob Gray (hca). 24/11/87 * MRD SR

IAN DURY AND THE BLOCKHEADS
12/12/77 Peel *Sex and drugs and rock and roll, Clevor Trever, Sweet Gene Vincent, Blockheads.* Ian Dury (v), Charlie Charles (d), Norman Watt-Roy (b), John Turnbull (g), Chas Jankel (gk), Mickey Gallagher (o). 30/11/77 MV4 MB NG

THE DYLANS
30/4/91 Goodier *Love vibration, Ocean wide†, L S O, Planet love.* Colin Gregory (bv), Quentin Jennings (o), Jim Rodger (lg), Garry Jones (d). 20/4/91 MV5 MC~

† On 'Best of Mark Goodier' Nighttracks Mark1.

DYNAMIC THREE
4/3/87 Peel *Beat like this, Ten M.C.s, Illing.* Dr Phibes, Capt. T.K., E.M.D; & Ricky Rennalls (k,perc), Damon Butcher (k). 17/2/87 * DG MR&FK
9/5/88 Peel *Def Stanza, I feel dynamic, Gangster.* Carlos Dennis (sc) credited instead of Dr. Phibes. 26/4/88 * DG TdB&PS

SNOOKS EAGLIN
22/7/90 Kershaw *Yours truly, Lavinia, Oh lawdy my baby, Talk to your daughter.* Snooks Eaglin (gv), George Porter Jr. (b,bkv), George Raines (d). 24/6/90 MV5 DG ME

STEVE EARLE
16/4/87 Kershaw *Good ole boys, Someday, Hillbilly highway, Little rock'n roller, Fearless heart.* Steve Earle (gv), Ken Moore (k), William Baxter (rg,sg), Ronald Kling (b), Harry Stinson (d), Michael McAdams (lg). 27/3/87 * RN SR

EAST OF EDEN
18/4/70 Top Gear *Nymphenburger, Sphinx (& It's the porridge they're after, 11/7/70).* Dave Arbus (vi,fl), Roy Caines (sx), Geoff Nicholson (lgv), Geoff Britton (d), Andy Sneddon (b). 6/4/70 PH JW BC
Group failed trial broadcast on R1 Club, 4/69; passed re-audition at end of year.
12/9/70 Top Gear *Scott of the Antarctic, Halloween.* David Jacks (b), Jeff Allen (d) r. Caines, Nicholson, Britton. 11/8/70 MV4 JW *
29/9/70 Harding *Here come the day, Jig-a-jig, Crazy daisy.* 22/9/70 MV5 MB MH&MF
4/6/71 Black *Alan Black goes quality surveying, Wonderful feeling, To Mrs V., Goodbye.* Jimmy Roche (lg) r. Sneddon. 6/5/71 AO2 JM JWH
8/11/71 Harris *Road song, Bradshaw the bison hunter, It ain't gonna do you no harm.* & Don Weller (sx). 19/10/71 T1 JM JWH [M]

EASTERHOUSE
22/8/84 Skinner *Coming up for air, Man alive, One more time, Evening watch.* Andrew Perry (v), Ivor Perry (g), Peter Vanden (b), Gary Rostock (d). 12/8/84 MV5 DG ME

CLINT EASTWOOD AND GENERAL SAINT
11/8/81 Skinner *Another one bites the dust, Run, Matilda, Barnyard.* General Saint (Winston Hislop) (v), Clint Eastwood (Robert Brammer) (v), Lloyd Donaldson (d), Stephen Baugh (b), John Kpiaye (g), Paget King (k), Mike Rose (al), Vin Gordon (tb). 6/8/81 MV4 MR
2/8/83 Jensen *Combination, Eternal love, Run, DJ power.* Eastwood, Saint, Courtney Pine (sx), Delroy Donaldson (gk), Dean Pierre (d), Cameron Pierre (lg), Freddie Gachette (b), Michael Spratt (perc). 21/7/83 MV4 JP *

ECHO AND THE BUNNYMEN
22/8/79 Peel† *Read it in books°, Stars are stars, I bagsy yours, Villiers Terrace.* Ian McCulloch (gv), Will Sergeant (g), Les Pattinson (b), Dave Balfe (k,perc) & (dm). 15/8/79 MV4 TVD NG

† On Strange Fruit SFPS060. ° Also on 'Winters of Discontent SFRCD204.

22/5/80 Peel *The pictures on my wall, All that jazz, Over the wall.* Pete Defreitas (d) r. Balfe & (dm). 13/5/80 MV4 JE MR
12/11/80 Peel *All my colours turn to clouds, That golden smile, Heaven up here, Turquoise daze.* Sargeant (p-1). 4/11/80 LH1 JS MR
8/2/82 Peel *Taking advantage, An equation, No hands.* 27/1/82 MV4 KH NG
These titles were written in on on the sheet at the last minute by Ian McCulloch: Kevin Howlett recalls the words to the songs being written in the studio. 'Taking advantage', was later retitled 'The back of love', and in May '82 became the band's first Top 20 hit. A genuine 'work in progress' session.

20/6/83 Peel *Silver, Seven seas, The killing moon.* 6/6/83 MV4 TW MC
24/10/83 Peel *Nocturnal me, Watch out below, Ocean rain, My kingdom.* 19/9/83 MV4 * *

THE ECLECTION
12/5/68 Top Gear *Mark time, In her mind, In the early days, Morning of yesterday, Confusion.* Mike Rosen (g,tp,v), Geoff Hultgren (bv), Trevor Lucas (g), Gerry Conway (d), Kerry Male (v). 30/4/68 PCI BA DT&AH
15/7/68 Symonds *Another time another place, Will tomorrow be the same (16/7), Nevertheless (17/7).* 9/7/68 MV5 * *
28/7/68 Top Gear *Another time another place, Nevertheless, St.Georg & the dragon, Will tomorrow be the same? (& Violet dew, 1/9/68).* 23/7/68 PCI BA PR&MR
Group also appeared on R1 Club, 12/8/68 PS; & again in October; & 2/69.
3/11/68 Henry *In the early days, Another time another place, Morning of yesterday, Confusion, Please.* 28/10/68 AO2 AD *
8/12/68 Top Gear *Please, If I love her, Days left behind, Time for love.* 19/11/68 PCI BA AH&BC
27/4/69 Top Gear *Both sides now, Restitution, Charity, Earth, Put on your face.* John Palmer, Gary Boyle, Dorris Henderson r. Male, Rosen [M]. 21/4/69 PH BA *
Although contracts don't suggest so, Henderson possibly also on 28/10 & 19/11/68 dates.

BIG ED AND HIS ROCKIN RATTLESNAKES
22/1/87 Kershaw *Do you think I look like Elvis Presley, The old home fill her up keep keep on truckin' caff, This town, Uncle Tom's cab.* Big Ed (v) & (g), (g), (d) unknown. 17/12/86 * DST SR

EDDIE AND THE HOT RODS
21/2/77 Peel *Keep on keeping on, Why can't it be, Teenage depression, On the run.* Barry Masters (v), Dave Higgs (g,bkv), Paul Gray (b), Steve Nicol (d). 15/2/77 MV4 JG MR
17/10/77 Peel *Life on the line, I don't know what's going on, Telephone girl, Beginning of the end.* & Graeme Douglas (g,bkv). 10/10/77 MV4 TW DD
5/3/79 Peel *Strangers on the payphone, Power and glory, Breathless, Living dangerously.* & Neil Burn ('extra high' bkv). 5/2/79 MV4 TW NBU
19/3/79 Peebles *Power and glory, Out to lunch (20/3), He does it with mirrors (21/3), Circles (22/3).* 8/3/79 * JG *

DUANE EDDY
30/7/74 Peel *Cannonball rag, Dance to the guitar man, The lonely one.* Duane Eddy (g) & Diane M. Abbate, & (o), (lg), (b), (d) unknown. 29/7/74 LH1 JW BAI
Previously appeared live on 'Monday Monday' 6/3/67 PH; Tony Brandon 27/1/69.

EDEN
15/8/85 Into The Music *Killer, Free, Child, Crying to you.* Darren Poole (v), Mark 'Micky' Poole (g), Pete Tasker (b), Mark Rose (k), Danny Parsons (d). 20/7/85 MV4 DG MC

THE EDGE
24/4/79 Peel *The edge (instrumental), Friday 17th, I give up, Who's your friend.* Lu (gv), Glyn (bv), Gavin (kv), Jon (d,perc,v). 18/4/79 MV4 JS NG

DAVE EDMUNDS' ROCKPILE
14/2/77 Peel *Down down down, TV TV man, Heart of the city, I knew the bride.* Dave Edmunds (gv), Billy Bremner (g,bkv), Nick Lowe (bv,lv-3,4), Terry Williams (d). 8/2/77 MV4 PR MR

DAVE EDMUNDS
8/3/82 Jensen *Your true love, Dear dad, Deep in the heart of Texas, From small things big things come, Crawling from the wreckage.* Dave Edmunds (vg), John David (b), Dave Charles (d), Geraint Watkins (p), Mickey Gee (g). 21/2/82 MV4 DG MC

238

EDSEL AUCTIONEER
8/2/89 PEEL *Brickwall dawn, Between two crimes, Place in the sun, Blind hurricane.* Chris Cooper (d), Ashley Horner (b,g), Aidan Winterburn (rgv). 24/1/89 MV4 DG MR

EDWARD II AND THE RED HOT POLKAS
29/10/87 KERSHAW *The Bromsberrow heath three-hand reel, Sophie Bourbons, Dawn run, Red Jenny land.* Jon Moore, Tom Greenhalgh & Barnaby Stradling (g), John Gill (b), Steve Goulding (d), David Haines & Rod Stradling (ml), Danny Stradling (perc).
15/10/87 * DG NG&MC
16/3/89 KERSHAW *The queen's jig, Just as the tide is flowing, Swedish polka, Swing easy.* Gill, Moore, Greenhalgh, Haynes (ml), D. Stradling (perc), Alton Zebbey (perc). 16/2/89 MV4 DG FK

DAVID HONEYBOY EDWARDS
16/5/92 KERSHAW *Big fat mama blues, Catfish blues, So long, Mother in law.* David Honeyboy Edwards (gv).
27/4/92 MV3 MHW MR

TERRY EDWARDS
2/2/92 PEEL *Four, Eighty One, Knife, You suffer/Your achievement/Dead/The kill, Lubbock Texas.* Terry Edwards (dm,g,bars,sx), Mark Bedford (b), Terry Underwood (ts), Dave Woodhead (tp). 15/12/91 MV3 DG JB
After dozens of session guest appearances with other acts, not to mention those as a founder member of the Higsons, Edwards chose his debut solo date to salute the magic of Miles Davis and Napalm Death.

EEK-A MOUSE
12/10/83 JENSEN *Peeni-walli (fire flies), Terrorists in the city, Noah's ark, Ganja smuggling.* Eek-A-Mouse (v) & Kalabash: Nastas Hackett (d), Hugh Miller (b), Kenneth Mackintosh (rg), Sidney Mills (lg,k), Winston Miller (p); & J.P. Palmer (perc). 9/10/83 MV4 DG ME
17/10/83 PEEL *Wa-do-dem, Hitler, Assassinator, Hire and removal.* Same studio, same line-up, next day:
10/10/83 MV4 TW MC
26/6/84 PEEL *Elizabeth, Safari, Mouse and man, Triple love.* 'and Jah Mullah': Noel Alphonso (d), Ronald Morris (b), Michael Ranglin (k), Ronald Butler (lg), Cleon Douglas (rg), Clifton Carnegie (perc).
16/6/84 MV5 DG MC

EGG
13/8/69 PEEL *Seven is a jolly good time, While growing my hair, The song of McGillicudie the Pusillanimous or don't worry James your socks are hanging in the coal cellar.* Mont Campbell (bv), Clive Brooks (d), Dave Stewart (o). 24/7/69 PH PR *
Pass from the panel, despite one comment: 'cleverness here, but no entertainment'.
21/9/69 HENRY *While growing my hair, Seven is a jolly good time, The song of McGillicudie the Pusillanimous.* 5/9/69 PCI MB *
12/2/71 BLACK *Part four of long piece three, A visit to Newport hospital, Part three of long piece three, Germ patrol.* 21/1/71 AO2 JM JWH
Group rec'd Peel Sunday Concert, 4/2/71 PS, TX 14/2/71.
7/3/72 PEEL *Germ patrol, Wring out the ground loosely now, Ennagram.* 22/2/72 MV4 * BC
23/3/72 DRUMMOND *Ennagram, Hoax.* 13/3/72 MV5 MB MH&MF

EINSTÜRZENDE NEUBAUTEN
5/9/83 PEEL *Kango licht, Sehnsucht zittern* Blixa Bargeld, N. U. Untuh, F. M. Einheit, Marc Chung.
24/8/83 BYA NG

EIRE APPARENT
20/4/69 TOP GEAR *Yes I need someone, Highway '61 revisited, Gloria.* Ernest Graham (lv,rg), David Taylor (lg,bkv), Chris Stewart (bv), David Lutton (d).
15/4/69 PH BA AH&BC
'Unanimous pass from the panel'. Twice on R1 Club in next few weeks.

JIM ELDON
25/2/90 KERSHAW *One door closes, Bridlington fishermens'* song, Dancing in the dark, Poor old horse, Rocking with the band, There isn't any superman. Jim Eldon (fd,v). 11/1/90 MV3 DG *
7/4/91 KERSHAW *Red leather shoes, The outlaw and the police chief's wife, Haircuts, Rocking at the end of time, I wish there was no prisons.* 'and Mike Hurst': (acc,p,ml). 21/2/91 MV5 DG NG&SA

ELECTRIBE 101
13/11/89 PEEL *Talking with myself, Tell me when the fever ended, Lipstick on my lover.* Brian Nordhoff (k), Les Fleming (k,bkv), Joe Stevens (k), Roberto Cimarosti (k), Billie Ray Martin (v). 24/10/89 * HP MA

ELECTRIC BOYS
17/4/92 FRI. ROCK *Groovus maximus, Knee deep in you, Mary and the mystery world, All lips and hips.* Conny Bloom (gv), Sandy Curistell (b), Franco Santonione (g), Nicholas Sigevall (d). 3/4/92 MV5 MC~

ELECTRIC GUITARS
15/12/81 JENSEN *Food, Language problems, Beat me hollow, Voice of sound.* Matthew Salt (d), Richard Halı (b), Dick Truscott (k), Andy Saunders (g), Neil Davenport (v), & Wendy Partridge (bkv).
6/12/81 MV4 DG ME
27/10/82 JENSEN *Scrap that car, Ja ja, Start up the new life.* & Martin Vesey (tp), Sarah Partridge (v).
13/10/82 PHM DS TWN

ELECTRIC LIGHT ORCHESTRA
14/2/72 HARRIS *10538 overture, Nellie takes a bow, Battle of Marston moor (& Whisper in the night, 20/3/72).* Roy Wood (rgv), Jeff Lynne (lv), Bev Bevan (dv), & 6 musicians. 4/2/72 BRM JG *
27/11/72 HARRIS *Kuiama, Roll over Beethoven.* Lynne, Bevan &: Mike D'Albuquerque (bv), Colin Walker (clo), Mike Edwards (clo), Richard Tandy (sy), Wilf Gibson (vi). 1/11/72 LHI JG *
30/4/73 HARRIS *Momma, From the sun to the world, In the hall of the mountain king.* 25/4/73 LHI PR *
Line-up also rec'd In Concert 19/4/73 PS, TX 12/5, prod. JG.
11/3/74 HARRIS *King of the universe, Daybreaker, Ma-ma-belle, New world rising (& Bluebird is dead, 22/4/74).* Hugh McDowell (clo), Mik Kaminsky (vi) r. Walker, Gibson. 13/2/74 LHI PR *
New line-up had rec'd 2nd In Concert 25/1/74 HP, TX 2/2/74, prod. JG.

THE ELECTRO HIPPIES
20/7/87 PEEL† *Sheep, Starve the city (to feed the poor), Meltdown, Escape, Deadend, Thought, Chickens, Mother, Mega-Armageddon death part three (part four).* Simon (dv), Dom (bv), Andy (gv). 12/7/87 * DG DD
† On Strange Fruit SFPS042. Most of this session is also on the two 'Hardcore Holocaust' albums.

ELEVEN
27/6/84 PEEL *If I was you and you were me, Drop that bomb, My metropolis, Perpetual emotion (love is a...).* Frederic Ravel (d), Michael Bradley (b), Damian O'Neill (g), David Drumbold (lv). 5/6/84 MV5 * TdB

STEVE ELGIN AND THE FLATBACKERS
23/5/79 PEEL *Agony column, Flatbacker, Miss world 79, Lies.* Steve Elgin (lv,k), Julie Usher (gv), Jeannie Hay (k,bkv,lv-2), Lucy Dray (b,bkv), Lynn Carol (d,perc,bkv).
16/5/79 MV4 JS NG

ELIXIR
28/2/86 FRI. ROCK *Hold high the flame, Pandora's box, Son of Odin, Star of Beshaan.* Paul Taylor (v), Kevin Dobbs (b), Phil Denton (g), Norman Gordon (g), Nigel Dobbs (d). 7/2/86 MV4 TW MC

THE ELIZABETHAN JAZZ TRIO
23/7/69 PEEL *A toye, Sick tune, Carmanns whistle, Lover and his lass.* * 19/6/69 * PR *

ELLERY BOP
29/10/81 PEEL *Ringing, Sharp star rising, Fight and desire.*

Jamie Farrell (gv), Mark Parry (d), Junior (perc); & Ian (b), Jonathan (k). 14/10/81 MV4 CL NG
1/7/82 JENSEN *Go forth, Hooded children, I fall, Hard from the start.* Farrell, Parry, Steve Johnson (b).
10/6/82 MV4 JS MC
13/12/82 PEEL *Jihad, Imperial way, 51st state, Guilt.* Johnson, Farrell, Tim Whittaker (perc), Rob Jones (d).
8/12/82 * RP NG
26/5/83 JENSEN *Caught up in blue, Sao'do, Fire in reflection.* Parry, Johnson, Farrell, Whittaker, Michael Jones (p). 22/5/83 MV4 DG ME
12/1/84 PEEL *Above the world, Scream to touch, Ourselves alone, Twisted.* Kevin Connelly (perc) r. Whittaker, Jones. 19/12/83 MV4 TW MC
4/9/84 LONG *Cut it, A chance, Torn apart, One girl.* Robbie Butcher (b) r. Johnson. 26/8/84 MV5 DG ME

MARC ELLINGTON
22/4/71 HENRY *Oh no! it can't be so, You ain't going nowhere, 40 years on, Song for a friend.* Marc Ellington (gv). 14/4/71 MV4 MB MH&MF
Passed audition 10/69.
17/11/72 SEQUENCE *Song for a friend, Jacobite lament, No deposit no return, Blue suede shoes.* & 3 (unknown).
5/10/72 LHI JM JWH&JS

ELLIS
4/9/72 FREEMAN *Morning paper, Leaving in the morning (5/9), Good to be alive (8/9).* Steve Ellis (lv) & Zoot Money (k), Emile Fataar (b), Andy Gee (lg), Dave Lutton (d). 30/8/72 AO2 * *
25/9/72 HARRIS *Morning paper, Miami mole, Good to be alive, Angela.* [M]. 13/9/72 AO2 JG BC
27/8/73 HARRIS *One scotch one bourbon one beer, Morning paper, We used the money, Loud and lazy love songs.* Nick South (b) r. Fataar. 8/8/73 LHI JG *

ELLIS, BEGGS AND HOWARD
8/6/88 L. KERSHAW *Bad times, Ju ju, Say a prayer, Where did tomorrow go.* Simon Ellis (k,bkv), Nick Beggs (b,bkv), Austin Howard (lv), Keith Airey (g), Paul Harvey (g), Robbie France (d). 27/5/88 MV4 TdB *

DAVE ELLIS
30/4/73 HARRIS *I have been amazed, Jitterbug, I don't know, Jingle.* Dave Ellis (g). 11/4/73 LHI PR *
29/6/73 SEQUENCE *I don't know, Jingle, Smile for me, Hawkwind dancer, Something wrong.*
7/5/73 LHI JM BAI&MG
3/9/73 HARRIS *Can you tell me, Song and dance, Hawkwind dancer, Nose rag.* 15/8/73 LHI JG *

MATTHEW ELLIS
25/7/72 PEEL *Missed you tonight, If the cap fits, Lady my lady.* * 10/7/72 * JW BC
8/9/72 PEEL *Sea horse, Who needs you, Waking to life.* & 2 (unknown). 22/8/72 TI JM *

ELOY
5/8/83 FRI. ROCK *On the verge of darkening lights, Through a sombre galaxy, Heartbeat, Fools.* Frank Borneman (gv), Hannes Folberth (k), Hannes Arkona (lgk), Klaus Peter Matziol (b), Fritz Randow (d).
1/7/83 Horus Studio, Hanover TW DD

ELTI FITS
26/9/79 PEEL *Factory room, Letter box, Reject, Song.* Sarah Keynes (v), Graham Ellis (g,bkv), Nigel Ross (b), Karl Burns (d). 4/9/79 MV4 BS MR

JOE ELY
27/1/91 KERSHAW *Row of dominos, For your love, Indian cowboy, Bamboo shade.* Joe Ely (gv). 10/1/91 OS * *

EMF
25/11/90 GOODIER *I believe†, Unbelievable, Lies, Girl of an age.* James Atkin (v), Ian Dench (g,bkv), Zachary Foley (b), Derry Brownson (k), Mark Decloedt (d), Gareth Milford (sc). 17/11/90 MV5 MC~
† On 'Best of Mark Goodier' Nighttracks MARK1.

THE END
11/6/66 SAT. CLUB *Until it's time for you to go, You don't*

know, You lie. Colin Giffin (ts,g), Gordon Smith (bars), David Brown (b), Hugh Attwooll (d), Nicky Graham (g,o). 6/6/66 AO1 * *

20/3/68 Night Ride Dream world, Introspection, Shades of orange, Mirror. John Horton, Hugh Grant r. Attwooll, Smith. 12/3/68 AO2 JM *

31/3/68 Top Gear Under the rainbow, Shades of orange, Mirror, Introspection. 18/3/68 PCI BA *

ENDGAMES
30/3/81 Peel Both of us, Fading away, Beauty #2, Pioneer. David Rudden (bv), Paul Wishart (sx,fl), David Murdoch (k), Willie Gardner (gv), David Wilde (d). 17/3/81 LH1 DG MR

26/5/82 Peel We feel good (future's looking fine), Darkness, First last for everything, You'll never walk alone. Rudden, Wishart, Murdoch, Gardner, Brian McGee (d), Douglas Muirden (sx). 10/5/82 MV4 TW DD

7/6/82 Jensen Both of us, First last for everything, Carousé, Cry for a woman. 30/5/82 MV4 DG ME

ENERGY ORCHARD
1/10/89 Kershaw Sailortown, Belfast, Somebody's brother. Bap Kennedy (agv), Spade McQuade (g,bkv), Paul Toner (g,bkv), Joby Fox (b,bkv), Brezzi Breslin (k), David Toner (d). 31/8/89 MV5 DG DD

16/7/90 Campbell Somebody's brother, King of love, Hard street, Sweet Irish rose. 27/6/90 MV5 MPK~ JSM

THE ENID
25/2/83 Fri. Rock In the region of the summer stars, Song for Europe, Something wicked. Robert John Godfery (kv), Chris Nortt (d), Steven Stewart (g). 4/2/83 * TW DD

ENJIN
5/6/70 Black Master of the rings, Who put the R in oven. Roger Bunn (gbv), Edward Ray-Smith (tb,db), Lyn Dobson (ts,fl), Alan Fealdman (o,p,rec), Ned Balen (d,perc). 29/4/70 AO2 JM *

ENO AND THE WINKIES
5/3/74 Peel The paw paw negro blowtorch, Baby's on fire/Totalled, Fever. Eno (v,sy), Mike Desmarais (d), Guy Humphreys (g), Philip Rambow (g), Brian Turrington (b). 26/2/74 LH1 TW BC&MR
Eno did synthesiser links for SEQUENCE 16/2/73, rec'd 25/1/73 LH1.

EON
29/6/91 Peel Fear the mindkiller, Infernal machine, Be cool, Basket case. Ian B, J. Saul Kane, Alan Scott (all: mx). 15/5/91 OS Eon *

THE EQUATORIAL GUINEA RECORDINGS
5/1/92 Kershaw Lament for our village, The illness, My mother, Antonio, Blessing of the village, We want to fly high like the eagle, We dance with the bells, Marie. Desmali y son grupo dambo de la costa (1-4 only), Bisila de malabo (5-7 only), The Guinea boys (8 only). 12/91 FR: Equatorial Guinea AK~

ERAZERHEAD
20/7/82 Peel I hate you, Teenager in love, Martian girl, No-one sees me now. Lee Drury (v), Jim Berlin (g), Billy Trigger (d), Gary Spanner (b). 14/6/82 MV4 KH DD

RANDY ERWIN
14/4/88 Kershaw My sweetheart's in love, Cattle call, T for Texas, Cannonball yodel. Randy Erwin (gv), Kim Platko (g), Dusty Rhodes (b), Gale Hess (fd). 31/3/88 * DG MWT&SA

ESPIONAGE
4/6/83 Long The great escape, Good things don't go on for ever, Your love for sale, Heartbeat. * 4/5/83 PHM c.JL TWN

THE ETCHINGHAM STEAM BAND
5/11/74 Peel The gypsy's wedding day, Orange in bloom, 2 polkas: Sheep shearing/Buttered peas, The hard times of old England. Ashley Hutchings (ab), Ian Holder (acc), Terry Potter (hca), Vic Gammon (wh,ml,cnc), Shirley Collins (v). 21/10/74 MV4 JW *
"Recorded in NEW 8-track Studio 4"- Ashley's diary.

MELISSA ETHERIDGE
19/7/88 L. Kershaw Bring me some water, Precious pain, Chrome plated heart, Occasionally, Don't you need. Melissa Etheridge (gv). 10/7/88 MV4 TdB~ JB

ETON CROP
15/11/83 Peel Gay boys on the battlefield, Boring isms, Explain, He didn't say anything. Ed Tuyl (d,tp), Corne Bos (b,sx), Erwin Blom (gv), Peter de Kwaasteniet (gp), Peter Verschueren (k), Leoneke Daalder (mel,perc), Ben Hoogendam (bkv-4 only). 9/11/83 MV4 RP NG

20/11/84 Peel Snobhill, Boy meets tractor, Get something for doing nothing, Quality in the Grooves. Lukas Daalder (mel-2, bkv-4), Frans Weeke (bkv-4) r. Hoogendam. 13/11/84 MV5 MRD MR

14/10/85 Peel† Cocacolanization, It's my dog maestro, You won't get me out in the rain, Harry Nelson Pillsbury. Bos, Blom, Verschueren, de Kwaatseniet, Le. Daalder, Weeke, Susie Honeyman (vi), Michael Harding (tp). 1/10/85 MV5 PWL TdB

† On Strange Fruit SFPS063.

19/11/86 Peel A bundle for a dead dog, Jolly adventures with Janus McManus, Banana battle, Paraffin brain. Lu. Daalder, Hoogendam return; Weeke, Harding out. 19/10/86 * DG ME

8/6/88 Peel A jolly cheerful crowd, Pavel Morozov the bastard!, Beating the Sicilian, Trivialities. Bos, Blom, de Kwaasteniet, Spike Daalder (sy), Ingmar van Wynsberge (g,bkv), Le. Daalder ('sound creator',bkv). 29/5/88 * DG ME&SC

EUGENIUS
3/8/92 Goodier Sex sux, One's too many, Here I go again, Oomalama. Eugene Kelly (lv), Gordon Keen (g), Raymond Boyle (b), Roy Laurence (d). 4/7/92 MV5 MC BJ

EUPHORIA
11/12/81 Fri. Rock Lookin' for you, Fight (for the world), No-one else but you, Don't want to lose you. Peter Leyden (g), Ken Donaldson (b), Alan Hepplewhite (d). 13/11/81 * TW DD

EUROPEANS
15/6/83 Jensen Spirit of youth, Falling, Going to work, Innocence. Fergus Marrer (lv,b), Steve Hoggarth (bkv,k), Colin Woore (bkv,g), Geoff Dugmore (bkv,d,perc). 2/6/83 MV4 JP MR

THE EURYTHMICS
29/7/82 Jensen Love is a stranger, I've got an angel, Somebody told me, 4:4 in leather. Annie Lennox (lv,k), Dave Stewart (kg,dm), Tim Wheater (fl,k,perc), Adam Williams (prg). 18/7/82 MV4 DG TdB

DAVE EVANS
10/1/72 Harris Only blue, Ten ten tasha, Grey lady morning, Now is the time, Magic man. Dave Evans (gv). 5/1/72 * JG *

15/5/72 Harris The words in between, That's my way, Insanity rag, Sailor, On the run. 25/4/72 * JG *

11/12/72 Harris Beauty queen, Sad pig dance, Lady Portia, Sunday's beautiful, Take me easy. 22/11/72 * JG *

25/11/74 Harris You and me, Every bad dog, Yesterday's rain, Illustrated man. 23/10/74 * JG *

EVEN AS WE SPEAK
16/2/92 Peel Falling down the stairs, Stay with me, Straight as an arrow, Sailor's graves. Anita (d), Rob (b), Paul (g,bkv), Matt (g), Mary (v). 9/1/92 MV4 DG NG&RJ

EVEREST THE HARD WAY
15/10/81 Jensen When you're young, Real escape, Jump the fiery hoop, Say nothing, Ice age. David Service (g,lv), Jim Telford (k), Michael Peden (b), Ian Stoddart (d). 4/10/81 MV4 DG ME

EVERYONE
3/10/70 Top Gear Midnight shift, Sitting on a rock, Too much a loser, Trio. Andy Roberts (gv), Bob Sargeant (p), John Porter (g), Dave Richards (b), John Pearson (d). 21/9/70 PH JW *

With hindsight, an all-star line-up; but only a 'Borderline pass' from the panel.

EVERYTHING BUT THE GIRL
28/6/84 Jensen Another bridge, Ballad of the times, This love (not for sale), Easy as sin. Ben Watt (g,o), Tracey Thorn (v), Phil Moxham (b), June Miles Kingston (d). 7/6/84 MV5 MHY MPK

30/8/84 Peel Ballad of the times, Riverbed dry, Never could have been worse, Don't you go. 18/8/84 MV5 DG MC

27/2/85 Peel Are you trying to be funny, Trouble and strife, Easy as sin, Sean. & Neil Scott (g). 19/2/85 MV5 MRD GP

24/9/88 Goodier Love is here where I live, Blue moon rose, Lonesome for a place I Know, Apron strings. Thorn, Watt, Steve Sanger (d), Damon Butcher (k), Steve Pearce (b), Pete King (sx). 10/9/88 MV4 DG MC

3/2/90 SAT. SEQ Driving, The road. Thorn, Watt, King. 30/1/90 T2, KH DM

EX POST FACTO
3/3/83 Jensen Daylight nightmares, Sombre soloist, Dancing child, Ruth Ellis. Frank Sparks (k), Chris Clarke (v), Mark Coleridge (d), Paul Reason (g), Bernie Carroll (b), Kenny Dawick. 6/2/83 MV4 DG *

10/4/84 Peel Actor's warning, Innonence, It's no show, The last four. Judith Laity (clo), Andy Warren (bkv) r. Dawick. 17/3/84 MV5 DG MC

THE EX
15/9/83 Peel Crap rap, Design for living, U.S. hole, Buy buy. Jos Kley (v), Sabien Witteman (d), Joke Laarman (b), Luc Klaassen (b,p-4 only), Terrie Hessels (g); & Wineke T. Hart (vi-4 only), Kees vanden Haak (ss-4 only), Dolf Planteydt (g-3 only), John Langford (acc-3 only). 7/9/83 MV4 RP NG

4/12/85 Peel Choice, Uh-oh Africa, Hands up! you're free, Butter or bombs. Klaassen, Hessels, Langford (blp-3 only), Katrin Bornfeld (d), Tom Greene (g-2), G.W.Sok (v), Susie Honeyman (vi-1). 24/11/85 MV5 DG ME

16/12/86 Peel Knock, Ignorance, Business as usual, A job/Stupid. Bornfeld, Klaassen, Hessels, Sok, John V. D. Weert (gv). 30/11/86 * DG ME&FK

EXCALIBUR
18/7/86 Fri. Rock Hot for love, Early in the morning, Death's door, Come on and rock. Paul McBride (v), Steve Blades (gk), Paul Solynskij (g), Martin Hawthorn (b), Mick Dobson (d). 20/6/86 MV4 DG MC
'Pleasant and very young band, none over 19! The next Def Leppard maybe?' DG on session sheet.

EXHIBIT B
23/7/85 Long The other side, Excerpt from a hippie opera, It's hypothetical, The escapology party. Howard Minns (dk), James Hughes (gb,v), Gerry Culligan (sx). 5/6/85 MV4 BYA MPK

EXIT CONDITION
2/6/91 Peel Learning the hard way, Strong & true, Slow reflex, Toiler on the sea. Richard Stanier (d), David Ellis (b), Darren Harris (gv). 5/5/91 MV3 DG ME&FK

THE EXPELAIRES
3/6/79 Peel Dashboard, It's alright mother, Nasty media, Frequency. Carl 'Tich' Harper (d), Mark Copson (b), David Wolfenden (g), Craig Adams (k), Grape (v). 25/6/79 * BS DD

THE EXPELLED
10/1/83 Peel Make it alone, This world, Government policy, What justice. Rick Fox (d), Macca (Craig McEvoy) (b), Tim Ramsden (g), Jewelie (v). 20/12/82 * TW DD

THE EXPLORERS
4/7/85 Into The Music Lorelei, Venus de Milo, Prussian blue, You go up in smoke. Blair Cunningham (d), John McKenzie (b), Nick Graham (k,bkv), Andy MacKay (sx,ob), Phil Manzanera (gv), James Wraith (v). 8/6/85 MV4 DG MC

8

EXTREME NOISE TERROR

17/11/87 Peel† *False profit, Another nail in the coffin, Use your mind, Carry on screaming, Human error, Conned through life, Only in it for the music part 2.* Mick Harris (d), Jerry Clay (b,bkv), Pete Hurley (g,bkv), Dean Jones (v), Phil Vane (v). 10/11/87 * DG SC&DD

11/5/88 Peel *Murder, Take the strain, No threat, Show us you care, Propaganda, System enslavement.* Mark Gardiner (b) r. Clay. 1/5/88 MV5 DG ME

8/3/90 Peel† *Work for never, Subliminal music (mind control), People not profit, Punk fact or faction, I am a bloody fool/In it for life, Deceived, Shock treatment.* Tony Dickens (d), Mark Bailey (b) r. Harris, Gardiner. 6/2/90 MV5 DG MR

† On Strange Fruit SFMCD208.

EYUPHURO

1/7/90 Kershaw *Orera korera, Namikopo, Wamphla.* Zena Bagar (lv), Gimo Abdul Remane (glv), Jorge Mabuza (sx), Chico Ventura Viola (g), Belarmino Rita & Mussa Abdala (perc). 7/6/90 MV5 DG NG

THE FABULOUS POODLES

27/10/76 Peel *Roll your own, Cherchez la femme, Grow too old, Pinball pinups, Opening finale, Acapella.* Richie C. Robinson (b,bkv), Bobby Valentino (vi,bkv), Bryn B. Burrows (d). 7/10/76 * TW *

27/4/77 Peel *Workday, On the street where you live, When the summer's through, Mr Mike.* & Tony Demeur (g,hca,lv). 18/4/77 MV4 TW DD

25/10/78 Peel *Convent girls, B movies, Mirror star, Toytown people, We'll meet again.* 3/10/78 MV4 BS MR

8/12/80 Read *Stomping with the cat, Talkin' trash, Poison pens, You ain't nothin' but fine.* 27/10/80 LHI CL *

THE FACES

15/3/70 Dlt *Three button hand me down, Flying, Wicked messenger.* Rod Stewart (v), Ron Wood (lg), Ronnie Lane (b), Ian McLagen (o,g), Kenny Jones (d). 10/3/70 CM c.PWI *

28/3/70 Top Gear *Wicked messenger, Devotion, Pineapple and the monkey, Shake shudder shiver.* 9/3/70 PH JW *
Rec'd Peel Sunday Concert 25/6/70 PS, TX 5/7/70.

1/9/70 Harding *All over now, Three button hand me down, Around the plynth.* 27/8/70 AO2 MB MH&MF

19/9/70 Top Gear *Had me a real good time, Around the plynth, Country comforts.* 15/9/70 MV4 PR *
Next, rec'd 2nd Peel Sunday Concert 19/11/70 PS, TX 29/11/70.

3/5/71 Harris *Had me a real good time, Love in vain, Browned off, Maybe I'm amazed.* 20/4/71 TI PD BH
Rec'd 3rd Peel Sunday Concert 13/5/71 PS, TX 23/5/71.

6/10/71 Peel *Stay with me, Miss Judy's farm, Maggie May.* 28/9/71 MV4 JW BC
...And fourth In Concert rec'd 17/2/72 PS, TX 26/2/72.

JOHN FAHEY

28/5/69 Peel *Buckingham stomp, Death of the Claytown peacock, Sunflower river blues, In Christ there is no east or west, Steel guitar rag (Dance of the inhabitants of the palace of King Philip XV, Some summer day, Poor boy, 22/6/69 TOP GEAR.* John Fahey (ag). 22/5/69 S2 PH MH?

15/10/87 Kershaw *On the sunny side of the ocean, The Spanish two-step, Nightmare/Summertime, The dance of death, St. Patrick's.* 8/10/87 * DG ME&FK

FAHRENHEIT

14/12/90 Fri. Rock *Don't wanna lose, Can't say no, Wait for the day, Hard to hold.* Dave Burley (v), Rick Lockwood (g,bkv), Nick Grayson (b,bkv), Adrian Hoe (k,bkv), Sam Carr (d). 30/11/90 MV5 DD~

FAIRFIELD PARLOUR

30/4/70 Henry *Soldiers of the flesh, By your bedside, Chalk on the wall, Bordeaux rose, Monkey.* Peter James Daltrey, Edward Pumer, Stephen Clark, Daniel Bridgeman. 23/4/70 AO2 MB MH&MF

Nearly the last of dozens of daytime pop sessions by this band.

FAIRGROUND ATTRACTION

5/4/88 Mayo *Moon on the rain, Find my love, A smile in a whisper, The moon is mine.* Eddi Reader (v), Mark Nevin (g), Simon Edwards (ab), Roy Dodds (d,perc); & Steve Forster (mnd). 20/3/88 MV4 PW TdB

FAIRPORT CONVENTION

10/12/67 Top Gear *Let's get together, One sure thing, Lay down your weary tune, Chelsea morning.* Judy Dyble (v), Ashley Hutchings (b), Martin Lamble (d), Simon Nicol (g), Richard Thompson (gv). 24/11/67 PH BA PR

3/3/68 Top Gear *If (stomp), If I had a ribbon bow, Time will show the wiser, Violets of dawn.* Ian Matthews (v) joins. 6/2/68 AO2 BA DT
BA submitted this second session as trial broadcast. 'Unanimous, enthusiastic pass' from panel; 'compared to Harpers Bizarre'.

18/3/68 Symonds *If (stomp), It takes a lot to laugh it takes a train to cry, It's alright ma it's only witchcraft, Chelsea morning.* 11/3/68 PS JW *
Contracts file suggests Matthews first appeared on this date, but Ashley Hutchings thinks it unlikely 'If (stomp)', a Matthews/Thompson song, would have been recorded on previous date without him.

2/6/68 Top Gear *Close the door lightly when you go†, Where I stand†, Nottamun town, You never wanted me (& Some sweet day†, 30/6/68).* Sandy Denny (v) r. Dyble. 28/5/68 PCI BA DT

24/6/68 Symonds *Marcie, Night in the city, Jack O'Diamonds, Morning glory.* 18/6/68 MV4 * *

1/9/68 Top Gear *If you feel good you know it can't be wrong†, Fotheringay, Gone gone gone†, Eastern rain (& Suzanne†, 29/9/68).* 26/8/68 PS BA PR

8/12/68 Henry *Meet on the ledge, Bird on a wire†, Reno Nevada, Mr. Lacey.* 2/12/68 AO2 AD *

15/12/68 Night Ride *Things you gave me, Meet on the ledge, Autopsy, Morning glory, Bird on a wire, Mr.Lacey.* 25/11/68 MV4 PC *

22/12/68 Top Gear *Meet on the ledge, She moves through the fair, Light my fire, I'll keep it with mine, Billy the orphan boy's lonely Christmas.* 9/12/68 PCI BA PR

6/1/69 Symonds *Reno Nevada†, Book song, I still miss someone†, Tried so hard†, Sandy.* 27/12/68 MV4 c.RB *
Band next appeared live from the Paris on R1 Club 6/1/69, playing 'Bird on a wire', 'Jack O'Diamonds', 'I still miss someone', 'You're gonna need my help'.

9/2/69 Symonds on Sunday *Fotheringay, Who knows where the time goes, Shattering live experience†, You're gonna need my help.* 4/2/69 PCI JW TW

6/4/69 Top Gear *Cajun woman, Percy's song†, Si tu dois partir va t'en°, Autopsy.* & guest Ric Grech (vi); Matthews out. 18/3/69 PH BA AH&BC
† on 'Heyday' album, Hannibal HNCD 1329. ° On 'I and only' BOJCD025.

27/9/69 Top Gear *Sir Patrick Spens, Jigs & reels medley, Tam Lin, The Lady is a tramp, Reynardine.* Dave Swarbrick (vi) r. Grech; & Dave Mattacks (d) r. Lamble [died 12/5/69, after M1 accident]. 23/9/69 MV4 JW TW

27/4/70 Symonds *Open the door Richard, The flatback caper, Sir Patrick Spens (& The bonny black hare, 25/5/70).* Dave Pegg (b,fd,mand) r. Hutchings, Denny, from 1/70. 21/4/70 PH BA NG

2/5/70 Top Gear *The deserter, Walk awhile, The flatback caper, Poor Will and the jolly hangman (& Doctor of physic, 1/8/70).* 20/4/70 PH JW TW

26/7/70 Folk On 1 *Sir Patrick Spens, Medley: jigs and reels, The deserter, Hangman's reel, Bonny bunch of roses (& Dirty linen, Flowers of the forest, Now be thankful, Tam Lin 2/8/70).* 7&9/7/70 AO2 FL *

19/11/70 Henry *Tunes my mother taught me, Sickness and diseases, Journeyman's grace, Now be thankful.* 12/11/70 AO2 MH&MF

Rec'd Peel Sunday Concert 15/10/70 PS, TX 25/10/70.

27/3/71 Folk On 1 *Sir William Gower, Banks of the sweet primroses, The journeyman's grace, Sickness and diseases, Instrumental medley, Lord Marlborough, Angel Delight.* Thompson still named on contract for '71, but probably out. 18/3/71 MV5 FL *

3/4/71 R2 Night Ride *Bridge over the River Danube, Sir William Gower, Sickness and diseases, Angel delight, Lark in the morning, Deserter, Lord Marlborough.* 8/3/71 AO2 DDR *

20/2/73 Peel *Tokyo, Matthew Mark Luke John, Rosie, Possibly parson's green.* Trevor Lucas (gv), Jerry Donahue (gv) r. Nicol. 5/2/73 TI PD ARV

10/9/73 Harris *Polly on the shore, The days of '49. The lass of Hexhamshire (& The brilliancy medley/Cherokee shuffle, 5/11/73).* 5/9/73 LHI JG *

6/8/74 Peel *John the gun, Fiddlesticks, Rising for the moon, Down in the flood.* Sandy Denny (pv) returns. 16/7/74 LHI TW BC

14/6/89 Skinner *Set me up, Matty Groves/Rutland reel/Sack the juggler, Red and gold, The noise club.* Nicol, Mattacks, Pegg, Ric Sanders (vi,k), Martin Allcock (g,k,bkv). 4/6/89 HP HP TdB&FK

ANDY FAIRWEATHER-LOW

19/10/74 Rock On *Mellow down, The light is within, Spider jiving, Dancing in the dark.* * 14/10/74 LHI BA MF&NGR

17/11/75 Peel *If I ever get lucky, Inner city highwayman, Jump up and turn around, Wide eyed and legless.* Dave Mattacks (d,perc), John David (bv), B.J. Cole (ps), Rabbit (kv), Andy Fairweather-Low (gv). 21/10/75 MV4 TW BAI

7/2/77 Peel *Checking out the checker, Lighten up, Ain't no fun, Be-bop'n' holla, Shimme doo wah sae.* Fairweather-Low, David (b,bkv), Cole, Mick Weaver (k,bkv), Henry Spinetti (d). 31/1/77 MV4 TW DD
Repeated on ALAN FREEMAN, 25/6/77, as 'Matrix H Quad Experiment'.

THE FAITH BROTHERS

14/3/85 Long *Eventide, A stranger on home ground, Tradesmen's entrance, Storyteller.* Lee Hirons (b), Steve Howlett (d), Billy Franks (gv), Henry Tresise (o,p), Will Tipper (tp), Mark Waterman (sx). 27/2/85 MV5 JS MPK
'Trumpet solo on 'Storyteller' played through BBC paper cup to create that "old" sound' JS.

TH' FAITH HEALERS

27/4/91 Peel† *Coffee commercial couples, Bobby Kopper, Jesus freak.* Joe Dilworth (d), Ben Hopkin (b), Tom Cullinan (gv), Roxanne Stephen (v). 24/3/91 MV3 DG ME&PA
† on Strange Fruit SFRCD119.

11/1/92 Peel *Hippy hole, This time, Reptile smile, SOS.* 24/11/91 MV3 DG ME&RK

24/7/92 Peel *Love in sesh, Moona inna Joona, I'm ready, Get th'f*** out of my face.* 5/7/92 MV4 SA~ NF

THE FALL

15/6/78 Peel *Rebellious juke box, Mother sister, Industrial estate, Futures and pasts.* Mark Smith (lv), Martin Bramah (g,b,bkv), Yvonne Paulette (k), Karl Burns (d); & Steve Davis (cga-1 only). 30/5/78 MV4 TW MR

6/12/78 Peel† *Put away, Mess of my°, No Xmas for John Key, Like to blow.* & Marc Riley (b), Davis out. 27/11/78 MV4 BS DD&BT
† on Strange Fruit SFPS028. ° On 'Winters of discontent' SFRCD204.

24/9/80 Peel *Container drivers, Jawbone and the air rifle, New Puritan, New face in hell.* Smith, Riley (g), Craig Scanlon (g,bkv), Steve Hanley (b), Paul Hanley (d). 16/9/80 MV4 JS *

31/3/81 Peel *Middlemass, Lie dream of a casino soul, Hip priest, C 'N' C/Hassle schmuk.* & Dave Tucker (cl). 24/3/81 LHI DG MPK

15/9/81 Peel *Deer park, Know look, Winter (Hostel Maxi), Who makes the Nazis?* Tucker out. 26/8/81 MV4 DG NG

23/3/83 PEEL *Smile, Garden, Hex knot, Eat yourself fitter†.*
Burns (d,b) returns, r. Riley. 21/3/83 MV4 JP DD
† On 'Manchester- so much to answer for'
SFRCD202.

3/1/84 PEEL *Pat trip dispenser, 2 by 4, Words of
expectation, Creep.* Brix Smith (gv) joins.
12/12/83 MV4 TW MC

1/3/84 JENSEN *God box, Lay of the land, Oh brother,
Creep.* 19/2/84 MV5 DG ME

17/9/84 LONG *No bulbs, Drago's guilt, Stephen song, Slang
king.* 9/9/84 MV5 DG ME

29/9/84 SAT. LIVE *Copped it, Elves, Fortress/Marquis Cha
Cha.* S. Hanley not credited on sheet.
Live from S2 MRD TdB

3/6/85 PEEL *Cruisers' Creek, Couldn't get ahead, Gut of the
quantifier, Spoilt Victorian child.* & Simon Rogers (g,k),
S. Hanley returns, P. Hanley out.
14/5/85 MV5 MRD MWT

7/10/85 PEEL *L A, Man whose head expanded, What you
need, Faust banana.* 29/9/85 MV5 DG ME

9/7/86 PEEL *Hot afternoon bop, R O D, Gross chapel/GB
grenadiers, U S 80s 90s.* Simon Wolstencroft (d) r.
Burns. 29/6/86 MV5 DG ME

11/5/87 PEEL *Australians in Europe, Twister, Guest
informant, Athlete cured.* 28/4/87 * * *

19/5/87 LONG *Frenz, There's a ghost in my house, Get a
hotel, Haf found Boorman.* Marcia Schofield (k,lv-4)
joins. 13/5/87 MV4 PW MPK&FK

31/10/88 PEEL *Kurious oranj, Dead beat descendant, Cab it
up, Squid lord.* Rogers out. 25/10/88 MV4 MR~
Also recorded live gig at Subterania on Peel's 50th
birthday party, 29/8/89, TX 30/8.

1/1/90 PEEL *Hilary, Black monk theme, Chicago now,
Whizz bang.* Martin Bramah (g) r. B. Smith, Kenny
Brady (fd) joins. 17/12/89 MV3 DG ME

23/3/91 PEEL *The war against intelligence, Idiot joy
showland, A lot of wind, The mixer, Everything hurts.*
Bramah, Schofield out. 5/3/91 MV5 MR~

15/2/92 PEEL *Freerange, Return, Kimble, Immortality.*
19/1/92 MV3 DG ME&JB
...and, after 19 sessions, 15 of them for Peel, it's
Smith, Scanlon, Hanley, Wolstencroft, and David Bush
(k) r. Brady. LATE NEWS: Band recorded their 20th
Radio 1 session, for Peel, after the 25th anniversary, in
early 1993 'Paranoia man in cheap shot room',
'Service', 'Strychnine', 'Lady bird green grass'. MORE
LATE NEWS: 'Kimble' became Strange Fruit's first 7-inch
release, SFPS787, in March '93, B-Side C'N'C/Hassle
schmuk, from 24/3/81. The 12-inch SFPS087 also
included 'Words of expectation' (12/12/83) and 'Spoilt
Victorian child' (14/5/85). On CD SFPCD087, 'Gut of the
quantifier' (14/5/85) replaced C'N'C/Hassle Schmuk'.

FAMILY

26/11/67 TOP GEAR *Piece of my mind, Scene through the
eyes of a lens, The voyage, The breeze, Winter.* Roger
Chapman (v), John 'Charlie' Whitney (g), Ric Grech
(vi,bv), Rob Townsend (d), Jim King (sx,fl,p). 20/11/67
PCI BA DT
'Unanimous, enthusiastic pass' from panel.

12/2/68 SYMONDS *Winter, Me my friend (13/2), See through
windows (16/2).* 5/2/68 PS * *

21/4/68 TOP GEAR *See through windows, Hey Mr.
Policeman, Three times time, Old songs new songs.*
16/4/68 PCI BA PR

22/7/68 SYMONDS *Hey Mr. Policeman, Me my friend (23/7),
The procession (24/7), Emotions (25/7).* 11/7/68 PS * *

4/8/68 TOP GEAR *The procession, The weaver's answer, Me
my friend, Three times time (& The breeze, 15/9/68).*
29/7/68 PCI BA *

7/9/68 SAT. CLUB *The breeze, The weaver's answer, See
through windows.* 3/9/68 TH KB *&BC

24/11/68 TOP GEAR *Dim, Second generation woman, How hi
the li, Observations (& Hometown, 5/1/69).*
11/11/68 PCI BA *
Group appeared live on R1 Club on 1/11/68 PS.

3/12/68 R1 CLUB *Observations from a hill, The weaver's
answer, How hi the li, Dim, Second generation woman.*
31/10/68 PS c.DGE *

16/12/68 SYMONDS *How hi the li, Second generation woman
(17/12), Observations (18/12), Dim (19/12).*
9/12/68 PH * *

9/3/69 SYMONDS ON SUNDAY *The procession, Hole in the
compass, How hi the li.* 3/3/69 AO2 JW TW

30/3/69 TOP GEAR *Love in a sleeper, I sing 'um the way I
feel, Bring it on home, A song for me.* 11/3/69 PH BA AH
Group had just been live on R1 Club again,
5/3/69 PS.

3/8/69 TOP GEAR *Drown in wine, Wheels, No mules' fool,
The cat and the rat.* John Weider (b,vi) r. Grech.
28/7/69 PH JW BC

5/9/70 TOP GEAR *Hole in the compass, Lives and ladies,
Bad news.* Poli Palmer (k,vib) r. King. 10/8/70 PH JW BC
This line-up had recorded the first ever Peel Sunday
Show concert, 1/1/70 PS, TX 4/1/70.

29/3/71 HARRIS *Strange band, The Procession, No mule's
fool, Part of the load, Home town (& Lives and ladies,
26/4/71).* 16/3/71 T1 JM *

17/7/71 TOP GEAR *Save some for thee, Burning bridges, In
my own time, Seasons.* Weider out. 2/7/71 T1 JM JWH
Muir recorded date for Walters (on leave), repeated
it on BLACK 13/8/71.

22/11/71 HARRIS *Children, Between blue and me, Hole in
the compass.* & John Wetton (b). 8/11/71 T1 PD *

27/1/72 DRUMMOND *Between blue and me, Children, Spanish
tide, Blind.* 17/1/72 MV5 MH&MF

23/10/72 HARRIS *Broken nose, Ready to go, Dark eyes,
Burlesque, My friend the sun (& Coronation, 18/12/72).*
Jim Cregan (bg) r. Wetton. Rec. date unknown OS * *

22/5/73 PEEL† *Buffet tea, Boom bang, Check out.* Tony
Ashton (k) r. Palmer. 8/5/73 LH1 JW *
† On Strange Fruit SFRCD061.

THE FAMILY CAT

4/10/89 PEEL *Remember what it is that you love, Octopus
Jr., From the city to the sea, Sandbag your heart.* Kev
(d), John (b), Tim (g), Jelb (g), Fred (gv).
10/9/89 MV3 DG DD

9/7/90 PEEL *With a war, Gameshow, Fearless, Streamroller.*
26/6/90 MV5 MC~ RPF
'It is 10.25pm & England have just won vs. Belgium.
We are all jumping up and down and shouting a lot.
The last note was mixed and lo and behold England
scored! I think they were waiting for us to finish.
Three of the songs we've done today were written
specially for this session. But honestly, what a night to
be trying to concentrate on songs, when England are
taking so long to score. Love from The Family Cat.'
Note to Peel on sheet.

20/3/92 PEEL *Too many late nights, Furthest from the sun,
Prog one, River of diamonds.* 30/1/92 MV4 DG NG&DMC

FAMOUS JUG BAND

11/6/69 PEEL *Going to Germany, Common or garden
mystery, Black is the colour, I don't need no orchestra.*
Pete Berryman (gv), Henry 'the Eighth' Bartlett (jug,v),
Jill Johnson (v), Wizz Jones (gv). 29/5/69 PS PR *

29/6/69 STAGE ONE *The only friend I own, Where are you
now, Common or garden mystery.* 24/6/69 PH c.DGE *
Failed unanimously by panel: 'very amateur' 'dull
lifeless sounds'.

19/4/70 COUNTRY MEETS FOLK *Deep minor rhythms, Where
are you now, Would you believe.* Jones out.
18/4/70 PH BB *
Passed by panel. Then on R1 Folk show
17/5/70, rec'd 12/5 S1 prod. FL.

18/6/70 HENRY *Golden years, Farmyard girl, Great western,
A taste of salt.* 11/6/70 AO2 MB MH&MF

8/7/70 R2 NIGHT RIDE *Here comes the dawn, Would you
believe, Sunshine possibilities, Great western, Raggin the
scale, Golden years, Chameleon, The road.* 8/6/70 AO2
c.DMY *

17/12/70 HENRY *The time is flying, Would you believe,
Surely she knows, The harvest song, From my
fingertips.* 10/12/70 AO2 MB MH&MF

2/1/71 FOLK ON 1 *Gabriel, The time is flying, Surely she
knows, A taste of salt, Would you believe, All my life,
One blue guitar, The road, No love for the lady,
Where are you now.* 22/12/70 AO2 FL *

FARENJI WARRIORS

22/8/83 JENSEN *Jungle call, Flying carpet, You got it,
Lookin' around.* Rose Minor (lv), Aswan Farenji (cga),
Chrissie Quayle (sx,fl,bkv), Ruben White (d), Leo Afolabi
(sx,bkv), Danny Vernege (b), Richard Booth (g), Steve
Kelly (elp). 18/8/83 MV4 JP KW

THE FARM

17/5/83 PEEL *Memories, No man's land, Information man.*
Peter Hooton (lv), Phil Stevenson (b), Steve Grimes (g),
Andy McVann (d), George Maher (tp), Tony Evans (tp),
Joe Musker (perc). 17/4/83 MV4 DG MC

19/3/84 PEEL *Hearts and minds, Too late, Somewhere,
Same old story.* Hooton, Grimes, John Melvin (g,bkv),
McVann, Maher, John Owens (b,p-3 only), Musker.
28/2/84 MV5 MRD TdB

12/2/85 LONG *Power over me, Living for tomorrow, Better,
Steps of emotion.* Carl Hunter (b) r. Owens, Steve Levy
(sx), Tony Evans (tb) join; Musker out.
20/1/85 MV4 BYA PW

9/12/85 PEEL *Some people, Sign of the cross, Little ol'
wine drinking me, Heart of the nation.* Hooton, Grimes,
McVann, Maher, Evans, Hunter, Melvin, Levy. 26/11/85
MV5 PWL MS&MR

20/8/86 PEEL *Worn out sayings, Power over me, Wearing
that smile, The Moroccan.* Keith Mullin (g,bkv) r.
Melvin. 10/8/86 * DG ME&FK

24/5/90 PEEL *Groovy train†, Very emotional (Ballad to Ray
Toohey), I don't know, Family of man.* Hooton, Grimes,
Hunter, Mullin, Roy Boulter (d), Ben Leach (k).
6/5/90 MV3 DG ME
† On 'New season' SFRCD205.

22/10/90 GOODIER *Higher and higher, Sweet inspiration,
Hearts and minds†, No man's land.* & Paula David
(bkv). 15/9/90 MV3&5 MC~
† on 'Best of Mark Goodier' Nighttracks Mark1.

8/4/91 CAMPBELL *Don't let me down, Stepping stone, How
long, Down on the farm.* 27/3/91 MV5 PW MPK

31/8/91 PEEL *Mind, Smile†, Love see no colour, News
International.* Rebecca Lee White (bkv) r. David.
21/7/91 MV3 MR~
† on Sony 12-inch of 'The rising sun' 658173.

THE FARMER'S BOYS

19/4/82 JENSEN *Funny old Mr Baz, I lack concentration,
Spring, Autumn, Or what.* Frog (dm), Stan (g,k), Baz
(v,k), Mark (b). 4/4/82 MV5 DG ME

14/9/82 PEEL *With these hands I built the world, Soft
drink, The country line, Drinking and dressing up,
Description of the River Waveney at Wortwell.* Billed as
'Kid Brian and his Farmer's Boys': & Kid Brian
('introductions'). 6/9/82 * TW MC

27/9/82 JENSEN *T.O.S.D, More than a dream, A promise you
can't keep, Funky combine John.* & Terry Edwards
(sx,tp). 19/9/82 MV4 DG ME

10/11/82 PEEL *I lack concentration, Muck it out, T.O.S.D
(The old spotted dog), I think I need help, A promise
you can't keep, More than a dream, Spring, Squit,
Whatever is he like?* * Rec. date unknown, recorded live at the
General Wolfe, Coventry * *
Recorded session for Peter Powell 29/3/83.

13/7/83 PEEL *The way you made me cry, Matter of fact,
Probably one of the best investments I ever made, I*

don't know why I don't like all my friends. Edwards out. 9/7/83 MV4 DG MC

Recorded session for Andy Peebles 20/7/83.

6/9/83 JENSEN *Apparently, Torn in two, The wailing wall, 'E woke up this morning.* 28/8/83 MV4 DG TdB

Recorded In Concert 7/9/83.

27/8/84 PEEL *Sport for all, Walk about, All of a sudden, Heartache.* 14/8/84 MV5 JWI TdB&PS

Two sessions for R1 tea-time show in 1984: 5/2 and 18/10.

6/4/85 SAT. LIVE *I built the world, Heartache.* Live from S2 MRD TdB

FASHION
2/2/82 JENSEN *Streetplayer, You only left your picture, It's allright, So you wana make love.* Dee Harris (gv), Salvator Mulligan (sy,k), Dik Davis (d,perc), Marlon Recci (b). 13/1/82 PHM * TWN

FAST KUTZ
26/6/87 FRI. ROCK *Driving me crazy, Looking for love, Midnight love, Playing with fire.* Kenny Nicholson (lg), Ian Gillson (g), Ian McLaughlan (b), Paul Fowler (d), Keith Davison (v). 5/6/87 MV4 TW DD

FASTWAY
29/4/83 FRI. ROCK *We become one, Easy livin', Give it all you got, You got me runnin'.* Jerry Shirley (d), Alfie Agius (b), David King (v), Eddie (g). 15/4/83 * TW DD

FAT AND FRANTIC
12/4/88 MAYO *Last night my wife hoovered my head, The senator's daughter, Waiting for the Queen to burp, Take me home.* Jim Harris (tp,v), John Soper (gv), Silas Crawley (wsh,v), Craig Tuff (bv), Simon Saunders (d). 10/4/88 MV4 PW TdB

FAT GRAPPLE
27/7/72 DRUMMOND *The ballad of the skinhead Sandy, Happy in the lord, Mister, Requiem.* Nick Liddell (b), Lionel Gibson (lg), Rob Wilkinson (d), Eddie Jobson (p,vi), John Saxby (perc,v), Phil Welton (gv). 12/7/72 * TW *

5/7/73 PEEL *Happy in the lord, The opener, The whaling song.* Steve Lee Bowers, John Pryor r. Wilkinson, Jobson. 2/7/73 LH1 BA *

THE FAT LADY SINGS
17/3/87 LONG *Border keep, Is this all there is, Contact, Not to touch.* Nick Kelly (v,g), Robert Hamilton (dv), Ali McMordie (b), Roger Pike (gv), Dave Field (sx). 8/3/87 MV4 PW *

FAT MATTRESS
19/10/69 DLT *Magic Forest, I don't mind, Naturally, Everything's blue.* Noel Redding (lg,bkv), Neil Lander (lv), Eric Dillon (d), Jimmy Leverton (bv). 13/10/69 AO2 c.PWI *

25/10/69 TOP GEAR *Naturally, Mr Moonshine, Magic forest, Happy my love.* 6/10/69 PS JW TW

2/11/70 RI CLUB *Highway, Black sheep (5/11), Lookout Cleveland (6/11). (Session may first have been TX 12-16/10/70).* Steve Hammond (gv), Mick Weaver (o) r. Redding. 14/9/70 PS RH *

THE FATIMA MANSIONS
28/3/89 PEEL *The day I lost everything, Only losers take the bus, The door to door inspector, What.* Billed as Cathal Coughlan (v,k) 'and the Fatima Mansions': Nick Allum (d), Seanathan O'Crocain (b), Andreas O'Gruama (g), Zac Woolhouse (k). 19/3/89 MV4 DG MA

19/4/90 PEEL *Mr Baby, It will be cold, Blues for Ceausescu, Broken radio No. 1.* Hugh Bunker (b) r. O'Crocain, & Nick Bunker (k-3 only). 25/3/90 MV3 DG ME

13/5/91 GOODIER *You're a rose†, Something bad is giving birth to something, 1000 per cent, Go home Bible Mike.* Nick Bagnall (k) r. Bunker. 27/4/91 MV5 MC~
† On 'Best of Mark Goodier' Nighttracks Mark1.

FAUST
5/6/73 PEEL *Just a second/Ask the cleaning woman she knows the subtitle/Foam rubber.* Werner Diermaier (d),

Hans-Joachim Irmier (k), Jean-Herve Peron (b), Rudolf Sosna (g), Gunther Wusthoss (k,sx). 22/5/73 LH1 JW *

'This didn't actually happen. When they turned up at the studio we found we didn't have enough plugs in Langham 1 for their equipment, synthesisers and stuff. Instead we bought in a tape they did for us in Germany' JW.

FAZE ONE
10/11/86 LONG *One and only, Layin' down a beat, Rhythm to the beat, Stronger than strong.* Lee Bennett (lv,d), Odell Johnson (k,lv), Michael Chinn (sc), Jay Jay Bell (g), Paul Phillips (k). 19/10/86 MV4 BYA *

11/12/86 KERSHAW *One and only, Laying down a beat, Rhythm to the beat.* Stepski (lv), Gino (kv), Chinn, Phillips. 27/11/86 * NB SR

CHARLIE FEATHERS, WARREN SMITH, JACK SCOTT, BUDDY KNOX AND THE ROGER JAMES GROUP
1/7/77 PEEL *Ubangi stomp, What in the world's came over you, Hula love, Too much alike, Leroy's back in jail again, Rock'n roll Ruby, Bottle to the baby, Goodbye baby bye bye, Rock your little baby, Blue suede shoes.* Warren Smith (lv-1,6,10), Jack Scott (lv-2,5,8), Buddy Knox (lv-3,9), Charlie Feathers (lv-4,7) & the Roger James Group. 3/5/77 * DP&MB *

DR. FEELGOOD
19/11/73 HARRIS *She does it right, I don't mind, Riot in cell block No. 9, Tore down.* Lee Brilleaux (v), Wilko Johnson (g), John Sparkes (b), The Big Figure (d). 24/10/73 LH1 JG *

11/5/74 ROCK ON *Twenty yards behind, Weekend love, Keep it out of sight, Matchbox.* 1/4/74 * BA *

9/12/74 HARRIS *The more I give, Boom boom, All through the city, Talk to me baby.* 13/11/74 * JG *

10/2/75 PEEL *I don't mind, I'm a hog for you, Keep it out of sight, Route 66.* 21/1/75 MV4 TW BC

10/10/77 PEEL *You upset me baby, She's a wind up, Baby Jane, 99 ¹/₂* 20/9/77 MV4 MB MR

18/9/78 PEEL *Nightime, Take a tip, Doctor, Sugar shaker.* 5/9/78 MV4 * *

FELT
9/4/83 LONG *Sunlight bathed the golden glow, Mexican bandits, Red indians.* * 21/3/83 PHM c.JL PSM

15/10/84 LONG *Crystal ball, Roman litter, Dismantled king is on the throne, Vasco da Gama.* Laurence (gv), Gary Ainge (d), Mick Lloyd (b), Morris Deebank (g). 30/9/84 HP BYA PW&MFA

19/2/86 LONG *Ballad of the band, The day the rain came down, I didn't mean to hurt you, Caspian see.* Marco Thomas (b) r. Lloyd. 12/2/86 MV5 BYA MPK

30/10/86 KERSHAW *When the dawn starts creeping in, All the people I like, Sophie Mansions/Rain of crystal spires.* * 27/8/86 * DST PSM

ANDY FERNBACH
10/9/69 PEEL *Mystic meaning, Woman goes from man to man, I feel like starting again, If you miss your connection.* Andy Fernbach (slg,v), Dave Fernbach, Ned Balen'. 27/8/69 S2 PR *

14/3/70 WS R&B *Kerb shuffling song, Movin' on, Woman goes from man to man, Friendship tree.* 4/3/70 * JG JY

6/9/70 RAVEN'S R&B *Thanksgiving, Honky tonk women, Childhood, Hell hound on my trail.* 19/7/70 MV4 JG JY

13/3/71 RAVEN'S R&B *Broke down engine, Bare feet on stone, Friendship tree, Is there time?, Movin' on.* 3/3/71 MV4 MB *

31/1/72 HARRIS *Chasing my tail, Coastin', If you miss your connection.* & Stan Gordon. 25/1/72 MV5 JM JWH&JE

FFLAPS
4/4/88 PEEL *Pethu piws, Llosg llech, Y dyn bun, Blodyn Tatws.* Ann Matthews (gv), Alan Holmes (vi,b), Johnny Evans (d). 13/3/88 MV4 DG ME

1/8/90 PEEL *Malltod, Rhowch hi i'r Belgwyr, Hyll eto, Arwyr duwiol.* 19/6/90 MV3 DG ME

FIAT LUX
26/2/83 LONG *Embers, Comfortable life, Aqua vitae, Feels like winter again.* * 21/2/83 PHM c.JL PSM

FICTION FACTORY
21/1/84 LONG *This is, Panic, Rise and fall.*
* 6/1/84 PHM c.PWL *

JOHN FIDDLER
4/11/90 KERSHAW *Time will tell, Let the kids grow, Only the roses, Strong heart, Walking blues.* John Fiddler (gv,hca) & Jay "right hand man". 16/8/90 MV5 DG NG

THE FIELDMICE
23/4/90 PEEL *Anoint, Sundial, Fresh surroundings, By degrees.* Michael McLennan (b), Robert (gv), Harvey Williams (g), Ian Cait (sy). 1/4/90 MV3 DG ME

FIELDS
3/1/72 HARRIS *Friend of mine, Wouldn't you agree, Over and over again.* Graham Field (o), Andy McCulloch (d,perc), Alan Barry (gbv). 23/12/71 PS JG *

52ND STREET
13/8/83 LONG *The rap, Look into my eyes, Cool as ice, Express.* Tony Thompson (d), Derek Johnson (b), Tony Henry (g), John Dennison (k), Beverly McDonald (lv). 10/8/83 PHM DS PSM

FILLER
10/11/90 PEEL *First out, Trapped then killed, Touched, Hurts to say.* Dave Skeen (dv), Jonathan Barry (bv), Richard Bramley (g). 4/11/90 MV3 DG ME&AA

FILTHKICK
18/9/89 PEEL *Lynching party/Bar room brawl/A ? Between the lines/Meat rack, The harder you fall/Drowning in affluence.* Ben (d), Jim (b), Mark (g), Leggo (v). 15/8/89 MV3 DG MR

17/9/90 PEEL *Rise/Gein within/Just another word, Mondo delirium/Cabin fever, Mind games/Kill kill kill, This void of ignorance, Brian Fry.* Daz (d), Pete (b), Steve (g), Leggo. 7/8/90 MV5 MR~

FINE YOUNG CANNIBALS
16/1/85 LONG *Move to work, Don't ask me to choose, Couldn't care more, Funny how love is.* Andy Cox (g), David Steele (b,p,o), Roland Gift (v), Martin Parry (d), Graham Hamilton (tp), Ragna Gift (bkv). 9/1/85 MV5 LM MPK

18/6/85 LONG *Blue, Time isn't kind, Johnny.* & Cara Tivey (k), Ragna Gift out. 19/5/85 HP BYA PW

FINGERPRINTZ
5/12/78 PEEL *Sean's new shoes (instrumental), Finger prince, Nervz, Who's your friend, Sync unit.* Step Ling (lv), Jinne O'Neill (r), Cha Burnz (lg), Kenny Dalglish (b), Bob Shilling (d). 28/11/78 MV4 MR~

FINI TRIBE
22/5/85 PEEL *Goose duplicates, An evening with clavichords, We're interested, Splash care.* Simon McGlynn (d), Philip Pinsky (b), John Vick (k), Andy McGregor (g), David Millar (gv), Chris Connelly (v). 12/5/85 MV5 DG ME

22/2/89 PEEL *Electrolux, Disturb, Swans.* Vick, Pinsky, Millar. 12/2/89 MV5 DG ME

FIRE ENGINES
9/3/81 PEEL *Untitled, Discord, Candy skin (We don't need this) Fascist groove thang.* David Henderson (gv), Russell Burn (d), Graham Main (b), Murray Slade (g). 23/2/81 LH1 TW DD

23/11/81 PEEL *The big wrong time, Young tongues need taste, Qualitamatic, Produced to seduce to.* & Miti Adhikari (k-4). 14/11/81 MV4 DG MC

FIRE PARTY
31/10/89 PEEL *Basis, How to, Are you on, Stray bullet.* Nicky Thomas (d), Kate Samworth (b), Natalie Avery (g), Amy Pickering (v,b-1 only). 17/10/89 MV5 DG MA

THE FIRE
13/3/84 PEEL *Stop, Dancing and laughing, Mothers and sons, Jimmy's grin (Song to this port).* David Wibberley

(g,lv), Jamie Dickie (b), Ian Bickle (d), Jill McCarthy (clo-3), David Dickie (k). 29/2/84 MV5 RP NG

FIREHOSE
22/6/88 PEEL *She paints pictures, Choose any memory, Makin' the freeway, Hear me.* Ed Crawford (gv), Mike Watt (b,bkv), George Hurley (d). 12/6/88 * DG DD&CBM

FIREWORKS
21/9/83 PEEL *Man of the times, Second eleven, Shall we all dance.* Moose (v), Steve Norris (g), Dave Griffiths (b), Martin Watts (d). 12/9/83 MV4 JP DD

FIRST OFFENCE
25/11/88 FRI. ROCK *Hold me, Night mare, The hand that rocks, Sacred heart.* Robin Hall (v), Neil Way (b), Colin Brown (d), Nick Beard (g). 12/8/88 * * MC

FIRST OFFENCE (91)
16/3/91 PEEL *Three steps, A brotherhood of man, Money, Drugs.* Steven Harris (v), Ian Bent ('cuts'), Billy Spiby (k), Carl Adesile (prd,prg), Eric Powell (prg). 19/2/91 MV5 MR~

FIRST STRIKE
4/1/91 FRI. ROCK *Love's on fire, Long way home, Just another night, Nasty.* Mick White (v), Billy Kulke (b), Dave Senzcak (g), Dee Dowling (g), Dave Anderson (d). 14/12/90 MV5 DD~

FISHBAUGH, FISHBAUGH AND ZORN
19/6/72 HARRIS *Beginnings, Wine, I owe her my life (& Everybody get out of bed, 31/7/72).* * 7/6/72 * JG *

FISHMONKEYMAN
27/5/91 GOODIER *Vote for us, If I told you once, Heads, Eyes peeled.* Paul Denheyer (gv), Ken Hancock (g,bkv-2), Jason Orr (b,bkv), Carl Henry (d). 11/5/91 MV5 MC~

FIST
30/7/82 FRI. ROCK *Dog soldier, Vamp, The wanderer, Lucy.* Dave Irwin (g), Norm Appleby (b), Harry Hill (d), Glen Coates (v). 9/7/82 * TW DD

PATRIK FITZGERALD
15/2/78 PEEL *Don't tell me because I'm young, Bingo crowd, Little dippers, Safety pin stuck in my heart, Back street boys.* Patrik Fitzgerald (gv). 8/2/78 MV4 MB NG
31/7/78 PEEL *No fun football, Little fishes, A mixed kid, The sound of my street, Jarvis.* 19/7/78 MV4 BS NG
17/4/79 PEEL *Suicidal wreck, Improve myself, Tonight, All the splattered children, Dance music/Late night.* 10/4/79 MV6 TVD MR

FIVE BLIND BOYS OF ALABAMA
11/7/92 KERSHAW *Deep river, Look where he brought me from, Didn't it rain, Changed man.* Jimmy Carter, Clarence Fountain, George Lewis Scott, Jerome Lee Monk, Curtis Stephen Foster, Caleb Butler, Johnny Lee Fields. 26/5/92 MV3 NG~

FIVE HAND REEL
25/11/75 PEEL *Campbell's farewell to Red castle/The Duchess of Perth/The lads of Mull, Slieve gallon braes, Wee wee German lairdie.* * 28/10/75 MV4 TW BAI
24/9/76 PEEL *Kempey's, When a man's in love [&? PasB damaged].* * 2/9/76 MV4 * *
3/6/77 PEEL *A man's a man for all that, Carrick Fergus, P stands for Paddy, Pinch of snuff.* Dave Tulloch (d), Barry Lyons (b), Tom Hickland (vi,v-3), Dick Gaughan (g,v, solo v-4), Bobby Eaglesham (dul,g,v-1,2). 25/5/77 MV4 MB NG
31/3/78 PEEL *The trooper and the maid, Jackson and Jane, My love is like a red red rose.* 22/3/78 MV4 DP NG

THE FIXX
25/2/82 JENSEN *Time in a glass, Cameras in Paris, Shuttered room, Red skies at night.* Adam Woods (d), Charlie Barrett (b), Jamie West (g), Rupert Greenall (k), Cy Curnin (v). 31/1/82 MV4 DG ME

THE FIZZBOMBS
1/7/87 LONG *Blue summer, It's not as simple as that, The Neil Diamond one (Cherry cherry), Beach party.* Katy Lironi (lv), Margarita Vazquez Ponte (g,bkv), Ann

Donald (b), Angus McCloud (dk), Fergus Anderson (sty). 24/6/87 MV4 PW MPK&TD

THE FLAMING MUSSOLINIS
16/4/85 LONG *Swallow glass, Masuka Dan, My Cleopatra, Ember days.* Alan Savage (lv,ag), Craig McClune (d), Jeff Fogarty (sx,k), Kit Haigh (g), Doug Maloney (b). 3/4/85 MV5 JS MPK
1/8/85 LONG *Holding sand, Long way to fall, Privilege, Catholic wedding.* 12/6/85 MV5 BYA MPK

FLARE
16/7/70 HENRY *The sunshine song, Message for you, The travelling song (& Epitaph, not broadcast).* Clive Chaman (b), Max Middleton (elp), Ed Spevock (d), Brian Short (v), Stanley Chaman (lg). 9/7/70 A02 * MH&MF

FLASH
9/3/72 DRUMMOND *Children of the universe, Black and white.* Peter Bank (g), Ray Bennett (b), Mike Huff (d), Colin Carter (v). 28/2/72 MV5 MB MH&MF

THE FLATBACKERS
21/8/80 PEEL *Gary, Never had nuffin', I know, Pumping iron.* Julie Usher (lg,lv-1), Lucy Dray (b,lv-2,3,4), Lynne Monk (d,perc,v, handclaps,chanting). 12/8/80 MV4 DG MR
15/9/80 READ *Pumping iron, Kid from Kibrooke, There's a buzz going round, Serenade of love.* 26/8/80 MV4 CL *
16/3/81 JENSEN *There's a buzz going round, It's your number, Little man, Making changes.* 17/11/80 * DG ME

THE FLATMATES
24/9/86 PEEL *Tell me why, Love cuts, Happy all the time, Thinking of you.* Sarah Fletcher (bkv,b), Debbie Haynes (lv), Martin Whitehead (g), Rocker (d,bkv,sty). 14/9/86 * DG ME
18/3/87 LONG† *I wanna be with him, My empty head, Every day, When I'm with you.* † On Nighttracks SFNT011. 1/3/87 MV4 HP *
16/9/87 PEEL *You're gonna cry too, Barbella blue, Sportscar girl, Shimmer.* Joel O'Beirne (d) r. Rocker. 6/9/87 * DG SC&JB

PETER GREEN'S FLEETWOOD MAC
12/11/67 TOP GEAR *Long grey mare, Baby please set a date, Looking for somebody, I believe my time ain't long, Got to move.* Pete Green (lgv), Jeremy Spencer (gv), Mick Fleetwood (b), John McVie (b). 7/11/67 MV4 BP PR
21/1/68 TOP GEAR *Can't hold out, Blue coat man, Sweet little angel, The stroller, Bee-I-bicky-bop blue jean honey babe meets high school hound dog hot rod man (& Where you belong, Don't be cruel, The sun is shining, The world keeps turning, 24/3/68).* & guest Eddie Boyd (v-2,4,6). 16/1/68 A02 BA DT
On 26/2, rec'd session for R3's *Blues in Britain,* MV5 prod. JG.
13/4/68 SAT. CLUB *Worried dream, Please find my baby, Black magic woman, Peggy Sue got married.* 9/4/68 PH BB *
17/4/68 NIGHT RIDE *How blue can you get?, My baby is sweet, Long grey mare, Buzz me, I'm so lonesome and blue.* 16/4/68 A02 DK *
2/6/68 TOP GEAR *That ain't it, Mean mistrusting mama, Psychedelic send-up number, Dead shrimp blues (& Sheila, 7/7/68).* Billed just as 'Fleetwood Mac' from now on. 27/5/68 PCI BA *
1/9/68 TOP GEAR *A mind of my own, I have to laugh, You're the one, Preachin' the blues (& You need love, A talk with you, Bo Diddley, Wine whisky women, 13/10/68; & Crutch and kane, If you be my baby, Crazy for my baby, 24/11/68).* Danny Kirwan (lg) joins; & guest Christine Perfect (v). 27/8/68 PCI BA AH
Group had appeared live for an interview on 'Radio 1 O'clock' PH the day before, 26/8/68.
5/11/68 RI CLUB *Like crying like dying, Albatross [on PasB as 'Albatratz'], Hang on to a dream, Baby don't you want to go.* As 27/8, without Perfect. 9/10/68 PH * *
26/11/68 WS R&B *Hard-hearted woman, Sweet home*

Chicago, *Crazy about my baby, Set a date.* 1/11/68 A02 JS JY
16/3/69 TOP GEAR *You'll never know what yu're missing until you try, Blues with a feeling, Heavenly, I can't believe you wanna leave (& Tallahassie lassie, Early morning come, 11/5/69).* 10/3/69 PH BA PR
23/3/69 SYMONDS ON SUNDAY *You'll be mine, Roll along blues, Peggy Sue got married, Albatross.* 17/3/69 A02 JW TW
On the same session, members of the band guested on an all-star recording led by Alexis Korner, for the same show (see Korner, below).
2/6/69 WS R&B *All over again, Talk with you, Just want to tell you.* 14/5/69 MV4 JG JY
15/6/69 CHRIS GRANT'S TASTY POP SUNDAE *Coming your way, Man of the world, Jumpin' at shadows, Linda.* 10/6/69 PCI c.PWI *
Grant was stand-in DJ for SYMONDS ON SUNDAY show in June 69.
12/10/69 DLT *Linda, Oh well pt.1, Although the sun is shining.* 6/10/69 A02 c.PWI *
23/5/70 TOP GEAR *Sandy Mary, World in harmony, Tiger, Only you, Leaving her blues.* & Nick Pickett (guest). 27/4/70 PH JW TW
Five-piece rec'd Peel Sunday Concert 9/4/70 PS, TX 19/4/70.
22/8/70 FIRST GEAR *Buddy's song, When will I be loved, Jenny Lee, When I see my baby, Honey hash.* Green out. 7/7/70 MV4 JW BC
1/12/70 HARDING *Down at the crown for now, Purple dancer, Station man.* Christine McVie (kv) joins. 24/11/70 MV5 MB MH&MF
14/12/70 RI CLUB *Sandy Mary, Crazy about you baby, Down at the crown for now (14/12), Turn me loose (16/12) (& Sandy Mary, Crazy about you baby, & Tell me all the things you do, not on PasBs as having been broadcast).* 10/11/70 PS * *
23/3/71 TOP GEAR *Start again, Teenage darling, Preaching, Get like you used to be (& Dragonfly, 27/3/71).* 5/1/71 MV4 * BC
23/7/71 BLACK *Woman of a thousand years, Show me a smile, Future games.* Bob Welch (gv) r. Spencer. 1/7/71 A02 JM JWH

FLESH FOR LULU
6/9/82 PEEL *Dancer, Walk tired, Missionary, Spy in your mind.* James Mitchell (d), Philip Ames (b,bkv), Mark Ambler (k), Nick Marsh (gv). 21/8/82 MV4 DG MR
15/12/83 JENSEN *Restless, Dog dog dog, Lame train, Hyena.* Mitchell, Marsh, Rocco Barker (lg), Glenn Bishop (b). 1/12/83 MV4 JP *
6/11/84 LONG *Black tattoo, Cat burglar, Peace and love, Endless sleep.* Kevin Mills (b) r. Bishop. 21/10/84 HP BYA PW

FLOAT UP CP
1/12/83 JENSEN *You make me wet, The loneliest girl in the world, Throw me to the lions, My memory scars deeply.* Derek Goddard (d), Sarah Sarbandi (vla), Sean Oliver (bg), Neneh Cherry (v), Gareth Sager (pg,cl), Flash (ts), Tessa Pollitt (clo). 24/11/83 MV4 JP SC
26/9/84 PEEL *Pray for this, Sexy bushes, You make me wet.* Cherry, Oliver, Sagar, Sarbandi, Bruce Smith (d), Oliver Moore (sx). 19/9/84 MV5 RP MPK
5/12/84 LONG *Loneliest girl blues, My guilty memory, The henchman, He loves me - no,no,no.* 21/11/84 MV5 JS MPK

A FLOCK OF SEAGULLS
12/5/81 PEEL *Messages from the rings of Saturn, Talking (it's not me talking), I ran, Committed.* Mike Score (sy,g,lv), Paul Reynolds (g), Frank Maudsley (b,bkv), Ali Score (d). 6/5/81 LH1 CL NG
10/9/81 SKINNER *Don't ask me, Messages from the rings of Saturn, I ran, Tangilamara (instrumental).* 6/9/81 MV4 DG ME

31/3/82 Jensen *DNA, I ran, Space age love song, Standing in the doorway.* 11/3/82 PHM * TWN

22/1/83 Long *Man made, I ran, Telecommunication, You can run.* 28/11or12/82? PHM cJL TWN

This could have been an early repeat transmission: PasBs claim session recorded 28/12/82, TX 28/11/82, impossible even for this band. Janice thinks this was her first session, so perhaps 1st TX 4/12/82?

18/4/83 Jensen *Over the border, What am I supposed to be?, Transfer affection.* 10/4/83 MV4 DG ME

FLOOD

4/11/91 Goodier *Shoulders, Electric start, Change the map, My girl's man.* Graham Parker (d), Danny Collier (b), Charlie Bloor (g,lv), Nigel Day (gv). 2/11/91 MV4 MC~

FLORISTS

25/7/83 Peel *Top models know, Our much loved daughter, Julia, The longest hour.* Sue Prior (v), Lawrence Diagram (g), Gary Terrell (b), Dick Harrison (perc), Andy Diagram (tp), Michael Pollard (d).
13/7/83 MV4 RP NG&EL

FLOWERED UP

16/7/90 Goodier *Sunshine, Phobia, It's on, Doris.* John Tovey (d), Andy Jackson (b), Tim Dorney (k), Joe Maher (g), Liam Maher (v). 7/7/90 MV5 MC~

2/4/91 Goodier *Crackerjack, Egg rush, Phobia.*
22/12/90 MV5 MC~

THE FLOWERPOT MEN

24/4/86 Long† *Sharpen my heart, Alligator bait, Beat city, Django.* Ben Watkins (gv), Adam Peters (clo); & Margo Buchanan & Sam Brown (bkv). 9/3/86 MV4 BYA *
† On Nighttracks SFNT007.

THE FLOWERS

12/9/79 Peel *Living doll, Tunnels, The deep end dance, Tear along.* Hill-ray (v), Andy Copland (g), Fraser Sutherland (b), Simon Best (d). 28/8/79 MV4 BS MR

FLOY JOY

17/9/84 Long *Baby you know I..., Into the hot, Mission, Operator.* Mike Ward, Shaun Ward, Carroll Thompson (lv), Des Campbell, Kenny Crawley, Colin Weavill, Mark Amblers. 23/8/84 MV5 MHY&DG MPK

FLUKE

25/11/90 Peel *Thumper, Taxi, Jig, Our definition of jazzi.* Jonathan Fugler (v), Michael Tournier & Mike Bryant (k,smp,prg). 18/11/90 MV3 DG ME&FK

26/1/92 Peel *The bells, Top of the world, The allotment of Blighty, The timekeeper.* 10/12/91 MV4 MR~ JB

At this point in the Sessionography, regular Peel listeners might expect to find a session by The Flying Creamshots. Mysteriously, I can find no trace of one; although Billy Bragg reportedly just missed them in San Fransisco.

THE FLYING PICKETS

6/4/83 Peel *Get off my cloud, Psycho killer, Disco down, Factory.* Ken Gregson, Red Stripe, Rick Lloyd, Gareth Williams, Brian Hibard, David Brett (all v).
30/3/83 MV4 RP TdB

THE FLYS

23/3/78 Peel *New hearts, Fun city, We don't mind the rave, Living in the sticks.* Dave Freeman (lg), Neil O'Connor (rgv), Joe Hughes (b), Pete King (d).
15/3/78 MV4 DP MR

21/11/78 Peel *Love and a molotov cocktail, Name dropping, I don't know, Waikiki beach refugees.*
14/11/78 MV4 MR~

8/10/79 Peel *Let's drive, Energy boy, Frenzy is 23, I'll survive.* Graham Deakin (d) r. King. 18/9/79 MV4 JS MR

FM

25/4/85 Into The Music *The other side of midnight, Face to face, That girl, Dangerous.* Pete Jupp (d,bkv), Merv Goldsworthy (b,nkv), Chris Overland (lg,bkv), Steve Overland (lvg), Didge Digital (k). 30/3/85 MV4 DG MC

FOCUS

2/3/73 Sequence *House of the king, Hocus pocus, Focus I,*

Improvisation of anonymous II, Sylvia/Hocus pocus.
* 30/1/73 * JM *

THE FOLK DEVILS

4/4/84 Peel *Where the buffalo roam, Beautiful monster, Tight sleep, What's that smell?* Kris Jozajtis (g,bkv), Al Cole (d), Ian Lowery (v), Mark Whiteley (b,bkv).
20/3/84 MV5 MRD TdB

17/9/84 Peel *Big car big car, Wail, Broken head, Ink runs dry.* 5/9/84 MV5 RP NG

8/7/85 Peel *This traitor hand, It drags on, Under the bridge, Dead heat.* 18/6/85 MV5 JWI MR

WAYNE FONTANA

24/4/73 Peel *The game of love, Um um um um um um, Pamela Pamela.* 2/4/73 T1 JW *
Last of dozens of pop sessions.

FORCE FED

18/4/90 Peel *Full up, Loaded, Claustrophobia, Can't get out.* Nigel Clark (d), Kalvin Piper (b), Nick Clark (g), Jamie Sims (v). 18/3/90 MV3 DG MR

2/2/91 Peel *I don't know, Burn my back, Fast forward, One million miles.* N. & N. Clark, Neil Pitfield, Mick Knowlton (v). 8/1/91 MV5 MR~ PY

FOREHEADS IN A FISHTANK

24/8/91 Peel *British Telecom, Happy shopper, Sex and drugs and, Sylvester's mother.* Adrian Leaman (d), Gavin Jones (b), Jeff Leahy (gv), Jez Watts (k), Matt Brewster (k). 7/7/91 MV3 DG MFA&PRB

FOREST

26/3/69 Night Ride *A glade somewhere, Pools of memory, Reflecting in the sea, Mirror of life, Smoke, Fading light.* Martin Welham (g,hca,v), Adrian Welham (g,mand,v), Derek Allenby (mand,hca,wh,v). 18/3/69 S1 PR *
Failed by panel: 'cacophony' 'appalling sound, raggy and amateur' 'messy, uninspiring, distasteful'.

19/11/69 Top Gear *Gipsy girl and ramble away, Autumn childhood, Love's memory gone, Mirror of life.*
16/9/69 MV4 JW *
2nd trial broadcast passed by panel. Did Peel Sunday Concert TX 1/3/70.

10/10/70 Top Gear *Hares on the mountain, Graveyard, Hermit/Guardian angel, Hawk the hawker (& Do not walk in the rain, 2/1/71).* 28/9/70 PH JW *

15/3/71 Harris *Hawk the hawker, You don't know, Graveyard.* 2/3/71 MV5 JM JWH
2nd Peel Sunday Concert TX 1/8/71.

24/4/72 Harris *March hare, You could have been a gypsy, I wrote (& Phoebe, 22/5/72).* 12/4/72 AO2 JG *

23/10/72 Harris *Leave my woman alone, Love's memory gone, Regarding, The turning of the day.* Dave Panton, Dave Statts r. Allenby. 27/9/72 AO2 JG *

THE FOREST IS CRYING:
BULGARIAN FRIVOLITIES

25/6/89 Kershaw *A boy was born, A full garden, The black eyes of my aunt, A bird is singing, Neno le, Bre varai, Mai furlinko, Ya denize, Gine gine, Sto e ogreala, Elenko mome malenko, Vazpelo e pile cheren garran.* Mitev brothers (1-3), Nadka Karadjova (4,5), Bisserov sisters (6-8 unaccompanied, 9-11 & instr. accompaniment), Mladen Koynarov (12-solo v, pp).
23/3/89 WX DG JB&JLO

A FORMAL SIGH

10/9/81 Peel *Looking at walls, Bleak intrusion, Ev rev, Ad nauseam.* Flo Sullivan (v), Greg Milton (g,b), Mark Peters (b), Roger Sinek (d), Robin Surtees (g).
5/9/81 MV4 DG MR

FORMERLY FAT HARRY

23/5/70 Top Gear *Honky tonk angel, Untitled, Seuble.* Phil Greenberg (gv), Gary Peterson (g,k), Bruce Barthol (b), Laurie Allan (d). 12/5/70 MV4 JW *
Rec'd Peel Sunday Concert 3/12/70 PS, TX 13/12/70 prod. JG.

30/12/71 Drummond *Tell me all about it, Goodbye for good, My friend was a pusher.* 15/12/71 MV4 MB MH&MF

CHRIS FOSTER

29/6/77 Peel *The golden glove, Lady Maisry, William Taylor, The famous flower of serving men, Unicorns.* Chris Foster (gv). 22/6/77 MV4 * NG

FOTHERINGAY

5/4/70 Folk On One *The way I feel, Nothing more, The sea, Ned Kelly, Banks of the Nile, Too much of nothing.* Sandy Denny (vgp), Trevor Lucas (g), Gerry Conway (d), Jerry Donahue (g), Pat Donaldson (b).
2/4/70 MV5 FL *&BC
Contracted for Folk on Friday, actually broadcast as a half-hour special after Pick of the Pops on a Sunday.

25/4/70 Top Gear *Banks of the Nile, Ned Kelly, The sea, Nothing more (& The way I feel, 4/7/70).* 13/4/70 PH JW *

18/5/70 Symonds *Silver threads and golden needles, Peace in the end, Too much of nothing (& Nothing more, 29/6/70).* 5/5/70 PH BA *

21/11/70 Folk On One *Eppy Moray, Gypsy Davy, Bold Jack Donahue, The lowlands of Holland*, Ned Kelly, The banks of the Nile.* Denny solo (4 only). 12/11/70 MV5 FL *

21/12/70 Harris *Gypsy Davy, Bold Jack Donahue, John the gun, Eppy Moray, Will ye go lassie go.*
15/11/70 CM JM JWH

THE FOUNDATIONS

14/1/68 Top Gear *A whole new thing, Back on my feet again, Help me, 96 tears.* Peter Macbeth (b), Alan Warner (gv), Pat Burke (sx), Tim Harris (sx), Eric Allandale (tb), Clem Curtis (v), Tony Gomez (o), Mike Elliott (sx). 8/1/68 PCI BA * [M: daytime]

THE FOUR BROTHERS

8/9/88 Kershaw *Serevende, Rudo chete, Rudo imoto, Rumbizayi.* Marshall Munhumumwe (d,lv), Never Mutare (b,bkv), Frank Sibanda (g,bkv). 25/8/88 * DG TdB&TD
In fact, only three: Aleck Chipaika (g,bkv) was delayed by an 'aeroplane seat deficiency' in Addis Abada. Nevertheless, a classic debut: repeated on 13/10, and then by Peel, 4/5/89.

26/9/88 Peel† *Rugare, Uchandifunga, Vimbayi, Pahukama.*
11/9/88 HP DG *
Chipaika (gv) gets a flight out of Ethiopia, and catches up with the band in time for this one. † On Strange Fruit SFPS070.

5/6/89 Peel *Rudo chete, Pasi pano pane zvidzo, Wakazvarwa seyi, Ngatipindukewo.* 23/5/89 MV3 DG MR

20/8/89 Kershaw *Zuro chisara, Nhaka yemusiiranwa, Siya zuiriko, Baba vanerusaruro.* 18/5/89 MV3 DG NG

400 BLOWS

16/2/84 Peel *Introduction, Conscience, For Jackie M, Still beating that devil.* Andrew Edward Beer, Robert Taylor, Tony Thorpe. 8/2/84 MV5 DG NG

14 ICED BEARS

26/11/86 Peel *Balloon song, Cut, Shy like you, Train song.* Robert Sekula (v), Kevin Canham (g), Nick Roughley (g,bkv), Dominic Mills (b), Nick Emery (d).
28/10/86 * DG TdB&TD

27/7/87 Peel *If I said, Spangle, Miles away, Hay fever.* Sekula, Canham, Steven Ormsby (b), William Cox (d).
21/7/87 MV4 DG MR&JB

14 KARAT SOUL

4/5/83 Jensen *Sixteen candles, Come go with me, Destination love, Why do fools fall in love, Goody goody.* Glenny T. Wright, David Thurmond, Brizz, Russell Fox II, Brian Simpson (all v). 28/4/83 MV4 JP *

14/10/86 Long *The wanderer, YMCA, Jump to the day, This boy.* Glenny T. Wright, Russell Fox II, Michael Alexander, Anthony Holding, Kevin Lucas (all v). Live from MV5 BYA *

MR. FOX

5/12/70 Top Gear *Mr Trill's song, The gay goshawk, Susan's song, Ballad of Noddy Nick (& Mr Fox, 27/2/71).* Bob Pegg (acc,ml,o,gv), Carole Pegg (fd,wh,v).
24/11/70 MV4 JW *

Debuted on Country Meets Folk PH 30/8/70
[M: Folk shows].

25/9/71 Top Gear *Silly Billy, HP source, Gypsy.* & Barry
Lyons (b), Alun Eden (d). 13/9/71 PH JW BC

BRUCE FOXTON

18/7/83 Jensen *Freak, Are you ready to talk?, Writing's on
the wall, This is the way.* Bruce Foxton (lv), Pete
Glennister (g), Adrian Lillywhite (d), Stan Shaw (k),
Roddy Lorimer (tp), Anthony Thistlethwaite (sx), Mae
McKenna & Lorenza Johnson (bkv). 3/7/83 MV4 DG TdB

FOXX

23/12/88 Fri. Rock *Unwanted life, Spontaneous Human
Combustion, Badlands, Living in Samson's dream.* Craig
Beattie (d), David Jay (b), Mark J Mynett (g), Danny
Foxx (v). 28/10/88 MV4 DD~

JOHN FOXX

20/6/85 Long *Lose all sense of time, Shine on, Stars on
fire, In mysterious ways.* John Foxx (kv), Randy Hope
Taylor (d), Paul Wickens (d), Robert Simon (g).
9/6/85 HP BYA PW

FOYER DES ARTES

17/11/86 Peel *Frauen in frieden und freiheit, Konnten
bienen fliegen, Einhaus aus den knochen von Cary
Grant, Schimmliges brot.* Gerd Pasemann (g), Max Goldt
(v), Terry Edwards (sx,k), Frog (b), Simon Charterton
(d). 12/10/86 * DG ME&SC

FRAMES

2/3/81 Peel *The shock of the new, Play it by fear, La
chanson ironique, Stingray.* Sue Jonas (v), Nick Radford
(g), Stephen Wood (d), Mike Marshfield (b).
24/2/81 LH1 DG MR

PETER FRAMPTON'S BAND

4/9/72 Harris *It's a plain shame, Fig tree bay, Do you feel
like I do, Jumping Jack Flash.* Peter Frampton (gv),
Mike Kellie (d), Mickey Gallagher (k), Rick Wills (b).
23/8/72 MV5 JG *
Line-up later rec'd In Concert
9/11/72 PS, TX 18/11/72.

THE FRANK & WALTERS

9/9/91 Goodier *Michael†, Fashion crisis in New York,
Walter's trip, Daisy chain.* Paul Linehan (lv,b), Ashley
Keating (d), Niall Lineman (g); & John Power (perc).
24/8/91 MV5 MC~
† On 'The Best of Mark Goodier' Nighttracks Mark1.
8/12/91 Peel *Fashion crisis in New York, Happy busman,
The world carries on.* 3/11/91 MV3 DG~ JLC

THE FRANK CHICKENS

30/5/83 Peel *Tokyo boogie, Sake ballad, We are ninja,
Woman in harbour, UFO.* Kazuko Hohki, Kazumi
Taguchi. 16/5/83 MV4 TW DD
5/10/83 Peel *Fujiyama mama, Night of Alaska, Monster,
Life theatre, Shellfish bamboo.* with David Toop & Steve
Beresford (k,dm). 28/9/83 MV4 DG AP
3/4/84 Peel *We are ninja, Blue canary, Dream theatre,
Yellow toast.* & Beresford only. 14/3/84 MV5 RP NG
13/8/84 Skinner *Blue canary, We are Frank Chickens, Black
Ship, Yellow toast.* Toop (g) returns; & Grant Cuncliffe
(d,perc), Justin Adams (g), Elliot Mackeral (vi), Dave
Defries (tp). 26/7/84 MV5 MHY *
27/11/84 Long *We say you say, We are ninja, Pikadon,
Green banana.* Four-piece again. 14/11/84 MV5 DG MPK
12/3/85 Peel *China night, Amy rang, Japanese rumba, Sake
ballad, Eightman.* & Elisabeth Perry (vi), Alexander
Balenescu (vla), Lol Coxhill (sx). 5/3/85 MV5 MRD MR
13/8/85 Long *Yellow detective, Madam fatal, China night.*
& Tony Coe (sx), Balanescu, Perry. 31/7/85 MV4 BYA *
18/8/86 Peel *Two little ladies, We say you say, Japanese
girls, Sacred marriage, Chicken ondo.* Four-piece.
5/8/86 * DG MH&MS
14/1/88 Kershaw *Yellow toast, Werewolf woman, One
million hamburgers.* Kazumi, Kazuko, Fred Hood
(d,perc), Nigel Frydman (b), Justin Adams (g,bkv),

Martin Belmont (g), Sianned Jones (vi,bkv), Grant
Cunliffe (prg). 17/12/87 * DG NG&MA
10/7/89 Peel *Jackie Chan, Want to see you again, Carmen
77, Do the karaoke.* Kazuko, Atsuko Kamara (v), Hood,
Adams, Cunliffe, Jah Wobble (b), David Harrow
(sy,smp), Clive Bell (acc,fl,wh). 25/6/89 MV3 DG MC&SA

JACKSON C. FRANK

9/10/68 Night Ride *Blues run the game, Jimmy Clay, Just
like anything, Carnival, You never wanted me.*
* 9/10/68 * PC *

FRANKFURTER

5/5/87 Peel *Inbred zombies, Gimme donuts, Hot babes,
We're gonna eat/John Peel.* Mean Tom (d,g,v), Angus
Tomahawk (bv), Nick Schozza (v), R.J. Justice (v).
16/4/87 * DG ME&FK

FRANKIE GOES TO HOLLYWOOD

2/12/82 Peel *Two tribes, The world is my oyster, Krisco
kisses, Disneyland.* Holly Johnson (v), Paul Rutherford
(v), Brian Nash (g), Peter Gill (d), Mark O'Toole (b).
24/11/82 * AP *
15/3/83 Jensen *Welcome to the pleasure dome, Relax
(shoot it in the right direction), The only star in
heaven, Invade my heart.* 24/2/83 MV4 MPK~
19/12/83 Peel *Junk funk (Get on down), The other side of
midnight, The power of love, Get it on.* & Andy
Richards (k). 3/12/83 MV4 DG MC

THE FRANTIC ELEVATORS

3/3/81 Peel *Ding dong, Searching for the only one,
Hunchback of Notre Dame†, I am the man, Production
prevention.* Neil Smith (g), Mick Hucknall (v), Brian
Turner (b), Kevin Williams (d). 25/2/81 LH1 DG NG
† On 'Manchester - so much to answer for'
SFRCD202.
30/3/81 Skinner *Searching for the only one, Hey! hey!, We
are going down, I wish I was king.* 13/3/81 LH1 DG HP
30/9/81 Peel *And I don't care (nobody stays here), After
hanging around, What to do?, I'm not to see her, Ice
cream and wafers.* 19/9/81 MV4 DG MR

ANDY FRASER BAND

17/4/75 Peel *Love train, Bring it on home, Ain't gonna
worry, Don't hide your love away.* Andy Fraser (bv),
Nick Judd (elp), Kim Turner (d). 10/4/75 MV4 PR BAI

FREAKS

20/3/71 Top Gear *Come out into the open, Music for
Rawlinson end, Rawlinson end, Bad blood, Watcher.* Viv
Stanshall (v,tp), Neil Innes (k), Andy Roberts (g), Keith
Moon (d), Denis Cowan (b), Bubs White (g), Shamsi
Sarumi (cga), Gaspar Lawal (bgo). 2/3/71 MV4 JW BC

FREE

21/7/68 Top Gear *Waiting on you, Walk in my shadow,
Moonshine, Free me.* Paul Rodgers (v,hca), Paul Kossoff
(g), Andy Fraser (bv), Simon Kirke (d). 15/7/68 PCI BA PR
17/12/68 WS R&B *Walk in my shadow, Moonshine, Rock
me, Sugar for Mr Morrisson.* 15/11/68 AO2 JG JY
23/3/69 Top Gear *I'm a mover°, Song of yesterday†, Over
the green hills, Broad daylight.* 17/3/69 PH BA AH&BC
† On 'Before the fall' SFRCD203.
9/6/69 WS R&B *Walk in my shadow, Free me, Born under
a bad sign.* 14/5/69 * JG *
13/12/69 Top Gear *Trouble on double time, Mr Big, I'll be
creeping', Mouthful of grass (& Woman, 7/3/70).*
8/12/69 PH JW TW
20/12/69 WS R&B *I'll be creepin', Mouthful of grass, Mr
Big.* 26/11/69 * JG *
Rec'd early Peel Sunday Concert, 15/1/70 PS, TX 18/1/70.
28/12/69 Henry *Mr Big, I'll be creeping, Woman, The
hunter.* 2/12/69 MV5 MB *
9/4/70 Henry *Alright now, Mr Big, Heavy load, Fire and
water.* 2/4/70 AO2 MB MH&MF
23/6/70 Harding *Fire and water, Alright now°, Heavy load,
Oh I wept.* 4/6/70 AO2 MB MH&MF
Rec'd 2nd Peel Concert 2/7/70 PS, TX 12/7/70.

27/4/71 Harding *My brother Jake, Ride on pony, Get where
I belong°.* 19/4/71 MV5 MB MH&MF
° On B side of 1991 CD re-release of 'Alright now'
CID486-878 809-2. This second BBC version of 'Alright
now' is also now on 'I and only' BOJCD025.
26/6/72 Harris *Guardian of the universe, Child, Little bit of
love, Travelling man, Catch a train.* 24/5/72 AO2 JG *

FREEFALL

4/4/92 Peel *Shine, Our eyes, Green and blue, Love in
idleness.* Sean Shaw (d), Charles Hankers (bv), Andrew
Abram (g,bkv), Stuart Johnson (g). 9/2/92 MV3 DG ME&AD

FREEZE

20/11/80 Peel *Quietly burning, And then we danced,
Sunday, Lullaby in black.* Gordon Sharp (v), David
Clancey (gk), Keith Grant (g), Graeme Radin (d).
27/10/80 MV4 TW TdB&NG
19/8/81 Peel *Building on holes, From the bizarre,
Location.* Sharp, Clancy, Neil Braidwood (d,k), Mike
Moran (b). 12/8/81 MV4 CL NG

FREEZE FRAME

31/3/83 Peel *Fox hole, Personal tough, Your voice, Today
tomorrow.* Ronnie Stone (k,d,gv), Steve Byrne (v).
26/3/83 MV4 DG MR
3/4/84 Jensen *Exit the happy halo, Every white flag, Only
a boy, Culture won't wait.* & Clive G. (k).
22/3/84 MV5 JP MPK

FREIWILLIGE SELBST-KONTROLLE (F.S.K.)

6/8/85 Peel° *A swingin' safari, Lieber ein glas zuviel,
Drunk, Trink wie ein tier.* Wilfred Petzi (tb,g,perc,v),
Thomas Meinecke (cnt,g,perc,v), Justin Hoffman
(elp,g,xyl,v), Michaela Melian (b,mel,v). 4/8/85 MV5 DG ME
° On 'Last orders' ZickZack ZZ1066 (German
release); 'Swingin safari' also on 'Continental breakfast'
Ediesta CALC LP 16.
13/8/86 Peel† *Am tafelberg von Kapstadt, I wish I could
'Sprechen sie Deutsch', Die musik findet immer nach
haus, Dr. Arnold Fanck.* 3/8/86 * DG MR
24/6/87 Peel† *Komm gib mir deine hand, Girl, Birthday,
Don't pass me by.* 21/6/87 * DG MR&MC
† On Strange Fruit SFMCD204.
19/4/88 Peel *In lauterbach, Stalinbart jodler, Die
Englishchen frauleins, Cannonball yodel.*
10/4/88 * DG ME&JBN
19/1/92 Peel *Black market, Ohne kapitalisten geht es
besser, Horsti Schmandhoff, Ostblockgirl '91.* & Carl
Oesterhelt (d). 3/12/91 JB~ MR

FRIENDS AGAIN

28/4/83 Jensen *Lullaby number two, Bird of paradise, Sun-
kissed, Vaguely yours.* Neil Cunningham (b), Chris
Thompson (gv), James Grant (g), Stuart Kerr (dv), Paul
McGeechan (elp). 17/4/83 MV4 DG ME

FRED FRITH

5/12/74 Peel *Please give it back, My need is greater than
yours, Noise Carruthers pure bloody noise, In which
case the anxiety, Narrow road.* Fred Frith (g,vi),
Anthony Moore (k), Dagmar Krause (v). 2/12/74 TW *

RAYMOND FROGGATT

10/6/68 Symonds *Callow-la-vita, Rosie's gonna get wed
(11/6), My back yard (12/6), Just a little bit of love
(14/6) (& Red balloon, not broadcast).* Raymond
Froggatt (v), Hartley G. Cain (g), Louis Clarke (bp),
Lenny Ablethorpe (d). 4/6/68 * * *
23/12/68 Night Ride *Always goodbye, Lay down your weary
tune, The girl who stood beside me, Roly, Bells of
Rhimney, Lonely old world, Corrina.* Stanley Southall
(g), r. Cain. 2/12/68 MV4 PC * [M: dozens of daytime sessions]
16/4/70 Henry *Sometimes I wonder, Hasn't the lord blessed
us, Sooner or later, Movin' down south (& Wild
mountain thyme, Home to Kathy, It's raining, 4/6/70).*
3/4/70 MV5 MB MH&MF
27/7/70 Symonds *It's raining, A matter of pride, She don't
care about me.* 15/7/70 MV4 BA NG
5/11/70 Henry *Tom Thumb blues, Nashville skyline, The*

246

boxer, It takes a lot to laugh (& Sometimes I wonder, 10/12/70). 29/10/70 AO2 MB MH&MF

7/9/72 DRUMMOND Heather, Come stay with me, Always goodbye (& Running water, It's raining, 28/9/72). Michael Hinks (b) r. Clarke. 21/8/72 MV5 MB MH&MF

FRONT 242
23/7/86 PEEL No shuffle, Funkadhafi, Don't crash, Body to body. R23 (dv), Patrick Coornys (k), Jean Luc de Meyer (v), Daniel B. (k,sfx). 13/7/86 MV5 DG ME&MA

FROZEN HEART
13/7/90 FRI. ROCK Remember, Shout it to the top, The knives are out, Between the crossfire. Paul Watkins (v), Kevin Skingley (gv), Nigel Hobbs (kv), Mike Parker (b), Steve Pierce (d). 29/6/90 MV5 MC~

THE FRUIT MACHINE
26/8/82 PEEL Take your medicine, I don't need no doctor, Trials of a physical jerk, I think there's something wrong. Ludi Andrews (v), Michelle Fagan (v), David Harkins (v), Robbie Harris (b), Chris Kant (g), Ian Fraser (d); & Chicken Supremes (bkv-l). 2/8/82 MV4 TW DD

FUDGE TUNNEL
21/5/90 PEEL Sweet meat, Boston baby, Bedcrumbs, Sex mammoth. Adrian Parkin (d), Dave Ryley (b,bkv), Alex Newport (gv), Fudge Bear ('spiritual advisor'). 22/4/90 MV3 DG ME

19/6/92 PEEL Ten percent, Good kicking, Tipper Gore, Stuck. Fudge Bear absent. 21/5/92 ME~ JB

FUGAZI
13/12/88 PEEL Waiting room, Break in, Merchandise, Glueman. Guy Picciotto (v), Ian MacKaye (gv), Joe Lally (b), Brendan Canty (d). 11/12/88 HP DG ME

FUMBLE
11/7/72 PEEL Take good care of my baby, Teddy bear, Teenagers in love, Breaking up is hard to do. Des Henly (glv), Sean Mayes (pv), Barry Pike (d), Mario Ferrari (b,gv). 27/6/72 MV4 * BC [M]
   Recorded sessions in 1970 to 71 as 'The Baloons'.
10/8/74 ROCK ON Here we go again, Keep on knockin', After the dance. David Christopher joins. 5/8/74 LH1 BA *
30/11/74 ROCK ON That's alright mama, The night has a thousand eyes, Free the kids, Weekend. 25/11/74 MV4 BA *
24/2/79 IT'S ROCK 'N' ROLL Mama don't you hit that boy, No money down, Tupelo Mississippi flash, Your mama don't dance. Christopher out. 13/2/79 MV5 DP *

FUN BOY 3
19/1/83 JENSEN Pressure of life, Tunnel of love, Going home, Well fancy that. Terry Hall (v), Lynval Golding (v), Neville Staples (v), June Miles Kingston (d), Annie Whitehead (tb), Nicky Holland (p,bkv), Bethan Peters (b), Caroline Levelle (clo), Ingrid Schroeder (bkv). 16/1/83 MV4 DG ME

THE FUNBOY FIVE
1/10/79 PEEL Life after death, Compulsive eater, Haircut Bob Dylan '66, Bleached roots of surf. Robert Radhall (d), Bob Brimson (b), Mick Sinclair (gv), John McCrae (k). 19/9/79 MV4 BS NG

THE FUNKEES
19/11/74 PEEL Abraka, Tule-tule, Life, Dancing in the nude. Tony Mallett, Danny Heibs (b), Jake N. Sollo (lg, kv), Chyke Madu, Harry Agada, Sonny Akpan (rga). 5/11/74 MV4 * *
14/7/75 PEEL Wine festival, Lobo, Too lay, Experience. Madu, Akpan, Sollo, Heibs, Harry Mosco (g,v,wooden gg). 1/7/75 MV4 TW *

THE FUNKY GINGER
15/8/88 PEEL Money passion vice, Jack the knife, Slaughter house. Funky Ginger (perc,'various'), Dr. Ross (g,k), Sedley Francis (b), Doby DJ (sc). 26/7/88 MV4 MR~

FINBAR AND EDDIE FUREY
27/6/72 PEEL The bonnet/Crowley's reel, Reynardine, Spanish cloak/Dingle regatta, Pretty Sara, Farewell to Tarwathy. 12/6/72 * * BC

R1 debut live on My Kind of Folk, prod. FL, 29/1/69. Then on Country Meets Folk, PH 6/12/69 [M: Folk shows].
9/1/73 PEEL Jennifer Gentle, Bobby and spikes reel, Life is just that way, Tattered Jack Walsh. * 7/11/72 * * BC
14/5/74 PEEL Peggy and the soldier, John Peel's favourite pipe jig, Lament for Anacuain/Ace and deuce of pipery, Sailor come home from the sea, Crowley's reel. * 5/11/74 * * *

FURIOUS PIG
18/8/80 PEEL Johnny's so long, I don't like your face, The king mother. Martin Kent, Stephen Kent, Jonathan (Cass) Davis, Dominic Weeks (all "vocal stylists"). 11/8/80 MV4 DG DD

FURNITURE
4/3/85 LONG I can't crack, Brilliant mind, It's the unspoken things, She gets out the scrapbook. Maya Gilder (o), Jim Irvin (v,perc), Hamilton Lee (d,perc), Larry N'Azone (sx,bcl,sy), Sally Still (bv), Tim Whelan (gpv). 20/2/85 MV5 DG MPK
12/6/86 LONG Shake like Judy, I miss you, Love your shoes, Escape into my arms. N'Azone out. 21/5/86 MV4 BYA PS
25/11/88 MAYO Slow motion kisses, You haven't learnt a thing, Subway to the beach, Friend of a friend. 10/1/88 MV4 PW TdB

THE FUTURE SOUND OF LONDON
18/9/92 PEEL Lifeforms, Expander, Papua New Guinea, Space hippy. Garry Cockbain & Brian Dougans (prg). 25/8/92 MR~ CML

THE FUZZTONES
5/6/85 PEEL She's wicked, Epitaph for a head, Bad news, Cinderella. Ira Elliott (bkv,d), Michael Jay (bkv,b), Rudi Protrudi (lv,g,hca), Elan Portnoy (g), Deb O'Nair (bkv,o). 26/5/85 MV5 DG ME

FUZZY DUCK
24/8/71 HARDING Double time woman, Time for changes, Country boy. Garth Watt-Roy (g), Mick Hawkesworth (b), Ray Sharland (o), Paul Francis (d). 16/8/71 MV5 JM *

GABBY & GRYNNER
21/4/91 KERSHAW (We want) More Grynner, Get out of de way, Chicken and ram, Easy come easy go. Gabby (v), Grynner (v), Perry Helius (d), Irvin Yarde (g), David Batson (tp), Gary Belfield (sx), Elaine James (bkv), Wayne Nunes (b), Tony Edmunds (sy), Steve Whelan (tp), Pat Bassbone (tb), Yvonne Brown (bkv). 15/3/91 MV3 DG MWT&RF

GAFFA
4/4/79 PEEL Baby sitting, Anna Nervosa, White but not quite, The rota, Gangster tendencies. Wayne Evans (bv), John Maslen (gv), Clive Smith (g), Mick Barratt (d). 20/3/79 MV4 TVD MR

GALAHAD
26/4/91 FRI. ROCK One for the record, Face to the sun, Room 801. Stuart Nicholson (v), Roy Keyworth (g), Tim Ashton (b), Karl Garrett (k), Spencer Luckman (d). 22/3/91 MV5 MC~

GALAXIE 500
17/10/89 PEEL Flowers, Blue thunder, Decomposing trees, Don't let our youth go to waste. Damon Krukowski (d), Naomi Yang (b), Dean Wareham (g,lv). 24/9/89 MV5 DG DD
4/11/90 PEEL Moonshot, Submission, When will you come home, Final day. 30/10/90 MWT~ AR

GALLAGHER AND LYLE
18/11/71 DRUMMOND Sparrow, Great Australian dream, City and suburban blues, Conversation (& To David, Charlie and Ian, Desiderata, Comfort and Joy, Heritage, 9/12/71). Benny Gallagher (kv), Graham Lyle (gv). 8/11/71 MB MH&MF
27/2/72 SPEAKEASY Conversation, Sparrow, Desiderata, Green fingers. 25/2/72 PS TB *

28/2/72 HARRIS Green fingers, International, Mrs Conattelis, Desiderata. 16/2/72 AO2 JG *
20/4/72 DRUMMOND Hello my America, Let it shine, Of a moment, Give the boy a break, Friday night. 0/4/72 MV5 MB MH&MF
4/9/72 HARRIS Great Australian dream, Among the birks, Home (& Give the boy a break, 9/10/72). 16/8/72 AO2 JG * [M: daytime].
8/6/73 SEQUENCE Willie, Dan, Among the birks, Seedy. 17/5/73 LH1 JM *
19/11/73 HARRIS Layna, I believe in you, Seeds of change, Shine a light. Jimmy Jewell, Bruce Rowlands join. 31/10/73 LH1 JG *
29/11/73 PEEL Shine a light, Randolph and me, Country morning, Misspent youth. 19/11/73 LH1 BA *
23/9/74 HARRIS Song and dance man, Keep your candle burning, Villain of the peace, We. 4/9/74 LH1 JG *
2/11/74 ROCK ON Rain, Song and dance man, King of the silents, We. Alan Hornall, Ray Duffy r. Rowlands. 28/10/74 MV4 BA * [M: daytime]

RORY GALLAGHER
14/5/71 BLACK Laundromat, Just the smile, Hands up, Sinner boy. Rory Gallagher (gv), Wilgar Campell (d), Gerry McAvoy (b). 15/4/71 AO2 JM *
27/7/71 HARDING In your town, I fall apart, Gypsy woman, It takes time (& It's the same thing, 17/8/71). 19/7/71 MV5 MB *
31/7/71 RAVEN'S R&B Sinner boy, Wave myself goodbye, Laundromat, Gypsy woman. 21/7/71 MV4 MB *
   Next, rec'd Peel Sunday Concert 12/8/71 PS, TX 22/8/71.
21/12/71 DRUMMOND Used to be, Crest of a wave, Should have learned my lesson. 24/11/71 MV4 MB MH&MF
   Rec'd 2nd In Concert 13/1/72 PS, TX 22/1/72.
15/6/72 DRUMMOND Messin' with the kid, Hoodoo man blues, Pistol slapper blues, Bullfrog blues. 2/6/72 * MB MH&MF
7/8/72 HARRIS Feels so bad, Could have had religion, Cuckoo, Messin' with the kid. 10/7/72 T1 PD *
   Rec'd 3rd In Concert 13/7/72 PS, TX 29/7/72.
8/2/73 PEEL Race the breeze, Hands off, Banker's blues, Walk on hot coals. Rod De'ath (d), Lou Martin (k) r. Campbell. 5/2/73 LH1 BA *
   Rec'd fourth In Concert 1/2/73 PS, TX 10/2/73.
26/2/73 HARRIS Seventh son of a seventh son, Daughter of the Everglades, If I had a reason. 21/2/73 LH1 PR *
7/1/74 HARRIS Tatoo'd lady, Cradle rock, A million miles away (2-1st TX 15/12/73, ROCK ON). 5/12/73 LH1 JG *
22/7/74 HARRIS Back on my stomping ground, I wonder who, They don't make them like you anymore (& As the crow flies, 16/9/74). 19/6/74 LH1 JG *
   Rec'd fifth In Concert 20/6/74 HP, TX 29/6/74.

GALLIARD
31/1/70 TOP GEAR Frog galliard, Wrapped her in ribbons, Near dawn breaking, Ask for nothing. Richard Pannell (lg), Geoff Brown (rg), Andrew Abbott (b), Leslie Podraza (d), Lyle Jenkins (ts), David Caswell (tp). 12/1/70 * JW *
23/4/70 HENRY Modern day fairy tale, I wrapped her in ribbons, Ask for nothing. Rec. date unknown * MB MH&MF

GALLON DRUNK
1/9/91 PEEL† Ruby, Some fool's mess, Drag '91, Two wings mambo. Max Decharne (d), Mike Delanian (b), James Johnston (g,o,v), Joe Byfield (maraccas). 14/7/91 MV3 DG DMC&JLB † On Strange Fruit SFMCD213.

MUSICIANS OF THE GAMBIA
15/1/87 KERSHAW Solo (The leopard), Massaneh ceesay, Saliya, Lambango. Dembo konte (kor,v: 1,3 only), Kausu Kouyate (kor,v: 1 only), Pa Jobarteh (2 only), Musicians of the compound of Amaudu Kanuteh (4 only). 12/87 FR: Gambia AK~

GANG OF FOUR
18/1/79 PEEL† I found that essence rare, Return the gift,

5.45, At home he's a tourist. John King (lv,mel), Andy Gill (gv), Dave Allen (bv), Hugo Burnham (dv). /1/79 MV4 BS BAI

9/7/79 PEEL† Natural's not in it, Not great men, Ether, Guns before butter. 2/7/79 * * *

12/3/81 PEEL† Paralysed, History's bunk, To hell with poverty. 9/3/81 LHI PS DD&MPK
    † On Strange Fruit SFRCD107.

12/8/82 JENSEN We live as we dream alone, World at fault, Good boy, History of the world. Gill, King, Burnham, Sara Lee (b,bkv), Edi Reader (v,sy,d). 1/8/82 MV4 DG ME

JESSE GARON AND THE DESPERADOES

11/11/86 LONG Laughing smiling and falling again, Leave you behind, Up on the big wheel, Hank Williams is dead. Frances Schoppler (v), Andrew Tully (g), Stuart Clarke (g), Kevin McMahon (g), Angus McPake (b), Margarita Vazquez Ponte (d). 8/10/86 MV4 BYA MPK&EL

GARRISON

6/7/84 FRI. ROCK On the run, Turn on the night, The first time. Tony Mitchell (bv), Dave Scott (g), Kevin Wilson (g), Mark Hutchinson (d). 8/6/84 * BYA&JWI *

GASS

29/5/70 BLACK Holy woman, Muddy waters, Kulusemama (& Everything's going my way, 24/7/70). Godfrey McLean (d), Robert Tench (v), DeLisle Harper (b), Derek Austin, Michael Piggot. 22/4/70 AO2 JM *
    Passed audition (prod. BA 15/6/66), 1st session for SAT. CLUB of 15/4/67 [M].

14/4/71 BLACK Goats and monkeys, Back to the roots, It could happen to you (& You'll never stop, 21/5/71). Lennox Langton r. Piggot. 18/3/71 T1 JM JWH

GASWORKS

22/1/69 NIGHT RIDE These things I remember, Frankie Rose. John Brown (g), Michael Draper (g). 10/1/69 S1 JM *
    Failed by Audition panel: 'a saddening waste of time'. Re-auditioned 4/9/70, failed again. Rec'd In Concert 15/3/73 PS as Trial Broadcast, TX 17/3/73.

13/9/73 PEEL We three kings, Don't push me, Share it out, I never knew. & Brian Scott (b) [This show presented by Alexis Korner, producer Clive Burrows]. 10/9/73 LHI CB *

18/5/74 ROCK ON We three kings, Keep on rollin', God's great space ship, So long. & Roger Chantler. 22/4/74 LHI BA * [M: Concerts]

DICK GAUGHAN

13/2/73 PEEL The Gillie Mhor, Rattling roaring Willie, Jock of Hazeldean, Fine flowers in the valley. Dick Gaughan (agv). 29/1/73 T1 JW * [M: Folk Shows]

21/11/74 PEEL Farewell to whiskey, Planxty Johnson, Farewell to Sicily, The gypsy laddie. 11/11/74 T1 JW *

2/8/77 PEEL Farewell to whiskey, Freedom come all ye, Rashie Moor, Boys of the Lough, My Donald. 27/7/77 MV4 MB NG

29/5/86 KERSHAW What you've got, Think again, Amandla, Hawks and eagles. 19/5/86 Y2 CG PSM

19/11/87 KERSHAW When I'm gone, Shipwreck, The worker's song, Fifty years from now. 12/11/87 * DG NG&EL

13/1/91 KERSHAW Childhood's end, Dark as a dungeon, Your daughters and your sons, Tom Joad. 4/10/90 MV4 DG TD&MR

GAYE BIKERS ON ACID

11/5/87 LONG† Don't be human Eric - let's be Frank, Ruby red lips, Get on up to get down, Space rape. Mary (Ian Garfield Hoxley) (v), Tony (Richard Anthony Horsfall) (g), Robber (Ian Michael Reynolds) (b), Kevin Hyde (d). 3/5/87 MV4 PW MS
    † On Nighttracks SFNT010.

RON GEESIN

3/7/68 NIGHT RIDE Pretty little faces, Off the left cuff, Yesterday's sheep, Very nostalgic piece, Devised now. Ron Geesin (all instruments, vocals, tapes, effects). 20/6/68 S2 DK *

18/9/68 MY KIND OF FOLK Piano invention, Banjo trilogy. 11/9/68 S2 FL *

9/4/69 NIGHT RIDE The first piece, John's title, Three-quarter-inch plywood cover for VOICE, Out of your time, Virtuoso piece for banjo. 1/4/69 S2 PR CL

11/10/69 TOP GEAR† Agitation in anticipation of offspring (2' 15"), Agitation in anticipation of offspring (3' 25"), Agitation in anticipation of offspring (4' 10"). 19/7/69 MV1 JW TW&MF
    † On 'TOP GEAR' LP BBC Records REC 52S.

19/6/71 TOP GEAR Twist and knit for two guitars, Duet for two and street market, Wrap a keyboard round a plant, The middle of whose night, Duet for one string banjo and water tank. & Geoffrey Mitchell (counter-tenor, 4-only). Rec. Date Unknown RGS RG~

15/11/71 HARRIS A cymbal and much electronics, Got ma black vest on, Which way out, Thank you, Two feet and a mouth. 2,4: 26/10/71; 1,3: Rec. Date Unknown. 2,4: T1; 1,3: RGS PD&RG

6/3/73 PEEL Geesin's 6/8ths, Roll 'em bowl 'em, On through out up, Mr. Peugeot's trot, Upon composition. Rec. Date Unknown RGS RG~

19/9/74 PEEL For sale, Where the daffodils do thrive (Two part beneficial flop), Two travel moments, Paddling steamers across high teacups, Nuts bolts several guitars, Animal autos, Evaporated ballroom, Jagged prance, Brain twirl. 1 & 9: poems; 2-7: film soundtrack excerpts. Rec. Date Unknown RGS RG~

20/2/76 PEEL Ab Db & Gb black major throb, White note of calm, Romanian ragtime strut, Smoked hips, Tomorrow's people on the move today (from ballet music for 'Spaceship Earth'). Rec. Date Unknown RGS RG~

GENE LOVES JEZEBEL

30/6/83 JENSEN Sticks and stones, Bruises, Upstairs, Scheming. Julie-Ann (b), Ian Hudson (lg), Dick Hawkins (d), Ja (gv), Mike Aston (lv), Kymille (v). 16/6/83 MV4 JP AP

26/9/83 PEEL Pop tarantula, Brittle punches, Upstairs, Screaming for Emmalene. Steve Radwell (b) r. Julie-Ann. 17/9/83 MV4 DG MC

24/5/84 PEEL Waves, Shame, Five below. Kymille out. 12/5/84 MV5 DG MR

GENERAL PUBLIC

13/3/84 JENSEN Hot you cool, Burning bright, As a matter of fact. Ranking Roger (v,perc), Dave Wakeling (gv), Horace Panter (b), Stoker (d), Micky Billingham (k), Mick Jones (g). 26/2/84 MV5 DG ME

GENERATION X

20/4/77 PEEL Day by day, Listen!, Youth youth youth, Your generation. Billy Idol (lv), Bob Andrews (gv), Tony James (bv), John Towe (d). 12/4/77 MV4 JG MR

21/7/77 PEEL From the heart, Rock on, Gimme some truth, No no no. Mark Laff (d) r. Towe; Idol (g-3 only). 12/7/77 MV4 JG MR

22/8/77 DLT Day by day, No no no, Your generation, Rock on. 12/8/77 MV5 PR *

27/6/78 JENSEN Shakin' all over, King Kong, One hundred punks. 12/6/78 MV5 PR ME

14/2/79 PEEL Paradise west, Love like fire, Night of the Cadillacs, English dream. 15/1/79 MV4 TW DD

GENESIS

1/4/70 NIGHT RIDE The Shepherd, Let us now make love, Stagnation, Looking for someone, Dusk, Pacidy. Peter Gabriel (v,fl), Tony Banks (k), Mike Rutherford (b,gv), Anthony Phillips (g), Jonathan Mayhew (d). 22/2/70 MV4 ARD NG
    'I rate this group very highly' wrote ARD on his report to the panel. They agreed: 'intriguing tone colours', 'enthusiastic' pass.

31/5/71 HARRIS Musical box, Stagnation. Steve Hackett (g), Phil Collins (d,bkv), r. Phillips, Mayhew. 10/5/71 T1 PD ARV

28/1/72 PEEL Return of the giant hogweed, Harold the barrel, The fountain of Salmacis (& Harlequin, 17/3/72). 9/1/72 T1 JM NG
    Rec'd In Concert 2/3/72 PS, TX 11/3/72.

7/11/72 PEEL Watcher of the skies, Twilight alehouse, Get them out by Friday. 25/9/72 T1 JW BC

GENEVA

23/3/90 FRI. ROCK† Shoot, Out of the fire, Don't listen, Coming home. Jamie Stewart (v), Don Doncaster (d), Ady Lawton-Taylor (b), Mick Forest (g), Richard Ashley (g). 9/3/90 MV5 TW DD
    † On SWIS52, 'Climbing the mountains'.

GENTLE GIANT

17/3/70 SYMMONDS Isn't it quiet and cold, City hermit, Freedom's child. Phil Shulman (ts,tp,fl,v), Derek Shulman (gbv,hca), Ray Shulman (gbv,vi,tp), Kerry Minnear (k,vi,clo,perc,v), Gary Green (lg), Martin Smith (d). 21/7/70 PH BA *
    Contracts file claims band did their first session for WOGAN, rec'd 29/6/70. Untraceable on PasBs.

8/12/70 HARDING Home town special, Nothing at all, Funny ways. 1/12/70 MV5 MB MH&MF

7/1/72 PEEL Alucard, Plain truth, Giant (& Funny ways, 4/2/72). Malcolm Mortimer (d) r. Smith. 12/12/71 T1 PD *

14/7/72 PEEL Mr Class and Quality, Prologue, Schooldays. John Weathers (d) r. Mortimer. 13/6/72 T1 JM *

5/9/72 PEEL Plain truth, The advent of Panurge, Funny ways. 8/8/72 MV4 PR BC

14/12/72 PEEL Prologue, The advent of Panurge, Cry for everyone. 11/12/72 LHI BA *

28/9/73 SEQUENCE Way of life, The advent of Panurge, The runaway. Phil Shulman out. 28/8/73 LHI JM *

8/1/74 PEEL Excerpts from Octupus, Way of life. 4/12/73 LHI TW BC

1/7/74 HARRIS So sincere, Aspirations, Playing the game, The face. 29/5/74 * JG *

17/12/74 PEEL Proclamation, Experience, Aspirations, Cogs in cogs. 10/12/74 * TW *

13/10/75 PEEL Just the same, Free hand, On reflection. 16/9/75 MV4 * BAI

GENTLEMEN

8/5/76 FREEMAN Waiting to die, No looking back, Just a child. Howard Kingston (lv), Roger Jackson (k,bkv), Rick Fenn (g), Roger Dann (b,bkv), David George (d). 22/4/76 MV4 TW *

THE GENTS

30/7/83 LONG Stay with me, Revenge, Cowboy, She's got something. * 18/7/83 PHM c.JL PSM

GEORDIE

27/4/73 SEQUENCE Don't do that, Hope you like it, Keep on rockin', Mercenary man. Vic Malcolm, Brian Gibson, Brian Johnson (v), Tom Hill. 3/4/73 T1 JM NG [M: daytime]

9/7/82 FRI. ROCK No sweat, So you lose again, Rock 'n' roll, Move away. Malcolm, Gibson, Hill, Rob Turnbull (v), David Stephenson (g). 25/6/82 * JW DD

GEORGE AND MARTHA

12/12/88 PEEL I understand, Burn, Machine, Wretch. Stephan M. (v), Chris M. (g), Stefan Muller (b), Frank Seele (d). 6/12/88 MV4 DG MR

ROBIN GEORGE

25/1/85 FRI. ROCK Dangerous music, Shoot on sight, Hit list, No news is good news. Robin George (gv), Hugh Lucas (g), Phil Soussan (b), Keks (d). 14/12/84 MV4 TW DD

GERRY AND THE PACEMAKERS

24/4/73 PEEL Ferry cross the Mersey, How do you do it, You'll never walk alone. Gerry Marsden (gv), Billy Kinsley (b), Joe McLaughlin (p), Pete Clarke (d). 17/4/73 LHI * *
    A one-off. 'Must have been one of Peel's funny periods' JW. Band did many Light Programme sessions in 60s.

GETTING THE FEAR

21/11/83 JENSEN *Fatal date, Death is bigger, Dune buggy attack, Last salute.* Bee (v), Aky (d), Barry (b), Buzz (g,cl,b). 10/11/83 MV4 JP GP

21/11/84 LONG *Yurune, Coming down fast, Sometimes, Swell.* 31/10/84 MV5 JS MPK

GHOST

15/10/70 HENRY *I wander in my garden, In heaven, Time is my enemy, Hearts and flowers.* Shirley Kent, Paul Eastment, Charlie Crima, Daniel MacGuire, Terry Guy. 8/10/70 AO2 MB MH&MF

GHOST DANCE

16/4/86 LONG *Last train, Can the can, Only the broken hearted, River of no return.* Anne Marie (v), Steve Smith (gv), Gary Marx (gv), Etch (b). 6/4/86 MV4 BYA *

28/10/87 LONG *Born to be your slave, I will wait, Dr Love (This heart's on fire), If only you were here now.* Anne-Marie, Marx, Etch, Richard Steel (g,bkv), John Grant (d,bkv). 14/10/87 MV4 PW MPK

GIANT

27/4/90 FRI. ROCK *I can't get close enough, It takes two, Stranger to me, No way out.* Daniel Huff, David Huff, Alan Pasqua, Michael Brignardello, Thomas Oakley. 13/3/90 BRM TW DD

GIANT SAND

11/3/90 KERSHAW *Searchlight, Trickle down system, Romance of falling, Still too far.* Howe Gelb (v,gp), Mark Walton (b,bkv), John Convertino (d,bkv). 8/2/90 MV5 DG MR

STEVE GIBBONS BAND

30/7/76 PEEL *Rollin', Tupelo Mississippi flash, Johnny Cool, Spark of love.* Steve Gibbons (lv), Bob Wilson (gv), Dave Carroll (gv), Trevor Burton (bv), Bob Lamb (d). 20/7/76 MV4 JG MR

3/3/77 PEEL *Right side of heaven/Rollin' on, Please don't say goodbye, One of the boys.* 21/2/77 MV4 TW DD

4/7/77 PEEL *Tulane, The music plays on, Gave his life to rock'n roll, Boppin' the blues.* 27/6/77 MV4 TW DD

GILBERT

19/5/68 TOP GEAR *You, What can I do, Disappear, My front door, Come on home (& I don't know what to do, Better than Valentino, 16/6/68).* Gilbert O'Sullivan (pv; solo-5,6,7), & The Keith Mansfield Orchestra (16). 14/5/68 PCI BA DT&AH

GILGAMESH

26/9/74 PEEL *One end more, Arriving twice, Lady and friend, Not withstanding.* * 19/9/74 LHI JM BAI&MG

3/11/75 PEEL *Jamo, Island of Rhodes.* Alan Gowen (k), Phil Lee (g), Jeff Clyne (b), Michael Travis (d,perc). 11/9/75 MV4 TW *

GILLAN

7/5/82 FRI. ROCK *No laughing in heaven, Hadely bop bop, Vengeance, M.A.D., Born to kill.* Ian Gillan (v), Colin Towns (k), Janick Gers (g), John McCoy (b), Mick Underwood (d). 23/4/82 Kingsway Studios TW DD

GIRL

25/1/80 FRI. ROCK *Do you love me, My number, Lovely Lorraine, You really got me.* Phil Collen (lg), Phillip Lewis (lv), Gerry Laffy (g), Simon Laffy (b), Dave Gaynor (d). 9/1/80 * TW *

GIRLS AT OUR BEST

23/2/81 SKINNER *Fast boyfriends, One hundred thousand pounds, I'm beautiful now, Pleasure.* Judy Evans (v), Gerard Swift (b), Carl Harper (d), James Allan (g). 13/2/81 LHI DG PW

23/2/81 PEEL† *China blue, This train, Getting beautiful warm gold fast from nowhere.* 17/2/81 LHI DG MR
† On Strange Fruit SFPS029.

GIRLSCHOOL

1/8/80 FRI. ROCK *Take it all away, Breakdown, Demolition, Nothin' to lose.* Kelly Johnson (lgv), Kim McAuliffe (gv), Denise Dufort (d), Di Williams (bv). 28/5/80 * TW *

26/1/81 SKINNER *Yeah right, The hunter, Kick it down, Watch your step.* 16/1/81 LHI DG *

14/11/86 FRI. ROCK *Play with fire, Turn it up, Never too late, All day all night.* McAuliffe, Dufort, Cris Bonacci (lg), Gil Weston-Jones (b). 17/10/86 MV4 TW *

22/5/92 FRI. ROCK *Good girl, One more, We came.* Jackie (b) r. Gil. 1/5/92 MV4 DD~ MC

GLASGOW

6/1/84 FRI. ROCK *Heat of the night, Shine on me, No way out, Stranded.* Mick Boyle (v), Archie Dickson (g), Neil Russell (b), Joe Kilna (d). 16/12/83 * TW DD

THE GLASS MENAGERIE

6/5/68 SYMONDS *Need somebody to love, She's a rainbow (7/5), Light my fire (8/5), Run out of time (9/5).* William Atkinson (d), Alan Kendall (lg), Keith O'Connell (o,p,v), John Medley (bv), Ian Stonebridge (lv,hca) [M]. 26/4/68 PCI * *

23/6/68 TOP GEAR *One more heartache, You didn't have to be so nice, Love me two times (& Dear Mr Fantasy, 21/7/68).* 5/6/68 MV4 BA *

9/3/69 TOP GEAR *Putting it off 'til another day, Do you ever think, Life is getting it together, She came from hell.* O'Connell out. 21/1/69 PCI BA AH

GLASS TORPEDOES

24/1/80 PEEL *Forced a smile, Something, Tall stories, This is the end.* Barbara Donovan (v), Mark Coleridge (dv), Gary Daly (b), Paul Reason (lg). 9/1/80 * JE NG

THE GLAXO BABIES

26/4/79 PEEL *It's irrational, Who killed Bruce Lee, Burning, She went to pieces.* Robert Chapman (rg,lv), Dan Catsis (g,bkv), Tom Nichols (b), Geoff Allsop (d), Tony Wraften (sx,bkv). 17/4/79 MV4 JS MR

Robert Chapman is now the author of the highly-recommended 'Selling the Sixties: The Pirates and Pop Music Radio' (Routledge, 1992).

4/3/80 PEEL *Jihad, Limited entertainment, Permission to be wrong, There'll be no room for you in the shelters.* Nichols, Catsis, Charlie Llewelyn (sy,d,v), Tim Aylett (v,perc), Alan Jones (g,sy,v). 19/2/80 MV4 JE MR

THE GLEE CLUB AND THE MATTERHORNS

25/3/87 LONG *Repo man, Glee bug, I've got you under my skin, She.* Adrian Utley (g), Steven Manley (g), Clive Deamer (d,lv), Neil Deamer (db). 18/3/87 MV4 DG MPK&FK

GLENCOE

17/10/72 PEEL *Airport, Look me in the eye, Telephonia, It's.* John Turnbull (g), Norman Watt-Roy (b), Graham Maitland (o,p), Stewart Francis (d). 12/9/72 MV4 PR BC

2/11/72 PEEL *Look me in the eye, Watching the rivers flow, Lifeline.* 16/10/72 LHI BA *

10/5/73 PEEL *Born in the city, Is it you, Roll on bliss (& Two on an island in search of a new world, 31/5/73).* 30/4/73 LHI BA *

15/11/73 PEEL *Roll on bliss, To divine mother, It's, Airport.* 5/11/73 LHI BA BAI

GLOBAL VILLAGE TRUCKING COMPANY

2/5/74 PEEL *Apple pie, The sun can always catch you with your trousers down, Watch out there's a mind about.* Jon Owen (lv,rg), Mike Medora (lg), Jimmy Lascelles (elp,o), Jon McKenzie (b), Simon Stewart (d). 11/4/74 LHI TW *

16/9/74 HARRIS *Smiling revolution, Short change/Tall story, Lasga's form.* 28/8/74 LHI JG *

7/11/74 PEEL *Sky train, On the judgement day, Down in the lowlands.* 24/10/74 MV4 * *

9/6/75 PEEL *Love will find a way, Cock of the rocks, I never knew.* Pete Kirtley (lg) r. Medora. 27/5/75 MV4 * *

GLORY

30/10/87 FRI. ROCK *Let me see, Dare I say, As it is, Never no, Sporting life.* Dough Palfreeman, Dave Burke, Paul Burns, Andy Rawmsley. 29/8/87 MV4 TW *

GMC

29/10/85 LONG *Shining star, GMC, Big bad cow, What you see is what you get.* Bruce Smith (d), David Wright (sx), Neneh Cherry (v), Nick Straker (k), Paget King

(k), Alan Dias (b), Francois Cuffy (g), David De Fries (tp). 23/9/85 MV5 BYA MPK

GNIDROLOG

24/4/71 TOP GEAR *My room, Time and space, Saga of Smith and Smythe.* Stewart Goldring (lg,mnd), Colin Goldring (rgv,hca,rec), Nigel Pegrum (d,fl,ob), Peter Cowling (b). 13/4/71 MV4 BC

Passed audition rec'd 7/12/70 (prod. PR)

9/3/72 DRUMMOND *Peter, Snails, In spite of Henry's toenail.* 1/3/72 MV4 MB MH&MF

GO HOLE

23/11/87 PEEL *Bayonet practice, Treacherous, I'll be waiting.* Les Clarke (g,lv), John Mason (b,bkv), Matt Wrigley (d,bkv). 17/11/87 * DG MC&JB

THE GO-BETWEENS

5/8/82 PEEL *Near the chimney, Metal and shells, Ask, A peaceful wreck.* Robert Forster (gv), Grant McLennan (bv), Lindy Morrison (d). 14/7/82 MV4 RP NG

5/1/84 JENSEN *Bachelor kisses, Part company, The old way out, Just a king in mirrors.* Robert Vickers (b) joins. 10/12/83 MV4 DG ME

29/10/84 PEEL† *The power that I now have, Secondhand furniture, Five words, Rare breed.* 21/10/84 MV5 DG ME
† On Strange Fruit SFPCD074.

6/5/86 LONG *Head full of steam, Casanova's last words, I work in a health spa, Apology accepted.* & Dean Brodrick (k). 9/4/86 MV4 BYA *

26/3/87 KERSHAW *Spirit of the vampyre, Don't call me gone, The house Jack Kerouac built, Bye bye pride.* * 13/3/87 * * *

GOBLIN

14/8/72 HARRIS *Take what you need, She's mine, Hammer falls, Grave robber.* Jeffrey Davis (gv), Roderick William Gordon (gv), Robin Sylvester (b,p). 11/7/72 MV5 JG *

GOD MACHINE

29/5/92 PEEL *Commitment, Desert song, Double dare, Pictures of a bleeding boy.* Ron Austin (d), Jimmy Fernandez (b), Robin Proper Sheppard (gv). 21/4/92 MV4 MR~

THE GODFATHERS

21/11/85 KERSHAW *John Barry, This damn nation, Lonely man, Sun arise.* George Mazur (d,perc,bkv), Mike Gibson (g,bkv), Kris Dolimore (g,bkv), Chris Coyne (b,bkv), Peter Coyne (lv). 31/10/85 Y2 CG PSM

19/5/86 LONG† *If only I had time, I want everything, I'm unsatisfied, I want you.* 4/5/86 MV4 AJ SC
† On Nighttracks SNTCD019.

6/10/87 LONG *S.T.B, The strangest boy, 'Cos I said so, It's so hard.* 27/9/87 MV4 HP TdB&SC

28/7/88 KERSHAW *Those days are over, Just because you're paranoid doesn't mean, Half paralysed, How low is low.* 14/7/88 MV4 DG NG

GODFLESH

27/9/89 PEEL *Tiny tears, Wound (not wound), Pulp, Like rats.* 'G' Christion Green (b), Justin Broadrick (g,v,prg), Kevin (sx-3 only). 27/8/89 MV3 DG ME

THE GOLDEN HORDE

9/6/86 LONG *Codeine, Cry baby, Paula, Gatecrashing your mind.* Simon Carmody (v), Bernie Furlong (bkv), Sam Steiger (g), Des O'Byrne (g), John Conners (b), Peter O'Kennedy (d). 28/5/86 MV5 BYA MPK

9/6/87 LONG *Endless weekend, Last night's fun, She's a wierdo, It is I/I live for the sun.* Furlong out. 24/5/87 MV4 HP TdB

JOHN GOLDING

2/7/74 PEEL *Oh boy, Here's to the summer day, Believe what you feel, Do you really need to keep on asking.* John Golding (gv), & (bj,mnd) unknown. 10/6/74 TI * &DD

15/7/74 HARRIS *Oh boy, It only hurts when you laugh, I might change, It's true.* 12/6/74 LHI JG *

20/2/75 PEEL *Loving is a one-sided thing, Good luck and*

love to you, What they say about you, Those "being
far away from you" blues. 13/2/75 MV4 * *

GONE TO EARTH
30/1/86 KERSHAW Lubyanka stomp, Gates of heaven, Never
come back, No work today. David Robinson (gv,perc),
Harry Hutchinson (d), David Thom (b,mnd,ag), David
Clarke (fd,v), Tudor (g), Brenda Kenny (v,perc).
10/1/86 Y2 SP SR

GONG
17/11/71 PEEL Magic brother, Clarence, Tropical fish.
Contracted as 'Kevin Ayers, Daevid Allen and The
Gong': Kevin Ayers (bgv), Daevid Allen (gv), Gilly Smith
(v), Pip Pyle (d), Didier Malherbe (sx), Christian Tritsch.
9/11/71 MV4 JW BC

12/6/73 PEEL Can't kill me, Radio gnome direct
broadcast/Crystal machine, Zero the hero and the
orgasm witch. Allen, Smith, Malherbe, Mike Howlett (b),
Steve Hillage (g), Pierre Moerlen (d), Tim Blake (sy).
29/5/73 MV4 PR BC

29/1/74 PEEL Radio gnome, Oily way. Rob Tate (d), Di
Stewart (perc,v) r. Moerlen. 15/1/74 LHI TW *

GONZALES
3/9/74 PEEL Put it where you want it, Ugly man, Run to
the nearest exit, Clapham South, A day in the life.
'with Viola Wills' (lv) & Roy Davies (elp), De Lisle
Harper (b), Gordon Hunte (lg), Steve Ferrone (d), Alan
Sharpe (cga,perc), Ron Carthy (tp), Steve Gregory
(sx,fl), Chris Mercer (ts), Geoff Beadle (bars), Michael
Eves (ts), (1,4-Wills out). 20/8/74 LHI PR *

21/11/74 PEEL Adelanto Nightride, No way, Skyscraper,
Pack it up. Davies, Harper, Hunte, Gregory, Mercer,
Beadle, Eves, Carthy, George Chandler (v), Glenn Le
Fleur (d), Robert Stignac (cga,perc), Robert Ahwai (rg).
7/11/74 MV4 TW *

11/11/75 PEEL Baby please rescue me, What's going on,
Stuck on you, Remember me. 'with Viola Wills' (lv);
Malcolm Griffiths, Larry Steele, Richard Bailey (d), r.
Harper, Sharpe, Ferrone, Gregory, Beadle. 2/10/75 MV4
TW BAI [M: daytime, minus Wills]

CELINA GONZALES
11/2/88 KERSHAW Mison es un misterio, Yo soy el punto
Cubano, Alla voy, A toda Cuba le gusta. Celina
Gonzalez (v), Reutilio Junior (v), Félix Martinez (b,md),
José Herrera (g), Francicso Rodriguez & Barbara Torres
(bkv), Raul Maria Rodriguez (tp,bkv), Mario Oropesa
(mrm), Rolando Garcia (ti), José Maria Rodriguez (bgo),
Calixto Campos (cga). 21/1/88 * DG MR&TD

GOOD HABIT
4/1/73 PEEL I am and so are you, I'm going down, Ship
of gold, The only place left to be. Ian Thomson (sx,fl),
Paul Steward (d), Alan Collier (gv), Philip Blackmore
(gv), John Roberts (sx), David Land (bv). 18/12/72 LHI BA *

GOODBYE MR MACKENZIE
2/12/86 LONG Born leaders, Goodbye Mr Mackenzie, Wake
it up, His master's voice. Martin Metcalfe (gv), Shirley
Manson (kv), Rhona Scobie (kv), Derek Kelly (d); &
Callum Slythe (b). 12/11/1986 MV4 BYA MPK

PHILLIP GOODHAND-TAIT
9/1/71 R2 NIGHT RIDE In my world, Oh Rosanna, Fire and
rain, One road, When tomorrow comes, Jeannie. Philip
Goodhand-Tait (pv), with Hookfoot. 11/12/70 * DDR BTN

13/3/71 R2 NIGHT RIDE In the old country, Oh Rosanna,
Children of the last war, Bird on a wire, Cold night.
27/1&5/2/71 AO2 DDR BTN

25/3/71 HENRY Silver wing, Cold night, When tomorrow
comes, Oh Rosanna (& In my world, 22/4/71) With
Hookfoot: Caleb Quaye (g), Ian Duck (v), Roger Pope
(d), Dave Glover (b), Peter Ross (unknown).
17/3/71 MV4 MB MH&MF

5/9/71 SPEAKEASY Everyday, I think I'll write a song, In the
old country, Who laid your living down. 3/9/71 S2 TBS *

17/8/72 DRUMMOND Child of Jesus, Everyday, City streets,
Moon. &2 (unknown). 7/8/72 * MB MH&MF

21/11/72 PEEL Child of Jesus, Leon, When will I be loved,
Raining rain. 24/10/72 * * BC

3/12/72 SPEAKEASY Will you still love me tomorrow?, When
that day comes, Sugar train. 1/12/72 PS TB *

1/4/73 SOUNDS ON SUNDAY Everyday, 5 flight walk up, You
are, Leon, Warm summer rain, Sugar train, When that
day comes. 16/3/73 PH TB *

21/9/73 SEQUENCE Warm summer rain, One more rodeo, I
think I can believe, Sugar train, You are.
7/8/73 T1 JM BAI&MG

12/3/74 PEEL Almost killed a man, Ready willing and able,
Jesus don't only love the cowboys, Everybody's gone
away. 12/2/74 LHI * * [M]

GORE
4/11/87 PEEL Axe of revenge, Loaded, Mean man's dream,
Chainsaw, The arena. Peter Deswart (g), Danny Arnold
(d), Marij Hel (b). 27/10/87 * HP TdB

6/12/88 PEEL The breeding, In the garden of evil. Arnold,
Hel, Joes Bently (g), Frankie Stoo (g).
29/11/88 MV4 DG MR

21/9/91 PEEL Rustproof rape, Waste taste, Treat, No
respect. Hel, Bardo Maria (d), Van Reede (g).
9/7/91 MV5 JB~ PA

THE GOSPEL
1/12/86 LONG Wear the right tag, Isolation, Spirit, Gospel.
Michael (bv), Gary (d,bkv), Will (lg,tp), John (k,perc).
9/11/86 MV4 AS MS

JOHN GOURD
6/11/68 NIGHT RIDE A funny love affair, Sitting in a den,
Small minority, Thank you kindly, Through the leaves.
John Gourd (agv). 6/11/68 S2 PC *

GRACE IN DANGER
31/1/92 FRI. ROCK Boom town, Gypsy's kiss, Valley of the
shadows, Trouble. Mark Garfield (d), Chris Powell (g),
Grahame Farr (g), William Garbutt, Keiran Shannon (v).
10/1/92 MV5 TW DD

GRAFFITI
7/9/90 FRI. ROCK If you want love, Shine a light, Is it
really love. Rick Chase (v), Marcus Flynn (g), Jim Page
(b), Tony Stock (k), Adrian Todd (d). 24/8/90 MV5 DD~

GRAPEFRUIT
21/1/68 TOP GEAR Breaking up a dream, Dear Delilah, The
dead boot, Trying to make it Monday. Peter
Sweetenham (rg), Geoffrey Sweetenham (d), John Perry
(lg,o), George Alexander (b); & David Katz for 11
musicians, Bill Shepherd (md).
15/1/68 PCI BA * [M: daytime]

GREGORY GRAY
26/3/86 LONG Sensual, Seatown, Johnny Purley, James
Bond. Gregory Gray (lv), Ivor Goldberg (g), Lyn
Edmondson (b), Kelvin Christiane (sx), Rodney Wallis
(k), Tony Scantilbury (d). 19/3/86 MV4 BYA MPK

THE GREASE BAND
11/6/71 BLACK Believe in what you believe, Willie and the
pig, Peyton Place boogie (& Let it be gone, 9/7/71).
Bruce Rowlands (d), Henry McCullough (g), Alan
Spenner (b), Neil Hubbard (g). 26/4/71 T1 PD BH

THE GREAT CRASH
14/8/73 PEEL She throws it all away, Hero of the beach,
Regimental reunion. Nick Smith (g), Al Grey (kv),
George Benn (bv), Piers Geddes (dv). 7/8/73 LHI JW *

THE GREAT LEAP FORWARD
8/6/87 PEEL Propping up the nose of the king, Hope's not
enough son - ask your parents, Haranguing the
boisterous buffoons, When it's cold in summer. Nobby
Normal (d), Arty Farty (bkv,hn), Padraig Byrne (b),
Helvetica Halbfett (gv). 24/5/87 * DG ME&MA

8/2/88 PEEL How to be successful in a world of failure,
Cursing this audacity, A peck on the cheek à la
politique, The original sin. Nobby Normal (d), John
Sargeant (b), Eileen Cox (k), Big Al (gv).
26/1/88 * DG MR&MC

GREAT NORTHERN ELECTRICS
10/12/90 GOODIER Rosemary, Sunday's child, Here come
that man, I want you. Tim Harrison (b), Nick King (g),
Simon Lacey (lv,k), Steven Sidelnyk (d).
28/11/90 MV5 MC~

GREATEST SHOW ON EARTH
5/5/70 HARDING Border line, Mountain song, Time. Laurent
'Tex' Philpotts (ts), Garth Watt-Roy (gv), Mick Deacon
(o), Ron Prudence (d), Dick Hanson (tp), Ian Aitcheson
(ts), Norman Watt-Roy (b), Colin Horton-Jennings
(lv,fl,g). 28/4/70 MV4 MB MH&MF
    Failed audition 27/8/68. Passed trial b'cast for
    WALKER 14/2/70 [M].

3/11/70 HARDING The leader, Check me into my life. *
27/10/70 * MB MH&MF

GREAVES-BLEGVAD
10/1/78 PEEL Mostly twins and trios, From the trees to the
wheel, Actual frenzy. Andy Ward (d,glo-3), John
Greaves (b,pv), Anthony Moore (sy), Peter Blegvad (gv),
Tom Newman (g). "All numbers specially written for
Peel". 13/12/77 MV4 MB MR

GREEN HOUSE OF TERROR
10/4/86 KERSHAW Black bugs blood, Ruth, Graveyard shift,
Anywhere out of this world. Guy Greenhough (lv),
James Harries (g,bkv), Pat Banning (g,bkv), Mark
Baines (d), Simon Shaw (b). 19/3/86 SS CG TWN

GREEN ON RED
14/11/85 KERSHAW Don't shine your light on me, Everybody
loves to play the fool, Mighty fine day, Down to the
bone. Dan Stuart (gv), Chris Cacavas (kv), Chuck
Prophet IV (gv), Jack Waterson (b), Keith Mitchell (d).
6/11/85 Y2 CG PSM

9/4/87 KERSHAW That's what dreams, We ain't free, Sorry
Naomi, Jimmy boy, No man's land. & Victoria & Breeze
(v). 24/3/87 * MRD SR

23/4/89 KERSHAW Busted, Are you sure Hank done it this
way, D T Blues, Fading away. Prophet, Stuart, Rene
Coman (b), Brent Newman (d), & Sally Burke (acc-1
only). 6/4/89 WX DG MWT
    'The band brought along a guest player, a 16-year-
old accordion player called Sally Burke. She played on
one song, "Busted" and made a major contribution to
that title. You may feel that this is worth a single
session fee" DG to JW on back of session sheet.

THE GREEN TELESCOPE
23/1/86 KERSHAW X+Y=13, Who knows, Horror asparagus
stories, Try to. Lenny Helsing (gd,v,perc), Bruce Lyall
(o,bkv), Alan McLean (b,bkv), Martin Montgomery
(bkv,perc). 11/1/86 Y2 CG SR

GREENHOUSE
3/3/91 PEEL Ban the car, Rules, New world order, Her too.
Tom Kincaid (d,bkv), Rob England (b,bkv), Simon King
(g,bkv), John Parkes (gv). 5/2/91 MV5 MR~

GREENSLADE
29/1/73 HARRIS Feathered friends, Temple song, An English
western. Dave Greenslade (k), Dave Lawson (elp,o),
Tony Reeves (b), Andy McCulloch (d). 10/1/73 LHI PR *

3/12/73 HARRIS Time to dream, Bedside manners are extra,
Pilgrim's progress. 31/10/73 LHI JG *

16/12/74 HARRIS Melange, Melancholic race, Red light.
6/11/74 MV4 JG *

MICK GREENWOOD
20/12/71 WALKER Taxi, To the sea, Charlie. Mick
Greenwood (agv), Jerry Donahue (lg), Pat Donaldson
(b), Tony Cox (p, VCS3 synthesiser), Barry De Sousa
(d). 3/12/71 MV4 PR *

20/1/72 DRUMMOND Friend of mind, To the sea, After the
First World War (& Charlie, 9/3/72). Gerry Conway r.
Donaldson. 10/1/72 MV5 MB MH&MF
    One more session for WALKER, rec'd 20/7/72 AO2, TX
7/8/72, on which Dave Peacock r. Conway.

CLIVE GREGSON AND CHRISTINE COLLISTER
9/1/86 KERSHAW That same mistake, Unlucky in love, All

because of you, It's all just talk. Clive Gregson (gv, lv-
1,3), Christine Collister (v,lv-2,4). 19/12/85 Y2 IW TWN

GREYHOUND
14/8/71 Viv Stanshall's Radio Flashes *54-46 was my number,
Moon walk, Black and white, Singer man.* Sonny Binns
(o,p), Trevor White (b), Earl Dunn (lg), Danny Smith
(d), Glenroy Oakley (v). 29/6/71 MV4 JW BC
    After failing two previous auditions under other
names, finally passed with this session [M: daytime].

GRIFFIN
1/11/69 Top Gear *What a day it's been, The shine, My
head your lies.* Peter Kirtley (g), Colin Gibson (b),
Graham Bell (pv), Kenny Craddock (o), Alan White (d).
21/10/69 MV4 JW BC

NANCI GRIFFITH
2/6/88 Kershaw *Listen to the radio, Trouble in the fields,
Love wore a halo, Love at the five and dime, I would
give you Ireland.* Nanci Griffith (gv) & Philip Donay,
James Breen, James Hooker Brown, Denny Biksby.
19/5/88 MV4 DG MR
17/8/91 Sat. Seq. *If wishes were horses, It's a hard life
wherever you go, It's too late, It's just another
morning here.* Solo. 7/8/91, Egton House.

CAROL GRIMES
18/7/74 Peel *Somebody's sleeping in my bed, That's what
it takes, Give it everything you've got, A change is
gonna come.* Carol Grimes (v), Tim Hinckley (p), Neil
Hubbard (g), Alan Spenner (b), Ian Wallace (d), Mel
Collins (sx). 4/7/74 LH1 TW *

GROOVALAX
1/5/84 Jensen *Tears, It couldn't happen here, Hot (Living
in England), More of a man.* Tim Brinkhurst (gv),
Jacqueline Cuff (v), Pauline Cuff (v), Bob Morris (bv),
Henry Morris (d). 19/4/84 MV4 MHY MPK

THE GROOVE FARM
8/4/87 Long *Captain Fantastic, Baby blue marine, Danny
says, Get out of my life, Turning me upside down.*
Darren (d), Chad (b), Jon (g), Andrew (g,lv).
25/3/87 MV5 DG MPK&SC

STEFAN GROSSMAN
5/6/68 Night Ride *Mississippi blues, I'm so glad, All my
friends are gone, Requiem (for Pat Kilroy), You're
gonna be sorry.* Stefan Grossman (g). 5/6/68 S1 DK *
5/12/70 Raven's R&B *Hot dog, Soldier's dream, Make
believe stunt, That's no way to get along, Mississippi
blues No. 2.* 28/10/70 * JG JY

GROUNDATION
16/4/81 Peel *Forward, Judgement, Rebel, Juganout.* Dave
Miller (d), Henry Forde (rg), George Jeffers (b), Ellis
Paul (k), Franklin Jeffers (lg), Terence Browne (lv),
Robert Charlse (sx). 23/3/81 LH1 PS DD

THE GROUNDHOGS
7/3/70 WS R&B *Mistreated, Garden, Eccentric man.* Tony
McPhee (gv), Peter Cruickshank (b), Ken Pustelnick (d).
4/2/70 MV4 JG JY
28/7/70 Harding *Cherry red, Still a fool, Garden.*
21/7/70 MV5 MB MH&MF
    Group's UK trial broadcast was John Peel Concert
rec'd 14/5/70 PS, TX 24/5/70.   .
12/9/70 Top Gear *Eccentric man, Mistreated, Strange town
(& Gasoline, 21/11/70).* 4/8/70 MV4 JW TW
24/10/70 Raven's R&B *Blind deaf and dumb, Groundhog
blues, No more doggin'.* 30/9/70 MV4 JG JY
20/2/71 Top Gear *Split pt.1, Split pt.2, A year in the life,
Split pt.4.* 16/2/71 MV4 * BC
27/2/71 Raven's R&B *Cherry red, Still a fool, Groundhog
blues.* 17/2/71 MV4 MB *
6/4/71 Harding *Cherry red, Eccentric, Split pt.1.*
29/3/71 MV5 MB MH&MF
17/8/71 Harding *Split pt.1, Cherry red, Eccentric (& Split
pt.2, Mistreated, 7/9/71).* 26/7/71 MV5 MB MH&MF
14/3/72 Peel *Earth is not room enough, Wages of peace,*

Music is the food of thought, Bogroll blues.
29/2/72 MV4 * *
6/4/72 Drummond *Earth is not room enough, Music is the
food of thought, Amazing grace.* 29/3/72 * MB MH&MF
2/2/73 Sequence *I love Miss Ogeny, Living in the past, Split
pt.3.* Clive Brooks (d) r. Pustelnick. 2/1/73 T1 JM&PD NG
13/3/75 Peel *Light my light, I love Miss Ogyny, Soldier.*
6/3/75 MV4 PR *
    Several In Concerts recorded in early 70s.

GROWN UP STRANGE
6/3/86 Kershaw *When you became that summer, My dream
and I, Kitty come home, Wing and a prayer.* Mokka
(gv), Bendy (b), Dave Williams (k), Michael Grant (d).
19/2/86 Y2 NB PSM

GRUPPO SPORTIVO
13/6/78 Peel *Beep beep love, Rock'n'roll, Girls never
know, I shot my manager.* Hans Vandenburg (g,lv), Eric
Whermeyer (b), Peter Calicher (k), Max Mollinger
(d),"the Gruppettes: Meiue Touw (bkv), Josee Van Iersel
(bkv)". 5/6/78 MV4 TW DD

GRYPHON
21/8/72 Harris *Kemp's jig, Sir Gavin Grimbold, Astrologer,
Estampie.* Brian Gullard (bsn,b,krumhorn), Graeme
Taylor (g,mnd), David Oberle (d,glo), Richard Harvey
(rec,k,hmn). 18/7/72 MV5 JG *
    Debuted live on Country Meets Folk 29/4/72, prod.
BB.
25/6/73 Harris *Pastime with good company, Tea wrecks,
The astrologer, Kemp's jig (& Mother nature's son,
30/7/73).* 13/6/73 LH1 JG *
12/8/74 Harris *The opening number, Midnight mushrumps
(1st, 2nd & 3rd movements).* & Philip Nestor.
10/7/74 LH1 JG *
    Had rec'd In Concert 3/5/74 HP, TX 18/5/74. 2nd In
Concert rec'd 13/11/75 PS, TX 13/12/75.

GUANA BATZ
1/2/84 Peel *Zombie walk, Jungle rumble, Train kept a
rollin', The cave.* Pip Hancox (v), Mick White (b),
Stuart Osborne (g), Dave Turner (d). 24/1/84 MV4 TW MPK
2/5/84 Peel *No particular place to go, Nightwatch, King
rat, The overture.* 24/4/84 MV5 MRD TdB
10/10/84 Peel *Dynamite, Brand new cadillac, Rockin' in
the graveyard, Nightmare fantasy, Rocking in my coffin.*
Sam Sardi (b) r. White. 30/9/84 MV5 DG GP
7/5/85 Peel *Endless sleep, Goofing around, Can't take the
pressure, Got no money.* 23/4/85 MV5 MRD MR

ISAAC GUILLORY
21/11/72 Peel *Hold on St. Peter, Movin' on, Brussels, The
Carbondale strut.* Isaac Guillory (agv).
31/10/72 LH1 JW BC&BAI
10/4/74 Harris *Sidewalks of America, Steamboat, Brussels,
St. Peter (& Movin' on, Staying awhile, 21/5/74 PEEL).*
& Dave Mattacks (d) & (b) unknown. 10/4/74 LH1 PR BAI

GUMBALL
15/12/90 Peel *All the time, This town, I want you,
Vietnam.* Jay Spiegel (d), Eric Vermillion (b), Don
Fleming (gv); & guest Norman Blake (g,bkv).
25/11/90 MV3 DG ME&JLY
29/7/91 Peel *39 lashes, Light shines through, Back off
boogaloo, Marilyn, High or low.* 20/8/91 MV5 MR~

GUN
26/5/84 Fri. Rock *Shame on you, Better days, Coming
home, Taking on the world.* Mark Rankin (v), Baby
Stafford (g), Scott Shields (d), Giuliano Gizzi (g), Dante
Gizzi (b). 5/5/89 WX TW *
26/6/89 Campbell *Shame on you, I will be waiting,
Something to believe in, Taking on the world.*
7/6/89 ED PW MPK
12/2/90 Goodier *Something to believe in, Can't get any
lower, Coming home, Taking on the world.*
/2/90 MV5 DG MC
28/2/92 Fri. Rock *Don't blame me, Shame on you,*

Welcome to the real world, Steal your fire. Alex
Dickson (g) r. Stafford. 7/2/92 MV4 * *
16/3/92 Campbell *Welcome to the real world, Higher
ground, Word up, Shame on you.* 26/2/92 MV4 PW MPK
30/3/92 Harris *Steal your fire, Welcome to the real world,
Watching the world go by, Better days.*
23/2/92 MV4 TdB~

THE GUN
12/11/67 Top Gear *Hold on, Stop in the name of love, The
lights on the wall, Most peculiar man.* Paul Curtis,
Louis Farrell, Timothy Mycroft, Gearie Kenworthy.
6/11/67 PCI BA *
17/11/68 Henry *I'm so glad, Railroad boy, The man who
paints the pictures, Race with the devil.* Adrian Curtis
r. Mycroft, Kenworthy. 11/11/68 AO2 AD *
18/11/68 Symonds *Race with the devil, Sunshine (19/11),
Take-off (20/11), Come with me (21/11).* 8/11/68 PCI * *
24/11/68 Top Gear *Sunshine, Race with the devil, Unlock
my door, The man who paints the pictures. & 3
trumpets & 3 trombones.* 4/11/68 PCI BA PR
29/1/69 R1 Club *Race with the devil, Sunshine, Yellow cab
man, Take-off.* 6/1/69 PS KB *

GUNSHOT
18/5/91 Peel *Construct/Destruct, Bullets entering chest, To
those who deserve it, Gunshot's history.* Mercury (rp),
Alkaline (rp), White Child Rix (ma), Alan Scott (prg).
21/4/91 MV3 DG ME&CML

GUNSLINGERS
26/4/85 Fri. Rock *Monster, There must be something we
ain't tried, Lies all lies, She got me covered.* *
22/3/85 MV4 TW DD

A GUY CALLED GERALD
7/11/88 Peel† *Time waits for no man, Rockin' Ricki°,
Emotions electric.* Gerald Simpson (prg,sy); & 'Chapter':
Aniff Cousins & Colin Thorpe (sy,smp); & Paulette
Blake (v). 30/10/88 HP DG ME
    † On Strange Fruit SFPS071; ° also on 'Manchester -
so much to answer for'.
6/9/89 Peel *Johnny roadhouse, Satisfaction, Bruford.*
Gerald, Edward Barton & Cola Nile (v). 6/8/89 MV5 DG PA

THE GYMSLIPS
20/5/82 Peel *Erika (with a k), Renées, Big sister, 48
Crash, You'll never walk alone.* Paula Richards (gv),
Suzanne Scott (bv), Karen Yarnell (dv).
12/5/82 MV4 JWI NG
16/9/82 Peel *Barbara Cartland, Pie and mash, Drink
problem, Thinking of you, Robot man.* 1/9/82 MV4 RP NG
20/12/82 Jensen *Miss Nunsweeta, Yo yo, Some girls, Dear
Marje. & Helen Ottaway (p,sy).* 9/12/82 MV4 JS MR
30/5/83 Peel *Silly egg, Wandering star, Up the wall, More
tea, vicar?* Kathy Barnes (k) r. Ottaway.
30/4/83 MV4 DG SC
7/12/83 Peel *Whirlwind flings, Love's not the answer,
Valley girl, Call again.* 28/11/83 MV4 DG MC
6/6/84 Peel *Leave me, Soldier, On the line, We're gonna
bring your empire down.* Richards, Karen Kay (bv), Sue
Vickers (k), Michelle Chowrimootoo (d).
22/5/84 MV5 MRD TdB

GYPSY
29/7/71 Henry *Pony ride, Don't cry on me, Changes
coming, Keep on trying.* Robin Pizer (lg), John Napp
(g), David Smith (d), David McCarthy (b), Rod Reed
(rg). 21/7/71 MV4 MB MH&MF
18/9/71 Top Gear *Don't cry on me, What a day, Let me
take you home (& I don't want to see you, 17/11/71).*
6/9/71 PH JW BC
7/12/71 Harris *Changes coming, Don't cry on me, Shame,
North country girl.* 2/2/72 AO2 JG *
26/6/72 Harris *Brand new car, There is a party, Oo's
cheatin', Shame.* Ray Martinez (g) r. Reed. 6/6/72 MV5 JG *
31/8/72 Drummond *You know better than me, Let's roll,
Brand new car.* 14/8/72 MV5 MB MH&MF

20/11/72 Harris *Changes coming, Brand new car, Let's roll, Shame.* 8/11/72 LH1 JG *

23/4/73 Harris *Keep on going, The loser, The jig (& Let's roll, 21/5/73).* 4/4/73 LH1 PR *

31/5/73 Peel *Let's roll, Still you're not sure, You got to me, The jig.* 21/5/73 LH1 BA *

9/7/73 Harris *You got to me, Wait, The loser, Don't cry on me.* 4/7/73 LH1 JG *

11/10/73 Peel *Slow down, Sorting it out, Still you're not sure, I'll be there (& You got to me, 8/11/73).* 8/10/73 LH1 BA *

STEVE HACKETT BAND
1/4/83 Fri. Rock *Cell 151, Walking through walls, Hackett to pieces, Please don't touch.* Steve Hackett (gv), John Hackett (fl,g), Nick Magnus (k), Ian Mosley (d), Chas Cronk (b). 4/3/83 MV4 TW DD

HAGAR THE WOMB
20/2/84 Peel *Today's "Miss World", Armchair observer, By force, A song of deep hate.* Chris Knowles (d), Mitch Flacko (b), Paul Harding (g), Janet Nassim (g), Ruth Ellis, Karen Amden & Elaine Reubens (v). 11/2/84 MV5 DG PW

PAUL HAIG
23/6/82 Jensen *Funky town, Shining hour, Luck, Heaven sent.* Paul Haig (b,g,kv), James Locke (perc,k), Karen Brown (v). 13/6/82 MV4 DG ME

20/6/83 Jensen *The freeway, On this night of decision, Good time living, All our love.* Haig, Ronnie Torrance (d). 19/5/83 MV4 JP *

29/10/84 Long *One lifetime away, Love eternal, Fear and dancing.* Haig, Donald Johnson, Alan Rankine. 7/10/84 HP BYA PW

THE CAST OF HAIR
26/1/69 Symonds on Sunday *Aquarius, Ain't got no... I got life, Air, Hare Krishna, Good morning sunshine, Let the sunshine in.* Vince Edward, Marsha Hunt, Linda Kendrick, Sonja Kristina, Annabel Leventon, Paul Nicholas, Peter Straker, Joan White; James Verner for 15 singers; & Derek Wadsworth for Hair Orchestra (10 musicians). 20/1/69 * JW *

HAIRCUT 100
29/6/81 Skinner *Baked beans, Favourite shirts, Fantastic day, Surprise me again.* Patrick Hunt (d), Les Nemes (b), Nick Hayward (gv), Graham Jones (g), Phil Smith (sx). 25/6/81 LH1 DG ME

'Tiny coincidence: this is my 100th BBC session' DG.

13/6/84 Jensen *High noon, Forty-forty home, Hidden years, It's immaterial.* Hayward out; & Graham Ward (d), Guy Barker (tp), Peter Beechill (tb). 13/5/84 MV5 DG ME

HALF MAN HALF BISCUIT
20/11/85 Peel† *D'ye ken Ted Moult?°, Arthur's farm°, All I want for Christmas is a Dukla Prague away kit°, The Trumpton riots, Ol'tige.* Paul Wright (d), Neil Crossley (bv), Nigel Blackwell (rg,lv), Simon Blackwell (lg), David Lloyd (k). 10/11/85 MV5 DG ME

† on Strange Fruit SFPCD057.

3/3/86 Peel *I left my heart in Papworth General, The continuous cremation of Hattie Jacques, Reasons to be miserable (part 10)°, The bastard son of Dean Friedman.* 23/2/86 MV5 DG ME

° On 'Back again in the DHSS' LP on Probe Plus.

8/9/86 Peel *Rod Hull is alive. . . why?, The best thing in life, Dickie Davies' eyes, I was a teenage armchair Honved fan.* 31/8/86 * DG ME&FK

4/4/90 Peel *Ordinary to enschede, Our tune, Yipps (My baby got the), Pragvec at the Melkveg.* 1/3/90 MV3 DG ME

27/6/92 Peel *Marsultras (you'll never make the station), 4AD 3D CD, Floreat interria, Goodnight Irene.* 2/6/92 MV4 MR~

HAMBI AND THE DANCE
28/10/81 Jensen *Living in a heartache, The world, Dancin' inside you, Madeline.* * 15/10/81 MV4 JS *

14/11/84 Long *Face me with a smile, War zones, Dancing with hearts in our hands, What have we got to lose.* Hambi Haralambous (v), Ronnie Eno (b), Sam Brew (g), Phil Coxon (k), Jackie Challener, Mae McKenna & Lorenza Johnson (bkv). 17/10/84 MV5 JS MPK

CLAIRE HAMMILL
20/3/72 Harris *When I was a child, Bardoll blues, Where are your smiles at today, Smile your blues anyway, I don't get any older.* Claire Hammill (gv). 7/3/72 * JG *

12/5/72 Peel *When I was a child, The big time kid, Speedbreaker.* * 14/4/72 * JM *

4/12/72 Harris *Wall to wall carpeting, The artist, Warrior of the water, Speadbreaker, Sidney Gorgeous.* Solo. 15/11/72 * JG *

19/1/73 SEQUENCE *Please stay tonight, Crying under the bedclothes, The artist, Luck of the draw, Peaceful.* 19/2/72 * JM NG

27/8/73 Harris *War going on, You know how ladies are, Nothing better to do, Postcards in 3D take a long time to arrive (& Full, 22/10/73).* 8/8/73 * JG *

PETER HAMMILL
24/7/73 Peel *Easy to slip away, German overalls, In the end, Time for a change.* Hammill (gpv). 9/7/73 T1 JW *

5/3/74 Peel *Rubicon, Red shift, A house is not a home.* & 2 (unknown). 18/2/74 T1 TW *

3/9/74 Peel *No more the sub-mariner, The emperor in his workroom, Faint heart and the sermon.* * 19/8/74 T1 TW *

21/4/77 Peel *Betrayed, Afterwards, Autumn.* & Graham Smith (vi). 13/4/77 MV4 * NG

24/9/79 Peel *Mister X (gets tense), Faculty X, Mediaevil/Time for a change.* Solo. 12/9/79 MV4 JE NG

BUTCH HANCOCK AND JIMMIE DALE GILMORE
25/8/88 Kershaw *Dallas, White freight liner blues, Leo and Leona, Already gone.* Jimmie Dale Gilmore (gv), Butch Hancock (gv,hca). 28/7/88 MV4 DG MA

27/5/90 Kershaw *Baby baby baby be mine, Don't look for a heartache, Deep eddy blues, Leo y Leona.* & Jesse Taylor (g). 29/4/90 MV3 DG ME

HANDSOME BEASTS
10/7/81 Fri. Rock *Local heroes, David's song, Another day, Sweeties.* Steve Hough (b), Phil Aston (g), Pete Malbasa (d), Gary Dallaway (v). 24/6/81 MV4 TW *

'1st session in SSL 24-track MV4' TW on session sheet.

JOSH HANNA'S BASIC TRUTH
11/11/74 Harris *David Whipp, Younger days, Christine.* Josh Hanna (glv), James Rigg (k), Philip Rigg (b), Rick Kent (d). 16/10/74 MV4 JG *

HANOI ROCKS
24/8/84 Fri. Rock *I can't get it, Underwater world, Don't you ever leave me, Boulevard of broken dreams.* Andy McCoy (lg), Nasty Suicide (g), Sam Yaffa (b), Razzle (d), Mike Monroe (v). 20/7/84 MV4 TW DD

THE HAPPY FEW
28/7/82 Peel *Seven years, 3am, Beg forgiveness, Bucket of ice.* Phil Emby (d,perc), David Cuff (g,b,v), Dominic Riley (g,v-1), Nick Green (g,b). 3/7/82 MV4 DG MR

THE HAPPY FLOWERS
11/7/90 Peel *My head's on fire, Mom and Dad like the baby more than me, Ruckwerts essen vetzt, I dropped my ice cream cone, These peas are so green.* John Beers (gv), Charlie Kramer (d,b,v). 28/6/90 MV5 DG NG&RPF

THE HAPPY MONDAYS
9/4/86 Peel† *Kuff Dam, Freaky dancin', Olive oil, Cob 20.* Shaun Ryder (v), Paul Ryder (b), Marc Day (g), Paul Davis (k), Gary Whelan (d), Mark Berisford (perc). 1/4/86 MV4 DG MR&JB

† on Strange Fruit SFPCD084.

27/2/89 Peel† *Tart tart, Mad Cyril, Do it better.* 21/2/89 * DG MR

† on Strange Fruit SFPCD077.

HARD CORPS
4/6/84 Peel *Sacred heart, To breathe, Metal and flesh,*

Dirty. Hugh Ashton (cmp), Clive Pearce, Robert Doran & Paul Davies (k), Régine Fetet (v). 26/5/84 MV5 DG MR

15/8/84 Skinner *Je suis passée, For pleasure, Metal and flesh, Dirty.* 29/7/84 MV5 DG MR

14/5/85 Long *Desolation land, The bell, Bravo!* Davies out. 1/5/85 MV5 BYA MPK

HARD MEAT
25/6/69 Peel *Walking up down street, Liquid boats, Run shaker life, Strange fruit.* * 6/6/69 * * *

21/9/69 Top Gear *Space between, Yesterday today and tomorrow, Most likely you'll go your way.* * 8/9/69 * * *

30/4/70 Henry *Through a window, Yesterday today tomorrow, Run shakes a life.* * 10/4/70 * MB MH&MF

7/1/71 Henry *Like a rolling stone, When your time is over, On the road.* * 23/12/70 * MB MH&MF

HARDIN AND YORK
14/6/69 Walker *Little miss blue, Candlelight, Can't keep a good man down, Tomorrow today.* Peter York (d), Eddie Hardin (kv). 4/6/69 AO2 cJBU *

30/7/70 Henry *Can't find my home, The pike, Just a case of time.* 23/7/70 AO2 MB MH&MF

29/4/71 Black *For the world, Tomorrow today, The pike (& Deep in my despair, 28/5/71).* 5/4/71 T1 PD *

12/8/71 Henry *Natural gas, For the world, Deep in my despair, The pike.* 28/7/71 MV4 MB *

TIM HARDIN
21/7/68 Henry *If I were a carpenter, If I knew, Don't make promises.* Tim Hardin (gpv), Brian Brocklehurst (b). 14/7/68 PS AD *

28/7/68 Top Gear *Reason to believe, Don't make promises, Danville Dan, Hang on to a dream.* Tim Hardin (gpv) & the Spike Heatley Quintet (1-solo). 15/7/68 PC1 BA PR&BC

Contracts suggest a recording for SPEAKEASY 19/4/74, but a broadcast has proved untraceable so far.

20/5/74 Harris *Reason to believe, Black sheep boy, Hang on to a dream.* & John Dylan, Dave King, Pete Dennis, John Mealing. 1/5/74 LH1 PR BAl&DD

JOHN WESLEY HARDING
27/8/90 Campbell *Here comes the groom, Spaced cowgirl, Scared of guns, The devil in me.* John Wesley Harding (agv), Steve Donelly (ag), Kenny Craddock (o,p), Bruce Thomas (b), Pete Thomas (d). 1/8/90 MV5 PW MPK

25/3/91 Campbell *The world (and all its problems), Save a little room for me, The person you are, Fifty-fifty split.* 'and the Folk Upstarts': Steve Donelly (ag), James Blennerhassett (db), Jody Linscott (perc). 6/3/91 MV5 PW MPK

1/5/91 Harris *The people's drug, The person you are, The devil in me, My nightmare scenario blues.* & Steve Donnelly (g), James Blenner Hassett (b), Jody Linscott (perc). 10/3/91 MV5 TdB PA

CHRIS HARDY
13/11/68 My Kind Of Folk *Richmond walking song* Chris Hardy (agv). 6/11/68 S2 FL *

'Jackson C. Frank arrived for a session with a young British student who had been accompanying him, Chris Hardy, a student at Canterbury University, and he recorded one solo item' FL; 'impressive first broadcast', said the Audition panel.

4/4/72 Peel *On the wall, Tightrope, You have found the way, Living ground.* 27/3/72 PH JW *

6/7/72 Drummond *Living a life a day, After all, July spirit, Escape boogie.* 21/6/72 MV4 MB MH&MF

28/6/73 Peel *Spinning slow, Food for the breeze, Jug up, Early in the morning.* & the Basement Blowers (unknown). 4/6/73 LH1 BA *

24/1/74 Peel *Cold steel rock, It's no crime, Nefarious doings, In the shadows.* 17/1/74 LH1 * *

DALE HARGREAVES' FLAMINGOS
11/12/82 Long *Zap international recruiting song, Lucky guy, Russian rain, Eastern side.* * 10/12/82 PHM cJL *

252

HARLEM SPIRIT
29/1/83 LONG *Love is the game, Universal man, Why can't we be lovers, Mek we rock.* ~ 24/1/83 PHM c.JL TWN

ROY HARPER
29/10/67 TOP GEAR *Forever, Zengem, Midspring dithering, Nobody's got any money.* Roy Harper (gv), Clem Cattini (d), Brian Brocklehurst (b). 16/10/67 PCI BA PR&AH
17/3/68 TOP GEAR *Life goes by, A beautiful rambling mess, Night fighter song writer, All you need is.* Roy Harper (gv), & Keith Mansfield Group, (9 musicians). 13/3/68 MV4 BA DT
8/6/69 TOP GEAR *Hey Francesca†, Hell's angels, She's the one†, I hate the white man (& It's tomorrow and today is yesterday†, 27/7/69).* Solo. 3/6/69 MV4 JW ~
 † On 'Come out fighting, Genghis Smith', Awareness AWCD1035.
3/1/70 TOP GEAR *Forever, I hate the white man, North country girl, Don't you grieve.* 15/12/69 PH JW ~
4/1/71 HARRIS *One man rock and roll band, Me and my woman (& The same old rock, 8/2/71).* 18/12/70 MV5 JM JWH
15/5/71 TOP GEAR *One man rock and roll band, The same old rock, Kangaroo blues.* 10/5/71 PH JW ~
13/12/71 HARRIS *Highway blues, North country, South Africa, The Lord's Prayer.* 29/11/71 T1 PD ARV
19/2/73 HARRIS *12 hours of sunset, Little lady, South Africa, All Ireland.* 14/2/73 LH1 PR BAI
19/3/74 PEEL *Too many movies, Commune, Forever, Highway blues, I'll see you again, North country.* 11/3/74 T1 JW ~
1/4/74 HARRIS *Forever, 12 hours of sunset, North country.* & 3 (unknown). 6/3/74 LH1 PR ~
12/12/74 PEEL *Too many movies, Home, Highway blues, 12 hours of sunset, One man rock and roll band.* 5/12/74 MV4 TW BAI
23/6/75 PEEL *Referendum, Hallucinating light, The spirit lives.* & Trigger: Chris Spedding (lg), Dave Cochran (b), Bill Bruford (d). 10/6/75 MV4 TW BC
18/2/77 PEEL *Another day, Cherishing the lonesome, These last days, Grown ups are just silly children.* & Chips: Andy Roberts (g), Henry McCullough (g), Herbie Flowers (b), John Hallsey (d), Dave Lawson (k). 14/2/77 MV4 TW DD
21/8/78 PEEL *The same old rock, Forget me not, I hate the white man.* & Andy Roberts (g). 7/8/78 MV4 TW DD

THE HARPOONS
4/9/85 LONG *Sea horses, Taking on the rubicon, The last man, Celebrate the ugly.* Peter Stillman (g), Steve Yabsley (g), Geoff Gorton (b), Scott Jarrold (v), Jon Brokenbrow (d). 14/8/85 MV5 BYA MPK

TIM HART AND MADDY PRIOR
30/10/68 MY KIND OF FOLK *Lish Young buy a broom, Adam & Eve, The horn of the hunter.* Tim Hart (gv,bj,dul), Maddy Prior (v,bj,sp). 23/10/68 S2 FL ~
 The rejection of this trial b'cast tape by the panel was over-ruled by Jimmy Grant [M: Folk Shows].
1/1/69 NIGHT RIDE *The horn of the hunter, Who's the fool now, Queen Eleonor's confession, Adam and Eve, Oats and beans and barley, Turkey and rhubarb.* 17/12/68 PCI JM ~
4/9/71 TOP GEAR *Serving girls' holiday, Seamus the showman, Saucey sailor, Polly on the shore (& I live not where I love, 3/11/71).* 27/7/71 MV4 ~ ~

MIKE HART
22/5/68 NIGHT RIDE *Elsie Straws, Spiders and larks, Is it true, The shelter song.* ~ 15/3/68 S1 DK ~

KEEF HARTLEY
30/12/68 WS R&B *Sinnin' for you, Highway child, Half breed.* Keef Hartley (d), Owen Finnegan (v), Spit James (lg), Peter Dines (o), Gary Thain (b). 29/11/68 AO2 JG JY
 Passed by panel: 'very wild R&B group'.
26/1/69 TOP GEAR *Think it over, Sinnin' for you, Half-breed.* 3/12/68 PCI BA AH

4/5/69 TOP GEAR *Waiting around, Too much thinking, Me and my woman, Sinnin' for you.* & Wynder K. Frog (k), Henry Lowther (tp,vi), Lyn Dobson (al), Harry Becket (tb), Barbara Thompson (ts); Dines out. 29/4/69 MV4 JW TW
28/7/69 WS R&B *Waiting around, Sinnin' for you, Me and my woman, Hartley's jam for bread.* 31/5/69 AO2 JG JY
25/10/69 TOP GEAR *Waiting around, Believe in you, Spanish fly, Too much thinking.* & Lowther, Thain & Miller Anderson (gv), James Jewell (ts) & 2 (tp), 2 (sx) (unknown). 14/10/69 MV4 JW ~
27/12/69 WS R&B *Spanish fly, Driftin' and driftin', Me and my woman.* 26/11/69 MV4 JG JY
 Rec'd Peel Sunday Show Concert 22/1/70 PS, TX 25/1/70 with 7-piece horn section.
24/4/70 BLACK *Me and my woman, Too much thinking, Not foolish not wise, Believe in you, Spanish fly.* As 26/11/69, & 3 (tp), 3 (sx), 2 (tb). 25/3/70 MV5 JM ~
30/6/70 HARDING *Sinnin' for you, You can't take it with you, Just a cry.* 23/6/70 MV5 MB MH&MF
13/9/70 RAVEN'S R&B *From a window, The time is near, Premonition.* & Thain, Anderson & Lyle Jenkins, Dave Caswell. 22/7/70 MV4 JG JY
 Rec'd 2nd Peel Sunday Concert 12/11/70 PS, TX 22/11/70, & Dines & 8-piece horn section. 3rd Peel Sunday Concert rec'd as 5-piece 25/3/71 PS, TX 11/4/71.
9/7/71 BLACK *Just a cry, Think it over, Shadows across a wall, Overdog/Roundabout.* & Thain, Anderson & Derek Austin (o), Lyn Dobson (al). 17/6/71 AO2 JM JWH
7/1/72 PEEL *Marin county, Thinking of you, Heartbreaking woman (& Don't you belong, 11/2/72).* & Thain, Pete Wingfield (pv), Chris Mercer (sx), Nick Newell (sx), Junior Kerr (lgv). 7/12/71 T1 JM JWH
1/2/72 PEEL *Don't sign it, Heart breaking woman, Don't you belong.* 25/1/72 MV4 ~ ~
25/2/73 SEQUENCE *I know something, Circles, Australian lady, You and me.* & Mercer, & Neil Hubbard (g), Phil Chen (b), Jess Roden (v), Elkie Brooks (v), Jean Rousell (k). 23/1/73 T1 PD ~

PHIL HARTLEY
21/11/88 PEEL *Lord smutty lips, Inspector of crime, Prepare to change sandals, Purchase nicely.* ~ 13/11/88 HP DG JB

THE SENSATIONAL ALEX HARVEY BAND
13/10/73 ROCK ON *Faith healer, Giddy up a ding dong, Teenager.* Alex Harvey (gv), Zal Cleminson (lg), Ted McKenna (d), Hugh McKenna (p,o), Chris Glen (b). 4/10/73 LH1 PR BAI&GB
 Alex Harvey's first broadcast was with his Soul Band on 7/11/64, on WS R&B, rec'd 15/10/64 PH, prod. JG: They did 'Watermelon man' & 'Bags Groove', and line-up included Bobby Wishart (ts,fl) [M]. 'Soul Band' contracted for RI In Concert 20/4/72 PS (TX 29/4). then SAHB debuted on In Concert 2/12/72 (rec'd 2/11 PS). Did another a year later, then this session.
26/10/75 SOUNDS ON SUNDAY *Money honey, Vambo marble eye, Give my compliments to the chef, Love story, Gamblin' bar room blues.* 25/9/75 MV5 MB ~

P J HARVEY
3/11/91 PEEL† *Oh my lover, Victory, Sheela na gig, Water.* Rob (d), Stephen Vaughan (b), PJ Harvey (gv). 29/10/91 MV4 MR~ JB
 † On Strange Fruit SFRCD119. Two more sessions already since 25th anniversary of Radio I; the third, 1st TX 12/3/93, with cover of 'Wang dang doodle' was extraordinary. Yet another classic, unique Peel Session.

HATFIELD AND THE NORTH
1/2/73 PEEL *Rifferama, Fol de rol de rol/Licks for the ladies, Finesse is for fairies/Nan True's hole/Lything and gracing.* Phil Miller (g), Pip Pyle (d), Richard Sinclair (bv), Dave Stewart (o,p) [NB: David Sinclair (k), not Stewart, is named on contract, dated 12/1/73, but

Stewart is listed on trial broadcast form filled-in at session]. 22/1/73 LH1 BA ~
31/7/73 PEEL *Medley: For Robert/For Cyrille/Son of 'There's no place like Homerton', Medley: To mum and the gongs/Lobster in cleavage probe/Invasion of the land crabs.* 24/7/73 LH1 TW BC
2/4/74 PEEL *Shaving is boring/Licks for the ladies, Your majesty is like a cream doughnut, Aigrette/Rifferama/Top Gear commercial.* & Mick Fox (hp-on TOP GEAR commercial). 19/3/74 LH1 TW BC
5/12/74 PEEL *Do the lethargy shuffle (yeah yeah), Let's eat (real soon), Fitter Stoke has a bath/Calyx.* 21/11/74 MV4 TW ~

RICHIE HAVENS
1/6/69 SYMONDS ON SUNDAY *Just above my hobby horse's head, Lady Madonna, Wear your love like heaven, Maggie's farm.* Richie Havens (gv), Brian Brocklehurst (b), Maurice Placquet (d). 26/5/69 AO2 c.PW1 ~
4/6/69 PEEL *From the prison, Maggie's farm, Just above my hobby horse's head, I can't make it anymore.* 30/5/69 S2 PR ~
 Recorded session for RI Club at PS same day as this broadcast.
8/6/69 TOP GEAR *Handsome Johnny, Things I used to do, High flying bird, Dolphin song.* 3/6/69 MV4 JW ~

TED HAWKINS
17/4/86 PEEL *Cold and bitter tears, Bring it home daddy.* Ted Hawkins (agv). 5/4/86 At Ted's house in LA AK~
10/7/86 KERSHAW *Ladder of success, Sorry you're sick, Bad Dog, Happy hour.* 26/6/86 Sunset Marquis Hotel, LA AK
12/11/87 KERSHAW *Just one look, Bring it home daddy, Happy hour, Today I started loving you again.* 5/11/87 ~ DG NG & SF.
20/8/89 KERSHAW *Who do you love, Dollar tree, Ain't got nothing yet, No other love for me, Nowhere to run.* 3/8/89 MV5 TdB~

HAWKWIND
19/9/70 TOP GEAR *Hurry on sundown, Seeing it as you really are, Some of that stuff.* Thomas Crimble (b), Terry Ollis (d), Huw Lloyd Langton (lg), Nik Turner (v,sx,fl), Dik Mik (el), Dave Brock (gv,o). 18/8/70 MV4 JW TW
 Recorded a Peel Sunday Concert 5/11/70 PS, TX 15/11/70 at which a roadie stole a mike, leading to the band temporarily being banned.
24/4/71 TOP GEAR *Inwards out, Dreaming/You shouldn't do that.* Dave Anderson (b) r. Crimble; Langton out. 19/4/71 PH JW BC&NG
27/5/71 HENRY *Master of the universe, Dreaming-You shouldn't do that.* 19/5/71 MV4 MB MH&MF
14/8/72 WALKER *Silver machine* [Network session]. Derek Dettmar (sy), Simon King (d), Ian Kilminster (b) r. Mik, Ollis, Anderson. 2/8/72 MV5 RP ~
 Rec'd 2nd In Concert 28/9/72 PS, TX 14/10/72.
2/8/85 FRI. ROCK *Magnu - dreamworker of time, They've got your number, Assault of the hawk.* Dave Brock (g), Huw Lloyd Langton (lg), Harvey Bainbridge (k), Alan Davey (b), Danny Thompson (d). 19/7/85 MV4 TW DD

BRYN HAWORTH
30/12/74 HARRIS *Anyway you want to be, Peace of mind, Miss Swiss, Give all you got to give.* Bryn Haworth (agv). 11/12/74 ~ JG ~
8/1/75 PEEL *Used, Pick me up, Darling Cory, Ee I love you.* 12/12/74 MV4 TW BAI
21/7/75 PEEL *Dance, Good job, How long, Make love your aim.* 8/7/75 MV4 ~ ~
29/11/76 PEEL *Send down the rain, We're all one, I just can't get used to your love.* & Rosh Kato (g), Gordon Haskell (b,bkv), Jim Russell (d). 16/11/76 MV4 JG MR

PETE HAYCOCK'S CLIMAX
29/8/85 INTO THE MUSIC *Young enthusiasts, Black Jack, Guilty, Scene of the crime.* Pete Haycock (gv), Keff

McCulloch (gk,bkv), Livingstone Brown (b,bkv), Pete Thompson (d,bkv). 3/8/85 MV4 DG MC

HAYSI FANTAYZEE
28/7/82 JENSEN *Chizoola, Shiny shiny, Holy Joe, Skinny boy groovy baby.* Kate (v), Jeremiah (v), Mick Green (g), Alfie Agius (b), Simon Henry (sx), Bobby Valentino (vi). 20/6/82 MV4 DG ME

HDQ
15/6/88 PEEL *Through my eyes, Those remembered times, Believe, Have faith.* Golly (v), Rob Berwick (b), Dickie Hammond (g), Lainey (d). 2/6/88 * DG MA&SC
6/2/89 PEEL *Leaving home, Just when I thought, If only/Sinking, All we knew.* 17/1/89 MV4 DG MR

HEAD CLEANER
4/7/92 PEEL† *XL5, Fear, Attitude, Ace of spades.* Martin Willis (gv), Guy Siddle (bv), Erick Legrande (dv). 14/6/92 MV3 ME~
† on Strange Fruit SFPCD086.

HEAD OF DAVID
30/4/86 PEEL† *Snuff rider M.C., Joyride burning X, Shadow Hills California, Newly-shaven saint.* Reuben Burroughs (v), Eric Jurenovski (g), Dave Cochrane (b), Sharp (d). 22/4/86 MV4 DG MR
† On 'LP' BFFP10.
6/10/86 PEEL *Jack Nicholson, Pierced all over, Metal Texas psych-out.* 23/9/86 * DG MR&JB
15/7/87 PEEL *Bugged, Snake domain, Tequila, Skindrill.* Justin Broadrick (d,bkv) r. Sharp. 7/7/87 * DG DD
15/6/89 PEEL *Moonshine, Caprice, Wildwood, Snake hands forever.* Cochrane, Jurenovski (g,dm), Burroughs. 28/5/89 MV3 DG MR

HEADHUNTERS
7/7/83 PEEL *Way of the South, Wipe out the funk, Disorder in the house, Landlord.* Finn (g), Nick (d), Servo (v), Bulldog (b). 29/6/83 * BYA NG

HEADS HANDS AND FEET
4/5/71 HARDING *Help, Country boy, Devil's elbow (& I wish you know me, 25/5/71).* Tony Colton (v), Ray Smith (gv), Pete Gavin (dv), Chas Hodges (bv), Mike O'Neill (o,pv), Albert Lee (gv). 21/4/71 MV4 MB MH&MF
Rec'd Peel Sunday Concert 17/6/71 PS, TX 11/7/71.
28/10/71 DRUMMOND *Warming up the band, Ain't going to let me down, How does it feel to be right all the time, Trying to put me on.* O'Neill out. 18/10/71 MV5 MB MH&MF
31/3/72 PEEL *I'm in need of your help, Trying to put me on, Safety in numbers, Road show (& Warming up the band/Hot property, 6/4/72).* 14/3/72 T1 JM *
2nd In Concert rec'd 27/4/72 PS, TX 6/5/72.
15/5/72 HARRIS *Hot property, Road show, Harlequin, Song and dance.* 2/5/72 MV5 JG *
11/7/72 PEEL *Hang me bang me, Dancer, Harlequin, Rhyme and time.* 23/5/72 MV4 PR *
14/5/73 HARRIS *Jack Daniels, Yakety yak, Gypsy man, Music to the man.* Lee, Hodges & Ray Smith (gv), Steve Simpson (g,fd,hca), Dave Peacock (b,bj), Ian Wallace (d). 2/5/73 LH1 PR BAI

HEADSTONE
30/12/74 HARRIS *Sunny days, Get through to you, Live for you, Take me down.* Mark Ashton (gv), Joe O'Donnell (vi), Steve Bolton (d), Jerome Impson (b), Peter Van Hoeck (gv). 27/11/74 MV4 JG *

THE JEFF HEALEY BAND
18/1/89 SKINNER *Confidenceman, See the light, All along the watchtower, My little gitl, I need to be loved.* Jeff Healey (gv), Joe Rockman (b), Tom Stephen (d). 6/12/88 MV4 PW TdB
1/5/89 CAMPBELL *Angel eyes, When the night comes falling, Roadhouse blues, Foxy lady.* 15/4/89 MV3 HP TdB&TD

THE HEART THROBS
16/3/88 MAYO *Here I hide, Cry hard cry fast, Come, I see danger.* Stephen Ward (k), Rose Carlotti (lv,g), Rachel Carlotti (b,bkv), Mark Side (d). 31/1/88 MV4 HP MA&TD

27/4/89 PEEL *In vain, Shut down, I wonder why.* Alan Barclay (g) joins. 11/4/89 WX DG MR
20/8/90 PEEL *Pumping, Slip and slide, Calavera.* 15/7/90 MV3 DG TD&DB

HEARTBEAT
16/11/82 JENSEN *Very much his baby, Shadow play, Hard caring, Spoox sex.* Hilary Morrison (kv), Nick Haines (g), James Locke (dk), David Henderson (g), Louise Drummond (bkv), Graham Main (perc). 26/9/82 MV4 DG ME

HEAVENLY
14/4/91 PEEL *And the birds aren't singing, So little deserve, Escort crash on Marston street.* Matthew Fletcher (d), Rob Pursey (b), Peter Momtchiloff (g), Amelia Fletcher (gv). 17/3/91 MV3 DG ME&CML

HEAVY METAL KIDS
23/7/74 PEEL *Rock and roll man, It's the same, Hanging on, Runaround eyes.* Ronnie Thomas (bv), Keith Boyce (d,perc), Micky Waller (g), Danny Peyronel (kv), Gary Holton (g). 2/7/74 LH1 TW *
9/9/74 HARRIS *It's the same, Crisis, Runaround eyes, Hanging on.* 7/8/74 LH1 JG * [M: daytime]

HEAVY METAL THUNDER
6/5/88 FRI. ROCK *HMT, What's left in you, The preacher, The kara.* Ian Crawford (d), Mick Hannaby (g), Mick Rutherford (bv), Paul Bainbridge (g). 22/4/88 * HP MC

HEAVY PETTIN'
11/6/82 FRI. ROCK *Shout it out, Love times love, Hell is beautiful, Roll the dice.* Gordon Bonnar (g), Punky Mendoza (g), Brian Wagh (b), Gary Moat (d), Steven Hayman (v). 25/5/82 * TW MC

HEERA
26/1/89 KERSHAW *Jind baliye, Bakhiyan to tang kurti, Raba ki kariye, Beat the rhythm balle balle.* Jaswinder Kumar & Palvinder Dhami (v), Bhupinder Roopra (vi), Gurnam Sagoo (k,smp), Deepak Khazanchi (g), Sidharth Khazanchi (b), Abbas Aheikh (dholak,cga), Mukesh Barot (d). 12/1/89 MV4 DG MWT
16/2/92 KERSHAW *Mahiya, Amb lad gaye, Boliya.* Kumar, Sagoo, Satwant Singh Taak (k), Hardev Singh Marwhay (electric perc), Pandit Dinesh (dholak), Sava Khazanchi (d). 28/1/92 MV4 DG NG

HEIST
27/3/86 LONG *Trapped, The chop, Feelings, Toot!* Paul Degnan (bv), Michael Bernard (b), Adam James (g), Dave Wilson (d). 2/3/86 MV4 BYA JB

HELEN AND THE HORNS
7/9/83 PEEL *Pioneer town, Footsteps at my door, Snakebite, Freight train.* Helen (gbv), Marc Jordan (tp), Dave Jago (tb), Paul Davey (sx). 31/8/83 MV4 BYA *
5/12/83 PEEL *Secret love, Twice brewed, I'd been hoping for a happy ending, Southern belle.* & Michael Riley (perc). 26/11/83 MV4 MR~
1/8/84 PEEL *Lonesome country boy, Two strings to your bow, Girl versus boy, Take five†.* Helen, Jago, Davey, Chris Smith (tp,flh), Simon Walker (vi). 25/7/84 MV5 SFX *
† On HELT2 12-inch.

HELMET
22/6/91 PEEL *Unsung°, Rude†, Sinatra†, Your head°.* John Stanier (d), Henry Bogdan (b), Peter Mengede (g), Page Hamilton (gv). 26/5/91 MV3 DG ME&AM
† On Strange Fruit SFMCD212; ° On Amphetamine Reptile SCALE 41.

HELP YOURSELF
8/5/71 TOP GEAR *Crazy Cajun cakewalk man, Running down deep, Old man.* Malcolm Morley (gv), Richard Treece (b), David Charles (d), Ernie Graham (gv), Jonathan Glemser (g). 26/4/71 PH JW BC
Rec'd Peel Sunday Concert 25/5/71 PS, TX 13/6/71.
10/4/72 HARRIS *Let it roll, Johnny B Goode, Half breed.* Paul Burton (b) r. Graham, Glemser (Treece now lg). 21/3/72 MV5 JG *

19/5/72 PEEL *Johnny B Goode, Re-affirmation, Let it roll (& While away, 30/6/72).* 25/4/72 T1 JM *
21/8/72 HARRIS *Alabama lady, Just passing through, She's my girl, American mother.* 15/8/72 MV5 JG *
17/11/72 SEQUENCE *Help yourself, The only one that gets me off is Frank Bough, Hello goodbye blue.* Morley out. 10/10/72 T1 PD *
17/4/73 PEEL *Amy, Blown away, Who killed paradise, Man-we're glad we know you.* Morley returns, r. Leonard; Ken Whaley (b) r. Burton. 10/4/73 T1 JW *

HEMLOCK
25/5/73 SEQUENCE *Mr Horizontal, Broken dreamer, The shape I'm in, Just an old friend.* Miller Anderson (gv), Mick Weaver (o,p), Jim Leverton (b), Eric Dillon (d), Pete Dines (k). 1/5/73 T1 JM *

THE JIMI HENDRIX EXPERIENCE
18/2/67 LIGHT. SAT. CLUB *Stone free†, Hey Joe [take #2]†, Foxy Lady†, Love or Confusion† (& Foxy Lady [alternate take], Hey Joe [take #1], both not broadcast).* Jimi Hendrix (gv), Noel Redding (bv), Mitch Mitchell (d). 13/2/67 S2 BB PH
1/4/67 LIGHT. SAT. CLUB† *Killin' floor, Fire, Purple haze.* 28/3/67 S2 BB PH&TW
15/10/67 TOP GEAR *Little miss lover, Driving south, Burning of the midnight lamp†, Hound dog†, Experiencing the blues† (& I was made to love her/Ain't too proud to beg [instrumental jam], Driving south [take #2]†, both not broadcast).* Stevie Wonder (d-6 only) r. Mitchell. 6/10/67 PH BP PR
13/11/67 WS R&B *Hoochie coochie man†, Can you please come crawl out your window, Driving South.* & Alexis Korner (sg-1). 17/10/67 AO2 JG JY
This take of Driving South is identifiable by Hendrix breaking a string, and the track consequently ending with Mitchell's drum solo.
24/12/67 TOP GEAR° *Day tripper†, Spanish castle magic†, Radio One jingle†, Getting my heart back together again†, Wait until tomorrow† (& Getting my heart back together again [take #1], not broadcast).* 15/12/67 PH BP PR
† on Castle Communications 'Radio One' CCSCD 212. But, as Harry Shapiro has pointed out in his discography in 'Electric Gypsy', the LP sleeve notes to 'Radio One' (sic: 3 sessions are *not* from Radio 1) are wrong on several points of detail: Redding sings on 'Day Tripper', not John Lennon; the track the LP calls 'Hear my train a comin' is actually 'Getting my heart back together again'; similarly, 'Experiencing the blues' is labelled 'Catfish blues'; and the 'Radio One' jingle was recorded at the start of the 15/12 session, not, as the notes claim, at the end. Although both *Saturday Club* broadcasts and the last TOP GEAR date are included complete, one wonders why several other tracks which survive were omitted. ° Final session as broadcast also on Strange Fruit SFRCD065.

CHRISTIE HENNESSY
26/2/74 PEEL *Far away in Australia, The wealthy squire, Casey's wake, Messenger boy.* Christie Hennessy (agv) & (dul), (fd) unknown. 11/2/74 T1 JW NG

HENRY COW
29/5/71 TOP GEAR *Hieronymo's mad again, Poglith drives a Vauxhall Viva.* Fred Frith (gpv,vi), Tim Hodgkinson (o,al,v), Sean Jenkins (d), John Greaves (bgv). 4/5/71 MV4 JW BC
'A winner in our new groups competition' JW to panel: unanimous pass for 'progressive programmes'.
14/3/72 PEEL *Teen beat, Rapt in a blanket, I came to see you.* Chris Cutler (d) r. Jenkins; & Geoff Leigh (ts,fl). 28/2/72 PH JW BC
14/11/72 PEEL *With the yellow half moon and blue star, With the yellow half moon and blue star pt 2.* & DJ Perry (speech) this date only. 17/10/72 LH1 JW BC

254

8/5/73 Peel *Guider tells of silent airborne machine, 9 funerals of the citizen king, Bee.* 24/4/73 LH1 JW *

9/5/74 Peel *Pidgeons: Ruins/Half awake half asleep/Bittern storm over Ulm.* Lindsay Cooper (ob) joins. 25/4/74 LH1 JW *

18/8/75 Peel *Beautiful as the moon terrible as an army with banners, Nirvana for mice, The Ottawa song, Gloria Gloom, Beautiful as the moon etc. (reprise).* & Dagmar Krause (v); Leigh out. 5/8/75 MV4 TW BC

THE HEPBURNS

17/4/89 Peel *Tonight the world of entertainment, Where you belong, Believe me, You must have had it all.* Les Mun (d), Mike Thomas (b), Nigel Boulton (g), Matt Jones (gv), Iain Davies (k). 21/3/89 WX DG MR

THE HERD

26/11/67 Top Gear *Mixed-up minds, Come on believe me, Paradise lost, She loves me she loves me not, I want you.* Peter Frampton (gv), Andy Bown (k), Gary Taylor (b), Andrew Steele (d). 22/11/67 MV4 BA *

  1st appeared on Pop North, PHM 11/5/67, prod. John Wilcox [M].

HERE AND NOW

16/11/78 Peel *This time, What you see is what you are, Oh my god can be so hard we tried and we tried but couldn't find it, Chicken marimba.* Gavin da Blitz (sy), Keith da Missile Bass (bv), Freddy Facetious (dv), Steffy Sharpsticks (gv), Suzz da Blooz & Annie Wombat ('choir of angels'). 8/11/78 MV4 MR~

HERE'S JOHNNY

5/1/84 Peel *Hellzapoppin', World in action, Every mirror I see, Your room.* Colin McKay (v), Dave Knowles (k), Andy Zsigmond (g), Steve Brown (d), Dave Whittaker (b); & Caroline McKinnon (bkv-4). 21/12/83 MV4 RP NG

HERESY

3/8/87 Peel *Flowers (in concrete), Belief/Network of friends, Sick of stupidity, Too slow to judge/A sense of freedom.* Steve Charlesworth (d), Calvin Piper (b), Mitchell Dickinson (g), John March (v). 26/7/87 * DG MA&ME

9/3/88 Peel *Consume/Face up to it, Into the grey, When unity becomes solidarity, The street enters the house/Cornered rat, Open up.* Steven Ballam (g) r. Dickinson. 1/3/88 MV4 DG MC

18/1/89 Peel *Everyday madness everyday, Break the connection/Ghettoised, Network ends, Release/Genocide.* 10/1/89 MV4 DG MR

HERON

28/8/72 Harris *Harlequin five, Big A, Friend, Me and my lady.* Steve Jones (kv), Gerald Moore (gv), Les Calvert (b), Roy Apps (rgv), Graham (surname unknown) (d), Bill Boazman (g). 10/8/72 PS JG *

  Original 4-piece debuted on Peel Sunday Concert 3/1/71, & did 2nd Concert on 20/6/71.

MIKE HERON'S REPUTATION

30/4/75 Peel *Draw back the veil, Sold on your love, & (unknown titles).* Mike Heron (gv), Malcolm Le Maistre (v), Graham Forbes (lg), David Barker (k), Mike Tomich (b), John Gilston (d). 15/4/75 MV4 * *

19/4/77 Peel *Do it yourself, Draw back the veil, Are you going to hear the music.* Frank Usher (lg), Dave Sams (k) r. Forbes, Barker. Now billed just as 'Heron'. 5/4/77 MV4 JG MR

HEY PAULETTE

1/8/89 Peel *Our immeasurable differences, I really do love Penelope, A pet day, Erstwhile wet blanket.* Darren Nolan (d), Colom Fitzpatrick (b), Derrick Dalton (g,bkv), Eammon Davis (gv). 25/6/89 MV3 DG MC

HEY! ELASTICA

27/9/82 Jensen *Barbarella, Elastican eyes, Clay hips, My kind of guy.* Barry McVicar (gv), Chez (g), George Cathro (b), Keith Burns (d), Giles De Mabrielle (v), Sam (v). 16/9/82 MV4 JS MR

HI FI

15/3/79 Peel *Movie condition, The silence, Feel naked, Black taxi.* Larry Berridge (g,lv), Doctor Jenkins (lg,bkv), Byron Conn (b), Steve Jones (d,perc). 7/3/79 MV4 JS NG

HIBISCUS

7/11/80 Fri. Rock *I see the sun, White knight, Quilta.* Bob Corner (k), Graham Close (g), Kevin Moore (b), Pete Saunders (d). 15/10/80 * TW DD

HIDING PLACE

5/1/78 Peel *Lucky seven, Roll it, The wanderer, Looking out.* Kenny Driscoll (v), Tich (lgv), Dave Dawson (bv), Robert Allen (dv), Paul Abrahams (k). 19/12/77 MV4 * *

THE HIGH FIVE

6/10/82 Peel *If they come in the morning, The curse of revolt, Turning, No guarantee.* Rob Jones (d), Phil Jones (b), Mark Braben (g), Aza (lv,g), Jake Waksten (perc). 11/9/82 MV4 DG MC

6/6/83 Peel *Cold steel gang, On the banks, Hand on my heart, Big village.* Hamish Cameron (k,hca) r. Waksten. 23/5/83 MV4 TW *

12/3/84 Peel *100 tons, Walk them back, Working for the man, Hard line.* John Hughes (p-3) r. Cameron. 3/3/84 MV5 DG MC

7/11/85 Kershaw *Please please don't pass me by, Who killed David Jones, All that is going down, Fortunate son.* Cameron returns. 24/10/85 Y2 SP PSM

HIGH LEVEL RANTERS

17/7/68 MY KIND OF FOLK *Cushy butterfield, Buy broom besoms, The girl with the blue dress, Davy Davy knick knack, (& 1 other, illegible on PasB).* Billed as 'Johnny Handle and The High Level Ranters'. 6/7/68 S2 FL *

  Group first broadcast on Midland service 7/66 [M: Folk shows].

18/4/72 Peel *A mile to ride/Jockey lay up in the hayloft, Plains of Waterloo, High level bridge hornpipe, Felton Lonnen, The hens march/The broken-legged chicken/The black cow of Whickam, Gillian the prover/Neil Gow's wife.* Johnny Handle, Tom Gilfellow, Alistair Anderson, Colin Ross. 10/4/72 PH JW *

13/7/72 Drummond *The shoemaker, Ship jigs: The wedding of Blythe/The peacock follows the hen/Andrew Carr, Cold and raw (& Dance to your daddy, Whinham's reel/Nancy Clough/Storres, 24/8/72).* * 26/6/72 MV5 MB MH&MF

18/7/74 Peel *Fenwick of Bywell, Marley hill ducks, Dance to your daddy, Hesleyside reel.* Johnny Handle (acc,pp,v), Colin Ross (pp,jh), Alistair Anderson (cnc), Tom Gilfellow (gv). 3/7/74 NW JW *

HIGH TIDE

21/5/69 Peel *Walking down their outlook, Pushed but not forgotten, Missing out.* Tony Hill (g), Simon House (vi), Peter Pavli (b), Rodge Cooper (d). 9/5/69 PS PR *

  'Borderline pass' from panel: 'I don't like this at all' said one producer.

17/8/69 Top Gear *Walking down their outlook, Nowhere, Futilist's lament, Dilemma.* 12/8/69 PH JW *

  Contracts file suggests a session for HENRY, rec'd 7/9/69, but I can find no trace of broadcast.

11/4/70 Top Gear *The joke, Saneonimous.* 24/3/70 MV4 JW *

THE HIGSONS

1/6/81 Peel *(I don't want to live with) Monkeys, Got to let this heat out, A dash to the shops, Surrender.* Switch Higson (v), Terry Edwards (g,sx,tp,bkv), Stuart McGeachin (g,bkv), Colin Williams (b,bkv), Simon Charterton (d,bkv). 25/5/81 LH1 CL NG

27/8/81 Skinner *The lost and the lonely, (My love is) Bent (at both ends), It goes wapp!, Crash.* 20/8/81 MV4 DG MR

4/11/81 Peel *We will never grow old, Conspiracy, Where have all the club a-go-go's went?, Touch down.* 21/10/81 MV4 * *

26/4/82 Jensen *Ha! ha!, Born blind, Our day now, Ylang ylang, Burn the whole thing down.* & Pip Cartwright

(tb), Jane Chettleburgh (cnt), Susie Cox (sx). 18/4/82 MV5 DG ME

11/10/82 Peel *John Peel's new sig tune, You should have run me down, Gangway, Annie and Billy, Put the punk back into funk.* Back to five-piece. 22/9/82 MV4 RP MC

6/12/82 Jensen *Where have all the club-a-gogo's went?, Somethin' gud, Music to watch girls by, One world.* 25/11/82 MV4 JS MR

22/6/83 Peel *Push out the boat, Clanking my bucket, Round and round, Attack of the cannibal businessman.* & Dan Higson (sx). 9/5/83 MV4 TW MC

20/12/83 Jensen *I can hear voices, Junk keeps piling up, Ice age, Do the jerk.* & Jane Chettelburgh (cnt,v). 20/11/83 MV4 JS MR

25/6/84 Peel *Walk on water, 1958, Keep the fire alight, It's a wonderful life.* Five-piece again. 13/6/84 MV5 RP NG

THE ROY HILL BAND

27/6/78 Peel *It can take a lifetime, Melody avenue, I like I like I like, More, It's only my life.* Roy Hill (g,lv), Colin Wilkinson (d), Gary Twigg (bv), Ross McGeeny (lgv), Mike Taylor (kv), Peter Acock (sxv) (4-Hill only). 20/6/78 MV4 MB MR

9/4/79 Peel *Baby don't pretend, Small adventurer, The loser, TV detective.* Hill, Taylor, Acock, John Knightsbridge (g), Tony Fernandez (d), Chas Cronk (b). 2/4/79 MV6 TW DD

HOLGER HILLER

25/3/87 Peel *Holger Hiller, Tiny little cloud, 48 kissen, Warm glas.* Holger Hiller (prg,smp,v), Izumi Kobayashi (k). 8/3/87 * DG NG&PS

HIPSWAY

29/7/85 Long *Ring of the bell, Set the world, Forbidden, Long white car.* Graham Skinner (v), Simon Jones (g), Harry Travers (d), John McElhone (b); & Craig Armstrong (k). 30/6/85 HP BYA SC

HIS LATEST FLAME

20/11/89 Campbell *Come on come on, Sporting life, Finest hour, Love's in the neighbourhood.* Irene Brown (g,bkv), Tricia Reid (g,bkv), Moira Rankine (lv), Tracy Gilbert (b,bkv), James Savage (k,bkv), Chris Sharrock (d), Dave Ritchie (hca,bkv). 1/11/89 MV5 PW MPK

ROBYN HITCHCOCK AND THE EGYPTIANS

15/9/84 Sat. Live *Sometimes I wish I was a pretty girl, Flavour of night, I often dream of trains, Ye sleeping knights of Jesus.* Hitchcock (p,gv) solo. Live from S2 MRD TdB

7/9/85 Kershaw *Brenda's iron sledge, My wife and my dead wife, Heaven (& The cars she used to drive 3/10/85).* Robyn Hitchcock (gv), Andy Metcalfe (b), Morris Windsor (d). 29/8/85 Y2 JL *

29/5/86 Kershaw *Bass, 52 stations, The president, Lady waters and the hooded one, Tell me about your drugs, The can opener.* Hitchcock, Windsor (dv), Metcalfe, Rodger Jackson (kv). 14/5/86 Y2 SP TWN

  Hitchcock apparently next recorded a three-song session on 25/10/86, 'Fun in the sun', 'Lock away your eyes', 'Where angels fear to tread', but the programme it was on has proved untraceable.

4/2/88 Kershaw *Tropical flesh mandala, Devil mask, Chinese bones, Listening to the Higsons.* Jackson out. 14/1/88 * DG NG&MFA

9/2/89 Kershaw *Madonna of the wasps, Superman, Veins of the queen, One long pair of eyes.* & Dave Woodhead (tp-3 only). 26/1/89 MV4 DG NG

19/1/92 Kershaw *Oceanside, So you think you're in love, Open the door Richard, Birds in perspex, Arms of love, Kung fu fighting, Banana boat song.* Hitchcock, Metcalfe, Windsor. Rec. date unknown KK AK~

  'Robyn used to live round the corner from me in Crouch End, and always thought my kitchen a good place to play; we'd had Baaba Maal, and Butch Hancock and Jimmie Dale Gilmore in there before. That afternoon, Juliette was making this huge pile of sandwiches on the worktop right near the mikes, and had to try and cut the bread without making any noise.'

HITS
23/6/78 PEEL *Bring me the head of Yukio Mashinaldi, Et moi et moi et moi, Only thirteen, Crossroads.* Giovanni Dadomo (v), Dave Fudger (g), Barry Myers (b), Nick Howell (d). 6/6/78 MV4 MB MR

HOCKETT
17/10/72 PEEL *When I was a little boy, Meri it is, Seven yellow gypsies.* Gary Carpenter (o,fl,p), Ian Cutler (vi), Andy Tompkins (g), Bernie Murray (d), Ray Warman (bv). 9/10/72 * JW *

HOCUS POKE
10/2/72 DRUMMOND *HP Beagle, Down in the street, The poke.* * 26/1/72 * MB MH&MF

HOLE
5/1/92 PEEL *Violet, Forming, Drown soda, Doll parts.* Caroline Rue (d), Jill Emery (b), Eric Erlandson (lg), Courtney Love (g,lv). 19/11/91 MV4 MR~ CML

HOLLE HOLLE
23/9/87 PEEL *Patli patang, Pind na challia, Ankhaa tunai haar, Holle holle.* Chandu & Arun (Indian drums), Inder (perc), Abass (cga), Ragen (b), Deepak (g), Shatish (k), Joe (sx), Manjeet (lv), Bina & Kum Kum (bkv-4 only). 15/9/87 * DG MR&JB

TIM HOLLIER
20/11/68 NIGHT RIDE *Bird of paradise, In silence, Song to a room, And I, I search for small distractions.* Tim Hollier (gv). 20/11/68 SI PC * [M: Folk Shows]

THE HOLLIES
22/10/67 TOP GEAR *Games we play, Step inside, King Midas in reverse, Postcard, Charlie and Fred, Away away away.* Graham Nash, Allan Clarke, Tony Hicks, Bobby Elliott, Bernard Calvert; & orchestra of 14, with Johnny Scott (md). 13/10/67 * * *
Group's first Broadcast was on 'The Talent Spot' Light Programme 7/6/63. Dozens of pop sessions followed.

HOLMES BROTHERS
15/9/91 KERSHAW *Please don't hurt me, Big boss man, None but the righteous, Walk with me.* Wendell Holmes (gv), Sherman Holmes (brs,v), Gib Whaton (ps), Willie (Popsie) Dixon (dv). 25/7/91 MV5 DG MA&AA

HOLOSADE
17/6/88 FRI. ROCK *Welcome to hell house, Look into the mirror, Computer world, Psycho.* Philip De Sade (v), Gary Thomas (g), Mike Lee (d), Jack Hammer (lg), Ian McDonald (b). 3/6/88 * PW DD

HOLY MACKEREL
16/11/72 PEEL *Waterfall, Spanish attraction, On, The boy and the mekon.* Terry Clark (v), Derek Smallcombe (lg), Anthony Wood (b), Chris Ware (lg), Roger Siggery (d). 13/11/72 LHI BA *
Rec'd daytime sessions under previous name 'Jason Crest' after passing audition 11/68 [M].

HOLY WILLIE'S PRAYER
16/1/71 TOP GEAR *Willow, Very good time, If you don't, Honesty.* Chris Hardy (g,vi,v), Rod Cameron (p,hmn,gv). 29/12/70 MV4 * *
'Booked as unknown duo after submitting tape' JW to panel.

HOME
3/6/71 HENRY *Tramps, Bad days, In my time, Red-E-Lewis and the red caps.* Laurie Wisefield (lgv), Michael Stubbs (lgv), Clifford Williams (bv), Michael Cook (d). 26/5/71 MV4 MB MH&MF
'I got the impression that when they really settle down they will become quite a force in the business... the guitarist is only 17' MB to panel: unanimous pass.
4/10/71 HARRIS *Moses, Red-E-Lewis and the red caps, (& My lady of the birds, 15/11/71).* 20/9/71 TI JM JWH

3/11/71 PEEL *Tramp, The idol, Mother, In my time.* 4/10/71 PH * *
30/12/71 DRUMMOND *Next one please, Mother, Lady of the birds.* 29/12/71 MV4 MB MH&MF
10/1/72 HARRIS *Captain Thimball, How would it feel? Next one please, Family.* 4/1/72 MV5 JG *
Rec'd In Concert 13/4/72 PS, TX 22/4/72.
23/5/72 PEEL *Rise up, Red-E-Lewis and the red caps, Baby friend of mine.* 9/5/72 MV4 * *
28/7/72 PEEL *Shady lady, Baby friend of mine, Knave, How would it feel?* 28/6/72 TI PD *
28/8/72 HARRIS *Lady of the birds, In my time.* 31/7/72 TI JG *
28/9/72 DRUMMOND *Knave, I like what you do to me, Dreamer, Fancy lady Hollywood child.* 18/9/72 MV5 MB MH&MF
5/1/73 SEQUENCE *I like what you do to me, In my time, Sunny side of the street, Dreamer.* 5/12/72 TI PD *
29/3/73 PEEL *Dreamer, I like what you do to me, How would it feel?* 26/3/73 LHI BA *
11/6/73 HARRIS *The alchemist.* 30/5/73 LHI JG *
1/11/73 PEEL *Red-E-Lewis and the red caps, Dreamer, Excerpt from The Alchemist.* & Dave Skillen (v), Jim Anderson (p). 22/10/73 LHI BA *
Rec'd 2nd In Concert & new 6-piece line-up 19/10/73 HP, TX 24/11/73.
20/4/74 ROCK ON *Green eyed fairy, Salad days, Excerpt from the alchemist 'Old man calling', Excerpts from the alchemist 'A secret to keep' '& The brass band played'.* Skillen out. 18/3/74 LHI BA *

A HOMEBOY A HIPPIE AND A FUNKY DREAD
25/11/90 KERSHAW *Freedom, Monkey flip, Rough & ready, Total confusion reprise.* Mark Williams (pv) credited only.
8/11/90 MV5 DG *
3/2/91 PEEL *Drop your soul, Vicious, Dream.* & Tony Winter. 13/1/91 MV3 DG MA

HOMESICK JAMES AND GRIZELDA
31/10/70 TOP GEAR *Got to move, Skies are crying, Crossroads, Dust my room.* Homesick James (gv) & unknown. 19/10/70 PH JW *

THE HONEY BUS
19/11/67 TOP GEAR *Maxine's parlour, Do I still figure in your life, Good day sunshine, Arise Sir Henry, Like an old time movie.* Pete Dello, Ray Cane, Colin Boyd, Peter Kircher; & strings. 15/11/67 MV4 BA PR
20/11/67 SYMONDS *Do I still figure in your life, Maxine's parlour (21/11), Arise Sir Henry (22/11).* [M: daytime]. 13/11/67 PS * *
18/2/68 TOP GEAR *Ain't that just bonnie for you, I can't let Maggie go, Francoise, She comes to me.* 7/2/68 MV4 BA PR
15/9/68 TOP GEAR *Looking down, Girl of independent means, Scarlet lady, How long, Warwick town.* & 3 extra musicians. 20/8/68 PCI BA AH
29/12/68 TOP GEAR *Black mourning band, Girl of independent means, She sold Blackpool rock, Would you believe?, Incredibly bad.* Jim Kelly r. Dello; & 2 violins, 1 viola, 2 trumpets/French horn, flugelhorn. 17/12/68 PCI BA *
1/6/70 SYMONDS *Follow the plan, Ceilings No 2, Melinda (& She said yes, 29/6/70).* & string quintet. 8/4/70 PH BA NG
5/10/72 PEEL *I can't say it but I can sing it, Big ship, The lady's not for burning, Writing's on the wall, Lady.* Dello returns, r. Kelly. 2/10/72 LHI BA *

THE HONEYMOON KILLERS
24/11/82 PEEL *Fonce a mort, Histoire a suivre, Reveillons-nous, Romantic evening.* Marc Hollander (k), Jean François Jones (d), Yves Flon (sx), Vincent Kenis (b), Yvon Kromman (v-1&4, g-2&3), Veronique Vincent (v-2,3), Gerald Fenerberg (g). 13/11/82 * DG MR

THE HONEYSMUGGLERS
19/11/90 GOODIER *Pie in the sky, Beautiful people, Apple*

tree, Listen. Steve Dinsdale (d), Chris Spence (b), Jed Murphy (g), Steve Cox (k). 3/11/90 MV5 MC~AA

THE HOODOO GURUS
1/9/87 LONG *Middle of the land, On my street, Come see me, Hayride to hell.* Dave Faulkner (gv), Brad Shepherd (g), Mark Kingsmill (g), Clyde Bramley (b). 15/8/87 Trafalgar studios, Sydney, Australia * *

THE HOOK 'N' PULL GANG
1/10/86 LONG *Footsie love, Pour it down yer throat, The family's in, I'd lick the pavements (if I thought it would help you).* Alan McDade (b), Eileen McMullan (d,lv), Rita Blazyca (gv). 21/9/86 MV4 KJ MC&JB

HOOKFOOT
18/5/71 HARDING *Mystic lady, The opener, Nature changes.* Caleb Quaye (g), Ian Duck (v), Roger Pope (d), Dave Glover (b), Peter Ross. 10/5/71 MV5 MB MH&MF
Debuted (without Ross) as solo band on Peel Sunday Concert TX 5/4/70 [M].
6/4/73 SEQUENCE *If I had the words, Cuckoo, Communication, Cruisin'.* Ross out; Fred Gandy (b) r. Glover. 13/3/73 TI PD *

THE HOOVERS
2/3/91 PEEL *Green, Comes a time†, Mr average, Big time.* Jo So (d), Phil (g), Granty (bv), Owey (gv). 29/1/91 MV5 MR~
† On 'New season' SFRCD205.

MARY HOPKIN
14/2/72 HARRIS *What a friend you are, International, Y Doryn Pur (& Sparrow, 13/3/72).* with Tony Visconti plus 7 musicians [Last of many appearances]. 8/2/72 MV5 JG *

HORSE
17/3/89 FRI. ROCK *Screwed blued and tattooed, She don't care, Life's a bitch, Good day to die.* Damon (b), Dave Hoyland (d), Gary Gene (v), Mark Perez (g). 17/2/89 MV4 TW *

HORSLIPS
24/9/73 HARRIS *Furniture, Flower any then all, Clergy's lamentation.* Barry Devlin (bv), Jim Lockhart (fl,kv), Johnny Fean (g), Eamonn Carr (d), Charles O'Connor (fd,mnd,v). 19/9/73 LHI JG *
16/10/73 PEEL *Bratach bana, Dearg doom, Knockeen free.* 1/10/73 TI JW *
19/2/74 PEEL *The silver spear, Charolet/The march/You can't fool the beast.* 28/1/74 TI JW *
4/3/74 HARRIS *More than you can chew, King of the fairies, Ferdia's song.* 13/2/74 LHI JG *
19/11/74 PEEL *Mad Pat/Blind man, Lonely hearts, Nightown boys.* 4/11/74 MV4 TW *
7/4/77 DLT *Warm sweet breath of love, The Power and the glory, The rocks remain, Trouble with a capital T.* 4/4/77 MV5 * *

HOT HOUSE
7/5/85 LONG *Shanty town, Evening with the blues, Same place same time, Don't come to stay.* Heather Small (lv), Mark Pringle (g), Robbie Taylor (k), Ian Maidman (b), Jamie Laine (d), Melissa Henry (bkv). 24/4/85 MV5 BYA PW
2/7/85 LONG *My boy's arms, Me and you, Love rich cash poor, Homeboy (a.k.a. Get lost).* Small, Pringle, Maidman, Laine, Henry, Steve Fletcher (k), Peter Veitch (k), Tom Fenner (perc). 26/5/85 MV4 BYA PW
10/2/87 LONG *Pull over, Catch before we fall, When push come to shove, Jealous kind.* Small, Pringle, Ian Prince (k), Ernie McKone (k), Western Foster (d), Graham Edwards (b). 4/2/87 MV4 BYA MPK

HOT WATER
13/9/78 PEEL *Boxer, Back to the beach, Motorway, Dark fooling man.* Ben (Brenda) Prescott (v), Sheila Macartney (v), John Lovering (g), Ann Williams (k), Paul Shroud (b), Jeff Taylor (sx), Roy Smith (cga,perc), Owen Hughes (d). 30/8/78 MV4 BS NG

THE HOTHOUSE FLOWERS
3/11/87 Long *Hydroman, The ballad of Katie (and the big man with the black horse), If you're happy, Mountains.* Liam O'Moinlai (vp), Leo Barnes (sx), Peter O'Toole (b), Fiachina O'Braonain (g), Gerry Fehily (d). 11/10/87 MV4 PW TdB

THE HOUSE OF LOVE
20/6/88 Peel *Destroy the heart, Nothing to me, Plastic, Blind.* Guy Chadwick (gv), Terry Bickers (g), Chris Groothuizen (b), Pete Evans (d). 7/6/88 MV4 DG DD

14/9/88 Peel *The Hedonist, Don't turn blue, Safe, Love in car.* 26/8/88 MV4 DG MA

12/4/89 Peel *In a room, The Beatles and the Stones, Christine, Loneliness is a gun.* Acoustic session. 2/4/89 MV4 DG MR
 Also recorded live gig at Subterania 29/8/89 for Peel's 50th Birthday Party, TX 30/8.

1/1/90 Peel *Se dest, 32nd floor, 7.45 am.* Bickers out. 12/12/89 MV5 DG ME

15/12/91 Peel *Into the tunnel, Fade away, High in your face.* Simon Fernsby (lg) joins. 5/11/91 MV4 MR~
 Booked for Jackie Brambles' tea-time show 20/4/92.

22/8/92 Peel *Cruel, Burn down the world, Crush me.* Simon Manby (g,bkv). 4/8/92 MV4 PL~ AA

A HOUSE
9/2/87 Peel *Call me blue, Y.O.U, Hit me over the head with your handbag dear, Heart happy.* David Couse (v,ag), Fergal Bunbury (g), Martin Healy (b), Dermot Wylie (d). 25/1/87 * DG ME&FK

18/6/87 Long *Only one thing wrong with perfect, Watch out you're dead, Clump of trees, Don't think you're different.* 7/6/87 MV4 HP TdB&MA

13/3/92 Peel *Endless art, Charity, Freakshow, Force feed.* Couse, Bunbury, Healy, Dave Dawson (d), Dave Morrisey (k), Susan Kavanagh (bkv). 2/2/92 MV3 DG ME&RF

THE HOUSEMARTINS
29/7/85 Peel *Drop down dead, Flag day, Stand at ease, Joy joy joy.* Hugh Whitaker (dv), Ted Key (bv), Stan Cullimore (gv), Paul Heaton (v); & Kevin Abbott (tp). 21/7/85 MV5 DG ME

20/11/85 Long *Anxious, We're not deep, Reverend's revenge, Freedom, People get ready.* Abbott out. 6/11/85 MV5 BYA MPK

14/4/86 Peel *Over there, Happy hour, Get up off our knees, Caravan of love.* Norman Cook (b,bkv) r. Key. 6/4/86 MV5 DG ME&FK

16/6/86 Peel *Happy hour, Heaven help us all, He ain't heavy he's my brother, When I first met Jesus, Peel show sig (a cappella).* Billed as 'The Fish City 5', a cappella session. 3/6/86 MV4 DG TdB&FK

24/6/86 Long *Sheep, Drop down dead, Think for a minute, Heaven help us all, Flag day, Anxious, Happy hour.* 10/6/86, live at the Town and Country Club DS SR
 Next, band did a cappella session on SATURDAY LIVE, 6/9/86 S2, prod. PRS & TdB.

23/12/86 Long *A friend in Jesus, Mercy, So glad, He brought me out, Heaven help us all.* A cappella session #2. 11/12/86 S2 BYA *

11/11/87 Peel *There is always something there to remind me†, Sunday isn't Sunday, Build.* Dave Hamingway (dv) r. Whitaker. 3/11/87 * DG *
 † On 'Now that's what I call quite good.' LP, Go! Discs.

THE DAVE HOWARD SINGERS
2/12/85 Long *Baby comeback, That guy everywhere, Camberwell, It's OK.* Dave Howard (v,o,dm), Nick Smash (perc). 20/11/85 MV5 BYA MPK

3/8/88 L. Kershaw *Chances, Mickey and Dee, God's god, Confused.* Howard only. 26/6/88 MV4 TdB~

HOWLIN' WILF
18/9/86 Kershaw *If I could, She moves me, Backstroke, Baby please don't go.* Howlin' Wilf (v,hca), Dot Hunt

(g), Tony Hilton (db), Keith Shepherd (d). 3/9/86 * RG PSM

15/10/87 Kershaw *Tell me baby, Wondrous place, What am I gonna do with you, Something moves me.* Wilf, Shepherd, Andy Neal (g), Matt Radford (db), Slim (o,p). 24/9/87 * DG JB&ME

12/1/89 Kershaw *Lights on nobody in, Don't make a prison out of love, Two can play, Dependent on you.* 'and the Vee-Jays': Neal, Shepherd, Jason Wilson (b). 8/12/88 MV4 DG MWT

HUDSON-FORD
29/6/74 Rock On *Free spirit, Floating in the wind, Take a little wood, Don't wanna be a star.* John Ford, Richard Hudson, Nicky Keene, Chris Parren, Ken Lews. 24/6/74 LH1 BA * [M]

HUG
16/9/91 Goodier *Mesmerized, Arctic, You should see me, Wake up.* Gemma Wilson (v), Ken Sakamoto (v,perc), Liam Gilfellow (b), Dave Curie (d), Ade Wollard (dj,smp), George Kitching (g). 7/9/91 MV5 MC~ DMC

MIKE HUGG
14/9/72 Drummond *Fool no more, Picture of you, Sad song, Don't keep me hanging on.* Mike Hugg (pv), David King (g), Mickey Waller (d), John Curtis (b). 6/9/72 MV4 MB *
 File suggests session for Jimmy Young recorded 15/8/72, untraceable.

HOWARD HUGHES AND THE WESTERN APPROACHES
7/4/86 Long *Plains, The wagon takes control, Buffalo Bill, Horsepower.* Howard Hughes (v), Steve Turner (g), Chris Pye (g,sy), Roberto Soave (b), Lennie Satch (d). 24/3/86 MV4 BYA SC

HULA
25/3/85 Peel *Freeze out†, Bad blood, Sour Eden, Gun culture.* Ron Wright (g,v,mel), Simon Crump (sx,bcl), John Avery (b,k,perc), Mark Albrow (k,tps), Nort (d,perc). 12/3/85 MV5 MR JB † On Red Rhino REDT64.

16/7/86 Peel *Burn it out, When that hammer starts to beat, Backwall blue, Church trumpet.* Darrell D'Silva (al,ts) r. Crump. 1/7/86 MV4 DG DD

ALAN HULL
18/1/73 Peel *The miller's song, Money game, Numbers, Tynemouth song (& Country gentleman's wife, 8/2/73).* Alan Hull (gpv). 8/1/73 LH1 BA NG
 Debuted as solo act live from PH on Country Meets Folk, 31/1/70.

6/8/73 Harris *Drug song, Down on the underground, Numbers, When the war is over (& United States of mind, 24/9/73).* 18/7/73 LH1 JG *

11/12/73 Peel *Take good care of business, Gin and tonics all round, Money game, Waiting.* 12/11/73 T1 * BC

14/1/74 Harris *Gin and tonics all round, Dealer's choice, Winter song, One more bottle of wine.* 28/11/73 LH1 JG *

29/5/75 Peel *Squire, Dan the plan, Money game, One more bottle of wine, City song.* 22/5/75 MV4 * *

6/4/76 Peel *Walk in the sea, Love is the answer, I wish you well, Somewhere out there.* & Robert Barton. 11/3/76 MV4 * *

THE HUMAN LEAGUE
16/8/78 Peel *Being boiled, No time, You've lost that lovin' feeling, Blind youth.* Ian Marsh (sy,k,v), Martyn Ware (sy,k,v), Philip Oakey (v), Adrian Wright (visuals). 8/8/78 MV4 BS MR

HUMAN ORCHESTRA
3/5/76 Peel *Games, Stop.* * 3/2/76 MV4 * *

HUMANOID
28/11/88 Peel *Orbital (feeling), Slam, Jet stream Tokyo.* Brian Douglas, John Lakker. 15/11/88 MV4 MR~

HUMBLE PIE
24/8/69 Symonds on Sunday *Desperation, Natural born boogie, Sad bag of Shakey Jake, Heartbeat.* Steve Marriott (gv) Peter Frampton (gv), Greg Ridley (b), Jerry Shirley (d). 17/8/69 MV5 c.PWI *

27/9/69 Top Gear *Shakin' all over, Shakey Jake/Walk on gilded splinters.* 9/9/69 MV4 JW TW&BC
 Group next rec'd Peel Sunday Concert 10/9/70 PS, TX 20/9/70.

9/8/70 DLT *One eyed trouser snake rhumba, Big Black dog, Four day creep.* 27/7/70 AO2 c.PWI *

26/3/71 Black *Four day creep, I'm ready, The light, I'm a rolling stone (& I don't need no doctor, 23/4/71).* 1/3/71 T1 JM JWH

17/2/72 Drummond *The road runner, Come on everybody, Sweet peace and time.* David 'Clem' Clempson (g) r. Frampton. 7/2/72 MV5 MB MH&MF

THE HUMBLEBUMS
7/3/70 Top Gear *Please sing a song for us, Harry, Rick rack, Mother (& Everybody knows that, 13/6/70).* Billy Connolly, Gerry Rafferty & Daryl Runswick, Bernie Holland, Mike Travis. 23/2/70 * * *
 Had previously done b'casts in Scotland. Rec'd Peel Sunday Concert 28/5/70 PS, TX 7/6/70; with Connolly, Rafferty, Jim Tagford, Barry Atkinson, Eileen Woodman.

6/8/70 Henry *Cruising, Mother, Keep it to yourself, Singing bird.* As 28/5/70. 30/7/70 AO2 MB MH&MF

19/10/70 Harris *Steamboat row, Her father didn't like me anyway, Oh no, A little of your time.* Connolly, Rafferty, Atkinson & Ian Campbell. 9/10/70 MV5 JM * [M]

HUNTER MUSKETT
14/9/73 Sequence *Leave the land, Cockfight, If I played a steel guitar, Scarecrow.* Terry Hiscock (agpv), Chris George (gv,hca), Douglas Morter (gv), Roger Trevitt (bg). 31/7/73 T1 JM NG
 1st b'cast was on Folk on 2, 19/12/71.

THE HUNTER'S CLUB
13/4/88 Mayo *Lightning strikes, Feel like making love, Gimme your soul, Angel.* Beast (b), Rikki Torrent (g), Christian Merciless (g,dm), Otis Oblivion (v). 27/3/88 MV4 HP TdB

HURRAH!
8/12/82 Jensen *Lonely room, Hip hip, This boy, Saturday's train.* Paul Handyside (lgv), Taff Hughes (rgv), Dave Porterhouse (b,bkv), Paul Damien Mahoney (d). 28/11/82 MV4 DG ME

HYPNOTONE
20/4/91 Peel *Paris, Hypnotonic, Yu yu, Sub.* Tony Martin (k,prg), Martin Duffy (k), Valerie Fisher (v), Carlos Manning (rp). 28/3/91 MV4 DG TdB&JMK

I'M SO HOLLOW
20/8/80 Peel *Fashion, Monotony, Dreams to fill the vacuum, Which way?* Gary Marsden (b), Jane Wilson (sy,v), Joe Sawicki (d), Rod Leigh (gv). 13/8/80 MV4 DG NG

I, LUDICROUS
16/6/87 Peel *Fabulous, Quite extraordinary, A pop fan's dream, Ridiculous.* Mark Crossley (b), John Procter (g,k,dm), David Rippingdale (v). 31/5/87 * DG ME&FK

I.Q.
11/5/84 Fri. Rock *Just changing hands, Awake and nervous, Widow's peak.* Mike Holmes (g), Paul Cook (d), Peter Nichols (v), Tim Esau (b), Martin Orford (k). 27/4/84 MV4 TW MC

ICARUS
11/12/80 Peel *Don't put reggae in a bag, Shall we roam, Tower block kid.* Cyril Charles (lv), Ashley Charles (v), Leroy Cyrus (k), Harold Cyrus (d), Leon Modeste (b), James Nagan (lg). 26/11/80 LH1 BS NG

ICE
18/11/67 Pete's People *Got to get you into my life, Anniversary (of love), It's alright, Mercy mercy mercy, Don't call me.* Lynton Naiff (o), Steve Turner, Grant Serpall, John Carter, Glyn James. 3/11/67 MV5 c.JHO *

4/12/67 Symonds *It's alright, Show me (6/12), Got to get you into my life (7/12), Don't call me (8/12).* & Linda Hoile (v). 27/11/67 PS c.RB *

24/12/67 Top Gear *Please don't cry, Open the door to your heart, Think, Walk on the water.*
19/12/67 AO2 BA DT

6/1/68 Pete's People *Open the door to your heart, Please don't cry, Day tripper, Show me, Time's fading fast.*
22/12/67 MV5 cJHO *

5/2/68 Symonds *Ice man, Maria Lane (6/2), Walk on the water (8/2).* 30/1/68 MV4 cRB *

15/4/68 Symonds *Day tripper, Ice man (16/4), Open the door to your heart (17/4), Wide blue yonder boy (19/4).* 29/3/68 PCI cRB *

THE ICICLE WORKS

26/1/82 Peel *In the cauldron of love, A factory in the desert, All is right, When winter lasted forever.* Robert Ian McNabb (gkv), Chris Layhe (bv), Chris 'Chas' Sharrock (d). 11/1/82 MV4 TW DD

25/11/82 Jensen† *(Birds fly) Whisper to a scream, Lover's day, As the dragon fly flies, Love hunt.*
14/11/82 MV4 DG ME † On Nighttracks SFNT015.

2/3/83 Peel *Love is a wonderful colour, Reverie girl, Reaping the rich harvest, In the dance the shaman led.* 26/2/83 MV4 DG MC

29/11/83 Jensen *Chop the tree, Nirvana, Mountain comes to Mohammed, Out of season.* 30/10/83 MV4 DG ME

3/3/84 Long *A factory in the desert, Scarecrow, Ragweed campaign, In the cauldron of love.* 13/2/84 PHM cPWL *

15/8/84 Peel *Hollow horse, Deep in the woods, Conscience of kings, When you hear the mission bells.*
8/8/84 MV5 BYA NG

24/4/85 Long *Perambulator, All the daughters (of her father's house), Diamond in the rough, Impossibly three lovers.* & Tony Whittingham (tb), Tony Kelly (ts), Philip Cesar (tp). 20/3/85 MV5 JS MPK

ICON A. D.

13/10/82 Peel *Cancer, Clockwork orange, Face the facts, Ransom, No hope.* Caroline & Bev Smith (v), Craig Sharp (g), Roger Turnbull (b), Mark Holmes (d).
25/9/82 MV4 DG MPK

IDIOT DANCERS

20/5/80 Peel *Imagination, True soul, 500 years, Jealousy.* Tatty (d), Mike Horsham (bv), Dave McCarthy (gv).
14/5/80 MV4 JE NG

IDLE RACE

8/10/67 Top Gear *I like my toys, Hey Grandma, Knocking nails into my house, Imposters of life's magazine, Here we go round the lemon tree.* Jeff Lynne (gv), Dave Pritchard (gv), Greg Masters (bv), Roger Spencer (dv).
2/10/67 PH BA PR [M: by '68, dozens of daytime sessions]

25/2/68 Top Gear *The lady who would fly, The skeleton and the roundabout, Tell me the time, Don't put your boys in the army Mrs Ward.* 19/2/68 MV4 BA PR

9/6/68 Top Gear *The end of the road, Blueberry blue, On with the show, The morning sunshine (& Follow me follow, Lucky man, 7/7/68).* 4/6/68 PCI BA DT

22/9/68 Top Gear *Follow me follow, The birthday, Told you twice, Pie in the sky.* 3/9/68 PCI BA AH

26/1/69 Top Gear *Mr Crowd and Sir Norman, Days of the broken arrows, Sea of dreams, Worn red carpet (& Frantic desolation, 9/3/69).* 20/1/69 PH BA *

29/6/69 Top Gear *Sea of dreams, Please no more sad songs, Someone knocking, Reminds me of you (& Come with me, 3/8/69).* 23/6/69 PH JW * [M]

IDOL RICH

14/8/87 Fri. Rock *IOU, Dirty dreams, Just when I thought I had it all, The first time.* Nick Burr (g), Nick Hughes (b), Kim Jones (g), Mike Fisher (d), Stuart Neill (v).
Rec. date unknown MV4 TW DD

IF

17/7/70 Black *Reaching out on all sides, Sinking, What can a friend say.* Jim Richardson (b), Terry Smith (lg), Dick Morrissey (sx,fl), Denis Elliott (d), Dave Quincy (ts,al), John Hodgkinson (v,perc), John Mealing (pv).
1/7/70 AO2 JM JWH

Rec'd Peel Sunday Concert 9/7/70 PS, TX 2/8/70.

15/1/71 Black *Tarmac T. Pirate and the lonesome nymphomaniac mealing, I couldn't write and tell you, The city is falling, Sunday sad.* 23/12/70 AO2 JM *

16/7/71 Black *Upstairs, Sweet January, Forgotten roads, Fibronacci's number.* 28/6/71 TI JM BH

14/9/71 Harding *Child of storm, Seldom seen Sam, Far beyond.* 6/9/71 MV5 MB MH&MF

Rec'd 2nd Peel Sunday Concert 15/7/71 PS, TX 5/9/71.

28/1/72 Peel *The city is falling, Box, (& Reaching out on all sides, 24/3/72).* 3/1/72 TI PD ARV

IF ONLY

12/10/90 Fri. Rock *Tumbling dice, All over, Ghost of you, Rock and a hard place.* Jackie Bodimead (v), Greg Hart (g), Martin Chaisson (g), Ian Edwards (b), Toby Sadler (k). Andy Elphick (g). 21/9/90 MV5 DD~

IFANGI BONDI

24/9/90 Peel *Sanjo, Faro, Sikarsi.* Momadou Nying (dv), Musa Mboob (Afd), Badou Jobe (b), Bai Janha & Aliey Dian (g), Adamu Sallah (k), Paps Touray (v), Ali Harb (v,fl). 29/7/90 MV3 DG ME&DTH

IJAHMAN

11/2/89 Miss P *Lend a hand, My summer time, Bear you in mind, Madgie.* Ijahman (v), Michael Nanton (k), Des Dale Wilmot (b), Marley (Steven) Wright (g), Asker (Noel Barnes) (perc), Dixie (Garthell Pinnock) (d).
28/10/88 MV5 PW NG

IN CAMERA

16/12/80 Peel *The fatal day, Co-ordinates, Apocalypse.* David Steiner (v), Andrew Gray (g), Pete Moore (b), Jeff Wilmott (d). 9/12/80 LHI JS MR

IN EXCELSIS

8/2/84 Peel *Fire, Love lies, Vows, Bonanza.* Roxy (d), Mark (b), Spon (g), Errol (v). 25/1/84 MV5 DG NG

INCA BABIES

6/2/84 Peel *Grunt cadillac hotel, Brother rat, Superior spectre, Big jugular.* Alan Brown (d), Bill Marten (b), Harry Stafford (g), Mike Keeble (v). 28/1/84 MV5 DG MC

28/8/84 Peel *The judge, She mercenary, Cactus mouth informer, Blind man (The chiller).* Stafford, Keeble, Peter Bogg (d), Bill Bonney (b). 21/8/84 * MRD TdB

26/6/85 Peel *Crawling garage gasoline, Doomed locustland, Daniella, No sacred sound.* Bill Marten (b) returns r. Bonney. 16/6/85 MV5 DG ME

21/7/86 Peel *Plenty more mutants, Opium den, The depths, Dresden.* Stafford, Bogg, Bonney, Darren Bullows (g). 8/7/86 MV5 DG MS&JB

THE INCREDIBLE BLONDES

16/10/85 Long *The morning after, Pin it up, White lies free, Ritzy girl.* Barry McLeod (gv), Sarah Flynn (k), Robert Campbell (d). 6/10/85 HP BYA *

INCREDIBLE STRING BAND

15/10/67 Top Gear *Painting box, Mercy I cry a city, Chinese white, Night fall.* Mike Heron (g,sit,hca,v), Robin Williamson (g,vi,mnd, perc,v). 10/10/67 AO2 BA *

6/3/68 Night Ride *You get brighter, All too much for me, Ducks on the pond.* 4/3/68 AO2 JM *

5/3/69 Night Ride *All sit down, Dust B Diamonds, Theta, Fine fingered hand.* & Christina 'Licorice' McKechnie, Rose Simpson. 5/2/69 SI JM *

24/8/69 Top Gear *The letter, This moment, Gather around, Waiting for you, (& Black Jack Davy, 1/11/69).*
5/8/69 MV4 JW *

25/7/70 Top Gear *Won't you come and see me, Empty pocket blues, Flowers of the forest, Beautiful stranger (& Dark-eyed lady, 3/10/70).* 20/7/70 PH JW *

24/9/70 Henry *Everything's fine right now, Coleman's fancy/Rakish Paddy/The wayward fox/Johnny Grey, Won't you come and see me, Raga phuti raga (& Ring dance, 29/10/70).* 17/9/70 AO2 MB MH&MF

9/1/71 Top Gear *Everything's fine right now, Long long road, The circle is unbroken, Raga phuti raga.*
6/10/70 MV4 JW *

13/10/71 Peel *You get brighter, Jigs, How we danced the lord of Weir, The actor.* Malcolm LeMaistre (mnd,gv), r. Simpson. 5/10/71 MV4 JW *

25/11/71 Drummond *The circle is unbroken, The sailor and the dancer, Living in the shadows, Tree.*
17/11/71 PH MV4 JW BC

17/3/72 Peel *Did I love a dream, Restless night, Down before Cathy.* 29/2/72 TI JM NG

29/8/72 Peel *Black Jack Davy, Rends moi†, Did I love a dream†, Witches hat†/Ladybird/I bid you good night/Long time sunshine.* Stan Lee (psg), Stuart Gordon, r. McKechnie; & Jack Ingram (g).
4/8/72 PH JW BC

6/3/73 Peel *Raga June, At the lighthouse dance, Saturday maybe, Maker of islands.* Gerard Dott r. Gordon.
26/2/73 TI PD&JW ARV

19/3/73 Harris *Cold days of February†, Little girl†, The sailor and the dancer†, At the lighthouse dance.*
27/2/73 LHI PR *

23/10/73 Peel† *Dreams of no return, Black Jack Davy, Jane, Dear old battlefield.* Mike Heron (g,sit,hca), Robin Williamson (mnd,g,vi), Graham Forbes, Jack Ingram (d), Stan Lee (b), Malcolm LeMaistre (gv). 9/10/73 LHI JW BC
†† On BOJCD004. Other titles on this release may be drawn from the above session tracks, but re-named.

NEIL INNES

4/8/72 Peel *How sweet to be an idiot, I give myself to me, Momma B, Every time, Children's song.* Neil Innes (o,pv), Tom McGuinness (lg), Hughie Flint (d), Dixie Dean (b), Tony White (rg). 11/7/72 TI JM *

7/2/74 Peel *Bandwagon, Twyford Vitromant, Momma B, Dream on/L'amour perdu, Disney waltz, This love of ours.* possibly & Alan Spenner (b), Ollie Halsall (g), & 2 (unknown). 31/1/74 LHI JG BAI

24/5/77 Peel *Drama on a Saturday night, Randy Raquel, Queen Elizabeth, Cheese and onions.* Neil Innes (pgv), Ollie Halsall (lg,o), Brian Hodgson (b), Pete Baron (d). 18/5/77 MV4 MB NG [M: R2, R4]

INSIDE OUT

19/5/91 Peel *Loss for words, I cut myself, Cold sterile, Get the funk out.* Cathy Carrell (d), Karen Neal (b,lv), Lynda Metz (g,bkv). 23/4/91 MV5 MPK~ JSM

THE INSPIRAL CARPETS

1/8/88 Peel *So far, Monkey on my back, Greek wedding song, Whiskey.* Craig Gill (d), Dave Swift (b), Graham Lambert (g), Clint Boon (o,bkv), Steve Holt (v).
17/7/88 MV5 DG MH&SG

5/4/89 Peel† *Out of time, Directing traffic, Keep the circle around, Gimme shelter.* Martin Walsh (b), Tom Hingley (v) r. Swift, Holt. 26/3/89 MV4 DG DD&MA
† On Strange Fruit SFRCD072.

9/10/89 Peel *Sun don't shine, She comes in the fall, Song for a family, So this is how it feels.*
17/8/89 MV5 NG&MR JLO

5/6/90 Peel† *Beast inside, Grip, Weakness, Keep it in mind.* 20/5/90 MV3 DG ME † On Strange Fruit SFRCD085.

9/3/92 Goodier *Smoking clothes, Two worlds collide, Sleep well tonight, Butterfly.* 29/2/92 MV4 MC~

INSTINCT

10/8/83 Jensen *Cool fool, Where time flies, Rip up the schedules, Ice-box eyes.* Angela Jaeger (v), Simon Underwood (bk), James Johnstone (gk,perc).
7/8/83 MV4 DG ME

15/5/85 Long *Sweat to pay, No soul in sight, Keep the dream, Over and over.* & Andy Richards (k).
17/4/85 MV5 BYA MPK&PW

INTASTELLA

17/6/91 Goodier *Are you happy, Overdrive, People.* Stella Grundy (v), Spencer Birtwhistle (d), Martin Wright (g), Martin Mittler (k), Anthony Green (perc). 6/4/91 MV5 MC~

INTENSE DEGREE

15/3/88 Peel† *Hangin' on/Vagrants/Skate-bored, Intense degree/All the guys/Daydreams, Take no chances/Future* shock/Politician, Allegiance/Bursting. Rich Hill (v), Rich Cutts (g), Rich Collins (g), Liz Thirtle (b), Frank Pendelbury (d,bkv). 28/2/88 * DG JB&SA

† On Strange Fruit SFPS053; Most of this session is also on the two 'Hardcore Holocaust' compilations.

INTO PARADISE
10/6/91 Goodier Dreaming, Angel, Gently Falls, Dive. Dave Long (v), James Eadie (g), Spike Mullins (k), Ronan Clarke (d), Rachael Tighe (b). 25/5/91 MV5 MC~

INTO THE WILDERNESS
22/9/87 Long Nightwatchman, Cruel world, Fallen soul, What they did. Tony Millward (g,lv), Mike Twisse (k), Hugh Stokes (b,bkv), George Cowley (d).
30/8/87 MV4 HP MS&FK

SWEETIE IRIE
14/7/91 Kershaw Maagda man, Call me, Winery, Push up. Sweetie Irie (v), Bluebird (v), Peter Albert (b), Clifton Morrison (k), Pauly Yebuah (d,md,k). 21/3/91 MV5 DG TdB

IRON MAIDEN
14/12/79 Fri. Rock Iron maiden, Running free, Transylvannia, Sanctuary. Paul Di'Anno (v), Steve Harris (b), Dave Murray (g), Tony Parsons (g), Doug Sampson (d). 14/11/79 * TW *

IRRESTIBLE FORCE
19/9/92 Peel Spiritual high, Space is the place, Mountain high. Mixmaster Morris. 30/8/92 MV3 ME~

GREGORY ISAACS AND ROOTS RADICS
5/11/81 Peel The front door, Permanent lover, Confirm reservation, Substitute. Gregory Isaacs (v), Dwight Pinkney (lg), Style Scott (d), Erroll Carter (b), Eric Lamont (rg), Anthony Johnson (k).
26/10/81 MV4 TW DD&MC
6/12/82 Peel That's not the way, Sad to know you're leaving, Cool down the pace, Night nurse.
27/11/82 MV4 DG MC

ISOTOPE
7/3/74 Peel Bite on this/upward curve, Windmills and waterfalls, Honkey donkey, Do the business. Gary Boyle (g), Jeff Clyne (b), Brian Miller (p,sy), Nigel Morris (d).
28/2/74 LH1 JW BC
Group had debuted on In Concert,
rec'd 12/10/73 HP, TX 17/11/73, prod. JG.
6/8/74 Peel Golden section, Spanish sun, Lilly Kong/E-Dorian, Illusion. Hugh Hopper (b), Lawrence Scott (k) r. Clyne, Miller. 23/7/74 LH1 TW *
7/7/75 Peel Fone bone, Atilla, Pipe dream. & Geoff Seopardie. 24/6/75 MV4 TW *

ISRAFEL
3/4/92 Fri. Rock Crime of passion, Skin deep, A tale from the city, Strength of heart. Andrew Chessworth (d), Chris Greenall (g), Mike Askew (bv). 6/3/92 MV4 TW MC

IT'S IMMATERIAL
19/11/81 Peel A gigantic raft, Imitate the worm, White man's hut, Rake. Paul Barlow (d), Jarvis Whitehead (g), Henry Priestman (g,k), Julian Scott (b), John Campbell (v). 11/11/81 MV4 RP NG
9/8/82 Peel Huzah huzah physic stick, Life's my favourite instinct, Speak, Washing the air. Scott out.
17/7/82 MV4 DG MR
17/1/83 Jensen Rake, White man's hut, Turkish fife and drum, Challo. & guest Mick Dempsey (perc).
30/12/82 MV4 JS TdB
18/6/83 Long Cruel issue, Let's murder the moonshine, Washing the air. 16/6/83 PHM c.JL *
21/11/83 Peel Let's murder the moonshine, Challo, White man's hut, The worm turns. 12/11/83 MV4 DG MC
14/5/84 Jensen Crocodile tears, Rope, Ed's funky diner, George. 26/4/84 MV5 MHY *
6/5/85 Peel Rope, Hang on sleepy town, Space, Festival time. Brenda Airturo (perc) r. Barlow. 21/4/85 MV5 DG ME
2/10/85 Long Happy talk, Several brothers, Fish waltz, The better idea. Brenda Kenny (perc,bkv), Gillian Miller (bkv) r. Airturo. 1/9/85 HP BYA PW

JAB JAB
6/1/86 Long Greenhouse, Flowers, Rub a dub, I'm in a dream. Joe Augustine (b), Ryan Noel (d), Thomas Joseph (v,perc), Martin Norton (g), Kevin McMillian (k). 8/12/85 HP BYA PW

JABULA
19/9/74 Peel Baclishi, Thandie, Naledi, Our forefathers. Lucky Rankhu (lg), Ennis Mothle (b), Graham Morgan (d), Julian Bahula (afd), Vicky Mhlongo (v), Dudu Pukwana (sx). 12/9/74 LH1 * *

THE JACK RUBIES
6/7/87 Long I saw the glory, Wrecker of engines, Over my head, Vegas throat. Lawrence Giltnane (d,perc), Ian Wright (gv), Stephen Ineson (gv,hca), Steve Brockway (b). 17/6/87 MV4 HP NG&PS

JACK THE LAD
29/5/73 Peel Boilermaker blues, One more dance, Rosa Lee, Draught genius. Simon Cowe (lg), Ray Laidlaw (d), Rod Clements (b,vi), Mitch Mitchell (g,mnd).
14/5/73 T1 JW&PD BC [M: daytime]
9/10/73 Peel Where the action is, Fast lane driver, Back on the road again. 17/9/73 T1 JW *
24/1/74 Peel Plain leaking, Lying in the water, Roadie, Turning into winter. 17/1/74 LH1 JW *
21/5/74 Peel Nancy, Oakey strike evictions, Peggy (overseas with a soldier) (& Weary whaling grounds, 25/6/74). Philip Murray, Ian Fairburn r. Clements.
2/5/74 LH1 JW BC
1/10/74 Peel Big ocean liner, The ballad of Tonto McGuire, The old straight track, The third millenium.
17/9/74 LH1 JW *
28/10/74 Harris Big ocean liner, Buy broom buzzems, Oakey strike evictions, Captain Grant. 2/10/74 MV4 JG *
20/3/75 Peel The gentleman soldier, Captain Grant, My friend the drink, Kojoke, Walters' drop. 13/3/75 MV4 * *
11/9/75 Peel Winston O'Flaherty, One for the boy, Baby let me take you home, Rocking chair. 4/9/75 MV4 * *
23/11/75 Sounds On Sunday Rocking chair, Baby let me take you home, One for the boy, Kojoke, Smoker's koffin, My friend the drink, Captain Grant, Captain Pugwash. 30/10/75 MV5 MB *
21/10/76 Peel Trinidad, 8 ton crazy, We'll give you the roll, Take some time. Cowe out. 28/9/76 MV4 JG MR

JACK THIGHS
6/6/80 Fri. Rock Shy girl, You know how I'm feeling, Fast car, Paper chaser. Terry Keegan (v), Nigel Brown (g), Terry Swain (g), Brian Tippey (b), Hugh McGouran (d) [Changed name to 'Taurus' before transmission].
30/4/80 * TW *

JACKDAW WITH CROWBAR
3/6/87 Peel Iceberg, Ignorant, Turkey shoot, Amarillo. Dan Morrison (d), David Tibbatts (b), Tim Ellis (g,bkv), Fergus Durrant (gv). 19/5/87 * DG TdB&MWT
12/10/87 Peel Tightrope, Stomach pump, Sailor soul survivor. 4/10/87 * DG ME&EL

J. J. JACKSON AND THE URCHINS
26/11/67 Top Gear Four walls, Sho nuff, Come see I'm your man, But it's alright, Change is gonna come. (unknown). 17/11/67 PH BA * [M]

JACKSON HEIGHTS
8/12/72 Harris Maureen, As she starts, A belly full of water, Sweet hill tunnel. Lee Jackson (bv), John McBurnie (agv), Brian Chatton (kv), Tony Connor (d).
31/10/72 T1 JM *

JOE JACKSON
3/11/78 Blackburn Is she really going out with him? [Network session]. Joe Jackson (pv), Graham Maby (b,bkv), Gary Sanford (lg), Dave Houghton (d,bkv).
19/10/78 MV4 *
26/2/79 Peel One more time, Got the time, Fools in love, I'm the man. 21/2/79 MV4 JS MR

Session repeated on Peebles' new evening show in week starting 6/3/79.
20/3/79 Jensen One more time, Sunday papers, Fools in love, Baby stick around. 8/3/79 PHM TH TWN

JACKTARS
20/11/89 Peel Pull the plug, Flower powder, Millions of grains, Things not seen. Huw Williams (d), Dave Morgan (b), Pete McPartland (g), Ian Travis (gv). 19/10/89 MV5 DG MWT

JACOB'S MOUSE
11/4/92 Peel Oblong, Fridge, Microflesh, Homophobe, A thin sound. Sam Marsh (dv), Jebb Boothby (b), Hugo Boothby (g). 24/2/92 MV3 MR~

JAGUAR
13/4/84 Fri. Rock Long shadows, Last flight, This time, Stand up. Gary Pepperd (g), Jeff Cox (b), Chris Lovell (d), Paul Merrell (gv). 16/3/84 MV4 TW DD

JAKKO
14/7/84 Long This is me, I can't stand this pressure, Dangerous dreams, Camera. * 12/5/84 * c.PWL *
13/12/84 Into The Music Cover up, In the meantime, Shout, Tell her. Jakko (gkv,dm, 4-all instruments), Lyndon Connah (k), Ed Poole (b). 1/12/84 MV4 DG MC

THE JAM
2/5/77 Peel† In the city, Art school, I've changed my address, Modern world. Paul Weller (g,lv), Bruce Foxton (b,bkv), Rick Buckler (d). 26/4/77 MV4 MB MR
† On Strange Fruit SFRCD080.
25/7/77 Peel All around the world, London girl, Bricks and mortar, Carnaby Street 19/7/77 MV4 JG MR
Rec'd In Concert 1/6/78 PS, TX 10/6/78.
12/6/78 Jensen News of the world, The night, A bomb in Wardour Street. 5/6/78 MV5 * ME
5/11/79 Peel Thick as thieves, The Eton rifles, Saturday's kids, When you're young. 29/10/79 MV4 TW BAI&TdB

JAMES
19/10/83 Peel Vulture, The chicken wire, Discipline, Hymn from a village. Tim Booth (lv), James Glennie (b), Paul Gilbertson (g), Gavan Whelan (d). 3/10/83 MV4 TW *
17/4/85 Long Tin can, Summer song, Folklore, Sili din. James Laurence Gott (g) r. Gilbertson. 7/4/85 BYA PW
20/1/86 Peel Insect, Scarecrow, Are you ready, Really hard. 12/1/86 MV5 DG MPK
9/9/87 Peel What for?, Ya ho, Stowaway, Whoops. 3/9/87 * DG TD&NG
20/10/88 Kershaw Medieval, Sit down, Strip mine. & Mike Armistead (sy). 6/10/88 MV4 DG ME
30/4/90 Peel How was it for you, Sunday morning, Come home. Booth, Gott, Glennie, David Baynton-Power (d), Saul Davies (rg,vi), Mark Hunter (k), Andy Diagram (tp). 10/4/90 MV3 MR~ FK
9/7/90 Goodier Hang on, Government walls, Don't wait that long. 30/6/90 MV5 DG MC
3/2/92 Goodier Seven, Heavens, Live a life of love, Protect me. 27/1/92 MV5 MC~ CML

NICKY JAMES BAND
30/8/73 Peel Rock 'n roll jamboree, I guess I've always loved you, A bottle of cheap red wine, My style. Nicky James (lv), John Weider (lg), Alan Fealdman (k), Barry Martin (sx), Brother Fataar (b), Chico Greenfield (d). 20/8/73 LH1 BA *

JOHN JAMES
2/10/68 Night Ride If only I, Slow fast dog trot, Lampeter, Girl from Liverpool, Victory rag. John James (gv).
2/10/68 S1 DK * [M: Folk shows]
31/10/70 Raven's R&B Ostrich walk, If you quit me baby, Once I lived by the sea, Ragtime millionaire. 30/9/70 MV4 JG JY
Second date for Raven rec'd 14/4/71, TX 24/4/71.
13/3/72 Harris Conquistador, The sky is my pie, The sailor's farewell, Easy street. & Pete Berryman. 29/2/72 MV5 JG *

5/11/73 HARRIS *Original rags, Ragtime millionaire.* Solo.
10/10/73 LHI JG *

JANE POW
13/4/92 GOODIER *Sanitised, It's on its way, Get by, 90s.*
Richard Starke (gv), Greg MacDermott (dv,sty), Rupert
Hanna (b), Andrew Starke (gv), Peter Dale (k).
21/3/92 MV4 MA~

THE JANITORS
17/7/85 PEEL *Nowhere, Mexican kitchen, Good to be the
king, Thunderhead Johnny.* * 7/7/85 MV5 * *
26/9/85 LONG *Both ends burning, Wall star, Primal cut,
Cockroach son.* Craig Hope (g), Pete Crow (b), Tim
Stirland (d), Dentover (v). 11/9/85 MV5 BYA PW
15/1/86 PEEL *Going to be, Really shrinking, Track eating
baby, Let's go home.* 7/1/86 MV5 MR~
20/1/87 PEEL *Booga dang thing, Gostaggerlee, Family
fantastic, It's a chrome ball.* Jeff (b) r. Crow.
6/1/87 * DG MR&MA

BERT JANSCH
18/12/68 NIGHT RIDE *Tree song, I loved a lass, I gotta
woman, Thames lighterman, Haitian flight song,
Birthday blues.* Bert Jansch (gv) & Danny Thompson
(b). 11/12/68 S2 JM *
    Jansch first broadcast on Home Service Guitar Club,
prod. BA, 16/12/66. Live on Country Meets Folk, 25/1/69
PH.
2/8/71 HARRIS *Twa Corbies, Nobody's bar, Bird song (&
Omie Wise, Tell me what is true love, 23/8/71).* Solo.
15/7/71 AO2 JM JWH
11/5/73 SEQUENCE *Oh my father, The wheel, Running from
home, Heart of Soho.* 19/4/73 LHI JM NG

JAOJOBY
14/4/91 KERSHAW *Tsaiky joby, Tsy zanaka mpanarivo, Come
on/Amy zaka tiana.* Jaojoby Eusebe (v), Zanfinera
Claudine Robert (v), Mahadimy Joseph (v), Totozanaka
Jean de Dieu (g), Andriamaro Rivo (k), Andriantsiferana
Joseph (k), Djaonarana Jean Claude (d). Rec. date unknown
FR: Madagascar by Ian A. Anderson

JASMINE MINKS
17/2/86 PEEL *The Ballad of Johnny Eye, Cry for a man,
You can take my freedom, I don't know.* Thomas Reid
(d,bkv), Martin Keene (b), Adam Sanderson (gv), James
Shepherd (gv), Derek Christie (tp). 4/2/86 MV5 MW *
24/11/86 LONG *Follow me away, Cut me deep, Traffic goes,
Ballad.* Duncan Walters (g) r. Sanderson.
15/10/86 MV4 AJ MC&FK

JASS BABIES
3/11/81 PEEL *Parable, Let me soak it up, My love make
you melt, Talk in tongues.* Steve Brown (d), Peter Coyle
(v), David Whittaker (b), Rob Boardman (g).
19/10/81 MV4 TW DD

JALI MUSA JAWARA
5/5/88 KERSHAW *Banna, Cherif barika, Subindor.* Jali Musa
Jawara (kor,v), Mariama Diabete (bkv), Maramagbe
Keita (bkv), Aboubakar Camara (g), Kalifa Camara (xyl).
24/4/88 * DG *

JAZAWAKI
27/8/84 SKINNER *Lessons from the cat, Smart tinned beaner,
Don't panic, Girl can't help it.* Stella R Toyx (sx,v),
Jane Jazawade (gv), Mrs Church (b), Yvonne De Caycay
(d). 16/8/84 MV5 MHY MPK
11/12/84 LONG *Strange kind of moon, Slingback, Chinese
whispers, Don't panic.* 28/11/84 MV5 BYA MPK

J C 001 & D J D-ZIRE
24/2/91 KERSHAW *Alone, Your fun, He could talk.* Billed as
'Part E. Unknown, ...' J C 001 (v), DJ D-Zire (dj),
Janet & Desy (v-2, 3), Yvonne (prg, v-3), Ian (sx),
Shaun (b). 3/1/91 MV5 DG ME & NG
24/11/91 KERSHAW *All my children, Build the mutha up,
Rob 'em 'n' rap 'em.* J Cool (v), DJ Dazire (dj), Richie
Stevens (d), Cain Austin (b), Glen Nightingale (g,bkv),
James Halliwell (o,sy). 17/10/91 MV4 DG NG&GPR

JELLYBREAD
18/10/69 WS R&B *Rivers invitation, Lost my heart, That's
all right, Chairman Mac's boogaloo.* Pete Wingfield (kv),
Paul Butler (gv), John Best (b), Chris Waters (d).
17/9/69 MV4 JG JY. Next, on R1 Club 1/70.
3/5/70 RAVEN's R&B *Don't pay them no mind, Rockin'
pneumonia and the boogie woogie flu, Evening, No
brag just facts.* 15/4/70 MV4 JG ;Y
18/9/70 BLACK *Got to forget you, Pity the fool, Don't pay
them no mind (& Evening, 16/10/70).* 7/8/70 MV5 JM *
7/11/70 RAVEN's R&B *Old before your time, Sally hotlips,
The missing link.* 14/10/70 MV4 JG JY
26/11/70 HENRY *Old before your time, Sally hotlips, Missing
link.* 19/11/70 AO2 MB MH&MF
25/1/71 R1 CLUB *Rockin' pneumonia and the boogie woogie
flu, Old man Hank (27/1), I'm ready (28/1).* 12/1/71 PH
* *
13/2/71 RAVEN's R&B *Boogie sandwich, I'm ready, Night
life, Rockin' pneumonia and the boogie woogie flu.*
27/1/71 MV4 MB *
24/2/71 R2 NIGHT RIDE *The missing link, Rivers invitation,
Sally hotlips, Old before your time, Boogie sandwich.*
17/2/71 MV5 c.DMY *
2/10/71 RAVEN's R&B *Delaware stomp, Which way, Night
life, I'm ready.* 22/9/71 MV4 KS *
15/2/72 PEEL *Down along the cove, Nadine, Sister Lucy,
Mynah bird.* 8/2/72 MV4 PR BC
28/4/72 PEEL *Sister Lucy, Hound dog, Green-eyed gypsy
queen (& Michigan drag, 23/6/72).* Kenny Lamb (k) r.
Wingfield, Rock Hayward r. Waters. 10/4/72 T1 JM NG

JELLYFISH KISS
12/3/90 PEEL *Crazy bong, Little red car, Premortem, I'm
sticking with U.* Rich (v-4 only), Jess (v-4 only), Dave
(g), Mark (g), Nik (b), Greg (d). 13/2/90 MV5 DG MR

THE JESUS AND MARY CHAIN
31/10/84 PEEL *In a hole, You trip me up, Never
understand, Taste the floor.* Jim Reid (v), William Reid
(g), Douglas Hart (b), Bobby Gillespie (d). 23/10/84 MV4
MRD MR
    'They were down to play their first London gig the
next night, the Wednesday, at the White Lion in
Islington, I think,' recalls Mark Radcliffe, 'and Alan
McGee and Slaughter Joe Foster came along to the
session. They all wanted to put all this feedback on
the tapes, and I kept saying "No, you don't want to
do that", and they kept saying "Oh yes we do". So in
the end we put it on, and of course they were right'.
13/2/85 PEEL† *The living end, Inside me, Just like honey.*
Karen Parker (bkv). 3/2/85 MV5 DG ME
11/11/85 PEEL *Some candy talking, Psycho candy, You trip
me up, Cut dead.* Billed as 'Jim and William Reid'
only. 29/10/85 MV5 * *
8/12/86 LONG *Darklands, Down on me, Deep one perfect
morning.* Reids only, says sheet. 23/11/86 MV4 produced
by Willie Dowling *
5/1/87 PEEL† *Fall, In the rain, Happy place.*
25/11/86 * DG SC&DD † On Strange Fruit SFMCD210.
13/6/88 PEEL *Side walking, Coast to coast, Take it, My girl.*
Hart returns. 31/5/88 MV4 MR~
12/12/89 PEEL *Far out and gone, Silverblade, Here comes
Alice.* 26/11/89 MV3 DG ME

JESUS JONES
9/7/89 KERSHAW *All the answers, Norman, Cut and dried,
What would you know.* Mike Edwards (g,lv), Al
Jaworski (b), Barry Dogg (smp), Jerry de Borg (g), Gen
(d). 25/5/89 MV3 DG TdB
5/11/90 GOODIER *Right here right now, International bright
young thing, Someone to blame†, Trust me.*
16/10/90 MV5 MC~ † On 'Best of Mark Goodier' .

JESUS LIZARD
17/3/91 PEEL *Wheelchair epidemic, Bloody Mary, Seasick,
Monkey trick.* Mac McNeilly (d), David Wm. Sims (b),
Duane Denison (g), David Yow (v). 24/2/91 MV3 DG JLC&MR

JET
19/6/75 PEEL *Brian damage, Diamonds are a girl's best
friend, Nothing to do with us, Around the world in 80
mins.* Andy Ellison (v), Peter Oxendale (k), Martin
Gordon (b), Dave O'List (g), Mike Nicholls (d).
12/6/75 MV4 TW *

JETHRO TULL
4/8/68 TOP GEAR *A song for Jeffrey, Serenade to a cuckoo,
My Sunday feeling, So much trouble (& Cat squirrel,
22/9/68).* Ian Anderson (fl,hca,v), Mick Abrahams (gv),
Glenn Cornick (b), Clive Bunker (d). 23/7/68 PCI BA
AH&BC
15/12/68 TOP GEAR *Love story, Dharma for one, Stormy
Monday, Beggar's farm.* 5/11/68 PCI BA DT
22/6/69 TOP GEAR *A new day yesterday, Fat man, Nothing
is easy.* Martin Barre (g), r. Abrahams. 16/6/69 MV4 JW
TW

JIM JIMINEE
20/1/88 MAYO *This is your life, Look to the sky, She's
coming back, A habit of you.* Kevin Jamieson (vpg,sx),
Delphi Newman (v), Peter Dyes (gk), Nick Hannan (b),
Lindsay Jamieson (d). 30/12/87 MV4 PW MWT&EL

FLACO JIMENEZ
3/12/87 KERSHAW *Did I tell you, La mucura, The border
line, Alabama jubilee, Rancho grande.* Flaco Jimenez
(acc,bkv), Oscar Tellez (bajo saxto,v), Marty David (b),
Bob Clouter (d), Vic Collins (ps), Snow boy (perc).
26/11/87 * DG NG&SC

JIVE TURKEY
21/12/87 LONG *Flipside, Operation martyrdom, Factory
faces, Trouble, True blue.* Sean Collingham (bgv), Nigel
Collingham (g), Joel Collingham (d).
6/12/87 MV4 PW MA&TD

PA JOBARTEH
14/7/88 KERSHAW *Kele faba, Sabunima, Kumusora, Tata din
din, Fisco Konate.* Pa Jobarteh (kor). 7/7/88 MV4 DG NG

ELTON JOHN
3/11/68 HENRY *All across the havens, Lady Samantha,
Skyline Pigeon.* Elton John (p,o,v); & Caleb Quaye (g),
Boots Slade (b), Malcolm Tomlinson (d).
28/10/68 AO2 AD PWH&MR
    'Male vocal in the 1968 feeling - thin, piercing voice
with no emotional appeal...dreary songs... one key
singer... pretentious material' Audition panel 12/12;
but, despite that, a pass: 'first class!' AD.
27/11/68 NIGHT RIDE *Lady what's tomorrow, Vall-hala,
Digging my grave, My first days at Hi Eaton, The
scaffold.* Solo (Contract says "sings and plays guitar").
27/11/68 MV4 PC *
20/7/69 SYMONDS ON SUNDAY *Son of your father, Lady
Samantha, Sails, Rock 'n' roll madonna.* & Roger Pope
(d), David Glover (b), Caleb Quaye (g). 11/7/69 AO2 c.PWI *
9/8/69 WALKER *Rock'n' roll madonna, Empty sky, Son of
your father, Sails.* 28/7/69 CM c.JBU *
11/10/69 SPEAKEASY *Border song, Rock 'n roll madonna.*
30/9/69 MV5 JG *
12/4/70 DLT *Ballad of a well-known gun, Border song.* &
Hookfoot & The Chanter Sisters (bkv) 6/4/70 AO2 c.PWI *
    The day before this recording, 5/4, the same line-up
had their 'John Peel Concert' broadcast; rec'd 26/3/70
PS, Produced JG. It's from this concert that 'Ballad of a
well-known gun' on 'Before the fall' SFRCD 203 is
taken.
2/7/70 HENRY *Country comfort, Take me to the pilot,
Amoreena, Burn down the mission.* & Dee Murray (b),
Nigel Olsson (d) & (bkv) unknown 25/6/70 AO2 MB MH&MF
26/8/70 HARRIS *Bad side of the moon, Border song,
Country comfort, My father's gun.* Line-up as 25/6.
13/8/70 PH JG *
    His last conventional pre-recorded session. Trio
appeared live on 'The Rosko Show', prod'd AD, 2/1/71
PS.

260

25/12/73 Peel *Rudolph the red-nosed reindeer/White Christmas/Jingle bells, Blowin' in the wind/She belongs to me/Mr. Tambourine man, Don't dilly dally on the way/Lilly of Laguna/Down at the old Bull and Bush/Knees up Mother Brown/Hokey Cokey, Daniel/Your song.* Elton John (pub piano), BBC Radio 1 staff (bkv-4 only). 18/12/73 LH1 JW BC

JOHNNY SAYS YEAH
1/1/87 Long *Johnny says yeah, Waiting here for me, Won't let you go, Better off dead.* Jason Wilson (lv), Jools Wilson (gv), Simon Preston (b), Nick Machin (d), Bruce Hosie (rg), Nick Stevens (tp), Sean Tranter (sx). 14/12/86 MV4 BYA MS

DAVY JOHNSON
22/6/73 Sequence *Smiling face, Save your soul, The boatman, Keep right on.* * 31/5/73 LH1 JM BAI&NG

JOHNNIE JOHNSON
23/2/92 Kershaw *Creek mud (instrumental), Tanqueray, Kansas City, Blues no. 572 (instrumental).* Johnnie Johnson (pv), Davis McLarty (d), Zonder Kennedy (g,bkv), Michael Merritt (b). 12/12/91 MV4 DG NG&JLC

LARRY JOHNSON
12/12/70 Top Gear *Sitting on the banks of the river, The beat from Rampart street, Broke and hungry, How long (& Things I need to do, 20/2/71).* Larry Johnson (gv). 7/12/70 PH * *

LINTON KWESI JOHNSON
8/5/79 Peel *Down di road, Want fi goh rave, It dread inna Inglan, Sonny's Lettah, Reality poem.* Linton Kwesi Johnson (v), & 'other musicians as on LP'. 1/5/79 MV4 TVD MR
27/10/81 Peel *Independent intavenshan, Reality poem, Reggae fi'peach, All wi' doin' is defendin'.* Johnson & Dennis Bovell (p,'vocal perc') (1,2,3 'pre-recorded backing tracks'). 3/10/81 MV4 DG MR
  'The musicians that Dennis Bovell had promised did not turn up,' says Johnson; 'but the atmosphere was nonetheless surprisingly relaxed. Dennis was very reassuring. There was no need to panic. We would do 'All wi doin is defendin' as planned. The electric piano provided bass and rhythm, played by Dennis. The drums and percussion were provided by Dennis' mouth: grunts for bass drum, tongue clapping for wood block, tongue and teeth for hi-hat, etc. The sound engineer and the producer were as astonished as I was. I did my vocals and that was that.'

PAUL JOHNSON
29/7/87 Long *Tell me something good†, Fear of falling†, Harvest for the world, Darling you send me.* Paul Johnson (lv), Dave Itall (gv), Gary Sanctuary (k), Hugh McKenna (pv), Paul Powell (b), Bobby Clarke (d). 22/7/87 MV4 PW MPK&TD
  † On CBS PJOHNQ4.
5/8/87 Peel *Fear of falling, Burning, Every kinda people, A song for you.* & Jordan Bailey & Jenny Evans (bkv). 28/7/87 * DG MR&SC

WILKO JOHNSON
28/9/78 Peel *Everybody's carrying a gun, Slipping and sliding, Blazing fountains, All right, Highway 61.* Wilko Johnson's (gv) 'Solid Senders': Stevie Lewins (b), John Denton (p), Alan Platt (d). 19/9/78 * MB MR
12/5/80 Read *When I'm gone, Cairo blues, Bottle up and go, Can you please crawl out your window.* Russel Strutter (b,bkv), Alex Bines (d,bkv) r. Lewins, Platt. 24/4/80 MV4 CL *
13/1/88 Mayo *Waiting for the rain, I keep it to myself, Turned 21, Back in the night, Barbed wire blues.* Johnson & Norman Watt-Roy (b,bkv), Salvatore Ramundo (d,bkv). 9/12/87 MV4 * MPK

SOPHIE AND PETER JOHNSTON
22/2/83 Peel *One face, Television/Satellite, Rain, Paradise.* Peter Johnston (sy,d,prg), Sophie Johnston (lv), Tom McCluskey (sy). 19/2/83 MV4 DG MC

26/10/83 Peel *Travel in time, Words and words, Open eyes.* McCluskey out. 15/10/83 MV4 DG MC

THE JOHNSTONS
14/4/72 Peel *Ready Teddy, Won't you come with me, Continental trailways bus, If I sang my song.* Probably Adrienne & Luci Johnston, Paul Brady (uncertain) * 27/3/72 * JM *
8/5/72 Harris *Continental trailways bus, The wind in my hands, Won't you come with me, If I sang my song (& Ready Teddy, 12/6/72).* * 18/4/72 * JG *

JOLLY BOYS
26/8/90 Kershaw *Two little girls from Kingston, Benwood Dick, Banana, Want more money, Mother and wife.* Moses Deans (gv), Joseph Bennet (rumble box,v), Noel Howard (bj,v), Allan Swymer (cga,v). 17/7/90 MV5 MA~

HOWARD JONES
21/3/83 Jensen *New song, Don't put these curses on me, Natural, Human's lib.* Howard Jones (kv), Phil Towner (d). 13/3/83 MV4 DG ME
5/2/85 Long *Things can only get better, Look Mama, Dream into action, No one is to blame.* Jones, Trevor Morais (perc), Martin Jones (b). 27/1/85 HP BYA PW
30/3/87 Long *The balance of love, Conditioning, Little bit of snow, Don't want to fight/Give me strength, IGY.* Jones, Morais, Derek Jhingoree (b), Roy Jones (k); & Afrodisiac - Naomi Osborne, Karen Wheeler & Claudia Fontaine (bkv). Live from the Hippodrome, Golder's Green BYA ME&MFA

NIC JONES
11/7/72 Peel *Donald the pride of Glencoe, The island of Helena, The harper of Loch Maben, The Ruffard Park poachers.* Nic Jones (agv). 5/6/72 MV4 JW *
7/12/72 Peel *The outlandish knight, The greeny mossy banks of the sea, Lakes of Shillin, William of Winesberry.* 27/11/72 * BA *
20/9/73 Peel *Isle of France, Lass of London city, The harper of Loch Maben, O'Caralan's concerto.* 6/8/73 * BA *
31/1/74 Peel *Ploughman lads, Isle of France, The drowned loves, Fare thee love.* 24/1/74 * JW *
7/11/74 Peel *The working lads of Russia, Dives and Lazarus, Jigs: Blackthorn stick/Dr O'Neill, Bonny banks of Fordie.* 28/10/74 * JW *
12/11/75 Peel *Bonny George Campbell, The wanton seed, Sammy's bar, Lakes of Shillin.* 14/10/75 MV4 * *
23/7/76 Peel *Billy don't you weep for me, Annachie Gordon, Ten thousand miles, My grandfather knew the plough.* 8/7/76 MV4 * *
26/4/77 Peel *William Glen, Annachie Gordon, Rose of Allandale.* 19/4/77 MV4 JG MR

PAUL JONES
4/5/72 Drummond *Construction workers song, Voices, And you say I'm too dependent on my mind (& It had to come, 29/6/72).* 19/4/72 MV4 MB MH&MF
  One-off night-time R1 appearance from R&B singer, veteran of hundreds of BBC sessions. Now presents R2 R&B show.

WIZZ JONES
4/12/68 My Kind Of Folk *The dazzling strange, Shuck'n sugar.* Wizz Jones (agv) [Had previously appeared as member of other acts]. 27/11/68 S2 FL *
9/7/69 Peel *If only I'd known, The time is flying, Weeping willow blues.* * 12/6/69 S2 PH *
16/1/71 Top Gear *The legendary me, Beggarman, Willie Moore, The time is flying (& If only I'd known, 13/3/71).* & Pete Berryman (g). 21/12/70 PH JW *
4/1/72 Peel *American Jones, First girl I loved, Mama let me lay it on you, No more time to try.* * 13/12/71 PH * *
26/3/73 Harris *Darlin' Cory, The banks of the Ohio, Portland town, The sky.* & Darrell Adams (v) [M: Folk shows]. 14/3/73 LH1 PR *

JOOLZ
30/7/84 Peel *At dawn, It's nothing, Tattoo, Mammy's boy,*

Violation. Joolz (v), Jah Wobble (b,k), Dave Maltby (g), Olly Marland (k). 21/7/84 * DG MC
6/5/85 Long *Deja vu, Housewife's choice, Paradise, Home sweet home.* Solo. 22/4/85 MV5 JS *

JOSEF K
24/3/81 Peel *No glory, Endless soul, Chance meeting, Pictures.* Paul Haig (g,voice), Malcolm Ross (g), David Weddell (b), Ron Torrance (d). Rec. date unknown PRIV * *
22/6/81 Peel† *The missionary, Heart of song, Apple brush, Heaven sent°.* 15/6/81 LH1 TW DD
  † On 'Young and stupid' LTMCD2307; ° also on Supreme International Editions 12-inch, EDITION 87/7.

JOY DIVISION
14/2/79 Peel† *Exercise one, Insight, She's lost control, Transmission.* Peter Hook (bgv), Ian Curtis (gv), Bernard Dickin (sy,g,b), Stephen Morris (d). 31/1/79 MV4 BS NG
10/12/79 Peel† *Love will tear us apart, 24 hours, Colony, Sound of music.* 26/11/79 MV4 TW DD
  † On Strange Fruit SFRCD111.

THE JOYCE MCKINNEY EXPERIENCE
17/8/88 Peel *Tanfastic, Lions and tigers, Walk on your own, In the pink.* Gigs (d), Robbie (b), Charlie (g) Sharon & Yvonne (v). 31/7/88 MV5 DG MA

JSD BAND
23/6/72 Peel *Open road, Peggy and the soldier, Barney Bralligan selection, Sylvie (& Down the road, 21/7/72).* Colin Finn (d), Jim Divers (b), Des Coffield (g,bj,v), Lindsay Scott (fd), Sean O'Rourke (bj,g,fl,v). 5/5/72 PH JM JWH&BAI
  Debuted live on 'Country meets folk' PH 25/3/72, prod. BB.
25/7/72 Peel *Sarah Jane, Betsy, Irish girl, Johnny O'Breadislee.* 25/7/72 MV4 * BC
31/7/72 Harris *Rakes O'Kildare, Honey babe, Sarah Jane, Dusty road.* 5/10/72 Peel *Fishin' blues, Groundhog, Paddy stacks, The dowie dens of Yarrow.* 2/10/72 LH1 BA *
19/11/72 Sounds On Sunday *As I moved out, Barney Brannigan, Honey babe, Johnny O'Breadislee, The Irish girl, Open road.* 1/11/72 MV5 FL *
24/11/72 Sequence *Going down the road, Irish girl, As I rowed out, Fishin' blues.* 3/10/72 T1 JM JWH
28/12/72 Peel *Young waters, Darlin' Corey, The Galway races, Dig's Paddy bar.* 4/12/72 LH1 BA *
1/5/73 Peel *Galway races, Castle Kelly, Travelling days.* Chuck Fleming (vi) r. Scott. 16/4/73 * JW *
1/6/73 Sequence *Galway races, The cuckoo, The king's favourite, Castle Keely.* 8/5/73 T1 JM *
19/7/73 Peel *Little Maggie, Tune your fiddles, Seamus' jig, Glasgow.* 16/7/73 LH1 BA *
3/9/73 Harris *Glasgow, Tune your fiddles, Seamus' jig.* 18/7/73 LH1 JG *
21/2/74 Peel *Railroad mama, Downfall of Paris, Sunshine life (& The fox, 2/5/74).* 14/2/74 LH1 * *
1/6/74 Rock On *Crow black children, The cuckoo, Rainy day, Medley: O'Carolan's draft, The Duke of Leinster, The girls of county Mayo.* 13/5/74 LH1 BA *

JU JU
27/4/82 Peel *Doreen, Hello good morning, Millionaire, Messages, Walk alone.* Alex Findlow (d), Celia Hemchen von Brockhorn (sx,v), Mark Fletcher (b), Paul Barns (g), Mark Illman (g). 19/4/82 MV5 TW MC
21/7/83 Peel *Mysterious, Tap on my brain, Zen master, Picture of Dorian Gray.* Ralph Derijke (sxv) r. Brockhorn. 27/6/83 MV4 TW MC

THE JUGGERNAUGHTS
2/1/85 Peel *Mystery train, The body of the Kirk, One thousandth part, Made my first million.* Nigel Seaford (bv), Gordon Kerr (rgv), Paul Haig (lg), James Locke (d). 11/12/84 MV5 MRD PW

JUICY LUCY
8/11/69 Top Gear *She's mine and she's yours, Just one time, Chicago North Western, Who do you love.* Glenn

Campbell (gv), Ray Owen (lv), Chris Mercer (ts), Neil Hubbard (g), Keith Ellis (b), Pete Dobson (d). 4/11/69 MV4 JW * [M: daytime]

26/5/70 HARDING *If I had possession, Terraplane blues.* 19/5/70 MV5 MB MH&MF

JUKE BOY BONNER
8/11/69 TOP GEAR *I know what's gonna happen, Smiling like I'm happy, People think they know me well well (& I didn't know, Jumping with Juke boy, 7/2/70).* * 8/11/69 MV4 JW TW

JULES VERNE
13/6/92 PEEL *Hollow tomorrow, Misadventure, Hang up, Celebrity twister/A wake.* Daniel Hunt (gv), Paul Winstanly (g,bkv), Kari Bailey (b), David Potts (d). 17/5/92 MV3 ME~

THE JUMPING BELAFONTES
8/6/83 JENSEN *Why did you do it?, Movement, Funky Uxbridge, Top cat.* Duncan Galloway (lv,al), Sean Maher (g), Anthony Adams (rg), Anthony Longden (b), Pete Mathews (d), Timothy Sayers (ts). 29/5/83 MV4 DG ME

THE JUNE BRIDES
20/11/84 LONG *On the rocks, No place called home, In the rain, I fall.* Phil Wilson (lv,g), Simon Beesley (gv), Ade Carter (b), Brian Alexis (d), Frank Sweeney (vla), Jon Hunter (tp), Reg Fish (tp). 7/11/84 MV5 JS MPK

5/11/85 PEEL† *This town, Waiting for a change, We belong, One day.* Dave Bickley (d) r. Alexis. 22/10/85 MV5 PWL ME † On Strange Fruit SFPS023.

THE JUNGLE BROTHERS
13/10/88 KERSHAW *Straight out the jungle, Promo, Freestyle, I'll house you.* Sammy B. (dj), Mike G. (v), Afrika (v). 29/9/88 MV4 DG NG

15/4/90 KERSHAW *J beez coming thru, Black woman, Feelin' alright, What U waitin' 4.* 15/3/90 MV5 DG MC

JUNIOR GEE AND THE CAPITAL BOYS
3/10/84 PEEL *Scratch, Have you got the time, Love money, Check us out.* Junior Gee (v), Ambassador (v), Scratch (v), Double D (sc,v); backed by the Funkmasters (unknown). 26/9/84 MV5 RP TD

JUNIORS EYES
10/11/68 TOP GEAR *By the tree (on the second dream on your right), White light, Hang loose, Imagination.* Mick Wayne (lg), Steve Chapman (d), John Redfern (o), John 'Honk' Lodge (b). 28/10/68 PCI BA *

4/5/69 TOP GEAR *Sing a song, So embarrassed, For Adam and Eve, Miss Lizzie (& Not far away, 8/6/69).* 28/4/69 PH JW TW

Files suggest new line-up, with Tim Renwick (g), Graham Kelly and John Cambridge, did two sessions for HENRY, 7&8/69, untraceable. Group did appear live from the Salutation Hotel, Perth on R1 CLUB 19/9/69. Last BBC date backing Bowie 20/10/69.

JUNK
5/6/85 LONG *The only place, No. 35, Kill for you, Bella Donna.* David Bloom (d), Alan Russell (g), Walter (gv), Andy Hobson (b). 22/5/85 MV5 BYA MPK

JUNKYARD ANGEL
17/4/72 HARRIS *Keep a warm fire burning, Need a woman, Bob and Robert Thack, Forbidden fruit.* * 29/3/72 * JG *

MICKEY JUPP
13/3/71 TOP GEAR *I can't lose, Further up on the road, Don't you never, It hurts me too (& Lorraine pt 1, 5/6/71).* 'Mickey Jupp's Legend' Jupp (lv,g) & (unknown). 2/3/71 * PR *

28/6/78 PEEL *Cheque book, Switchboard Susie, Anything you do, Daisy Mayes.* Jupp, Mick Grabham (g), John Gordon (b), Ron Telemacque (d). 19/6/78 MV4 TW TdB&MPK

JUST US
2/1/73 PEEL *La Roca, Nameless, Forsoothe, Vehim.* Elton Dean (al), Nick Evans (tb), Mark Charig (cnt), Louis Maholo (d), Jeff Green (g), Neville Whitehead (b). 11/12/72 * JW *

JUSTINE

4/9/70 BLACK *Unknown journey, Is that good that's nice.* Valerie Cope (v), Bethlyn Bates (v), Chris Gibb (d), Jerry Hovrell (bv), John McBurnie (gv), Keith Trowsdale (g). 4/8/70 PS JM *

Passed by panel, despite comments like 'another dreary heavy pseudo-jazz-influenced group'.

DOCTOR K
3/3/69 WS R&B *Watch yourself, One more mile.* Richard Kay (p), Geoff Krivit (lg), Roger Rolt (rg), Harold Vickers (b), Eric Peachey (d), Mick Haase (lv,hca). 5/2/69 MV4 JG *

18/10/69 TOP GEAR *Country boy, For Caroline, I've been here before, Sugar moon.* 30/9/69 JW *

15/11/69 WS R&B *Bring it on home, Five long years, Caroline.* 15/10/69 MV4 JG JY

KALEIDOSCOPE
3/1/68 TOP GEAR *A dream for Julie, Dive into yesterday, Faintly blowing, (Further reflections) in the room of percussion.* * 13/12/67 * * *

KALIMBA
18/12/84 LONG *Breakaway, Sun city, Spiteful, Precious.* Andrea Oliver (v), Guy Batey (b), Andy Norton (g), Tintin (d), Pete Durgerian (sx,hca,gv). 5/12/84 MV5 JS MPK

KAN KAN
26/4/82 PEEL *Apartment 100, Shot in the dark, Somethings never change, Deja vu.* Patrick Deneen (v,d,k,b), Graham McGill (b,g), Flavia Malim (v). 7/4/82 MV5 RP NG

KANDA BONGO MAN
3/3/88 KERSHAW *Djessy, Iyole, Amour fou, J.T.* Kanda Bongo Man (v), Remy Salomon (b), Dally Kimoko (lg), Mimi Kazidona (rg), T. Jan (d), Kilesa (bkv). 18/2/88 * DG ME&JBN

7/1/90 KERSHAW *Sai, Bedy, Bayembi.* K. B. Man, Kimoko, Salomon, Martin Miabanzila (g), Komba Mafwala (d). 14/11/89 MV5 DG MR&TD

THE KANE GANG
11/8/83 JENSEN *Amusement park, Smalltown creed, You make him cry, Mighty day.* Dave Brewis (kgb), Graham Lant (d,perc), Martin Brammer (v), Paul Woods (v). 4/8/83 MV4 JP KW

AMORY KANE
13/11/68 NIGHT RIDE *Four ravens, Reflections, Physically disqualified blues, Night, Evolution.* Amory Kane (v) & unknown British backing band. 13/11/68 MV4 PC *

KARRALLON
8/5/92 FRI. ROCK *Livin' up, Bad boys, Let the love lie, Double trouble.* Gary Platts (g), Andy Rochelle (d), Paul Manara (v), Dave Deeley (d), Mike Clemens (k), Nic (g). 17/4/92 MV5 MC~

KATCH 22
2/11/91 PEEL *Mindfield, Service with a smile, The jam, State of meditation.* Hunt Kill Bury Finn (rp), Mad Marka (dj), DJ Brainiac (dj), DJ Kill A Man Twice (dj), Cavey ('dancer'). 17/9/91 MV5 TdB DMC

ALIAS RON KAVANA
30/9/90 KERSHAW *Ain't that peculiar/Fox hunter's reel, Hand me down, This is the night, Pennies for black babies.* Ron Kavana (gv,mnd), Mick Molloy (g), Richie Robertson (b), Les Morgan (d), Geraint Watkins (acc,pv), Fran Byrne (acc,perc). 2/9/90 MV4 DG ME&FK

KEANAN
3/12/85 LONG *Sister satellite, Marine boy, World war rockets, Take me to the love shop.* Keanan (lv), Angie Giles (bkv), Sam Harley (b), Bill Woods (lg), Martin Turner (prg,k). 24/11/85 HP BYA PW

ROBERT EARL KEEN JR.
29/4/90 KERSHAW *Rollin' by, Mariano, The road goes on forever, Fuel for a fool.* Robert Earl Keen Jr. (gv). 29/3/90 MV5 DG NG

SALIF KEITA
16/7/89 KERSHAW *Koyan/Prim prim, Nous pas bouger.* Salif Keita (v), Jean Francois Kellner (g), Herve Bouffartigues

(sy), Doumb N'Djengue (b), Brice Wouassi (d), Souleyman Doumbia (perc), Keletigui D'Abate (blp), Nicholas Guerre (sx), Ron Mesa (tp), Mark Sims (tb), Assitan Keita & Djene Doumbouya (bkv). 1/6/89 MV3 DG TdB

DAVE KELLY
18/9/68 NIGHT RIDE *A few short lines, Arkansas woman, When you've got a good friend, Hard times, Travelling blues.* Dave Kelly (agv). 13/9/68 MV5 DK *

17/10/70 RAVEN'S R&B *It's you, The way I feel today, Ain't no fun for me, Hello L.A. Bye-bye Birmingham.* 'The Dave Kelly Band': Kelly & (d), (b), (p), (sx) unknown. 5/8/70 MV4 JG JY

19/11/87 KERSHAW *A few short lines, Sus blues, Crossroad blues, Mean ol' Frisco, 32-20.* Dave Kelly (gv). 6/8/87 * DG DD&TD

JO-ANN KELLY
4/9/68 NIGHT RIDE *Rock me, Since I first met you baby, Shine on rising sun, Louisiana blues, Roll and tumblin' blues.* with Bob Hall (p-on all sessions below) & Steve Rye (hca). 3/9/68 S2 DK *

Jo-Ann Kelly was unanimously rejected by the panel after an audition in 3/67. Comments ranged from 'a sincere attempt' to 'discordant' 'very depressing' 'monotonous dirge' and 'who knows or cares what she's singing about?' 1st b'cast for R3's Blues in Britain, rec'd 19/2/68 [M].

19/11/68 WS R&B *Rock me, Louisiana blues, Custard pie, Since I first met you baby, Early in the morning.* & Steve Rye: (1,4,5-JK&BH), (2-JK solo), (3-JK,BH,SR). 25/10/68 AO2 JG JY

7/2/70 WS R&B *Jump steady daddy, Moon going down, Alabama women, Baby what you want me to do.* & Dave Kelly (g); (1-JK & BH), (2-JK & DK), (3-BH & DK), (4-all). 7/1/70 MV4 JG JY

20/9/70 RAVEN'S R&B *Moon going down, Jump steady daddy, Black rat swing, We'll let you know.* & Matthew Kelly; (1,2-JK & BH), (3,4-JK, BH, MK). 22/7/70 MV4 JG JY

30/1/71 RAVEN'S R&B *You win again, I've been scorned, Can I get a witness, Rolling log blues, Louisiana blues, Can't be satisfied.* & Bob Hall only. 13/1/71 MV4 MB *

6/10/71 R2 NIGHTRIDE *Make me a palate on your floor, Nothing in ramblin', Detroit stomp, Pinetops boogie, Sugar babe, Travelling blues, Louisiana blues, It'll be me.* 5/7/71 AO2 DK *

JONATHAN KELLY
27/3/72 HARRIS *Madelaine, Sligo fair, Ballad of cursed Anna, Rock you to sleep.* Jonathan Kelly (agv) & 4 (unknown). 8/3/72 AO2 JG *

Trial b'cast on Stage One 14/9/69 passed by panel [M: daytime, In Concerts].

20/7/72 DRUMMOND *You are what you feel, Mother moon, Ballad of cursed Anna, Dedicated to Mary unlimited.* Solo. 5/7/72 MV4 MB MH&MF

24/8/73 SEQUENCE *Sensation street, Beautiful eyes, All in a new light, I'll never find another love.* & (ag) unknown. 12/7/73 LH1 JM *

SHIRLEY KENT
25/2/71 HENRY *Wicker basket weaver, Wild August, Hiding there, Who am I now (& Song of the ill-loved, 25/3/71).* Shirley Kent (agv). 17/2/71 * MB MH&MF

25/11/71 DRUMMOND *Comical wise, November night, Sleep good (& Golden horses, 23/12/71).* 15/11/71 * MB MH&MF

BENNY KERN
30/12/71 DRUMMOND *The musical man, A man in a suit/Capri, Buffalo song/Rock and roll man, Music sweet music/Tell my friend (& The athlete, 17/2/72).* Benny Kern (agv). 8/12/71 MV4 MB MH&MF

KEYTONES
17/5/88 L. KERSHAW *Over the hill, Good to be alive, Ghost of lonely heart, The swallows desert the skies.* Jarrod Coombes (b,lv), Jim Knowler (g,bkv), Shaun O'Keefe (d). 8/5/88 MV4 TdB~

IMRAT KHAN
6/7/69 Top Gear *Kalarati, Tori*. Imrat Khan (sit), Vilayat Khan (su). 1/7/69 MV4 JW TW
The Khans previously appeared on R3 in Spring 69.
18/4/70 Top Gear *Bihag, Aheer Bnaero*. Imrat Khan (sit,su), Latif Ahmed Khan (tab). 14/4/70 MV4 JW TW

NUSRATH FATEH ALI KHAN
10/3/88 Kershaw *Allah hoo, Yannabee noor hotum*. Nusrat Fateh Ali Khan (lv), Farouk Ali Khan & Atta Fario (hmn,v), Kobab Ali Khan (v), Duldar Hussein (tab), Mohammed Medkeen, Nefees Ahmed & Asad Ali (bkv), Mujaid Ali Khan (v). 25/2/88 * DG MC&GJ
10/9/89 Kershaw *Allahoo allahoo, Mastue Nazaran, Unke darpe Panchine, Nit khair mangin*. Khan, Farouk Ali Khan, Kobab Ali, Asad Ali, & Rahmat Ali (v,hmn), Mohamad Iqbal, Khalid Mahmood, Gholam Farid (v), Didar Khan (tab). 20/7/89 * DG TdB

VILAYAT KHAN
1/9/68 Top Gear *Shankara, Snudh malu*. Vilayat Khan & I (possibly brother Imrat). 2/8/68 AO2 BA *

KHARTOMB
13/12/82 Peel *Swahili lullaby, Sanatogen, Daisy high, Tribal man*. Paula Crolla (v), Caroline Clayton (v,b,fl), Ali Barnes (d), Ian Christie (g,b). 4/12/82 * DG MR

KICK PARTNERS
28/3/83 Peel *Steel workers, Granston Villas, It's too late, The beats in your heart*. Wayne Allen (gv), Chris Pearson (b), Linda Hamblin (v), Rose Eyre (sy,o,v), Paul Hardy (d), Kev Sanderson (perc). 16/3/83 MV4 RP NG

KICK REACTION
30/1/86 Long *When the picture's looking good, Rescued by romance, Your favourite song, Berwickshire gazette*. Stephen Barker (d), Stuart Thorn (b), Peter Lyon (gv), Jimmy Campbell (k), Mark Milner (tp), Stephen Brown (tb), Bill Innes (sx). 22/1/86 MV5 BYA MPK

KICKS
1/1/83 Long *Confusion, The wall, Slow motion, Girls talk*. * 30/12/82 PHM cJL PSM

ANGELIQUE KIDJO
6/6/92 Kershaw *Batonga, We we, Logozo, Ekoleya*. Angelique Kidjo (v), Djahuno Carlos Dabo (bkv,perc), Joao Manuel Mota (g,bkv), Alain Ednin (sy), Jean Hebrail (b), David Fall (d). 7/5/92 MV5 DG NG&PA

KILLING FLOOR
5/5/69 WS R&B *The sun keeps shining, Leo's blues, Something, Nobody by my side*. Mick Clarke (lg), Stuart McDonald (b), Bill Thorndycraft (v,hca), Bas Smith (d), Lou Martin (p). 14/5/69 MV4 JG JY
5/7/69 Walker *Nobody by my side, Lost alone, My mind can ride away*. 30/6/69 CM cJBU *
20/7/69 Top Gear *Mind can ride easy, Louis blues, The sun keeps shining*. 14/7/69 PH JW *
29/11/69 WS R&B *Lost alone, Bedtime blues, Back in the chicken shack*. Paul Turner (p) r. Martin, McDonald out. 29/10/69 MV4 JG JY
5/6/71 Raven's R&B *Driftin' and driftin', Darlin' Corey, Louis' thing, You need love*. Billed as 'K. Floor'. 26/5/71 MV4 MB *

KILLING JOKE
29/10/79 Peel *Pssyche, Wardance, Nuclear boy, Malicious boogie*. Jazz Coleman (kv), Geordie aka A. Lizzard (gv), Big Paul (dv), Youth (bv); & roadie Alex Paterson ('disco whoop' bkv-4 only). 17/10/79 MV4 BS NG
17/3/80 Peel *Change, Tomorrow's World, Complications*. 5/3/80 MV4 JE NG
27/4/81 Peel *The fall of because, Tension, Butcher*. 14/4/81 LHI DG MR&MFA
10/6/81 Skinner *Tension, Unspeakable, Exit*. 29/5/81 LHI DG *
16/12/81 Peel *The hum, The empire song, We have joy, Chop chop*. 11/12/81 MV4 JWI TdB
12/7/83 Peel *Willful days, Frenzy, Dominator, Harlequin*. Paul Raven (b) r. Youth. 4/7/83 MV4 JP MC
17/4/84 Jensen *Eighties, New Culture, Blue feathers, All*

play rebel. Jaz, Raven, Kevin Walker (g), Paul Ferguson (d). 5/4/84 MV5 JP MPK

THE KILLJOYS
18/10/77 Peel *Recognition, At night, Back to front, Naive*. Kevin Rowland (v), Mark Phillips (g), Ghislaine Weston (b), Lee Burton (d), Heather (bkv-4). 11/10/77 MV4 JG MR
13/2/78 Peel *All the way, Smoke your own, Spit on me, Ghislaine*. Bob Peach (d) r. Burton; & Keith Rimell (g,b-4); Rowland (g-4), Weston (v-4). 1/2/78 MV4 MB NG

WILLIAM E. KIMBER AND THE IAN GREEN ORCHESTRA
5/11/67 Top Gear *Lazy life, A day of love, Molehill is not a mountain, Crazy how love slips away*. * 27/10/67 * * *

KING
20/7/78 Peel *Antipope†, Jet boy jet girl, My baby don't care, Baby sign here with me*. Captain Sensible (g,bkv; p,cel-3), Henry Badowski (v,k,sx), Kim Bradshaw (b), Dave Berk (d), Alex K. (vi). 11/7/78 MV4 MR~
† On 'Winters of discontent,' SFRCD204.

KING ('83)
27/8/83 Long *Unity song, Trouble, Don't stop, I kissed the spikey fridge*. * 24/8/83 PHM cJL TWN

B. B. KING
30/3/89 Kershaw *When it all comes down, Go on, Paying the cost to be the boss, The thrill is gone, Ain't nobody's business*. B B King (gv), Caleb Emphrey Jr. (d), Michael Doster (b), Leon Warren (g), James Toney (o,p), Walter King (sx,md), Edgar Synigal Jr. (sx), James Bolden (tp). 9/3/89 MV4 DG NG

JAMES KING AND THE LONEWOLVES
4/6/84 Jensen *Chance I can't deny, Born to lose, Step away, Happy home*. Mick Price (d), Colin Neil (b), James King (gv), Jake Mason (g), Patti Palladin (bkv-4 only). 20/5/84 MV5 DG ME

KING BISCUIT BOY
8/12/71 Peel *Boom boom (out goes the light), Biscuit's boogie, Hey hey, Cross my heart*. Canadian soul singer. No contract survives. 7/12/71 * * BC

KING BUFFALO
26/5/88 Kershaw *Kissing sweet, Shoot a little light, One day, The gambler*. Paul Smith (gv), Warren Kennedy (g), Richard Vernon (b), Bob Andrews (k), Chris Smith (d). 24/3/88 * DG JB&REL

KING CRIMSON
11/5/69 Top Gear *The court of the crimson king, 21st century schizoid man, Talk to the wind*. Michael Giles (dv), Greg Lake (bv), Robert Fripp (lg), Ian McDonald (al,fl,k), 6/5/69 MV4 JW TW
7/9/69 Top Gear *The court of the crimson king, Epitaph, Bearings (get thy)*. 19/8/69 MV4 JW *

KING MISSILE
4/4/92 Kershaw *The love song, Pickaxe, The sandbox, It's*. John S. Hall (v), Dave Rich (g,bkv), Chris Xefos (b,sy,bkv), Roger Murdoch (d). 15/3/92 MV3 DG ME&GB

KING OF THE SLUMS
26/4/88 Peel *Big girl's blouse, Fanciable headcase, Venerate me utterly, Leery bleeder*. Charley Keigher (gv), Sarah Curtis (vi), Jon Chandler (b), Ged O'Brian (d). 12/4/88 MV4 DG MR

KINGMAKER
7/10/91 Goodier *Really scrape the sky, Hard times, When Lucy's down, Join the human race*. John Andrew (d), Myles Howell (b), Laurence Hardy (gv), Nick Muir (o), Paul Kegg (clo). 28/9/91 MV5 MC~

KINGS OF OBLIVION
25/4/90 Peel *Pay, Fear trade, Much too much two faced, Ghost*. Neil Humphries (d,bkv), Darren Smith (bv), John Harris (g,bkv). 3/4/90 MV3 MR~

KINGTRIGGER
15/3/82 Jensen *Vodka, The sight of blood, River, Walking poison*. Sam Hodgkin (v), Martin Clapson (gv), Ian Cleverly (perc), Trudi Baptiste (pv), Stuart Kennedy (bv). 4/3/82 MV4 JS *

3/11/82 Jensen *Lay your hands on me, Fever, Walk the plank, Temptation*. Chris Bell (d) r. Baptiste; & Jackie Challenor, Lorenza Johnson & Mae McKenna (bkv). 17/10/82 MV4 DG ME

THE KINKS
29/10/67 Top Gear *David Watts, Sunny afternoon, Suzannah's still alive, Autumn almanac, Mr Pleasant, Harry Rag*. Ray Davies (gv), Dave Davies (gv), Mick Avory (d), Peter Quaife (b); & (tp) (o,p) unknown. 25/10/67 MV4 BA *
Trial broadcast was on Saturday Club on 19/9/64. Dozens of dates followed.
7/7/68 Top Gear *Days, Monica, Love me till the sun shines, Waterloo sunset*. & Nicky Hopkins (o). 1/7/68 PCI BA *
16/5/72 Peel *Holiday, Supersonic rocket ship, Acute schizophrenia paranoia blues, Skin and bone*. R. & D. Davies, Avory &: John Dalton (b), John Gosling (p), John Beecham (tb), Mike Rosen (tp), Alan Holmes (fl). 5/5/72 TI JW BC
11/7/74 Peel *Money talks, Demolition, Mirror of love*. Eight musicians & 2 (unknown). 6/6/74 LHI TW BAI

KISS AMC
3/7/89 Peel *Rawside†, Yakety yak, Doc martens*. Anne-Marie (v), Christine (v); & the Ruthless Rap Assassins: Kermit le Freak (prg), Dangerous Hinds (kv), Carsonoba (sc,v), Paul Roberts (g). 18/6/89 ED DG SA
† On 'Manchester - so much to answer for' SFRCD202.

KISS THE BLADE
9/4/85 Long *Subterfuge, Wheels of fortune, Like a vice, Final sunrise*. Barry Phillips (rgv), Vince Jones (d), Ollie Cherer (lg), Andy Jones (b). 27/3/85 MV5 JS MPK

KISSING THE PINK
30/7/83 Long *Maybe this day, Big man, Restless*. * 25/7/83 PHM cJL TWN

KIT
3/1/90 Peel *How to break this, Up on a wire, Cheatin' my heart, What if I fell*. Lin Sangster (gv), Michelle Brown (b), Tony Smith (d), Kenny Manson (g), Phil Luckin (tp). 28/11/89 MV5 DG MR

KITCHENS OF DISTINCTION
12/9/92 Peel *Four men, Mad as Snon, When in heaven, Blue pedal*. Patrick Fitzgerald (bv), Julian Swales (g,hca), Dan Goodwin (d). 23/8/92 MV3 ME~DMC

THE KLEZMATICS
1/8/92 Peel *Doyne/Freyt aykh yidelekh, Klezmatics khosidl/Fisher lid, Keyser tartar/Terkish yale veyve tamts, Honikzaft*. Matt Darriau (cl,sx), David Licht (d), Frank London (tp,k,bkv), Paul Morrissett (b), Lorin Sklamberg (v,acc,k), Alicia Svigals (vi,bkv). 14/7/92 MV4 MR~ MA&RJ

GLADYS KNIGHT AND THE PIPS
10/12/67 Top Gear *Take me in your arms and love me, I heard it through the grapevine, Just walk in my shoes, Everybody needs love*. Gladys Knight (lv), the Pips (bkv), & the Johnny Watson Concept, incl. Jimmy Page (g), Jim Sullivan (g). 1/12/67 PH 8A PR

KNIVES
24/5/84 Jensen *Someone of steel, The secret, Eldorado, First light*. Scott Addison (bp), Ben Addison (d), Mick Fox (g), Barry Goddard (v). 10/5/84 MV5 MHY *

KNOX
31/3/80 Read *Love is burning, Dream factory, Last broken heart, Going uptown*. Ian M. Carnochan (gv), Nicky Hallam (g), Matthew Seligman (b), Nick Gibson (dv). 22/2/80 MV4 BS *

BUDDY KNOX AND BAD RIVER
16/5/70 Top Gear *Party doll, Hula love, Somebody touched me, Rock your little baby to sleep (& Muddy water, 8/8/70)*. Buddy Knox (US singer) & British backing band Bad River (unknown). 11/5/70 PH * *

SPIDER JOHN KOERNER
17/7/68 Night Ride *Things ain't right, Eugene C from*

Tennessee, I ain't blue, Running jumping standing still, I don't wanna be terrified. * 25/6/68 * DK *

AMI KOITA
17/3/91 KERSHAW Siraman Jjeli, Tounga, Djanfan Magni, Sosso. Ami Koita (v), Mariame Kouyate (v), Mamaye Kouyate (ng), Boubecar Diabate (kor,v).
28/2/91 MV5 DG PA&TdB

KOKOMO
22/8/74 PEEL I'm sorry babe, Forever, It ain't cool to be cool, Angel. Neil Hubbard (g), Alan Spenner (b), Tony O'Mally (kv), Frank Collins (v), Paddie McHugh (v), Dyan Birch (v), John Sussewell (d), Jim Mullen (g), Jody Linscott (cga). 15/8/74 LH1 TW *
27/2/75 PEEL Good to be alive, Oo-ee-baby, Cos we've ended now as lovers, New morning. Terry Stannard (d) r. Sussewell; & Chris Mercer (sx). 20/2/75 AO2 TW BAI
8/9/75 PEEL Do it right, Kitty, Pinch of salt, Happy birthday. Sussewell r. Stannard, Mullen out. 2/9/75 MV4 PR *

DEMBO KONTE AND KAUSU KOUYATE
23/4/87 KERSHAW Mama sawu, Saliya, Yeyengo, Sira la julo. Dembo Konte (kor,v), Kausu Kouyate (kor,v). 15/4/87 * MRD SR
30/6/88 KERSHAW Oumie haydara, Dembou boujang, Sanneh jobe. 16/6/88 MV4 DG MR
2/10/89 PEEL Amadou fall, Sane jobe, President Diawara, Alla lakhe. with the Three Mustaphas Three rhythm section: Houzam (d), Sabah Habas (b), & Hijaz Mustapha (g,md). 5/9/89 MV3 DG MR
21/7/91 KERSHAW Chidou, Yaiyango, Momodou betticky, Sanneh jobe. Duo only. 27/6/91 MV5 DG NG&PA

KOOGA
3/1/86 FRI. ROCK Across the water, Lay down your love, She walks in beauty, Gabrielle. Martin Williams (d), Dave Howells (b), Neville MacDonald (gv), Neil Garland (k). ?/12/85 MV4 TW DD

ALEXIS KORNER
5/11/68 WS R&B You don't know, Do you mind, You are my sunshine, Streamline train, Why did you waste my time. Alexis Korner (gv), Robert Plant (hca), Steve Miller (p). 11/10/68 AO2 JG JY
Alexis had many previous BBC radio appearances, both as host of this show, and a musician.
2/2/69 TOP GEAR The clapping song, Please don't say no, You don't know my mind. & Nick Smith (bv). 14/1/69 PC1 BA AH&BC
30/3/69 SYMONDS ON SUNDAY Shady little baby, Hot rodding, New worried blues. Alexis with guests Fleetwood Mac, Tony 'Duster' Bennett, and Christine Perfect: Korner (g,lv-1,3), Bennett (lv-2), Peter Green (lg), Christine Perfect (pv), Mick Fleetwood (d), John McVie (b). 17/3/69 AO2 JW TW
Famous one-off all star line-up session, recorded by Walters and Tony Wilson on same day as a normal session by Fleetwood Mac, broadcast on the previous week's show, 23/3. The week after this went out, Walters was made Peel's producer.
7/4/69 WS R&B The clapping song, Will the circle be unbroken, Chain of fools, This little light of mine. & Martin Hummingbird. 19/3/69 MV4 JG JY
20/9/69 WS R&B Rosy, Mary, Soul twist. & New Church: Nick South (bv), Peter Thorop, Sappho Korner, Ray Worley. 20/8/69 MV4 JG JY
26/4/70 WS R&B Looking for fun, I'm coming home, Jesus is just alright, Worried blues, Sunrise. & New Church. 1/4/70 MV4 JG JY
28/5/70 HENRY I don't know, Will the circle be unbroken, Jesus is just alright, Voodoo queen. & New Church. 21/5/70 AO2 MB MH&MF
29/10/70 HENRY Mighty mighty, That's all, 32/20 blues, Stop playing games. & New Church: Colin Hodgkinson (b) r. South, S. Korner, Worley; & Zoot Money (k). 22/10/70 AO2 MB MH&MF

14/11/70 RAVEN'S R&B Stump blues, Just the blues, Go down sunshine, Sweet home Chicago. & Colin Hodgkinson (b) only. 14/10/70 MV4 JG JY
20/3/71 RAVEN'S R&B Vicksburg blues, Going down slow, Sweet home Chicago, Precious lord. & friends: Zoot Money. Paul Rowan, Sappho. 17/3/71 MV4 MB *
2/6/71 R2 NIGHTRIDE Opening sig., Cannonball blues, Make me a cat on your floor [I think: PasB very feint], The Vicksburg blues, The love you save, Spoonful, Lo and behold, Kid man blues, That's all. Solo. 19/5/71 PH DK *
16/10/71 RAVEN'S R&B Lo and behold, Going down slow, Evil hearted blues, Doggone my good luck soul, You are my sunshine, Gospel ship. & friends. 6/10/71 * KS * [M]
11/6/79 PEEBLES Honky tonk woman, You are my sunshine, Bourgeois blues, Bye baby bye, Here comes the sun, My chicken shack back home. & Rod Dawes (gv). 31/5/79 MV4 CL MR

LEO KOTTKE
10/2/77 PEEL Scarlatti rip off, Easter, San Antonio Rose/America the beautiful/Machine gun, Mona Ray/Morning, Pamela Brown. Leo Kottke (ag). 7/2/77 MV4 TW DD

BILLY J. KRAMER
24/4/73 PEEL I'll keep you satisfied, Trains, boats and planes, Little children, From a window. Billy J. Kramer (v), Frank Davis (g), Sandy Byers (d), Ken Buckley (b), Mick Green (g). 17/4/73 * JW *

THE KRISPY THREE
3/7/90 PEEL Mentally appetising, Natch it up, E I. Wiz (ma,v), Sonic (v), Don (v). 10/6/90 MV3 DG MA&JB
7/12/91 PEEL Answer me will ya, Where we going, Too damn ignorant, Hard times. 24/10/91 MV4 DG NG&CML

KROKUS
18/7/80 FRI. ROCK Lady double dealer, Shy kid, Back seat rock and roll, Mad racket. Marc Storace (v), Fernando Von Arb (rg), Freddy Steady (d), Tommy Keifer (lg), Chris Von Rohr (b). 21/5/80 * TW *

ALI HASSAN KUBAN AND THE NUBIAN BAND
27/6/92 KERSHAW Amira, Nubia, Tamin galbak, La ya habibi la. Ali Hassan Kuban (v), Abdel Razik (v), Hassan Meky (sy), Bibi Hammond (b), Ahmed Attiat Allah (al), Mohamed Fathi (d,peerc), Mahmoud Fadl & Hassan Mahoud (d,perc). 30/4/92 MV4 NG&GT

THE KURSAAL FLYERS
13/2/75 PEEL Tennessee, Route 66, Yellow sox, Foggy mountain breakdown (version). Graeme Douglas (g), Vic Collins (ps), Richie Bull (b,bj), Paul Shuttleworth (v), Will Birch (d). 30/1/75 MV4 TW BAI

FELA RANSOME KUTI
24/7/73 PEEL Fefenene, Gentleman. 16 musicians (unknown). Rec. date unknown OS * *

L KAGE
27/8/91 GOODIER Head on fire, She is, Dumb dumb, Passion. Dean O'Loughlin (gv), John Morrison (b), Andy Pell (g), Hendricks (d). 17/8/91 MV5 MC~

THE LA'S
2/9/87 LONG Doledrum, Way out, Freedom song, Come in come out. Lee Mavers (gv), Paul Hemmings (g), John Power (b,bkv), Timo Timson (d). 23/8/87 MV4 PW PS&FK
31/5/88 L. KERSHAW Son of a gun, There she goes, I can't sleep, Over. Mavers, Power, Ian Templeton (d). 18/5/88 MV4 PW MPK
13/3/89 CAMPBELL Feelin', Timeless melody, Callin' all, IOU, Way out. Mavers, Powers, Chris Sharrock (d), Barry Sutton (g). 1/3/89 MV4 HP MPK
20/3/89 CAMPBELL Feelin', Timeless melody, Callin' all, IOU, Way out. 1/3/89 MV4 HP MPK
Broadcast date untraceable HARRIS Feelin', Callin' all, Timeless melody, I can't sleep. Mavers, Powers, Neil Mavers (d), Peter Camille (g). 7/10/90 MV5 MA~PA

COLIN LACHLAN
7/12/83 JENSEN Spirits making music, Paper tiger, Promises you can't keep, Angels of Mons. Colin Lachlan (gv), Phil Dines (b), Jerry Chapman (sy,p,bkv), Ray Wells (d), Geraldo Darbilly (perc). 27/11/83 MV4 DG ME

LAIBACH
24/6/86 PEEL Krvava gruda-plodna zemlda, Krst, Live is life. Eber, Dachauer, Keller, Saliger. 15/6/86 MV4 DG MR
27/4/87 PEEL Leben-tod, Trans-national, Krvoprelitze. * 7/4/87 * DG MR

DENNY LAINE AND THE ELECTRIC STRING BAND
8/10/67 TOP GEAR Say you don't mind, Why did you come, Reason to believe, Catherine wheel, Ask the people, Guilty mind. Denny Laine (gv), John Stein (vi), Nigel Pinkett (clo), Andy Leigh (b), Peter Trout (d). 4/10/67 MV4 BA *
Group first appeared live from PH on Light Programme's Monday Monday, 19/6/67, prod. KB.
28/1/68 TOP GEAR Catherine wheel, Machine song, Too much in love, Masks, Sally free and easy. 24/1/68 MV4 BA *

ANNABEL LAMB
4/10/83 JENSEN Hands of the hunter, Sacraments of Love, Missing, The flame. Alan Hodgson (d), Chris Jarret (g), Steve Greetham (b), Robin Langridge (p,sy), Annabel Lamb (v,sy,p). 22/9/83 MV4 JP TdB

KEVIN LAMBE
24/7/72 HARRIS Road to Antibes, Far betwen the morning, Who's the hero, Who am I. Kevin Lambe (ag,v) & I, (unknown). 27/6/72 MV5 JG *
Five days before, Lambe was contracted to record a session for HARRIS with 'backing provided by session unit directed by Ed Welch', but there is no trace of this having been broadcast, or recorded.

LANCASTER
12/3/71 BLACK Moon's dawn, Sail away, Lovely lady, Getting straight. Jack Lancaster (ts,fl,vi), David Cakebread (b,clo), Alan Powell (d), Barry Reynolds (g). 18/2/71 AO2 JM JWH
Rec'd Peel Sunday Concert 27/5/71 PS, TX 13/6/71.

LANDSCAPE
19/4/78 PEEL Kaptin Whorlix, Gotham City, Lost in the small ads, Workers' playtime. John Walters (el-ss,perc), Peter Thoms (el-tb,perc), Andy Pask (b), Christopher Heaton (elp), Richard Burgess (d). 12/4/78 MV4 MB NG
15/3/82 JENSEN It's not my real name, Manhattan boogie woogie, Colour code (Tell me something new), Eastern girls. 25/2/82 MV4 JWI *

RONNIE LANE'S SLIM CHANCE
11/12/73 PEEL Ooh la la, Careless love, Flags and banners, How come. Ronnie Lane (gv), Bruce Rowlands (d), Chrissie Stewart (b), Billy Livsey (k), Jimmy Jewell (sx), Graham Lyle (mnd,v), Benny Gallagher (gv). 27/11/73 LH1 JW BC
Then rec'd Sounds on Sunday 27/2/74 LH1, TX 10/3/74.
3/12/74 PEEL Sweet Virginia, Lovely, Anniversary. Lane & Ruan O'Lochlainn (sx,k), Steve Simpson (g), Charlie Hart (k,vi), Jim Frank (d), Brian Belsham (b). 19/11/74 MV4 TW *
Line-up rec'd In Concert 13/12/74 HP, TX 21/12/74; and Speakeasy 10/4/75 CH, TX 13/4/75.
15/1/76 PEEL Don't try and change my mind, One for the road, Steppin' and reelin', All or nothing. Lane, Simpson, Hart, Belshaw, Colin Davey (d), Chris Thomas (p-2). 8/1/76 MV4 TW *
Line-up (minus Thomas) rec'd In Concert 12/2/76 PS, TX 13/3/76; and last session, for JENSEN, rec'd 31/10/79 TX 5/11/79.

HUW LLOYD LANGTON
16/5/86 FRI. ROCK Like an arrow (through the heart), I could cry, So long waiting, Take a back step. John Clark (d), Kenny Wilson (b), Huw Lloyd Langton (g). 25/4/86 MV4 TW DD

LASH LARIAT AND THE LONG RIDERS
19/1/85 PEEL *Oh baby, Bitter tears, Feel like yelling, Never been so weary.* Lash Lariat (gv), Luke Lariat (db), Johnny T. (fd), Matt Black (bj), Elmer Thudd (d,bkv). 13/1/85 MV5 DG ME

30/12/85 PEEL *Think about me, Change, Devil's dancer, Eloise.* 10/12/85 MV5 HP~

LAST FLIGHT
20/3/81 FRI. ROCK *Dance to the music, I am ready, Everybody fight some, Headlines.* Bob Hawthorn (lv), Paul Murray (g), John Sinfield (b), Graham Waxman (d). 18/2/81 * TW DD

LAST PARTY
30/3/87 PEEL *Bigger things, Autumn acre, Don't even consider it, Tin foil mountain.* Simon Rivers (gv), Kim Ashford (sy), Daniel Ashkenazy (b), Neil Palmer (d). 17/3/87 * DG MR&MA

9/1/89 PEEL *Purple Hazel, A full English breakfast, Platforms and trains, Creature lakes.* 3/1/89 MV4 DG MR

LATIN QUARTER
9/4/86 LONG *Sandinista, The night, The men below, America for beginners.* Steve Skaith (gv), Greg Harewood (b), Dave Charles (d), Martin Lasalles (k), Richard Wright (g), Yona Dunsford (kv), Carol Douet (v). 30/3/86 MV4 BYA TdB

LAUGH
17/3/86 PEEL *Never had it so bad, Paul McCartney, Hey I'm still thinking, Take your time yeah.* Spencer Birtwhistle (d), Martin Mittler (b), Martin Wright (gv), Craig Gannon (g). 9/3/86 MV5 DG ME&MFA

7/9/87 PEEL *Time to lose it, Interlove, Come on come out, The Wright experience.* Ian Bandelow (g) r. Gannon. 25/8/87 * DG MWT&SC

LAUGHING CLOWNS
8/12/82 PEEL *Theme from mad flies man flies, Nothing that harms, The year of the bloated goat, Every dog has its day.* Jeff Wegener (d), Edmund Kuepper (gv), Louise Elliot (sx), Peter Doyle (tp), Leslie Millar (db). 29/11/82 MV4 TW DD

LAUGHTER IN THE GARDEN
22/9/82 JENSEN *Nightmare, Such fun, Clutch tight, Desperate remedies.* Andy Wallace (gv), Pauline Mayers (kv), Roselyn Journeaux (v,cl), Mark Cross (d), Tom (b), Victoria Doyle (al), Richard Webb (ts). 12/9/82 MV4 DG ME

LAUREL AND HARDY
4/11/82 PEEL *Tell her sey me sorry, You're nicked, Toast one quick, Speeding.* Laurel (v), Hardy (v), John Kpyaie (g), Spy (b), Angus Gaye (d), Reg Graham (k), Annie Whitehead (brs), Chris Layne (v). 20/10/82 MV4 RP NG

24/3/83 JENSEN *Video trafficking, Lots of loving, Dangerous shoes, In by a certain time.* Laurel, Hardy, Lane, Spy, Graham, Whitehead, Richie Stevens (d), Alun Lane (perc). 20/3/83 MV4 DG ME

GASPAR LAWAL BAND
28/8/71 VIV STANSHALL'S RADIO FLASHES *Ye ye oro, Jankulubo.* Terry Poole (b), Gaspar Lawal (d,perc,v), Graham Bond (o,v), Shamsi Surami (afd,cga), Pug Weathers (xyl,cga), Derick (surname unknown) (afd,cga), Liz Wilson, Jillian, Kareen & Diane Stewart (bkv), Malcolm (surname unknown) (ts,fl). 23/8/71 PH JW *&PK

JULIET LAWSON
11/5/72 DRUMMOND *I won't get my feet wet again, Frog in the jam, Let me not put you down (& Playing is no song, 6/7/72).* Juliet Lawson (ag,v). 6/3/72 * MB *

LAZY LESTER
26/11/87 KERSHAW *Strange things, Tell me pretty baby, The same thing could happen to you, Patrol wagon.* Lazy Lester (v,hca), John Bruce (g), Sean Scott (d). 12/11/87 KK DG AK

LE RUE
6/8/87 KERSHAW *Tit galop, Lafayette, Wheel, Billy the kid, Hey baby.* Pierre Le Rue (fd,acc,v), Phillipe Le Rue

(bj,g-5), Lonzo McShane (d), Fergus Feely (mnda), Dennis Calloway (b,accv-5). 16/7/87 * MRD SR

28/4/88 KERSHAW *Come see come saw, Hellbound train, Hey Joe, Honky tonk woman.* P. & P. Le Rue, McShane, Jeff Mead (b). 7/4/88 * DG NG&MFA

15/10/89 KERSHAW *Tell me ma, Sourwood MT, Walkin' to New Orleans, Mardi Gras.* P. & P. Le Rue, Feely, Donal McGrath (b). 7/9/89 MV3 DG NG

THE LEAGUE OF GENTLEMEN
17/11/80 PEEL *Inductive resonance, Heptaparaparshinokh, Farewell Johnny Brill, Dislocated.* Robert Fripp (g), Barry Andrews (o), Sara Lee (b), Johnny Toobad (d). Rec. date unknown PRIV * *

THE LEATHER NUN
29/7/86 LONG† *Lust for love, Pure heart, Desolation avenue, Prime mover.* Gert Claesson (d), Vengt Aronsson (g), Nils Wohlrage (g), Jonas Almquist (v), Anders Ollson (b). 13/7/86 MV4 BYA TdB
  † On Nighttracks SFNT014.

LEATHERFACE
4/1/92 PEEL *I want the moon, Springtime, Dreaming, Peasant in paradise.* Andrew Karzi-Lang (d), Stuart Raymond (b), Dicky Kadogo-Hammond (g), Frankie Stubbs (gv). 12/11/91 MV4 MR~

LED ZEPPELIN
23/3/69 TOP GEAR *Communication breakdown, You shook me, I can't quit you baby.* Jimmy Page (g), Robert Plant (v), John Paul Jones (b,p,o), John Bonham (d). 3/3/69 PH BA PR&BC
  This trial broadcast tape was passed unanimously by Audition panel 22/4/69: 'Excellent', Jimmy Grant.
14/4/69 WS R&B *Sunshine woman, I can't quit you baby, You shook me.* 19/3/69 MV4 JG JY
22/6/69 CHRIS GRANT'S TASTY POP SUNDAE *The girl I love she got long black wavy hair, Communication breakdown.* 16/6/69 AO2 c.PWI *
  Grant was stand-in DJ for Symonds on Sunday show in June 69.
29/6/69 TOP GEAR *What is and what should never be, Whole lot of love, Travelling riverside blues†, Communication breakdown.* 24/6/69 MV4 JW TW
10/8/69 TOP GEAR *Communication breakdown, Can't quit you baby, Dazed and confused, White summer†, You shook me, How many more times.* 27/6/69 PH JG TW
  Billed as 'One Night Stand', this was the pilot for Jeff Griffin's Radio 1 Concert series. Group later recorded a second live concert for the series, 1/4/71 PS, TX 4/4/71. † On 4 CD Box Set 'Re-Masters', Atlantic 7567-82144-2.
  'As we were not doing singles as such, the only way we could get airplay was to do these sessions; so they were very important, plus they were very enjoyable as well. Certainly at the BBC the guys were very good balancers and knew their stuff; it was very different to being thrown into a TV studio in Munich. 'Travelling riverside blues' was made up in the studio, there and then'. Jimmy Page, interviewed by R1, 1993.

ALVIN LEE & MYLON LEFEVRE
14/1/74 HARRIS *Let 'em say what they will, Rockin' till the sun goes down, So sad (no love of his own), We will shine.* * Rec. date unkown PRIV * *

ADRIAN LEGG
24/8/85 KERSHAW *Cajun interlude, Wreckless love (& Pass the valium, Widdershins 10/10/85).* Adrian Legg (gv). 5/8/85 Studio 3, BHM c.JL RYK

24/7/86 KERSHAW *Cuckoo shuffle, Divorcee's waltz, The itchy pig, Cajun interlude, Bayou belles II.* Rec. date unknown SS CG TWN

21/1/88 KERSHAW *The Irish girl, Tracy's big moment, Trump the clouds, Waiting for a dancer.* 3/12/87 * DG FK&MWT

LEISURE PROCESS
22/3/82 PEEL *Sweet vendetta, Gimme that sax boy, The*

erection set. Ross Middleton (v,g,b), Gary Barnacle (k,sx). 10/3/82 MV4 RP NG

THE LEMONHEADS
17/7/89 PEEL *Clang bang clang, Circle of one, The door, Mallo cup.* * 4/7/89 * DG *

DEKE LEONARD AND ICEBERG
24/5/73 PEEL *Hard way to live, Razor blade and rattle snake, Jayhawk special, Four corners of hell.* Deke Leonard (gv), Brian Breeze (g), Paul Burton (b), Keith Hodge (d). 14/5/73 LHI BA *

26/9/73 HAMILTON *A hard way to live* [Network session]. Leonard, Breeze, David Charles (d), Martin Ace (b). 17/9/73 AO1 c.PWI *

20/12/73 PEEL *7171 511, In search of Sarah and 26 horses, Daughter of the fireplace, Eddy Waring.* 26/11/73 LHI BA *

27/2/78 PEEL *Map of India, Oh!, Big hunk of love, Dirty dirty feelin'.* Leonard, Lincoln Carr (b), Howard Hughes (p), Anthony Stone (d). 15/2/78 MV4 MB NG

LOS LEONES DE LA SIERRA & EL MONO BLANCO
1/4/90 KERSHAW *Soy Latin d'Americano soy Argullo, Queiereque/El herradero/As alasanas, La leva, La bamba, El dajaro cu/El pesro.* Eusebio Mendez & Leonardo Lara (v), Guillemo Velasques (gv), Marie Isabel Flores (v), Jose Inez Suarez (vihuela,v); & Patricia Hidalgo (hp,quijada,v) & Guilberto Guitierre (jarana, pandeiro,v) (both 5-only); & El Mono Blanco (4-only). 20/2/90 MV5 DG MR

LES THUGS
16/11/87 PEEL *Intro/Les thugs/Little kiddy, Bulgarian blues, Legal drugs, About your life.* * 1/12/87 * DG JB

LEVELLERS FIVE
16/5/90 PEEL† *Warning Shadows, Mister tell me, Home, Shell.* Ian Almond (afd,perc), Carole Fleck (perc), Terry Walsh (b), Steven Lindley (g), John Donaldson (gv). 19/4/90 MV3 DG *
  † On Strange Fruit SFPCD083.

6/10/90 PEEL *Somewhere, What's the matter, Clatter, Love thing ha.* 11/9/90 MV4 MR~

23/5/92 PEEL *Pressure drop, Messelina, Mass, Everyone for themselves.* 12/4/92 MV4 ME~

THE LEVELLERS
25/11/91 GOODIER *England my home, I have no answers, Barrel of the gun, Carry me.* Simon Friend (g), Charles Heather (d), Mark Chadwick (gv), Jonathan Sevink (vi), Jeremy Cunningham (b). 15/11/91 MV4 MC~JMK

LEVITATION
18/5/92 GOODIER *Resist, Evergreen, Hang nail, Mary.* Bob White (bk), Terry Bickers (gv), Bill Hayes (g), Dave Franklin (d). 28/3/92 MV4 MC~AA

BARRINGTON LEVY
13/3/85 LONG *Here I come, Under me sensi, Prison oval rock, Money move.* Barrington Levy (v) & Larry Basie (b), Michael Martin (k), Stanley Andrews (g), Drummie Zeb (d), Jah Bunny (perc), Paget King (o), Eddie Thornton (tp), Michael Rose (sx). 10/2/85 HP JWI PW

24/6/85 LONG *You say you love me, Cool and loving, Murderer, Give me your love.* & Angus Gaye (d), Larry Silvera (b), Stanley Andrews (lg), Toulon Clen (rg), Michael Martin (k), Carlton Olgilvie (o,sy), Lloyd Donaldson (perc). 29/5/85 MV5 BYA MPK

G. LEWIS & D.C. GILBERT
7/10/80 PEEL *Anchors, Norde, Quicken your step.* G.Lewis, B. Gilbert (g,b,k,perc). 22/9/80 MV4 TW DD

LINDA LEWIS
6/7/73 SEQUENCE *Iris, Hampstead way, Bless them all, The spring song, The lark.* * 14/6/73 LHI JM BAI&MG

THE LEYTON BUZZARDS
1/8/78 PEEL *Through with you, I don't want to go to art school, Can't get used to losing you, 17 and mad.* Kevin Steptoe (d), Vernon Austin (gv), David Jaymes (bv), Geoff Deane (lv). 26/7/78 MV4 BS NG

22/1/79 PEEL *Saturday night beneath the plastic palm trees, Baby if you love me say yes if you don't say no, The greatest story ever told, Love is just a dream.* 18/12/78 MV4 BS DD

27/6/79 PEEL *Sharp young men, Last tango (in Leyton), People in the street, Sweet dreams little one.* 6/6/79 MV4 TW NG

21/1/80 PEEL *When you walk in the room, Telephone, Jealousy, Swanky pop.* & Milton Reame James (k); Tony Gainsborough (d) r. Steptoe. 14/1/80 MV4 TW DD

LFO

20/10/90 PEEL *Take control, To the limit, Rob's nightmare, Lost world.* Mark Bell & Jez Varley (k,prog), Susie Thorpe (v). 7/10/90 MV3 PW TD&JL

THE LIGGERS

20/10/80 PEEL *Pretty girls, Dreams die first, Me and Mary Jane.* Patti Owens (k,v), Gina Sobers (b,k), Neil Anderson (g,d), Andrew (g), Donna Sullivan (b,k). 30/9/80 MV4 JS MR

LIGHT A BIG FIRE

17/3/86 LONG *Who would believe, Here comes my girl, Driving thru Nevada, Women.* Thomas McLaughlin (v), Pete Dench (g), Pat Diskin (b), Neville Seventeen (kv), Eamonn Ryan (d). 26/2/86 MV5 BYA MPK

GORDON LIGHTFOOT

19/3/69 NIGHT RIDE *If I could, Affair on Eighth Avenue, Pussywillow Cat's tails, The circle is small, Railroad trilogy, The leaves of grass, For loving me, Bitter green.* Gordon Lightfoot (ag,v). 11/3/69 SI JM *

LIGHTNIN' SLIM

24/2/72 DRUMMOND *Sugar mama, Big boss man/Sometime, Rooster blues (& Don't let it get you down, 20/4/72).* Lightnin' Slim (ag,hca,v). 14/2/72 * MB *

20/10/73 ROCK ON *Short dress woman, Miss Sarah, I'm my own boss.* & Whispering Smith. 11/10/73 * PR *

LIGHTNING STRIKES

21/10/87 LONG *Get ready, Beatbox international, Going for gold, America's calling.* Dave Earl, Eddie Auffray (g), Jon Brooder (bv), Sten (k,bkv), Teb Colville-Scott (d). 7/10/87 MV4 PW TdB&JB

THE LILAC TIME

1/3/88 MAYO *The king and queen of the carioca, Streetcorner, Take time, Hargeesha.* Stephen Duffy (g,perc,hca,v), Nick Duffy (bj,g,acc), Michael Weston (k). 24/1/88 MV4 PW TdB

THE LINDEN TREE

6/5/91 GOODIER *Sun rose, Rollin', Same old pain, Walk your way†.* Len Lawson (gv), Steve Nicklin (g), Andy Kirkland (b), Mark Kerr (d), Johnny Deas (o,p). 23/3/91 MV5 MC~
† On 'Best of Mark Goodier' Mark1.

LINDISFARNE

6/1/71 R2 NIGHTRIDE *Road to kingdom come, Lady Eleanor, Winter song, Nothing but the marvellous is beautiful, Meet me on the corner, Dingley Dell.* Alan Hull (vgk), Rod Clements (b,vi), Simon Cowe (gv,mand), Ray Jackson (v,hca,mand), Ray Laidlaw (d,perc). 14/12/70 MV5 ARD NG
Tape passed by panel, with proviso 'there doesn't seem to be a lot of call for this type of ingredient in our general output'.

30/1/71 TOP GEAR *Positive earth, Knacker's yard blues, Lady Eleanor, Dream within a dream (& Psalm to a secret, 10/4/71).* 12/1/71 MV4 JW BC

1/2/71 HARRIS *From a window, Why can't I be satisfied, Scarecrow song, We can swing together.* 19/1/71 MV5 JM JWH

6/3/71 FOLK ON 1 *Road to kingdom come, Positive earth, Winter song, Jack Hammer blues, January song, down, Lady Eleanor, Jack Hammer blues (reprise).* 10/2/71 AO2 FL *

6/5/71 HENRY *Walking blues, Turn a deaf ear, Meet me on the corner.* 28/4/71 MV4 MB PK

22/5/71 RAVEN'S R&B *Walking blues, Knacker's yard blues,*

Jack Hammer blues, Train in G major, I'm coming home. 12/5/71 MV4 MB *

21/6/71 HARRIS *Lady Eleanor, City song, The fog on the Tyne, Scotch mist.* 8/6/71 T1 JM JWH
Three days after this broadcast, group recorded first 'John Peel Concert' PS 24/6/71, TX 18/7/71.

11/9/71 TOP GEAR *Meet me on the corner, Uncle Sam, Alright on the night, Fog on the Tyne (& Together forever, 10/11/71).* 31/8/71 MV4 JW BC

7/10/71 DRUMMOND *Train in G major, January song, Fog on the Tyne.* 20/9/71 MV5 MB MH&MF

10/11/71 WALKER *Fog on the Tyne, No time to lose (11/11), Lady Eleanor (12/11).* 21/10/71 AO1 cJBE *

4/2/72 PEEL *Dancing Jack Peel, Together forever, No time to lose, Alright on the night, Meet me on the corner (& Poor old Ireland, 10/3/72).* 17/1/72 T1 PD ARV

6/3/72 WALKER *Mandolin King, Meet me on the corner (7/3), Together forever (8/3), Fog on the Tyne (9/3).* 2/2/72 MV5 RP *
Also appeared live on 'Country meets folk' 19/2/72 PH, prod. BB.

15/5/72 WALKER *Lady Eleanor, Scarecrow song (16/5), Together forever (18/5).* 4/5/72 AO1 RP *

25/5/72 DRUMMOND *Lady Eleanor, Love me do, Uncle Sam, Road to Kingdom come.* 10/5/72 MV4 MB *

13/6/72 PEEL† *Mandolin king, Poor old Ireland, Road to kingdom come, Lady Eleanor.* 8/5/72 T1 JW BC?
† On Strange Fruit SFPS059; 'Lady Eleanor' also on 'Before the Fall' SFRCD203.

10/7/72 HARRIS *Drug song, Passing ghosts, Country gentleman's wife, Turn a deaf ear.* 14/6/72 AO2 JG *

18/1/73 PEEL *Oh no not again, Train in G major, Uncle Sam, Court in the act.* 8/1/73 LH1 BA *

4/4/74 PEEL *No need to tell me, Taking care of business, In your head, North country boy.* Hull, Jackson, Charlie Harcourt (gv), Kenny Craddock (gkv), Tommy Duffy (bv), Paul Nichols (d). 28/3/74 LH1 JW *

5/8/74 HARRIS *Dealer's choice, You put the laugh on me, In your hand, Tonight.* 3/7/74 LH1 JG *

THE LINES

17/1/80 PEEL *Don't need surgery, Time to go, Two split seconds, False alarm.* Richard Conning (gv), Mick Lineham (g), Joe Forty (b), Nicholas Cash (d). 8/1/80 MV4 JS MR&MPK

27/1/81 PEEL *Bliss-tability, Transit, Bucket brigade, Nerve pylon.* 20/1/81 LH1 BS MR

THE LINKMEN

31/5/84 JENSEN *Alcohol malice, Every inch a king, Perfect caper, She holds me in flames.* Nick Bates (v), Will Hoon (b), Olly Hoon (g), Giz (d). 17/5/84 MV4 MHY MR

ERROL LINTON

10/6/90 KERSHAW *Don't you love me babe, Just keep loving her, Low down blues, Don't pay your poll tax, My babe.* Errol Linton (hca,v). 10/5/90 MV5 DG NG

9/5/92 KERSHAW *Love you true, Love that woman, So many women, Clash of the cans.* & Tyrone Balkissoon (bkv,wsh,tamb), Pigmeat Pete Smith (gv). 16/4/92 MV4 DG NG&NF

23/5/92 SAT. SEQ *Clash of the cans, Love me true, Lowdown blues, Polly put the kettle on.* Live from on-air studio, EG5 PRS SA

ROARING LION AND LORD PRETENDER

22/9/91 KERSHAW *Caroline, I ain't going to do it no more, Jouvert, God made us all, True true calypsonian.* Winston Matthews (d), Michael Ruiz (b), Theron Shaw (sy), Hendren Boucard (sx), Adrian Philbert (perc), Theron Shaw (g). 1/8/91 MV5 DG NG&CML

LIONHEART

29/3/85 FRI. ROCK *Wait for the night, Hot tonight, Tower of silver, Give me the light.* Dennis Stratton (g), Steve Mann (gkv), Rocky Newton (bv), Chad Brown (v), Andy Bierne (d), Phil Lanzon (k). 22/2/85 MV4 TW MC

LIONSHEART

26/10/90 FRI. ROCK *World of pain, So cold, Stealer, Portrait.* Steve Grimmett (v), Mark Owers (g), Steve Owers (b), Anthony Christmas (d), Graham Collett (k). 5/10/90 MV5 DD~

LISTEN

13/7/72 DRUMMOND *Astral boogie, The coming (& After all, All your rock and roll is dead, 17/8/72).* Paul Abrahams (o,p), David Worth (b), Roger `Cairns (o,v), Edward Durbron (lg), Mike Anscombe (d), Linda Sukenik (lv). 28/6/72 MV4 MB *

JAMES LITHERLAND'S BROTHERHOOD

28/6/70 RAVEN'S R&B *Elegy, What's this I hear, Dreams of glass and sand.* James Litherland (g), Malcolm Duncan (ts), Roger Ball (ss,al,bars), John Wetton (b), Bill Atkinson (d), Michael Rosen (tp,g). 10/6/70 MV4 JG JY

14/8/70 BLACK *Elegy, What's this I hear, Going north (& Something sad 9/10/70).* 8/7/70 AO2 JM *
Rec'd and billed as 'Brotherhood' but renamed Mogul Thrash by repeat on 9/10/70 (see below).

LITTLE ANGELS

20/5/88 FRI. ROCK *I can't wait, Big bad world, She's a little angel, No solution.* * 7/5/88 * PW MWT

LITTLE BIG DIG

17/7/84 SKINNER *The day my girlfriend died, I got the fear, You are my sweetie shop, Nothing much at all.* Tom Murray (v,cl), Jack Crawford (d,perc), Colin Cairns (b), Suzie Hope (v), Mark Fleming (gk). 24/6/84 MV5 DG PS

LITTLE BIG HORN

10/5/91 FRI. ROCK *No surrender, All god's children, 21st century, So the story goes.* Ivan Norris (v), Nic Slater (lg), Steve Young (rg), Redverse (b), Ian Chas (d). 5/4/91 MV5 TW DD&MC

LITTLE BOB STORY

21/1/77 PEEL *Like a rock'n roll, Baby don't cry, So bad, High time.* Robert Piazza (v), Dominique Lelan (bv), Dominique Quertier (d), Dominique Guillon (rg,bkv), Guy George Gremy (lg). 11/1/77 MV4 TW *

22/7/77 PEEL *Mr Tap, Nothing else (can give it to me), All or nothing, Little big boss.* 13/7/77 MV4 * MR

LITTLE RED DUFFLE COATS

7/2/81 PEEL *Mountains, Sky the pitch, Natasha Rumbova buys a kite, Enrolment.* Billy Muir (d), Nick Prescott (b), Tommy McGregor (pv), Ian Macleod (g). 19/12/80 MV4 DG PS

LIVE SKULL

22/3/89 PEEL *Safe from me, Someone else's sweat, Adema, Amputease.* Rich Hutchins (d), Sonda Andersson (b), Mark C. (g), Tom Paine (g), Thalia Zedek (v,g-2 only). 14/3/89 WX DG ME

THE LIVERPOOL SCENE

19/1/69 TOP GEAR *Wild west, All around my grandmother's floor, Tramcar to Frankenstein, The entry of Christ into Liverpool (& The raven, Colours, 23/2/69).* Adrian Henri (v), Andy Roberts (g), Percy Jones (b), Brian Dodson (d), Mike Evans (sx). 6/1/69 MV4 BA PR
Passed by panel, despite following comments: 'entertaining I should imagine to devotees to self-pitying ideas on current society'; 'not accurate poetry'; 'one assumes this is suitable for Top Gear - certainly it would be unsuitable for anything else'.

20/7/69 TOP GEAR *I've got the Fleetwood Mac Chicken Shack John Mayall can't fail blues, Winter poem, G.B.S. blues.* 15/7/69 MV4 JW TW
Had also appeared on R3 31/5/69, as part of the 'Poetry Marathon' programme produced by George Macbeth at the Roundhouse; and Henri, Roberts & Evans were Led Zeppelin's interval act at Concert pilot, 27/6/69 PH.

3/1/70 TOP GEAR *Home grown, Boathouse, Night song, Tractor.* 29/12/69 PH JW TW
After this, the group did 4 weekly specials produced by Frances Line, rec'd in S2 over 4 days in Jan & Feb 70, TX from 1/2/70.

ROBERT LLOYD

23/3/87 PEEL *Something nice, Tocatta and fatigue, Of course you can't, The part of the anchor.* Robert Lloyd (v) 'and the New Four Seasons': Cara Tivey (k,bkv), Dave Lowe (g,bkv), Micky Harris (b), Mark Fletcher (d). 10/3/87 * DG MS&MR

19/10/87 PEEL *Top floor to let, Sweet Georgia Black, Half a heart.* Mark Tibenham (dm,v) r. Fletcher. 11/10/87 * DG ME&PS

18/7/88 L. KERSHAW *Mr Superior, Nothing matters, Sweet Georgia Black, Toccata and fatigue.* Lloyd, Lowe, Tibenham, Roger Morton (sx,bkv), Tracey Lee (bkv). 8/6/88 MV4 HP TdB

13/2/89 PEEL *Mama nature's skin, Nothing matters, The funeral stomp, Ta love.* Lloyd, Lowe, Tibenham, Magda (g,v,bj), Bobby Bird (g), Susanne Unruh (d). 31/1/89 MV4 DG ME

26/3/90 PEEL *The race is on, Grown so ugly, The man who couldn't afford to orgy, Good boy.* Lloyd, Magda, Wendy Harper (vi,sy,tamb,bkv), Nick Small (b,bkv), Peter Byrchmore (g,brs), Daniel S. (d). 4/3/90 MV3 DG ME

13/1/91 PEEL *Here comes Mimi, Go forth and multiply, Kiss me stupid, Slags and angels.* Lloyd, Byrchmore, Small, Daniel S., Cath Eburne (k,bkv), Kerry Lloyd (bkv). 11/12/90 MV5 MR~. See also 'Terminal Hoedown'.

LLWYBR LLAETHOG

5/1/88 PEEL *Tour de France 87, Cyfundrefn gyfalafol, Megamicks.* John (dv,g-1 only), Kevs (gv,d-1 only), Ben (b), Debs (perc). 20/12/87 * DG ME&PS

11/10/89 PEEL *Dinas fawr, Trachwant, Byd mor wahanol, Fyw dy fywyd.* 17/9/89 MV3 DG ME

ANNA LOCKWOOD

5/2/69 NIGHT RIDE *Talk and sounds.* Anna Lockwood (v). 22/1/69 SI JM *

LOERMEL

12/6/92 FRI. ROCK *Heat part II, Hold me down, Lean, Sheepy thing.* Vicki Horobin (lv), Nick Roach (b), Nigel Gregory (g), Gary White (g), Eric Porter (k). 22/5/92 MV5 TW MC

THE LOFT

3/1/85 LONG *The canal and the big red town, Skeleton staircase, Lonely street, On a Tuesday.* Peter Astor (gv), David Morgan (d), Bill Prince (b), Andy Strickland (g); [See 'Weather Prophets' (below)]. 9/12/84 VS BYA *

LAURA LOGIC

21/2/79 PEEL *Wake up, Alkaline loaf in the area, Quality crayon wax OK, Shabby abbott.* Billed as 'Essential Logic'. 'Lora' Logic (sx,v), Phil Lip (g), William Charles (g), Mark Turner (b), Dave Wright (sx), Richard Thompson (d). 6/2/79 MV4 BS MR

2/6/81 PEEL *Pedigree charm, Martian man, Rat alley.* Laura Logic (v,al,ts), Phil Legg (g,b), Duncan McDonald (d,perc). 26/5/81 LHI DG DD

3/12/81 JENSEN *Horrible party, May in June, No more records, Radio three and a third.* Logic, Legg, Charles Heywood (d), Ben Anneseley (b). 22/11/81 MV4 DG *

JACKIE LOMAX AND HEAVY JELLY

4/6/70 HENRY *You'd better let me know, F.F.F.Females, Watch your step, Bio blues.* Jackie Lomax (gv), John Morshead (lg), Steve Thompson (b), Bruce Rowland (d) [Lomax had previous sessions with other backing bands in 69]. 28/5/70 AO2 MB *

LONDON BEAT

26/7/84 L. KERSHAW *Please baby (can I have my heart back please), Falling in love again, Drop, Katey.* Willy M. (ag), George Chandler (v), Jimmy Helms (v), Jimmy Chandler (v). 20/7/88 MV4 HP MPK

THE LONDON POSSE

22/10/87 LONG *'Cos I'm from London, We rule, We're the dett, Freestyle.* Bionic MC (rp), MC Rodie Rok (rp), DJ Business (mx), Sipho (hbb). 30/9/87 MV4 HP MPK

LONE STAR

24/2/76 PEEL *Flying in the reel, A million stars, She said.*

Tony Smith (g), Kenny Driscoll (lv), Rick Worsnop (k), Paul Chapman (g), Pete Hurley (b), Dixie Lee (d). 29/1/76 MV4 TW *

5/8/76 PEEL *Hypnotic mover, Spaceships.* 15/4/76 MV4 TW BAI

25/6/77 FREEMAN *Bells of Berlin, From all of us, Lonely soldier.* John Sloman (v) r. Driscoll. 28/2/77 MV6 TW BAI Recorded and broadcast as Matrix 'H' Quad experiment.

LONG TALL TEXANS

1/2/88 MAYO *Your own way, The Indians, Saints and sinners, Should I stay or should I go.* Mark Carew (db,lv), Mark Denman (g,bkv), Anthony Theodotou (d,bkv). 12/1/88 MV4 HP MWT

LONGDANCER

22/12/72 SEQUENCE *How soon, Ballad to highway, Silent emotions.* Dave Stewart (g,mnd,v), Brian Harrison (g,bv,o), Kai Olsson (gv), Steve Sproxton (gv,rec,hca). 21/11/72 TI JM * [M: daytime]

LOOP

19/8/87 PEEL† *Soundhead°, Straight to your heart, Rocket USA.* Robert Wills (gv), Glen Ray (b), James Dillon (g), John Wills (d). 11/8/87 * DG ME&MP
    ° On 'New Season' SFRCD205.

27/6/88 PEEL† *Pulse, Collision, This is where you end.* Neil McKay (b) r. Ray. 14/6/88 MV4 TdB~

31/1/90 PEEL† *Afterglow, From centre to wave, Sunburst.* Scott (g) r. Dillon. 21/1/90 MV3 HP ME
    † All sessions on 'Wolf Flow' Reactor CD3.

LORNA G

22/7/87 MISS P *Why, Don't go crazy, Many years ago, Lyrics to kill.* Lorna G (v), Bernard Cumberbatch (b), Black Steel (k), The Mad Professor (d), Jerry Lyons (g), Chris Scully (perc). 8/7/87 MV4 HP MPK

THE LOTUS EATERS

18/10/82 PEEL *Can you keep a secret?, Stranger so far, When you look at boys†, The first picture of you.* Peter Coyle (v), Gerry Kelly (g), Phil (b), Alan Wills (d), Gerard Quinn (k). 2/10/82 MV4 DG *
    † On band's debut album 'No sense of sin' Arista 206263.

10/10/83 PEEL *Alone of all her sex, German girl, You fill me with need, Love still flows, Signature tune (instrumental).* Coyle, Kelly, Quinn, Michael Dempsey (b), Steve Creese (d). 5/10/83 MV4 RP NG

LOUD

24/8/90 FRI. ROCK *This time, Black hysteria, Explosive, D generation.* Chris McLaughlin (gv), Martin Hawthorn (b), Ricky Howard (d), Colin Clarkson (g). 10/8/90 MV5 MC~

LOUDSPEAKER

22/2/92 PEEL *Knockout, It wasn't me, Stripmind, No time.* Chris Douglas (d), Charles Hanson (b), Kurt Wolf (g), Matt Burruso (gv). 26/1/92 MV3 DG JB

LOUISIANA RED

8/11/77 PEEL *Intro, I wonder who, The whole world, When my mama was living, My heart's a loser, Look at the children run, I walked all night long.* Louisiana Red (gv). 2/11/77 MV4 JG *

LOUVIN AND WHITSTEIN

11/8/88 KERSHAW *What about you, Ruby's song, The family who prays, Alabama.* Charlie Louvin (gv), Charles Whitstein (gv), Tim Davies (db). 7/8/88 HP DG DD

LOVE BLOBS

4/9/92 PEEL *Blood control, Soul station, Peanuts, Two down.* Paul Thorpe (gv), Colin Todd (b,bkv), Tim Holdcraft (g), Tim Cedar (d). 16/8/92 MV3 ME~ FK

THE LOVE BRIGADE

9/11/87 LONG *Western laughter, Hello we're back again, Fresh adventures, The love brigade.* Paul Arnall (g), Paul Richards (d), Sarah Simonds (v). 25/10/87 MV4 PW TdB

LOVE SCULPTURE

21/4/68 TOP GEAR *Brand new woman, River to another day, Do I still figure in your life, Stumble, Sweet little*

---

rock'n roller. Dave Edmunds (gv), John Williams (b), Bob 'Congo' Jones (d). 2/4/68 PCI BA DT&AH

6/10/68 TOP GEAR *The rebel, Wang dang doodle, Promised land, Sabre dance (broadcast twice) (& Don't answer the door, 3/11/68).* [M]. 16/9/68 PCI BA AH

9/3/69 TOP GEAR *Farendale, Great balls of fire, Evening, Inner light.* 28/1/69 PH JG AH

LYLE LOVETT

21/4/88 KERSHAW *If I had a pony, She's no lady, Father down the line, You can't resist it.* Lyle Lovett (gv), John Hagen (clo). 3/4/88 MV5 DG MA

LENE LOVICH

27/11/78 PEEL *Monkey talk, Home, Lucky number, Say when.* Lene Lovich (v), Les Chappell (gv), Don Snow (k), Bob Irwin (d), Ron Francois (b). 21/11/1978 MV4 MR~

10/12/79 PEEL *Angels, One in a million, Birdsong.* Lovich, Chappell, Justin Hildreth (d), Mark Chaplin (b), Dead Kelvatt (k). 3/12/79 MV4 TW DD

13/4/81 SKINNER *Rocky road, Maria, Savages, Details. &* Thomas Dolby (sy). 26/3/81 LHI JS *

L7

18/11/90 PEEL *Scrap, Packin' a rod, Shove, Let's lynch the landlord.* Dee Plakas (d), Jennifer Finch (bv), Suzi Gardner (gv), Donita Sparks (gv). 1/11/90 MV5 DG NG&JSM

THE LUCY SHOW

24/8/87 LONG *Melody, View from the outside, Shame, Sun and moon.* Rob Vandevan (bv), Mark Bandola (gk,dm,v). 12/8/87 MV4 HP *

THE LUCYS

11/3/81 PEEL *No door, Lost animal, The right man, Perfect marriage.* Ann Paley (bv), Colin McMahon (bv), Joanne Melvin (v), Pete Drew (dv), Bee Berwick (perc,v), Mike Hobbs (sx), Pete Boyse (gv). 3/3/81 LHI DG MR

LUDDITES

19/9/83 PEEL *Just to return, Letters, See these, 7.7.3.3. (instrumental).* Steve McDermott (v), Mike Stead (g), Lawrence Gill (b), Dave Stead (d). 10/9/83 MV4 DG MR

LUDUS

18/8/82 PEEL *Too hot to handle, Wrapped in silence, Covenant, (Pride below the navel) Vagina gratitude.* Linder (v), Ian (g), Paul (b), Lee (ts), Graham (ss), Roy (d), Dave (k). 4/8/82 MV4 JWI NG

16/4/83 LONG *Let me go where my pictures go, Breaking the rules, Little girls, Mirror mirror.* * 11/4/83 PHM cJL TWN

LULU

19/11/67 TOP GEAR *Higher and higher, Love loves to love love, To love somebody.* Lulu (v) & The George Bean Group. 14/11/67 * BA DT

LE LULUS

4/11/86 LONG *Down my spine, Love attack, Junk love, Techno fear.* Yoyo (v), Dr J (sfx), Steviepoos (dm,smp,sy), Denise Gibson (v), David Elgee (sfx), Steve Boyce Buckley (k,prg). 29/10/86 MV5 AJ MC

LUNA

24/4/92 PEEL *Crazy people, Slide, That's what you always say, I can't wait.* Stanley Demeski (d), Justin Harwood (b), Dean Wareham (gv). 1/3/92 MV3 DG ME&PL

LUNACHICKS

30/5/89 PEEL *Binge and purge, Mabel rock, Rip you to shreds, Public school hell.* Becky (d), Squid (b,bkv), Gina (g), Sindi (g), Theo (v). 7/5/89 HP DG MA

THE LURKERS

27/10/77 PEEL *Freakshow, Total war, I'm on heat, Then I kissed her, Be my prisoner.* Nigel Moore (b), Esso (d), Pete Stride (g), Howard Wall (lv). 18/10/77 MV4 MB MR

24/4/78 PEEL *Ain't got a clue, Pills, Tell her, Jenny. & Plug* (bkv). 18/4/78 MV4 MB MR

7/8/78 PEEL *Here come the bad times, God's lovely men, In room 309, Countdown.* 25/7/78 MV4 BS MR

30/1/79 PEEL *Whatever happened to Mary, Take me back to Babylon, Out in the dark, See the world.* 24/1/79 MV4 BS NG

LUSH

19/2/90 PEEL *Hey hey Helen, Leaves me cold, Breeze†.* Christopher Alland (d), Steve Rippon (b), Emma Anderson (g,bkv), Miki Berenyi (gv). 23/1/90 * DG MR
† On 'New Season' SFRCD205.

LYIN' RAMPANT

14/6/85 FRI. ROCK *Time again, Promises, Crazy, Kill them all.* Eddie Trainer (g,bkv), George Pringle (b), Stewart Adams (g), Tam Creamer (d), Gordon Thompson (v).
Rec. date unknown MV4 TW DD

THE JACKIE LYNTON GRANDE

21/10/74 HARRIS *I don't need you, Bendy Wellingbox, Coming down your way, Jimmy and Jock, Put it there (& Roll me, ROCK ON 12/10/74).* Jackie Lynton (v; 2,4-solo), Mick J. Gunn, Keith Purnell, Roger Groom, John Sinclare, Bob Young. 10/10/74 MV4 JG *
[M: this date is in File no. 4 in archive!]

BAABA MAAL

19/5/88 KERSHAW *Bamba, Meyabe, Kasanoura.* Baaba Maal (lv), Assan Ndoye Cisse (rg), Sidiki Kouyate (b), Bada Sek (perc), Masamba Diop (afd), Mbaye Nyass (d), Hilare Charby (k), Alasan Ran Jallow (sx), Seydina Dieme Tonya (sx). 10/5/88 * MR~
10/11/88 KERSHAW *Yela, Polet dieri, Mamadou Moussa, Delouya.* Baaba Maal '& Mansur Sek' (agv), B. Sek, M. Diop, Tonya Lo (bkv), Niane Limar (bkv). 3/11/88 MV4 DG NG

KIRSTY MACCOLL

4/12/89 CAMPBELL *Don't come the cowboy with me Sonny Jim, What do pretty girls do, Don't run away from me now, Still life.* Kirsty MacColl (v), Phil Rambow (ag), Martin Belmont (g), Pete Glenister (g), Bobby Valentino (vi), Gavin Povey (p), Paul Riley (b), Pete Thomas (d). 8/11/89 MV5 PW MPK

MACKA B & ROBOTICS

18/11/90 KERSHAW *Gone home, Get conscious, Cameroon (pam pam), Blackman.* Macka B (v), John McLean (v), Neil Fraser (d,perc), Steel (b), Dave (g), Fish (sy). 18/10/90 MV5 DG NG

ANDY MACKAY

16/7/74 PEEL *The hour before dawn, Ride of the Valkyries, Walking the whippet.* Mackay (sx,cl) & 4 (unknown). 24/6/74 TI JW *

BILLY MACKENZIE

12/9/83 PEEL *Since when do you cook breakfast, This flame, God bless the child.* * 3/9/83 * * *

MACKENZIES

10/2/86 PEEL *New breed, Man with no reason, Give me everything, Gobstopper.* Iain Beveridge (g), Gary Weir (v), Paul Turnbull (d), Peter Gilmour (b); & David Allen (g), Peter Ellen (sx), Scott Brown (perc). 21/1/86 MV5 MW *
30/7/86 PEEL *Milk, Big Jim (there's no pubs in heaven), Mealy mouths, Jingle (slight return).* Four-piece & Ellen, Brown, Ann Quinn (perc). 20/7/86 * DG ME

THE MAD PROFESSOR

4/10/82 PEEL *Beyond the realms of dub, Ghetto pace/Elastic plastic, John Peel dub, In fine style, Funking in the capital dub.* Mad Professor (sy), Garnett Cross (v,p,d), Preacher (b), Jah Shaka (perc), Billy Cross (d). 23/9/82 OS * *

MADNESS

27/8/79 PEEL† *The prince°, Bed and breakfast man, Land of hope and glory, Stepping into line.* Mike Barson (k), Suggs (lv), Mark Bedford (b), Woody (d), Chris Foreman (gv), Lee Thompson (sx,v). 14/8/79 MV4 BS MR
† On Strange Fruit SFRCD007; ° Also on '1 and only' BOJCD025.
21/1/80 READ *Deceives the eye, Don't quote me on that!, My girl, Young and the old.* 3/1/80 MV4 CL JE
1/10/81 SKINNER *Missing you, Sign of the times, Tiptoes.* Chas Smash (tp,perc,v) first credited on this one. 27/9/81 MV4 DG ME
26/7/82 JENSEN *Rise and fall, Tomorrow's just another day,*

Calling cards, Are you coming with me?
24/6/82 MV4 JS MR&MA

EDDIE MAELOV AND SUNSHINE PATTESON

6/7/81 SKINNER *Times are hard, Man for sale, The boy, All I see is you.* Eddie Maelov (v), Sunshine Patteson (kv), Bob Barnett (g), Dave Ravelle (b), Nick Dodd (d). 5/6/81 LHI DG AP

MAGAZINE

20/2/78 PEEL *Touch and go, The light pours out of me, Real life, My mind ain't so open.* Howard Devoto (lv, g-3 only), Martin Jackson (d), Barry Adamson (b), John McGeoch (g), Dave Formula (k). 14/2/78 MV4 MB MR
31/7/78 PEEL *Give me everything, Burst, Big dummy, Boredom.* 24/7/78 MV4 TW DD
Next, rec'd In Concert 22/12/78 PS, TX 16/12/78.
14/5/79 PEEL *T.V. baby, Thank you for letting me be myself again, Permafrost.* Jackson out. 8/5/79 MV4 TW MR
14/1/80 PEEL *A song from under the floorboards, 20 years ago, Look what fear has done to my body, Model worker.* & John Doyle (d). 7/1/80 MV4 TW DD

MAGIC CARPET

22/6/72 DRUMMOND *Father time, Peace song, The phoenix, Thanks be.* Alisha (g,dul), Clem Afford (sit), Keshaw Sathe (tab), James Moyes (g). 7/6/72 MV4 MB MH&MF

MAGMA

21/3/74 PEEL *Kohntarkosz, Theusz Hamtaahk.* Christian Vander (d), Jannick Top (b), Klaus Blasquiz (v), Michel Graillier (p), Gerrard Bikialo (p), Claude Almos (lg). 14/3/74 LHI BA&DD

MAGNA CARTA

28/5/69 NIGHT RIDE *Sea and sand, Spinning wheels of time, Emily, Shades of grey, You don't know what love is, I am no more, Times of change, Old John Parker, Going back, Daughter daughter.* Chris Simpson (gv), Lyell Tranter (g), Glen Stuart (real name Alastair Urquhart) (v). 15/5/69 S2 PR *
Trial broadcast live on Country Meets Folk, PH 10/5/69, prod. IG. Then appeared often on this show and Folk on 1.
11/6/69 NIGHT RIDE *Elizabethan, Midwinter, Romeo Jack, I don't want to know, If I were free.* 19/5/69 PCI PR AH
16/4/70 HENRY *Emily, Sea and sand, Romeo Jack, Seven o'clock hymn (& Old John Parker, 14/5/70).* 26/3/70 MV5 MB * [M]
3/8/70 SYMONDS *Airport song, The spinning wheels of time, Elizabethan (& Ring of stones, Harris 2/11/70).* 2/7/70 AO2 BA PK&NG
10/9/70 HENRY *Airport song, Ring of stones, Daughter daughter, Elizabethan.* 3/9/70 AO2 MB MH&MF
14/1/71 HENRY *Bridge at Knaresborough town, Down along up, Beyond the Isle of Skye, Seven o'clock hymn.* Davey Johnson (g) r. Tranter. 13/1/71 MV4 MB MH&MF [M]
5/8/71 HENRY *Old John Parker, Lords of high degree, Sponge, Seven o'clock hymn.* 19/7/71 MV5 MB MH&MF
29/6/72 DRUMMOND *Faulkland green, Time for the leaving, I am no more (& Way farin', 10/8/72).* Stan Gordon (g) r. Johnson. 14/5/72 TI MB MH&MF
30/3/73 SEQUENCE *Emily thru' the window pane, Song of evening, Father John.* [M] 27/2/73 TI JM *

MAGNUM

27/5/83 FRI. ROCK *The prize, Breakdown, Vicious companions, Road to paradise.* Tony Clarkin (g), Mark Stanway (k), Wally Lowe (b), Bob Cately (v), Kex Gorin (d), Robin George (g). 13/5/83 * TW DD

MAHLATHINI AND THE MAHOTELLA QUEENS

16/6/88 KERSHAW *Stokfel jive no.1, Melodi yalla, Lilizela Mlilizeli, Thokozile.* Simon Mahlathini Nkabinbe (v), Hilda, Mildred & Nobesuthu (v), West Nkosi (sx,wh), Mzwandile David (acc), Sipho Madendo & Marks Mankwane (g), Joseph Makwela (b), Philemon Hamole (d). 9/6/88 MV4 DG MC

MALAGASY ALL-STARS
(MUSICIANS FROM MADAGASCAR)

4/12/86 KERSHAW *Mifohaza, Kondray Tsikitsiky, Batrelaka, Marovoay, Manadala, Madiroualo.* Rakoto Frah (sodina), Justin Rakotomavo (acc,fl), Colbert (valiha,g), Dama Mahaleo (kabosy), Zeze (valiha), Pana (perc). 30/11/86 * AS TdB

MALARIA

3/8/81 PEEL *I will be your only one, Geh duschen, Nimm mich schnell in deine arme, How do you like my new dog?* Gudrun Gut (d,g,bkv), Bettina Köster (sx,v), Christine Hahn (b,d), Manon Duursma (g), Susanne Kuhnke (sy,bkv). 25/7/81 MV4 DG MR
29/3/83 JENSEN *The original meeting, Jealousy, You you, Thrash me.* 10/3/83 MV4 JS HPK

MALICORNE

20/6/74 PEEL *La fille soldat, Pierre de Grenoble, Les livres, Dame Lombarde, Martin.* Gabrielle Yacoub, Marie Yacoub, Hughes de Courson, Laurent Ver Cambre. 13/6/74 LHI * BAI
7/8/75 PEEL *J'ai vu le loup le renard et la belette, La peronelle, Le mariage Anglais.* 31/7/75 MV4 * BAI

MAMA'S BOYS

19/2/82 FRI. ROCK *Straight forward, The heat of the night, Runaway dreams, Belfast city blues.* Pat McManus (gv), John McManus (b), Tommy McManus (d), Philip Begley (o-4 only). Rec. date unknown Lombard Studios, Dublin TW DD & Philip Begley

MAMMOTH

7/4/89 FRI. ROCK *Can't take the hurt, Political animal, Long time coming, Piggin' out.* John McCoy (g), Mack Raker (g), Colin Pincott (g), Vini Reed (d), Nicky Moore (v). 31/3/89 * TW *

BATTI MAMZELLE

30/5/74 PEEL *Lament, San Juan, Get out of my way, I see the light.* Miguel Baradas (pn), Russel Valdez (pn), Ralph Richardson (pn), Winston Delandro (g), Peter Earl Duprey (b), Richard Bailey (d), Frank Ince (bgo,perc), James Chambers (v). 16/5/74 LHI TW BAI

MAN

13/1/72 DRUMMOND *Angel easy, Many are called but few get up/Dance of the mushrooms.* Clive John (gv), Mick Jones (gv), Martin Ace (b), Terry Williams (d), Deke Leonard (gv). 3/1/72 MV5 MB MH&MF
Jones and John's previous band, The Bystanders, recorded many sessions in the 60s, after passing a trial broadcast for Sat. Club, 30/7/66. Changed name 12/68.
12/9/72 PEEL *Come on, Life on the road.* Jones, John, Williams, Will Youatt (bv), Phil Ryan (k). 29/8/72 MV4 PR *
9/3/73 SEQUENCE *It ain't their fight, Life on the road, The Brazilian cucumber meets the Deke's new nose.* 6/2/73 TI PD *
2/10/73 PEEL *A night in Dad's bag (1st TX ROCK ON, 29/9), Ain't their fight.* Alan Lewis (g) r. John. 18/9/73 LHI TW BC
1/4/74 HARRIS *Romain, God gave us turtles, Blowing away.* Jones, Leonard (returns), Williams, Ken Whaley (b), Malcolm Morley (k). 27/2/74 LHI PR *
14/11/74 PEEL *Many are called but few get up, A hard way to die, Day and night.* Morley out. 31/10/74 MV4 TW BAI

THE MAN FROM DELMONTE

24/8/88 L. KERSHAW *Patient, Australia fair, Big noise, Like a millionaire.* Howard Goody (d), Sheila Seal (b,bkv), Martin Vincent (gk,bkv), Mike West (ag,lv). 7/8/88 MV4 MR~

MANDRAKE PADDLE STEAMER

6/4/69 TOP GEAR *The ivory castle of Solitaire Huske, Cooger and dark, Senila lament, Janus suite.* John Web, Peter Frohlich, Michael Hutton, David Moses, Martin Woodward. 25/3/69 PH BA AH
File suggests, oddly, that a 100 per cent different

line-up under this name had debuted on R1 CLUB 31/1/69.

KABA MANE
6/5/90 KERSHAW *Kunga kungake, Tchossa massante, Lantendam, Deardja.* Kaba Mane (gv), Juonito Lima Pires (g), Joao Emmanuel Motta (g), Eddy Edoute (b), Christian Siba (d), David Lewis (tp), Marino Zapdellini (sx), Pierre Chabrele (tb), Ansoumane Mane (bkv). 27/3/90 MV3 DG *

MANFRED MANN
7/1/68 TOP GEAR *Every day another hair turns grey, Mighty Quinn, Handbags and gladrags, Sleepy hollow, Cubist town.* Manfred Mann (k), Tom McGuiness (g), Mike Hugg (d), Mike D'Abo (v), Klaus Voormann (b). 3/1/68 MV4 BA DT

Dozens of Light Programme sessions after previous, original line-up passed audition in 9/63.

22/12/68 TOP GEAR *Abraham Martin and John, Fox on the run, Clair, So long (& Orange peel, 19/1/69).* 25/11/68 PCI BA PR

24/1/70 TOP GEAR *Kone kuf, Time, Sometimes.* Manfred Mann's Chapter Three: Mann, Hugg, & Steve York (b), Bernie Living (sx), Craig Collinge (d), Sonny Corbett (tp), Derek Coxhill (bars), Clive Stevens (ts), Carl Griffiths (ts). 19/1/70 PH JW *

MANFRED MANN'S EARTH BAND
4/7/71 DLT *Mighty Quinn, Big Betty, Living without you.* Mann & Mick Rogers (lg), Chris Slade (d), Colin Pattenden (b); & Lisa Strike, Barry St. John. 23/6/71 MV5 c.PWI *

Rec'd In Concert 7/10/71 PS, TX 19/10/71.

1/12/71 PEEL *Happy being me, Captain Bobby Stout, One way glass.* 29/11/71 PH JW DG

28/1/72 PEEL *Meat, Captain Bobby Stout, Ashes in the wind (& Mighty Quinn, 10/3/72).* 10/1/72 TI PD ARV

29/9/72 PEEL *Messin', Dealer, Glorified magnified.* 5/9/72 TI JM *

17/4/73 PEEL *Father of day, Bubblegum and Kipling, Get your socks off.* 3/4/73 LHI TW *

4/5/73 SEQUENCE *Get a lot, Get your socks off, Cloudy eyes, Father of day.* [M: daytime]. 10/4/73 TI JM NG

THE MANGROVE STEEL BAND
1/4/87 PEEL *I shot the sherrif, Sonata in C, Josephine, Ah want it back.* Austin Gachette (d), Victor Alleyene (cga), Laramie Green, Christopher Hunter, Annalyn Lazardi, Robert Thompson, Emery Russell, Franky Martin, Tony Andrews, Paul Joseph, Harrison Thomas, Jason Holmes, Justin Russell, Matthew Philip, Julian Green, Wayne Andain (all pn), Tony Francis (perc), Raymond Joseph (md). 22/3/87 * DG ME&JB

MANIC STREET PREACHERS
4/2/91 GOODIER *Motown junk, Do you love us, Generation terrorists, Methadone pretty.* Sean Moore (d), James Bradfield (g), Nicky Wire (b), Richie James (Edwards) (v). 19/1/91 MV5 MC~

14/2/92 FRI. ROCK *Do you love us, Under my wheels, Slash and burn, Natwest Barclays Midland Lloyds.* Wire only appears on 2nd session sheet. 24/1/92 MV5 TW DD

MANKIND
22/5/70 BLACK *The voice, Flood tide, Mr Loneliness, The world.* Robin Lipsey (o,clav), Stuart Henderson (b), Michael Ashcroft (lg), Adrian Ashcroft (d). 15/4/70 AO2 JM *

7/8/70 BLACK *Allow me to go, Far away is a party, You're tired of living in peace.* 17/6/70 AO2 JM *

MANTAS
6/1/89 FRI. ROCK *Deceiver, Let it rock, Winds of change, Tonight.* J. Dunn (gk), Mark Savage (d), Keith Nichol (k), Al Barnes (g), Pete Harrison (v). 11/11/88 MV4 MC~

MACHANIC MANYERUKE
10/12/89 KERSHAW *Maiwa muponso wangu, Zaxewu, Regai ndinamate, Chirema patember, Wazwarirwepe Jesu.* Machanic Manyeruke (gv). 23/11/89 MV5 DG NG

PHIL MANZANERA AND 801
22/11/77 PEEL *Law and order, Falling feeling, Remote control, Out of the Blue.* Phil Manzanera (gv), Simon Ainley (gv), Bill MacCormick (bv), Dave Skinner (kv), Paul Thompson (d). 14/11/77 MV4 TW DD

THOMAS MAPFUMO
12/8/90 KERSHAW *Mutandarika, Muchadura, Chitima Nditakure.* Thomas Mapfumo (v), Ephrain Karimaura (g), Washington Kavhayi (b), Sabastian Misata (d), Chartwell Dutiro (sx,mbi), Charles Makokwe (sy), Taurayi Nayanzira (mbi), Everson Chibami (tp), Lancelot Mapfumo (cga), Kudzayi Chiramusen & Tendai Ruzvidzo (bkv). 21/6/90 MV5 DG NG

MIKE MARAN
11/2/72 PEEL *Please come in we know you're out there, Tiger's looking back, The life and death of Arthur Perkins, Fair warning (& Red school uniform, 7/4/72).* Mike Maran (agv). 18/1/72 TI JM *

Debuted on Country Meets Folk 7/2/71 PH [M: Folk shows].

18/8/72 PEEL *Please keep the rain away, Lady in black, Fool's castle, Magic moon song (& Hell bent, 29/9/72).* 18/7/72 TI JM *

30/11/72 PEEL *It all goes to show, Tiger's looking back, Daughter of time, Monday boy.* 6/11/72 LHI BA *

15/12/72 SEQUENCE *It all goes to show, Please come in we know you're out there, Monday boy, The life and death of Arthur Perkins, Sometime child.* 18/11/72 LHI JM NG

16/8/73 PEEL *Wouldn't it be nice, Crazy days, Brave new world, Unchained, Ducks and snowmen.* 23/7/73 LHI BA *

28/9/73 SEQUENCE *Goodbye horseshoes, Dobidubidoo, The trees they did grow high, Wouldn't it be nice.* 30/8/73 LHI JM NG

28/2/74 PEEL *Crovie, Pax vobiscum, Crazy days, Goodbye horseshoes and black cats (& Eyes like Steve McQueen, 2/5/74).* 21/2/74 LHI JW *

THE MARCH VIOLETS
2/8/82 PEEL *Radiant boys, Steam, 1-2-I love you, Grooving in green.* Laurence Elliott (b), Tom Ashton (g), Simon Denbigh (v), Rosie Garland (v), Kevin Lycett (perc). 10/7/82 MV4 DG MC

24/3/83 PEEL *Strange head†, Slow drip lizard, The undertow†, Crowbaby.* Denbigh, Ashton, Garland, Hugh (b), Steve Atkinson (k), Chris Shoel (sx), & the Violettes: Sara James & Michaela Sanderson (bkv). 19/3/83 MV4 DG *

† On LP 'Rebirth' Natural History VRB25.

28/2/84 JENSEN *Walk into the sun, Deep, Kill the delight, Big soul kiss.* Denbigh, Ashton, Elliot (b,dm), Jean Murray (v), Eric Bellis (p). 12/2/84 MV5 DG ME

19/6/84 PEEL *Lights go out, Love hit, Electric shades, Don't take it lightly.* Bellis out. 12/6/84 MV5 MRD TdB

13/1/86 LONG *Close to the heart, South country, High times, Avalanche of love.* Ashton, Elliott, Cleo (v), and Andy Tolson (d). 15/12/85 HP BYA *

MARDEN HILL
24/2/88 MAYO *Satellite, The execution of emperor Maximillian, Oh Constance, Citadel.* Guy Evans (d,perc), Ian Smith (b), Peter Moss (gv), Charlie Philips (kv), Matt Lipsey (fl,v), Christa Jones (bkv), James McMillans (tp,flh). 13/12/87 MV4 HP TdB

MARILLION
26/2/82 FRI. ROCK *Forgotten sons, Three boats down from the candy, The web.* Fish (v), Diz Minnitt (b), Steve Rothery (g), Mark Kelly (k), Mick Pointer (d). 29/1/82 * TW DD

THE MARINE GIRLS
16/2/82 PEEL *Don't come back, Love to know, Place in the sun, He got the girl, Fever.* Tracey Thorn (gv), Jane Fox (b), Alice Fox (v,perc). 1/2/82 * DG DD

19/4/83 PEEL *Love you more, Lazy ways, Seascape, That day.* & Tim Hall (sx,cl). 16/4/83 MV4 DG TdB

MARK ALMOND
30/11/70 HARRIS *Tramp and the young girl, The city, Two together, All you can do is try (& The ghetto, Once I loved a girl, 11/1/71).* Jon Mark (ag), Johnnie Almond (fl,sx), Tommy Eyre (o,p), Roger Sutton (b). 20/11/70 MV5 JM *

26/7/71 HARRIS *Sparkey, Once I loved a girl, The Little prince, The organ grinder, The body shop (& The city, 30/8/71).* 13/7/71 TI JM JWH

21/7/72 PEEL *The 11-4, Morning always comes too soon, The little prince.* 27/6/72 TI JM *

BOB MARLEY AND THE WAILERS
15/5/73 PEEL *Slave driver, Rasta man, Concrete jungle.* Bob Marley (ag,v), Bunny Livingstone (cga,bgo,v), Peter Mackintosh (gv), Aston Barrett (b), Carlton Barrett (d), Earl Lindo (k). 1/5/73 LHI JW BC&MR

Rec'd In Concert 24/5/73 PS, TX 23/6/73.

25/12/73 PEEL *Kinky reggae, Can't blame the youth, Get up stand up.* Livingstone out. 26/11/73 TI JW&PD ARV

MAROON TOWN
15/10/87 LONG *How long?, Stand up and listen, Fire, Man in the street.* Jan Hewison (d), Rajan Datar (b), Devan German (rg), Glynis German (kv), Goran Selby (lg), Caroline McCookweir (al,v), Mike Firn (ts), Kay Charlton (tp,v), Pablo (perc). 4/10/87 MV4 HP TdB&SC

BERNIE MARSDEN
28/8/81 FRI. ROCK *Look at me now, Who's fooling who, Byblos shack, Shakey ground.* Bernie Marsden (gv), Don Airey (k), Neil Murray (b), Simon Phillips (d), David Coverdale (v). 7/8/81 * TW *

MARTIAN DANCE
18/9/80 PEEL *Stand alone, Two sides one story, The situation, Transformed.* Jerry Lamont (lv), Duncan Greig (d), Daniel Grahame (b), Kevin Addison (g). 8/9/80 MV4 TW DD

21/4/81 PEEL *Roses to Reno, Party games, Claudine's.* 6/4/81 LHI TW DD

JOHN MARTYN
10/7/68 NIGHT RIDE *Come along and sing of summer, Fairytale lullaby, The gardeners, Memphis blues, The river.* John Martyn (agv). 13/6/68 S2 DK *

Next appearance was live on Country Meets Folk, 9/11/68 PH.

11/12/68 NIGHT RIDE *Different from the back, Mr. Jelly roll baker blues, Dusty, Hello train, Flying on home, Seven black roses.* & Harold McNair (fl). 9/12/68 PCI JM *

Next, three live appearances on Country Meets Folk at PH: 28/12/68; 15/3/69; 7/6/69.

4/6/69 MY KIND OF FOLK *Mr. Jelly roll baker blues, Fairytale lullaby.* 29/5/69 S2 FL *

4/4/70 TOP GEAR *Traffic light lady, Give us a ring, Road to ruin, Tomorrow time (& Seven black roses, 18/7/70).* & Beverley Martin (v). 23/3/70 * * * TW

Also sang 'Back to stay' as guest on Bridget St John's R1 Folk Show, 20/9/70

20/10/71 PEEL *May you never, Bless the weather, Inside of him, Singing in the rain.* 20/9/71 PH JW *

22/11/71 HARRIS *Would you believe me, Sugar cube, Road to ruin, A man walks inside (& May you never, 27/12/71).* 2/11/71 TI JM NG

23/10/72 HARRIS *Go down easy, Glory of love, Rather be the devil, May you never.* 4/10/72 LHI JG *

Next, on R2's MUSIC TO MIDNIGHT, TX 17/1/73.

4/6/73 HARRIS *Devil got my woman, Inside.* 23/5/73 LHI PR *

15/10/73 HARRIS *May you never, Make no mistake, Eibhli Gheal Chiuinn ni Chearbhaill, Fine lines.* & I (unknown). 10/10/73 LHI JG *

13/1/75 PEEL *One day (without you), Discover the lover, My baby girl, The message, Spencer the rover.* 7/1/75 MV4 TW MR

4/2/77 PEEL *May you never, Certain surprise/Couldn't love you more, Over the hill, One day without you.* 18/1/77 MV4 JG MR

16/1/78 PEEL *Small hours, Big muff.*
9/1/78 MV4 TW DD&M[M]

BRETT MARVIN AND THE THUNDERBOLTS

30/5/70 TOP GEAR *Too many hotdogs, So tired, Crazy with the blues (& Going back, 19/9/70).* John Lewis (pv), Graham Hine (g), Jim Pitts (mnd), John Randall (wsh), Peter Gibson (tb), Keith Trussell ('zob stick').
18/5/70 PH JW TW

    Rec'd Peel Sunday Concert 23/7/70 PS, TX 26/7/70.

3/10/70 RAVEN'S R&B *Drop down mama, County jail, When I woke up, Thoughts on you.* 5/8/70 MV4 JG JY

20/2/71 RAVEN'S R&B *Milkcow blues, Come in my kitchen, Little red caboose, Take your money and go down the road, I'm ready.* 10/2/71 MV4 MB *

22/3/71 R1 CLUB *Little red caboose, Take your money and go down the road (23/3), I'm ready (24/3), Stuck at home (25/3).* 2/3/71 PH * *

15/4/71 HENRY *Little red caboose, The blues ain't nothing but, Phonograph, Lost lover blues.*
7/4/71 MV4 MB MH&MF

1/12/73 ROCK ON *Bay roller, Blow me down, Make it to the woods, On the hook.* Gwynn 'Taffy' Davies, Mick Hodgkinson r. Lewis, Pitts. 27/9/73 LH1 PR BAI

MASASU

11/6/90 PEEL *Mbokoshi ya lufu, Litande, Chimbayambaya.* Evans Bwalya (d,bkv), Abuild Madichi (b), John Melemena (lg,v), Oswald Mwelwa (rg), Henry Lwanga (bkv), P.K. Chishala (rg,v). 22/5/90 MV3 MR~

HUGH MASEKELA

5/11/84 LONG *Pula ea na (It's raining), Motlalepula (Rainmaker), Serafina, Johannesburg.* Hugh (flh), Barney (sx), Johnny (gv), Banjo (rg), Obri (b), Buli (d), Francis (perc), Tsepo (perc,v), Ruby, Felicia & Sonti (bkv).
24/10/84 MV5 BYA MPK

MASON, CAPALDI, WOOD AND FROG

16/2/69 SYMONDS ON SUNDAY *World in changes, Waiting on you, Born under a bad sign, Feeling alright.* Dave Mason (gv), Jim Capaldi (dv), Chris Wood (sx,fl), Wynder K. Frog (real name, Mick Weaver) (k). 10/2/69 AO2 JW TW

2/3/69 TOP GEAR *Waiting on you, Crying to be heard, World in changes, Leaving blues.* 25/2/69 PH BA AH

DAVE MASON

14/1/74 HARRIS *Just a song, Silent partners, Everywoman, Baby please (& World in changes, 23/5/74).* *
4/1/74 Recorded specially at CBS Studio 3, London * *

MASS

12/1/91 PEEL *Sado seduction, Someone else, Medusa, Unnamed.* Steve Beatty (d), Daz Fralikc (b,bkv), Nick Ryall (g), E (v). 16/1/90 MV3 DG ME&SA

DOROTHY MASUKA

30/6/91 KERSHAW *Pata pata, Manyere, Magumede, Ngotsotsi.* Dorothy Masuka (lv), Mary Hlabi (bkv), James Manyungwa (d), Ashton Mutauiri (b), Jonah Sithole (g), Moses Nyaruka (g). 13/6/91 MV5 DG NG

MATCHING MOLE

25/1/72 PEEL *Immediate kitten, Brandy* [re-named 'Part of the dance']. Robert Wyatt (d), Bill MacCormick (b), Phil Miller (g), Dave Sinclair (o), Dave McRae (elp,p). 17/1/72 PH JW BC

24/3/72 PEEL *No 'alf measures, Lything and gracing.* Sinclair out. 6/3/72 T1 JM JW

9/5/72 PEEL *Marchides/Instant pussy (& Smoke signal, 6/6/72)* [complete 19' 35" medley of all 3 items TX only on 6/6/72]. 17/4/72 T1 JW *

6/7/72 DRUMMOND *Gloria Gloom/[Nan True's Hole]/Brandy for Benj.* 21/6/72 MV4 MB MH&MF

    Rec'd In Concert 27/7/72 PS, TX 9/9/72.

MATTHEWS' SOUTHERN COMFORT

14/2/70 TOP GEAR *My front pages, Blood red roses, Uncle Joe, Reagan's rag, What we say.* Ian Matthews (lv), Peter Watkins (b), Gordon Huntley (ps), Carl Barnwell

(g,bj,v), Roger Swallows (d), Mark Griffiths (lg).
2/2/70 PH JW BC

13/4/70 FERRIS *Ballad of Obray Ramsey, Johnson, Something in the way she moves (& Touch her if you can, 4/5/70).* 7/4/70 PH BA NG

9/5/70 EDMONDS *Ballad of Obray Ramsey, Darcy Farrow, Something, I wanna be your mama again.*
4/5/70 CM JW (or JBU) *

11/6/70 HENRY *Bitter green, Ballad of Obray Ramsey, I wanna be your mama again, Woodstock.* 2/6/70 MV5 MB MH&MF

    Rec'd Peel Sunday Concert 18/6/70 PS, TX 26/6/70.

12/7/70 FOLK ON 1 *Woodstock, I wanna be your mama again, Old Rudd, Tale of the trial, D'Arcy Farrow, Ballad of Obray Ramsey, Touch her if you can, Blood red roses. & Tom Paley* (bj). 4/6/70 MV5 FL *

23/8/70 R2 COUNTRY MEETS FOLK *Old Rudd, Scion, I wanna be your mama again, Please be my friend.* Andy Leigh, Ray Duffy r. Watkins, Swallow [Rec. date uncertain: PasB says 22/8 only; for pre-recording of whole live show; could be partial repeat of 4/6 date]. MV5 FL *

22/10/70 HENRY *Brand new Tennessee waltz, Belle, Tell me why, Touch her if you can.* 15/10/70 AO2 MB *

28/11/70 TOP GEAR *I believe in you, Sylvie, And when she smiles, And me.* 17/11/70 MV4 JW BC

5/12/70 FOLK ON 1 *Old Rudd, Yankee lady, Touch her if you can, Road to Ronderlin, Blood red roses, Tale of the trial, Tell me why, And when she smiles, And me.* 24/11/70 MV5 FL * [See 'Southern Comfort' below]

IAN MATTHEWS

26/4/71 HARRIS *It takes a lot to laugh it takes a train to cry, Not much at all, Hearts, Baby Ruth.* Solo.
13/4/71 T1 JM *

5/6/71 TOP GEAR *Home, There's a Woody Guthrie song, Through my eyes, Hearts, Never ending.*
17/5/71 PH JW BC [M: daytime '78]

MATUMBI

3/5/78 PEEL *Music in the air, Rock, Chatty-chatty.* Euton Jones (perc), Glaister Fagan (tamb, bkv), Bunny Donaldson (d), Jah Blake (b), Dennis Bovell (g,bkv), Webster Johnson (k), Lannie Fagan (lv).
28/2/78 MV4 MB MR

13/11/78 PEEL *Empire road, Bluebeat and ska, Money, Hook deh.* Bagga Love (v), More Ears (v), Blackbeard (gv), Taz (k,v), Jah Blake (b), Jah Bunny (d), Fergus (perc), Buttons and Zeb (horns). 17/10/78 MV4 MB MR

HARVEY MATUSOW'S JEWS HARP BAND

18/12/68 NIGHT RIDE *Talk and instrumental, 18 nuns, Walking toenail blues, Clootchunt, War between fats and thins.* * 18/12/68 * JM *

MAXIMUM JOY

17/9/81 PEEL *Caveman fly, Slip into the fit, Open your heart.* Dan Catsis (b,sx,p), Tony Wrafter (sx,tp), John Waddington (g), Janine Rainforth (v,vi), Dan Shields (d), Sandy Smith (perc,v). 12/9/81 MV4 DG RA

8/3/82 PEEL *In the air, All wrapped up, Dancing on my boomerang.* Rainforth, Wrafter, Waddington, Shields, Charlie Llewellin (d), Kevin Evans (b). 22/2/82 * TW DD

27/4/82 JENSEN *Searching for a feeling, In the air, Up yer egos, Silent street.* Shields out. 15/4/82 MV5 JS MR

JOHN MAYALL'S BLUESBREAKERS

5/11/67 TOP GEAR *The last time, Suspicious, Worried love, Supermarket day, Snowy word (& Jenny, 11/2/68).* John Mayall (v,hca), Mick Taylor (lg), John McVie (b), Keef Hartley (d), Rip Kent, Chris Mercer (sx).
30/10/67 PCI BA *

    Original band passed audition 7/64. 1st b'cast session Sat. Club 30/10/65; several BBC dates followed.

    Despite contract, line-up more likely to have had Paul Williams (b) not McVie, and Hunt out; and possibly Henry Lowther (tp) and Dick Heckstall-Smith (sx). Same, save Andy Fraser (b) on date below. This info courtesy of Pete Frame's Mayall family tree.

31/3/68 TOP GEAR *Picture on the wall, Knockers step forward, The last time, Rock me baby.* & 1 (unknown). 26/3/68 PCI BA * [M]

BIG MAYBELLE AND THE SENATE

1/10/67 TOP GEAR *Mellow yellow, Top gear, Show me, Mean to me, Skate, Baby please don't go, Sweet thing, Every day I get the blues.* Big Maybelle (v) & The Senate (2, 3, 5, 7, The Senate only). 21/9/67 PCI BA DT

MZWAKHE MBULI

20/10/91 KERSHAW *Uyeyeni, Emandulo, Pitoli.* Mzwakhe Mbuli (lv,cga), Matome Rachbane (sx,fl,v), Steve Zulu (sy,v), Floyd Manana (g), Kenneth Nkonki (b), Bigboy Ditle (d). 29/8/91 MV5 DG NG&AA

MC 900 FOOT JESUS & DJ ZERO

1/3/90 PEEL *Truth is out of style, Slippin', Real black angel.* M.C. 900 Foot Jesus (v,ma), D.J. Zero (tt, sc).
18/2/90 MV3 DG JB

MCCARTHY

12/11/86 PEEL *A child soon in chains, Frans Hals, An M.P. speaks, Anti-nature.* Gary Baker (d), John Williamson (b), Tim Gane (g), Malcolm Eden (gv).
7/10/86 * DG ME&SC

8/1/87 LONG *The wicked palace revolution, The vision of Peregrine Worsthorne, The well of loneliness, Monetaries.* 31/5/87 MV4 PW TdB&JB

28/10/87 PEEL *Charles Windsor, The funeral, Should the Bible be banned?, This Nelson Rockefeller.*
20/10/87 * DG MR&TD

1/11/88 PEEL *The myth of the North/South divide, I'm not a patriot but..., Keep an open mind or else, The lion will lie down with the lamb.* Gary Brewer credited for (d). 23/10/88 HP MA~FK

IAN MCCULLOCH

4/12/89 PEEL *Faith and healing, The flickering wall, Damnation, Candleland.* Ian McCulloch (gv), Steve Humphreys (d,prg), Edgar Summertime (b), John McCevoy (g), Mike Mooney (g,k). 28/9/89 * DG NG

COUNTRY JOE MCDONALD

4/7/70 TOP GEAR *Hold on it's coming, Balancing on the edge of time, It's so nice to have love, Maria, Tell me where you're bound.* Country Joe McDonald (gv).
29/6/70 PH JW *

2/6/72 PEEL *Hold on it's coming, Colleen Ann, Fantasy (& Memories, 28/7/72).* 8/5/72 PH JM JWH

    Rec'd In Concert 4/5/72 PS, TX 13/5/72. Came back in 1975, rec'd 2nd In Concert with Barry Melton 28/1/75 PS, TX 1/3/75.

11/7/77 PEEL *Sweet Lorraine, The man from Atharbaska, Get it together, La-di-dar, Tricky Dicky, Interlude with son and heir, Save the whales.* Solo. 29/6/77 MV4 MB MR

SHELAGH MCDONALD

16/12/71 DRUMMOND *Lonely king, For you, Odyssey (& Spin, 27/1/72).* * 1/12/71 * MB MH&MF

MISSISSIPPI FRED MCDOWALL

5/3/69 NIGHT RIDE *Louise, Burying ground blues, Glory hallelujah, Jesus on the main line, Way out on the Frisco line, Keep your lamps trimmed and burning, Good morning little schoolgirl.* * 26/2/69 AO1 JM *

WES MCGHEE

13/12/76 PEEL *Midnight moon, Rosemary, Long nights and banjo music.* * 18/11/76 MV4 * *

MCGUINESS FLINT

29/11/70 DLT *Who you got to love, When I'm dead and gone, Mister mister, (& Bodang buck, not broadcast).* Tom McGuiness (g), Hughie Flint (d), Benny Gallagher (g,b,p,al,hca), Graham Lyle (g,mnd,b), Dennis Coulson (acc,pv). 9/11/70 AO2 c.PW1 *

14/12/70 HARRIS *Bodang buck, Heritage, Who you got to love, I'm letting you know, Dream darling dream* [M: daytime 71]. 4/12/70 MV5 JM JWH

22/8/72 PEEL *Let me die in my footsteps, Lo and behold, Get your socks off.* Disbanded 12/71, re-formed as

'Coulson, Dean, McGuiness & Flint': Dixie Dean (b) r. Gallagher & Lyle. 1/8/72 MV4 * BC [M: daytime 73]

30/9/74 HARRIS *Siren Sadie, Ride that horse (I don't like you), Country music.* Jim Evans (g), Lou Stonebridge (k) r. Coulson. 14/8/74 LHI JG *

JOHN MCLAUGHLIN AND SHAKTI

13/5/77 PEEL *Kriti, Two sisters, La danse du bonheur.* John McLaughlin (g), L. Shankar (vi), Zakir Hussain (tab), T. H. Vinayakram (gha), Nancy and Poona (dro). 9/5/77 MV4 TW BAI

RALPH MCTELL

28/2/70 TOP GEAR *Clown, Michael in the garden, Daddy's here, Eight frames a second.* Ralp McTell (gv). 9/2/70 * * *

Debuted live at PH on Country Meets Folk 24/8/68 [M: Folk shows; hundreds of sessions, and still counting].

19/12/70 TOP GEAR *Spiral staircase, The ferryman, Too tight rag, Chalk dust.* 9/11/70 PH * BC

8/3/71 HARRIS *Claudia, The ferryman, Lay your money down (& You well meaning brought me here, 5/4/71).* 23/2/71 MV5 JM JWH

20/9/71 HARRIS *In some way I loved you, Bird man, First and last man (& Claudia, Lay your money down, 11/10/71).* 13/9/71 T1 JM NG&ARV

9/12/71 DRUMMOND *Nettle wine, Bird man, Cocaine, Pick up the gun.* 1/12/71 MV4 MB MH&MF

15/12/71 PEEL *Genesis i. 20, The ferryman, Nettle wine, Bird man (& In some way I loved you, 8/2/72).* 6/12/71 PH * *

12/5/72 PEEL *When I was a cowboy, Small voice calling, A woman with one leg, Honey baby now.* 24/4/72 PH JM JWH

22/5/72 HARRIS *Truckin' little baby, When I was a cowboy, Viola Lee blues, Small voices calling (& First song, 3/7/72).* &1 jug player (unknown). 3/5/72 AO2 JG *

24/10/72 PEEL *When I was a cowboy, Zimmerman blues, Barges, First song.* 3/10/72 LHI * *

3/11/72 SEQUENCE *When I was a cowboy, Tea-pot blues, Gypsy, First song.* & Maddy Prior (v). 26/9/72 T1 JM JWH&JE

9/4/73 HARRIS *When I was a cowboy, Zig zag line, Lunar lullaby, First song.* Solo. 4/4/73 LHI PR *

19/2/74 PEEL *When Maddy dances, Secret mystery, Let me down easy.* & Danny Thompson (b). 5/2/74 LHI * *

6/3/75 PEEL *Interest on the loan, El progresso, Would I lie to you, Country boys.* & 4 (unknown). 27/2/75 MV4 * *

6/12/76 PEEL *1913 massacre, Drybone rag, Rizak-laru, Naomi, Vigilante man, From Clare to here, Summer lightning.* 2/12/76 MV4 TW *

DAVID MCWILLIAMS

27/11/68 NIGHT RIDE *Redundancy blues, Lady Helen of the laughing eyes, Echo of my heart, Twilight, In the early hours of the morning.* David McWilliams (agv). 26/11/68 S2 PC *

First session was for Light Programme's Roundabout 7/67 [M].

5/2/73 HARRIS *The gypsy, Lord o'folly, She was a lady, The stranger.* & (g), (b) unknown. 24/1/73 LHI PR *

15/6/73 SEQUENCE *Nark, Leave the bottles on the floor, Pharisee, Redundancy blues.* Solo. 24/5/73 LHI JM NG

8/7/74 HARRIS *Twenty golden years, Singer in the band, You've only been a stranger.* & 3 (unknown). 8/5/74 PR *

MDC

2/11/87 PEEL *Chock full of it, Multi-death-dead cops, Millions of damn Christians/Bye bye Ronnie, South Africa is free.* Dave Dictor (v), Gordon Fraser (g), Franco (b,v-4), Al Schvitz (d,v-4). 25/10/87 * DG ME&TD

THE MEAT PUPPETS

8/3/92 KERSHAW *Attacked by monsters, Lake of fire, Automatic wood, Leaves, Another moon.* Curt Kirkwood

(g,lv), Chris Kirkwood (bv), Derrick Bostrom (d). 3/3/92 MV4 MR~

MEAT WHIPLASH

28/10/85 PEEL *Loss, Walk away, Eat me to the core, She comes tomorrow.* Edward Connelly (b), Steve McClean (g), Michael Kerr (d), Paul McDermott (v), Elaine Wornock (bkv-4), Leslie McKay (bkv-4), Richard Green (o-4). 15/10/85 MV5 PWL MR

MEDICINE HEAD

10/1/70 TOP GEAR *His guiding hand, Walkin' blues, Be blessed to your heart, Ooee baby (& Goin' home, 9/5/70).* John Fiddler (v,g,d,wb), Peter Hope-Evans (hca,jh,perc). 15/12/69 PH JW TW [M: daytime]

9/7/70 HENRY *Thou shalt not pass, There's always a light, Coast to coast.* 2/7/70 * MB MH&MF

24/10/70 TOP GEAR *But the night is young, Sing with the drum, Hungry eye, To train time (& Once there was a day, 23/1/71).* 13/10/70 * JW *

26/10/70 HARRIS *His guiding hand, Home's Odyssey, Sing with the drum, Once there was a day.* 16/10/70 T1 JM NG

12/6/71 TOP GEAR *Pictures in the sky, You get the rockin' and rollin', Don't you worry, Medicine pony (& But the night is young, 24/7/71).* 24/5/71 * JW BC

17/6/71 HENRY *Pictures in the sky, To train time, Coast to coast, Have no fear (& Expectation blues, 30/8/71 HARRIS).* 9/6/71 * MB MH&MF

11/10/71 HARRIS *All the world is bright, That is that, Don't you worry, The night is long (& On the road, 8/11/71).* 27/9/71 T1 PD BH

14/1/72 PEEL *Kum on, Rain, You and me, Only to do what is true.* 21/12/71 T1 JM JWH&JS

21/2/72 HARRIS *Back to the wall. On the land, You can make it here.* 9/2/72 * JG *

20/4/72 DRUMMOND *You can make it here, You're not here, Magic prize, Back to the wall.* 12/4/72 * MB MH&MF

2/5/72 PEEL *Back to the wall, Magic prize, You're not here.* 25/4/72 MV4 * JWH&BAI

25/8/72 PEEL *Not like a soldier but like an old love song, Approximately blue suede shoes, Rock & roll kid, Through a hole.* 14/8/72 T1 JM JWH

18/9/72 HARRIS *Roch 'n' roll kid, How does it feel, Rainy day blues, You and me.* 12/9/72 * JG *

29/1/73 HARRIS *That ain't jive, All the fallen teen angels (& Some of us said, 26/3/73).* 17/1/73 LHI PR BAI

11/5/73 SEQUENCE *Rising sun, Morning light, Rock 'n' roll kid, I know why, Be my flier.* 17/4/73 LHI JM *

2/7/73 HARRIS *Rising sun, Be my flier, Rock'n' roll kid (& Come on over, 13/8/73).* 27/6/73 * JG *

18/9/73 HARRIS *Rainy day blues, In the palm of your hand, Be my flier, How's it feel.* 21/8/73 * * *

29/4/74 HARRIS *Epitaph Blues, White dove, & ?* (PasB damaged). 17/4/74 * JG *

5/12/74 PEEL *Walkin' blues, It's got to be alright, I just wanna make love to you, Can't live a lie.* & Roger Saunders (lg), Rob Townsend (d), Charlie McCracken (b). 28/11/74 LHI TW *

15/7/76 PEEL *Over you, It's natural, Sun sinking low.* & Saunders (bv) only. 29/6/76 MV4 JG *

3/5/77 PEEL *His guiding hand, Slip and slide, Pictures in the sky†, It's natural.* & Morgan Fisher (o,p,wb). 27/4/77 MV4 JG NG

† On 'Before the Fall' SFRCD203. 'The ultimate session!' JG on sheet.

MEGA CITY 4

2/8/88 PEEL *Severe attack of the truth, Clear blue sky, January, Distant relatives, Alternative arrangements.* Chris Jones (d), Jerry Bryant (b), Danny Brown (g,bkv), Wizz (g,lv). 19/7/88 MV4 MR~

THE MEKONS

14/3/78 PEEL *Garden fence of sound, Where were you, Letters in the post, Lonely and wet, Dance and drink the Mekons, Dan Dare-out of space (it's a really nice place).* John Langford (dv), Roz Allen (b), Kevin Lycett

(g,lv-3 only, bkv), Tom Greenhalgh (g,bkv), Andy Corrigan (lv, bkv-3 only), Andy Sharp (bkv-1,5 only), Mark White (lyrics,v). 7/3/78 MV4 MB MR

2/10/78 PEEL *Like spoons no more, Trevira trousers, What are we going to do tonight, Rosanne, I'll have to dance then (on my own).* Mary Jenner (bv) r. Allen; & Martin Culverwell, Jo Barnett, Simon Best, and Mick Wixey (bkv). 25/9/78 MV4 BS DD

19/11/79 PEEL *I saw you dance, Watch the film, After 6, Beetroot.* 5/11/79 MV4 TW DD

5/1/81 PEEL *East is red, Weak chain, The building, English white boy engineer.* Lycett, White, Langford, Greenhalgh, Pete Barker (g), Mark Wilson (v), Minou Myling (v), Jackie Fleming (v), Brendan Peacock (gv); & Bob Sargeant (p-1 only). 17/12/80 LHI MS NG

16/9/85 PEEL *Hey Susan!, Beaten and broken, Deep end, Chop that child in half.* Langford, Stoke Newington Jr. (vi), Tommy Greene (v), Lou Edmonds (b), Ken Lite (g), Dick Taylor (lg), Rob Worry (k), Sally Smitter (bkv). 3/9/85 * MR~

31/7/86 KERSHAW *After six, The story of nothing, I can't find my money, Hole in the ground.* Langford, Lycett, Greenhalgh, Steve Goulding (d), Suzie Honeyman (vi), Brendan Croker (g), Rico Bell (acc). 8/7/86 * CG TWN

23/2/87 PEEL *Danton, Skid row, Revenge, Sophie.* Langford, Greenhalgh, Goulding, Lycett, Honeyman, Bell, John Gill (b,fd), Dick Taylor (g), Sally Timms (v); & Michelle Shocked (v,mnd). 10/2/87 * DG MR&MS

Broadcast date unknown MAYO *Hole in the ground, Fantastic voyage, Oblivion, You wear it well.* Langford, Greenhalgh, Goulding, Timms, Taylor, Honeyman, Bell, Robert Worby (o), Ken Lite (g), & Lu Edmonds (b-3 only). 24/2/88 MV4 PW *

THE MEL-O-TONES

27/8/85 PEEL *Machines, Weekend in suburbia, Wigs on the green, Posh.* Frank Martin (v), Martyn Dempsey (g), Bob Parker (b), Jon Neesan (d), David Dickie (p,k). 13/8/85 MV5 JWI TdB

MELANIE

21/9/69 TOP GEAR *Visit my dreams, Up town and down, Baby guitar, Beautiful people, Tuning my guitar.* Melanie (gv). 15/9/69 PH JW TW

15/5/89 CAMPBELL *Ruby Tuesday, Rock 'n' roll heart, Racing heart, Apathy.* Melanie Schekeryk (v), Alan Ross (g,bkv), Justin Myers (b), Pete Thompson (d), Chris Staines (bkv), Kay Langfield (bkv), Neil Palmer (k). 26/4/89 WX PW MPK

GEORGE MELLY

26/12/72 PEEL *If you're a viper, Trouble in mind, Gimme a pig foot.* George Melly (v) with Fawkes-Chilton Feetwarmers. 18/12/72 T1 JW *

Melly's BBC contract files date from 1954 and currently stand six inches high.

THE MELVINS

10/3/91 PEEL *Leech, Euthanasia, Theme, Way of the world.* Dale Croven (d,bkv), Lori Black (bv), Buzz Osborne (gv). 17/2/91 MV3 DG MR

THE MEMBERS

23/1/79 PEEL *Love in a lift, Phone-in show, At the Chelsea nightclub, Sound of the suburbs.* Jean-Marie Carroll (gv), Nigel Bennett (gv), Chris Payne (bv), Adrian Lillywhite (d), Nick Tesco (lv). 17/1/79 MV4 BS NG

19/2/79 PEEBLES *Soho a go go, Physical love (20/2), Solitary confinement (21/2), Handling the big jets (22/2).* 15/2/79 * JG *

1/10/79 PEEL *Muzak machine, Killing time, Romance, Gang war.* 24/9/79 MV4 BS DD

28/4/80 READ *Muzak machine, Physical love, Brian was, The gean men.* 10/4/80 MV4 CL *

13/4/81 PEEL *Boys like us, Chairman of the board, Working girl, Birmingham.* Rudi Thompson (ts), Adam Maitland (al) join. 1/4/81 LHI CL NG&MR

4/5/81 SKINNER *Going west, Nobody, At the arcade, Everyday's a holiday.* 24/4/81 LH1 DG ME

24/9/81 SKINNER *Family, Boys like us, Radio, Against the world.* Simon Lloyd (al) r. Maitland. 17/9/81 MV4 JS *

MEMBRANES

30/5/84 PEEL *Shine on pumpkin moon, Big nose and howling wind, Great mistake, Spike Milligan's tape recorder.* Coofy Sid (d), John Robb (bv), Mark Tilton (gv); & Nick Brown (vi), Mark Waring (perc), David Payne (perc). 19/5/84 MV5 DG MC

THE MEN THEY COULDN'T HANG

12/7/84 PEEL *Walkin' talkin', The men they couldn't hang, The green fields of France, Boy named Sue.* Swill Meateater (Phil Odgers) (gv), Shanne Veg (b), Stephen Cush (gv), Jon Odgers (d), Possum Wayne (g,p); & guests Chicken Kev, Carol & Frances (bkv). 4/7/84 MV5 BYA *

6/2/85 PEEL *The ironmasters, Night to remember, Scarlet ribbons, Donald where's your trousers?* Swill, J. Odgers, Shanne, Laughing Dog Brand (Cush) (gv), Paul Simmonds (g); & Merrills (bkv), Slim (p,cnt). 21/1/85 MV5 MRD MR

24/7/85 PEEL *Shirt of blue, Where have all the flowers gone?, Greenback dollar, Kingdom come.* & Neil Simmonds (sx), Bobby Valentino (vi), Merrill & Wendy (of the Boothill Foot-tappers) (bkv). 16/7/85 MV5 JWI MR

18/9/85 LONG *Walkin' talkin', The Green fields of France, Ironmasters, Green back dollar, Night to remember, The day after.* Five-piece. Live from MV5 BYA TdB

25/6/86 LONG† *Going back to Coventry, Ghosts of Cable Street, Dancing on the pier, Tiny tin soldiers.* 15/6/86 MV4 BYA TdB

   † On Nighttracks SFNT012.

10/9/90 CAMPBELL *Australia, The man in the corner shop, The family way, Handy man.* & Nick Muir (k,bkv), Ricky McGuire (b) r. Shanne. 29/8/90 MV4 PW MPK

D. L. MENARD

12/5/88 KERSHAW *The back door, Cold cold heart, Green oak tree, Jambalaya.* D. L. Menard & others unknown. Recorded by Andy Kershaw outside D. L. Menard's hopuse in Erath, Louisiana, April 1988.

13/5/90 KERSHAW *Wildwood flower, The mistake I made, The back door, J'ete au bal.* Billed as 'D. L. Menard, Eddie LeJeune & Ken Smith'. Menard (g,lv-1,3), Eddie Le Jeune (acc,lv-2), Ken Smith (fd). 26/4/90 MV3 DG ME

MERCURY REV

5/10/91 PEEL *Chasin' a bee, Syringe mouth, Coney Island cyclone, Fritterin',* Jim Chambers (d), Dave Fridmann (b), John Donahue (gv), Sean Grasshopper (g,bkv,cl), Sue Thorpe (fl), Dave Baker (v). 27/8/91 MV3 MR~

MERCYFUL FATE

22/4/83 FRI. ROCK *Curse of the pharoahs, Evil, Satan's fall.* King Diamond (v), Timi Grabber (b), Michael Denner (g), Hank Shermann (g), Kim Ruzz (d). 18/3/83 * TW DD

MAX MERRITT AND THE METEORS

5/5/72 PEEL *Morning glory, Good friend of mine, Ain't you glad, Everybody try (& Dedicated to a friend, 16/6/72).* Max Merritt (gv), Stewart Steer (d), Bob Bertles (sx,fl), Dave Russell (b). 18/4/72 T1 JM JWH&BAI
1st b'cast in file was In Concert, rec'd 2/3/72 PS, TX 11/3/72.

27/11/75 PEEL *King size rosewood bed, Wrong turn, Long time gone, Slipping away.* Merritt, Steer, Barry Duggan (sx,fl), Fuzz Deniz (b), John Gourd (g,k). 23/10/75 MV4 TW BAI

11/6/76 PEEL *Let it slide, Rosie, Tell me mama, Midnight man.* Lance Dixon (k) r. Duggan. 18/5/76 TW MR

MERRY BABES

20/6/88 L. KERSHAW *Cold and bare, The one I love, Take my word for it, Melanie from another planet.* John Houston Irvine (d,prg,bv), Paul Kennedy (g), Marijne Van De Vlugt (v). 12/6/88 MV4 TdB~

THE MERTON PARKAS

20/8/79 PEEL *A face in the crowd, Plastic smile, Empty room, You need wheels.* Mick Talbot (kv), Danny Talbot (gv), Neil Hurrell (b), Simon Smith (d). 13/8/79 MV4 TW DD

MICHAEL MESSER BAND

22/8/88 L. KERSHAW *I can't be satisfied, Rolling in my sweet baby's arms, Lone wolf blues, Minnetonka shake.* Michael Messer (ps,lsg), Ed Genis (g), Andy Crowdy (b), Jeffro Robertson (d). 10/8/88 MV4 PW MPK

METAL MESSIAH

16/9/88 FRI. ROCK *Intro/Metal messiah, Nightwing, Curse of the king.* Kevin Frost (d), Graham Kerr (b), Biff (g,bkv), Grem Darroch (g,bkv), Phil Ayling (v). 1/7/88 * HP DD

METAL URBAIN

19/1/78 PEEL *Atlantis, E-202, Hysterie connective, Ghetto.* Nancy Luger (g), Hermann Schwartz (g), Eric Debris (dm,sy), Clode Panik (lv). 16/1/78 MV4 TW DD

25/10/78 PEEL *Futurama, Numero zero, Anarchie au palace, 50/50.* 11/10/78 MV4 TW NG

THE METEORS

23/6/81 PEEL *Voodoo rhythm, Love you to death, Rockabilly psychosis, My daddy is a vampire, Rockhouse.* P. Paul Fenech (gv), Nigel Lewis (bv), Mary Robertson (d). 16/6/81 LH1 DG ME

5/11/81 JENSEN *Insight, Blue sunshine, Teenagers from outer space, Graveyard stomp.* 29/10/81 MV4 DG PS

13/12/83 PEEL *Ain't gonna bring me down, You crack me up, Lonesome train, Long blonde hair.* Fenech, Rick Ross (b), Matthew Fraser (d). 30/11/83 MV4 RP NG

9/7/84 PEEL *Stampede, Deep dark jungle, Surf city, I'm just a dog.* Fenech, Ross, Ian Cubitt (d,bkv); & Steve Andrews (bkv-1,3). 27/6/84 MV5 RP NG

30/10/85 PEEL *Torture, Meat is meat, Bertha lou, Maniac.* Fenech, Nev Hunt (b), Spider (d). 20/10/85 MV5 DG ME

METHOD ACTORS

22/7/81 PEEL *Round World, My time, E-y-e, Strictly gossip/Repetition.* Vic Varney (gv), David Gamble (dv). 18/7/81 MV4 DG MR

MIAOW

18/6/86 PEEL *Did she?, Following through, Three quarters of the way to paradise, Cookery casualty.* Cath Carroll (g,lv), Andy Winters (g), Ron Caine (bv), Chris Fenner (d); & Jonathan Bedford (o-4). 8/6/86 MV5 DG ME

11/2/87 PEEL *Just keep walking, Thames at high water, The dreamers' death, Fate.* Steve Maguire (g) r. Winters; & Terry Edwards (ss,tp). | 27/1/87 * DG MR&MA

MICKEY DREAD

23/8/82 PEEL *Parrot jungle, Problems, Zodiac sound, Heavy weight sound, Rub a dub.* * Rec. date unknown OS * *

MICRODISNEY

10/8/83 PEEL *Sleepless, Moon†, Sun†, Before famine†.* Sean O'Hagan (g,b), Cathal Coughlan (kv). 3/8/83 MV4 BYA *

23/1/84 PEEL *This liberal love, Escalator in the rain, Dolly, Everybody is dead†.* John Watt (b), Tom Fenner (d) join. 14/1/84 MV4 DG MC

1/5/84 PEEL *Dreaming drains†, A friend with a big mouth†, Teddy dogs†, Loftholdingswood†.* Jonathan Fell (b) r. Watt. 14/4/84 MV5 DG MC

10/10/84 PEEL *Genius†, Horse overboard†, 464†, Goodbye - it's 1987.* & Nick Montgomery (k-1 only). 2/10/84 MV5 MRD NG

3/11/84 SAT. LIVE *A friend with a big mouth, Loftholdingswood, 464.* Live from S2 MRD TdB

11/12/85 PEEL *Town to town†, Bullwhip road†, People just want to dream, Begging bowl†.* James Compton (k) r. Montgomery. 3/12/85 MV5 PWL MR

   † On Strange Fruit SFRCD 105.

6/8/86 PEEL *Armadillo man, Half a day, Soul boy, And he descended into hell.* Compton out, says sheet. 27/7/86 * DG ME&SC

MIDNIGHT CHOIR

16/12/87 PEEL *Idle, Balsawood Bob, Pig-man, Country-death-clown.* Matt (d), Simon (b), Nick (g), Duncan (g,o), Ziggy (v). 8/12/87 * DG MR&MC

MIDWAY STILL

6/10/91 PEEL *Wish, Come down, What you said, Making time.* Declan Kelly (d), Jan Konopka (b), Paul Thomson (gv). 1/9/91 MV3 DG ME&SA

13/7/92 GOODIER *Lies, Me in you, J and G, Sweat.* 5/6/92 MV4 MC PA

MIGHTY BABY

20/12/69 TOP GEAR *I'm from the country, India, House without windows.* Ian Whiteman (p), Mike Evans (b), Roger Powell (d), Martin Stone (g) Alan King (v). 2/12/69 MV4 JW *

MIGHTY BALLISTICS HI POWER

1/5/86 KERSHAW *Remembrance day, Black gold, Englishman abroad (whiskey galore), Woman of straw.* Chris Maund (v,g,b,o), Gary Taylor (g,b,p,o,bkv), Trevor Shepherd (v), Steve Napper (d,bkv), Kim Pooley (v). 16/4/86 Y2 CG PSM

MIGHTY FORCE

17/11/90 PEEL *Dive, Antarctica, Freebass.* Adam West & Simon Davies (prg). 6/11/90 MV5 MR~ JSM

THE MIGHTY LEMON DROPS

5/12/85 KERSHAW *Pass you by, Like an angel, All the way, Something happens.* Paul Marsh (v), David Newton (g), Tony Linehan (b), Keith Rowley (d). 14/11/85 Y2 DST TWN

5/2/86 LONG† *The other side of you, Now she's gone, Waiting for the rain, When I dream.* 26/1/86 HP BYA SC
   † On Nighttracks SFNT004.

27/8/86 PEEL *Open mind, Take me up, Behind your back, Up tight.* 19/8/86 * DG MR&PS

27/9/86 SAT. LIVE *Behind your back, Out of hand.* Live from S2 TdB~

13/4/87 LONG *Going under, Fall down (like the rain), Up and away, Out of hand.* Barry Douce (k) joins. 5/4/87 MV4 PW DD&FK

19/1/88 MAYO *Shine, World without end, In everything you do, Paint it black.* 3/1/88 MV4 HP TdB

30/10/89 CAMPBELL *Written in fiction, Into the heart of love, Beautiful shame, Sometimes good guys don't wear white.* Marcus Williams (b,bkv) r. Linehan. 18/10/89 MV5 PW MPK

MIGHTY MIGHTY

2/4/86 PEEL *Throwaway, Is there anyone out there?, Ceiling to the floor, Settle down.* Hugh Harkin (v,hca), Russell Burton (b,bkv), Michael Geoghegan (g), Peter Geoghegan (g,o), 'H' (David Hennessey) (d). 25/3/86 MV4 DG *

3/9/86 PEEL *I don't need you anymore, Little wonder, One way, Gemini smile.* 24/8/86 * DG ME

19/1/87 PEEL *I'll get you back, I never imagined, Yours truly, Built like a car.* 4/1/87 * DG ME&FK

28/1/87 LONG *Maisonette, Blue and green, Law, Biddy Baxter.* 21/1/87 MV4 BYA MPK

MILAN STATION

9/7/81 PEEL *Imaginary baby, This room is strange, Men in the rain, Chapter two.* Denny Pooley (gv), Colin Bendelow (b), Neil Henderson (lv), Grahame Cusack (dv), Norman (g,bkv). 4/7/81 LH1 DG MR

MILK

5/1/92 PEEL *Wrong again, Pyrosulphate, Wings, Would the real Jesus Christ please stand up.* Steven Keeler (d), Duncan Brown (b), Victor Kemlicz (gv). 14/11/91 MV4 DG NG&NK

THE MILK MONITORS

26/5/87 PEEL *Don't lean on me, Yo! dance with me, Revenge, When all else fails.* Jason Basin (Wood) (d), Max Yobitch (b), Jake Jams (g), Keef Creole (g), Marc Monitor (v). 10/5/87 * DG ME&FK

7/10/87 PEEL *The way you move, Max ray traitor, Drag you down, Hey! hey! hey! we're the Milk Monitors.* 29/9/87 * DG *

FRANKIE MILLER

5/2/73 Harris *Wild night, Ann Eliza Jane, You don't need to laugh, In no resistance.* Frankie Miller (v) & Brinsley Schwartz. 17/1/73 LHI PR BAI

3/5/73 Peel *I'm ready, It's all over, It takes a lot to laugh it takes a train to cry, After all (& Ann Eliza Jane, 31/5/73).* 30/4/73 LHI BA *

25/6/76 Peel *The Doodle song, Ain't got no money, Sail away, Brickyard Blues.* Miller, James Hall (p), Graham Deakin (d), Chrissie Stewart (b), Ray Minhinnet (g). 10/6/76 MV4 TW *

23/5/77 *Ain't got no money, Be good to yourself, Jealous guy, Down the honky tonk.* 16/5/77 MV4 TW DD

5/6/78 Peel *Have you seen me lately Joan?, Good time love, Stubborn kinda fella, Breakaway.* & Tony O'Malley (p), Ray Russell (g), Chrissy Stewart (b), B.J. Wilson (d), Martin Drover (tp), Chris Mercer (ts), Dyan Birch (bkv), Bonnie Wilkinson (bkv). 22/5/78 MV4 TW DD

2/4/79 Peel *Good to see you, A woman to love, Papa don't know, Is this love?, Falling in love with you.* & Steve Simpson (g, acc), Ed Dean (lg), Nick Judd (p), Tex Comer (b), Fran Byrne (d). 19/4/79 MV4 TVD DD

MILLTOWN BROTHERS

3/12/90 Goodier *Which way should I jump, When it comes, Where I stand, Sally Ann†.* Matt Nelson (lv,ag), Simon Nelson (g,bkv), Barney James (k,bkv), Nian Brindle (d), James Fraser (b). 20/10/90 MV5 MC~

† On 'Best of Mark Goodier' Mark1.

MINIMAL COMPACT

16/1/85 Peel *The well, Nada, Not knowing, Introspection.* Max Franken (d,b), Malka Spigel (b,k,bkv), Rami Fortis (g,k,bkv), Vincent Kenis (g,k), Luc van Lieshout (tp,mel,hca), Samy Birnbach (v,perc). 6/1/85 MV5 DG ME

MINNY POPS

2/12/80 Peel *Mono, Goddess, Jets, Ice-cube wall.* Wim Dekker (sy), Wally Van Middendorp (v,tps), Gerard Walhof (g), Lion Van Zoeren (b). 12/11/80 LHI DG NG

THE MINT JULEPS

21/5/85 Long *Ain't we got nerve, Don't let your heart, I don't need your love, Move in closer, I'm so sorry.* Marcia, Sandra, Debbie & Lizzie Charles, Julia Isaac, Debbie Longworth. 8/5/85 MV5 BYA NPK

22/1/86 Long *Baby baby, Monkey man, Think, Let me in, Only love can break your heart, Jesus gave me water.* & Jools Holland (p-5 only). Live from S2 * *

MIRACLE LEGION

6/8/89 Kershaw *Valentine's day, With a wish, Six months, Homer.* * 29/6/89 * DG *

13/6/92 Kershaw *Reel around the fountain, Snacks and candy, Good for her, Everything is rosy.* Mark Mulcahy (v), Ray Neal (g), Dave McCaffrey (b), Scott Boutter (d). 5/4/92 MV4 MA~

MISSING PRESUMED DEAD

14/1/81 Peel *You always say no, What she wants, 0.5 alive, Schlimm, Walkie talkie eyes.* Michael Ikon (g,tp), Tim Whelan (g,v,fl), Julian Treasure (d), Ian Hawkridge (b,k), Vince Cutcliffe (g). 6/1/81 LHI BS MR

THE MISSION

3/2/86 Long *Sacrilege, And the dance goes on..., Severina, Like a hurricane.* Wayne Hussey (gv), Mick Brown (d), Craig Adams (b), Simon Hinkler (g); & Paul Gregory (perc,bkv). 19/1/86 HP BYA MA

6/10/86 Long *Wasteland, Shelter from the storm, Tomorrow never knows, Wishing well.* 24/9/86 MV4 BYA MPK

28/9/88 L. Kershaw *Disease, Belief, Deliverance, Kingdom come.* 21/9/88 MV4 PW MPK

10/2/90 Sat. Seq. *Butterfly on a wheel, Bird of passage,* [& *Butterfly* take no. 2, not broadcast]. Hussey (agv), Hinkler (p) only. 7/2/90 SI KH TdB

MISTY

13/6/79 Peel *Oh wicked man, Rich man, Salvation, Babylon's falling.* Walford Tyson (lv), Delvin Tyson

(bkv), Antoinette McCalla (bkv), Chesley Samson (lg), Joe Brown (lg), Delbert McKay (rg,bkv), Vernon Hunt (k), Tony Henry (b,bkv), Julian Peters (d). 5/6/79 MV4 TVD MR

6/12/79 Peel *True rasta man, Judgement coming on the land, Sodom and Gomorrah.* D.Tyson, Henry, Samson, Kong (lv), Duxey (lv), Barry Facey (lg), Dennis Augustine (rg), Ras Bedeau (tp), Bampy (d), Sam (o), Joe Brown (p), General Spearhead (tst-2 only). 27/11/79 MV4 JS MR

29/9/80 Peel *Bale out, Peace and love, Wise and foolish.* D. & W. Tyson, McKay, Henry, Augustine, Samson, Brown, B. Facey (lg), Bolo (p), Bampy (d), Biddu (sx), Smokes (perc). 15/9/80 MV4 TW DD

1/6/81 Peel *Live up jah life, Life boat, Big city blues, Africa.* Tysons, McKay, Henry, Samson, Brown, Augustine, Peters, Godson Bedean (sx), Brother D. (lg). 12/5/81 LHI DG MR

3/1/83 Peel *New day, Can't stand it, Earth, Own them control them.* Tysons, MacKay, Henry, Augustine, Brown, Lorrance Crossfield (lg), Delford Brisco (k), Noi Norty (sx), Gilbert Sylvester (perc). 15/12/82 * RP NG

13/7/83 Jensen *Slavery days, City blues, Poor and needy.* Tysons, Brown, Henry, Augustine, Crossfield, Tawanda (k), Niinoi (sx), Ngoni (v), Duxie (v). 19/6/83 MV4 DG GP

29/2/84 Peel *West livity, City runnings, The wanderer.* Tysons, Henry, Augustine, Crossfield, Munya (d), Tawanda (k), Duxie (v) Ngoni (v). 22/2/84 MV5 DG NG

20/5/85 Peel *Hawks on the street, Thought for the children, Horizon.* Tysons, McKay, Henry, Brown, Crossfield, Augustine, D. Briscoe (k), A. Hayward (sx-3), Steve Williamson (sx-3). 7/5/85 MV5 MRD MWT

20/5/86 Peel *Envy us, Just a festa, Own them control them†, Together.* Tysons, MacKay, Henry, Crossfield, Augustine, Tawanda (k), Steve Williamson (sx). 29/4/86 MV4 DG MS&MR

† On 12-inch People Unite PU00712, with two 'versions' not broadcast.

JONI MITCHELL

29/9/68 Top Gear *Chelsea morning, Galleries, Night in the city, Cactus tree.* Joni Mitchell (agv) & the John Cameron Group (5). 23/9/68 PCI BA PR

Mitchell was booked for several other R1 sessions during tours in 1968 & 69, but all were cancelled, for various reasons.

SAM MITCHELL

3/2/72 Drummond *Terraplane blues, Love's prayer, Come on in my kitchen, Me and uncle dog and hambone (& Bootin' me about, 13/4/72).* * 26/1/72 * MB MH&MF

MOBY GRAPE

16/2/69 Top Gear *If you can't learn, Trucking man, Ain't that a shame, Five to eight (& I am not willing, 16/3/69).* Jerry Miller (gv), Peter Lewis (gv), Bob Mosley (bv), Don Stevenson (dv). 4/2/69 PH BA AH

THE MODELS

13/7/77 Peel *Man of the year, Censorship, Brainwash, Freeze.* Cliff Fox (glv), Marco (lg), Mick Allen (bv), Terry Day (d). 4/7/77 MV4 MB DD

MODERATES

20/4/81 Peel *Housewife for life, Nightlife, What's that sound (for what it's worth), Emile.* Bob Carr (g,vi), John Brady (v,k), Heidi Kure (v), John Potter (d), Tom Gould (g), Mike Pursey (b). 25/3/81 LHI DG PW

MODERN ENGLISH

25/11/80 Peel *Mesh and lace, A viable commercial, Black houses, Sixteen days.* Rob Gray (v), Gary McDowell (g,bkv), Mick Conroy (b,bkv), Richard Brown (d), Stephen Walker (sy). 11/11/80 LHI JS MR

13/10/81 Peel *Someone's calling, Face of wood, Being peeled.* 7/10/81 MV4 RP NG

MODERN EON

5/2/81 Peel *Real hymn, Grass still grows, High noon, Mechanic.* Alix Johnson (gv), Bob Wakelin (k,sy), Cliff

Hewitt (d), Danny Hampson (b), Tim Lever (g,sx). 28/1/81 LHI CL NG

9/2/81 Skinner *Watching the dancers, Second still, Mechanic, Cardinal signs.* 29/11/81 LHI DG MR

14/9/81 Skinner *The foist, Garland leaves, From the window, After the party.* 10/9/81 MV4 JS MR

THE MODERNAIRS

20/4/82 Peel *In order to change, Bantustan, Land of my fathers.* Dave Baynton-Power (d,bkv), Hugh Hughes (lv,k), Phil Bradley (lv,g), Heather Jades (bkv), John Adams (sx), Claire Thompson (vi), Phil Lucking (tp,tb). 5/4/82 MV5 DG *

THE MO-DETTES

4/2/80 Peel *Norman (he's no rebel), Dark park creeping, Kray twins, Bitter truth.* Jane Crockford (b, lv-3 only), Kate Corris (gv), June Miles-Kingston (d), Ramona Carlier (lv). 28/1/80 MV4 TW DD

29/9/80 Peel *Two can play, Raindrops and roses (My favourite things), The Sparrow, Bedtime stories.* 26/8/80 MV4 BS MR

3/11/80 Read *Foolish girl, Bedtime stories, Dark park creeping, Bitter truth.* 17/10/80 MV4 BA *

13/7/81 Skinner *The waltz, Vicious circle, Nasty children, Yellow smile, Tonight (version).* Jane Woodgate (bv) r. Crockford. 5/7/81 MV4 DG ME&PW

21/7/81 Peel *Nasty children, L'intro, White rabbit, Yellow smile.* 11/7/81 MV4 DG MR

MOGUL THRASH

29/1/71 Black *Sleeping in the kitchen, Conscience, St Peter, Can't live without you.* James Litherland (g), Malcolm Duncan (ts), Roger Ball (ss,al,bars), John Wetton (b), Bill Harrison (d), Michael Rosen (tp,g). 7/1/71 AO2 JM JWH&MF

13/4/71 Harding *Fuzz box (the bust), Conscience, What's this I hear.* 5/4/71 MV5 MB MH&MF

Rec'd Peel Sunday Concert 15/4/71 PS, TX 25/4/71.

THE MOLESTERS

19/10/78 Peel *Commuter man, Disco love, End of civilization, Girl behind the curtain.* Stella Anscombe (v), Leoni Nicol (v), John Ellis (v), Paul Heyward (g), Mark Gresty (b), Wayne Calcutt (d). 4/10/78 MV4 BS NG

6/2/79 Peel *Miss U.S.A., What's the time, Latex darling, P.M.W./Young and rich.* Carole Brooks & Tracy Spencer (v) r. Anscombe, Nicol. 30/1/79 MV4 BS MR

MONEY

22/2/80 Fri. Rock *Man in a subway, Leo the jester, Fast world, Another case of suicide.* David West-Mullen (v), John Overton (g), Larry Phillips (b), Tony Bowden (d). 6/2/80 * TW *

ZOOT MONEY

19/5/72 Peel *It ain't easy, Good to be alive, My father (& Three times corner, 7/7/72)* (Show presented by Alexis Korner). Zoot Money (p,o). 16/4/72 CM JM PK

Did many sessions in 60s with his Big Roll Band.

23/8/73 Peel *Good to be alive, Open road, Up to now, Three times corner (& Heaven and earth, 13/9/73).* 13/8/73 LHI BA *

MONGREL

8/2/73 Peel *The road, Melting away, Lost, Last night.* Robert Brady (pv), Stuart Scott (g), Jimmy Phillips (g), Megan Davies (bv), Vo Fletcher (d). 22/1/73 LHI BA *

Had rec'd a R1 Network session on 9/1/73, prod TW, 'Last night', 'Lonely stars'.

THE MONITORS

5/7/79 Peel *Telegram, All the help I can get, Believe in you, Token gesture.* Lee Wellbrook (gv), Chris Kitchen (glv), Nick Bidgood (b), Gary Porter (d). 26/6/79 MV4 TVD MR

MONKEY MESSIAH

9/12/91 Goodier *Sugary sweet lies of gold, Can't let go, Strangest things, Wheels in motion.* Adey (gv), Jeff Connor (gv), Dave Bates (k), Paul Prior (b), Bal Stevens (d,bkv). 30/11/91 MV4 MC~BJ

THE MONKEY RUN
15/7/87 Long *Inferior life, Resurrection, Big love thing, The evil deceiver.* Jim Stringer (bv), Mark Hodkinson (g,bkv), Terry Eves (k,bkv), Craig Henderson (d,bkv).
28/6/87 MV4 HP TdB&FK

MONO MONO
3/7/73 Peel *Make you realise, Awareness.*
* Rec. date unkown. OS * *

THE MONOCHROME MEN
10/4/87 Fri. Rock *Jump back, Songs of madness, Dig deep, Harder to love.* Kofi Baker (d), John Bentley (b), Brian Johnson (k), Ant Glynne (gv), Danique Osborne & Goodi Laos (bkv). 27/3/87 MV4 DG DD

THE MONOCHROME SET
22/2/79 Peel *Espresso, Noise, Love goes down the drain, Ici les enfants†/ Fat fun†.* Bid (lv,rg), Lester Square (lg,bkv, laughing box), Jeremy Harrington (b,bkv), John D. Haney (d,perc). 14/2/79 MV4 JS NG
6/9/79 Peel *Fallout, Martians go home, Viva death row†, Goodbye Joe/The strange boutique.* & Tony Potts (films). 21/8/79 MV4 BS MR
23/4/80 Peel *4.0.5. lines, B.i.d. spells bid, Apocalypso, Love zombies†.* Andy Warren (b,bkv) r. Harrington; & Bob Sargeant (mrm-3 only). 15/4/80 MV4 BS MR
  † On LP 'Volume, Contrast and Brilliance' Cherry Red Records.
6/8/83 Long *That creepy feeling, The twitch, Don't touch, Sugar plum.* * 22/7/83 PHM cJL PSM

MONOCONICS
21/5/80 Peel *Exit stage left, People will talk, Such a shame (about you), Vox pop.* Denny Pooley (glv), Grahame Cusack (d,bkv), Dave Green (b,bkv).
12/5/80 MV4 TW DD

GRUPO CIUDAD SEGUNDO MONTES
24/3/91 Kershaw *El Desarollo, Segundo Montes, La desmilitarizacion, Queremos la paz.* Neftali Hernandez Perez (v,timbales), Meymis Elizabeth Guevara Serpas (v,cga), Neftali Hernandez Gomez (b), Omar Guevara (gv), Efrain Amaya (gv), Misael Hernandez Perez (v,vi).
14/3/91 MV5 DG JB&SBR

MOOD ELEVATORS
28/7/81 Skinner *Metro girl, Jungle dance, Georgie girl, Waiting for Jane, I can't take it.* David Ditchfield (gv), Jenny Jones (dv,perc), Ian Ditchfield (b).
19/7/81 MV4 DG ME

MOODISTS
21/5/84 Peel *Some kinda Jones, You could be his killer, Who's the chicken hawk, Phantom flight.* Dave Graney (v), Mick Turner (g), Steve Miller (g), Chris Walsh (b), Clare Moore (d). 9/5/84 MV5 RP NG
10/7/85 Peel *Other man, Bullet train, Take the red carpet out of town, Justice and money too.* Turner out.
2/7/85 MV5 JWI TdB

THE MOODY BLUES
3/12/67 Top Gear *Another morning, Twilight time, Time to get away, Nights in white satin, Forever afternoon* Justin Hayward (gv), John Lodge (bv), Ray Thomas (v,fl), Graeme Edge (kv), Mike Pinder (d). 13/11/67 PClorPS BA PR
  Original line-up, with Denny Laine & Clint Warwick, lst appeared live on Joe Loss Show 5/3/65 PH, Light Programme. Dozens of sessions followed.
4/2/68 Top Gear *Forever afternoon, Nights in white satin, Dawn is a feeling, What am I doing here?*
29/1/68 PCl BA DT
21/7/68 Top Gear *Voices in the sky, The best way to travel, Ride my see-saw, Dr Livingstone I presume.*
16/7/68 PCl BA AH
23/2/69 Top Gear *Send me no wine, To share our love, Lovely to see you, Never comes the day.*
18/2/69 PH BA AH
24/8/70 Symonds *And the tide washes in, Don't you feel*

small, Melancholy man, Minstrel song, It's up to you.
28/7/70 PH BA NG [M]

MOODY BOYS & SCREAMER
18/8/91 Peel *140 Bpm & running, Centre of the world.* Tony Thorpe (prg), Nick Coler (prg), Rico (tb), Tony Poddie (rp). 2/7/91 MV5 TdB~

MOON ('70)
13/6/70 Top Gear *Mississippi woman, Voodoo child, Making a name.* Ian McLane (d), Sid Gardner (b), Dick Stubbs (lg), Ray Owen (gv). 1/6/70 PH JW *

MOON
28/7/75 Peel *Lone ranger, My old friend, Don't let me be lonely tonight, You've got the love.* Noel McCalla (v), Louis Salvoni (d), Laurence Netto (lg), Graham Collyer (rg), Ronald Lawrence (b), Douglas Bainbridge (cga,fl,al), Nicky Payn (ts,fl). 15/7/75 MV4 TW *
20/1/76 Peel *My kinda music, Makin' love, It's getting better, Don't wear it.* 13/1/76 MV4 TW *
23/8/76 Peel *Too close for comfort, Day dreaming, Cold nights.* 27/7/76 MV4 TW *
20/6/77 Peel *Only sad boys cry, Name of the game, This is your life (take 2) (& This is your life-(take 1), not broadcast).* John Shearer (d) r. Salvoni. 8/6/77 MV4 MB NG

THE MOONDOGS
10/4/80 Peel *School girl crush, Who's gonna tell Mary, Talking in the canteen, Roddie's gang.* Jackie Hamilton (bv), Gerry McCandless (gv), Austin Barrett (d).
1/04/80 MV4 MR~
18/5/81 Peel *Dream girl, Home is where the heart is, That's what friends are for, I'm not sleeping.*
27/4/81 LHI TW DD

MOONFLOWERS
16/2/91 Peel *My baby, Groove power, Back where we belong, Higher.* Toby Paso (d), Dave Vernon (g), Adam Pope (perc), Paul Waterworth (b), Sam Burns (o,sx), Sean O'Neill (lv). 23/1/91 MV5 DG NG&RPF

MOONRIDER
4/8/75 Peel *Our day's gonna come, Danger in the night, Gold digger.* Line-up unknown: possibly Keith West (v), John Weider (g), Bruce Thomas (b), Chico Greenwood (d). Show presented by Bob Harris.
24/7/75 MV4 * *

CHRISTY MOORE
24/6/91 Campbell *Welcome to the cabaret, Ride on, Smoke and strong whiskey, Green island, Whacker Humphries/Singing bird.* Christy Moore (g).
/6/91 MV5 PW MPK

GARY MOORE
10/2/84 Fri. Rock *Shapes of things, Hold on to love, Empty rooms.* Gary Moore (lgv), Neil Carter (kg), Craig Gruber (g), Ian Paice (d). 27/1/84 MV4 TW DD

MOOSE
9/6/91 Peel *Susanne, In every dream home a heartache, Je reve†, Do you remember?†* Damien Warburton (d), Jeremy Tishler (b), Moose McKillop (g), Russell Yates (gv), Timbo Gane (g), Laetitia Sadier (v-3 only).
16/4/91 MV5 MWT~ DMC
1/2/92 Peel *1 2 X U, Ace Conroy, Hell is, Orange peel†.* Warburton, Yates, McKillop, Stephen Young (b).
17/12/91 MV4 MR~ LS
  † On Strange Fruit SFMCD214.

MORE
23/5/80 Fri. Rock *I have no answers, Soldier, Way of the world, Atomic masters.* Kenny Cox (g), Paul Todd (g), Brian Day (b,bkv), Frank Darch (d), Paul Day (v).
16/4/80 * TW *

MORE 'N' MORE
12/4/91 Fri. Rock *Play dirty, Hot wired, Dreaming, Turning point.* Nicky Moore (v,hca), Kenny Cox (g), Craig Plummer (d), Big Mac Baker (g), Sarah Boyd (b).
15/3/91 MV5 TW DD

MORE FIENDS
8/11/89 Peel *Vinyl grind, Fatty humps, Yellow spades, Slug*

juice. Rich Poor (dv), Ron Fiend (bv), Allen Fiend (gv), Elizabeth Fiend (gv). 22/10/89 * DG MC

THE MOSS POLES
8/9/87 Long *Take it or leave it, I hear you scream, Underground, Little prince.* Nick Potter (gv), Shaun Bergin (b,bkv), Vick Edwards (d).
9/8/87 MV4 PW TdB&MA

THE MOTHMEN
3/3/82 Jensen *Temptation, Wadada, One black dot, Gosub.* Rob Harding (g,lv), Tony Bowers (g,sx,v), Charlie Griffiths (kv), Chris Joyce (d), Ronnie Hardman (b).
28/1/82 PHM * *

MOTOR BOYS MOTOR
1/9/81 Peel *Little boy and fatman, Hooves, Clean shirt and a shave, Here come the Flintstones.* * 24/8/81 MV4 TW *
12/11/81 Jensen *One down one down, Drive friendly, Yes indeedy, Hot and cold, Freeze up the truth.* Bill Carter (g,bkv), Chris Thompson (b,bkv), John Kingham (d), Tony Moon (v,hca). 1/11/81 MV4 DG MR

MOTORCYCLE BOY
14/9/87 Peel *Scarlet, Some girls, I could make you happy, Under the Bridge.* Alex Taylor (v), David Scott (g), Michael Kerr (g), Eddie Connelly (b), Paul McDermott (d); & Frank Sweeney (vla-2 only). 30/8/87 * DG ME&TD

MOTORHEAD
25/9/78 Peel *Louie-louie, Tear ya down, I'll be your sister, Keep us on the road.* Phil 'Philthy Animal' Taylor (d), Fast Eddie Clarke (gv), Lemmy (bv). 18/9/78 MV4 BS DD
6/10/81 Jensen *Fast and loose, Live to win, White line fever, Like a nightmare, Bite the bullet/The chase is better than the catch.* 1/10/81 MV4 JS *

THE MOTORS
22/4/77 Peel *Emergency, Bringing in the morning light, Dancing the night away.* Nick Garvey (gv), Rob Hendry (gv), Andy McMasters (bv), Ricky 'Slaughter' Wernham (d). 22/3/77 MV4 JG MR
21/9/77 Peel *Phoney heaven, Freeze, You beat the hell out of me, Dancing the night away.* Bram Tchaikovsky (g,bkv) r. Hendry. 12/9/77 MV4 TW DD

MOTT THE HOOPLE
21/2/70 Top Gear *Laugh at me, At the crossroads, Thunder buck ram.* Ian Hunter (elp,lv) Mick Ralphs (lg,v), Verden Allen (o), Overend Watts (b), Dale Griffin aka. 'Buffin'. 3/2/70 MV4 JW *
  'Unanimous pass' from panel for this 'Dylan-influenced group'. Next, rec'd Peel Sunday Concert 23/4/70 PS, TX 3/5/70; & 2nd Concert, rec'd 15/10/70 PS, TX 25/10/70. Years later, Dale Griffin was to produce more than a thousand of the other sessions listed in these pages.
16/3/71 Harding *Whisky woman, Angel of 8th Avenue, Keep a knockin', Original mixed up kid.*
8/3/71 MV5 MB MH&MF
24/7/71 Top Gear *Midnight lady, Like a rolling stone, Angel of 8th Avenue.* 6/7/71 MV4 * BC
  Also live on Rosko Show, 17/7/71 PS.
4/11/71 Drummond *Moon upstairs, Darkness darkness, The journey.* 25/10/71 MV5 MB MH&MF
  3rd In Concert, rec'd 30/12/71 PS, TX 8/1/72.
16/10/72 Harris *Ready for me, Jerking crows, Sweet Jane, One of the boys.* Rec. date unknown OS * *

MOURNBLADE
14/7/89 Fri. Rock *If you can't be good, Whizz kid, American dream, Red hot reputation.* Steve Tallens (g), Dunken F. Mullet (lv,hca), Magpie (d), Blacken (b,bkv).
2/6/89 MV3 HP DD

MOUSEPROOF
18/12/70 Black *Growing leaves and blowing leaves and sticky leaves that burn, Song of the mouse.* Geoff Fitzgerald (g), Tony Turnball (d), Alan Smith (b), Alan Place (g), Geoff Leigh (sx,fl). 2/12/70 AO2 JM JWH

MOUTH MUSIC
1/9/91 Kershaw *Mile marabhaisg air a ghaol, S muladach*

mi's mi air m'aineol, Fraoch a Ronaigh. Mairi Macinnes & Jaq Ferry (v), Martin Swan (k), Quee Macarthur (b), James Mackintosh (d), Chic Medley (perc). 23/7/91 MV5 MR~

THE MOVE

1/10/67 Top Gear *Cherry blossom clinic, Hey grandma, Stephanie knows who, Flowers in the rain, Do ya wanna be a rock 'n' roll star, Kilroy was here.* Roy Wood (gv), Carl Wayne (v), Bev Bevan (dv), Trevor Burton (gv), Ace Kefford (bv). 21/9/67 MV4 BA PR
Passed audition 20/7/66. Innumerable sessions followed.

28/1/68 Top Gear *Cherry blossom clinic, Weekend, Fire brigade, It'll be me, Walk on the water.* 22/1/68 MV4 BA *

20/4/70 Ferris *Brontosaurus, What, Lightening never strikes (& Looking on, 18/5/70).* Jeff Lynne (gv), Rick Price (b) r. Wayne, Kefford, Burton. 18/3/70 PH BA *

4/8/70 Harding *When Alice comes back to the farm, Looking on, She's a woman.* 28/7/70 MV5 MB MH&MF

23/12/71 Drummond *Message from the country, Words of Aaron, Ben Crawley steel co, Ella James.* Price out. Last session in BBC studios. 15/12/71 MV4 MB MH&MF

THE MOVIE STARS

5/11/82 Fri. Rock *No time to kill, It's your life, Waking up, Eye of the storm.* Larry Lamborne (k), Andy Brown (b), Clive Wagerfield (g), Mick Gardener (d), Robbie Matthews (v). 22/10/82 * * *

THE MOVIES

7/7/77 Peel *Yo-yo, Big boys' band, Heaven on the street.* John Cole (slg,lv), Gregg Knowles (lg), Mick Parker (k), Dave Quinn (b), Jamie Lane (d,bkv), Julian Diggle (perc,bkv). 28/6/77 MV4 JG MR

JONAH MOYO

18/6/87 Kershaw *Solo na Mutsai, Sugar daddy, We sing for peace, Lekani kulila.* Jonah Moyo (gv), Joshua Dube (g), Standrick Zaranyika (v), Jonah Mugona (b), Papa Manda (sx,cga), Job Ncube (tp), Patrick Zhiwayo (d). 4/6/87 * DG MG&MA

1/12/88 Kershaw *Makeyi wakakanya, Happiness overflowing, Ndiwe, We can do it.* Zaranyika out; & Priscilla Masarira & Nicholas Kunaka (v). 10/11/88 MV4 DG NG

OLIVER MTUKUDZI

4/11/90 Kershaw *Psss psss hallo, Haungadaro, Dzvene reseri, What's going on.* Oliver Mtukudzi (g,lv), Picky Kasamba (bkv), Florence Tinabwo & Buba Ngobani (bkv), Robert Mtukudzi (sy), Moses Nyaruka (lg), Ashton Mtaviri (b), James Nyungwa (d). 2/6/90 MV5 DG DD&AA

MUDHONEY

24/5/89 Peel *By her own hand, If I think/Here comes sickness, You make me die.* Dan Peters (d), Matt Lukin (b), Steve Turner (g), Mark Arm (g). 9/5/89 WX DG MR

LA MUERTE

19/2/86 Peel *I put the blame on you, I'm a man, Motor gang, Wild thing.* Thierry (d), Sisco (b), Didier (g), Marc (v). 9/2/86 MV5 DG TdB

MULTI STORY

25/10/84 Into the Music *I Marcus, Ahead of your time, Willow and the sun.* Paul Ford (v,ag), Andy Carney (g), Rob Wilsher (k), Roger Nasey (b), Steve Byrne (d). 13/10/84 MV4 DG MC

MUMMY CALLS

25/10/84 Long *Under your spell, Chestnut tree, Sexual desire, Deadly night.* David Banks (v), Andrew Ainsley (b), Brook (d), Alan Adair (k), Paul Howard (sx), Elisa Richards (v) & Billy Hamilton (bkv). 14/10/84 MV5 BYA PW

PAULINE MURRAY

31/3/80 Peel *Sympathy, When will we learn, Dream sequence, Shoot.* Pauline Murray (v), Peter Howells (d), Robert Blamire (b), Alan Rawlings (g). 19/3/80 MV4 JE NG

MUSICAL YOUTH

29/4/81 Peel *Johnny too-bad, Can't fight it, Don't blame the youth, Culture.* Fred Waite (Father of Patrick, below) (v,lg), Michael Grant (k 'age, 11'), Kelvin Grant

(rg '9'), Patrick Waite (b '12'), Frederick Waite (d '13'). 22/4/81 LH1 DG NG

28/9/82 Peel *Young generation, Children of Zion, Heartbreaker, Rub 'n' dub.* Dennis Seaton (v-2,3) r. Waite senior. 18/9/82 MV4 DG MR

THE MUTE DRIVERS

21/8/89 Peel *Frustration, Burning burning, Happy birthday, Twenty thousand millionaires.* David Rogers (bv), Steve Wright (g,perc,v). 8/8/89 MV5 DG TdB

MY BLOODY VALENTINE

5/10/88 Peel *I can feel it but I can't see it, Lose my breath, Colm's song, Feed me with your kiss.* Debbie Googe (b), Kevin Shields (gv), Bilinda Butcher (gv). 25/9/88 HP DG ME

MY DAD IS DEAD

26/6/90 Peel *Without a doubt, Water's edge, Nothing special.* Mark Edwards (v,g,d), Doug Gillard (d,g), Tim Gilbride (g), Chris Burgess (b). 27/5/90 MV3 DG ME

MY JEALOUS GOD

12/11/90 Goodier *Carol caviar, Everything about you, Pray, Anything.* Jim Melly (gv), Danny Burke (g), Chris O'Donnell (b), Andrew Berkely (d). 25/8/90 MV5 MC~

HEATHER MYLES

25/11/92 Kershaw *Love lyin' down, Playing in the dirt, That's why I'm walking, Changes.* Heather Myles (v), Roger Rettig (ps,g), Robert Bond (d), Paul Riley (b,bkv), Bob Loveday (fd), Phil Rambow (ag). 21/5/92 MV4 NG~ SCO

MYTHICA

10/5/70 R1 Folk Show *Proclamations: a sequence of songs, poems and prose.* Peter Dobson (agv), Peter Lynch (agv,vi), Arf Billington (hca,v) [M: Folk shows]. 23/4/70 MV5 FL *

15/2/71 Harris *Hayrick, Song of wandering Aengus, Red white and blue, Sally.* 2/2/71 MV5 JM JWH

NA FILI

17/7/73 Peel *Ar Eirinn, Jigs: Gander in the pratie hole/Humours of Donnybrock/Why so?, Caitlin triall, Mary from Ballyhaumis.* Tomas O'Canainn (pp), Tom Barry (wh), Matt Cranitch (fd). 2/7/73 T1 JW ARV
Group first appeared on R2's Folk on Sunday, 3/9/72, prod. FL [M: R2].

25/7/74 Peel *Polkas, Kitty Tyrrel, Slip jigs and reel, ?* (PasB illegible). 13/7/74 AO2 JW *

20/7/76 Peel *Trip to Athlone, Deus meus, Dalaighs, Calt nt dhuirhir.* 6/7/76 MV4 * *

NAJMA

17/9/87 Kershaw *Karoon na yad magar, Dill laga ya tha, Lodi hai jamalo.* Najma Akhtar (v), Talvin Singh (tb,perc), Lazar Gregorian (b), Ian Terry (k), Ray Carless (ss). 27/8/87 * DG NG&MWT

NAMES

3/3/82 Peel *Discovery, Life by the sea, This is harmony, Shanghai Gesture.* Michel Smordynia (bv), Marc Deprez (g), Christophe den Tandt (k), Luc Capelle (d). 17/2/82 MV4 KH NG

NAPALM DEATH

22/9/87 Peel† *The kill/Prison without walls/Dead, Deceiver/Lucid fairytale/In extremis, Blind to the truth/Negative approach/Common enemy, Obstinate divide/Life/You suffer.* Michael Harris (dv), Shane Embury (b), Bill Steer (g), Lee Dorrian (v). 13/9/87 * DG ME&EL

20/4/88 Peel† *Multi national co-operations/Instinct of survival, Moral crusade/Worlds apart/Mad, Divine death/C9/Control, Walls/Raging in hell/Conform or die/SOB.* 8/3/88 MV4 DG MR

† On Strange Fruit SFMCD201.

10/9/90 Peel *Unchallenged hate/Murdered mentally, From enslavement to obliteration/Suffer the... (title obliterated), Retreat to nowhere/Scum, Deceiver/Social*

sterility. Harris, Embury, Jesse Pintado (g), Mitch Harris (g), Barny (Mark Greenway) (lv). 12/8/90 MV3 DG MR&AA

PETER NARDINI

16/1/86 Kershaw *The happy hippy, Nightmares in G major, The new ice age, Radio waves, Glasgow cathedral.* Peter Nardini (gv). 7/1/86 Y2 SP PSM

NASMAK

8/6/82 Peel *Plaster, No touch and go, Heartache blow up, Walkman.* Joop van Brakel (g,perc,v), Toon Bressers (v), Theo van Eenbergen (b,perc, v). 19/5/82 MV4 RP MC

NASTY POP

24/11/75 Peel *Stage 'n' plays, Crow, Lonely king.* * 4/11/75 MV4 * *

NASTY ROX INC

16/6/87 Long *Set, Say it mean it, Nasty Rox Inc, Burn rubber.* Daniel Fox (v), John Waddell (g), Mark Townsend (b), Ian Roberts (d), Tony Spiker (perc), CJ Mackintosh (sc,mx). 29/4/87 MV4 PW MPK

NATIONAL HEAD BAND

6/2/71 Top Gear *Country water, Hey look at you now, Listen to the music (& Buttocks, not broadcast).* Jan Schelhaas (o,p), Dave Paul (bv), Lee Kerslake (dv), Neil 'Rusty' Ford (lgv). 18/1/71 PH JW BC
'Specialist programmes only' Audition panel. Did Peel's Sunday Concert, 1/7/71 PS, TX 25/7/71, prod JG.

NATIONAL HEALTH

1/3/76 Peel *Paracelsus, Agrippa, Excerpt from lethargy shuffle and mind your backs tango.* Phil Miller (g), Dave Stewart (k), Mont Campbell (b,frh), Alan Gowen (k), Bill Bruford (d,perc), Steve Hillage (g). 17/2/76 MV4 JG MR

12/10/76 Peel *Clocks and clouds, Brujo.* & Amanda Parsons (v); Neil Murray (b) r. Campbell; Hillage out. 21/9/76 MV4 JG MR

16/11/77 Peel *A legend in his own lunchtime, The collapso.* & Richard Sinclair (lv-1 only); Pip Pyle (d) r. Bruford; Parsons, Gowen out. 9/11/77 MV4 MB NG

NATURAL ACOUSTIC BAND

20/8/70 Henry *All I want is your love, Subway Cinderella, Cocaine boy, First boy.* Robin Thynne (agv), Krysia Kocjan (agv), Tom Hay (d,perc,glo). 13/8/70 * MB MH&MF

4/3/71 Henry *Learning to live, February feeling, Running into changes, Waiting for the rain.* 24/2/71 * MB MH&MF

5/6/72 Harris *Learning to live, Echoes, Midnight study, Subway Cinderella, Dying bird.* 16/5/72 MV5 JG *

11/12/72 Harris *All I want is your love, Echoes, Moontime writer.* & Mohammed Amin (b). 15/11/72 LH1 JG * [M: Speakeasy]

NATURAL GAS

10/11/71 Peel *How long were you there?, The jailer, Bad man.* Terry Samde (dv), Steve Dale (lv), Alex Sinclair (g), Tony Phillips (b,bkv). 18/10/71 PH JW BC

30/6/72 Peel *Jumping Jack flash, Long hot days, Little small time, Mastermind.* 22/5/72 MV5 JM *

NATURAL LIFE

28/10/91 Goodier *Natural life, Love, Deb & Duff, Into your skin.* Jon Spong (v), Ray Wilson (k), Mark Matthews (b), Darren Hunter (g), Peter Holdforth (d), John Locko (g), Andrew Lovell (perc). 12/10/91 MV4 MA~

NATURAL SCIENTIST

12/10/81 Peel *Seven not seventeen ways, No direction home, I'm reading this Concise Oxford Dictionary, See through you.* Dave Willan (d), Iggy (bv), Stuart Baldwin (g), Neil Crossley (k), Boris Forrest (g,lv). 5/10/81 MV4 TW MR&MC

THE NATURALITES

13/6/83 Peel *Jah love this, Jah holy hills, I want your love, Suffer.* Ossie Samms, Neil I. & Jah P. (rgv), Bimus I (lg), Marcus Naphtali (o,p), Lenroy Judah (b), Alton Ricketts (d), Simba (perc), Junior Lindo (ts), Hugh Daffus (al), Eitiko (tp). 4/6/83 MV4 DG MC

11/6/85 Peel *Pull together, Rastafari, Your love, Guide me*

with the tide. Samms, Daffus, Wilf Fearon (d), Percy McLeod (rgv), Lenroy Guiste (b), Paul Prince (lg), Albert Barnes (tp), Winston Williams (k).
21/5/85 MV5 MRD MR

16/9/86 Long *Upside downside, Last days, Jah love is so fine, Rasta youths*. Samms, Fearon, McLeod, Guiste, Prince, Johnny White (perc), Winston Squires (k), Marcus Hodge (k), Chris Whiteley (g). 17/8/86 MV4 BYA *

NAZARETH
8/6/72 Drummond *Called her name, Spinning top, Morning dew, Fool about you*. Dan McCafferty (v), Pete Agnew (b), Manny Charlton (g), Darrell Sweet (d).
31/5/72 MV4 MB MH&MF

Original audition tape rec'd in Glasgow failed by panel 10/70: 'very low standard' 'out of tune singer'. First b'cast was In Concert rec'd 13/1/72 PS, TX 22/1/72. 2nd In Concert rec'd 8/6/72 PS (day of this session broadcast), TX 17/6/72.

2/11/72 Peel *Ruby baby, Black-hearted woman, Fool about you (& Red light lady, 30/11/72)*. 30/10/72 LHI BA *

13/11/72 Harris *Woke up this morning, Hard living, Country girl, Goin' down*. 18/10/72 LHI JG *
Rec'd 3rd In Concert 4/1/73 PS, TX 13/1/73.

26/3/73 Harris *Razamanaz, Night woman, Broken down angel, Vigilante woman*. 14/3/73 LHI PR BAI

5/4/73 Peel *Alcatraz, Broken down angel, Razamanaz, Bad bad boy*. 2/4/1973 LHI BA *

13/8/73 Harris *Razamanaz, Too bad too sad, Turn on your receiver, Bad bad boy* (3-used as Harris Sig. from 27/8/73). 1/8/73 LHI BA *
Rec'd 4th In Concert 17/5/73 HP, TX 16/6/73; then on Sounds on Sunday 30/12/73 rec'd 27/11/73 LHI.

8/4/74 Harris *Silver dollar forever, Light my way, Shapes of things, Jet lag*. 27/3/74 LHI PR *

NED'S ATOMIC DUSTBIN
19/11/90 Goodier *Cut up, Nothing like, Aim, Happy*. Jonathan Penney (v), Alexander Griffin (b), Daniel Worton (d), Gareth Pring (g), Matthew Cheslin (b).
10/11/90 MV5 MA SA

8/12/90 Peel *Selfish, Throwing things, You, What gives my son*. 13/11/90 MV5 MR~

11/5/92 Goodier *Suave and suffocated, Legoland, You don't want to do that, Intact*. 18/4/92 MV4 MA RF

BILL NELSON
15/6/81 Peel *Rooms with brittle views, Stay young, Sleep cycle, Jazz*. Bill Nelson (g,perc,v), Ian Nelson (sx,k), Don Snow (k), Alan Quinn (bv), Bogdan Wiczling (d), Richard Jobson (v-4 only). 2/6/81 LHI DG ME

22/2/83 Jensen *Dancing on a knife's edge, Time tracking, Contemplation, Indiscretion*. Nelson (v, all instruments), Jan Nelson (bkv). 15/1/83 Recorded at the Echo Observatory.

NEMESIS
4/5/90 Fri. Rock *Out from the inside, Static, Game that never ends, Overshadow*. David Brown (d), Jon-Paul Sherlock (bv), Joe Ivory (gv), Cameron Dunham (g,lv).
20/4/90 MV4 TW MC

NEON
22/3/79 Peel *Confuse the news, Eyeing up diddies, Plum plum crazy, Exterminate*. * 14/3/79 MV4 JS NG

THE NEON HEARTS
5/4/79 Peel *The other great sex prose, Roll on deodorant, Body language, Rings of confidence*. Tony Deary (lgv), Steve Heart (sx), Paul Raven (b), Mark Fuller (d).
21/3/79 MV4 JS NG

NERVOUS GERMANS
14/10/80 Peel *Waiting for the next wave, Watch out, Love letter, Bogart*. Micky Meuser (bv), Manni Hollander (gv), Edgar Liebert (dv), Grant Stevens (lv). 8/10/80 MV4 BS NG

THE NEUTRONS
31/10/74 Peel *Take you further, Living in the world today, Welsh R Blunt*. * 17/10/74 * * *

NEW AGE
16/11/81 Jensen *All I want, Living for now, All there is,*

First to live first to die. Barry Morris (v,sx), Ian Morris (g), Neil Battle (b), Nigel Loxley (k), Martin Burbage (k), Andy Hendry (d). 8/11/81 MV4 DG ME

22/4/82 Peel *On the inside, Ideals, Progression, Accption*.
10/4/82 MV6 DG PS

NEW FAST AUTOMATIC DAFFODILS
9/1/90 Peel† *Purple haze, Man without qualities II, Jagger bog, Big (instrumental)*. Andy (v,mel), Dolan (g), Justin (b), Icarus (perc), Perry (d). 19/12/89 MV5 DG JB

24/11/90 Peel† *Get better, Part 4, Man without qualities I*. 11/11/90 MV3 DG MA&AR
† On Strange Fruit SFMCD209.

THE NEW GENERATION
10/3/68 Top Gear *She's a soldier boy, Sadie and her magic Mr Galahad, I saw you (at skippy fair), A brush with sister Jo, Eleanor Rigby (& Smokey blues away, 28/4/68)*. * 28/2/68 * * *

NEW HEARTS
14/10/77 Peel *Revolution-what revolution? Love's just a word, Here come the ordinaries, Just another teenage anthem*. Matt MacKintyre (d), John Harty (b,bkv), Dave Cairns (lg,bkv), Ian Paine (lv). 3/10/77 MV4 MB DD

NEW MODEL ARMY
26/7/83 Jensen† *Notice me, Liberal education, I wish, Great expectations*. Justin Sullivan (Slade) (gv), Stuart Morrow (bv), Rob Heaton (d). 17/7/83 MV4 DG ME

4/1/84 Peel† *Christian militia, Small town England, Running, Falklands spirit*. 14/12/83 MV4 RP HP

21/1/85 Long *Frightened†, No rest, Drag it down†, The attack†*. 30/12/84 MV5 PW&TD PW&TD
†† On 'Radio Sessions 83-84' Abstract LP ABT017.

NEW ORDER
16/2/81 Peel† *Truth, Senses, I.C.B., Dreams never end*. Peter Hook (bv), Bernard Dicken (gv), Gillian Gilbert (g,sy), Stephen Morris (d). 26/1/81 LHI TW DD

1/6/82 Peel† *Turn the heater on, We all stand, Too late, 5-8-6*. Rec. date unknown PRIV * *
† On Strange Fruit SFRCD110.

25/8/84 Sat. Live *Sooner than you think, Age of consent, Blue Monday, In a lonely place, Temptation*. Live from S2 MRD TdB

THE NEW YOU
30/3/88 Mayo *The wedding, Charged, Close up, Depend on it*. Marie Malone (v,perc), David Westmore (b), Ian Cleverly (d,bkv), Paul Hazel (g,perc), Nigel Buckner (al,bars). 16/3/88 MV4 HP MPK

RANDY NEWMAN
18/6/74 Peel *Leave your hat on, Louisiana, I think it's gonna rain today, Political science, Birmingham, Simon Smith and the amazing dancing bear/Albanian wedding day (& My old Kentucky home, 22/6/74, ROCK ON)*. Randy Newman (pv). 3/6/74 LHI JW BC&MF

THE NEWS
7/6/79 Peel *Fifty per cent reduction, High society, Advertise, Brain drain*. Ivor Drawmer (k,bkv), Roger Harrison (d,perc,bkv), Alan Quinn (b,lv), Trevor Midgley (gv). 30/5/79 MV4 JS NG

NEWTOWN NEUROTICS
21/3/83 Peel *Wake up, Agony, Life in their hands, March, Jimi jingle Peel*. Steve Drewett (gv), Colin Dredd (Masters) (b), Simon Lomond (O'Brien) (d).
7/3/83 MV4 TW *

NIAGARA
24/7/81 Fri. Rock *Across the bridge, Victim of love, Crossfire, Cold eyes*. Bobby Harrison (v), Gus Isador (g), Greg Dortch (b), Billy Carson (d), Paul Nicholas (k).
10/7/81 * TW DD

THE NICE
22/10/67 Top Gear *The Flower king of flies, Azrial, Sombrero Sam, Tantalising Maggie, Rondo, The thoughts of Emerlist Davjack*. Ian Hague (d), Keith Emerson (k), Lee Jackson (bv), David O'List (g). 18&19/10/67 MV4 BA PR

28/1/68 Top Gear *Daddy where did I come from, For no-*

---

one, La aresa dia conte, She belongs to me. Brian Davison (d) r. Hague. 17/1/68 MV4 BA DT

16/6/68 Top Gear *Get to you, The diamond hard blue apples of the moon, The Brandenburger, Little Arabella (& Sorcery, 14/7/68)*. 10/6/68 PCI BA PR

4/8/68 Henry *Little Arabella, Rondo, The flower king of flies*. 29/7/68 MV4 AD *

25/8/68 Top Gear *America, Lumpy gravy, Aries, Ars longa vita brevis*. 6/8/68 PCI BA AH

29/8/68 Pop North *Hang on to a dream, Little Arabella, America*. 26/8/68 PHM JWX *

1/12/68 Top Gear *Happy friends, The Brandenburger, Hang on to a dream, Intermezzo from the Korelia suite (& Walter's Handel music, 12/1/69)*. O'List out.
26/11/68 PCI BA AH&BC
Group next appeared live on R1 Club 28/11/68 PS.

20/4/69 Top Gear *I'm one of those people my father tells my sister not to go out with, Azrial revisited, Blues for the prairies, Diary of an empty day (& Top Gear Sig., 16/3/69)*. 4/3/69 PH BA AH&BC
Group received special extra payment of £50, for re-recording 'Top Gear' sig. on this session.

8/6/69 Top Gear *Get to you, Country pie, For example, St. Thomas. & Roy Harper (4 only)*. 2/6/69 PH JW TW

6/4/70 Ferris *Country pie, Excerpts from five bridges suite (& My back pages, The Pathetique 3rd movement, 27/4/70)*. 25/3/70 PH BA NG

ROGER NICHOLSON
29/5/72 Harris *Nonesuch, Spring season, Medieval garden, Appalachian two-step*. Roger Nicholson (dul).
10/5/72 MV5 JG *

NICKY AND THE DOTS
18/7/79 Peel *Can't touch anything, She walks there, Sitting next to Susan, Girl gets nervous*. Nick Dwyer (lv), Chris Douseley (g), Paul Clark (o), Dave Williams (b), Ken Hogg (d). 11/7/79 MV4 TVD NG

NICO
11/2/71 Henry *Aris song, My only child, O Konig (& Abschied, 11/3/71)*. Nico (hmn,v). 3/2/71 MV4 MB MH&MF
Rec'd Peel Concert the day after this recording, at The Paris.

20/2/71 Top Gear† *No one is there, Janitor of lunacy, Secret side, Frozen warnings*. 2/2/71 MV4 JW BC
Next, on R2's Nightride 27/3/71, rec'd 19/2/71 A02. † On Strange Fruit SFRCD064.

3/12/74 Peel *We've got the gold, You forgot to answer, Janitor of lunacy, The end*. 18/11/74 MV4 JW *

THE NIGHTBLOOMS
12/6/90 Peel *Afraid, One week moment, Let me, Butterfly girl*. Leon Morselt (d), Petra Van Tongeren (b), Harry Otten (g), Michel Vander Woude (g), Esther Sprikkelman (v). 15/5/90 MV3 MR~

NIGHTDOCTOR
3/11/80 Read *Joe Frazier, Should I?, Tune in, Music like dirt*. Charles Wood (g), Ivan Lampkin (gv), Richard Maun (al), Alan Deval (ts), Vincent Gordon (tb), Robbie Coombes (v), Roger Haires (b), George Young (d), Caroline Williams (k), Lynford Joshua (perc).
23/10/80 MV4 DG MR

29/12/81 Jensen *High fashion, Menelik, Jah light, Too late*. Young, Haires, Wood, Williams, Coombes, Deval, Freddie Cruickshank (g), Annie Whitehead (tb), Terry Allen (perc), Noel Job (v,perc). 11/12/81 MV4 DG ME

THE NIGHTINGALES
13/10/80 Peel† *Start from scratch°, Butter bricks, Torn, 12 years*. Robert Lloyd (lv), Joe Crow (gv), Paul Apperley (d), Eamonn Duffy (b). 1/10/80 MV4 BS NG
† On Strange Fruit SFPS052; ° also on 'Winters of Discontent' SFRCD204.

7/7/81 Peel *Return journey, (One) Mistake, Bush beat, Inside out*. Lloyd, Apperley, Steve Hawkins (b), Andy Lloyd (g,bkv), Nick Beales (g,bv). 6/7/81 LHI TW DD

18/3/82 PEEL† *Give 'em time, Which Hi-Fi, My brilliant career, The son of God's mate.* 3/3/82 MV4 RP NG
† On Cherry Red 12-inch Cherry 44.

4/4/83 PEEL *Urban ospreys, Yeah it's okay, The bending end, The whys of acknowledgement, Only my opinion.* John Nester (b) r. Hawkins. 28/3/83 MV4 JP MC

12/12/83 PEEL *Look satisfied, All talk, This, Not man enough.* 5/12/83 MV4 DG MC

11/3/85 PEEL *How to age, Heroin, First my job, Part-time moral England.* Howard Jenner (b), Pete Byrchmore (g,k) r. Nester, Beales. 3/3/85 MV4 DG ME

26/3/86 PEEL *Down in the dumps, Coincidence, At the end of the day, Rockin' with Rita.* Lloyd, Byrchmore, Jenner, Ron Collins (d,bkv), Maria Smith (vi,bkv). 18/3/86 * DG MR&MC

NIGHTSTALKER
24/7/92 FRI. ROCK *Take my stage, War, Reaper, Stand proud and tall.* Rhys Jones (v), Bambi (b), Ben Creasey (g), Ade (d). 3/7/92 MV5 MC~

NINE BELOW ZERO
29/3/82 JENSEN *Eleven plus eleven, True love is a crime, You can't say yes and you can't say no, Sugarbeat (and rhythm sweet).* * 11/3/82 MV4 JS MR

999
1/11/78 PEEL *Subterfuge, Homicide, Soldier, Let's face it.* Pablo Labritain (d), Guy Days (gv), Nick Cash (gv), Jon Watson (b). 25/10/78 MV4 MR NG

1919
12/5/82 PEEL *After the fall, Caged, The ritual, Slave, Repulsion.* Mark Tighe (g), Mick Reed (d), Ian Tilleard (v), Nick Hiles (b), Sputnik (sy). 8/5/82 MV4 DG MR

11/5/83 PEEL *Alien, Storm, Cry wolf, Control.* Sputnik out; & Steve Madden (b-1). 4/5/83 MV4 RP NG

NIRVANA ('67)
10/12/67 TOP GEAR *Take this hand, Pentecost hotel, Wings of love, We can help you, Satellite jockey.* Alex Spyropoulos, Patrick Campbell-Lyons (others unknown), & The Syd Dale Orchestra. 4/12/67 * BA DT

NIRVANA
22/11/89 PEEL *Love buzz, About a girl, Polly, Spanx thru'.* Kurt Cobain (gv), Chris Novoselic (b), Chad (d). 26/10/89 MV4&S DG TdB

3/11/90 PEEL *Son of a gun†, Molly's lips†, D7, Turnaround†.* Dave Grohl (dv) r. Chad. 21/10/90 MV3 DG ME&FK

3/11/91 PEEL *Dumb, Drain, 'No title as yet'.* 3/9/91 MV5 DG ME&TD

18/11/91 GOODIER *Polly†, Been a son†, Something in the way, Aneurysm†.* 9/11/91 MV4 MA~JT
† On Geffen 'Insecticide' GED24504.

NO MEANS NO
25/5/88 PEEL *Little creep, Body bag, Stop it, Mamma's little boy.* John Wright (d,bkv), Rob Wright (b,bkv), Andy Kerr (g,lv). 17/5/88 * MR~

19/6/89 PEEL *The day everything became nothing, The tower, Two lips/Two lungs and one tongue/Rags & bones.* 30/5/89 MV3 DG MR

NO QUARTER
16/4/82 FRI. ROCK *Power and the key, Racing for home, C'mon, The last song, Calling.* Snappi (v), Dave Young (g), Robert Palmer (b), Steve Chard (d). 12/3/82 * TW DD

RAB NOAKES
6/6/72 PEEL *Half a mile from nowhere, Drunk again, Good night loving trail, Winter song (& Hard on you, 1/8/72).* Rab Noakes (agv). 15/5/72 PH JW *
It's possible Rab's second RI session was rec'd 25/10/72 LHI for HARRIS, TX 6/11/72, but this cannot be confirmed, because PasB is missing.

23/11/72 PEEL *The way you know, A long time ago, One bed one purse, Wait a minute.* & Robin McKidd (agv). 30/10/72 * BA *

4/5/73 SEQUENCE *There's always tomorrow, Sitting in a*

corner blues, The sketcher and the last train, Wrong joke again. & McKidd. 12/4/73 * JM NG

5/2/74 PEEL *Wrong joke again, As big as his size, Branch, Clear day.* & Mark Griffiths (lg), (b), (d) (uncertain). 21/1/74 * * BC

18/2/74 HARRIS *Diamond ring, Tomorrow's another day, Sitting in a corner, The sketcher and the last train.* Solo. 30/1/74 * JG *

22/10/74 PEEL *Memories, Slob, Stepping stone, Never too late.* 7/10/74 MV4 JW *

12/6/75 PEEL *Stepping stone, Early morning friends, Somebody counts on me, Do-re-mi.* & Pick Withers (d), Charlie Harcourt (lg), Rod Clements (b). 5/6/75 MV4 TW *

5/7/78 PEEL *She's all I see, I won't let you down, It'll be me, See me again.* & Richard Brunton (b), Steve Whalley (g), Terry Stannard (d). 5/7/78 MV4 MB MR

NOIR
30/8/70 RAVEN's R&B *How long, Hard labour, Beggar man.* Gordon Hunte (gv), Roy Williams (b), Berry Ford (dv), Tony Cole (elp,o,v). 19/7/70 MV4 JG JY
Passed by panel: 'jungle drums and chanting'.

20/11/70 BLACK *Lady X, Indian Rope man, Hard labour (& The system, 11/12/70).* 4/11/70 AO2 JM BC
Group did Peel's Sunday Concert, Rec'd 26/11/70 PS, TX 6/12/70, prod. JG.

NORMIL HAWAIINS
19/6/80 PEEL *Uncle green genes, The Beat goes on, Memories, Levels of water.* Brian Kealy (d), Laurence Henderson (b), Jim Lusted (gv), Guy Smith (gv,p), Sue Leeves (bkv), Nick Rose (b-3 and 4 only). 20/5/80 MV4 BS MR

JIMMY NORTON'S EXPLOSION
6/8/79 PEEL *Getting away with murder, Just like Lazarus, Ambition, Lost in a landslide.* Glen Matlock (b,lv), Danny Kustow (g,bkv), Budgie (d). 30/7/79 TW DD

THE NOSEFLUTES
11/9/85 PEEL *Taking out the creases, Worthy pious, Let me in to beg, Love endures the Autumn, Bullet enters Brad.* Ron Collins (d), Chris Horton (b), John Horton (g), Dave Pritchard (g), Chris Long (vi), Martin Longley (v). 1/9/85 MV5 DG ME

25/8/86 PEEL *History of heart disease, Serving in paradise, Catcheel maskhole, Leg full of alcohol, The ravers.* & Mark Rowson (d), Roger Turner (perc) for Collins. 17/8/86 * DG ME&FK

20/5/87 PEEL *Body hair, Rotting honeymoon, Spitball on my kisser, Thug thug thug.* Collins returns. 5/5/87 * DG MR&MFA

16/1/89 PEEL *Born in the last ditch, Ossified, Rum ship, Much decorated.* Desperate Din (k) r. Long. 8/1/89 MV3 DG MA

NOTSENSIBLES
17/12/79 PEEL *Because I'm mine, King Arthur, I thought you were dead, I'm in love with Margaret Thatcher.* Haggis (Michael Hargreaves) (lv), Sage (Steven Hartley) (g), R.C. Rawlinson (k), Gary Brown (b), Kevin Hemmingway (d), Dan the Sessionman ("No relation."-TVD) (guest appearance-3 only). 28/11/79 MV4 TVD NG

NOUS SOMMES
25/8/89 FRI. ROCK *Near dark, Perfect pride, Under my eyes, Glory gods.* Paul Kettley (v), Nick Dunn (g), Grant Kirkhope (gv), Gareth Baybutt (b), Brian Wilson (d). 16/6/89 ED PW MWT&DD

NUCLEAR SOCKETTS
6/8/81 PEEL *Riot squad, Honour before glory, Pretender's zeal, Play loud.* Phil Malone (d), Brett Gurney (b), Mark Howling (g). Kes (v). 1/8/81 MV4 DG MR

NUCLEUS
7/3/70 TOP GEAR *Elastic rock, 1916, Orpheus, Persephone's jive, Twisted track.* Ian Carr (tp,flh), Brian Smith (ts,ss,fl), Karl Jenkins (elp,ob), Chris Spedding (g), Jeff Clyne (b), John Marshall (d). 2/3/70 PH JW BC
[M: Jazz shows] Not to be confused with previous

Nucleus (Duffy Power, John McLoughlin, Danny Thompson, Terry Cox) who did WS R&B session 20/1/67, TX 13/2/67.

24/7/70 BLACK *Never carry, Ballad of the pimp, Morning call, 1916.* 24/6/70 * JM *

27/3/71 TOP GEAR *Snakeskin dream, Bearded lady, Morning call.* 15/3/71 PH JW *

17/11/71 PEEL *Feel it first, Belladonna, Tall grass, Pieces of me.* Dave MacRae (elp) & Clive Thacker (d) r. Spedding, Marshall. 2/11/71 MV4 JW *

7/11/72 PEEL *Belladonna, Suspension, Mayday (& Summer rain, 9/1/73).* Alan Skidmore (ts,ss), Gordon Beck (elp), Alan Holdsworth (g), Roy Babbington (b) & Aurio de Sousa (perc) r. Smith, Jenkins, Clyne. 10/10/72 LHI JW *

GARY NUMAN
25/6/79 PEEL† *Cars, Airlane, Films, Conversation.* Gary Numan (lv), Chris Payne (k), Billy Currie (k), Paul Gardiner (b), Cedric Sharpley (d). 29/5/79 MV4 TW MR
† On Strange Fruit SFMCD202.

NUTZ
15/6/74 ROCK ON *Round and round, As far as the eye can see, Joke, Light of day.* David Lloyd (v), Mick Devonport (lg), Keith Mulholland (b), John Mylett (d). 10/6/74 LHI BA *

5/8/74 HARRIS *Poor man, Ain't no thanks to you, I can't unwind, Can't tell her why.* 10/7/74 LHI JG *

SINEAD O'CONNOR
18/1/88 MAYO *Just call me Joe, Jump in the river, Still listening.* Sinead O'Connor (v), Marco Perroni (g), Kevin Mooney (b). 18/11/87 MV4 PW MPK

MARY MARGARET O'HARA
22/3/89 SKINNER *Year in song, Body's in trouble, Walk that way, Dark dear heart.* Mary Margaret O'Hara (v), Rusty McCarthy (g), Don Rooke (ag,lsg), David Piltch (b), Hugh Marsh (vi), Kevan McKenzie (d). 26/2/89 MV4 PW TdB & TD

25/11/89 SAT. SEQ. *Dear darling, Have you gone, Blue Christmas.* O'Hara, Rooke, McCarthy only. 20/11/89 EG2 KH DMC

28/1/90 KERSHAW *When you know why you're happy, A new day, Nothing is wrong, Blue Christmas.* Full band as 26/2/89. 9/11/89 MV5 DG MR

A BAND CALLED O
3/10/74 PEEL *No manners, Angelica, Sidewalk ship.* Derek Ballard (d), Mark Anders (b), Craig Anders (lg), Pix (gv), Peter Filleul (elp). 24/9/74 MV4 TW BC

24/3/75 PEEL *Nothing I wouldn't do, Fine white wine, Sleeping, Some people.* 18/3/75 MV4 * BC?

6/5/76 PEEL *Still burning, Paradise blue, Feel alright, A smile is diamond.* Jeff Bannister (kv) r. Filleul. 23/3/76 MV4 TW MR

18/3/77 PEEL *The knife, Time seems to fly, Back alley lightning.* 22/2/77 MV4 * MR

OCCAPELLA
18/7/84 SKINNER *Facts of life, No adulation in the valley, Don't change your ways, All hung up on you.* James Locke (d), Nico Vitto (b), Tony de Winton Puller (gk), Bill Innes (sx), Jackie Joyce (v), Liz Curtis (v). 17/6/84 MV5 DG ME

OCCASIONAL WORD ENSEMBLE
24/7/68 NIGHT RIDE *Brownville blues, George King, I'm so glad, Mrs Jones, Georgia skin game.* Ric Sanders, Mitch Howard, John Brown, Richard Sylvester. 24/7/68 S2 DK *

OCEAN COLOUR SCENE
8/10/90 GOODIER *Fly me, Yesterday today, Blue deep ocean, Sway.* Simon Fowler (v), Stephen Cradock (g,bkv), Damon Minchyela (b), Oscar Harrison (d,bkv). 29/9/90 MV5 MC~

OFFSPRING
5/5/83 PEEL *One more night, Beautiful eyes, Baby, Round and round.* Les Paul Morrison (bv), Alan Williams (g), Sean Jones (g), Hefyn Hughes (dv). 27/4/83 MV4 RP NG

AYUB OGADA
23/3/89 KERSHAW *Obiero, Ondiek, Dala.* Ayub Ogada (nyatiti,lv), Nana Tsiboe (gonge), Nana Appaih (mpintintua, odukroga, suitcase,lv), Edwardo Periera (perc). 23/2/89 MV4 DG MWT

OK JIVE
18/5/81 SKINNER *To you, Not tonight, Where ya bin?, Lose control.* Ruby Jive (v), Bavon Wayne-Wayne (lg), Datsun Cherry (rg,bkv), Chopper (b,bkv), Lee (d,perc). 14/5/81 LHI JS *

OLDHAM TINKERS
13/1/75 PEEL *A man like thee, Signora, Charlie Chaplin, Oldham's burning sands.* John Howarth (bj,v), Gerry Kearns (gv), Larry Kearns (mnd,v). 30/12/74 * JW *
9/6/91 KERSHAW *Oldham's burning sands, Come whome to thi childer an me, The Rochdale mashers, John Willie's horse.* * Rec. date unknown * c. JL *

DR. OLOH & HIS MILO JAZZ BAND
9/11/91 PEEL *Cobbah me, Yawohammi, Aleluyah tumbay, Ajuba.* Mohammed Dean (perc,bkv), Abdul Bangura (d,bkv), Brima Kamara (d), Dr Oloh (lv), Mohammed Kamara (d,bkv), Sineh Konika (lead d), Alie Kamara (tr,bkv). 10/10/91 MV4 DG NG&JT

OMAR
19/8/91 GOODIER *Positive, Your loss my gain, Walk in the park, Serious style.* Phil Hudson (g), Darren Abraham (d), Greg Harwood (b), Brian Henry (k), Omar Hammer (kv). 29/6/91 MV5 MC~

THE ONANS
29/12/87 LONG *Train to Scotland, Breast-fed, Moment, Bigot on a horse.* Neil Herd (gv), Julian Crouch (bv), Roy O'Shea (d). 20/12/87 MV4 PW MA&TdB

ONE
15/5/70 BLACK *Stop pulling and pushing me, It's all up to you, Near the bone, Cautiously.* Alan Marshall (gpv,tamb,cga,hp), Bobby Sass (g), Kevin Fogarty (g), Brent Forbes (b), Norman Leppard (fl,ts), Conrad Isidore (d). 8/4/70 AO2 JM *

ONE BY ONE
3/8/91 PEEL *Spineless/Kneejerk, Power of lump/World on fire, Satan in the grooves/Tell me, Weakness (night & day).* Big Bad Sned (bv), Alec (b), Micky McGuiness (gv), Fazzy (bv,'road machine'). 18/6/91 MV5 MR~

1,000 VIOLINS
25/9/85 PEEL *Why is it always December, The candle man, Though it poured the next day I never noticed the rain, The sun ain't gonna shine anymore.* Sean O'Neill (d), Colin Gregory (g,b,bkv), Dave Walmsley (k,g,tp,bkv), John Wood (v). 15/9/85 MV5 DG ME
2/12/86 PEEL *Almost dead and nigh on forty years to go, I was depending on you to be my Jesus, If I were a bullet then for sure I'd find a way to your heart, No-one was saving the world.* Darren Swindle (b), Peter Day (d) r. O'Neill. 4/11/86 * DG ME
14/9/87 LONG *Hey man that's beautiful, The only time I got to rock was in my granny's chair, Poet, A place to surf.* Jan Addey (d) r. Day. 2/9/87 MV4 PW MPK&FK

ONE TO ONE
9/3/88 MAYO *Sweet love, Slow down, Only you, Tracks of my tears.* Andy Cleall (gv), Vince Randall (lg), Mickey James (k), Grant Bowden (b,bkv), Dennis Dance (d). 3/2/88 MV4 HP MPK

REMMY ONGALA
4/8/88 KERSHAW *Nasikitika, Nifanyenini, Dole tupu, Usingizi.* Remmy Ongala (gv) 'and Orchestra Super Matimila': Muhindi Haji (b), Freddy Mwalasha (g), Ayas Hassan (g), Matu Dikwndia (sx), Saidi Jumanna (perc), Lawrence Chuki (d). 21/7/88 MV4 DG MR
2/5/92 KERSHAW *Narudi nyumbani, Bwana mdogo, Nisemenini, Dunia.* Ongala 'and the Super Matimila Band': Haji, Cosmos Chidumule (lv), Mjusi Shemboza (g), Yussuph (d), Batii Osenga Ipopolipo. 5/4/92 MV3 DG SA&JT

THE ONLY ONES
20/9/77 PEEL *Lovers of today, Oh no, Telescopic love, In betweens.* Peter Perrett (lv,rg), John Perry (lg), Mike Kellie (d), Alan Mair (b). 13/9/77 MV6 MB MR
14/4/78 PEEL *Another girl another planet, The beast, No peace for the wicked, Language problem.* 5/4/78 MV4 MB NG
3/1/79 PEEL† *Miles from nowhere, Flaming torch, From here to eternity, Prisoner.* 19/12/78 MV4 TW MR
2/6/80 PEEL† *The happy pilgrim, The big sleep, Oh Lucinda (love becomes a habit), Why don't you kill yourself?* 21/5/80 MV4 DG NG
   † All sessions on Strange Fruit SFRCD102.

ONWARD INTERNATIONAL
13/2/84 PEEL *Nebuchadnezar, Pe'no gelo, Sambo Doobonnay.* Simon Edwards (b,perc,v), Kim Burton (p,perc), Bosco (perc,v), Roberto Pla (perc), Dave Patiman (perc), Peter Thomas (perc,tb,v), Paul D'Oliveira (tp,perc,v), Paul Spong (tp,perc), Dave Bitelli (sx,cl,fl,perc,v). 1/2/84 MV4 DG NG
28/11/84 PEEL *Lagrimas, Calix bento, Ponteio, Onward international calypso.* Bitelli, Bosco, Pla, Burton, Edwards, Patiman, Rick Taylor (tb), Mike O'Gorman (tp,flh), Steve Sidwell (tp,flh), Dawson Miller (perc). 20/11/84 MV5 DG MR

ORANGE JUICE
30/10/80 PEEL† *Poor old soul, You old eccentric you, Falling and laughing, Lovesick.* Edwyn Collins (gv), James Kirk (gv), David McClymont (b,bkv), Steven Daly (d,perc,bkv). 21/10/80 MV4 JS MR
   'By the time our single 'Blue boy' appeared we were being investigated for fraud by the Social Security in Glasgow. They'd gathered together a lot of press cuttings and taped this Peel session,' says Edwyn Collins. † On CD version of 'Ostrich Churchyard' compilation, Postcard DUBH 922CD.
19/1/81 READ *Upwards and onwards, Wan light, Felicity.* 9/1/81 LHI DG *
10/8/81 PEEL *Dying day, Holiday hymn, Three cheers for our side, Blokes on 45.* 3/8/81 MV4 TW DD
4/5/82 JENSEN *Mud in your eye, I can't help myself, In spite of it all, Turn away.* Collins, McClymont, Malcolm Ross (g,kv), Zeke Manyika (d). 25/4/82 MV5 DG ME
5/3/83 LONG *Lovesick, Flesh of my flesh, Rip it up.* 14/2/83 PHM c.JL PSM
22/2/84 JENSEN *What presence?, Salmon fishing in New York, Bridge.* Collins, Manyika, Clare Kenny (bv). 9/2/84 MV5 JP MPK

THE ORB
19/12/89 PEEL† *A huge ever-growing pulsating brain that rules from the centre of the ultraworld (Loving you).* Jimmy Cauty (pd,mx), Alex Paterson (sc,dj). 3/12/89 MV3 DG Engineered by Jimmy Cauty
13/10/90 PEEL† *Backside of the moon (Tranquility lunar orbit), Into the 4th dimension (Essenes in starlight).* Paterson, Thrash (mx), Miquette Giraudy (k), Steve Hillage (g,k,prg), Andy Falconer (k,prg). 2/10/90 MV4 MR~ † On StrangeFruit SFRCD118.
5/6/92 PEEL *Oobe, No fun.* Paterson, Thrash, Simon Phillips (b), Nick Burton (b), Greg ('engineer'). 12/5/92 MV4 MR~

ORCHESTRA JAZIRA
18/7/83 PEEL *Money, Sakabo.* Kwadwo Oteng (k), Fish (tb), Jane Shorter (ts), Nicky Scott Francis (al), Isaac Tagoe (cga,v), Emanuel Odi (perc), Martin Nimoy (perc,v), Folo Graaf (rg), Ben Mandelson (lg), Opata Azu (b), Nigel Watson (d). 20/6/83 MV4 TW MC

ORCHESTRAL MANOEUVRES IN THE DARK
3/9/79 PEEL *Julia's song, Messages, Red frame white light, Bunker soldiers.* Andy McCluskey (bv,dm), Paul Humphries (kv). 20/8/79 MV4 TW DD
21/4/80 PEEL *Pretending to see the future, Enola Gay†, Dancing, Motion and heart.* & David Hughes (k), Malcolm Holmes (d). 14/4/80 MV4 TW DD

   † On 'I and only' BOJCD025.
6/10/80 PEEL *Annex, The Misunderstanding, The more I see you.* Martin Cooper (sy-2 only) r. Hughes. 29/9/80 MV4 TW DD
21/2/83 PEEL *Genetic engineering, Of all the things we've made, ABC auto-industry, Bunker soldiers.* 29/1/83 MV4 DG HP&MC

THE ORCHIDS
8/5/90 PEEL *Dirty clothing, Frank Desalvo, And when I wake up, Caveman.* James Hackett (v,ag), Matthew Drummond (g), John Scally (g), Chris Quinn (d). 8/4/90 MV3 DG MWT

THE ORIGINAL MIRRORS
7/2/80 PEEL *Reflections, Flying, Boys cry.* Steve Allen (lv), Ian Broudie (g,bkv), Jonathan Perkins (k,bkv), Phil Spalding (b,bkv), Pete Kircher (d,bkv); & Chris Hunter (al-2,3 only). 22/1/80 MV4 JS MR
21/4/80 READ *Sharp words, Could this be heaven?, Chains of love, Feel like a train.* 27/3/80 MV4 CL *

ORIGINAL SINNERS
7/8/92 FRI. ROCK *Shoot it up, 123 for love, Love or the money, Heartbreak road.* Paul Ratcliffe (b), Richard Elliott (g), Pete Stevens (v), Dan Turner (g), Dave Axford (d). 17/7/92 MV5 DD MC

THE ORSON FAMILY
25/10/83 PEEL *Wear that pointed bra, Snakin' along, Big red gretsch, Crawdad hole.* Vernon (g), Ruby (g), Skully (v), Brewster (d). 19/10/83 MV4 RP NG
11/6/84 JENSEN *In the courtyard, Sweetest embrace, Rock 'n' roll with you, Tear in the heart.* Ruby, Vernon, John Orson (v) David O. (d), Vincent (b). 24/5/84 MV5 MHY MPK

JOHNNY OSBOURNE AND THE INSTIGATORS
26/3/84 JENSEN *Give a little love, Water pumpin', Truth and rights, Get crackin'.* Johnny Osbourne (v), Dingle (rg), Dave (d), Oliver (perc, bkv), Conway (lg), Leroy (b), Tony (k), Courtney (perc, bkv). 15/3/84 MV4 JP MPK

OSENI
3/7/73 PEEL *Naira & Kobo, In praise of Sonny Ade.* 6-piece African group, line-up unknown. Rec. date unknown OS * *

OSIBISA
1/8/70 TOP GEAR *Aiyko bia, Music for gong gong, Black ant.* Files missing, but line-up probably Teddy Osei (sx,fl,dv), Mac Tontoh (tp,flh), Sol Amarfio (d,bgo), Lasisi Amoa (cga,sx), Spartacus R (bn), Wendell Richardson (g), Robert Bailey (k). 27/7/70 * * BC
26/2/71 BLACK *The dawn, Think about the people, Akwaba, Spirit up above.* 10/2/71 T1 JM JWH
20/5/71 HENRY *Survival, Kotoko, X sharp, Phallus C.* 12/5/71 MV4 (or AO2) MB MH&MF
10/7/71 TOP GEAR *Oranges, Phallus C, Woyaya.* 14/6/71 * * BC
11/1/72 PEEL *Woyaya, Survival, Akwaba.* 4/1/72 * * *
16/3/74 ROCK ON *Happy children, Fire, Bon bon, Music for gong gong.* * 11/3/74 * BA *

JOHN OTWAY AND WILD WILLY BARRETT
26/6/78 PEEL *Place farm way, Oh my body is making me, Can't complain, The Alamo.* John Otway (lv,ag), Andrew Thomas (g), Paul Sandeman (b), Dave Holmes (d). 14/6/78 MV4 JG NG
   Wild Willy Barrett, booked to appear, was 'fired by telegram for saying he had measles when he was probably watching the World Cup'-JG on sheet.
8/6/81 SKINNER *Landslide, Best dream, Oh! my body is making me, (Give it) Head butts, Baby's in the club.* John Otway (gv), Wild Willy Barrett (gb,dm). 22/5/81 LHI DG ME

OUT ON BLUE SIX
16/9/80 PEEL *Johnny, Mascara, Soft sarcasm, Party mood.* Kate Sekules (v,b), Sarah Cramp (bkv), Tim Oliver (bkv), Nigel Holland (b,v), Carl Marsh (g), Geoff Woolley (k), Mike Daly (d). 9/9/80 MV4 JS MR
24/6/81 PEEL *I'm the man, Personal politics, Examples, Just one face.* Cramp, Oliver out. 17/6/81 LHI CL NG

THE OUTCASTS

25/5/81 PEEL *Gangland warfare, The end of the rising sun, Programme love, Machine gun.* Greg Cowan (b,lv), Martin Cowan (gv), Colin Cowan (d), Raymond Falls (d), Colin Getgood (g). 13/5/81 LHI CL NG

29/9/82 PEEL *Winter, Magnum force, Sex and glory, Frustration.* Ross Graham (perc,bkv) r. C. Cowan. 15/9/82 MV4 RP NG

OVERLORD X

1/12/87 PEEL *I'm deaf, X in effect, Lyrical content.* Overlord X (dj,prd), The Don (prd). 24/11/87 * DG MR&MC

15/8/88 PEEL *The hard core, X posse, The dedication, Bax the place.* Sir Premetee (sc,dj) r. The Don. 2/8/88 MV4 MR~

THE OYSTER BAND

2/7/87 KERSHAW *Jacky Robinsons and all a'siden, Pigsty Billy, The early days of a better nation, The Oxford girl.* John Jones (v,ml), Ian Telfer (fd,k), Alan Prosser (g,bkv), Ian Kearey (b,g,bkv), Russell Lax (d). 11/6/87 * DG NG&FK

16/10/89 CAMPBELL *I fought the law, Love vigilantes, Too late now, Polish plain.* Rec. date unknown PRIV * *
[See 'June Tabor']

PALADIN

22/7/71 HENRY *Give me your hand, Bad times, Watching the world pass by.* Keith Webb (d), Lou Stonebridge (lv,p,hca), Derek Foley (gv), Pete Becket (v), Peter Solley (g,bv). 14/7/71 MV4 MB MH&MF

Debuted live from the Paris on Rosko Show 27/3/71, prod. AD. Next appeared on Peel Sunday Concert, rec'd 10/6/71 PS, TX 27/6/71.

21/10/71 DRUMMOND *Third world, Watching the world pass by, Fill up your heart.* 11/10/71 MV5 MB MH&MF

26/5/72 PEEL *Well we might, Sweet music, Get on deck (& Get one together, 7/7/72).* Joe Jammer r. Stonebridge, Foley. 2/5/72 T1 JM JWH&ME

PALAIS SCHAUMBURG

9/12/82 PEEL *3 nach 9, Pack die herzenaus, Hocke(e)y, Swingin' safari.* * 28/11/82 OS * *

PALE FOUNTAINS

3/8/82 PEEL *Lavinia's dream, (I'm a) Long shot for your love, Thank-you, The Norfolk Broads.* Michael Head (gv). Chris McCafferty (b), Thomas Whelan (d), Nathan Baxter (perc), John Millor (perc), Andy Diagram (tp). 19/7/82 * TW DD

14/5/83 LONG *Hey there Fred, Louisiana, Something on my mind.* * 9/5/83 PHM cJL PSM

PALE SAINTS

17/8/89 PEEL *She rides the waves, You tear the world in two, Way the world is, Time thief†.* Chris Cooper (d), Ian Masters (bv), Graeme Naysmith (g), Ashley Horner (g). 23/7/89 MV5 JW MA
† On 'New Season' SFRCD205.

PALLAS

30/3/84 FRI. ROCK *Cut and run, Shock treatment, Rise and fall/Heart attack.* Euan Lowson (v), Graeme Murray (b,bkv), Ronnie Brown (k,bkv), Niall Mathewson (lg,bkv), Derek Forman (d,bkv). 9/3/84 MV4 DG DD

PRAMJIT PAMMI

18/2/90 KERSHAW *Gabhroo Jawaan, Shankan churre laal, Video wala.* Pramjit Pammi (v), Inder Kalsi (b), Harjeet (sy), Kally Kalyan (dholak), Bina Mistry (bkv), Bindi Sagoo (d), Dhirin (g), Nawaazish Ali Khan (vi,md), Sunil Kalyan (tab). 25/1/90 * DG *

PANAMA JUG BAND

20/3/68 MY KIND OF FOLK *Whitewashed station, Going to Germany.* Ron Needes (mnd,jug), Anthony Ralph, Brian Strachan (lgbd), Dennis Parker (lv), Chris Anderson. 15/3/68 PCI FL *

20/8/69 PEEL *38 plug, Canned heat, Jailhouse, Going to*

Germany, Round and round. Needes, Strachan, Parker, Gary Compton (sp,wsh), Liz Harris (v). 31/7/69 PH PR *

PAPA FACE

23/2/84 PEEL *Hot hot hot, Skidip, MC Jamboree, Dedicated to I.* Donald Facey with the Reprobates: Riche Stevens (d), Alan Lane (g), Chris Lane (g), Ian Austen (b), Reg Graham (p), Angus Gaye (perc); & Bionic Rhona (bkv-I). 14/2/84 MV5 MRD TdB

12/11/84 LONG *Loafter, Face 'pon the Muke Line, Now you know, Gone continental.* 28/10/84 HP BYA&CLN PW&TD

PAPA LEVI

18/6/84 PEEL *Mi God mi king, The hit, Bonnie and Clyde.* Paul Robinson (d), George Oban (b), J. J. Belle (g), Carlton Ogilvie (k), Papa Levi (v). 9/6/84 MV5 DG MC

PAPA SPRAIN

21/3/92 PEEL *Time bath, I got stop, You are ten million needless people, Cliff tune.* Gary McKendry (b,g,v,p), Joseph Cassidy (g), Rudy Tambala (prg). 5/1/92 MV3 DG ME&RJ

See also BUTTERFLY CHILD: same studio, same producer, same engineer, same musicians; one week later, different name!

PAPA'S NEW FAITH

22/12/87 LONG *Through the roof, Every trip, Gather up, Bring you.* Martyn Jensen (v), Kevin Jensen (kg), Alex Silva (g,rec,bkv), Mike Ormsby (b,bkv), Kris Ayre (d). 2/12/87 MV4 SF MPK&TD

IVO PAPASOV

3/12/89 KERSHAW *Kopanitza, Stanke le konak sajbijke, Zaplakala e gorata, Stoyan ne majka dumashe, Smes'eno horo/Rachenitza.* Ivo Papasov (cl), Stefan Angelov (d), Radi Kazakov (b), Andrei Kamzamalov (g), Nesho Neshev (acc,sy), Yuri Yunakov (sx), Mariya Karafizieva (v). 31/10/89 MV5 DG TdB

PARIS ANGELS

27/9/90 PEEL *Scope, Smile, Stay†.* Simon Worrall (d), Scott Carey (b), Paul Wagstaff (g), Mark Adge (g), Steven Tajti (k), Rikki Turner (v), Jane Gill (bkv). 26/8/90 MV3 DG MA&FK
† On 'New Season' SFRCD205.

7/1/91 GOODIER *Perfume, Oh yes†, What goes on, Scope.* 27/10/90 MV5 MC~
† On 'Best of Mark Goodier' Nighttracks Mark1.

27/10/91 PEEL *Slippery man, Chaos, Breathless, GBF.* 10/9/91 MV5 PW ME&AM

GRAHAM PARKER AND THE RUMOUR

16/6/76 PEEL *White honey, Back door love, Don't ask me questions, Soul shoes.* Graham Parker (ag,lvg), Brinsley Schwarz (g,bkv), Martin Belmont (g,bkv), Bob Andrews (o,p,bkv), Andrew Bodnar (b,bkv), Stephen Goulding (d,bkv). 1/6/76 MV4 JG MR

15/11/76 PEEL *Hotel chambermaid, Pouring it all out, Help me shake it, Heat treatment.* 2/11/76 MV4 JG MR

DAVID PARKER

12/6/71 TOP GEAR *Lazy, If I ever, Conclusions, Dark-eyed lady.* * 24/5/71 * * *

PARTNERS IN CRIME

29/11/84 INTO THE MUSIC *Hollywood dreams, Gypsy tricks, She's got eyes for you, What does it take?* John Coghlan (d), Mac Macaffrey (b), Ray Major (g), Mark de Vanchque (k), Noel McCalla (v). 17/11/84 MV4 DG MC

DON PARTRIDGE

11/2/68 TOP GEAR *I'm a goin' away, Old Joe Clark, The wayward boy.* Don Partridge (gv).

Debuted live from PH on Country Meets Folk, 20/1/68 [M]. 30/1/68 AO2 BA *&BC

PARTY DICTATOR

13/7/91 PEEL *Pressure, Bagger, Dreamland, Beam me up.* Popel (d), Matthias (b,bkv), Ole (g,bkv), Nick (lv). 19/5/91 MV3 DG ME&GPR

THE PASSAGE

27/11/80 PEEL *Dark times†, Shave your head, Devils and angels, The Shadows.* Joey McKechnie (d,bkv), Dick

Witts (k,bkv), Andy Wilson (g,sy,bkv), Lizzy Johnson (lv). 18/11/80 LHI DG MR
† On 'Manchester- so much to answer for' SFRCD202.

14/10/81 PEEL *Rod of iron, Form and void, Man of war, Love is as.* Wilson, Witts only. 30/9/81 MV4 CL NG

7/6/82 PEEL *A day, Empty words, Horse play.* & Paul Mahoney (d). 24/5/82 MV4 TW AP

27/10/82 PEEL *Watching you dance, Dark times, Man of war, Love is as, Horseplay, Empty words.* McKechnie (d) returns. 11/10/82 Recorded at The Ritz, Manchester. JL *

12/2/83 LONG *Clear as crystal, Angleland, Dogstar, Sing the praise.* * 7/2/83 PHM cJL PSM

THE PASSIONS

29/11/79 PEEL *Snow, Man on the tube, Oh no it's you, Why me?* Barbara Gogan (lv,g), Clive Timperley (gk,bkv), Clare Bidwell (b,bkv), Richard Williams (d). 19/11/79 MV4 TW DD

14/5/80 PEEL *Hunted, Real mean, Absentee, Lies.* 7/5/80 JE NG
'On my walk round the building at 20.30 last night, I head female voices coming from the Gents toilet. I went to investigate and found two young ladies by the Gents' stand-up having their photographs taken in a most unfemale fashion. I told them to leave immediately. Outside the toilet, I told them in no uncertain manner that they were behaving in a most disgusting manner. I told the photographer what trouble he could be in for taking these pictures without permission on BBC premises, and also the group could be banned from all future recordings. The group then became most concerned over the whole incident'. Memo from House Foreman, Maida Vale Studios, to his superiors, 8/5/80.

17/11/80 PEEL *Someone special, The Swimmer, Bachelor girls, German film star.* David Agar (b,bkv) r. Bidwell. 5/11/80 LHI DG NG

5/1/81 READ *Oh no it's you, Hunted, German film star, I radiate.* 28/11/80 LHI DG AP

13/8/81 SKINNER *Runaway, The square, Into the night, Some fun.* 30/7/81 MV4 DG MR

16/3/82 JENSEN *Hold on don't go, Jump for joy, Small talk, White lies.* Kevin Armstrong (g), Jeff Smith (k) r. Timperley. 18/2/82 MV4 JS *

THE PASSMORE SISTERS

5/8/85 PEEL *Shatter, Story of a working man, Goodbye to the girl, Red.* Adrian Lee (d), Howi Taylor (b), Peter Richardson (g), Martin Sadofski (v). 28/7/85 MV5 DG ME

11/11/86 PEEL *Strong for Europe, Sally why?, Goodbye Billy Wild†, Hit the ground.* Brian Roberts (g,bkv) r. Richardson. 5/10/86 * DG MK

28/7/87 LONG *These things I feel, Foundry of lies†, Steven's story, All I need is change.* Sadofski, Taylor, Roberts, Richardson, Robert Grace (d). 5/7/87 MV4 HP TdB&MPK
† On LP 'First love, last rites', Sharp Records CALP1, plus possibly one other session track re-titled.

THE PASTELS

7/2/84 PEEL *Something going on, Stay with me till morning, Tomorrow the sun will shine, Trains go down the track.* Stephen Pastel (gv), Brian Superstar (g), Martin (bv), Bernice (d); & Aggie (v,o), Joe (from Hendon) (gv). 17/1/84 MV4 MRD MPK

31/7/84 SKINNER *She always cries on Sundays†, Twenty-five unfinished plays, Million tears, Baby honey.* Joe out; & David Keegan (vi). 1/7/84 MV5 DG MPK
† On LP 'Stuck on The Pastels' Creation CRELP031.

PATRICK STREET

20/10/88 KERSHAW *McKenna's jigs, East Clare reel, Holy ground, Facing the chair.* Andy Irvine (v,mnd,hca), Gerry O'Bierne (g), Arty McGlynn (g), Kevin Burke (fd), Jackie Daly (acc). 22/9/88 MV4 DG TdB

THE PATTERSONS
17/8/85 KERSHAW *Chords of fame, Crazy love.* Billy Bragg (v) & others unknown (v). Rec. date unknown Y2 * SR

PATTO
17/4/70 BLACK *When they beat the drum, Hanging rope (& Red glow, 29/5/70).* Mike Patto (g), Ollie Halsall (g), Clive Griffiths (b), John Halsey (b). 11/3/70 AO2 JM *
    As The Time Box, did many pop sessions in late 60s. Changed name in '70 [M].
12/5/70 HARDING *Time to die, Hold me back, Hanging rope.* 27/3/70 MV4 MB (or PR) MH&MF
10/11/70 HARDING *Government man, Hard life, Love me.* 3/11/70 MV5 MB (or PR) MH&MF
5/4/71 HARRIS *Money bag, The man, Alright.* 30/3/71 MV5 JM *
6/7/71 HARDING *Give it all away, You you point your finger, Air raid shelter.* 28/6/71 MV5 MB MH&MF
    Group later banned, after failing to turn up for a *Sounds of the Seventies* session in October 1971. Ban lifted early in 1973.
5/2/73 HARRIS *Flat-footed woman, General Custer, Singing the blues on reds.* & Dave Brooks (ts). 24/1/73 LH1 PR *
27/2/73 PEEL *Holy Toledo, San Antone, Loud green song.* 12/2/73 T1 JW *
16/3/73 SEQUENCE *Sausages, Hold me back, Landlord, I got rhythm.* 13/2/73 T1 JM NG

OWEN PAUL BAND
13/11/84 LONG *Pleased to meet you, Bring me back that spark, Prime time, Somewhere South of Africa.* Owen Paul (v), Ritchie Williams (g), Mark Radcliffe (b), Martin Saunders (d), Steve French (k), Phil Smith (sx). 3/10/84 MV5 JS MPK

PAVEMENT
10/7/92 PEEL *Circa 1762, Kentucky cocktail, Secret knowledge of backroads, Here.* Gary Young (d), Mark Ibold (b,bkv), Bob Nastanovich (d), Spiral Stairs (gv), Stephen Malkmus (gv). 23/6/92 MV4 MR~

PEACE
22/12/71 PEEL *Heartbreaker, Like water, Seven angels.* Paul Rodgers (gv), Stuart MacDonald (b), Mick Underwood (d). 30/11/71 MV4 JW BC

PEACHES
5/9/74 PEEL *B for Charlie, Methley, Street finding man.* Nick Shillito (gv), Roger Davis (gv), Nick Howard (k), Lucian Camp (b), Jim Bamber (d). 29/8/74 LH1 TW *
6/2/75 PEEL *Who dunnit, Fings, The Sturmey Archer kid, Never look back.* Thomas Atley (k) r. Howard. 23/1/75 MV4 TW *
22/1/76 PEEL *Wild man, Lucy and the tiger, Heart of steel, Just another song.* Martin Isaacs (gv) r. Davis, Atley; & Art Gar-Belcher (sx). 15/1/76 MV4 TW *

THE PEARLFISHERS
8/7/91 GOODIER *Sacred, A bottle of the best, Heaven help the child, You want love.* David Scott (gv,ag), Mil Stricevic (b), Jim Gash (d,b,bkv), Brian McAlpine (k). 30/3/91 MV5 MC~

ANN PEEBLES AND THE RED DOG BAND
10/10/74 PEEL *You keep me hanging on, Slipped tripped and fell in love, Do I need you, I can't stand the rain.* Ann Peebles (lv) & 6-piece Red Dog Band (unknown). 9/10/74 MV4 TW BAI

BOB PEGG AND NICK STRUTT
10/7/73 PEEL *Kirbstall forge, Baroque's off, The wild man of the hill, Headrow song.* * 3/7/73 * * *

PELE
12/8/91 GOODIER *Megalomania, Raid the palace, Name and number, Time is money.* Ian Prowse (g), Andrea Nicholson (vi), Paul Dallison (d), Andrew Roberts (o,p,g), James MacAllister (b). 3/8/91 MV5 MA PA

PENDRAGON
25/11/83 FRI. ROCK *Victims of life, Pleasure of hope, The black knight.* Nick Barrett (gv), Nigel Harris (d), Peter Gee (b), John Barnfield (k). 11/11/83 * TW DD

PENETRATION
10/7/78 PEEL *Future daze, Vision, Stone heroes, Movement.* Pauline Murray (lv), Fred Purser (lg,bkv), Neil Floyd (rg), Robert Blamire (b), Gary Smallman (d). 5/7/78 MV4 BS NG
7/3/79 PEEL *Danger signs, Last saving grace, Coming up for air.* 28/2/79 MV4 JS NG
15/10/79 READ *Shout above the noise, Lifeline (16/10), On reflection (17/10), Last saving grace (18/10).* 21/9/79 * * *

PENTANGLE
18/2/68 TOP GEAR *Travelling song, Turn your money green, Soho, Let no man steal your thyme.* John Renbourn (gv), Bert Jansch (gv), Jacqui McShee (gv), Terry Cox (d), Danny Thompson (b). 29/1/68 PC1 BA PR
    'Unanimous, enthusiastic pass' from panel. Next, contracted for NIGHT RIDE date 9/5/68, TX 29/5/68 (untraceable); then live on Country Meets Folk 15/6/68 PH.
7/7/68 TOP GEAR *Every night, I'm lonely, Forty-eight, Orlando (& No more my lord, Bransle gay/La rotta/The Earl of Salisbury, 4/8/68).* 2/7/68 PC1 BA DT
    2nd live appearance on Country Meets Folk, PH 17/8/68.
3/11/68 TOP GEAR *Sovay, Sweet child, I loved a lass, In your mind (& I've got a feeling, 15/12/68).* 23/9/68 PC1 BA *
    3rd Country Meets Folk show, Live at PH 7/12/68.
18/5/69 TOP GEAR *Once I had a sweetheart, Hunting song, Bruton town, Sally go round the races.* 12/5/69 PH JW *
    Live on R1 Club, PS 15/5/69; & Country Meets Folk, PH 7/6/69 [M: dozens, including own series in Dec/Jan 69/70].
12/11/70 HENRY *Wedding dress, Maid in love, Lord Franklin, Sally free and easy.* 5/11/70 AO2 MB MH&MF
20/2/71 R2 NIGHT RIDE *Train song, Helping hand, Way behind the sun, Hunting song, Sally free and easy, Will the circle be unbroken.* 8/2/71 AO2 DDR *
19/4/71 HARRIS *Circle, When I get home, Helping hand, Wedding dress.* 6/4/71 T1 JM JWH
29/11/71 HARRIS *Lord Franklin, Willie of Winsbury, Lady of Carlisle, Will the circle be unbroken.* 9/11/71 T1 JM NG
17/7/72 HARRIS *Cherry tree carol, Jump baby jump, Lady of Carlisle (& People on the highway, No love is sorrow, 9/10/72).* 19/6/72 T1 JG&PD *

PERE UBU
7/8/89 PEEL *We have the technology, Miss you, Bus called happiness.* Scott Krause (d), Tony Maimone (b,bkv), Jim Jones (g,bkv), Eric Feldman (k,bkv), David Thomas (v,acc). 27/6/89 ED DG MR

PERFECT DAZE
25/7/88 PEEL *Break it away, Another kind of view, The back of the line, Ticket don't go.* Timi Ramm Bamm (b), Wolfie Retard (b), Wild Johnny Rescoe (g), Scruff Setzer (gv), Laurence Repo (v). 10/7/88 MV5 DG ME

PERFECT STRANGERS
8/8/83 JENSEN *Pain and pleasure, Without you, This blue, Over and over.* Roderick Syers (kgv), Martha McGowan (kv): & Anne Dudley (k), Hugh Ashton (d,prg). 31/7/83 MV4 DG ME

PERFECT VISION
23/8/84 PEEL *On edge, Biff baff, Somersault of love, Laugh at breakage.* Steve Xerri (kv), Giles Thomas (g), James Daniel (b), John Lewin (gv). 15/8/84 MV5 JWI NG

CHRISTINE PERFECT
1/11/69 TOP GEAR *No road is the right road, When you say, Sunshine hours, Pen in hand.* Christine Perfect (pv) & The Derek Wadsworth Orchestra. 13/10/69 * * *

PERSIAN RISK
11/7/86 FRI. ROCK *Break free, One day one night, Women and rock, Jane.* Steve Hopgood (d), Nick Hughes (b),

Phil Vokins (g), Carl Sentance (v), Philip James (k). 6/6/86 MV4 DG DD

PERSONAL COLUMN
23/11/82 PEEL *The same old situation, Friction, Red, Dangerous places.* Terry Sterling (d), Marc Vormawah (g,lv), Mike Hayes (b). 10/11/82 * RP *
28/7/83 PEEL *Strictly confidential, Sleight of hand, Ignorance is bliss, Crusade.* Colin Brown (k), Rob Boardman (g) join. 16/7/83 MV4 DG MR
4/8/83 JENSEN *A woman's place, Dangerous places, Point of no return, What am I doing here?* Phil Hargreaves (sx) joins. 24/7/83 MV4 DG ME
16/4/84 PEEL *World in action, British style, Cosmetic surgery, The price you pay.* Tom Fenner (d) r. Sterling. 4/4/84 MV5 PSI NG

THE PERSUADERS
30/1/85 PEEL *Captain of the ship, Great expectations, Music for pleasure, Somethings.* Brian Farrell (d), Dave Price (b), John Gillin (g), John Jenkins (k), Tony Upham (v); & the Brett Sinclair horns: Tony Peers & Tony Griffiths (tp), Andy Herd (tb), Paul Thomas (al), Karen Pettigrew (ts), & Marc Vormawah (bkv). 16/12/84 MV5 DG ME
28/5/85 LONG *Day after day, To be free, Another time another place, A night on the town.* Five-piece plus Peers, Pettigrew, Robert Yates (tb), Steven Yates (al). 15/5/85 MV5 BYA MPK

PET HATE
12/4/85 FRI. ROCK *Girls grow up too fast, Cry of the wild, Love me madly, Wreck the radio.* Steve Roberts (d), Dave Roberts (b), Jimmy Beatson (lg), James Page (g), Alistair Terry (agv). 8/3/85 MV4 DG DD

PETER AND THE TEST TUBE BABIES
27/10/80 PEEL *Moped lads, Beat up the Mods, Elvis is dead, Maniac.* Peter Bywaters (lv), Derek Greening (g,bkv), Chris Marchant (b,bkv), Nick Loizides (d,bkv). 14/10/80 MV4 JS MR

THE PETTICOATS
23/10/80 PEEL *Dream, Paranoia, Life-no.* Stef Petticoat (d,b,g,lv). 15/10/80 MV4 BS NG

PFM
14/6/73 PEEL *Photos of ghosts, Mister nine till five, Celebration, River of life.* Mauro Pagani (vi,ww), Franco Mussida (gv), Flavio Premoli (kv), Giorgio Piazza (b), Franz Di Gioccio (dv). 11/6/73 LH1 BA *
22/11/73 PEEL *Il banchetto, La carrozza di hans, Dove e quando.* Yan Patrick Djivas (b) r. Piazza. 12/11/73 LH1 BA *

THE PHARAOHS
13/10/80 READ *Same dream, Even on eleven, Berta, Sometimes think of you.* Thompson Smurthwaite II (lv), Bernie Kelly (d), Pete Fitton (g), Dusty Hall (al), James Mackie (ts,k), Paul Boardman (tb), Phil Boardman (tp), Adam Williams (b). 3/10/80 MV4 DG PS&MC

DR. PHIBES
11/5/91 PEEL *Burning cross, Dreaming/Insomnia, L.A. woman.* Keith York (d), Lee Belsham (b), Howard King (gv). 18/4/91 MV5 DG MWT&JB

PHILISTINES JR.
7/8/92 PEEL *Big chief, Happy birthday Captain Columbus, Army song, Thank you John Peel.* Adam Pierce (d), Tarquin Katis (bv), Peter Katis (gv). 21/7/92 MV4 TdB PA&TdB

SHAWN PHILLIPS
29/5/71 TOP GEAR *Hey Miss Lovely, Spring wind, Salty tears, Withered roses (& L. Ballad, 11/9/71).* Shawn Phillips (agv). 10/5/71 PH JW *
19/3/73 HARRIS *Took a walk, Anello, Dream queen.* & Pete Walmesley (g), Barry de Souza (d), Pete Robinson (k). 7/3/73 LH1 PR BAI&MG
27/3/73 PEEL *Troof.* 19/3/73 T1 JW *
8/10/74 PEEL *See you/Planscape, 92 years, Talking in the garden/Furthermore, January 1st.* Jon Gustafson (b) r.

Walmesley (backing band is original line-up of Quatermass). 1/10/74 MV4 TW *

STEVE PHILLIPS
23/7/87 KERSHAW *Let's get drunk again, Broke and hungry, The panic is on, I'm running wild.* Steve Phillips (gv). 18/6/87 * DG NG&MC

4/3/90 KERSHAW *Wake up Mary, Don't forget it, I just telephone upstairs, 125 express, Crossroad blues.* 21/12/89 MV5 DG TD

PHOENIX
16/5/74 PEEL *Double whammy, Way behind the moon, Warm warm sweet thing.* David Rohoman (d), Chris Birkin (b), Chris Smith (pv), Adrian Pietryga (g), Mick Paice (hca,sx), Roy St. John (v). 7/5/74 LH1 * BC

PIANO RED
10/10/77 PEEL *Shake rattle and roll, Pinetop boogie, Dr. Feelgood, St. Louis blues, I'm leaving, Goodbye, Please don't talk about me when I'm gone, It's a sin to tell a lie, Blues blues blues, The right string but the wrong yo-yo.* Piano Red (p). 28/9/77 MV4 DP NG

PIGBAG
21/7/81 SKINNER *Vile in, Human race, Eating burgers, Honk wild.* Simon Underwood (b,vi), Chris Leigh (tp), Ollie Moore (ts), Roger Freeman (perc,o,tb), James Milton-Johnstone (gb,al), Chip Carpenter (d,perc). 12/7/81 MV4 DG ME&HP

15/9/81 PEEL *Me and your shadow, You can wiggle my toe to that, The dug-out.* 9/9/81 MV4 DG NG

18/3/82 JENSEN *En ti la tierra (in the earth), Caldonia (your feet's too big), Jack Frost (we don't need you).* 14/2/82 MV4 DG *

3/2/83 JENSEN *Ubud, The bank song, Can't see for looking, Smiling faces.* Underwood, Leigh, Johnstone, Moore, Oscar Verden (k), Brian Nevill (d,sx,perc), Angela Jaeger (v,perc), Kofi-Adu (d). 27/1/83 MV4 JS MPK

PIGBROS
21/8/85 PEEL *Cheap life, Hedonist hat, Lick bones, War food.* Fuzz (d), Jonathan (b), Nick (gv), Richard (sx,g). 11/8/85 MV5 DG MR

6/5/86 PEEL *Bad attitude, In doubt, Immensity home, What counts?* Svor Naan (g,sx,cl) r. Richard. 27/4/86 MV5 DG ME&TD

PIL
17/12/79 PEEL *Pop tones, Careering, Chant.* John Lydon (lv), Keith Levine (g,sy), Jah Wobble (b), Martin Atkins (d). 10/12/79 MV4 TW DD

25/2/92 GOODIER *Cruel, Acid drops, Love hope, Think tank.* Lydon, John McGeogh (g), Mike Joyce (d), Alan Dias, Ted Chau. Live from MV5 TdB PL&AA

PINK FAIRIES
28/11/70 TOP GEAR *Lucille, The snake, 3/5 of a mile in 10 seconds.* John 'Twink' Alder (dv), Russell Hunter (d), Paul Rudolph (lgv), Duncan Sanderson (b). 10&24/11/70 MV4 JW BC&IS

Passed by panel, despite comments like 'a most ugly heavy noise', and 'not for general use'.

16/2/71 HARDING *Do it, Uncle Harry's last freakout, Tomorrow never knows.* 8/2/71 MV5 MB MH&MF

Rec'd In Concert 14/10/71 PS as 3-piece, after Twink's departure, TX 16/11/71.

6/4/72 DRUMMOND *I saw her standing there, Portobello shuffle, Walk don't run.* Twink out. 29/3/72 MV4 MB MH&MF

15/12/72 SEQUENCE *I saw her standing there, Well well well, Marilyn, Big-legged woman.* Contract still has Rudolph, but more likely Mick Wayne (gv) or Larry Wallis (gv). 4/11/72 T1 JM NG

THE PINK FLOYD
1/10/67 TOP GEAR *The gnome, Scarecrow, Set the controls, Matilda mother, Reaction in G, Flaming (& Apples and oranges, 5/11/67).* Syd Barrett (gv), Nick Mason (d), Richard Wright (k), Roger Waters (bv). 25/9/67 PH BA DT
First broadcast was live on 'Monday Monday' ('Arnold

Layne', 'Candy and a currant bun'), 3/4/67 PH. Bill Bebb commissioned a session at PH on 28/7 for SAT. CLUB, but not completed after Syd Barrett's 'freak-out'. This, therefore, is the first complete Pink Floyd session. Tracks later repeated on SYMONDS, 13-17/11/67.

31/12/67 TOP GEAR *Vegetable man, Scream thy last scream, Jug band blues, Pow R Toc H.* 20/12/67 MV4 BA *

11/8/68 TOP GEAR *The murderotic woman or careful with that axe Eugene, The massed gadgets of Hercules, Let there be more light, Julia dream.* Dave Gilmore (gv) r. Barrett. 25/6/68. PC1 BA DT

Yes, those are the titles on the PasB: 'The murderotic...' is 'Murderistic woman', an early name for the piece re-titled 'Careful with that axe Eugene' — hence the hybrid BBC title. 'Massed gadgets' is another name for the piece 'A saucerful of secrets'. These details courtesy of Andy Mabbett, co-editor of the independent Pink Floyd magazine The Amazing Pudding.

15/12/68 TOP GEAR *Point me at the sky, Baby blue shuffle in D major, The embryo, Interstellar overdrive.* 2/12/68 MV4 BA *

Group also appeared live on R1 Club from the Paris, 20/12 playing 'Let there be more light', 'Set the controls' 'Point me at the sky' and 'Careful with that axe Eugene' (Prod: BP, Eng: PR).

14/5/69 NIGHT RIDE *Daybreak, Cymbaline, Green is the colour, The narrow way.* 12/5/69 PS PR CL&AH
'Daybreak' became 'Grantchester Meadows'. 'The narrow way' became part 3 of that piece on 'Ummagumma' LP ('Baby blue shuffle' evolved into 'Narrow way' pt 1). All tracks repeated on TOP GEAR 1/6/69. Group had not turned up for booked 2nd live performance on R1 Club 9/4/69. Only two subsequent BBC studio dates: Peel Sunday Concert rec'd 16/7/70 PS, TX 19/7/70 (the Atom Heart Mother first broadcast); & In Concert, rec'd 30/9/71 PS, TX 12/10/71. ('Echoes' first broadcast). Also: 'Dark side of the Moon' performance at Wembley Empire Pool 16/11/74, TX 11/1/75. Knebworth concert 30/6/90 broadcast live on R1 FM.

PINK INDUSTRY
18/1/82 PEEL *Enjoy the pain, The final cry, Tomorrow.* Jayne (v), Ambrose (b,k,clo), Dave (g,k), Tin Tin (d), Kif Cole (perc), Phil (perc). 4/1/82 MV4 TW DD

16/11/82 PEEL *Creaking doors, Holy shit-there's a survivor, I've lost my mind, New thing.* Jayne, Ambrose only. 25/10/82 MV4 TW DD

23/8/83 PEEL *Don't be anyone's fashion, This is the place, Send them away, Taddy up, Two cultures.* Tadzio Jodlowski (g) joins. 13/8/83 * DG MC

8/5/84 PEEL *Pain of pride, No defence, Piano ping, Don't let go.* 25/4/84 MV5 PSI NG

PINK MILITARY
26/11/79 PEEL *Wild west, Did you see her?, Stand alone.* Jayne Casey (lv), Roy White (g,bkv,p), Steve Torch (b,bkv), Nicky (sy,v), Budgie (d), Jackie (bkv). 14/11/79 MV4 BS NG

5/6/80 PEEL *Everyday, Pilgrim forest, Dance of the waning moon.* Jayne, Nicky, Martin Dempsey (b), Charlie Griffiths (k), Neil (perc), Dave Baynton-Power (d). 27/5/80 BS MR

PINK PEG SLAX
3/7/84 PEEL *Bippo bippo (bop man bop), Self pitying Stan, Cajun feast, Lonely afternoon.* Abner Cavanagh (d), Chet Taylor (b), Vince Berkley (gv), Martin Lefou (fd,p); & Andrew (ag), Ade & Wink (bkv). 23/6/84 MV5 DG MC

1/5/85 PEEL *I saw the light, Ooh my little mama, Buzz saw fiddle, Excuses at a dollar a throw.* Colin Moderne (ag,p) joins. 16/4/85 MV5 AJ *

27/11/86 KERSHAW *Down the hoochie coochie, One spark became a dud, Such a fool, Chastity Chet.* Lefou out; & Simon Anderson (v), Andrew Ffoulkes (v), Andy Holdall (tb), Nick McCoy (tp), Ron Swift (cl). 12/11/86 * DST SR

THE PIRANHAS
21/2/79 PEEL *Coloured music, Jilly, Saxophone, Cheap and nasty.* Alan Bines (sx), John Helmer (lgv), Bob Grover (rgv), Reg Hornsbury (b), Richard Adland (d). 7/2/79 MV4 BS NG

26/7/79 PEEL *Boyfriend, Getting beaten up, Yap yap yap, Happy families.* 17/7/79 MV4 BS MR&MPK

28/1/80 PEEL *Anything, Final straw, Something, Green don't suit me.* 16/1/80 MV4 JE NG

15/9/80 READ *Two time Sally, Pay back, Green don't suit me, Final straw.* 5/9/80 MV4 CL *

THE PIRATES
12/1/77 PEEL *Drinking wine spodeodee, Let's talk, Talking about you, Cat clothes.* Mick Green (g,bkv), Johnny Spence (b,lv), Frank Farley (d,bkv). 4/1/77 MV4 JG MR

14/11/77 PEEL *I can tell, Gibson Martin Fender, Four to the bar, Shakin' all over.* 8/11/77 MV4 JG MR

19/6/78 PEEL *Johnny B. Goode's good, Shake hands with the devil, Voodoo, Long journey home.* 9/5/78 MV4 * MR

PITCH SHIFTER
25/5/91 PEEL *Gritter, Tendrill, Dry riser inlet.* Mark Clayden (b), Stuart Toolin (g), Johnathan Carter (g,bkv), Jonathan Clayden (v). 28/4/91 MV3 DG ME&DMC

THE PIXIES
6/1/88 MAYO *Here comes your man, Subbacultcha, Down to the well, Break my body.* Black Francis (gv), David Lovering (d), Mrs John Murphy (Kim Deal) (bv), Joey Santiago (lg). 20/2/87 Fort Apache studios, Boston, USA. Producer, Gary Smith *

16/5/88 PEEL *Levitate me, Hey, In heaven (Lady in the radiator song), Wild honey pie, Caribou.* 3/5/88 MV4 MR~

18/10/88 PEEL *Dead, Tame, There goes my gun, Manta ray.* 9/10/88 HP DG JB

2/5/89 PEEL *Down to the well, Into the white, Wave of mutilation.* 14 or 16/4/89 MV3 DG MWT

20/8/90 GOODIER *This monkey's gone to heaven, Ana, Allison, Wave of mutiliation.* 18/8/90 MV5 MA~

4/8/91 PEEL *Palace of the brine, Letter to Memphis, Motorway to Roswell, Subbacultcha.* & Bobby Santiago ('3rd guitar'). 23/6/91 MV3 DG JB&PRB

ROBERTO PLA
16/9/90 KERSHAW *El mundo de las locas, Colombia tierra querida, Alma mia, Andro a Colombia.* Roberto Pla (timbale), Peter Eckford (cga), Conal Fowkes (p), Ian Wood & Sid Gaulo (tp), Julian Arguelles (sx), Paul Taylor (tb), Barbara Snow (tp,bkv), Lisandro Zapata (b,bkv), Tomas Dyani Akurul (bgo), Luis Avendano (lv,perc). 21/8/90 MV3 MR~

PLACEBO
5/5/82 JENSEN *Poppy dance, Gita, Big apple, Blot.* Michelle Wild (v), Gary Wild (g), Freddie Roberts (g), Steve Wheatley (d), Phil Armstrong (b). 29/4/82 MV5 JS MR

PLAIN CHARACTERS
2/12/81 PEEL *Hideaway, O, Menial tasks, Fingerprint city.* Colin Tucker (v), Paul Johnstone (g), John Hyde (b), Tim Broughton (d). 23/11/81 MV4 TW DD

PLAINSONG
1/2/72 PEEL† *Tigers will survive, Seeds and stems again, Spanish guitar, Any day woman.* Ian Matthews (gv), Andy Roberts (gv), Bob Ronga (gv), Dave Richards (bv). 24/1/72 PH JW BC&NG

21/2/72 HARRIS *Time between†, Raider, Call the tune.* 15/2/72 MV5 JG *

6/6/72 PEEL *Truck driving man†, Amelia Earhardt's last flight†, Yo yo man†, I'll fly away (& The true story of Amelia Earhardt†, not broadcast).* 24/4/72 T1 JW&PD BC?

15/6/72 DRUMMOND *Diesel on my tail, For the second time, Me and Mr Holmes, Poison apple lady.* 31/5/72 MV4 MB MH&MF

7/8/72 HARRIS *I'm so lonesome I could cry†, Miss the Mississippi†, Old Kent Road, Carolina moon, Louise† (& Wreck of the old '97†, 11/9/72).* 19/7/72 AO2 JG *
†† 'On Air' BOJCD005.

30/11/72 PEEL *Nobody eats at Lineburgh anymore, Old man at the mill/Charlie, Save your sorrows, Home.* Ronga out. 27/11/72 LHI BA *
Day of this b'cast, 30/11/72, group rec'd In Concert at PS, TX 16/12/72.

7/1/73 SOUNDS ON SUNDAY *Seeds and stems, Any day woman, I'll take you to the movies, Blue blue day, Miss the Mississippi, I work for Jesus, I don't want to talk about it, Save your sorrows, I don't want to talk about it (reprise).* 3-piece, as 27/11. 29/12/72 MV5 FL *

PLANT BACH OFNUS
2/3/88 PEEL *Aflan, Llwyd, Awst, Pydredd.* Fiona Owen (v), Gorwel Owen (v,tps,vi), Robin Griffith (sy). 16/2/88 MV4 DG MC

27/1/91 PEEL *Saith, Curiad & bas groove, Cyfnod pump, Ailenedigaethyllygaidmennol.* Fiona, Gorwel only. 6/1/91 MV3 DG ME&FK ·

PLANXTY
8/8/72 PEEL *Planxty Irwin, Merrily kiss the quaker, West coast of Clare, The raggle taggle gypsy.* Christy Moore (gv,hmn,bh), Donal Lunny (bz), Liam Og Flynn (pp), Andy Irvine (mnd,v). 24/7/72 PH JW *
1st B'cast was live from PH on Country Meets Folk 6/5/72; followed by session on R2's Folk on Sunday 4/6/72.

12/3/73 PEEL *Cunla, Bean Phaidin, The hare in the corn, The rambles of Kitty (& Two reels, 14/5/73).* 28/2/73 LHI PR *

29/10/73 HARRIS *The hare in the corn/Kitty rambles, The cliffs of Dooneen, The jolly beggar, As I rowed out.* 17/10/73 LHI JG *

6/11/73 PEEL *Bean Phaidin, Kid on the mountain/Fishbuck, As I rowed out (1), As I rowed out (2).* 15/10/73 TI JW * [M: R2, BBC Local radio]

PLASTIC PENNY
14/1/68 TOP GEAR *Turning night into day, Everything I am, Take me back, No pleasure without pain my love, Mrs Grundy.* Brian Keith (lv), Paul Raymond (o), Tony Murray (b), Nigel Olsson (d), Mick Grabham (lg), & Tony Gilbert for 4 musicians (String Quartet). 10/1/68 MV4 BA DT [M: daytime]

PLAY DEAD
28/1/82 PEEL *Effigy, Metallic smile, Pray to Mecca, Propaganda.* Rob Hickson (lv), Steve Green (lg), Pete Waddleton (b), Mark Smith (d). 13/1/82 MV4 KH NG

23/6/83 PEEL *The tennant, Total decline, Gaze.* 'Wiff' credited for (d). 15/6/83 MV4 RP NG

18/1/84 PEEL *Break, Return to the east, No motive.* 11/1/84 MV4 RP NG

PLEASUREHEADS
25/5/89 PEEL *She said, There's no chance, Frankly, Twirling tranquiliser chair.* Joe MacColl (d), Dave Colton (b), Andy Donovan (g), Kevin Murphy (g), Pete Elderkin & Dean Nicholls (v,perc). 30/4/89 MV3 DG ME

PLUG UGLY SWELL HEADS
17/12/86 LONG *Upside down, Wipe out, Circle of lies, Twenty four hours from Kalmekak.* Peter Coyle (v), Steve Cummerson (g), Dave Whittaker (b), Steve Brown (d). 19/11/86 MV4 BYA MPK

PLUMMET AIRLINES
14/9/76 PEEL *Don't give a damn, You're keeping us talking, Water to wine, Stars will shine.* Harry Stevenson (g,lv), Daryl Hunt (b,bkv), Richard Booth (g), Duncan Kerr (g,bkv), Keith Gotheridge (d). 31/8/76 MV4 TW MR

28/2/77 PEEL *Our last dance, Call out the engine driver, Since I left you, Doctor Boogie.* & Gaspar Lawal (perc), Derek Quin (perc). 24/1/77 MV4 TW DD

THE POGUES
17/4/84 PEEL *Streams of whiskey, Greenland whale fisheries, The boys from the county Hell (not broadcast), The auld triangle.* Billed under their original name of 'Pogue Mahone' for this first session only:
Shane MacGowan (lv,g), Jem Finer (bj,v,g-4 only), Andrew Ranken (d,bkv), Spider Stacy (wh), James Fearnley (acc), Cait O'Riordan (b). 10/4/84 MV5 MRD TdB

9/7/84 JENSEN *Dingle regatta/Holly Johnsons, Poor Paddy on the railway, The boys from the county hell, Connemara let's go!* 21/6/84 MV5 MHY *

12/12/84 PEEL *Whiskey you're the devil, The navigator, Sally McLannan, Danny boy.* 4/12/84 MV5 MRD MR

13/5/85 SAT. LIVE *Repeal of the licensing laws, Streams of whiskey, A pair of brown eyes.* Live from S2 TdB~

11/7/85 LONG *Wild cats of Kilkenny, Billy's bones, The old main drag, Dirty old town.* Philip Chevron (g) joins; & Tommy Kene (pp), Henry Thomas (fd). 3/7/85 MV5 BYA MPK

5/11/86 LONG *If I should fall from grace with God, Lullaby of London, Rake at the gates of hell, Turkish song of the damned.* MacGowan, Finer, Fearnley, Stacey, Ranken, Chevron, Terry Woods (ci), Daryl Hunt (b). 22/10/86 MV4 BYA MPK&EL

THE POLECATS
9/3/81 SKINNER *Pink and black, Please give me something, Miss Bobby Sox, High school baby.* Tim Worman (v), Martin Boorer 'Boz' (g), Philip Bloomberg (b), Neil Rooney (d). 19/2/81 LHI JS *

THE POLICE
24/10/78 JENSEN *Can't stand losing you†, Hole in my life, Truth hits everybody, Next to you.* Sting (b,lv), Stewart Copeland (d) and Andy Summers (g). 16/10/78 MV5 BS ME
Shows that week hosted by Gambaccini in Jensen's absence. † On 'I and only' BOJCD025.

29/1/79 PEEBLES *So lonely, Roxanne (30/1), Truth hits everybody (31/1), Next to you (1/2).* 23/11/78 MV4 MB BAI&DD

30/7/79 PEEL *This bed's too big without you, Message in a bottle, Next to you, Can't stand losing you ('the bit we left out').* 23/7/79 MV4 TW DD

THE POLITBURO
5/3/87 LONG *Seraph, Conspiracy theories, Tear it down, UK on holiday, Blue movies on the backs of my eyelids.* Bill Austin (d), Stephen Dowsett (bv), Hugh Poulton (gv). 22/2/87 MV4 JE TdB

POND
25/9/92 PEEL *Cinders, Spots, Snowing, Pretty thing.* Charlie Campbell (gv), Chris Brady (bv), David Triebwasser (d,bkv). 11/9/92 MV4 JB~ KR

PONDEROSA GLEE BOYS
25/7/81 PEEL *Scream or change your mind, Creation, Ritual.* Tomo (v), Brian Swenson (gv), Carl Eaton (bv), Steve Coy (dv). 15/7/81 MV4 CL NG

THE POOH STICKS
3/5/88 PEEL† *On tape, Alan McGee, Heartbreak, Indiepop ain't noise pollution.* Paul (g,bkv), Alison (b), Stephanie (b,d,g), Hue Pooh Sticks (Williams) (v); & Amelia Fletcher (bkv). 19/4/88 * DG *

18/5/89 PEEL† *Desperado, Young people, Hard on love, Dare-True-Kiss-Promise.* Hue, Stephanie, Paul, Geraldine (g,bkv). 9/4/89 MV3 DG MWT
† On eponymous LP on Overground Records OVER018.

11/11/91 GOODIER *Who loves you, Young people, Crazy love, When Sunny gets blue.* Hue, Paul, Fletcher (returns), Alison Vannigen (b), Mick Gant (g), Trudy Gregory (v,bkv). 19/10/91 MV4 MC~

THE POP GROUP
10/8/78 PEEL *We are time, Kiss the book, Words disobey me.* Mark Stewart (lv), Garreth Sager (g,k), John Waddington (g,bkv), Simon Underwood (b), Bruce Smith (d). 3/7/78 MV4 TW BAI

THE POP GUNS
23/1/90 PEEL *Someone you love, Bye bye baby, Put me thru it, Where do you go.* Greg Dixon (g), Pat Walkington (b), Shaun Charman (d), Wendy Morgan (v), Simon Pickles (g). 9/1/90 MV5 DG MR

30/9/90 PEEL *Going under, I'm spoiling everything, Those other things, A world away (it's grim up north).* Pickles out. 4/9/90 MV5 JB~

THE POP RIVETS
13/2/80 PEEL *Where have all the good times gone, Going nowhere, Beatle boots, Empty sounds.* (Wild) Billy Childish (lv), Nobby Stiles (b,bkv), Zoony the Lazoon (g,bkv), Cecil Batt (d). 29/1/80 MV4 JS MR

POP WALLPAPER
22/1/85 LONG *What did you do, Nothing can call me back, Our way, Headache-heartache.* Audrey Redpath (v), David Evans (g), Miles Raymond (b), Joh McVay (sx,k), Les Cook (d), Evan Henderson (g). 2/12/84 VS BYA HP&PW

POP WILL EAT ITSELF
30/6/86 PEEL *Inside out, Demolition girl, Oh Grebo I think I love you, Sweet sweet pie.* Adam Mole (g,o), Clint Mansell (gv), Richard March (b), Graham Crabb (d,bkv). 17/6/86 DG TdB&MA

5/1/87 LONG *Love missile F1-11, Ugly, Ha ha empty head, Picnic in the sky, Illusion of love.* 10/12/86 MV4 BYA *

6/7/87 PEEL *There is no love between us anymore, Grebo guru, Beaver patrol, Razor blade kisses (Evelyn).* 14/6/87 * DG ME&FK

6/4/92 GOODIER *Eat me drink me love me kill me, Mother, The Scottish song, Bullet proof.* & Fuzz (d). 14/3/92 MV5 MC AR

MALDWYN POPE
17/7/73 PEEL *Truly, Couldn't be wrong, Shall we go to sea, Dream castle, That is the question, How can I forget you?* * 10/7/73 LHI JW BC

26/3/74 PEEL *Maybe it's wrong, Gunfighter, All day, Autumn.* * 4/3/74 * * *

17/10/74 PEEL *Lazy country days, Don't say, Don't you know.* * 5/8/74 TI * *

THE POPINJAYS
21/9/88 PEEL *Perfect dream home, Dr. Fell, Fine lines, Backward daydream.* Polly Hancock (g,k), Wendy Robinson (v,hca). 4/9/88 HP DG TdB

POPPI UK
1/3/88 PEEL *Post modern sex jogger, Chinese apple belt, You're not the same, Rambo's girlfriend.* Tony Sikkes (d), Hans Pieters (bv), Ger Laning (gv), Frank van den Elzen (g). 14/2/88 * DG ME&MC

POPPY FACTORY
14/1/91 GOODIER *Stars†, 7 x 7, Drug house, Looking up.* Jonathan Binns, Jock Cotton (gv), Michael Dale (b,k). 15/12/90 MV5 MC~
† On 'Best of Mark Goodier'.

10/7/91 HARRIS *Stars, Fabulous beast, Good time, Submarine.* John McDonald (k) r. Binns. 5/5/91 MV5 TdB~

THE POPTICIANS
27/7/83 PEEL *Hello everybody, Brown paper bag, Mobile home, Song about losing your glasses.* John Hegley (gv), Russell Greenwood (dv), Susan Norton (sxv), Keith Moore (cl,v). 20/7/83 MV4 RP ME

12/11/84 PEEL *Scoutmaster, Song about the misery of human existence, Private, Song about John's brother's glasses, Red Ken, Somehow you look different tonight.* 4/11/84 MV5 DG ME

A POPULAR HISTORY OF SIGNS
18/10/83 PEEL *Stigma, House, Christmas island, Comrades.* Andrew Jarman (bv), Pete Scammell (sy,g), Paul Clarke (perc), Mark Dean (electronic perc,seq). 12/10/83 MV4 RP NG

POPULAR VOICE
27/7/82 PEEL *Home for the summer, Keep Winning, Possession, That sound is pain.* Barry Derbyshire (v), Michael Byles (sx,g), Mark Gardner (sy), Chalky Keelian (d), Daley (p). 28/6/82 MV4 TW DD

22/9/83 JENSEN *Can it be me, Living dangerously, Live on the edge of town, Awake all night.* Byles, Daley, Bill (d), Tim (sy), Joe (v). 1/9/83 MV4 JP *

PORCH PARTY
11/6/83 LONG *Deep inside of me, How much more, Dreams can be broken, Frustration.* * 3/5/83 PHM c.JL *

PORTION CONTROL
11/1/84 PEEL *Go talk, Rough justice, Scramble.* Dean Piavani (v), Ian Sharp, John Whybrew, Pat Bermingham. 4/1/84 MV4 RP NG

7/8/85 LONG *Cut and thrust, Bolted, Taste of love, Havoc man.* Peter Ware r. Bermingham. 19/6/85 MV5 BYA *

POSITIVE NOISE
27/8/80 PEEL *Give me passion, Down there, End of a dream, Ghosts.* Ross Middleton (g,lv), Graham Middleton (k), Fraser Middleton (b), Les Gaff (d). 19/8/80 MV4 DG MR

25/3/81 PEEL *Charm, Love like property, Treachery, 1917 (I'm in the mood).* Russell Blackstock (lgv) joins. 16/3/81 LH1 PS DD&MPK

9/4/81 SKINNER *Hypnosis, Love is a many splintered thing, Blood and soil, And yet again.* & Gary Barnacle (sx). 20/3/81 LH1 DG ME

THE POSTMEN
11/12/80 PEEL *Fishman, Mouse etc., Uncle, Henry's coming.* * 25/11/80 LH1 JS MR

THE POTATO FIVE
8/1/86 LONG *Babylon, Fish, Mr Yo Yo, Sweet lady, Kenny Achampong.* Andy Minnion (sx), Malcolm Buck (sx), Richard Walker (sx), Simon Driscoll (tb), Trevor Gardiner (d), David Driscoll (b), Martin Aberdeen (g), Julie Liggett (k), Floyd Lloyd (v). Live from MV5 BYA HP

COZY POWELL
29/10/74 PEEL *Keep your distance, Foolish girl, Superstrut, Hold on.* Bernie Marsden (g), Don Airey (k), Clive Chapman (b), Frank Siello (v), Cozy Powell (d). 15/10/74 MV4 TW *

POWER
3/10/85 LONG *Don't kick me down, Crying out for more, Callous love, My luck is bad luck.* Richard Jackman (v), Mark Lewis (g); & Don Snow (k), Clive Byron (d), Ron Bentley (bk), Ronnie Asprey (sx), Roy Gayle (bkv). 22/9/85 HP BYA PW

POWER HOUSE
14/6/91 FRI. ROCK *All you can say, Without love, Love is a weapon, Anything you want.* Paul Davis (v), Billy Frank (b,bkv), Peter Frank (g), Phil Studdart (g), Phil Armorgie (d). 17/5/91 MV5 TW MC

DUFFY POWER
2/8/70 RAVEN'S R&B *Baby baby baby, That's alright, Love song, Hell hound on my trail, Everyday since you've been gone.* 8/7/70 MV4 JG JY

27/3/71 RAVEN'S R&B *Lordy Miss Claudie, Little boy blue, Man in the sky, Love song, Sally plain.* Duffy Power, Rod Argent (k). 10/3/71 * MB *

6/9/73 PEEL *Dusty road, Love is gonna go, Glad that you're not me, Little soldiers.* Power, Graham Quinten Jones (g,p), Chris Bailey, Peter Kirk. 3/9/73 LH1 BA BC

PRAGVEC
29/8/78 PEEL *Nervous, Bits, Ruby, Stay.* Nick Cash (d), David Boyd (bv), John Studholme (gv), Susan Gogan (lv,sy). 23/8/78 MV4 BS NG

7/2/79 PEEL *Toast, Expert, The follower, Hijack.* 29/1/79 MV4 BS DD

THE PRATS
13/9/79 PEEL *Jesus had a Pa, Prats 2, Strange Interlude, A day in the life of me, Poxy pop groups, Nothing, You're nobody, Prats 1.* Greg MacGuire (lv,g), Paul McLaughlin (lg), Tom Robinson (b), Dave MacGuire (d). Rec. date unknown PRIV * *

PRAYING MANTIS
9/11/79 FRI. ROCK *Captured city, Lovers to the grave, Johnny cool.* Tino Neophytou (lgv), Peter Moore (rgv), Chris Neophytou (b), Chris Hudson (d). 31/10/79 * TW *

PREFAB SPROUT
28/8/85 PEEL *Cars and girls, Rebel land, Lions in my*

garden. 'with Kevin Armstrong' (g) is all sheet says. 18/8/85 MV5 DG *

THE PREFECTS
21/8/78 PEEL *Things in general, Escort girls, The Bristol road leads to Dachau, Agony Column.* Robert Lloyd (lv,hca), Roots Apperley (lg,bkv), Joe Motivator (rg,bkv), Ted Ward (b), Ada (d). 11/8/78 MV4 TW NG

15/1/79 PEEL† *Motions, Faults, Total look, Barbarellas.* Lloyd, Apperley, Eamon Duffy (b), David Twist (d); & Andy Burchell (cl), Dave Whitton (sx, 'plastic squeak'). 8/1/79 MV4 TW DD

† On Strange Fruit SFPS025.

PREMI
11/8/87 PEEL *Paliye panjeba waliye, Nach di di godthkhulgaye, Jago aya, Terj ni kali gooth goriye.* Chani (d), Kala (cga), Jassi Lota (dholka,v), Digsy (tamb), Mike (b), Gareth (g), Thomas (ss), Raju & Jittu (k), Johal (v). 4/8/87 * DG MR&ME

THE SID PRESLEY EXPERIENCE
12/6/84 JENSEN *Hup two three four, Gone to Texas, Rock and roll traitor, Gold turkey.* Peter Coyne (v), Chris Coyne (v), Del Bartle (g), Kevin Murphy (d), Ron Carthy (tp), Emma Burnham (bkv). 31/5/84 MV5 MHY MR

14/8/84 JENSEN *Firewater, Take a chance, Jealously, Can't leave her alone.* Carthy, Burnham out. 4/8/84 MV5 DG MC

PRESS ANY KEY
17/1/85 INTO THE MUSIC *Tokyo girl, She looks he looks, Is this our world?, A long long way.* Chris Buck (d), Tim Harries (b), John Russell (g,lv-1,2), Richard Taylor (k), Neddy Fender (k,lv-3,4). 15/12/84 MV4 DG MC

THE PRETENDERS
12/2/79 BURNETT *Stop your sobbing* [Network session]. Chrissie Hynde (lv,g), James Honeyman-Scott (g), Pete Farndon (b), Martin Chambers (d). 18/1/79 MV4 * *

3/4/79 JENSEN *Up the neck, Private life, Stop your sobbing.* 5/2/79 MV5 PR ME

17/7/79 JENSEN *The Cuban slide, Mystery achievement, Kid, I need somebody, Tattooed love boys.* 2/7/79 MV5 PR ME

30/7/79 READ *Mystery achievement, I need somebody (31/7), The Cuban slide (1/8), Tattooed love boys (2/8).* 13/7/79 MV4 JS *

8/11/83 JENSEN *Stop your sobbing, Ohio - my city has gone, Message of love, Money.* * 30/5/83 * * *

PRETTY MAIDS
9/12/83 FRI. ROCK *City light, Fantasy, Cold killer, Queen of dreams.* Phil Moorhead (d), John Darrow (b), Ken Hammer (g), Piet Collins (g) Alan Owen (k), Ronnie Atkins (v). 25/11/83. * DG *

THE PRETTY THINGS
3/12/67 TOP GEAR *Turn my head, Defecting grey, Talking about the good times, Walking through my dreams.* Phil May (lv), Dick Taylor (lg), Skip Alan (d), John Povey (o,pv), Alan Waller 'Wally Allen' (b). 27/11/67 PCI BA DT

1st TX for group was live on 'Parade of the Pops' (Light) 8/7/64 PH [M: Sat. Club, WS R&B 64,65].

17/11/68 TOP GEAR *S.F. sorrow is born, She says good morning, Balloon burning, Old man going.* John 'Twink' Alder (d) r. Skip Alan. 21/10/68 PCI BA PR

Next, live on R1 Club 21/1/69 PS; & pre-rec 7/2/69 PS, TX 28/2/69 R1 Club.

25/5/69 TOP GEAR *Send you with loving, Alexander, The loveliest person, No more Spring, Marilyn.* 20/5/69 MV4 JW TW

Live on R1 Club again on 2/12/69 PS.

6/7/70 SYMONDS *In the square, The letter, Rain, She's a lover, Sickle clowns.* Skip Alan returns r. Alder, Peter Tolson (lg) r. Taylor. 23/6/70 PH BA PK&NG

Had recently done Peel's Sunday Concert, rec'd 11/6/70 PS, TX 21/6/70, prod. JG. Next, on R1 Club yet again, from 3-7/8/70, rec'd 15/6/70 PS.

11/9/70 BLACK *Sickle clowns, She's a lover, Cries from the midnight circus (& Grass, 18/12/70).* 2/9/70 AO2 JM JWH

15/5/71 TOP GEAR *Stone hearted mama, Circus mind, Slow beginning (& Summertime, 14/8/71).* 27/4/71 MV4 JW BC

29/6/71 HARDING *Summertime, Cries from the midnight circus, Slow beginnings.* 21/6/71 MV5 MB MH&MF

4/8/72 PEEL *Love is good, Spider woman, Don't bring me down, Onion soup.* Stuart Brooks (b) r. Wally Allen. 17/7/72 T1 JM JWH&JS

15/8/72 PEEL *Rosalyn, Onion soup, All night sailor (& Love is good, not broadcast).* & Dick Taylor (g-1 only). 25/7/72 PR JWH&JS

30/10/72 HARRIS *Religion's dead, Peter/Rip off train, Road runner, Havana bound.* 4/10/72 LH1 JG *

15/2/73 PEEL *Religion's dead, Love is good, Defecting grey, Old man going, Havana bound.* 29/1/73 LH1 BA *

27/8/73 HARRIS *Route 66, Onion soup, Peter/Rip off train, Atlanta.* 15/8/73 LH1 JG *

Had rec'd In Concert 9/8/73 HP, TX 15/9/73.

6/1/75 PEEL *Bridge of God, Silk torpedo, Come home momma, Dream/Joey.* Jack Green (bv) r. Brooks; & Gordon Edwards (gkv). 17/12/74 MV4 TW BC

Had rec'd another In Concert 28/11/74 HP, TX 14/12/74, prod. JG. '1st session with new speakers in MV4, used unequalised. Last regular session with Bob Conduct' TW on session sheet.

24/7/75 PEEL *Belfast cowboy/Bruise in the sky, Big city, Dream/Joey, Not only but also.* 17/7/75 MV4 TW *

I'm afraid someone else will have to take this from here, and find out which of these takes, and which from their several broadcasts before Radio 1, have survived and made it onto 'On Air' BOJCD003.

MAXI PRIEST
6/3/85 PEEL *Should I (Put my trust in you), Throw my corn, In the Springtime.* Maxi (lv), Paul Robinson (dv), Errol Robinson (b), Jerry Robinson (p), Ewan Robinson (o), Trevor Robinson (perc), Jerry Fulgence (lg), Frank End (rg), Al Deval (sx), Peter Lamont (tb), Kevin Robinson (tp), Carroll Tompson (v), Candy McKenzie (v), Jane Eugene (v). 26/2/85 MV5 MRD MR

21/3/85 LONG *Dancing mood, Hey little girl, Caution, Should I.* Maxi; P., K., Er., & Ew. Robinson, Deval, Lamont. 17/3/85 HP BYA PW

13/7/88 L. KERSHAW *You're my angel, Marcus, Let me know, Goodbye to love.* Maxi, P. Robinson, Clifton Morrison (k), Duncan Bridgeman (prg), Leroy Hayward (b), Martin Augustin (g), Belva Haney (bkv). 6/7/88 MV4 HP MPK

PRIMAL SCREAM
10/12/85 PEEL *Crystal crescent, Aftermath, Subterranean, I love you.* Thomas McGurk (d), Robert Young (b), James Beattie (lg), Paul Harte (rg), Martin St. John (tamb), Bobby Gillespie (v). 1/12/85 MV5 DG ME

14/5/86 PEEL *Tomorrow ends today, Leaves, Bewitched and bewildered.* Stewart May (rg) r. Harte. 6/5/86 MV4 DG MR&JB

7/7/86 LONG *Silent spring, Velocity girl, Imperial, Feverclaw.* 22/6/86 MV4 BYA AG

THE PRIMEVALS
18/9/85 PEEL† *Saint Jack, See that skin, Spiritual, Dish of fish.* Lefty Burnett (d), John Honeyman (b), Brother Malcolm (McDonald) (g), Don Gordon (g), Michael Rooney (v). 8/9/85 * DG MA

† On Strange Fruit SFPS014.

17/12/85 LONG *Primeval call, Lonesome weeping blues, Prairie chain, Fire and clay.* Tom Rafferty (rg) r. Gordon. 4/12/85 MV5 BYA MPK

17/4/86 KERSHAW *Fertile mind, Early grave, Hey sister, Elixir of life.* Rafferty out. 9/4/86 Y2 SP PSM

12/8/87 LONG *My dying embers, Follow her down, Cotton head, Heya.* Rooney, Honeyman, McDonald, Paul Bridges (d), Gordon Goudie (g). 1/7/87 MV4 HP MPK&MP

22/10/87 KERSHAW *One sweet drink, Bleeding black, Let's get natural, Burden of the debt.* 1/10/87 * DG *

THE PRIMITIVES

17/6/86 Long *Nothing left, Run baby run, Really stupid, I'll stick with you.* Paul Court (g,bkv), Tracy Cattell (lv), Pete Tweedie (d), Stephen Dullaghan (b). 4/6/86 MV4 BYA MPK

17/7/86 Kershaw *Where the wind blows, Across my shoulder, Spacehead, Crash.* 18/6/86 * SP SR

15/10/86 Peel *Stop killing me, Shadow, Buzz buzz buzz, As tears go by.* 30/9/86 * DG MR&MWT

13/4/87 Peel *Dream walk baby, Ocean blue, Everything's shining bright, She don't need you.* 31/3/87 * DG MR&TD

30/7/87 Long *Out of reach, Don't want anything to change, Carry me home, Ticket to ride.* 15/7/87 MV4 PW MPK

25/4/88 Peel *Things get in your way, Keep me in mind, Way behind me.* Richard Tig Williams (d) r. Tweedie. 17/4/88 MV5 DG *

PRINCE FAR I AND CREATION REBEL

4/7/78 Peel *Spoken introduction, Black man's land, No more war, The dream, Foggy road, Front line.* Prince Far I (lv), Vernon (g), Clifton Morrisson (k), Clinton Jack (b), Dr. Pablo (mel), Charley (d). 7/6/78 MV4 JG NG

PRINCIPAL EDWARD'S MAGIC THEATRE

31/7/68 Night Ride *51st day of Spring, Motel song, Buckle my knee, Hey Joe, To a broken guitar.* Vivien MacAuliffe (v), Martin Stellman (v), Michael 'Root' Cartwright (g,mnd), Lyn Edwards (perc), Belinda Bourquin (vi,rec,k). 16/7/68 MV5 DK *

Overwhelming 'No' of panel over-ruled, made a 'Yes', by Jimmy Grant. Some of the other producers' comments: 'who can like this, if they don't come from New Delhi?' 'ugly tuneless voice... the pseudo-eastern influence I find offensive' 'could it not be useful to the Birmingham Pakistani programme?'

30/3/69 Top Gear *Lament for the earth, The ballad of the big girl now and the mere boy, Third sonnet to sundry notes of music, Pinky: a mystery cycle.* & Jeremy Ensor, David Jones, Monica Mettles. 24/2/69 PH BA *

17/1/70 Top Gear *Thus making a change, Autumn lady travelling song, Plague of birds, King of the.* Ensor, Cartwright, MacAuliffe, Edwards, Stellman, Bourquin. 13/1/70 MV4 JW *

10/4/71 Top Gear *Kettering song, Weasel, Freef'rall.* Ensor, Cartwright, Stellman, Bourquin, John Jones, Roger Swallow, Catherine Freckingham. 23/3/71 MV4 JW BC

18/10/73 Peel *Juggernaut, Milk and honey land.* Cartwright, Bourquin & Nick Pallett (gv), Richard Chipperfield (bv), David Jones (perc), Geoff Nicholls (d). 17/9/73 LH1 BA *

9/3/74 Rock On *The whizzmore kid, The glass-white gangster, Average chap, Juggernaut.* 4/3/74 LH1 BA *

JOHN PRINE

23/1/73 Peel *Clocks and spoons, Flag decal, Angel from Montgomery, Everybody.* John Prine (gv). 22/1/73 T1 PD (for JW) *

On back of session sheet, someone has scribbled "Nominee for Grammy Award". Rec'd In Concert 18/1/73 PS, TX 11/2/73.

28/5/87 Kershaw *Aimless love, The oldest baby in the world, The bottomless wake, Unwed fathers.* Solo, and sole session, 14 years later. 21/5/87 * DG TdB&PS

MADDY PRIOR AND JUNE TABOR

20/10/75 Peel *Four loom weaver, The seven joys of Mary, Singing the travels, The doffin' mistress.* Maddy Prior (v), June Tabor (v). 23/9/75 MV4 JW BC?&NG

THE PROCLAIMERS

7/1/87 Long *Letter from America, Beautiful truth, Throw the 'R' away, Joyful Kilmarnock blues.* Craig Reid (v,perc), Charlie Reid (v,ag). 4/1/87 MV4 JE MS

Also appeared on SAT. LIVE later that year.

PROCOL HARUM

8/6/67 Light Pop North *A whiter shade of pale, Conquistador, Lime Street Blues.* Matthew Fisher (o), Gary Brooker (pv), Ray Royer (g), Dave Knights (b), Bobby Harrison (d). 5/6/67 PHM JWX *

18/6/67 Light Easy Beat *Morning dew, Mabel, Whiter shade of pale.* [M: daytime]. 14/6/67 PS * *

8/10/67 Top Gear *She wandered through the garden fence, Good Captain Clack, Homburg, Kaleidoscope, Repent Walpurgess.* Robin Trower (g), Barry 'B. J.' Wilson (d), r. Royer, Harrison. 27/9/67 MV4 BP PR

16/10/67 Symonds *Conquistador, Good Captain Clack (19/10), Homburg (20/10).* 3/10/67 MV4 * *

25/2/68 Top Gear *Quite rightly so, Shine on brightly, Rambling on, Skip softly my moonbeams.* 14/2/68 MV4 BA *

8/9/68 Top Gear *Wish us well, Skip softly my moonbeams, Long gone geek, In held 'twas in I.* 19/8/68 PCI BA *

25/5/69 Symonds *On Sunday Homburg, A salty dog, Milk of human kindness, Pilgrim's progress.* Chris Copping (o) r. Fisher, Knights out. 20/5/69 PCI c.PW1 *

1/6/69 Top Gear *A salty dog, Juicy John pink, Devil came from Kansas, Too much between us.* 27/5/69 MV4 JW *

8/6/70 Symonds *Your own choice, Dead man's dreams, About to die.* 12/5/70 PH BA PK&NG

Rec'd Peel Concert 4/6/70 PS, TX 14/6/70.

2/10/70 Black *Whiskey train, Juicy John pink, Nothing that I didn't know.* 16/9/70 AO2 JM JWH

25/10/71 Harris *Simple sister, Power failure, Quite rightly so, Broken barricades.* Dave Ball (g) r. Trower; & Alan Cartwright (b). 6/10/71 T1 JM&PD ARV&JWH

19/3/74 Peel *Butterfly boys, The idol, Beyond the pale, Nothing but the truth.* Mick Grabham (g) r. Ball. 12/3/74 LH1 TW BC

THE PROFESSIONALS

10/11/80 Peel *Join the professionals, All the way with you, Crescendo, Kick down the doors.* Paul Cook (d,bkv), Steve Jones (lg,lv), Paul Myers (b,bkv), Kid McVeigh (g,bkv). 3/11/80 LH1 TW ME

15/12/80 Read *Join the professionals, Mad house, Crescendo, Kick down the doors.* 6/11/80 LH1 CL *

PRONG

1/2/89 Peel† *Defiant, Decay, Senseless abuse, In my veins.* Ted Parsons (d,bkv), Mike Kirkland (b,lv-2,4), Tommy Victor (g,lv-1,3). 22/1/89 MV3 DG ME

† On Strange Fruit SFPCD078.

PROPHECY OF DOOM

14/2/90 Peel† *Insanity reigns supreme, Earth reality victim, Rancid oracle, Hybrid thought.* Dean (d), Martin (b), Shrub (g), Tom (g), Shrew (v). 28/1/90 MV3 DG MA

† On Strange Fruit SFRCD079.

1/6/91 Peel *Raze against time, Onward ever backward, Acknowledge the confusion master, The voice of Tibet/Our shame & hypocrisy.* 7/4/91 MV3 DG ME&AA

THE PSYCHEDELIC FURS

30/7/79 Peel *Imitation of Christ, Fall, Sister Europe, We love you.* 'Butler Rep' (Richard Butler) (lv), John Ashton (g), Roger Morris (g), Duncan Kilburn (sx), Tim Butler (b), Rod Johnson (d). 25/7/79 MV4 TVD NG

28/2/80 Peel *Soap commercial, Susan's strange, Mac the knife.* 'Uncle Ely' (Vince Ely) (d) r. Johnson. 18/2/80 MV4 TW DD

10/2/81 Peel *Into you like a train, On and again, All of this and nothing.* 2/2/81 LH1 TW DD

21/4/81 Skinner *Pretty in pink, She is mine, All of this and nothing, Dumb waiters.* 9/4/81 LH1 JS *

19/2/90 Campbell *Entertain me, Book of days, Torch, Pretty in pink.* R. & T. Butler, Ashton, Knox Chandler (g,clo), Joe McGinty (k), Vince Davey (d). 7/2/90 MV5 PW MPK

THE PSYLONS

9/6/86 Peel *Remembrance, Clearer skies, Mockery of Decline, Landmark.* Keith Wyatt (gv), Jack Packer (g), Warren Grech (b), Carl Edwards (d). 1/6/86 MV5 DG MS&ME

13/11/86 Kershaw *Separate ways, All the things we need, She said, Keyhole Joe.* 5/11/86 * DST SR

PULP

18/11/81 Peel *Turkey mambo momma, Please don't worry, Wishful thinking, Refuse to be blind.* Jarvis Cocker (gv,perc), Peter Dalton (sy,o,g,bkv, xyl,cnt,perc), Jamie Pinchbeck (b,perc), Wayne Furniss (d,perc). 7/11/81 MV4 DG PW

30/6/92 Goodier *Babies, Live on, She's a lady, Glass.* Ten years later, it's... Cocker, Russell Senior (g,vi), Candida Doyle (k,sty), Stephen Mackey (b), Nicholas Banks (d). 30/5/92 MV4 MA PA

PUNISHMENT OF LUXURY

30/8/78 Peel *Funk me, Babalon, Let's get married/You're so beautiful.* Brian Bond (lv), Jeff Thwaite (d), Malla Cabbala (gv), Nevil Luxury (lgv), Jimmy Giro (bv). 22/8/78 MV4 BS MR

30/5/79 Peel *Radar bug/Metropolis, British baboon, Secrets.* Steve Secret (d,bkv) r. Thwaite; Cabbala out. 22/5/79 MV4 TVD MR

PURPLE HEARTS

16/7/79 Peel *Beat that, Millions like us, Nothing's left, Frustration.* Simon Stebbing, Jess Shadbolt, Gary Sparks, Bob Manton. 10/7/79 * * *

PUSSY GALORE

25/7/90 Peel *Dead meat, Understand me, Nothin' can bring me down, New breed.* John Spencer, Bob Best, Neil Hagerty, Kurt Wolf. Rec. date unknown, tape from USA

Q TIPS

14/4/80 Read *The dance, S.Y.S.L.J.F.M. (the letter song), A man can't lose what he don't have, Down in the valley.* Paul Young (lv), John Gifford (gv), Mick Pearl (b), Barry Watts (d), Ian Kewley (o,p), Stewart Blandameer (al,v), Steve Farr (bars,v), Tony Hughes (tp,v). 14/3/80 MV4 CL *

QAX

9/1/85 Long *Driving heart, Skin deep, Look at me, No dice.* Nicki Smith (v), Jacky Smith (k), Steve Harrington (k,sx), Rob Lamb (b). 2/1/85 MV5 JS MPK

QUADRILLE

18/6/71 Black *The game, Deaf dumb and blind but still driving, Time machine (& Like the sea, not broadcast).* Robin Lipsey (o), Mike Ashcroft (g), Peter Miles (d), Mike Hewlett (b). 3/6/71 AO2 JM *

QUADS

10/9/79 Peel *Revision time blues, I know you know, There's never been a night, There must be thousands.* Josh Jones (lvg), Jack Jones (gv), Jim Doherty (bv), Johnny Jones (dv). 29/8/79 MV4 TVD MR

QUANDO QUANGO

1/12/83 Peel *Love tempo, Go exciting, Triangle.* Mike Pickering (sx,v), Gonnie Rietveld (syv), Barry Johnson (b,d), Simon Topping (perc). 23/11/83 MV4 RP TdB

29/3/84 Jensen *Swampland, Triangle, Atom rock, S.T. &* Derek Johnson (g), Bernard Sumner (prd), Tony Thompson (d). 8/3/84 MV4 JP MPK

QUARTET

7/5/70 Henry *Who's there, Over and over again, Lotus.* Kevin Peek (g), Terry Britten (g), Alan Tarney (b), Trevor Spencer (d). 30/4/70 AO2 MB MH&MF

This Australian band rec'd a trial b'cast for Dave Cash show 11/12/69, passed, TX 5/1/71 [M: daytime]. Years later, Peek ended up in Sky with John Williams.

8/10/70 Henry *You've got me wondering, Mama where d'ye fail, I wish you'd change your mind.* 1/10/70 AO2 MB MH&MF

QUATERMASS

1/8/70 Top Gear *One blind mice, Laughing tackle, Make up your mind.* Pete Robinson (k), John Gustafson (bv), Mick Underwood (d). 28/7/70 MV4 JW *

11/8/70 Harding *Up on the ground, Gemini (& One blind mice, 22/9/70).* 14/7/70 MV5 MB MH&MF

23/2/71 Harding *One blind mice, Monster in paradise, Laughing tackle.* 15/2/71 MV5 MB MH&MF

QUE BONO
16/6/81 PEEL *Burton wood, Houses, Twister, Siren's scream.*
Pete Mulvihill (d), Jane Mulvihill (v), Alan Maskell (g),
Simon Hall (b). 9/6/81 LH1 DG MR

QUEEN
15/2/73 PEEL† *My fairy king, Keep yourself alive, Doing
alright, Liar.* Freddie Mercury (pv), Brian May (g,bkv),
John Deacon (b,bkv), Roger Taylor (d,bkv).
5/2/73 LH1 BA JE
13/8/73 HARRIS *See what a fool I've been, Liar, Son and
daughter (& Keep yourself alive, 24/9/73).*
25/7/73 LH1 JG CL&JE
6/12/73 PEEL† *Ogre battle, Great king rat, Modern times
rock'n' roll, Son and daughter.* 3/12/73 LH1 BA MF&NGR
† On Band of Joy 'Queen at the Beeb' BOJCD001.
15/4/74 HARRIS *Modern times rock'n' roll, March of the
black queen, Nevermore, White queen.* 3/4/74 LH1 PR *
4/11/74 HARRIS *Now I'm here, Stone cold crazy, Flick of
the wrist, Tenement funster.* 16/10/74 MV4 JG *
14/11/77 PEEL *Spread your wings, It's late, Melancholy
blues, We will rock you.* 28/10/77 MV4 JG MR

THE QUESTIONS
6/4/83 JENSEN *All the time in the world, Body and soul,
Month of Sundays, Give it up.* John Robinson (gv), Paul
Barry (bv), Frank Mooney (d), Mike Talbot (p).
31/3/83 MV4 JS MR

QUICKSAND
29/9/73 ROCK ON *Time to live, Hide away my song.* James
Davies (gv), Phil Davies (bv), Robert Collins (o,v),
Anthony Stone (dv). 20/9/73 LH1 PR *

PAUL QUINN AND EDWYN COLLINS
20/8/84 SKINNER *Different drum, It had to happen, Louise
Louise, Ain't that always the way.* Paul Quinn (vk),
Edwyn Collins (g,bkv), Chris Bell (d), Paul Heard (b),
Craig Gannon (g). 5/8/84 MV5 DG ME

QUINTESSENCE
21/8/70 BLACK *Pearl and bird/Brahmin, Jesus Buddah,
Twilight zones.* Ronald Rothfield 'Raja Ram' (fl), Phil
Jones (v), Richard Vaughn (b), Alan Mostert (lg), Jeremy
Milton (d), David Codling (rg). 15/7/70 AO2 JM JWH
Rec'd Peel Sunday Concert 24/9/70 PS, TX 4/10/70.
19/3/71 BLACK *You'll never stay the same, Dive deep.*
25/2/71 AO2 JM JWH
10/2/72 DRUMMOND *Cosmic surfer, Ganga mai.*
2/2/72 MV4 MB MH&MF

QUIVER
13/2/71 TOP GEAR *Back on the road again, Ballad of
Barnes county, Down your way.* Calvin Batchelor (lgv),
Bruce Thomas (b), Tim Renwick (g), John 'Willie'
Wilson (d). 19/1/71 MV4 * BC
'Unanimous pass with no reservations... Should be
used on quite a lot of Radio 1 programmes' Audition
panel. Group recorded John Peel's Sunday Concert
18/2/71 PS, TX 28/2/71, prod. JG.
13/7/71 HARDING *Once in the morning with the sun, Just
loving you.* 5/7/71 MV5 MB MH&MF
27/9/71 HARRIS *Take a train, She's a lady, Glad I came
around (& Back on the road again, 29/11/71).*
23/8/71 TI PD *
8/5/72 HARRIS *I might stumble, She's a lady, I know you
so well, Gone in the morning.* 26/4/72 AO2 JG *
16/5/72 PEEL *Green tree, Gone in the morning, Love/No
boundaries.* 2/5/72 MV4 * RC
16/6/72 PEEL *I might stumble, Love/No boundaries, Take a
train.* 8/5/72 PH JM JWH
29/6/72 DRUMMOND *Don't make me nervous, Back on the
road again, I know you as well, Route 66.*
19/6/72 TI MB MH&MF
22/11/73 HARRIS *Something else, Meadowland magic,
Highway shoes, Feel so down.* 10/1/73 LH1 PR *

RACING CARS
22/3/76 PEEL *Pass the bottle, Calling the tune, They shoot
horses don't they?, Rhondda reggae.* Gareth Mortimer

(lv,ag), David Land (b), James Dodd (d), Ray Ennis
(lg,slg,bkv), Hedley Grosvenor (lg,bkv). 2/3/76 MV4 JG MR
20/9/76 PEEL *Four wheel drive, Moonshine fandango, Hard
working woman, Down town tonight.* Graham Williams
(g), Robert Wilding (d) r. Grosvenor, Dodd.
9/9/76 MV4 TW *
12/4/77 PEEL *Breaking the rules, Tickin' over, Travelling
mood, Swampy.* 4/4/77 MV4 TW DD
14/9/77 PEEL *Nobody's business, Standing in the rain,
Weekend rendezvous, Clever girl.* & Geraint Watkins
(acc-1 only). 5/9/77 MV4 TW DD
11/9/78 PEEL *Second best, When I'm walking home, Takin'
on the world, Bring on the night.* 14/8/78 MV4 BS DD

RADIO 5
13/5/80 PEEL *True colours, Animal connections,
Expressionless, Dancing with Germany.* Jock Cotton
(v,g), Don Hayes (b), Geoff Haran (g), Chris Groves (d),
(dm). 6/5/80 MV4 BS MR

RADIO STARS
20/5/77 PEEL *Horrible breath, Dirty pictures, Dear
Prudence, No Russians in Russia.* Andy Ellison (lv,hca),
Ian McLeod (g), Martin Gordon (b,o), Gary Thompson
(d). 17/5/77 MV4 JG MR
18/11/77 PEEL *Good personality, The beast of Barnsley,
Don't waste my time, Is it really necessary?* Steve Parry
(d) r. Thompson. 7/11/77 MV4 TW DD
4/10/78 PEEL *Boy meets girl, Radio stars, Sex in chains,
Sitting in the rain.* Jamie Crompton (d) r. Parry.
4/9/78 MV4 TW DD
17/10/78 JENSEN *Radio stars, Baffin island, Norwegian
wood, Rock and roll for the time being.* 22/9/78 * * *

RADIOHEAD
22/6/92 GOODIER *Prove yourself, Creep, I can't, Nothing
touches me.* Thom Yorke (lv,g), Ed O'Brien (bkv,g),
Colin Greenwood (b), Jon Greenwood (g), Phil Selway
(d). 13/6/92 MA~JMK

JESSE RAE
13/6/85 LONG *Scotland funk, Tomorrow, Get ready,
Chainsaw.* Jesse Rae (v,b,k), Calum McNair (g), Michael
Peadon (b), Lesley Farm (v), Leigh Murray (v), Graham
Weir (tb), Neil Weir (tp), Steve Ferrone (d).
22/5/85 S2G JS *

GERRY RAFFERTY
6/2/73 PEEL *Over my head, Singing bird, Don't get me
wrong.* Gerry Rafferty (all instruments, v). 15/1/73 JW *

THE RAGGA TWINS
16/6/91 PEEL *Spliffhead & jugglin', Wipe the
needle/Hooligans.* Flinty Badman, Smiley PJ, Deman
Rocker. 14/5/91 MV5 MR~AR
23/2/92 PEEL *Bring up the mic some more/Ragga trip, The
truth/Tansoback.* The Ragga Twins (rp), Shut Up &
Dance (mx,tt). 21/1/92 MV4 MR~PA

THE RAILWAY CHILDREN
24/11/86 PEEL† *Consider, Any other town, Listen on, Big
hands of freedom.* Gary Newby (gv), Brian Bateman
(g), Stephen Hull (b), Guy Keegan (d).
21/10/86 * DG MA&FK
18/5/87 LONG† *Merciless, Monica's light, In the meantime,
Go ahead.* 6/5/87 MV4 HP MPK&SC
Broadcast date unknown L. KERSHAW *Somewhere South, Over
and over, After the rain†, Hours go by†.* & Tony
Martin (k). 20/4/88 MV4 MPK&JBN
23/4/90 CAMPBELL *What she wants†, Won't be long†, Every
beat of the heart, Music stop.* 18/4/90 MV5 PW MPK
10/10/90 HARRIS *Everybody, So right†, Kinds of fuel†,
Strange attractor†.* 26/8/90 HP TdB~SA
† On Nighttracks CDNT002.

RAIN
18/3/91 GOODIER *Lemonstone desired, Drive on, All I want,
Going.* Ned Murphy (gv), Colin Clark (gv), Martin
Campbell (bv), Tony McGuigan (d). 16/2/91 MV5 MC~

THE RAINCOATS
1/5/79 PEEL *In love, You're a million, Adventures close to
home, Fairy tale in the supermarket.* Anna (gv), Vicki
(vi,gv), Gina (bv), Palmolive (d). 6/3/79 MV4 TVD MR
18/12/80 PEEL *Using my eyes, Family treet, Baby song.*
Charles Hayward (d) r. Palmolive. 10/12/80 MV4 BS NG
17/8/82 JENSEN *Dance of hopping mad, Honey-mad women,
Ooh ooh la la la.* Ana, Vicky, Gina, Richard Dudanski
(d), Derek Goddard (perc), Mac O'Connell (sx).
8/8/82 MV4 DG ME

RAINER AND DAS COMBO
5/2/87 KERSHAW *Sleepwalk, Last fair deal gone down, Meet
me in the morning, Funny how time slips away, I am
a sinner.* Rainer (g,slg,v) & (b), (ps), (d), unknown.
2/11/86 * JL SR

THE RAINMAKERS
16/2/88 MAYO *Tornado of love, Snakednce, Rainmaker, One
more summer.* Rich Ruth (b,bkv), Bob Walkenhorst
(g,lv,k), Steve Phillips (lg,bkv), Pat Tomek (d).
15/1/88 New York * *

THE RAMONES
20/7/85 KERSHAW *Go home Annie, Too tough to die,
Chasing the night.* * Rec. date unknown Y2 * *

RANDY
24/6/74 HARRIS *Lady Luck, Got a feeling, Take me back,
Crazy love.* Brian Wallis (bv), Mark Hankins (gv),
George Lloyd (gv), Neil Coleman (dv). 15/5/74 LH1 PR *

ALAN RANKINE
unknown LONG *The sandman, Your very last day, Break for
me.* Chris Whitten (d), Dorreen Chanter (v), Alan
Rankine (b,g,kv). 16/11/86 MV4 AS MS

RANKING ANN
28/8/85 LONG *Feminine gender, Right to fight, Something
fishy going on, Awa do men.* Bernard Cumberbatch (b),
Black Steel (k), Ranking Ann (v). 4/8/85 HP BYA TdB

RANKING ROGER
15/6/88 L. KERSHAW *One minute closer (to death), Time to
mek a dime, In conversation, Your problems.* Ranking
Roger (v,perc), Bobby Bird (g), Fuzz Townshend (d),
Horace Panter (b), Nigel Darvill (k). 1/6/88 MV4 HP MPK

RARE BIRD
4/5/70 SYMONDS *Beautiful scarlet, You went away, As your
mind flies by.* Graham Field (o), David Kaffinetti (elp),
Steve Gould (bv), Mark Ashton (d). 14/4/70 PH BA NG&PR
9/9/74 HARRIS *All that I need, Last tango in Beulah, Turn
your head around, Hard time.* Gould, Kaffinetti & Fred
Kelly (d), Mick Fiat (b), Kevin Lamb (perc,v).
28/8/74 LH1 JG *

MOSES RASCOE
22/12/88 KERSHAW *Deep sea diver, John Henry, Bright lights
big city.* Moses Rascoe (gv). Recorded by Andy Kershaw in a
New Orleans hotel room, late 1988 * * *

RAVEN
29/1/82 FRI. ROCK *Lambs to the slaughter, Hold back the
fire, Hard ride, Chainsaw.* Mark Gallagher (g), John
Gallagher (b,lv), Rob Hunter (d).
15/1/82 Jam Studios & MV4 (mix) TW DD

RAVISHING BEAUTIES
29/4/82 PEEL *Arctic death, Futility, We will meet them
again, No need to cry.* Virginia Astley (lv), Kate St.
John (bkv,co,ob,fl), Nicky Holland (bkv,k), Ben Hoffnung
(perc). 14/4/82 * CL *

RAW DEAL
31/1/85 INTO THE MUSIC C *Easy-lovin' man, Rollin' on, A
little understanding, Your love, Secondtime around.*
Kevin Thompson (d), Steve English (b), Regan Cairns
(g), Des Horsfall (v). 12/1/85 MV4 DG DD

THE RAW HERBS
27/5/87 LONG *Holland, Bless this day, Syd's late night,
Don't bury me yet.* Derek Parker (v), Kevin Backe (g),
Arch (Steven Archibald) (b), Brian Alexis (d).
17/5/87 MV4 PW MA&DD

RAW NOISE

14/9/91 Peel *Stench of death (metal), Making a killing, Under the influence, Ratfink, Waste of life.* Niall Carr (d), Martin Peck (b), Alo Firouzbakht (g,bkv), Tony Doy (lg), Dean Jones (v). 4/8/91 MV3 DG MA&JRS

LOU RAWLS, MAXINE BROWN & THE JOHNNY WATSON CONCEPT

8/10/67 Top Gear *Hold on I'm coming, Yesterday's heroes, I was made to love, Street of dreams, Oh no not my baby, It's an uphill climb to the bottom, One step at a time, On Broadway, In the midnight hour, Love is a hurting thing.* Lou Rawls (lv-2, 4, 6, 8, 10), Maxine Brown (lv-1, 3, 5, 7, 9) '& guitarist' & 10 & 5 extra musicians. 3/10/67 * * *

MR. RAY'S WIG WORLD

29/8/92 Peel *Faster kittykat, Synapse/Sharon loves Charlie, Beverley heavenly, Mad Dog.* Colin Cooper (gv), Robert Cross (g), Roger Sinek (d), Michael Corcoran (b). 11/8/92 MV4 MA~PA

RAYMONDE

13/2/86 Long *Raymonde, The milk train doesn't stop here anymore, I predict, Son of the soil.* James Maker (v), Phil Huish (g), Derek Thompson (b), Leslie Westlake (d). 5/2/86 MV5 BYA MPK

23/4/86 Long *Every good boy deserves a favour, I'll always shoot them down in flames, Speeding heart, Torch of liberty.* 26/3/86 MV4 BYA *

REAL PEOPLE

21/1/91 Goodier *I can't wait, Window pane, Wonderful†, Open up your mind (let me in).* Tony Griffiths (bv), Chris Griffiths (gv), Sean Simpson (gv), Tony Elson (d). 12/1/91 MV5 MA~

† On 'Best of Mark Goodier' Nighttracks Mark1.

THE REAL SOUNDS OF AFRICA

6/8/87 Kershaw *Dynamos and Caps, Sophie, Murrume, Poto.* Joseph Kabange (d), Jack Malosa (b), Gaby Mumba (g), Modest Badi Banga (g), Modest Mwandwe (g) Sam Ilunga (sx) Geoff Kumwamba (sx) Charles Kalenga (tp) Gilbert Sangana (tp) Ghaby Mutumbo (v), Jojo Kavund (v); & Coco Kanyinda (cga), Mashua Nzou (v). 23/7/87 * DG SC&TD

19/1/89 Kershaw *Maifa, Umwelezeye, Mujinga, Oye oye.* 11-piece above; & John Posani (perc). 1/12/88 MV4 DG SC

3/9/89 Kershaw *Omna, Musao, Egalite, Ou est le problems.* & Lucas Mashura (v), John Muyambo (perc). 13/7/89 MV5 DG NG

8/4/90 Kershaw *Soccer fan, Free Nelson Mandela, Tornados, Dynamos.* & John Posani (cga), Mumba out. 16/11/89 MV5 DG NG

REBEL DA FE

12/4/83 Peel *Ascension, Hideaway, Alter and correct, Yangtse Kiang.* Brian Ellis (v), Jarvis Whitehead (g), Karen Halewood (kv), Gary Williams (b), Mark Robson (d). 6/4/83 JS *

THE REBIRTH BRASS BAND

4/8/91 Kershaw *Bourbon Street parade, Paul Barbarin's second line, When the saints go marching in, Second line.* John Gilbert & Roderick Paulin (sx), Kermit Ruffins (tp,v), Glen Andrews (tp), Stafford Agee & Keith Anderson (tb), Philip Frazier (tu), Keith Frazier (bass drum), Ajay Mallery (snare drum). 11/7/91 MV5 DG PA&AA

THE RECORDS

9/7/79 Peebles *Teenarama, Starry eyes, All messed up and ready to go, Girl.* Will Birch (dv), John Wicks (gv), Phil Brown (bv), Huw Gower (gv). 6/7/79 MV4 BS *

RED BEANS AND RICE

3/3/80 Read *Throw it in the grass, That driving beat, Everybody wants to go to heaven, Everybody needs somebody.* Mike Paice (sx,hca), Tom (d), Benny Harbert (b), Leverne Brown (v), Geoff Coleman (g). 7/2/80 MV4 CL *

THE RED BEARDS FROM TEXAS

1/7/85 Peel *Party on the patio, I saw her standing there,*

Automobile, Ain't that a shame. Morton Pinkley (gv), Wild Hoss Maverick III (bv), Bud Weiser (g), Duke Delight (d). 25/6/85 MV5 JWI MR

RED BEAT

15/12/80 Peel *See, Child, Tribe, The wheel.* Roy Jones (lv), Kevin Keane (g), Chris Thompson (b), Paul Jones (d). 2/12/80 MV4 JS MR

THE RED GUITARS

11/8/83 Peel *Fact, Marimba jive, Paris France, Dive.* Jerry Kidd (v), Louise Barlow (b), Hallam Lewis (lg), Matt Higgins (d), John Rowley (rg). 6/8/83 MV4 DG MC

14/11/83 Jensen *Sting in the tale, Heartbeat go, Slow to fade, Steeltown.* 3/11/83 MV4 JP MR

24/7/84 Peel *Within four walls, Shaken not stirred, Crocodile tears, Remote control.* 14/7/84 MV5 DG MR

1/10/84 Long *Seven types of ambiguity, Crocodile tears, Astronomy, Jamaican homecoming.* 16/9/84 MV5 DG ME

13/2/85 Long *Be with me, Clean up, Trains on time, Marianne.* Robert Holmes (v) r. Kidd. 3/2/85 HP JWI PW

RED HARVEST

24/3/88 Mayo *In my heart, Runaway, Heaven, Out of this world.* Andy Sandom (hca), Steve Morris (v), Philip Martin (g,bkv), Christine Ellis (k), Tony Barnard (b), Mark Higgett (d); & Adrian Borland (lg). 9/3/88 MV4 PW MPK

RED HOUR

4/1/92 Peel *Almost there, All I need, Free fall, William Jailor.* Geoff Cooke (d), Chris Hughes (b), Roger Birby (lg), Roger Lindsay (rg), Dave Canavan (lv). 17/11/91 MV3 DG MA&PA

RED LETTER DAY

21/4/86 Peel *Spark of love, Coming home, Killing ground, Pictures.* Ade (lv,g), Davie (lg,bkv), Keith (b,bkv), Daryn (d). 13/4/86 MV5 DG ME

RED LORRY YELLOW LORRY

13/1/83 Peel *Sometimes, Happy, Silence, Conscious decision.* Chris Reed (g), Martin Fagen (g), Mick Brown (d), Steve Smith (b), Joanna Dobson (sx). 22/12/82 MV4 * NG&AM

16/11/83 Peel *See the fire, Strange dream, Monkeys on juice.* Reed, Brown, Dane Wolfenden (g), Paul Southern (b,bkv). 5/11/83 MV4 DG TdB

27/9/84 Long *Sometimes, This today, Head all fire, Secret.* 6/9/84 MV5 BYA *

19/4/88 L. Kershaw *Big stick, Hands off me, The rise, Chance.* Reed, Wolfenden, Leon Phillips (b). 13/4/88 MV4 HP MA&FK

RED NINJA

1/12/91 Peel *Trenton job, Bad voicemen of the apocalypse, Killing at hellz gate, Look black in anger.* Motion (v), Loop T (prg,b), Sex Ninja (v), DJ Stix (bkv), Wadlow (bkv,smp), Peter Peter (bkv,smp), Gadjet (mel), IQ (k,smp). 22/10/91 MV4 MR~ AR

RED STAR BELGRADE

3/9/81 Skinner *New adventures, Streetcar, Zero heroes, Human camera.* Rick Hammerton (v,sy), Bruno Brown (lg), Paul Webb (b), Neil Youngs (d). 23/8/81 MV4 DG ME

THE REDSKINS

20/10/82 Peel† *The peasant army, Kick over the statues°, Reds strike the blues, Unionize & Pickin' the blues (outro).* Chris Dean (gv), Nick King (d), Millicent Martin (Hewes) (b) Steve Nichol (tp), Lloyd Dwyer (sx); & guests Dagenham Pete Pixie (bkv), John Mekon (bkv), Colin Car (bkv). 9/10/82 MV4 DG MR

† On Strange Fruit SFPS030; ° also on 'Winters of Discontent' SFRCD204.

15/8/83 Peel *Young and proud, Hold on, 99-and-a-half, Take no heroes.* Five-piece. 8/8/83 MV4 TW *

9/2/84 Jensen *Keep on keeping on, It can be done, A plateful of hateful.* 16/1/84 MV4 DG ME

REFRESHERS

5/4/82 Jensen *One step ahead, Gentle with the knife, Ambition, All night success.* Hazel Jones (v), Dai Chatley

(d), Bryn Williams (b), Paul Weston (g), Steve Rose (sy), Jonathan Gibb (tp). 21/3/82 MV4 DG ME

REGGAE REGULAR

3/7/78 Peel *Weed stalk, Fool's game/Fool's game (dub version), Where is Jah?, Not any more.* Junior Ewbanks (lg), Patrick Donnegan (rg,bkv), George 'Flee' Clarke (k), Trevor 'Seal' Salmon (b), Errol Francis (d), Tony Rookwood (lv-1and 4 only), Alan King (lv-2 and 3 only). 12/6/78 MV4 TW DD

10/10/78 Peel *Never needed nobody, That little girl, Ital club, Victim of life.* 27/9/78 MV4 MR NG

REGINALD

31/7/71 Top Gear *The weaver, Half the story, Seelookhearfeel.* John Horne (bgv), Roger Greenwood (gv), Brian Howe (o,tp,v), Walter Day (dv), Dave Almond (lg,sx,v). 20/7/71 * JW *

TERRY REID

1/6/68 SAT. CLUB *Penny, Without expression, Better by far, Summertime blues.* Terry Reid (lgv), Eric Leese (o), Keith Webb (d). 28/5/68 PH KB *&BC

Panel failed this trial b'cast: 'nothing exceptional'.

2/3/69 Top Gear *Tinker tailor, Writing on the wall, Marking time, Without expression.* Pete Shelley (o,p) r. Leese. 11/2/69 PH BA AH

2nd trial b'cast, this time, just passed by panel.

19/10/69 DLT *Marking time, May fly, Superlungs.* 13/10/69 AO2 c.PWI *

10/11/71 Peel *Anyway, Thine to try, Dreamin'.* Reid & David Lindeley (psg,v), Lee Miles (b) & (d) unknown. 19/10/71 MV4 * BC

THE RELATIONS

23/4/86 Peel *Come back home, Mr Wonderful, Holy water, You can call me anything.* Neil (d), Vinny (b), Kelly (g), Gerry (v). 15/4/86 MV4 DG MR&MWT

RELUCTANT STEREOTYPES

29/9/80 Read *M.O.D, Visual romance, Plans for today, The label.* Winston (v), Steve (cd), Paul (b), Tony (g), Colin (d). 25/9/80 MV4 CL *

REM

13/3/91 Campbell *World leader pretend, Fretless, Half a world, Radio song, Losing my religion, Love is all around.* Michael Stipe (v), Peter Buck (ag,mnd), Mike Mills (bv), Bill Berry (perc); & Peter Holsapple (various). All acoustic set, promoting then new album 'Out of Time'. Live from MV5 MPK~SA&SB

THE REMAYNES

2/1/86 Kershaw *Space hopper, The 15th, Tainted love, Outside your door.* Cally (dv), Joss Cope (k), Barry Dance (b), Donald Ross Skinner (g). 12/12/85 Y2 SP TWN

THE REMIPEDS

25/8/81 Peel *Keep me hanging on, Snooky, Bodily contact, Ain't no day.* Ozzie Orzell (lv-2,4), Rick Kulak (g,bkv,lv-3), Eddie K (k,bkv,lv-1), Dave Hughes (b,bkv), Sugar Ray McKnight (d,bkv), Glynn Bartlett (tp), Alphonso Augusto Montuori (sx). 17/8/81 MV4 CL DD

JOHN RENBOURN AND TERRY COX

4/12/68 NIGHT RIDE *Moondog, Sally free and easy, Lady nothing toye foux, Lamente di Tristram, La rotta, Melancholy galliard, Earl of Salisbury.* John Renbourn (g), Terry Cox. 28/11/68 PC1 JM *

Renbourn debuted with a solo session on the Light Programme's Folk Room, TX 28/8/65, prod. BA [M: Folk shows].

JOHN RENBOURN AND JACQUI MCSHEE

11/12/68 NIGHT RIDE *Watch the stars. Crying sometime, Every night when the sun goes in, My Johnny was a shoeman, The lags' song.* John Renbourn (g), Jacqui McShee (v). 10/12/68 SI JM *

7/5/73 Harris *Wedding dress, Melancholy galliard/Der judens tanz, Lord Franklin, Flower of Northumberland.* 25/4/73 * JG *

24/7/73 Sequence *Portland town, Reynardine, The silkie, Willie o' the Winsborough.* 5/4/73 LH1 JM BAI&MG

RENEGADE SOUND WAVE
22/6/87 Peel *Kray twins, Traitor, How to be hard, Blue-eyed boy.* Gary Asquith (v), Danny Briottet (b), Carl Bonnie (g). 2/6/87 * DG MA&ME

RENIA
1/10/73 Harris *Cowboy's dream, Love ticket, Shelter (& With what you say,* not broadcast). Peter Sutherland (k,bkv), Malcolm Sutherland (b), Dave Matthew (d), John Robinson (lg), Kenny Stewart (lv). 29/8/73 LH1 JG *

RENAISSANCE
18/10/69 Top Gear *Island, Bullet, Innocents.* Keith Relf (gv,hca), Jim McCarthy (dv), Jane Relf (v), John Hawken (pv), Louis Cennamo (b). 7/10/69 MV5 JW *
Rec'd Peel Concert 26/3/70 PS, TX 5/4/70.
14/5/70 Henry *The sea, The face of yesterday, Bullet.* 7/5/70 AO2 MB MH&MF

REPETITION
17/8/81 Peel *Carnival, Autumn, On the other side, Enchantment.* Andy Hooper (k), Steve Musham (v), Jim Solar (b,g,k), Tim Transe (d). 8/8/81 MV4 DG MR

REPUBLIC
23/9/92 Goodier *Forty years, Everybody's killed somebody, Red, Awayday.* Nigel Potter (d), Darren Betts (b), Simon Hawes (g), Charlie Robinson (lv). 22/8/92 MV4 MC~

RESISTANCE
9/5/79 Peel *Incognito, Walking talking abstract man, Svengali number two, Closet kings.* Mark Damron (lv,g), John O'Leary (b,bkv), Iain Reid (k,bkv), Martin Saunders (d,perc). 2/5/79 MV4 JS NG
6/1/81 Peel *Don't fraternise with the fraternity, Ego, Black comedy, Nuclear family.* 15/12/80 LH1 TW DD

RESTRICTED CODE
17/3/81 Peel *Monkey monkey monkey, We know we know, Yakov bok, Shake your body.* Tom Cannavan (v,g), Frank Quadrelli (gv), Kenny Blythe (bv), Stephen Lironi (d,perc); & Ian Duff (p). 10/3/81 LH1 DG MR
13/5/81 Skinner *Day after day, Ghost story, Dancin' in the streets, I never needed anyone as much as you.* 1/5/81 LH1 DG AP

RESTRICTION
21/8/84 Skinner *Irie feeling, Hazy skies, Sister, Callin' for mercy.* Andrew Clarke (d), Mark Spence (b), Rob Smith (g), Charlie Clarke (sx), Basil Anderson (k), Jenny Allison (v), Eric 'The General' McCarthy (v). 2/8/84 MV5 SFX MC

ORQUESTA REVE
23/7/89 Kershaw *Suave suave, Agui todo se resueve, Oye mira y calla.* Elio Reve (timb), Antonio Gomez (p), Gilberto Oviedo (tres), Romil Travieso (tb), Rene Garcia (vi), Moises Valle (v), Juan M. Dias (v), Odelquis Reve (cga), Roberto Flores (b), Fidel Laniel (tb), Marcello Cruz (tb), Raul Martinez (guiro), William Padrino (v). 8/6/89 ED DG NG

THE REVILLOS
25/9/79 Jensen *Where's the boy for me, Scuba scuba, Motorbike beat, Jukebox sound.* * 10/9/79 MV5 * *
29/10/79 Read *Motor bike beat, Where's the boy for me (30/10), Scuba scuba (31/10), Juke box sound (1/11).* * 4/10/79 MV4 CL ME
17/3/80 Peel *Scuba-scuba, You were meant for me, Rock-a-boom, Voodoo.* Hi Fi Harris (g), Felix (b), Rocky Rhythm (d), Fay Fife (lv), Eugene Reynolds (lv), Revettes (Babs and Cherie) (bkv). 10/3/80 MV4 TW DD
13/5/81 Peel *Caveman raveman, She's fallen in love with a monster man, Snatzo mobile, Man attack.* Kid Krupa (g), Vince 'Spik' Santini (b) r. Harris, Felix 29/4/81 LH1 CL *
23/6/81 Skinner *Bongo brain, Your baby's gone, Do the mutilation, The big shot.* 18/6/81 LH1 DG MR
17/3/84 Long *Big boss, Midnight, The vampire strikes, Devil in the new man.* * 27/2/84 * c.PWL *

REVOLVER
29/7/91 Goodier *Crimson, Heaven sent an angel, Nothing*

without you, Headfall. Mat Flint (gv), Hamish Brown (b), Nick Dewey (d). 20/7/91 MV5 MC~
23/11/91 Peel *Crimson, Drowning inside, Wave†, John's not mad†.* 12/9/91 MV5 DG NG&SA
† On Strange Fruit SFMCD214.

THE REZILLOS
30/12/77 Peel *(My baby does) good sculptures, No, Fight amongst yourselves, Top of the Pops.* Angel Paterson (d,bkv), William Mysterious (b,bkv), Luke Warm (Jo Callis) (g,bkv), Fay Fife (lv), Eugene Reynolds (lv). 12/12/77 MV4 CL BAI
8/6/78 Peel *Cold wars (have cooled me down), Destination Venus, Somebody's gonna get their heads kicked in tonight, I can't stand my baby (soul version).* Simon Templar (b) r. Mysterious. 31/5/78 MV4 BS NG
22/8/78 Jensen *Getting me down, Top of the pops, Glad all over, It gets me.* 14/8/78 MV5 PR ME

STEVE RHODES SINGERS
17/7/73 Peel *Akoi moi, Prayer for a traveller, Ibo native air, Adukpo no mo.* 25 singers (unknown).
Rec. date unknown OS * *

EMITT RHODES
24/11/71 Peel *Bubblegum cruiser, Birthday lady, Love will scare you, Really wanted you.* * 23/11/71 PH JW BC&IS

RHYTHM ETERNITY
26/6/92 Peel *Hold on tight, Freedom, Pink champagne.* Lynsey Davenport (v), Scott Rosser & Paul Spencer (k,prg). 24/5/92 MV3 ME~

THE RHYTHM METHOD
15/1/85 Long *Femme fatale, Red trees, Another notch on your sex gun, Softly in the morning.* Patrick Fitzsymons (v), Simon Thomson (g), Paul Kelly (d), Martin O'Kane (b), Chris Leggit (k); & Brian Carson (sx-4 only). 13/1/85 BEL * *

THE RHYTHM PIGS
9/11/87 Peel *Killer beat, New saviour, Simple, Satan tuned my snare.* Greg Adams (gv), Ed Ivey (bv), Bill Atwell III (d); & Terry Edwards (ts,al-4). 1/11/87 * DG ME&FK

THE RICH KIDS
7/11/77 Peel *Young girls, Rich kids†, Burnin' sounds, Bullet proof lover.* Midge Ure (g,lv), Steve New (g), Glen Matlock (bv), Rusty Egan (d). 31/10/77 MV4 TW DD
† On 'Winters of Discontent' SFRCD204.
3/4/78 Peel *Ghosts of princes and towers, Lovers and fools, Empty words, Here comes the nice.* Matlock (lv-3 only). 20/3/78 TW DD

RICHMOND
16/7/73 Harris *Raise your head to the wind, Work for my baby, Leaving again, Sitting on a cliff top.* Charles Seward (agv), Steve Hall (g) & (b), (d) unknown. 4/7/73 LH1 JG *

RIDE
26/2/90 Peel *Like a daydream, Dreams burn down, Perfect time, Sight of you.* Laurence Colber (d), Stephen Queralt (b), Andy Bell (g), Mark Gardner (gv). 4/2/90 MV3 DG MR
29/9/90 Peel *Severance, Here and now, All I can see, Decay.* 16/9/90 MV3 DG ME&FK
2/3/92 Goodier *Urgent rush, Moosecrap, Ride on time, The amazing adventures of Jellyhead.* 22/2/92 MV5 MA PA

RIFF
3/8/90 Fri. Rock *Promise don't cry, Ride the rainbow, No mercy, Singing the blues.* Frank Becking, Volker Britz, William Lennox, Burkherd Westerhoff. 13/7/90 MV5 MC~

JOSHUA RIFKIN
27/12/73 Peel *Searchlight rag, Sugar love, Country club, Weepin' willow.* Joshua Rifkin (p). 17/12/73 LH1 BA MF

MARC RILEY AND THE CREEPERS
29/11/83 Peel *Cure by choice, Location Bangladesh, Baby paints, Blow your own trumpet, Pickin' the nose.* Marc Riley (o,gv), Paul Fletcher (o,g), Jim Khambatta (k,bkv), Eddie Fenn (d), Pete Keogh (b). 21/11/83 MV4 TW MC

23/7/84 Peel *Snipe, Hole 4 a soul, Shirt scene, Shadow figure.* Clive Stewart (sx-1,4) r. Khambatta. 26/6/84 MV5 MRD TdB
26/2/85 Long *Breakneck sideswipe, Poop scoop, Harry's chin, Breakneck sideswipe pt 2.* Riley, Fenn, Fletcher, Keogh. 6/2/85 MV5 JS MPK
4/9/85 Peel *Black dwarf, Bard of Woking, Goin' rate, Cold fish.* & Jim Khambatta (o), Mike Gallagher (sx), Jon Hunter (tp). 25/8/85 MV5 DG ME
4/6/86 Peel *Another song about motorbikes, The adventures of Brian Glider, Bank of horrors, Stroke of genius.* Riley, Fenn, Gallagher, Phil Roberts (b,hca), Mark Tilton (g). 27/5/86 MV4 DG MR&MA
25/2/87 Peel *Lucky, Yea heavy and a bottle of bread, Sparks, Tearjerker.* Billed as 'The Creepers': same line-up. 8/2/87 * DG ME&TD

STEVE RILEY AND THE MAMOU PLAYERS
29/8/92 Kershaw *Mardi gras jig/Scott playboys special, Mon vieux wagon, Tit galop pour la pointei aux pains, La valse a defunt pepere.* Steve Riley (acc), Michael Chapman (d), David Greely, Kevin Barzas. 26/7/92 MV3 ME~

RIOT OF COLOUR
15/4/86 Peel *Skink, Watching, Cold hands.* Alex Osman (d), Dominic Blaazer (bv,g), Alistair Jackson (g). 8/4/86 MV4 DG MR&MS

RIP RIG AND PANIC
21/9/81 Peel *Symphony in Dave's flat, A grand grin and a shaky smile please Mr Barman, Pullover no sox.* Lambkin Shnod (vi,v), Finklebaum (ww), Miss Pib (d,perc), The Stinking Hog (b,ag), Nico (v-3). 14/9/81 MV4 DG AP
12/7/82 Peel *What are the toads doing so far from the swamp?, Instant sin sheds skin, Blasé.* Gareth Sager (g), Mark Springer (p), Sean Oliver (b), Andrea Oliver (v-3), Jez, Flash & Weasel (rd), David De Fries (tp), Steve Noble (perc), Giles Leaman (perc). 19/6/82 MV4 DG MR

RIPCORD
27/7/88 Peel *Barriers/Get away, Existence without cause/So strong/Aim to please, Collision of vision/No effort no thought, Vivisection/Passer by.* John Miller (d), Jim Whiteley (b), Steve Ballam (g), Steve Hazzard (v). 12/7/88 * MR~

RITUAL
14/12/81 Peel *Playtime, Mind disease, Human sacrifice, Brides.* Jamie Stewart (g), Mark Bond (b), Errol Blyth (v), Steve Pankhurst (sx), Ray Taylor-Smith (d). 7/12/81 MV4 TW DD

RITZEN RATZEN ROTZER
20/3/86 Kershaw *Ten bob haircut, Dog dog, Spice of life, Hairy Hungarian buttock dance.* Gordon Farago, Paul White, T. W. Milne, Peter, Kevin Evans, Emmylou, Michael Hurst. 13/3/86 Y2 NB PSM
16/10/86 Kershaw *Jingle, Stylish man, On thee hard, You can't polish a ****, Middle man.* Kev Sexual (v), Curly Hertzog (hca,g), Meccano Mule (acc,bj,tp), Little Miss Motormouth (sx), Blind Reverend Capstan Filter (b), Laughing Gravy (d). 1/10/86 Y2 DST TWN

RO RO
12/2/73 Harris *Help me understand, Blackbird, Travelling man.* 4 (unknown). 31/1/73 * JG *

ROADSIDE PICNIC
21/4/89 Skinner *Never too late, You get wet sleeping in the park, Kindred spirit, Steve on the beach.* Mario Castronari (b), Dave O'Higgins (ss,ts), John G. Smith (p,k,sy), Mike Bradley (d,perc). 5/3/89 * * *

ROADSIDE THEATRE
27/8/79 Kershaw *Pretty Polly, Dreams (I dreamed were mine), Cities of gold, Open door, Winter time in the mountain.* Ron Short (g,fd,v), Tommy Bledsoe (bj,v), Nancy Jeffrey & Kim Cole (v). 6/7/89 ED DG NG

ANDY ROBERTS AND ADRIAN HENRI
27/3/68 Night Ride *64 Canning street, Tonight at noon,*

8

287

Burdock river ran, Love story. Andy Roberts (gv), Adrian Henri (v). 19/3/68 S1 DK *

30/10/68 NIGHT RIDE See the conquering heroine comes, Galactic love poem, Hull poem. 30/10/68 S1 PC *

21/1/72 PEEL Ballad of chairman Shankly, One of those days, Morning song, Peter Pan man. 7/1/72 AO2 JM *

11/8/72 PEEL Winter song, The green green grass of London, I suppose you think it's funny (& King for a day, 15/9/72; & Galactic Love Poem SEQUENCE 3/11/72). 27/7/72 CM JM *

ANDY ROBERTS

28/3/70 TOP GEAR Just for the record, Creeping John, John the revelator, Cocaine (& You're a machine, 13/6/70). Andy Roberts (gv). 10/3/70 MV4 * BC

22/3/71 HARRIS Radio lady, Welcome home, Keep my children warm, I've seen the movie. Roberts, Bob Sargeant (p), John Porter (g), John Pearson (d), Dave Richards (b) (formerly known as Everyone, see above). 9/3/71 MV5 JWH

6/12/71 HARRIS Poison apple lady, Richmond, I work for Jesus in the personnel department, Elaine. Roberts, Bob Ronga (b), Ian Whiteman (p), Roger Powell (d). 15/11/71 T1 PD BH

16/4/73 HARRIS The song of the stars, Home at last, Break my mind (& The new Karensky, 16/7/73). & Neil Innes (g,pv). 21/3/73 LH1 PR GB

21/6/73 PEEL Harvest of tears, All around my grandmother's floor, Hobo Bill's last ride, Living in the halls of Zion. Solo. 11/6/73 LH1 JG *

7/9/73 SEQUENCE The great stampede, Kid jealousy, Lord of the graves, Clowns of the road. 26/7/73 LH1 JM BAI&MG

28/3/74 PEEL Rootie tootie, Havin' a party, I've got mine, From brown to blue, The great stampede, Speedwell. & 3 (unknown). 21/3/74 LH1 * *

See Roberts' other Peel gigs with Liverpool Scene, Plainsong, Viv Stanshall, Roy Harper, everyone and his dog...

THE TOM ROBINSON BAND

1/11/77 DLT 2-4-6-8 Motorway [Network session]. Tom Robinson (b,lv), Danny Kustow (lg,bkv), Brian 'Dolphin' Taylor (d,bkv), Mark Ambler (k). 24/10/77 MV5 PR *

7/11/77 PEEL Long hot summer, Don't take no for an answer, We ain't gonna take it, Martin. 1/11/77 MV4 JG MR

12/3/79 PEEL Black angel, Blue murder, All right all night, Crossing over the road, Law and order. Robinson, Kustow, Ian Parker (k, bkv,lv-5 only), Preston Hayman (d,perc). 5/3/79 MV4 TW DD

15/1/90 CAMPBELL 2-4-6-8 motorway, Blood brother, Glad to be gay, Boom time. Robinson, Kustow, Ambler, Steve Creese (d). 10/1/90 MV5 PW MPK

TOM ROBINSON AND JAKKO JAKSZYK

14/1/91 CAMPBELL We never had it so good, The baby rages on, What have I ever done to you, Blood brother. Tom Robinson (lv), Jakko Jakszyk (k,bkv), Gavin Harrison (d). 28/11/90 MV5 PW MPK

ROCK GODDESS

26/11/82 FRI. ROCK Take your love away, To be betrayed, Satisfied then crucified, Back to you, The love lingers still. Jody Turner (g,lv), Julie Turner (dv), Tracey Lamb (bv). 5/11/82 * TW&AP *

ROCKS

14/2/78 PEEL Firefly, Spectrum, Ready for Freddie, Horn song (who put the shanty on the shimmy loo). Mike Patto (lv, p-1,2), Chris Stainton (p-3,4; o-1,2), Fred Gandy (b), Bernie Holland (g), John Halsey (d). 7/2/78 MV4 MB MR

JESS RODEN

10/9/74 PEEL What the hell, Live love and learn, Reason to change, Feelin' easy. Jess Roden (v) & Iguana, to be the J. R. Band henceforth: John Cartwright (b), Pete Hunt (d), Bruce Roberts (g), Steve Webb (g), Ron Taylor (al), Chris Gower (tb). 27/8/74 LH1 TW *

30/12/74 HARRIS Sad story, Trouble in the mind, Celebrate. 20/11/74 * JG *

1/5/75 PEEL Lies, Honey don't worry, Under suspicion, What took me so long. 24/4/75 TW *

1/4/76 PEEL Blowin', In a circle, You can leave your hat on, On a winner with you. Billy Livsey (k) joins. 18/3/76 MV4 *

17/12/76 PEEL Stay in bed, The Ballad of big Sally, U.S. dream, Me and crystal eye. 7/12/76 MV4 JG MR

S. E. ROGIE

24/3/88 KERSHAW Koneh Pelawoebeh, Don't touch me tomatoe, Nyalima Nyapoi, Passion. S. E. Rogie (gv). 17/3/88 * DG NG&JB

9/3/89 KERSHAW Clue koondi, Ndma neneekpa, Please go easy with me, Keke kekefarana. 2/3/89 MV4 DG TdB

23/6/91 KERSHAW Song of unity, Stop backbiting, Recipe for true and lasting happiness. Rogie 'and his Palm Wine Trotters': Gideon Rogers (d), Aston Martin (b), Leonard S. Jones (g), David Oladunni (cga). 23/5/91 MV5 DG MA&AA

ROGUE MALE

20/9/85 INTO THE MUSIC Dressed incognito, On the line, Get off my back, Rough tough. Steve Kingsley (dv), Kevin Collier (bv), Jim Lyttle (g,lv), Johnny Frazer-Binnie (lgv). 6/9/85 MV4 DD~

ABDUL TEE-JAY ROKOTO

30/7/89 KERSHAW Kanka kuru, Fire dombolo, Salay matu, Kondi call. Abdul Tee-Jay (glv), Zozo Mohammed (b,bkv), Sidik Fofana (d,bkv), Sam Maitland (g,bkv), David Oladunni (perc,bkv), Denis Otunni (ts), Colin Graham (tp). 30/7/89 ED DG MA

ROMA

9/11/90 FRI. ROCK Feeling for love, Dancing under neons, Too much, Wasted. Mark Smith (v), Tony Watkins (gv), Rob Clewley (bv), Mic Smith (d). 19/10/90 MV5 MC~

ROMAN HOLIDAY

17/8/82 PEEL Motor maniac, One more jilt, Jive dive, Standby. Steve Lambert (lv), John Durno (b,bkv), Brian Bonhomme (g,bkv), Simon Cohen (d), Mike Deacon (p), Robert Lambert (sx), John Eacott (tp), Bob Fish (v). 31/7/82 MV4 DG MR

25/1/83 PEEL Furs and high heels, Chartreuse, No ball games. Fish out; Adrian York (k) r. Deacon. 17/1/83 * TW MC

ROMEO'S DAUGHTER

1/9/89 FRI. ROCK Heaven in the back seat, Velvet tongue, Wild child, I cry myself to sleep. Leigh Matty (v), Andy Wells (v), Craig Joiner (g), Ed Poole (b), Tony Mitman (k). 21/7/89 MV5 TW *

THE ROOGALATOR

31/5/76 PEEL Ride with the Roogalator, All aboard, Tasty two, Cincinnati fatback. Daniel Adler (g,lv), Nick Plytas (k), Jeff Watts (b), Bobby Irwin (d). 13/5/76 MV4 TW *

11/11/76 PEEL Sock it to my pocket, Walkin' in the heat, If you don't like smelling it you'd better stop selling it. Julian Scott (b), Justin Hildreth (d) r. Watts, Irwin. 28/10/76 MV4 TW *

1/9/77 PEEL Love and the single girl, Easy talk, Mind breeding, Sweet Moma. Adler (lv-3, 4 only), Plytas (lv-1 only). 16/8/77 MV4 MB MR

ROOM 101

28/9/83 PEEL 101, I've got your number, Rivers, I'm not your kind. Danny Senninger (kgb,v-3,4), Mae Fortune (k,sy,v-1,2). 21/9/83 MV4 RP TdB

THE ROOM

13/1/81 PEEL Who are your friends, Waiting room, Fever, Crash. Becky Stringer (b), Dave Jackson (v), Clive Thomas (d), Robyn Odlum (b). Rec. date unknown PRIV * *

5/10/81 PEEL Heat haze, Bated breath, Escalator, Rewind, Conversation. 26/9/81 MV4 DG AP

30/6/82 PEEL No dream, Chat shows, Candle, Summer sex signals. 22/5/82 MV4 DG MR

9/7/83 LONG Ringing, Never, On the beach. 13/6/83 PHM cJL *

16/10/84 LONG The friendly enemy, Crying red, A shirt of fire, Naive. Jackson, Stringer, Peter Baker (k), Alan Wills (d), Paul Cavanagh (g). 23/9/84 MV5 DG ME

29/4/85 PEEL† The storm, Here comes the floor, But when do we start to live?, Jeremiah. 14/4/85 MV5 DG ME
Jackson, Stringer & Baker re-formed as Benny Profane (see above). † On Strange Fruit SFPS062.

THE ROSE OF AVALANCHE

12/6/85 PEEL Goddess, A thousand landscapes, Gimme some lovin', Rise to the groove. Philip Morris (v), Alan Davis (b), Paul Berry (g), Glenn Schultz (g); & Steve Allen (k). 28/5/85 MV5 MR~

11/3/86 LONG Velveteen, A stick in the works, Too many castles, Never another sunset. & Mark Thompson (d). 5/3/86 MV4 BYA MFA

ROSE TATTOO

15/5/81 FRI. ROCK Bad boy, Nice boys, Butcher and fast Eddy, Rock 'n' roll outlaws. Angry Anderson (v), Peter Wells (slg,v), Mick Cocks (g), Geordie Leech (b), Digger Roxal (d). 22/4/81 * TW DD

TIM ROSE

1/10/67 TOP GEAR Hey Joe, Come away Melinda, You're slipping away from me, Morning dew, Fare thee well. Tim Rose (ag,v), Alan Weighall (b), Dougie Wright (d). 25/9/67 PC1 BA DT

22/10/67 TOP GEAR When I was a young man, Another side to this life, I gotta do things my way, Morning dew, Hello sunshine. & David O'List (g), '& 3 musicians, drums, bass, guitar, organ [ie. The Nice], & Madeline Bell, Lesley Duncan, Kay Garner' (all bkv). 16/10/67 AO2 BA *

22/2/68 POP NORTH I got a loneliness, Morning dew. & (b), (d) unknown. 19/2/68 PHM JWX *

25/2/68 TOP GEAR King lonely the blue, Cobwebs, I got a loneliness, Come away Melinda, Memory pain, Long time man. & The Aynsley Dunbar Retaliation, '& Lesley Duncan for 3 singers' (2 & 5: Aynsley Dunbar Retaliation only). 20/2/68 AO2 BA PR

The day after this live on R1 Club at PH.

2/3/68 SAT. CLUB Roanoke, I got a loneliness, Eat drink and be merry, Morning dew. * 27/2/68 PH BB *

7/7/68 TOP GEAR I guess it's over, Long-haired boy, Roanoke, Foggy mountain breakdown. & 2 musicians, including Roger Coulam (o,md). 1/7/68 PC1 BA

28/7/68 HENRY I got a loneliness, Long-haired boy, Dim light. 21or22/7/68 PS AD *

Next, live on Radio One O'Clock from PH 12/8/68.

22/9/68 TOP GEAR When I was a young man, Angela, Kangaroo, Dim light, Long-haired boy. & (d), (b), (o) unknown. 16/9/68 PC1 BA *

9/11/70 HARRIS Sympathy, I've got to get a message to you, Georgie by morning, You can't stop yourself. * 30/10/70 MV5 JM JWH

15/11/70 DLT You can't stop yourself, Morning dew. & 5 musicians (unknown). 2/11/70 PS c.PWI *

DR. ROSS

12/1/73 SEQUENCE My little woman, Dr Ross boogie, Cat squirrel. Dr. Ross. 8/12/72 LH1 JM *

ROTE KAPELLE

3/12/86 PEEL† Marathon man, Sundays, Acid face baby, Jellystone park. Jonathan Muir (d), Malcolm Kergan (b), Chris Henman (g), Ian Binns (k), Margarita Vazquez Ponte & Andrew Tully (perc,v). 9/11/86 * DG SC
† On In-Tape Records IT44.

ROUEN

1/8/85 INTO THE MUSIC Run with you, Hold me, No better place to die, Ordinary life. Nick Allsopp (bkv), 'J' Johnson (d), Mark 'Roz' Roslanowski (g), Nick Sellers (k), Nik Cox (v). 6/7/85 MV4 DG ME&MC

ROUGH JUSTICE

27/11/81 FRI. ROCK Motorway mad, 90 000 miles, Hey you, Bad luck. Paul Edwards (v), Geoff Taylor (g), Russ Middleton (g), Nick Downes (b), Paul Graham (d). 23/10/81 * TW DD&AP

ROXY MUSIC

21/1/72 Peel *Remake remodel, B.O.B. medley, Would you believe, If there is something (& Sea breezes, 18/2/72).* Bryan Ferry (kv), Andy Mackay (sx,cl,ob), Eno (sy,el,bkv), David O'List (g), Graham Simpson (b), Paul Thompson (d). 4/1/72 T1 JM JWH&BAI

23/6/72 Peel *Bitters end, 2HB, Chance meeting, Ladytron.* Phil Manzanera (g), Peter Paul (b), r. O'List, Simpson. 23/5/72 T1 JM NG&BAI

1/8/72 Peel *Virginia Plain (& If there is something,* not on *PasB* possibly not broadcast). Rik Kenton (b), r. Paul. 18/7/72 MV4 PR MF

9/11/72 Peel *The B.O.B. medley, For your pleasure, The bogus man pt. II.* 6/11/72 LH1 BA *

8/3/73 Peel *Editions of you, Pyjamerama, In every dream home a heartache.* Sal Maida (b), r. Kenton. 5/3/73 LH1 BA *

Contract file suggests group's only other BBC studio session might have been 'Pyjamerama' as a Network session 28/2/73 PH, prod PWI. John Porter credited as (b). As to whether this actually transpired...

RUBELLA BALLET

6/7/82 Peel *Slant and slide, Belfast, Ballet dance, T, Me.* Sid Attion (d,bkv), Gem Stone (b,bkv), Peter Fender (g,bkv), Zillah Minx (v). 29/5/82 MV4 DG MR

8/2/83 Peel *Love life, Newz, Exit, Blues.* Mark Adams (g) r. Fender. 26/1/83 * RP MC

RUBY BLUE

7/5/89 Kershaw *Take your money, Not alone, Somebody say something, The song of the mermaid to Mr Levy the sailor.* Rebecca Pidgeon (lv,ag), Chris Buck (d,bkv), Anthony Coote (b,bkv), Roger Fife (g,bkv), Erika Spotswood (v). 13/4/89 WX DG MA

24/9/90 Campbell *Can it be, Take your money, Something's gone wrong, Bloomsbury blue.* Pascal Consoli (d) r. Buck. 22/8/90 MV4&5 PW MWT

DAVID RUDDER & TAMBU

2/9/90 Kershaw *One more officer, No no we ain't going home, Down at the shebeen, The journey.* David Rudder (v), Tambu (v), Vonrick Maynard (d), Anthony Voisin (g), Pelham Goddard (k), Edward Elliott (tb), Michael Lindsay & Haydn Robin (tp), Albert Bushe (b,bkv), Louis Wharwharwood (g,bkv), Leo Stephenson (sx), Winston Matthe (perc). 23/8/90 MV5 DG MA&FK

RUDI

23/6/80 Read *Time to be proud, Without you, The pressure's on, Yummy yummy.* Brian Young (gv), Ronnie Matthews (bv), Graham Marshall (d). 29/5/80 MV4 CL *

28/9/81 Peel *Crimson, Tiger land, When I was dead, Excitement.* 21/9/81 * DG HP&GP

16/12/81 Jensen *Frozen by your touch, Toy town, Crimson, Life.* & Paul Martin (k). 3/12/81 MV4 JS *

THE RUDIES

26/12/70 Top Gear *Moon bug, You make me so very happy, Patches (& Oh me oh my,* not broadcast). Danny Smith (d), Trevor Donnelly (b), Sonny Binns (o), Erroll Dann (g), Glenroy Oakley (v). 23/11/70 PH JW *

Auditioned 7/68 as Glenroy Oakley and the Oracles, failed. This trial b/cast failed too: 'Badly played' 'wrong chords' 'pseudo-reggae' 'out of tune' said panel. Reformed as Greyhound May 1971.

RUEFREX

24/9/85 Long *In the traps, By the shadowline, The Ruah, Even in the dark hours.* Paul Burgess (d), Jackie Forgie (g), Gary Ferris (g), Tom Coulter (b), Allan Clarke (v), Cathal Coughlan (k). 15/9/85 BYA JB

RUMILLAJATA

11/2/90 Kershaw *La guambrita, Karallanta, Tempestad, Corti poncho.* Jorge Laura (mnd), Hugo Rodriguez (gv), Adrian Villanueva (fl,d), Miguel Puna (pp), Nestor Tintaya (pp,dv). 7/12/89 MV5 DG *

THE RUMOUR

3/6/77 Peel *Something's going on, Do nothing 'til you*

hear from me, I'm so glad, Lookin' after number one. Brinsley Schwarz (g), Martin Belmont (g,v), Andrew Bodnar (b), Steve Goulding (d), Bob Andrews (p,v), Paul Carrack (o,v), John Earle (ts), Mick Hanson (tp). 23/5/77 MV4 TW DD

RUN FOR FUN

21/8/85 Long *This time, Friends again, Only to a memory, A new evening gone.* Craig Lindsay (bv), David Wren (k), Glen Massey (g), Steve Simmons (d). 24/7/85 MV4 BYA MPK

RUNRIG

2/1/84 Jensen *Night fall on Marsco, Fuaim a bhlar, Skye, Toll dubh.* Donnie Munro (lv), Malcolm Jones (lg), Rory MacDonald (b,bkv), Richard Cherns (k), Ian Bayne (d), Calum MacDonald (perc,bkv). 15/12/83 MV4 DG DD

TODD RUNDGREN

24/7/72 Harris *I saw the light, A dream goes on forever, I'm so proud, Hello it's me.* Todd Rundgren (p,gv). 3/7/72 T1 JG *

Rec'd In Concert 6/7/72 PS, TX 15/7/72.

THE RUNNING MAN

4/11/71 Drummond *Hope place, If you like, Find yourself, Another.* Ray Russell & (tp) (ts,fl), (b), (d), (v) unknown. 27/10/71 MV4 MB MH&MF

17/2/72 Drummond *Smile, Spirit, Electric lady.* 9/2/72 MV4 MB MH&MF

TOM RUSH

21/1/68 Top Gear *Sunshine sunshine, No regrets, Something in the way she moves, Tin angel.* Tom Rush (gv) & 'The Bob Potter 12'. 10/1/68 * * *

RAY RUSSELL'S ROCK WORKSHOP

10/4/70 Black *Spine cop, Wade in the water, Buy me a bluebird, He looks at me, Ice cold (& Theme for freedom, 8/5/70).* Ray Russell (md) & (tp), 2 x (ts), (tb), (o,p), (b), (d), (perc) unknown, but including Alex Harvey. 6/3/70 PH JM *

Russell's Quartet first appeared on the Light Programme's Jazz Scene, 14/5/67 [M: R1 Jazz shows].

19/6/70 Black *You to lose, Born in the city, Primrose hill (& Spine cop, Hole in my stocking, 10/7/70).* & Alex Harvey & large band. 5/6/70 AO1 JM *

18/8/70 Harding *Theme for freedom, Wade in the water, Ice cold.* & Alex Harvey. 4/8/70 MV5 MB MH&MF

3/9/70 Henry *Just to be apart, Time of the last persecution, Inside the keeper's pantry (& Plan D, 8/10/70).* Bill Fay & Ray Russell's Trio. 25/8/70 MV5 MB MH&MF

9/3/71 Harding *What's mine is mine, Living reason, Forgotten to live, Street war.* Ray Russell & 9-piece band 1/3/71 MV5 MB MH&MF

[M: R3 Jazz shows; & links for SEQUENCE].

THE RUSSIANS

19/7/79 Peel *Can't explain, Meet me after school tonight, Manic depression, Stop you're killing me.* John Brassett (b,bkv), Dusty Miller (v), John Lucibello (d), Julie Rebelovitch (v). 9/7/79 MV4 TW DD

RUTHLESS RAP ASSASSINS

26/6/89 Peel *Three the hard way†, Posse strong, Just mellow.* Dangerous Hinds (kv), Dangerous 'C' Carsonova (tt,v), M.C. Kermit le Freak (v), Paul Roberts (g). 4/6/89 MV3 DG ME

† On 'Manchester- so much to answer for' SFRCD202.

THE RUTS

29/1/79 Peel† *Savage circle, Babylon's burning, Dope for guns, Black man's pinch, Criminal mind.* Malcolm Owen (lv), Paul Fox (g,bkv), Vince 'Segs' Jennings (b,bkv), Dave Ruffy (d,bkv). 23/1/79 MV4 * MR

9/3/79 Jensen *In a rut, Babylon's burning, Something that I said.* 26/2/79 * JG *

21/5/79 Peel† *Sus, Society, You're just a..., It was cold, Something that I said.* & Mannah (bkv-1 only). 14/5/79 MV4 TW DD

18/2/80 Peel† *Staring at the rude boys, Demolition dancing, In a rut, Secret soldiers.* 11/2/80 MV4 TW DD

† On Strange Fruit SFRCD109.

10/3/81 Peel *Different view, Parasites, Fools lead the fools, Mirror smashed.* Billed as 'Ruts DC' from now on: Segs, Ruffy, Fox, & Gary Barnacle (sx,k). 16/2/81 LH1 TW DD

31/3/81 Skinner *Different view, Dangerous minds, Fools lead the fools, Despondency.* 6/3/81 LH1 DG AP

SABBAT

27/2/87 Fri. Rock *A cautionary tale, For those who died, The 13th disciple.* Andy Sneap, Martin Walkyer, Fraser Craske, Simon Negus. 6/2/87 MV4 * *

SAD LOVERS AND GIANTS

3/12/81 Peel *Alice isn't playing, There was no time, Sex without gravity, Clint.* Garcon (v), Tristian Garel-Funk (g), Cliff Silver (b), Nigel (d), David (k,sx). 25/11/81 MV4 RP NG

SADE

12/3/84 Jensen *Sally, Smooth operator, When am I going to make a living?, Hang on to your love.* Sade (v), Stuart Matthewman (g,sx), Andrew Hale (k), Paul Denman (b), Blair Cunningham (d), Dave Early (perc). 23/2/84 MV5 DG MPK

SAFFRON

14/4/73 Night Ride *Hear now, Streets of London, Day is done.* Karen Chapman (v,tamb), Michael Welch (bv), Michael Nuttall (gv), Brian Knowles (gpv). 21/2/73 AO1 cCCM * [M: R2]

18/3/74 Harris *Salisbury plain, Meet you there, Will the ploughman ever return.* 6/2/74 LH1 PR NG

BRIDGET ST. JOHN

28/8/68 Night Ride *To be without a hitch, Ask me no questions, Many happy returns, Rochefort, Lizard-long-tongue boy.* Bridget St. John (agv). 21/8/68 S1 DK *
'Borderline pass' from Audition panel: critical comments included 'pretentious rubbish' 'her guitar-playing is inaccurate and uninspired and her voice dull'.

27/4/69 Night Ride *I like to be with you in the sun, The curious crystals of unusual purity, Turquoise, Don't think twice it's alright, Night in the city, Autumn Lullaby.* 9&11/4/69 S1 JK *

24/8/69 Top Gear *Curl your toes, Night in the city†, Hello again (of course) (& Song to keep you company†, The river†, Lazarus†, Like never before, 18/10/69).* 21/7/69 MV1 JW TW&MF

† On 'Top Gear' LP BBC Records REC 52S. Also appeared on 'The Peter Sarstedt Programme' R1 19/10/69.

21/11/70 Top Gear *Back to stay, The leaves of lime, City crazy, If you'd been there.* 9/11/70 PH JW *
Appeared on Peel Sunday Concert 17/5/70 PS; & her own R1 folk show, 20/9/70 with guests Kevin Ayers and John Martyn.

10/12/70 Henry *The lady and the gentle man, Down Derry daye, The river, Flying.* 3/12/70 AO2 MB *

10/5/71 Harris *City crazy, Thank you for, The pebble and the man, Making losing better, Song for the laird of Connaught hall (& Oh my, 31/5/71).* & Kevin Ayers (v-6). 27/4/71 MV5 JM *
Had also done 2nd Peel's Sunday Concert, TX 31/1/71.

25/10/71 Harris *Happy day, Celine, Early morning song, Lazarus (& City crazy, 22/11/71).* 5/10/71 T1 JM JWH ·
Did 3rd Peel Sunday Concert, TX 19/9/71.

10/4/72 Harris *To leave your cover, Fly high, Thank you for, Nice (& Lazarus, 15/5/72).* & (b), (d) unknown. 22/3/72 AO2 JG *

25/4/72 Peel *Thank you for, Happy day, Silver coin, Fly high.* & 1 (unknown). 27/3/72 PH JW BC

7/7/72 Peel *Fly high, To leave your cover, If you've got money in your pockets, Ask me no questions.* & 3 (unknown). 5/6/72 MV5 JM *

24/8/72 DRUMMOND *Love minus zero, Nice, Every day, Song for the laird of Connaught hall.* 31/7/72 MV5 MB *

19/2/73 HARRIS *Last goodnight, The road was lonely on my own, Head and heart, Keep smiling.* 7/2/73 LH1 PR *

30/4/73 SEQUENCE *Last goodnight, Sparrow pit, Jumble queen, Head & heart.* 29/3/73 LH1 JM BAI&MG

7/6/73 PEEL *Sparrow pit, Passing thru, Jumble queen, The road was lonely on my own. & 3 (unknown).* 7/5/73 LH1 BA *

18/12/73 PEEL *Curious & woolly, Choosing you lose one, Jumble queen; Sparrow pit, In the bleak midwinter.* 3/12/73 TI TW *

10/6/74 HARRIS *I don't know if I can take it anymore, Some kind of beautiful, Song for the Waterden widow, Want to be with you.* 1/5/74 LH1 PR *

29/8/74 PEEL *Want to be with you, Song for the Waterden widow, Some kind of beautiful, I don't know if I can take it anymore, Present song.* 12/8/74 LH1 JW *

Did 4th In Concert, rec'd 1/8/74 HP, TX 14/9/74, & (p,clav), (lg), (b), (d) unknown.

7/1/76 PEEL *Come up and see me sometime, Catch a falling star, Untitled song, Bumper to bumper. & 1 (unknown).* 11/12/75 MV4 * *

5th In Concert rec'd 18/4/75 PS, TX 3/5/75; & twice on R2 Folkweave '75.

26/11/76 PEEL *Moody, grow, Crazy have you Eton, Song for you.* 4/11/76 MV4 * *

SALFORD JETS

10/3/80 READ *Gina, Who you looking at?, I want my girlfriend back, Cops and robbers.* Diccon Hubbard (bv), Rod Gerrard (lgv), Geoff Kerry (elp,o,v), Dave Morris (dv), Mike Sweeney (lv). 8/2/80 MV4 JS *

15/12/80 READ *Lookin' at the squares, The lonely one, Little girl it's you, Keep away from my baby.* 5/12/80 LH1 DG AP

SALLY ANGIE

4/12/68 NIGHT RIDE *Children of the sun, Song of the healer, Flee the melancholy flower, Lady Mary, Midsummer night happening.* Sally Oldfield (gpv), Mike Oldfield (g). 3/12/68 PC1 PC *

In 7/69, Sally Oldfield re-auditioned as a solo act, but was 'not considered suitable'.

SALVATION SUNDAY

12/2/86 LONG *Hide your heart, Shades of blue, In and out of love, Heart in motion.* Joanne Winterbottom (v), Steve Winterbottom (rg), David Rowley (d), Marvin Naylor (lg), Robert Mingo Talbert (k), Martin Baker (b). 2/2/86 HP BYA NG

SAM APPLE PIE

24/8/69 STAGE ONE *Tiger man, Uncle Sam's blues, Wandering.* Sam Sampson (v,hca,fl), Mick 'Tinkerbell' Smith (lg), Andy 'Snakehips' Johnson (slg), David Charles (d), Bob Renny (b). 19/8/69 PH c.DGE *

15/9/70 HARDING *Listen to me, Do the toilet (convenience rock), You can't tell me.* Michael Stuart, Derek Smith r. Smith, Charles. 1/9/70 MV5 MB MH&MF

11/5/71 HARDING *Blackhearted woman, Goodbye my friend, King Kong's breath.* 3/5/71 MV5 MB MH&MF

16/2/73 SEQUENCE *Old Tom, Another Orpheus, Call me boss, Flying.* Sampson, Renny, Johnson & Denny Barnes (lg), Lee Baxter Hayes Jr. (d). 16/1/73 TI JM *

SAMSON

2/11/79 FRI. ROCK *Big brother, Six foot under, Hammerhead, Take it like a man.* Paul Samson (g), Chris Aylmer (b), Thunderstick (d), Bruce Dickinson (v). 17/10/79 * TW DD

16/3/84 FRI. ROCK *Don't get mad get even, Doctor ice, Love hungry, Are you ready?* Samson & Dave Colwell (g), Merv Goldsworthy (b), Pete Jupp (d), Nicky Moore (v). 24/2/84 MV4 TW DD

6/6/86 FRI. ROCK *Tomorrow, One day heroes, A matter of time, Turn on the lights.* Billed as 'Paul Samson's

Empire': Samson & Kevin Riddles (bk), Mark Brabbs (d), Dave Colwell (gk), Sam Blue (v). 23/5/86 MV4 TW *

11/8/89 FRI. ROCK *Love this time, State of emergency, Look to the future, Someone to turn to.* Samson & Toby Sadler (k), Peter Scallan (v), Dave Boyce (b), Charlie Mack (d). 7/7/89 MV3 TW *

OUMOU SANGARE

6/10/91 KERSHAW *Moussolou, Ah N'diya, Diaraby Nene, Sadionna (trad. hunter's song).* Oumou Sangare (lv), Mabintou Diakite & Alima Toure (bkv), Brehima Diakite & Kamalen Ngoni (unknown), Alou Outtapa (b), Aliou Traoare (vi), Boubacar Diallo & Tolo Schiaka (g,djembe). 12/8/91 MV5 MR~

THE SAPPHIRES

5/7/83 JENSEN *Don't say nuthin' bad about my baby, What's easy for two, Shoppin' around, Piece of my heart.* Ruby (v), Sylvia (v), Vicky (v), Pete Gage (g), John McKenzie (b), Keith O'Connell (k), Les Circle (d), Pete Thomas (sx). 30/6/83 MV4 JP MR

SARACEN

15/1/82 FRI. ROCK *Flame of youth, Jekyll and Hyde, Equinox, Crusader.* John Thorne (d), Barry Yates (b), Richard Lowe (k), Robert Bendelow (g), Steve Bettney (v). 9/12/81 * TW DD

14/2/85 INTO THE MUSIC *Cheatin', A face in the crowd, Love on sight, It's not over.* Bettney, Lowe, Danny Spencer (d), Jason Gardner (b), Haydn Conway (g). 18/1/85 MV4 DG MC

BOB SARGEANT

10/4/73 PEEL *King of the night, Love of a kind, Situation.* Bob Sargeant (kgv), Walt Monohan (b), Ritchie Dharma (d), Jack Lancaster (ts,ss,fl). 27/3/73 * JW *

1/1/74 PEEL *Sunshine blue, Between you and me, Situation, The waiting game. &* Jeff Sharkey (g). 11/12/73 LH1 JW *

13/6/74 PEEL *Let yourself go, Never again, First starring role.* Sargeant & John Woods (d), Robin Lumley (k). 30/5/74 LH1 TW *

2/6/75 PEEL *Situation, Can you feel it, Everyday's a lonely day, Sunshine blue/First starring role. & 3 (unknown).* 21/5/75 * TW *

29/4/76 PEEL *Broadway, Prisoner of love, The radio goes on forever, Here we go again. &* Monahan, Clive Bunker (d). 6/4/76 * JF MR

21/6/77 PEEL *Dancing at the jook joint, City kids, Life theme/Story of my life, Open up your heart. &* Sharkey, Monahan, Bunker, Barbara Sargeant (bkv), Pat Sharkey (bkv,rec). 14/6/77 MV4 JG MR

PETER SARSTEDT

25/9/68 NIGHT RIDE *Steel Flamingos, I am a cathedral, Blagged, Time love hope life, The artist.* * 25/9/68 S1 * * [M]

SASSAFRAS

18/6/73 HARRIS *Electric chair, Schooldays, Sea of stars, Busted country blues.* Terry Bennett (v), David Shell (g), Richard Holt (k), Ralph Evans (g), Peter Stroud (d). 13/6/73 * JG *

Group did audition tape in Birmingham 1/72; 'borderline pass' from R1 Audition panel. Files missing, no subsequent line-up or recording details available.

26/7/73 PEEL *Busted country blues, Expecting company, Beans and things, Goose that lays the golden egg (& School days, 30/8/73).* 23/7/73 * BA *

28/9/73 SEQUENCE *Kansas city, Wine, Electric chair, I am the Walrus.* 16/8/73 LH1 JM JE&GB

29/10/73 HARRIS *The way of me, Busted country blues, Expecting company.* 17/10/73 * JG *

17/1/74 PEEL *Box car hobo, To Ethel, Ohio, Schooldays.* 14/1/74 * BA *

SATISFACTION

22/6/70 WS R&B *Afterwards Autumn, You upset the grace of living, Cold summer.* Mike Cotton, & (g), (sx), (tb), (b), (d) unknown. 27/5/70 * JG JY

A possibly earlier first session, also for WS/RAVEN, contracted in 1/70, has proved untraceable.

12/12/70 RAVEN's R&B *Don't rag the lady, My fixation, Just lay back and enjoy it.* 11/11/70 MV4 JG JY

Next, another session was booked for RAVEN, rec'd 20/1/71, TX 26/2/71, but PasB is missing.

2/3/71 HARDING *Your love is it, My fixation, Just like friends.* 22/2/71 MV5 MB MH&MF

PAUL SAVAGE AND JOHN HEWITT

19/6/71 TOP GEAR *Blue, Carry on, It's been a long time.* Paul Savage (gv), John Hewitt (gv). 7/6/71 * JW *

SAVAGE PROGRESS

27/7/84 PEEL *Reclaim the night, Burning bush, Hip parade, Ball and chain.* Glynis Thomas (v), Rik Kenton (b), Ned Morant (perc), Carol Isaacs (k), Stewart Elliott (d). 18/7/84 MV5 RP NG

30/7/84 SKINNER *Reclaim the night, Etty, Tin man, Burning bush.* 22/7/84 MV5 DG ME

SAVOY BROWN BLUES BAND

30/6/68 TOP GEAR *Louisiana blues, Walkin' by myself, Gnome sweet gnome, Mr Down Child.* Chris Youlden (v), Kim Simmonds (g), David Peverett (g), Roger Earl (d), Bob Hall (p), Rivers Jobe (b). 20/5/68 PC1 BA *

Verdict of panel? 'Regretfully, yes'.

1/10/68 WS R&B *Louisiana blues, Worried mind, I'll gamble with my woman, Buchanan's blues.* 23/8/63 AO2 JG JY

19/5/69 WS R&B *Ring in his nose, I want you to love me, Train to nowhere.* 30/4/69 MV4 JG JY

25/5/69 TOP GEAR *Ring in his nose, I've made up my mind, Train to nowhere, Don't turn me from your door (& Life's one act play).* 19/5/69 PH JW TW

6/12/69 WS R&B *You don't have to go, Driftin' and driftin', Back home.* Tony Stevens r. Jobe, Hall; Simmonds out, says contract. Cut name to just 'Savoy Brown' from this session. 12/11/69 MV4 JG JY

10/1/70 TOP GEAR *You'd better pray for the Lord to guide you, A hard way to go, When I was a young boy.* Simmonds returns. 6/1/70 MV4 * *

Rec'd Peel Sunday Concert 15/1/70 PS, TX 18/1/70.

12/7/70 RAVEN's R&B *Lookin' in, Money can't save your soul, Leavin' again.* Youlden out, before 10/6/70 (below). 24/6/70 MV4 JG JY

31/7/70 BLACK *Lookin' in, Money can't save your soul, It hurts me too, Leavin' again.* 10/6/70 AO2 JM JWH

2/2/71 HARDING *Street corner talkin', Blues in king, Blues on the ceiling.* Simmonds & Paul Raymond (o), Ron Berg (d), Peter 'Scott' Ainsworth (v), Andy Pyle (b), according to contract. 25/1/71 MV5 MB MH&MF

SAXON

15/2/80 FRI. ROCK *Backs to the wall, Stallions of the highway, Motorcycle man, Still fit to boogie, Strangers in the night.* Biff Byford (v), Paul Quinn (g), Graham Oliver (g), Steve Dawson (b), Frank Gill (d). 23/1/80 * TW *

25/4/82 STUDIO B15 *20 000 ft, Dallas 1 pm, The eagle has landed, 747 strangers in the night.* * Live from LH1 TW *

LEO SAYER

20/9/73 PEEL *Tomorrow, Innocent bystander, Why is everybody going home.* Leo Sayer (v), James Litherland (g), Dave Rose (k), Bill Smith (b), John Dentith (d). 3/9/73 LH1 BA MF

'Must have a Top 3 hit in the next few months' wrote BA in his report to Audition Unit.

SCAFFOLD

10/3/68 TOP GEAR *Yellow book, Do you remember, Carry on Krow, Please don't run too fast.* Mike McGeer, Roger McGough, John Gorman, Dave Mason (bkv) & The John Cameron Group. 5/3/68 AO2 BA *

1st broadcast was on Light Programme's Pop Inn 10/5/66 [M].

SCALA TIMPANI

20/2/85 PEEL *Crazy, Utopian Sunday, The underlined

reaction. Russel Courtenay (d), Alistair Broadhead (b), Chesh Wegrzynski (g), Simon Elliott-Kemp (k), Russell Bonnell (v). 10/2/85 MV5 DG ME

THE SCARECROWS
1/5/85 Long *The deep end, Plain boyish, Take it up, Submission.* James Cotterill (b), Mandy Darlington (v), Jerry Thirlby (g), Adrian Shepherd (k), David Twist (d), Billy Paul (sx). 21/4/85 HP BYA *

SCARLET FANTASTIC
16/7/86 Long *No memory, Plug me in, Lucky seven, Follow that star.* Rick P. Jones (gk), Maggie De Monde (kv). 9/7/86 MV5 BYA MPK

25/8/87 Long *Film star kiss, Stay, Rhythm of resistance.* 16/8/87 MV4 HP TdB&PS

THE SCARS
6/3/80 Peel *She's alive, So strong, Author! author!, Je t'aime c'est le mort.* Bobby King (v), Paul Research (gv), John Mackie (b), Calumn Mackay (d). 20/2/80 MV4 JE NG

4/6/81 Peel *Remember me, Turn me on, Vanishing, They came and took her.* Steve McLaughlin (d) r. Mackay. 20/5/81 LH1 PS NG&GP

SCHLAFLOSE NACHTE
11/11/81 Peel *Same mistake twice, Touch me, Recall.* Gila Mousson (v,b,perc), Bernie von Braun (sy,g,b,perc), Peter Prima (d). 2/11/81 MV4 TW DD

SCIENTIST
6/1/91 Peel *The bee, The exorcist, The circle.* * 13/12/90 MV5 DG NG&DTH

SCORCHED EARTH
24/6/83 Fri. Rock *Where do we go from here, Tomorrow never comes, Shangri la.* Dave Cooper (kv), Paul Bodley (g), Dave Matthews (g), Tony Badger (b), Tim Kristic (d). 10/6/83 * TW DD

SCORPIO RISING
16/12/91 Goodier *Saturnalia, Water melon, Disturbance, Freedom thirteen.* Michael Banks (v), Steve Soar (b), Martin Atherton (g), Colin Owens (d), David Smart (g). 7/12/91 MV4 MA~

ROBIN SCOTT
23/4/69 Night Ride *The sun, Morning rain, Mara's supper, Penelope, Port of leaving, I am your suitcase lover.* Robin Scott (gv). 21/4/69 S1 PR *
Passed audition 3/69. [M].

SCREAM AND DANCE
25/3/82 Peel *Giacometti, Cat scat, Sumo man, Slow movement.* Amanda Stewart (v), Ruth George-Jones (v), John Langley (d), Julian Dale (db), John Carley (cga), Simon Preston (perc). 27/2/82 MV4 DG MR

20/5/82 Jensen *We must go back, Rubber girdles, Crow, Mr Tom Narrow.* 6/5/82 MV4 JS MR

1/2/83 Peel *Proverbs, I get this, Unequal portions, Let me out.* George-Jones & Sarah Gagg (v), Marco (d), Preston & Kenny Bongo Lacey (perc), Dan Catsis (bg). 19/1/83 MV4 RP NG

THE SCREAMING ABDABS
6/11/86 Long *Rifle range, Grounded, Happy heads, Everybody's got a girlfriend.* Mick Jackson (v), John Fay (d), August Finer (b), Ben Davies (g). 12/10/86 MV4 BYA MWT

THE SCREAMING BLUE MESSIAHS
2/8/84 Peel† *Good and gone, Someone to talk to, Tracking the dog, Let's go down to the woods and pray.* Bill Carter (gv), Chris Thompson (b,bkv), Kenny Harris (d). 24/7/84 MV5 MRD MR
† On Strange Fruit SFPS003.

6/7/85 Kershaw *Good and gone, Tracking the dog, Talking doll.* 14/6/85 Y2 cJL SR

12/11/87 Long *Sweet water pools, I wanna be a Flintstone, Big brother muscle.* 4/11/87 MV4 HP MPK&FK

SCREAMING JETS
11/10/91 Fri. Rock *Come on, No point, Starting out, Better.* Brad Heaney (d), Paul Woseen (b), Grant

Walmsley (g), Rich Lara (g), Dave Gleeson (v). 20/9/91 MV5 * *

SCREAMING LORD SUTCH AND THE NEW SAVAGES
7/9/72 Drummond *Bye bye Johnny, Gotta keep rocking, Hands off Jack the ripper, Good golly Miss Molly.* *
16/8/72 * MB *

SCREAMING TARGET
5/8/91 Goodier *Fallout, This town, Who killed King Tubby, Bedazzled.* Don Letts (v), Leo Williams (b), Steve Roberts (g), Greg Roberts (d), Dan Donovan (k), Chez (v). 27/7/91 MV5 MC~AM

SCREEN 3
26/1/82 Jensen *Hearts in limbo, Nuts and berries, Come into my jungle, Family.* Brett Cooper (d), Richard Kett (b), Neil Dyer (gv), Peter Jay (tp), Jason Votier (tp). 10/1/82 MV4 DG ME&GP

16/2/83 Peel *Red dust, Wet playtime, Refugee, Wonders of wildlife.* 9/2/83 MV4 RP NG

2/11/83 Peel *Broke and in love, I'm not impressed, There she goes again, The visitor.* & Steve Osbourne (tb). 24/10/83 MV4 TW MC

SCRITTI POLITTI
13/12/78 Peel *The humours of Spitalfields, Knowledge and interest, Doubt beat, '5/12/78'.* Green (g), Tom (d), Nial (b). 5/12/78 MV4 TW MR

4/7/79 Peel *Messthetics, Hegemony, Scritt locks door, The new one.* 26/6/79 MV4 JS NG

24/5/82 Peel *Asylums in Jerusalem, A slow soul, Jacques Derrida.* Green, Tom & Joe Cang (b), Mike McAvoy (k); & Jackie Challenor, Lorenza Johnson & Mae McKenna (bkv). 15/5/82 MV4 DG MC

2/8/82 Jensen *Asylums in Jerusalem, Gettin' havin' and holdin', Jacques Derrida, Lions after slumber, Slow soul.* Green, Joe, Tom, & Django Bates (k), Jamie Talbot (sx); Lorenza, Mae & Jackie (bkv). 15/7/82 MV4 JS *

SEALS AND CROFTS AND ZOOT MONEY
11/4/71 DLT *Tin town, Ridin' thumb, Hand-me-down shoe (& Granny will your dog bite, 19/4/71 R1 CLUB).* James Eugene Seals (gv), Darrell George Crofts (mnd,v) & (d), (p), (b) unknown. 5/4/71 A02 c.PWI *
Rec'd session for R1 CLUB the next day, 6/4. TX 19/4.

7/5/71 Black *Hand-me-down shoe, Freaks fret, The prisoner, Granny will your dog bite, A boy down the road.* & Zoot Money (p,o). 8/4/71 A02 JM JWH [M: daytime]

SEAWEED
31/7/92 Peel *Squint, Sit in class, She's cracked, Bewitched.* Clint Werner (g), John Akins (b), Wade Neal (g), Bob Bulgrien (d), Aaron Staupfer (v). 12/7/92 MV3 ME~SA

SEBADOH
28/8/92 Peel *Pot doesn't help, Close enuff, Circle game, Slints, Mouldy bread.* Eric Gaffney (d), Lou Barlow (gv), Jason Loewenstein (bv). 9/8/92 MV4 TdB~ SA

SEBASTIAN'S MEN
18/4/84 Peel *Hurt so frighten so hate so, Horizon, Forever and ever in the icehouse, A solo prodigy.* Mike McCaroll (d), Tony Elliott (b), David Hogg (g), Ian Cowpland (lg), Margie Henderson (v). 27/3/84 MV5 MRD TdB

MARTA SEBESTYEN
13/4/88 Peel *Csardas, The train, Dunantuli tancok, Szeki tancok, Szeress egyet.* Marta Sebestyen (v) 'and Muzsikas': Damiel Hamar (b,cymbalon), Peter Eri (hca,tarogata), Mihaily Sipas (vi), Sandor Csoori (bpp,vla). 5/4/88 MV4 DG HA

24/9/89 Kershaw *Negotinka and cigancica, Croatian folk songs from Drava region, The fishlake of Szeged, The bride's farewell.* Marta Sebestyen (v,solo-4) 'and Vujicsics': Ka'roly Gyori (tmbu), Ferenc Szendrodi (tmbu), Ga'bor Eredics (db), Miha'ly Borbe'ly (tmbu brac), Miroslav Brcza'n (tmbu cello). 29/8/89 MV3 DG DD

SECRET AFFAIR
25/7/79 Peel *I'm not free (but I'm cheap), Glory boys, My world, Goin' to a go-go.* Ian Page (v,tr), Dave Cairns

(g,bkv), Dennis Smith (b,bkv), Seb Shelton (d). 18/7/79 MV4 TVD NG

26/11/79 Peel *I'm not free (but I'm cheap), Get ready, New dance.* & Dave Winthrop (sx). 7/11/79 MV4 DS NG

SECTION 25
20/1/81 Peel *Babies in the bardo, Hit, One true path.* Larry Cassidy (bv), Vincent Cassidy (d), Paul Wiggin (g,tps). 13/1/81 LH1 BS HP

10/5/84 Jensen *Reflection, Looking from a hilltop, Warhead.* L. & V. Cassidy & Angela Flowers (kv), Jenny Ross (kv), Lee Shallcross (d,k). 1/4/84 MV5 DG ME

SIDI SEDDIKI
2/12/90 Kershaw *Haram aliq, Shove fin quona, Liam.* Sidi Seddiki (agv), Charlie Hart (b), Aziz Ben Salem (fl), Hagag Kenway (perc). 22/11/90 MV5 DG ME&NF

PEGGY SEEGER
15/1/69 Night Ride *My love and I are one, The children, The song of choice, Che Guevara, Fill up your glasses.* Peggy Seeger (agv). 13/1/69 S1 JM *

THE SEERS
27/4/88 L. Kershaw *Wildman, Girl in action, Freedom trip, Breathless.* Age Blackmore (d), Jason Kidd (bv), L.A. Wildman (g), Kat Day (g), Spider (pv). 17/4/88 MV4 HP TdB

THE SELECTER
22/10/79 Peel *They make me mad, Carry go bring come, Street feeling, Danger.* Pauline Black (lv), Neol Davies (gv), Gappa Hendrickson (v), Compton Amanor (g), Desmond Brown (k), Charley "Ironfinger" Anderson (b,bkv), Charlie Bembridge (alias Charley H) (d). 9/10/79 MV4 JS MR

1/12/80 Peel *Selling out your future, Deep water, Tell what's wrong, Washed up and left for dead.* James Mackie (o) Adam Williams (b). r Brown, Anderson. 10/11/80 LH1 TW AP

SEND NO FLOWERS
1/7/82 Peel *Days of rage, Caprice, Ashes, Beneath the dreams.* Lyn (gv), Timmo (g,k), Paul (b), Jake (d), Alan (perc). 26/5/82 * * *

THE SENSELESS THINGS
27/4/88 Peel *Passions out of town, I've lost my train, When you let me down, The only one.* Cass Cade (d), Morgan Plusfour (b), Ben S. Thing (g), Mark Oblivion (gv). 27/3/88 * DG ME&JBN

21/3/90 Peel *Tangled lines, Leo/It is too late, Tell me what is on your mind, Someone's talking 'bout you.* 27/2/90 MV5 DG MR

THE SENSIBLE JERSEYS
19/6/85 Peel *Wasting my time, Crucial information, People all around the world, Two-way radio.* Simmy Richman (d), Stephen Booker (bkv,b), Andrew Cunningham (gv), David Clifton (bkv,g,o). 9/6/85 MV4 DG ME

SERIOUS DRINKING
6/5/82 Peel *Spirit of '66, Love on the terraces, Hangover, He's an angry bastard but I like him, Walk alone.* Jem Moore (b), Andy Hearshaw (g), Eugene McCarthy (v), Martin Ling (v), Simon (d). 26/4/82 MV5 TW DD

27/9/82 Peel *R.G.B, Countdown to Bilko, 12 x u/Bobby Moore was innocent, Drugs, Yours or mine.* Lance Dunlop (d) r. Simon. 13/9/82 MV4 TW DD

13/1/83 Peel *Don't shoot me down, Revolution starts at closing time, Wonderful world beautiful people, Baby I'm dying a death.* 10/1/83 * TW DD

16/6/83 Jensen *Really good bloke, Time is tight, Winter's over, TV song.* Pete Saunders (k) joins. 12/6/83 MV4 DG ME

3/10/83 Peel *Closer closer, Go for the burn, Wierd son of angry bastard, Our time.* 26/9/83 MV4 TW MC

THE SERVANTS
24/3/86 Peel *A fleeting visit, Rings on her finger, You'd do me good, She whom once I dreamt of.* David Westlake (gv), John Mohan (lg), Philip King (b), John Wills (d). 16/3/86 MV5 DG ME&FK

SET THE TONE
18/1/83 JENSEN *Prove it, Skin me, Grind.* Kenny Hyslop (d,dm), Kendall Stubbs (bg), David Allen (k), Steve Doyle (k), Evelyn Asiedu (v), Chris Morgan (gv). 13/1/83 MV4 JS *

SEVENTH SEANCE
8/9/84 LONG *My death, Anguish of love, Another empty face, Dorian.* Winston Detliev (gv), Caroline Taylor (vi), Ian Smith (bkv), Phil Steriopulos (db,b), Dave Adams (d), Garfield (sx), Rachel Taylor (p,fl). 30/8/84 PHM IW TWN

70 GWEN PARTY
26/5/91 PEEL *This new model England, Hiding in the wall, Deviling hour, Peeping stick.* Victor N'dip (gv), Lurgin Pin (b,k,v). 30/4/91 MV5 MR~
20/6/92 PEEL *Auto killer UK, Howard Hughes, Stop resurrect & fire, Smash.* 26/5/92 MV4 MR~

SEVERED HEAD
18/3/83 FRI. ROCK *Heavy metal, God of my father, Killing the kidz, Two wheel mistress.* Danny Morris (lv,g), Ian Dixon (b), Lawrence Pledger (d), Mark Squire (g), Liz Morris (bkv, dancing), Cindy Dilling (bkv). 18/2/83 * TW DD

THE SEX CLARK FIVE
18/7/90 PEEL *Microwave music, Modern fix, Netta grew up last, Mongol song, America under the Mongol yoke prelude, Can't shake loose.* James Butler, Rick Storey, Joy Johnson, Trick McKaha. Rec. date unknown, at Birland Studio, Alabama, USA * *

SEX GANG CHILDREN
11/11/82 PEEL *Kill machine, German nun, State of mind, Sebastiane.* Andi (v), Rob Stroud (d), Terry MacLean (g), Dave Roberts (b). 27/10/82 MV4 RP MC

SEX GODS
18/11/87 LONG *Fluency, Fat pocket justice, McHelicopter, Rings of Saturn.* Stephen Johnson (g), Michael Mooney (g), Carl Washington (b), Gary Dwyer (d), Andy Eastwood (v). 1/11/87 MV4 HP TdB

THE SHADOWS
25/12/73 PEEL *Nivram, Jungle jam, Turn around and touch me, Wonderful land.* '4 & I, Mo Foster (b)' says sheet. 10/12/73 TI JW MR&ARV

SHAKE
30/4/79 PEEL *(But) Not mine, Glasshouse, Night by night, Teenbeat.* Angel Patterson (d), Simon Templar (bv), Troy Tate (g), Jo Callis (gv). 23/4/79 MV4 CL DD&MPK

SHAKE SHAKE
2/9/81 SKINNER *I plus I (yellow lines), Wonderland of wire, This way that way, Shuttle service.* Jacqui Hamlin (v), Jo Dworniak (bv), Blair Cunningham (d), Nigel Roberts (kv), Duncan Bridgeman (kv). 30/8/81 MV4 DG *

THE SHAKIN' PYRAMIDS
23/3/81 SKINNER *Cry cry kitten, Let's go, Connie Lou, I knocked bim bam.* Davie Duncan (v,hca,perc), Jamie Creighton (g), Railroad Ken (g). 5/3/81 LHI JS *

SHALAWAMBE
12/9/88 PEEL *Mulemena, Samora Machel, Mulamu.* Julius Kabwe (d), Claudie Kabwe (b), Ricky Chota (rg), Dolenzy Kabwe (lg,lv), Gerard Bwalanda (k); & Victoria, Beatrice & Agnes (cga,perc,bkv). 23/8/88 * MR~

SHAM 69
6/12/77 PEEL *Borstal breakout, Hey little rich boy, They don't understand, Rip off, What 'av we got.* Jimmy Pursey (lv), Dave Parsons (b,bkv), Dave Treganna (g,bkv), Mark Cain (d), various others (bkv). 28/11/77 MV4 TW DD

THE SHAMEN
13/1/87 PEEL *Strange day's dream, Passing away, Through my window, Where do you go?* Keith (d), Colin (bv), Derek (k), Peter (k). 14/12/86 * DG ME&TD
12/4/88 PEEL *Knature of a girl, War prayer, Nothing, Misinformation.* Will (b) r. Derek; Colin (g). 29/3/88 * DG DD&JB

2/8/89 PEEL *Transcendental, What's going down, Negation state, Phorward.* Colin, Will, John Delafons (d). 13/6/89 ED DG MR
23/3/91 PEEL *Hyperreal, Make it mine, Possible worlds†, In the bag.* Colin, Will, Plavka (v), Ley Icon (tt,rp), Mr. Mr. Man (sfx,mx). 12/2/91 MV5 MR~ † On 'New Season'.
28/9/92 GOODIER *Make it mine, Space time, Boss drum, Ebenezer Goode.* Colin, Richard West (rp,tt), Bob Brecks (k). 12/9/92 MV4 MC~RF

SHANGHAI
16/2/76 PEEL *Shakin' all over, Candy eyes, Over the wall, Let's get the hell off the highway.* Cliff Bennett (v), Mick Green (g), Brian Alterman (g), Speedy King (b,bkv), Pete Kircher (d,bkv). 5/2/76 MV4 MB *

THE SHAPES
10/4/79 PEEL *Airline disaster, Business calls, Beans/Bedtime stories, Leamington.* Seymour Bybuss (v), Steve Richards (g), Tim Jee (g), Bryan Helicopter (b), Dave Gee (d). 3/4/79 MV6 TVD MR

DAVE SHARMA
20/1/89 FRI. ROCK *Torch the tower, Flight 212, Spellbinder, Pandora's box.* Dave Sharma (g), Martin Connolly (b), Neil Huxtable (d), Don Airey (k). 25/11/88 MV4 TW *

EMMA SHARPE AND THE FEATURES
10/3/82 JENSEN *Chinese ladies, I'm not crying, Ludo in the summerhouse, Cindy, Wonderland.* Emma Sharpe (v), Bruce Main (b), Alan Hall (g), Dave Edge (d), Steve Tatler (gk). 28/2/82 MV4 DG MR

SANDIE SHAW
14/5/86 LONG† *Frederick, Are you ready to be heartbroken?, Steven, Girl don't come.* Sandie Shaw (v), Steve Näive (k), Neil Conte (d), Kevin Armstrong, Chris Bostock (b). 7/5/86 MV4 BYA MPK † On Nighttracks SFNT002.
20/9/88 L. KERSHAW *Nothing less than brilliant, Hello angel, Lover of the century, I love peace.* & Armstrong; Richard Coles (k), Stephen Street (b), Andrew Paresi (d), Mark Nevin (ag-3 only). 24/8/88 MV4 PW MPK
5/12/88 PEEL *Girl called Johnny, Cool about you, Flesh and blood, Strange bedfellows.* & Armstrong, Coles, Paresi, Phil Sewell (b,bkv), Clare Hirst (sx,bkv). 27/11/88 HP DG ME

PETE SHELLEY
21/12/81 JENSEN *I generate a feeling, Witness the change, Yesterday is not here.* Pete Shelley (gkv), Barry Adamson (b), Alan Dalgleish (k). 15/11/81 MV4 DG ME
14/2/83 JENSEN *Many a time, Telephone operator, I just want to touch.* & Adamson, Gerrard Cookson (g), Mel Wesson (k), Jim Russell (d). 10/2/83 MV4 JS TdB
2/7/83 LONG *If you ask me, What was heaven, You and I, XLI.* * 23/6/83 PHM c.JL *
3/10/84 LONG *Never again, Waiting for love, Life without reason, Give it to me.* & Adamson, G. Cookson, Francis Cookson, Steve Turley. 20/9/84 MV5 MHY *
26/2/86 LONG *I surrender, Blue eyes, They're coming for you, On your own.* & G Cookson, Norman Fisher-Jones (g), Jim Gardiner (k), Simon Hoare (d), Peter Thomas (b). 9/2/86 HP BYA *

SHELLEYAN ORPHAN
27/6/84 JENSEN *Cavalry of cloud, Tangled perpetual, Melody of birth, Midsummer pearls and plumes.* Jemaur Tayle (gv), Mark Davies (clo,p), Caroline Crawley (v), Tom Davey (ob), Richard Tomes (vi), Desné Gobie (vla). 3/6/84 MV5 DG ME

ANDY SHEPPARD
6/4/89 SKINNER *Optics, Forbidden fruit, Carla Carla Carla.* Andy Sheppard (sx), Pete Maxfield (db), Simon Gore (d), Dave Buxton (p), Orphy Robinson (vib,mrm), Mamadi Kamara (perc). Live after midnight from MV3 KH TdB

THE SHILLELAGH SISTERS
14/3/84 PEEL *Beetle bug bop, Black cadillac, Romp and stomp.* Jacquie O'Sullivan (lv), Lynder Halpin (db),

Tricia O'Flynn (sx), Mitzi Ryan (d), Boz Boorer (g). 6/3/84 MV5 RP TdB

JOHNNY SHINES
21/3/70 TOP GEAR *Kind hearted woman, Ramblin', No mail today, Dynaflow (& I tried and I tried, 20/6/70).* Johnny Shines (gv). 17/3/70 MV4 JW *

SHIVA
14/1/83 FRI. ROCK *Borderline, User, Stranger lands, How can I?* John Hall (gv), Andy Skuse (b), Chris Logan (d). 3/12/82 * TW DD

MICHELLE SHOCKED
25/9/86 KERSHAW† *5 a.m. in Amsterdam, The incomplete image, Who cares, The secret to a long life (is knowing when it's time to go).* Michelle Shocked (agv). 31/5/86 Recorded at the Kerville Folk Festival, Texas * * † Later released on Cooking Vinyl, CD 002 as part of 'The Texas Camp Fire Tapes'.
14/5/87 KERSHAW *Contest comin', Woody's rag medley, Strawberry jam, Leavin' Louisiana.* & John Gill (fd), Mike Hirst (ml), Brendan Croker (g). 30/4/87 MV4 PLA *
15/9/88 KERSHAW *Anchorage, Must be luff, A wintersong, Sleep, Russian roulette.* Solo. 1/9/88 MV4 DG MR
20/2/89 SKINNER *Memories of East Texas, On the greener side, Grafitti limbo, Ballad of Penny Evans.* Solo. Live from on-air studio, Prod. KH.

SHOES FOR INDUSTRY
25/9/79 PEEL *Devil dogs, War of the potatoes, Shell shock, Fear of wages.* John Schofield (d), Steve Lonnen (b), Andy Leighton (g), Steve Franklin (k), Paul B. Davies (v,sx). 10/9/79 MV4 JE DD&MPK

SHONEN KNIFE
25/1/92 PEEL *Flying jelly attack, Watchin' girl, Tortoise brand pot cleaner's theme, Antonio baka guy, Boys, Chinese song.* Atsuko Yamano (dv), Michie Nakatani (bv), Naoko Shibata (gv). 8/12/91 MV3&4 DG ME

SHOOT
21/12/72 PEEL *Ships and sails, Neon life, Stars and sorrows (& Living blind, 18/1/73).* Jim McCarty (pv), Craig Collins (d), Bill Russell (b), Dave Green (lgv). 4/12/72 LHI BA BC
28/8/73 HAMILTON *On the frontier* [Network session]. McCarty, Green, Tim Posford (bv), Peter Woolf (d). 15/8/73 PH c.PWI *

SHOOT! DISPUTE
9/2/84 PEEL *Lack lustre, Can't believe, The great explainer, Fun time.* Cathy Lomax (v), Mark Charles (d), Steve Smith (b,bkv), Denzil Daniels (perc), Scampi (sx). 4/2/84 MV5 DG PW
13/6/84 PEEL *Monkey, Power of persuasion, Gatgun, Love for sale.* & Dylan (g,bkv). 6/6/84 MV5 RP DD
22/9/84 LONG *Don't colour my mind, Hazy days.* * 10/9/84 c.PWL *

THE SHOP ASSISTANTS
21/10/85 PEEL *Safety net, All that ever mattered, Almost made it, Somewhere in China.* Alex Taylor (v), David Keegan (g), Sarah Kneale (b), Laura McPhail (d), Ann Donald (d). 8/10/85 MV5 PWL MR
20/2/86 LONG *Home again, All of the time, Looking back, What a way to die, Nature lover.* Joan Bride r. Donald. 16/2/86 MV4 BYA SC
8/12/86 PEEL *Fixed grin, I don't wannna be friends with you, Ace of spades, Before I wake.* Bride out. 11/11/86 * DG MFA&JB

SHORT COMMERCIAL BREAK
14/10/82 PEEL *Oxo, Yorkie, Smarties, Bran Flakes.* Kirsty (bkv,g), Effy (d,bkv), Bernie (lv), Allan (b). 18/8/82 * CL * 'Not to be broadcast' is written over the sheet, although the TX date written in suggests that it was.

THE SHREW KINGS
22/8/85 LONG *Losing my cool, Sitting here, The bird has flown, Dr Love.* Bill Tidnam (v), Jef Harvey (v), Noel Dyde (g), Michael Hughes (g), Mark Clarke (db), Eoin Shannon (d). 28/7/85 MV4 BYA SC

SHRIEKBACK
8/2/82 JENSEN *A kind of fascination, All the Greek boys (do the hand walk), Sexthink one.* Barry Andrews (kv), Carl Marsh (gv), David Allen (b,bkv), Brian Nevill (d,bkv), Clare Hirst (sx-1 only), Linda Nevill (bkv-1 only). 28/1/82 MV4 JS *

11/8/82 PEEL *All the Greek boys (do the hand walk), My spine (is the base line), Feelers.* Allen, Andrews, Marsh (all-b,k,g,vi,v); Martyn Barker (d,perc-1) joins; & Stephanie Nuttall (d,perc-2), John Murphy (d,perc-3). 26/7/82 MV4 TW DD

22/3/83 JENSEN *Brink of collapse, Considerable, (Grapes into) Lettuce, Despite dense weed.* & Pedro Ortiz (perc). 3/3/83 MV4 JS MPK

15/3/84 PEEL *New home, Under the lights, Suck.* Barker out; & Emma Burnham, Linda Neville, Helen Musto (bkv-1,3). 7/3/84 MV5 MRD NG

10/12/84 LONG *White out, Holy water boiling oil, Health and knowledge, Feelers.* Barker returns; & Lou Edmonds. 18/11/84 MV5 BYA PW

10/6/85 PEEL *Everything that rises must converge, Fish beneath the ice, Faded flowers.* & Clare Torry (bkv). 2/6/85 MV5 DG ME

THE SHRUBS
2/7/86 PEEL *John Corpse, Black mailer, Animal, Assassin.* John Bentley (d), Stephen Brockway (b), Julian Hutton (g), Micheal Ricketts (g), Mick Hobbs (v). 22/6/86 HP DG FK&PS

26/8/87 PEEL *Sullen days are over, King Urn, Papa Chaperon, Ballet gorilla.* Mark Grebby (b) r. Brockway. 26/8/87 * DG *

SHUT UP AND DANCE
29/8/90 PEEL *White white world, A change soon come, Lamborghini, 5 6 7 8.* DJ Hype (tt), PJ (v), Smiley C (v). 5/8/90 MV3 DG ME&FK

28/3/92 PEEL *Autobiography of a crack head, Love is all we need, Strut your stuff, Green man.* 23/1/92 MV5 DG MA&AR

SHY
25/5/84 FRI. ROCK *Throwing it all away, My Apollo, Was I wrong, Behind closed doors.* Tony Hills (v), Paddy McKenna (k), Alan Kelly (d), Steve Harris (g), Mark Badrick (b). 11/5/84 MV4 TW MC

5/6/87 FRI. ROCK *Telephone, Can't fight the nights, Young heart, Break down the wall.* Roy Davis (b) r. Badrick. 22/5/87 MV4 DG DD&TdB

SIAN
12/1/90 FRI. ROCK *Loser in love, Little miss innocent, Had enough, Don't say it's over.* David Shields (lv), Simon Dodd (g,bkv), Peter Frank (g), Jay Keenan (b), Norman Walker (d). 24/11/89 MV5 PW DD

THE SIDDELEYS
28/9/88 PEEL *Something almost brilliant happened last night, You get what you deserve, I wish I was good, Every day of every week.* Allan Kingdom (g), Johnny Johnson (v), David Clynch (d), Andrew Brown (b). 13/9/88 MV4 MC~

23/5/89 PEEL *My favorite wet Wednesday afternoon, Theft, Love with blood, When I grow up I'll be a god.* & Jonathan Stein (sy). 18/4/89 WX DG MR

SIEGE
6/2/87 FRI. ROCK *Wait for me, Red light, How does it feel, Wasted time.* Sharon Thompson (v), Les Black (g), Mark Conquer (b), Ray Lawrence (d). 16/1/87 MV4 TW DD

LABI SIFFRE
26/2/73 HARRIS *Saved, Blue lady.* Labi Siffre (gv). 21/2/73 LHI PR *

Panel had rejected an Audition tape in 2/68, as 'simply not up to any kind of broadcasting standard'. One year later, trial b'cast on Dave Cash show 3/69 passed 'enthusiastically' by panel [M: daytime].

SIGNORINAS
12/11/81 PEEL *Neutral, Cocktail party, Escalator, City*

golfer. Richard Wise (d), Doug Hendrey (perc), Patrick Hawkins (b), Andrew White (g), Artemis Pittas (v), Iliona Outram (v). 4/11/81 MV4 RP NG

JUDEE SILL
17/4/72 HARRIS *Jesus was a cross-maker, Enchanted sky machines, The kiss, The phoenix, Lady-O.* Judee Sill (agv). 5/4/72 AO2 JG *
Rec'd In Concert 23/3/72 PS, TX 1/4/72.

12/3/73 HARRIS *The kiss, Soldiers of the heart, There's a rugged road (& The phoenix, 14/5/73).* 14/2/73 LHI PR BAI

MIKE SILVER
17/9/73 HARRIS *Riverside, Life on the old same railway, Pictures (& Pioneers return, 19/11/73).* Mike Silver (agv). 12/9/73 LHI JG *

SILVERFISH
2/11/89 PEEL *Driller, (Shed) Out of luck, Fat painted carcass.* Fuzz Duprey (g), Les Rankin (v), Chris P. Mowforth (b,bkv), Stuart Watson (d). 5/10/89 MV3 DG DD

28/4/91 PEEL *Harry Butcher, Pink & lovely, Big bad baby pig squeal, 3 puppy pie.* 2/4/91 MV5 MR~

12/1/92 PEEL *Jimmy, Crazy, Vitriola, Rock on.* 26/11/91 MV4 MR~

SIMBA WANYIKA
19/8/90 KERSHAW *Mwenda pole, Mapenzi yaniua, Hasira ni hasara.* George Peter Fkinyonga (gv), Wilson Peter Kinyonga (gv), Victor Boniface (b), Mike Beche (d,bkv), Hassan Mwachimwengu (cga). 19/7/90 MV5 DG MA

13/9/90 PEEL *Shillingi, Sikujva vtabadilika, Mama Maria, Pamela.* 24/7/90 MV5 MR~

SIMPLE MINDS
10/4/79 JENSEN *Life in a day, Chelsea girl, No cure.* Jim Kerr (v), Charlie Burchill (g), Mick McNeil (k), Derek Forbes (b), Brian McGee (d). 2/4/79 * * ME

7/1/80 PEEL *Changeling, Premonition, Citizen (Dance of youth), Room.* 19/12/79 MV4 TVD NG

23/2/82 JENSEN *I promised you a miracle, In trance as mission, King is white (and in the crowd).* Kenny Hyslop (d) r. McGee. 11/2/82 MV4 JWI MR

13/8/82 JENSEN *Summer song, Glittering prize, Hunter and the hunted.* Mike Ogletree (d) r. Hyslop. 26/8/82 MV4 JS MR

3/10/83 JENSEN *Waterfront, Kick inside, New gold dream†.* Mel Gaynor (d) r. Ogletree. 11/9/83 MV4 DG ME
† On 'I and only' BOJCD025.

MARTIN SIMPSON
15/7/77 PEEL *Soldier's joy/Did you ever see a devil Uncle Joe?/Fly around my pretty little miss, You win again, Green fields of America, The wild Bill Jones medley/Georgia railroad/Cluck old hen, Satan your kingdom must come down.* Martin Simpson (g,bj,v). 6/7/77 MV4 MB NG

11/6/87 KERSHAW *My crown, The swastika song, Hardtime killing floor, The new kitchen blues.* 14/5/87 * DG MR

THE SINATRAS
7/12/81 PEEL *Finding your own level, That shape, New clothes, The chameleon complex.* Neil Pearson (d), Tom Hamilton (v), Nick Hunt (g,bkv), Nick Hannah (k,bkv); & John Barrow (sx), Dean Sargent (tp). 28/11/81 MV4 DG MR

13/4/82 JENSEN *She asked me how I feel, Passion is the key, Drowning not waving, The girl of my dreams.* & Barry Morris (sx). 26/3/82 MV4 JWI *

24/5/83 JENSEN *Betrayal, Try a little tenderness, More than four walls, But still says love.* Hamilton, John Fraser (g), Lee Sussenbach (d), Mark Astley (perc), Adam Ireland (tb), Mark Rouse (tp). 12/5/83 MV4 JP MR

14/1/84 LONG *Only takes a minute, Shout it from the rooftops, God knows when, Kissed again.*
* 29/12/83 PHM c.PWL *

PETE SINFIELD AND A BOWL OF SOUP
24/8/73 SEQUENCE *Wholefood boogie, Envelopes of*

yesterday, Song of the seagoat, Night people. & 11 (unknown). 10/7/73 TI JM NG
Sinfield had previously done solo links for SEQUENCE.

SINK
14/12/87 PEEL *Re-begin, Chocolate love, I hate yourself, Baby.* Ed Shred (gv), Sunil Kittur (b-3,4), Purple Paul (b-1,2), Tommy Stupid (g), Pete Whitehouse (d). 6/12/87 * DG ME&PL

20/9/88 PEEL *Birthday song, Diamonds, For want of..., Perspective.* Shred, Paul, Def Metro Pete-Gnome (d), Blind Lorenze Hoss Cash (v), Red Wood Jim (hca,vib), Legs (tamb). 21/8/88 HP DG ME

20/6/90 PEEL *Echo, One final kick in the head, Amanush, Walking with me blues.* Shred, Kermack (d), Paul Sky (hca,b), John Ruscoe (g). 8/5/90 MV3 MR~

SIOUXSIE AND THE BANSHEES
5/12/77 PEEL† *Love in a void, Mirage, Metal, Suburban relapse.* Siouxsie (lv), Kenny Morris (d), Steve Severin (b), John McKay (g). 29/11/77 MV4 MB MR
† On Strange Fruit SFPCD012.

23/2/78 PEEL† *Hong Kong garden, Overground, Carcass, Helter skelter.* 6/2/78 MV4 TW DD
† On Strange Fruit SFPCD066.

16/4/79 PEEL *Placebo effect, Playground twist, Regal zone, Poppy day.* 9/4/79 MV6 TW BAI&MPK

18/2/81 PEEL *Halloween, Voodoo dolly, But not them, Into the light.* John McGeoch (g), Budgie (d) r. McKay, Morris. 10/2/81 LHI DG MR

16/6/81 SKINNER *Arabian nights, Red over white, Headcut, Supernatural thing.* 4/6/81 LHI DG MR

24/5/82 JENSEN *Coal mind, Greenfingers, Painted bird, Cascade.* 13/5/82 MV4 JS MR

3/2/86 PEEL *Candy man, Cannons, Lands End.* John Valentine-Carruthers (g) r. McGeoch. 28/1/86 MV5 MR~

2/2/87 LONG *Shooting sun, Song from the edge of the world, Little Johnny Jewel, Something blue.* 11/1/87 MV4 JE TdB

SIREN
27/8/70 HENRY *Cheat me, God bless the bride, Lonesome ride, Soon.* Kevin Coyne (v), David Clague (b), Martin Sax (lg), Nick Cudworth (p), Tat Meager (d). 20/8/70 AO2 MB MH&MF

THE SISTERS OF MERCY
7/9/82 PEEL *1969, Alice, Good things, Floor show.* Ben Gunn (rg), Gary Marx (lg), Craig Adams (b), Andrew Eldritch (g,v,dm). 25/8/82 * RP MWT

10/3/83 JENSEN *Heartland, Jolene, Valentine, Burn.* 6/3/83 MV4 DG ME

13/7/84 PEEL *Walk away, Emma, The poison door, No time to cry.* Wayne Hussey (g) r. Gunn; & Doctor Avalanche (d,bkv). 19/6/84 MV5 MRD TdB

SIXMYTH
15/3/91 FRI. ROCK *Got it bad, Pushing up roses, Jazzed down, The way you were.* Chief Twose (lv), Bram Damein (g), Gypsy (g), Jade Junkii (b), Dazzle (d). 22/2/91 MV5 DD~

SKAGARACK
7/11/86 FRI. ROCK *Gigs, I'm alone, Damned woman, Always in a line, Victim of the system, Double crossed.* * 23/8/86 MV4 * *

SKAT
10/3/82 PEEL *Honcho, Sleeping dogs lie, Sad boy style, Just a word.* Russell Greenwood (d), Helen McCookerybook (b,lv), Jim McCallum (rg), Carl Evans (lg,bkv). 8/3/82 MV4 JWI *

SKELETAL FAMILY
19/5/83 PEEL *Black ju-ju, The wind blows, Someone new, And I.* Anne Marie Hurst (v), Stan Greenwood (g), Howard Daniels (d), Roger Nowell (Trotwood) (b). 11/5/83 MV4 RP NG

30/4/84 JENSEN *Don't be denied, 11:15, Burning oil, Promised land.* Martin Henderson (d) r. Daniels. 8/4/84 MV5 DG ME

8/10/84 PEEL *Far and near, Hands on the clock, Move, No chance.* Karl Heinz (sx) joins. 22/9/84 MV5 DG MC

19/3/85 LONG *Waltz, Mixed feelings, Watch me, Trees.* 6/3/85 MV5 JWI MPK

25/11/85 LONG *What goes up, Restless, Split him in two, The wizard.* Trotwood, Greenwood, John Clarke (g), Kevin Hunter (d), Katrina Phillips (v). 10/11/85 HP BYA *

24/6/86 LONG *Just a minute, Now, Big love, Put it on brown.* Clarke out. 14/5/86 MV4 BYA *

SKI PATROL

22/1/81 PEEL *Extinguish, Where the buffalo roam, Cut.* Nick Clift (g), Francis Cook (b), Alan Cole (d), Ian Lowery (v). 19/1/81 LH1 TW DD

SKID ROW

25/7/70 TOP GEAR *After I'm gone, Felicity, An awful lot of women.* Gary Moore (lg), Brendan Shiels (b), Noel Bridgeman (d). 21/7/70 MV4 JW *

Had rec'd Peel Sunday Concert as trial b'cast 11/7/70 PS, TX 21/6/70.

25/8/70 HARDING *Maggie's farm, Un co-op show, Band blues, Girl (I'm never going to leave you).* 18/8/70 MV5 MB MH&MF

27/2/71 TOP GEAR *Ramblin', If you dip your wick you've got to pay for the oil.* 9/2/71 MV4 JW BC

Recorded 2nd Peel Concert 7/1/71 PS, TX 17/1/71.

20/7/71 HARDING *Ma, Cherry wine, It'll be me.* 12/7/71 MV5 MB MH&MF

THE SKIDS

19/5/78 PEEL *Of one skin†, Open sound, Contusion, Night and day, TV stars.* Richard Jobson (v), Stuart Adamson (lg), William Simpson (b), Thomas Kellichan (d). 16/5/78 MV4 * MB MR

† On 'Winters of Discontent' SFRCD204.

1/9/78 PEEL *Dossier of fallibility, Hope and glory, Six times, The saints are coming.* 29/8/78 MV4 TW MR

26/2/79 PEEL *Summer, Hang on to the shadows, Zit, Walk on the wild side.* 19/2/79 MV4 TW DD

7/5/79 PEEL *War poets, Withdrawal symptoms, Hymns from a haunted ballroom, Masquerade.* 30/4/79 MV4 TW DD

15/9/80 PEEL *Filming in Africa, An incident in Algiers, Circus games, Snakes and ladders (instrumental).* Richard Jobson (v,g-4), Russell Webb (bg), Mike Baillie (d), John McGeoch (g-1,2,3, v-1,3; Stuart Adamson ill), Steve Severin (v-1,3). 1/9/80 MV4 DG MPK&HP

SKIFF SKATS

23/5/84 PEEL *Cripple creek, Hickory-holler, Long tall Texan, Maybelline, Jingle-Night time Radio One (Parody of 'Relax').* Earnshaw Cods (bj,g), Funky Texas (g), Buck Harder (wsh), T-Box Tone (b), Ringo Feathers (sx), The Old Hired Hand (dobro,fd,mnd). 16/5/84 MV5 RP NG

26/2/85 PEEL *Split personality, Hill billy boogie, Glendale train, Barefoot Nelly.* Pete Smith (gv), Rob Smith (bj,v), Tony Hilton (db), Tony McFadzean (lsg,dob), James Cooke (fd,mnd), John Hasler (wsh), Hector Walker ('zob stick'). 12/2/85 MV5 MRD HP

SKIN ALLEY

6/12/69 TOP GEAR *Country air, All alone, Marsha.* Thomas Crimble (bv), Krzysztof Henryk Juszkiewicz (o,v), Bob James (fl,sx,gv), Giles Alvin Pope (d). 22/9/69 PH * *

2/4/71 BLACK *Reflections, Skin Valley, Serenade (& Dick's seven, Goodbye, 30/4/71).* 4/3/71 AO2 JM JWH

16/12/71 DRUMMOND *Bad words and evil people, A final coat, So many people.* Nick Graham (bv), Tony Brown (d) r. Crimble, Pope. 29/11/71 MV5 MB MH&MF

SKIN GAMES

29/9/87 LONG *Precious, Public life, Skin games, No criminal mind.* Wendy (v), Johnny Willett (g), Jim Marr (b), Dave Innes (d). 20/9/87 MV4 PW TdB

SKIP BIFFERTY

15/10/67 TOP GEAR *Yours for at least 24, On love, Money man, Orange lace, I don't understand it.* Graham Bell

(lv), Tom Jackman (d), John Turnbull (g), Mickey Gallagher (p), Colin Gibson (b). 29/9/67 PH BA *

11/2/68 TOP GEAR *When she comes to stay, In the morning, Follow the path of the stars, The other side of Jesus Smith.* 5/2/68 PCI BA *

14/7/68 TOP GEAR *Once, Man in black, Don't let me be misunderstood, The Hobbit.* 9/7/68 PCI BA DT

SKODAS

30/6/81 PEEL *Dog, Do it yourself, Mouth, I'm not going to give a thing, Everybody thinks everybody else is dead.* Annie Lacey (v), Andy Moule (g,bkv), Jason Pitchers (b,bkv), Richard Nelson (d,bkv). 24/6/81 LH1 CL NG

SKREWDRIVER

28/10/77 PEEL *Street fight, Unbeliever, The only one, Anti-social.* John Grinton (d), Kevin McKay (b), Ron Hartley (g), Ian Stuart (v). 19/10/77 MV4 MB NG

PATRICIA SKY

2/4/69 NIGHT RIDE *Silly song, Jimmy Clay, Modern Major General, She's up for grabs, The dance of death, Many a mile, Hangin' round.* * 26/3/69 S1 * *

30/7/69 PEEL *Separation blues, Love will endure, To Keith, Ira Hayes, Spencer the Rover.* * 29/7/69 * * *

SKYCLAD

11/9/92 FRI. ROCK *The widdersmins jig, Spinning Jenny, The declamation of indifference, Emerald.* Keith Baxter (d), Dave Pugh (g), Fritha Jenkins (k,vi), Graeme English (b), Steve Ramsey (g), Martin Walkyier (v). 21/8/92 MV5 MC~

SLAB!

22/9/86 PEEL *Mars on ice, Painting the Forth bridge, Dust, The animals are all eating people pie.* Stephen Dray (v,sx), Paul Jarvis (g), Bill Davies (b), Robin Risson (d), Neill Woodger (tb), Hugh Rawson (tp). 12/8/86 ~ DG MR&MC

16/2/87 PEEL *Undriven snow, Mining town in Lotusland, Blood flood, Parallax avenue.* Dave Morris (g) joins; & Margaret Ward (bkv,tps). 1/2/87 * DG ME&MPK

7/3/88 PEEL *Big sleeper, Last detail, Killer for a country, Bride of sloth.* Scott Kiehl (d) r. Risson; Woodger out. 21/2/88 ~ DG ME&FK

SLADE

8/6/69 SYMONDS ON SUNDAY *Everybody's next one, C'mon C'mon, Good old desk, (& The raven, not broadcast).* Noddy Holder (lvg), Dave Hill (lg), Jim Lea (b), Don Powell (d). 2/6/69 AO2 c.PWI *

Recorded as 'Ambrose Slade'. 'Entertaining, fresh musical sounds': passed by the panel [M: daytime].

28/4/70 HARDING *The Shape of things to come, Omaha, Sweet box and remember.* 25/3/70 MV5 MB MH&MF

12/1/71 HARDING *Man who speaks evil, Dirty joker, The gospel according to Rasputin, Just the way.* 11/1/71 MV5 MB MH&MF

13/5/71 HENRY *Get down and get with it, Man who speaks evil, My life is natural, In like a shot.* 5/5/71 MV4 MB MH&MF

27/1/72 DRUMMOND *In like a shot, My life is natural, The shape of things to come (& Look wot you dun, 16/3/72).* 12/1/72 MV4 MB MH&MF

26/5/72 PEEL *Move over baby, Let the good times roll, Bye goodbye, Darlin' be home soon (& Keep on rockin').* 9/5/72 T1 JM *

SLAMMER

22/1/88 FRI. ROCK *Born for war, Hellbound, If thine eye offend thee.* Andy Gagic (d), Dean Wilson (b), Enzo Annecchini (g), Milo Zivanovic (g), Paul Tunnicliffe (v). 8/1/88 ~ HP DD

SLAPP HAPPY

16/7/74 PEEL *Europa, Me and Parvati, Little something, War is energy enslaved.* Anthony Moore (k), Peter Blegvad (gv), Dagmar Krause (lv), Geoff Leigh (sx), Robert Wyatt (perc,v), Lyndsay Cooper (ob,perc), Fred Frith (g), Jeff Clyne (db). 25/6/74 LH1 TW BC

THE SLITS

27/9/77 PEEL† *Love and romance, Vindictive, New town, Shoplifting.* Ari Up (v), Tessa (b,bkv), Viv Albertine (rg,bkv), Palmolive (d,bkv). 19/9/77 MV4 TW BAI&NG

22/5/78 PEEL† *So tough, Instant hit, FM.* 17/4/78 MV4 TW *

† On Strange Fruit SFMCD207.

26/10/81 PEEL *Difficult fun, In the beginning, Earthbeat & wedding song.* Ari, Tessa, Viv & Neneh (bkv), Bruce (d), Steve (k), Sean (b-2 only). 12/10/81 MV4 TW DD

SLOW BONGO FLOYD

15/7/91 GOODIER *Doors of perception, Chemistry, Heaven, River of love.* Phillip Wilkes (d), Michael Jones (rgv), Ian Fletcher (g), Fernando Teste (k,sx), John Walsh (b,bkv), John Holmes (k,bkv). 6/7/91 MV5 MA~JT

SLOWDIVE

21/4/91 PEEL *Catch the breeze, Song 1, Golden hair.* Simon Scott (d), Nick Chaplin (b), Christian Savil (g), Neil Halstead (gv), Rachel Goswell (gv). 26/3/91 MV4 DG ME&SA

SLOWEST CLOCK

6/9/88 L. KERSHAW *Where's Andi, Desert mouth, Rejoice the burning, Turning green.* Dave Burke (d), Frank Price (v), Gerry Fahy (g), Brian Neavyn (b,bkv). 31/8/88 MV4 HP MPK

SLOWJAM

22/9/91 PEEL *Tex Wade, Steel bridges, Funny face, Little fick.* Darren Davies (bv), Matt Gray (gv), David Aldermen (gv); & Andrea (of the Darling Buds) (ag). 11/8/91 MV3 DG MA

THE SMALL FACES

14/4/68 TOP GEAR *If I were a carpenter, Lazy Sunday, Get ready, Every little bit hurts.* Steve Marriott (gv), Ian McLagan (k), Kenny Jones (d), Ronnie Lane (bv), P.P Arnold (v-1, 4). 9/4/68 PCI BA DT&AH [M: previous Light programme, not all contract files traceable].

SMALL FACTORY

14/8/92 PEEL *Suggestions, Hopefully, Friends, Lose your way.* Phobe Summersquash (dv), Alex Kemp (bv), David Auchenbach (gv). 16/7/92 MV4 DG NG&JLC

SMASHING ORANGE

8/2/92 PEEL *Just before I die, Cherry rider, Highway, Not very much to see.* Tim Sippke (d), Stephen Wagner (b), Rick Hodgson (g), Rob Montejo (gv). 21/11/91 MV4 DG NG&JB

SMASHING PUMPKINS

13/10/91 PEEL† *Siva, A girl named Sandoz, Smiley.* Jimmy Chamberlain (d), Darcy (b), James Iha (g), William Corgan (gv). 8/9/91 MV3 DG ME&RM

† On Strange Fruit SFMCD214.

SMIGGS BAND

21/5/76 PEEL *Going down south, Just for you, Nadine, Mean Street.* Gordon Smith (g,vhp), Ruan O'Lochlainn (k,sx), Tony Cousins (b), Tim Penn (k), Bunt (d). 20/4/76 * TW *

SMILEY CULTURE

7/1/85 LONG *Lyric designer, Vocalist operation, Entertainer entertainer.* Smiley Culture (v,rp) & unknown. 16/12/84 VS BYA *

THE SMIRKS

26/4/78 PEEL *Fool, Banking with the bankers, OK UK, The island sea.* Simon Milner (lv,g), Neil Fitzpatrick (lgv), Ian Morris (bv), Mike Doherty (d). 19/4/78 MV4 MB NG

T.V. SMITH'S EXPLORERS

12/1/81 PEEL *The servant, Walk away, The last words of the great explorer.* Eric Russell (g), Mel Wesson (k), Colin Stoner (b), David Sinclair (d), T.V. Smith (v). 5/1/81 LH1 TW AP

2/2/81 SKINNER *Have fun, I live for everything, The perfect life, Looking down on London.* 22/1/81 LH1 DG MR

T.V. SMITH'S CHEAP

25/1/88 PEEL *Third team, Silicon valley holiday, Luxury in exile, Buried by the machine.* T.V. Smith (v), Mik Helsin (g), Andy Bennie (b), Fuzz Deniz (d). 5/1/88 * DG MR&FK

GORDON SMITH
14/8/68 NIGHT RIDE *Pearlie blues, Worried life blues, Highway 51, Walkin' blues, Rollin' and tumblin'.* * 31/7/68 SI * *
26/2/69 NIGHT RIDE *Rollin' and tumblin', Pearlie blues, Diving duck, Walkin' blues.* * 4/2/69 SI * *

MICHAEL SMITH
4/5/82 PEEL *Long time/Black and white, Roots, It a come/Stuck/Picture or no picture, Me can't believe it, Trainer.* Michael Smith (v), Tony Uter (perc). 24/4/82 MV5 DG MC

THE SMITHS
31/5/83 PEEL† *What difference does it make°, Miserable lie, Reel around the fountain°, Handsome devil°.* Morrissey (v), Johnny Marr (g,hca), Andy Rourke (b), Mike Joyce (d). 18/5/83 MV5 RP NG
 † Complete session on Strange Fruit SFPCD055.
4/7/83 JENSEN *You've got everything now°, Wonderful woman, These things take time°.* 26/6/83 MV4 DG MC
 'Hand in glove', also broadcast on 4/7, was Rough Trade single RT132, not a BBC session recording.
5/9/83 JENSEN *I don't owe you anything, Accept yourself°, Pretty girls make graves (& Reel around the fountain, 12/8/86).* 25/8/83 MV4 JP MR
21/9/83 PEEL° *This night has opened my eyes, Still ill, This charming man, Back to the old house.* 14/9/83 MV4 RP TdB
 ° on 'Hatful of Hollow' Rough 76. 'This night has opened my eyes' is also on 'Louder than Bombs' Rough 255.
9/8/84 PEEL *William it was really nothing, Nowhere fast, Rusholme ruffians´, How soon is now.* 1/8/84 MV5 JP NG
 ´ on 12-inch of 'Last night I dreamt that somebody loved me' RTT200.
17/12/86 PEEL *Is it really so strange√, London, Half a person, Sweet and tender hooligan√.* 2/12/86 MV4 JP *
 √ on 12-inch of 'Sheila Take a Bow' RTT 196, and album 'Louder than bombs' Rough 255.

SNAFU
19/1/74 ROCK ON *That's the song, Country west, Funky friend, Jessie Lee.* Bobby Harrison (lv,bj), Micky Moody (g,mnd,v), Pete Solley (kv), Colin Gibson (b), Terry Popple (d). 10/1/74 LH1 PR *
28/1/74 HARRIS *Said the judge, Long gone, Goodbye USA, Get back to the country, Monday morning.* 9/1/74 LH1 PR BAI
21/10/74 HARRIS *Lock and key (1st TX ROCK ON, 5/10), Jessie Lee, Playboy blues.* 25/9/74 MV4 JG *
4/9/75 PEEL *Lock and key, Every little bit hurts, Bloodhound, Hard to handle.* Tim Hinkley (kv) r. Solley. 28/8/75 MV4 TW *

THE SNAPDRAGONS
29/2/88 MAYO *The dead, Once a millenium, Dare, Things you want.* James Taylor (agv), John Sullivan (gp), Spike Mullings (b), Pel Riccardi (d). 7/2/88 MV4 PW TdB
25/10/89 PEEL *Truth is never more than an opinion, Girl's blouses, Eternal in a moment, Quick to the dead.* 1/10/89 MV3 DG DD

SNOWBLIND
22/2/85 FRI. ROCK *Losing my place, Hold on, Chasing the dragon, Walk the line.* Tony Mason (v), Andy Simmons (g), Ross Bingham (k), Kevin Baker (d), Geoff Gillespie (b). 25/1/85 MV4 TW DD

SNUFF
30/1/89 PEEL *Win some, For both sides/I think we're alone now, Another girl, Now you don't remember/No one home.* Duncan (dv), Andy (b,bkv), Simon (gv). Rec. date unknown * DG ME&MFA

SNYPER
10/2/89 FRI. ROCK *Beginning of the end, Deathrite at sunset, No death so sad, Manifestations.* Cyd Hessin (v), Carl Dwyer (lg), Colin Newsom (rg), Mark Fletcher (b), Paul English (d). 13/1/89 MV4 PW DD

SO WHAT
13/12/85 FRI. ROCK *I've got to go, I'll be your friend, Promises, I don't know why.* Tom Smillie (bv), Rod Earl (g), Des Duffy (lg), Jerry Duffy (d). 13/11/85 MV4 TW DD

SO YOU THINK YOU'RE A COWBOY?
18/8/83 PEEL *Poor John, Smoke smoke smoke, Orange blossom special, Don't come back/I don't need you.* Annie Foy (v), Alan McDowall (gv), Tony Pilley (hca,bkv,perc), Kenny Brady (fd), Robbie Bain (d), Fraser Sutherland (b). 23/7/83 MV4 DG MR

S.O.B
27/10/90 PEEL *Over the line, Humanity of stupidity, Obsessed with wickedness, What's the truth, Unseen terror, Why.* Yoshitomo Suzuki (v), Toshimi Seki (g), Daisuke Kawataka (b), Satdshi Yasue (d). 11/10/90 MV3 PW JLO&DB

SOFA HEAD
11/1/90 PEEL *It doesn't work, Invitation to dinner/Infanticide, Fill, Valium housewife.* Lainey A. (dv), Ian (b), Wal (gv), Claire (v). 10/12/89 MV3 DG JB

SOFT CELL
3/8/81 SKINNER *Bedsitter†, Chips on my shoulder, Seedy films, Youth, Entertain me.* Marc Almond (v,perc), David Ball (sy,perc); & Robert & Fifi 'the Vicious Pink Phenomena' (bkv). 26/7/81 MV4 DG ME
 † On 'I and only' BOJCD025.
10/2/83 JENSEN *Soul inside, Her imagination, Where was your heart when you needed it most!, Memorabilia (medley).* 6/1/83 MV4 JS ME

THE SOFT MACHINE
17/12/67 TOP GEAR *Clarence in wonderland, We know what you mean, Hope for happiness, Certain kind (& Strangest scene, not broadcast).* Kevin Ayers (gb,lv-1,2), Mike Ratledge (o,p), Robert Wyatt (d,lv-3,4). 5/12/67 AO2 BA DT
 Widely-diverging opinions from panel on this trial broadcast tape: 'pretentious rubbish' 'neat, pretty and charming'. Borderline pass: 'a rather ordinary contemporary pop group'.
15/6/69 TOP GEAR† *Face lift/Mousetrap/Backwards/ Mousetrap reprise, The moon in June.* Hugh Hopper r. Ayers; extra instrumentation: Hopper (al-1), Ratledge (fl,vib-1) & Brian Hopper (ss-1). 10/6/69 MV4 JW TW
29/11/69 TOP GEAR *Instant pussy, Mousetrap/Noisette/ Backwards ballad/Mousetrap reprise/Pig/Orange skin food/A door opens and closes/10.30 returns to the bedroom†* ['Pig' onwards is actually 'Esther's nose job']. H. Hopper, Ratledge, Wyatt (1-Wyatt pv solo); & Elton Dean (al), Lyn Dobson (ss), Nick Evans (tb), Mark Charig (flh). 10/11/69 PH JW TW
16/5/70 TOP GEAR† *Slightly all the time/Out bloody rageous/Eamonn Andrews.* & Elton Dean (al) only. 4/5/70 PH JW TW
 This 4-piece rec'd John Peel Concert, 21/5/70 PS, TX 31/5. Also Prom Concert live on R3 13/8/70 from Royal Albert Hall.
25/9/70 BLACK *Out bloody rageous/Slightly all the time/Mousetrap (& Esther's nose job, 30/10/70).* 17/9/70 CM JM JWH
2/1/71 TOP GEAR *Virtually†, Fletcher's blemish.* Four-piece. 15/12/70 MV4 JW *
 In March 1971, 10-piece rec'd 2nd John Peel Concert 11/3 PS, TX 21/3. Included Ronnie Scott, Phil Howard, Neville Whitehead, Roy Babbington, Mark Charig, Paul Nieman.
26/6/71 TOP GEAR *Grides†, Dedicated to you but you weren't listening†, Eamonn Andrews/All white.* 1/6/71 MV4 JW BC
24/11/71 PEEL *As if†, Drop†, Welcome to Frillsville.* Phil Howard (d) r. Wyatt. 15/11/71 PH JW BC
 †† On Strange Fruit SFRCD201.
20/12/71 HARRIS *From a work in progress, As if/Pigling*

blond (& Grides, All white, Slightly all the time, 10/1/72). 16/11/71 TI JM JWH&JS
18/7/72 PEEL *Stumble/Lbo/As if, Fanfare/All white/Me/Drop.* John Marshall (d), Karl Jenkins (p,sx) r. Howard, Dean. 11/7/72 MV4 * *
 3rd In Concert rec'd 20/7/72 PS, TX 2/9/72.
24/11/72 SEQUENCE *The softweed factor, Fanfare/All white/Between/Riff, Ceseurehh/EPV/Stumble. I* 7/10/72 TI JM *
20/11/73 PEEL *Stanley stamp's gibbon album, Hazard profile, Down the road.* Roy Babbington (b) r. Hopper. 30/10/73 LH1 TW BC
 Subsequent work on R3: Jazz in Britain Rec'd 10/6/74 LH1, & Alan Holdsworth (g), TX 26/8/74; & Newcastle Jazz Festival gig, TX 13/11/76, Rec'd 29/10/76, Newcastle University Theatre (after Ratledge quit).

MICK SOFTLEY
23/11/70 HARRIS *Time machine, You go your way I'll go mine, The eagle, Caravan, The ship.* Mick Softley (gv), Ned Balen (trombone), Lyn Dobson (ts,fl,sit). 13/11/70 MV5 JM *
18/10/71 HARRIS *Hello little flower, Caravan/The Eagle, Good morning Mr Sunshine, Hey hey mama (& Time machine, 15/11/71).* * 21/9/71 TI JM JWH
18/2/72 PEEL *I'm so confused, If wishes were horses, Travelling man, Just flew in on a jet plane (& The land of the crab, 14/4/72).* & 5 musicians (unknown). 31/1/72 TI JM *
1/5/72 HARRIS *A traveller's song, Me and Lady Willow, From the land of the crab, Magdalene song, The great wall of Cathay.* Solo. 4/4/72 MV5 JG *
12/7/73 PEEL *Weeping willow, From the land of the crab, Gypsy, Me and Lady Willow (& Waterfall, If you're not part of the solution you must be part of the problem, If wishes were horses, 30/7/73 HARRIS; & Just flew in on a jet plane, 4/10/73).* 2/7/73 LH1 BA *
31/8/73 SEQUENCE *From the land of the crab, Julie Anyone, Waterfall.* 19/7/73 LH1 JM *
21/10/74 HARRIS *Stable yard, Windsor, Hansard.* 11/9/74 LH1 JG *

SOHO
14/12/87 LONG *Piece of you, Soul thing, I'm a receiver, Sweet thing, Blonde on black.* Jackie Soho (v), Pauline Soho (v), Timothy London (gv), Nigel Lackey (dm,seq). 8/11/87 MV4 PW TdB&MA

SOLSTICE
12/8/83 FRI. ROCK *Peace for the new age, The sea, Canibalise legaliss, Find yourself.* Sandy Leigh (v), Andy Glass (g), Mark Hawkins (b), Martin Wright (d), Marc Elton (k,vi). 29/7/83 * TW DD

SOMEONE'S BAND
23/10/70 BLACK *How it began, Molin, Aunt Anna.* Mel Buckley (lg), Dave Barber (d), John Coxon (rg), Terry Powney (b), Ses James (perc,v). 7/10/70 AO2 JM *

SOMETHING HAPPENS
2/8/88 L. KERSHAW *Here comes the only one again, Esmerelda, Over, Got you.* Tom Duanne (v), Ray Harman (g), Alan Byrne (b), Eamonn Ryan (d). 27/7/88 MV4 PW MPK

SOMO SOMO
14/8/86 KERSHAW *Mele, Kizolele, Kilema, Poleni.* Mose Se Sengo (lgv), Nsimba Bitendi Foquis (v), Nya Etana Mokwaka (cga), T. Daniel Howard (d), Mark Turner (g), Herman Asafo Agyei (b), John Telfer (sx), Paul Dias Jayasinna (tp). 23/7/86 SS CG TWN

SON HOUSE
11/7/70 TOP GEAR *My good gal, Spoken intro/Death letter, Spoken intro/Don't you mind people grinnin' in your face.* Son House (gv). 6/7/70 PH JW PR
 Repeated on RAVEN'S R&B 9/8/70.

SONIC YOUTH
19/5/86 PEEL *Come and smash me, Expressway to your skull, Moonbeam magic in a glass head cage, Hallowed*

be thy name. Steve Shelley (dv), Kim Gordon (bv), Thurston Moore (gv), Lee Ranaldo (gv). Rec. date unknown PRIV * *

Peel had previously broadcast a concert tape recorded at the Hammersmith Palais 28/4/85.

19/10/88 PEEL *Psycho mafia, My new house, Rowche Rumble, Victoria.* & Epic Soundtracks (perc,v). 11/10/88 MV4 MA~

20/3/89 PEEL *Corporate ghost, Rubin's beard, Major label chicken feed, Clippers.* 12/3/89 MV4 DG JB&FK

20/7/92 GOODIER *Purr, Youth against fascism, Burning spear, Creme brulee.* 7/7/92 MV4 MA~

LA SONORA DINAMITA
22/4/90 KERSHAW *La bamba, El cu cu, A mover la colita, El preso.* Melida Yara Yanguma (v), Omar Dario Viloria (tb,perc), Brigido Antonio Chaberra (bkv), Carlos Enrique Escobar (tb), Jorge Enrique Calderon (v), Julio Ennesto Estrada Rincon (b), Carlos Dario Pina Diaz (sx,perc), Neil Eduardo Benitez (cga), Rafael Emilio Benitez (timb,cowbell), Jose Enrique Carrillo (p), William Rafael Calderon (v). 8/3/90 MV5 DG NG

SOPHISTICATED BOOM BOOM
7/10/82 PEEL *Don't love me, Hearts on skates, Stalemates, Instant appeal.* Libby McArthur (v), Tricia Reid (lg, bkv), Irene Brown (g), Jacquie Bradley (d), Laura Mazzolini (b). 20/9/82 MV4 TW DD

15/6/83 PEEL *Singing today, Jimmy's in love, The next time, Courage.* & Nick Clark (sy,g). 11/6/83 MV4 DG MR

THE SOUL SISTERS AND THE CLOCKWORK ORANGE
22/10/67 TOP GEAR *You got 'em beat baby, Three time loser, Hold on, Blueberry hill, Bring me home love, Soulful dress, I can't stand it.* Teresa Cleveland (v), Ann Gissendammer (v), & The Clockwork Orange, (2&5: Clockwork Orange only). 16/10/67 PCI BA *

THE SOUND
6/10/80 READ *Jeopardy, Unwritten law (7/10), I can't escape myself (8/10), Heartland (9/10).* Adrian Borland (gv), Graham Green (b), Bi Marshall (k), Michael Dudley (d). 26/9/80 MV4 DG AP&MFA

16/11/81 PEEL *Fatal flaw, Skeletons, Hot house, New dark age.* Max Mayers (k) r. Marshall. 9/11/81 MV4 TW AP

SOUNDGARDEN
7/6/89 PEEL *Flower, Thank you, Everybody's got something to hide.* Chris Cornell (gv), Kim Thayil (lg), Hiro Yamamoto (b), Matt Cameron (d). 14/5/89 HP DG MWT

10/7/92 FRI. ROCK *I can't give you anything, I don't care about you, Can you see me, Homicidal suicidal.* Ben Shepherd (b) r. Yamamoto. 12/6/92 MV5 MC~

THE SOUP DRAGONS
24/2/86 PEEL *Whole wide world, Too shy to say, Learning to fall, Just mind your step girl.* Ross Sinclair (d), Sushil Dade (b), Jim McCulloch (g), Sean Dickson (gv); & Jacqueline (bkv). 16/2/86 MV5 DG ME&FK

1/9/86 LONG *Slow things down, The same old story, Lindy's realised, Make my day.* & Joe McAlinden (vi). 20/8/86 MV4 BYA MPK

6/1/87 PEEL *Our lips are sealed, The kids are alright, Purple haze, Listen to this.* 7/12/86 * DG ME

30/6/87 LONG *Kingdom chairs, Can't take no more, Cow nest, Turning stone.* 21/6/87 MV4 HP TdB&FK

TIM SOUSTER
17/9/69 PEEL *Sonata 2 & 4, Sonata 5 & 6, 2nd interlude, Sonata II (all by John Cage).* Tim Souster (p). 27/8/69 S2 PR *

Sole R1 appearance [M: R3].

SOUTHERN COMFORT
20/3/71 TOP GEAR *Roses (sleepwalk), The dreadful ballad of Willy Hurricane, April lady, Get back home.* Andy Leigh (bv), Gordon Huntley (ps), Carl Bamwell (gv), Ray Duffy (d), Mark Griffiths (g). 9/3/71 MV4 * BC

Live on Rosko show 29/5/71 PS; & rec'd Peel Sunday Concert 24/6/71 PS, TX 18/7/71.

18/10/71 HARRIS *Lilly Brown, Old Rudd, I wanna be your mama again, Ain't no sunshine.* 4/10/71 T1 PD *

16/1/72 SPEAKEASY *Oklahoma hills, I wanna be your mama again, Cosmic jig, Mare take me home.* 14/1/72 PS TB *

25/1/72 PEEL *Old Rudd, Harlem girl, Cosmic jig, Lilly Brown.* 18/1/72 MV4 * *

31/1/72 HARRIS *I wanna be your mama again, Josephine's biscuit, Travelling light (& You should have been a car salesman, 20/3/72).* 26/1/72 A02 JG *

31/1/72 R2 NIGHT RIDE *I wanna be your mama again, Good old 2-6-2, To love (1/2), Morning has broken (3/2), Josephine's biscuit (4/2).* 22/11/71 A02 DK *

4/12/72 HARRIS *Stir don't shake, You're telling those lies again, St Anne's well, Yankee lady, I need help.* 8/11/72 LH1 JG *

4/6/73 HARRIS *Something in the way she moves, I sure like your smile, Hey hey good morning (& Sweet columbine, 30/7/73).* Huntley & Terry Brown (agv), Chris Macauley (d), Dave Coomber (bv), Dave Stamp (agv), Andy Holland (agv). 23/5/73 LH1 PR *

SOUTHERN DEATH CULT
10/6/82 PEEL *Fat man, Today, False faces, Or glory.* Ian Astbury (v), Haq Qureshi (d), David 'Buzz' Burrows (g), Barry Jetson (b). 21/5/82 MV4 JWI MC

24/1/83 JENSEN *Apache, The patriot, Flower in the desert, False faces.* 20/1/83 MV4 JS *

SOUTHSIDE JOHNNY AND THE ASBURY JUKES
20/4/89 SKINNER *Trapped again, On the air tonight, Ain't that peculiar, Let the good times roll, Hard to find, The fever.* John Lyons (lv,hca), Bobby Bandiera (g), George Ruiz (b,bkv), Kevin Kavanagh (k), Wes Nagy (k), Tom Major (d), Joey Stan (sx), Dan Levine (tb,bkv), Barry Danellion (tp,bkv). Live, after midnight, from MV3 HP TdB

OTIS SPANN
2/7/69 PEEL *Lucille, I'm not going to sell you my thing, Back alley blues.* * 1/7/69 * PR *

SPARE RIB
13/2/73 PEEL *Hear me calling, Making light, Little Miss Femme Fatale, Probably do.* Jo Ann Kelly (v), Roger Brown (gv), Adrian Pitryga (lg), Bruce Rowlands (d), John Atkinson (b), Nick Judd (p). 6/2/73 LH1 * BC

Rec'd In Concert as trial b'cast 11/1/73 PS, TX 20/1/73.

THE MIGHTY SPARROW
17/9/89 KERSHAW *Jean & Dinah, Mange, All in the game.* Mighty Sparrow (lv), Julien Martin (lg), Elston Nero (k), Winstone Rollins (tb), Avelia Moisey (tp), Ray Carless (sx), M. T. Williams (perc), Don Diaz (b), Tony Mason (d), Colin Graham (tp), Elaine Wellington & Pauline Oduro (bkv). 24/8/89 OD DG TdB

In February 1963 the BBC Radio Popular Music Committee had ruled that a track on his RCA LP 'Sparrow Come Back' was NTBB 'not to be broadcast', on grounds of taste. The track was called 'Number 69'!

ROGER RUSKIN SPEAR AND HIS GIANT ORCHESTRAL WARDROBE
26/6/71 TOP GEAR *On her doorstep, Mattress man, Call of the freaks.* Roger Ruskin Spear (various) [& others: 'I can't remember the full line-up, but Thunderclap Newman was definitely there, playing the contra-bass saxophone' JW]. 8/6/71 MV4 JW BC

SPEAR OF DESTINY
29/11/82 PEEL *Black madonna, O-men of the times, The wake, Judgement hymn.* Kirk Brandon (gv), Stan Stammers (b), Chris Ball (d), Lascelles James (sx). 22/11/82 * TW MC

5/1/83 JENSEN *Roof of the world, The Flying Scotsman, The grapes of wrath, The man who tunes the drums.* 12/12/82 MV4 DG ME

24/1/84 JENSEN *Attica, The liberator, Rainmaker, Young men.* Brandon, Stammers, Dolphin Taylor (d), Neil Pyzer (k,sx), Alan St. Clair (gv). 8/1/84 MV4 DG ME

14/8/85 LONG *Somewhere in the East, Up all night, Harlan county, Rocket ship.* & Micky Donnelly (sx). 21/7/85 HP BYA SC

THE SPECIALS
29/5/79 PEEL† *Gangsters, Too much too young°, Concrete jungle, Monkey man.* Jerry Dammers (k,bkv), Roddy Radiation (lg), Terry Hall (lv), Sir Horace Gentleman Panter (b), Lynval Golding (lg,bkv), John Bradbury (d,perc), Neville Staples (v,perc). 23/5/79 MV4 JS NG
† On Strange Fruit SFPS018; ° also on 'I and only' BOJCD025.

22/10/79 PEEL *Rude boys outa jail, Rat race, Long shot kick the bucket/Liquidator/Moon stomp (The skinhead symphony in three movements).* 15/10/79 MV4 TW DD
'Skinhead Symphony - Live take, no overdubs'-TW on sheet.

1/12/80 PEEL *Sea cruise, Stereotypes, Raquel.* & Rico Rodriguez (tb), Dick Cuthell (cnt). 29/10/80 MV4 BS NG

12/9/83 PEEL *Alcohol, Lonely crowd, Bright lights.* Now billed as 'The Special A.K.A': Dammers, Bradbury, Gary McManus (b), John Shipley (g), Andy Aderinto (sx), Rhoda Daker, Egidio Newton & Stan Campbell (v). 22/8/83 MV4 TW MC

SPECIMEN
14/7/83 JENSEN *Lovers, Syria, Stand up stand out, Wolverines.* Ollie Wisdom (v), Kevin Mills (b), Jonathan Trevisick (d), Jonathan Klein (g,ag), Jonathan Melton (k). 7/7/83 MV4 JP MR

SPECTRUM
27/7/92 GOODIER *How you satisfy me, True love, Revolution, Set me free.* Pete Kember (v,kg), Mike Stour (b), Kev Cowan (gk), Tony Lambert (d). 26/6/92 MV4 MA~

CHRIS SPEDDING
27/11/70 BLACK *The one lick I know, Everything I do (is gonna be funky), Honky tonk blues, A hard woman is good to find.* Chris Spedding (gv) & unknown 11/11/70 A02 JM JWH
[M: session guitarist for everyone].

1/10/71 BLACK *The only lick I know, Sunshades, At the dark end of the street (& White lady, 25/10/71).* & 4 (unknown). 7/9/71 T1 JM JWH

4/4/72 PEEL *The only lick I know, Dock of the bay, A piece of pre-recorded music, A hard woman is good to find.* & (b), (d), & 1 other (unknown). 21/3/72 MV4 PR *

4/1/77 PEEL *Hurt by love, Pogo dancing, Get out of my pagoda, Misunderstood, Motor bikin'.* Chris Spedding (gv) and the Vibrators: Ian Carnochan (gv), John Ellis (gv), Pat Collier (b), Jon Edwards (d). 16/12/76 MV4 TW BAI

JOHN B. SPENCER
5/3/87 KERSHAW *Promises, Don't get hit by a train, Poor little rich boy, Will this house be blessed.* Billed as 'The John Spencer Group': John Spencer (gv) & Graeme Taylor (g), Paul Hughes (db,jh), Laurie Harper (fd,mnd,jh). 18/2/87 * CG SR

2/3/89 KERSHAW *One way flight, Drive-in movies, Poor man on the cross, Break and entry.* & Taylor, Andy Hamilton (sx), Winston Bussett (b), Howard Tibble (d). 2/2/89 MV4 DG NG

2/6/91 KERSHAW *Cry baby cry, Fond goodbye, Mad man in Memphis, Cruisin'.* & Mick Moody (g), Bernard O'Neill (db), Alan Dunn (acc), Jamie Matthews (hca,uk,v). 14/2/91 MV5 DG SB&MR

SPIDER
19/6/81 FRI. ROCK *What you're doing to me, Nine to five, Rock & roll forever will last, Awol.* Brian Burrows (bv), Robby Burrows (d), Sniffa Bryce (lg), Colin Harkness (g,lv). 10/6/81 * TW DD

31/1/86 FRI. ROCK *Gimme gimme it all, I'm not the only one, Need to know about you, Mind heart body & soul.* 10/1/86 MV4 TW DD

DAVY SPILLANE
31/3/88 KERSHAW *Atlantic bridge, The storm, River of gems,*

Daire's dream. Davy Spillane (pp,fl), Paul Moran (d,cga), Tony Molloy (b), Anthony Drienhan (g), James Delaney (k). 3/3/88 * DG NG&MA

SPIN

10/2/92 Goodier *Beautiful thing, Easy number, I'm getting out, Not just anyone*. Matt James (d,bkv), Kevin Miles (b), Steve Mason (g), Martin Falls (v). 28/12/91 MV4 MC~AR

SPIREA X

17/12/90 Goodier *Revolution, Sisters and brothers, Chlorine dream†, Jet pilot*. Jim Beattie (gv), Robert McGovern (rg), Anthony McGovern (b), Judith Boyle (bkv,perc), Andrew Kerr (d), Dave Morgan (cga). 8/12/90 MV5 MA~
† On 'Best of Mark Goodier' Nighttracks Mark1.

SPIRITUALIZED

14/3/92 Peel *Angel sigh/Feels so sad, Smiles*. Johnny Mattock (d), Willie B. Carruthers (b), Jason 'Spaceman' Pierce (gv), Mark Refoy (g), Kate Radley (o); & 'the Kick Horns': Simon Clarke (sx,fl), Tim Sanders (sx), Roddy Lorimer (tp). 7/1/92 MV5 MR~ JB

SPIROGYRA

15/11/71 Harris *Captain's log, Forest of dear, Love is a funny thing, Duke of Beaufort*. Martin Cockerham (agv), Barbara Gaskin (v), Steve Borrill (b), Julian Cusack (vi,p). 1/11/71 T1 PD ARV

SPITFIRE

16/11/91 Peel *Fluid, Dive, Firebird, Hotlegs*. Justin (d), Nick (b), Matt (lg), Steve (rg), Jeff (v). 15/9/91 MV3 DG ME&RJ

SPIZZ OIL...

7/8/78 Peel† *Cold city, 6000 crazy, Pure noise/Alien Language/Protect from heat, Platform 3/Switched off*. Spizz (lv,g,kazoo), Pete Petrol (lg), Frank Guest (p,perc). 1/8/78 MV4 BS MR&MPK
† On Strange Fruit SFPS022.

...SPIZZ ENERGI...

21/3/79 Peel *European heroes, Energy crisis, Soldier soldier, Life's so safe*. Alpha Scanner (b), Mark Coalfield (k), Paul Guest (g), Spizz (gv). 12/3/79 MV4 TVD MR
27/11/79 Peel *New species, Touched, Intimate, Effortless, Where's Captain Kirk*. Spizz, Coalfield, Scott (g,bkv), Jim Solar (b), Hero Shima (d). 13/11/79 MV4 JB MR

and... ATHLETICO SPIZZ 80

12/5/80 Peel *Red and black, Rythem inside, Hot deserts, Central park*. C.P. Snare (d), Jim Solar (b), Scotty (g), Coalfield, Spizz. 30/4/80 MV4 JE NG
6/10/80 Read *Scared, Brainwashing time (7/10), Melancholy (8/10), Central Park (9/10)*. Scotty, Coalfield out. 2/10/80 MV4 CL *

SPK

31/8/83 Peel *Metal dance, The sandstorm method, Metal field, Will to please*. Sinan (v), Derek Thompson (tp,b,k,perc), Graham (perc,el). 20/8/83 MV4 DG TdB
1/11/83 Jensen *But can you dance to it?, The shape of things to come, One world, The kill*. 23/10/83 MV4 DG ME

SPLASH

20/3/85 Long *Dancing in circles, Felicity, Religioh on Sundays, Heaven sent*. Simon Taylor (lv,g), Colin Murden (bv), Ian Gillott (gv), Gary Holmes (d,perc). 22/9/85 HP PWL *

SPLINTER

14/9/74 Rock On *The place I love, China light, Lonely man, Costafine town, White shoe weather*. Bob Purvis (gv), Bill Elliott (gv). 2/9/74 LH1 BA *
30/12/74 Harris *China light, Peace and love, What is it, Somebody's city*. 27/11/74 MV4 JG *
[M: daytime].

SPLINTERED

27/3/92 Peel *Godsend, Kill the body so the head will die, Breakdown pt. 3, Judas cradle*. Paul Dudeney (dv), Paul Wright (b), James Machin (gv), Richard Johnson (g,sy). 16/2/92 MV3 DG ME&JRS

SPLIT ENZ

18/10/78 Peel *I see red, Mind over matter, Frenzy, Semi-detached*. Malcolm Green (d), Eddy Rayner (k), Nigel Griggs (b), Neil Finn (g), Noel Grombie (perc), Tim Finn (v). 26/9/78 MV6 MB TdB

SPLODGENESSABOUNDS

24/11/80 Peel *Rolf, Richard Freak, Malcolm's Mum parts 1-3, Desert Island Joe*. Max Splodge (v), Fred Winston Forbe (k), Miles Flat ("worst guitar"), Pat Thetic (rg), Roger Over-and-out Rodent ("attempted bass"). Baby Greensleeves (v), Whiffy Archer (sx), Desert Island Joe Lurchslive (d). 28/10/80 MV4 DG MR&HP

SPONTANEOUS MUSIC ENSEMBLE

14/5/71 Black *Rhythm on, Sustained*. John Stevens (d), & 3 others: (agv, unknown), Barry Guy (b), & possibly Trevor Watts or Evan Parker (al,ss). 25/4/71 CM JM *
1st b'cast under this name on WS BANDBEAT, TX 8/10/66, prod. JG [M: Jazz shows].

SPOOKY TOOTH

17/3/68 Top Gear *It hurts you so, Too much of nothing, Sunshine help me, Tobacco road*. Gary Wright (o,v), Greg Ridley (b), Mike Harrison (pv), Mike Kellie (d), Luther Grosvenor (g). 21/2/68 MV4 BP PR
Passed by panel, but comments ranged from 'I liked this group, loads of attack and screaming feeling' to 'loud and pretentious psychedelic rubbish'.
23/6/68 Top Gear *Love really changed me, Evil women, I can't quit her*. 17/6/68 PC1 BA PR
20/7/68 Sat. Club *Morning dew, New York mining disaster, Tobacco Road*. 16/7/68 PH KB *
5/8/68 Symonds *The weight, Society's child (6/8), It's all about a roundabout (7/8)*. 26/7/68 PC1 * *
6/10/68 Top Gear *Feelin' bad, The weight, I can't quit her, Blues town*. 30/9/68 PC1 BA *
7/10/68 Symonds *The weight, Blues town (8/10), Feelin' bad (9/10), Sunshine help me (11/10)*. 1/10/68 MV4 * *
10/10/68 Pop North *Blues town, The weight, Feelin' bad*. 7/10/68 PHM JWX *
20/10/68 Henry *Morning dew, The weight, Feelin' bad*. 14/10/68 MV4 AD *
21/10/68 R1 Club *Feelin' bad, The weight, Garden gate, Blues town, I can't quit her*. 15/10/68 PS KB *
Next broadcast live on same show from the Paris, 4/12/68.
20/1/69 Symonds *Better by you better than me, When I get home (21/1), Feelin' bad (22/1), I've got enough heartache (23/1)*. 13/1/69 PH KB *
Files suggest part of session repeated on R1 Club 7/2/69.
23/2/69 Top Gear *Better by you better than me, Waitin' for the wind, When I get home, That was only yesterday*. 3/2/69 PH BA * [M: daytime]
17/3/69 Young *That was only yesterday, Better by you better than me (19/3)*. 3/3/69 MV4 * *
26/4/69 Walker *Pretty woman, Feelin' bad, Better by you better than me*. 23/4/69 MV4 cJBU *
1/6/69 Symonds On Sunday *Nobody's there at all, Better by you better than me, The weight*. 27/5/69 PC1 c.PW1 *
6/7/69 Henry *Bring us salvation, Better by you better than me, Son of your father*. 27/6/69 PC1 MB *

SQUEEZE

29/8/77 Peel *Cat on the wall, Model, All fed up, Sex master*. Glen Tilbrook (lg), Harry Kakoulli (b), Gilson Lavis (d), Julian Holland (p), Chris Difford (rg). 17/8/77 MV4 MB NG
15/5/78 Peel *Bang bang, Ain't it sad, I must go, The knack*. 3/5/78 MV4 JG NG
71/3/79 Peebles *Slap 'n' tickle, Up the junction, Cool for cats, Hop skip jump*. Johnny Bentley (b) r. Kakoulli. 2/3/79 MV4 JG *
8/4/82 Jensen *Onto the dance floor, Elephant girl, I can't hold on, The apple tree*. Donald Snow (k) r. Holland. 18/3/82 MV4 JS MR

Difford and Tilbrook recorded an acoustic set 19/10/89 for Sat. Seq., TX 18/11/89: *'She doesn't have to shave', 'Footprints in the frost', 'Is that love', 'Melody motel'*. Prod. KH.

STACKRIDGE

8/7/71 Henry *Grand piano, 32 Westmore, Dora the female explorer, Every man*. James Warren (b), Michael Slater (fl), William Bent (d), Andy Davis (gp), Mike Evans (vi). 30/6/71 MV4 MB MH&MF
Borderline pass from Audition panel: 'Amateur group with limited musical knowledge' 'Just about adequate' 'No real musical policy'.
2/8/71 R1 Club *Dora the female explorer, Harzo plod, Grand piano (3/8), Norwegian wood (5/8)*. 16/7/71 AO1 cJBE *
20/10/71 Peel *3 legged table pt.3, Slark*. 21/9/71 MV4 JW BC
4/4/72 Peel *Lummy days, The story of my heart, Syracuse the elephant*. 20/3/72 PH JW BC
12/10/72 Peel *Anyone for tennis?, There is no refuge, Friendliness, Teatime*. James Walter joins. 9/10/72 LH1 BA *
25/1/73 Peel *Keep on clucking, Fourposter bed/Orange blossom special, Do the Stanley, Purple space ships over Yatton*. 15/1/73 LH1 BA *
5/3/73 Harris *The Lyder loo, Road to Venezuela, God speed the plough, The galloping gaucho*. 7/2/73 LH1 PR *
6/7/73 Sequence *The galloping gaucho, Fundamentally yours, Dolores, Road to Venezuela*. 12/6/73 T1 JM *
22/11/73 Peel *McGregor/Zorgon's daughter, The laughing policeman, February in Shropshire, The volunteer*. Rod Bowkett, Keith Gemmell r. Slater, Bent. 19/11/73 LH1 BA *
23/2/74 Rock On *Dangerous bacon*. 11/2/74 LH1 BA *
24/8/74 Rock On *Galloping gaucho, Pocket billiards, Rufus T. Firefly*. Paul Karas, Roy Morgan, Mutter Slater r. Walter, Warren, Evans. 19/8/74 LH1 BA *
30/1/75 Peel *Dancing on air, Spin round the room, No one's more important than the earthworm, Benjamin's giant onion*. 22/1/75 MV4 JG *
2/3/76 Peel *Hold me tight, Hey good looking, Save a red face, Steam radio song*. James Walter (b), Peter Van Hooke (d), Dave Lawson (k), Mutter Slater (v). 19/2/76 MV4 TW *

STACKWADDY

16/10/70 Black *Road runner, Ginney Joe, Klinkers*. Mick Stott (lg), John Knail (v,hca), Stuart Banham (b), John Groom (d). 30/9/70 T1 * *
'Appalling lead voice... a lunatic shout... sounds as if he's being sick... screaming, toneless and distorted' Fail: Audition panel.
18/2/72 Peel *Hoochie coochie man, Rock me baby, You really got me, Willie the pimp*. * 24/1/72 T1 JM *

STAMPEDE

28/5/82 Fri. Rock *Shadows of the night, Photographs, Moving on, The other side*. Reuben Archer (v), Laurence Archer (g), Alan Wilson (k), Colin Bond (b), Frank Noon (d). 16/4/82 MV4 TW DD

VIV STANSHALL

21/3/70 Top Gear *Cyborg signal, Blind date, Eleven moustachioed daughters, The strain*. 'Viv Stanshall's Big Grunt': Roger Ruskin Spear (sx), Dennis Cowan (b), Ian Wallace (d), Bubs White (g). 16/3/70 AO1 JW *
27/10/75 Peel *Trail of the lonesome pine, The unbridled suite/In the final analysis, Aunt Florrie remembers (from 'Giant whelks at Rawlinson end')*. Viv Stanshall (g,eu,pp, dum dum, talking drum, perc), Pete Moss (b,p,acc,vi,cel), Mox (hca,fl), Bubs White (b,uk,g). 16/10/75 MV4 TW BAI
22,23,24,26/12/75 Peel *Christmas at Rawlinson End parts 1-4; including musical backing tracks: Aunt Florrie recalls, Convivial vivisectionist, The party's over now, Uncle Otto, Roar of the end, A half for chuck*. Stanshall, Moss, Julian Smedley (vi,mnd), Andy Roberts (dul). 2/12/75 MV4 TW BAI&ME

6/4/77 PEEL *Part 34: An Absence of Whelks, Aunt Florrie recalls Dan, Nice and tidy.* * 21/3/77 MV4 MB DD

23/5/77 PEEL *Part 35: Spades balls and sausage trees, Wheelbarrow, Aunt Florrie recalls.* Stanshall, Zoot Money (g,p,v), Barry Dransfield (vi,clo). 11/5/77 MV4 MB NG

19/12/77 PEEL *The road to unreason pt. 37, Aunt Florrie recalls, Three vivisectionists, Mrs Radcliffe.* Stanshall, Money, Mox (hca,fl). 24/8/77 & 14/12/77 MV4 MB NG

5/4/78 PEEL *Florrie's waltz, Fool and bladder, Interlewd, Smeeton.* Stanshall, Smedley, Jim Cuomo (cl,rec,cel,leg). 29/3/78 MV4 * NG

25/7/78 PEEL *Ginger Geyser, Socks, Stripe me a pinky, Fresh faced boys, Aunt Florrie, Piece in toto.* Moss r. Cuomo. 18/7/78 MV4 MB MR

24/12/79 PEEL *Gooseflesh steps pt.1: Sig./Cracks are showing/Swelter/End roar/Cums.* John Kirkpatrick (acc,cnc,jh,bkv) r. Smedley. 11/12/79 MV4 MB MR

18/4/88 PEEL *The crackpot at the end of the rainbow, Florrie's waltz/Under the sea, In the pipes, Murder living next door, Private rhythms, In the pipes (reprise), Cackling gas, Florrie's waltz/Under the sea.* Stanshall, Moss (p,d,acc), Kenny Baldock (b), Dave Swarbrick (vi, mnd). 23/2/88 * DG ME&SA

23/11/88 PEEL *The eating at Rawlinson End.* Stanshall, Swarbrick, Tony Roberts, Moss, Danny Thompson. 9/8/88 MV4 MR~

6/4/91 PEEL *Cackling gas capers, Octavio, Tour de farce, Achmedillo, Peristaltic waves.* Viv Stanshall, Swarbrick, Roberts, Thompson, Rodney Slater, Roger Ruskin Spear, Henry Lowther, John Megginson, Les Cirkel. 29/5/91 MV5 MR~

STARFIGHTERS

4/9/81 FRI. ROCK *Killing time, Devil's drivin', Power crazy, Alley cat blues.* Steve Burton (lv), Stevie Young (rg), Pat Hambly (lg), Doug Dennis (b), Steve Bailey (d). 21/8/81 * TW DD

STARRY EYED AND LAUGHING

1/8/74 PEEL *Money is no friend of mine, Chimes of freedom, See your face, Fifty-fifty.* Tony Poole (gv), Ross McGeeney (lgv), Iain Whitmore (bv), Mike Whackford (d). 18/7/74 LH1 * BAI

14/12/74 ROCK ON *Never say too late, Nobody home, Living in London, Closer to you now.* 9/12/74 MV4 BA MF&NGR

16/1/75 PEEL *Nobody home, Thought talk, Don't give me a hard time, Since I lost you.* 9/1/75 MV4 * *

11/8/75 PEEL *Down the street, Good love, Swarthfell rock, Flames in the rain.* 29/7/75 MV4 TW BAI

2/5/77 DLT *Lonely love, Lost without you, Suzy blue eyes, Jealous mind.* Arthur May (g), David Pomeroy (b), Paul Turner (d), r. Whitmore, Whackford. 25/4/77 MV5 TB *

THE STARS OF HEAVEN

22/1/86 PEEL† *Sacred heart hotel, Talk about it now, Moonstruck, So you know.* Stanley Erraught (g), Peter O'Sullivan (b,bkv), Stephen Ryan (gv), Bernard Walsh (d). 14/1/86 MV5 PRS MR

† released as side one of mini-album 'Sacred Heart Hotel', Rough Trade RTM173.

26/5/86 PEEL *28, Every other day, What else could you do?, Paradise of lies.* 13/5/86 MV4 DG MR

4/8/86 LONG *Little England, Unconscious, All about you, Never saw you.* 23/7/86 MV4 BYA MPK

17/2/87 PEEL *Wheels, Calvary cross, Can't seem to make you mine, Still feeling blue.* 3/2/87 * DG MR&PS

27/1/88 PEEL *Two o'clock waltz, Ammonia train, Northern isles, Unfinished dreaming.* 17/1/88 * DG ME&FK

STATE OF SHOCK

5/7/91 FRI. ROCK *Walls of fear, Summer fate, Lucid sleep, Dead end maze.* Mark Robinson (lv,g), Graham Williamson (b), Rick Cross (g), Ronnie McLean (d). 14/6/91 MV5 DD~

STATETROOPER

14/2/86 FRI. ROCK *Set fire to the night, Too late (for love),*

Faster than light, She's got the look. Gary Barden (v), Jeff Summers (gv), Jeff Brown (bv), Steve Glover (k), Martin Bushell (g), Bruce Bisland (d). Rec. date unknown MV4 TW *

STATUS QUO

22/1/68 SYMONDS *Pictures of matchstick men, Judy in disguise (25/1), Spicks and specks (23/1).* Francis M. Rossi (lg), Alan Lancaster (b), John Coghlan (d), Roy Lynes (o), Ricky 'Harrison' aka Parfitt (rg). 16/1/68 MV4 * *

'Enthusiastic pass' from panel.

17/2/68 SAT. CLUB *Spicks and specks, Judy in disguise, Pictures of matchstick men, Things get better.* 13/2/68 AO2 BB DT

Original line-up, joined by Bob Young (k, r Lynes) in June 1970, went on to do an astonishing 42 live and new session appearances on R1 daytime shows, all before Autumn 1970.

3/3/72 PEEL *Mean girl, Na na na, Railroad, Someone's leaving.* Young out. 7/2/72 T1 PD ARV

7/12/72 PEEL *Don't waste my time, Unspoken words, O baby, Paper plane, Softer ride.* 20/11/72 LH1 BA *

16/1/73 PEEL *Paper plane, Don't waste my time, Softer ride.* 8/1/73 T1 JW *

Last R1 studio date was In Concert, rec'd 1/3/73 PS, TX 24/3/73. After that, all contracts marked 'Own Studio'.

STEALER'S WHEEL

15/11/71 PEEL *Make you break you, Can I have my money back? (16/11), Long way round (18/11), Didn't I (19/11).* Gerry Rafferty (gv) &: Tom Parker (p,o), Roger Brown (g), Gary Taylor (b), Andrew Steele (d). 20/10/71 MV5 PR *

Unanimous pass from Panel: 'impeccable'. 1st R1 date with: Joe Egan (ag), Ian Campbell (b), Paul Pilnick (lg) & Peter Clarke (d), was In Concert TX 7/12/71.

12/12/71 SPEAKEASY *Steamboat row, I get by, Maybe tomorrow, Please sing a song for us.* Rafferty, Egan etc, as In Concert. 10/12/71 PS TB *

17/1/72 HARRIS *I get by, Please sing a song for us, You put something better inside of me.* 11/1/72 MV5 JG *

29/2/72 PEEL *We're on the right track, I get by, Jose, Mary Skeffington.* 14/2/72 PH JW *

29/5/72 HARRIS *Heart of stone, Can I have my money back, Can't believe you want to leave.* Tony Williams (b), Rod Coombes (d) r. Campbell, Clarke. 10/5/72 AO2 JG *

5/12/72 PEEL *Late again, Midnight rider, Chevrolet, I get by.* Luther Grosvenor (gv), De Lisle Harper (b) r. Williams. 21/11/72 LH1 * BC

18/12/72 HARRIS *I get by, You put something better inside of me, Chevrolet.* 22/11/72 LH1 JG * [M: daytime]

11/1/73 PEEL *Gets so lonely, You put something better inside of me, Here comes the queen, Outside looking in.* 1/1/73 LH1 BA *

7/6/73 PEEL *Johnny's tune, Everything will be alright, I get by, Late again.* 4/6/73 LH1 BA *

10/4/75 PEEL *Wishbone, This morning, Monday morning, Right or wrong.* Rafferty, Egan &: Peter Robinson, Andrew Steele (d), Dave Wynter, Ken Elliott. 3/4/75 MV4 TW BAI

STEAMHAMMER

13/7/69 TOP GEAR *When your friends are gone, Passing through, Louisiana blues, 6/4 for Amiran.* Kieran White (gv,hca), Martin Pugh (lg), Steve Joliffe (sx,fl), Steve Davy (b), Rob Tait (d). 8/7/69 MV4 JW *

27/9/69 WS R&B *Junior's wailing, When your friends are gone, Riding on the L&M.* 3/9/69 MV4 JG JY

28/2/70 WS R&B *Junior's wailing, On the tide, Another travelling tune.* Mick Bradley (d) r. Tait. 4/2/70 MV4 JG JY

STEEL PULSE

29/9/77 PEEL *Prodigal son, Ku Klux Klan, Bad man, Prediction.* Steve Nesbitt (d), Ronnie McQueen (b),

David Hinds (g,lv), Basil Gabbidon (lg), Selwyn Brown (o), Michael Riley (perc,bkv), Alfonso Martin (perc). 31/8/77 MV4 MB MR

27/4/78 PEEL *Hansworth revolution, Rock against racism, Makka splaff.* 4/4/78 MV4 MB MR

13/8/79 PEEL *Unseen guests, Uncle George, Reggae fever.* Riley out. 16/7/79 MV4 TW BAI

7/5/80 PEEL *Drug squad, Shinin', Nyahbinghi.* 9/4/80 MV4 JE NG

6/1/82 PEEL *Ravers, Man no sober, Blues dance.* 5/12/81 MV4 DG MR

9/4/84 JENSEN *Chant a psalm, Steppin' out, Throne of gold, Roller skates.* Alvin Ewen, Carlton Brian r. McQueen, Gabbidon. 1/3/84 MV5 JP MPK

STEELEYE SPAN

11/4/70 TOP GEAR *A calling-on song, The blacksmith, The hills of Greenmore, All things are quite silent, Dark-eyed sailor.* Ashley Hutchings (b), Maddy Prior (v), Gay Woods (cnc,v), Terry Woods (mand,gv), Tim Hart (g,mnd,dul,v). 31/3/70 MV4 JW *

27/6/70 TOP GEAR *The blacksmith, Female drummer, Rave on, I was a young man, Lark in the morning.* Peter Knight (fd), Martin Carthy (g) r. Terry & Gay Woods 23/6/70 MV4 JW *

23/7/70 HENRY *Cold haily windy night, The king, Prince Charlie, Bold poachers.* 16/7/70 AO2 MB *

17/10/70 FOLK ON 1 *Silver spear/College grove, Lay down your weary tune, False knight on the road, Hitler's downfall/Hag with the money, Female drummer (mk 2), Lovely on the water, Wee weaver.* 29/9/70 AO2 FL JWH

4/2/71 HENRY *Reel, Female drummer (mk 2), General Taylor, Farther along (& Lark in the morning, 2nd reel, not broadcast).* 27/1/71 MV4 MB & MF*

27/3/71 TOP GEAR *Two reels, Let's dance, Prince Charlie Stuart, Bring 'em down/A hundred years ago.* 16/3/71 MV4 JW *

30/9/71 DRUMMOND *Cold haily windy night, Long lankin/Lark in the morning, Wee poor labouring man, Adieu sweet lovely Nancy, Uncle Tom Cobley and all/Tom Pierce.* Knight ill. 22/9/71 MV4 MB MH&MF

Five-piece recorded Peel's Sunday Concert 15/9/71 PS, TX 26/9/71.

8/2/72 PEEL *Reels: The oak tree/Pigeon on the gate, Ups and downs, Spotted cow, Rosebud in June, Sheepcrook and black dog.* Rick Kemp (b) & Bob Johnson (gv) r. Hutchings, Carthy. 31/1/72 PH JW *

10/3/72 PEEL *Jigs, Royal forester, John Barleycorn (& The gamekeeper, 28/4/72).* 21/2/72 T1 PD ARV

1/6/72 DRUMMOND *King Henry, Dancing at Whitsun, Gaudete, Jigs.* 17/5/72 MV4 MB *

28/7/72 PEEL *Rag doll, Cam'ye o'er fra' France, False knight on the road, Saucy sailor.* 4/7/72 T1 JM JWH&NG

15/10/72 SOUNDS ON SUNDAY *Ups and downs, John Barleycorn, Cam'ye o'er fra'France, Parcel of rogues, King Henry, Cam'ye o'er fra'France (reprise).* 19/9/72 PH FL *

24/10/72 PEEL *New reels: The Bank of Ireland/Lucy Campbell, Gaudete, Truck driving man, Weaver.* 2/10/72 T1 JW&PD ARV

10/11/72 SEQUENCE *Bonnie moormen, Aitken prawn, A parcel of rogues, Jacobite rock.* 18/9/72 T1 PD ARV

27/11/72 HARRIS *John Barleycorn, General Taylor, Sheepcrook and black dog, Reels: The Bank of Ireland, Lucy Campbell.* 11/10/72 LH1 JG *

6/2/73 PEEL *Hello Mary Lou, Misty moisty morning, Three drunken maidens.* 16/1/73 LH1 JW BC

22/2/73 PEEL *Ups & downs, Misty moisty morning, Hares on the mountain, Lots is a bun dance.* 12/2/73 LH1 BA *

3/6/73 SPEAKEASY *Misty moisty morning, Gaudete, Hornpipes and jigs.* 1/6/73 PS TBS *

26/2/74 PEEL *Thomas the rhymer, Edwin, Long-a-growing.* & Nigel Pegrum (d). 19/2/74 LH1 TW *

11/3/74 Harris *Two magicians, Summer is a' coming, The Lykewake dirge, Misty moisty morning.*
20/2/74 LH1 PR * [M: daytime]

STEREOLAB
8/9/91 Peel† *Super electric, Changer, Doubt, Difficult fourth title.* Joe Dilworth (d), Martin Kean (b), Tim Gane (g), Laethia Sadier (lv), Gina Morris (v).
30/7/91 MV5 MR~
  † On Strange Fruit SFRCD119.
11/7/92 Peel *Laissez faire, Revox, Peng, John Cage bubble gum.* Kean, Gane, Sadier, Andy Ramsey (d), Mick Conroy (k), Mary Hansen (v). 28/6/92 MV3 ME~FK

STEREO MCS
3/5/88 L. Kershaw *G street, It's groovy, What is soul, On the go.* Rob B, Head, Cesare (dj). 24/4/88 MV4 PW TdB
2/2/89 Kershaw *On the mic, Toe to toe, Neighbourhood, Out of touch.* 5/1/89 MV4 DG NG
21/10/90 Peel *Lost in music, The other side, Going back to the wild, Scene of the crime.* Rob B, Head, Owen If (d), Paul O (perc). 9/10/90 MV5 JB~DB

CAT STEVENS
17/12/67 Top Gear *I love them all, Kitty, Sun's in the sky, I'm gonna be King, Blackness of the night.* Cat Stevens (ag,v), & the Art Greenslade Orchestra. 8/12/67 * BA PR
  Many appearances on Light Programme in mid-60s.
2/3/68 Sat. Club *Mighty peace, Lovely cities, Image of hell, I'm so sleepy.* with the Johnny Arthey Orchestra.
19/2/68 PH BB *
10/10/68 Pop North *Here comes my wife, It's a supa (dupa) life.* with The Mal Craig Three and The Northern Dance Orchestra. 7/10/68 PHM JWX *
19/10/68 Sat. Club *It's a supa (dupa) life, Here comes my wife, Northern wind (& Sun's in the sky, 18/11 SYMONDS).* with The Des Champ Orchestra.
15/10/68 PH BB *
22/6/70 Symonds *Katmandu, Tea for the tiller man, Trouble, Lady D'Arbanville.* & Alun Davies (g), Brian Dobson (d), John Ryan (b). 16/6/70 PH BA PK&NG
28/6/70 DLT *Maybe you're right, Lady D'Arbanville, Fill my eyes.* As 16/6. 24/6/70 MV5 c.PWI *
25/10/70 Cash at Four *Lady D'Arbanville, Wild world, Father and son.* & (g) unknown. 21/10/70 PS c.JBU *
17/5/71 Harris *Peace train, Can't think of right words to say, Moon shadow, Tuesday's dead.* & Davies, Larry Steele. 23/3/71 T1 PD&JM JWH&BH&ARV
  Every Transcription Service engineer remembers this one, because it was the first proper eight-track recording at Ken. House.

JIMMY STEVENS
19/10/72 Peel *Happy birthday Sam, Allerton towers, Paid my dues, Tears behind my eyes.* * 9/10/72 * BA *
6/12/73 Peel *Won't you be my Yoko, Please don't let it be, Thank you for being a woman, L.O.L.A.*
  * 21/11/73 * BA *

JOHN STEVENS
7/6/76 Peel *Anni, Can't explain, Spirit of peace.*
  * 27/5/76 MV4 * *

AL STEWART
29/5/68 Night Ride *The Carmichaels, Swiss cottage maneeuvres, Room of roots, Song for Jim, Samuel oh how you've changed.* Al Stewart (agv). 8/5/68 S1 DK *
  First broadcast singing his song 'Do I love my neighbour' on the Light Programme's religious slot Five To Ten, 15/4/65. First proper solo session in Light's Folk Room, 11/9/65, prod. BA; & live on Country Meets Folk, PH 2/3/68.
18/8/68 Top Gear *Swiss cottage manoeevres, You should have listened to Al, I don't believe you, Old Compton St. blues (& Good as gone, In Brooklyn, 15/9/68).* Al Stewart (ag,v), Steve Gray (o), & 3 (unknown).
12/8/68 MV4 PH
18/9/68 My Kind of Folk *You should have listened to Al, Manuscript, Old Compton St. Blues, Room of Roots, In*

Brooklyn. Backed by Giles, Giles & Fripp: Michael Giles (d), Peter Giles (bv), Robert Fripp (g,o), Ian McDonald (p,g,sx); (2,4-Stewart solo). 11/9/68 S2 FL *
  Four more appearances on this show in Spring/Summer 1969, all from S2, prod. FL [M: Folk shows].
20/8/69 Peel *The sparrow, My enemies have sweet voices, Memphis Tennessee, Clifton in the rain, Gethsemane again, Swiss cottage maneouvres, Burbling.*
8/8/69 S2 PR MH
27/8/69 Night Ride *I don't believe you, The ballad of Mary Foster pt 1, The ballad of Mary Foster pt 2, Blessed, Zero she flies, Scandinavian girl, Ivich.* 15/8/69 S2 PR MLH
  Also, live on Country Meets Folk 23/8/69 PH.
13/12/69 Top Gear *Zero she flies, Burbling, Electric Los Angeles sunset (& Manuscript 2/5/70).* 1/12/69 PH * *
  Rec'd Peel Sunday Concert 7/5/70 PS, TX 17/5/70.
7/2/72 R2 Night Ride *Lullaby of Birdland, A small fruit song, I'm falling, My enemies have sweet voices (8/2), Electric Los Angeles sunset & Songs out of clay (9/2).* *
18/11/71 S2 DK *
24/3/72 Peel *A small fruit song, You don't even know me, Old Compton St. blues, Zero she flies (& Absolutely sweet Marie, I'm falling, 28/4/72). & 4 (unknown).*
8/3/72 T1 JM JWH&JS
  Files next suggest a daytime session for WALKER, rec'd 26/4/72, which is untraceable on PasBs.
18/5/72 Drummond *A small fruit song, I'm falling, Amsterdam, Just like Tom Thumb's blues (& Songs out of clay, 13/7/72).* * 8/5/72 MV5 MB *
8/10/72 Sounds on Sunday *Amsterdam, I'm falling, Clifton in the rain, Electric Los Angeles sunset, Nostradamus, Small fruit song.* * 29/9/72 AO2 FL *
18/5/73 Sequence *Song, Electric Los Angeles sunset, Once an orange always an orange, Post WWII blues, Nostradamus.* * 26/4/73 LH1 JM BAI&MG
10/1/74 Peel *Post WW II blues, Soho needless to say, Roads to Moscow.* & Francis Monkman (k), Isaac Guillory (g), Florian Pilkington Miksa (b), Pete Zorn (sx,fl), Annie Haslam (v). 7/1/74 LH1 BA *
  Rec'd In Concert 27/6/74 PS, TX 13/7/74.
29/7/74 Harris *Soho needless to say, Terminal eyes, Post WWII Blues (& Right now, 7/10/74).* & friends from Home: Laurie Wisefield (g), Francis Monkman (k), Clifford Williams (b), Michael Cook (d). 3/7/74 LH1 JG *

STICHED-BACK FOOT AIRMAN
Broadcast date unknown Long *It's a real skyve, Careful balance, Acid rain, Worm's head.* Mike Farmer (dk,bkv), Simon Vincent (gbv), Robin Vincent (gbv).
25/11/87 MV4 MR *

STICKY GEORGE
22/6/72 Drummond *Daddy gone Zanzibar blues, Me and thee, Smile like a rainbow, All you are.* * 5/6/72 * MB *

STIFF KITTENS
9/9/86 Long *Happy now, Killing time, Our shadows fall, An end to this.* Steve McKee (b), Sean Arnold (d), Steve Dodds (g), Sarah Lee (rg), Ian Scarlet (v).
20/7/86 MV4 BYA *

STIFF LITTLE FINGERS
13/4/78 Peel *Alternative Ulster, Wasted life, Johnny was, State of emergency.* * Rec. date unknown DWN SN SN
18/9/78 Peel† *Johnny was, Law and order, Barbed wire love, Suspect device.* Jake Burns (lg,lv), Henry Cluney (rg,bkv), Ali McMordie (b,bkv), Brian Faloon (d,concussion). 12/9/78 MV4 MB MR
17/9/79 Peel† *Wait and see, At the edge, Nobody's hero, Straw dogs.* Jim Reilly (d) r. Faloon. 3/9/79 MV4 BS DD
25/2/80 Peel† *No change, I don't like you, Fly the flag, Doesn't make it all right.* Cluney (lv-1).
12/2/80 MV4 JE MR
  † On Strange Fruit SFRCD106.
3/3/80 Read *Fly the flag, At the edge, Gotta gettaway, Wait and see.* 1/2/80 MV4 JS *

30/11/81 Jensen *Sad-eyed people, Listen, That's when your blood bumps, Two guitars clash.* Dolphin Taylor (d) r. Reilly. 19/11/81 MV4 JS *

THE STIFFS
14/2/80 Peel *Let's activate, Brookside riot squad, Best place in town, Innocent bystander.* Phil Hendriks (gv), Ian Barnes (g,bkv), John McVittie (b,bkv), Tommy O'Kane (d,bkv), Rankin' Juice (perc,wh,"disco cowbells and bluffing"). 5/2/80 MV4 JS MR
10/3/82 Peel *Standing ovation, Over the balcony, Hook in your heart, Child's play.* Hendriks, Barnes, Billy Rumour (b), Bloody Rich (d). 20/2/82 MV4 DG MR&MC

STILETTO
10/11/80 Read *Reckless, Jealous, Canadian boy, You better hang on.* Alan 'Dix' Dixon (d), Derek Nattress (b), Steve Daggett (rg,sy), Bren Laidler (v), Paul Dean (lg).
30/10/80 MV4 DG TdB

STIMULIN
27/8/81 Peel *Sex object, You get everything, Vacuum, The game is up.* Alix Sharkey (lv,lg), Tony McDermott (b), John Scofield (vib,bkv), Thoby Young (tp), Roger Hilton (d), Justin Langlands (cga). 22/8/81 MV4 DG MR

ALAN STIVELL
11/6/73 Harris *Suite sad Americaine, Tri Martolod, Susie McGuire, Silvestrig, Suite Irlandaise/King of the Fairies.* Alan Stivell (hp,fl,bpp), Michel Santangeli (d), Gerard Levasseur (b), Dan Ar Bras (lg), Gabriel Yacoub (dul,ag), Rene Werneer (fd), Pascal Stive (o).
6/6/73 LH1 PR BC
  Rec'd In Concert 7/6/73 PS, the following day.
3/12/73 Harris *Tri Martolod, Suite Irlandaise, An Hani a garan, Ian Morrison reel.* 14/11/73 LH1 JG BC
  Recorded 2nd In Concert 30/11/73 HP, TX 22/12/73.

THE STOAT
17/10/78 Peel *Tears run dry, No way to say goodbye, Don't say nothing, Escorts.* Richard Wall (bv), John Waters (gv), George Decsy (d). 2/10/78 BS DD

STONE THE CROWS
6/12/69 Top Gear *Raining in your heart, Friend, Blind man, Touch of your loving hand.* Maggie Bell (v), Leslie Harvey (g), Jimmy Dewar (bv), Colin Allen (d), John McGuinnis (k). 24/11/69 PH JW *
  Passed by panel: 'excellent'.
21/2/70 WS R&B *Raining in your heart, Blind man, Friend.* 21/1/70 MV4 JG JY
30/5/70 Top Gear *Fool on the hill, Freedom road, Hollis Brown (& Danger zone, 12 /9/70).* 19/5/70 MV4 JW *
26/6/70 Black *Friend, The touch of your lovin' hand, The ballad of Hollis Brown (& Raining in your heart, 31/7/70).* 13/5/70 AO2 JM *
  Rec'd Peel Sunday Concert 28/5/70 PS, TX 7/6/70.
14/7/70 Harding *Sad Mary, I saw America pt.1, pt.3.* 7/7/70 MV5 MB MH&MF
16/8/70 Raven's R&B *I saw America (parts 1,2 & 3).* 4/7/70 AO1 JG JY
13/11/70 Black *Dwarfburger, Sad Mary, Love 74, Mad dogs and Englishmen, Danger zone (& Things are getting better, 4/12/70).* 28/10/70 AO2 JM JWH
  Rec'd 2nd Peel Concert 26/11/70 PS, TX 6/12/70.
1/1/71 Lulu's Back In Town *Mad dogs and Englishmen, Blind man, Love 74.* 11/12/70 PH c.DGE *
21/1/71 Henry *Love 74, Sad Mary.* 20/1/71 MV4 MB MH&MF
2/7/71 Black *Let it down, Freight, Freedom road (& Faces, 30/7/71).* 7/6/71 T1 PD BH
16/9/71 Drummond *Keep on rolling, Don't think twice it's alright, Aileen Mochree, Big Jim Salter.* Ronnie Leahy (k), Steve Thompson (b), r. McGuinnis, Dewer.
6/9/71 MV4 MB MH&MF
18/9/71 Top Gear *Keep on rolling, Aileen Mochree, Big Jim Salter, Don't think twice it's alright* 8/9/71 MV4 JW BC
1/11/71 Harris *Big Jim Salter, Faces, Mr. Wizard (& Aileen Mochree, 29/11/71).* & 3 guest musicians: Average White Band horns. 12/10/71 T1 JM JWH

Rec'd 3rd In Concert 4/11/71 PS, TX 16/11/71.

28/4/72 PEEL *Going down, On the highway, Mr. Wizard, Penicillin blues.* 11/4/72 TI JM NG

11/5/72 DRUMMOND *Niagara, Keep on rolling, Penicillin blues.* 1/5/72 MV5 MB *

Les Harvey died, electrocuted on stage in Swansea, 4/5/72, between recording and broadcast of this session.

18/9/72 HARRIS *On the highway, Good time girl, Penicillin blues.* Jimmy McCulloch (g) r. Harvey. 6/9/72 A02 JG *

Rec'd 4th In Concert 12/10/72 PS, TX 28/10/72.

STONEGROUND

27/10/71 PEEL *Rock and roll tonight, Super clown, Sad man, You must be one of us.* Sal Valentino (gv), Tim Barnes (lv), John Blakeley (rg), Cory Lerios (o,p), Brian Godula (b,clo), Steve Price (d) & Lyn Hughes, Diedre La Porte, Lydia Phillips, Annie Sampson. 26/10/71 MV4 TW BC

11/11/71 DRUMMOND *If you gotta go, Corrina, Passion flower, You must be one of us.* 1/11/71 MV5 MB MH&MF

Rec'd In Concert 11/11/71 PS, TX 23/11/71.

STORYTELLER

28/6/70 FOLK ON 1 *Song for Buster, Man in the moon passage song, For really - truly, Love's a blind, Has been, Vestapol, The lake, The ballad of old three laps, Story, First week in January.* Mike Rogers (gv), Caroline Attard (v), Terry Durham (v), Roger Moon (gv), Rod Clarke (bv). 9/6/70 MV3 FL *

6/7/70 SYMONDS *Love's a blind, The ballad of old three laps, Has been (& First week in January, 10/8/70).* 30/6/70 PH BA PK&NG

17/9/70 HENRY *Remarkable, Crystal telephone, Gipsy Woman, Bosworth field.* 10/9/70 A02 MB MH&MF

6/2/71 R2 NIGHT RIDE *High in the sky, Time for a little something, Vestapol, Remarkable, Bull Jack, Night games, Goin' back.* Chris Belcher (b) r. Clarke. 18&25/1/71 A02&MV5 DDR *

27/2/71 FOLK ON 1 *Time for a little something, Beautiful affair, A pale shadow of his former self, High in the sky, The name certainly rings a bell, Vestapol, Night games, Remarkable.* 3/2/71 A02 FL *

18/3/71 HENRY *Four or five lines/Home to you, P.S. get lost, Please remember me, Fair at the zoo.* Andy Bown r. Durham. 10/3/71 MV4 MB MH&MF

STP 23

3/4/90 PEEL *I'm gonna love you a little more, Faithful, Good times.* Clune (k), Tim (k), Jane (v), David (g). 6/3/90 MV5 DG MR

THE STRAITJACKET FITS

29/11/89 PEEL *Quiet come, Bad note for a heart, Hand in mine, Roller ride.* Shayne Carter (gv), Andrew Brough (gv), David Wood (b), John Coulie (d). 12/11/89 * DG MC

RICHARD STRANGE AND THE ENGINE ROOM

12/9/88 L. KERSHAW *Inch' Allah, Endless winter, The ghost of Brian Jones.* Richard Strange (v), James T. Ford (k,prg), Steve Bolton (g), Pedro Ortiz (perc), David Coulter (dig,hca,dul). 16/8/88 MV4 HP MPK

STRANGE LOVE

17/7/92 PEEL *Visionary, Hopeful, Fire, Snakes.* John Langley (d), Joe Allen (b), Julian Poole (g), Alex Lee (g,bkv), Patrick Duff (lv). 30/6/92 MV4 MR~ CML

DR. STRANGELY STRANGE

6/6/70 TOP GEAR *Jove was at home, Ashling, Mary Malone.* * 26/5/70 * * *&BC

THE STRANGLERS

7/3/77 PEEL *Hangin' around, I feel like a wog, Goodbye Toulouse, Somethin' better change†.* Hugh Cornwell (gv), Jean-Jacques Burnel (bv), Dave Greenfield (o,pv), Jet Black (d). 1/3/77 MV6 JG MR

† On 'Winters of Discontent' SFRCD204.

13/9/77 PEEL *Dead ringer, No more heroes, Burning up time, Bring on the nubiles.* 30/8/77 MV4 TW MR

11/2/82 JENSEN† *The man they love to hate, Nuclear device/Genetix, Down in the sewer.* 24/1/82 MV4 DG *

† on Nighttracks SNTCD020.

STRAWBERRY SWITCHBLADE

5/10/82 PEEL *10 James Orr Street, The little river, Secrets, Trees and flowers.* Rose McDowall (gv), Jill Bryson (g,bkv); & James Kirk (b), Shahid Starwars (d), Alex Fergusson (p,g), Babs Shores (bkv-4). 4/10/82 MV4 TW DD

7/10/82 JENSEN *Dance, Another day, By the sea, Linda.* Fergusson, Babs out. 3/10/82 MV4 DG HP

11/2/84 LONG *Who knows what love is, Poor hearts, Deep water.* * 23/1/84 PHM c.PWL *

24/10/84 LONG *Beautiful end, Michael who walks by night, Black taxi, Jolene.* McDowall, Bryson & David Balfe (sy) 'Gunter Lemon' (dm). 27/9/84 MV5 MHY *

15/4/85 PEEL *Cut with the cake knife, 60 cowboys, Nothing changes, Life full of wonders.* McDowall, Bryson, Balfe. 5/2/85 MV5 MRD *

THE STRAWBS

12/1/69 TOP GEAR *I'll show you where to sleep, Poor Jimmy Wilson, The battle, That which once was mine.* Dave Cousins (gv,dul,bj), Tony Hooper (gv), Ron Chesterman (b), & Tony Visconti (md,rec). 10/12/68 PCI BA AH

Had previously appeared on R1 folk shows earlier in 1968, and more followed in '69. [Files for any sessions before '68 untraceable].

7/9/69 TOP GEAR *We'll meet again sometime, Another day, Till the sun comes shining through.* & Claire Lowther (clo). 25/8/69 PH JW TW

9/4/70 HENRY *When you and I were young, Another day, Where is the dream of your youth? (& We'll meet again sometime, 28/5/70).* Rick Wakeman (k) r. Lowther; Lindsay Cooper (b), r. Chesterman; & John Marshall (not on contract). 30/3/70 A02 MB MH&MF

New line-up had also rec'd special folk show for R1, 14 & 25/3/70, TX 22&29/3/70.

31/10/70 TOP GEAR *Canon Dale, The reaper/Antiques and curios/Hey it's been a long time, Song of a sad little girl.* John Ford (b) r. Cooper; & Richard Hudson (perc). 5/10/70 PH JW *

7/11/70 FOLK ON 1 *Martin Luther King's dream, Song of a sad little girl, It's in your hands, Temperament of mind, Antique suite.* 6/10/70 A02 FL *

Next, on 8/10/70, group rec'd Peel's Sunday Concert, TX 18/10/70; then Night Ride, Christmas Day 1970.

1/7/71 HENRY *Witchwood, Sleep.* 23/6/71 MV4 MB MH&MF

Next, 2nd Peel's Sunday Concert, rec'd 5/8/71 PS, TX 15/8/71 [M: daytime].

13/12/71 HARRIS *Benedictus, The journey's end, New world, On growing older, The flower and the young man.* Derek 'Blue' Weaver (k) r. Wakeman 30/11/71 TI JM NG&MF

[M: Speakeasy].

20/1/72 DRUMMOND *New world, Tomorrow, Is it today lord, The flower and the young man (& Benedictus, 9/3/72).* 12/1/72 MV4 MB MH&MF

Rec'd 3rd In Concert 27/1/72 PS, TX 5/2/72.

1/5/72 HARRIS *Heavy disguise, Here it comes, New world, Is it today lord, Tomorrow.* 19/4/72 A02 JG *

9/2/73 SEQUENCE *Lady Fuschia, The river, The winter and the summer, Down by the sea.* David Lambert (g) r. Hooper 9/1/73 TI JM NG [M].

STRAY

23/9/71 DRUMMOND *Queen of the sea, Sister Mary, After the storm.* Steve Gadd (v), Ritchie Cole (d), Gary Giles (b), Del Bromham (lg). 15/9/71 MV4 MB MH&MF

21/1/72 PEEL *Mr. Hobo, Leave it out, How could I forget you.* 29/12/71 TI PD *

Rec'd In Concert 10/2/72 PS, TX 19/2/72.

26/10/72 PEEL *Cross country, Alone again, I believe it.* 23/10/72 LHI BA *

17/5/73 PEEL *It's alright ma, Pretty thing, Come on air.* 7/5/73 LHI BA *

15/7/73 SEQUENCE *Crazy people, Hallelujah, It's alright ma, The gambler.* 19/6/73 TI JM *

17/11/73 ROCK ON *Crazy people, Move it, Down down down, Jump back.* 25/10/73 LHI PR *

9/7/74 PEEL *Mystic lady, Right from the start, Times like these, Give it up.* 18/6/74 LHI * *

Rec'd 2nd In Concert 25/4/74 PS, TX 4/5/74.

STRAY CATS

29/12/80 READ *Rock this town, Stray cat strut, Bonneville bonnie, Rumble in Brighton.* Brian Setzer (gv), Lee Drucker (b), Jim McDonnell (d). 19/12/80 LHI DG PW

STREETS ON FIRE

18/10/85 FRI. ROCK *Home to you tonight, Breakin' out, Blown away, Take you home.* Aidan Keenan (g,lv), Barry Keenan (d), Simon Fox (lg), Robert Gatcum (bk). 27/9/85 MV4 TW DD

STRESS

17/9/90 GOODIER *Flowers in the rain, Father once said, Beautiful people, Daytime believer.* Wayne Binitie (gv), Ian Mussington (lv,g,d), J.E. Rod (g), Mitch Ogugua (b), Simon Stewart (g), Alex Mungo (k,bkv). 1/9/90 MV5 MC~

STRETCH

12/12/75 PEEL *Can't judge a book, Hold on, Living on the highway, Miss Jones.* Geoff Rich (d), Steve Emery (b), Kirby (g), Elmer Gantry (v). 25/11/75 MV4 TW BAI

24/5/76 PEEL *Feelin' sad, Fixin' to die, That's the way the wind blows, Showbiz blues.* & Phil McDonnell (o-1). 29/4/76 MV4 TW BAI

18/10/76 PEEL *Can't get enough, Hold up the light, Rock'n roll hoochie-coo, The way life is.* McDonnell out. 30/9/76 MV4 TW *

THE STRETCHHEADS

27/11/91 PEEL *Anal beard, Skinrip, Afghanistan bananastan, Filthy great yarblockodes.* Mr. Jason (d), Mofungo Diggs (b), Dr. Technology (g), Wilberforce (v), Mr. Martin (b), Mr. Marcus (tp). 16/6/91 MV3 DG ME&AC

STRING DRIVEN THING

17/8/70 BRANDON *That's my lady, I'll be your baby tonight (18/8), Way down town (19/8), Magic Garden (20/8), California dreaming.* Chris Adams (gv), John Mannion (gv), Pauline Adams (tamb). 5/8/70 PS PR *

Unanimous pass of this trial broadcast by Audition panel.

19/9/72 PEEL *Regent Street incident, Circus, Let me down, Jack Diamond.* Graham Smith (vi), Colin Wilson (b), r. Mannion. 11/9/72 PH JW *

28/11/72 PEEL *Hooked on the road, My real hero, Regent street incident, Let me down.* 6/11/72 TI JW BC

1/10/73 HAMILTON *It's a game [network session].* Bill Hatje (b), r. Wilson, & Colin 'Billy' Fairley (d). 19/9/73 A02 c.PWI *

8/11/73 PEEL *Two timing rama, Night club, The machine that cried, To see you.* 24/9/73 LHI BA *

15/8/74 PEEL *Overdrive, Keep on moving, To know you, Man of means, Black eyed queen.* Jim Exell (b), Andy Roberts (g), Kim Beacon (v), r. Hatje, C & P Adams. 8/8/74 LHI * * [M]

29/3/76 PEEL *Things we said today, But it do, Starving in the tropics.* 4/3/76 MV4 * *

THE MIKE STUART SPAN

26/5/68 TOP GEAR *My white bicycle, Children of tomorrow, Through the looking-glass.* * 7/5/68 PCI BA DT

STUD

6/3/71 TOP GEAR *Sail on, 1112235, Turn of the pages.* Jim Cregan (lgv), Richard McCracken (ag,b), John Wilson (d). 8/2/71 PH *

25/5/71 HARDING *Sail on, Harpo's head, Song.* 17/5/71 MV5 MB MH&MF

21/3/72 PEEL *Good things, Red wine, Samurai.* 7/3/72 MV4 * *

THE STUKAS

24/1/78 PEEL *Dead lazy, Big boy, Motor bike, Sport.* John Mackie (d), Mick Smithers (lg), Raggy Lewis (rg), Kevin Allen (b), Paul Brown (v), John Mac and Raggy L. (bkv). 17/1/78 MV4 MB MR

STUMP

5/2/86 Peel| Down on the kitchen table, Orgasm way, Grab hands, Buffalo. Robert McKahey (d), Kevin Hopper (b), Chris Salmon (g), Mick Lynch (v). 26/1/86 MV5 DG ME † on Strange Fruit SFPS019.

7/7/86 Peel Tupperware stripper, Big end, Satisfaction, Bit-part actor. 24/6/86 MV4 DG TdB&MC

28/1/87 Peel Living it down, The eager bereaver, Alcohol, Bone. 13/1/87 * DG MFA&MR

13/9/88 Peel The song remains, Thelma, Strayte 'n' narrow, Seven sisters. 14/8/88 HP DG *

THE STUPIDS

12/1/87 Peel Layback session, Jesus do what you have to do, Root beer death, Memory burns/Slumber party. Tommy Stupid (d,v,g), Pauly Pizza (b), Marty Tuff (g). 9/12/86 * DG MR&MA

27/5/87 Peel† Life's a drag, Heard it all before, Shaded eyes, Dog love, Stupid Monday. Ed (b,bkv), Tommy (d,b,g,lv), Nick (bv). 12/5/87 * DG MR&TD † on Strange Fruit SFPS054. Most of this session is also spread over the two 'Hardcore Holocaust' albums.

21/10/87 Peel You die, You'll never win, Pasta boy, Your little world, You don't belong. Tommy, Ed, Stevie Snacks (b); & The Sugarbeat Crew (perc-3 only). 13/10/87 * DG MR&JB

THE STYLE COUNCIL

10/5/83 Jensen Headstart for happiness, Mick's up, Here's one that got away, The Paris Match. Paul Weller (v), Mick Talbot (k), Chris Josephs (perc), Paul Taylor (tb), Steve White (d), Breeze James (bkv), Albaie Johnson (bkv). 5/5/83 MV4 JP *

13/8/83 Sat. Live Le depart. * Live from S2 MRD TdB

31/12/83 Sat. Live My ever changing moods, Mick's blessings, Paris match, Head start for happiness, Long hot summer. Paul Weller (gv), Mick Talbot (k), DC Lee (v). Live from S2 MRD TdB

SUBSONIC 2

9/11/91 Peel Unsung heroes of hip hop, Doom of the sonic boom, Dedicated to the city, Tower of Babel. Robin Morley (v), Donald Brown (v), Colin Elliot (perc,g), Steve Heyliger (k,perc), Darren Campbell (b), Simeon Lister (sx). 15/10/91 MV4 MR~

SUBURBAN STUDS

2/12/77 Peel Suburban studs, I hate school, Necro, No faith. Eddy Zipps (lv,g), Keith Owen (g), Paul Morton (b), Steve Pool (d). 22/11/77 MV4 TW MR

SUBWAY SECT

24/10/77 Peel† Chain smoking, Parallel lines, I don't split it, Nobody's scared. Vic Goddard (v), Rob Miller (g), Paul Myers (b), Bob Ward (d). 17/10/77 MV4 TW DD

4/12/78 Peel† Watching the devil, Stool pigeon, Double negative, Head held high. Goddard, Ward, Colin Scot (b), John Bristol (g), Steve Atkinson (k). 29/11/78 MV4 MR NG † Both sessions on Rough Trade 'Retrospective' album.

SUDDEN AFTERNOON

20/2/86 Kershaw Dancing in the flowers, Walking on stony ground, State of mind, Acid rain, Andy Kershaw jingle. * Rec. date unknown Y2 * PSM

SUDDEN SWAY

24/11/83 Peel† Let's evolve, Relationships. Simon Childs (g), Peter Jostins (b), Michael McGuire (kv), Lee Shale (perc), Colin Meech (perc), Karole Meech (bkv). 16/11/83 MV4 JP NG † on Strange Fruit SFPS005.

21/11/84 Peel In the park, A problem solving broadcast (pt 1), A problem solving broadcast (pt 2), T minus tranquility. McGuire, Jostins, Childs, Shale, Shawn Foreman (rg), Susan McClean (b), Lee Bailey (rg), Eliza Egee (rg,v,p,bkv). 11/9/84 MV5 MRD TdB

SUEDE

27/4/92 Goodier Metal Mickey, The drowners, Sleeping pills,

Moving. Brett Anderson (v), Bernard Butler (g), Mat Osman (b), Simon Gilbert (d). 5/4/92 MV4 MA~ DMC

SUGAR

24/8/92 Goodier If I can't change your mind, Hoover dam, The slim, Where diamonds are halos. Bob Mould (g), David Barbe (b), Malcolm Travers (d). 1/8/92 MV4 MC~

THE SUGARCUBES

9/12/87 Peel Motor crash, Cold sweat, Delicious demon, Deus, Mama. Bjork Gudmundsdottir (v), Einar Benediktson (v,tp), Siggi Baldursson (d), Erikki Erlingsson (g), Bragi Olasson (b), Thor Eldon Jonsson (g). Rec. date unknown Berry St. Studios, London Produced by Ray Shulman

6/4/88 Mayo Polo, Cat, Sick for toys, (& Traitor, Blue-eyed pup, not broadcast). Bjork, Einar, Bragi, Thor; & Einar Mellaxson (k). 12/3/88 Gramm studios, Iceland * *

17/2/92 Goodier Hit, Lucky night, Walkabout, Heteroscum. & Siggi Baldursson (d), Magga (k). 11/1/92 MV5 MC~GPR

SULTANS OF PING F.C.

8/3/92 Peel Kick me with your leather boots, He thought I was your best friend, Give him a ball and a yard of grass, Karaoke queen. Morty McCarthy (d), Alan Macfeely (b), Pat O'Connell (g), Niall O'Flaherty (v). 5/3/92 MV4 DG NG&BJ

SUMMERHILL

8/8/88 L. Kershaw I'll keep you in mind, Hold back the heartache, Rosebud, Knew I would return. Seori Burnett (gv), Neil Scott (g), Keith Giles (b), Iain Sheddon (d); & B.J. Cole (ps). 13/7/88 MV4 PW SC

15/12/88 Kershaw Our friends are dead, Please don't go away, River blue, Static. 17/11/88 MV4 DG NG

2/10/89 Campbell Don't let it die, Here I am, If I knew better, Lately. Mike Strugis (d) r. Sheddon. 27/9/89 MV5 PW DD

SUMO GIANTS

9/5/85 Into The Music Living on the airwaves, Wishing I could be, Tower of Babel, Fe fi fo fum. Ray Fullard (d,bkv), John Barry (b,bkv), Andy Ford (g,bkv), Allan Fullard (k,bkv), Adrian Lynden (v). 13/4/85 MV4 DG MC

SUN CARRIAGE

28/7/91 Peel Sick dog crawling can't see love, B.A.B.E, Kiss to tell, Written by. Michael (d), Sarah (b), Mathew (gv). 9/6/91 MV3 DG ME&PA

SUNBURST

22/1/71 Black Cheese wire, Two finger funk, Dicky bird. * 7/1/71 T1 JM JWH

THE SUNCHARMS

5/6/92 Peel Magic carpet, Into the sun, Spaceship, On reflection. Richard Farnel (b), Matt Neale (g), John Malone (g), Chris Ridley (d), Marcus Palmer (v,tamb,hca). 26/4/92 MV3 ME~

THE SUNDAYS

6/3/89 Peel I won, My finest hour, Skin and bones. Harriet Wheeler (v), David Gavurin (g), Paul Brindley (b), Patrick Hannan (d). 28/2/89 MV3 DG MR

SUNSET GUN

28/3/84 Jensen Be thankful, Change, Hand jive, Stay with me. Deidre Rutkowski (v), Louise Rutkowski (v), Ross Campbell (k), Jim Williams (g), Simon Rogers (b). 18/3/84 MV5 DG ME

SUNSHINE

3/8/72 Drummond Advert, When will I see the light, Long-haired lady, Relics. Ethel Coley (v), Joanne White (v), Gordon Edwards (lgv,o), Jack Green (bv), Terry Slade (d), Bill Roberts (lg). 19/7/72 MV4 MB MH&MF Rec'd In Concert as trial b'cast 22/6/72 PS, TX 15/7/72.

SUPERCHARGE

1/9/75 Peel I believe in you, Don't let go, We are free. Dave Irving (d), Ozzie Yue (gv), Tony Dunmore (b), Iain Bradshaw (k), Graham Robertson (al,bars), Albie Donnelly (ts). 19/8/75 MV4 TW *

14/6/76 Peel Only you, Funkier than thou, Back on my

feet. & Les Karski (g,v); Bob Robertson (sx) r. Robertson. 20/5/76 MV4 TW *

17/3/77 Peel Last train, Really quite easy, Mess you made. & Andy Parker (ts); Bradshaw out. 8/3/77 MV4 JG MR

SUPERCHUNK

30/5/92 Peel Let it go, Tie the rope, Fishing, United. Mac McCaughan (gv), Jim Wilbur (g,bkv), Laura Ballance (b), Jon Wurster (d). 14/4/92 MV4 JB~PA

15/6/92 Goodier Throwing things, For tension, Punch me harder, Cool. 15/5/92 MV4 MA~PL

SUPERSISTER

3/4/73 Peel Pudding and yesterday. Robert Jan Stips (k), Sacha Van Geest (fl,sx), Marco Vrolyk (d), Ron van Eck (b). 20/3/73 * JW BC

SUPERSTAR

1/9/92 Goodier Barfly, I can't help it, She's got everything now, Trudy you're a go go. Joe McAlinden (g,lv), Mark Hughes (g), Raymond Prior (bv), Neil Grant (dv). 8/8/92 MV5 MA~ AA

SUPERTRAMP

18/7/70 Top Gear It's a long road, Try again, Birds of prey. Richard Davies (o,v), Richard Palmer (gv), Dave Winthrop (sx,v), Robert Millar (d), Roger Hodgson (bv). 30/6/70 MV4 JW PR 'Enthusiastic pass' from Audition panel. Group soon did John Peel Sunday Concert, rec'd 1/10/70 PS, TX 11/10/70, prod. JG.

12/9/72 Peel Pony express, School, Everyone is listening, I can see. Frank Farrell, Kevin Currie r. Palmer, Millar. 22/8/72 MV4 * BC

23/11/72 Peel Summer romance, Rudy, Pony express, Dreamer. Farrell out. 20/11/72 LH1 BA *

22/3/73 Peel Dreamer, Black cat, Hey Laura, Bloody well right. & Dougie Thompson (b). 12/3/73 LH1 BA *

25/6/73 Harris School, And the light, Down in Mexico. 20/6/73 LH1 PR BAI

5/7/73 Peel Chicken man, Down in Mexico, Just a normal day (& Land ho, 2/3/74 ROCK ON). 25/6/73 LH1 BA *

6/6/74 Peel Bloody well right, If everyone was listening, School. Bob C. Benberg (d) r. Currie, John Anthony Helliwell (sx,cl,v) r. Winthrop. 23/5/74 LH1 TW *

5/10/74 Rock On Dreamer, Rudy, Crime of the century. 30/9/74 MV4 BA MF&NGR

THE SURF DRUMS

9/1/86 Long What's the difference, Stop, Soft embrace, Sing weep no more. Dave Kehoe (gv), Rich Left (g), Colin Packwood (b), Mick Lafolley (d), Annie Taylor (k); & Martin Phillips (fl). 22/12/85 MV5 BYA PW

11/6/87 Long Black tambourine, Nothing at all, All there is, Love chain. & Joe Foster (sit-3). 27/5/87 MV4 PW MPK&MFA

SURFIN' DAVE

10/10/85 Kershaw Living white hell, Do the bus stop, State side, Exchange & Mart. Surfin' Dave (gv), Chris Haskit (g,bkv), Jeremy Willis (b,bkv), Mick Green (d,bkv). 25/9/85 Y2 RG SR

SURGERY

23/6/91 Peel D nice†, Dear sweet Laura†, Brazier, Locust. John Leamy (d), John Lachapelle (b), M. Scott Kleber (g), Sean McDonnell (v). 28/5/91 MV5 MR~ LS 'Dear John Peel, thanks for the opportunity to record in the excellent BBC studios. Mike, the engineer/producer/magician, treated us like kings, sincerely, Surgery.' on sheet. † On Strange Fruit SFMCD212.

SURREAL ESTATE

13/5/86 Long The messenger, Peppermint and ivory towers, The weight of the world, Northern lights. John Potter (gv), Bobby Carr (lg), Anthony Wilding (b), Alan McLaughlin (d); & Peter Higgin (k). 16/3/86 MV4 BYA TdB

SUS

6/10/83 Peel She seems all right, Mr DJ, Society says, Yearning for your love. Junior Bailey & Hopeton McLean (lv), Paul Hamer (tb), Baba Williams (ts), Sorenson Bellot (d), Derwent Bent (b), Len Jones (lg), Errol Shorter (rgv), Eddie Williams (perc), Franklin Fraser (k). 24/9/83 MV4 DG AP

JALI NYAMA SUSO
2/10/86 KERSHAW *Kuruntu kelefa, Lucy, Jali Nyama Suso, Sunkariba.* Jali Nyama Suso (kor,v). 10/9/86 * RG SR

THE SUTHERLAND BROTHERS BAND
14/10/71 DRUMMOND *Sleeping dog, Wars of the roses, The pie, I was in chains.* Iain Sutherland (gv), Gavin Sutherland (gv), Kim Ludman (b), Neil Hopwood (d). 6/10/71 MV4 MB MH&MF
13/3/72 HARRIS *The pie, Skid row, I was in chains, Change the wind.* 1/3/72 AO2 JG * [M: daytime]
5/9/72 PEEL *Sailing, Space hymn, Sleeping dog, Who's crying now (& Change the wind, not broadcast).* Ludman out. 7/8/72 PH JW *
30/10/72 HARRIS *Flying down to Rio, Who's crying now, Sorrow, Space hymn.* 27/9/72 AO2 JG *
8/12/72 SEQUENCE *Space hymn, Flying down to Rio, All I got is you, Change the wind, Don't forget.* 7/11/72 TI JM NG

THE SUTHERLAND BROTHERS AND QUIVER
6/3/73 PEEL *Real love, You get me anyway, Rock and roll show, Love is my religion.* Iain & Gavin Sutherland, & Tim Renwick (lgv), John Wilson (d), Bruce Thomas (b), Peter Wood (p) 19/2/73 TI PD (for JW) ARV [M: networks]
17/8/73 SEQUENCE *Bad loser, Don't mess up, You and me, Champion the underdog.* 3/7/73 TI JM *
5/1/74 ROCK ON *Dream kid, I hear thunder, You and me, It's a bluesy world.* 3/1/74 LH1 PR *
22/1/74 PEEL *Real love, Dream kid, It's a bluesy world, I hear thunder.* 8/1/74 LH1 * *
18/2/74 HARRIS *I hear thunder, Champion the underdog, Dream kid (& Rolling away/Rocky road/Saved by the angel of rock and roll, It's a bluesy world, Seagull/Lonely love, 3/6/74).* 23/1/74 LH1 PR *
13/8/74 PEEL *World in action, Beat of the street, Saviour in the rain, Annie.* Thomas out. 30/7/74 LH1 TW BC
23/1/75 PEEL *Devil are you satisfied, Silver sister, Something special, Last boy over the moon.* 16/1/75 MV4 TW *
30/6/75 PEEL *Dirty city, Little bit something else, Somebody buy the band a drink, Laid back in anger.* Wood out. 17/6/75 MV4 * *
24/11/75 DLT *Ain't too proud, Doctor dancer (25/11), Arms of Mary (26/11), Dirty city (27/11).* 19/11/75 MV4c.TB *
4/12/75 PEEL *Mad trail, When the train comes, Love on the moon, Ain't too proud.* 18/11/75 MV4 TW * [M]

SWAMPTRASH
22/3/88 MAYO *Bone, The cullin', Glasnost, Ring of fire.* Billy Joe (v,bj), Doc (bj), Cal (vi,g), Dexter (mnd), Coolhand (ag), Elmore James (d). 6/3/88 MV4 PW MA&TD

SWAN ARCADE
27/2/73 PEEL *Let bucks a-hunting go, Babylon, He'll have to go/Lunatic asylum, Salmon tails (& Last Valentine's day, 1/5/73).* David & Heather Brady (v), Royston Wood. 13/2/73 * JW *
9/4/74 PEEL *A long time ago, Deliverance will come, So from my window, Peat bog soldiers.* Miller r. Wood. 25/3/74 * JW *
8/10/74 PEEL *The weary whaling growds, Down in the valley to pray, Foster's mill, The battle of Sowerby Bridge.* Jack French (gv), Kevin Hingston (bv), Chris Taylor (dv) r. Miller. 23/9/74 MV4 JW *

SWANS WAY
16/5/83 JENSEN *When we dance (it's not enough), Life and times, The blade, Soul train.* Maggie Edmund (bkv,d,p,fl), Robert Shaw (lv,sx,g,perc), Rick P. Jones (ab,vi,cga,bkv); & Joshua Fifer (tp). 8/5/83 MV4 DG ME
15/2/84 JENSEN *Club secrets, Illuminations, Stay, The trance.* 23/1/84 BRM GH *

10/9/84 LONG *Je jové, Valentine, When the wild calls (ballad version), Salmon are jumping.* 30/8/84 MV5 MHY MPK

SWEET ADDICTION
3/11/89 FRI. ROCK *Down to the bone, Broken bottles, Putting you wrong, Little too easy.* Matt Wolff (v), Dave Airey (g), Jo Johnson (b), Gavin Johns (d). 6/10/89 MV5 PW DD&PA

SWEET MARRIAGE
17/8/69 TOP GEAR *Titania†, Mort†, Annie's sister.* Tony Merrick (lv), Alan Doyle (g), Keith Lawless (bv), Ronald Walker (lg), Anthony McDonald (d). 11/8/69 MV1 JW TW&MF
† On 'Top Gear' LP BBC Records REC 52S

SWEET SAVAGE
19/12/80 FRI. ROCK *Into the night, Queen's vengence, Killing time, Eye of the storm.* Vivian Campbell (lg), Raymond Hatler (b), David Bates (d), Trevor Fleming (rg). 3/12/80 * TW DD

SWEET WATER CANAL
17/4/70 BLACK *Comin' on, Easy to be hard, Rise and shine (& Train, 22/5/70).* * 20/3/70 * * *

SWELL
6/6/92 PEEL *Every day any day, Tell them why, Life's great, There's always one thing.* Sean Kirkpatrick (d), Monte Vallier (b), Pete Vogl (g), David Freel (v,ag). 28/4/92 MV4 MR~

THE SWELL MAPS
27/10/78 PEEL *Read about Seymour, Harmony in your bathroom, Full moon in my pocket/Blam/Full moon etc, International rescue, Another song.* Epic (drums), Jowe (b), Nikki (g), Biggles (g). 16/10/78 MV4 TW DD
22/5/79 PEEL† *Bandits, Vertical slum/Forest fire, Armadillo, Midget submarine.* & Laura Logic (sx-2,4 only). 15/5/79 MV4 TVD MR&MPK
† On LP 'Whatever happens next' Rough Trade ROUGH21.
1/4/80 PEEL *Big empty field, Bleep and Booster come round for tea/Secret island, (Let's) Buy a bridge, The helicopter spies/A raincoat's room.* 18/3/80 MV4 BS MR

SWERVEDRIVER
3/9/90 PEEL *Out, Over, Volcano trash, Zed head.* Graham Bonnar (d), Adi Vines (b), Jim Hartridge (g), Adam Franklin (gv). 31/7/90 MV5 MR~
16/3/92 GOODIER *Pile up, Hands, Glow, Feeling.* 23/11/91 HP MC~

SWIMMING IN SAND
15/9/86 LONG *Lunatics, Climbing, Happy sad, You and I.* Meira Shore (lv), Bob Taylor (gv), Mike Benn (kv), Sue Hewitt (dv), Mike Turtle (b), Bill Pamplin (perc), Alan Tidbury (tb), Nicky Tidbury (tp). 3/9/86 MV4 BYA MPK

SWIMMING IN THE SEA
3/11/82 JENSEN *Bloodstream, What is and what's over, Bluenotes, Where the spies are.* Gary Leach (d), Graham Andrew (g), Nel (b), Aaron Davidson (k), Tracey Payne (v). 21/10/82 MV4 JWI MR

THE SWINGING LAURELS
28/6/82 PEEL *Rodeo, Murder mile, Swing the cat, Beating heart.* Gary Birtles (v,sx,k,perc), John Barrow (sx,bkv,perc), Dean Sargent (b,tp), Mark O'Hara (k). 2/6/82 MV4 RP NG
20/8/83 LONG *Falling, Stay with me.* * 17/8/83 PHM c.JL TWN

SYMBIOSIS
30/1/71 TOP GEAR *NTU, Volume 4: Be bop, Bass variations on standfast, Aura, Standfast.* Robert Wyatt (d), Roy Babbington (b), Nick Evans (tb), Gary Windo (ts,fl), Mongezi Feza (tp,fl), Steve Florence (g). 11/1/71 PH JW BC 'Yes for limited use': Audition panel.

SYNCBEAT
24/9/84 PEEL *Khamsin, 52nd beat, Dominance.* Andy Connell (k), Martin Jackson (d,smp), Derek Johnson (b). 15/9/84 MV5 DG MC

SYNCOPATION
10/5/82 JENSEN *Strangest things, Nothing changes, Marking time, Rain.* James Carter (g,lv), Michael Calderbank (bv), Craig Rostock (d), Pete Hawksworth (sy,v). 24/2/82 PHM * TWN
11/12/82 LONG *Confusion, Sometimes, Shadows, Down.* * 7/12/82 PHM c.JL *

SYNDICATE
6/3/85 LONG *Don't get me down, Burning sound, Nostalgia locomotion, The golden key.* Jamo Stewart (gv), Robert Anderson (k), Breave (b). 13/2/85 MV5 JS MPK

SYSTEMS
17/11/81 PEEL *Total recall, Can you imagine, Wishful thinking, Falling up.* John Hawkins (v), Kevin Brown (k), Bazz Hughes (b), Jeremy Kelly (g), Tony Elson (d), Mike Nelson (sx). 31/10/81 MV4 DG ME

JUNE TABOR
10/3/75 PEEL *Seamus the showman, Scarborough fair town, Dancing at Whitsun, And the band played "Waltzing Matilda".* June Tabor (v); 'and Tim Hart (g-1,3 only; 3-solo). 4/3/75 MV4 * *
13/9/76 PEEL *Young waters, Pull down lads, Young Allan, Short jacket and white trousers.* & John Gillaspie (k). 26/8/76 MV4 TW *
22/2/77 PEEL† *Lord Bateman, The banks of the sweet Dundee, The fiddle and the drum, Donal Og.* Solo. 25/1/77 MV4 PR MR
† on Strange Fruit SFPS015.
19/7/77 PEEL *Derry Jail, Riding down to Portsmouth, The devil and the bailiff McGlinn, Streets of Forbes, No man's land, A Taboresque Utterance.* 11/7/77 MV4 MB DD 'A Taboresque utterance' according to Malcolm Brown on the session sheet, was 'written in indignation upon hearing of John Peel's broadcast sexual and sadistic desire to bite into her neck'.
1/2/78 PEEL *The overgate, Now I'm easy, Unicorns, Flash company, Furze field.* & Martin Simpson (g,bj), John Gillaspie (p,sy,rec,o). 24/1/78 MV4 MB MR
7/7/88 KERSHAW *Where are you tonight, As I roved out, The terror time, Mayn rue plats, Joe Peel.* & Huw Warren (p,sy). 23/6/88 * DG DD&MA
5/1/91 PEEL *White rabbit†, Anarchy Gordon, Wheels on fire, All along the watchtower†.* June Tabor (v) '& the Oyster Band': Lee (d,tamb), Chopper (b,clo), John Jones (ml), Ian Telfer (fd,cnc), Alan Prosser (g,bkv). 27/11/90 MV5 MR~
† Pressed up on a promotional release [See also under 'Prior, Maddy'].

TAD
2/1/90 PEEL *Nuts 'n' bolts, Daisy, Helot, Wood goblins.* Steve Wiederhold (d), Kurt Danielson (b,bkv), Gary Thorstensen (g), Tad Doyle (gv). 5/12/89 MV5 DG MR
5/7/90 PEEL *3D witch hunt, Delinquent, Plague years, Jack Pepsi.* 19/6/90 MV3 MR~

TAGGETT
2/4/73 WALKER *Time, Save a happy song for tomorrow, Magic woman touch.* Tim Wheatley (b), Terry Fogg (d), Peter Hansen (k), Tont Hicks (g), Colin Horton-Jennings (g). 23/3/73 AO2 c.PWI *
26/4/73 PEEL *Squares to a circle, Lonely nights lonely days, Buster, Time.* 16/4/73 LH1 BA BC
18/3/74 HAMILTON *(I'll be your) Anchor man* [Network session]. & 3 musicians & 3 singers (unknown). 13/3/74 PH c.PWI *

SHUNG TAIN
18/3/90 KERSHAW *Posterity of the Chinese dragon, Little boat on the river, Cantonese music, Dancing and singing in the village.* Guo Yi Wang Shunxin, Zhao Zheng Ren, Chang Gui Duo, Jiang Du. 22/2/90 MV5 DG NG

TALIESIN
15/2/91 FRI. ROCK *Taliesin, Twice born, Die by the sword,*

From a distant world. Glen Tharia (bv), Simon Godwin (g), Mark Coleman (d). 25/1/91 MV5 DD~

TALISKER
5/3/76 PEEL Diddlin' for the Bairns/The dark isle, Dreaming of Glenisla, The black bear, Tha cu ban againn (We have a white dog), Hey Mandu. John Rangecroft (ts,cl), Davie Webster (as), Lindsay Cooper (db), Marc Meggido (db), Ken Hyder (d,perc). 24/2/76 MV4 * MR

TALISMAN
14/7/81 SKINNER Nitty gritty, Nothing change, Slow poison, Run come girl. Donald De Cordova (d), Dennison Joseph (b), Leroy Forbes (lg,bkv), Desmond Taylor (lv,rg), Brendan Whitmore (ts), Bill Bartlett (o,p). 2/7/81 MV4 DG MR
9/9/81 PEEL Wicked dem, Run come girl, Nothing change. 7/9/81 MV4 TW DD

TALK TALK
18/11/81 JENSEN Renée, It's so serious, Talk talk, Magic moments. Mark Hollis (v), Paul Webb (bv), Simon Brenner (k), Lee Harris (d). 5/11/81 MV4 JS *
19/4/83 JENSEN For what it's worth, Night boys, Again a game, Why is it so hard? Phil Ramacon (k) r. Brenner. 27/3/83 MV4 DG ME

TALULAH GOSH!
7/8/86 LONG† Looking for a rainbow, Do you remember, Talulah gosh, Sunny inside. Amelia Fletcher (gv), Liz Pebbles (v,vi), Chris Scott (b), Peter Punk (g), Matthew (d), Gregory (g). 30/7/86 MV5 BYA MPK
11/1/88 PEEL† World's ending, Be your baby, I don't want to have to break your face, In love for the very first time, Spearmint head. Pebbles, Gregory out; & Eithne Farry (bkv). 29/12/87 * DG *
    † On Sarah Records 604.

TAM LINN
3/3/75 PEEL Tam Linn's opener, Gypsy Davey, Ask me father, Hearts lament. 4 (unknown). 25/2/75 MV4 * *

SHARON TANDY AND THE FLEUR DE LYS
29/10/67 TOP GEAR Go go power, Crosscut saw, There's always something there to remind me, Our day will come, Hold on. Sharon Tandy (v) & Fleur de Lys: Bryn Haworth (g) & others (unknown) (2-Fleur de Lys only). 11/10/67 * BA *

TANGERINE DREAM
21/2/74 PEEL Mysterious semblance at the strand of nightmares, Movements of a visionary, Sequent C, Phaedra. * Edgar Froese, Chris Franke, Peter Baumann. Rec. date unknown PRIV * *
11/7/74 PEEL Overture, Zeus, Baroque.
    * Rec. date unknown PRIV * *

TANK
30/4/82 FRI. ROCK Hammer on, Don't walk away, Heavy artillery, He fell in love with a Stormtrooper. Mark Brabbs (d), Algy Ward (b), Pete Brabbs (g). 25/3/82 * JS&TW DD

TANZ DER YOUTH
9/8/78 PEEL I'm sorry, Why I die, Mistaken, Delay. Brian James (g,lv), Andy Colquhoun (b,v), Tony Moore (k,v), Alan Powell (d). 2/8/78 MV4 BS NG

TAPESTRY
7/6/71 HARRIS Sea suite, Aquarian (& Time of man, not broadcast). Herbie Fennel (fl,d), Pete Stone (bv,vi,glo), Angie Britten (kgv), Chris Chandler (lg,clo). 11/5/71 TI JM JWH
17/1/72 HARRIS Betrothal, Time of man (& Aquarian, 14/2/72). & Bob Critchley, Trevor Davies. 12/1/72 AO2 JG *

TAR
7/7/91 PEEL Viaduct removal†, Walking the king, Ballad of the storyteller†, Play to win. Mike Greenless (d), Tom Zalucki (b), Mary Zablucki (g), John Moho (gv). 16/5/91 MV5 DG TdB&DMC
    † On Strange Fruit SFMCD212.

TARA ZARA
19/7/85 FRI. ROCK The time is right, Wake up, Hold me tonight, Behind the mask. Danielz (v), Jeff Williams (gv), Andy Street (k), Mike Lever (b), Simon Henderson (d). 7/6/85 MV4 TW DD

TARIKA SAMMY
3/3/91 KERSHAW Firaisankina, Pelika, Zanahary, Kilalao, Andao Hihira, Ramiaramila, Mila namana. Sammy, Solomon Ratianarinaivo, Hanitra Razanarimialy. Rec. date unknown FR: Madagascar IA *
25/4/92 KERSHAW Transport, Misy kalo, Soa ny manakavan, Taralila Saraka, Siloka. Sammy, Hanitra, Tiana (adonua, kabosy,v), Noro (perc,v). 19/4/92 MV4 ME~

TARZAN 5
11/5/81 SKINNER This week, Clean weekend, In his camera, Ten days in Corfu. Andrea Simpson (v), Sue McGhie (bkv), Craig Eastwood (sx), Steven Blacklidge (g), Phil Cullingford (b), Andrew Cullingford (d). 30/4/81 LH1 JS *

TASTE
25/8/68 TOP GEAR Same old story, Blister on the moon, Dual carriageway pain, Norman invasion (& Born on the wrong side of time, 27/10/68). Rory Gallagher (gv), Eric Kittrington (b), Norman Damery (d). 5/8/68 PC1 BA *
30/10/68 NIGHT RIDE Same old story, Dual carriageway pain, Born on the wrong side of time, Wee wee baby. Richard McCracken (b), John Wilson (d) r. Kittrington, Damery. 3/10/68 MV5 DK *
12/11/68 WS R&B Walking blues, Sugar mama, Same old story. 25/10/68 AO2 JG JY
9/3/69 TOP GEAR I'm moving on, Sugar mama, Leaving blues, Hail (& Wee wee baby, 20/4/69). 17/2/69 PH BA *
10/3/69 WS R&B Leaving blues, Hail, Wee wee baby, Catfish. 19/2/69 MV4 JG JY
13/7/69 SYMONDS ON SUNDAY Dual carriageway pain, Same old story, Walking blues. 8/7/69 PC1 c.PWI *
22/11/69 WS R&B What's goin' on, Railway and gun, I got my brand on you, Eat my words. 29/10/69 MV4 JG JY
10/5/70 RAVEN's R&B Morning sun, Walking blues, Eat my words. 15/4/70 MV4 JG JY
    Rec'd John Peel Concert 2/4/70 PS. TX 12/4/70.
23/6/70 HARDING Morning sun, Railway and gun, Eat my words. 16/6/70 MV5 MB MH&MF

TROY TATE
24/9/83 LONG Ten feet tall, Leave that girl alone, Love is, Girl on a ferry. & Ten Feet Tall (unknown). 22/9/83 MR c.JL *
23/1/85 LONG God's puppet/Liberty, Tomorrrow I'll be gone, Airport of silence, Sorrow. Troy Tate (kv), Malcolm Mortimer (d), Pete Risingham (b), Jéz Foden (g). 6/1/85 HP BYA PW

TAXI PATA PATA
12/2/87 KERSHAW Melodie K, Mbongo ekeyi, Independence, Kanina. Nsimba Foguis & Terry Mhuriro (v), Steve Buckley (sx), Chris Batchelor (tp), Mamadi Kamara (cga), Lucky Mupawaende & Zak Siboke (g), Apache Dee (b), Frankie Müller (d). 2/2/87 * DG DD&TdB

THE JAMES TAYLOR QUARTET
29/4/87 PEEL Blow-up, Goldfinger, Hump-backed bridge, One-way street. Simon Howard (d), Allan Crockford (b), David Taylor (g), James Taylor (o). 21/4/87 * DG MA&ME
3/2/88 MAYO The spyder, No moon at all, The girl from Ipanema, All about mine. & Harriet Victor (v-2) & Kyra De Coninck (v-3). 17/1/88 MV4 HP TdB&MFA
23/11/88 SKINNER Down by the river, Breakout, Summer song, Bossa palante. Taylor, Chris Jenkins (perc), Robert Bedwell (b), Lawrence Parry (tp), John Wallace (bars), John Wilmott (ts), Paul Carr (g), Steve White (d), Andrew Stex (v-3). 13/11/88 MV4 PW MA&TdB
8/6/89 SKINNER Groovin' home, It don't matter, Mon oncle, Round midnight. Taylor, Carr, White, Wallace, Paul

Francis (b), Cleveland Watkiss (v). Live from MV3 HP TdB&TD

THE TEA SET
3/4/80 PEEL Keep on running (big noise from the jungle), Nelson was a nance, Sawtooth, Contract killer. Cally (d), Nick Haeffner (g), Nic Egan (lv), Ron West (b), Mark Wilkins (sy). 25/3/80 MV4 BS MR

TEACHER
23/9/90 KERSHAW You can't step twice on the same piece of water, The problem, Wizard jam. Michael Whyte (g,prg), The general (prg). 6/9/90 MV5 DG PA&MR

THE TEARDROP EXPLODES
15/10/79 PEEL Brave boys keep their promises, Ha ha I'm drowning, Went Crazy, Chance. Michael Finkler (g), Julian Cope (b,lv), Ged Quinn (k,bkv), Gary 'Rocky' Dwyer (d,bkv). 2/10/79 MV4 JS MR
24/4/80 PEEL Thief of Baghdad, When I dream, The poppies in the field. David Balfe (k) r. Quinn. 16/4/80 MV4 JE NG
27/10/80 READ Reward, Suffocate, For years, The great dominions. Cope, Dwyer, The Emotional Jungle (g), The Evil Wasp (k), The Legendary Eric Batchelor (sx). 16/10/80 MV4 CL *
    Contracts index next suggests session recordings for 'Radio 1 show' 13/1/81; Peter Powell 23/2/81; 'live' for Skinner 19/3/81.
17/8/81 SKINNER And the fighting takes over, Better scream, Bent out of shape, Screaming secrets. Cope, Dwyer, Alfie Agius (b), Troy Tate (g), Jeff Hammer (k), Bimbo Lexington & the 500 ('ambient sound'), Ted Emmett (tp). 13/8/81 MV4 DG MR
    Files say another session recorded the next day, 14/8/81, for Peter Powell; then 25/10/81 for Simon Bates.
22/12/81 PEEL Soft enough for you, Sex, The challenger. Cope, Balfe, Dwyer, Tate, Ron (b). 16/11/81 MV4 TW DD&MC
    Further contracts issued: 23 or 28/5/82 for Peter Powell; 9/6/82 for Simon Bates & Steve Wright.
8/7/82 JENSEN Serious danger, Log cabin, Buchanan, You disappear from view. Cope, Dwyer, Balfe. 27/6/82 MV4 DG ME

THE TEARJERKERS
25/3/80 PEEL Is it art, I'm sorry, Jenny Jenny, Comic book heroes. Paul Maxwell (lv), The Groover (g), Brian Ranson (g), Howard Ingram (b), Nigel Hamilton (d). 12/3/80 MV4 JE NG

TEARS FOR FEARS
1/9/82 PEEL Ideas as opiates, The hurting, Suffer the children, The prisoner. Curt Smith (bv), Roland Orzabal (g,kv), Chris Hughes (dm). 14/8/82 MV4 DG MR
20/10/82 JENSEN Memories fade, The prisoner, The start of the breakdown, The hurting. Ian Stanley (k) joins. 10/10/82 MV4 DG ME
23/7/84 SKINNER Head over heels, The working hour, Broken. Smith, Orzabal, Stanley, Andy Davis (k), Manny Elias (d), William Gregory (sx). 8/7/84 MV5 DG ME

TEENAGE FANCLUB
30/9/90 PEEL† God knows it's true°, So far gone, Alcoholiday, Longhair. Norman Blake (gv), Raymond McGinley (g,bkv), Gerard Love (bv), Brendan O'Hare (d,bkv). 28/9/90 MV4 MWT~
    † On Strange Fruit SFPCD081; ° also on 'New Season' SFRCD205.
23/9/91 GOODIER The concept/Satan, What you do to me, Everything flows, Starsign. 31/8/91 MV5 MA~PA

THE TELESCOPES
13/6/89 PEEL Sadness pale, There is no floor, Suffocation, Silent water. Stephen Lawrie (v), Dave Fitzgerald (g), Joanna Doran (g), Dominic Dillon (d), Robert Brooks (b). 16/5/89 MV3 DG MR
15/9/91 PEEL Please tell mother, Splashdown, Prescence of your grace, To the shore. 6/8/91 MV5 MR~

TELEVISION PERSONALITIES

1/9/80 Peel *Silly girl, Picture of Dorian Gray, La grande illusion, Look back in anger.* Empire (d), Joe from Hendon (b,bkv), Dan (g,lv). 20/8/80 MV4 DG NG

27/2/86 Kershaw *Paradise is for the blessed, My conscience tells me no, I still believe in magic, Salvador Dali's garden party.* Dan, Mr Head (bv), Jeffrey Loom (d). 13/2/86 Y2 NB SR

TEMPEST

8/6/73 Sequence *Foyers of fun, Grey and black, Up and on, Stranger.* Jon Hiseman (d), Allan Holdsworth (lgv), Mark Clarke (bv), Paul Williams (lv). 15/5/73 T1 JM *

THE TEMPEST

18/8/83 Jensen *Obscenities, Which one, Five against the house, ABC.* Alex Novak (lv), Mark Refoy (g), Alan Emptage (b), Mick Packwood (d), John Luccibello (perc). 11/8/83 MV4 JP MR

10 CC

20/1/74 Sounds On Sunday *Oh effendi, Sand in my face, Somewhere in Hollywood, Rubber bullets, Headline hustler, The worst band in the world.* Eric Stewart (gv), Graham Gouldman (bv), Kevin Godley (dv), Lol Creme (gv). Introduced by Stuart Henry. 7/1/74 Studio 3, MCR TH *

13/5/74 Harris *Hotel, Old wild man, Clock work creep, Silly love, Oh effendi.* 8/5/74 LH1 PR *

10,000 MANIACS

1/7/85 Peel *Just as the tide was a' flowin', Lily dale, Maddox table, Back o' the moon.* Natalie Merchant (v), Robert Buck (lg,mnd), John Lombardo (ag), Steven Gustafson (b), Dennis Drew (k), Jerry Augustyniak (d). 23/6/85 MV5 DG SC

10/9/87 Kershaw *What's the matter here, Don't talk, Gun shy, Poison in the well.* Lombardo out. 1/9/87 * DG ME&SC

25/5/89 Skinner *What's the matter here, Eat for two, Dust bowl.* Merchant, Julia Palmer (clo) & Buck only, says sheet. 19/5/89 MV3 KH MA

  † on 10-inch single of 'Eat for two', Elektra EKR100TE.

9/12/90 Kershaw *The Latin one, Cotton alley, Orange, Tension.* Lombardo back; & Mary Ramsey (vla-4 only). 29/11/90 MV5 DG NG

TEN YEARS AFTER

10/12/67 Top Gear *Love until I die, Don't want you woman, Sometimes I feel like going home, Loosin' the dogs (& The sounds, 14/1/68).* Alvin Lee (gv), Leo Lyons (b), Ric Lee (d), Chick Churchill (o). 21/11/67 A02 BP PR

  Passed audition as 3-piece 'The Jaybirds' 2/66 (without Churchill).

7/4/68 Top Gear *Rock your mama, Portable people, I ain't seen no whisky (& I may be wrong but I won't be wrong always, 14/1/68).* 13/3/68 MV4 BA PR

8/4/68 Symonds *Portable people, Rock your mama (9/4), Love until I die (11/4), Hold me tight (12/4)..* 1/4/68 PH * *

18/8/68 Top Gear *Woman trouble, Woodchoppers' ball, No title blues, I'm going home (& Spider in my web, 29/9/68).* 14/8/68 PH BA AH&BC

23/12/68 Symonds *I'm going home, Hear me calling (24/12), Crossroads (25/12), Woman trouble (26/12).* 13/12/68 MV5 * *

5/1/69 Top Gear *Don't want you woman, Speed kills, A sad song, No title (& Woman trouble, 2/3/69).* 30/12/68 MV4 BA *

26/1/69 Symonds On Sunday *Hear me callin', Woodchoppers ball, I'm going home, Speed kills.* 21/1/69 PH TW

17/2/69 WS R&B *Crossroads, Spider in my web, Loosin' the dogs.* 22/1/69 MV4 JG JY

15/6/69 Top Gear *Good morning little schoolgirl, Woke up this morning, I can't keep from crying sometimes (& Crossroads, 27/7/69).* 9/6/69 PH JW TW

THE TENDER LUGERS

29/9/86 Peel *Johnny/Joanne, Enjoy yourself, A little protection, Teenage cream.* Tim Lewis (d), Gary Oliver (b), Jason Collingwood (g), Bruce McGregor (gv). 16/9/86 * DG MFA&MC

TERMINAL CHEESECAKE

4/6/90 Peel *Pony boy, Blowhound, Stinky beads, Inbreds '80.* Gary (bv), Russdancrane (g,b), Ghed (perc,tab), Rudy (d). 20/4/90 OS * *

TERMINAL HOEDOWN

9/2/92 Peel *Superwoman, Fear eats the soul, Yeah, Go-go juice.* Ernie Hendricks (d), Eamonn James Duffy (b), Peter Byrchmore (lg,bkv), Joe Crow (rg,bkv), Robert Lloyd (v). 22/12/91 MV3 DG ME&SBR

TERRANOVA

21/12/79 Fri. Rock *Saints and sinners, White rose, Calling lady love, Dirty love.* Colin Pattenden (b), Chris Slade (d), Dave Fishel (k), Peter Cox (v), Chris West (g). 28/11/79 * TW *

TERRAPLANE

20/8/82 Fri. Rock *Let the wheels go round, The beginning of the end, Gimme the money, If you could see yourself.* Luke Morley (g), Danny Bowes (v), Nick Linden (b), Gary James (d). 6/8/82 * TW DD

SONNY TERRY & BROWNIE MCGHEE

19/6/73 Peel *Walkin' my blues away, Rock island line, Walk on, Life is a gamble.* 5/6/73 PH JW BC

TERRY AND GERRY

23/7/84 Peel *Hello, Wolfman's request, Clothes shop close, Butter's on the bread, Wait until you're older.* Terry Lilley (db,v), Gerry Colvin (gv), Andy Downer (gv), Doreen de-Ville (Sue Richardson) (wsh). 11/7/84 MV5 RP GP

10/4/85 Peel *Simon, Kennedy says, Armchair terrorist song, A shanty for the gravy boat.* 24/3/85 MV5 DG ME

9/10/85 Peel *Reservation, The last bullet in the gun, The ballad of a nasty man, Fashion rodeo, Peel jingle.* Terry, Gerry, 'Doreen', Jeremy Page (gv), Chris Davies (bars), Alistair Robertson (ts), Chris Bowden (al). 24/9/85 MV5 JWI TdB

TEST DEPARTMENT

22/8/83 Peel *Shockwork, State of Affairs, Hunger.* Angus Farquhar, Paul Jamrozy, Graham Cunnigton, Toby Burdon. 15/8/83 MV4 TW MC

4/2/85 Peel *Operation prayer power, Massive kamikaze attack.* * Rec. date unknown * * *

TESTCARD F

3/1/83 Peel *Bandwagon tango, Blanket expression, Ransom, Unfamiliar room.* Sue Hope (v), Pete Roberts (sy), John Hartwell (electric d), Vince Rogers (o). 18/12/82 MV4 DG MC

LES TETES BRULEES

27/10/90 Peel *Oyili, Ekye, Ziliyan, Mindzug.* Andre Afata (dv), Martin Maam (bv), Roger Bexongo (perc,gv), George Essono (kv), Jean-Marie Ahanda (tp,v). 16/10/90 MV5 * MWT&JLO

JAKE THAKRAY

31/8/72 Drummond *Sister Josephine, Gorilla, The Barntown cock, Country boy (& Old Molly Metcalfe, Fine bay pony, The jolly captain, 21/9/72).* Jake Thakray (agv). 2/8/72 * MB MH&MF

THAT PETROL EMOTION

24/6/85 Peel† *V2, Lettuce, Blind spot, Can't stop.* John O'Neill (g), Ciaran McLaughlan (d), Raymond Gorman (g), Damian O'Neill (b), Steve Mack (v). 11/6/85 MV5 JWI MR

18/11/85 Peel† *Tight lipped, Circusville, Cheapskate, Mouth crazy.* 5/11/85 MV5 PWL MR

  † on Strange Fruit SFMCD205.

5/5/86 Long *Zig zag wanderer, Belly bugs, For what it's worth, Spin cycle.* 16/4/86 MV4 BYA MPK

14/1/87 Peel *Big decision, Swamp, Inside, Chester Burnette.* 16/12/86 * DG MR

4/5/87 Long *Genius move, Here it is take it!, Me and baby brother, Party games.* 26/4/87 MV4 HP JB

THE THE

5/11/83 Long *Twilight hour, This is the day, Giant, Soul mining.* 6 musicians (uncertain). 20/7/83 * c.PWL *

THEATRE OF HATE

9/12/80 Peel *Rebel without a brain, The wake, 63, It's my own invention.* Kirk Brandon (lv), Steve Guthrie (g), Stan Stammers (b), Luke Rendall (d), John Boy (sx). 1/12/80 LH1 TW DD&JB

24/8/81 Peel *Love is a ghost, Conquistador, Propaganda, Do you believe in the westworld?* Guthrie out. 15/8/81 MV4 DG MR

18/2/82 Peel *Dreams of the poppy, Incinerator, The hop, The klan.* Brandon, Stammers, Boy, Nigel Preston (d), Billy Duffy (g). 8/2/82 MV4 DG DD

24/6/82 Jensen *Legion, The solution, The Americans, Anniversary.* John Lennard (sx) credited, instead of 'Boy'. 17/6/82 MV4 JS MR

THEE HYPNOTICS

10/4/89 Peel *Soul trader, Love in a different vein, Nine times, Let's get naked.* Mark Thompson (d), Will Pepper (b), Ray Hanson (g), James Jones (v,hca). 28/3/89 WX DG MR

THEN JERICO

18/2/87 Long *Let her fall, Muscle deep, Blessed day, The hitcher.* Steve Wren (d), Jasper Stainthorpe (b), Scott Thomas (g), Alex Mungo (k), Mark Shaw (v). 28/1/87 MV4 DG MPK

10/8/87 Long *Play dead, Quiet place, Electric, Searching.* Shaw, Stainthorpe, Wren, Scott Taylor (g); & Rob Downes (g), Alex Wright (k). 12/7/87 MV4 PW TdB&MA

THERAPY

28/9/91 Peel *Innocent X/Meat abstract, Prisonbreaker, Perversonality.* Fyfe (dv), Michael (b), Andy (gv). 15/8/91 MV5 DG TdB&JLO&SCO

THEY MIGHT BE GIANTS

30/4/89 Kershaw *Nightgown of the sullen moon, Kiss me son of god, It's not my birthday, She was a hotel detective.* John Flansburgh (gv), John Linnell (o,p,acc,v). 22/2/89 Dubway Studios, NY, NY, USA * *

4/2/90 Kershaw *Where your eyes don't go, Particle man, Maybe I know, Chess piece face.* 18/1/90 MV3 DG MWT

THIN LIZZY

15/7/71 Henry *Look what the wind's just blown in, Eire, Return of the farmer's song, Things aren't working out down at the farm.* Phil Lynott (bv), Brian Downey (d), Eric Bell (g). 7/7/71 MV4 MB MH&MF

  'Steam-rollered through the session...very strong... I think they'll make a big name for themselves': from MB's report to Audition unit. Passed: 'well-executed... limited appeal'.

3/11/71 Peel *Raygun, The rise and demise of the funky nomadic tribe, Dublin, Clifton Grange Hotel.* 12/10/71 MV4 *

2/3/72 Drummond *Call the police, Baby face, Buffalo gal (& Sarah, 27/4/72).* 23/2/72 MV4 MB MH&MF

2/6/72 Peel *Call the police, Things aren't working out down at the farm, Chatting today.* 26/4/72 T1 JM *

28/11/72 Peel *Whiskey in the jar, Suicide, Black boys on the corner, The saga of the ageing orphan.* 14/11/72 LH1 TW BC

4/6/73 Hamilton *Randolph's tango* [Network session]. 21/5/73 PH c.PWL *

7/8/73 Peel *Gonna creep up on you, Litle girl in bloom, Vagabonds of the western world.* 31/7/73 LH1 JW *
  Also rec'd In Concert 26/7/73 HP, TX 1/9/73.

16/8/73 Peel *Randolph's tango, The rocker, Slow blues.* 6/8/73 LH1 BA *

17/9/73 Harris *Randolph's tango, Slow blues, Little girl in bloom, The rocker.* 29/8/73 LH1 JG *

2/3/74 Rock On *Little girl in bloom, Little darling, Showdown.* Gary Moore (g), r. Bell. 25/2/74 LH1 BA *

1/4/74 HARRIS *Slow blues, Sitamoia, Little darling, Showdown.* 6/3/74 LH1 JG *

11/4/74 PEEL *Little darling, Sitamoia, It's only money, Black boys on the corner, Still in love with you.* 4/4/74 LH1 TW BAI

24/10/74 PEEL *Philomena, It's only money, Sha la la, She knows.* Scott Gorham (g) & Brian Robertson (g) r. Moore. 3/10/74 MV4 TW BAI

25/11/74 HARRIS *She knows, Banshee, Philomena (& Dear heart, Last shelf along, possibly not broadcast, or PasB incomplete).* 23/10/74 MV4 JG *
  Rec'd In Concert 27/11/74 HP, TX 7/12/74.

5/6/75 PEEL *Rosalie, Freedom song, Half caste, Suicide.* 29/5/75 MV4 TW BAI

9/3/76 PEEL *Jailbreak, Emerald, Cowboy song, The warrior.* 12/2/76 MV4 TW BAI

11/10/76 PEEL *Don't believe a word, Johnny the fox meets the weed, Fool's gold, Johnny.* 23/9/76 MV4 TW BAI

22/8/77 PEEL *Killer without a cause, Bad reputation, That woman's gonna break your heart, Dancing in the moonlight†, Downtown sundown.* & (sx) unknown. 1/8/77 MV4 TW BAI
  † On 'Before the Fall' SFRCD203. Rec'd In Concert 26/11/81 Hammersmith Odeon (Snowy White, Darren Wharton r. Robertson).

THIN MEN

13/4/83 JENSEN *Too many times, Jump for joy, Moving room, Centre of attention.* Neil (v), Gary (gv), Malcolm (kv), Korda (d), Tim (b). 7/4/83 MV4 JP *

THING

9/3/91 PEEL *Blu 4 U, Kiss the sun, All will be revealed, It's so easy.* Jesse Obstbaum (v), Jake Ottman (g), Salvatore Canzorieri (g), Sean Bolivar (b), Andrew Nelson (d). 10/2/91 MV3 DG ME&JLO

THIRD EAR BAND

1/1/69 NIGHT RIDE *The grove, Stone circle, Egyptian book of the dead, Pierrot.* Glen Sweeney (d), Richard Coff (vi), Paul Minns (ob), Benjamin Courtland (vi). 31/12/68 AO2 PR *

27/7/69 TOP GEAR *Hyde park raga, Druid, Ghetto raga.* 21/7/69 PH JW *

12/6/70 BLACK *Earth, Downbone raga, Water (& Festival, 17/7/70).* Ursula Smith r. Courtland. 20/5/70 AO2 JM *

20/6/70 TOP GEAR *Downbone raga, Feel your head, Hyde park raga.* 8/6/70 PH JW *

11/2/72 PEEL *Air, I the key.* Denim Bridges (g), Simon House (vi), Michael Marchant (gv), Peter Pavli (b), r. Smith. 25/1/72 T1 JM&PD *

21/3/72 DRUMMOND *Groan's dance, Fleance's song, Hierophant.* 21/2/72 MV5 MB MH&MF

18/5/73 SEQUENCE *I the key, The magus, Ten dimensional landscape.* 24/4/73 T1 JM NG

35 SUMMERS

19/1/91 PEEL *Come together, Good morning and goodbye, Discotheque.* Andy Hignett (d), Robbie Fay (b), Duncan Lomax (rg,bkv), Ian Greenwood (lg), Jamie Southern (k), David Pichilingi (v). 20/12/90 MV5 DG MWT&RPF

20/10/91 PEEL *Loyality, Really down, Candy, Sheep.* Alan Curry (d) r. Hignett. 22/8/91 MV5 DG NG&PA

THIS FINAL FRAME

18/5/82 JENSEN *The mask falls away, My disguise, Eden, One step away.* Carl Henry (d), Pete McAsey (b), Paul Skillen (gv), Eamonn Sale (k,v-2 only), Jim Shaw (tp), Mike Cobb (hp). 9/5/82 MV4 DG ME

THIS HEAT

22/4/77 PEEL *Fall of Saigon, Not waving but drowning, Horizontal hold.* Charles Bullen (g), Charles Hayward (d,k), Gareth Williams (o,b). 28/3/77 MV4 TW DD

24/11/77 PEEL *Makeshift, Rimp romp ramp, Sitting, Slither, Basement boy.* 26/10/77 MV4 MB NG

THIS PICTURE

28/7/88 L. KERSHAW *Naked rain, Offering, Blacker than.*

Duncan Forrester (d,perc), Steve Hughes (b), Robert Forrester (g), Symon Bye (pv). 24/7/88 MV4 TdB SC

THIS POISON

30/11/87 PEEL *Question mark, St.Johnstoun, Driving skills, It'll all work out.* Derek MacMoir (g), Saigz MacTaylor (gv), Alistair MacDonald (b), Steve MacGray (d). 22/11/87 * DG ME&FK

THE THOMPSON TWINS

23/2/81 SKINNER† *A product of..., The price, Could be her could be you, Oumma aulareso.* Tom Bailey (bv), John Roog (g), Peter Dodd (g), Jane Shorter (sx), Chris Bell (d), Joe Leeway (perc). 12/2/81 LH1 JS *
  † On Nighttracks SFNT005.

7/2/83 JENSEN *Kamikaze, Judy do, If you were here, Tears.* Bailey, Leeway, Alannah Currie (perc,v), Andrew Bodnar (b), Boris Bransby-Williams (d). 3/2/83 MV4 JS TdB

RICHARD & LINDA THOMPSON

25/1/73 PEEL *The little beggar girl, Dragging the river, The great Valerio, Medley: The Neasden hornpipe; The Avebury particle accelerator; The flowing tide.* Richard Thompson (agv), Linda Peters (v). 1/1/73 * BA *

12/2/74 PEEL *Hokey pokey, Georgie on a spree, I'll regret it all.* 4/2/74 T1 JW *

24/2/75 PEEL *A heart needs a home, Wishing, I'm turning off a memory.* & Ian Whitman (p), Pat Donaldson (b), Dave Mattacks (d) ['All vocals Linda, Richard had flu'-TW]. 11/2/75 MV4 TW *

RICHARD THOMPSON

20/7/85 KERSHAW *You don't say (& She twists the knife again, When the spell is broken 3/8/85).* Solo. 1/7/85 SS CG PSM

29/1/87 KERSHAW *Valerie, Turning of the tide, Simple again, Shoot out the lights, End of the rainbow.* 7/1/87 SS CG PSM

3/3/88 KERSHAW *The killerman gold posse, Waltzing, Pharoah, Push and shove, Killing jar.* 28/1/88 * DG NG

19/10/88 SKINNER *Turning of the tide, Two left feet, Valerie, Waltzing for dreamers..* 16/9/88 Talks Studio PP2, Broadcasting House KH TdB

A THOUSAND MILES OF SUNSHINE

21/5/84 JENSEN *Jimmy Highlife, For liberty, Follow me, Spring has yet to smile.* Christopher Jerome (k), Benjamin Coles (perc), Gregory Orford (g), Tim Sewell (b), Chris Gorgier (g), Tammy Foster (bkv), Julie Gardiner (bkv), Steve Parkinson (d). 3/5/84 MV5 MHY *

THOUSAND YARD STARE

3/6/91 GOODIER *Buttermouth, Wish a perfect, This ness, Cottager.* Stephen Barnes (v), Sean McDenough (b), Giles Duffy (lg), Kevin Moxon (rg), Dominic Bostock (d,bkv). 4/5/91 MV5 MC~

THE THRASHING DOVES

24/10/85 KERSHAW *Biba's basement, The spirit of Rochdale house, Beautiful imbalance, Northern civil war party.* Ken Forman (gv), Brian Forman (kv), Ian Button (gv), Harry Sajjan (b), Kevin Sergeant (d,perc,v). 17/10/85 Y2 DST TWN

3D

5/4/82 PEEL *Houdini, Some die for money, Alone, The orchard.* Billed as '3D a Fish in Sea': Fred Palethorpe (d), Roy Campbell (b), John Reynolds (g), Steve Spurgin (k), Phil Martin (sx), Richie Holmes (v). 27/3/82 MV4 DG MR

9/11/82 PEEL *Dreaming of you, A child's toy, Red wine.* Palethorpe, Reynolds, Spurgin, Dave Edge (b), John Corner (v,sx). 23/10/82 MV4 DG MR

13/9/83 PEEL *Pantau, Brave boys' paradise, Stay, Loveliest world.* Edge out. 30/7/83 MV4 DG MR

360S

30/3/92 GOODIER *Illuminated, Free, Glob, Dead 1970.* Audrey Clark (gv), Eric Russell (g), Brian Evans (b), Johnny Grady (d). 7/3/92 MV4 MA RC

THE THREE JOHNS

10/8/82 PEEL *Pink headed bug, Lucy in the rain, Heads

like convicts, No place, You'll never walk alone.* John Langford (d,g), John Hyatt (v), John Brennan (bv), John Henry (tu,p), Tom Greenhalgh (g-2), Mark White ('screaming'-3), Stuart Curley & Jeremy Gilpen (bkv-4,5). 21/7/82 MV4 RP AP

9/3/83 PEEL *Fruit flies, Marx's wife, Windolene, Men-like monkeys, Sad house.* Langford, Hyatt, Brennan; & Greenhalgh, Curley, Sally Timms (v), David Spencer (v). 5/3/83 MV4 DG MC

7/11/83 PEEL *Sun of mud, The day industry decided to stop, A public song for a friend under suspicion of fire bombing a private shop, Poo-poo-poodle Bourgeois/Mouths to feed.* & Greenhalgh, Dave Hunt (dm), John Ridley (hca-3,4 only). 26/10/83 MV4 RP NG

12/11/83 LONG *Teenage nightingales, Lucy in the rain, Kick the dog, Fruitless.* 6 musicians (uncertain); & Martin Pasek (hca-3). 27/10/83 PHM c.PWL *

30/4/84 PEEL *Nightingales, Train, Junk, Bloop.* & Greenhalgh, Mitch Hagar (bkv), Karen Hagar (bkv), Paul Griffiths (hca), Jeanie O'Toole (perc). 17/4/84 MV5 BYA *

23/7/85 PEEL *Demon drink, Coals to Newcastle, King car, Torpedo, Third world war.* & Kate Morath (ob), Tom Greenford (p), John Ridley (hca), John Spence (v-5). 14/7/85 MV5 DG ME

2/3/87 PEEL *Key Largo, The book of the dead, Computer, Never and always.* & Greenhalgh, Steve Goulding (d), Sally Timms (bkv-2 only). 15/2/87 * DG ME&MFA

THREE MUSTAPHAS THREE

20/1/83 PEEL *Intro/Dobrodolska horo/O haralambis, Si vous passait par la, Tria pedia voliotika/Freylich un liebedike, O memetis, Czay calypso.* Hijaz (vi), Housack (d), Niaveti (acc), Ousack (clo,v), & Patrel Mustapha (lv,bz). 12/1/83 * RP NG

6/7/83 PEEL *Mustapha introduction/Pefida, A chilling tale pt.2, Valjare grave kosovare, Haspiko grigoro.* 2/7/83 MV4 DG MR

30/1/84 PEEL *Bam/Teteli, Introduction/Schnabbelleh freilach, To tilefono tis xenitias, Belz, Jingle, Theme tune.* & Isfa'ani Mustapha (perc). 21/1/84 MV4 DG MC

24/4/85 PEEL *Svadba, Singe tema, Grigoro noz - a chilling tale part 5, Ya habaybi ya ghaybine.* & Fat'mah Mustapha (tb). 7/4/85 MV5 DG ME

2/12/85 PEEL† *Niska banja, Besarabia, Hora lui marin, Ainy la la/Ah ya assmar el lawn, Vranjanski ekspres, O memetis, Cabra.* 'L'Orchestre "Bam" de Grand Mustapha International and Party': Uncle Patrel (bz,v), Isfa'ani (perc,md), Houzam (d,bkv), Hijaz (hawaiian g,vi), Sabah Habas H. (b,bkv), & Niaveti Mustapha III (fl,acc,picc); & Laura Daviz (v), Kem Mustapha (p,acc), Yheric Mustapha (tp), Andreos Blake (cl,sx), Telor Borrachon Pavel (tb); '& the string ensemble "Fat'mah", complete with EEC names and passports' Anne Stephenson & Sally Herbert (vi), Joss Pooke (vla), Rachel Maguire (clo). 19/11/85 MV5 MR~
  † released as LP 'Local Music' on Globestyle Records Fez 003.

21/9/87 PEEL *A ova/Valle epogradecit, Musafir, Xamenhevtexia/Fien, Gankino Horo, Selver.* Hijaz, Isfa'ani, Kemo (k,kaval), Sabah H. (bv), Houzam, & Niaveti Mustapha. 8/9/87 * DG ME&MPK

28/8/90 PEEL *Sitna Lisa, Buke e kripe/Kalazhojne, Taxi driver/Benga taxi, Kopanitsa.* Sabah Habas, Houzam, Niaveti, Dadudi (sx,cl), Kemo (p,qiftgli,acc), & Hijaz Mustapha. 10/7/90 MV5 MR~

25/1/92 KERSHAW *Turisticka pjesma, Selma, Urbas voda/Prepisor.* Dadudi (cl,sx), Sabah Habas, Houzam, Niaveti, Kemo, & Hijaz Mustapha. 5/12/91 MV5 DG *

THREE WISE MEN

10/12/86 PEEL *Cruising for a bruising, Urban hell, Refresh, Hard bop.* Jemski, Danny 'D' & A.J. (rp), Cybotron (sc,dj), Phil Chil (prg). 18/11/86 * DG ME&SC

THRILLED SKINNY

3/10/88 PEEL *Social climbing, So happy to be alive, Love

rut/Neigh on sea, Eat my hat. Elliot Smoke (d,bkv), Simon Goalpost (b,lv-2,3), Andy Furniture (g,lv-1,4), Utensil Realname (elp,bkv). 18/9/88 HP DG MA

THROWING MUSES
18/5/88 L. KERSHAW *Santa Claus, Mania, Soap and water, The burrow.* David Narcizo (d), Leslie Langston (b), Kristin Hersh (gv), Tanya Donelly (gv). 4/5/88 MV4 HP MPK

ADMIRAL TIBBETT
2/1/89 MISS P *Serious time, Leave people business, Babylon war, Keep a telling me.* Admiral Tibbett (v), Jerry Fulgfence (g), Gregory Assing (k), Philip Poleon (b), Derek Leroy Elsey (d,prg). 28/10/88 MV4 HP MA

KATHRYN TICKELL
22/1/87 KERSHAW *Border spirit/Untitled, Rothbury hills/J.B. Milne/The Carrick hornpipes, Brafferton village/The grey bull hornpipe, Remember me hornpipe/Madame Bonaparte.* Kathryn Tickell (pp,fd). 10/12/86 Y2 CG TWN

8/10/87 KERSHAW *The A.B. hornpipe/Billy Pigg's hornpipe, Roly gentle/Mrs. Bolowski's, The Redesdale hornpipe/Bill Charlton's fancy, Sir Sidney Smith's march, Sweet Hesleyside/Wark football team, Wild hills of wannies.* 10/9/87 * DG NG&MFA

23/2/89 KERSHAW *Glenaln hornpipe/Tyne bridge hornpipe, Otterburn, Fenham/Catch a pennyfox, Floating from Skerry/Farewell to Edinburgh.* & Ian Carr (g). 9/2/89 MV4 DG DD&FK

TIE THE BOY
3/9/86 LONG *Save it for a rainy day, Orgy, Pink flamingo, Now you're gone.* Peter Cunnah (g), Kevin Williams (gv), Tim Hegerty (d), Jerry Daver (b). 24/8/86 MV4 BYA *

TIGERS
7/4/80 READ *Fall for you, Ska trekking, Worlds to conquer, Religion for the hungry.* Tony Jacks (lv,g), Nick Potter (b), Ross McGeeney (gv), Nick Cola (sy,kv), Peter Dobson (d). 6/3/80 MV4 CL *

TIGERTAILZ
25/5/90 FRI. ROCK *Love overload, For a few dollars more, I can fight dirty too, Rock 'n' roll damnation.* Kim Hooker (gv), Jay Pepper (g), Pepsi Tate (b), Ace Finchum (d), Martin Shellard (k). 4/5/90 MV5 MC~

TANITA TIKARAM
7/4/88 KERSHAW *Poor cow, Rose on wood, Cathedral song, Sighing innocents.* Tanita Tikaram (gv). 10/3/88 MV4 DG NG

'This is the first Radio One Maida Vale recording to be re-mastered onto R-DAT cassette: far better quality than quarter-inch @ 15 ips!' Dale Griffin on sheet.

29/1/90 CAMPBELL *Sunset's arrived, Thursday's child, Once and not speak, Little sister leaving town.* & Mark Cresswell (g), Helen O'Hara (vi), Bob Noble (k), Andy Brown (b), Nick France (d). 24/1/90 MV5 PW MPK

STEVE TILSTON
27/10/71 PEEL *The highway, Reaching out, Don't let it get you down (& All in a dream, 29/12/71).* Steve Tilston (ag,v). 20/9/71 PH JW BC [M: R2]

24/2/72 DRUMMOND *One man band, I feel fine, Falling, Coming into love (& Mama please talk to your daughter, 20/4/72).* 16/2/72 MV5 MB MH&MF

1/6/73 SEQUENCE *Room with a view, Money honey, City life, Time is your jailer.* 10/5/73 LH1 JM *

8/10/73 HARRIS *Make time for love, The greening wind, Here you go again (& Do what you please, Scrape off the paint, 26/11/73).* & 2 (unknown). 3/10/73 LH1 JG * Later recorded three In Concerts.

TIME FLIES
26/1/81 SKINNER *Change, Losing sleep, Dancing tonite, Go.* Rob Parnell (bv), Mark Longden (lgv), Peter Newton (rgv), Paul Mullineux (dv). 2/1/81 LH1 DG PW

TIME UK
17/10/83 JENSEN *All quiet on the western front, Puppets don't bleed, Seeds of the new frontier, You make it sound easy.* Rick Buckler (d), Jimmy Edwards (g,lv),

Danny Kustow (g), Ray Simone (g,bkv), Nick South (b). 6/10/83 MV4 JWI KW

TIMON
20/4/70 FERRIS *I'm just a travelling man, Better not say you love me now, The eye in the pond (& Who needs a king, 15/6/70).* Timon (gv) '& Ronald Cole for 2 musicians'. 31/3/70 PH BA *

Trial broadcast TX 27/12/69 had been as guest on Moody Blues Show, prod JG.

22/2/71 HARRIS *I'm not important, Who's been knocking at my window, Who are you with your magic blowing.* & (b), (d) unknown. 9/2/71 MV5 JM JWH

TIN MACHINE
13/8/91 GOODIER *A big hurt, Baby universal, Stateside, If there was something, Heaven's in here.* David Bowie (gv), Reeves Gabrels (lg), Tony Sales (bv), Hunt Sales (d). Live from MV5 MR~PL&AA

TINTAGEL
20/1/71 NIGHT RIDE *Eastern queen, Where the boats land, Adult tree ballad.* Jed Stone (p), Robin Stone (g), Len Platt (perc), Dick Jones (b), Keith Washington (gv), Alison Martin (v), P.J. (v). 30/12/70 PS ARD *

16/3/72 DRUMMOND *Cain again, In space, In honour of Sykes, The cold song.* Kent Parker (lgv) r. R. Stone, Platt, Martin. 6/3/72 MV5 MB MH&MF

21/9/72 DRUMMOND *I know how you feel, Salt sea ploughman, Banks of green willow, Captain's all.* Steve Moorby (g) r. Parker; & Vern Cochrane. 6/9/72 MV4 MB MH&MF

TIPPA IRIE
8/7/85 LONG *Is it really happening to me, Football hooligans, Lyric maker, Complain neighbour.* Tippa Irie (v), Trevor 'Seal' Salmon (b), Patrick Donegan (g), Brian Campbell (k), Anthony Ward (d). 26/6/85 MV5 BYA MPK

KEITH TIPPETT
26/9/70 TOP GEAR *Thoughts to Geoff/Five. after dawn/Green and orange night park.* Keith Tippett (p), Mark Charig (cnt), Elton Dean (al,sxl), Nick Evans (tb), Roy Babbington (b), Brian Spring (d). 25/8/70 MV4 JW *

Tippett's original group had debuted live on R1 Jazz Club 8/1/69.

21/1/72 PEEL *Chugging brown, Yellow buzz, Mauve ballade (& Topless air-pockets, 3/3/72).* Trio. 5/1/72 T1 JM *

Muir had recorded Tippett 4/1/71 CM, TX 26/4/71 Jazz in Britain R3.

TIR NA NOG
26/8/71 HENRY *Maggie's farm, Five a day, Dante, Boatsong.* Leo O'Kelly (g,bjv), Sonny Condell (g,bjv). 18/8/71 MV4 MB MH&MF

Duo's debut rec'd 6/5/71 PS, TX 16/5 John Peel's Sunday Concert; then 31/7, live on Country meets folk.

9/6/72 PEEL *Blue bottle star, Piccadilly, Come and see the show, The same thing happening.* 1/5/72 PH JM JWH

25/9/72 HARRIS *Sad old Kristina, So freely, Aberdeen Angus, Strong in the sun.* 5/9/72 MV5 JG *

17/10/72 PEEL *Teeside, Going away, Strong in the sun, In the morning, I wanna roo you.* 4/9/72 PH JW BC

1/2/73 PEEL *Cinema, Free ride, Most magical, In the morning.* 15/1/73 LH1 BA *

23/4/73 HARRIS *Cinema, The wind is high, Free ride (& Love lost, 2/7/73).* 28/3/73 LH1 PR *

13/11/73 PEEL *Free ride, Today we flew, Backwater a while, Better off at home.* 23/10/73 LH1 TW *

TOAD THE WET SPROCKET
27/6/80 FRI. ROCK *Just another game, Rock and roll runner, One glass of whiskey, Big deal.* Mick Mustafa (v), Martin Wightwick (d), Peter Austin (b), Curly (g). 14/5/80 * TW *

TOBRUK
22/10/82 FRI. ROCK *Wild on the run, Motel love, Rage of angels, The show must go on.* Alan Vallance (d), Mick

Newman (g), Nigel Evans (g), Jem Davis (k), Steve Woodward (bv), Snake (v). 8/10/82 * TW DD

TOE FAT
2/3/70 CASH *Bad side of the moon, I done told ya (3/3), Turns out like the heat (4/3), That's my love for you (5/3).* Cliff Bennett (v), Lee Kerslake (d), John Glasscock (g), Ken Hensley (g). 19/2/70 MV5 c.RB *

23/3/70 WOGAN *Bad side of the moon, I can't believe (24/3), Born to be wild (25/3).* 11/3/70 AO2 c.DMI *

21/4/70 HARDING *The idol, Nobody, I love everybody, Gone.* 14/4/70 MV5 MB MH&MF

13/10/70 HARDING *Three time loser, A new way, Midnight sun.* Alan Kendall (lg), Brian Glasscock (d) r. Kerslake, Hensley. 6/10/70 MV5 MB MH&MF

TOKYO BLADE
19/10/84 FRI. ROCK *Someone to love, Lovestruck, Breakout, Night of the blade.* Vic Wright (v), John Wiggins (g), Andy Boulton (g,bkv), Steve Pierce (d), Andy Writon (b,bkv). 14/9/84 MV4 TW DD

TOMORROW, FEATURING KEITH WEST
1/10/67 TOP GEAR *Three jolly little dwarfs, My white bicycle, Revolution, Real life penut dream.* Keith West (v), John 'Twink' Alder (d), Steve Howe (lg), John Wood (b). 21/9/67. (contract says 18/9) MV4 BP PR

West & Wood's previous band, The In Crowd, passed a trial b'cast on Sat. Club 5/65; then no bookings until this.

4/2/68 TOP GEAR *Blow up, Strawberry fields forever, Now your time has come, The incredible journey of Timothy Chase.* 31/1/68 MV4 BP PR

TOO MUCH TEXAS
8/8/88 PEEL *Jayne, Anchor, Rogue, Harp.* Tom (gv), Gordon (g), Raymond (b), Lawrence (d). 24/7/88 MV5 DG MA

TOOLS YOU CAN TRUST
12/10/83 PEEL *The feud, Working and shopping†, Show your teeth, Houses and tools.* Ben Stedman (bg,d,tps), Rob Ward (v,perc,tps); & Eddie Fenn & Colin Larn (d). 8/10/83 MV4 DG MR

† On 'Manchester - so much to answer for' SFRCD202.

11/4/84 PEEL *Ranters and preachers, Messy body thrust, Cut a new seam, Blowin' up a storm.* & Fenn (d), Claire Wilkinson (perc). 21/3/84 MV5 PSM NG&TD

5/12/84 PEEL *A knock for the young, Crammed down the throat, Shazam/Sign of the swinging lightbulb.* & Phil Hughes (g,tp,perc), Jill Richardson (d,perc), Martin Herring (d,perc). 27/11/84 MV5 MRD *

TOOTS AND THE MAYTALS
31/8/87 LONG *You know who I am, The whole world turning, Hard road, Daddy.* Toots Hibbert (v), Prof. Memphis Foley (g), Webster Brixton (k), Franklyn Dunn (d), Winston Grennan (d), & Leba, Melanie & Jenieve Hibbert (bkv). 19/8/87 MV4 PW MPK&FK

TOP
17/2/91 PEEL† *No 1 dominator, Feel good, When the summer's gone.* Alan Wills (d), Paul Cavanagh (gv), Joe Fearon (b). 31/1/91 MV5 DG MWT&PL

† On 10-inch of 'Buzzin' Island 10ISP504.

TORANAGA
8/7/88 FRI. ROCK *Sentenced, Execution, Soldiers be brave, Dealers in death.* Mark Duffy (v), Andy Mitchell (g), 'Burt' Burton (b), Steve Todd (d). 17/6/88 * PW DD

TORMÉ
8/11/85 FRI. ROCK *Wild west, Turn out the lights, My baby loves a vampire, Teenage kicks.* Bernie Tormé (gv), Ian Whitewood (dv), Chris Heilmann (bv), Phil Lewis (lv). 18/9/85 MV4 TW MC

TORTOISE CORPSE
15/6/90 FRI. ROCK *Efnisien, The legacy, Loony tune (wake up mad), Atomic attack.* Tony Calvert (v), Steve Hammill (b), Tim Hamill (g), Ivan Hoe (d). 18/5/90 MV4 HP DD

TOT
7/12/87 PEEL *Barney O, The bell, To add up, Cling.* Tony Martin (ma), Debbie Turner (v), Rachel George (v). 29/11/87 * DG ME&PS

DIE TÖTEN HOSEN
10/7/84 PEEL *Hip hop bommi bop, Spiel mir das lied vom tod†/Es is vorbei†, Reisefieber†, Bis zum bitteren ende†, Hofgarten.* Trini (d), Andi (b), Breiti (rg), Kuddel (k,v,lg), Campi (v), Freddy Love (rp-1). 30/6/84 MVS DG MC
† On LP 'Liebespieler' Virgin TOT88

ALI FARKA TOURÉ
24/9/87 KERSHAW *Timbarma, Yulli, Kadi kadi, Laleyché.* Ali Farka Touré (gv,perc). 17/9/87 * DG MFR&NG
A 'dynamite' tape also exists of four songs recorded by Ali Farka in Andy Kershaw's kitchen, says Andy, probably in November that year, which he thinks was broadcast around about that time, but we haven't found a date yet.

FRANK TOVEY
23/5/88 L. KERSHAW *Hard times in the cotton mill, John Henry, The Blantyre explosion, Ricky's hand, 31 depression blues.* Frank Tovey (v), Jean-Marie Carroll (acc,g), Paul Rodden (bj), Elliot Machard (vi), Mark Jeffrey (d). 15/5/88 MV4 TdB~

TOXIC REASONS
18/11/86 PEEL *White noise, Break the bank, No pity, Harvest.* Bruce Stuckey (gv), Tufty (bv), J. J. Pearson (dv). 14/10/86 * DG MFA&TD

TRACIE
23/1/84 JENSEN *Mama never told me, Can't hold on till summer, Far from the hurting kind, Nothing happens here but you.* Tracie (v), Helen Turner (k), John Robinson (g), Steve Sidelnyk (d), Kevin Miller (b), Barbara Shaw (tp), Hilary Seabrook (sx). 12/1/84 MV4 JP *

THE TRACTORS
1/7/87 PEEL *Caesar/Caesar, Joe, Postcard story, Undertaker's waltz.* Andrew Cave (v), David Evans (g), Ian O'Connor (g), Jeffery Fitzhenry (b), Peter Ludden (d), Edwina Allcock (clo), Paul Boyce (cl). 7/6/87 * DG ME&FK

TRAFFIC
1/10/67 TOP GEAR *Smiling phases, A house for everyone, Hole in my shoe†, Coloured rain, Paper sun (& Mr Fantasy, 29/10/69).* Steve Winwood (ov), Dave Mason (gv), Jim Capaldi (dv), Chris Wood (sx,fl,v). 25/9/67 MV4 BP PR
Session later repeated on Symonds, 23-27/10/67.
† On 'I and only' BOJCD025.
24/12/67 TOP GEAR *Here we go round the mulberry bush, Heaven is in your mind, No face no name no number, Dealer, Hope I never find me there.* 11/12/67 PCI BA DT
3/3/68 TOP GEAR *Heaven is in your mind, No face no name no number* (written on PasB as 'No force...'), *Roamin' thru the gloamin' with 40,000 headmen, Blind man (& Dear Mr Fantasy, 7/4/68).* 26/2/68 PCI BA DT
Session repeated on SYMONDS week beginning 11/3/68.
30/6/68 TOP GEAR *You can all join in, Who knows what tomorrow may bring?, Feelin' alright (& Pearly Queen, 28/7/68).* 24/6/68 PCI BA *
20/7/68 SAT. CLUB *Who knows what tomorrow may bring? (& Pearly Queen, All join in, Feelin' alright, 4/8/68 HENRY.)* 15/7/68 PS KB *

THE TRANSMITTERS
21/11/79 PEEL *Dirty Harry, I fear no-one but my friends, Bird in the house, Blankety blank.* John Grimes (lv), Sam Dodson (g), Amanda de Grey (k), Sid Wells (b), Jim Chase (d). 30/10/79 MV4 JS MR
29/7/81 PEEL *Joan of Arc, Love factory, Voodoo woman in death plunge/The rent girls are coming, Dance craze.* Wells, Dodson, Dave Baby (sx), Julian Treasure (d), Rob Chapman (v). 22/7/81 MV4 DG NG

TRANSVISION VAMP
21/7/88 L. KERSHAW *Trash city, Andy Warhol's dead, Sweet thing, Sex kick.* Wendy James (v), N.C. Sayer (g), Tex Axile (kg), Dave Parsons (b), Pol Burton (d). 15/6/88 MV4 PW MPK

BOUBACAR TRAORE
13/10/91 KERSHAW *Mariamba, Kevale, Rayes ba, Adieu Pierrette.* Boubacar Traore (gv) 1/10/91 MV5 TdB~

TRAPEZE
20/7/70 SYMONDS *Your love is alright, It makes you want to cry (& Medusa,14/9/70).* Dave Holland (d), Mel Galley (gv), Glenn Hughes (bv). 7/7/70 PH BA PK&NG

THE TRASHCAN SINATRAS
27/2/90 GOODIER *Circling the circumference, Only tongue can tell, Best man's fall.* Steven Douglas (d), George Midaid (b), John Douglas (g,bkv), Paul Livingston (g), Frank Read (v). 26/2/90 MVS DG MC

TREEBOUND STORY
12/3/86 PEEL *Your kind, Forever green, My life's example, Something.* Rob Gregory (d), Paul Infanti (b), Paul Currie (gv), Richard Hawley (g). 4/3/86 MV4 DG ME

TREES
21/5/70 HENRY *Glasgarian, Nothing special, Great Silkie.* Unwin Browne (v), Barry Clarke (g), David Costa (g,bj), Bias Boshell (b), Celia Humphries (v). 14/5/70 AO2 MB MH&MF
Interesting fact #652: Celia Humphries later became Mrs Pete Drummond.
30/8/70 FOLK ON 1 *Nothing special, Streets of Derry, Polly on the shore, Little Sadie, The great silkie.* 6/8/70 MV5 FL NG
21/9/70 SYMONDS *Glasgarian, Polly on the shore, Little Sadie.* 1/9/70 PH BA NG&PK
27/1/71 R2 NIGHTRIDE *Pool, Adam's tomb/Soldiers three, Garden of Jane Delawney, Sally free and easy, Little Sadie.* 22/1/71 AO2 ARD *
8/2/71 HARRIS *Forest fire, Adam's toon, Soldiers three, Sally free and Easy.* 4/2/71 AO2orT1 JM JWH
3/2/72 DRUMMOND *Prince heathen, Tom o'bed bun, Cry of morning, Bergen polka.* Humphries, Clarke, Chuck Fleming (fd), Alan Eden (d), Barry Lyons (d), John Lifton (el). 19/1/72 MV4 MB MH&MF
Recorded another one for DRUMMOND 20/3/72, TX 30/3/72, but unfortunately that PasB is missing.
26/6/72 HARRIS *Friar Tuck gets his, The innocent hare, Van Dieman's land.* Joe O'Donnell, Chas Ambler r. Fleming, Eden, Lifton. 13/6/72 MV5 JG *

TRESPASS
2/5/80 FRI. ROCK *Stormchild, Visionary, One of these days, Live it up.* Mark Sutcliffe (lg,bkv), Paul Sutcliffe (d), Dave Crawte (rg), Chris Linscott (b), Steve Mills (lv). 2/4/80 * TW *

THE TRIFFIDS
13/11/84 PEEL *Bright lights big city, Monkey on my back, Field of glass.* Allan MacDonald (d,bkv), Martyn Casey (b), Jill Birt (o), David McComb (lv,g), Rob McComb (g,bkv,perc). 6/11/84 MV5 MRD MR
14/5/85 PEEL† *Life of crime, Lonely stretch, Chicken killer.* Graham Lee (ps) joins; & Fiona Franklyn & Sally Collins (bkv). 5/5/85 MV5 DG ME
† On Strange Fruit SFPS036.
27/5/86 PEEL *Kelly's blues, Wide open road, Kathy knows, Keep your eyes on the hole.* Six-piece. 20/5/86 MVS DG MR&JB
12/9/88 L. KERSHAW *Rent, Go home Eddie, Into the groove.* 7/9/88 MV4 PW MPK

TRILOGY
11/2/83 FRI. ROCK *Arctic life, Necrosleep, A legion in Morocco, Dark hunter.* Paul Dennis (gv), Mark Bloxsidge, Nick Szymanek. 28/1/83 * TW DD

TRIXIE'S BIG RED MOTORBIKE
24/8/82 PEEL *Invisible Boyfriend, Whatever happened to the treetops, You took him away from me, Splash of red.* Mark Litten (dm,b,g), Jim Bycroft (k,sx), Melanie Litten (v). 28/07/82 MV4 RP MR
25/8/83 PEEL *That's the end of that, One nation under a brolly, Norman and Narcissus, In Timbuktu, White Horses.* Jane Fish (clo, bkv,'claps') r. Bycroft. 17/08/83 MV4 BYA AP

THE TROJANS
7/10/87 LONG† *Maggie meets ska-gill, Jericho battle, My last meal (death row blues), Acid rain.* Peter Lambert (d), Andrew Crawford (b), Crispin Gill (g), J.T. (vi), Rudi Jones (ts), Colin Humphries (ts), Paul Besterman (hca,flg), Gary Mayall (vp,mel). 23/9/87 MV4 HP MPK&FK
† On Phoenix IZGA2006.

ROBIN TROWER
12/4/73 PEEL *Twice. removed from yesterday, Man of the world, Daydream, Summer song.* Robin Trower (g), James Dewar (bv), Reg Isidore (d). Files missing. 26/3/73 * BA BC
22/10/73 HARRIS *Day of the eagle, A little bit of sympathy, Lady love, Daydream.* 26/9/73 * JG *
18/3/74 HARRIS *The fool and me, Alathea, Rolling stoned, I can't wait much longer.* 20/2/74 LHI PR *
26/3/74 PEEL *A little bit of sympathy, Bridge of sighs, In this place, Alathea.* 5/3/74 LHI TW *
3/2/75 PEEL *Fine day, Confessing midnight, It's only money, Gonna be more suspicious.* Bill Lordan (d) r. Isidore. 28/1/75 MV4 TW *

TRUDY
5/5/88 L. KERSHAW *Countdown, Fireball, Kiss kiss kiss, Holiday planet.* Melissa Heathcote (v), Victor Champion (v), Lana Anderson (v,perc,sx), Richard Targett (d,perc,prg), Vic Austin (g), Jim Ferranti (g), Dingo McCloud (b), Graham Simmond (k,prg). 1/5/88 MV4 TdB FK

T2
30/10/70 BLACK† *Questions and answers, C.D, In circles.* Keith Cross (lg), Bernard Jinks (b), Peter Bunton (d). 14/10/70 AO2 JM JWH
† Available on Worldwide Records.

TUBEWAY ARMY
16/1/79 PEEL† *Me I disconnect from you, Down in the park, I nearly married a human.* Gary Numan (k,g,lv), Paul Gardiner (b), Jess Lidyard (d). 10/1/79 MV4 BS NBU
† On Strange Fruit SFMCD202.

MOE TUCKER
3/4/92 PEEL *Blue all the way to Canada, Fired up, Trains, Too shy.* John Sluggett (d), Daniel Hutchens (b), Sonny Vincent (g), Sterling Morrison (g), Moe Tucker (gv). 18/2/92 MV4 MR~

CHRIS STAINTON'S TUNDRA
20/8/74 PEEL *They don't know, Double crossed, The calling of the wind, I want to tell you (& Think like a child, 29/10/74).* Chris Stainton (kg), Glen Turner (g,lv), Charlie Harrison (b), Henry Spinetti (d). 6/8/74 LHI TW *
2/9/74 HARRIS *'Ard nut, What else can I say, Say you don't want it, I don't want to play.* 21/8/74 LHI JG *

THE TUNNEL FRENZIES
14/11/89 PEEL *Turn the screw, Drowning school, Getta grip, Fast dream speeding.* Simon Haden (d), Jason Bellman (bv), Mark McClenan (gv), Gary Fox (v). 29/10/89 MV3 DG ME

PIERCE TURNER
15/4/87 LONG *Going on going down, Wicklow hills, Manana Manhattan, How it shone.* Pierce Turner (kv), Schaun Tozer (k), Glyn Perrin (k), Jim Williams (g), Simon Limbrick (d), Sonia Morgan (bkv). 1/4/87 MV4 DG MPK&JB

THE TURNPIKE CRUISERS
7/12/87 LONG *Singing about war, Sleaze attack at the edge city drive in, Eddie's ghost, Assault and battery.* Richard King (v,hca), Greg Slater (g), Jim Marino (b), Kevin Andonegui (d), Karen Bentham (sx), Steven Borsley (tp). 22/11/87 MV4 PW TdB&PL

TV 21

30/10/80 PEEL *This is zero, It's me, Waiting for the drop, On the run.* Norman Rodgers (g,lv), Ally Palmer (g,bkv), Neil Baldwin (b), Colin MacLean (d). 22/10/80 MV4 BS. NG

2/2/81 SKINNER *Snakes and ladders, Change, Instinct (the hidden voice), When I scream.* Rodgers, Palmer, Baldwin, Ali 'Angel' Paterson (d,bkv), Troy Tate (g,bkv). 23/1/81 LH1 DG TdB

14/10/81 SKINNER *Something's wrong, Attention span, It feels like it's starting to rain, Ideal way of life.* Dave Hampton (k,tp) r Tate. 13/9/81 MV4 DG MPK

21/12/81 PEEL *All join hands, My chance, Omei, BB's in town.* 12/12/81 MV4 DG MR

TWA TOOTS

31/10/83 PEEL† *A new depression, Yo-yo, Don't play 'A rainy night in Georgia', It's a lovely day.* Philippa Richmond (gv), Sara Brown (bv); & Will Cassell (d), Frank Brown (Sarah's Father) (tb). 22/10/83 MV4 DG MR
† On Strange Fruit SFPS010.

TWANG

12/2/86 PEEL *Big dry out†, Eight at a time, Lawsuit man, Cold tongue bulletin.* Leonard Penrose (d), John Sargeant (b), David Hindmarsh (g), Andy Ladd (v). 2/2/86 MV5 DG ME
† On 'Manchester - so much to answer for' SFRCD202.

17/9/86 PEEL *Every home should have one, This is intrusion, What's the rap?!, Here's lukewarm.* 7/9/86 * DG ME

3/2/88 PEEL *Work the word, Snapback, Yo-ho-delic.* Albert Walton (d) r. Penrose. 24/1/88 * DG MA&ME

TWELFTH NIGHT

23/11/84 FRI. ROCK *Kings and queens, C.R.A.B., The creepshow, Take a look.* Brian Devoil (d), Andy Revell (g), Andy Sears (v), Rick Battersby (k), Clive Mitten (b). 12/10/84 Great Yarmouth TW DD

20TH CENTURY STEEL BAND

19/12/75 PEEL *Heaven and hell is on earth, Endless vibrations, Number one, Love's theme.* Luciano Bravo (pn), Gideon Rodgers (pn) Bubbles Oliver (pn, md, lv-2 only)), Winston Finlay (pn), Godfrun Moore (pn), Martin Farren (pn), Mikey Brumont (pn), Colin Moore (d), Trampas Williams (cga,perc,lv-1 only). 11/11/75 MV4 TW *

TWENTY FLIGHT ROCKERS

9/10/85 LONG *Fall in love with you, Dreams that kill, Everybody knows, Tower block rock, Punishment and crime, Weekend revolution.* Gary Twinn (lv), Mark Laff (d), Ian McKean (g), Jeff Vine (b). Live from MV5 BYA *

21 GUNS

2/2/81 PEEL *21 guns, Dark night, Ambition rock.* Trevor Evans (k), Johnny Rex (d) Kevin Turner (b), Stuart (g), Gary 'Judge' Chambers (v). Rec. date unknown. Produced by Neville Staples PRIV * *

25TH OF MAY

24/6/91 GOODIER *What's going on, It's all right, Don't sit down, Things are getting better.* Steve Swindelli (v), Ed Garbett (gv), Nigel Cope (b), James Mathias (sc), Jabba (perc,d), Steve Cowell (k). 1/6/91 MV5 MC~

10/8/91 PEEL *Made in the USA, Crackdown, Stuff the right to vote.* 2/6/91 * DG AM&ME

23 SKIDOO

23/9/81 PEEL *Retain control, Macaw gungah, View from here, Four note base.* Fritz, Alex, Johnny, Sam, Tom, Tim, Tim, Richard. 16/9/81 MV4 CL NG

THE TWINKLE BROTHERS

1/10/81 PEEL *I'm longing for you, Rasta pon top, Me no you, Never get burned.* Norman Grant (dv), Eric Bernard (kv), Derrick Brown (bv), Ralston Grant (rgv), Karl Hyatt (perc,v), Ashton Grant (lg), Lloyd Willacy (lg), Donovan Black (perc,v). 23/9/81 MV4 CL NG

THE TWINSETS

20/1/82 PEEL *Stranded in the jungle, Johnny come home,*

I'll remember you, Suspicious minds. Rory Hall (g), Norman Bell (b), Stuart Wright (d), Gay & Rachel Spankie (v). 6/1/82 MV4 KH NG

4/11/82 PEEL *Zippo, Sophisticated boom boom, Talk, Out of nowhere, Heartbeat.* Gaye & Rachel, Hall, Nick Haines (g,p), Dru Farmer (d). 16/10/82 * DG MR

9/11/83 PEEL *Too too much, Glittering new day, Crush, Meant to be, Girl on her own.* G. & R. Bell, Hall, Mike Berry (g), Dave Mack (d). 29/10/83 MV4 DG MR

TWISTED NERVE

2/11/81 PEEL *When I'm alone, Never say goodbye, Indecision, Five minutes of fame, We don't need them.* Keith Hamilton (d), Gordon Munro (v), Bill McNair (g), Norbert Bass-Bin (b). 17/10/81 MV4 DG TdB

TWO TRIBES

7/2/92 FRI. ROCK *Groove, Truth to come, File under rock, What do they want from us.* Ashton (v), Paul Gold (b), Jon McLoughlin (g), Rod Quinn (d). 25/10/91 MV5 TW DD&MC

2TV

5/9/79 PEEL *Mary Thompson, Dear heart, Johnny plays up, Kids on the street.* Steve Speight (gv), Steve Barrass (g,bkv), Chris Speight (b), Steve Gale (d). 22/8/79 MV4 TVD NG

TWO TWO

8/1/83 LONG *Africa, (Ngine Nawma Hii) Kwagayo, Just us three, Pijin Billy, Two Two jingle, Janice Long.* * 6/1/83 PHM cJL *

TYGERS OF PAN TANG

11/4/80 FRI. ROCK *Euthanasia, Don't take nothing, Wild catz, Don't touch me there.* Jess Cox (v), Robert Weir (g), Brian Dick (d), Rocky (b). 5/3/80 * TW *

6/9/85 FRI. ROCK *Waiting, Desert of no love, Women in cages, The wreck-age.* Dick, Jon Deverill (v), Steve Lamb (g), Neil Shepherd (g), Dave Donaldson (b), Pete Whalan (k). 23/8/85 MV4 TW DD

THE TYLA GANG

6/6/77 PEEL *Young lords, Don't shift the gear, Wizz kid, Speedball morning.* * 30/5/77 MV4 CL *

20/10/77 PEEL *On the street, Dust on the needle, Styrafoam, Don't turn your radio on.* Sean Tyla (g,v), Bruce Irvine (lg), Brian Turrington (b), Michael Desmarais (d). 4/10/77 MV4 JG MR

15/8/78 PEEL *It's gonna rain, Moonlight ambulance, Spanish Streets, No roses.* Ken Whaley (b) r. Turrington. Billed as 'Sean Tyla' only. 9/8/78 MV4 BS NG

TYRANNOSAURUS REX

5/11/67 TOP GEAR *Scenscof † Child star, Highways, Hot rod mama, Dwarfish trumpet blues (& Pictures of purple people, 4/2/68).* Marc Bolan (gv), Steve Peregrine-Took (perc). 30/10/67 PCI BA PR

13/3/68 NIGHT RIDE *Beginning of doves, The wielder of words, The wizard, Afghan woman, Hippy gumbo, Frowning Atuahallpa.* 28/2/68 S2 JM RD

24/3/68 TOP GEAR *Knight, Debora, Afghan woman, Frowning Atuahallpa (& Mustang, Strange orchestra, 3/5/68).* 11/3/68 PCI BA *

14/7/68 TOP GEAR *Stacey Grove, One inch rock, Salamanda palaganda, Eastern spell (& Wind quartets, 25/8/68).* 11/6/68 PCI BA DT

10/11/68 TOP GEAR *The friends, Conesuela, The seal of seasons, The evenings of damask (& The travelling tragition, Trelawny lawn, 22/12/68).* 14/10/68 PCI BA *
Next, contracted to record R1 Club 21/11/68 PS, no TX date in records.

11/5/69 TOP GEAR *Once upon the seas of Abyssinia†, Nijinsky hind, Misty coast of Albany†, Chariots of silk† (& Iscariot†, 15/6/69).* 5/5/69 PH JW TW

22/11/69 TOP GEAR† *Fist heart mighty down dart, Pavilions of the sun, A day laye, By the light of the magical moon.* Mickey Finn (perc) r. Peregrine-Took. 17/11/69 PH JW TW

Next appeared as last minute guests on 1st ever Peel Sunday Show Concert, rec'd 1/1/70 PS, TX 4/1/70.

25/6/70 HENRY *One inch rock, Jewel, Elemental child.* 18/6/70 AO2 MB MH&MF

7/11/70 TOP GEAR° *Ride a white swan†, Jewel†, Elemental child, Sun eye†.* Band re-named itself 'T-Rex' at the time of this session 26/10/70 MV4 JW *
° On Strange Fruit SFPS031; 'Sun eye' also on 'Before the Fall' SFRCD203.

16/11/70 HARRIS *My baby's like a cloud form, The visit, Elemental child, Ride a white swan, Is it love, Funk music.* & Tony Visconti (b). 6/11/70 MV5 JM JWH

19/12/70 DLT *Summertime Blues†, Ride a white swan, Jewel (& Hot love†, 21/12/70 R1 CLUB).* Visconti out. 9/12/70 MV5 c.PWI *.
Recorded 2nd Peel Sunday Concert 10/12/70 PS, TX 20/12/70.

29/3/71 R1 CLUB *Beltane Walk†, Hot Love, Seagull woman* (2-'Network' session: based on Private Tape). 9/3/71 PH PR DP

23/8/71 HARRIS *Sailors of the highway†, Girl†, Cadillac, Jeepster, Life's a gas†.* 3/8/71 T1 JM *
†† On 'Across the airwaves' Cube/Dakota Records. The session dates in the sleeve notes are incorrect in several places [M: daytime network sessions only, reworking of own studio master tapes].

THE TYRREL CORPORATION

6/7/92 GOODIER *Lies before breakfast, The bottle, Cheated, Ballad of British justice.* Joe Watson (lv), Niel Robinson (d), Tony Barry (k), Paul Moran (k), Paul Gendler (g), Laurence Parry (perc,md), Valerie Chalmers & Emma Whittle (bkv). 23/5/92 MV5 MC AR

TYTAN

26/3/82 FRI. ROCK *Cold bitch, The watcher, The far side of destiny, Blind men and fools.* Dave Dufort (d), Kevin Riddles (bk), Gary Owens (g), Stevie Gibbs (g), Kal Swan (v). 26/2/82 * TW DD

UB40

2/1/80 PEEL *Food for thought, 25 per cent, King†.* Jimmy Brown (d,bkv), Alistair Campbell (rg,lv), Robin Campbell (lg,bkv), Earl Falconer (b), Norman Hassan (perc), Brian Travers (sx), Micky Virtue (k). 12&18/12/79 MV4 JS NG&MR
† On 'I and only' BOJCD025. Next bookings, recording for David Jensen 11/2/80, and Andy Peebles 20/3/80.

5/5/81 SKINNER *One in ten, Present arms, Neon haze, Sardonicus.* Astro (tp) joins. 23/4/81 LH1 JS *

25/1/82 PEEL *Politician, I won't close my eyes, Love is all is all right, Prince Baldhead meets gymslip and the school girls at the chemist.* 9/1/82 MV4 DG MR

27/7/82 JENSEN *So here I am, Forget the cost, The prisoner, Don't do the crime.* 8/7/82 MV4 JS *

25/4/83 JENSEN *Red red wine, Please don't make me cry, Nkomo ago go (instrumental).* 14/4/83 MV4 JP GP
Several other bookings, mainly Network sessions and concerts, contracted 1982-83.

UFO

21/10/70 NIGHT RIDE *Loving cup, Follow you home, Come away Melinda.* Michael Bolton (lg), Pete Way (b), Andy Parker (d), Phil Mogg (v). 30/9/70 AO1 ARD *
'Borderline pass' from panel.

13/7/74 ROCK ON *Doctor doctor, Built for comfort, Give her the gun, Oh my.* Paul Chapman (g), Michael Schenker (g) r. Bolton. 8/7/74 LH1 CL MF&NGR
Group rec'd In Concert at HP 6/6/74, TX 15/6/74.

28/10/74 HARRIS *Time on my hands, Give her the gun, Rock bottom.* 2/10/74 MV4 JG *

17/6/77 PEEL *Too hot to handle, Lights out, Try me.* Paul Raymond (kg) r. Chapman. 1/6/77 MV4 MB NG
This line-up, according to contracts, had done 2nd In Concert at PS, 11/12/75, TX 24/1/76.

UGLY MUSIC SHOW
20/1/91 PEEL *Been here before, White horses, Basted, The pie is the limit.* Jim Robinson (lg,dm), Angus Jenner (rgv), Mike Hammer (b). 18/12/90 MV5 MR~

UK DECAY
29/4/80 PEEL *Rising from the dead, Unwind tonight, Sexual, For my country.* Abbo (v), Steve Spon (gk), Martyn 'Segovia' Smith (b), Steve Harle (d). 22/4/80 MV4 BS MR

5/8/81 PEEL *Last in the house of flames, Stage struck, Glass ice, Duel.* Dutch (b) r. Smith. 27/7/81 MV4 TW *

UK SUBS
31/5/78 PEEL *I couldn't be you, Tomorrow's girls, Disease, C.I.D., Stranglehold.* Charles Harper (v), Pete Davies (d), Paul Barker (b), Nick Garratt (g). 23/5/78 MV4 MB MR

15/9/78 PEEL *World war, TV blues, Another kind of blues, All I wanna know, Totters.* 6/9/78 MV4 MR~

28/6/79 PEEL *Killer, Crash course, Lady Esquire, I.O.D., Emotional blackmail.* 19/6/79 MV4 BS MR

THE UKELELE ORCHESTRA OF GREAT BRITAIN
5/11/87 KERSHAW *Born to be wild, Presto tange, Candy says, Orange blossom special.* George Hinchcliffe, Andy & Jo Astle, Marianne Lux, Brian Stapleton, Nony Ardill, Caroline Fitton, Mandy Fitton, Dave Suich, Liane Kordan, James Marsh (uk), Simond Edwards (bass uk). 22/10/87 * DG NG&SC

12/11/89 KERSHAW *Silver machine, In C, A perfect day, I who have nothing.* Dave (lv-1), Liane, George (lv-4), Mary, Andy, Jo, Kitty (lv-3), Brian, Caroline, Hank (b) (all-uk). 10/8/89 MV3 DG NG

THE UKRAINIANS
16/11/91 PEEL *Rospryahaite, Ti Moyi Radoshchi, Dity Plachut, Teper Hovorymo.* Len Liggins (vi,v), Roman Remeynes (mnd,v), Stephen Pasicznyk (acc,v), Peter Solowka (g,mnd,v), Chris Harrap (b), Dave Lee (d). 24/9/91 MV3 JB~PL

ULI JON ROTH
8/3/85 FRI. ROCK *Starlight, Neptunian love.* Uli Jon Roth (g). 8/2/85. MV4 TW DD

FRANCISCO ULLOA
18/7/92 KERSHAW *Canto de hacha, Majando cafe, Norcita, Arturo al monte, Cuantas veces he sufrido.* Francisco Ulloa (acc,lv), Jose Batista Rafael Tupete (sx), Giovanni de Susus Arias (cga), Juan Felipe Rozon (guirra), Jesus Juan Antonio (tmba,v), Rafael Peralta Lopez (pinguino bass,v). 10/5/92 MV3 ME~

ULTRA MARINE
22/5/92 PEEL *Saratoga, Nova Scotia, Honey, Pansy.* Ian Cooper (g), Paul Hammond (b), Charlie May (k), Paul Johnson (d), Phil James (hca). 7/4/92 MV4 MR~ SA

ULTRAVOX
28/11/77 PEEL† *My sex, The man who dies every day, Artificial life, Young savage.* Stevie Shears (g), Chris Cross (b,bkv), Warren Cann (d,bkv), Billy Currie (k,vi), John Foxx (v). 21/11/77 MV4 TW DD
   † On Strange Fruit SFPS047.

UNCLE DOG
16/12/71 DRUMMOND *Mystery truth, Smoke, Old hat.* John Pearson (d), Phil O'Crookes (lg), Carol Grimes (v), John Porter (b) David Skinner (p). 8/12/71 MV4 MB MH&MF

28/3/72 PEEL *Boogie with me, You need somebody, Old hat, Sweet white wine.* O'Crookes out; Terry Stannard (d) r. Pearson. 14/3/72 MV4 * *

1/9/72 PEEL *River road, Boogie with me, Sometimes.* George Butler (d) r. Stannard; Paul (surname unknown) (b) r. Porter; & Dick Horner (lg), Martin Stone (g), Humphrey Curtis (sx,fl). 21/8/72 T1 JM *

16/11/72 PEEL *River road, We got time, Old hat (& Lose me, 7/12/72).* 13/11/72 LH1 BA BC

UNDER NEATH WHAT
24/2/89 FRI. ROCK *Straight ahead money, Painted ID, Like an animal, Eggs bacon coffee and suicide.*
   * 27/1/89 MV4 TW *

UNDER TWO FLAGS
29/9/83 JENSEN *Land of the rising guns, Masks, Can't take love, The feeling of resistance.* Gavin (v), Soapy (gv), Didz (g), Martin (b), Wendy (d). 15/9/83 MV4 JP MR

UNDERGROUND ZERO
17/8/84 FRI. ROCK *Never reach the stars, 7 light years, Between worlds.* Carl Dawson (g), Andrew Rix (bv), Adrian Rix (k), Paul Holden (g), Sean Holden (d), Judi Griggs (v). 3/8/84 MV4 TW DD

THE UNDERTONES
16/10/78 PEEL *Get over you, Top 20, She can only say no, Male model.* Feargal Sharkey (lv), John O'Neill (rg), Damian O'Neill (lg,bkv), Billy Doherty (d), Mickey Bradley (b,bkv). Rec. date unknown. DWN SN~

5/2/79 PEEL† *Listening in, Family entertainment, Billy's third, Here comes the summer.* 22/1/79 MV4 BS DD

23/1/80 PEEL† *Girls that don't talk, Tear proof, What's with Terry?, Rock'n roll.* 21/1/80 MV4 BS DD

9/12/80 PEEL *The positive touch, You're welcome, When Saturday comes.* Rec. date unknown PRIV * *

26/8/81 SKINNER *Song number one, Bye-bye baby blue, Beautiful friend, Just like Romeo and Juliet.* 16/8/81 MV4 DG ME

7/12/82 PEEL† *Untouchable, The love parade, Luxury, The sin of pride.* 8/11/82 * * *
   † On Strange Fruit SFRCD103.

UNHOLY TRINITY
6/2/86 KERSHAW *Don't ask me, Hey momma keep your big mouth shut, No respect, Can't you say goodbye.* Del Bartle (g), Jeff Lucas (b), Kevin Murphy (d). 16/1/86 Y2 SP PSM

UNICORN
10/12/73 HARRIS *Brand new bag, Sleep song, Ballad of John and Julie.* Patrick Martin, Kenneth Baker, Pete Perrier, Kevin Richard Smith (g,mnd). 28/11/73 LH1 JG *
   Previously recorded In Concert, 10/71.

8/7/74 HARRIS *Ooh mother, In the gym, Electric night.* 5/6/74 LH1 JG *

24/9/74 PEEL *Nightingale crescent, Take it easy, Autumn wine, Electric night.* [M]. 3/9/74 LH1 * BC

UNITED NATIONS
6/6/85 INTO THE MUSIC *You cheated, Sound of the 1980s, Welcome to the real-time world, The first move.* Christopher Mooney (d), Peter Hankey (b), Gary Davies (g), Christopher Stonier (k), Paul McCafferty (v). 11/5/85 MV4 DG MC

UNITY
24/8/82 JENSEN *Crab race, Culture them, Reggae music, Mark of the Nazarene.* Andrew Griffiths (d), Anthony Swanson (b,bkv), Tracey Whittingham (rg,bkv), Danny McCoy (lg), Owen Bloomfield (k,bkv), Ivor Dowdie (perc,bkv), Lloyd Pusey (lv). 15/8/82 MV4 DG ME

UNSANE
14/7/91 PEEL *Organ donor/Street sweeper/Jungle music/Exter ...?, Bath.* Charlie Ondras (d), Pete Shore (bv), Chris Spencer (gv). 21/5/91 MV5 TdB~ DMC

UNSEEN TERROR
11/4/88 PEEL† *Incompatible/Burned beyond recognition, Oblivion descends/Divisions, Voice your opinion, Strong enough to change/Odie's revenge/It's my life.* Shane Embury (d), Mitchell Dickinson (bg,v-4,5,7), Micky Harris (v-1,2,3,6,8). 22/3/88 * DG MR&SC&FB
   † On Strange Fruit SFPS069.

UPP
3/4/74 PEEL *Bad stuff, I give it to you, It's a mystery, Get down in the dirt.* Jim Copley (d), Andy Clarke (kv), Stephen Amazing (b), Andy Powell (g-4 only). 27/3/75 TW *

UPTOWN HAWAIIANS
29/10/89 KERSHAW *Sweet Leilani, Hawaiian bathtub melody, Moana chimes, Blues for Honolulu.* Mike Cooper (slg,mnd,v), Cyril Lefebvre (dob), Lol Coxhill (sx), Olly Blanchflower (db), Steve Beresford (p,sy,v). 3/10/89 MV5 DG MR&JB

URIAH HEEP
12/5/70 HARDING *Dreamare, Gypsy, Come away Melinda.* Mick Box (gv), David Byron (lv), Paul Newton (b), Ken Hensley (k), Nigel Ollson (d). 5/5/70 MV5 MB MH&MF
   'Competent rather progressive hard rock group'; passed by Audition panel.

12/10/70 HARRIS *Salisbury, Bird of prey.* 2/10/70 MV4 JM *

1/6/71 HARDING *I wanna be free, Love machine, Shadows of grief.* Ian Clarke (d) r. Ollson. 24/5/71 MV5 MB MH&MF
   Despite contracts, Clarke more likely than Ollson to have appeared 2/10/70; could also have been Keith Baker. (source: Pete Frame's Rock Family Trees).

28/10/71 DRUMMOND *Look at yourself, What should be done, July morning.* 20/10/71 MV4. MB MH&MF

UROPA LULA
3/8/82 JENSEN *Talking loud and saying nothing, Timber fall I, Here's a medal, Fell upon a jewel.* Andrew Edge (d), Alan Dias (b), David Lloyd (gkv). 25/7/82 MV4 DG MFA

USI
6/10/89 FRI. ROCK *Step inside love, Get up and Dance, In love again, The 2nd time.* Steve Johnson (g,lv), Paul Johnson (b), Neil Anthony (d). 22/9/89 MV5 TW&HP DD&EL

UT
29/5/84 PEEL *Confidential, Absent farmer, Tell it (atomic energy pattern), Phoenix.* Nina Canal (gbdv), Jacqui Ham (vgd), Sally Young (vgd). 15/5/84 MV5 MRD TdB

6/1/88 PEEL *Evangelist, Hotel, Safe burning.* 22/12/87 * DG DD&PL

U2
Late 79? Or recorded 26/11/80 POWELL *Father is an elephant, I will follow, Twilight, 11 o'clock tick-tock.* Bono (v), The Edge (g), Adam Clayton (b), Larry Mullen (d). Rec. date unknown. PHM TH DFW
   How Bono made his first broadcast from a disused gents toilet in Hulme. A date for this (possibly) first session has proved elusive so far, but it definitely happened. Tony Hale booked them on the strength of '11 o'clock tick-tock', and persuaded Dave Atkey, Peter Powell's producer, to take the session. 'No-one much except Tony was behind them then', recalls their Northern plugger Tony Michaelides. Bono wandered round the upper circle of the Playhouse, and found the old gents. Then DFW pointed out it had once been used as the echo chamber for the Northern Dance Orchestra (a mike would pick up the sound from a speaker). Cables were run up there, and Bono was shut in with nothing save the mike and the old wall tiles for company.

22/9/80 READ *I will follow, Electrico (23/9), An Cat Dubh (24/9), Into the heart (TX date unknown).* 18/9/80 * * *
   Files suggest a session booked for POWELL, recorded on 26/11/80, but broadcast has so far proved untraceable. It is possible, despite TH & DFW's memories, that this was the Manchester session.

8/12/80 BURNETT *I will follow†* [Network session]. 2/12/80 MV5 PW *
   † on 'I and only' BOJCD025.

8/9/81 SKINNER *Boy girl, With a shout, I threw a brick through a window, Scarlet.* 3/9/81 MV4 DG MR&MFA
   Following week, 16/9, recorded In Concert PS, TX 3/10. And a contract exists for a recording for POWELL at BBC Birmingham on 28/9/81, but, again, broadcast is untraceable.

31/1/83 JENSEN *Like a song, Sunday bloody Sunday, Surrender.* Extra instrumentation: Bono (g), The Edge (k,bkv). 23/1/83 MV4 DG ME

17/10/90 CAMPBELL *Desire, Under a blood red sky.* 7/10/88 MV4 c.PWI MWT

THE V CORPORATION
18/6/86 Long *Wonderful thing, Cry king, Destruction business.* Anna Ross (v), Nick Bagnall (b), Ali Reay (g), Stu Haikney (d), Pete Greenaway (sx,perc), Gary Cowey (k). 11/6/86 MV4 BYA MPK

VACANT HEARTS
29/3/82 Jensen *Dream delay, I say it's wrong, You are my revolution, Leisure zone.* Russ Harrison (gv), Roger Crombie (g),Ian Roberts (d), Peter Fry (b), John Slater (perc), Peter Barratt (k). 22/1/82 PHM * *

VAMPIRE BATS FROM LEWISHAM
19/2/82 Jensen *Ordinary scheme, Real lovers, Petrol, Milk with knives (instrumental).* Steve Bolton (gv), Bernie Clarke (k), Bill Wainwright (b), Laurie Latham (perc), Mark Pinder (d). 4/2/82 MV4 JS *

VAN DER GRAAF GENERATOR
29/12/68 Top Gear *People you were going to, Afterwards, Necromancer, Octopus.* Peter Hammill (v), Keith Ellis (b), Hugh Banton (o), Guy Evans (d).
18/11/68 MV4 BA PRorBC
7/9/69 Symonds On Sunday *Reawakening, Afterwards.*
26/8/69 PCI c.PWI *
7/2/70 Top Gear *Darkness, After the flood.* 27/1/70 MV4 JW *
24/10/70 Top Gear *Lost, Killer.* David Jackson (ts,al,fl,v) r. Ellis. 12/10/70 PH JW BC
25/6/71 Black *Theme I, Darkness, Man erg (& Vision, 23/7/71).* 10/6/71 TI JWH&ARV
29/12/71 Peel *An epidemic of Father Christmasses, Lemmings, Refugees.* 14/12/71 MV4 *
10/7/75 Peel *Scorched earth, Sleepwalkers.* 3/7/75 MV4 TW *
20/4/76 Peel *Still life, La rossa.* 1/4/76 MV4 TW *
22/11/76 Peel *When she comes, Masks.* 11/11/76 MV4 TW *
2/11/77 Peel *(Fragments of) A plague of lighthouse keepers/Sleepwalker's end, Cat's eye/Yellow Fever (running), The sphinx in the face.* Graham Smith (vi), Charles Dickie (clo,elp,sy,v), Nic Potter (b), r. Banton, Jackson. 24/10/77 MV4 JG *

MARINA VAN ROOY
10/4/92 Peel *All heaven's open, Honey Drip, Staying with me.* Marina Van Rooy (v), Ian Martin Wright (k), Peter Gyle (bkv), Steven Cummerson (dm,prg).
23/2/92 MV3 DG ME&GT

THE VAPORS
11/7/79 Peel *Turning Japanese, Trains, Waiting for the weekend, Cold war.* Dave Fenton (g,lv), Ed Bazalgette (gv), Steve Smith (bv), Howard Smith (d). 4/7/79 MV4 TVD NG
18/2/80 Read *America, Turning Japanese, Waiting for the weekend, Spring collection.* 18/1/80 MV4 JS *

VARDIS
29/5/81 Fri. Rock *Power under foot, Steamin' along, Love is dead, Let's go.* Steve Zodiac (gv), Alan Selway (b,bkv), Gary Pearson (d). 13/5/81 * TW *

SUZANNE VEGA
20/8/92 Campbell *Rock in this pocket†, In Liverpool†, Gypsy, When heroes go down.* Suzanne Vega (agv). Live from on-air studio, Egton House KH NF
† on CD single '99.9°F'

THE VEIL
5/11/85 Long *Twist, Is this sin, Enchanting, Heavy heart.* James Christopher (b), Andy Dakeyne (g), Marcus De Mowbray (d), Andrella (v). 23/10/85 MV5 BYA MPK

CHAMPION DOUG VEITCH
4/9/84 Peel *One black night, Banks of marble, Not the heart, Another place.* Doug Veitch (v), Tony McDermott (b), Roger Hilton (d), Bobby Valentino (fd), Alan Dunn (acc), Jim Craig (ps), James McMillan (tp), Dave Killen (tb). 7/8/84 MV5 BYA TdB
17/10/85 Kershaw *Jumping into love, Rodgers and out, Marguarita.* Martin Bell (fd), Chris Hall (acc,ml), Mick McDermott (b), Simon Elms (tp) r. Valentino, Dunn, Killen. 10/10/85 PHM DST TWN
19/3/86 Peel *Marguarita, Tears on my pillow, Rodgers and*

out, *Sweet bacchanal* & M. & T. McDermott, Craig, Hall, George Hinchcliffe (p,o), Bell (fd), Lawrence Woods (sx), Elms, Killen. 18/2/86 MV5 DG TdB

VELVET CRUSH
8/6/92 Goodier *Blind faith, Atmosphere†, Slip away†, Drive me down†.* Ric Menck (d), Paul Chastain (b,lv), Jeffrey Borchardt (g), David Gibbs (gv). 2/5/92 MV4 MA~DMC
† On EP 'Drive me down' Creation CRESCD139.

ELMER GANTRY'S VELVET OPERA
26/11/67 Top Gear *Dream starts, Reaction of a young man, Flames, Mother writes (& Long nights of summer, 7/1/68).* David Terry (v), Colin Forster (lg), Richard Hudson (d), Roy Stacey (b). 3/11/67 PH BP PR
With James Horrocks (o), group had passed audition early in 67 as 'Five Proud Walkers'.
18/12/67 Monday, Monday *Flames, I was cool, Something else.* 8/12/67 AO2 c.DGE *
27/1/68 Sat. Club *Mother writes, Flames, Mary Jane.* 16/1/68 PH BB *
8/4/68 Symonds *Air, Mary Jane (9/4), Looking for a happy life (10/4), Turn on your love light (11/4).* 22/3/68 AO2 c.RB *
27/4/68 Mark Roman *Dreamy.* 4/4/68 AO2 MB *
19/5/68 Top Gear *Fixin' to die, Mary Jane, Dreamy, Air (& Codine, 23/6/68).* 22/4/68 PCI BA PR [M]

VELVET OPERA
11/9/69 RI Club *Gypsy Fantasies, Statesboro' blues, Black Jack Davy, Hurdy gurdy man, Anna dance square.* Paul Brett (g), Johnny Joyce (gv), John Ford (b), Richard Hudson (d,sit) [Formed out of split of Elmer Gantry's Velvet Opera, 4/69]. 13/8/69 PS KB *
8/6/70 Symonds *Rattler run, Statesboro' blues, Water wheel (& Gypsy fantasy, 13/7/70).* Mickie Keen (gv) r. Brett. 19/5/70 PH BA PK&NG
New line-up had also appeared live on RI Club PS 24/2/70 & PS 29/4/70.
4/1/71 RI Club *She keeps giving me these feelings, Munich city, Move it.* Dave McTavish (v), Colin Bass (b), Mick Fincher (d), Colin Forster (lg). 24/11/70 PS PR *
Completely new line-up, save Forster, had to submit tape as Trial Broadcast. Passed.

VENOM
16/8/85 Fri. Rock *Black metal, Nightmare, Too loud for the crowd, Bloodlust.* Cronos (bv), Mantas (g), Abaddon (d). 2/8/85 MV4 TW DD

VENTURE
14/3/85 Into The Music *Herats on fire, Nightlife, Miss you, So long.* John T. Burke (d), Pete Earle (b), Oliver Wright (g), Ian Gosling (g), Mick Railton (k), Rob Cass (v). 16/2/85 MV4 DG MC

JOHN VERITY
24/3/85 Into The Music *Looking for love, Honesty and emotion, Only in a dream, Hold on to love.* John Verity (vlg), Steve Rodford (d,bkv), Terry Uttley (b,bkv), John Neill (g,bkv), Steve Thompson (k). 2/3/85 MV4 DG MC

VERVE
7/3/92 Peel† *Slide away, Superstar, 'Title unknown', Already there.* Peter Salisbury (d), Simon Jones (b), Nick McCabe (g), Richard Ashcroft (v).
13/2/92 MV5 DG NG&JB
† on Strange Fruit SFMCD214.

THE VERY THINGS
9/1/84 Peel† *Message from Disneytime, Down the final flight, Phillip's world service, Wall of fir°.* Robin Raymond (g), The Shend (bv), Disneytime (d).
17/12/83 MV4 DG MR
† On Strange Fruit SFPS0046; ° also on 'Winters of Discontent' SFRCD204.
8/12/87 Peel *Let's go out, There's a ghost in my house, She's standing still, Walking in the sand.* & Robert Holland (k), Vincent (b). 30/10/87 Rerry Street Studios, produced by Smuff & Ray Shulman. * *

THE VIBES
22/4/85 Peel *Inside out, Looking in the mirror, Egyptian thing, Judgement day.* Johnny J. Beat (d), Lloyd (b), Fuzz Fury (g), Johnny "Mother" Johnson (lg), Gaz Voola (v). 2/4/85 MV5 AJ MR

THE VIBRATORS
28/10/76 Peel *Dance to the music, Sweet sweetheart, Jenny Jenny, I'm gonna be your nazi baby, We vibrate.* Ian 'Knox' Carnochan (gv), John Ellis (g), Pat Collier (b), Jon Edwards (d). 12/10/76 MV4 JG MR
22/6/77 Peel *Petrol, Keep it clean, Baby baby, London girls, She's bringing you down.* 13/6/77 MV4 TW DD
6/3/78 Peel *Automatic lover, Destroy, Troops of tomorrow, Fall in love.* Gary Tibbs (b,bkv), Eddie (d) r. Collier, Edwards. 27/2/78 MV4 TW DD

VICE SQUAD
3/6/81 Peel *Coward†, It's a sell out†, 1981, Times they are a changing.* Beki Bondage (v), Dave Bateman (g), Mark Hambly (b), Shane Baldwin (d). 1/6/81 LHI TW DD
† On 'Riotous Assembly' LP.
21/8/81 Skinner *Living on dreams, Evil, Coward, Still dying, Resurrection.* 9/8/81 MV4 DG ME
10/5/82 Peel *Humane, Propaganda, No right of reply, Sterile.* 28/4/82 MV4 RP MC
14/3/84 Jensen *Saviour machine, You'll never know, Rest of your life, Scarred for life.* 'Lia' (v), Hambly, Bateman, Baldwin, & 'Sooty' (lg). 4/3/84 MV5 DG ME

VICTIM'S FAMILY
8/8/89 Peel *Luv letters/Balderdash, As it were/God Jerry and the PMRC, Burly Jalisco, Corona belly.* Eric (d), Larry (b), Ralph (gv). 11/7/89 MV5 DG DD

VIEW FROM THE HILL
24/7/85 Long *I want you back, No conversation, Heart to heart, Lovers confession.* Pat Patterson (gv), Steve Scipio (g,perc), Sam Kelly (d), Trevor White (bv), Angie Wynter (v). 7/7/85 MV4 BYA TdB
22/9/86 Long *On the corner, Turn out the light, For the sake of love, I'm no rebel.* Vic Martin (k) r. Scipio. 3/8/86 MV4 BYA MS

GENE VINCENT
23/11/69 DLT *Say momma, Be bop a lula, Rocky road blues, Pistol packin' mama.* Gene Vincent (v) & The Wild Angels. 16/11/69 MV4 c.PWI *
Session repeated on Dave Cash 29/12/70, & First Gear 22/8/70. Vincent previously recorded several sessions at The Playhouse, particularly for Saturday Club in 1963.
6/2/71 Top Gear *Whole lotta shakin', The day the world turned blue, Rocky road blues, Say mama.* & The Houseshakers. 25/1/71 PH JW BC
14/2/71 All Our Yesterdays *Say mama, Rocky road blues, Baby blue.* & Earl Sheridan & the Houseshakers. 3/2/71 AO2 BA NG
8/11/71 Walker† *Be bop a lula, Say Mama, Roll over Beethoven, Whole lotta shakin' going on, Distant drums.* & Richard Cole (g), Dave Bailey (k), Bob Moore (d), Charlie Harrison (b). 1/10/71 MV4 DT BTN
Vincent died 13/10/71, before session broadcast. † On Nighttracks SFNT001.

VINEGAR JOE
9/12/71 Drummond *Early Monday morning, Circles, Ride me easy, Never met a dog that took to me.* Robert Palmer (v), Elkie Brooks (v), Pete Gage (g), Tim Hinkley (p), Rob Tate (d), Terry Poole (b). 6/12/71 MV5 MB MH&MF
10/3/72 Peel *Ain't it peculiar, Leg up, Rusty red, Early morning Monday.* 22/2/72 TI JM JWH&PK
10/7/72 Harris *Bathtub pirate, What in the world are we coming to, Angel, I saw her standing there.* 20/6/72 MV5 JG *
22/11/72 Harris *Falling, So long, Whole lotta shakin', Rock and roll gypsies.* Jim Mullen (g), Mike Deacon (p), John Woods (d), Steve York (b) r. Hinkley, Tate, Poole. 1/11/72 LHI JG *
25/2/74 Harris *Dream your own dreams, Giving yourself*

away, Hunky woman (& Jesus gonna make it alright, 24/4/74) (*1, 3- 1st TX 19/1/74, ROCK ON). Pete Gavin (d), r. Woods, Mullen. 16/1/74 LHI JG *

THE VIPERS
13/2/79 PEEL *You're on your own kid, Too rough, You're so strange, Playin' the game.* Paul Boyle (lv,rg), George Sweeney (lg), Dolan (b,bkv), Dave Moloney (d). 27/2/79 MV4 TVD MR

VIRGIN DANCE
25/12/82 LONG *Are you ready, Overload, Sometimes, Time pain and tears.* * 21/12/82 PHM IW *

17/3/83 PEEL *Facts, Barriers, No disguise, Love's friends.* Kenny Dougan (rg), Graham McMaster (b), Cliff Hewitt (d), Lorraine Gardner (k), E. Hind (gv). 12/3/83 MV4 DG MC

28/7/83 JENSEN *Desire, Strangers, Overload, Night call.* David Noels (k) r. Gardner. 10/7/83 MV4 DG ME

VIRGINIA DOESN'T
18/10/79 PEEL *Sanctuary, Telephone box, Tuesday night (on a housing estate), (I'd rather) die, The smurf song, Peely.* Kev Robinson (v), Tweets Bird (g), Ratch Tuffin (g,bkv), Craig Lindsay (b,bkv), Chris Corner (d). 3/10/79 MV4 TVD NG

VIRGINIA WOLF
18/10/84 INTO THE MUSIC *Goodbye don't mean forever, Only love, For all we know, Are we playing with fire?* Dave Irving (d), Jeff Watts (b), Nick Bold (g), David Hinton (k), Chris Ousey (v). 6/10/84 MV4 DG MC

ORCHESTRE VIRUNGA WITH SAMBA MAPANGALA
5/5/91 KERSHAW *Malako, Vunjamilpa, Yembele, Marina.* Samba Mapangala (lv), Rama Athumani (sx), Nyimbi Bin Rissasi (cga,bkv), Mokili Mbenga (g), Masudi Bin Lisambola (g), Juma Abasi Maina (b), Abdalia Kodi Kassim (d). 25/4/91 MV4 DG NG&AA

26/9/92 KERSHAW *Sungura, Ikolo kolo, Unisamehe.* Mapangala, Athumani, Maina, Kassim & Twaniri Mohamed (sx), Syan Mbenza (lg), Masoudi Bavon (g), Pepe Nsunda (perc). 23/7/92 MV4 DG MPK&AA

VIRUS
14/10/88 FRI. ROCK *Testify to me, No return, Holy are the blind, Justifiable.* Coke McFinlay (g), John D. Hess (b), Tez Taylor (d), Henry Heston (gv). 15/7/88 * HP DD

VISAGE
23/6/83 JENSEN *Questions, Can you hear me?, The promise, Only the good (die young).* Steve Strange (v), Rusty Egan (d), Steve Barnacle (b,k), Andy Barnet (g,bkv), Mulligan (k). 15/5/83 MV4 DG ME

VISIONS OF CHANGE
12/5/87 PEEL *Teepees in limbo, More than now, Reciprocate, Visions of change.* Gigs (d), Spencer (b), Lee Go-Go (g), Ian (v). 21/4/87 * DG MR&TdB

THE VISITORS
14/2/80 PEEL *Pattern, Exploiting the masters, Our glass, The Orcadian.* John McVay (kv), Colin Craigie (gv), Derek McVay (bv), Keith Wilson (dv). 6/2/80 MV4 BS NG

8/1/81 PEEL *Poet's end, Compatibility, Distance.* 16/12/80 LHI JS MR

25/2/82 PEEL *Flow, Third base, Unit of acceptance.* Malcolm Green (g,p) r. Craigie. 10/2/82 MV4 KH NG

VITAL EXCURSIONS
17/11/82 PEEL *Just a little blurred, Live show, Cat with vertigo, Sleep.* Anthony Wraster (tp,sx,fl), Angela Stewart (v), John Fairbrother (tb), Danny Sheals (d), Steven Lewis (perc), Fiona Fleck (p), Simon Edwards (b). 30/10/82 MV4 DG MR

VITUS DANCE
4/10/79 PEEL *Down at the park, Disgusting, Inter city living, I'm in control (I think), Problem parade.* Kevin McFadden (lgv), Mark Byrne (lgv), Malcolm Young (bv), Kearin Wright (d). 25/9/79 MV4 JS MR

VIXEN
9/1/87 FRI. ROCK *Call of the wild, High school fox, Silver*

arrow, The Midas touch. Roxy Petrucci, Share Pendersen, Jan Kuehnemund, Janet Gardener. Rec. date unknown MV4 TW DD

VOICE OF THE BEEHIVE
2/3/87 LONG *Any day of the week, What you have is enough, Man works hard, Sorrow floats.* Tracy Bryn (gv), Melissa Brooke (v), Mike Jones (gv), Mark (b), Dan 'Woody' Woodgate (d). 24/2/87 MV5 BYA ME

7/5/87 KERSHAW *Uh love, I say nothing, Beat of love, When you don't have your gun.* Martin Brett (b) r. 'Mark'. 23/4/87 * DG NG&MFA

2/6/87 LONG *Man in the moon, Trust me, It's a good thing, There's a barbarian in the back of my car.* 10/5/87 MV4 HP MS

7/3/88 MAYO† *Jump this way, Independence day, No green blues, Jesus.* 26/2/88 MV4 HP MA
   † On Nighttracks SNTCD017.

10/8/91 SAT. SEQ.† *Say it, Don't call me baby.* Acoustic session. 8/8/91, Egton House, KH *
   † On 12-inch of 'I think I love you', London LONX308.

VOODOO CHILD
15/5/87 FRI. ROCK *Voodoo child, Lost in heart, In shadows, Free the spirit.* Ricky Powell (g), Chris Morris (d), Steve Moulton (b). 8/5/87 MV4 TW DD

VOW WOW
30/1/87 FRI. ROCK *You know what I mean, Nightless city, Hurricane, Shot in the dark.* Genki Hitomi (v), Kyoji Yamamoto (g), Ken Sano (b), Rei Atsumi (k), Toshi Niimi (d). 2/1/87 MV4 TW DD

4/12/87 FRI. ROCK *Don'tcha wanna come, Siren song, Running wild, Nightless city, Shot in the dark, Hurricane.* Neil Murray (b), r. Sano. 30/8/87 * * *

VOYAGER UK
28/8/87 FRI. ROCK *Don't hold back, Razor's edge, Line of fire, Rock this town.* Andy Wells (k), Ian Markovic (v), Rick Smith (d), Paul Smith (b), Dave Thompson (g), Pauk Harkin (g). 24/7/87 MV4 * *

VULTURES
16/6/88 L. KERSHAW *I'll kill that girl, I go ape, Good thing, Something new.* Janie Nichol (v), Andy Clement (d), Allison Young (b), Anna Watkins (g). 5/6/88 MV4 TdB~

WAH! HEAT
10/6/80 PEEL *7 minutes to midnight, Don't step in the cracks, Somesay, Other boys.* Pete Wylie (gv), Colin Redmond (g), Oddball Washington (b,bkv), Rob Jones (d), K.J.Tyrer (sy). 19/5/80 TW DD&MPK

14/4/81 PEEL *Cut out, Sleep, The checkmate syndrome, Forget the down.* Wylie, Washington, King Bluff (k), Jungle Beat Joe Musker (d). 30/3/81 LHI TW DD

4/8/81 SKINNER *Forget the down, Otherboys, Some say, Better scream.* Billed just as 'Wah!': Wylie, Washington, John Maher (d), Steven Johnson (g), Mick Jones (o,str). 23/7/81 MV4 JS *

18/5/82 PEEL *Papa crak, 8-8.3 or 10 'til 12, Satie's faction, You'll never walk alone/You'll never walk again.* Billed as 'Shambeko! Say Wah!': Wylie ('everything except...'), Washington (b); & Alan Peters (tp-1). 5/5/82 RP NG
   The rendition here of 'You'll never walk alone' was in response to an injunction typed across the top of session sheets in Spring 1982: "Please supply verse and chorus of You'll never walk alone for archives". 'At one point I'd hoped to make an album out of it, but it didn't last,' says Peel. Among those who complied were Amazulu, The Diagram Brothers, The Gymslips, Serious Drinking, Ju Ju, Endgames, Kevin Coyne, The Crabs, and The Three Johns, "but Wah's was the best," says Peel.

18/10/82 JENSEN *You better get ready, Ever wanna, Hope, The truth about Eddie.* Now, 'Wah!' again: Wylie, Washington, Chris Joyce (d), Charlie Griffiths (k). 30/9/82 JS&DG *

13/4/83 PEEL *Hope (I wish you'd believe me), Sleep (Lullaby for Josie), Year of decision, Silver and gold).* & Jay Naughton (k), Ruby, Sylvie & Shirly (bkv). 14/2/83 MV4 TW DD

17/9/84 PEEL† *Better scream, Weekends, Basement blues/The story of the blues, Yuh learn.* Billed as 'The Mighty Wah!': Wylie, Phil Wylie (g,bkv), Josie Jones (bkv), Eugene 'Redman' Lange (bkv,lv-4 only), Jay Naughton (k), Henry Priestman (k), Paul Steven-John Ballow (d), Joey Musker (perc), Dickie Rude (b). 22/8/84 * RP NG
   † On Strange Fruit SFPS035.

THE WAILING COCKS
29/11/78 PEEL *Positive loving, Raffles, Listen to the wailing cocks, Rockin youth.* Andy Growcott (d), Alan Boyle (g,bkv), Ian Rowley (b), Andde Leek (k,lv). 22/11/78 MV4 MR~

THE WAILING SOULS
7/11/84 PEEL *Firehouse rock, Bredda Gravalcious, Stop red eye, Bandits taking over.* Bread, Garthy, Pipe & Buddy (v), backed by the Reggae Regulars: Patrick Donegan (g), Brian Campbell (k), Trevor 'Seal' Salmon (b), Winston Williams (d). 30/10/84 MV5 MRD TdB

LOUDON WAINWRIGHT III
22/5/71 TOP GEAR *Sink the Bismark!, School days, Be careful there's a baby in the house, East Indian princess (& Four is a magic number, 17/7/71).* Loudon Wainwright III (ag,v). 18/5/71 MV4 JW *

13/10/71 PEEL *Say that you love me, Samson and the warden, Motel blues, Trilogy (circa 1967), Plane too.* 11/10/71 PH JW *
   Recorded In Concert 14/10/71 PS, TX 26/10/71.

8/11/71 HARRIS *Drinking song, Glenville reel, Bronx girl Eileen, Hey Packey, Motel blues, Dead skunk in the middle of the road, Four is a magic number.* 25/10/71 TI PD *

12/6/73 PEEL *Clockwork chartreuse, A.M. World, Drinking at the bar, Jerusalem town, Lullabye.* 11/6/73 TI JW *

12/5/75 PEEL *Bi-centennial anniversary, Detroit's a dying city, Unrequited to the nth degree, Hollywood hopeful, Have you ever been to Pittsburgh, Five gold stars.* 6/5/75 MV4 TW *

26/8/76 PEEL *Ingenue, Golfing blues, Swimming song, Prince Hal's dirge.* 9/8/76 MV4 TW DD

9/12/76 PEEL *Natural disaster, Air travel, Monkey in my closet, Dick and Jane, It's over the hill/My girl.* 23/11/76 MV4 JG MR

13/8/79 PEEL *Saturday morning fever, The acid song, Vampire blues, April fools' day morn, Dump the dog and feed the garbage.* 1/8/79 MV4 TVD NG

14/4/83 PEEL *Outsidey, I'm all right, Screaming issue, Career moves, Not John.* 9/4/83 MV3 DG GP

30/9/85 PEEL *Expatriot, No , You kids today, I wanna be on MTV, Hard day on the planet, Little did I know.* 17/9/85 MV5 JWI NG

1/10/87 KERSHAW *Me and all the other mothers, Aphrodisiac, You don't want to know, What's his name.* 13/8/87 * DG NG&MS

14/10/89 SAT. SEQ. *Nice guys, School days, They spelled my name wrong again, Harry's wall.* 13/10/89 BS, BHouse kH *

19/10/89 PEEL *They spelled my name wrong again, Jesse don't like it, Sunday time, Sometimes I forget.* 8/10/89 MV3 DG ME

THE WAKE
14/7/83 PEEL *Uniform, The drill, Here comes everybody.* Caesar (gv), Robert Gillespie (b), Carolyn Allen (sy,bkv), Steven Allen (d). 6/7/83 BYA PS

23/2/84 JENSEN *Talk about the pest, Rise and shine, Make you understand, The calendar.* Alexander Macpherson (b) r. Gillespie. 16/2/84 MV4 JP MPK

JOE LOUIS WALKER
5/1/89 KERSHAW *I-don't know why, Moanin' news.* Joe Louis Walker (gv) & unknown. Rec. date unknown * * *

THE WALKING SEEDS
26/1/87 PEEL *Huge living creature, Junior acid bait, Mark Chapman, Blathering out.* Tony Mogan (d), Lol Geoghegan (perc), Robert Parker (b), Barry Sutton (g,bkv), Frank Martin (v). 11/1/87 * DG ME&FK
30/9/87 PEEL *Transmaniacon M.C, Eyes too big, El sexorcist, Schoolfinger.* Geoghegan out. 22/9/87 * DG ME&EL
19/4/89 PEEL *Matchsticks, Gates of freedom, Cave woman, Shaved beatnik.* Andy Rowan (b) r. Sutton; Parker (g). 4/4/89 WX JW MR
22/2/90 PEEL *Mortal Blues, Hairy who, Broken cup.* Lee Webster (b) r. Rowan. 30/1/90 DG MR

THE WALLACE COLLECTION
22/6/70 SYMONDS *Dear beloved secretary, We gotta do something new, Serenade, Bruxelles.* Sylvain van Holmen, Freddy Nieuland, Raymond Vincent, Marc Herouet, Jean Valcke, Guido Everact, Serge Ghasarion. Belgian band. 26/5/70 PH BA PK&NG

THE WALLFLOWERS
16/12/86 LONG *Thank you, You are the one, 83.7 degrees, That girl.* Peter D Brickley (gv), Stephen Bywater (lg), John Strachan (b), Patrick Hunt (d). 26/11/86 MV4 BYA SC

WALLY
11/6/73 HARRIS *Black crow.* Roy Webber (agv), Paul Gerrett (p), Pete Cosker (lg), Paul Middleton (ps), Pete Sage (b,vi), Mike Smith (d). 11/6/73 LHI PR *
10/9/73 HARRIS *Your own way, Phil's song (& See you, Sunday walking lady, 5/11/73).* Roger Narraway (d) r. Smith. 22/8/73 LHI JG *
4/3/74 HARRIS *Right by me, The martyr, Giving.* 2/1/74 LHI JG *

WALRUS
7/8/70 BLACK *Who can you trust, Rage and old iron, Blind man.* Noel Greenaway (v), Steve Hawthorne (b), John Scates (g), Bill Hoad (sx), Roy Voce (sx), Barry Parfitt (o), Roger Harrison (d), Don Richards (tp). 21/7/70 AO2 JM *
'Borderline pass' from panel. Later, did R1 Club session, PH 5/1/71.
9/2/71 HARDING *Who can you trust, Blind man, Road aide, Never let my body touch the ground.* 1/2/71 MV5 MB MH&MF

THE WALTONES
24/8/88 PEEL *When you smile, Miles different ways, She's everywhere but here, Deepest.* Alex Fyans (d), Many Lee (b), Mark Collins (g), James Knox (v). 16/8/88 MV4 MR~

THE HANK WANGFORD BAND
19/12/85 KERSHAW *Never wear mascara, Cowboys stay on longer, Cowcow boogie, End of the road.* Hank Wangford (gv), Bobby Valentino (fd,mnd,v), Big Mac (dv), Sissi Footwear (perc,v), George Hamilton VI (b,acc,hca,v), Jet Atkins (gv). 5/12/85 Y2 CG *

CLIFFORD T. WARD
21/8/72 WALKER *Carrie, God help me, Sam, Coathanger.* Clifford T. Ward (pv), Ken Wright (d), Derek Thomas (lg), John Pasternak (b), David Skinner (p), Paul Lockey (rg). 14/8/72 AO2 CB *
26/10/72 PEEL *Coathanger, Sam, Anticipation, Gaye, The Open University.* Bev Pegg, Paul Booton r. Pasternak, Lockey [M: daytime]. 16/10/72 LHI BA *
19/4/73 PEEL *Crisis, Gaye, Where's it going to end, Wherewithal (& The magician 17/5/73).* & 4 (unknown). 9/4/73 LHI BA * [M: DAYTIME]

WARFARE
8/4/88 FRI. ROCK *Revolution, Death charge, Burn down the Kings Road, Ebony dreams.* Evo (d,lv), Gunner (g), Zlaughter (b), Algy Ward (k-4 only). 18/3/88 * HP DD

WARHORSE
22/12/70 HARDING *St. Louis, Ritual, No chance.* Ged Peck (lg), Nick Simper (b), Mac Poole (d), Ashley Holt (v), Frank Wilson (p,o). 15/12/70 MV5 MB MH&MF
19/8/71 HENRY *Red sea, Back in time, Woman of the devil.* Peter Parks (lg), r. Peck. 11/8/71 MV4 MB MH&MF

THE WASPS
22/2/78 PEEL *Teenage treats, J-J-J-Jenny, She made magic, Something to tell you.* Gary Wellman (g,bkv), Steve Dominic (b), Jimmy Rich (d), Jessie Lynn-Dean (lv). 13/2/78 MV4 TW DD
20/2/79 PEEL *Angelica, Rubber cars, She's alarming, This time.* Neil Fitch (gv), Dave Owen (bv), Tiam Grant (d), Jesse Lynn-Dean (lv). 13/2/79 MV4 BS MR

THE WATERBOYS
13/2/84 JENSEN *All the things she gave me, Savage earth heart, A pagan place, License to kill.* Mike Scott (gv), Karl Wallinger (k,bkv), Anthony Thistlethwaite (sx), Martin Swain (b), Chris Whitton (d), Anthony Hepworth (tp), Ingrid Schroeder (bkv). 19/1/84 MV4 JP HP
Contracts index suggests previous recording for Peter Powell 3/5/83, and two later in 1984: 29/4 'Tea-time Show' and 30/4 Andy Peebles.
3/3/84 SAT. LIVE *Trumpets, The 3 day man.* Live from S2 MRD TDB
Two more for SAT. LIVE the next year: 16/2/85 and 19/10/85; and 20/11/85 'Tea-time Show'.
15/7/89 SAT. SEQ. *In search of a rose, Sharon's tune, When will we be married, And a bang on the ear, Room to roam.* Scott, Anthony Thistlethwaite (hca,mnd), Steve Wickham (fd), Trevor Hutchinson (b), Colin Blakey (fl), Nigel Bridgeman (d), Sharon Shannon (bkv). Live from MV3 PW FK

THE WATERMELON MEN
8/5/86 KERSHAW *You should be mine, Pouring rain, Tonight, Back in my dreams.* Eril Illes (agv,o), Imre Von Polgar (g), Johan Lundberg (g), Hans Sacklen (b), Erik Westlin (d). 2/5/86 Y2 CG PSM

THE WATERSONS
7/8/86 KERSHAW *The jolly waggoner, The prickle holly bush, The king's song, Young banker.* Norma, Mike & Rachael Waterson, Martin Carthy (all-v). 17/7/86 SS CG TWN
18/2/88 KERSHAW *The Derby ram, Adieu adieu ('The flash lad'), The poacher's lament.* 28/1/88 * DG NG

WAY OF THE WEST
1/6/81 SKINNER *Monkey love, See you shake, Number three, Front door.* Pete Carney (gv), Reid Savage (g), Liz Weller (b), Dave Bonnefoy (d,perc), Jason Warre (sx). 21/5/81 LHI JS *

WE FREE KINGS
28/7/86 PEEL *Motorcycle rain, Stupidity street, Brilliant, Big heat.* Joe (v), Seb (g), Kenny (d), Aidan (mnd), Pam (ml), Phil (clo), Jeff (fd). 16/7/86 MV4 BYA *

WE'VE GOT A FUZZBOX AND WE'RE GONNA USE IT
10/3/86 PEEL *Aaarrrggghhh!!! (Don't let us die), Fever, Rules and regulations, Justine.* Tina (d,sx), Jo (b,g), Magz (vi,perc,d), Vix (v). 2/3/86 MV5 DG ME&MS
10/4/86 LONG *Aaarrrggghhh!!!, Love is the slug, Hollow girl, Console me, Spirit in the sky.* 2/4/86 MV4 BYA *
11/8/86 PEEL *You got me, Preconceptions, Jackie, She, Bohemian rhapsody.* 29/7/86 * DG MR&MS
12/1/87 LONG *Wait and see, Self, What's the point?, High hopes.* & The Walsall Heavy Drinkers' Brass Ensemble: Karen, Phillipa, Penny & Sue (bars,ts,tb,tp; all on-1,3 only). 7/1/87 MV4 BYA MPK

THE WEATHER PROPHETS
10/10/85 LONG *Love song no.1, 24 years, I almost prayed, Lighthouse room.* Peter Astor (gv), Oisin Little (g), Greenwood Golding (b), Dave Morgan (d); & Dave Evans (perc). 2/10/85 MV5 BYA MPK
3/7/86 KERSHAW *Walking under a spell, Mayflower, Can't*

keep my mind, Why does the rain? Evans out. 11/6/86 Y2 CG PSM
17/7/86 LONG *Hill house, Midnight mile, The key to my love is green, You're my ambulance.* 2/7/86 MV4 BYA MPK
1/12/86 PEEL *Swimming pool blue, Hollow heart, She comes from the rain, Faithful.* 2/11/86 * DG FK&SC
4/3/87 LONG *Hill house, Mayflower, You upset the grace of living when you lie, Poison mind.* 18/2/87 MV4 BYA MPK&EL
25/6/87 KERSHAW *Sleeping when the sun comes up, Hollow heart, You bring the miracles.* 28/6/87 * DG NG&MA

THE WEB
19/5/70 HARDING *I love you, I spider, Concerto for bedsprings.* Lennie Wright (d), John Eaton (g), Tom Harris (sx,fl), Kenny Beveridge (d), Tony Edwards (g), Dave Lawson (k). 12/5/70 MV5 MB MH&MF
Failed audition 5/3/68. Passed trial b'cast on R1 Club rec'd 20/1/69. DAYTIME SESSIONS FOLLOWED.
20/10/70 HARDING *Concerto for bedsprings, Face in the mirror.* 13/10/70 MV5 MB MH&MF

AJ WEBBER
28/1/74 HARRIS *Jam jars, Let me in on your secret (& Get back to the country, 25/3/72).* Aj Webber (ag,v) & 3 (unknown). 2/1/74 LHI JG *
Rec'd In Concert 27/6/74 HP, TX 15/7/74.
9/12/74 HARRIS *The gardener, That's life, I'd like to play guitar like John McLaughlin, While you're being so good to me.* & (b), (p) unknown. 6/11/74 MV4 JG *

THE WEDDING PRESENT
28/11/85 KERSHAW *My favourite dress, At the edge of the sea, Once more, Living and learning.* David Gedge (gv), Keith Gregory (b), Pete Solowka (g), Shaun Charman (d); & Andrew Middleton ('feedback guitar'-3,4 only). 7/11/85 Y2 CG PSM
26/2/86 PEEL† *Felicity, What becomes of the broken hearted, You should always keep in touch with your friends, This boy can wait.* & Mike Stout (g-1 only); Charman (bkv-1 only). 11/2/86 MV5 MW MR
† On Strange Fruit SFPCD009.
15/5/86 LONG° *Everyone thinks he looks daft, Shatner, My favourite dress, I found that essence rare.* & Mike Stout (g-4 only); Charman (bkv-4 only). 20/4/86 MV4 BYA TdB
° On Nighttracks SNTCD016.
25/11/86 PEEL *All about Eve, Don't be so hard, Room with a view, Never said, Kozayok [Hopak].* Stout (b) stands in for Gregory. 26/10/86 * DG ME&MA
18/3/87 PEEL *Give my love to Kevin, Getting nowhere fast, Something and nothing, A million miles.* & Mike Stout (g-2 only). 3/3/87 * DG MR&MC
14/10/87 PEEL† *Ukrainian Session #1: Tiutiunyk, Yichav Kozak za Dunai, Hude Dnipro hude, Katrusya/Svitit Misyats.* Solowka (acc,mnd); & The Legendary Len Liggins (vi,lv), Ron Rom (handclaps). 6/10/87 MV4 DG MR&FK
5/4/88 PEEL† *Ukrainian Session #2: Minnooli dnee, Vasya vasyl'ok, Zadumav didochok, Verkhovyna.* Simon Smith (d) r. Charman; Solowka (acc,mnd); & Len Leggins (vi,v,bal), Roman Remeynes (mnd,v). 15/3/88 MV4 DG MR
† First two Ukrainian sessions make up 'Ukrainski Vistupi Y Johna Peela', RCA 10-inch LP PL74104.
30/5/88 PEEL *Unfaithful†, Why are you being so reasonable now, Take me I'm yours, Happy Birthday.* all (bkv-4). 24/5/88 MV4 DG *
'My main memories? ...erm, the vending machines,' says David Gedge; 'one spends fairly long intervals hanging around the little waiting room. Groups are faced with the prospect of inventing little japes like buying a fiver's worth of products and then putting it all back into one section of the revolving compartment model, so that the first bright-and-early BBC staffer wins themselves a couple of sandwiches, three Mars bars and various other edibles, for a princely 20p!' †
on free 7-inch with an issue of HOD magazine.
15/5/89 PEEL *Ukrainian Session #3: Cherez richku cherez*

hai, Zavtra ya budu pid nebom chuzhim, Sertsem I
dusheyev. Solowka (acc,mnd); & Len Liggins (vi,v),
Roman Remeynes (mnd,v). 2/5/89 WX DG MR
    Also recorded live gig at Subterania 29/8/89 at Peel's
50th birthday party, TX 30/8.
28/10/90 PEEL Dalliance, Blonde, Niagara, Heather.
14/10/90 MV3 PW NG&MFA
2/5/92 PEEL Flying saucer†, Softly softly, Come play with
me†, California†. Paul Dorrington (g) r. Solowka.
17/3/92 MV4 MA~ RJ
    † On extra CD included in Hit Parade 2, RCA
Records, January 1993. Band recorded their 12th
session, for GOODIER, after Radio 1's 25th anniversary.
Thanks to David Gedge for contributions.

WEE PAPA GIRL RAPPERS
4/8/87 LONG Flaunt it, Don't talk that rap, He's mine, Hut
hut the beat. Sandra Lawrence (v), Timmie Lawrence
(v); & Bob Harman (k), Simon Bailey (k), Def Con Beat
(dm,hbb). 19/7/87 MV4 PW TdB
21/3/88 MAYO You got the beat, Heat it up, The beat the
rhyme the noise, Wash that man. & Jim Baker (k),
Hamish McDonald (prg), Sam Allen (dj), Andy Dewar
(perc), Jeremiah Healy (dj). 13/3/88 MV4 HP *

WEEKEND
22/11/82 JENSEN View from her room, The end of the
affair, Woman's eyes, Weekend off (instrumental). Alun
Mark Williams (Spike) (g,vla), Simon Booth (g), Alison
Statton (v,b-4 only), Phil Moxham (b), Dawson Millar
(perc), Roy Dodds (d), Harry Beckett (tp,flh), Annie
Whitehead (tb). 4/11/82 MV4 RP MR

WEEN
17/4/92 PEEL Pork roll egg and cheese, Nan, Captain
Fantasy, Don't get too close to my fantasy. Claude
Coleman Jr. (d), Kramer (p,b), Mickey Melchiondo (g),
Aaron Freeman (gv). 20/2/92 MV4 DG NG&AA

WELFARE STATE
21/2/70 TOP GEAR Lot's song, Silence is requested in the
ultimate abyss†, Rat race. Rec. Date unknown PRIV * *
    † on 'Top Gear' LP BBC Records REC 52S.

SEETHING WELLS
18/11/82 PEEL Titles unknown. Seething Wells ('ranting!'),
Chris Moore (g), Jon Langford (g), Martin Leon (b),
Nick King (d). 7/7/82 MV4 RP MC

PAPA WEMBA
16/3/89 KERSHAW M'fono yami, Hambayi Ede, Bokulaka.
Papa Wemba (lv), Mufela Kalonga (b), Christian Polloni
(g), Maika Munan (g), Boffi Bayengola (d), Philippe
Marais (sy), Xavier Jouvelet (perc), Iknola Isibangi (cga),
Mubi Majadi (bkv), Mela Amissi (bkv). 27/2/89 HP HP DD
5/9/92 KERSHAW Le voyageur, Lingo lingo, Matinda, Annah
(& Madilamba, Zero, Maria Valencia, Ombela; on PEEL
later same night). Papa Wemba (lv), Amisi Mela (bkv),
Patick Mazie Magdelaine (g), Magid Mahdi (b), Heire ra
Kotofizinga & Jean Philippa Dary (k), Roger Raspail &
Lauzent Coatalen (perc), Joseph Kuo (d).
19/8/92 MV3 NG~ PL

THE WEREFROGS
1/5/92 PEEL Spinning felt clouds, Sheila, Cry, Don't slip
away. Steve Frog (d), Matthew Frog (b), Marc Frog
(gv). 10/3/92 MV4 MR~

WESTERN PROMISE
4/6/85 PEEL All the king's horses, Running with the saints,
Burning and looting, My war. Sean Butler (d), Dave
King (b), John McGlone (rg,lv), Phil Fowler (lg).
19/5/85 MV5 DG ME

DAVID WESTLAKE AND THE GO-BETWEENS
25/2/87 LONG Faithful to three lovers, The word around
town, Dream come true, Everlasting. David Westlake
(gv), Robert Forster (g), Robert Vickers (b), Amanda
Brown (vi,ob); & John Wills (d) 'courtesy of The
Wishing Stones'. 14/1/87 BYA MPK

WESTWORLD
29/1/87 LONG King Creole, Insection 123, Where the action

is. Nick Burton (b), Elizabeth Westwood (v), Derwood
Andrews (lg). 18/1/87 MV4 JE DD

WHAT? NOISE
9/5/90 PEEL Anybody, Crash, Shit, George. Chris Nagle,
Julia Nagle, Timothy Harris. 12/4/90 MV3 DG *

WHERE'S THE BEACH?
31/8/89 PEEL Tripping the love fantastic†, Suakin,
Deliciously deranged. Peter Jones & Adam Marshall
(ma), Chloe Mac (v). 1/8/89 MV5 DG MR
    † On 'New Season' SFRCD205.
26/9/90 PEEL Feed the fire, Chaos at the axe factory
(instrumental), Mega Armageddon death/Yankamantra.
Angie Simmons (v) r. Mac. 19/8/90 * DG PL

WHIPPED CREAM
17/11/91 PEEL Explosion, Whatever, Wait for a minute.
Lars-Erik Grimelund (d), Jonas Sonesson (b), Elisabeth
Punzi (gv), Jorgen Cremonese (gv). 25/8/91 HP DG ME&TBK

WHIRLWIND
10/4/80 PEEL Oakies in the pokey, Cruising around,
Nervous breakdown, Staying out all night. Nigel Dixon
(g), Mick Lewis (g), Chris Emo (b), Gary Hassett (d).
2/4/80 MV4 JE NG

WHITE AND TORCH
20/3/84 PEEL Don't be shot, Heartbreak, No not I, Bury
my heart. Roy White (kv), Steve Torch (v), Charlie
Morgan (d), Dave Levdy (b), Jackie Robinson (bkv).
10/3/84 MV5 DG MC

ANDY WHITE
16/1/86 LONG Rembrandt hat, The big rain, Vision of you,
The walking wounded. Andy White (g,bv), Rod McVey
(acc,p,o). 5/1/86 BYA PW
13/2/86 KERSHAW Religious persuasion, Things start to
unwind, The price is high, Tuesday apocalypse no. 13.
23/1/86 Y2 NB SR
29/9/86 LONG Reality row, There were roses, Marion girl. &
Brendon McGarrity (d). 17/9/86 MV4 BYA *

SNOWY WHITE
1/11/84 INTO THE MUSIC The water's edge/Stepping stones,
Fortune, Chinese burn, Lucky star. Snowy White (lgv),
Kuma Harada (b), Winston Delandro (g), Godfrey Wang
(k), Richard Bailey (d,perc). 20/10/84 MV4 DG MC

THE WHITECATS
3/4/78 PEEL Escalator of love, Second time around,
Teenage dream. Kelvin Blacklock (v), Eddie Cox (g),
Steve Turner (b), Rat Scabies (d). Rec. Date unknown PRIV BS
25/8/78 PEEL Junkyard angels, Detectives, Here I go again,
Shotgun lovers. & Bob Sargeant (k,gv). 16/8/78 MV4 BS NG

BARRENCE WHITFIELD AND THE SAVAGES
20/11/86 KERSHAW Girl from outer space, The apology line,
I don't dig your noise. * ?/10/86 Fort Apache Recording
Studio, Boston, Mass * MCO
19/2/87 KERSHAW Brainwashed, Juicy fruit, Runnin' and
hidin', Madhouse, Iron curtain. Bruce Katz (k), Barrence
Whitfield (v), Richie Robertson (b), Lorne Entress (d),
Milton Reder (g), David Sholl (sx). 19/2/87 * DST DFW
28/4/91 KERSHAW† Juicy fruit, The doctor Knows his
business, Dust on my needle, (There's a) Hole in my
heart & my love leaked. Whitfield, Reder, Sholl, Seth
Pappas (d), Dean Cassell (b). 14/4/91 MV3 DG ME&AA
    † on LP 'Savage Tracks', New Rose Records, 1992.

JACKI WHITREN
28/8/72 HARRIS As the evening sun goes down, Give her
the day, Once I loved a love song, 'Fore you walk out
the door. Jacki Whitren (gv) & 4 (unknown). 8/8/72 MV5
JG *
8/10/72 SPEAKEASY Ain't it funny, To a friend through a
friend, As the evening sun goes down. 6/10/72 PS TB *
25/3/73 SOUNDS ON SUNDAY I can see a new horizon, Country
life, A little extra please, Give her the day, To a friend
through a friend, I'll give it a miss, Running all the
time, As the evening sun goes down. & Pat Donaldson
(b), Gerry Conway (d), Ivan Chandler. 20/3/73 PS CB *

7/5/73 FREEMAN Give her the day, New horizon, But which
way do I go? 2/5/73 LHI TW *
28/5/73 HARRIS Ain't it funny, New horizon, Give her the
day, To a friend through a friend (& I've thought
about it, 23/7/73). 16/5/73 LHI PR *
    Next, rec'd In Concert 7/6/73 PS, TX 30/6/73.
17/8/73 SEQUENCE Lost love blues, Ain't it funny, Give her
the day, To a friend from a friend. 5/7/73 LHI JM *
10/9/73 HAMILTON Human failure [Network session]. 31/8/73
LHI c.PWI *
9/12/73 SOUNDS ON SUNDAY Lost lover blues, Give her the
day, To a friend through a friend, Ain't it funny, White
road, With your last thoughts for Anna, A little bit
extra please. & 2 (unknown). 3/12/73 B6 JM *

THE WHO
15/10/67 TOP GEAR Pictures of Lilly, Our love was, I can
see for miles, Relax, I can't reach you, A quick one
while he's away, & Jingles: Top Gear #1 & #2, Radio
1 #1 & #2, Happy Jack, Jingle (& My way, Someone's
coming, 19/11/67). Pete Townsend (gv), Roger Daltrey
(v), Keith Moon (d), John Entwhistle (bv). 10/10/67 De
Lane Lea Studios, Wembley, London BA *
    Failed 1st audition (applied as 'The Detours' but
recorded as 'The Who') 9/4/64 S2 & Doug Sandon (d).
Re-auditioned & Moon 12/2/65, S2, after release of 'I
can't explain'. 3 'no' 4 'yes' votes: 'lead guitar seemed
more sure of himself than the rest. Overall not very
original and below standard'. Passed. 1st appeared
2/4/65 live at PH on Joe Loss Show [M]. This Top Gear
session repeated on SAT. CLUB & SYMONDS.
19/4/70 DLT I'm free, Heaven & hell, The seeker, Shakin'
all over. Repeated on SYMONDS, WALKER etc.
13/4/70 OS * * Other 'own studio' sessions followed.

WIDOW MAKER
27/4/76 PEEL Such a shame, Leave the kids alone, When I
met you. Steve Ellis (v), Ariel Bender (g), & (b), (d),
(g) unknown. 30/3/76 MV4 JG MR

THE WIGS
7/4/87 LONG In your shadow, World service, George's
dream, Storm inside. Glen Morten (d), Mark Rozario
(g), Mick James (gv), Keith Cockburn (bv), Keith Jones
(v). 25/2/87 MV4 BYA MC

THE WILD FLOWERS
7/5/86 LONG Godsend, A kind of kingdom, The welcome
son, Station. Dave Fisher (d), Dave Atherton (g), Pete
Waldron (b), Neil Cook (v). 7/5/86 MV4 BYA MPK
12/6/86 KERSHAW Where my heart lies, It ain't so easy,
Seventh canyon, A kind of kingdom. 28/5/86 Y2 SP *

WILD STRAWBERRIES
21/3/86 FRI. ROCK Sheyla, Fire on the water, Snakes can't
dance, Wild boys. Zlatan Cehic, Sead Lipovaca, Nasko
Dudimlic, Alen Islamovic. 21/2/86 MV4 * *

THE WILD SWANS
23/3/82 JENSEN Opium, Flowers of England, The iron bed,
Now you're perfect. Alan Wills (d), Phil Lucking (b),
Jeremy Kelly (g), Gerard Quinn (k), Paul Simpson (v).
7/3/82 MV4 DG ME
13/5/82 PEEL† No Bleeding, Enchanted°, Thirst. Baz
Hughes (b) r. Lucking (indisposed). 1/5/82 MV4 DG MR
    † On Strange Fruit SFPS006; ° also on 'Winters of
Discontent' SFRCD204.
8/10/86 LONG Northern England, Now and forever,
Crowning glory, Holy spear. Joseph Searon (b) r.
Hughes. 28/9/86 BYA TdB

WILD TURKEY
9/11/72 PEEL Good old days, Chuck Stallion & the
mustangs, Tomorrow's friend, Eternal mothers/The
return. Glenn Cornick (b), Gary Pickford-Hopkins (v),
Jeffrey Jones (d), Alan Lewis (lg), Stephen Gurl (p),
Michael Dyche (g). 23/10/72 LHI BA MH&MF
1/3/73 PEEL The sole survivor, Butterfly, See you next
Tuesday. 26/2/73 LHI BA *

21/5/73 HARRIS *Good old days, Butterfly, If you see Kate.*
16/5/73 LH1 PR *
Rec'd In Concert 10/5/73 HP, TX 9/6/73.

8/11/73 PEEL *Sweet talking woman, Soldier Boy, Social World.* Bernie Marsden (lg), r. Lewis. 29/10/73 LH1 BA *
Rec'd 2nd In Concert 12/10/73 HP, TX 17/11/73.

WILD WEEKEND
12/8/82 PEEL *Hungry, Janine and the razor man, Scarecrow, Swimming in mud.* Ade Sleigh (d), Al Roberts (b), Keith Holian (g), Gary Horabin (k), Dave Candler (v). 24/7/82 MV4 DG MR

WILD!
11/9/87 FRI. ROCK *Don't look back, Love games, Starlight, Babee.* Nikki Brooks (lv), Dave Wild (g,bkv), Bob Skeat (b), Steve Hopgood (d). 31/7/87 * PW DD

WILDFIRE
9/11/84 FRI. ROCK *Summer lightning, The key, Nothing lasts forever, Jerusalem.* Paul Mario Day (v), Martin Bushell (lg), Jeff Summers (g), Jeff Brown (b), Bruce Bisland (d), Austin England (k-2,4 only). 5/10/84 MV4 DG MC

22/7/83 FRI. ROCK *One last chance, Shot in the dark, Just a friend, Takin' a chance.* Steve Overland (g), Chris Overland (g), Phil Soussan (b), Mark Booty (k), Simon Kirke (d). 24/6/83 * TW DD

JOHN WILLIAMS
16/7/69 PEEL *Courant/Ballet/La Volta, Sonata, Asturias, Miller's dance, Sonata.* John Williams (ag). 17/6/69 B15 PR *
The classical guitarist's 1st BBC date was in 1957.

12/4/71 HARRIS *Two dances by Michael Protonas, Little Prelude, Asturias, El Colibri, Study by Villa Lobos, Scherzino Mexicano.* 1/4/71 AO2 JM JWH

LUCINDA WILLIAMS
9/7/89 KERSHAW *Something about what happens, Disgusted, Wild and blue, Sunday song.* Lucinda Williams (gv), Gurf Morlix (g), Jim Leslie (b), Donald Lindley (d). 4/5/89 WX DG MA

22/6/89 SKINNER *Motherless children, Am I too blue, Nothin' and ramblin', Price to pay.* Williams, Morlix only. 22/6/89 Egton Studio 5B KH ME&SA

PAUL WILLIAMS
3/7/72 HARRIS *Waking up alone, That's enough for me, A perfect love, We've only just begun.* Paul Williams & 11 (unknown). 26/6/72 * JG *

STEVE WILLIAMSON
25/6/90 CAMPBELL *Awakening, Down, Straight ahead, How high the bird, Mandy's mood.* Steve Williamson (sx), Joe Bashorun (k), Tony Remy (g), Gary Crosby (b), Steve Washington (d). 6/6/90 MV5 PW MPK

THE PHIL WILSON QUINTET
16/4/87 LONG *Ten miles, Joy will find you out, Even now, Small town.* Phil Wilson (gv), Paul Strudwick (g,bkv), Pete Waldron (b), Paul Mulreany (d), Frank Sweeney (vi), Joanne Lilley (bkv). 8/4/87 MV5 HP *

MARI WILSON
29/4/82 JENSEN *Rave, Ecstasy, Dance card, Love man.* Mari Wilson (v), Can Dide & Kurt Lamour (bkv), Harry (k), Jim (g), Cary Staccato (b), Barry (sx), Gary (d). 22/4/82 MV5 JS MR

WIN
17/6/85 LONG *Un-American broadcasting, Way we think that, Rewop!, Empty holsters.* Russell Burn (d), Davey Henderson (gv), Ian Stoddard (k); & Emanuelle Shoniwa (gb,bkv). 2/6/85 HP BYA MS

THE WINKIES
15/4/74 HARRIS *Trust in Dick, Moan like a man, Davy 'o blowtorch.* Guy Humphreys (g), Brian Turrington (b), Mike Desmarais (d), Philip Rambow (gv). 13/3/74 LH1 PR *
Rec'd In Concert as trial b'cast 25/1/74 HP, TX 2/2/74; then backed Eno for Peel Session.

WIRE
31/1/78 PEEL† *Practice makes perfect, I am the fly,*

Culture vultures, 106 beats that. Colin Newman (gv), Graham Lewis (b), Robert Gotobed (d), Bruce Gilbert (g). 18/1/78 MV4 MB NG

3/10/78 PEEL† *The other window, Mutual friend, On returning, Indirect enquiries.* 20/9/78 MV4 BS NG

18/9/79 PEEL† *Crazy about love.* 11/9/79 MV4 JE MR
† On Strange Fruit SFRCD108.

10/5/88 PEEL *German shepherds, Boiling boy, Drill.* 24/4/88 * DG SC&SA

WISHBONE ASH
19/8/70 HARRIS *Errors of my ways, Phoenix (& Blind eye, not broadcast).* Andy Powell (gv), Ted Turner (gv), Martin Turner (bv), Steve Upton (d). 6/8/70 PS JG *

11/1/71 HARRIS *Queen of torture, Errors of my ways, Was dis (& Lullaby, 15/2/71).* 1/1/71 MV5 JM JWH

29/4/71 HENRY *Blind eye, Lullaby, Phoenix.*
21/4/71 MV4 MB MH&MF

10/7/71 TOP GEAR *Jailbait, The pilgrim, Lady Whiskey, Lullaby.* 5/7/71 PH JW *

1/11/71 HARRIS *Jailbait, The Pilgrim, Lullaby.*
18/10/71 T1 PD ARV

25/4/72 PEEL *Blowing free, Warrior, The King will come.* 18/4/72 MV4 * *

18/5/72 DRUMMOND *Throw down the sword, Warrior, Time was.* 10/5/72 MV4 MB MH&MF

3/7/72 HARRIS *Blowing free, Leaf and stream, The King will come, Sometime world.* 31/5/72 AO2 JG *

5/7/85 ROCK *Cell of fame, People in motion, Love is blue, Long live the night.* Andy Powell (gv), Melvin Spence (b,lv), Steve Upton (d), Laurie Wisefield (g). Rec. date unknown MV4 TW DD

WITCHFYNDE
13/2/81 FRI. ROCK *Give 'em hell, Getting heavy, Belfast, Moon magic.* Gray Scoresey (d), Pete Surgery (b,bkv), Montalo (g), Chalky White (v). 21/1/81 * TW DD

WITNESS
4/3/91 GOODIER *Sail on down, Loverman, Light at the end of the tunnel, House called love or.* Simon 'Pim' Jones (g), Grahame 'Skin' Skinner (v), Andy Carr (b), Jim Kimberley (d), James Haliwell (k). 23/2/91 MV5 MC~

A WITNESS
6/1/86 PEEL *The loud hailer song, Smelt like a pedestrian, O'Grady's dream, Sharpened sticks.* Vince (b), Rick (g), Keith (v) & 'Dr. Umatix' (d). 15/12/85 MV5 DG ME

9/12/86 PEEL *Faglane morris wind, Nodding dog moustache, Raw patch, Hard day's love.* 'Nobby Normal' (d). 16/11/86 * DG NG&FK

19/1/88 PEEL† *Zip up, Sunbed sentimental, Take me up to the earth, McManus octaphone.* 'Fred Harris' (d,bkv). 10/1/88 * DG ME&FK

30/11/88 PEEL† *Life the final frontier, I love you Mr Disposable Razors°, Helicopter tealeaf, Prince Microwave Bollard.* Alan (d) r. Harris. 20/11/88 HP DG ME
† On Strange Fruit SFMCD206; ° also on 'New Season' SFRCD205.

JAH WOBBLE AND INVADERS OF THE HEART
1/12/91 KERSHAW *Saeta†, Moroccan, Emigre.* Jah Wobble (bv), Justin Adams (gv), Mark Ferda (sy,bkv), Neville Murray (perc,bkv), Ali Slimoni (perc,v). 10/11/91 MV5 DG SA&JMK
† On 'Ungodly kingdom' EP Oval 107.

WOLF
29/6/73 SEQUENCE *Cadenza, Isolation valley, The ache, McDonald's lament.* Darryl Way (elp,sy,vi,vla), John Etheridge (g), Dec Messicar (b), Ian Mosley (d). 5/6/73 T1 JM BAI&MG
Had rec'd In Concert 5/4/73 PS, TX 5/5/73, as trial b'cast.

16/7/73 HARRIS *Bunch of fives, Jack, Saturation Point.* 11/7/73 LH1 JG *

THE WOLFHOUNDS
1/4/86 PEEL *Me, Anti-Midas touch, Hand in the till, Whale on the beach.* Dave Callahan (v), Paul Clark (g), Andy

Golding (g), Andy Bolton (b,sy), Frank Stebbing (d). 23/3/86 MV5 DG ME&TD

10/6/87 PEEL *Rule of thumb, Sandy, Boy racers RM1, Disgusted E7.* 26/5/87 * DG ME&MFA

1/2/88 PEEL *Happy shopper, Non specific song, Son of nothing, William Randolf Hearse.* Martin Stebbing (b) r. Bolton. 19/1/88 * DG MR&JB

WOLFSBANE
26/2/88 FRI. ROCK *Paint the town, Money to burn, Fell out of heaven, Can't stop shaking.* Blaze Bayley (v), Jase (g,bkv), Jeff (b,bkv), Steve Danger (d). 5/2/88 * PW DD

WOMMET
31/10/70 TOP GEAR *The way you look, How can you love me so, City of gold, Greyhound bus.* Mick Abrahams (gv) & unknown. 20/10/70 * * *

THE WONDER STUFF
23/11/87 LONG *Mother and I, Poison, Ooh she said, Rue the day.* Martin Gilkes (d), Miles Hunt (lv,g), Malcolm Treece (g,bkv), Bob Jones (b,mel). 28/10/87 MV4 HP MPK

CHRIS WOOD AND ANDY CUTTING
12/1/92 KERSHAW *Brandy a ouellete, Homage a musiciens, When Chloe/Ville de Quebec, The history man/Roseville fair.* Chris Wood (vi,gv), Andy Cutting (acc). 3/10/91 MV4 DG NG&AA

THE WOOD CHILDREN
2/12/87 LONG *Happens every day, Important in your life, Imaginary trap, Vat of tea.* Nick Stockman (agv), Richard Kirkland (b), Jeff St. Pierre (d,bkv), Andy Shelley (g). 11/11/87 MV4 HP MPK&FK

BRENTON WOOD
11/2/68 TOP GEAR *The Oogum boogum song, Gimme little sign, Baby you've got it, My girl.* Brenton Wood (v), & 'Tony Gilbert for the services of 3 musicians, Roger Coulam (md/o)'. 30/1/68 * * *

WOODEN HORSE
3/1/72 WALKER *East Bound train, Wake me in the morning, This is a song.* Dave Mateer (gv), Susan Traynor (v), Malcolm Harrison (gv), Stephen Marwood (gv), Neil Brockbank (b). 9/12/71 AO1 RP * [M: DAYTIME]

27/4/72 DRUMMOND *Letter, Northern beaches, Kali.* [M]. 17/4/72 MV5 MB MH&MF

THE WOODENTOPS
19/9/84 PEEL *Get it on, Well well, Everything breaks, The last time.* Rolo McGinty (v), Simon Mawby (g), Paul Holliday (d), Fraser Cheney (b), Alice Goodhead (k). 8/9/84 MV5 DG MC

8/5/85 LONG *It will come, Hear me James, Last time, Good thing.* Rolo, Mawby, Alice Thompson (k), Paul Hookham (d), Frank De Freitas (b). 28/4/85 MV4 BYA TdB

9/9/85 PEEL *It will come, Plenty, So good today, Plutonium rock (Godzilla).* Benny Staples (d) r. Hookham. 27/8/85 MV5 DG MR

7/4/86 PEEL *Give it time, Move me, Special friend, Have you seen the lights.* 30/3/86 MV5 DG ME

16/6/86 LONG *Love train, Why, Travelling man, Shout.* 1/6/86 MV4 BYA TdB

17/2/88 MAYO *Wheels turning, They can say what they want, Maybe it won't last, Heaven.* Stephenson (k,bkv) r. Thompson. 27/1/88 MV4 PW MWT

GAY AND TERRY WOODS
21/11/70 TOP GEAR *A nobleman's fair daughter, I feel concerned, January snows, Van Dieman's land.* Terry Woods, Gay Woods. 3/11/70 MV4 JW BC&IS

16/6/75 PEEL *Blackbird, Winter poem, When the time is right, Song for the Gypsies, Country girlie, The hymn.* * 3/6/75 MV4 * *

4/4/78 PEEL *We can work this one out, Full moon, Dream come true, Lonesome blue.* Gay Woods (dul, v-1,2,4), Terry Woods (rg, v-3), Jim Russell (d), Kuma Hara (b), & unknown (lg). 28/3/78 MV4 CL MR

WORKFORCE
17/4/85 PEEL *Theories, Drowning pool, Compromise.* Paul

Wheatcroft (v), Rod Leigh (g,k), Tim Owen (sx,perc), Terry Todd (b), Alan Fish (d). 31/3/85 MV5 DG ME

13/1/86 Peel *Cut to pleasure, Rope dancer, Say it again.* Clive Rowat (b) r. Todd. 5/1/86 MV5 DG ME

WORKING WEEK
14/5/84 Peel *Venceremos/We will win, Stella marina, Soul of light.* Simon Booth (g), Larry Stabbins (sx,fl), Annie Whitehead (tb), Dick Pearce (tp), Bosco, Dawson, & Neville Murray (perc), Roy Dodds (d), Kim Burton (p), Ernest Mothle (b), Claudia Figuera (lv-1 only), Julie Tippett (lv-1,3 only). 1/05/84 MV5 MRD TdB

WORLD OF TWIST
15/10/90 Goodier *Sons of the stage, Jelly baby, Fire, I'm a teardrop.* Tony Ogden (v), Gordon King (g), Julia McShells (bkv), D.J. Bluc (prg). 22/9/90 MV5 MC~

11/8/91 Peel *Untitled, St. Bruno, Kick out the jams, Blackpool tower.* Ogden, King, Nicholas Sanderson (d), Pete Smith (ma). 25/6/91 MV5 MR~

THE WORLD
10/8/70 Symonds *Not the first time, Angelina, Things I could have said (& Lead up, 21/9/70).* Neil Innes (g,pv), Dennis Cowan (b), Ian Wallace (d), Roger Mckew (lg). 14/7/70 PH BA NG&PK

THE WOULD BE'S
19/3/90 Peel *All this rubbish is true, Must it be, Funny ha ha, My radio sounds different in the dark.* Julie McDonnell (v), Aidin O'Reilly (tb,ts), Mattie Finnegan (lg), Paul Finnegan (g-'14 years old!'-DG), Eamonn Finnegan (b), Pascal Smith (d). 25/2/90 MV3 DG ME

WRECKAGE
9/12/88 Fri. Rock *Fifth avenue, Dogs of war, Hanging town, Blood on our hands.* Mike Jurgens (v), Jamie Laird (b), Charlie X (g), Stuart Ricks (g), Jammer (d). 14/10/88 MV4 TW *

WRECKLESS ERIC
11/10/77 Peel *Whole wide world, Semaphore signals, Personal hygiene, Rags and tatters, Reconnez cherie.* * 25/9/77 MV4 * DD

8/3/78 Peel *Semaphore signals, Waxworks, Grown ups, Brain thieves.* Eric (gv) & New Rockets: Davy Lutton (d), Barry Payne (b), Charlie Hart (o,vi), John Glyn (sx). 1/3/78 MV4 MB NG

17/3/80 Read *It'll soon be the weekend, Out of the blue, Broken doll, A popsong.* Eric & Colin Fletcher (g), Walter Hacon (g), John Brown (b), Dave Otway (d). 14/2/80 MV4 CL *

29/12/80 Read *(I'd go the) Whole wide world, I saw her standing there, Reconnez cherie, Feelings.* Malcolm Morley (g,o,p) r. Hacon. 18/12/80 LH1 CL *

GARY WRIGHT'S WONDERWHEEL
3/2/72 Drummond *Two-faced man, For a woman, The wrong time, I know.* Gary Wright (o,pv), Bryson Graham (d), Archie Legget (b), Micky Jones (lg). 19/1/72 MV4 MB MH&MF

Gary Wright's Expansion had passed trial b'cast on Rosko Show 20/3/71.

22/2/72 Peel *I know, Yesterday's tomorrow, Whether it's right or wrong.* 15/2/72 MV4 * *

8/6/72 Drummond *Love takes, Somebody, Ring of changes, Set on you babe.* 22/5/72 T1 MB (or PD) MH&MF

18/8/72 Peel *Something for us all, Old as I was born, By tomorrow, Gimme the good earth.* 25/7/72 T1 JM (or PD)*

WRITING ON THE WALL
8/12/68 Top Gear *Tasker's successor, Shadow of man, Profile of a door, Felicity Jane (& Sha la la la la le, 2/2/69).* William Finlayson (lg), John Scott (b), William Scott (o), Linton Patterson (v), James Hush (d). 12/11/68 PCI BA AH

'For Bernie Andrews, yes, but 5¹/₂ minute numbers are not for us... we have no discotheques': pass from panel for Top Gear only.

13/2/71 Top Gear *Lucifer, Father time, Mrs Cooper's pie.* 26/1/71 * * BC

ROBERT WYATT
19/12/72 Peel *We got an Arts Council grant/Righteous rhumba, Little child, Godsong/Hatfield* [Fol de rol]. Robert Wyatt (v,po,perc,d), Francis Monkman (p,sy). 5/12/72 LH1 JW *

26/9/74 Peel† *Alifib, Soup song, Sea song, I'm a believer.* Solo (v,p,o,mrm,perc). 10/9/74 LH1 JW BC
† On Strange Fruit SFPS037.

X MEN
13/9/84 Peel *The witch, Little girl, Xtramental, Count von Black.* Mark Stollar (v), Miles Aldridge (g), Tim Hosking (b), Debbie Green (bkv,tamb), Susan Feighery (bkv,tamb), Tom Cullinam (d,g-3), Joe Foster (g). 4/9/84 MV5 MRD TdB

X RAY SPEX
6/3/78 Peel *Genetic engineering, Artificial, I am a poser, Identity.* Poly Styrene (v), Jak Airport (g), Paul Dean (b), Paul Heardin 'B.P'. (d), Steve Rudi (sx). 20/2/78 MV4 TW DD

13/11/78 Peel *Germ free adolescents, Warrior, Age.* 6/11/78 MV4 TW DD

XDREAMYSTS
10/11/80 Peel *Pardoned cry, I don't wanna go, One in every crowd, Reality blues.* Vel Walls (v), John 'Doc' Doherty (g), Roe Butcher (b), Brian Moffatt (d). 5/12/79 MV4 TVD NG

XENTRIX
19/1/90 Fri. Rock *Nobody's perfect, Dark enemy, Interrogate, Ghostbusters.* Chris Astey (gv), Paul McKenzie (b), Christian Havard (g), Dennis Gasser (d). 1/12/89 MV5 TW DD

XERO
10/4/81 Fri. Rock *Don't you think it's time, Lone wolf, Can you see me, Cuttin' loose.* Moon Williams (lv), Barry Fitzgerald (d), Bill Liesgang (g), Tony Murphy (g), Peter Solinsky (b). 1/4/81 * TW DD

XL
4/11/88 Fri. Rock *Headstrong, Anthem, Purple hearts, Fashion by force, Let it loose.* Chris Bradley (bv), Stewart Whawell (g), Richard Kirk (d), Andy Dawson (g). 29/7/88 * PW DD

XMAL DEUTSCHLAND
25/11/82 Peel *Incubus succubus, Geheimnis, Qual, Zinker.* Fiona Sangster (k), Anja Huwe (v), Manuela Rickers (g), Manuela Svingman (d), Wolfgang Ellerbrock (b). 17/12/82 * RP NG

27/6/83 Peel *In motion, Vito, Reigen, Sehnsucht.* 22/6/83 MV4 RP AP

24/4/84 Peel *Nachtschatten, Tag fuer tag, Mondlicht, Augen-blick.* Peter Bellendir (d) r. Svingman. 11/4/84 MV5 DG NG

13/5/85 Peel† *Polarlicht, Der wind, Jahr um Jahr, Autumn.* 30/4/85 MV5 MRD MR
† On Strange Fruit SFPS017.

24/9/86 Long *Ozean, If only, Sicklemoon, Eisengrav.* 14/9/86 BYA TdB

XTC
24/6/77 Peel *She's so square, Crosswires, Radios in motion, Science friction.* Andy Partridge (gv), Colin Moulding (bv), Barry Andrews (k,sxv), Terry Chambers (d). 20/6/77 MV4 MB DD

26/9/77 Peel *Into the atom age, Heatwave mark 2, I'm bugged, Dance band.* 21/9/77 MV4 MB DD

25/10/77 DLT *She's so square, Science friction, Dance band, Heatwave Mk II.* 21/10/77 MV5 * *

7/2/78 DLT *Statue of liberty, This is pop, Into the atom age, Radios in motion.* 30/1/78 MV5 * *
Next, rec'd Sight and Sound In Concert 9/3/78 HP. TX 25/3/78.

23/11/78 Peel *Meccanik dancing, The rhythm, New town animal in a furnished cage, Super thief.* 13/11/78 MV4 TW DD

2nd In Concert rec'd 17/1/79 PS, TX 27/1/79.

26/2/79 Peebles *Life is good in the greenhouse, Heatwave (27/2), Spinning top (28/2), Instant tunes (1/3).* Dave Gregory (gkv) r. Andrews. 8/2/79 MV4 JG *

'That was my audition,' says Dave Gregory; 'I hadn't actually joined the band, and still had a day-job. I drove up to London after finishing work at 4.30pm, and met the band in the studio. Perhaps we'd had one rehearsal, but I was certainly very nervous. I suppose I must have passed.'

31/5/79 Jensen *Life begins at the hop, When you're near me I have difficulty, Making plans for Nigel.* 21/5/79 MV5 * BAI&NG

1/10/79 Read *Making plans for Nigel, Helicopter (2/10), When you're near me I have difficulty (3/10), Outside world (4/10).* 7/9/79 MV4 CL *

15/10/79 Peel *Opening sig. and speech, Scissor man†, Roads girdle the globe, Ten feet tall, Real by reel.* 8/10/79 MV4 TW DD
† Originally B-side in double-pack single 'Towers of London', now on compilation LP 'Rag and Bone Buffet' (Virgin). Recorded 3rd In Concert at Hammersmith Palais, 22/12/80, TX Jan 1981.

25/1/82 Jensen *Runaways, Jason and the Argonauts, No thugs in our house, Snowman.* 14/1/82 LH1 JS MR

19/11/84 Brookes *You're the wish you are I had, This world over (20/11), Seagulls screaming (21/11), Reign of blows (22/11).* Partridge, Moulding, Gregory only. 10/84 MV4or5 * TdB

22/2/87 Sunday Live *Another satellite, The Meeting place, Earn enough for us.* Live from MV3 c.PRS *

'I used a guitar sample on "Satellite" instead of a real one,' recalls Andy Partridge, 'and my toy sampler made the song better.' The band also rehearsed a special arrangement of 'Sacrificial bonfire', but the show ran out of time, and it was not taped.

5/4/89 Skinner *King for a day, Poor skeleton steps out, Scarecrow people (& Here comes President Kill again, 3/5/89; & One of the millions, Garden of earthly delights, KERSHAW 11/6/89).* 16/3/89 WX PW TdB&TD

'Possibly the worst day of my life,' says Dave Gregory. Driving all the band's gear up to London, he was involved in a horrific motorway accident. The car was a write-off, but fortunately both he and the gear seemed OK. 'And it rained non-stop that day, I decided if I was ever to face the ultimate challenge of my character, this was probably it.' 'Several hours late, this bedraggled figure stumbled into the studio,' says Andy, 'shouting "the car's a wreck, but the drum programs are safe!"'.' The only damage was a cracked printed circuit board in one of Dave's sequencers. A BBC engineer fixed it with superglue. Thanks to Andy Partridge, Dave Gregory and John Dredge (XTC's fan in BBC radio programme registry), for help getting this straight.

XYMOX
17/6/85 Peel *Stranger, Muscoviet Mosquito, Seventh time.* Ronnie Moerings (g,kv), Anke Wolbert (k,bv), Pieter Nooten (kv), Frank Weizig (k,g), Peter Haartsen (g,sfx,tps). 4/6/85 MV5 MRD MR

13/11/85 Peel *After the call, Agonised by love, Mesmerised.* 3/11/85 MV5 DG MS

YA YA
11/10/84 Into the Music *Body rock, Those eyes, Don't think, We've only tonight.* Lea Hart (lv,g), Ray Callcut (g), Graham Garrett (d), Terry Stevens (b). 29/10/84 MV4 DG MC

THE YACHTS
24/10/78 Peel *Mantovani's hits, Yachting type, Look back in love (not in anger), Then and now.* Martin Watson (gv), Henry Priestman (o,pv), Martin Dempsey (bv), Bob Bellis (dv). 9/10/78 MV4 BS DD

2/7/79 PEEL *Then and now, In a second, Love you love you, March of the moderates.* * *4/6/79* MV4 JS DD

STOMU YAMASHTA'S EAST WIND
14/3/74 PEEL *Hey man, One by one, Optical dream, Wind words.* Stomu Yamashta (perc), Hugh Hopper (b), Brian Gascoigne (k), Sammi Abu (fl), Mike Travis (d), Frank Tankowski (g). *7/3/74* LH1 JW BAI

THE YARDBIRDS
10/3/68 TOP GEAR *Think about it†, Goodnight sweet Josephine†, White Summer, Dazed and confused.* Keith Relf (v,hca), Jimmy Page (g), Jim McCarty (d), Chris Dreja (b). *6/3/68* PH BA PR
  Last of dozens: Last Sat. Club session recorded previous day, 5/3/68. 1st session recorded 29/10/64 PH (prod JG) TX 21/11/64 on World Service Rhythm and Blues. *†* On 'On Air' BOJCD200.

YARDSTICK
3/7/92 PEEL *Blind eye, Brutal deluxe, Double zero, Twenty three.* Kevin Young (v), Ian O'Hare (g), Grease (b), Jim Harley (d). *9/6/92* MV4 JB~ PA

YAZOO
19/7/82 PEEL *Don't go, Midnight, In my room, Winter kills.* Vince Clarke (k,dm,g), Alison Moyet (pv). *16/6/82* MV4 RP TdB
16/9/82 JENSEN *Situation, Bring your love down, In my room, Too pieces.* *2/9/82* MV4 JS *

YEAH JAZZ
10/9/86 LONG *She said, Make a fist, Step into the light, Travel scrabbler, Bob's song.* Kevin Hand (agv), Mark Chatfield (g), Ian Hitchens (d), Stuart Ballantyne (b), Terry Edwards (sx,p). *27/8/86* MV4 BYA MPK
27/1/88 MAYO *Freeland, Billy comes of age, Heaven, 24 hours from Tulsa.* Kevin Tucker (d) r. Hitchens. *6/1/88* MV4 HP MPK&MFA

YEAH YEAH NOH
7/8/84 PEEL† *Prick up your ears, Beware the weakling lines, Starling pillow-case, Jigsaw.* Graham Summers (d), Adrian Crossan (b), John Grayland (g), Sue Dorey (perc), Derek Hammond (v). *28/7/84* MV5 DG MC
23/4/85 PEEL† *Temple of convenience, See through nature, Crimplene seed lifestyle, Another side to Mrs Quill.* Craig (slg), Andrew Nicholls (p) r. Summers. *9/4/85* MV5 AJ *
27/1/86 PEEL†° *The superimposed man, Blood soup, Stealing in the name of the lord, (It's) Easier to suck than sing.* Tom Slater (g) r. Craig; & Julie Dennis (bkv). *19/1/86* MV5 DG ME
  † All three sessions on 'Fun on the lawn lawn lawn' Vuggum BAD002. *°* Final session also on Strange Fruit SFPS026.

YES
12/1/69 TOP GEAR *Dear Father, Everydays, Sweetness, Something's coming.* Jon Anderson (v), Pete Banks (g), Chris Squire (b), Tony Kaye (o), Bill Bruford (d). *7/1/69* MV4 BA AH
14/6/69 WALKER *Looking around, Sweetness, Every little thing.* *4/6/69* MV4 c.JBU *
10/8/69 HENRY *Then, Beyond and before, No experience necessary.* *3/8/69* MV4 MB *
10/8/69 SYMONDS ON SUNDAY *Every little thing, Everydays, Looking around, (& possibly Sweetness, Something's coming,* not broadcast). *4/8/69* AO2 c.PWI *
25/1/70 DLT *Astral traveller, Sweet dreams, (& Then, Looking around, Everydays:* no record of broadcast). *19/1/70* AO2 c.PWI *
14/4/70 HARDING *Sweet dreams (& For everyone, 26/5/70).* Steve Howe (g) r. Banks. *7/4/70* MV5 MB MH&MF
  Previous month, recorded concert 12/3 PS (prod JG), TX 15/3/70 John Peel's Sunday Show.
27/10/70 HARDING *America.* *20/10/70* MV5 MB MH&MF
23/4/71 BLACK *The clap.* *12/4/71* T1 JM BH
  Remembered by everyone at Transcription as a total disaster. 'They wanted to do "Starship Trooper", but

after six hours we gave up,' recalls Bob Harrison; 'when they got it right, my mix wasn't right, and vice-versa. Even their own engineer, Eddie Offord, who came along, couldn't seem to get them what they wanted. Eventually they just did the one acoustic number.'
10/11/73 ROCK ON *Dance of the Dawn (& Ritual, 24/1/74; & The remembering, FREEMAN 19/1/74; & The revealing science of god, HARRIS 25/2/74).* Rick Wakeman (k), Alan White (d), r. Kaye, Bruford. *1/11/73* LH1 PR *

YIP YIP COYOTE
2/6/83 PEEL *Pioneer girl, Wagon train, Dream of the west, Red bandanna.* Fifi (v), Carl Evans (g,bkv), Eg White (b), Volker Vonhoff (d). *28/5/83* MV4 DG MC
16/1/84 PEEL *Sho' thing boss, Cry like the wind, Son of a gun, Delray.* *10/1/84* MV4 MRD MPK
25/7/84 PEEL *The Cowboy Lament, Road to hell, Burn the barn down, In the name of God.* Tom (k) r. Vonhoff. *12/7/84* MV5 MRD MR
3/9/84 LONG *Kiss me, My heart broke down in two, I always got my man!, Cry like the wind.* & Clif (d). *9/8/84* MV5 MHY *

YO YO HONEY
1/7/91 GOODIER *What's on your mind, Get it on, So so soft.* Emanuelle (k,prg,v), Chidi Chickwe (perc,v), Anita Jarrett (lv). *18/5/91* MV5 MC~

YOU'VE GOT FOETUS ON YOUR BREATH
4/1/83 PEEL *Today I started slogging again Mk.2, Clothes hoist, Wash it all off Mk.2, Ignorance is bliss (or is it?).* Jim Thirlwell (all instruments).
  Rec. date unknown PRIV self-produced by Jim Thirlwell *

JESSIE YOUNG AND THE WORD
15/10/67 TOP GEAR *Spring fever, Geno's gone walkabout, Come on up, Hold on, Every Christian.* * *9/10/67* * * *

THE ROY YOUNG BAND
13/9/70 DLT *Searchin', Keep a knockin', Oh my sould/Reddy Teddy, Turn on your love light.* Roy Young (pv) & Howie Gray (sx), Alan Townsend (tp,tb), Dave Wendell (lg), Paul Simmonds (b), Clifford Davies (d). *7/9/70* AO2 c.PWI *
31/12/70 R2 NIGHT RIDE *Dizzie Miss Lizzie, Tutti Frutti, Revelation, Maybe I'm amazed, Granny's got a painted leg, Follow me my friends, She said yeah.* & Jon Lee (tb). *17/12/70* AO1 LP *
  Group also appeared live on several Rosko and R1 Clubs 70/71.
5/1/71 HARDING *Turn on your love light, She's gone away, Granny's got a painted leg, Fortune teller.* *28/12/70* MV5 MB MH&MF
7/9/71 HARDING *Wild canty wire, New sun-new horizon, Lady.* Owen 'Onnie' Mcintyre (lg), Nick South (b), Rick Dodd (sx), Eddie Thornton (tp) r. Wendell, Simmonds, Gray, Townsend. *30/8/71* MV5 MB MH&MF [& many daytime sessions 71-72]
25/2/72 PEEL *Rag mama rag, Roll it on, Slow down, Mr Funky (& Nowhere to go, 31/3/72).* *8/2/72* T1 JM JWH&NG
22/9/72 PEEL *Back up train, Boney moronie, Annie's back, All around the world (& I can't believe it, 12/10/72).* Denis Elliott, Nick Clark, George Ford, Howie Casey, Dave Casewell r. Mcintyre, South, Dodd, Davies, Thornton. *28/8/72* T1 PD *

YOUNG GODS
12/10/88 PEEL *L'amourir, Jimmy, The Irrtum boys, Fais la mollette.* Use Heistand (d), Cesare Pizzi (k,smp), Franz Treichler (v). *2/10/88* HP DG *

YOUNG MARBLE GIANTS
26/8/80 PEEL *Searching for Mr. Right, Brand new life†, Final day, Nita, Posed by models.* Philip Moxham (b,dm), Alison Statton (v), Stuart Moxham (g,o). *18/8/80* MV4 DG DD
  † On 'Winters of Discontent' SFRCD204.

YOUNG TRADITION
12/2/69 PEEL *John Barleycorn, Wondrous love, Banks of the Nile, 3 traditional airs, 5 cuts jig, En vrai amour, Bright morning star, The rolling of the stones, What if a day.* Pete Bellamy (v), Royston Wood (v), Heather Wood (v), 'with Chris Hogwood & David Munro.' *29/1/69* PH JM *
  Unaccompanied trio had previously recorded for The Light Programme and folk shows.
27/8/69 PEEL *My dancing day, The husband man & the serving man, Bright morning stars are rising, The shepherd's hymn, Claudy banks.* Munro out. *12/8/69* MV5 PR~

JESSIE COLIN YOUNG
10/6/74 HARRIS *Sunlight/Barbados, Morning sun, Savoy for Julie, Ridge top (& Grey day, T-bone shuffle, Miss hesitation, Light shine, 17/6/74).* Jesse Colin Young (gv) & 4. *Rec. date unknown* OS * *

ZEITGEIST
12/1/82 JENSEN *Ripped, Summer blaze, Don't hold on, Pack up and go!* H (d), Detroit (b,bkv), Tex (g), Spegos (perc), Jaf (v), Zaz (v). *3/1/82* MV4 DG ME

BENJAMIN ZEPHENIAH
10/1/83 PEEL *Problems, I Christmaas poem, Uganda's what I mean.* * *7/1/83* B6 CL *
7/2/83 PEEL *Dis policeman, Riot in progress, The boat, Uprising downturn, 13 dead, Fight them not me.* Benjamin Zepheniah (v), Spartacus R (perc), Moses Valley (perc), Angie Parkinson (perc). *1/2/83* * RP NG

ZERO ZERO
19/10/91 PEEL *Maximum violence, Here's the news, The sanity clause.* Simon Robinson, Mark Grant. *22/9/91* MV3 DG AR&ME

THE ZEROS
30/11/77 PEEL *Nice girls, Hungry, Easy way out, Solid state.* Phil Gaylor (d), Steve Cotton (b), Steve Godfrey (g). *23/11/77* MV4 MB NG

ZERRA I
16/5/83 PEEL *Cry, Let's go home, Nothing, Diaries.* Andreas Grimminger (g), Paul Bell (kv), Korda (d). *7/5/83* MV4 DG MC
23/11/83 PEEL *The other side, I know, Dangerous vision, Children.* & Alison Kelly (clo), Adrian Wyatt (b). *14/11/83* MV4 TW *
26/4/84 JENSEN *Rain, I feel it, Mountains and water, Shaoirse I do cheann (instrumental).* Bell, Grimmo, Wyatt, Mike Mesbur (d). *25/3/84* MV4 DG ME

TUCKER ZIMMERMAN
30/10/72 HARRIS *Face that hasn't sold out, The girl who cried my tears, (It all depends upon) the pleasure man, Waltzing heroes come and go.* Tucker Zimmerman (gv). *18/10/72* * JG *

ZINICA
29/6/87 PEEL *Faya Bulinky†, Mr. John†, Jacket tail†, Found you to lose you.* John Herbert (v-3,4), Anthony Nash (g,v-1,2), Landiman Omeil (acc), John Palmer (tp), Victor Perry (lead bj), Walter Lackwood (2nd bj), Edward Cattuse (b), Winston Perry (d). *23/6/87* * DG MR&SC
9/7/87 KERSHAW *Jackass with the tail†, Stone bass†, Rum and coke, Johnny's life†.* *25/6/87* * DG ME
  † On LP 'Bluefields express', Club Sandino NSC001.

ZIP
16/5/88 L. KERSHAW *I'm never going to give it up, Serious game, The way you are is not the way you were, Why compromise.* Pete Shelley (v,prg), Gerard Cookson (g,prg), Mark Sanderson (b). *11/5/88* MV4 HP MPK

ZODIAC MINDWARP
21/5/86 LONG *Dangerous, Kickstart for love, Hymn of the speed kings, High priest of love.* Zodiac Mindwarp (v), Cobalt Stargazer (g), Kid Chaos (b), Slam Thunderhide (d). *11/5/86* MV4 BYA SC

THE ZONES

23/5/78 PEEL *Sign of the times, Away from it all, No sense of humour, Tough at the bottom.* Willie Gardner (lg,v), Russell 'Spyder' Webb (b), Billy McIsaac (k,bkv), Kenny Hyslop (d). 17/5/78 MV4 MB NG

22/9/78 PEEL *Anything goes, Deadly dolls, The end, It's only fashion.* 13/9/78 MV4 BS NG

30/5/79 JENSEN *Looking to the future, You're not fooling me, Mainman, Morning star.* 14/5/79 * * *

ZU ZU SHARKS

25/12/82 LONG *Big boys, Love tumbles down, When the hammer falls, Highlife.* * 22/12/82 PHM c.JL *

ZVUKI MU

8/5/89 PEEL *Zima, Crazy queen, Forgotten sex, Gadopiatikna.* Alexei Pavlov (d,tp), Alexander Lipnitsky (b), Alexei Bortnichuk (lg), Pavel Hotin (sy,bkv), Peter Mamanov (gv). 23/4/89 MV3 DG ME

DIE ZWEI AT THE RODEO

7/6/84 PEEL *River of no return, Fairhaired squaws, Western union, Grapsch!* Gerd Strass (v), Udo Strass (v), Holger Hiller (g). 23/5/84 MV5 RP PS&TD

... and in case you were wondering ...

There are 5850 sessions listed above, of which 2984 are 'Peel Sessions'. Of this 5850, Dale Griffin produced the greatest number, 1212; then comes Tony Wilson on 563 (although he probably did many more of those that remain uncredited); John Walters, 364; Jeff Griffin, 352; Malcolm Brown, 347; and Bernie Andrews, 339.

The most prolific 'SM' here is Mike Robinson, who is definitely credited as having engineered 684 of these sessions; followed by Nick Gomm, on 447; Mike Engles, 438; Dave Dade, 388; Martin Colley, 280; and Ted de Bono, 221.

The most popular studio by far was the old Maida Vale 4, where 2168 of these sessions were recorded. Maida Vale 5 has hosted 899, and Langham 1, 548; with the other old, closed studios all below that figure.

Late News

The PasBs of three early editions of John Peel's 'Night Ride' have so far proved untraceable, those of 3/4, 1/5 and 15/5/68; but I am indebted, as this book goes to press, to Simon Black for the following details of sessions on two of these missing programmes:

3/4/68 Mabel Greer's Toyshop *Beyond and before, Electric funeral, Images of me and you, Janetta.* Probably Pete Banks (g), Chris Squire (b), Jon Anderson (v), Clive Bailey (g), Tub Thumper (d). Recording details unavailable.

1/5/68 Davy Graham *Bruton town, Tristano, I'm ready, Rock me, Good morning blues.* Graham (gv, 2-instrumental). Live in on-air studio.

ACKNOWLEDGEMENTS

I should like to thank the following:

At BBC Radio 1: Controller Johnny Beerling and former Executive Producer Stuart Grundy, first of all for the germ of the idea, and inviting me to pitch for something I'd long fancied having a go at, and then for their help once I'd begun, providing me with use of an office, phone and photocopier. Thanks also to their staff: Bill Morris, Mandy Salvoni, Jo Grace and Jenny Pitt; Head of Music Chris Lycett; Senior Producers Jeff Griffin, Mike Hawkes, Kevin Howlett and Tony Wilson; Producers John Leonard, Pete Ritzema, Phil Ross and Jeff Smith; DJs John Peel, Bob Harris, Tommy Vance, Andy Kershaw, Mark Radcliffe and Mark Goodier; Archivist Phil Lawton; Pinky for putting up with me getting in the way in the office; everyone else in 306, in particular Sue Baines, Lee Hancock and Julie Laird; Clare Marvin at Reception, and Alec and James, the messengers.

BBC Radio 1 (retired or left): Bernie Andrews, Bill Bebb, Alan Black, Tim Blackmore, Malcolm Brown, Trevor Dann, Pete Drummond, Jimmy Grant, Tony Hale, Janice Long, Donald MacLean, John Muir, Bev Phillips, Roger Pusey, Mary Ramonde, Robin Scott, David Symonds, John Walters, Teddy Warrick and Mark White.

Elsewhere in the BBC: Jackie Kavanagh, Jeff Walden and, in particular, Fiona Brazil at Written Archives, Caversham; Kay Green, John Dredge, Vicky Winch and Chris Pullen in Programme Registry, both groups of archivists being quite the nicest people to work with in the BBC; Richard Addison of Radio Drama, for his help printing out *Sounds of the Seventies* PasBs; Pete Dauncey, Spot Mulkeen, Bob Harrison, Paul Kent, Adrian Revill and John Thomason, all now or once of the Transcription Service; Bob Conduct and everyone, past and present, in Sound Ops Group 2, in particular today's SMs Miti Adhikari, James Birtwistle, Graham Bunce, Martin Colley, Dave Dade, Ted de Bono, Mike Engles, Nick Gomm and Mike Robinson; Manchester SMs Tony Worthington, Dave Fleming Williams and Paul Smith; and former balancers/ tape ops Bill Aitken, John Etchells, Mike Franks, Allen Harris, Ian Sharpe and John White; Dave Tate at World Service; Mike Harding in International Recordings; Maggie Brown of Programme Contracts and the Light Entertainment Index; her colleagues Angela Horseman (Contracts, Birmingham) and Lindsay Ross (Contracts, Glasgow); the staffs of the BBC Radio Reference Library and the Popular Music Library; Sue Falconer at BBC Enterprises; and Dave Taylor in Despatch.

Former freelance session producers Bob Sargeant, John Porter and John Williams.

For band contacts and other inside information: Clive and Shurley Selwood, and Brian O'Reilly, at Strange Fruit Records; John Walters; Scott Piering; Geoff Travis; Joan Murphy of Windsong; Mike Heatley; Ian A. Anderson of *Folk Roots*; Joe Boyd; Phil Smee; Earache Records; Mike King, author of a forthcoming biography of Robert Wyatt, *Wrong Movements*; Geoff Barton and Neil Jeffries of *Kerrang!*; Jon Lewin of *Making*

Music; Wendy Pilmer, BBC Radio Features Manchester; and Stewart Cruickshank, BBC Radio Scotland, whose boundless knowledge and enthusiasm helped me enormously.

Bands and musicians: I am grateful to all the musicians who replied to my letters and phone calls about their sessions, but I should like to thank in particular Viv Albertine, Ian Anderson, Joan Armatrading, Tony Banks, Maggie Bell, Pauline Black, Mick Box, Lee Brilleaux, Dave Brock, Mark Burgess, Brian Burrows, Ian Carr, Jimmy Cauty, Edwyn Collins, Phil Collins, the Cookie Crew, Mike Cooper, Ivor Cutler, Michael Dempsey, John Fiddler, Fish, David Gedge, Ron Geesin, Lynval Golding, Scott Gorham, Roy Harper, Mick Harris, Mick Harvey, Alan Hempsall, Jon Hiseman, Ashley Hutchings, Linton Kwesi Johnson, Jim Kerr, Ray Laidlaw, Len Liggins, Jeff Lynne, Nick Mason, Kim McAuliffe, Raymond McGinlay, Simon Nicol, Rab Noakes, Andy Partridge, Alex Paterson, John Perry, Jason Pierce, Noel Redding, Craig and Charlie Reid, Andy Roberts, Michael Rooney, Mike Rutherford, Peter Solowka, Paul Samson, Feargal Sharkey, Richard Sinclair, Viv Stanshall, Darrell Sweet, Ed Wenn, Karl Willetts and Robert Wyatt.

For help on the Sessionography: Alistair Calder, Tunde Cockshott, Sharon Fitzgerald and Jem Taylor (University of Glasgow Computer Services department) for database and computer advice; for helping me key the original raw data on the sessions into my database, three M.Phil postgraduates in the John Logie Baird Centre for Research in Film, Television and Music, University of Strathclyde: Kerry Musselbrook (*Sounds of the Seventies,* 1980s *Evening Show*), Ciaran McGonachy (*Friday Rock Show,* late 1980s *Peels*), and Jane McWilliams (1980s *Peels*) and for keying some punk sessi... and offering choice contextual recoll... tions while doing so, A.J. Hull, of th... Economic History department, University of Glasgow.

Mark Melton at the Musicians' Union.

The staff of the Music & Arts, and General Reference Sections of the Mitchell Library, Glasgow.

Heather Holden-Brown, commissioning editor at BBC Books, and editor Julian Flanders, for their instant and continuing enthusiasm for the project.

Nicola for putting me up on my research trips to London; my wife Magda; and, finally, the people without whom this book could not have been written, and without whose words and deeds I would certainly have had much, much less to type up: Bernie Andrews, Jeff Griffin, John Walters and John Peel.

Bibliography

Stephen Barnard, *On the Radio: Music radio in Britain* (Milton Keynes, 1989)

Robert Chapman, *Selling the Sixties: The pirates and pop music radio* (London, 1992)

Pete Frame's *Rock Family Trees* (Omnibus, 1980; & Volume II, London, 1983).

Bob Geldof, *Is that it?* (London, 1986)

John Hind and Stephen Mosco, *Rebel Radio* (London, 1985)

Kevin Howlett, *The Beatles at the Beeb* (London, 1982)

James Maw, *The Official Adam Ant Story* (London, 1981)

Noel Redding and Carol Appleby, *Are you experienced?* (London, 1990)

Johnny Rogan, *Morrissey & Marr: The severed alliance* (London, 1992)

Jon Savage, *England's Dreaming: Sex Pistols and punk rock* (London, 1991)

Also invaluable were Mark Paytress and Cliff McLenehan's occasional articles in *Record Collector* magazine.